International Conference on Recent Advances in Natural Language Processing

(RANLP 2013)

Hissar, Bulgaria
9 – 11 September 2013

Editors:

G. Angelova
K. Bontcheva
R. Mitkov

ISBN: 978-1-62993-555-3

Printed from e-media with permission by:

Curran Associates, Inc.
57 Morehouse Lane
Red Hook, NY 12571

Some format issues inherent in the e-media version may also appear in this print version.

Printed by Curran Associates, Inc. (2014)

Association for Computational Linguistics
209 N. Eighth Street
Stroudsburg, Pennsylvania 18360

Phone: 1-570-476-8006
Fax: 1-570-476-0860

acl@aclweb.org

Additional copies of this publication are available from:

Curran Associates, Inc.
57 Morehouse Lane
Red Hook, NY 12571 USA
Phone: 845-758-0400
Fax: 845-758-2634
Email: curran@proceedings.com
Web: www.proceedings.com

Preface

Welcome to the 9th International Conference on "Recent Advances in Natural Language Processing" (RANLP 2013) in Hissar, Bulgaria, 9–11 September 2013. The main objective of the conference is to give researchers the opportunity to present new results in Natural Language Processing (NLP) based on modern theories and methodologies.

The conference is preceded by two days of tutorials (7-8 September 2013) and the lecturers are:

- Preslav Nakov (Qatar Computing Research Institute, Qatar Foundation)
- Vivi Nastase (Fondazione Bruno Kessler)
- Diarmuid Ó Séaghdha (Cambridge University)
- Stan Szpakowicz (University of Ottawa)
- Iryna Gurevych (Technical University Darmstadt)
- Judith Eckle-Kohler (Technical University Darmstadt)
- Violeta Seretan (University of Geneva)
- Dekai Wu (Hong Kong University of Science & Technology)

The conference keynote speakers are:

- Nicoletta Calzolari (Institute of Computational Linguistics "Antonio Zampolli", Pisa)
- Iryna Gurevych (Technical University Darmstadt)
- Horacio Saggion (University Pompeu Fabra, Barcelona)
- Violeta Seretan (University of Geneva)
- Mark Stevenson (University of Sheffield)
- Dekai Wu (Hong Kong University of Science & Technology)

This year 22 regular papers, 36 short papers, and 41 posters have been accepted for presentation at the conference. In 2013 RANLP hosts 3 workshops on influential NLP topics, such as NLP for medicine and biology, Linked Open Data (LOD) for NLP, semantic web and information extraction, and adaptation of language resources.

The proceedings cover a wide variety of NLP topics: part of speech tagging, language resources, semantics, opinion mining and sentiment analysis, multilingual NLP, language modelling, word sense disambiguation, information extraction, term extraction, parsing, text summarisation, machine translation, question answering, temporal processing, text simplification, named entity recognition, text generation, text categorisation, NLP for special languages, morphology and syntax, etc.

We would like to thank all members of the Programme Committee and all additional reviewers. Together they have ensured that the best papers were included in the proceedings and have provided invaluable comments for the authors.

Finally, special thanks go to the University of Wolverhampton, the Bulgarian Academy of Sciences, the ACOMIN European project, Ontotext, the Association for Computational Linguistics – Bulgaria for their generous support for RANLP.

Welcome to Hissar and we hope that you enjoy the conference!

The RANLP 2013 Organisers

The International Conference RANLP–2013 is organised by:

Research Group in Computational Linguistics, University of Wolverhampton, UK

Linguistic Modelling Department, Institute of Information and Communication Technologies, Bulgarian Academy of Sciences, Bulgaria

RANLP–2013 is partially supported by:

AComIn (Advanced Computing for Innovation, FP7 Capacity grant 316087)

Ontotext AD

Programme Committee Chair:

Ruslan Mitkov, University of Wolverhampton

Organising Committee Chair:

Galia Angelova, Bulgarian Academy of Sciences

Workshop Coordinator:

Kiril Simov, Bulgarian Academy of Sciences

Publication Chair:

Kalina Bontcheva, University of Sheffield

Tutorial Coordinator:

Preslav Nakov, Qatar Computing Research Institute

Proceedings Printing:

Nikolai Nikolov, Association for Computational Linguistics, Bulgaria

Programme Committee Coordinators:

Ivelina Nikolova, Bulgarian Academy of Sciences
Irina Temnikova, Bulgarian Academy of Sciences
Natalia Konstantinova, University of Wolverhampton

Program Committee:

Guadalupe Aguado de Cea (Polytechnic University Madrid, Spain)
Roberto Basili (University of Roma, Tor Vergata, Italy)
Jerome Bellegarda (Apple Inc., USA)
Chris Biemann (TU Darmstadt, Germany)
Kalina Bontcheva (University of Sheffield, UK)
Svetla Boytcheva (American University in Bulgaria, Bulgaria)
António Branco (University of Lisbon, Portugal)
Jill Burstein (Educational Testing Service, USA)
Nicoletta Calzolari (National Research Council, Italy)
Kevin Bretonnel Cohen (University of Colorado School of Medicine, USA)
Ken Church (The Johns Hopkins University, IBM Research, USA)
Dan Cristea ("Al. I. Cuza" University of Iasi, Romania)
Ido Dagan (Bar Ilan University, Israel)
Anne De Roeck (The Open University, UK)
Richard Evans (University of Wolverhampton, UK)
Antonio Ferrández Rodríguez (University of Alicante, Spain)
Joey Frazee (University of Texas at Austin, USA)
Fumiyo Fukumoto (Yamanashi University, Japan)
Alexander Gelbukh (Nat. Polytechnic Inst., Mexico)
Ralph Grishman (New York University, USA) Patrick Hanks (University of the West of England and University of Wolverhampton, UK)
Kris Heylen (University of Leuven, Belgium)
Graeme Hirst (Univ. of Toronto, Canada)
Veronique Hoste (University College Ghent, Belgium)
Mans Hulden (University of Helsinki, Finland)
Diana Inkpen (University of Ottawa, Canada)
Hitoshi Isahara (Toyohashi University of Technology, Japan)
Ali Jaoua (Qatar University, Qatar)
Mijail Kabadjov (DaXtra Technologies Ltd., UK)
Dimitar Kazakov (University of York, UK)
Alma Kharrat (Microsoft, USA)
Udo Kruschwitz (University of Essex, UK)
Hristo Krushkov (University of Plovdiv, Bulgaria)
Sandra Kuebler (Indiana University, USA)
Lori Lamel (LIMSI - CNRS, France)
Chew Lim Tan (National University of Singapore, Singapore)
Qun Liu (Chinese Academy of Sciences, China)
Suresh Manandhar (University of York, UK)
Yusuke Miyao (National Institute of Informatics, Japan)
Johanna Monti (University of Sassari, Italy)
Alessandro Moschitti (University of Trento, Italy)
Rafael Muñoz Guillena (University of Alicante, Spain)
Preslav Nakov (QCRI, Qatar)
Roberto Navigli (University di Roma La Sapienza, Italy)
Vincent Ng (The University of Texas at Dallas, USA)
Kemal Oflazer (Carnegie Mellon University, Qatar)
Constantin Orasan (University of Wolverhampton, UK)

Sebastian Pado (University of Heidelberg, Germany)
Karel Pala (Masaryk University, Czech Republic)
Martha Palmer (University of Colorado, USA)
Stelios Piperidis (ILSP, Greece)
Simone Paolo Ponzetto (University of Heidelberg, Germany)
Gábor Prószéky (Pázmány University & MorphoLogic, Hungary)
Allan Ramsay (Univ. of Manchester, UK)
Horacio Rodriguez (Universitat Politècnica de Catalunya, Spain)
Paolo Rosso (University of Valencia, Spain)
Vasile Rus (University of Memphis, USA)
Horacio Saggion (Universitat Pompeu Fabra, Spain)
Patrick Saint-Dizier (IRIT-CNRS, France)
Satoshi Sakine (New York University, USA)
Doaa Samy (University Autonomous of Madrid, Spain)
Violeta Seretan (University of Geneva, Switzerland)
Khaled Shaalan (Cairo University, Egypt)
Kiril Simov (Bulgarian Academy of Sciences, Bulgaria)
Keh-Yih Su (Behavior Design Corp., Taiwan)
Stan Szpakowicz (University of Ottawa, Canada)
John Tait (Johntait.net Limited)
Josef van Genabith (Dublin City University, Ireland)
Dan Tufis (RIAI, Romanian Academy, Romania)
L. Alfonso Ureña López (University of Jaen, Spain)
Paola Velardi (University of Roma "La Sapienza", Italy)
Suzan Verberne (Radboud University Nijmegen, The Netherlands)
Piek Vossen (VU University Amsterdam, The Netherlands)
Yorick Wilks (Univ. of Sheffield, UK)
Dekai Wu (HKUST, Hong Kong)
Torsten Zesch (TU Darmstadt, Germany)
Min Zhang (University of Michigan, USA)

Additional Reviewers:

Karteek Addanki (HKUST, Hong Kong)
Itziar Aldabe (Univ. of Basque Country, Spain)
Hadi Amiri (National University of Singapore)
Marilisa Amoia (Saarland University, Germany)
Wilker Aziz (University of Wolverhampton, UK)
Nguyen Bach (Carnegie Mellon University, USA)
Daniel Bär (TU Darmstadt, Germany)
Eduard Barbu (Universiy of Jaén, Spain)
Leonor Becerra (Laboratoire Hubert Curien, France)
Cosmin Bejan (University of Washington, USA)
Asma Ben Abacha (CRP Henri Tudor, Luxembourg)
Boryana Bratanova (University of Veliko Turnovo, Bulgaria)
Erik Cambria (National University of Singapore, Singapore)
Marie Candito (Univ Paris Diderot - INRIA, France)
Miranda Chong (University of Wolverhampton, UK)
Marta R. Costa-Jussa (Barcelona Media Innovation Center, Spain)

Eugeniu Costetchi (CRP Henri Tudor, Luxembourg)
Raquel Criado (University of Murcia, Spain)
Noa Cruz (University of Huelva, Spain)
Daniel Dahlmeier (National University of Singapore, Singapore)
Kareem Darwish (QCRI, Qatar Foundation, Qatar)
Orphee De Clercq (University College Ghent, Belgium)
Gerard de Melo (ICSI Berkeley, USA)
Leon Derczynski (University of Sheffield, UK)
Liviu Dinu (University of Bucharest, Romania)
Son Doan (UC San Diego, USA)
Iustin Dornescu (University of Wolverhampton, UK)
Brett Drury (LIAAD-INESC, Portugal)
Kevin Duh (Nara Institute of Science and Technology, Japan)
Isabel Durán Muñoz (University of Wolverhampton, UK)
Chris Dyer (Carnegie Mellon University, USA)
Ismail El Maarouf (University of Wolverhampton, UK)
Maria Eskevich (Dublin City University, Ireland)
Mariano Felice (Cambridge University, UK)
Mark Fishel (University of Zurich, Switzerland)
Wei Gao (QCRI, Qatar Foundation, Qatar)
Albert Gatt (University of Malta, Malta)
Matthew Gerber (University of Virginia, USA)
Goran Glavaš (University of Zagred, Croatia)
José Miguel Goñi-Menoyo (Politechnical University of Madrid, Spain)
Brian Harrington (University of Toronto Scarborough, Canada)
Laura Hasler (University of Strathclyde, UK)
Hany Hassan (Microsoft Research, USA)
Kai Hong (University of Pennsylvania, USA)
Ales Horak (Masaryk University, Czech Republic)
Young-Sook Hwang (SK Telecom, South Korea)
Iustina Ilisei (University of Wolverhampton, UK)
Sujay Kumar Jauhar (Carnegie Mellon University, USA)
Minwoo Jeong (Microsoft, USA)
Kristiina Jokinen (University of Helsinki, Finland)
David Kauchak (Middlebury College, USA)
Jin-Dong Kim (Database Center for Life Science, Japan)
Natalia Konstantinova (University of Wolverhampton, UK)
Zornitsa Kozareva (USC Information Sciences Institute, USA)
Laska Laskova (Sofia University, Bulgaria)
Junyi Li (University of Pennsylvania, USA)
Maria Liakata (University of Warwick, UK)
Ting Liu (Google, USA)
Elena Lloret (University of Alicante, Spain)
Chi-kiu LO (HKUST, Hong Kong)
Oier Lopez de Lacalle (Basque Foundation for Science, Spain and University of Edinburgh, Scotland)
Annie Louis (University of Pennsylvania, USA)
Wei Lu (University of Illinois at Urbana-Champaign, USA)

Yapomo Manuela (University of Strasbourg, France)
Maite Martin (Univeristy of Jaén, Spain)
Eugenio Martinez-Camara (University of Jaén, Spain)
Bonan Min (New York University, USA)
Wolfgang Minker (Ulm University, Germany)
Olga Mitrofanova (St. Petersburg State University, Russia)
Makoto Miwa (National Centre for Text Mining, University of Manchester, UK)
Behrang Mohit (Carnegie Mellon University, Qatar)
Michael Mohler (University of North-Texas, USA)
Manuel Montes (INAOE, Mexico)
Vlad Niculae (University of Wolverhampton, UK)
Ivelina Nikolova (Bulgarian Academy of Sciences, Bulgaria)
Petya Osenova (Sofia University and IICT-BAS, Bulgaria)
Diarmuid Ó Séaghdha (University of Cambridge, UK)
Georgios Paltoglou (University of Wolverhampton, UK)
Alexander Panchenko (Universite catholique de Louvain, Belgium)
Katherin Pérez (University of Wolverhampton, UK)
Vinodkumar Prabhakaran (Columbia University, USA)
Carlos Ramisch (Université Joseph Fourier, France)
Luz Rello (Universitat Pompeu Fabra, Spain)
Miguel Angel Rios Gaona (University of Wolverhampton, UK)
Raphael Rubino (Dublin City University, Symantec, Ireland)
Pavel Rychlý (Masaryk University, Czech Republic)
Gerold Schneider (University of Zurich, Switzerland)
Lane Schwartz (Air Force Research Laboratory, USA)
Avirup Sil (Temple University, USA)
Yvonne Skalban (University of Wolverhampton, UK)
Jan Snajder (University of Zagred, Croatia)
Sanja Stajner (University of Wolverhampton, UK)
Ekaterina Stambolieva (euroscript Luxembourg S.à. r.l., Luxembourg)
Sebastian Stüker (Karlsruhe Institute of Technology)
Ang Sun (inome Inc, USA)
Yoshimi Suzuki (University of Yamanashi, Japan)
Irina Temnikova (Bulgarian Academy of Sciences, Bulgaria)
Joel Tetreault (Nuance Communications, USA)
Katerina Raisa Timonera (University of Wolverhamtpon, UK)
Maria Cristina Toledo Baez (University of Murcia, Spain)
Marco Turchi (Fondazione Bruno Kessler, Italy)
Paola Valli (University of Trieste, Italy)
Andrea Varga (The University Of Sheffield, UK)
Aline Villavicencio (Federal University of Rio Grande do Sul, Brazil)
Veronika Vincze (University of Szeged, Hungary)
Haifeng Wang (Baidu, China)
Stephanie Weiser (Knowbel Technologies, Belgium)
Sandra Williams (The Open University, UK)
Victoria Yaneva (University of Wolverhampton, UK)
Heng Yu (Chinese Academy of Sciences, China)
Wajdi Zaghouani (Carnegie Mellon University, Qatar)

Table of Contents

Conference Programme

Monday September 9, 2013

Session 1a: (10:10 - 11:10) Part-of-Speech Tagging

Twitter Part-of-Speech Tagging for All: Overcoming Sparse and Noisy Data
Leon Derczynski, Alan Ritter, Sam Clark and Kalina Bontcheva

Exploiting Synergies Between Open Resources for German Dependency Parsing, POS-tagging, and Morphological Analysis
Rico Sennrich, Martin Volk and Gerold Schneider

Session 1b: (10:10 - 11:10) Language Resources

DutchSemCor: in Quest of the Ideal Sense-tagged Corpus
Piek Vossen, Rubén Izquierdo and Attila Görög

Beyond the Transfer-and-Merge Wordnet Construction: plWordNet and a Comparison with WordNet
Marek Maziarz, Maciej Piasecki, Ewa Rudnicka and Stan Szpakowicz

Session 1c: (10:10 - 11:10) Semantics

Using a Weighted Semantic Network for Lexical Semantic Relatedness
Reda Siblini and Leila Kosseim

Capturing Anomalies in the Choice of Content Words in Compositional Distributional Semantic Space
Ekaterina Kochmar and Ted Briscoe

Monday September 9, 2013 (continued)

Session 2a: (11:40 - 13:00) Opinion Mining and Sentiment Analysis

Semi-supervised vs. Cross-domain Graphs for Sentiment Analysis
Natalia Ponomareva and Mike Thelwall

Sentiment Analysis of Reviews: Should we Analyze Writer Intentions or Reader Perceptions?
Isa Maks and Piek Vossen

Improving Web 2.0 Opinion Mining Systems Using Text Normalisation Techniques
Alejandro Mosquera and Paloma Moreda Pozo

Mining Fine-grained Opinion Expressions with Shallow Parsing
Sucheta Ghosh, Sara Tonelli and Richard Johansson

Session 2b: (11:40 - 13:00) Multilingual NLP

Acronym Recognition and Processing in 22 Languages
Maud Ehrmann, Leonida della Rocca, Ralf Steinberger and Hristo Tannev

Sense Clustering Using Wikipedia
Bharath Dandala, Chris Hokamp, Rada Mihalcea and Razvan Bunescu

A Pilot Study on the Semantic Classification of Two German Prepositions: Combining Monolingual and Multilingual Evidence
Simon Clematide and Manfred Klenner

Temporal Relation Classification in Persian and English contexts
Mahbaneh Eshaghzadeh Torbati, Gholamreza Ghassem-sani, Seyed Abolghasem Mirroshandel, Yadollah Yaghoobzadeh and Negin Karimi Hosseini

Session 2c: (11:40 - 13:00) Language Modelling

Segmenting vs. Chunking Rules: Unsupervised ITG Induction via Minimum Conditional Description Length
Markus Saers, Karteek Addanki and Dekai Wu

CCG Categories for Distributional Semantic Models
Paramita Mirza and Raffaella Bernardi

Identifying Social and Expressive Factors in Request Texts Using Transaction/Sequence Model
Daša Munková, Michal Munk and Zuzana Fráterová

Realization of Common Statistical Methods in Computational Linguistics with Functional Automata
Stefan Gerdjikov, Petar Mitankin and Vladislav Nenchev

Monday September 9, 2013 (continued)

Session 3a: (15:30 - 16:30) Information Extraction

Confidence Estimation for Knowledge Base Population
Xiang Li and Ralph Grishman

TwitIE: An Open-Source Information Extraction Pipeline for Microblog Text
Kalina Bontcheva, Leon Derczynski, Adam Funk, Mark Greenwood, Diana Maynard and Niraj Aswani

Session 3b: (15:30 - 16:30) Term Extraction

Context Independent Term Mapper for European Languages
Mārcis Pinnis

Automated Learning of Everyday Patients' Language for Medical blogs Analytics
Giovanni Stilo, Moreno De Vincenzi, Alberto E. Tozzi and Paola Velardi

Session 3c: (15:30 - 16:30) Parsing

magyarlanc: A Tool for Morphological and Dependency Parsing of Hungarian
János Zsibrita, Veronika Vincze and Richárd Farkas

Incremental and Predictive Dependency Parsing under Real-Time Conditions
Arne Köhn and Wolfgang Menzel

Session 4: (16:30 - 18:30) Methods, Resources and Language Processing Tasks (Posters)

Tuesday September 10, 2013

Session 5a: (10:00 - 11:00) Text Summarisation and Tables-of-Content Generation

Introducing a Corpus of Human-Authored Dialogue Summaries in Portuguese
Norton Trevisan Roman, Paul Piwek, Ariadne M. B. Rizzoni Carvalho and Alexandre Rossi Alvares

Hierarchy Identification for Automatically Generating Table-of-Contents
Nicolai Erbs, Iryna Gurevych and Torsten Zesch

Session 5b: (10:00 - 11:00) Translation Technology / MT-inspired Approaches

High-Accuracy Phrase Translation Acquisition Through Battle-Royale Selection
Lionel Nicolas, Egon W. Stemle, Klara Kranebitter and Verena Lyding

Normalization of Dutch User-Generated Content
Orphée De Clercq, Sarah Schulz, Bart Desmet, Els Lefever and Véronique Hoste

Session 5c: (10:00 - 11:00) POS Tagging and Parsing

Combining POS Tagging, Dependency Parsing and Coreferential Resolution for Bulgarian
Valentin Zhikov, Georgi Georgiev, Kiril Simov and Petya Osenova

How Symbolic Learning Can Help Statistical Learning (and vice versa)
Isabelle Tellier and Yoann Dupont

Tuesday September 10, 2013 (continued)

Wednesday September 11, 2013

Wednesday September 11, 2013 (continued)

Session 8a: (11:40 - 13:00) Text categorisation

Headerless, Quoteless, but not Hopeless? Using Pairwise Email Classification to Disentangle Email Threads
Emily Jamison and Iryna Gurevych

A Boosting-based Algorithm for Classification of Semi-Structured Text using the Frequency of Substructures
Tomoya Iwakura

Authorship Attribution in Health Forums
Victoria Bobicev, Marina Sokolova, Khaled El Emam and Stan Matwin

Linguistic Profiling of Texts Across Textual Genres and Readability Levels. An Exploratory Study on Italian Fictional Prose
Felice Dell'Orletta, Simonetta Montemagni and Giulia Venturi

Session 8b: (11:40 - 13:00) NLP for Specialised Languages

Closure Properties of Bulgarian Clinical Text
Irina Temnikova, Ivelina Nikolova, William A. Baumgartner, Galia Angelova and K. Bretonnel Cohen

Measuring Closure Properties of Patent Sublanguages
Irina Temnikova, Negacy Hailu, Galia Angelova and K. Bretonnel Cohen

Grammar-Based Lexicon Extension for Aligning German Radiology Text and Images
Claudia Bretschneider, Sonja Zillner and Matthias Hammon

Domain Adaptation for Parsing
Eric Baucom, Levi King and Sandra Kübler

Session 8c: (11:40 - 13:00) Morphology and Syntax

ASMA: A System for Automatic Segmentation and Morpho-Syntactic Disambiguation of Modern Standard Arabic
Muhammad Abdul-Mageed, Mona Diab and Sandra Kübler

PurePos 2.0: a Hybrid Tool for Morphological Disambiguation
György Orosz and Attila Novák

Sequence Tagging for Verb Conjugation in Romanian
Liviu Dinu, Octavia-Maria Şulea and Vlad Niculae

History Based Unsupervised Data Oriented Parsing
Mohsen Mesgar and Gholamreza Ghasem-Sani

Wednesday September 11, 2013 (continued)

Session 9: (15:30 - 17:30) Applications (Posters)

More than Bag-of-Words: Sentence-based Document Representation for Sentiment Analysis
Georgios Paltoglou and Mike Thelwall

How Joe and Jane Tweet about Their Health: Mining for Personal Health Information on Twitter
Marina Sokolova, Stan Matwin, Yasser Jafer and David Schramm

What Sentiments Can Be Found in Medical Forums?
Marina Sokolova and Victoria Bobicev

Opinion Learning from Medical Forums
Tanveer Ali, Marina Sokolova, David Schramm and Diana Inkpen

Towards Fine-grained Citation Function Classification
Xiang Li, Yifan He, Adam Meyers and Ralph Grishman

Automatic Extraction of Contextual Valence Shifters.
Noémi Boubel, Thomas François and Hubert Naets

Improving Sentiment Analysis in Twitter Using Multilingual Machine Translated Data
Alexandra Balahur and Marco Turchi

Evaluation of Baseline Information Retrieval for Polish Open-domain Question Answering System
Michał Marcińczuk, Adam Radziszewski, Maciej Piasecki, Dominik Piasecki and Marcin Ptak

Automatic Cloze-Questions Generation
Annamaneni Narendra, Manish Agarwal and Rakshit shah

An NLP-based Reading Tool for Aiding Non-native English Readers
Mahmoud Azab, Ahmed Salama, Kemal Oflazer, Hideki Shima, Jun Araki and Teruko Mitamura

Did I Really Mean That? Applying Automatic Summarisation Techniques to Formative Feedback
Debora Field, Stephen Pulman, Nicolas Van Labeke, Denise Whitelock and John Richardson

A Feature Induction Algorithm with Application to Named Entity Disambiguation
Laura Toloşi, Valentin Zhikov, Georgi Georgiev and Borislav Popov

A Clustering Approach for Translationese Identification
Sergiu Nisioi and Liviu P. Dinu

Wednesday September 11, 2013 (continued)

ASMA: A System for Automatic Segmentation and Morpho-Syntactic Disambiguation of Modern Standard Arabic

Muhammad Abdul-Mageed
Indiana University
Bloomington, IN, USA
mabdulma@indiana.edu

Mona Diab
George Washington University
Washington DC, USA
mtdiab@email.gwu.edu

Sandra Kübler
Indiana University
Bloomington, IN, USA
skuebler@indiana.edu

Abstract

In this paper, we present ASMA, a fast and efficient system for automatic segmentation and fine grained part of speech (POS) tagging of Modern Standard Arabic (MSA). ASMA performs segmentation both of agglutinative and of inflectional morphological boundaries within a word. In this work, we compare ASMA to two state of the art suites of MSA tools: AMIRA 2.1 (Diab et al., 2007; Diab, 2009) and MADA+TOKAN 3.2. (Habash et al., 2009). ASMA achieves comparable results to these two systems' state-of-the-art performance. ASMA yields an accuracy of 98.34% for segmentation, and an accuracy of 96.26% for POS tagging with a rich tagset and 97.59% accuracy with an extremely reduced tagset.

1 Introduction

Arabic raises various challenges to natural language processing (NLP): Arabic is a morphologically rich language (Tsarfaty et al., 2010), where significant information concerning syntactic units is expressed at the word level, which makes part of speech (POS) tagging a challenge since it involves morpho-syntactic disambiguation, including features like voice, number, gender (Diab, 2007; Diab et al., 2007; Habash et al., 2009).

We address the problem of full morpho-syntactic disambiguation of words in context. We devise a system, ASMA, that performs both inflectional morpheme segmentation and agglutinative clitic segmentation. For example, given a surface word in context such as وَبِحَسَنَاتِهِم (*wabiHasanaAtihim*, Eng. 'and by their virtues')[1], ASMA provides the following segmentation: وَ بِ حَسَن اَتِ هِم *wa bi Hasan aAti him*, with the prefixal clitics وَ بِ (*wa bi*, Eng. 'and' 'by'), the stem حَسَن (*Hasan*), the inflection morpheme اَتِ (*aAti*), and the suffixal pronominal morpheme هِم (*him*). ASMA then assigns each one of these resulting morphemes a POS tag. For an explanation of Arabic morphology, cf. section 2.

The most successful approaches to date that render this level of morphological segmentation (addressing both inflectional as well as agglutinative boundaries) typically rely on employing a morphological analyzer in the process (Habash et al., 2009). We show that it is possible to efficiently perform full morpho-syntactic disambiguation employing language-independent methods that are not based on a morphological analyzer. Our motivation is that dependence on a morphological analyzer comes at the cost of development since such an analyzer is generally based on manually written rules and an extensive lexicon.

ASMA performs both inflectional morpheme segmentation and agglutinative clitic segmentation, as well as fine grained POS tagging of Modern Standard Arabic (MSA). In ASMA, a *segment* is a stem, an inflectional affix, or a clitic. ASMA does not handle morphotactic boundaries, thereby potentially deriving stems which may not be smoothed into correct lexemic forms for the POS process. An example of the result of the *segmentation* in ASMA is as follows: the surface form الوِلَايَات (*AlwilaAyaAt*, Eng. 'the states') is segmented into ال + وِلَاي + اَت (*Al+wilaAy+aAt*) where *wilaAy* is a stem, *Al* is a clitic, and *At* is an affixival inflectional suffix. It should be noted that *wilaAy* is not a valid Arabic lexeme. For ASMA to convert it into a lexeme, it would have to process the morphotactics on the stem and render it as وِلَايَة

[1] For Arabic examples, we use both the Arabic script and the Buckwalter Arabic transliteration scheme (Buckwalter, 2004).

(*wilaAyap*) restoring the lexeme/lemma final ة *p*.

The remainder of the paper is structured as follows: Section 2 describes the pertinent facts about Arabic morphology. Section 3 describes related work, namely on AMIRA 2.1 and MADA+TOKAN 3.2. In section 4, we describe ASMA, the overall system, in section 5, we report results on the segmentation task, and in section 6 on the POS tagging task. In section 7 we provide an error analysis, and conclude in section 9.

2 Arabic Morphology

Arabic exhibits derivational, inflectional, and agglutinative morphology. Derivational morphology is mostly templatic where a word is made up of a root and a pattern, along with some idiosyncratic information. For example, a root such as ك ت ب (*k t b*) if combined with the pattern *1a2a3*, where the numbers [1,2,3] designate the root radicals, respectively, it results in the derivational form كَتَب (*katab*, Eng. 'to write'). Likewise for the same root when it combines with the pattern *1A2a3*, it result in the word كاتَب (*kaAtab*, Eng. 'to correspond'). All derivation forms undergo inflection reflecting various types of functional features such as voice, number, aspect, gender, grammatical case, tense, etc. The resulting word is known as a *lexeme*. Therefore a lexeme such as كَتَبَت (*katabat*, Eng. 'she wrote') reflects feminine [gender], singular [number], past [tense], perfective [aspect], 3rd [person] inflections for the verb. Typically, one of the fully inflected lexemes is considered a citation form, and it is known as the *lemma*. The choice of a specific lexeme as a citation form is a convention, and it is typically the 3rd person masculine singular perfective form for verbs and the 3rd person singular form for nouns. Hence in this case the lemma is كَتَبَ (*kataba*, Eng. 'he wrote'). Arabic words often undergo clitic agglutination to form surface words. For example, the lexeme كاتَبَت (*kAtabat*, Eng. 'she corresponded') could have an enclitic/suffixal pronoun as follows: كاتَبَتهُم (*kAtabathum*, Eng. 'she corresponded with them'). The agglutination process results in morphotactic variations at the morpheme boundaries where the orthography is changed for the underlying lexeme. For example, in a noun such as وَبِحَسَنَتهِم (*wabiHasanathim*, Eng. 'and by their virtue'), the underlying lexeme (same as lemma in this case) is the noun حَسَنَة (*Hasanap*), where the lexeme final Taa-Marbuta ة (*p*) is changed into a regular ت (*t*) when followed by a pronominal clitic. Accordingly, segmenting off agglutinative clitics without handling boundary morphotactics to restore the underlying lexeme form results in *stems*.

3 Related Work

AMIRA 2.1 (Diab et al., 2007; Diab, 2009) is a supervised SVM-based machine learning algorithm for processing MSA, including clitic tokenization and normalization, POS tagging, and base phrase chunking. Diab. et al. adopt the inside-outside-beginning (IOB) chunk approach (Ramshaw and Marcus, 1995) for clitic tokenization, i.e., each letter in a word is labeled as being at the beginning (B), the inside (I), or the outside (O) of a chunk. Note that the tokenization by Diab et al. does not split off inflectional morphology. For example, while ASMA would segment وبحسناتهم (*wbHsnAthm*) into *w+b+Hsn+At+hm*, AMIRA 2.1 would output *w+b+HsnAt+hm*, i.e., it does not split off the number and gender inflectional suffix ات *At* from the stem حسن (*Hsn*).

One advantage of ASMA over AMIRA 2.1 is thus that ASMA identifies inflectional morpheme boundaries. Similar to AMIRA 2.1, ASMA employs an IOB chunking approach on the character level for segmentation of words into morphemic chunks (clitics, stems, and inflectional affixes). AMIRA 2.1 achieves an F-measure of 99.15% for the entire word being segmented correctly. AMIRA 2.1 also performs POS tagging. It uses multiple POS tagsets ranging from a basic 24 tagset called Reduced TagSet (RTS) to an enriched tagset (ERTS) of 75 tags. AMIRA 2.1. achieves an accuracy of 96.6% for RTS and 96.13% for ERTS. ASMA, in contrast, uses a fuller tagset of 139 POS tags, which includes morphological information, e.g., on gender and number.

MADA+TOKAN 3.2 Habash et al. Habash and Rambow (2005; Habash et al. (2009) developed MADA, a system for the morphological disambiguation of MSA. MADA relies on the output of the Buckwalter Arabic Morphological Analyzer (BAMA) (Buckwalter, 2004) and uses 14 individual SVM classifiers for learning individual features, which makes it computationally costly compared to ASMA which uses a single classifier for each of the two tasks of segmentation and morphological disambiguation. TOKAN, a separate tool, performs tokenization on the output of MADA. For tokenization, Habash et al. report 98.85% word level accuracy and for POS tagging, 96.1% accuracy. MADA+TOKAN 3.2 perform segmentation similar to ASMA. However, MADA+TOKAN 3.2 depend on the underlying morphological analyzer. In contrast to ASMA, MADA+TOKAN 3.2 perform POS tagging yielding the fully specified morphological analysis in the ATB, which comprises 440 unique tags.

4 ASMA

4.1 Method: Memory-Based Learning

For both segmentation and POS tagging, we use *memory-based learning* (MBL) (Aha et al., 1991) classifiers. MBL is a lazy learning method that does not abstract rules from the data, but rather keeps all training data. During training, the learner stores the training instances without abstraction. Given a new instance, the classifier finds the k nearest neighbors in the training set and chooses their most frequent class for the new instance. MBL has been shown to have a suitable bias for NLP problems (Daelemans et al., 1999; Daelemans and van den Bosch, 2005) since it does not abstract over irregularities or subregularities. For each of the two classification tasks (i.e., segmentation and POS tagging), we use MBT (Daelemans et al., 1996), a memory-based POS tagger that has access to previous tagging decisions in addition to an expressive feature set.

4.2 Data Sets and Splits

We use segmentation and POS data from the Penn Arabic Treebank (PATB) (Maamouri et al., 2004), specifically, we use the following parts: ATB1V4, ATB2V3, ATB3V3.1 and ATB3V3.2 with different splits as described below. The textual basis of the treebank consists of newswire articles covering political, economic, cultural, sports, etc. topics. Table 1 presents for each part the number of words, the number of tokens (i.e., only clitics are split off), the number of segments (i.e., clitic and inflectional morphology is split off), the number of news reports, and the source of the reports (i.e., the news agency)[2]. As mentioned above, Arabic is generally written without diacritics. While the ATB does have a version with diacritics restored, for our experiments, we use the version without diacritics, for both segmentation and POS tagging.

For a fair comparison of ASMA to both AMIRA and MADA, we adopt two different data splits, AMIRA-SPLIT and MADA-SPLIT, with each split corresponding to the data splits used in the evaluations of these systems. The same splits are used both for segmentation and POS tagging. For the AMIRA-SPLIT, we follow the procedure by Diab et al. (2004), but we use more recent releases of the ATB than Diab et al. We split each of the first three parts into 10% development data (DEV), 80% training data (TRAIN), and 10% test data (TEST). We then concatenate the respective splits from each part. For example, to create a single DEV set from the three parts, we concatenate the 10% DEV data from ATB1V4, ATB2V3, and ATB3V3.2, etc. For MADA-SPLIT, we follow the MADA manual[3]. For this split, ATB1V4 and ATB2V3 and the first 80% of ATB3V3.1 are used as the TRAIN set, the last 20% of ATB3V3.1 are divided into two halves, i.e. DEV and TEST (each making up 10% of ATB3V3.1) respectively. The development sets are used for parameter and feature optimization.

5 Segmentation

5.1 Setup

We define segmentation as an IOB classification task, where each letter in a word is tagged with a label indicating its place in a segment. The tagset is {*B-SEG, I-SEG, O*}, where B is a tag assigned to the beginning of a segment, I denotes the inside of a segment, and O spaces between surface form words.

Procedure: We performed a non-exhaustive search for optimal settings for the following MBT parameters: the MBL *algorithm*, the *similarity* metric, the *feature weighting* method, and the *value* of the k nearest neighbors. The best setting used the IB1 algorithm with *weighted overlap* as the similarity metric, gain ratio (GR) as a feature weighting method, and a value of $k = 1$.

[2] The information is based on the LDC documentation at `http://www.ldc.upenn.edu/Catalog/docs/*`.

[3] `http://www1.ccls.columbia.edu/MADA`

Data set	# words	# tokens	# segments	# texts	Source
ATB1V4	145,386	167,280	209,187	734	AFP
ATB2V3	144,199	169,319	221,001	501	UMMAH
ATB3V3.1	340,281	402,291	551,171	600	An Nahar
ATB3V3.2	339,710	402,291	512,932	599	An Nahar

Table 1: Data statistics and sources

Our complete feature set comprises the six preceding characters, the previous tag decisions of all the six preceding characters except the character immediately preceding the focus character, the focus character itself and its ambiguity tag (*henceforth, ambitag*), and the seven following characters. For features, we tested (1) left only, right only, and left and right contexts across various *window sizes* and (2) different *types of information*, e.g., feature sets with/without previous tag decisions for left context, feature sets with/without ambitags of right context. An ambitag is a combination of all tags of the ambiguity set of a word.

Evaluation: We evaluate segmentation in terms of character-based accuracy, word level accuracy, and precision, recall, and F-measure for segments. For example, the word الولَايَات (*AlwlAyAt*, Eng. 'the states') has the correct segmentation ال + ولَاي + ات *Al+wlAy+At* and comprises 8 characters. If it is segmented incorrectly as الولَاي + ات (*Al-wlAy+At*), one of the 8 characters, the 'w' is incorrectly classified as I as opposed to B, and consequently, we have a character based accuracy of 7/8, a word level based accuracy of 0/8. On the segment level, precision is 50%, recall 33.33%, and the F-measure 41.65.

5.2 Segmentation Results

Table 2 shows the results for segmentation on the two data splits, AMIRA-SPLIT and MADA-SPLIT. For both data splits, the best features are the six preceding characters, the previous tag decisions of all the six preceding characters except the character immediately preceding the focus character, the focus character itself and its ambitag, and the seven following characters.

AMIRA-SPLIT: On the TEST data for this split, we reach an accuracy of 99.53%, a precision of 97.97%, a recall of 98.04% and an F of 98.01%. The segmentation accuracy is at 98.34% for words.

MADA-SPLIT: For this data set, we achieve an accuracy of 99.49%, precision of 97.72%, a recall of 97.85% and an F of 97.79%. Segmentation accuracy for words is at 98.10%

These experiments show that on the segmentation level, the MADA split is slightly more complex than the AMIRA split.

Our segmentation results are not fully comparable to the tokenization performance of AMIRA (Diab et al., 2004) since AMIRA does not split off inflectional morphology. MADA (Habash and Rambow, 2005; Habash et al., 2009), in contrast, does perform segmentation, but it is based on a morphological analyzer. ASMA, without the use of any external resources, achieved a word accuracy of 98.10% on the MADA-SPLIT, which is only slightly lower than MADA's 98.85% word accuracy.

6 POS Tagging

POS tagging is defined here so that each segment, rather than a full word (as in (Kübler and Mohamed, 2012)) or a token (as in (Diab et al., 2004)), is assigned a POS tag. For the experiments reported here, we modify the ATB tagset such that case and mood tags are removed since those are syntactic features that cannot be determined based on a local context. While AMIRA, similar to ASMA, does not predict case and mood, MADA does at the cost of some performance loss. The remaining tagset comprises 139 segment-based tags. The input for the POS tagger consists of gold segmented data. The reasons for this decision are mainly to allow us to compare our system to AMIRA, which also uses gold segmentation.

6.1 Setup

Procedure: We performed a non-exhaustive search for the best parameters described in section 5. We use the IGTREE algorithm. We identified the *modified value difference metric* (MVDM) as similarity metric, gain ratio (GR) as a feature weighting method, and $k = 1$ for known words

System	Split	Acc.	Precision	Recall	*F*	Word Acc.
ASMA	AMIRA-SPLIT	99.53	97.97	98.04	98.01	98.34
	MADA-SPLIT	99.49	97.72	97.85	97.79	98.10
MADA 3.2						98.85

Table 2: Segmentation results

and $k = 30$ for unknown words as optimal parameters. For both data splits, the following feature sets give optimal results on the DEV set: For known segments, the best feature set uses the focus segment, its ambitag, two previous segments, and the predicted tag of three previous segments. For unknown segments, the feature set consists of the five previous segments and their predicted tags, the focus segment itself and its ambitag, the first five characters and the last three characters of the focus segment, and six following segments and their ambitags.

Evaluation: We evaluate based on segments, i.e. on the units which were used for POS tagging, rather than on full words. We report overall accuracy as well as accuracy on known segments and on unknown segments.

6.2 POS Tagging Results

Table 3 shows the results for POS tagging on the two data sets given the settings and the feature set described above.

AMIRA-SPLIT: Using the feature set described above, we reach an accuracy of 96.61% on known words and 74.46% on unknown words, averaging 96.26% on all words.

MADA-SPLIT: We reach an accuracy of 94.61% on known words and of 86.00% on unknown words, averaging 94.67% on all words. In comparison, the results for unknown words are much higher. This is due to the fact that in the MADA split, we only have 593 unknown words while the AMIRA split has more than twice as many (i.e. 1261 unknown words).

These experiments show that for POS tagging, the MADA split is considerably more challenging than the AMIRA split. This means that even if results reported for MSA are based on the same sub-word analysis, the data splits have to be taken into account in a comparison as well.

Our POS tagging results are not directly comparable to AMIRA, because of the differences in segmentation and because of the different POS tagsets. They are comparable to those obtained with MADA using tokenization by TOKAN. Roth et al. (2008) report 94.7% accuracy on predicting 10 morphological types of features, the closest setting to our tagset. This is very close to the 94.67% we report using the MADA-SPLIT. Roth et al. report a slight improvement for an extended system using diacritic markers as additional input, but as Kübler and Mohamed (2012) have shown, automatic diacritization must be extremely accurate in order to be useful for POS tagging.

6.3 Experimenting with Other Tagsets

We also ran experiments with two other tagsets, the standard RTS tagset, which is composed of 25 tags, and the CATiB tagset (Habash and Roth, 2009), which comprises only 6 tags, in order to investigate the effect of using different levels of morphological and morpho-syntactic information in the tagset. The full tagset, as mentioned above, includes all morphological information, except for case and mood markers. The RTS tagset is a reduced version, resulting in a tagset that is similar to the English Penn Treebank tagset (Santorini, 1990). Using the RTS tagset also allows us to make our results more comparable to AMIRA. The CATiB tagset represents only the major word classes, such as noun or verb. We used CATiB because its tagset corresponds to traditional notions in Arabic grammar and because it was used in the Columbia Arabic Treebank (Habash and Roth, 2009).

For this set of experiments, we use the same parameters and feature settings as described in section 6.2 above. Thus, the results reported on this set of experiments are potentially suboptimal. In the future, we plan to tune the performance of ASMA with each of these tagsets. Table 4 shows the results of these experiments.

6.3.1 RTS

AMIRA-SPLIT: Using RTS, we reach an accuracy of 96.28%. This is very slightly higher than our results for the full POS tagset (96.26%), and it is very close to AMIRA's results when using

System	Split	Acc: known	Acc: unknown	Acc: all
ASMA	AMIRA-SPLIT	96.61	74.46	96.26
	MADA-SPLIT	94.80	86.00	94.67
MADA 3.2				94.70
AMIRA 2.1 - ERTS				96.13

Table 3: POS tagging results

Tagset	System	Split	Acc: known	Acc: unknown	Acc: all
RTS	ASMA	AMIRA-SPLIT	96.56	77.79	96.28
	ASMA	MADA-SPLIT	94.20	84.99	94.06
	AMIRA 2.1				96.60
CATiB	ASMA	AMIRA-SPLIT	97.88	79.27	97.59
	ASMA	MADA-SPLIT	96.04	88.36	95.92

Table 4: POS tagging results with the RTS and CATiB tagsets

the RTS. But note that AMIRA uses tokenization rather than segmentation; thus the results are not directly comparable. We also notice that ASMA's performance on unknown words improves by almost 3 percent points to 77.79%, as opposed to 74.46% using the full tagset. This is to be expected since guessing the morphological information for an unknown word is more difficult than guessing only the main category in RTS.

MADA-SPLIT: Here, ASMA reaches an overall accuracy of 94.06%. This is slightly lower than for the full tagset (94.67%), due to a drop in accuracy on unknown words, from 86.00% to 84.99% and a slight drop in accuracy on known words from 94.80% to 94.20%.

The results for the RTS on both data splits show that ASMA reaches state-of-the-art results, without using morphological analysis and while using a classifier not optimized for sequence handling, but which has access to previous classification decisions. The results also show that, in general, using the reduced tagset does not significantly change the difficulty of the task. In other words, giving up morphological information in the tagset in this specific case does not lead to higher tagging accuracy.

6.3.2 CATiB

AMIRA-SPLIT: With the CATiB tagset, ASMA reaches an overall accuracy of 97.59%, showing that an extreme reduction of the tagset to one completely devoid of morphological information increases tagging accuracy.

MADA-SPLIT: With the CATiB tagset used with this split, ASMA reaches an overall accuracy of 95.92%.

Tag	Conf. %	% of Error
NOUN	3.6	1.05
NOUN_PROP	8.16	0.62
ADJ	7.64	0.59
PV	7.76	0.30
PV_PASS	45.54	0.13
IV_PASS	45.23	0.12
ADJ.VN	43.23	0.11
IV	3.38	0.10
PVSUFF_SUBJ:3FS	7.36	0.10
NOUN.VN	31.14	0.09

Table 5: Example results per POS category and their respective confusable modified ATB POS tag

Both sets of experiments show that the amount of morphological and morpho-syntactic information present in the POS tagset has an influence on the difficulty of the POS tagging step, even though the connection is not always a direct one. Thus, if ASMA is used as a preprocessing system for upstream modules, it is necessary to choose the tagset with regard to the upstream task.

7 Error Analysis

We performed an error analysis to see which types of errors ASMA makes. Table 5 presents a confusion matrix for the ATB tagset we used in section 6.2. We provide results only with the AMIRA split, as the results for the MADA split are similar. The table is sorted based on the contribution the confusion pair makes towards the overall error rate.

The table shows that because of the high number of POS labels, each confusion case contributes only marginally to the overall error rate. The most likely errors involve nouns (NOUN), proper nouns (NOUN_PROP), and adjectives (ADJ). These errors can be explained via the characteristics of Arabic: Proper nouns in Arabic are generally standard nouns used as names. Thus, the same word can be used as either noun or proper noun, depending on the context. Additionally, unlike English, Arabic proper nouns are not marked by capitalization or other orthographic means. The noun-adjective distinction is not clear in Arabic: Adjectives can be used as nouns, and they share the same morphological patterns as nouns.

The next set concerns the POS tags PV_PASS, IV_PASS, and ADJ.VN. With the lack of diacritics, the classifier is prone to erring with regard to cases where diacritics play a crucial factor in carrying the grammatical function. Since passivization is marked using diacritics in Arabic, passive verbs also suffer from the lack of diacritics, both in the perfective (i.e., PV_PASS) and imperfective (i.e., IV_PASS) cases, and hence the misclassification and high percent of confusion between passive and active verbs in the data. Adjectival verbal nouns – i.e., ADJ.VN as in مُعلِن (*mu'lin*, Eng. 'announcing') – are also confused with adjectives as these two parts of speech have very similar contexts, especially given the lack of diacritic *nunation*[4] characteristic of the adjectival verbal noun.

8 ASMA in Comparison

As described above, ASMA performs both inflectional morpheme segmentation and agglutinative clitic segmentation, as well as fine grained POS tagging of Modern Standard Arabic (MSA). Compared to AMIRA, ASMA performs more fine grained morphological disambiguation due to ASMA's identification of inflectional morpheme boundaries. Compared to MADA, ASMA performs the same tasks, however without using a morphological analyzer. Given that restriction, it still achieves state-of-the-art results, only minimally lower than MADA's. One major advantage of ASMA is the high speed with which it operates: On a PowerPC 970 machine, with a Darwin Kernel Version 8.11.0 and 2GB memory, it takes ASMA about 5 minutes to process 100 000 words. Although we have not had the chance to compare ASMA and MADA in terms of the speed with which each operates, we believe that ASMA is significantly faster than MADA. After all, whereas MADA employs 14 individual SVM classifiers to learn individual features, ASMA employs a single classifier per task, segmentation and morpho-syntactic disambiguation. AMIRA is observably slower than ASMA. In addition, while the MBL framework in ASMA uses virtually no time to train, SVMs (which AMIRA and MADA use) are known for long training times. Its speed makes ASMA valuable especially for real-world tasks, such as information retrieval and extraction, and tasks depending on big data processing.

ASMA is flexible in terms of the granularity of its output as it renders morphological disambiguation with three different tagsets (i.e., the full ATB 139 tagset, the RTS, and the reduced CATiB tagset). As such, ASMA can be customized to different NLP tasks depending on the specific needs of each task. Both AMIRA and MADA also employ different tagsets. In the context of our introduction of ASMA, we have shown how it is that performance varies according to the size of the tagset used. To the best of our knowledge, this is the first report exploiting the CATiB tagset.

9 Conclusion and Future Work

In this paper, we have presented ASMA, a system for automatic segmentation and morpho-syntactic disambiguation of Modern Standard Arabic (MSA). We compared ASMA to the two most popular Arabic processing suites, AMIRA and MADA, and showed ASMA's advantages. ASMA has the advantages of speed as well as non-dependence on an external morphological analyzer (unlike MADA). It also identifies morpheme boundaries at a level more fine grained than AMIRA. Moreover, ASMA performs POS tagging with different degrees of granularity and hence can be customized according to an upstream task if used as a preprocessing system. For the future, we plan to investigate the utility of using a conditional random fields classifier either to complement or replace ASMA's current memory-based classifier. In addition, we will attempt to improve ASMA's performance based on our error analysis.

[4] *Nunation* indicates indefiniteness and refers to word-final diacritics occuring as a short vowel followed by an unwritten /n/ sound.

References

David Aha, Dennis Kibler, and Marc K. Albert. 1991. Instance-based learning algorithms. *Machine Learning*, 6:37–66.

Tim Buckwalter. 2004. Arabic morphological analyzer version 2.0. Linguistic Data Consortium.

Walter Daelemans and Antal van den Bosch. 2005. *Memory Based Language Processing*. Cambridge University Press, Cambridge, UK.

Walter Daelemans, Jakub Zavrel, Peter Berck, and Steven Gillis. 1996. MBT: A memory-based part of speech tagger-generator. In *Proceedings of the 4th Workshop on Very Large Corpora*, pages 14–27, Copenhagen, Denmark.

Walter Daelemans, Antal van den Bosch, and Jakub Zavrel. 1999. Forgetting exceptions is harmful in language learning. *Machine Learning*, 34(1-3):11–43. Special Issue on Natural Language Learning.

Mona Diab, Kadri Hacioglu, and Daniel Jurafsky. 2004. Automatic tagging of Arabic text: From raw text to base phrase chunks. In *Proceedings of the 5th Meeting of the North American Chapter of the Association for Computational Linguistics and Human Language Technologies Conference (HLT-NAACL)*, pages 149–152, Boston, MA.

Mona Diab, Kadri Hacioglu, and Dan Jurafsky. 2007. Automatic processing of Modern Standard Arabic text. *Arabic Computational Morphology*, pages 159–179.

Mona Diab. 2007. Towards an optimal POS tag set for Modern Standard Arabic processing. In *Proceedings of Recent Advances in Natural Language Processing (RANLP)*.

Mona Diab. 2009. Second generation AMIRA tools for Arabic processing: Fast and robust tokenization, POS tagging, and base phrase chunking. In *2nd International Conference on Arabic Language Resources and Tools*, Cairo, Egypt.

Nizar Habash and Owen Rambow. 2005. Arabic tokenization, part-of-speech tagging and morphological disambiguation in one fell swoop. In *Proceedings of the 43rd Annual Meeting of the Association for Computational Linguistics (ACL)*, pages 573—580, Ann Arbor, MI.

Nizar Habash and Ryan Roth. 2009. CATiB: The Columbia Arabic Treebank. In *Proceedings of the ACL-IJCNLP 2009 Conference Short Papers*, pages 221–224, Suntec, Singapore.

Nizar Habash, Owen Rambow, and Ryan Roth. 2009. MADA+TOKAN: A toolkit for Arabic tokenization, diacritization, morphological disambiguation, POS tagging, stemming and lemmatization. In *Proceedings of the Second International Conference on Arabic Language Resources and Tools*, pages 102–109, Cairo, Egypt.

Jan Hajič. 2000. Morphological tagging: Data vs. dictionaries. In *Proceedings of the1st conference of the North American Chapter of the Association for Computational Linguistics*, pages 94–101.

Sandra Kübler and Emad Mohamed. 2012. Part of speech tagging for Arabic. *Natural Language Engineering*, 18(4):521–548.

Mohamed Maamouri, Anne Bies, Tim Buckwalter, and W. Mekki. 2004. The Penn Arabic Treebank: Building a large-scale annotated Arabic corpus. In *NEMLAR Conference on Arabic Language Resources and Tools*, pages 102–109.

Emad Mohamed and Sandra Kübler. 2010. Is arabic part of speech tagging feasible without word segmentation? In *Human Language Technologies: The 2010 Annual Conference of the North American Chapter of the Association for Computational Linguistics*, pages 705–708. Association for Computational Linguistics.

Lance A. Ramshaw and Mitchell P. Marcus. 1995. Text chunking using transformation-based learning. In *Proceedings of the ACL 3rd Workshop on Very Large Corpora*, pages 82–94, Cambridge, MA.

Ryan Roth, Owen Rambow, Nizar Habash, Mona Diab, and Cynthia Rudin. 2008. Arabic morphological tagging, diacritization, and lemmatization using lexeme models and feature ranking. In *Proceedings of ACL-08: HLT, Short Papers*, pages 117–120, Columbus, Ohio.

Beatrice Santorini. 1990. Part-of-speech tagging guidelines for the Penn Treebank Project. Department of Computer and Information Science, University of Pennsylvania, 3rd Revision, 2nd Printing.

Reut Tsarfaty, Djamé Seddah, Yoav Goldberg, Sandra Kübler, Marie Candito, Jennifer Foster, Yannick Versley, Ines Rehbein, and Lamia Tounsi. 2010. Statistical parsing of morphologically rich languages (SPMRL): What, how and whither. In *Proceedings of the NAACL Workshop on Statistical Parsing of Morphologically Rich Languages*, Los Angeles, CA.

Optimising Tree Edit Distance with Subtrees for Textual Entailment

Maytham Alabbas
Department of Computer Science,
College of Science, Basrah University,
Basrah, Iraq
maytham.alabbas@gmail.com

Allan Ramsay
School of Computer Science,
University of Manchester,
Manchester, M13 9PL, UK
Allan.Ramsa@manchester.ac.uk

Abstract

This paper introduces a method for improving tree edit distance (TED) for textual entailment. We explore two ways of improving TED: we extend the standard TED to use edit operations that apply to subtrees as well as to single nodes; and we use the 'artificial bee colony' algorithm (ABC) to estimate the cost of edit operations for single nodes and subtrees and to determine thresholds. The preliminary results of the current work for checking entailment between two texts are encouraging compared with the common bag-of-words, string edit distance and standard TED algorithms.

1 Introduction

One key task for natural language systems is to determine whether one natural language sentence entails another. *Entailment* can be defined as a relationship between two sentences where the truth of one sentence, the entailing expression, forces the truth of another sentence, what is entailed. Many natural language processing (NLP) tasks such as information extraction and question answering have to cope with this notion.

An alternative formulation for the entailment between two texts is given by the *recognising textual entailment* (RTE) paradigm, which contrasts with the standard definition of entailment above. Dagan et al. (2005) describe RTE as a task of determining, for two sentences *text T* and *hypothesis H*, whether *"...typically, a human reading T would infer that H is most likely true."* According to these authors, entailment holds if the truth of *H*, *as interpreted by a typical language user*, can be inferred from the meaning of *T*. This notion of entailment is less rigorous, and less clearly defined, than the standard notion, but it can be useful for a number of tasks, and has been investigated very extensively in recent times.

Tree edit distance (TED), which models *T-H* pairs by explicitly transforming *T* into *H* via a minimal cost sequence of editing operations, has been widely used for this task. Using TED poses two challenges: the standard three operations (i.e. deletion, insertion and exchange) apply only to single nodes, rather than to subtrees; and estimating a combination of costs for these operations with threshold(s) is hard when dealing with complex problems. This is because alterations in these costs or choosing a different combination of them can lead to drastic changes in TED performance (Mehdad and Magnini, 2009).

In order to overcome these challenges, we have extended the standard TED to deal with subtree operations as well as operations on single nodes. This allows the algorithm to treat semantically coherent parts of the tree as single items, thus allowing for instance entire modifiers (such as prepositional phrase (PPs)) to be inserted or deleted as single units. We have also applied the artificial bee colony (ABC) algorithm (Akay and Karaboga, 2012) to estimate costs both of edit operations (single node and subtree) and of threshold(s).

The work was carried out as part of an attempt to build a textual entailment (TE) system for modern standard Arabic (MSA)(Alabbas, 2011). MSA poses a number of problems that, while familiar from other languages, make tasks such as TE particularly difficult for this language–the lack of diacritics in written MSA combines with the complex derivational and inflectional morphology of the language to produce worse levels of lexical ambiguity than occur in many other languages; the combination of free word-order, pro-drop, verbless sentences and complex nominals produces higher levels of syntactic ambiguity than occur in many other languages; and the combination of these combinations makes things even worse. We have tested our algorithms on a corpus of MSA *T-H* pairs. This corpus contains 600 pairs, binary annotated as 'yes' and 'no' (a 50%-50% split). The average length of sentence in this dataset is 25 words per sentence, with some sentences containing 40+ words (see (Alabbas, 2013) for further details of this dataset and description of the methodology used for collecting it). In order to maintain comparability with work on TE for English, in Section 4 we have replicated a number of standard techniques (bag-of-words, Levenshtein distance on strings, standard TED). These experiments show that the extended version of TED, ETED, improves the performance of our technique for Arabic by around 3% in f-score and around 2% in accuracy compared with a number of well-known techniques. The relative performance of the standard techniques on our Arabic testset replicates the results reported for these techniques for English testsets. We have also applied our ETED to the English RTE2 testset, where it again outperforms the standard version of TED.

2 TED for RTE

The idea here is to convert both *T* and *H* from natural language expressions into parse trees through parsing and then to explicitly transform *T*'s parse tree into *H*'s parse tree, using a sequence of edit operations (Kouylekov and Magnini, 2005; Bar-Haim et al., 2007; Harmeling, 2009; Mehdad and Magnini, 2009; Wang and Manning, 2010; Heilman and Smith, 2010; Stern et al., 2012). If a low-cost transformation sequence can be found then it may be that *T* entails *H*. Dependency parsers (Kübler et al., 2009) are popular for this task, as in other NLP areas in recent years, since they allow us to be sensitive to the fact that the links in a dependency tree carry linguistic information about relations between complex units.

Different sets of operations on trees, using various types of transformations in order to derive *H* from *T*, have been suggested. Herrera et al. (2005), for instance, used the notion of tree inclusion (Kilpeläinen, 1992), which obtained one tree from another by deleting nodes. Herrera et al. (2006) and Marsi et al. (2006) used a tree alignment algorithm (Meyers et al., 1996), which produces a multiple sequence alignment on a set of sequences over a fixed tree. TED (Zhang and Shasha, 1989; Klein et al., 2000; Pawlik and Augsten, 2011) is another example of a transformation-based model in that it computes the minimum cost sequence of transformations (e.g. insertion, deletion and exchange of nodes) that turns one tree into the other. To obtain more accurate predictions, it is important to define an appropriate inventory of edit operations and assign appropriate costs to the edit operations during a training stage (Kouylekov and Magnini, 2005; Harmeling, 2009). For instance, exchanging a noun with its synonyms or hypernyms should cost less than exchanging it with an unrelated word. Heilman and Smith (2010) extended the above mentioned operations (e.g. move-sibling, relabel-edge, move-subtree, etc.), since the available edit operations are limited in capturing certain interesting and prevalent semantic phenomena. Similarly, a heuristic set of 28 edit operations, which include numbers of node-exchanges and restructuring of the entire parse tree, is suggested (Harmeling, 2009).

TED-based inference requires the specification of a cost for each edit operation and a threshold for the total cost of the edit sequence. Selecting a best set of costs and a suitable threshold is challenging. Some researchers have defined costs manually (Kouylekov and Magnini, 2005), but they are usually learned automatically (Harmeling, 2009; Wang and Manning, 2010; Heilman and Smith, 2010; Stern and Dagan, 2011), e.g. Mehdad and Magnini (2009) have used particle swarm optimization (PSO), which is a stochastic technique that mimics the social behaviour of bird flocking and fish schooling (Russell and Cohn, 2012), for estimating and optimising the cost of each edit operation for TED.

2.1 Standard TED

In this paper we will use Zhang and Shasha (1989)'s TED algorithm (henceforth, ZS-TED), which is an efficient technique based on dynamic programming to calculate the approximate tree matching for two rooted ordered trees, as a starting point. Ordered trees are trees in which the left-to-right order among siblings is significant. Approximate tree matching allows us to match a complete tree with just some parts of another tree. There are three operations, namely deleting, inserting and exchanging a node, which can transform one ordered tree to another. A nonnegative real cost is associated with each edit operation. These costs are changed to match the requirements of specific applications. Deleting a node x means attaching its children to the parent of x. Insertion is the inverse of deletion, with an inserted node becoming a parent of a consecutive subsequence in the left-to-right order of its parent. Exchanging a node alters its label. Detailed presentation of ZS-TED can be found in (Bille, 2005): the main change that we make to the basic algorithm is to include extra tables for recording *which* operations were performed rather than simply recording their cost.

2.2 Extended TED

The main weakness of ZS-TED is that it is not able to perform transformations on subtrees (i.e. delete subtree, insert subtree and exchange subtree). In order to make ZS-TED deal with subtree operations, we need to follow two stages:

1. Run ZS-TED (without entire subtree operations) and compute the standard alignment from the results;
2. Go over the alignment and group subtrees operations (e.g. every consecutive *k* deletions that correspond to an entire subtree reduces the edit distance score by $\alpha \times k + \beta$ for any desired α and β in interval [0,1]).

We have applied this technique on Zhang and Shasha (1989)'s $O(n^4)$ algorithm but it will also work for Klein (1998)'s $O(n^3 log_n)$ algorithm, Demaine et al. (2009)'s $O(n^3)$ algorithm or Pawlik and Augsten (2011)'s $O(n^3)$ algorithm. The additional time cost of $O(n^2)$ can be ignored since it is less than the time cost for any available TED algorithm.

2.2.1 Find a sequence of single operations

In order to find the sequence of edit operations that transforms one tree into another, such as the pair shown in Figure 1, the computation proceeds as follows: create a new matrix called δ_2, which has the same dimensions as the matrix δ which is used to store the forest costs during ZS-TED to store the sequence of edit operations as a list. In particular, when the values of δ are computed, the values of δ_2 are computed, by using the edit operation labels: "i" for an insertion, "d" for deletion, "x" for exchange and "m" for no operation (matching). So, the final edit sequence to transform T_1 into T_2 in Figure 1 is **dddmmiiimm**.

The final mapping between T_1 and T_2 is shown in Figure 1. For each mapping figure the insertion, deletion, matching and exchange operations are shown with single, double, single dashed and double dashed outline respectively. The matching nodes (or subtrees) are linked with dashed arrows.

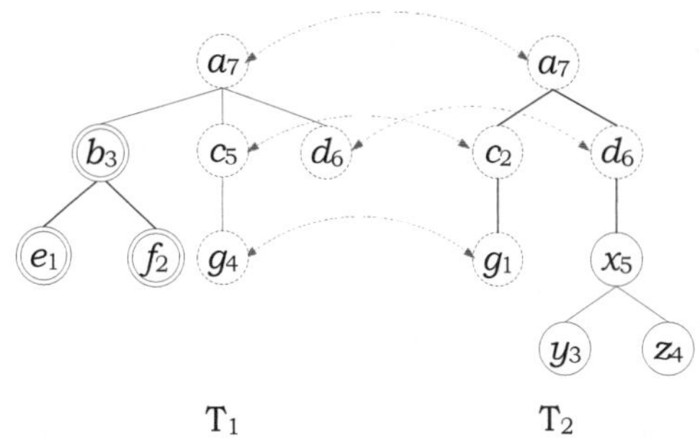

Figure 1: Standard TED, mapping between T_1 and T_2.

2.2.2 Find a sequence of subtree operations

Extending TED to cover subtree operations will give us more flexibility when comparing trees (especially linguistic trees). Thus, we have extended the TED algorithm to allow the standard edit operations (insert, delete and exchange) to apply both single nodes *and subtrees*.

Let $E_{p=1..L} \in \{$"d", "i", "x", "m"$\}$ be an edit operation sequence that transforms T_1 into T_2 by applying the technique in Section 2.2.1. Suppose that S^1 and S^2 are the optimal alignment for T_1 and T_2 respectively, when the length of $S^1 = S^2 = L$.

To find the optimal single and subtree edit operations sequence that transform T_1 into T_2, each largest sequence of same operation is checked to see whether it contains subtree(s) or not. Checking whether such a sequence corresponds to a subtree depends on the type of edit operation, according to the following rules: (i) if the operation is "d," the sequence is checked on the first tree; (ii) if the operation is "i," the sequence is checked on the second tree; and (iii) otherwise, the sequence is checked on both trees. After that, if the sequence of operations corresponds to a subtree, then all the symbols of the sequence are replaced by "+" except the last one (which represents the root of the subtree). Otherwise, checking starts from a new sequence as explained below. For instance, let us consider $E_h, ..., E_t$, where $1 \leq h < L$, $1 < t \leq L$, $h < t$, is a sequence of the *same* edit operation, i.e. $E_{k=h..t} \in \{$"d", "i", "x", "m"$\}$. Let us consider $h0 = h$, we firstly check nodes $S^1_h, ..., S^1_t$ and $S^2_h, ..., S^2_t$ to see whether they or not are subtrees. If E_k is "d," the nodes $S_h^1, ..., S_t^1$ are checked, whereas the nodes $S_h^2, ..., S_t^2$ are checked when E_k is "i." Otherwise, the nodes $S_h^1, ..., S_t^1$ and $S_h^2, ..., S_t^2$ are checked. All edit operations $E_h, ..., E_{t-1}$ are replaced by "+" when this sequence is corresponding to a subtree. Then, we start checking from the beginning of another sequence from the left of the subtree $E_h, ..., E_t$, i.e. $t = h - 1$. Otherwise, the checking is applied with the sequence start from the next position, i.e. $h = h + 1$. The checking is continued until $h = t$. After that, when the $(t - h)$ sequences that start with different positions and end with t position do not contain a subtree, the checking starts from the beginning with the new sequence, i.e. $h = h0$ and $t = t - 1$. The process is repeated until $h = t$.

So, the final edit sequence to transform T_1 into T_2 in Figure 1 is **++d+m++imm**.

The final mapping between T_1 and T_2 according to the extended TED is shown in Figure 2.

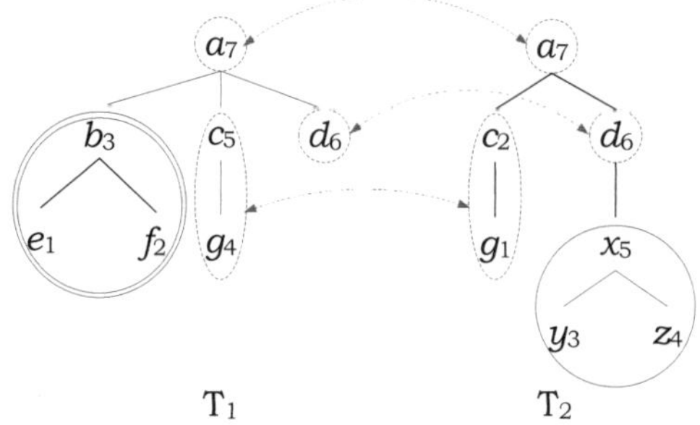

Figure 2: Extended TED with subtree operations, mapping between T_1 and T_2.

3 Optimisation algorithms

We used two optimisation algorithms, genetic algorithm (GA) and artificial bee colony (ABC), to estimate the cost of each edit operation (i.e. for single nodes and for subtrees) and threshold(s) based on application and type of system output.

3.1 GA

The GA starts with an initial population of solutions (known as chromosomes). In each generation, solutions from the current population are taken and used to form a new population by modifying the selected solutions' genome (recombined and possibly randomly mutated). This is motivated by a hope that the new population will be better than the old one. Solutions which are selected to form new solutions (offspring) are selected according to their fitness–the more suitable they are the more chances they have to reproduce. The algorithm terminates when either a maximum number of generations has been produced, or a satisfactory fitness level has been reached for the population. The main steps of the algorithm are shown in Algorithm 1.

Algorithm 1 The basic algorithm for GA.

```
1: Initialise population;
2: repeat
3:     Evaluation;
4:     Reproduction;
5:     Crossover;
6:     Mutation;
7: until (termination conditions are met);
```

3.2 ABC algorithm

In the ABC algorithm, the colony of artificial bees consists of three groups. First, employed bees going to the food source (a possible solution to the problem to be optimised) that they have visited previously. Second, onlookers waiting to choose a food source. Third, scouts carrying out random search. The first half of the colony consists of the employed artificial bees and the second half includes the onlookers and scouts. The number of employed bees is equal to the number of food sources. The employed bee of an abandoned food source becomes a scout. The main steps of the algorithm are shown in Algorithm 2.

ABC follows three steps during each cycle: (i) moving both the employed and onlooker bees onto the food sources; (ii) calculating their nectar amounts (fitness value); and (iii) determining the scout bees and then moving them randomly onto the possible food sources.

The ABC algorithm has been widely used in many optimisation applications, since it is easy to implement and has fewer control parameters.

4 Experimental results

To check the effectiveness of the extended TED with subtree operations, ETED, we used it to check the entailment between *T-H* Arabic pairs of text snippets and compared its results with a simple bag-of-words, Levenshtein distance and ZS-TED on the same set of pairs.

4.1 Systems

We have investigated different approaches that can be divided into two groups as follow.

Algorithm 2 Pseudo-code of the ABC algorithm (Akay and Karaboga, 2012).

SN size of population.
D number of optimisation parameters.
x_{ij} solution i,j, i = 1 ...SN, j = 1 ...D

Initialise the population of solutions $x_{i,j}$, i = 1...SN, j = 1...D, $trial_i$ = 0;
Evaluate the population;
cycle = 1;
repeat
  Produce new solutions v_{ij} for the employed bees (using $v_{ij} = x_{ij} + \phi_{ij}(x_{ij} - x_{kj})$, where $k \in \{1, ..., SN\}$ and ϕ_{ij} is a random number between [-1,1]) and evaluate them;
  Apply the *greedy selection* process for the employed bees (if the new solution v_{ij} has an equal or better nectar (fitness) than the old source, it is replaced with the old one in the memory. Otherwise, the old one is retained in the memory);
  Calculate the probability values $p_i = fit_i / \sum_{i=1}^{SN} fit_i$ for the solutions x_i;
  Produce the new solutions v_{ij} for the onlookers from the solutions x_i selected depending on p_i and evaluate them;
  Apply the greedy selection process for the onlookers;
  Determine the abandoned solution for the scout, if exists, and replace it with a new randomly produced solution x_i by $x_i^j = x_{min}^j$+rand[0,1]$(x_{max}^j - x_{min}^j)$;
  Memorise the best solution achieved so far;
  cycle = cycle+1;
until (cycle = Maximum Cycle Number);

Surface string similarity approaches

We tested the following approaches:

BoW: this approach uses the bag-of-words, which measures the similarity between *T* and *H* as a number of common words between them (either in surface forms or lemma forms), divided by the length of *H*, when the highest similarity is better.

LD$_1$: this approach uses the Levenshtein distance with 0.5, 1, 1.5 for cost of deleting, inserting and exchanging a word respectively.

LD$_2$: the same as for LD$_1$ except that the cost of exchanging non-identical words is the Levenshtein distance between the two words (with lower costs for vowels) divided by the length of the longer of the two words (derived and inflected forms of Arabic words tend to share the same consonants, at least in the root, so this provides a very approximate solution to the task of determining whether two forms correspond to the same lexical item).

Syntactic similarity approaches

These approaches follow three steps:

1. each sentence is preprocessed by a tagger and a parser in order to convert them to dependency trees, using a combination of taggers (i.e. AMIRA (Diab, 2009), MADA (Habash et al., 2009) and maximum-likelihood (MXL) tagger (Ramsay and Sabtan, 2009)) and parsers (i.e. MALTParser (Nivre et al., 2007) and MSTParser (McDonald et al., 2006)), which give around 85% for labelled accuracy (Alabbas and Ramsay, 2012; Alabbas and Ramsay, 2011), which is the best result we have seen for the Penn Arabic treebank (PATB). We use these combinations in series of experiments which involve;
2. pairs of dependency trees are matched using the ZS-TED/ETED to obtain a score for the pair;
3. either one threshold (for simple entails/fails-to-entail tests or two (for entails/unknown/fails-to-entail tests) are used to determine whether this score should lead to a particular judgement.

We tested the following approaches:

ZS-TED$_1$: this system uses ZS-TED with a manually determined set of fixed costs. The cost of deleting a node, inserting a node or exchanging a node are 0, 10 and 10 respectively.

ZS-TED$_2$: this system uses ZS-TED with a manually determined intuition-based set of costs that depend on a set of stopwords and on sets of synonyms and hypernyms, obtained from Arabic WordNet (AWN) (Black et al., 2006), as explained in Figure 3 (column A). These costs are an updated version of the costs used by Punyakanok et al. (2004).

ZS-TED+GA: this system uses a GA to estimate the costs of edit single operations and threshold(s) for ZS-TED. The chromosome for binary decision output is *{cost of deleting a node, cost of inserting a node, cost of exchanging a node, threshold}*, and the fitness is *a**f-score+*b**accuracy, where *a* and *b* are real numbers in the interval [0,1]. Providing different values for

a and b makes it possible to optimise the system for different applications–in the experiments below a is 0.6 and b is 0.4, which effectively puts more emphasis on precision than on recall, but for other tasks different values could be used. For three-way decisions, the chromosome is the same as for binary decisions except that we add a second threshold, and the fitness is simply the f-score. We used the steady state GA with the following settings: 40 chromosomes as population size, uniform crossover (UX), Gaussian mutation and maximum number of generations is 100.

ZS-TED+ABC: the same as ZS-TED+GA except using ABC instead of GA as the optimisation algorithm. We used the ABC algorithm with the following settings: 40 as the colony size and the maximum number of cycles for foraging is 100.

ETED$_1$: this system uses ETED with manually assigned costs. The costs for single nodes are the same for the ZS-TED$_1$ experiment and the costs for subtrees are half the sum of the costs of their parts.

ETED$_2$: this system uses ETED with the intuition-based costs for single nodes given in Figure 3 (column A) and the costs for subtrees given in Figure 3 (column B).

ETED+ABC: this system uses the ABC algorithm to estimate the costs of edit single operations and threshold(s) for ETED. For binary decision output, the chromosome is *{cost of deleting a node, cost of inserting a node, cost of exchanging a node, multiplier for the sum of the costs of the deletions in a deleted subtree, multiplier for the sum of the costs of the insertions in an inserted subtree, multiplier for the sum of the costs of the exchanges in an exchanged subtree, threshold}*. For three-way decisions the chromosome also contains the second threshold. For both cases the fitness is as for ZS-TED+GA. We do not include GA results for ETED, as extensive comparison of the standard GA algorithm and ABC on the ZS-TED experiments shows that ABC consistently produces better results for the same initial seeds and the same number of iterations.

The BoW algorithm and the basic string-edit algorithm are supplemented by the first two of the three procedures listed below and the others by all three, to ensure that we get the best possible performance at each stage:

- use AWN, OpenOffice Arabic dictionary and others as a lexical resource in order to take account of synonymy, antonym and hyponymy relations when comparing two words and when calculating the cost of an edit;
- take into consideration the POS tag when comparing two similar words (i.e. they should have the same POS tag);
- use a list of stopwords that contains some of the commonest Arabic words, which are treated specially when comparing words (e.g. by using different edit costs for them in distance-based approaches).

4.2 Results

We carried out experiments using the approaches above with two types of decisions as below.

Simple binary decision ('yes' and 'no'): *T* entails *H* when the cost of matching is less (more in case of bag-of-words) than a threshold. The results of this experiments, in terms of precision (P), recall (R) and f-score (F) for 'yes' class and accuracy (Acc.), are shown in Table 1. ETED shows a substantial improvement over bag-of-words and Levenshtein distance (around 19% in f-score and 6% in total accuracy) and over ZS-TED (around 2% in f-score and 2% in total accuracy).

Although we are primarily interested in Arabic, we have carried out parallel sets of experiments on the English RTE2 parsed testset,[1] using the Princeton WordNet (PWN) as a lexical resource, with the input text converted to dependency trees using Minipar (Lin, 1998). The pattern in Table 1 for English is similar to that for Arabic. ZS-TED is better than bag-of-words, ETED is a further improvement over ZS-TED.

Making a three-way decision ('yes,' 'unknown' and 'no' (not 'contradicts')): for this task we use two thresholds, one to trigger a positive answer if the cost of matching is lower than the lower threshold (exceeds the higher one for the bag-of-words algorithm) and the other to trigger a negative answer if the cost of matching exceeds the higher one (*mutatis mutandis* for bag-of-words). Otherwise, the result will be 'unknown.' The reason for making a three-way decision is to drive systems to make more precise distinctions. There is a difference between knowing that *H* does not

[1] http://u.cs.biu.ac.il/~nlp/RTE2/Datasets/RTE-2\%20Preprocessed\%20Datasets.html

Cost	(A) Single node	(B) Subtree (more than one node)
Delete	if X is a stop word =5, else =7	0
Insert	if Y is a stop word =5, else =100	double the sum of the costs of its parts
Exchange	if X subsumes Y =0, if X is a stop word =5, if Y subsumes or contradicts X=100 else =50	if a subtree S1 is identical to a subtree S2=0 else half the sum of the costs of its parts

Figure 3: Intuition-based edit operation costs for the systems ZS-TED2 and ETED1 (X in T, Y in H).

		Binary decision					Three-way decision		
Dataset	Approach	P_{yes}	R_{yes}	F_{yes}	Acc.	$F_{yes}\times$ 0.6+ Acc.$\times$ 0.4	P	R	F
ArbDS	BoW	63.6%	43.7%	0.518	59.3%	0.548	59.0 %	57.3%	0.581
	LD_1	64.7%	44%	0.524	60%	0.554	61.4%	58.0%	0.597
	LD_2	65%	47.7%	0.550	61%	0.574	62.9%	58.3 %	0.605
	ZS-TED_1	57.7%	64.7%	0.61	58.7%	0.601	64.3%	58.4%	0.612
	ZS-TED_2	61.6%	73.7%	0.671	63.8%	0.658	64.8%	58.3%	0.614
	ZS-TED+GA	59.2%	92%	0.721	64.3%	0.690	65.5 %	58.6 %	0.619
	ZS-TED+ABC	60.1%	91%	0.724	65.3%	0.696	67.8 %	58.2 %	0.626
	$ETED_1$	59%	65.7%	0.621	60%	0.613	65.3%	58.3%	0.616
	$ETED_2$	63.2%	75%	0.686	65.7%	0.674	66.7%	60%	0.632
	ETED+ABC	**61.5%**	**92.7%**	**0.739**	**67.3%**	**0.713**	**70.7%**	**62.4%**	**0.663**
RTE2	BoW	53.1%	49.9%	0.514	52.9%	0.520	50.8%	48.3%	0.495
	ZS-TED_2	52.9%	62.5%	0.573	53.5%	0.558	52.3%	50.2%	0.512
	$ETED_2$	54.2%	66.6%	0.598	55.2%	0.580	54.3%	52.7%	0.535
	ETED+ABC	**55.4%**	**70.1%**	**0.619**	**56.8%**	**0.599**	**55.7%**	**56.1%**	**0.559**

Table 1: Comparison between ETED, simple bag-of-words, Levenshtein distance and ZS-TED.

entail T and not knowing whether it does or not. Note that answering 'no' here means "I believe that H does not entail T", **not** "I believe that H contradicts T."

The results of this experiment, in terms of precision, recall and f-score for 'yes' class, are shown in Table 1. Again, ETED shows a worthwhile improvement bag-of-words and Levenshtein distance (around 6% in f-score) and over ZS-TED (around 4% in f-score).

5 Summary

We have described an extended version of tree edit distance (TED) that allows operations (i.e. delete, insert and exchange) both on single nodes and on subtrees. The extended TED with subtree operations, ETED, is more effective and flexible than the ZS-TED, especially for applications that pay attention to relations among nodes (e.g. in linguistic trees, deleting a modifier subtree should be cheaper than the sum of deleting its components individually).

We have also investigated the use of different optimisation algorithms, and have shown that using these produces better performance than setting the costs of edit operations by hand, and that using the ABC algorithm produces better results for the same amount of effort as traditional GAs.

The current findings, while preliminary, are quite encouraging. The fact that the results on our original testset, particularly the improvement in f-score, were replicated for a testset where we had no control over the parser that was used to produce dependency trees from the *T-H* pairs provides some evidence for the robustness of the approach. We anticipate that in both cases having a more accurate parser (our parser for Arabic attains around 85% accuracy on the PATB, Minipar is reported to attain about 80% on the Suzanne corpus) would improve the performance of both ZS-TED and ETED.

Acknowledgements

Maytham Alabbas owes his deepest gratitude to Iraqi Ministry of Higher Education and Scientific Research for financial support in his PhD study. Allan Ramsay's contribution to this work was partially supported by the Qatar National Research Fund (grant NPRP 09 - 046 - 6 - 001).

References

B. Akay and D. Karaboga. 2012. A modified artificial bee colony algorithm for real-parameter optimization. *Information Sciences*, 192(0):120 – 142.

M. Alabbas and A. Ramsay. 2011. Evaluation of combining data-driven dependency parsers for Arabic. In *Proceeding of 5th Language & Technology Conference: Human Language Technologies (LTC'11)*, pages 546–550, Poznań, Poland.

M. Alabbas and A. Ramsay. 2012. Improved POS-tagging for Arabic by combining diverse taggers. In L. Iliadis, I. Maglogiannis, and H. Papadopoulos, editors, *Artificial Intelligence Applications and Innovations (AIAI)*, volume 381 of *IFIP Advances in Information and Communication Technology*, pages 107–116. Springer Berlin Heidelberg, Halkidiki, Thessaloniki, Greece.

M. Alabbas. 2011. ArbTE: Arabic textual entailment. In *Proceedings of the Second Student Research Workshop associated with RANLP 2011*, pages 48–53, Hissar, Bulgaria. RANLP 2011 Organising Committee.

M. Alabbas. 2013. A dataset for Arabic Textual Entailment. In *Proceedings of the Second Student Research Workshop associated with RANLP 2013*, Hissar, Bulgaria. RANLP 2013 Organising Committee.

R. Bar-Haim, I. Dagan, I. Greental, and E. Shnarch. 2007. Semantic inference at the lexical-syntactic level. In *Proceedings of 22nd AAAI Conference on Artificial Intelligence (AAAI-07)*, pages 871–876, Vancouver, British Columbia, Canada. The AAAI Press.

P. Bille. 2005. A survey on tree edit distance and related problems. *Theoretical Computer Science*, 337(1-3):217–239.

W. Black, S. Elkateb, H. Rodriguez, M. Alkhalifa, P. Vossen, A. Pease, and C. Fellbaum. 2006. Introducing the Arabic WordNet project. In *Proceedings of the 3rd International WordNet Conference (GWC-06)*, pages 295–299, Jeju Island, Korea.

I. Dagan, O. Glickman, and B. Magnini. 2005. The PASCAL recognising textual entailment challenge. In *Proceedings of the 1st PASCAL Recognising Textual Entailment Challenges*, pages 1–8, Southampton, UK.

E. Demaine, S. Mozes, B. Rossman, and O. Weimann. 2009. An optimal decomposition algorithm for tree edit distance. *ACM Transactions on Algorithms (TALG)*, 6(1):2:1–2:19.

M. Diab. 2009. Second generation tools (AMIRA 2.0): fast and robust tokenization, POS tagging, and base phrase chunking. In *Proceedings of the 2nd International Conference on Arabic Language Resources and Tools*, pages 285–288, Cairo, Eygpt. The MEDAR Consortium.

N. Habash, O. Rambow, and R. Roth. 2009. MADA+TOKAN: a toolkit for Arabic tokenization, diacritization, morphological disambiguation, POS tagging, stemming and lemmatization. In *Proceedings of the 2nd International Conference on Arabic Language Resources and Tools*, Cairo, Eygpt. The MEDAR Consortium.

S. Harmeling. 2009. Inferring textual entailment with a probabilistically sound calculus. *Natural Language Engineering*, 15(4):459–477.

M. Heilman and N. Smith. 2010. Tree edit models for recognizing textual entailments, paraphrases, and answers to questions. In *Human Language Technologies: The 2010 Annual Conference of the North American Chapter of the Association for Computational Linguistics*, pages 1011–1019, Los Angeles, California, USA. Association for Computational Linguistics.

J. Herrera, A. Peñas, and F. Verdejo. 2005. Textual entailment recognition based on dependency analysis and WordNet. In *Proceedings of PASCAL Workshop on Recognizing Textual Entailment*, pages 21–24, Southampton, UK.

J. Herrera, A. Peñas, A. Rodrigo, and F. Verdejo. 2006. UNED at PASCAL RTE-2 challenge. In *Proceedings of the 2nd PASCAL Challenges Workshop on Recognising Textual Entailment*, pages 38–43, Venice, Italy.

P. Kilpeläinen. 1992. Tree matching problems with applications to structured text databases. Technical Report A-1992-6, Department of Computer Science, University of Helsinki, Helsinki, Finland.

P. Klein, S. Tirthapura, D. Sharvit, and B. Kimia. 2000. A tree-edit-distance algorithm for comparing simple, closed shapes. In *Proceedings of the eleventh annual ACM-SIAM symposium on Discrete algorithms*, pages 696–704. Society for Industrial and Applied Mathematics.

P. Klein. 1998. Computing the edit-distance between unrooted ordered trees. In *Proceedings of the 6th Annual European Symposium on Algorithms (ESA '98)*, pages 91–102, Venice, Italy. Springer-Verlag.

M. Kouylekov and B. Magnini. 2005. Recognizing textual entailment with tree edit distance algorithms. In *Proceedings of the 1st PASCAL Recognising Textual Entailment Challenge*, pages 17–20, Southampton, UK.

S. Kübler, R. McDonald, and J. Nivre. 2009. *Dependency Parsing*. Synthesis Lectures on Human Language Technologies. Morgan & Claypool Publishers.

D. Lin. 1998. Dependency-based evaluation of MINIPAR. In *LREC'98: Workshop on the Evaluation of Parsing systems*, pages 317–330, Granada, Spain.

E. Marsi, E. Krahmer, W. Bosma, and M. Theune. 2006. Normalized alignment of dependency trees for detecting textual entailment. In *Proceedings of the 2nd PASCAL Challenges Workshop on Recognising Textual Entailment*, pages 56–61, Venice, Italy.

R. McDonald, K. Lerman, and F. Pereira. 2006. Multilingual dependency parsing with a two-stage discriminative parser. In *10th Conference on Computational Natural Language Learning (CoNLL-X)*, New York, USA.

Y. Mehdad and B. Magnini. 2009. Optimizing textual entailment recognition using particle swarm optimization. In *Proceedings of the 2009 Workshop on Applied Textual Inference (TextInfer '09)*, pages 36–43, Suntec, Singapore. Association for Computational Linguistics.

A. Meyers, R. Yangarber, and R. Grishman. 1996. Alignment of shared forests for bilingual corpora. In *Proceedings of the 16th Conference on Computational Linguistics*, volume 1, pages 460–465, Copenhagen, Denmark. Association for Computational Linguistics.

J. Nivre, J. Hall, J. Nilsson, A. Chanev, G. Eryigit, S. Kübler, S. Marinov, and E. Marsi. 2007. MaltParser: a language-independent system for data-driven dependency parsing. *Natural Language Engineering*, 13(02):95–135.

M. Pawlik and N. Augsten. 2011. RTED: a robust algorithm for the tree edit distance. *Proceedings of the VLDB Endowment*, 5(4):334–345.

V. Punyakanok, D. Roth, and W. Yih. 2004. Natural language inference via dependency tree mapping: An application to question answering. *Computational Linguistics*, 6:1–10.

A. Ramsay and Y. Sabtan. 2009. Bootstrapping a lexicon-free tagger for Arabic. In *Proceedings of the 9th Conference on Language Engineering (ESOLEC'2009)*, pages 202–215, Cairo, Egypt.

J. Russell and R. Cohn. 2012. *Particle Swarm Optimization*. Book on Demand Ltd.

A. Stern and I. Dagan. 2011. A confidence model for syntactically-motivated entailment proofs. In *Proceedings of Recent Advances in Natural Language Processing (RANLP 2011)*, pages 455–462, Hissar, Bulgaria. RANLP 2011 Organising Committee.

A. Stern, R. Stern, I. Dagan, and A. Felner. 2012. Efficient search for transformation-based inference. In *Proceedings of the 50th Annual Meeting of the Association for Computational Linguistics*, volume 1, Jeju Island, Korea. The Association for Computer Linguistics.

M. Wang and C. Manning. 2010. Probabilistic tree-edit models with structured latent variables for textual entailment and question answering. In *Proceedings of the 23rd International Conference on Computational Linguistics (Coling 2010)*, pages 1164–1172, Beijing, China. Association for Computational Linguistics, Tsinghua University Press.

K. Zhang and D. Shasha. 1989. Simple fast algorithms for the editing distance between trees and related problems. *SIAM Journal of Computing*, 18(6):1245–1262.

Opinion Learning from Medical Forums

Tanveer Ali
University of Ottawa
tali028@uottawa.ca

Marina Sokolova
University of Ottawa & CHEO
sokolova@uottawa.ca

David Schramm
University of Ottawa & CHEO
dschramm@ottawahospital.on.ca

Diana Inkpen
University of Ottawa
Diana.Inkpen@uottawa.ca

Abstract

Our study focuses on opinion mining of several medical forums dedicated to Hearing Loss (HL). Surgeries related to HL are the most common surgeries in North America; thus, they affect many patients and their families. We have extracted the opinions of people from these forums related to stigma of HL, consequences of HL surgeries, living with HL, failures of HL loss treatments, etc. We performed a manual annotation first with two annotators and have 93% overall agreement with kappa 0.78 and then applied Machine Learning methods to classify the data into opinionated and non-opinionated messages. Using our feature set, we achieved best F-score 0.577 and 0.585 with SVM and logistic-R classifier respectively.

1 Introduction

The development of the Internet and of the user-friendly Web technologies profoundly changed the ways the general public can express their opinions on a multitude of topics. In order to make informed decisions, there is a necessity to develop methods that adequately – efficiently and effectively – extract new knowledge from the online messages (Bobicev et al., 2012). Opinions depend on individual's personality, culture and expectations of the society. Thus, opinions are challenging for independent external evaluation and categorization.

Natural language statements can be divided into two categories: facts and opinions. Facts can be expressed with topic keywords, while opinions are more difficult to express with a few keywords. They are the words of mouth on the web, e.g.,

Factual Sentence:
Most things come in somewhere between 40 and 105, depending on the frequency.

Opinionated Sentence:
I don't think you will find anyone who this level of amplification is undamaging, but the option is to not hear.

In this work, we have performed opinion mining of message posted on medical forums dedicated to Hearing Loss. Surgeries related to HL are the most common surgeries in North America; thus, they affect many patients and their families. Our current work aims to provide a tool that can extract opinions expressed by the general public. Understanding of what people think about the surgeries and their consequences helps health care providers to develop better health care policies and the general public outreach.

We collected data from web forums and we invited two annotators to manually annotate texts gathered from medical forums. We obtained the overall agreement of 93% and kappa was 0.78. Then we used a subjectivity lexicon and machine learning algorithms to automatically classify the posts. Our experiments with different combinations of features using different classifiers, i.e., Naïve Bayes, SVM and Logistics-R have shown significant improvement in F-score performance (55.7%, 56.8% and 57.8%, respectively) over the majority class baseline, which was 47.6%.

2 Related Work

A very limited work has been done on opinion mining on health related forums. Sokolova and Bobicev (2011) analyzed opinions posted on a general medical forum (i.e., the forum where the users discussed different health problems). The messages discussed health-related topics: medications, treatment, illness and cure, etc. The authors constructed a set of sentences manually labeled as positive, negative and neutral opinions. Among the three opinion categories, better results were obtained for the negative category (kappa = 0.365). For external evaluation of the labeling results, Machine Learning methods were applied on the annotated data. The best F-score = 0.839 was achieved by SVM. However, the authors used a small and imbalanced dataset, i.e., 169 positive and 74 negative sentences. Thus, the data had an inheritably high major class baseline of Accuracy = 70% and F-score = 57%. In our case, we used a considerably bigger and completely balanced data set having 93% overall agreement and 0.78 kappa between two annotators, with the majority class baseline of accuracy = 50% and F-score = 47.6%.

In (Goeuriotet al., 2012), the authors have built a medical domain lexicon in order to perform classification on a dataset that they collected from a website called Drug Expert. The dataset contains user reviews on drugs with ratings from 0 to 10 (negative to positive). The authors have performed the polarity detection on this dataset which already contains subjective information (opinions) about users' experience with particular drugs. However, in our case, we have extracted messages from health forums which publish both opinionated and non-opinionated posts.

3 Building the Dataset

We wanted our data be specific to the problem at hand. This is why we concentrated only a few health forums dedicated to Hearing Loss (HL). Although the very specific topic prevented us to have access to a high volume of data, at the same time, focusing on relevant forums only helped us to reduce the volume of unrelated messages. Also, we wanted to analyze the forum discussions, i.e., threads, which consist of more opinionated messages rather than questions and answers about the medical problems.

For the opinion mining, we have chosen a critical domain of HL problems: opinions about Hearing Aids. To the best of our knowledge, no relevant previous work was done in this area. For our dataset; we have collected individual posts from 26 different threads on three health forums[1].

3.1 Data Description

The initial collection of data contains about 893 individual posts from 34 threads. They were extracted using the XPath query by using the Google Chrome extension "XPathHelper".

This data was filtered and reduced to 26 threads by removing the threads in which people did not discuss Hearing Aids. The threads contained 607 posts in them. Table 1 lists the forum web sites, the number of threads collected from each forum, the number of posts gathered from each forum, and an average number of posts written by each author.

[1] http://www.medhelp.org, http://www.alldeaf.com, http://www.hearingaidforums.com

Forums	Threads	Posts	Avg. posts per person
www.hearingaidforums.com	7	185	2.9
www.medhelp.org	9	105	2.77
www.alldeaf.com	10	317	1.93
Total	26	607	2.53

Table 1. Filtered dataset collection statistics

We split the data from individual threads into sentences using our version of a regular expression based sentence splitter. We partly removed noise from the text by removing sentences containing very few words (4 in our case) as they did not convey well-formed opinions, for example:

Sentence: *No, educate me.*
Sentence: *Max AVERAGE SPL.*
Sentence: *Am I right ?*
Sentence: *It is permanent.*

The remaining sentences from the 26 threads were manually annotated by two independent annotators into two classes (opinionated and non-opinionated). There were several categories of opinionated and non-opinionated sentences. We provide the examples below.

Non-opinionated about Hearing Aids:

Factual on Hearing Aids:

So a doubling of 'power' equates to a 3dB rise in measured output.

Not relevant to Hearing Aids:

Lots of jobs in that field and I was pleased that I have met all of the qualifications.

Opinionated about Hearing Aids:

Positive

The aids you see discussed on this forum are designed with limiting factors intended to keep sound from being amplified to damaging levels.

Neutral/Unknown

I have yet to see an ENT indicate that properly adjusted hearing aids will either cause or not cause ear damage.

Negative

"I was referring to perception and in my understanding, even a duration of a few minutes can damage the ears."

In this paper, however, we work only with two broad message categories: opinionated about Hearing Aids and non-opinionated about them.

3.2 Subjectivity Lexicon

For our experiments, we used the Subjectivity Lexicon (SL) built by Wilson, Wiebe, and Hoffman (2005). The lexicon contains 8221 subjective expressions manually annotated as strongly or weakly subjective, and as positive, negative, neutral or both. We have chosen this lexicon over other large automatically generated dictionaries like SentiWordNet (Baccianella, Esuli, and Sebastiani, 2010), as it has been manually annotated and provides rich information with the subjectivity strength and prior polarity for each word considering the context of the word in the form of part of speech information.

The quality of this Subjectivity Lexicon is higher than the quality of other large automatically generated dictionaries; for example, SentiWordNet (Baccianella, Esuli, and Sebastiani 2010) includes more than 65,000 entries. Some papers (Taboada et al., 2011) have shown that larger dictionaries contain information which is not detailed and include more words which may lead to more noise.

Below is the sample entry from the lexicon:

type=strongsubj len=1 word1=boundless pos1=adj stemmed1=n priorpolarity=positive

This entry contains the term *boundless*, which is an adjective. Its length is 1 (single term), it is not stemmed; it is strongly subjective and positive. Similarly following are other entries from lexicon:

type=weaksubj len=1 word1=buckle pos1=verb stemmed1=y priorpolarity=negative

type=strongsubj len=1 word1=desiccated pos1=adj stemmed1=n priorpolarity=negative

Table 2 shows the relation between strong and weak subjectivity with the polarity lexicon.

	Strong Subj	Weak Subj	Total	Percent
Positive	1717 (30.8%)	1001 (37.74%)	2718	33.06
Negative	3621 (65%)	1291 (48.6%)	4912	59.75
Neutral	231 (4.14%)	360 (13.57%)	591	7.18
Total	5569	2652	8221	100
Percent	67.74	32.26	100	

Table 2. Distribution among subjectivity and polarity in the lexicon

4 Methodology

In this work, we have used several different features for the opinion mining of the sentences. Section 4.1 discussed the use of parts of speech in opinion mining. Section 4.2 lists all these features. These features are computed and presented for each sentence in a data file format used by the WEKA suite (Hall et al., 2009). Classification is performed based on the computed features and accuracy is measured using for different combinations of features in order to improve the classification performance.

4.1 Lemmatization

For all nouns and verbs, we have used the lemmatization using the GATE [2] morphological plugin which provides the root word. In case of noun the root word is the singular form of the plural noun, e.g., bottles becomes bottle, etc. In the case of verbs, the plugin provides the base form for infinitive, e.g., helping becomes help, and watches become watch. After performing lemmatization, we found 158 more words that were detected with same part of speech considered as the original. There were still 175 words which were found with the root word in the lexicon, but with different part of speech, e.g., *senses* was used as nouns in the data, after lemmatization it becomes *sense*, which exists as verb in the lexicon. Therefore it cannot be matched as the context and meaning of the word is different.

4.2 Features

All the features considered for the experiment are based on sentence level. Table 3 shows the final features selected for the experiments. The most common features were pronouns, followed by weak subjective clues, adjectives and adverbs.

STRONGSUBJ	# of words found as strong subjective in current sentence
WEAKSUBJ	# of words found as weak subjective in current sentence
ADJECTIVE	# of adjectives
ADVERBS	# of adverbs
PRONOUN	# of pronouns
POSITIVE	# of words found having prior polarity as positive
NEGATIVE	# of words found having prior polarity as negative
NEUTRAL	# of words found having prior polarity as neutral
PRP_PHRASE	# of phrases containing pronouns found in current sentence

Table 3. Final features considered for the experiments

[2] http://gate.ac.uk/sale/tao/splitch21.html#x26-52600021.11

5 Experiments

5.1 Manual Annotation

The dataset of 3515 sentences from 26 threads were manually annotated by two annotators. The annotators were asked to tag a sentence as opinionated if it conveys positive, negative or mixed opinions on hearing aids. All the sentences which do not contain any opinions are left blank and they are considered as non-opinionated. According to Table 4, annotator1 and annotator 2 did not put the opinionated label a large number of sentences, i.e., 2939 and 2728 respectively. We further considered them as non-opinionated.

	Annotator 1		
Annotator 2	Opinionated	Non-opinionated	Total
Opinionated	557		787
Non-		557	2728
Total	576	2939	3515

Table 4. Annotations statistics of Sentences between the two annotators

To evaluate the annotator agreement, we calculated *kappa* as in (Sokolova & Bobicev, 2011):

$$\text{kappa} = \frac{\frac{a+d}{N} - \frac{f1g1+f2g2}{N^2}}{1 - \frac{f1g1+f2g2}{N^2}}$$

The overall percentage agreement between the annotators for the dataset was 93% and kappa was 0.78. This indicates a substantial agreement between the taggers in both the cases.

5.2 Dataset preprocessing

Due to the large number of irrelevant sentences, the dataset is very much imbalanced. A balanced dataset is necessary for accurate classification, as in the case of imbalanced dataset as this, if all sentences are considered as non-opinionated, the accuracy of the system is very high (83%), as the non-opinionated class dominates the opinionated class in the dataset. To be exact, there are 557 opinionated sentences and 2728 non-opinionated sentences. For this purpose, we reduce the non-opinionated sentences by applying a version of the under-sampling technique (Barandela et al., 2004).

In contrast with a commonly applied random under-sampling, our under-sampling method selects only certain sentences to keep them in the data set. For each occurrence of an opinionated sentence, the next non-opinionated sentence is chosen to be kept, and the rest are discarded. The final dataset contains 1152 total sentences with 576 opinionated and non-opinionated sentences each.

5.3 Classification results

The output files generated by the system for both the datasets are classified using the WEKA (Hall et al., 2009). For our evaluation, we used 10-fold cross validation which is a standard classifier selection for classification purpose. Experiments were performed using three different classifiers: Naïve Bayes, support vector machine (SVM) and logistic regression (logistic-R). Performance was evaluated using the F1-measure between the three classifiers on the given datasets. The best performance for Naïve Bayes and support vector machine were 55.7% and 56.7% respectively with (strongsubj, weaksubj) feature. With Logistics-R the best performance was 57.8% with (strongsubj, weaksubj, pronoun) feature. It was found that the performance of logistic regression was the best on the features selected for our evaluation.

For the baseline, we considered the majority class baseline having 50% accuracy and achieved F-score 47.6%. For the gold classification standard, the feature vector of bag of words is considered. We have not considered the unique words for the bag of words because eliminating the words that appeared only once reduces the size of the vectors to half, and it makes it easier for the classifier to handle them. Also, these words do not contribute much to the post classification since they appear only once, i.e., in one post, and cannot be used to analyze other posts. From experiments, it was found that the gold standard result for our dataset was rather high for each classifier. Still, all the classifiers improved the results over the majority class baseline.

Opinionated vs. non-opinionated classification									
	Naive Bayes			SVM			Logistic-R		
	P	R	F-1	P	R	F-1	P	R	F-1
strongsubj,weaksubj	0.599	0.579	**0.557**	0.602	0.585	**0.567**	0.573	0.572	0.57
strongsubj,weaksubj,neutral	0.593	0.573	0.548	0.603	0.586	0.568	0.568	0.567	0.566
strongsubj,weaksubj,pron	0.583	0.565	0.539	0.586	0.574	0.557	0.585	0.582	**0.578**
all features	0.600	0.578	0.554	0.584	0.571	0.554	0.574	0.571	0.566
Gold Standard	0.628	0.626	0.624	0.628	0.626	0.624	0.590	0.590	**0.589**

Table 5. Comparison of performance between different features among three classifiers

Table 5 shows that the improvement was 8.1% for Naïve Bayes, 9.2% for SVM and 10.2% for logistic-R. We evaluated different sets of features for the classification performance. Table 5 shows that the best performance of all classifiers was with different feature sets, as for Naïve Bayes it was with (strongsubj, weaksubj) at 55.7%, for SVM it was with (strongsubj, weaksubj, neutral) at 56.8% and for logistic-R it was with (strongsubj, weaksubj, pron) at 57.8%. It was assumed that neutral word clues should indicate non-subjectivity, as they are neutral in polarity; however, the results did not show improvement with neutral features. This may be due to very limited neutral words in the lexicon, i.e., only 7.18%. The best classifier was logistic regression with the feature set (strongsubj, weaksubj, pron) with F1-measure 57.8%, which is slightly lower than the gold standard of 58.9% with logistic-R.

Opinionated vs. non-opinionated classification with lemmatization									
	Naive Bayes			SVM			Logistic-R		
	P	R	F-1	P	Re	F-1	P	R	F-1
Strongsubj,weaksubj,prp_phrase	**0.596**	**0.58**	**0.562**	**0.604**	**0.591**	**0.577**	**0.586**	**0.58**	**0.57**
strongsubj,weaksubj	0.604	0.58	0.554	0.605	0.591	0.576	0.584	0.58	0.57
strongsubj,weaksubj,neutral	0.600	0.582	**0.562**	0.597	0.583	0.568	0.584	0.58	0.58
strongsubj,weaksubj,pron	0.602	0.578	0.552	0.586	0.575	0.561	0.592	0.58	**0.58**
all features	0.602	0.58	0.556	0.593	0.582	0.569	0.582	0.57	0.57
Gold standard	0.628	0.626	0.624	0.628	0.626	0.624	0.590	0.59	**0.58**

Table 6. Comparison of performance with lemmatization between different features among three classifiers

As most opinions are expressed with the use of personal pronouns, we extracted the phrases that contain pronouns within sentences, e.g., I would assume, I feel as, I could sympathize. We consider the number of such phrases within sentences and evaluated the performance using combinations with other features. Also, to increase the number of matched words in the lexicon, all the nouns and verbs were lemmatized to see if the classification performance increases. The classification results show improvement for all the classifiers. It is interesting to note that Naïve Bayes and SVM both have shown their best performance with the feature combining subjectivity clues and phrases with pronouns, which indicate the significance of pronouns for subjectivity; however logistics-R performed best with subjectivity and phrases with pronoun features, but in this case pronoun phrase features show the 2nd best performance.

The classification performance in Table 6 increased with Naïve Bayes, SVM and logistic-R with 0.5%, 0.9% and 0.7%, respectively. Also note that the gold standard representation exceptionally performed better with Naïve Bayes and SVM, but with the logistic-R it was relatively comparable to our previous results and the performance with best features (strongsubj, weaksubj, pron) was just 0.4% less than the gold standard; so the results with (strongsubj, weaksubj, pron) are equivalent with the gold standard.

6 Analysis

The results from the experiments have provided various insights about opinion mining in health-related forums. For classification, the bag-of-words representation provided higher results than the other feature sets. We interpret this result an indication of the importance of the word meaning. The words were more important than their semantic orientation or polarity. We noticed that the subjectivity clues such as strong subjective or weak subjective labels from the lexicon have not increased the performance for identifying opinionated and non-opinionated sentences; they performed equivalently to the gold standard (i.e., bag-of-words). Also note that the bag-of-word representation (BOW) is a high gold standard that is hard to beat in many texts classification problems. In our case, a simple baseline of classifying every sentence into the most frequent class is outperformed by the BOW representation by 13.6% on average among all the three classifiers. This difference indicates how difficult the opinion mining task is. The personal pronouns such as *I, me, ours, yours,* etc. also play an important role, as these are commonly found in subjective sentences and the results have shown some improvement for features with pronouns. However, subjective clues and phrases that contain pronouns can lead to false prediction, e.g.:

Sentence 1:
I can understand *that once the lost gain has been reapplied, techniques such as compression can reduce the additional amount of SPL DB that is required.*

Sentence 2:
I understand *you will have to practice for some time with any type of hearing aid.*

Sentence 1 from our data is labeled by both annotators as non-opinionated but it contains ***understand*** which is strong subjective in lexicon; also ***I can understand*** contains a pronoun. At the same time, Sentence 2 contains the same strong subjective word and the same pronoun, but it is labeled by both annotators as opinionated in the data. It has been noted that **understand** has occurred more in non-opinionated sentences, which in part provides the reason for the high performance of the baseline.

Our results are comparative to other related studies. We achieved Precision = 0.604, Recall = 0.591 and F-score = 0.577 with (strong-subj,weaksubj,prp_phrase) feature set using the support vector machine classifier.

In general, for consumer reviews, opinion-bearing text segments are classified into positive and negative with Precision 56%–72% (Hu & Liu 2004). For online debates, the complete texts (i.e. posts) were classified as positive or negative stance with F-score 39%–67% (Somasundaran & Wiebe, 2009); when those posts were enriched with preferences learned from the Web, F-score increased to 53%–75%.

7 Conclusion and Future Work

In this work, we performed opinion mining of online messages related to Hearing Loss. We used several lexicon-based features together with the rule based features like pronoun phrases classification of opinionated and non-opinionated sentences. As categories, we considered sentences being opinionated if they contained opinions about Hearing Aids. Other sentences were considered as non-opinionated. Evaluations have been made using three different classifiers and it is shown that our proposed features outperformed the baseline classifier which uses only bag-of-word features.

In future work, we could use structural features, dialogue act features, and sentiment features (Biyani & Bhatia, 2012) for the subjectivity classification of sentences. The lexicon could be improved, as the domain lexicon created in (Goeuriot et al., 2012) has shown better results over other dictionaries for polarity detection.

Acknowledgements

This work was supported by NSERC and by the CHEO Department of Surgery Research. We thank Brian Dewar for his assistance in finding medical forums.

References

Baccianella, S., Esuli, A., &Sebastiani, F. (2010, May).*Sentiwordnet 3.0: An enhanced lexical resource for sentiment analysis and opinion mining.*In Proceedings of the 7th conference on International Language Resources and Evaluation (LREC'10), Valletta, Malta, May.

Barandela, R., Valdovinos, R. M., Sánchez, J. S., & Ferri, F. J. (2004). *The imbalanced training sample problem: Under or over sampling?.* In Structural, Syntactic, and Statistical Pattern Recognition (pp. 806-814). Springer Berlin Heidelberg.

Biyani, P., Caragea, S. B. C., & Mitra, P. (2012) *Thread specific features are helpful for identifying subjectivity orientation of online forum threads.*COLING.

Bobicev, V., Sokolova, M., Jafer, Y., & Schramm, D. (2012).*Learning sentiments from tweets with personal health information.*In Advances in Artificial Intelligence (pp. 37-48).Springer Berlin Heidelberg.

Eysenbach, G. (2009). *Infodemiology and infoveillance: framework for an emerging set of public health informatics methods to analyze search, communication and publication behavior on the Internet.* Journal of medical Internet research, 11(1).

Gillick, D. (2009, May). *Sentence boundary detection and the problem with the US.* In Proceedings of Human Language Technologies: The 2009 Annual Conference of the North American Chapter of the Association for Computational Linguistics, Companion Volume: Short Papers (pp. 241-244). Association for Computational Linguistics.

Goeuriot, L., Na, J. C., Min Kyaing, W. Y., Khoo, C., Chang, Y. K., Theng, Y. L., & Kim, J. J. (2012, January). *Sentiment lexicons for health-related opinion mining.*In Proceedings of the 2nd ACM SIGHIT International Health Informatics Symposium (pp. 219-226).ACM.

Hall, M., Frank, E., Holmes, G., Pfahringer, B., Reutemann, P., & Witten, I. H. (2009).*The WEKA data mining software: an update.* ACM SIGKDD Explorations Newsletter, 11(1), 10-18.

Hu, M., & Liu, B. (2004, August).*Mining and summarizing customer reviews.*In Proceedings of the tenth ACM SIGKDD international conference on Knowledge discovery and data mining (pp. 168-177).ACM.

Kennedy, A., & Inkpen, D. (2006).*Sentiment classification of movie reviews using contextual valence shifters.* Computational Intelligence, 22(2), 110-125.

Newman, M. L., Pennebaker, J. W., Berry, D. S., & Richards, J. M. (2003).*Lying words: Predicting deception from linguistic styles.* Personality and Social Psychology Bulletin, 29(5), 665-675.

Rhodewalt, F., & Zone, J. B. (1989). *Appraisal of life change, depression, and illness in hardy and nonhardy women.* Journal of Personality and Social Psychology, 56(1), 81.

Sokolova, M., &Bobicev, V. (2011).*Sentiments and Opinions in Health-related Web messages.*In Recent Advances in Natural Language Processing (pp. 132-139).

Somasundaran, S., &Wiebe, J. (2009, August).*Recognizing stances in online debates.* In Proceedings of the Joint Conference of the 47th Annual Meeting of the ACL and the 4th International Joint Conference on Natural Language Processing of the AFNLP: Volume 1-Volume 1 (pp. 226-234). Association for Computational Linguistics.

Taboada, M., Brooke, J., Tofiloski, M., Voll, K., &Stede, M. (2011).*Lexicon-based methods for sentiment analysis.* Computational linguistics, 37(2), 267-307.

Wilson, T., Wiebe, J., & Hoffmann, P. (2005, October).*Recognizing contextual polarity in phrase-level sentiment analysis.*In Proceedings of the conference on Human Language Technology and Empirical Methods in Natural Language Processing (pp. 347-354).Association for Computational Linguistics.

Yi, J., Nasukawa, T., Bunescu, R., &Niblack, W. (2003, November). Sentiment analyzer: Extracting sentiments about a given topic using natural language processing techniques. In *Data Mining, 2003.*ICDM 2003. Third IEEE International Conference on (pp. 427-434).

Annotating Events, Time and Place Expressions in Arabic Texts

Hassina Aliane
Research Center on Scientific and Technical Information, Algeria
haliane@hotmail.com

Amina Guendouzi
USTHB, Algeria
etudiantmil@yahoo.fr

Amina Mokrani
USTHB, Algeria
amina_mokrani@hotmail.fr

Abstract

We present in this paper an unsupervised approach to recognize events, time and place expressions in Arabic texts. Arabic is a resource –scarce language and we don't easily have at hand annotated corpora, lexicons and other needed NLP tools. We show in this work that we can recognize events, time and place expressions in Arabic texts without using a POS annotated corpus and without lexicon. We use an unsupervised segmentation algorithm then a minimalist set of rules allows us to get a partial POS annotation of our corpus. This partially annotated corpus will serve as a basis for the recognition process which implements a set of rules using specific linguistic markers to recognize events, and expressions of time and place.

1 Introduction

The considerable development of information and communication technology has fundamentally changed the way we access knowledge. To deal with the huge volumes of information, constantly increasing, efficient and robust technologies are needed. In this context, named entities (persons, places, organizations, dates ...) are requested in order to categorize, index, summarize, this information.

A very useful resource for conducting research in the area of NLP is an annotated corpus which can be used as data in the development of algorithms and as data in the evaluation of those algorithms (Mazur, 2012). However, natural languages are not all equal regarding the availability of such corpora. Arabic is among the resource-scarce languages and the Arabic NLP (ANLP) community still suffers from the lack of free available annotated corpora, electronic lexicons and other needed NLP tools. Moreover, there are no established (theoretical) linguistic studies to rely on, in the field of NER though there is recently an increasing interest from the ANLP community. We propose in this work a minimalist approach that allows recognition and annotation of key expressions in a raw corpus using only formal indices in the texts. This is not an exhaustive annotation of NEs but rather an empirical approach to provide a useful ANLP resource. The rest of the paper is organized as follows: section 2 is a survey of related work, section 3 describes our minimalist approach to event, time and place expressions recognition in Arabic texts, section 4 reports the results and evaluation of the approach and finally, we end with a conclusion and future work in section 5.

2 Related work

In the growing field of Information Extraction (IE), Named Entity Recognition (NER) refers to the recognition and categorization by types of person names, organizations, locations, numerals as well as time/dates. Nadeau and Sekine (2009) provide a pretty large survey of work on NER where we can find a large variety of NER tools for a few widely used languages. There are generally three main approaches to NER. Linguistic rule based, statistical based, and hybrid.

Rule-based methods are usually based on an existing lexicon of proper names and a local grammar that describes patterns to match NEs using internal evidence (gazetteers) and external evidence provided by the context in which the NEs appear (Zaghouani, 2012). Statistical and machine learning approaches generally require a large amount of manually annotated training data. Hybrid methods are a combination of the statistical and the rule-based approaches. A remaining challenge in the field is how to develop such systems quickly with minimal costs.

Unfortunately, the main efforts to build reliable NER systems for Arabic has been conducted in a commercial framework and the approach used as well as the accuracy of the performance are not known. Nevertheless, we can find recently interesting research works in this topic. Zaghouani (2012) surveys the most significant works in the field. Most of the reported work concerns recognition of proper names of persons and organizations. In (Traboulsi, 2006), we find a rule-based named-entity recognition model using local grammar and dictionaries and which gives good results when tested in a small- scale experiment with a Reuter corpus. Shaalan and Raza (2009) presented an Arabic NER system based on a rule-based approach, a dictionary of names, a local grammar and a filtering mechanism that rejects the incorrect NEs. The system obtained an F-measure of 87.7% for persons, 85.9% for locations, 83.15% for organizations and 91.6% for dates. Zaghouani (2012) described a rule-based system for Arabic NER which adapts a multilingual NER system to Arabic. The system obtained an F-measure of 61.54% for persons and 52.23% for organizations.

On the machine learning side, Zitouni *et al* (2005) developed a system which allows recognition of nominals, pronominals, references to entities and named entities. They used a maximum entropy markov model and the evaluation of their system on the ACE data set gave an F-measure of 69%. Benajiba also has a continuing work in this approach: Benajiba *et al* (2008) proposed a system that combines Support Vector Machine and Conditional Random Fields approaches. The system also used lexical, morphological and syntactic features and a multi- classifier approach where each classifier was designed to tag a NE class. The system obtained an F-measure of 83.5%. In his thesis, Benajiba (2009) concluded that no single Machine Learning approach is better than another for the Arabic NER task and that the best results were obtained when he used a multi- classifier approach where each classifier used the best ML technique to specific NE class. In another experiment, Benajiba *et al* (2009) explored a combination of lexical, contextual and morphological features. The impact of the different features has been measured in isolation and combined and an F-measure of 82.71% was obtained.

Related to event extraction, Abuleil (2007) presented a work for event detection in Arabic texts that is based on collecting key-word events like in natural disasters, bombing, elections ... The system was able to identify 439 events out of 467 on the test corpus.

Saleh *et al* (2011) described a Machine Learning approach to automatic detection of temporal and numerical expressions in Arabic texts based on processing the dashtag- TMP used in the Arabic tree- bank. The system obtained an F-measure of 73.1% for temporal expressions and 94.4% for numerical expressions.

3 A minimalist approach to recognition of event, time and place expressions in Arabic texts

3.1 Arabic Language

Arabic is a Semitic language spoken by more than 330 million people as a native language, in an area extending from the Arabian/Persian Gulf in the East to the Atlantic Ocean in the West. Arabic is a highly structured and derivational language where morphology plays a very important role. Arabic NLP applications must deal with several complex problems pertinent to the nature and structure of the Arabic language. For instance, Arabic is written from right to left. Like Chinese, Japanese, and Korean there is no capitalization in Arabic. In addition, Arabic letters change shape according to their position in the word. Modern Standard Arabic (the modern version of classical Arabic) does not have orthographic representation of short letters which requires a high degree of homograph resolution and word sense disambiguation.

3.2 Detecting Key expressions in Arabic texts

In order to provide an Arabic resource that will be useful for our NLP applications such as text summarization and question- answering, we propose an approach which is minimalist in the sense that it allows annotation of key expressions in a raw corpus of Arabic texts without any exhaustive pre- processing like POS tagging and without using dictionaries.

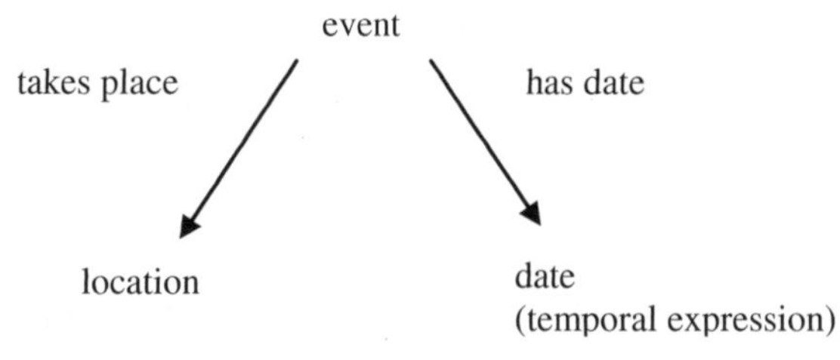

Figure1: structure of an event

The structure of event is relevant since at a conceptual point of view a structure of event engages participants such as actor, time and location. In this work, we adopt the conceptual event scheme as defined by Saval *et al* (2009) who built an ontology for natural disasters and which is shown in figure above.

We then, try to identify events, time and place expressions using surface indices from the texts. We don't deal with named entities of persons yet.

Segmentation and Partial POS tagging: As we have chosen to work by using only surface indices from the texts, we opted to adapt to our needs the algorithm described in (Aliane, 2011) which is an algorithm of segmentation based on Arabic linguistic theory. It is an unsupervised, knowledge-free discovery algorithm in the sense of (Bieman, 2006). It allows the discovery of the morphemes and affixes of the corpus without using lexicons or predefined tables of affixes as schematized in figure 2:

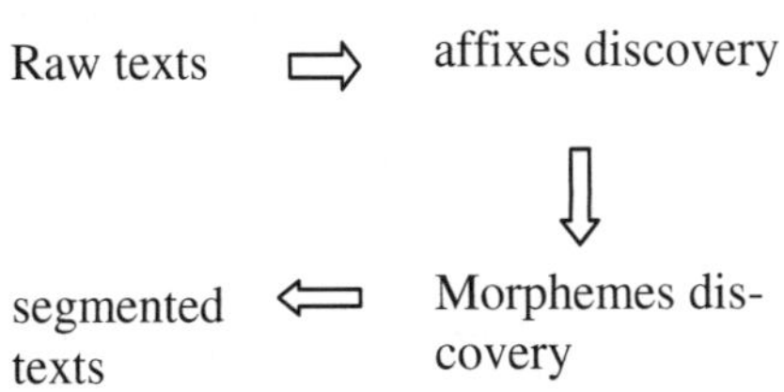

figure2: the segmentation algorithm

Nevertheless, this algorithm doesn't give the categories of the segmented units. It aims to simulate the underlying distributional analysis of the Arabic linguistic theory in a larger work (Aliane, 2011). The result of the segmentation process is [left affix +morpheme+ right affix]$_{<Lexie>}$; a lexie here, is a word between two pauses (a blank or a punctuation sign).

Then, our idea is that we can detect significant key expressions in the texts by adding to such segmented corpus some POS tagging by observing the texts in order to build a minimal set of rules depending on the form of the affixes. Arabic linguistic theory defines three part of speech which are: Noun (ism), Verb (fi'l) and Particle (harf) (Sibawayh, 77). Further sub- categorization can be found in (Ghoul, 2011). However, we don't aim at an exhaustive tagging so we manually build using the right and left affixes obtained by the segmentation process and other surface indices, a set of rules to annotate verbs and nouns in the corpus. From the indication of the affixes we obtained four rules, one for Noun (ism) and three for verbs: past, present and future. Nouns are labeled as <LN> for nominal lexie and verbs are labeled as <LV> for verbal lexie. We don't use the tense indication in this paper but we've made it for later work.

Besides the rules induced from the affixes, we have also two contextual rules which are:

R1/ if a lexie is preceded by "سوف" then annotate the lexie as verb at present time.

R2/ if a lexie is preceded by lexie$_1$ ϵ L then annotate the lexie as noun. L= { إلى، في، من، عن، على، عدا، حاشا، غير، إلا، لولا ،غير، إلا، لولا، سوى }.

Verbal Event detection: We are interested in this work only in the annotation of verbal events. Arabic grammarians define a verb as a form denoting "a happening" (حدث). This definition is sufficient to assume that any verb denotes à priori an event. Nevertheless, there are some lexies that have the form of verbs but that rather denotes modalities. The study of the classification and semantic of Arabic modalities is out of the scope of this work, thus, we apply a filtering rule to exclude the lexies which belong to the list of modalities and then every lexie annotated as verb in the partial POS tagging step described in the precedent sub-section will be annotated as a verbal event by adding the label <event>.

Temporal expressions detection: In this step, we identify non verbal linguistic units that convey temporal information by detecting temporal markers and then applying a contextual analysis right and left of the identified markers. This approach is inspired from (Vazov, 2001) and (Décles *et al*,1997). The detection phase looks for a particular set of markers (regular expressions) encoding temporal information. These markers can be stand- alone or trigger markers. The stand- alone markers represent autonomous temporal expressions. The contextual analysis is launched if the system identifies a trigger marker. A trigger marker signals the presence of a larger temporal expression and triggers a rule for the limitation and annotation of this expression. The contextual analysis determines the boundaries of the temporal expression in the analyzed utterance. The trigger markers are of two kinds:

M1 contains the markers which are linguistic units always appearing in the most right position in the temporal expression and that trigger a contextual analysis from right to left like: حين، منذ (when, since).

M2 contains markers which can be involved in any position in the temporal expression and that trigger contextual analysis both from right to left and from left to right such as: يوم، جانفي، دقيقة، (day, January, minute,).

We have grouped the observed stand- alone markers in Arabic texts in the set £ shown in table1. example: جاء صباحا. (he came morning.)

£
صباحا،مساءا،ظهرا،عصرا،عشاءا، مغربا، نهارا، ليلا، سحرا، فجرا، امسا، زوالا، غدا، ابدا، برهة، غدوة، الان، قط، هنيهة، قرنا، اسبوعا، يوما، عاما، خريفا، ربيعا، صيفا، شتاءا.

Table1: Stand-alone markers

The trigger markers are grouped in two sets M1 and M2 shown in Table2.

M1	M2
منذ حين	فترة، يوم، شهر, قرن، سنة،
مدة،	عام، ساعة، دقيقة،
غداة	عصر، ظهر، فجر، زوال، صباح،
طوال،	مساء، ليلة، ليل، نهار، أمسية،
طيلة	عشية، أمس، مساء، صبيحة،
بتاريخ	البارحة، ربيع، شتاء، صيف، خريف،
	السبت، الأحد، الاثنين، الثلاثاء،
	الأربعاء، الخميس، الجمعة
	جانفي، فيفري، مارس، افريل،
	ماي، جوان، جويلية، اوت، سبتمبر،
	أكتوبر، نوفمبر، ديسمبر
	تاريخ مثل: 15/ 12/ 2012، 10-12-2010

Table2: Trigger markers

Besides the markers in M1 and M2, we use some "heuristic" other markers which may determine the search space for the context analysis rules and they are the following sets:

D1 contains some adverbs that may precede a temporal expression as well as a location expression like: قبل، بعد (before, after)

D2 contains words that we find near to temporal expressions like: منتصف، بداية، (middle, beggining)

D3 contains words that denote numerals like: سبعة، ثمانية،

Context analysis rules: We have two rules: Rule1 which is triggered by markers from M1. On encountering a marker from M1, a left context analysis is launched (from right to left) by adding all encountered lexies left to the marker until we find a punctuation sign or a lexie which is labeled <LV> (verbal lexie) or a lexie labeled <L> (this means it remains ambiguous from the partial POS tagging step) and that does not belong to **£.**

example1: temporal expression detected by Rule1, a left context analysis is performed on encountering the trigger marker منذ.

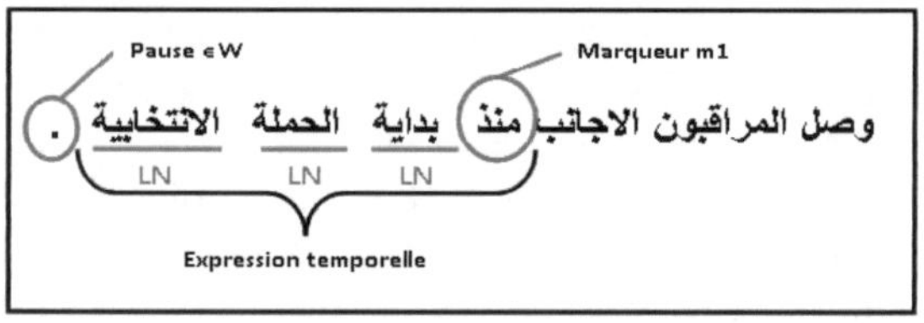

Rule2 is triggered on encountering a marker from M2, both left and right context of the marker are scanned. Analyzing the left context consists in building a larger temporal expression by adding all the lexies encountered until finding a punctuation sign or a lexie which is labeled <LV> (verbal lexie) or a lexie labeled <L> and that does not belong to **£.** The right context analysis adds all the lexies that are right to the marker if they belong to one of M1, M2, D1, D2, D3 and until encountering a lexie that doesn't belong to one of these sets.

Example2: temporal expression recognized when Rule2 is triggered by the marker العام (year)

Example3: Rule2 is triggered on encountering the marker يوم (day).

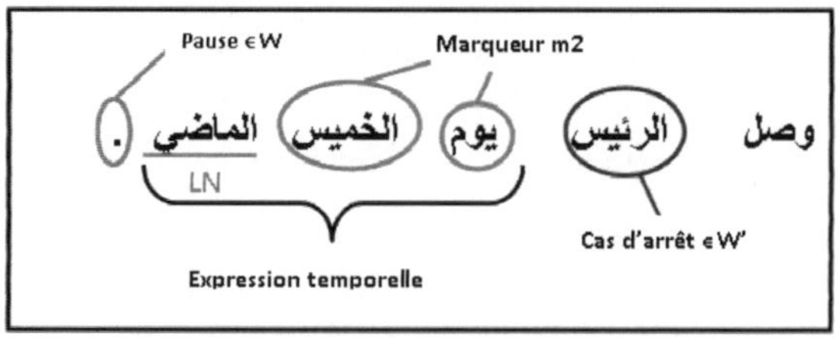

Place expressions detection: In order to detect location expressions, we also use surface markers from the texts. These markers are stand-alone markers or trigger markers. The trigger markers are lexies that always come in the most right position of the expression and trigger a contextual analysis from right to left. The location markers are shown in table3 below:

£	M
شرقا، غربا، شمالا، جنوبا، يسارا، يمينا	خلف، أمام، فوق، تحت، جنب، بجنب، قدام، وراء، اسفل، خارج، داخل، اتجاه، باتجاه، قرب، شرق، غرب، شمال، جنوب، وسط، يمين، يسار، في، بين

Table3: Stand-alone and trigger markers for place expression recognition

Then, we have one contextual analysis rule which is Rule3 and which principle is:

On encountering a marker *m* from M, a left contextual analysis is launched that builds a larger location expression by adding all the words encountered left to the marker until finding a punctuation sign or a lexie which is labeled <LV> (verbal lexie) or a lexie labeled <L> (this means it remains ambiguous from the partial POS tagging step) and that does not belong to £.or a particle (lexie which length is<3).

example4: place expression detected by rule3, the left context analysis here stops on encountering the two letter word ثم.

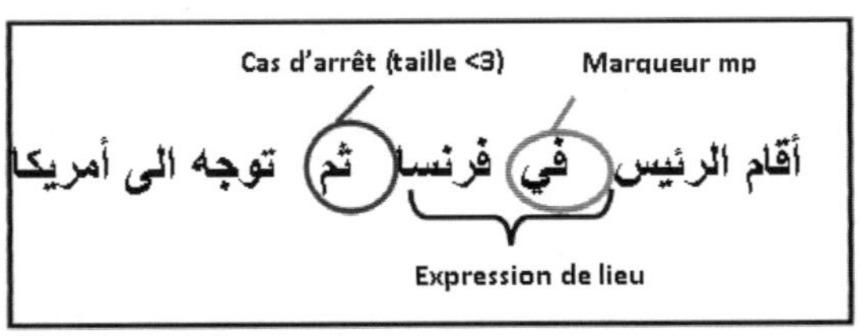

The overall approach is resumed in figure3

4 Results and evaluation

We have tested our system on a corpus of 30 articles from the web, written in Modern standard Arabic. The texts are not vowelized. The corpus is annotated by the tags <event> for verbal events detected, <Timex> for time expressions and <Pl> for place expressions, example is given in appendix1. The system was able to recognize 168 verbal events out of 268 and shows an F-measure of 84% for temporal expressions and 45% for place expressions. These recognition rates are influenced by the ambiguities left from the partial POS tagging step which didn't detect all the verbs and the nouns of the corpus.

Appendix1 shows an example of annotated text after processing.

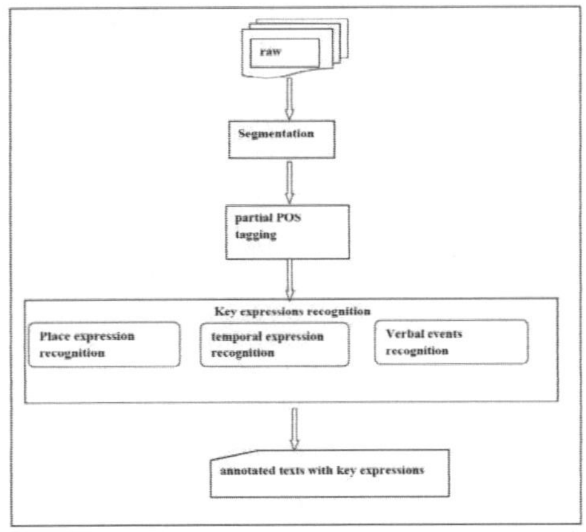

Figure 3 Architecture of the approach

5 Conclusion

We have shown in this work that we can perform annotation of key expressions in Arabic texts without any resources at hand. We have proposed a minimalist approach that uses only surface indices from the texts. We used those indices as markers to manually build a minimal set of general rules: two rules for time expressions recognition and one rule for location expression recognition.

This approach is independent from the nature of the texts. The results are encouraging and competitive with other works which use lexical resources or machine learning techniques. We aim to use these results to get further recognition and annotation by building contextual analysis rules where the time and location expressions already recognized help recognizing verbs and nouns that have not been annotated in the partial POS tagging step. This is possible by enlarging the conceptual schema of an event to involve the actor of the event. Hence, we can reiterate the whole annotation process to improve the scores.

References

Abuleil S. 2007. Using NLP Techniques for Tagging Events in Arabic Text. *the 19th IEEE International Conference on Tools with Artificial Intelligence.*

Aliane H. and Alimazighi Z. 2011. Discovering Arabic Structures: What a formal analysis can tell us?"

Special Issue on: "Computer Applications in Intelligent Natural Language Processing" of IJCAT, inderscience publisher Volume 40 n4.

Benajiba Y. 2009. *Named entity recognition*. Doctoral dissertation, Universidad Politecnica de Valencia.

Benajiba Y., Diab M., and Rosso P. 2008. Arabic named entity recognition using optimized feature sets. In *Proceedings of the Joint Meeting of the Conference on Empirical Methods in Natural Language Processing:* 284–293.

Benajiba Y., Diab M., and Rosso, P. 2009. Using language independent and language specific features to enhance Arabic NER. *Int. Arabic J. Inf. Technology:* 463–471.

Biemann C. 2007. *Unsupervised and Knowledge-free Natural Language Processing in the Structure Discovery Paradigm".* PHD Thesis, Leipzig university.

Desclés J.P, Cartier E, Jackiewicz E, and Minel J.L. 1997. Textual processing and contextual exploration method. *In CONTEXT'97, pages 189–197.*

Ghoul D. 2011. *Outils génériques pour l'étiquetage morphosyntaxique de la langue arabe : segmentation et corpus d'entraînement.* Mémoire de Master, Université Sthendal, Grenoble.

Mazur P. 2012. *Broad- coverage rule based processing of temporal information.* PHD thesis, Marcquarie University.

Nadeau D. and Sekine S. 2009. *A survey of named entity recognition and classification.* In Named Entities – Recognition, Classification and Use. S. Sekine and E. Ranchhod Eds., Benjamins Current Topics, Vol. 19, John Benjamins Publishing Company, Amsterdam.

Saleh I., Tounsi L. and J. Van Genabith ZamAn and Raqm: Extracting Temporal and Numerical Expressions in Arabic in Information Retrieval, Lecture notes in computer science vol. 7097, pp562-573.

Saval A., Bouzid M. and Brunessaux S. A semantic extension for event modelisation. *21st IEEE International Conference on Tools with Artificial Intelligence*

Shaalan K. and Raza, H. 2009. NERA: Named entity recognition for Arabic. *J. Amer. Soc. for Inf. Science .Technology. 60*, 8, 1652–1663.

Sibawayhi.1977. *"Al-Kitab",* in Haruin, al-hay'a al-misriyya l-amma li-l- kitab editions, le Caire.

Traboulsi H. N. 2006. *Named Entity Recognition:* A local grammar-based approach. Doctoral dissertation, Department of Computing, Surrey University, Guildford, U.K

Vazov N. 2001. A System for extraction of temporal expressions from French texts. proceedings of TALN 2001.

Zaghouani W. , 2012. a Rule- Based Arabic Named Entity recognition System. *in ACM Transactions on Asian Information Processing Vol. 11, No 1 Article2.*

Zitouni I., Sorensen J., Luo X., and Florian, R. 2005. The impact of morphological stemming on Arabic mention detection and coreference resolution. In *Proceedings of the Workshop of Computational Approaches to Semitic Languages (ACL'05).* 79–86.

Appendix1. Example of annotated text after key expressions recognition

واشنطن من كريغ غوردون : لقد مثل البيان الذي <EVENT> قدمته <EVENT/> هيئة الاستخبارات للرئيس بوش بخصوص <EVENT>تنظيم<EVENT/> القاعدة قبل وقوع هجمات <TIMEX> الحادي عشر من سبتمبر<TIMEX/> محك اختبار للرئيس بوش<EVENT> وادارته <EVENT/>. وقد اتضح بعد وقائع جلسة استماع <TIMEX> امس الاول<TIMEX/> ان هيئة لاستخبارات الاميركية كانت قد اكدت للادارة الاميركية احتمال قيام <EVENT> تنظيم <EVENT/> القاعدة بحملات اختطاف وشن بعض الهجمات الارهابية على الاراضي الاميركية.

وحسبما ذكر احد اعضاء هيئة المستشارين<PL> في لجنة التحقيق فقد اكد البيان الذي قدمه جورج <EVENT> <PL/> تينيت<EVENT/>للرئيس الاميركي<TIMEX> في السادس من اغسطس عام 2001 <TIMEX/> على ان اعضاء<EVENT> تنظيم <EVENT/>القاعدة كانوا<EVENT> يعيشون <EVENT/><PL> في الولايات المتحدة <PL/> <TIMEX> لسنوات عديدة <TIMEX/>وقد<EVENT> تمكنوا <EVENT/> لابعد من ذلك من تنظيم شبكة للدعم والتمويل <PL> في الولايات المتحدة .
<PL/>وكان مكتب التحقيقات الفيدرالي قد ابدى قلقا بالغا ازاء <EVENT> تواجد <EVENT/>اعضاء القاعدة <PL> في اميركا لدرجة <PL/><EVENT> جعلت<EVENT/> المكتب<EVENT> يوظف <EVENT/> نحو 70 من المحققين الميدانيين لتعقب اعضاء القاعدة <TIMEX> في صيف 2001 <TIMEX/>.

<EVENT> واوضحت <EVENT/> مذكرة هيئة الاستخبارات الاميركية ايضا ان اهتمام القاعدة بالخطف كوسيلة من وسائل الارهاب لم <EVENT> يتوان <EVENT/> للحظة وقال ريتشارد<PL> بين <PL/> <EVENT> فينسيت <EVENT/> عضو لجنة التحقيق <PL> في احداث <PL/> <TIMEX>الحادي عشر من سبتمبر<TIMEX/> ان مكتب التحقيقات الفيدرالي كان <EVENT>يقوم <EVENT/> بتعقب الانشطة المشتبه<PL> في صلتها<PL/> مع حوادث الاختطاف<TIMEX> في شهر اغسطس عام 2001 <TIMEX/>.

وبالرغم من تأكيدات ادارة الرئيس بوش على ان المصادر الاستخباراتية التي <EVENT> قدمت<EVENT/>لها <TIMEX> في صيف 2001<TIMEX/> قد اكدت فقط على الهجمات المحتملة لتنظيم القاعدة <PL> خارج الاراضي الاميركية بيد <PL/> ان عنوان البيان الذي<EVENT> قدمت <EVENT/> هيئة الاستخبارات الاميركية للرئيس الاميركي كان <EVENT> يتضمن<EVENT/> معلومات اخرى وهو <EVENT> تصميم <EVENT/> القاعدة على القيام بمهاجمة الاهداف الاستراتيجية <PL> داخل الاراضي الاميركية <PL/>وهذا ما<EVENT> يمكن<EVENT/>ان <EVENT> نلحظه<EVENT/> من ثنايا <EVENT> تصريحات <EVENT/> كوندوليزا رايس مستشارة الامن القومي الاميركي خلال مثولها للشهادة <PL> امام لجنة التحقيق <PL/> <PL> في اعتداءات <PL/> < TIMEX>الحادي عشر من سبتمبر يوم الخميس الماضي <TIMEX/> وذلك بالاضافة الى التصريحات والبيانات التي ادلى بها اعضاء هذه اللجنة. وقد<EVENT> اظهرت<EVENT/> هذه التصريحات والبيانات ان هيئة الاستخبارات الاميركية ومكتب التحقيقات الفيدرالية كانا على علم باحتمال وقوع بعض الهجمات الارهابية على الاراضي الاميركية ومحاولة هيئة الاستخبارات الاميركية لفت نظر الرئيس بوش الى وقوع هذه الاحتمالية وذلك من خلال التأكيد عليها<PL> في البيان <PL/> <EVENT>قدمته <EVENT/>الهيئة للرئيس الاميركي <TIMEX> السادس من اغسطس عام 2001<TIMEX/> والذي كان <EVENT>يسمى<EVENT/> بالبيان الرئاسي اليومي وقد<EVENT> تسلم<EVENT/> بوش هذا البيان بعد طرحه بوش لتساؤل عن احتمالية قيام القاعدة بمهاجمة الولايات المتحدة.

<EVENT> ومالت<EVENT/> رايس الى التأكيد على الاعتقاد السائد لدى البيت الابيض ان البيان ما هو الا معلومات قديمة قائمة على تقارير قديمة جدا<EVENT> وقالت<EVENT/> ان المذكرة لم <EVENT> تحذر <EVENT/> من هجمات محتملة على الولايات المتحدة الاميركية.

وقد فند اعضاء لجنة التحقيق من الديمقراطيين من الاعتقاد والادعاء ولكنهم<EVENT> اتفقوا<EVENT/> على ان البيان لم يكن <EVENT>يحتوي<EVENT/> على معلومات<TIMEX> دقيقة بشأن<TIMEX/> موعد مكان الهجمات .وعلى الرغم من ذلك فقد <EVENT> طرحت<EVENT/> جلسات الاستماع للجنة التحقيقات بعض المسائل المهمة والمركزية وهي ما هي المعلومات التي <EVENT>نقلت<EVENT/> لبوش عن التهديدات الارهابية ومتى اخبر بوش بهذه المعلومات وهذا هو سبب التركيز على بيان <TIMEX>السادس من اغسطس <TIMEX/> الذي قدم للرئيس بوش اثناء قضائه لاجازته السنوية<PL> في ولاية <PL/><EVENT>تكساس<EVENT/> وينظر البيت الابيض الآن <PL> في مسألة اعادة <PL/><EVENT> تقييم <EVENT/>ودراسة هذه المذكرة بيد ان رايس وبعض اعضاء لجنة التحقيق<EVENT> قاموا<EVENT/> بالكشف عن بعض من محتويات هذه المذكرة <TIMEX> يوم الخميس الماضي <TIMEX/>.وقد<EVENT> اوضحت <EVENT/> جلسة الاستماع ان ادارة الرئيس بوش كانت على علم بثلاث حقائق قبل احداث <TIMEX> الحادي عشر من سبتمبر<TIMEX/> فقد كانت الادارة الاميركية<EVENT> تعلم <EVENT/> بتواجد اعضاء القاعدة<PL> في الاراضي الاميركية وهذا<PL/> ما كان<EVENT> ينبئ <EVENT/>بحدوث بعض الهجمات الارهابية على الاراضي الاميركية وان القاعدة كانت<EVENT> تخطط<EVENT/> لمهاجمة الولايات المتحدة عن طريق انتهاج اسلوب الاختطاف لتنفيذ هذه المخططات. ولكن رايس اكدت على ان التهديدات التي يتم <EVENT> تحذيرنا <EVENT/> منها لم تكن محددة<PL> في الوقت ولا <PL/><PL>في المكان ولا<PL> <PL/>في اسلوب الهجمات وعليه فلم تكن هذه البيانات ذات جدوى واضحة <PL/> <EVENT> واوضحت <EVENT/> جلسة الاستماع ايضا الخلل الرهيب <PL>في التنسيق والتواصل بين البيت الابيض ومكتب التحقيقات الفيدرالي <PL/> <EVENT>وقالت<EVENT/> رايس ان مكتب التحقيقات الفيدرالي كان قد قام بجهود مضنية لتعقب اعضاء القاعدة <PL> في الاراضي الاميركية بيد<PL/> ان هيئة المستشارين <EVENT>قامت<EVENT/> بتنفيد ونفى<EVENT> تصريحات <EVENT/> رايس.

A Semi-supervised Learning Approach to Arabic Named Entity Recognition

Maha Althobaiti, Udo Kruschwitz, and Massimo Poesio
School of Computer Science and Electronic Engineering
University of Essex
Colchester, UK
{mjaltha, udo, poesio}@essex.ac.uk

Abstract

We present ASemiNER, a semi-supervised algorithm for identifying Named Entities (NEs) in Arabic text. ASemiNER does not require annotated training data, or gazetteers. It also can be easily adapted to handle more than the three standard NE types (Person, Location, and Organisation). To our knowledge, our algorithm is the first study that intensively investigates the semi-supervised pattern-based learning approach to Arabic Named Entity Recognition (NER). We describe ASemiNER and compare its performance with different supervised systems. We evaluate this algorithm by way of experiments to extract the three standard named-entity types. Ultimately, our algorithm outperforms simple supervised systems and also performs well when we evaluate its performance in order to extract three new, specialised types of NEs (Politicians, Sportspersons, and Artists).

1 Introduction

Named Entities (NEs) are textual references via proper names, such as first and last names, locations, and companies. Detecting NEs within unstructured text and classifying them into predefined categories of names is known as Named Entity Recognition (NER) (Grishman and Sundheim, 1996).

Arabic NER has been given great amount of attention over the past fifteen years. A number of Arabic NER systems have been developed using three approaches, which have been investigated thoroughly in the literature of NER. These approaches are rule-based (Shaalan and Raza, 2007; Shaalan and Raza, 2009), Machine Learning (ML) (Benajiba et al., 2007; Benajiba and Rosso, 2007; Benajiba and Rosso, 2008; Abdul-Hamid and Darwish, 2010) and hybrid (Abdallah et al., 2012; Oudah and Shaalan, 2012).

Over the past decade, some studies have explored the possibility of solving the problem of NER with a reduced level of supervision. These studies proposed semi-supervised and unsupervised systems, which no longer require annotated datasets and can be easily adapted to new types (Nadeau et al., 2006; Etzioni et al., 2005; Liao and Veeramachaneni, 2009; Liu et al., 2011).

This paper introduces ASemiNER, an Arabic semi-supervised NER system built under minimal supervision. Gazetteers (predefined lists of NEs) and annotated corpora are not required by ASemiNER. That is, ASemiNER is a bootstrapping algorithm that takes a few examples of a particular NE type as input and iteratively induces and learns patterns, which are used to extract more examples. Extraction patterns are induced and generalised automatically from data using very general criteria that require no human intervention, and no prior knowledge of the language or the corpus domain. In addition to the fact that ASemiNER extracts and recognises the three standard NEs (Person, Location, and Organisation names), it has proven to be an adaptable system that can be easily modified to extract new NEs without the need for analysing the dataset or collecting and tagging new large corpora.

The remainder of this paper is structured as follows: Section 2 includes background information on Arabic NER, including recent work. Section 3 illustrates the architecture of the proposed algorithm. Section 4 describes the corpora used in the experiments and the preprocessing steps used to prepare them. The experimental setup and the evaluation results are reported and discussed in Section 5. Finally, the conclusion features comments regarding our future work.

2 Background

2.1 State-of-the-art Arabic NER

Arabic has started to gain a significant amount of focus in large-scale projects, such as Global Autonomous Language Exploitation (GALE)[1] (Nadeau and Sekine, 2007). In addition, researchers have been making an effort over the past fifteen years to boost the performance of Arabic NER task.

Many Arabic NER researchers have employed rule-based techniques (Mesfar, 2007; Shaalan and Raza, 2009) that require experts. Thus, many ML methods, including Supervised Learning (SL) techniques, have been investigated in order to learn NE annotated decisions from training data. The most common SL techniques used for NER are Maximum Entropy (Benajiba et al., 2007), Support Vector Machine (Benajiba et al., 2008), and Conditional Random Fields (CRF) (Benajiba and Rosso, 2008)

Abdallah et al. (2012) proposed a hybrid NER system for Arabic in which they integrate the rule-based approach with the ML-based approach in order to optimise overall performance. Oudah and Shaalan (2012) contribute to the Arabic hybrid NER approach by investigating three different ML approaches including Decision Trees, SVM, and Logistic Regression, along with different features. Their system outperforms the state-of-the-art Arabic NER when applied to ANERcorp.

AbdelRahman et al. (2010) presented an integration approach between two machine learning techniques, CRF and semi-supervised pattern generation where the generated patterns were used as CRF features. Mohit et al. (2012) also investigated the problem of NER in Arabic Wikipedia using semi-supervised domain adaptation technique. They trained a model on newswire text based on standard supervised method. Then, they adapted the model with self-training on unlabeled target-domain data.

2.2 Semi-supervised techniques

Semi-supervised learning (SSL) is a relatively recent approach in the NLP community. It is still active and is likely to be improved and tested with various NLP tasks, including NER. The most common SSL technique is bootstrapping, which only requires minimal supervision, namely, a set of seeds in order to initiate the learning process (Nadeau and Sekine, 2007).

An early study that influenced later works (Riloff and Jones, 1999) propounds that the algorithm begins with a set of seed examples of a particular entity type (e.g., London is entity of type city). Then, all contexts (e.g., "State of <X >", "seminars in <X >") found around these seeds in a large corpus will be gathered, ranked, and used to find new examples. Pasca et al. (2006) used the same bootstrapping technique employed in (Riloff and Jones, 1999), but they applied the technique to very large corpora and managed to generate one million facts with a precision rate of about 88%.

Etzioni et al. (2005) proposed a system called "KnowItAll" that aims to automate the process of extracting large collections of facts, such as names of cities or movies from the web, in a domain-independent and scalable manner, starting with a set of predicates (e.g., City, and Country) and a set of generic extraction patterns. Furthermore, Nadeau et al. (2006) proposed a named-entity recognition system that combines named entity extraction inspired by the study of Etzioni et al. (2005) with a simple form of named-entity disambiguation. Their study's remarkable performances compete with baseline supervised approaches.

In 2009, Liao and Veeramachaneni proposed a simple semi-supervised learning algorithm using CRF. the algorithm starts with a small amount of labeled data (L) and a classifier that is trained on L. Then, the data D are extracted from unlabeled data using the trained classifier. The extracted data D with high confidence are added to the training data. At each iteration, the classifier trained on the previous training data is used to tag unlabeled data and so on (Liao and Veeramachaneni, 2009). Baroni et al. (2010) presented an algorithm that induces semantic information from naturally occurring text without supervision and requiring a small amount of pre-encoded knowledge, POS tagging, lemmatization of the corpus, and a set of extraction templates defined over POS sequences.

3 Methodology

Like most other semi-supervised algorithms, our algorithm contains 3 components, as shown in Figure 1.

[1] http://projects.ldc.upenn.edu/gale/

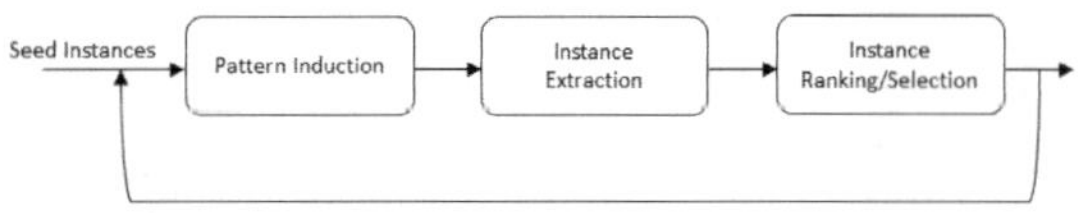

Figure 1: The Three Components of ASemiNER

Our algorithm begins with a seed list of a few examples of a given NE type (e.g., ‘Muhammad’ and ‘Obama’ can be used as seed instances for entity of type person) and learns patterns that are used to extract more examples (candidate NEs). These examples will be sorted and used again as seed instances for the next iteration.

3.1 Pattern Induction

3.1.1 Initial Patterns

ASemiNER uses a similar approach to that which was adopted in Baroni et al. (2010) to infer patterns, but with some modifications. Our algorithm infers a set of surface patterns that contain seed instances in the training corpus. So, for each seed instance x, we first retrieve all sentences containing the term x. Since words preceding or following the target word may be useful for determining its category, the algorithm extracts a number of tokens[2] on each side of the seed x without crossing sentence boundaries. Figure 2 is an example of initial patterns containing the seed instance (Muhammad) and its surrounding tokens.

Arabic Pattern:

- الدكتور/NN محمد/NNP البشر/NNP سفير/NN المملكة/NN العربية/JJ السعودية/JJ في/IN المغرب/NNP نوه/VBD

English Gloss:

- Dr. /NN Mohammed/NNP Albshr/NNP the/DT ambassador/NN of/IN Saudi/NNP Arabia/NNP in/IN Morocco/NNP indicated/VBD that/DT

Figure 2: Example of Initial Pattern

We will refer to each “Token/POS-tag” pair as “TP pair” (e.g., ‘indicated/VBD’ represents one TP pair). Noun tokens in TP pairs are kept in their inflected form, while verb tokens are replaced with their roots. For example, (*katabt* ‘wrote’)[3] and (*taktub* ‘writes’) will be changed to (*katab* ‘write’).

For each particular type of NEs (e.g., Person), lists of “trigger” words[4] (nouns and verbs) are provided as input. The lists of trigger nouns are semi-automatically extracted from randomly selected Arabic Wikipedia articles. Specifically, we extract nouns that appear most frequently before or after the NE and stored them as trigger nouns. Trigger verbs are the most frequent verbs (stems) that appear before or after NE in the Arabic Wikipedia articles. Trigger verbs and nouns, which surround NEs, are identified in order to find the most common Arabic NE indicators. Some examples of trigger nouns are: (*alsayd* ‘Mr.’), (*alsaydh* ‘Mrs.’), and (*bn* ‘the son of’) for a person’s name; (*madynah* ‘city’), and (*wilaayah* ‘state’) for location.

3.1.2 Generalisation

In the next step, the initial patterns are generalised. Therefore, all extracted initial patterns should complete the following steps in order to generate the final patterns:

1. TP pairs that contain nouns, and verbs are stripped of their “Token” parts, unless they are in the corresponding lists of trigger words. For example, TP pair (*alsayd/NN* ‘Mr./NN’) will stay unchanged since (*alsayd* ‘Mr.’) is in the list of trigger nouns, while (*qalam/NN* ‘pen/NN’) will be changed to only ‘ */ NN*’ as (*qalam* ‘pen’) is not among trigger nouns.

2. TP pairs that contain prepositions are not changed.

3. TP pairs that contain other parts of speech categories (e.g., proper noun, adjective, coordinating conjunction) are stripped of their “Token” parts. For instance, the token (*mufyd/JJ* ‘useful/JJ’) will be converted to only ’ */JJ*’ without the “Token” part.

4. All POS tags used for verbs (e.g., *VBP, VBD, VBN*) are converted to one form: *VB*.

5. All POS tags used for nouns (e.g., *NN, NNS*) are converted to one form: *NN*.

6. All POS tags used for proper nouns (e.g., *NNP, NNPS*) are converted to one form: *NNP*.

[2] Following a few trials, we found that a suitable number of tokens is 7.

[3] Throughout the entire paper, Arabic words are represented as follows: (*Qalam transliteration* ‘English translation’).

[4] Also known as keywords or indicators that form a window around the NE.

7. The seed instance is replaced with NE class tag (e.g., <PersonName>, <Location>, <Organisation>).

Figure 3 shows the final pattern resulting from the initial pattern, after the constrained processes mentioned above are applied:

Arabic Pattern

- /VB الدكتور/NN <PersonName>/NNP /NNP سفير/NN /NN /JJ /JJ في/IN /NNP

English Gloss

- Dr./NN <PersonName>/NNP /NNP /DT ambassador/NN of/IN /NNP /NNP In/IN /NNP /VB that/DT

Figure 3: Example of Final Pattern Produced by ASemiNER

All final patterns that are generated from the algorithm and their frequencies are first computed, and then gathered to form the pattern set (*P*). In the final step, two more patterns were generated from every pattern in *P*. Therefore, the algorithm split every final pattern into two parts, where each seed instance is located in the leftmost or rightmost position in the pattern. The two patterns generated from our previously mentioned example can be seen in Figure 4.

1- Rightmost position:

- /VB الدكتور/NN <PersonName>/NNP (Arabic Pattern)
  Dr. /NN <PersonName>/NNP (English Gloss)

2- Leftmost position:

- <PersonName>/NNP /NNP سفير/NN /NN /JJ /JJ في/IN /NNP
  <PersonName>/NNP /NNP /DT ambassador/NN of/IN /NNP /NNP

Figure 4: Two More Patterns Generated from the Final Pattern

The rationale behind this is to increase the generality of the patterns by making them shorter in length, thus increasing their ability to collect more candidate NEs in the matching process against the text. For example, the short pattern "*Dr./NN <PersonName >*" might successfully match more NEs in the text than the long pattern illustrated in Figure 3. However, short patterns, which have TP-pairs containing no "Token" parts at all, but POS-taggings, are a source of noise. Therefore, the final patterns set (*P*) is filtered every time a new pattern is added to it. Thus, repeated patterns are not added. In addition, any pattern consisting of less than 6 TP-pairs[5] should contain at least one TP-pair with "Token" part. Consequently, the pattern "*/VB /NN <PersonName >/NNP /NNP*" is rejected and not added to the set (*P*).

3.2 Instance Extraction

In this phase, ASemiNER retrieves the set of instances *I* from the training corpus that match any of the patterns in *P*. First of all, we should make sure that the generalisation steps used in inducing patterns are applied to the training corpus in order to prepare it for the matching process (e.g., VBD, VBP, and VBN are converted to VB and so on). The matching final patterns in *P* against the corpus is conducted using regular expressions (regex). For example, the regex for the pattern " */VB alductur/NN <PersonName >/NNP*" is depicted in Figure 5.

```
Arabic Regex: [^/]*/VB\s\bالدكتور\b/NN\s([^/]*)/NNP
English Gloss: [^/]*/VB\s\bDr.\b/NN\s([^/]*)/NNP
```

Figure 5: Regex Automatically Generated from a Final Pattern

Since the absence of capitalisation in Arabic, Arabic POS taggers might mistake some organisations and locations for nouns (*NN*) or adjectives (*JJ*), especially meaningful names. For example, (*alwlaayaat almutHdah alamrykyh* 'United States of America') might be tagged as *alwlaayaat/NNS almutHdah/JJ alamrykyh/JJ*. The ASemiNER system automatically generates regexes from final patterns without modifying them, regardless of whether the POS tags assigned to the proper nouns by POS tagger are accurate or not.

An informal experiment showed that most proper Arabic names are 2 or 3 tokens in length. Therefore, in order to increase the number of NEs collected in each iteration, we allowed the ASemiNER system to automatically add the information of average NE length to the produced regexes, as seen below:

```
Arabic Regex: [^/]*/VB\s\bالدكتور\b/NN(\s([^/]*)/NNP){1,2}
English Gloss: [^/]*/VB\s\bDr.\b/NN(\s([^/]*)/NNP){1,2}
```

Figure 6: Regex with Average NE Length

We have also noticed that increasing the average length of proper names to more than 2 tokens increases the recall but negatively affects the precision and quality of the collected NEs.

[5] Informal experiments show us that a pattern with less than six TP-pairs is more likely to be a noisy pattern, especially if its TP-pairs do not contain "Token" parts at all.

3.3 Instance Ranking/Selection

ASemiNER ranks all examples[6] in *I* according to the number of different patterns that are used to extract them (Baroni et al., 2010). For example, candidate NE that is extracted by 5 distinct patterns will be ranked before the one that is extracted by only 2 distinct patterns. We avoid the use of plain frequencies as a criterion since some bad examples appear more in the text in a relatively similar context and can be extracted by only one pattern in (*P*). Meanwhile, the good examples might appear less in the text, but in different contexts, and can be extracted by more than one pattern in (*P*). Therefore, the high frequency threshold does not always produce good examples. In addition, pattern variety is a better cue to semantics than absolute frequency.

ASemiNER ranks the examples according to distinct patterns, and discards all but the top *m*, where *m* is set to the number of examples from the previous iteration, plus one. These *m* instances will be used in the next iteration, and so on. For example, if we start the algorithm with 10 seed instances, the following iteration will start with 11, and the next one will start with 12, and so on. This procedure is necessary in order to ensure that bad instances from the previous iteration are not included in the next one.

Moreover, information theory approaches is commonly used in text mining (Turney et al., 2010). For that reason, we tried to apply an Information-theory approach to examine the plausibility of candidate NEs, which are extracted by our system. Hence, we used Pointwise Mutual Information (PMI) statistics to measure the association strength of the instance i in (*I*) across each pattern in (*P*). A reliable instance is one that is associated with as many patterns in *P* as possible.

$$pmi(i) = \sum_{p \epsilon P} log \frac{|i,p|}{|i| * |p|}$$

In this case, $|i,p|$ is the frequency of the instance *i* extracted by pattern *p*. $|i|$ is the frequency of the instance in the corpus. The corpus should be decliticized, clitics should be separated from words, in order to reduce data sparseness and to compute the correct frequencies for each word in the corpus text sequence. $|p|$ is the frequency of the pattern *p* in the corpus.

[6] Also known as instances or candidate NEs.

4 Datasets

ASemiNER does not require any kind of annotated corpora or any type of gazetteers. However, our selection of corpora was based on the intention to compare ASemiNER with other systems. We chose two commonly used corpora in order to evaluate and compare our system with existing systems. These datasets are ANERcorp and ACE 2005.

ANERcorp contains more than 150,000 tokens (11% of the tokens are NEs). It is composed of a training corpus and a test corpus built and tagged especially for the NER task by Benajiba et al. (2007). We chose to evaluate our proposed system with the ANERcorp test corpus because it is commonly used in literature for comparing with existing systems. More details about ANERcorp are given in (Benajiba et al., 2007).

The second dataset used in the training phase is ACE 2005. It is available from the Linguistic Data Consortium (LDC) and has more than 113,000 tokens. The genres utilised in ACE 2005 are Broadcast News, NewsWire, and WebLogs.

Ten percent of the training data was dedicated to the validation set which was used to validate the effectiveness of the trained models. It also helped assign appropriate values to several parameters in our system, such as the number of initial seeds, the criterion to stop the training process, and so on.

ANERcorp and ACE corpora were preprocessed in order to prepare them for our proposed algorithm. Thus, sentence detection was applied to the corpora. Then, we conducted clitic tokenization, since neglecting clitics may cause a loss of important information when generating the patterns. We chose decliticization scheme 'D2' in which conjunctions, prepositions, and future marks are separated from each token (Habash and Sadat, 2006).

Each verb in the corpus is changed to its root from which it is derived. We used root stemmer, namely Khoja's stemmer (Khoja and Garside, 1999), instead of using a light stemmer, which sometimes fails to conflate related forms that should group together, as our goal was to produce a sound set of general patterns.

Regarding POS-tagging, we used AMIRA toolkit (Diab, 2009) and chose Reduced Tag Set (RTS), which neglects inflections in Arabic word categories, since our proposed method does not require any deep morphological information related to gender, number, or definiteness. This information is unnecessary, considering our aim is to make the algorithm generally applicable to languages other than Arabic.

5 Experiments & Results

We developed several experimental models according to three parameters that are defined in our proposed algorithm: the number of initial seeds, the ranking measure, and the number of iterations. The ANERcorp test corpus was used to evaluate every trained model. Regarding the NE type, we had two levels of experiments: in Experiment 1 we trained models to identify the standard NEs (Person, Location, Organisation) in order to compare our system with existing systems; Experiment 2 involved the identification of specialised NEs (Politicians, Sportspersons, and Artists).

5.1 Experiment 1: Standard NEs

We started with a simple model, which was trained on the ANERcorp corpus and passed through the three components only once. For each NE class, we only started with five seed instances. We referred to this model as 'Simple-Model-5'. We also trained two more models, Simple-Model-10 and Simple-Model-20, which only differed from Simple-Model-5 in the number of seed instances for each NE class; the number of seeds were 10 and 20 respectively.

Table 1 shows the precision and recall of these models for each NE class when applying them to the ANERcorp test corpus.

		Simple-Model-5	Simple-Model-10	Simple-Model-20
Person	Precision	88.09	88.46	86.32
	Recall	36.01	39.06	43.20
	F-measure	51.12	54.19	57.58
Location	Precision	89.96	86.80	90.55
	Recall	51.88	55.10	55.45
	F-measure	65.81	67.41	68.78
Organisation	Precision	85.95	83.87	84.35
	Recall	22.38	23.66	27.67
	F-measure	35.51	36.91	41.67

Table 1: Results of Simple-Model-5, Simple-Model-10, and Simple-Model-20

Based on these results, the number of iterations was set to ten for all coming experiments, because we recognised that increasing the number of iterations to more than ten loops makes no significant improvement in the performance of the system (improvement <0.01). We started with 20 seed instances for each NE class and the training corpus was ANERcorp. Candidate NEs were ranked according to the number of distinct patterns in order to select those that ranked the highest as seeds for the next iteration, as explained in section 3.3. We referred to these trained models, one model for each NE class, as 'Model-A(NE class)'.

We also used Pointwise Mutual Information (PMI) as a ranking measure for candidate NEs instead of using the number of distinct patterns. Table 2 shows the outcome of evaluating the trained models on the ANERcorp test corpus.

The results obtained using PMI as a measure to select the seed instances for the next iteration revealed generally low performance and particularly low recall. This can be attributed to the PMI's biased towards infrequent words (Turney et al., 2010), which means less patterns are extracted for the next iteration. Using PMI, the precision was not affected at all, since very few patterns are added into set *P* in each iteration. In general, PMI results in a performance lower than that achieved when using the number of distinct patterns as a reliable measure for seed selection.

		Model-A	Model-A (PMI)
Person	Precision	85.91	85.97
	Recall	51.17	44.64
	F-measure	64.14	58.77
Location	Precision	87.96	90.62
	Recall	62.48	56
	F-measure	73.06	69.22
Organisation	Precision	84.27	85.54
	Recall	40.30	33.80
	F-measure	54.52	48.45

Table 2: The Performance of Model-A on the ANERcorp Test Corpus and the Effect of Using PMI

In the next step, a large corpus, which is a combination of the ANERcorp training set and ACE 2005, was used in the training phase. We referred to the trained models resulting from this experiment as 'Model-B(NE class)'. Using large training data increases the recall of the trained models with a small negative effect on precision. However, the total F-measure is better when using a large corpus, rather than training our model on small training data.

Table 3 summarises the trained models with their values for each parameter. It also shows the performance of each model when applying them to the ANERcorp test corpus by computing its average F-measure for the three standard NEs: person, location, and organisation.

Trained Models	Training Corpus	Ranking measure	No. of initial seeds	Avg. F-measure
Simple Model-5	ANERcorp	--	5	50.81
Simple Model-10	ANERcorp	--	10	52.83
Simple Model-20	ANERcorp	--	20	56.01
Model-A	ANERcorp	Number of distinct Patterns	20	63.91
Model-A (PMI)	ANERcorp	Pointwise Mutual Information (PMI)	20	58.81
Model-B	ANERcorp + ACE 2005	Number of distinct Patterns	20	64.26

Table 3: Different Trained Models with their Parameters and their Performance on the ANERcorp Test Corpus

Based on all of our previous experiments, we have concluded that the following parameters give the best results: the number of initial seeds is 20, the number of iterations is 10, and the ranking measure is the number of distinct patterns used in extraction candidate NEs. Therefore, for the sake of simplicity, we refer to our system that used the trained models with the previously mentioned parameters as "ASemiNER".

In comparison with different supervised NER systems (Benajiba et al., 2007; Benajiba and Rosso, 2007; Benajiba and Rosso, 2008) when applied on the ANERcorp test corpus, ASemiNER can outperform a sensible supervised system, which depends on maximum entropy and a set of features. It still cannot compete, however, with more complex supervised systems. Table 4 shows the results of the comparison.

	Person	Location	Organisation
	F-measure	F-measure	F-measure
ANERsys 1.0	46.69	80.25	36.79
ANERsys 2.0	52.13	86.71	46.43
CRF-based System	73.35	89.74	65.76
Our System(ASemiNER)	64.14	73.06	54.52

Table 4: The Comparison Between Three Different Supervised Systems and our System when Applied on the ANERcorp Test Corpus

5.2 Experiment 2: Specialised NEs

Although most common types of entities investigated in literature are names of people, organisations, and locations, there are many specialised domains that require new annotated corpora and systems to recognise their special NEs (Althobaiti et al., 2012). The recent increase in the number of social networks and specialised domains shows the need to obtain systems that can be easily adapted to identify different, new types of NEs, regardless of the domains.

In this section, we show how well the system recognises new types of NEs, politicians, sportspersons and artists. These new types have been chosen because they constitute the largest percentage of persons' names in ANERcorp. Thus, all annotated persons' names in ANERcorp must be re-annotated using one of four tages: POL, ART, SPORT, and Other. First of all, a guideline was formulated to distinguish the attributes of each class where each new type has been defined, described, and determined. After that, one of the authors re-annotated test corpus for evaluation purposes.

Unlike supervised learning, which may require additional examples in the training data for new categories of NE, our semi-supervised approach used the ANERcorp training data without any addition or modification. The methodology was applied without any major modifications. The modification is only related to generating new lists of trigger nouns and verbs for each type of new NEs (i.e., politicians, sportspersons, artists). They were generated in the same way explained in section 3.1. We manually checked each list to retain only verbs that have a high probability to indicate a specific type of NE. So, verbs like (*entakhab* 'elect'), and (*Swwat* 'vote') can be useful in the case of politician entities.

The performance in this task is comparable to that of standard named entities. Table 5 compares the performance of ASemiNER when extracting standard NEs and the three specialised NEs.

		Precision	Recall	F-measure
Specialised types of NE	Politicians	82.87	50.72	62.93
	Sportspersons	86.56	42.14	56.68
	Artists	82	47.14	59.86
Classic types of NE	Person	85.91	51.17	64.14
	Location	87.96	62.48	73.06
	Organisation	84.27	40.30	54.52

Table 5: The Performance of ASemiNER on the ANERcorp Test Corpus in order to Extract Both Standard & Specialised NEs

For sportspersons, the low recall is possibly due

to the impact of the lower number of varied contexts in which seeds occur. So, sportspersons constitute only 19% of all person names that exist in the training corpus, and they occur in a few contexts. Thus, the diversity of contexts in which seeds appear plays an important role in obtaining a trained model with good performance. The remaining recall errors can be attributed to the diversity of categories. Accordingly, sportspersons can be broken down into other categories, such as "football players", "golfers" and "wrestlers". In contrast, politician entity recognition has a higher recall than sportspersons. This can be attributed to two facts: 1) Politicians make up 44% of the people names in the training corpus, and 2) An efficient model results from using initial seeds like 'Bush' or 'Muhammad', since such examples occur frequently and in a variety of contexts in the training corpus. Overall, our semi-supervised system proved to be easily adaptable when extending the NE hierarchy. In addition, ASemiNER performs just as well when recognising the standard person category. Even more, our system highlighted the importance of the manner in which initial seeds are chosen in any semi-supervised approach.

6 Conclusion

All in all, we advance the the state-of-the art Arabic NER by avoiding the need for supervision, adopting a novel solution for the Arabic NER problem, and handling specialised NE types. Our solution is a semi-supervised approach in which our system (ASemiNER) produces semantic information from naturally occurring text with limited supervision. Each NE type, therefore, only requires a seed list made up of a few examples. Furthermore, in terms of experiments, ASemiNER outperforms sensible supervised systems. Admittedly our algorithm does not perform as well as complex supervised systems, however, its extremely limited dependence on supervision more than compensates for this point. Moreover, ASemiNER can be easily adapted to identify new types of NEs and does not generate problems typical of supervised methods that require annotated training data, and demand more effort and time to extract specialised types of NEs.

References

Sherief Abdallah, Khaled Shaalan, and Muhammad Shoaib. 2012. Integrating rule-based system with classification for arabic named entity recognition. In *Computational Linguistics and Intelligent Text Processing*, pages 311–322. Springer.

Samir AbdelRahman, Mohamed Elarnaoty, Marwa Magdy, and Aly Fahmy. 2010. Integrated machine learning techniques for arabic named entity recognition. *IJCSI*, 7:27–36.

Ahmed Abdul-Hamid and Kareem Darwish. 2010. Simplified feature set for arabic named entity recognition. In *Proceedings of the 2010 Named Entities Workshop*, pages 110–115. Association for Computational Linguistics.

Maha Althobaiti, Udo Kruschwitz, and Massimo Poesio. 2012. Identifying named entities on a university intranet. In *Computer Science and Electronic Engineering Conference (CEEC), 2012 4th*, pages 94–99. IEEE.

Marco Baroni, Brian Murphy, Eduard Barbu, and Massimo Poesio. 2010. Strudel: A corpus-based semantic model based on properties and types. *Cognitive Science*, 34(2):222–254.

Yassine Benajiba and Paolo Rosso. 2007. Anersys 2.0: Conquering the ner task for the arabic language by combining the maximum entropy with pos-tag information. In *IICAI*, pages 1814–1823.

Yassine Benajiba and Paolo Rosso. 2008. Arabic named entity recognition using conditional random fields. In *Proc. of Workshop on HLT & NLP within the Arabic World, LREC*, volume 8, pages 143–153.

Yassine Benajiba, Paolo Rosso, and José Miguel Benedíruiz. 2007. Anersys: An arabic named entity recognition system based on maximum entropy. In *Computational Linguistics and Intelligent Text Processing*, pages 143–153. Springer.

Yassine Benajiba, Mona Diab, Paolo Rosso, et al. 2008. Arabic named entity recognition: An svm-based approach. In *Proceedings of 2008 Arab International Conference on Information Technology (ACIT)*, pages 16–18.

Mona Diab. 2009. Second generation amira tools for arabic processing: Fast and robust tokenization, pos tagging, and base phrase chunking. In *2nd International Conference on Arabic Language Resources and Tools*.

Oren Etzioni, Michael Cafarella, Doug Downey, Ana-Maria Popescu, Tal Shaked, Stephen Soderland, Daniel S Weld, and Alexander Yates. 2005. Unsupervised named-entity extraction from the web: An experimental study. *Artificial Intelligence*, 165(1):91–134.

Ralph Grishman and Beth Sundheim. 1996. Message understanding conference-6: A brief history. In *COLING*, volume 96, pages 466–471.

Nizar Habash and Fatiha Sadat. 2006. Arabic preprocessing schemes for statistical machine translation. In *NAACL*. ACL.

Shereen Khoja and Roger Garside. 1999. Stemming arabic text. *Lancaster, UK, Computing Department, Lancaster University*.

Wenhui Liao and Sriharsha Veeramachaneni. 2009. A simple semi-supervised algorithm for named entity recognition. In *Proceedings of the NAACL HLT 2009 Workshop on Semi-Supervised Learning for Natural Language Processing*, pages 58–65. Association for Computational Linguistics.

Xiaohua Liu, Shaodian Zhang, Furu Wei, and Ming Zhou. 2011. Recognizing named entities in tweets. In *ACL*, pages 359–367.

Slim Mesfar. 2007. Named entity recognition for arabic using syntactic grammars. In *Natural Language Processing and Information Systems*, pages 305–316. Springer.

Behrang Mohit, Nathan Schneider, Rishav Bhowmick, Kemal Oflazer, and Noah A Smith. 2012. Recall-oriented learning of named entities in arabic wikipedia. In *Proceedings of the 13th Conference of the European Chapter of the Association for Computational Linguistics*, pages 162–173. Association for Computational Linguistics.

David Nadeau and Satoshi Sekine. 2007. A survey of named entity recognition and classification. *Lingvisticae Investigationes*, 30(1):3–26.

David Nadeau, Peter Turney, and Stan Matwin. 2006. Unsupervised named-entity recognition: Generating gazetteers and resolving ambiguity. *Advances in Artificial Intelligence*.

Mai Oudah and Khaled F Shaalan. 2012. A pipeline arabic named entity recognition using a hybrid approach. In *COLING*, pages 2159–2176.

Marius Pasca, Dekang Lin, Jeffrey Bigham, Andrei Lifchits, and Alpa Jain. 2006. Organizing and searching the world wide web of facts-step one: the one-million fact extraction challenge. In *AAAI*, volume 6, pages 1400–1405.

Ellen Riloff and Rosie Jones. 1999. Learning dictionaries for information extraction by multi-level bootstrapping. In *AAAI*, pages 474–479.

Khaled Shaalan and Hafsa Raza. 2007. Person name entity recognition for arabic. In *Proceedings of the 2007 Workshop on Computational Approaches to Semitic Languages: Common Issues and Resources*, pages 17–24. Association for Computational Linguistics.

Khaled Shaalan and Hafsa Raza. 2009. Nera: Named entity recognition for arabic. *Journal of the American Society for Information Science and Technology*, 60(8):1652–1663.

Peter D Turney, Patrick Pantel, et al. 2010. From frequency to meaning: Vector space models of semantics. *Journal of artificial intelligence research*, 37(1):141–188.

An NLP-based Reading Tool for Aiding Non-native English Readers

Mahmoud Azab   Ahmed Salama   Kemal Oflazer
Carnegie Mellon University-Qatar
Doha, Qatar
{mazab,ahmedsaa,ko}@qatar.cmu.edu

Hideki Shima   Jun Araki   Teruko Mitamura
Carnegie Mellon University,
Pittsburgh, PA, USA
{hideki,junaraki,teruko}@cs.cmu.edu

Abstract

This paper describes a text-reading tool that makes extensive use of widely-available NLP tools and resources to aid non-native English speakers overcome language related hindrances while reading a text. It is a web-based tool, that can be accessed from browsers running on PCs or tablets, and provides the reader with an intelligent e-book functionality.

1 Introduction and Motivation

In this paper, we describe our approach in building a NLP-powered tool to aid in reading texts in English by non-native readers of the language, especially in an educational setting. Text, being bland, is hardly a conducive and motivating medium for learning, especially when the reader does not have access to aids that would enable her to get over minor and not-so-minor roadblocks ranging from unknown vocabulary to unrecognized and forgotten names, hard-to-understand sentences, issues with the grammar and lack of or forgetting the prior context in a former session of reading. We aim to make reading an active and interactive experience by enabling the user to interact with the text in a variety of ways using anytime-anywhere contextually guided access to textual information.

Our system is based on significant preprocessing and annotation of a library of texts using many publicly available NLP components for English, integrated in a UIMA (Unstructured Information Management Architecture) based server (Ferrucci and Lally, 2004). These annotated documents are then accessed via browser-based clients which essentially look like traditional e-book reading environments but with a much richer set of user accessible functionality. Thus our system can also be seen as a *showcase application for demonstrating English NLP tools and resources.* Our contribution is the integration of many publicly available tools and resources for English into a large-scale usable application implemented in a client-server software architecture structured around UIMA, along with work on development of some annotation components and/or combination of available ones.

In the rest of this paper, after a brief review of the use of NLP to help for reading, we will elaborate on the user visible functionality of our system and then present the software architecture and the implementation. Our system has been implemented save for a couple of features and we are now in the process of planning an intrinsic evaluation followed by a deployment to have it be used to gauge if student users find it effective.

2 Using NLP in Reading Aids

Recently, Computer Assisted Language Learning (CALL) systems have started making use of advanced language technology to build intelligent systems to aid and assess reading comprehension. An early project, GLOSSER Project (Nerbonne et al., 1997) developed a system that aids readers of foreign language text, by providing access to a dictionary, exploiting morphological analysis and part-of-speech disambiguation. The Free-Text Project (Hamel and Girard, 2000), developed a NLP-based CALL system for intermediate to advanced learners of French. The LISTEN project at CMU on the other hand, has aimed to tutor elementary school students in reading English text by using speech technology (Mostow and Aist, 2001).

The REAP (Reader Specific Lexical Practice) project (Heilman et al., 2006), aimed at selecting individualized practice reading documents from the web using lexical, syntactic and readability levels. REAP chooses documents that contain certain target vocabulary words that a student needs to learn. It also presents the documents within a web browser-based application along with a dictionary to provide word meanings and a set of automatically generated set of closed questions as an exercise. Recently, Eom et al. (2012) presented a system that incorporates word sense disambiguation for vocabulary assistance. Maamouri et al. (2012) presents, ARET (Arabic Reading Enhancement Tool) that aids the readers of Arabic as a second language. It provides the user with the morphological analyses, the meanings of the words and a text-to-speech module to pronounce the word. ARET also has an assessment tool that asks the user several kinds of questions to evaluate reading comprehension.

Our system currently targets English and offers a wider set of functionalities to users, in addition to a software architecture which can be extended very easily with more annotation components complying with UIMA interfaces. However, *our system architecture is language-independent*; adopting new languages is a fairly easy process as long as the relevant annotation tools and their UIMA interfaces are available.

3 User Functionality

From a reader's perspective, our tool is a web-based browser application. It runs in a multitude of browsers ranging over various platforms including touch tablets. It has a intuitive web interface to sign up, sign in, and browse available texts in the system's library. The reader has the option either to select a text from the library to read or to upload text she wants to read using the tool by including it in the library. If the reader chooses to submit her own text, the submitted text goes through several stages of real-time annotations that are used by the tool to make the text interactive. The tool then opens the text in a distraction-free tab.

The reader can interact with the text either by clicking on a word or selecting any segment of text. The system in turn takes into account the clicked/selected word's/segment's contents and its annotations by querying the server, highlights the segment (or something slightly and meaningfully larger, depending on the context) and presents a response, which most likely fits the reader's intent at the click position, as a default answer, along with a menu of other options. For instance,

- if the reader clicks on a content word, its meaning will be the most likely information she wants to know about i.e., the system presents the word meaning as the default response.
- if the reader clicks one of the words making up a named-entity, the system will extend and highlight the whole named-entity and present its type (e.g., person, location, etc.)
- if reader clicks on a pronoun, the system will display to who/what this pronoun refers by highlighting both the pronoun and the antecedent in context.
- the reader can explore beyond the default response by using the additional menu items provided: for instance she may ask about the grammatical role of a word in the sentence or get a list of questions involving a named entity and then select one and get it answered.

The tool provides all the available information to the reader but it orders these options according to an intention recognition module based on the annotations at the selected position. In the following sections, we describe the relevant details of the basic functions that our system provides.

3.1 Lexical Information

The current application provides the reader with the ability to inquire about lexical information such as word meaning, word type, sentence examples including the inquired word. Clicking on a word is the easiest and fastest way to access all the lexical information that is available for this word. In order to provide this lexical information we are making use of several tools which are fairly mature and can be used off-the-shelf.

Content Words: While there are many studies in second language acquisition on providing vocabulary and reading assistance (Prichard, 2008) and (Luppescu and Day, 1992). These studies showed that dictionaries can help in improving comprehension and efficient vocabulary acquisition. Luppescu and Day showed that the readers who use a printed dictionary have improved comprehension and acquisition, but negatively affect their reading speed.

Our tool provides vocabulary assistance to learners of English as a Second Language (ESL). When the reader selects a content word from the text, the tool provides the reader with the word definition and sentence examples including this word. We use WordNet (Fellbaum, 1998) as a broad-coverage machine-readable dictionary of English. Many words in WordNet have more than one sense. Currently, we incorporate morphological analysis, part-of-speech filtering to narrow down the available senses and then present the user with the first WordNet sense under the selected part-of-speech, as shown in Figure 1.

Phrasal Verbs and Compound Nouns: Multiple word expressions may include phrasal verbs (e.g., reach into) and compound nouns. The meaning of these types of expressions often differ considerably from that of the underlying verb/noun and maybe unfamiliar to non-native english readers, and so they may interfere with content comprehension. In case the reader inquires about a word which is a part of a (possibly discontinuous) compound verb/noun, the tool highlights the whole compound structure and provides its meaning and also the meaning of the clicked word in case that the reader is interested in this specific word. Figure 2 shows the response to the reader on clicking the word *break* which is part of compound verb *break through*.

Function Words: Function words such as *though*, *whether*, *beyond*, etc., and other functional elements such as prepositions and determiners, can be confusing to a non-native English readers (Felice, 2008) . For function words (other than pronouns), the tool provides the reader with the word type, the part-of-speech of the word with some additional explanation. Figure 3 shows an example when the reader selects a function word.

Named Entities: One important function our tool provides, is identifying named-entities in the text. If the reader clicks/selects a name or part of it, the full span of the named entity is highlighted along with its category as shown in Figure 4.

Pronouns and Coreference Resolution: If a reader clicks on a pronoun, our tool presents the reader with the nearest previous named-entity for the pronoun and provides menus to navigate all previous and future coreferences. This would help the reader use nonlinear reading strategies and facilitate the extraction of information about the selected named entity through the document without reading through the whole text. Thus the reader can get an immediate flashback to the first time the person was encountered so she can re-read or remember more about this person, or see nearby references to get more recent context, and when done can snap back to the query point and continue reading. See Figure 5 for a sample interaction possibilities with pronouns.

3.2 Syntactic Information

Sometimes understanding the words meaning are not enough to fully understand the sentence. In order to help the user to understand the grammatical relations in a sentence, our tool provides the reader with the ability to inquire about the grammatical role of a word within the sentence. The sentences in the documents are previously annotated with dependency relations and when a word is clicked, one of the other menu items the user is presented with is the option to view the grammatical role of the word (shown with the button "Role" in the figures). When requested, we present the grammatical role in a user-friendly fashion by mapping dependency labels to more descriptive and meaningful labels as shown in Figure 6.

3.3 In-text Question Answering

Sometimes the reader may want to learn additional information about a named entity. Asking questions and getting answers may help in comprehension of the text and is a good way to get a flashback about the selected entity. If the user clicks on a named entity or a pronoun referring to it, the tool provides the reader with a short list of related questions that are automatically generated (at annotation time) involving the selected/referenced named entity, from previous sentences in the text. These questions are then ranked based on length, proximity and whether or not it or its answer involves another named entity, and a short list of questions are presented to the user. The user can then click on a question she is interested in, and immediately get the corresponding answer, *which is also generated at annotation time in parallel with question generation.* Figure 7 shows an example of this functionality.

3.4 Other Functionalities

Text summarization has been used to improve reading comprehension (Dermody and Speaker Jr, 1999) as well as document understanding (Wang et al., 2008) since it reduces information overload and provides a reader with a concise and informative text. Our tool provides the reader with a different levels of text summarization such as paragraph, multi-section, chapter and whole document summarization. The reader can select one or more paragraphs and ask the tool to summarize it for her. She can also ask the tool to summarize all the text before her selection which helps her to refresh her mind with the highlights of the preceding text. For this purpose, we use the Mead toolkit (Radev

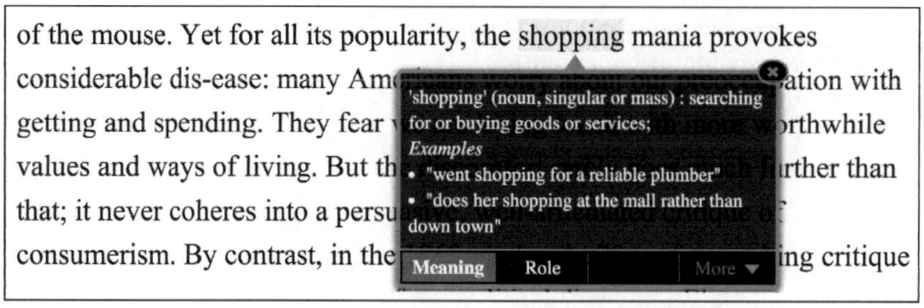

Figure 1: Looking up content word meaning

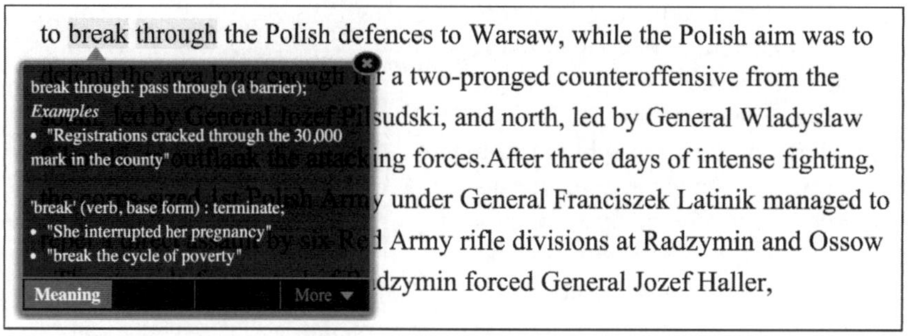

Figure 2: Response to selecting a compound verb

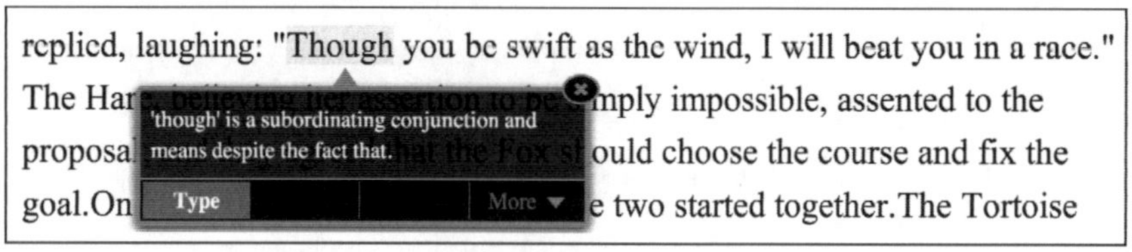

Figure 3: Response for a function word

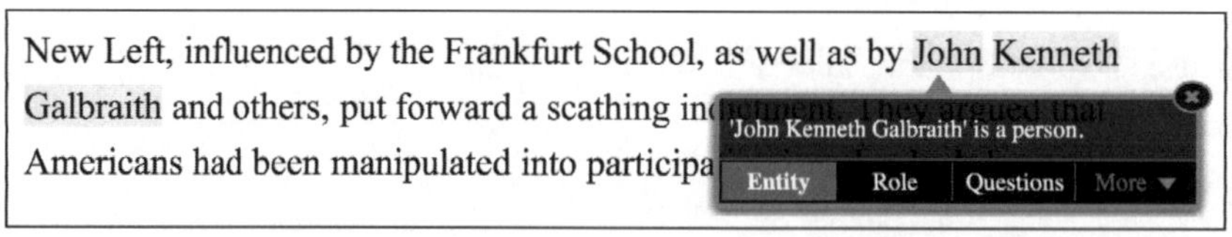

Figure 4: Response to selecting a portion of named-entity

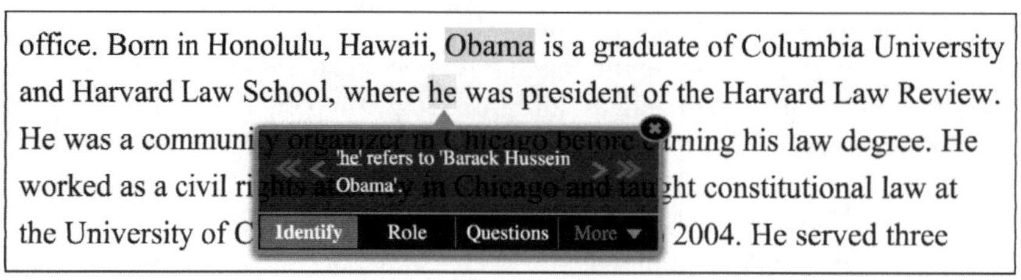

Figure 5: Identifying and Tracking named-entity mentions

et al., 2004) for English to provide the summarization functionality.

Another useful feature the tool also provides is logging the queries performed by a user together with data presented in response to the queries. At anytime, the reader can review the words she had problems with and asked about.

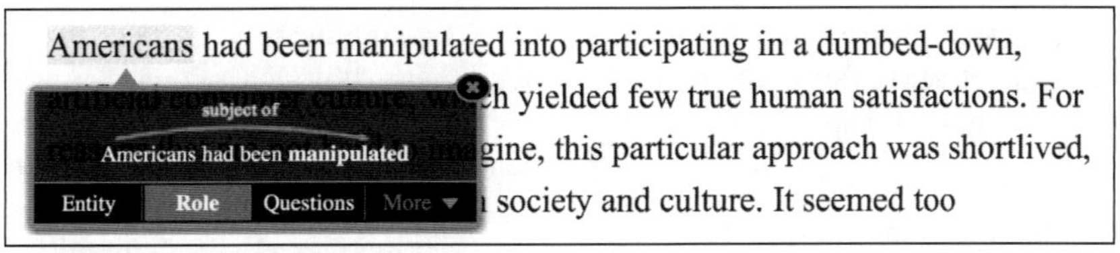

Figure 6: Showing the grammatical role of a word within the sentence

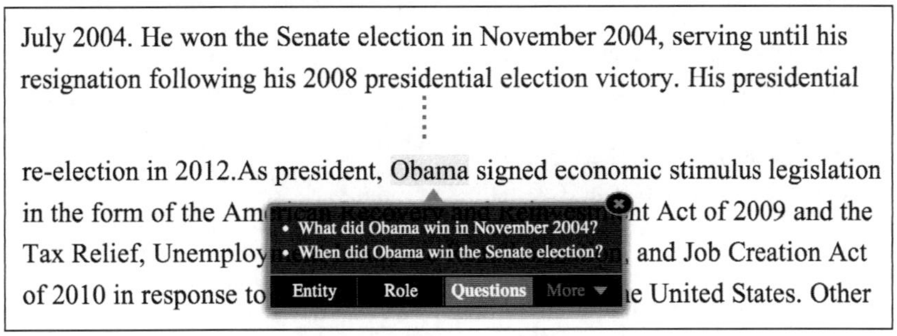

Figure 7: Presenting questions involving a named entity

4 System and Software Architecture

Our system follows a client-server paradigm where the server is responsible for all NLP-functionality, enriching plain text with annotations and retrieving them , while the client receives a version of the text that the user can interact and query the server with. The client here is a standard web browser, that can be accessed from browsers running on PCs or tablets, so on the reader's side no additional software is needed. The server processes and responds to requests received from these thin-clients.

All annotations that are needed to respond to user requests (except for summarization), are stored within a UIMA file produced by our annotators. The UIMA framework facilitates developing and integrating different text analysis engines and annotators in an extensible way and provides very powerful querying and search mechanisms for retrieving the annotations of the annotated documents.

4.1 Client Side

On the client side, the presentation layer is responsible for (i) keeping track of the user status and the opened documents, (ii) displaying the opened documents (iii) handling user-interactions, and (iv) sending queries to the server. The presentation layer is designed to be light and fast, with all the heavy processing to be done on the server side.

4.2 Server Side Query Processing

On the server side, the server receives requests and passes each request to the corresponding handler. These handlers in turn make use of two main units: the **data manager**, is responsible for all the database interactions on different data, the **query processing unit**, is responsible for extracting and reordering all the information related to a user query.

All documents in the system's library are all annotated with a series of NLP annotation tools and stored as a UIMA file. When UIMA is queried with a character position, it returns efficiently all the annotations associated with the word overlapping with that position which are then interpreted by the query processing unit.

During annotation, we segment the text into sentences, tokenize and run a POS tagger using Stanford CoreNLP.[1] We then use the following NLP components with appropriate UIMA wrappers to annotate our texts:

Stanford Dependency Parser (De Marneffe et al., 2006), provides grammatical relation annotations.

Stanford Named Entity Recognizer and **Stanford Co-reference Resolution** (Lee et al., 2013; Lee et al., 2011; Raghunathan et al., 2010) are used to determine the entities in the text and the relationships between them.

[1] http://nlp.stanford.edu/software/corenlp.shtml

Word Sense Annotator currently assigns the most frequent WordNet senses to content words by filtering the senses by just using the POS tag.

Compound Annotator identifies the phrasal verbs and the compound nouns in the text and adds additional annotation to words of a compound.

In-text Question Answering Annotator assigns the questions to the related named entities, and ranks them. The questions are generated using Heilman's question generator tool (Heilman and Smith, 2010).

For more details on the use of UIMA and the server architecture, please see Azab et al. (2013).

5 Evaluation

As we are using many tools and resources that have been developed for use on usually one genre of text, it will be an interesting experiment to see how they perform on the texts we will select for our library. We are currently in the process of preparing several short test documents for intrinsic evaluation of the performance of the annotation tools and reporting on their recall and precision. Manual evaluation of some of the components for one such document of about 1000 words is presented in Table 1.

We are also planning an extrinsic evaluation of the tool by having a group of non-native English speaking students use it and evaluate their experience. We are working together with a colleague who delivers a critical reading course who has provided us with a set of texts that students can read using our tools. He will then construct several evaluation experiments to see if our tool helps the students or not.

	Precision	Recall	F-score
NER	0.909	0.869	0.888
POS Tagger	0.986		
Coreference Resolution	0.679	0.63	0.653
Word Meaning	0.861	0.831	0.845
In-text Question Answering	0.62		

Table 1: Intrinsic evaluation of different NLP tools used.

6 Ongoing Work

We are currently working on improving our word sense identification annotator and implementing an additional sentence level annotation components:

Word-sense disambiguation : Word-sense disambiguation is a notoriously difficult problem and systems developed over the years have not been able to significantly exceed the most-frequent sense heuristic. Our current plan is to incorporate multiple word-sense disambiguators (e.g., Pedersen and Kolhatkar (2009)) along with super-sense taggers Ciaramita and Altun (2006), to build a system combination that can hopefully do a better job than the baseline, at least on our intrinsic test sets.

Lexical simplification : Text simplification can be defined as any process that reduces the syntactic or lexical complexity of a text while attempting to preserve its meaning and information content. The aim of text simplification is to make text easier to comprehend for a human user, or process by a program (Siddharthan, 2004). Text simplification has been studied for both human text readers and programs that process text. We are specifically concerned with students who try to acquire English as a second language (Petersen, 2007). Approaches for this target audience use simplification techniques as a preprocessing step to reduce complexity of sentence, mainly with respect to syntax (e.g., sentence decomposition on subordinate clause) and discourse structure (e.g., coreference resolution).

We are developing a sentence simplification module that addresses both lexical and limited syntactic simplification problems to help improve reading skills of non-native English learners. Our current focus is on developing a lexical simplification module that can identify the "difficult" vocabulary items or idiomatic uses in text, and annotate with their simpler versions.

7 Conclusion

We have presented our tool for helping non-native readers of English text to overcome language related hindrances while reading text. Our tool is also a showcase of English NLP and resources that have been built by the NLP community, integrated into an e-book reader application that can be adapted to more languages, provide resources are available. Our tool is based on a client-server software architecture, with the UIMA-framework being used for both annotation of documents and querying of annotations based on textual selections from the client applications running in browsers. We are also in the process of planning a test deployment for students for extrinsic experimentation.

Acknowledgments

This publication was made possible by grant NPRP-09-873-1-129 from the Qatar National Research Fund (a member of the Qatar Foundation). The statements made herein are solely the responsibility of the authors.

References

Mahmoud Azab, Ahmed Salama, Kemal Oflazer, Hideki Shima, Jun Araki, and Teruko Mitamura. 2013. An English reading tool as a NLP showcase. In *Proceedings of IJCNLP – System Demonstration*, Nagoya, Japan.

Massimiliano Ciaramita and Yasemin Altun. 2006. Broad-coverage sense disambiguation and information extraction with a supersense sequence tagger. In *Proceedings of EMNLP'06*, EMNLP '06, pages 594–602, Stroudsburg, PA, USA.

Marie-Catherine De Marneffe, Bill MacCartney, and Christopher D Manning. 2006. Generating typed dependency parses from phrase structure parses. In *Proceedings of LREC*, volume 6, pages 449–454.

Margaret M Dermody and Richard B Speaker Jr. 1999. Reciprocal Strategy Training in Prediction, Clarification, Question Generating and Summarization to Improve Reading Comprehension. *Reading Improvement*, 36(1):16–23.

Soojeong Eom, Markus Dickinson, and Rebecca Sachs. 2012. Sense-specific lexical information for reading assistance. In *Proceedings of the Seventh Workshop on Building Educational Applications Using NLP*, pages 316–325, Stroudsburg, PA, USA.

Rachele De Felice. 2008. *Automatic Error Detection in Non-native English*. Ph.D. thesis, St Catherines College, University of Oxford.

Christiane Fellbaum. 1998. WordNet: An electronic lexical database. *The MIT Press*.

David Ferrucci and Adam Lally. 2004. UIMA: an architectural approach to unstructured information processing in the corporate research environment. *Natural Language Engineering*, 10(3-4):327–348.

Marie-Jose Hamel and Marie-Christine Girard. 2000. FreeText - an advanced hypermedia CALL system featuring NLP tools for a smart treatment of authentic documents and free production exercises. In *Proceedings of EuroCALL-2000*.

Michael Heilman and Noah Smith. 2010. Extracting simplified statements for factual question generation. In *Proceedings of the 3rd Workshop on Question Generation*.

Michael Heilman, Kevyn Collins-Thompson, Jamie Callan, and Maxine Eskenazi. 2006. Classroom success of an intelligent tutoring system for lexical practice and reading comprehension. In *Proceedings of the Ninth International Conference on Spoken Language Processing*.

Heeyoung Lee, Yves Peirsman, Angel Chang, Nathanael Chambers, Mihai Surdeanu, and Dan Jurafsky. 2011. Stanford's multi-pass sieve coreference resolution system at the conll shared task. In *Proceedings CONLL'11*, pages 28–34.

Heeyoung Lee, Angel Chang, Yves Peirsman, Nathanael Chambers, Mihai Surdeanu, and Dan Jurafsky. 2013. Deterministic coreference resolution based on entity-centric, precision-ranked rules. *Computational Linguistics*, pages 1–54.

Stuart Luppescu and Richard R. Day. 1992. Reading, Dictionaries, and Vocabulary Learning. *Language Learning*, 43(2):263–279.

Mohamed Maamouri, Wajdi Zaghouani, Violetta Cavalli-Sforza, Dave Graff, and Mike Ciul. 2012. Developing ARET: an NLP-based educational tool set for Arabic reading enhancement. In *Proceedings of the Seventh Workshop on Building Educational Applications Using NLP*, pages 127–135, Stroudsburg, PA, USA.

Jack Mostow and Gregory Aist. 2001. Evaluating tutors that listen: An overview of project listen. In K. Forbus andP. Feltovich, editor, *Smart Machines in Education: The coming revolution in educational technology.*, pages 169 – 234. MIT/AAAI Press.

John Nerbonne, Lauri Karttunen, Elena Paskaleva, Gabor Proszeky, and Tiit Roosmaa. 1997. Reading more into foreign languages. In *Proceedings of ANLP'97*, pages 135–138.

Ted Pedersen and Varada Kolhatkar. 2009. Wordnet::senserelate::allwords: a broad coverage word sense tagger that maximizes semantic relatedness. In *Proceedings of HLT/NAACL'06, Companion Volume: Demonstration Session*, NAACL-Demonstrations '09, pages 17–20, Stroudsburg, PA, USA.

S. Petersen. 2007. *Natural language processing tools for reading level assessment and text simplification for bilingual education*. Ph.D. thesis, University of Washington, Washington, USA.

Caleb Prichard. 2008. Evaluating l2 readers vocabulary strategies and dictionary use. *Reading in a Foreign Language*, 20(2):216–231.

D. Radev, T. Allison, S. Blair-Goldensohn, J. Blitzer, A. Çelebi, S. Dimitrov, E. Drabek, A. Hakim, W. Lam, D. Liu, J. Otterbacher, H. Qi, H. Saggion, S. Teufel, M. Topper, A. Winkel, and Z. Zhang. 2004. Mead - a platform for multidocument multilingual text summarization. In *Proceedings of LREC 2004*, Lisbon, Portugal.

Karthik Raghunathan, Heeyoung Lee, Sudarshan Rangarajan, Nathanael Chambers, Mihai Surdeanu, Dan Jurafsky, and Christopher Manning. 2010. A multipass sieve for coreference resolution. In *Proceedings of EMNLP'10*, pages 492–501.

Advaith Siddharthan. 2004. Syntactic simplification and text cohesion. Technical Report 597, University of Cambridge.

Dingding Wang, Shenghuo Zhu, Tao Li, Yun Chi, and Yihong Gong. 2008. Integrating clustering and multi-document summarization to improve document understanding. In *Proceedings of the 17th ACM conference on Information and knowledge management*, CIKM '08, pages 1435–1436, New York, NY, USA. ACM.

Improving Sentiment Analysis in Twitter Using Multilingual Machine Translated Data

Alexandra Balahur
European Commission Joint Research Centre
Via E. Fermi 2749
21027 Ispra (VA), Italy
alexandra.balahur@jrc.ec.europa.eu

Marco Turchi
Fondazione Bruno Kessler-IRST
Via Sommarive, 18
Povo, Trento, Italy
turchi@fbk.eu

Abstract

Sentiment analysis is currently a very dynamic field in Computational Linguistics. Research herein has concentrated on the development of methods and resources for different types of texts and various languages. Nonetheless, the implementation of a multilingual system that is able to classify sentiment expressed in various languages has not been approached so far. The main challenge this paper addresses is sentiment analysis from tweets in a multilingual setting. We first build a simple sentiment analysis system for tweets in English. Subsequently, we translate the data from English to four other languages - Italian, Spanish, French and German - using a standard machine translation system. Further on, we manually correct the test data and create Gold Standards for each of the target languages. Finally, we test the performance of the sentiment analysis classifiers for the different languages concerned and show that the joint use of training data from multiple languages (especially those pertaining to the same family of languages) significantly improves the results of the sentiment classification.

1 Introduction

Sentiment analysis is a task in Natural Language Processing whose aim is to automatically detect and classify sentiments in texts. Generally, the "positive", "negative" and "neutral" classes are considered, although other scales have also been used (e.g. from 1 to 5 "stars" - according to the reviewing systems put at the disposal of clients or users by amazon.com, booking.com, etc.; adding the "very positive" and "very negative" classes, scales from 1 to 10, etc.).

In this article, we deal with the issue of sentiment analysis in tweets, in a multilingual setting. We employ machine translation - which was shown to be at a sufficiently high level of performance (Balahur and Turchi, 2012) - to obtain data in four languages. Our goal is to test if the use of multilingual data can help to improve sentiment classification in tweets (as shown to be the case in formal texts - (Banea et al., 2010)) and if the joint use of data coming from similar languages or languages that are different in structure can influence on the final result.

The main problem when designing automatic methods for the treatment of tweets is that they are highly informal texts, i.e. they contain slang, emoticons, repetitions of letters or punctuation signs, misspellings (done on purpose or due to writing them from mobile devices), entire words in capital letters, etc.

In order to test our hypotheses, we first design a simple tweet sentiment analysis system for English, taking into account the specificity of expressions employed, but without using language-specific text processing tools. The motivation is related to the fact that: a) such a distinction would require the use of language identifiers and would need the data from the different languages to be separated; b) We would like to apply the same techniques for as many languages as possible and for some of these languages, no freely-available language processing tools exist. We test this system on the SemEval 2013 Task 2 - Sentiment Analysis in Twitter (Wilson et al., 2013) - training data and test on the development data. The choice of this test set was motivated by the fact that it contains approximately 1000 tweets, being large enough to be able to draw relevant conclusions and at the same time small enough to allow manual correction of the translations, to eliminate incorrect translations being present in both training and test data.

Subsequently, we employ the Google machine translation system[1] to translate the SemEval 2013 training and development tweets in Italian, Spanish, German and French. We manually correct the translated development data (which we use for testing, not for parameter tuning) to produce a reliable Gold Standard.

Finally, we apply the same sentiment classification system to each of these languages and test the manner in which the combined datasets (from pairs of two languages, families of languages and all the languages together) perform. We conclude that the joint use of training data from different languages improves the classification of sentiment and that the use of training data from languages that are similar in structure helps to achieve statistically significant improvements over the results obtained on individual languages and all languages together.

The remainder of this article is structured as follows: Section 2 gives an overview of the related work. In Section 3, we present the motivations and describe the contributions of this work. In the following section, we describe in detail the process followed to pre-process the tweets, build the classification models and obtain tweets for four other languages. In Section 5, we present the results obtained on different languages and combinations thereof. Finally, Section 6 summarizes the main findings of this work and sketches the lines for future work.

2 Related Work

The work described herein is related to the development of multilingual sentiment analysis systems and sentiment classification from tweets.

2.1 Methods for Multilingual Sentiment Analysis

In order to produce multilingual resources for subjectivity analysis, Banea et al. (Banea et al., 2008) apply bootstrapping to build a subjectivity lexicon for Romanian, starting with a set of 60 words which they translate and subsequently filter using a measure of similarity to the original words, based on Latent Semantic Analysis (LSA) (Deerwester et al., 1990) scores. Another approach to mapping subjectivity lexica to other languages is proposed by Wan (2009), who uses co-training to classify un-annotated Chinese reviews using a corpus of annotated English reviews. (Kim et al., 2010) create a number of systems consisting of different subsystems, each classifying the subjectivity of texts in a different language. They translate a corpus annotated for subjectivity analysis (MPQA), the subjectivity clues (Opinion Finder) lexicon and re-train a Naive Bayes classifier that is implemented in the Opinion Finder system using the newly generated resources for all the languages considered. (Banea et al., 2010) translate the MPQA corpus into five other languages (some with a similar ethimology, others with a very different structure). Subsequently, they expand the feature space used in a Naive Bayes classifier using the same data translated to 2 or 3 other languages. Finally, (Steinberger et al., 2011a; Steinberger et al., 2011b) create sentiment dictionaries in other languages using a method called "triangulation". They translate the data, in parallel, from English and Spanish to other languages and obtain dictionaries from the intersection of these two translations.

2.2 Sentiment Classification from Tweets

One of the first studies on the classification of polarity in tweets was (Go et al., 2009). The authors conducted a supervised classification study on tweets in English, using the emoticons (e.g. ":)", ":(", etc.) as markers of positive and negative tweets. (Read, 2005) employed this method to generate a corpus of positive tweets, with positive emoticons ":)", and negative tweets with negative emoticons ":(". Subsequently, they employ different supervised approaches (SVM, Naïve Bayes and Maximum Entropy) and various sets of features and conclude that the simple use of unigrams leads to good results, but it can be slightly improved by the combination of unigrams and bigrams.

In the same line of thinking, (Pak and Paroubek, 2010) also generated a corpus of tweets for sentiment analysis, by selecting positive and negative tweets based on the presence of specific emoticons. Subsequently, they compare different supervised approaches with n-gram features and obtain the best results using Naïve Bayes with unigrams and part-of-speech tags.

Another approach on sentiment analysis in tweet is that of (Zhang et al., 2011). Here, the authors employ a hybrid approach, combining super-

[1] http://translate.google.com/

vised learning with the knowledge on sentiment-bearing words, which they extract from the DAL sentiment dictionary (Whissell, 1989). Their pre-processing stage includes the removal of retweets, translation of abbreviations into original terms and deleting of links, a tokenization process, and part-of-speech tagging. They employ various supervised learning algorithms to classify tweets into positive and negative, using n-gram features with SVM and syntactic features with Partial Tree Kernels, combined with the knowledge on the polarity of the words appearing in the tweets. The authors conclude that the most important features are those corresponding to sentiment-bearing words. Finally, (Jiang et al., 2011) classify sentiment expressed on previously-given "targets" in tweets. They add information on the context of the tweet to its text (e.g. the event that it is related to). Subsequently, they employ SVM and General Inquirer and perform a three-way classification (positive, negative, neutral).

3 Motivation and Contribution

The work presented herein is mainly motivated by the need to: a) develop sentiment analysis tools for a high number of languages, while minimizing the effort to create linguistic resources for each of these languages in part; b) study the manner in which the use of machine translation systems to produce multilingual data performs in the context of informal texts such as tweets; and c) evaluate the performance of sentiment classification when data from different languages is combined in the training phase. We would especially like to study the effect of using data from similar languages versus the use of data from structurally and lexically-different languages. The advantage of such an approach would be that if combined classifiers perform better, then the effort of separating tweets in different languages at the time of analysis (which in the case of streaming data is not negligeable) can be reduced or eliminated entirely.

Unlike approaches we presented in Related Work section, we employ fully-formed machine translation systems.

Bearing this in mind, the main contributions we bring in this paper are:

1. The creation of a simple tweet sentiment analysis system, that employs a pre-processing stage to normalize the language and generalize the vocabulary employed to express sentiment. At this stage, we take into account the linguistic peculiarities of tweets, regarding spelling, use of slang, punctuation, etc., and also replace the sentiment-bearing words from the training data with a unique label. In this way, the sentence "I love roses." will be equivalent to the sentence "I like roses.", because "like" and "love" are both positive words according to the GI dictionary. If example 1 is contained in the training data and example 2 is contained in the test data, replacing the sentiment-bearing word with a general label increases the chance to have example 2 classified correctly. In the same line of thought, we also replaced modifiers with unique corresponding labels.

2. The use of minimal linguistic processing, which makes the approach easily portable to other languages. We employ only tokenization and do not process texts any further. The reason behind this choice is that we would like the final system to work in a similar fashion for as many languages as possible and for some of them, little or no tools are available.

3. The use of a standard news translation system to obtain data in four other languages - Italian, Spanish, German and French;

4. The evaluation of different combinations of languages in the training phase and the effect of using languages from the same family versus the use of individual or all languages in the training phase on the overall performance of the sentiment classification performance.

We show that using the training models generated with the method described we can improve the sentiment classification performance, irrespective of the domain and distribution of the test sets.

4 Sentiment Analysis in Tweets

Our sentiment analysis system is based on a hybrid approach, which employs supervised learning with the Weka (Weka Machine Learning Project, 2008) implementation of the Support Vector Machines Sequential Minimal Optimization (Platt, 1998) linear kernel, on unigram and bigram features, but exploiting as features sentiment dictionaries, emoticon lists, slang lists and other social media-specific features. We do not employ any specific language analysis software. The aim is to be able to apply, in a straightforward manner, the same approach to as many languages as possible. The approach can be extended to other languages by using similar dictionaries that have been created in our team. They were built using the same dictionaries we employ in this work and their corrected translation to Spanish. The new sentiment dictionaries were created by simultaneously translating from these two languages to a third one and considering the intersection of the translations as correct terms. Currently, new such dictionaries have been created for 15 other languages.

The sentiment analysis process contains two stages: pre-processing and sentiment classification.

4.1 Tweet Pre-processing

The language employed in Social Media sites is different from the one found in mainstream media and the form of the words employed is sometimes not the one we may find in a dictionary. Further on, users of Social Media platforms employ a special "slang" (i.e. informal language, with special expressions, such as "lol", "omg"), emoticons, and often emphasize words by repeating some of their letters. Additionally, the language employed in Twitter has specific characteristics, such as the markup of tweets that were reposted by other users with "RT", the markup of topics using the "#" (hash sign) and of the users using the "@" sign.

All these aspects must be considered at the time of processing tweets. As such, before applying supervised learning to classify the sentiment of the tweets, we preprocess them, to normalize the language they contain. The pre-processing stage contains the following steps:

In the first step of the pre-processing, we detect repetitions of punctuation signs (".", "!" and "?"). Multiple consecutive punctuation signs are replaced with the labels "multistop", for the fullstops, "multiexclamation" in the case of exclamation sign and "multiquestion" for the question mark and spaces before and after.

In the second step of the pre-processing, we employ the annotated list of emoticons from SentiStrength[2](Thelwall et al., 2010) and match the content of the tweets against this list. The emoticons found are replaced with their polarity ("positive" or "negative") and the "neutral" ones are deleted.

Subsequently, the tweets are lower cased and split into tokens, based on spaces and punctuation signs.

The next step involves the normalization of the language employed. In order to be able to include the semantics of the expressions frequently used in Social Media, we employed the list of slang from a specialized site [3].

At this stage, the tokens are compared to entries in Rogets Thesaurus. If no match is found, repeated letters are sequentially reduced to two or one until a match is found in the dictionary (e.g. "perrrrrrrrrrrrrrrrrrfeeect" becomes "perrfeect", "perfeect", "perrfect" and subsequently "perfect"). The words used in this form are maked as "stressed".

Further on, the tokens in the tweet are matched against three different sentiment lexicons: GI, LIWC and MicroWNOp, which were previously split into four different categories ("positive", "high positive", "negative" and "high negative"). Matched words are replaced with their sentiment label - i.e. "positive", "negative", "hpositive" and "hnegative". A version of the data without these replacements is also maintained, for comparison purposes.

Similar to the previous step, we employ a list of expressions that negate, intensify or diminish the intensity of the sentiment expressed to detect such words in the tweets. If such a word is matched, it is replaced with "negator", "intensifier" or "diminisher", respectively. As in the case of affective words, a version of the data without these replacements is also maintained, for comparison purposes.

Finally, the users mentioned in the tweet, which are marked with "@", are replaced with "PERSON" and the topics which the tweet refers to (marked with "#") are replaced with "TOPIC".

4.2 Sentiment Classification of Tweets

Once the tweets are pre-processed, they are passed on to the sentiment classification module. We employed supervised learning using SVM SMO with a linear kernel, based on boolean features - the presence or absence of n-grams (unigrams, bigrams and unigrams plus bigrams) determined from the training data (tweets that were previousely pre-processed as described above). Bigrams are used specifically to spot the influence

[2]http://sentistrength.wlv.ac.uk/

[3]http://www.chatslang.com/terms/social_media

of modifiers (negations, intensifiers, diminishers) on the polarity of the sentiment-bearing words.

4.3 Obtaining Multilingual Data for Sentiment Analysis in Tweets

Subsequent to the tweet normalization, we translate the Twitter data (the training and development data in the SemEval Task 2 campaign) using the Google machine translation system to four languages - Italian, Spanish, French and German. The reason for choosing the development dataset for testing is that this set is smaller and allows us to manually check and correct it, to obtain a Gold Standard (and ensure that performance results are not biased by the incorrect translation in both the training, as well as the development data).

Further on, we extract the same features as in the case of the system working for English - unigrams and bigrams - from these obtained datasets. We employ the features to train an SVM SMO classifier, in the same manner as we did for English.

5 Evaluation and Discussion

Although the different steps included to eliminate the noise in the data and the choice of features have been refined using our in-house gathered Twitter data, in order to evaluate our approach and make it comparable to other methods, we employ the data used in an established competition, allowing subsequent comparisons to be made.

5.1 Data Set

The characteristics of the training (T*) and development (test in our case) - t*- datasets employed are described in Table 1. On the last column, we also include the baseline in terms of accuracy, which is computed as the number of examples of the majoritary class over the total number of examples:

Data	#Tweet	#Pos.	#Neg.	#Neu.	Bl%
T*	6688	2450	956	3282	49%
t*	1051	386	199	466	44%

Table 1: Characteristics of the training (T*) and testing (t*) datasets employed.

5.2 Evaluation and Results

In order to test our sentiment analysis approach, we employed the datasets described above, for each of the languages individually, all the two-languages combinations, combinations of languages from the same linguistic family and all languages together.

The results are presented in Table 2. We consider the measure of accuracy and do not compare to the SemEval official results, because in the competition, the results did not take into account the "neutral" class.

Language(s)	Accuracy
English	64.75
Italian	60.12
French	62.31
German	61.32
Spanish	62.66
English + French	65.91
English + German	63.98
English + Italian	64.78
English + Spanish	68.23
Spanish + Italian	70.45
Spanish + French	67.14
Spanish + German	65.64
Italian + German	63.29
Italian + French	63.95
German + French	62.66
Italian + French + Spanish	68.53
All 5 languages	69.09

Table 2: Results obtained classifying each language individually versus on pairs and families of languages, respectively.

5.3 Discussion

From the results obtained, we can draw several conclusions.

First of all, we can see that using tweet normalization and employing machine translation, we can obtain high quality training data for sentiment analysis in many languages. The machine-translated data thus obtained can be reliably employed to build classifiers for sentiment, reaching a performance level that is similar to the results obtained for English and significatly above the baseline.

Secondly, seeing the performance of the different pairs of languages compared to individual results, we can: a) on the one hand, see that combining languages with a comparatively high difference in performance results in an increase of the lower-performing one and b) on the other hand, in some cases, the overall performance is improved on both systems, which shows that combining this data helps to disambiguate the contextual use of specific words.

Finally, the results show that the use of all the languages together improves the overall classification of sentiment in the data. This shows that a multilingual system can simply employ joint training data from different languages in a single classifier, thus making the sentiment classification straightforward, not needing any language detection software or training different classifiers.

By manually inspecting some of the examples in the datasets, we could see that the most important causes of incorrect classification were the word orders and faulty translations in context. Another reason for incorrect sentiment classification was the different manner in which negation is constructed in the different languages considered. In order to improve on this aspect, we will include language-specific rules by adding skip-bigrams (bigrams made up of non-consecutive tokens) features in the languages where the place of the negators can vary.

6 Conclusions and Future Work

In this article, we presented a method to create a simple sentiment analysis system for English and extend it to the multilingual setting, by employing a standard news machine translation system. We showed that using twitter language normalization, we can obtain good results in target languages and that the joint use of training data from different languages helps to increase the overall performance of the classification. Finally, we showed that the joint training using translated data from languages that are similar yield significantly improved results.

In future work, we plan to evaluate the use of higher-order n-grams (3-grams) and skip-grams to extract more complex patterns of sentiment expressions and be able to identify more precisely the scope of the negation. In this sense, we plan to take into account the modifier/negation schemes typical of each of the languages, to consider (further to translation) language-specific schemes of n-grams.

We also plan to test the performance of sentiment classification using translations *to* English and employing classifiers trained on English data. In order to do this, we require lists of slang and digital dictionaries to perform normalization. We would like to study the performance of our approach in the context of tweets related to specific news, in which case these short texts can be contextualized by adding further content from other information sources. In this way, it would be interesting to make a comparative analysis of the tweets written in different languages (from the same or different regions of the globe), on the same topics.

References

Alexandra Balahur and Marco Turchi. 2012. Multilingual sentiment analysis using machine translation? In *Proceedings of the 3rd Workshop in Computational Approaches to Subjectivity and Sentiment Analysis*, pages 52–60, Jeju, Korea, July. Association for Computational Linguistics.

C. Banea, R. Mihalcea, and J. Wiebe. 2008. A bootstrapping method for building subjectivity lexicons for languages with scarce resources. In *Proceedings of the Conference on Language Resources and Evaluations (LREC 2008), Maraakesh, Marocco.*

C. Banea, R. Mihalcea, and J. Wiebe. 2010. Multilingual subjectivity: are more languages better? In *Proceedings of the International Conference on Computational Linguistics (COLING 2010), Beijing, China.*, pages 28–36.

S. Deerwester, S. Dumais, G. W. Furnas, T. K. Landauer, and R. Harshman. 1990. Indexing by latent semantic analysis. *Journal of the American Society for Information Science*, 3(41).

Alec Go, Richa Bhayani, and Lei Huang. 2009. Twitter sentiment classification using distant supervision. *Processing*, pages 1–6.

Long Jiang, Mo Yu, Ming Zhou, Xiaohua Liu, and Tiejun Zhao. 2011. Target-dependent twitter sentiment classification. In *Proceedings of the 49th Annual Meeting of the Association for Computational Linguistics: Human Language Technologies - Volume 1*, HLT '11, pages 151–160, Stroudsburg, PA, USA. Association for Computational Linguistics.

J. Kim, J.-J. Li, and J.-H. Lee. 2010. Evaluating multilanguage-comparability of subjectivity analysis systems. In *Proceedings of the 48th Annual Meeting of the Association for Computational Linguistics*, pages 595–602.

Alexander Pak and Patrick Paroubek. 2010. Twitter as a corpus for sentiment analysis and opinion mining. In Nicoletta Calzolari (Conference Chair), Khalid Choukri, Bente Maegaard, Joseph Mariani, Jan Odijk, Stelios Piperidis, Mike Rosner, and Daniel Tapias, editors, *Proceedings of the*

Seventh conference on International Language Resources and Evaluation (LREC'10), Valletta, Malta; ELRA, may. European Language Resources Association. 19-21.

John C. Platt. 1998. Sequential minimal optimization: A fast algorithm for training support vector machines. Technical report, Advances in Kernel Methods - Support Vector Learning.

Jonathon Read. 2005. Using emoticons to reduce dependency in machine learning techniques for sentiment classification. In *Proceedings of the ACL Student Research Workshop*, ACLstudent '05, pages 43–48, Stroudsburg, PA, USA. Association for Computational Linguistics.

J. Steinberger, P. Lenkova, M. Ebrahim, M. Ehrman, A. Hurriyetoglu, M. Kabadjov, R. Steinberger, H. Tanev, V. Zavarella, and S. Vazquez. 2011a. Creating sentiment dictionaries via triangulation. In *Proceedings of the 2nd Workshop on Computational Approaches to Subjectivity and Sentiment Analysis*, Portland, Oregon.

J. Steinberger, P. Lenkova, M. Kabadjov, R. Steinberger, and E. van der Goot. 2011b. Multilingual entity-centered sentiment analysis evaluated by parallel corpora. In *Proceedings of the Conference on Recent Advancements in Natural Language Processing (RANLP)*, Hissar, Bulgaria.

Mike Thelwall, Kevan Buckley, Georgios Paltoglou, Di Cai, and Arvid Kappas. 2010. Sentiment in short strength detection informal text. *J. Am. Soc. Inf. Sci. Technol.*, 61(12):2544–2558, December.

Weka Machine Learning Project. 2008. Weka. URL http://www.cs.waikato.ac.nz/~ml/weka.

Cynthia Whissell. 1989. The Dictionary of Affect in Language. In Robert Plutchik and Henry Kellerman, editors, *Emotion: theory, research and experience*, volume 4, The measurement of emotions. Academic Press, London.

Theresa Wilson, Zornitsa Kozareva, Preslav Nakov, Sara Rosenthal, Veselin Stoyanov, and Alan Ritter. 2013. SemEval-2013 task 2: Sentiment analysis in twitter. In *Proceedings of the International Workshop on Semantic Evaluation*, SemEval '13, June.

Ley Zhang, Riddhiman Ghosh, Mohamed Dekhil, Meichun Hsu, and Bing Liu. 2011. Combining lexicon-based and learning-based methods for twitter sentiment analysis. Technical Report HPL-2011-89, HP, 21/06/2011.

Domain Adaptation for Parsing

Eric Baucom
Indiana University
Bloomington, IN, USA
eabaucom@indiana.edu

Levi King
Indiana University
Bloomington, IN, USA
leviking@indiana.edu

Sandra Kübler
Indiana University
Bloomington, IN, USA
skuebler@indiana.edu

Abstract

We compare two different methods in domain adaptation applied to constituent parsing: parser combination and co-training, each used to transfer information from the source domain of news to the target domain of natural dialogs, in a setting without annotated data. Both methods outperform the baselines and reach similar results. Parser combination profits most from the large amounts of training data combined with a robust probability model. Co-training, in contrast, relies on a small set of higher quality data.

1 Introduction

Research on parsing has mostly concentrated on parsing the Penn Treebank (Marcus et al., 1993). As a consequence, most parsers have probability models that are optimized for the syntactic annotations in this treebank and more generally for the language in the treebank. This means that a parser trained on the Penn Treebank will show a severe degradation in performance when used for parsing data from another domain (McClosky et al., 2010). More recently, research has started on adapting parsers to new domains so that the degradation in parsing is minimized. One of the first venues at which domain adaptation was targeted was the 2007 CoNLL shared task on dependency parsing (Nivre et al., 2007).

One of the challenges in domain adaptation for parsing is the lack of annotated data in the target domain. Research has covered a range of different approaches, all geared towards providing automatically labeled data in the target domain to add as training data. Approaches include ensembles of parsers, self-training, and methods for selecting high quality sentences to reduce the noise (see section 2 for details). The most promising approach at present is an approach by McClosky et al. (2010), which automatically selects a domain that is the most similar to the target domain.

In our current work, we investigate domain adaptation for constituent parsing, in a setting where no labeled data in the target domain is available. More specifically, we compare two different approaches: One approach is based on an ensemble of parsers, the other one uses co-training with two different parsers. Both approaches reach moderate improvements over the baseline, and we are interested in seeing the advantages and disadvantages of those two promising methods. The source domain for our experiments is the Penn Treebank; the target domain consists of spontaneous dialogs based on cooperative tasks involving navigation on a map or in a search environment. For the unlabeled target domain data, we use the Edinburgh Map Task (HCRC) corpus (Thompson et al., 1996), and the Indiana Cooperative Remote Search Task (CReST) corpus (Eberhard et al., 2010) as test set.

The remainder of the paper is structured as follows: In section 2, we discuss related work. Section 3 introduces the two methods that we will compare, and section 4 describes the experimental setup. In section 5, we first discuss the results of the individual approaches, and then attempt a comparison and an error analysis. In section 6, we conclude and describe future work.

2 Related Work

Domain adaptation can be divided into two different scenarios: one where a small set of annotated data from the target domain is available, and one where no annotated target data is available. Early work on domain adaptation for parsing shows that not having target domain data makes the task extremely challenging: In the CoNLL 2007 shared task on dependency parsing (Nivre et al., 2007), no team submitting results for the out-of-domain setting improved much over the baseline. Dredze et al. (2007), for example, presented three approaches to domain adaptation: modifications to the feature set, using a parser ensemble, and target focused learning, but they reached the best results by using all the available data. The best performing system (Sagae and Tsujii, 2007) used a combination of two different models of an LR parser and then selected identically parsed target sentences to add to the training set of the final parser. This approach outperformed the baseline of Dredze et al. (2007) by approximately 1%.

McClosky et al. (2006) use self-training in combination with a PCFG parser and reranking. They train the parser and reranker on the Penn Treebank, then parse and rerank a small set of target domain data. They reach an error reduction of 28% in the target domain. However, Sagae (2010) shows that while the reranking approach by McClosky et al. (2006) reaches higher F-scores than a self-training approach without reranking, the latter actually performs better in a semantic role labeling task.

Reichart and Rappoport (2007), in contrast, use a small annotated data set in the target domain for self-training without reranking. I.e., they train the parser on their small target domain data set and then perform self-training on more unlabeled data. They evaluate their parser in terms of annotation cost, and they show a 50% reduction in annotation cost.

Chen et al. (2008) work on domain adaptation without labeled target data: They parse the target data with a dependency parser. But rather than using the full parses as additional training data, they only add short-distance dependencies, which can be parsed more reliably. They gain approx. 1% over adding all sentences in Chinese. Kawahara and Uchimoto (2008) use a similar approach: They train a classifier to recognize reliably parsed sentences to add to the training set. This method outperforms the source domain baseline as well as all CoNLL 2007 systems by approx. 1%.

Finkel and Manning (2009) extend the work by Daume III (2007), who investigated a method for selecting general features that hold across domains. Finkel and Manning (2009) apply this method to dependency parsing, by using a hierarchical Bayesian model. They show an improvement of their approach over training on data from all domains in 4 out of 6 domains.

McClosky et al. (2010) investigate the automatic selection of source domains that are useful for parsing a target domain. Thus, the parser can adapt per document to a new target domain. They use different similarity metrics to determine the similarity of different source domains to the target domain and feed those into a regression model. They show that their model outperforms self-training, a uniform model as well as the best single domain for training selected by an oracle.

Miceli Barone and Attardi (2012) perform domain adaptation for dependency parsing using unannotated data. They integrate a transductive SVM as classifier, which can handle labeled and unlabeled examples as training data, into a shift-reduce dependency parser. They also reach an improvement in the area of 1% on Italian.

This overview shows that most work concentrates on domain adaptation when no annotated data in the target domain is available or when the target domain is unknown. Our work also focuses on a scenario where there is only unlabeled target domain data available. We compare co-training, a method that has not been used successfully for domain adaptation in parsing before, and a simpler approach based on an ensemble of three different parsers.

3 Domain Adaptation Methods

3.1 Parser Combination

A simple way of creating additional, labeled training data in a new domain is to use an ensemble of parsers and then select the sentences on which the parsers agree. This parser combination method takes advantage of the different biases built into different parsing algorithms; agreement between parsers should translate into a greater likelihood that the agreed upon parse will be correct.

In practice, the ensemble of parsers is trained on an available annotated data set in the source domain, i.e., the Penn Treebank (PTB) for parsing. They are then used to parse a corpus of unannotated data in the target domain. The sentences from the unannotated target domain on which the parsers agree are added to the original source domain gold-standard annotated data, and one (or more) parser is retrained on the resulting union.

Originally, this method was used by van Halteren et al. (2001) to improve part of speech taggers. Following Sagae and Tsujii (2007) and (Chen et al., 2008), we adapt the approach to the task of parsing by retraining with agreed upon parses from only a part of the ensemble as well as with partial trees. This will lead to more training data, though potentially of a lower quality.

3.2 Co-Training

Co-training, as proposed by Blum and Mitchell (1998), is a semi-supervised machine learning approach that uses two different "views" of the data to train two specialized classifiers, which provide additional training data for each other. In co-training for domain adaptation of parsers, we follow Goldman and Zhou (2000) in assuming two different parsers rather than two different feature sets. In other words, the different views come from two parsers built on different parsing algorithms, i.e., with different biases. The source-trained parsers are used to parse the unlabeled target data, providing a confidence score with each parse. The parsers each parse sentences from a pool of m randomly selected sentences from the set of unlabeled target domain data. The output of each parser is ranked by confidence scores, and the n-best parsed sentences from each parser are added to the original training data for the next cycle. Then the set of sentences is replenished from the unlabeled data set. This process is repeated until no further improvement on the development set is observed. Because the parsers have different algorithms and, theoretically, different strengths, each should be able to learn from highly-confident training data provided by the other.

4 Experimental Setup

4.1 Data Sets

We use the following data sets: The Penn Treebank (PTB) (Marcus et al., 1993) serves as the training set from the source domain. The PTB training files were modified to remove any grammatical functions not present in our target domain (see below). All experiments use either sections 2-11 (as in the 2007 CoNLL shared task on domain adaptation), or sections 2-21 (the standard training set for parsing).

Our target domain is dialog text taken from cooperative map tasks. The test corpus consists of Cooperative Remote Search Task (CReST) dialogs, in which a *searcher* collects and deposits items throughout a search location (a series of connected offices) at the guidance of a *director*, who has a map of the location and communicates instructions remotely by mobile telephone. The original CReST corpus contains a small number of novel tags to handle phenomena that are common in dialog data but not in newspaper text, such as imperative verbs. These tags were converted to their closest equivalents in the PTB tagset. The syntactic annotation of the CReST corpus includes constituent and dependency annotations. We use the constituent annotation, which follows the PTB annotation (Santorini, 1991). In contrast to the PTB, the CReST annotations use a subset of the grammatical functions from the Penn Treebank: subject, predicate, location, direction, and temporal modifications. For our experiments, 5 dialogs (1 137 sentences) of the CReST corpus were reserved for development, and 18 dialogs (4 518 sentences) were used as the test set.

The Human Communication Research Center Map Task Corpus (HCRC, also known as the Edinburgh Map Task) (Thompson et al., 1996) is used as the unlabeled target domain set. HCRC consists of 128 dialogs. In each dialog, both participants had a map of the same area, but the maps differed in the landmarks featured in given locations, and participants could not see their partners' maps. One map included a route, and the holder of that map was asked to verbally guide the other participant to redraw the route on his or her map. We ignore all annotations in the corpus and only use the transcribed sentences. The full corpus contains 27 084 sentences. When one-word sentences are removed (as described below), 18 738 sentences remain. Note that this corpus shares many characteristics with the CReST corpus, but there are differences in the domain: the environments, landmarks, and the task itself are different, and in HCRC, neither participant is physically present in the mapped location. Furthermore, dialectal differences exist, in that 61 of the 64 HCRC participants were from the Glasgow, Scotland area, while the 46 CReST participants were from the US.

4.2 Parsers

Both experiments use the Berkeley Parser (Petrov et al., 2006). For parser combination, we also use the Bikel Parser (Bikel, 2004) and LoPar (Schmid, 2000), and for co-training, the Stanford Parser (Klein and Manning, 2003).

Bikel's parser is a probabilistic context-free (PCFG) parser with a probability model based on Collins's model 2 (Collins, 1999); the Berkeley parser performs split-merge cycles on the training data to automatically induce a PCFG with optimized syntactic categories. Collins' model 2 (Collins, 1997) is a generative model based on bigram probabilities, dependencies between pairs of words, as well as sub-categorization frames for head-words. LoPar was used in concert with these two parsers for the parser combination experiments due to its human accessible grammar files: rule counts can be directly modified and new rules added to the LoPar grammar. Thus, we can add partially agreeing sentences, in the form of individual rules, from the HCRC data. For the co-training experiments, we used the Stanford parser instead of Bikel's because the co-training experiments require the parsers to generate confidence scores for each parse. The Berkeley parser produces such scores, Bikel's does not. The Berkeley parser's training was limited to 5 split-merge cycles in order to avoid overfitting to the PTB.

In all experiments, sentences longer than 40 words were excluded from training and testing. All parsers were trained on the source domain training sets of PTB sections 2-11 and 2-21. All experiments use gold POS tags for the PTB and CReST. HCRC is tagged with TnT (Brants, 2000), trained on the full PTB.

4.3 Parser Combination

The three parsers were used to parse the HCRC corpus. Agreement among the three was determined by bracketing alone (unlabeled condition), and bracketing along with node labels (labeled condition). For the unlabeled condition, the labels to add to training are simply taken from the parser with the highest overall baseline, i.e. Berkeley.

LoPar alone was chosen as our test parser for the experiments that involve adding agreeing rules directly to the training. For the other experiments, we also used the Berkeley parser and Bikel's parser as final parsers.

4.4 Co-Training

For co-training, the value of the n best sentences added to the training set per cycle was chosen between 20 and 500, and a minimum of four co-training cycles were performed. The size of the pool of randomly selected sentences to parse, m, was chosen from values ranging from 250 to 1500. Optimal combinations of n and m were determined by a non-exhaustive search on the PTB 2-11 training set and the CReST development set. The optimal values for n and m were found to be 20 and 500, respectively. Then, we repeated the experiment with the PTB 2-21 training set.

We used a single training set for both parsers; i.e., after each cycle, the n-best parsed sentences from each parser were added to a common training set, rather than passed to a unique training set for the opposite parser. Initial experiments showed that the set of n-best ranked sentences was comprised almost entirely of single-word sentences, leading to a decrease in performance from the baselines. Consequently, we removed all one-word sentences from the raw target domain data.

4.5 Evaluation

For evaluation, we used the standard evalb software[1] and report F_1-scores, based on labeled precision and recall. We performed significance tests using Dan Bikel's Randomized Parsing Evaluation Comparator[2].

5 Results

5.1 Parser Combination

For the experiments on parser combination, we report three baselines, one baseline per parser. Then, we investigate agreement across 3 parsers and across 2 parsers.

Agreement across 3 parsers. Here, we report results for the following experiments:

1. SENTLAB adds HCRC sentences on which the 3 parsers agree on labeled analyses.
2. SENTUNLAB adds HCRC sentences on which the 3 parsers agree on bracketing but not necessarily on labels.
3. RULES adds individual context free rules to training on which the 3 parsers agree.

The third condition can only be used with LoPar as the final parser, the other two conditions are used in combination with each parser.

In table 1, we present the results for these experiments. We also experimented with conditions where we removed one-word HCRC sentences from the additional training data. However, the F-scores with one-word sentences removed were very close to their counterparts, if not somewhat lower. For this reason, we do not report them.

[1] http://nlp.cs.nyu.edu/evalb/

[2] http://www.cis.upenn.edu/~dbikel/software.html#comparator

Experiment	sec. 2-11	sec. 2-21
Berkeley baseline	71.30	**72.24**
Bikel baseline	**71.93**	71.94
LoPar baseline	70.41	70.75
Berk.+SENTUNLAB	65.86	69.46
Berk.+SENTLAB	70.49	69.41
Bikel+SENTUNLAB	67.16	69.36
Bikel+SENTLAB	68.04	68.64
Lo.+SENTUNLAB	70.37	*72.15*
Lo.+SENTLAB	70.50	71.42
Lo.+RULES	*70.58*	71.37

Table 1: Results of the parser combination on the CReST test set (F_1). We report labeled F_1.

The results show that the baseline parsers profit only marginally from the larger training set in the second column. Note that the results are lower than normally reported for in-domain parsing. This is due to the fact that the two domains are very different. LoPar performs lower than its two counterparts, the Berkeley parser and Bikel's, as is expected, since it is a PCFG parser with a straightforward probability model.

When we add the training data from HCRC to the source training, both the Berkeley parser and Bikel's parser degrade in performance while LoPar's performance increases over its baseline. A major source of error lies in CReST's many one-word sentences: 1 638 out of 4 518. In CReST, the vast majority (1 580) of the one-word sentence parses have INTJ as the unary node. The extended grammars used by LoPar closely matches this distribution, with a majority of the one-word sentence parses being dominated by the INTJ unary node. The Berkeley and Bikel parsers, in contrast, have a strong preference to label the unary nodes as FRAG. Despite being trained on the same additional data, LoPar is not as subject to this errant distribution. This may be due to the fact that the probability models in the Berkeley and Bikel parsers are more finely tuned to the PTB and thus more brittle to noisy data, whereas LoPar uses a simpler model and is more robust.

For LoPar, providing additional training data from HCRC in all 3 variants improves the F-scores by a small margin over its baseline, with only one exception: In the experiment where we train LoPar on the small training set and add all sentences on which all three parsers agree, we see a small loss in the F-score. The second trend that can be observed is that LoPar trained on the large source domain data set profits more from the additional target domain data than when it is trained on the smaller source domain set.

The best performing condition given the small source domain training set is the one in which we add individual rules, RULES. Given the larger source domain training set, the best performing condition is the one using sentences with unlabeled agreement, SENTUNLAB. Thus, if the parser has a solid, large grammar from the source domain, it can use the large but noisy addition to its grammar while the smaller source domain grammar requires more high quality additions. In the setting with the small source domain grammar, RULES adds 8 966 additional rules, SENTLAB adds 3 135 rules, and SENTUNLAB adds 25 764 rules. However, note that even the best performing LoPar variant cannot outperform the results by the Berkeley baseline (or the Bikel baseline, in the setting with the smaller source domain training set).

Agreement across 2 parsers. We now turn to the experiments with enforced agreement based on a dyad of parsers. In table 2, we present results from the experiments with the relaxed condition, for each possible dyad of parsers, combined with LoPar as the final parser. We also retrained the Berkeley and the Bikel parser on the extended data sets, but the results were far below the ones for LoPar. This is interesting in itself because LoPar, as the weakest baseline parser, is capable of profiting the most from the additional target domain data. We assume that this is a consequence of LoPar's simple, but robust probability model.

The best performer for both sizes of source domain data is the combination of the Berkeley parser and Bikel's in the unlabeled sentence condition (BERKELEY/BIKELSENTUNLAB), which is also the experiment where LoPar has the most additional training, adding either 50 050 rules (sec. 2-11 experiments) or 53 123 rules (sec. 2-21 experiments) (cf. 312 614 rules in sec. 2-11 baseline, 662 266 in sec. 2-21 baseline). Also worth noting is the fact that LoPar is taking training from the agreements from the *other two* parsers. LoPar profits the most from the sentences selected by the combination of parsers that have different biases. In this way, the parser combination approach is similar to co-training. Note that when we enforce agreement between two parsers only, the addi-

Experiment	F_1 (sec. 2-11)	F_1 (sec. 2-21)
Berkeley baseline	71.30	72.24
Bikel baseline	71.93	71.94
LoPar baseline	70.41	70.75
LoPar+BERKELEY/BIKELSENTLAB	71.26	72.77†
LoPar+BERKELEY/LOPARSENTLAB	70.51	71.36
LoPar+BIKEL/LOPARSENTLAB	70.15	71.10
LoPar+BERKELEY/BIKELSENTUNLAB	**73.41**†	**73.66**†
LoPar+BERKELEY/LOPARSENTUNLAB	70.43	72.22
LoPar+BIKEL/LOPARSENTUNLAB	72.87‡	73.29†
LoPar+BERKELEY/BIKELRULES	71.52	72.22
LoPar+BERKELEY/LOPARRULES	70.62	71.20
LoPar+BIKEL/LOPARRULES	70.49	71.35

Table 2: Results for LoPar with HCRC training, based on 2 parsers, on the CReST test set. †=significance at $p < 0.001$ over the best performing baseline, ‡ at $p < 0.005$.

tional training data boosts LoPar's accuracy to improve over both the Berkeley and the Bikel baselines. We also see that in this condition, there is only a minimal difference between the small and the large source domain training set.

We also looked at the influence of quantity of (additional) training data on the results. In general, more training data leads to better results. As expected, PTB sections 2-21 perform better than sections 2-11, but as more and more data is added, the results converge, leading us to the conclusion that as more reliable target domain training data is available, the size of the initial source domain training set becomes less important. However, there must be a critical mass of additional training data before results start to improve, with more data required for a smaller source domain training set. This might suggest that the other parser combinations may not have resulted in this critical mass; in other words, that the HCRC corpus may be too small as a target domain data set given a parser combination setting.

5.2 Co-Training

In the co-training setting, the additional training set is produced by two individual parsers, the Berkeley and Stanford parser. The selection of reliable sentences is based on parser confidence values, i.e., the probabilities associated with parses. The additional sentences are added in cycles. We stopped the co-training process after 10 cycles. The results on the CReST development set for 6 cycles are given in Table 3.

The results show that both parsers reach lower

Training	PTB 2-11		PTB 2-21	
Parser	Berk.	Stan.	Berk.	Stan.
Baseline	68.24	67.83	69.18	68.39
Cycle 1	68.06	67.89	**70.04**	68.40
Cycle 2	69.68	68.10	69.49	68.40
Cycle 3	69.29	68.03	68.64	68.40
Cycle 4	**70.40**	68.25	68.68	**68.51**
Cycle 5	68.35	**68.37**	69.21	68.46
Cycle 6	70.31	68.36	69.97	68.43

Table 3: F-scores for 6 cycles (development data).

baseline results on the development set than in parser combination. It is also obvious the Berkeley parser outperforms the Stanford parser and that the larger, source domain training set has only a minimal effect on parser accuracy.

For the smaller training set, the Berkeley parser reached optimal results in the fourth co-training cycle and the Stanford parser in the fifth cycle. With n set at 20, these scores represent the addition of 160 and 200 target domain sentences to the training set, respectively. For the larger training set, the Berkeley parser reached optimal performance in the first cycle, and the Stanford parser in the fourth cycle, meaning 20 and 160 sentences were added, respectively.

We then used the grammars from the optimal cycle and PTB training set in order to parse the test set using both parsers. The results of these settings, along with the parsers' baselines on the test set are shown in Table 4. These results show that both parsers reach higher F-scores than on the development set. Moreover, the development set

Training	sec. 2-11		sec. 2-21	
Parser	Berk.	Stan.	Berk.	Stan.
Baseline	71.30	70.58	72.24	71.48
Optimized	**72.11**†	70.63†	**73.11**†	71.60†

Table 4: F-scores for co-training on the test set. †=significance at $p < 0.001$ over the baseline.

scores saw significantly higher improvements; the greatest improvement overall came from the combination of Berkeley and PTB 2-11, which rose from a baseline of 68.24 to 70.40 in the fourth cycle. The best results on the test set, for both PTB training sizes, are reached by the Berkeley parser, with an F-score of 72.11 given the small training set and an F-score of 73.11 given the larger training set. The results are surprising given that only a very small number of target domain sentences was added to the source domain training set.

5.3 Discussion

We are now in a position to compare the results of the two domain adaptation methods. A first comparison shows that both methods reach a similar performance: Given the larger PTB training set, the parser combination method reaches an F-score of 73.66 while co-training reaches 73.11. However, these results are obtained by different parsers and by training on different amounts of target domain training sentences: While the parser combination approach reaches the highest results based on using LoPar, co-training favors the Berkeley parser. And while parser combination adds 15 200 sentences from the HCRC corpus (including one-word sentences), the best co-training results are reached by adding only 20 sentences. Also, the best performing parser combination took approximately 3.5 hours while the best performing co-training experiment (which took only 1 cycle) required 2.5 hours on the same cluster.

Error analysis. In examining the results of our two approaches, unsurprisingly, we found that a large proportion of the errors are related to the considerable differences between the source and target domain. Newspaper text is more formal than spontaneous dialogs. Moreover, some phenomena that occur frequently in CReST are absent or rare in the PTB training data. For example, sentence-initial "and" is a prominent feature of CReST, but naturally, not so frequent in the PTB. There are no sentences that begin with "and" in the training set, which makes them a challenge for the parsers. Thus, in our best co-training experiment, the Berkeley parser relied heavily on the generic `X` label. However, this label is not used in this context in the gold standard. Notably, the distribution of these labels in the Stanford parses as well as in the parser combination parses is similar to that of the gold standard. However, all parse models have a tendency to assume such sentences are fragmentary and thus should be grouped under the `FRAG` label.

In general, fragmentary cases, which are abundant in CReST, are difficult for parsers to learn since they often require global information to decide that a constituent is incomplete. All parsers tend to either posit an extra element `FRAG` where there should be none, or omit it when it should be there. This can have a devastating effect on the F-scores of short sentences, which are extremely frequent in CReST.

6 Conclusion and Future Work

We performed domain adaptation for constituent parsing using two different methods. Our target domain consists of spontaneous dialogues involving collaboration between speakers. In the comparison of parser combination versus co-training, both methods outperform their respective baselines, and they reach a similar performance on the test set. We can conclude that the best parser combination adds more target domain sentences to the source domain training set while the co-training technique is faster. Potentially, LoPar could also profit from the small number of sentences chosen in the co-training experiment, but we assume that their number is too small to have an effect on the rather robust probability model.

For the future, we are planning to extend our experiments: First, we are planning to add the Stanford parser to the parser combination experiments. Then, we will use both domain adaptation methods for dependency parsing. Since both the Penn Treebank and CReST are available in dependency format, we can perform these experiments on the same data sets.

Acknowledgment

This work is based on research supported by the US Office of Naval Research (ONR) Grant #N00014-10-1-0140.

References

Daniel M Bikel. 2004. *On the parameter space of generative lexicalized statistical parsing models*. Ph.D. thesis, University of Pennsylvania.

Avrim Blum and Tom Mitchell. 1998. Combining labeled and unlabeled data with co-training. In *Proceedings of the Eleventh Annual Conference on Computational Learning Theory*, pages 92–100.

Thorsten Brants. 2000. Tnt: A statistical part-of-speech tagger. In *Proceedings of the Sixth Conference on Applied Natural Language Processing*, pages 224–231, Seattle, WA.

Wenliang Chen, Youzheng Wu, and Hitoshi Isahara. 2008. Learning reliable information for dependency parsing adaptation. In *Proceedings of the 22nd International Conference on Computational Linguistics (COLING)*, pages 113–120, Manchester, UK.

Michael Collins. 1997. Three generative, lexicalised models for statistical parsing. In *Proceedings of the Eighth Conference of the European Chapter of the Association for Computational Linguistics (EACL)*, pages 16–23, Madrid, Spain.

Michael Collins. 1999. *Head-Driven Statistical Models for Natural Language Parsing*. Ph.D. thesis, University of Pennsylvania.

Hal Daume III. 2007. Frustratingly easy domain adaptation. In *Proceedings of the 45th Annual Meeting of the Association of Computational Linguistics*, pages 256–263, Prague, Czech Republic.

Mark Dredze, John Blitzer, Partha Pratim Talukdar, Kuzman Ganchev, João Graca, and Fernando Pereira. 2007. Frustratingly hard domain adaptation for dependency parsing. In *Proceedings of the CoNLL Shared Task Session of EMNLP-CoNLL 2007*, pages 1051–1055, Prague, Czech Republic.

Kathleen Eberhard, Hannele Nicholson, Sandra Kübler, Susan Gunderson, and Matthias Scheutz. 2010. The Indiana "Cooperative Remote Search Task" (CReST) Corpus. In *Proceedings of the Seventh International Conference on Language Resources and Evaluation (LREC)*, Valetta, Malta.

Jenny Rose Finkel and Christopher Manning. 2009. Hierarchical Bayesian domain adaptation. In *Proceedings of Human Language Technologies: The 2009 Annual Conference of the North American Chapter of the Association for Computational Linguistics*, pages 602–610, Boulder, CO.

Sally Goldman and Yan Zhou. 2000. Enhancing supervised learning with unlabeled data. In *Proceedings of the 17th International Conference on Machine Learning (ICML)*, pages 327–334, Stanford University, CA.

Daisuke Kawahara and Kiyotaka Uchimoto. 2008. Learning reliability of parses for domain adaptation of dependency parsing. In *Proceedings of the Third International Joint Conference on Natural Language Processing (IJCNLP)*, Hyderabad, India.

Dan Klein and Christopher Manning. 2003. Accurate unlexicalized parsing. In *Proceedings of the 41st Annual Meeting on Association for Computational Linguistics*, pages 423–430, Sapporo, Japan.

Mitchell Marcus, Mary Ann Marcinkiewicz, and Beatrice Santorini. 1993. Building a large annotated corpus of English: The Penn Treebank. *Computational Linguistics*, 19(2):313–330.

David McClosky, Eugene Charniak, and Mark Johnson. 2006. Reranking and self-training for parser adaptation. In *Proceedings of the 21st International Conference on Computational Linguistics and 44th Annual Meeting of the Association for Computational Linguistics (COLING-ACL)*, Sydney, Australia.

David McClosky, Eugene Charniak, and Mark Johnson. 2010. Automatic domain adaptation for parsing. In *Human Language Technologies: The 2010 Annual Conference of the North American Chapter of the Association for Computational Linguistics*, pages 28–36, Los Angeles, CA.

Antonio Valerio Miceli Barone and Giuseppe Attardi. 2012. Dependency parsing domain adaptation using transductive SVM. In *Proceedings of the Joint Workshop on Unsupervised and Semi-Supervised Learning in NLP*, pages 55–59, Avignon, France.

Joakim Nivre, Johan Hall, Sandra Kübler, Ryan McDonald, Jens Nilsson, Sebastian Riedel, and Deniz Yuret. 2007. The CoNLL 2007 shared task on dependency parsing. In *Proceedings of the CoNLL 2007 Shared Task. Joint Conference on Empirical Methods in Natural Language Processing and Computational Natural Language Learning (EMNLP-CoNLL)*, pages 915–932, Prague, Czech Republic.

Slav Petrov, Leon Barrett, Romain Thibaux, and Dan Klein. 2006. Learning accurate, compact, and interpretable tree annotation. In *Proceedings of the 21st International Conference on Computational Linguistics and the 44th Annual Meeting of the Association for Computational Linguistics*, pages 433–440, Sydney, Australia.

Roi Reichart and Ari Rappoport. 2007. Self-training for enhancement and domain adaptation of statistical parsers trained on small datasets. In *Proceedings of the 45th Annual Meeting of the Association of Computational Linguistics*, pages 616–623, Prague, Czech Republic.

Kenji Sagae and Jun'ichi Tsujii. 2007. Dependency parsing and domain adaptation with LR models and parser ensembles. In *Proceedings of the CoNLL Shared Task Session of EMNLP-CoNLL 2007*, pages 1044–1050, Prague, Czech Republic.

Kenji Sagae. 2010. Self-training without reranking for parser domain adaptation and its impact on semantic role labeling. In *Proceedings of the 2010 Workshop on Domain Adaptation for Natural Language Processing*, pages 37–44, Uppsala, Sweden.

Beatrice Santorini. 1991. Bracketing guidelines for the Penn Treebank Project. Department of Computer and Information Science, University of Pennsylvania.

Helmut Schmid. 2000. LoPar: Design and implementation. Technical report, Universität Stuttgart.

Henry Thompson, Anne Anderson, Ellen Gurman Bard, Gwyneth Doherty-Sneddon, Alison Newlands, and Cathy Sotillo. 1996. The HCRC Map Task Corpus: Natural dialogue for speech recognition. In *Proceedings of the ARPA Human Language Technology Workshop*, Plainsboro, NJ.

Hans van Halteren, Walter Daelemans, and Jakub Zavrel. 2001. Improving accuracy in word class tagging through the combination of machine learning systems. *Computational Linguistics*, 27(2):199–229.

Towards a Structured Representation of Generic Concepts and Relations in Large Text Corpora

Archana Bhattarai
Department of Computer Science
The University of Memphis
abhattar@memphis.edu

Vasile Rus
Department of Computer Science
The University of Memphis
vrus@memphis.edu

Abstract

Extraction of structured information from text corpora involves identifying entities and the relationship between entities expressed in unstructured text. We propose a novel iterative pattern induction method to extract relation tuples exploiting lexical and shallow syntactic pattern of a sentence. We start with a single pattern to illustrate how the method explores additional paterns and tuples by itself with increasing amount of data. We apply frequency and correlation based filtering and ranking of relation tuples to ensure the correctness of the system. Experimental evaluation compared to other state of the art open extraction systems such as Reverb, textRunner and WOE shows the effectiveness of the proposed system.

1 Introduction

Traditional information extraction methodologies tend to extract a predefined relation between named entities annotated in a different process. While this method might be useful and accurate for smaller data with limited entity types and relations, it cannot scale to extract entities and their relationships in web due to the sheer volume and heterogeneity of data. Thus open domain information extraction systems such as Reverb (Fader et al., 2011), TEXTRUNNER (Yates et al., 2007) and NELL (Carlson et al., 2010) have received added attention in recent times. Extracting machine readable structured information from free text is the basis of most of the semantic analytical systems. With these units of semantic information, a lot of applications requiring semantic information processing such as finding the semantic similarity between two unit of texts, semantic inference, automated question-answering etc can be visualized with better performance.

Existing work on pre-defined relation extraction have implemented methods of supervised, semi-supervised, bootstrapped and unsupervised classification(Zhao and Grishman, 2005), (Kambhatla, 2004) (Bunescu and Mooney, 2006) (Zelenko et al., 2003). For open information extraction methods, since they do not have predefined relations, it is very hard if impossible to generate labeled data for all potential relations in large text corpora. In this paper, we propose an iterative pattern induction based extraction system CREATE (Concept Representation and Extraction through Heterogenous Evidence), to extract relation tuples from large text corpora. We will start with a single selective pattern and iteratively add tuples and patterns in the corresponding collection. This method is easily usable in any domain since it does not require any labeled data. We ensure the selectivity of the pattern by filtering the patterns with statistics such as frequency and average pointwise mutual information (PMI) and specificity of the pattern. CREATE works under the assumption that sentences have a pattern of expressing information and this pattern is followed by multiple sentences. If we can explore these patterns in a language, we can extract tuples from all the sentences to build an automated system. One of the simplest cases of such a pattern is a sentence that only has two nouns and a verb in between. For example, for the sentence *"Google bought Youtube"*, the part-of-speech structure will be "NNP VBD NNP" and hence it is easy to identify two nouns as concepts and the verb as a relation between these two concepts. Thus, the tuple, *bought(Google, Youtube)* can be extracted with high confidence. The beauty of this system is that it gracefully identifies such patterns without requiring any human input and expands itself with the addition of every sentence on the system. The state of the art system that is closest to CREATE in terms of tuple generation is Reverb (Fader et al., 2011). The core idea of

Reverb is to identify a relation and extract concepts in the immediate left and right of the relation to form a tuple. The system takes a greedy approach where it only considers concepts that are adjacent to relations. Moreover, they also ignore the information that might change the context of the tuple in the sentence. For example, for the sentence *"RSV in older children and adults causes a cold."*, Reverb extracts tuple *causes(adults, a cold)* with confidence 0.6799. This approach has two disadvantages, first; it extracts invalid tuple as it ignores complete sentence context, second; it misses correct tuple *causes(RSV, cold)* because of its greedy nature. We overcome both the disadvantages in CREATE. Although, Reverb does not require training data to extract tuples, it does require labeled data to determine the confidence of a tuple. CREATE does not require labeled data other than the seed pattern at any stage of the process. With enough iterations and larger corpus, CREATE is able to extract the tuple *causes(RSV, cold)* correctly with high confidence.

Few of the properties that we exploit for the filtering of tuples are as follows:

- Patterns and tuples have dual dependence. Patterns can be used to extract tuples and tuples can be used to identify patterns.
- If a tuple is generated from two different sentences using two different patterns, then the confidence of the tuple is highly increased.
- If a pattern only produces high quality tuples, then the pattern is considered to be of high confidence.
- Web is highly redundant. This redundancy can be exploited to evaluate the correctness of a tuple.

Our approach is to learn the patterns in an iterative manner as in DIPRE (Brin, 1999) and Snowball (Agichtein and Gravano, 2000). We extend the work one step further to iteratively extract tuples with open relations from large text corpora. We follow the standard step of extracting patterns based on known tuples, extracting tuples based on known patterns and evaluating and refinining patterns based on inherent statistics to obtain high precision tuples and patterns.

We make the following contributions in this paper.

- We extend and adapt pattern based tuple extraction to perform open information extraction.
- We propose a method of domain independent pattern generation.
- With the patterns generated in step 2, we propose a method of relation tuple extraction.
- We propose an effective method to refine/rank extracted tuples and patterns without human supervision.

2 Related Work

One of the major goals of open information extraction is to build automated system that can read textual data to a deeper extent compared to bag of words model. Carlson et. al (Carlson et al., 2010) use semi-supervised bootstrapping approach to continuously read and update the knowledge base with an Expectation Maximization like algorithm. Other systems that are tied to a particular structure are (Suchanek et al., 2007), (Auer et al., 2007), (Wu and Weld, 2010) which focus on more structured part of large factual collections such as Wikipedia based on wikipedia-centric properties. The first true open information extraction system TEXTRUNNER, obtained training data applying some heuristics rules over dependency parsing of the training corpus. Using these training samples, sequence based classifiers were trained and more tuples were extracted. The WOE systems (Wu and Weld, 2010) introduced by Wu and Weld make use of Wikipedia as a source of training data for their extractors, which leads to further improvements over TEXTRUNNER (Yates et al., 2007). Wu and Weld also show that dependency parse features result in a dramatic increase in precision and recall over shallow linguistic features, but at the cost of extraction speed. Semisupervised methods start with a few manually provided domain independent extraction patterns that will extract training tuples. Statsnowball works under the principle of iterative pattern and tuple generation using Markov Logic Network (Zhu et al., 2009) and show improved extraction compared to TEXTRUNNER. Reverb (Fader et al., 2011) extracts on simple logic of extracting probable entities/concepts connected with a relation term adjacently. While it does not require seed data or training data to extract relation tuples, it depends on manually analysed data for the confidence evaluation of a tuple. Unsupervised methods generally exploit the characteristic of the text source, perform deep or shallow parsing and extract the patterns and cluster these patterns to extract relations. Yan et. al. (Yan et al., 2009) used the characteristics of wikipedia and performed clustering of patterns to extract relations without human supervision. They report a precision as high as 84% with deep linguistic parsing. Other works (Syed and Finin, 2010) also use wikipedia for ontology development for entities. (Min et al., 2012) extract relation tuples based on entity similarity graph and pattern similarity. Probabilistic topic based models (Chang et al., 2009) (Yao et al., 2011) have also been used to infer relation between entity-pairs. These models assume relation tuples as atomic observations in documents rather than word observations in standard LDA model.

3 Problem Definition

We formulate the problem of relation tuple extraction as a binary classification problem. Given a sentence $S = (w1; w2; ..; e1..; wj; ..r1; wk..; e2; ::; wn)$ where $e1$ and $e2$ are the entities of interest, $r1$ is the relation of interest, and $w1, w2....wj...wk$ is the context of the tuple in the sentence s, the classification function,

$$f(T(S)) = \begin{cases} 1 & \text{if } e1 \text{ and } e2 \text{ are related by } r1 \\ -1 & \text{otherwise} \end{cases}$$

Here $T(S)$ is a feature set extracted from the sentence as a context. The classification model is built based on context, independent of entities and relations. A context or a pattern of a tuple in a sentence is a 4-tuple $(left, middle\_left, middle\_right, right)$ where $left$ is the sequential list of entities and words that occur before first argument in the tuple, $middle\_left$ is the list of words that occur between first argument and relation, $middle\_right$ is the list of words that occur between relation and second argument and $right$ is the list of words that occur after second argument in the sentence unless another relation is detected.

The classification function $f(T(S)) = 1$ if the pattern of the tuple T in the sentence S exists in pattern database.the degree of similarity of the context of probable tuple is greater than threshold similarity with one of the contexts existing in context-base.

4 Create Tuple/Pattern Extraction Methodology

Given a set of documents containing sentences, our goal is to extract relation tuples with highest recall and precision. As explained earlier, our system is designed to utilize the dual dependence of tuple with pattern and pattern with tuple. As a starting point, we use a seed pattern $p = (\phi, \phi, \phi, \phi)$ that will generate tuples from text corpus. These tuples are then used to generate extraction patterns which in turn generate more tuples just like in Snowball. All the extracted tuples and patterns in the process are not guaranteed to be correct. A good tuple should be syntactically and semantically correct as well as articulate, autonomous and informative. Similarly, a good pattern should achieve a good balance between two competitive criteria; specificity and coverage. Specificity means the pattern is able to identify high-quality relation tuples; while coverage means the pattern can identify a statistically non-trivial number of good relation tuples. Hence, in the process, we have a self evaluating system which evaluates and filters out invalid tuples and patterns based on their statistical properties. The overall system can be broken down into several modules, each of which perform an isolated task such as concept extraction, relation extraction, probable tuple generation, tuple verification etc. The system architecture of the overall system has been depicted in figure 1 and the algorithm is shown in Table 1. The sub-modules are explained in detail in the subsequent sub-sections.

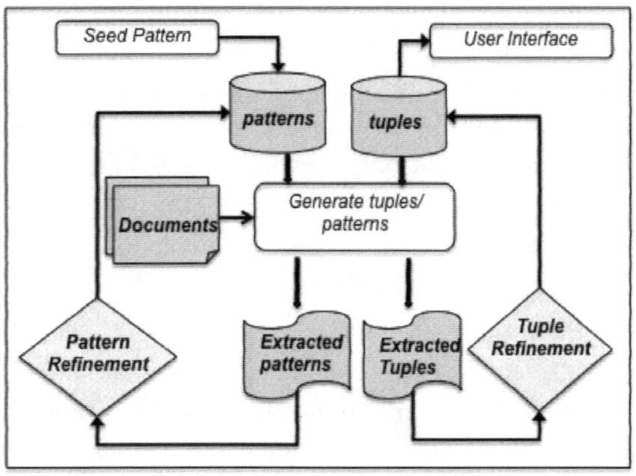

Figure 1: Overall System Architecture

Feature:We consider lexical and shallow parse information as features for relation extraction.

Lexical and shallow NLP techniques are robust and fast enough for a problem like ours where extraction needs to be performed at web scale. Although, our concept extraction module can be easily replaced with named entity extractor, we primarily use part-of-speech tagging and chunking results for concept/relation extraction. All the sentences in our data sets are parsed using a opennlp (Baldridge et al., 2004) part-of-speech tagger.

Seed Pattern: We start with a fairly general and yet very strict pattern that will extract tuples from a sentence. The seed pattern, $p_s = \{\phi, \phi, \phi, \phi\}$ meaning there is an empty left context, empty middle left context, empty middle right context and empty right context. As an example, let us consider a sentence "Temperature is ultimately regulated in the hypothalamus", our process extracts two concepts "Temperature" and "the hypothalamus" and relation "is ultimately regulated in". The left context (context before concept 1) in this case is empty, middle left context (context between concept 1 and relation) is also empty and similarly, middle right and right contexts are empty. This is a fairly specific pattern for a tuple to be valid and moreover, this pattern is domain independent and can be applied to any domain for english language. We have a running example showing the steps in table 2.

Concept Extraction Module: We extract concepts in the sentence based on noun phrases. We remove starting and trailing stopwords in noun phrases. If noun phrases contain conjunction, we break down noun phrase into two concepts.

Relation Extraction Module: To extract relations, we extract the longest sequence of words such that it starts with verb or is a sequence of noun, adjective, adverb, pronoun and determiner or a sequence of preposition, particle and infinitve marker. If any pair of matches are adjacent or overlap in a sentence, we merge them to a single relation. This method has been proven to be effective in (Fader et al., 2011).

Probable Tuple Extraction: For each relation $r \in R$ and for every combination of $c_i and c_j \in C$, such that c_i occurs before r and no other relation occurs between c_i *and* r and c_j occurs after r and no other relation occurs between c_j *and* r in the sentence, we create a probable tuple $t = (c_i, r, c_j)$.

Tuple Pattern Extraction: For each tuple $t = (c_i, r, c_j)$ in sentence s, we extract the sequence of words in sentence that occurs between beginning of sentence and concept c_i. If a relation occurs before c_i, we start with the end of closest relation. This is the left context. Similarly we extract middle_left context as the sequence of words between c_i and relation r. Middle_right context is the sequence of words between relation r and c_j. Right context is the sequence of words between c_j and either another relation r_p (if exists) or end of the sentence. We experiment with three types of patterns, first: purely lexical(only use lexicons for pattern generation), second: purely syntactic (only use part of speech tags for pattern generation) and third: mixed pattern(a combination of lexicons and part of speech tags. For mixed pattern, we replace all nouns, verbs, adjectives and adverbs with their part of speech tags and leave preposition, particle and other words to use lexicons.

Iteration: Our system is an iterative process and gets better qualitatively and quantitatively with each iteration. The number of iteration is highly dependent on the application of interest, pattern database size, size of corpus and time sensitivity of the system. We experimented on a smaller sample of data to see the convergence of the algorithm. We also iterated over a large corpus to see the effect of iteration on number of patterns and tuples. Since the extraction algorithm is based in active learning methodology, the system can perform quite well with iteration count as small as 2 in large corpus.

Algorithm 1 Iterative Pattern Induction

Input: $Pattern, P = \{seed\_pattern\}$,
$Tuples, T = \{\phi\}$
$Sentences, S = \{s_1, s_2, ...s_n\}$

Output: $Patterns, P = \{p_1, p_2, ...p_x\}$,
$Tuples, T = \{t_1, t_2, t_3......t_y\}$

for every $S_i \in S$ **do**
  $C_{prob} = \{c_1, c_2, ..c_j\} \leftarrow extractConcepts(S_i)$
  $R_{prob} = \{r_1, r_2...r_h\} \leftarrow extractRelations(S_i)$
  $p_{sent} = replaceConceptsRelations(C_{prob}, R_{prob})$
  $T_{prob} = \{t_1, ..t_u\} \leftarrow extractProbableTuples(C_{prob}, R_{prob})$
end for
for every $t_j \in T_{prob}$ **do**
  $pattern, p_i = extractPatternFor(S_i, p_s)$
if $p_i \in P \&\& t_j \notin T$
  $T.add(t_j), P.update(p_i)$
else if $p_i \notin P \&\& t_j \in T$
  $P.add(p_i), T.update(t_j)$
else if $p_i \in P \&\& t_j \in T$
  $P.update(p_i), T.update(t_j)$
end if
end for

Table 1: Iterative Pattern Induction Algorithm

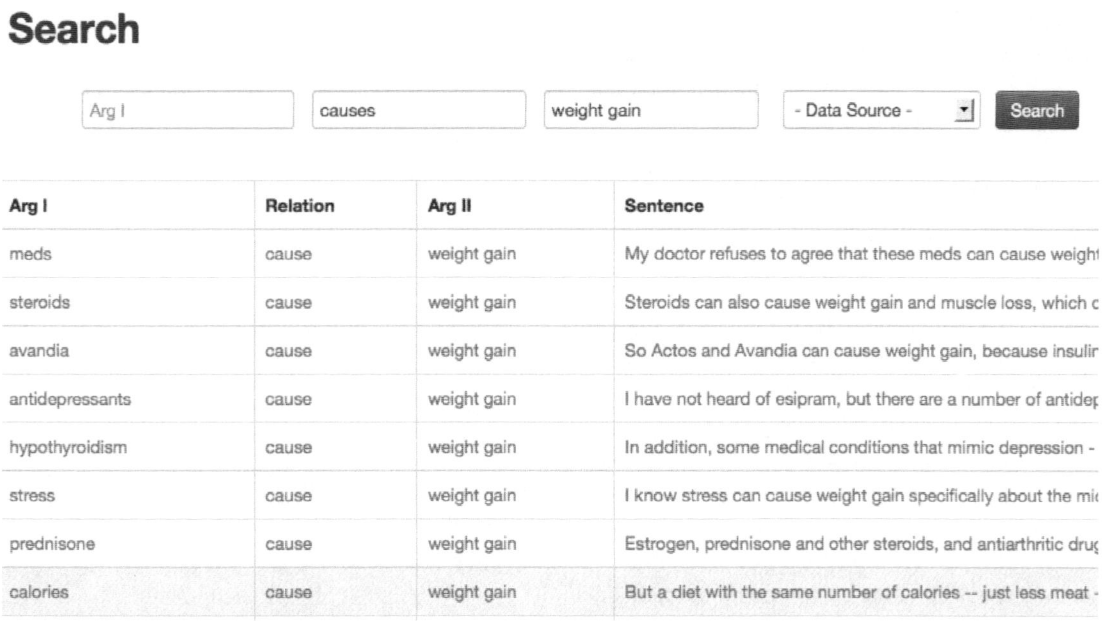

Figure 2: Concept based Search User Interface

Parameter	Value
seed pattern	$(\phi, \phi, \phi, .)$
sentence	Sunscreen may also cause drying of skin.
concepts	Concept1=Sunscreen, Concept2=skin
relations	relation=may also cause drying of
sentence pattern	Concept1 relation Concept2.
probable tuple	may_also_cause_drying_of(sunscreen, skin)

Table 2: Running Example of Tuple and Pattern Extraction

5 Tuple Refinement

5.1 Tuple and Pattern Filtering

We employ a holistic approach for concepts and relations extraction that enforces coherence in relations and concepts in tuples . To ensure validity of extracted tuples, we select patterns and tuples that occur more than α (3 in our experiments) and β (2 for medical and 1 for wikipedia for our experiments) times respectively. Also, total frequency of a pattern p in a relation r is defined as the sum of the frequencies of p in all entity pairs that have relation r. We define confidence of a tuple as follows:

$$Conf(t) = \frac{\sum_{p \in P_t} f(p_i)}{f(p_{max_t}) log(N)} \quad (1)$$

where $f(p_i)$ is the frequency of pattern p_i for relation r such that tuple t also has relation r. Here, $f(p_{max_t})$ is the frequency of pattern that has maximum frequency for relation r and N is the total number of distinct patterns that match tuple t. Note here that confidence conf(t) can be greater than 1 depending on the number of patterns that extract tuple t.

5.2 Tuple relevance

Traditional vector space model based relevance cannot be applied to concept based relevance paradigm. Hence we employ PMI based relevance for tuple retrieval. If e1 is the query entity for which search is executed, then the relevance of a tuple is calculated in terms of PMI between query entity e1 and second argument in tuple that contains e1 as first argument. PMI between entities e1 and e2 is defined as

$$\begin{aligned} PMI(e_1, e_2) &= log\frac{P(e_1, e_2)}{P(e_1, e)P(e_2, e)} \\ &= logN\frac{n_{12}}{n_1.n_2} \end{aligned} \quad (2)$$

$$NPMI(e_1, e_2) = \frac{PMI(e_1, e_2)}{-logP(e_1, e_2)} \quad (3)$$

where N: the total number of tuples in the corpus, $P(e_1, e_2) = n_{12}/N$=the number of sentences containing tuples that have e_1 and e_2 as arguments, $P(e_1, e) = n_1/N$: the probability that the entity e_1 cooccurs with entity e in tuples, $P(e_2, e) = n_2/N$: the probability that the entity e_2 cooccurs with entity e in tuples.

6 Prototype and Experiments

6.1 System Prototype

We built the system prototype based on the process explained in this paper for two datasets, namely; wikipedia and medical sites. We crawled 10 medical information sites and collected sentences talking about medicine. The prototype provides a tuple searching interface and a concept-graph based navigation system. We demonstrate the usefulness of the system with medical information and evaluate against few relations in wikipedia. Figure 2 shows a snapshot of the prototype for medical data for another example.

6.2 Comparison with Open Information Extraction Systems

We compared the result of our system with other systems such as Reverb, TextRunner and WOE. For evaluation purpose, we used the test set of 500 sentences used in Reverb system evaluation(Fader et al., 2011). The figures shows the quantitative comparison of our system compared to reverb and woe. It has to be noted however that this result does not evaluate the iterative process of create. The distinctive advantage of create is seen when applied to a relatively larger corpus where the system is applied iteratively.

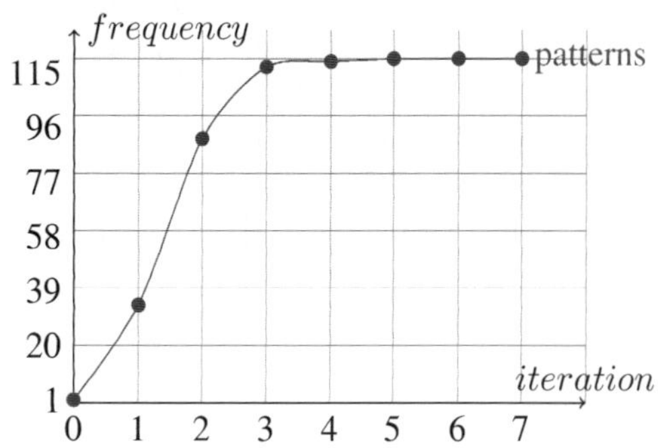

Figure 3: Effect of Iteration on Number of patterns

Figure 3 and figure 4 show the effect of iteration with the CREATE algorithm. It shows that in initial iterations, there is a rapid increase in number of patterns and tuples. However it starts to converge with higher iterations. For proof of concept,

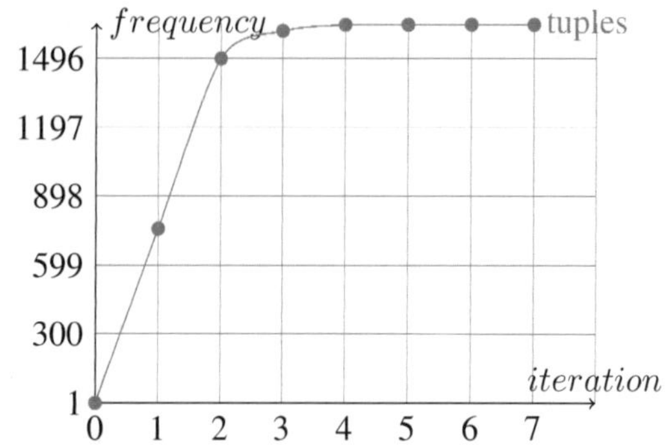

Figure 4: Effect of Iteration on Number of tuples

we experimented with a sample data that we created with medical sentences. It shows that tuple and pattern generation converges in 5 iterations.

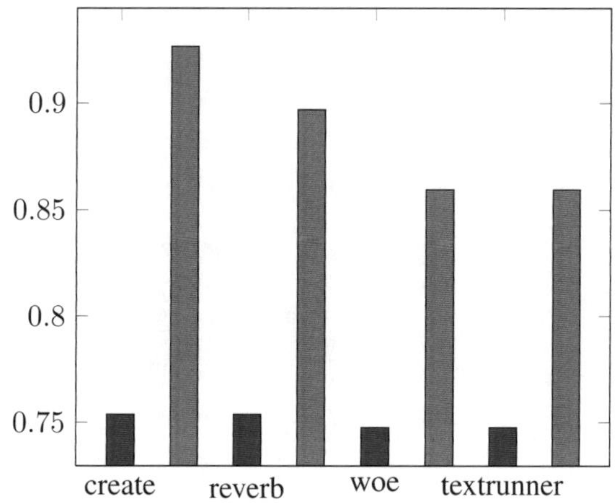

Figure 5: Comparison of CREATE performance with Reverb, WOE and TextRunner

Figure 5 shows the comparison of CREATE with Reverbm WOE and TextRunner. We see improved recall at around 92% and precision around 75% for create which outperforms all other systems. Similarly, figure 6 shows the effect of iteration on the performance of CREATE system. We see the same effect of rapid increase in performance in initial iterations and then it gets stabilized after few iterations.

We also experimented with the performance based on different patterns. Figure 7 shows that recall for POS pattern is the highest but the precision is highest with mixed pattern.

6.3 Wikipedia Tuple Extraction

We used Semantically Annotated Snapshot of the English Wikipedia (Atserias et al., 2008) to extract

Relation	Gold Data	Create (total/correct)	Precision	Recall
bornIn(x,Atlanta)	440	341/303	88.8	68.8
bornIn(x,Zurich)	108	87/75	86.23	69.4
graduatedFrom(x,Stanford)	456	403/345	85.6	75.6
graduatedFrom(x,Princeton)	582	464/385	82.9	66.1
presidentOf(x,United States)	44	65/39	60	88.86

Table 3: Data statistics for wikipedia.

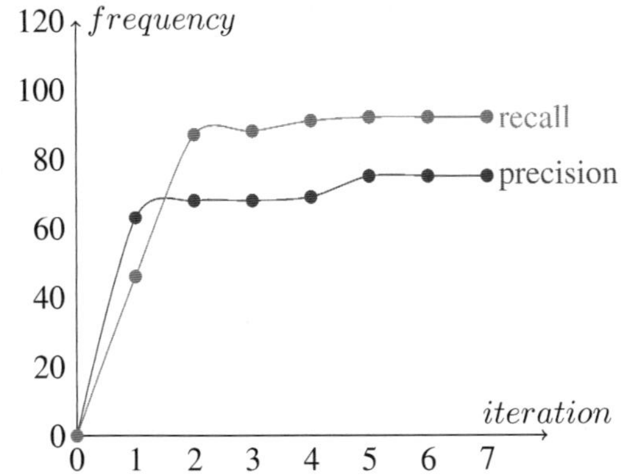

Figure 6: Effect of Iteration on Tuple Extraction Performance with confidence 0.6

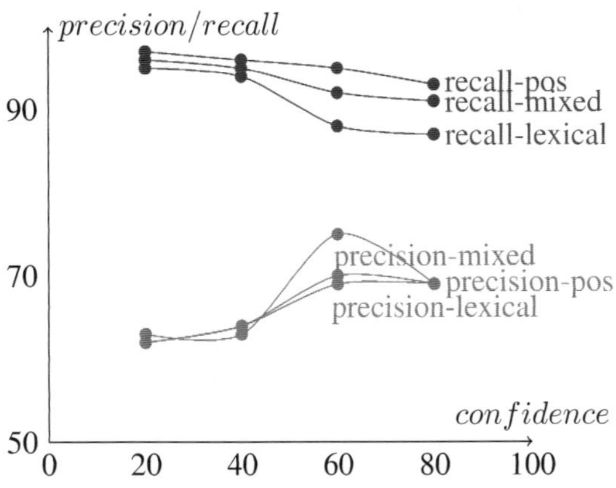

Figure 7: Precision/ Recall variance with Confidence

relation tuples as the first large dataset. The SW1 corpus is a snapshot of the English Wikipedia dated from 2006-11-04 processed with a number of public- available NLP tools. We chose to use this data as it has been processed and has information on shallow parsing such as POS tags and named entities on seven categories. To demonstrate the interchangeability of concept extraction module , we used the named entities as concepts

Data	Wikipedia	Medical
Document count	1431178	348284
Sentence count	36117170	4049238
Tuple count	6945440	1535293
Relation count	1847116	706359
Relation with freq > 9	1131	1865
Concept count	2673192	106263
Extraction latency (for single iteration)	5 hrs	2hrs

Table 4: Data Statistics.

for relation extraction. We then generated tuples from data. Since it is not possible to evaluate all the relation tuples extracted from wikipedia, we performed samples evaluation of the system for few sampled relations and tuples. We compared the performance of our system based on precision and recall compared to Dbpedia. The evaluation in terms of precision and recall is shown in Table 4. Precision and recall are given by the following equations

$$precision = \frac{|(correct\ docs) \bigcap (retrieved\ docs)|}{|(retrieved\ docs)|} \quad (4)$$

$$recall = \frac{|(correct\ docs) \bigcap (retrieved\ docs)|}{|(relevant\ docs)|} \quad (5)$$

7 Conclusion

We have qualitatively and quantitavely demonstrated the effectiveness and usefullness of our system and overall relation extraction systems. With increasng data being available, the value and importance of systems such as CREATE is ever increasing. We have demonstrated the prospects of relation extraction systems. At the same, we also need to be aware of the challenges that need to be solved before we can realize a fully functional machine reading system.

References

Eugene Agichtein and Luis Gravano. 2000. Snowball: Extracting relations from large plain-text collections. In *Proceedings of the fifth ACM conference on Digital libraries*, pages 85–94. ACM.

Jordi Atserias, Hugo Zaragoza, Massimiliano Ciaramita, and Giuseppe Attardi. 2008. Semantically annotated snapshot of the english wikipedia. *Proceedings of the Sixth International Language Resources and Evaluation (LREC'08).*

Sören Auer, Christian Bizer, Georgi Kobilarov, Jens Lehmann, Richard Cyganiak, and Zachary Ives. 2007. Dbpedia: A nucleus for a web of open data. In *The semantic web*, pages 722–735. Springer.

Jason Baldridge, Tom Morton, and Gann Bierner. 2004. The opennlp maxent package in java. *URL: http://maxent. sourceforge. net.*

Michele Banko, Michael J Cafarella, Stephen Soderland, Matt Broadhead, and Oren Etzioni. 2009. *Open information extraction for the web.* University of Washington.

Sergey Brin. 1999. Extracting patterns and relations from the world wide web. In *The World Wide Web and Databases*, pages 172–183. Springer.

Razvan Bunescu and Raymond Mooney. 2006. Subsequence kernels for relation extraction. *Advances in neural information processing systems*, 18:171.

Andrew Carlson, Justin Betteridge, Bryan Kisiel, Burr Settles, Estevam R Hruschka Jr, and Tom M Mitchell. 2010. Toward an architecture for never-ending language learning. In *Proceedings of the Twenty-Fourth Conference on Artificial Intelligence (AAAI 2010)*, volume 2, pages 3–3.

Jonathan Chang, Jordan Boyd-Graber, and David M Blei. 2009. Connections between the lines: augmenting social networks with text. In *Proceedings of the 15th ACM SIGKDD international conference on Knowledge discovery and data mining*, pages 169–178. ACM.

Nilesh Dalvi, Ravi Kumar, Bo Pang, Raghu Ramakrishnan, Andrew Tomkins, Philip Bohannon, Sathiya Keerthi, and Srujana Merugu. 2009. A web of concepts. In *Proceedings of the twenty-eighth ACM SIGMOD-SIGACT-SIGART symposium on Principles of database systems*, pages 1–12. ACM.

Anthony Fader, Stephen Soderland, and Oren Etzioni. 2011. Identifying relations for open information extraction. In *Proceedings of the Conference on Empirical Methods in Natural Language Processing*, pages 1535–1545. Association for Computational Linguistics.

Nanda Kambhatla. 2004. Combining lexical, syntactic, and semantic features with maximum entropy models for extracting relations. In *Proceedings of the ACL 2004 on Interactive poster and demonstration sessions*, page 22. Association for Computational Linguistics.

Bonan Min, Shuming Shi, Ralph Grishman, and Chin-Yew Lin. 2012. Towards large-scale unsupervised relation extraction from the web. *International Journal on Semantic Web and Information Systems (IJSWIS)*, 8(3):1–23.

Fabian M Suchanek, Gjergji Kasneci, and Gerhard Weikum. 2007. Yago: a core of semantic knowledge. In *Proceedings of the 16th international conference on World Wide Web*, pages 697–706. ACM.

Zareen Syed and Tim Finin. 2010. Unsupervised techniques for discovering ontology elements from wikipedia article links. In *Proceedings of the NAACL HLT 2010 First International Workshop on Formalisms and Methodology for Learning by Reading*, pages 78–86. Association for Computational Linguistics.

Fei Wu and Daniel S Weld. 2010. Open information extraction using wikipedia. In *Proceedings of the 48th Annual Meeting of the Association for Computational Linguistics*, pages 118–127. Association for Computational Linguistics.

Yulan Yan, Naoaki Okazaki, Yutaka Matsuo, Zhenglu Yang, and Mitsuru Ishizuka. 2009. Unsupervised relation extraction by mining wikipedia texts using information from the web. In *Proceedings of the Joint Conference of the 47th Annual Meeting of the ACL and the 4th International Joint Conference on Natural Language Processing of the AFNLP: Volume 2-Volume 2*, pages 1021–1029. Association for Computational Linguistics.

Limin Yao, Aria Haghighi, Sebastian Riedel, and Andrew McCallum. 2011. Structured relation discovery using generative models. In *Proceedings of the Conference on Empirical Methods in Natural Language Processing*, pages 1456–1466. Association for Computational Linguistics.

Alexander Yates, Michael Cafarella, Michele Banko, Oren Etzioni, Matthew Broadhead, and Stephen Soderland. 2007. Textrunner: open information extraction on the web. In *Proceedings of Human Language Technologies: The Annual Conference of the North American Chapter of the Association for Computational Linguistics: Demonstrations*, pages 25–26. Association for Computational Linguistics.

Dmitry Zelenko, Chinatsu Aone, and Anthony Richardella. 2003. Kernel methods for relation extraction. *The Journal of Machine Learning Research*, 3:1083–1106.

Shubin Zhao and Ralph Grishman. 2005. Extracting relations with integrated information using kernel methods. In *Proceedings of the 43rd Annual Meeting on Association for Computational Linguistics*, pages 419–426. Association for Computational Linguistics.

Jun Zhu, Zaiqing Nie, Xiaojiang Liu, Bo Zhang, and Ji-Rong Wen. 2009. Statsnowball: a statistical approach to extracting entity relationships. In *Proceedings of the 18th international conference on World wide web*, pages 101–110. ACM.

Authorship Attribution in Health Forums

Victoria Bobicev
Technical University of Moldova
Chisinau, Moldova
vika@rol.md

Marina Sokolova
CHEO Research Institute, Ottawa
University of Ottawa, Ontario, Canada
sokolova@uottawa.ca

Khaled El Emam
CHEO Research Institute, Ottawa
University of Ottawa, Ontario, Canada
kelemam@uottawa.ca

Stan Matwin
Dalhousie University, Halifax, Canada
Polish Academy of Sciences, Warsaw, Poland
stan@cs.dal.ca

Abstract

The emergence of social media (networks, blogs, web forums) has given people numerous opportunities to share their personal stories, including details of their health. Although users mostly post under assumed nicknames, state-of-the-art text analysis techniques can combine texts from different media and use that linkage to identify private details of an individual's health. In this study we aim to empirically examine the accuracy of identifying authors of on-line posts on a medical forum.[1] Our results show a high accuracy of the authorship attribution, especially when text is represented by the orthographical features.

1 Introduction

Emergence of social media (networks, blogs, web forums) has given people numerous opportunities to share their personal stories, including details of their health (e.g., disease diagnosis, symptoms, treatment) (Velden and Emam, 2012; Bobicev et at, 2012):

- The transfer went well - my RE did it himself which was comforting. 2 embies (grade 1 but slow in development) so I am not holding my breath for a positive.
- I've had 7 IUI and one ivf all cancelled due to not ovulating. I am a poor responder. What bothers me the most is never getting to the point of actually going thru the procedure.[2]

Sharing personal health information (PHI) is a behavior that can be seen in 80% of Internet users, or in 59% of all adults, who reported searching for health information (Fox, 2011).

Although users mostly post under assumed nicknames, state-of-the-art text analysis techniques can combine texts from different forums and then use that linkage to identify private details of an individual's health. Aggregating and mining posts from five forums, Li et al. (2011) identified the user's full name, date of birth, spouse's name, home address, home phone number, cell phone number, email, occupation and the lab test results. The latter are highly indicative of the suspected disease, and hence, of the health conditions of the said individual.

In order to gauge how best to protect internet user anonymity, we first wanted to know the ability of Text Mining techniques in authorship attribution on medical forums, i.e. the task of identification of an author among other authors posting on the same forum. The attribution is based on comparison of a new text to texts previously written by known authors.

We obtained the empirical evidence on the posts from an on-line community of IVF (In Vitro Fertilization) patients. We achieved a highly accurate authorship attribution: up to 90% when the text is represented by the orthographical features.

---

[1] This work had been done when the first author was a visiting professor at CHEO Research Institute.

[2] The messages have an original spelling and punctuation.

2 Related works

Authorship attribution has been intensively investigated by Computational Linguistics. Starting 2007, an annual competition on author attribution has been organized in conjunction with CLEF. [3]

Accuracy of the authorship attribution depends on features extracted from the analyzed text. Vocabulary features used in various research are word length (Brinegar, 1963), sentence length (Morton, 1965), vocabulary richness (Tweedie and Baayen, 1998), word n-gram frequencies (Hoover, 2003), errors and idiosyncrasies (Koppel and Schler, 2003), synonyms and semantic dependencies (Afroz et al., 2012).

A few studies used syntactic features, e.g. parts of speech and part of speech sequences (Zhao and Zobel, 2007), chunks of text (Stamatatos et al, 2001), syntactic dependencies of words (Gerritsen, 2003), and syntactic structures (Hirst and Feiguina, 2007).

The use of orthographical features in the attribution task was studied in Abbasi and Chen (2008). The features included characters, characters bigrams and trigrams, punctuation and special characters, as well as common vocabulary features. 88-96% accuracy was achieved on several data sets including e-bay comments, Java forum, email and chat corpora. Narayanan et al. (2012) adapted this feature set in the author classification of 100,000 blogs where the average length of each blog was 7500 words. The paper's authors correctly identified an anonymous author in >20% of cases; in approximately 35% of cases the correct author was one of the top 20 guesses. At the same time, Koppel (2009) had shown that 1000 character trigrams with highest information gain helped SVM to obtain 80-86% in attribution accuracy on literature corpus, email and blog corpora.

With the emergence of user-written Web content, authorship analysis is often done on online messages (Zheng et al., 2006; Narayanan et al., 2012). Large numbers of candidate authors, small volumes of training and test texts, and short length of messages makes the online authorship analysis exceptionally challenging (Juola, 2006; Koppel, 2009; Luyckx and Daelemans, 2008; Madigan et al., 2005; Stamatatos, 2009).

In Koppel et al. (2006), 10,000 blogs were used in the task of author attribution. The test data was built from 500-word snippets, one for each author. 20-34% of texts were classified with average accuracy of 80%; the rest of texts were considered unknown. In Koppel et al. (2011), on the same dataset, a 500-word snippet was attributed to one of 1,000 authors with *Coverage* = 42.2% and *Precision* = 93.2%. Consequently, the remaining 57.8% of snippets were considered unknown.

None of these cited works, however, considered authorship analysis of messages posted on medical forums or other online venues that are dedicated to discussions of personal health information.

3 The Forum Data

We focused on the authorship attribution on medical forums where the authors may post sensitive PHI, e.g., problems with conception. In particular, we worked with data from IVF.ca, an infertility on-line community created by prospective, existing and past IVF (In Vitro Fertilization) patients. The IVF.ca website includes forums: *Cycle Friends*, *Expert Panel*, *Trying to Conceive*, *Socialize*, *In Our Hearts*, *Pregnancy*, *Parenting*, and *Administration*.

The forums listed above consist of several sub-forums, e.g., the *Cycle Friends* forum consists of *Introductions*, *IVF/FET/IUI Cycle Buddies*, *IVF Ages 35+ and other*. Every sub-forum contains of a number of topics initiated by a forum participant, e.g. the "*IVF Ages 35+*" sub-forum contains 506 topics such as "*40+ and chances of success*", "*Over 40 and pregnant or trying to be*", etc. Depending on the topic itself and the amount of interest among participants, different numbers of posts are associated with each topic. For example, "*40+ and chances of success*" has four posts and "*Over 40 and pregnant or trying to be*" has 1136 posts.

Note that differentiation between the authors of posts is easier when the authors exhibit contrasting writing styles. The style dissimilarity usually comes with diversity among the author population and the topics they write about (Koppel et al., 2009).

We, on the other hand, worked with the forum posts that lack such diversity. Hence, the texts are more complex in differentiation between the authors. Specifically:

a) the posts have a unified content (i.e., all posts are about infertility treatment);

b) the same gender of authors (i.e., participants are overwhelmingly women);

[3] http://pan.webis.de

c) a small age range (most authors are 35-40 years old);

d) the same geographic location (most are Canadians and a few USA);

e) the same time of posting (2008 - 2012).

We intended to use posts as analysis units, i.e. our goal was to identify the author of each post individually. We assumed that the length of the texts written by an author would be sufficient for a meaningful analysis and that we needed a substantial number of posts per author. Two sub-forums *IVF Ages 35+* and *Cycle Buddies* satisfied our criteria better than other sub-forums.

We grouped posts by the authors to estimate the amount of text every author wrote and sorted these estimates according to the number of posts written by each author in descending order. Only a small number of authors had many posts. The post-per-author distribution for the first 100 of the most prolific authors in both forums is presented on Figure 1.

Only the first 30 authors in the *Age 35+* sub-forum had more than 100 posts; in the *Cycle Buddies* sub-forum situation was a little better, as almost all the 100 first authors had more than 100 posts. However, many posts contained citations of other authors and only short replies and we had to remove such posts from further studies.

The average length of posts was also important as shorter messages were harder to identify. The average length of posts in the *Ages 35+* sub-forum was about 750 characters (approx. 150 words) and in the *Cycle Buddies* subforum - about 600 characters or approx. 100 words. The larger number of posts in this sub-forum allowed us to remove the shortest posts and posts with citations.

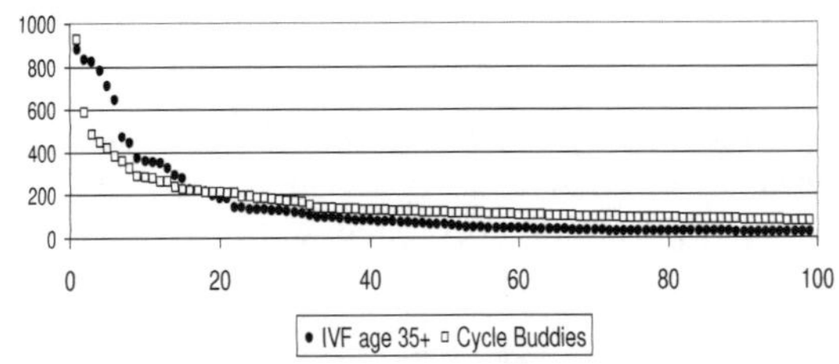

Figure 1: The number of posts per author distribution for the first 100 authors

For the empirical experiments, we harvested 18685 messages from the most prolific 30 authors from every forum, i.e. 60 authors in total, and selected 100 messages per an author for future analysis. We worked exclusively with the message contents. No author metadata was used in the file analysis.

It should be noted that most of the selected authors posted in many different topics and we collected posts without exclusion of any topics. Thus author classification had no influence of topic differences. Figure 2 presents the numbers of topics in which the 30 authors whom we selected for the experiments from *Age 35+* sub-forum posted.

Figure 2: The number of topics the authors posted in for the first 30 authors of Age 35+ sub-forum.

4 Stylistic Features and Authorship Attribution

The authorship attribution task traditionally relies on

- a statistical analysis of the author's vocabulary, e.g., the number of distinct words, occurrences of words, identification of most frequent words and phrases;
- the analysis of the composition style, e.g., position of words in sentences, type and length of sentences, paragraph formation (Oakes, 2005).

Provided there was enough data for quantitative analysis, the results of these analyses were able to accurately attribute authorship. The requirement usually implied a minimum of five occurrences of a feature.

Texts gathered from the web forums were usually short. In our data, an average post had one or two paragraphs and 50-250 words. A small number of occurrences of words determined the type of features we could use in our authorship attribution task. For example, even after combining all the posts of the same author in one document, we still could not meaningfully use the composition-style features for authorship attribution.

Choosing from the vocabulary features, we could use the most frequent words but not phrases. The vocabulary statistics would not be reliable as well, due to a small corpus size for each author.

At the same time, we had sufficient quantities of the orthographical features per author to use them in the authorship attribution. These features included alphabetic and non-alphabetic characters, capitalization, and punctuation. Currently, the orthographical features were often used to analyze short text messages, e.g. tweets. Common tasks included named entity recognition (Ritter et al., 2011) and text normalization (Han and Baldwin, 2011). The features were used in the authorship attribution through language modeling (Peng et al., 2003) and machine learning (Koppel and Schler, 2003).

4.1 Vocabulary features

Our initial word set was the same for both subforums. The set of the most frequent words consisted of 50 words that sometimes are referred to as 'stop' or 'short' words (me, of, get, have). Such words are often removed in text classification. However, they played an important role in the authorship attribution task (Zhao and Zobel, 2005). The rest of the used 3796 words (egg, wish), were salient words with frequency > 3 in the frequency dictionary for the joint sub-forum data.

To reduce redundancy of the features, we removed words that did not discriminate between the authors. The resulting feature sets considerably varied.

Table 1 shows the numbers of the vocabulary features for both sub-forums. We introduced the features' ID for the further reference.

Features	ID	Cycle Buddies	Age 35+
Frequent words	I	50	50
Salient words	II	3583	3788
All words	III	3633	3838

Table 1: The vocabulary features for the Cycle Buddies and Age 35+ subforums.

Features	ID	Cycle Buddies/Age 35+
Lower case letters	IV	26
Capital and low letters	V	52
Punctuation	VI	24
Numbers and punctuation	VII	34
All characters	VIII	86

Table 2: The orthographical features for the data.

4.2 Orthographical features

We used standard orthographical features, such as lower-case letters (a - z), capitalization (C, c), punctuation (;,!), etc. Table 2 reports the categories of the features and the number of features in each category. Feature numbers were the same for both subforums. Again, we introduced the features' ID for further reference in machine learning experiments.

4.3 Combined features

We used two feature sets that were combined from the vocabulary and the orthographical features.

The first set was an unaltered combination of all the features without useless features (i.e., features that did not discriminate among classes were removed). Another set was an outcome of the BestFirst selection algorithm; this set included punctuation (?, ., !), letters (e, n) and words (ladies, thanks, two, transfer).

Features	ID	#
Useless features removed	IX	3719
BestFirst selected features	X	73

Table 3: Combined features for the Cycle Buddies data.

Tables 3 and 4 list the number of features for the *Cycle Buddies* and the *Age 35+* sub-forums.

Features	ID	#
Useless features removed	IX	3924
BestFirst selected features	X	75

Table 4: Combined features for the Age 35+ data.

5 Machine Learning Experiments

In our previous work in classification of short texts (Bobicev et al., 2012), Naïve Bayes had been shown as highly accurate when compared with other ML algorithms. Due to NB's high efficiency we opted to apply it as well as KNN, another highly efficient algorithm. This task was solved as a multi-class classification problem, where one class represented one author. There were 30 authors in each subforum, hence that data sets were categorized into 30 classes.

We assessed the learning methods by computing multi-class *Precision (Pr), Recall (R), F-score (F)* and *Accuracy (Acc)*:

$Precision = \sum_{i=1}^{n} \frac{tp_i}{tp_i + fp_i}$ is the ratio of texts belonging to categories $c_1,...,c_n$ to all texts classified to these categories.

$Recall = \sum_{i=1}^{n} \frac{tp_i}{tp_i + fn_i}$ is the percentage of texts belonging to categories $c_1,...,c_n$ that are indeed classified into these categories.

We use the balanced *F-score* which is the harmonic mean of *Precision* (P) and *Recall* (R):

$$F\text{-}score = 2PrR / (Pr + R)$$

$Accuracy = \frac{1}{n}\sum_{i=1}^{n} \frac{tp_i + tn_i}{tp_i + fn_i + tn_i + fp_i}$ is the average *Accuracy* obtained on all the categories.

In these formulae, tp_i is the number of texts classified into the category c_i that indeed belong to c_i, fp_i is the number of texts classified into c_i that do not belong to c_i, fn_i is the number of texts that indeed belong to c_i but were not classified into it, tn_i is the number of texts that do not belong to c_i and were not classified into it.

Data	Pr	R	F	Acc (%)
Cycle Buddies	0.002	0.043	0.040	4.33
Age 35+	0.001	0.034	0.020	3.37

Table 5: Baseline classification results.

Featu-res	Naïve Bayes			
	Pr	R	F	Acc (%)
I	0.385	0.386	0.380	38.64
II	**0.714**	**0.635**	**0.648**	**63. 55**
III	***0.683***	***0.580***	***0.594***	***57.98***
IV	0.212	0.225	0.213	22.45
V	0.374	0.360	0.359	35.96
VI	0.379	0.365	0.354	36.45
VII	0.403	0.370	0.365	36.97
VIII	0.564	0.541	0.533	54.11
IX	0.648	0.524	0.520	52.44
X	***0.625***	***0.557***	***0.544***	***55.73***

Table 6: NB classification of the Cycle Buddies data.

For the baseline performance evaluation, we chose classification of all authors into the largest class. Table 5 presents the baseline classification results for the subforums.

We applied 10-fold cross-validation for the best classifier selection. Each post was used as an independent element. Thus, in each run of 10-fold cross-validation for each author 90 posts were used for training and 10 posts functioned as test items. The author was identified for each of them; hence we had 30 classes with 90 posts for training and 300 test posts. Tables 6 and 7 report the best classification results of both algorithms on each feature set for the Buddies subforum. Tables 8 and 9 report the best classification results for the both algorithms on the Age 35+ subforum. We put the top result for each classifier in **this font**. We mark the second and the third best results with ***this font.***

Featu-res	K-Nearest Neighbor			
	Pr	R	F	Acc (%)
I	0.266	0.218	0.223	21.85
II	0.374	0.125	0.131	12.50
III	0.350	0.130	0.134	12.96
IV	0.185	0.160	0.159	16.04
V	0.293	0.259	0.261	25.89
VI	***0.375***	***0.352***	***0.354***	***35.15***
VII	0.355	0.322	0.327	32.24
VIII	**0.413**	**0.381**	**0.382**	**38.07**
IX	0.360	0.137	0.140	13.65
X	***0.420***	***0.364***	***0.372***	***36.36***

Table 7: KNN classification of the Cycle Buddies data.

Featu-res	Naïve Bayes			
	Pr	R	F	Acc (%)
I	0.399	0.411	0.400	41.08
II	**0.770**	**0.681**	**0.696**	**68.08**
III	***0.730***	***0.622***	***0.639***	***62.19***
IV	0.215	0.233	0.216	23.30
V	0.331	0.342	0.330	34.24
VI	0.382	0.359	0.351	35.86
VII	0.387	0.372	0.364	37.17
VIII	0.544	0.539	0.527	53.87
IX	***0.680***	***0.560***	***0.561***	***55.99***
X	0.611	0.549	0.532	54.95

Table 8: NB classification of the Age 35+ data.

The presented results show that NB performs better than KNN on both forums. Moreover, this holds true for all the 10 feature sets in the forums.

From the combined features only the set X (i.e., BestFirst selected features) provided reasonably good results. The set IX (i.e., all features but useless) did not provide a reliable classification.

Featu-res	K-Nearest Neighbor			
	Pr	R	F	Acc (%)
I	0.317	0.282	0.279	28.25
II	0.419	0.140	0.127	14.04
III	0.375	0.144	0.129	14.38
IV	0.197	0.185	0.180	18.52
V	0.310	0.285	0.280	28.49
VI	***0.323***	***0.304***	***0.298***	***30.44***
VII	0.298	0.279	0.273	27.90
VIII	***0.400***	***0.363***	***0.359***	***36.33***
IX	0.431	0.145	0.132	14.55
X	**0.459**	**0.423**	**0.425**	**42.26**

Table 9: KNN classification of the Age 35+ data.

The most striking difference in the classifier performance is found on Features II, i.e. low and capital letters. On this feature set, NB achieves its best performance on both forums (F = 0.648 for the *Cycle Buddies*, F = 0.696 for the *Age 35+*), while KNN has its worst performance on the forums (F = 0.131 for the *Cycle Buddies*, F = 0.127 for the *Age 35+*).

6 Model-based Authorship Attribution

In this part of our work,we the language model-based attribution. We used Prediction by Partial Matching (PPM statistical model) for authorship classification. Prediction by Partial Matching (PPM) is an adaptive, finite-context method for text compression (Cleary, Witten, 1984).

An example of the general method of context probability interpolation is the probability of character *'l'* in the context of the word *'medical'* calculated as a sum of conditional probabilities of this character in dependence of different context length up to the limited maximal length in this particular case equal to 5:

$$P_{blended}('l') = \lambda_5 \cdot P('l' \mid 'edica') + \lambda_4 \cdot P('l' \mid 'dica') + \lambda_3 \cdot P('l' \mid 'ica') + \lambda_2 \cdot P('l' \mid 'ca') + \lambda_1 \cdot P('l' \mid 'a') + \lambda_0 \cdot P('l')$$

where λ_i (i = 1…5) are normalization coefficients; some of them can be equal to zero and $\sum_{i=1}^{5} \lambda_i = 1$, where 5 is the maximal length of the context.

Bratko and Filipic (2005) used letter-based PPM models for spam detection. In this task there existed two classes only: spam and legitimate email (ham). The created models showed strong performance in Text Retrieval Conference competition, indicating that data-compression models are well suited to the spam filtering problem.

Teahan et al. (2000) used a PPM-based text model and minimum cross-entropy as a text classifier for various tasks including the author attribution for the well known Federalist Papers.

Bobicev and Sokolova (2008) applied the PPM algorithm for text categorization. They used character-based and word-based PPM. The character-based PPM outperformed the word-based PPM.

In the current work we applied PPM to the orthographical features described in Section 4.2.

6.1 Classification Experiments

As in previous experiments, we used 10-fold cross-validation for the best model selection.

Tables 10 and 11 present results for the both sub-forums. We put the top results for each forum in **this font**. We mark the second and the third best results with ***this font.***

Featu-res	Pr	R	F	Acc (%)
IV	***0.851***	***0.822***	***0.836***	***82.2***
V	***0.882***	***0.857***	***0.869***	***85.7***
VI	0.400	0.363	0.380	36.3
VII	0.391	0.387	0.389	38.7
VIII	**0.911**	**0.893**	**0.902**	**89.4**

Table 10: Classification of the Cycle Buddies data.

Featu-res	Pr	R	F	Acc (%)
IV	***0.761***	***0.743***	***0.752***	***74.3***
V	***0.797***	***0.777***	***0. 787***	***77.7***
VI	0.331	0.325	0. 328	32.5
VII	0.368	0.357	0.362	35.7
VIII	**0.836**	**0.817**	**0.826**	**81.7**

Table 11: Classification of the Age 35+ data.

The empirical results show that model-based classification of authors significantly outperforms probability-based and prototype-based classification when applied to both the letter and all the characters features. All three algorithms achieve approximately the same accuracy when applied to punctuation and number features.

7 Discussion

We have shown empirically that stylistic features can help to identify an author among a large group of authors. Solving 30-class classification problems for two subforums, we constantly outperformed the baseline classification. Application of Naïve Bayes on the vocabulary features gave the best overall results for authorship attribution on the both subforums.

In general, Naïve Bayes performed better on the vocabulary features than on the orthographical ones; the reverse was true for KNN. However, Naïve Bayes outperformed K-Nearest Neighbor on the orthographical features as well.

Comparison of the best performance of the two algorithms showed that a probabilistic algorithm significantly outperforms a prototype algorithm in the authorship attribution on the medical subforum data.

The most impressive *Accuracy* and *F-score* gains were obtained by application of the model-based PPM on the letter and all-character features. The algorithm outperformed NB and KNN on both the forums. However, the specific PPM methodology of feature use makes much more difficult the comparison of the influence of specific text features on the author attribution task performance.

It should be noted that we obtained these results using internet forum posts and the length of these posts varied considerably. There were posts consisting of two or three words, e.g. "good luck!". We were able to identify the authors of the longer texts with an accuracy of 90%.

We also noticed that longer posts often contained important and sensitive information about person's health. If accessed and generalized from several posts, this extensive health information can be potentially harmful for the author. Personal and health information can be too extensive if, for example, it reveals the location, the diagnosis, and contains a possibility to identify the name. For example, in one post a patient says in what hospital she has a treatment, i.e. identifying the location. In another posts she specifies the treatment (this can also hint on the costs, hence, the income/money range) and she refers to a friend/relative giving their names. Or a patient complains about a specific condition (e.g., being overweight), telling others in what area she lives in and to what specialist (e.g., obesity doctor) she goes for treatment. These facts can be combined to create an accurate estimation of the poster's identity. Both listed scenarios present real cases that we've found in the data.

8 Conclusions

In this study we empirically examined the accuracy of identifying authors of online posts on a medical forum. Given that individuals may be reluctant to share personal health information on online forums, they may choose to post anonymously. The ability to determine the identity of anonymous posts by analyzing the specific features of the text raises questions about users posting anonymously as a method to control what is known publicly about them.

We have shown that the application of learning methods, especially NB and PPM, makes an automated identification of the author of an online post possible. Our method was able to correctly attribute authors with high confidence.

The focus of this work has been to show that the vocabulary and orthographical features can help to identify authors with a degree of high accuracy. Our experiments show that the author ship attribution based on orthographical features can be more effective that the authorship attribution based on the vocabulary features. We hypothesize that the use of orthographical features reflects on the author's personality. For example, in emotionally rich posts, the authors excessively use punctuation to emphasize their sentiments (e.g., question and exclamation marks, emoticons); those features are specific for each author.

To reduce the risk of a possible identification, we can suggest the author to change his or her habits of capitalization and the use of punctuation marks, as well as the use of emoticons.

These results are novel for the forum analysis, as the usual text analysis methods are based on semantics and analyze the use of words, phrases and other text segments.

The main implication of our results is that managers of online properties that encourage user input should also alert their users about the strength of anonymity. They should also caution users from posting sensitive information anonymously.

Acknowledgments

This work has been funded by the NSERC Discovery and Strategic Projects Research Grants. The authors thank Brian Dewar for his help with editing the manuscript.

References

Abbasi A. and Chen H. 2008. *Writeprints: a stylometric approach to identity-level identification and similarity detection in cyberspace.* ACM Transactions on Information Systems 2008; 26(2):1-29.

Afroz S., Brennan M., Greenstadt R. 2012. *Detecting Hoaxes, Frauds, and Deception in Writing Style Online.* IEEE Symposium on Security and Privacy 2012: 461-475.

Argamon S., Koppel M., Pennebaker J. and Schler J. 2008. *Automatically Profiling the Author of an Anonymous Text.* Communications of the ACM Association for Computing Machinery. 1983. *Computing Reviews*, 24(11):503-512.

Bobicev V. and Sokolova M. 2008. *An effective and robust method for short text classification.* Proceedings of the 23rd national conference on Artificial intelligence - Volume 3, 2008, pp. 1444–1445.

Victoria Bobicev, Marina Sokolova, Yasser Jafer, David Schramm. 2012. *Learning Sentiments from Tweets with Personal Health Information.* Canadian Conference on Artificial Intelligence 2012: 37-48.

Bratko A. and Filipic B. 2005. *Spam Filtering Using Compression Models.* Department of Intelligent Systems, Jozef Stefan Institute, Ljubljana, Slovenia, IJS-DP-9227.

Michael Brennan and Rachel Greenstadt. 2009. *Practical Attacks Against Authorship Recognition Techniques.* Proceedings of the Twenty-First Conference on Innovative Applications of Artificial Intelligence (IAAI).

Brinegar C. S. 1963. *Mark Twain and the Quintus Curtius Snodgrass Letters: A Statistical Test of Authorship.* Journal of the American Statistical Association 58, pp. 85–96.

Cleary J. and Witten I. 1984. *Data Compression Using Adaptive Coding and Partial String Matching.* IEEE Transactions on Communications, vol. 32, no. 4, pp. 396 – 402.

Bo Han and Timothy Baldwin. 2011. *Lexical normalisation of short text messages: Makn sens a #twitter.* ACL 2011.

Fox S. 2011. *The Social Life of Health Information, 2011.* the survey report http://www.pewinternet.org/Reports/2011/Social-Life-of-Health-Info.aspx.

Gerritsen C. M. 2003. *Authorship Attribution Using Lexical Attraction.* M.S. Dissertation, Massachusetts Institute of Technology.

Hirst G. and Feiguina O. 2007. *Bigrams of syntactic labels for authorship discrimination of short texts.* Literary and Linguistic Computing, 22(4), pp. 405-417.

Hoover D. L. 2003. *Frequent Collocations and Authorial Style.* Literary and Linguistic Computing 18: 261–286.

Patrick Juola. 2006. *Authorship Attribution.* Foundations and Trends® in Information Retrieval: Vol. 1: No 3, pp 233-334.

Koppel M. and Schler J. 2003. *Exploiting Stylistic Idiosyncrasies for Authorship Attribution.* Proceedings of IJCAI'03 Workshop on Computational Approaches to Style Analysis and Synthesis, pp. 69-72.

Koppel M. and Schler J. 2004. *Authorship verification as a one-class classification problem.* Proceedings of the 21st International Conference on Machine Learning.

M. Koppel, J. Schler, S. Argamon, and E. Messeri. 2006. *Authorship attribution with thousands of candidate authors.* Proceedings of the 29th annual international ACM SIGIR conference on Research and development in information retrieval, USA, 2006, pp. 659–660.

Koppel M., Schler J. and Argamon S. 2009. *Computational methods in authorship attribution.* JASIST 60 (1): 9–26.

M. Koppel, J. Schler, and S. Argamon. 2011. *Authorship attribution in the wild.* Lang Resources & Evaluation, vol. 45, no. 1, pp. 83–94.

Kukushkina O.V., Polikarpov A.A., and Khmelev D.V. 2001. *Using literal and grammatical statistics for authorship attribution.* Problems of Information Transmission, 37(2), 172-184.

F. Li, X. Zou, P. Liu, and J. Y. Chen. 2011. *New threats to health data privacy.* BMC Bioinformatics, vol. 12 Suppl 12, p. S7.

Kim Luyckx and Walter Daelemans. 2008. *Authorship Attribution and Verification with Many Authors and Limited Data.* Proceedings of the 22nd International Conference on Computational Linguistics (COLING 2008), 513-520.

D. Madigan, A. Genkin, D. D. Lewis, S. Argamon, D. Fradkin, and L. Ye. 2005. *Author Identification on the Large Scale.* Joint Meeting of the Interface and Classification Society of North America.

Andrew McDonald, Sadia Afroz, Aylin Caliskan, Ariel Stolerman and Rachel Greenstadt. 2012. *Use Fewer Instances of the Letter "i": Toward Writing Style Anonymization.* PETS 2012.

Morton A.Q. 1965. *The Authorship of Greek Prose.* Journal of the Royal Statistical Society (A), 128, 169-233.

A. Narayanan, H. Paskov, N. Gong, J. Bethencourt, E. Stefanov, R. Shin, and D. Song. 2012. *On the feasibility of internet-scale author identification.* Proceedings of the 33rd conference on IEEE Symposium on Security and Privacy.

Oakes M. 2005.*Statistics for Corpus Linguistics.* Edinburgh University Press.

F. Peng, D. Scuurmans, V. Keselj, and S. Wang. 2003. *Language Independent Authorship Attributions using Character Level Language Models.* Proc. of the 10th Conference of the European Chapter of the Associations for Computational Linguistics (EACL'03).

Marius Popescu, Liviu P. Dinu. 2007. *Kernel methods and string kernels for authorship identification: The Federalist Papers case.* Proceedings International Conference RANLP - 2007, pp 484-487.

Alan Ritter, Sam Clark, Mausam and Oren Etzioni. 2011. *Named Entity Recognition in Tweets: An Experimental Study.* Empirical Methods in Natural Language Processing, 2011.

Stamatatos E., Fakotakis N. and Kokkinakis G. 2001. *Computer-based authorship attribution without lexical measures.* Computers and the Humanities 35, pp. 193-214.

Stamatatos E. 2009. *A survey of modern authorship attribution methods.* J. Am. Soc. Inf. Sci. Technol., vol. 60, no. 3, pp. 538–556.

W. Teahan, R. McNab, Y. Wen, and I. H. Witten, 2000. *A compression-based algorithm for Chinese word segmentation.* Comput. Linguist., vol. 26, no. 3, pp. 375–393.

Tweedie F. J. and Baayen R. H. 1998. *How Variable May a Constant Be? Measures of Lexical Richness in Perspective.* Computers and the Humanities, 32 (1998), 323-352.

M. van der Velden, K. El Emam. 2012. *Not all my friends nee to know: A qualitative study of teenage patients, privacy and social media.* Journal of the American Medical Informatics Association, Published Online First, doi:10.1136/amiajnl-2012-000949.

Zhao Y. and Zobel J. 2007. *Searching with style: authorship attribution in classic literature.* Proceedings of 30th Australasian Conference on Computer Science, Vol. 62, pp. 59-68.

Zheng R., Qin Y., Huang Z., & Chen H. 2006. *A Framework for Authorship Analysis of Online Messages: Writing-style Features and Techniques.* Journal of the American Society for Information Science and Technology 57(3): (2006), 378-393.

TwitIE: An Open-Source Information Extraction Pipeline for Microblog Text

Kalina Bontcheva, Leon Derczynski, Adam Funk,
Mark A. Greenwood, Diana Maynard, Niraj Aswani
University of Sheffield
`Initial.Surname@dcs.shef.ac.uk`

Abstract

Twitter is the largest source of microblog text, responsible for gigabytes of human discourse every day. Processing microblog text is difficult: the genre is noisy, documents have little context, and utterances are very short. As such, conventional NLP tools fail when faced with tweets and other microblog text. We present TwitIE, an open-source NLP pipeline customised to microblog text at every stage. Additionally, it includes Twitter-specific data import and metadata handling. This paper introduces each stage of the TwitIE pipeline, which is a modification of the GATE ANNIE open-source pipeline for news text. An evaluation against some state-of-the-art systems is also presented.

1 Introduction

Researchers have started recently to study the problem of mining social media content automatically (e.g. (Rowe et al., 2013; Nagarajan and Gamon, 2011; Farzindar and Inkpen, 2012; Bontcheva and Rout, 2013)). The focus of this paper is on information extraction, but other active topics include opinion mining (Maynard et al., 2012; Pak and Paroubek, 2010), summarisation (e.g. (Chakrabarti and Punera, 2011)), and visual analytics and user and community modelling (Bontcheva and Rout, 2013). Social media mining is relevant in many application contexts, including knowledge management, competitor intelligence, customer relation management, eHealth, and eGovernment.

Information extraction from social media content has only recently become an active research topic, following early experiments which showed this genre to be extremely challenging for state-of-the-art algorithms (Derczynski et al., 2013a). Simple domain adaptation techniques (e.g. (Daumé and Marcu, 2007) are not so useful on this genre, in part due to its unusual structure and representation of discourse, which can switch between one-to-one conversation, multi-party conversation and broadcast messages. For instance, named entity recognition methods typically have 85-90% accuracy on longer texts, but 30-50% on tweets (Ritter et al., 2011; Liu et al., 2012).

This paper introduces the TwitIE information extraction system, which has been specifically adapted to microblog content. It is based on the most recent GATE (Cunningham et al., 2013) algorithms and is available as a GATE plugin available to download from `https://gate.ac.uk/wiki/twitie.html`, usable both via the GATE Developer user interface and via the GATE API. Comparisons against other state-of-the-art research on this topic are also made.

2 Related Work

In terms of Named Entity Recognition (NER), and Information Extraction (IE) in general, microblogs are possibly the hardest kind of content to process. First, their shortness (maximum 140 characters for tweets) makes them hard to interpret. Consequently, ambiguity is a major problem since IE methods cannot easily make use of coreference information. Unlike longer news articles, there is a low amount of discourse information per microblog document, and threaded structure is fragmented across multiple documents, flowing in multiple directions.

Second, microtexts also exhibit much more language variation, tend to be less grammatical than longer posts, contain unorthodox capitalisation, and make frequent use of emoticons, abbreviations and hashtags, which can form an important part of the meaning.

To combat these problems, research has focused on microblog-specific information extraction algorithms (e.g. named entity recognition for Twitter using CRFs (Ritter et al., 2011), Wikipedia-based topic and entity disambiguation (van Erp et al., 2013)). Particular attention is given to microtext normalisation, as a way of removing some of the linguistic noise prior to part-of-speech tagging and entity recognition (Derczynski et al., 2013a; Han and Baldwin, 2011; Han et al., 2012).

Named entity recognition of longer texts, such as news, is a very well studied problem (cf. (Nadeau and Sekine, 2007; Roberts et al., 2008; Marrero et al., 2009)).

For Twitter, some approaches have been proposed but often they are not freely available. Ritter et al. (Ritter et al., 2011) take a pipeline approach performing first tokenisation and POS tagging before using topic models to find named entities. Liu (Liu et al., 2012) propose a gradient-descent graph-based method for doing joint text normalisation and recognition, reaching 83.6% F1 measure.

We have also included in our evaluation of TwitIE, a Twitter-adapted version of the state-of-the-art Stanford NER (Finkel et al., 2005), which we trained using both tweets and newswire. It uses a machine learning-based method to detect named entities, and is distributed with CRF models for English newswire text.

NER apart, other actively researched IE topics are entity disambiguation (e.g. (Davis et al., 2012; van Erp et al., 2013)), event extraction and summarisation (e.g. (Becker et al., 2011b; Becker et al., 2011a; Chakrabarti and Punera, 2011)), and opinion mining (e.g. (Maynard et al., 2012; Pak and Paroubek, 2010)) to name just a few. Since at present, TwitIE's focus is currently on named entity recognition, we will not compare against these methods. In future work, TwitIE will be extended towards entity disambiguation and relation extraction.

3 The TwitIE IE Pipeline

The open-source GATE NLP framework (Cunningham et al., 2013) comes pre-packaged with the ANNIE general purpose IE pipeline (Cunningham et al., 2002). ANNIE consists of the following main processing resources: tokeniser, sentence splitter, POS tagger, gazetteer lists, finite state transducer (based on GATE's built-in regular expressions over annotations language), orthomatcher and coreference resolver. The resources communicate via GATE's annotation API, which is a directed graph of arcs bearing arbitrary feature/value data, and nodes rooting this data into document content.

The ANNIE components can be used individually or coupled together with new modules in order to create new applications. TwitIE re-uses the sentence splitter and name gazetteer components unmodified, though we re-trained and adapted all other components to the specifics of this genre.

The rationale behind adopting the sentence splitter unmodified, is that in most cases it tends to consider the text of the entire tweet as one sentence. Due to the limited local context, this did not present problems for the later components. Nevertheless, a more in-depth evaluation of the sentence splitter errors is necessary and envisaged as part of future work.

Similarly, the reuse of the ANNIE gazetteer lists was sufficient for the time being, due to their very generic nature (e.g. country names, days of the week, months, first names). However, the TwitIE POS tagger does come with customised in-built gazetteer lists, used for tagging unambiguous named entities, e.g. YouTube, Twitter, Yandex (see (Derczynski et al., 2013b) for details on the lists and how they were created and used).

For the rest of the TwitIE components, adaptation to the specifics of the microblog genre is required, in order to address the genre-specific challenges of noisiness, brevity, idiosyncratic language, and social context. General-purpose tools (e.g. POS taggers and entity recognisers) do particularly badly on such texts (see Sections 3.5 and 3.6).

Therefore, we have developed TwitIE – a customisation of ANNIE, specific to social media content, which has been tested most extensively on microblog messages.

Figure 1 shows the TwitIE pipeline and its components. TwitIE is distributed as a plugin in GATE, which needs to be loaded for these processing resources to appear in GATE Developer. Re-used ANNIE components are shown in dashed boxes, whereas the ones in dotted boxes are new and specific to the microblog genre.

The first step is language identification, which is discussed next (Section 3.2), followed by the TwitIE tokeniser (Section 3.3).

The **gazetteer** consists of lists such as cities, organisations, days of the week, etc. It not only consists of entities, but also of names of useful *indicators*, such as typical company designators (e.g. 'Ltd.'), titles, etc. The gazetteer lists are compiled into finite state machines, which can match text tokens. TwitIE reuses the ANNIE gazetteer lists, at present, without any modification.

The **sentence splitter** is a cascade of finite-state transducers which segments text into sentences. This module is required for the POS tagger. The ANNIE sentence splitter is reused without modification, although when processing tweets, it is also possible to just use the text of the tweet as one sentence, without further analysis.

The normaliser, the adapted POS tagger, and named entity recognition are discussed in detail in Sections 3.4, 3.5, and 3.6 respectively.

3.1 Tweet Import

The ability to collect corpora is particularly important with social media. Twitter, for example, currently forbids distribution of whole tweets, and so instead tweet corpora are distributed via tweet ID. Data is delivered from the Twitter API in JSON format. This is currently a process external to GATE, although we plan to address this in future work.

In the most recent GATE codebase, we added a new `Format_Twitter` plugin, which coverts automatically tweets in JSON, into fully-annotated GATE documents.

The JSON format ceonvertor is automatically associated with les whose names end in .json; otherwise the user needs to specify `text/x-json-twitter` as the document mime type. The JSON import works both when creating a single new GATE document and when populating a corpus.

Each tweet objects text value is converted into the document content, which is covered with a Tweet annotation whose features represent (recursively when appropriate, using HashMap and List) all the other key-value pairs in the tweet JSON object.

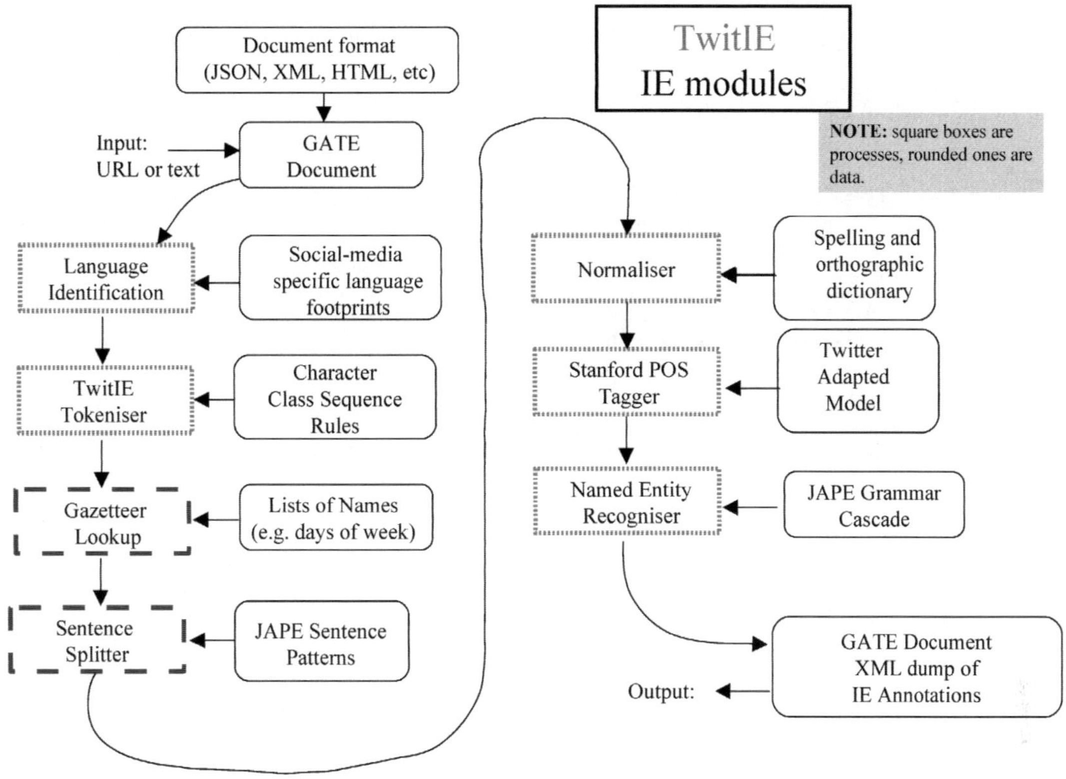

Figure 1: The TwitIE Information Extraction Pipeline

Multiple tweet objects in the same JSON le are separated by blank lines (which are not covered by Tweet annotations.

3.2 Language Identification

The TwitIE system uses the TextCat (Cavnar and Trenkle, 1994) language identification algorithm, which relies on n-gram frequency models to discriminate between languages. More specifically, we have integrated the TextCat adaptation to Twitter (Carter et al., 2013) which works currently on five languages. It is 97.4% accurate overall, with per language accuracy ranging between 95.2% for French and 99.4% for English (Derczynski et al., 2013a). These results demonstrate that language identification is hard on tweets, but nevertheless, can be achieved with reasonable accuracy.

Due to the shortness of tweets, TwitIE makes the assumption that each tweet is written in only one language. The choice of languages used for categorisation is specified through a configuration file, supplied as an initialisation parameter.

Figure 2 shows three tweets – one English, one German, and one French. TwitIE TextCat was used to assign automatically the lang feature to the tweet text (denoted by the Tweet annotation).

Given a collection of tweets in a new language, it is possible to train TwitIE TextCat to support that new language as well. This is done by using the Fingerprint Generation PR, included in the `Language_Identification` plugin. It builds a new ngerprint from a corpus of documents.

Reliable tweet language identification allows us to only process those tweets written in English with the TwitIE English POS tagger and named entity recogniser. This is achieved by making the execution of these components conditional on the respective tweet being in English, by using a Conditional Corpus Pipeline. GATE also provides POS tagging and named entity recognition in French and German, so it is possible to extend TwitIE towards these languages with some training and adaptation effort.

3.3 Tokenisation

Commonly distinguished types of tokens are numbers, symbols (e.g., $, %), punctuation and words of different kinds, e.g., uppercase, lowercase, mixed case. Tokenising well-written text is generally reliable and reusable, since it tends to be domain-independent, e.g. the Unicode tokeniser bundled with the ANNIE system in GATE.

However, such general purpose tokenisers need to be adapted to work correctly on social media, in order to

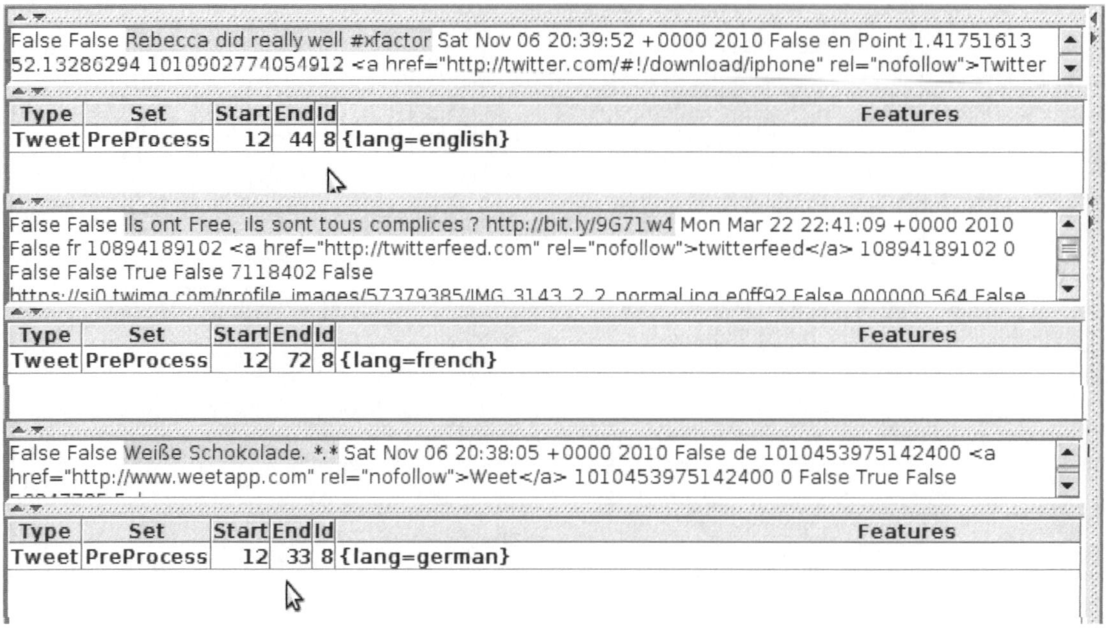

Figure 2: Example Tweets Annotated for Language

handle specific tokens like URLs, hashtags (e.g. #nlproc), user mentions in microblogs (e.g. @GateAcUk), special abbreviations (e.g. RT, ROFL), and emoticons. A study of 1.1 million tweets established that 26% of English tweets have a URL, 16.6% – a hashtag, and 54.8% – a user name mention (Carter et al., 2013). These elements prove particularly disruptive to conventional NLP tools (Derczynski et al., 2013a). Therefore, tokenising these accurately is important.

To take part of a tweet as an example:

```
#WiredBizCon #nike vp said when @Apple
saw what http://nikeplus.com did,
#SteveJobs was like wow I didn't...
```

One option is to tokenise on white space alone, but this does not work that well for hashtags and username mentions. In our example, if we have #nike and @Apple as one token each, this will make their recognition as company names harder, since the named entity recognition algorithm will need to look at sub-token level. Similarly, tokenising on white space and punctuation does not work well since URLs become split into many tokens (e.g. http, nikeplus), as do emoticons and email addresses.

The TwitIE tokeniser is an adaptation of ANNIE's English tokeniser. It follows Ritter's tokenisation scheme (Ritter et al., 2011). More specifically, it treats abbreviations (e.g. RT, ROFL) and URLs as one token each. Hashtags and user mentions are two tokens (i.e., `\#` and `nike` in the above example) with a separate annotation HashTag covering both. Capitalisation is preserved and an orthography feature added. Normalisation and emoticons are handled in optional separate modules, since information about them is not always needed. Consequently, tokenisation is fast and generic, while tailored to the needs of named entity recognition.

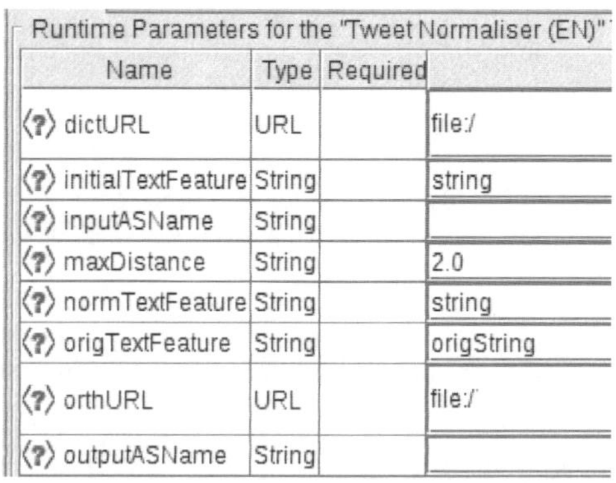

Figure 3: Configuration options for the TwitIE normaliser

3.4 Normalisation

Noisy environments such as microblog text pose challenges to existing tools, being rich in previously unseen tokens, elision of words, and unusual grammar. Normalisation is commonly proposed as a solution for overcoming or reducing linguistic noise (Sproat et al., 2001). The task is generally approached in two stages: first, the identification of orthographic errors in an input discourse, and second, the correction of these errors.

The TwitIE Normaliser is a combination of a generic spelling-correction dictionary and a spelling correction dictionary, specific to social media. The latter contains entries such as "2moro" and "brb", similar to Han et al. (2012). Figure 4 shows an example tweet, where the abbreviation "Govt" has been normalised to government.

Instead of a fixed list of variations, it is also possible to use a heuristic to suggest correct spellings. Both text edit distance and phonetic distance can be used to find candidate matches for words identified as misspelled. (Han and Baldwin, 2011) achieved good corrections in many cases by using a combination of Levenshtein distance and double-metaphone distance between known words and words identified as incorrectly entered. We also experimented with this normalisation approach in TwitIE, and provide a toy corpus of various utterances that require normalisation. This method has higher recall (more wrong words can be corrected by the resource) but lower precision (some corrections are wrong).

3.5 Part-of-speech Tagging

Accuracy of the general-purpose English POS taggers is typically excellent (97-98%) on texts similar to those on which the taggers have been trained (mostly news articles). However, they are not suitable for microblogs and other short, noisy social media content, where their accuracy declines to 70-75% (Derczynski et al., 2013a).

TwitIE contains an adapted Stanford tagger (Toutanova et al., 2003), trained on tweets tagged with the Penn TreeBank (PTB) tagset. Extra tag labels have been added for retweets, URLs, hashtags and user mentions. We trained this tagger using hand-annotated tweets (Ritter et al., 2011), the NPS IRC corpus (Forsyth and Martell, 2007), and news text from PTB (Marcus et al., 1993). The resulting model achieves 83.14% token accuracy, which is still below that achieved on news content.

The most common mistakes (just over 27%) arise from words which are common in general, but do not occur in the training data, indicating a need for a larger training POS-tagged corpus of social media content. Another 27% of errors arise from slang words, which are ubiquitous in social media content and are also often misspelled (e.g. *LUVZ*, *HELLA* and *2night*) and another 8% from typos. Many of these can be addressed using normalisation (see Section 3.4). Close to 9% of errors arise from tokenisation mistakes (e.g. joined words). Lastly, 9% of errors are words, to which a label may be reliably assigned automatically, including URLs, hash tags, re-tweets and smileys, which we now pre-tag automatically with regular expressions and lookup lists.

Another frequently made mistake is tagging proper noun (`NN`/`NNP`) – an observation also made by (Ritter et al., 2011). Therefore, we use ANNIE's gazetteer lists of personal first-names and cities and, in addition, a list of unambiguous corporation and website names frequently-mentioned in the training data (e.g. *YouTube*, *Toyota*).

By combining normalisation, gazetteer name lookup, and regular expression-based tagging of Twitter-specific POS tags, we increase performance from 83.14% accuracy to 86.93%. By generating additional 1.5M training tokens from tweets annotated automatically using two existing POS taggers (namely (Ritter et al., 2011) and (Gimpel et al., 2011)), we further improve the performance of our Twitter-adapted tagger to 90.54% token accuracy using the PTB tagset (better than state-of-the-art).

Figure 4 shows an example tweet, which has been tagged both without normalisation (upper row of POS tags) and with tweet normalisation (the lower row of POS tags). The word *"Govt"* is normalised to government, which is then tagged correctly as `NN`, instead of `NNP`.

3.6 Named Entity Recognition

Named entity recognition (**NER**) is difficult on user-generated content in general, and in the microblog genre specifically, because of the reduced amount of contextual information in short messages and a lack of curation of content by third parties (e.g. that done by editors for newswire). In this section, we examine how the default ANNIE named entity recognition pipelines performs in comparison to a Twitter-specific approach, on a corpus of 2 400 tweets comprising 34 000 tokens (Ritter et al., 2011).

We did not consider Percent-type entity annotations in these evaluations because there were so few (3 in the whole corpus) and they were all annotated correctly. Note also that twitter-specific UserID annotation as a Person annotation is *not* included in these results, as they can be matched using a simple, public regular expression provided by Twitter, and as a result were all 100% correct.

As we can see in Table 1, the performance of ANNIE and the Stanford NER tagger degrades significantly on microblog content, in comparison to newswire, which motivates the need for microblog domain adaptation. Thanks to adaptation in the earlier components in TwitIE (especially the POS tagger (Derczynski et al., 2013b)), we demonstrate a +30% absolute precision and +20% absolute F1 performance increase, as compared to ANNIE, mainly with respect to Date, Organization and in particular Person. TwitIE also outperforms Ritter's Twitter NER algorithm (Ritter et al., 2011) and our adaptation of the Stanford NER, which we trained using both tweets and newswire (see (Derczynski et al., 2013a) for details).

However, as shown in Table 1, when compared against state-of-the-art NER performance on longer news content, an overall F1 score of 80% leaves notable amounts of missed annotations and false positives.

Labelling Organizations in tweets proved particularly hard, where errors were often caused by miscategorisations. For example, *Vista del Lago* and *Clemson Auburn* were both labelled as Organizations, when they should have been Locations. Polysemous named entities were also handled poorly, due to insufficient surrounding disambiguating context (typical in microblogs). For example, *Amazon* was labelled as a Location when it should have been an Organization.

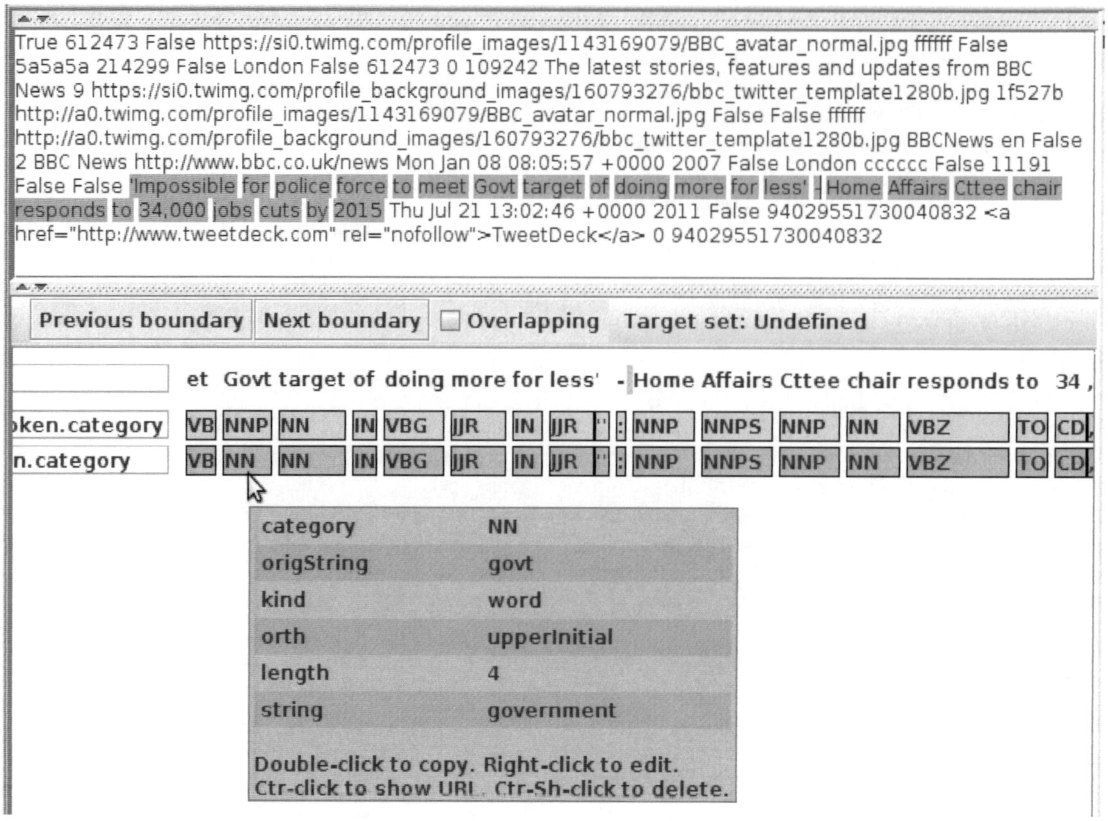

Figure 4: Comparing POS Tagger Output: A Normalisation Example

System	Precision	Recall	F1
	Newswire		
ANNIE	78%	74%	77%
Stanford	-	-	**89%**
	Microblog		
ANNIE	47%	**83%**	60%
TwitIE	**77%**	**83%**	**80%**
Stanford	59%	32%	41%
Stanford-twitter	54%	45%	49%
Ritter	73%	49%	59%

Table 1: Whole-pipeline named entity recognition performance, before and after genre adaptation. Newswire performance is over the CoNLL 2003 English dataset; microblog performance is over the development part of the Ritter dataset.

NEs represented in lowercase (e.g. *skype*) were frequently ignored. However, handling capitalisation is hard from trivial (Derczynski et al., 2013a) and this is an area where we plan more future work, combined with the creation of a larger, human-annotated corpus of NER-annotated tweets.

4 Conclusion

This paper presented the TwitIE open-source NER pipeline, specifically developed to handle microblogs. Issues related to microblog NER were discussed, and the requirement for domain adaptation demonstrated. As can be seen from the evaluation results reported here, significant inroads have been made into this challenging problem. By releasing TwitIE as open source, we hope to give researchers also an easily repeatable, baseline system against which they can compare new Twitter NER algorithms.

As already discussed, there is still a significant gap in NER performance on microblogs, as compared against news content. This gap is due to some degree to insufficient linguistic context and the noisiness of tweets. However, there is also a severe lack of labeled training data, which hinders the adaptation of state-of-the-art NER algorithms, such as the Stanford CRF tagger. These are all areas of ongoing and future work, as well as the adaptation of the entire TwitIE pipeline to languages other than English.

Acknowledgments

This work was supported by UK EPSRC grants Nos. EP/I004327/1 and EP/K017896/1 uComp,[1] and by the European Union under grant agreement No. 270239 Arcomem.[2]

References

H. Becker, M. Naaman, and L. Gravano. 2011a. Selecting Quality Twitter Content for Events. In *Pro-*

[1]http://www.ucomp.eu

[2]http://www.arcomem.eu

ceedings of the Fifth International Conference on Weblogs and Social Media (ICWSM).

H. Becker, M. Naaman, and L. Gravano. 2011b. Beyond Trending Topics: Real-World Event Identification on Twitter. In *Proceedings of the Fifth International Conference on Weblogs and Social Media (ICWSM).*

K. Bontcheva and D. Rout. 2013. Making sense of social media through semantics: A survey. *Semantic Web - Interoperability, Usability, Applicability.*

S. Carter, W. Weerkamp, and E. Tsagkias. 2013. Microblog language identification: Overcoming the limitations of short, unedited and idiomatic text. *Language Resources and Evaluation Journal.*

W. Cavnar and J. Trenkle. 1994. N-gram-based text categorization. In *Proceedings of the Annual Symposium on Document Analysis and Information Retrieval*, pages 161–175.

D. Chakrabarti and K. Punera. 2011. Event Summarization Using Tweets. In *Proceedings of the Fifth International Conference on Weblogs and Social Media (ICWSM).*

H. Cunningham, D. Maynard, K. Bontcheva, and V. Tablan. 2002. Gate: an architecture for development of robust hlt applications. In *Proceedings of the 40th Annual Meeting on Association for Computational Linguistics*, pages 168–175.

H. Cunningham, V. Tablan, A. Roberts, and K. Bontcheva. 2013. Getting more out of biomedical documents with gate's full lifecycle open source text analytics. *PLoS Computational Biology*, 9(2):e1002854, 02.

H. Daumé and D. Marcu. 2007. Frustratingly easy domain adaptation. In *Proceedings of the Annual meeting of the Association for Computational Linguistics.*

A. Davis, A. Veloso, A. Soares, A. Laender, and W. Meira Jr. 2012. Named entity disambiguation in streaming data. In *Proceedings of the 50th Annual Meeting of the Association for Computational Linguistics*, pages 815–824, Jeju Island, Korea, July. Association for Computational Linguistics.

L. Derczynski, D. Maynard, N. Aswani, and K. Bontcheva. 2013a. Microblog-Genre Noise and Impact on Semantic Annotation Accuracy. In *Proceedings of the 24th ACM Conference on Hypertext and Social Media.* ACM.

L. Derczynski, A. Ritter, S. Clark, and K. Bontcheva. 2013b. Twitter Part-of-Speech Tagging for All: Overcoming Sparse and Noisy Data. In *Proceedings of Recent Advances in Natural Language Processing (RANLP).* Association for Computational Linguistics.

A. Farzindar and D. Inkpen, editors. 2012. *Proceedings of the Workshop on Semantic Analysis in Social Media.* Association for Computational Linguistics, Avignon, France, April.

J. Finkel, T. Grenager, and C. Manning. 2005. Incorporating non-local information into information extraction systems by Gibbs sampling. In *Proceedings of the 43rd Annual Meeting of the Association for Computational Linguistics*, pages 363–370. Association for Computational Linguistics.

E. Forsyth and C. Martell. 2007. Lexical and discourse analysis of online chat dialog. In *International Conference on Semantic Computing*, pages 19–26. IEEE.

K. Gimpel, N. Schneider, B. O'Connor, D. Das, D. Mills, J. Eisenstein, M. Heilman, D. Yogatama, J. Flanigan, and N. Smith. 2011. Part-of-speech tagging for twitter: annotation, features, and experiments. In *Proceedings of the 49th Annual Meeting of the Association for Computational Linguistics: Human Language Technologies*, pages 42–47. ACL.

B. Han and T. Baldwin. 2011. Lexical normalisation of short text messages: makn sens a #twitter. In *Proceedings of the 49th Annual Meeting of the Association for Computational Linguistics: Human Language Technologies*, HLT '11, pages 368–378.

B. Han, P. Cook, and T. Baldwin. 2012. Automatically constructing a normalisation dictionary for microblogs. In *Proceedings of the conference on Empirical Methods in Natural Language Processing*, pages 421–432. ACL.

X. Liu, M. Zhou, F. Wei, Z. Fu, and X. Zhou. 2012. Joint inference of named entity recognition and normalization for tweets. In *Proceedings of the Association for Computational Linguistics*, pages 526–535.

M. Marcus, B. Santorini, and M. Marcinkiewicz. 1993. Building a Large Annotated Corpus of English: The Penn Treebank. *Computational Linguistics*, 19(2):313–330.

M. Marrero, S. Sanchez-Cuadrado, J. Lara, and G. Andreadakis. 2009. Evaluation of Named Entity Extraction Systems. *Advances in Computational Linguistics, Research in Computing Science*, 41:47–58.

D. Maynard, K. Bontcheva, and D. Rout. 2012. Challenges in developing opinion mining tools for social media. In *Proceedings of @NLP can u tag #usergeneratedcontent?! Workshop at LREC 2012*, Turkey.

D. Nadeau and S. Sekine. 2007. A survey of named entity recognition and classification. *Lingvisticae Investigationes*, 30(1):3–26.

M. Nagarajan and M. Gamon, editors. 2011. *LSM '11: Proceedings of the Workshop on Languages in Social Media*, Stroudsburg, PA, USA. Association for Computational Linguistics.

A. Pak and P. Paroubek. 2010. Twitter as a corpus for sentiment analysis and opinion mining. In *Proceedings of the Seventh conference on International Language Resources and Evaluation (LREC)*.

A. Ritter, S. Clark, Mausam, and O. Etzioni. 2011. Named entity recognition in tweets: An experimental study. In *Proc. of Empirical Methods for Natural Language Processing (EMNLP)*, Edinburgh, UK.

A. Roberts, R. Gaizauskas, M. Hepple, and Y. Guo. 2008. Combining terminology resources and statistical methods for entity recognition: an evaluation. *Proceedings of the Conference on Language Resources and Evaluation (LRE'08)*.

M. Rowe, M. Stankovic, A. Dadzie, B. Nunes, and A. Cano. 2013. Making sense of microposts (#msm2013): Big things come in small packages. In *Proceedings of the WWW Conference - Workshops*.

R. Sproat, A. Black, S. Chen, S. Kumar, M. Ostendorf, and C. Richards. 2001. Normalization of non-standard words. *Computer Speech & Language*, 15(3):287–333.

K. Toutanova, D. Klein, C. D. Manning, and Y. Singer. 2003. Feature-rich part-of-speech tagging with a cyclic dependency network. In *Proceedings of the 2003 Conference of the North American Chapter of the Association for Computational Linguistics on Human Language Technology*, NAACL '03, pages 173–180.

M. van Erp, G. Rizzo, and R. Troncy. 2013. Learning with the Web: Spotting Named Entities on the intersection of NERD and Machine Learning. In *Proceedings of the 3rd Workshop on Making Sense of Microposts (#MSM2013)*.

A Unified Lexical Processing Framework Based on the Margin Infused Relaxed Algorithm. A Case Study on the Romanian Language

Tiberiu Boroş
Research Institute for Artificial Intelligence, "Mihai Drăgănescu", Romanian Academy
tibi@racai.ro

Abstract

General natural language processing and text-to-speech applications require certain (lexical level) processing steps in order to solve some frequent tasks such as lemmatization, syllabification, lexical stress prediction and phonetic transcription. These steps usually require knowledge of the word's lexical composition (derivative morphology, inflectional affixes, etc.). For known words all applications use lexicons, but there are always out-of-vocabulary (OOV) words that impede the performance of NLP and speech synthesis applications. In such cases, either rule based or data-driven techniques are used to automatically process these OOV words and generate the desired results. In this paper we describe how the above mentioned tasks can be achieved using a Perceptron with the Margin Infused Relaxed Algorithm (MIRA) and sequence labeling.

1 Introduction

Natural Language Processing (NLP) applications and Text-to-Speech (TTS) synthesis systems require a set of pre-processing steps that include tasks such as lemmatization, syllabification, lexical stress prediction and phonetic transcription. Because these all these tasks require knowledge of the word composition (derivative morphology, inflectional affixes, part of speech, etc.) we will refer to them as lexical processing steps.

This paper presents a *unified lexical processing framework* based on the Margin Infused Relaxed Algorithm (MIRA) (Crammer and Singer, 2003) designed to solve the basic text-preprocessing tasks involved in both text-to-speech (TTS) synthesis and general NLP applications. Assuming that all existing systems use lexicons for known words, we focused our research in handling the difficult problems generated by presence of out-of vocabulary (OOV) or previously unseen in the training data words that negatively impact the performance of the above mentioned tasks. Our current research is focused on the Romanian language, but the methods presented here are data-driven and with proper lexicons and feature templates, *they can be used for other (Latin based) languages as well*. We show how we achieved state-of-the-art results on Romanian by using the MIRA framework.

2 Lexical processing with MIRA

There are various methods proposed in the literature for each of the previously mentioned lexical subtasks. For each of them, we will offer a short literature review of available methods and we will compare our results with the current state-of-art systems.

The previously proposed methods vary from rule-based to data-driven and different authors employ different classifiers (in data-driven approaches), such as Maximum Entropy Classifiers, Classification and Regression Trees, Support Vector Machines (SVM), Structured SVMs, Conditional Random Fields, etc. While these are all powerful methodologies, we chose the *Perceptron classifier with the MIRA update learning* as our sequence labeling classifier because of its robustness and its ability to obtain highly accurate results that compare to the ones obtained using CRFs. All the lexical processing methods that we propose, share the following similarities:

- All of them are reformulated as sequence labeling tasks;
- We use the same classifier for all our tasks (MIRA);

- The classification context is based on different and mostly lexical (except for lemmatization and lexical stress prediction, which use the morpho-syntactic) feature sets;
- The performance is measured in terms of word accuracy rates (WAR);
- All the tests are reported on OOV words, as we assume that all systems use lookup lexicons for known words;
- All our tests are performed on Romanian and we report the feature sets that yielded the best results.

3 Syllabification

Syllabification is the process of decomposing words into their phonological units, which is an important requirement in modern approaches to TTS synthesis and speech recognition.

All languages have phonetic rules that govern the syllabification process, but it is often the case that these rules are contradicted by etymological principles, a fact which complicates the task of automatic syllabification. Phonetic transcription (letter to sound – L2S) or the position of the lexical stress both provide useful information for syllabification, but more often than not, L2S and lexical stress are not accurate enough on OOV words to help the syllabification process. Also, syllabification lexicons are usually larger than L2S lexicons, thus providing more training data, which helps the syllabification system obtain better results than L2S. Because of the above mentioned reasons, we strictly based our method on purely lexical features (i.e. the word's letters).

Several algorithms have been proposed for the syllabification task divided between rule-based and data-driven. While, rule-based methods are centered on theoretical aspects of the syllabification problem, data-driven methods are usually preferable, since they are language independent and they only require the construction of syllabified words lexicons.

In the following description, we use the term *juncture point* to denote the places where hyphen marks (syllable breaks) are placed within a word.

The look-up procedure was introduced by Weijters (1991). It constructs a table of n-grams from the training corpus and uses this table to predict juncture points. Each n-gram contains the *focus character* (the character that is being analyzed to determine if a juncture point should or should not occur after) with left and right context, including hyphen marks. When syllabification is performed on a new word, the algorithm determines if a focus character should be followed by a hyphen, using the majority of similar n-grams.

The IB1 (Daelemans et al., 1997) algorithm creates n-grams (of predetermined size) from word juncture points and stores them into a database. When a new word has to be split into syllables, every n-gram around the word's possible junctures is matched against the n-grams already available from the training step. N-grams are compared using a distance measure to determine how similar two n-grams are to one another.

Marchand and Damper (2007) introduced Syllabification by Analogy (SbA) which follows the principles of the Pronunciation by Analogy (PbA) algorithm. It works by applying a "full pattern match" on the input string using entries in a dictionary compiled from the training corpora. Marchand and Damper also investigate the possibility of using syllabification to improve grapheme to phoneme performance on English words.

Barlett et al. (2008) use structured SVMs to predict tags for letters in a given word and compare results obtained using different tagging strategies. Their method outperforms the results of the SbA method.

3.1 Syllabification with MIRA

Our sequence labeling approach is inspired after Barlett et al. (2008). In their paper they experimented with different tagging strategies and according to their results, the numbered ONC (onset-nucleus-coda) achieved the highest performance. This is why we employed the same tagging strategy for our system. *The main difference between our approach and theirs, is the features set we designed and the classifier we used (MIRA).*

A widely accepted fact is that a syllable is composed of a *nucleus* vowel with or without surrounding consonants which are divided into the *onset* (the consonants preceding the vowel) and the *coda* (the consonants succeeding the vowel). The ONC tagging strategy assigns a tag to every letter of a word based on its role inside the parent syllable. There are three types of tags: O-onset, N-nucleus and C-coda. The numbered ONC makes every tag unique, *inside a syllable*, by adding an index to the tag. To exemplify, we will use the syllabification of the Romanian word "avertisment" (English "warning"). The correct tag sequence for this word is:

$N_1O_1N_1C_1O_1N_1C_1O_1N_1C_1C_2$. Determining where the junctures appear inside the word is easily attained by looking for tag sequences that are unacceptable inside the same syllable such as: C_i-O_j, N_i-N_1, C_i-N_j, N_i-O_j etc. (for whatever indexes i and j). By doing so, we obtain the break sequence: N_1-$O_1N_1C_1$-$O_1N_1C_1$-$O_1N_1C_1C_2$, and with a 1-1 correspondence between tags and letters, we get the sequence “a-ver-tis-ment”, which is the correct syllabification of the word.

After iterating through several feature sets we selected the one that yielded the highest results: (l_{-2},l_{-1},l), (l_{-3},l_{-2},l_{-1},l), $(l_{-4},l_{-3},l_{-2},l_{-1},l)$, $(l,l_1,l2)$, (l,l_1,l_2,l_3), (l,l_1,l_2,l_3,l_4), (l_{-1},l,l_1), $(l_{-2},l_{-1},l,l_1,l_2)$, where l is used to mark the current letter and l_i is used to denote the letter at relative distance i from the current one.

3.2 Experiments and results

To test this approach we used a training corpus consisting of 600K syllabified words, compiled from the Romanian Academy Explanatory Dictionary. Using 10-fold validation we obtained and accuracy of **99.01%** on **OOV** words**.** To our knowledge, the best performing system for Romanian syllabification is presented in Ungurean et al. (2011). In their approach, they use Katz-Backoff for determining the most probable n-gram letter split sequence using the output of a stochastic search algorithm. Their method obtained a maximum accuracy of **97.04%** using a window of 5 letter n-grams.

4 Lemmatization

Lemmatization is the process of determining a word’s canonical form from its inflectional form. It is a technique useful in various natural language processing applications such as data-mining and document classification. Lemmatization is related to the technique called stemming, which is the process of extracting the longest common subsequence between word forms.

In the case of English, the lemmatization process is fairly simple, but for highly inflectional languages, such as Romanian, this process poses a series of challenges. There are several approaches to this task, with a trend toward rule-based transformations applied to the sequence of characters. The best-performing Romanian lemmatizer [1] (to the best of our knowledge) is implemented after the methodology proposed in Ion (2007). The method builds a lookup table storing for each POS tag (named CTAG), the transformations required for word form to canonical form conversion. When the method has to predict the lemma for a previously unseen word with an associated CTAG (supplied by the POS tagging process), it searches the lookup table for the transformation rules of the CTAG and applies all of them to the unseen word, thus obtaining a set of candidate lemmas from which it probabilistically chooses the most likely one.

4.1 Lemmatization with MIRA

In order to use the MIRA framework, we had to reformulate lemmatization as a sequence labeling task. Our labels are designed to encode the following transformations:

- ‘*’ – means leave current letter *unchanged*
- ‘*_nil_*’ – means that the current letter must be *removed* from the word’s lemma
- ‘*_r(<character sequence>)* –means that the current letter has to be *replaced* with the character sequence in brackets (*<character sequence>*).

To exemplify, we will use the 2nd person, plural verb “îmbrăcați” (English “dressed”), which has the canonical form “îmbrăca” (“*to* dress”). The letter tag sequence is shown in Table 1.

î	m	b	r	ă	c	a	ț	i
*	*	*	*	*	*	*	_nil_	_nil_

Table 1 - Lemmatization example for word "îmbrăcați"

Lemmatization has to take into account the information provided by the word’s morpho-syntactic-description (MSD) tag (Ion, 2007). This means that we either have to train different models for different MSDs or we have to incorporate the MSD information inside the features we use. The Romanian MSDs inventory is very large (more than 600 MSDs) and consequently, the MIRA model obtained by training with MSDs is extremely large, difficult to train and use. Tufiş (1999) presents a strategy for coping with the large Romanian MSD inventory, in which he eliminates lexicon-recoverable morpho-syntactic attributes from the MSDs. The resulting tagset is much smaller and the resulting POS tags are called CTAGs (from Corpus POS tags).

[1] http://ws.racai.ro:9191

In order to reduce our lemmatization model size, we converted every word's MSD from our training set into a CTAG, based on the above mentioned methodology. This reduced our model size about 5 times.

The context used by the labeler is composed of both *lexical* and *morpho-syntactic* features (CTAGs): (l_{-2},l_{-1},l,C), $(l_{-3},l_{-2},l_{-1},l,C)$, $(l_{-4},l_{-3},l_{-2},l_{-1},l,C)$, (l,l_1,l_2,C), (l,l_1,l_2,l_3,C), (l,l_1,l_2,l_3,l_4,C), (l_{-1},l,l_1,C), $(l_{-2},l_{-1},l,l_1,l_2,C)$, where l is used to mark the current letter, l_i is used to denote the letter at relative distance i from the current one and C is used to denote the word form's CTAG.

4.2 Experimental results

Using a training corpus composed of 1M words we withheld 10% for each individual CTAG as the test set. The results of our experiments are shown in Table 1. The overall accuracy of **94%** which is **12%** higher than the results presented in Ion (2007).

In Table 1, all CTAGS beginning with an "N" are nouns, "A" are adjectives and "V" are verbs. The best result (100%) is for invariant adjectives ("A") for which the lemma is the word form. This behavior is preserved for all CTAGs for which lemma is equal to the word form: NSRN (noun, singular, nominative/accusative, non-definite form) with 99.5%, ASN (adjective, singular, non-definite form) with 98.95%, etc. At the opposite pole we find words with CTAGs that are harder to lemmatize: NPN (noun, plural, non-definite form) with 81.51% or NPOY (noun, plural, dative/genitive, definite form) with 83.01% due to their root alternation when going from singular (the number of the lemma) to plural, e.g. for "*stadioan***elor**" (NPOY, English "to the stadiums") lemma is "*stadion*" (English "stadium") where in bold we have the inflectional ending corresponding to the CTAG NPOY and in italic we have the root of the word.

CTAG	# of tokens	# of errors	Accuracy %
A	16	0	100
VN	871	47	94.6
NSON	4223	190	95.5
APOY	5078	99	98.05
NSVN	79	3	96.2
ASN	6205	65	98.95
VPSM	1178	77	93.46
NSOY	6761	279	95.87
ASRY	5121	67	98.69
NP	263	35	86.69
NPRY	6443	884	86.28
VG	2973	118	96.03
NN	263	3	98.86
VPSF	748	15	97.99
APN	6062	127	97.9
NSN	2591	6	99.77
V2	8195	664	91.9
NPOY	6427	1092	83.01
V3	7312	629	91.4
ASON	3030	43	98.58
VPPM	797	58	92.72
NSRY	6701	104	98.45
VPPF	747	15	97.99
V1	6180	455	92.64
APRY	5119	95	98.14
NSRN	4244	19	99.55
ASOY	5122	59	98.85
NPN	6615	1223	81.51
NPVY	28	3	89.29
NSVY	2225	31	98.61
ASVY	626	12	98.08
AN	106	6	94.34
Overall	**112349**	**6523**	**94.19**

Table 2 - Lemmatization results

5 Phonetic transcription

Phonetic transcription (PT; also referred to as grapheme-to-phoneme (G2P) or letter-to-sound (L2S)) can be formalized as finding a relation between letters and corresponding phonemes, which is not a straightforward task and may pose some challenges for languages such as English. For Romanian, phonetic transcription rules are relatively simple compared to English or French (Burileanu, 1999), but there are several exceptions that need to be managed. For the purpose of language independence, data-driven methods are preferable as they only require words and their phonetic transcription equivalents for training, which are easier to obtain than wide coverage set of phonetic transcription rules.

Several Machine Learning (ML) methods have been proposed for the PT task: Black et al. (1998), Jiampojamarn et al. (2008), Pagel et al. (1998), Bisani and Ney (2002), Marchand and Damper (2000) and Demberg (2007).

Jiampojamarn et al. (2008) presented a MIRA based method for L2S conversion of words. Their best result on the English CMU lexicon was 71%. However, the feature template provided in their paper did not turn out to be suitable in our tests. Instead we came up with a different one, which turned out to be the most discriminative for Romanian L2S: (l_{-2},l_{-1},l), (l_{-3},l_{-2},l_{-1},l), $(l_{-4},l_{-3},l_{-2},l_{-1},l)$, (l,l_1,l_2), (l,l_1,l_2,l_3), (l,l_1,l_2,l_3,l_4), (l_{-1},l,l_1), $(l_{-2},l_{-1},l,l_1,l_2)$, (l_{-2},l_{-1},l,l_1), (l_{-1},l,l_1,l_2), where l is used to mark the current letter, l_i is used to denote the letter at relative distance i from the current one.

All the data-driven methods for phonetic transcription require alignments between letters and phonemes. For so-called phonetic (or pseudo-phonetic) languages (e.g. Romanian), the task of grapheme to phoneme conversion is significantly easier and more accurate than for many other languages (such as English). However, there are several issues, common to several languages. The simplest example is that not all words have the same number of phonemes and letters and even if this condition is satisfied, it still does not imply a one-to-one alignment (e.g. experience - IH K S P IH R IY AH N S, where the letter x spawns two phonemes "K" + "S" and the ending "e" is silent; a similar phenomenon happens when we phonetically transcribe the word Romanian "experienţă" (experience) into e k s p e r i e n ts @, where again x spawns "k"+"s"). Expectation-Maximization (EM) can be used to find one-to-one or many-to-many alignments between letters and phonemes (Black et al., 1998; Jiampojamarn et al., 2008; Pagel et al. 1998). Although it is arguable that in the case of Romanian such alignments can be easily attained using simple heuristics, we preferred to use EM on our training data, *to keep our system portable to other languages*.

5.1 Experiments and results

Our training data was extracted from the Romanian Speech Synthesis Corpus (RSS) (Stan et al., 2011) and it is comprised of a small number of words (8K). However, due to the preponderantly phonetical nature of Romanian, this number seems to be sufficient for training a highly accurate L2S data-driven method. Using 10-fold validation we obtained an accuracy of **96.29%** on OOV words, which is comparable to the state-of-the art results (**96.99%**) of a rule-based system reported in Ungurean et al. (2011).

6 Lexical stress prediction

In natural speech certain syllables inside a word have a higher prominence compared to the neighboring syllables of the same word. When this phenomenon occurs, it is said that the syllable is carrying lexical stress. Lexical stress prediction is critical in prosody generation for TTS systems as it governs the correct pronunciation of diverse words and it is used to discriminate between homographs.

6.1 Related work

Oancea and Bădulescu (2003) introduced their rule-based method for lexical stress prediction on Romanian. They trained and tested their method on the same lexicon (4500 words) achieving a **94%** accuracy. Ungurean et al. (2009) used Katz back-off smoothing, for lexical stress assignment based on letter n-grams. Their algorithm works by calculating the probability of every possible combination of stress pattern on an input string. According to their evaluation, this method achieves an accuracy of over **99%** for OOV words.

6.2 Lexical stress prediction with MIRA

Our tagging strategy is inspired after the numbered ONC style encoding used for syllabification. In this case we designed a numbered tagging strategy, in which the "BPS" tag used to label letters which appear before the primary lexical stress; "APS" was used on letters that appear after the primary lexical stress and "PS" to label the letter which carries the primary lexical stress. To exemplify, we will show the labels for the word "îmrăc**<u>a</u>**ţi" (bolded and underlined *a*, receives the primary lexical stress). This type of encoding is available for Romanian, which only uses primary lexical stress. For other languages, which support multiple degrees of lexical stress, the encoding requires adaptations.

î	m	b	r	ă	c	a	ţ	i
BPS 1	BPS 2	BPS 3	BPS 4	BPS 5	BPS 6	PS	APS 1	APS 2

Table 3 – Lexical stress tagging for the word "îmbrăcaţi"

6.3 Experiments and results

Franzén and Horne (1997) conducted a study on stress patterns in Romanian. They showed that stress is rather influenced by derivational affixes than by inflectional ones, especially for nouns and verbs. Since the vast majority of derivational affixes change the grammatical category of a word, we were motivated to split our training data into 5 categories: nouns (N), verbs (V), adjectives (A), adverbs (R) and mixed (M). This is where the main difference between our approach and other methods can be seen: *splitting the training data based on the part-of-speech increases the overall accuracy by **3.9%*** (see Table 3).

POS	# tokens	# errors	Accuracy
V	11403	42	99.63%
A	11180	55	99.50%
R	52	10	80.77%
N	11060	296	97.32%
Ignored (M)	**33695**	**1718**	**94.90%**
Overall	**33695**	**403**	**98.80%**

Table 4 - Lexical stress accuracy

When predicting the primary lexical stress position for a given word, a model is chosen based on the POS tag of the given word. If the POS is different from the first four categories or if it is unknown (if there is no context available), the system uses the *mixed model*, which is a model created by training on the entire lexicon regardless of the POS.

The lexical feature templates we used for lexical stress prediction are identical to the ones we used for lemmatization.

7 Conclusions

In this paper we addressed the task of lexical processing for OOV words, which are one of the main sources of errors in both speech synthesis and natural language processing applications. We presented a unified data-driven framework that is designed to accurately handle the lemmatization, syllabification, phonetic transcription and lexical stress prediction of *OOV words*. Although, our main focus was on Romanian, the advantage of using data-driven methods is that with proper training lexicons and, in some cases, with minor adjustments, they *can be applied to any other language*.

Our results are better than state-of-the-art results cited for Romanian in the case of syllabification (99% vs. 97%) and lemmatization (94% vs. 82%), and only slightly worse for phonetic transcription (96.3% vs. 97%) and lexical stress prediction (98.8% vs. 99%), which can be explained by the fact that we did not incorporate any explicit knowledge of Romanian into our algorithms. In this context, we should emphasize that we successfully employed the MIRA framework described in this paper (without any modifications) to do phonetic transcription for English, French, German and Dutch and lemmatization for Serbian with very good results.

The methods we presented are already implemented in a natural language pre-processing tool written entirely in JAVA for portability and available as an open-source package.

Acknowledgments

The work reported here was funded by the project METANET4U by the European Commission under the Grant Agreement No 270893

References

Bartlett, S., Kondrak, G., & Cherry, C. 2008. Automatic syllabification with structured SVMs for letter-to-phoneme conversion. *Proceedings of ACL-08: HLT*, 568-576.

Black, A. W., Lenzo, K., & Pagel, V. 1998. Issues in building general letter to sound rules. In *The Third ESCA/COCOSDA Workshop (ETRW) on Speech Synthesis*.

Burileanu, D., Sima, M., & Neagu, A. 1999. A phonetic converter for speech synthesis in Romanian. In *Proc. of the XIVth International Congress on Phonetic Sciences ICPhS'99* (pp. 503-506).

Crammer, K. and Singer, Y. 2003. Ultraconservative online algorithms for multiclass problems. The Journal of Machine Learning Research, 3:951–991.

Daelemans, W., Van Den Bosch, A., & Weijters, T. 1997. IGTree: Using trees for compression and classification in lazy learning algorithms. *Artificial Intelligence Review*, 11(1), 407-423.

Demberg, V., Schmid, H., & Mohler, G. 2007. Phonological constraints and morphological preprocessing for grapheme-to-phoneme conversion. In *Annual Meeting-Association for Computational Linguistics* (Vol. 45, No. 1, p. 96).

Franzén, V., & Horne, M. 2009. Word stress in Romanian. *Lund Working Papers in Linguistics*, *46*, 75-91.

Ion, R. 2007. Word Sense Disambiguation Methods Applied to English and Romanian. PhD thesis (in Romanian). Romanian Academy, Bucharest.

Jiampojamarn, S., Cherry, C., & Kondrak, G. 2008. Joint processing and discriminative training for letter-to-phoneme conversion. Proceedings *of ACL-08: HLT*, 905-913.

Kahn, D. 1976. Syllable-based generalizations in English phonology (Vol. 156). Bloomington: Indiana University Linguistics Club.

Lafferty, J., McCallum, A., & Pereira, F. C. 2001. Conditional random fields: Probabilistic models for segmenting and labeling sequence data.

Oancea, E., & Badulescu, A. 2002. Stressed syllable determination for Romanian words within speech synthesis applications. *International Journal of Speech Technology*, *5*(3), 237-246.

Stan, A., Yamagishi, J., King, S., & Aylett, M. 2011. The Romanian Speech Synthesis (RSS) corpus: building a high quality HMM-based speech synthesis system using a high sampling rate. *Speech Communication*, 53(3), 442-450.

Tufiş, D. 1999. Tiered tagging and combined language models classifiers. *Text, Speech and Dialogue* (pp. 843-843). Springer Berlin/Heidelberg.

Ungurean, C., Burileanu, D., Popescu, V. and Derviş, A. 2011. Hybrid Syllabification and Letter-To-Phone Conversion For TTS Synthesis. In *U.P.B. Sci. Bull.*, Series C, Vol. 73, Iss. 3, 2011, ISSN 1454-234x

Weijters, A. 1991. A simple look-up procedure superior to NETtalk?. In *Proceedings of the International Conference on Artificial Neural Networks - ICANN-91*, Espoo, Finland

Automatic Extraction of Contextual Valence Shifters

Noémi Boubel **Thomas François** **Hubert Naets**
Cental, ILC (Université catholique de Louvain)
{noemi.boubel,thomas.francois,hubert.naets}@uclouvain.be

Abstract

In opinion mining, many linguistic structures, called contextual valence shifters, may modify the prior polarity of items. Some systems of sentiment analysis have tried to take these shifters into account, but few studies have focused on the identification of all these structures and their impact on polarized words.

In this paper, we describe a method that automatically identifies contextual valence shifters. It relies on a chi-square test applied to the contingency table representing the distribution of a candidate shifter in a corpus of reviews of various opinions. The system depends on two resources in French – a corpus of reviews and a lexicon of valence terms – to build a list of French contextual valence shifters. We also introduce a set of rules used to classify the extracted contextual valence shifters according to their impact on polarized words. They make use of the Pearson residuals in contingency tables to filter candidate shifters and classify them. We show that the technique reaches an F-measure of either 0.56 or 0.66, depending on how the categories of shifters are defined.

1 Introduction and State of the Art

Most opinion mining systems rely on the extraction of sentiment words to detect opinions. These words, which we will rather refer to as polarized words, convey useful information about the semantic orientation (positive or negative) of a text. However, the context in which these words appear may modify their valence in many ways. Although being of importance, this issue has been investigated only recently and is now the object of an increasing attention.

Polanyi and Zaenen (2004) first postulated the existence of *contextual valence shifters*, which are contextual phenomena altering the prior polarity of a term. Afterwards, some of these phenomena (such as negative or conditional syntactic structures) were dealt with on a case by case basis (Das and Chen, 2001; Na et al., 2004; Popescu and Etzioni, 2005; Pang et al., 2002; Wilson et al., 2005; Wilson et al., 2006; Councill et al., 2010). Studies addressing the phenomenon as a whole flourished later. They aimed at best modelling the expression of opinions (Polanyi and Zaenen, 2004; Taboada et al., 2011; Hatzivassiloglou and Wiebe, 2000; Morsy and Rafea, 2012; Musat and Trausan-Matu, 2010), before embedding those in a classification system. The main purposes of these studies are to determine a list of contextual valence shifters that impact the polarity of a term as well as to define the nature of this impact. However, these lists are often manually built from linguistic intuitions and not learned from language data. Works relying on a corpus of texts to develop resources that best reflect the actual role played by the linguistic context for opinion mining are few. Li et al. (2010) suggested a technique to automatically select polarity-shifting features in order to improve a sentiment classification system based on a machine-learning approach.

All these studies agree that contextual valence shifters can have diverse impacts on polarized words. They classify them according to the nature of this impact (Polanyi and Zaenen, 2004; Quirk et al., 1985; Kennedy and Inkpen, 2006): *inversers* invert the polarity of a polarized item, *intensifiers* intensify it and *attenuators* diminish it.

This study, based on a French corpus, focuses on the issue of contextual valence shifters and pursues two main objectives: (1) propose an automatic method that efficiently models contextual valence shifters, with the aim of improving performance of opinion mining systems (especially those based on a term-counting method); (2) clarify the linguistic structures constituting a hindrance to current classification systems. From these two perspectives, our approach differs from the work of Li et al. (2010). Moreover, we are interested in describing the effect of all kind of modifiers (inversers, but also intensifiers and attenuators). We restricted our study to all lexico-syntactic patterns located in the immediate context of a polarized term and impacting the valence of this term. This restriction means dealing with individual words. However, it should be noted that contextual shifters may sometimes be phrases too. Our approach also relies on the assumption that contextual shifters are in direct syntactic relation with the polarized word, which has to be confirmed.

Based on the results of previous works (Boubel, 2012; Boubel and Bestgen, 2011), we propose here a system that automatically extracts modifiers (in the form of lexico-syntactic patterns) and classifies them according to their semantic impact. The general methodology is detailed in Section 2 and we report the evaluation of the method in Section 3. The paper concludes with Section 4, discussing some issues we faced, in particular the problem of the attenuating valence shifters.

2 Methodology

2.1 Key principle

In order to identify valence shifters along with their semantic impact on polarized words, we propose to exploit two different pieces of information regarding the expression of polarity in a text: (1) the overall polarity t of the text, i.e. the score assigned to it on a scale from very negative to very positive, and (2) the polarity p (positive or negative) of a polarized word which appears in the text. We noticed that the distribution of the patterns related to polarized words (i.e. potential modifiers) is influenced by the values of p and t. Intuitively, we can consider three cases:

- patterns in which p is of opposite polarity than t will mitigate or reverse the valence of their associated term;
- patterns that reinforce the polarity of a word will appear especially when p and t share the same polarity;
- finally, a larger number of expressions having an attenuating effect on p will be found when t is around the middle of its scale (texts presenting a nuanced view).

2.2 The system

Based on this principle, we developed a system able to automatically detect and classify modifiers. It relies on two resources: (1) a corpus containing evaluative texts whose global polarity t is known and (2) a lexicon of terms whose polarity p is also known.

Our system performs a two-fold process. First, applying a parser to a corpus, we extract all syntactic dependency relationships that links a polarized term with another term (see Section 2.3). A statistical analysis is then performed to detect, among those, valence shifter candidates (see Section 2.3).

In the second step (see Section 2.4), a rule-based classifier further removes bad candidates and assigns a label to remaining modifiers that should correspond to their impact on polarized terms.

2.3 Statistical processing

In order to identify valence shifter candidates using statistical tests, the initial corpus – made up of evaluative texts whose polarity t is known – is first processed by a syntactic parser to obtain the list of all syntactic dependency relationships including a polarized term. Such relationships take the form of a pair of words (the polarized term and the candidate modifier), along with the nature of this relation (*e.g. NP(<NOM:déception>,<ADJ:total>)*). For each element of the list, three pieces of information are available: (1) the pattern itself, (2) the valence p of the term included in the structure, and (3) the score t of the text.

Then, we generalize over the relationships extracted, removing the polarized term and keeping only the valence shifter candidate and the syntactic relation linking it to its polarized term (*e.g. NP(<NOM:>,<ADJ:total>)*). This allows us to determine the frequency of each of these patterns in our corpus, in relation to two variables: the type of the pattern and the score t of the text. Based on these two variables, we build a contingency table for the patterns associated with positive terms and a second table for patterns in the context of a negative term [1].

Then, for a given pattern g, we compute a chi-

[1]We only keep patterns with a frequency higher than 20.

square test (Agresti, 2002) [2] where the distribution of g over the five possible values of t is compared with the distribution of all patterns except g. The chi-square value obtained is then used to decide whether the distribution of pattern g in the evaluative texts (t) is independent from the type of pattern. When the chi-square score is significant (based on a threshold α_1), we consider the pattern as a valuable valence shifter candidate.

Table 1 examplifies this analysis for the adjective *total* modifying a positive noun (*e.g.* "C'est une *réussite totale*.", *it is a total success.*). This pattern gets a chi-square of 139.67 ($p < 0.001$) and it stands out even more clearly when associated to a negative noun ($\chi^2 = 741.35$; $p < 0.001$), which confirms its interest as a good valence shifter candidate (*e.g.* "*déception totale.*", *a total disappointment.*).

2.4 Validation and classification of the candidates

At the end of our first step, we obtain a list of valence shifter candidates, selected on the basis of their chi-square score. In the second phase of our method, we apply rules primarily to identify the impact of each candidate on valence terms, but also to further filter the candidate list.

The idea is to rely on the adjusted residuals (Agresti, 2002), computed for the two contingency tables available for a candidate pattern (with negative and positive terms). Adjusted residuals corresponds to a z-score, and high values (based on a threshold α_2) means that the pattern g is either over-represented in texts with a given value of t, or is under-represented. These residuals can sometimes display specific and interesting patterns of under-representation or over-representation throughout the range of scores t possible for the texts. In previous work (Boubel, 2011), we analyzed the distributions of the adjusted residuals and we identified three typical profiles. Then, we were able to connect these profiles with their semantic role in the language, distinguishing three groups of modifiers: (1) "intensifiers", (2) "inversers", and (3) "concessive structures".

These findings were translated into a set of rules that automatically classify valence shifter candidates according to their impact on polarized terms.

[2] We used chi-square test as a first approach. However, it would be valuable to try other statistical tests in the future.

Rules are based on the patterns of over-/under-representation and assign a score for each of the three classes of modifiers described above. At this stage, it is possible to apply a filtering threshold fs to remove the patterns that received a low score for all classes.

We can summary the whole set of rules as the three following trends :

1. Structures that are over-represented in situations where the valence of p is similar to that of t, regardless of the nature of the term polarity p (positive or negative), obtain a high score in the intensification category;

2. Structures that are over-represented in situations where p is the opposite of t obtain a high score in the inversion category (attenuating or an inversing role);

3. Finally, structures over-represented in reviews reporting a nuanced view (*e.g.* when $t = 3$ for texts rated on a scale from 1 to 5) obtain a high score in the concession category.

Following this method, the adjective "total" modifying a noun phrase is given a score of 8 as an "intensifier", 0 as an "inverser" and 2 as a "concessive". It is indeed under-represented with a positive noun while the text is negative and over-represented while it is positive (see Table 1). As a consequence, this pattern is classified as an intensifier.

It is worth noting that the classification underlying this approach does not match the one commonly used in the field, which draws a distinction between intensifiers, shifters, and diminishers. Our second category "inversers" includes both shifters and diminishers, since these two classes have similar statistical properties according to our method. On the contrary, the analysis of the statistical behavior of some valence shifter candidates highlights a particular semantic behavior which is not dealt with as such in the literature: it corresponds to patterns connecting several polarized terms of different polarities and having an impact on the polarity value of the whole expression. These are the patterns gathered in the third category: the "concessive structures". We observe that using statistical properties from the contingency tables to identify categories of valence shifters has limitations in terms of qualitative approach of the

Score of texts (from 1 to 5) (t)	1	2	3	4	5	
[total-positive noun]	21 (0.74)	24 (-3.90)*	66 (-6.09)*	400 (4.65)*	536 (11.10)*	1,047
other patterns with positive noun	283,069	588,073	1,507,934	5,454,541	4,188,908	12,022,525
	283,090	588,097	1,508,000	5,454,941	4,189,444	12,023,572

Table 1: A contingency table for the adj. *total*. The adjusted residuals are significant for $\alpha_2 = 0.05$

task, but also helps to uncover interesting phenomena. We will come back to the insightful of this classification further in the paper.

3 Evaluation

The evaluation of our technique was carried out according to three steps. First, we collected the resources required by the approach, namely a corpus of evaluative texts classified according to their judgment (t), a valence lexicon, and a list of dependencies relationships in which modifiers have been annotated (our gold standard). They are further described in Section 3.1. Then, we carried out a quantitative evaluation of the technique, comparing its predictions to our gold standard (see Section 3.2). Finally, in Section 3.3, we conducted a qualitative analyse of the results, in order to better understand the way our technique works.

3.1 Resources

To implement our approach, the first resource needed is a corpus of texts ranked according to the opinion they express (t). The corpus we used was provided by the *NOMAO* company [3], which proposes a web and mobile application helping people to find, share and discover new places. It is made of 2,200,000 internet user reviews in French relative to restaurants or hotels (7,571,730 sentences). Every text has been given a score from 1 (very bad) to 5 (very good) by the author of the text.

The second resource needed is a valence lexicon, in which the polarities p of words are labelled. *NOMAO* also provided us with a such lexicon. It has been manually built and it includes 3,683 polarized French words relative to the domain of restaurant reviews (2,425 negative words and 1,258 positive words).

Finally, for evaluation purposes, a gold standard "corpus" was required, in which dependencies relationships containing a polarized words and a contextual valence shifter have been annotated. Since, there was no such corpus available, we randomly selected 500 sentences from the whole *NOMAO* corpus and discarded them from this corpus, that was therefore considered as the training corpus. The 500 sentences contained abount 2,000 dependency relationships including a polarized word [4]. These relationships were manually annotated with a two-fold procedure: (1) decide whether the term associated to a polarized word is a contextual valence shifter or not, and (2) describe its impact on the polarized word, according to one of the available categories.

Regarding the categories, we decided to use a finer-grained system than the one based on statistical properties (see Section 2.4), because the category of *attenuators*, introduced in previous studies, intuitively stood out. This allowed us to discuss in Section 4 the relevance of the concession category we had statiscally identified. We therefore defined the four following classes: (1) intensifiers (INT) emphasize the valence of their associated term; (2) inversers (INV) inverse the valence of their associated term; (3) attenuators (ATT) mitigate the valence of their associated term; and (4) concessives (CONC) articulate terms or phrases of opposite polarities.

The list of dependency relationships were annotated by two experts in accordance with these four categories. In order to estimate their interrater agreement, we computed the Fleiss' kappa (Fleiss, 1971) and obtained a substantial agreement ($kappa = 0.716$) for the annotations. Finally, this corpus was equally divided into a development set – used to select the best set of parameters – and a test set, to assess the performance of the best model.

3.2 Results

Regarding the evaluation, the first issue was to define an adequate evaluation metric, since the task is a multiclass case. We opted for two different

[3] http://fr.nomao.com/

[4] It is worth noting that each relationship was considered in the context of the sentence it was extracted from. Therefore, a pattern repeated in the gold standard could be annotated in more than one way. Moreover, since we only dealt with the structures that our methodology can extract, modifiers not syntactically related with a polarized word were not annotated.

approaches commonly used in the literature. The first split the problem into a detection problem and a classification problem. It computes classic measures such as precision, recall, and F-measure (to which we will refer to as the F-measure 1) regarding the model's ability to detect a modifier, whatever its label. Then, the classification rate is computed through conditional accuracy (Abney, 2008). The second approach consists in computing the precision, recall and F-measure for each category independently, before averaging them to obtain a global estimation (we will refer to as the F-measure 2).

Another issue was the slight discrepancy between the set of labels from the manual annotation and the models. Manual annotation uses INT, ATT, INV, CONC, while the automatic classification uses INT, INV, CONC. For evaluation purposes, we had to project the four-label system onto the three-class one, considering that the category ATT (attenuator) was included into the category INV (inverser) (as it is already supposed in Section 2.4).

Once these two problems were sorted out, we had to perform an optimization step. Three meta-parameters can indeed be manipulated: α_1, α_2, and fs. α_1 is the criterion for the selection of candidate modifiers, since it determines the significance level of the chi-square test. α_2 is the significance threshold for the residuals; decreasing it makes it more difficult for a given structure to match a classification rule. fs is the filtering score assigned for each structure.

In order to limit the number of experiments, the following values were tested for both α_1, α_2: 0.0001, 0.0005, 0.001, 0.005, 0.01, and 0.05, while fs was kept constant ($fs \geq$ **5**). Once the best model according to α_1, α_2 was selected, values ranging from 5 to 9 were experimented for fs. The evaluation metric for all models were computed as follows: a list of modifiers included in a dependency relationship were extracted from the training corpus and used to classify the relationships from the development set. It appeared that the optimal parameters are $\alpha_1 = 0.05$ and $\alpha_2 = 0.005$, as long as we want to exploit the whole training corpus.

These optimal parameters were used to select 10,503 patterns, whose chi-square scores were significant among a total of 328,308 patterns. Then, the application of our classification rules further filtered those patterns, yielding a list of 6,612 contextual valence shifter candidates: 2,607 were labeled as INT, 2,677 were identified as INV, 1,328 were classified as CONC, and 216 were assigned to more than one categories [5]. However, among those candidates, only 1,147 structures received a score of 5 or higher. More strikingly, if we set fs to 9, then no more than 113 patterns are selected, among which are 66 INT and 47 INV, but no CONC.

Manipulating the filtering score fs reveals that the number of extracted valence shifters largely varies. We used the test corpus from Section 3.1, which contains 171 valence shifters (102 INT, 16 CONC and 23 INV or ATT), to estimate the recall, the precision, the conditional accuracy, and the two F-measures for our model trained on the training corpus (see Table 2).

The F-measure 1 (which represents the capacity of the model to rightly detect shifters) starts from 0.49 for patterns with a score of 5 or higher and reaches 0.64 when $fs \geq 9$. This corresponds to a recall of 0.86 and a precision of 0.37. It is obvious that our system considers too many patterns as valence shifters. This F-measure can however be improved if we use a stricter filtering score. It appears that the chi-square is less efficient than the classification rules to filter valence shifters.

The F-measure 2 is globally better than F-measure 1 and reaches 0.57 when filtering the patterns with intermediate scores. Interestingly, it decreases strongly for $fs \geq 9$. This can be explained by the fact that the system extracts less "concessive structure" and globally assigns a lower score to that type of structure. Only 6 CONC patterns are correctly classified for $fs \geq 5$ and the system does not detect any patterns of this type when $fs \geq 9$. As a result, the recall and precision for this category equals 0.

Finally, it is worth noting that the system obtains a very good conditional accuracy (85.9 for $fs \geq 5$ and 97.6 for $fs \geq 9$). This is a very interesting finding, since it shows that the classification rules we developed are relevant.

3.3 Qualitative analysis

To further analyze the efficiency of our extraction method, we submitted the list of the 260 shifters with a score of 8 or higher to a qualitative evalua-

[5] When the score used for filtering is low, a few structures can receive a same score for two classes. However, these cases disappear as soon as we filter with a score of 5.

Score (fs)	≥ 5	≥ 6	≥ 7	≥ 8	≥ 9
F-Measure 1 (recall, prec.)	0.49(.86, .34)	0.51(.84, .37)	0.55(.82, .42)	0.52(.67, .43)	0.64(.60, .69)
Conditional accuracy	85.9%	85.5%	86%	92.5%	97.6%
F-Measure 2 (recall, prec.)	0.56(.51.62)	0.55(.50.62)	0.56(.50.63)	0.49(.38.69)	0.40(.32.56)

Table 2: Evaluation measures for the model with filtering scores ranging from 5 to 9.

tion. The analysis confirms the conclusions drawn above: the system tends to consider too many patterns as shifters, but most of the actual shifters get the correct label, according to experts judgment. After cleaning manually the list, it appears that the system has correctly classified 85 patterns among 260, most of them being incorrectly recognized as valence shifters. Some limitations of our method could explain these errors.

First, it happens that the object of the judgment, also associated with polarized words, is extracted (*e.g.* NP(<ADJ:>,<NOM:accueil>)).

Second, grammatical words, such as articles, auxiliary verbs, etc. tend to be captured by the system because they are very frequent in texts. Most of these patterns are not relevant, but some others are important to extract because they can negate or reverse the valence of a polarized word (e.g. NP(<NOM:>,<_DET:aucun>)).

Also, the choice of using syntactic dependency relationships entails some limitations: the expression acting as the valence shifter is sometimes not extracted as a wole. Moreover, parsing errors frequently happen, extracting wrong patterns.

Finally, it happens that some words incorrectly recognized as valence shifters are actually polarized words missing from the valence lexicon.

To conclude this analysis, some characteristics emerge out of the correctly-classified structures. On the one hand, intensifiers (mostly adverbs and adjectives) often have a direct semantic impact on the polarized word to which they are related. On the other hand, the patterns belonging to the INV and CONC categories are more complex and heterogeneous (*e.g.* AP(<ADJ:loin de>,<ADV:>)) and often impact a phrase or a whole sentence, not directly a lexical item. As a consequence, the effect can be hard to model and it is sometimes difficult to distinguish between the patterns from these two classes, either manually or automatically.

4 Discussion and conclusion

In this paper, a new methodology for the automatic extraction and classification of valence shifters has been proposed. It reaches a very good accuracy for the classification, although it tends to extract too many structures. An interesting side of the method lies in its ability to identify relevant structures that are often not considered in other studies. In further work, it will be necessary to integrate the lexicon we obtained into a sentiment analysis system to check whether or not taking modifiers into may improve the performance.

Beyond this applicative goal, our methodology also stressed issues in the categories used to organize contextual valence shifters. The class of diminishers (or downtoners), as it is commonly referred to in the opinion mining domain, is difficult to capture in an automatic way. In our system, we defined three classes of shifters on the basis of three different statistical profiles. The INV class includes both diminishers and inversers, since their statistic profiles are very similar. The CONC class contains structures that often relates terms with different polarities. However, it is worth considering that diminishers are often used in concessive or rhetorical structures and assign them to the class CONC rather than to the class INV. The F-measure 2 for our model in this condition is interestingly better than the one reported above: 0.66 instead of 0.56 for the structures kept when $fs \geq 5$.

In view of these results, it appears that ATT can belong either to the INV class or to the CONC. Our assumption on this matter is that there is actually two types of diminishers: (1) diminishers modifying the valence of a single lexical item, that have statistical profiles closer to the INV category, and (2) diminishers used in concessive structure to attenuate the overall polarity of a phrase or a sentence, which should be included in the CONC class. This hypothesis will be tested in further work, through the analysis of the statistical profiles of manually annotated diminishers.

Acknowledgments

We thank the *NOMAO* company who kindly provide their resources. This research is supported by Wallonie-Bruxelles International.

References

S.P. Abney. 2008. *Semisupervised Learning for Computational Linguistics*. Chapman and Hall/CRC, Ann Arbor, U.S.

A. Agresti. 2002. *Categorical Data Analysis. 2nd edition*. Wiley-Interscience, New York.

Noémi Boubel and Yves Bestgen. 2011. Une procédure pour identifier les modifieurs de la valence affective d'un mot dans des textes. In *Actes de TALN11*, volume 2, pages 137–142, Montpellier.

N. Boubel. 2011. Extraction automatique de modifieurs de valence affective dans un texte. Étude exploratoire appliquée au cas de l'adverbe. In *Travaux du Cercle belge de Linguistique*, volume 6.

N. Boubel. 2012. Construction automatique d'un lexique de modifieurs de polarité. In *Actes de TALN12*, Grenoble.

Isaac G Councill, Ryan McDonald, and Leonid Velikovich. 2010. What's great and what's not: learning to classify the scope of negation for improved sentiment analysis. In *Proceedings of the workshop on negation and speculation in natural language processing*, pages 51–59. Association for Computational Linguistics.

S. Das and M. Chen. 2001. Yahoo! for amazon: Extracting market sentiment from stock message boards. In *Proceedings of the 8th Asia Pacific Finance Association Annual Conference*, pages 37–56.

J.L. Fleiss. 1971. Measuring nominal scale agreement among many raters. *Psychological bulletin*, 76(5):378–382.

V. Hatzivassiloglou and J. M Wiebe. 2000. Effects of adjective orientation and gradability on sentence subjectivity. In *Proceedings of the 18th conference on Computational linguistics-Volume 1*, pages 299–305.

A. Kennedy and D. Inkpen. 2006. Sentiment classification of movie reviews using contextual valence shifters. *Computational Intelligence*, 22(2):110–125.

S. Li, S.Y.M. Lee, Y. Chen, C.R. Huang, and G. Zhou. 2010. Sentiment classification and polarity shifting. In *Proceedings of the 23rd International Conference on Computational Linguistics*, pages 635–643. Association for Computational Linguistics.

S. Morsy and A. Rafea. 2012. Improving document-level sentiment classification using contextual valence shifters. *Natural Language Processing and Information Systems*, pages 253–258.

C. Musat and S. Trausan-Matu. 2010. The impact of valence shifters on mining implicit economic opinions. *Artificial Intelligence: Methodology, Systems, and Applications*, pages 131–140.

J.C. Na, H. Sui, C. Khoo, S. Chan, and Y. Zhou. 2004. Effectiveness of simple linguistic processing in automatic sentiment classification of product reviews. *Advances in Knowledge Organization*, 9:49–54.

B. Pang, L. Lee, and S. Vaithyanathan. 2002. Thumbs up?: sentiment classification using machine learning techniques. In *Proceedings of the ACL-02 conference on Empirical methods in natural language processing-Volume 10*, pages 79–86.

L. Polanyi and A. Zaenen. 2004. Contextual valence shifters. In *Proceedings of AAAI Spring Symposium on Exploring Attitude and Affect in Text*, pages 106–111.

A.M. Popescu and O. Etzioni. 2005. Extracting product features and opinions from reviews. In *Proceedings of the conference on Human Language Technology and Empirical Methods in Natural Language Processing*, pages 339–346. Association for Computational Linguistics.

R. Quirk, S. Greenbaum, G. Leech, J. Svartvik, and D. Crystal. 1985. *A comprehensive grammar of the English language*, volume 397. Cambridge Univ Press.

M. Taboada, J. Brooke, M. Tofiloski, K. Voll, and M. Stede. 2011. Lexicon-based methods for sentiment analysis. *Computational Linguistics*, 37(2):267–307.

T. Wilson, J. Wiebe, and P. Hoffmann. 2005. Recognizing contextual polarity in phrase-level sentiment analysis. In *Proceedings of the conference on Human Language Technology and Empirical Methods in Natural Language Processing*, pages 347–354.

Theresa Wilson, Janyce Wiebe, and Rebecca Hwa. 2006. Recognizing strong and weak opinion clauses. *Computational Intelligence*, 22(2):73–99.

Grammar-Based Lexicon Extension for Aligning German Radiology Text and Images

Claudia Bretschneider[1,2]
[1]Center for Information and Language Processing, University Munich
claudia.bretschneider.ext@siemens.com

Sonja Zillner[2]
[2]Corporate Research, Siemens AG
sonja.zillner@siemens.com

Matthias Hammon[3]
[3]Department of Radiology, University Hospital Erlangen
matthias.hammon@uk-erlangen.de

Abstract

For efficient diagnosis processes, the multitude of heterogeneous medical data requires seamless integration. In order to automatically align radiology reports and images based on the pathological anatomical entities they describe, a preceding sentence classification is necessary. However, the lexical resource used has to contain semantic information about the pathological classification of each entity. We introduce an approach to extend medical lexical resources with pathology classification information and, at the same time, with new classified vocabulary. Our algorithm is based on a semi-supervised learning algorithm and incorporates a semantic context-free grammar combined with a RadLex-based lexicon.

1 Introduction

In radiology, the health status of a patient is described using a multitude of formats. During the examination process, a radiologist creates machine readable descriptions such as radiology images, dictated reports about the image findings and written texts. Although, most of the radiology data are related via the anatomical entities shown or described, there is no link between them, since the information pieces are stored in distributed systems. This absence of links between the items is hindering the radiologist's workflow. Especially when reading reports, radiologists want to reference back from the described finding (in the text) to the correlating body location (in the images). Without automatically created links, this resolution is obviously time-consuming when dealing with images taken with modalities that deliver a mass of stacked images.

Today, radiologists add alignment information to the text that names the image that contains the described findings. But still, the resolution of these textual links requires manual interventions to find the correct image and detect the described finding in the image.

To simplify this workflow, we introduce a mechanism that automatically aligns pathological anatomical entities in radiology text and images based on semantic annotations. Figure 1 shows our concept of linking anatomical concepts from image and text: Both the images and the texts are annotated with the anatomical concepts that they describe. Combining annotations with the same RadLex ID (RID), the link from one format to the other can be established. As a result, the radiologist can easily navigate from the pathological *Leber* [liver] (RID58) described in the text to the correlating position in the images.

For the integration, the necessary semantic annotations of the images have been made available as a result of a previous project (Seifert et. al., 2009; Seifert, 2010). In order to align these RadLex-based annotations with anatomical entities described in radiology reports, our text analysis system has to annotate the texts with RadLex-based annotations, too. Our established mechanism operates in two steps: First, we identify the relevant sentences that describe pathological findings and, second, extract the anatomical annotations only from these sentence.

We include a preceding sentence classification step, because according to the radiologists we worked with, the extraction of *all* anatomical entities from the text to link them with the image annotations is inappropriate. A large portion of the findings is included in the reports in order to exclude differential diagnoses. These are normal or absent findings that do not describe pathologies. But radiologists are rather interested in automated alignment of images of anatomical entities described with pathological findings.

The sentence classification is conducted based

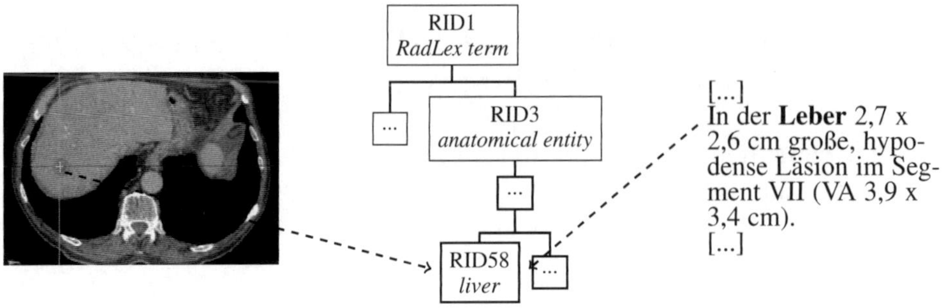

Figure 1: Aligning the anatomical concept *liver* from radiology text to image using RadLex-based annotations

on a lexicon and probabilistic semantic grammar rules (P-CFG). For parsing, we apply the standard probabilistic CKY algorithm (Kasami, 1965). During parsing, the most likely parse tree for the given sentence is determined. The topmost constituent in the resulting parse tree can be used to determine the pathology classification of the report sentences.

The chosen approach requires a full coverage lexicon including pathology classification of the entities. An initial linguistic resource based on the German RadLex taxonomy is provided. However, the German RadLex is lacking in terminology and pathology classification. The contribution of this paper is the description of a process to extend the German RadLex-based lexicon with vocabulary and pathology classification information in order to link heterogeneous medical data sources.

2 Related work

Medical grammar-based text analysis systems Theoretical work on the linguistic characteristics of the medical sublanguage has been conducted on the adaption of theories of Harris by (Friedman et. al., 2002). Early systems of (Sager et. al., 1994; Friedman et. al., 1994) are adaptations of the theories and implement own (context-free) medical language grammar for radiology reports. They show that parsing of medical texts based on a combined semantic-syntactic grammar can be successfully conducted. Even today, advances in grammar-based parsing of medical texts are reached (Fan et. al., 2011).

More recently, semantic text analysis systems have integrated the idea of parsing for medical text understanding for more sophisticated information extraction tasks (Savova et. al., 2010).

All those systems work with the advantage of elaborated lexicons that fully cover the vocabulary used in English report.

Terminology acquisition and semantic classification Semantic classifications beyond the hypernym information of taxonomies are still rare. Several approaches address this lack: Corpus-based approaches based on statistical analyses about the coverage and frequency of UMLS ontology concepts (Liu et al., 2012; Wu et al., 2012). (Johnson, 1999) derives semantic classes from ontology mapping and disambiguates multiple senses in contexts of discharge summaries. Limited to noun phrases, (Campbell et al., 1999) applies pattern-based rules and combines them with UMLS concepts to acquire new and semantically classified terminology. Finally, (Zweigenbaum et al., 2003) introduce a statistical approaches to automatically extending the UMLS ontology with French concepts.

Gap analysis While the grammar-based analysis of radiology reports has shown to be successful with complete lexical resources, we have to face the shortcomings of an incomplete lexicon. Furthermore, in other systems the grammar is used as mean for syntactic analysis of the content of the reports. Our approach to use it for pathology classification is novel and has not been applied so far.

Working with German clinical texts is another challenge in the field. English texts have been made available by a number of shared tasks and gained more and more interest in the last decade. Medical corpora in languages other than English are not available to that extend. At the same time, German language versions of medical ontologies are rare. Semantic classifications such as pathological information are particularly missing so far.

3 Corpus analysis

Our semi-supervised learning approach relies on a reference corpus, whose features are described shortly in the following section.

3.1 Reference corpus and development set

Since a publicly available corpus of German radiology reports is missing, we build our own annotated corpus. Our clinical partner, the University Hospital Erlangen, allocates the necessary texts: 2713 de-identified reports spanning the period from April 2002 until July 2007.

From this corpus, we selected 174 representative reports for a development set. Based on the findings described in the sentence, a radiologist classified each sentence. Sentences describing normal or absent findings are classified as 'non-pathological' and those containing descriptions of abnormalities are classified as 'pathological'.

3.2 Syntactic characteristics

One of the most apparent syntactic characteristics of the reports is their telegraphic style. The texts are rich in omission of verbs; the verbs are dispensable as they do not add semantics to the sentences. They are used to underline the absence or presence of symptoms - but are not necessary. Instead of noting

> *In der Lunge sind keine Ergüsse zu finden.* [In the lung, there are no effusions available.]

radiologists simply state

> *Lunge: Kein Erguss.* [Lung: No effusions.]

The average sentence length listed in Table 1 underline this finding.

3.3 Statistical characteristics

We annotated 4295 sentences in the development set of which less than half are classified as 'pathological'. This ratio is in line with the radiologists' experience. Table 1 shows further results of the statistical corpus analysis.

From comparing the numbers of word types, we conclude that the description of pathological findings requires a richer language than those of normal states and absent findings in non-pathological sentences. The linguistic resource has to cover this richness, which means that the multitude of entities should be classified as describing pathological findings.

	Sentence class	
Corpus characteristic	*PATH*	*NOPATH*
Sentences	1,943	2,352
Tokens	16,437	11,572
Average sentence length	8.46	4.92
Word types	2,398	1,581

Table 1: Results of statistical analysis of the development set

4 Analysis of controlled vocabulary in RadLex

Furthermore, we use the vocabulary from the German RadLex taxonomy as initial linguistic input. What information is already available is analyzed in the following section.

4.1 RadLex taxonomy

RadLex (RSNA, 2012) is a taxonomy published by the Radiological Society of North America (RNSA) in order to deliver an uniform controlled vocabulary for indexing and retrieval of radiology information sources. The current English version 3.8 (n=39,542) contains terms organized in 13 main categories: anatomical entity as one among others such as treatment, image observation and imaging observation characteristics. A German version (Marwede et. al., 2009) has been worked-out in 2007. However, as the maintenance of this language version has been stopped, the latest version 2.0 contains only a subset of terms (n=10,003). Our approach covers this lack in terminology and extends the resource.

For a structured analysis of the controlled vocabulary, we filtered an initial lexicon containing 9,479 entries.

4.2 Vocabulary coverage

The 9,479 entries in the linguistic resource contain 23,588 tokens of which 6,326 are distinct. Comparing this number with the word types used in the development set (n=3,172), the first assumption is that the lexicon covers the vocabulary used in the reports without problems. However, we discovered that this is not the case. We identified the three major problems:

1. The lexicon contains quite rare terminology which is not used in the development set, e.g., *absorbierbarer Gelatineschwamm* (RID11213) [absorbable gelatin sponge].

2. Additionally, important terms that have both a high occurrence in the development set and relevance for the pathology classification are either not included in the lexicon (e.g. *Läsion* [lesion]) or are included but are not classified (e.g. *vergrößert* | RID 5791 [enlarged]).

3. As learned from the corpus analysis, the description of pathological findings requires a rich vocabulary. However, the lexicon entries classified initially as 'pathological' represent only 18.1% of the whole resource (Table 1; We deduce this number from an initial analysis and pathology classification of the topmost hypernyms and its substructures.). Our initial lexicon is obviously lacking a high amount of vocabulary to describe those pathologies.

Classification	#	
non-pathological	6,001	63.3%
pathological	1,714	18.1%
not to be determined	1,764	18.6%
	9,479	100%

Table 2: Pathology classification of RadLex entries

The analysis reveals that the initial lexicon does not fully cover the whole range of vocabulary used in the reports. Furthermore, not all words in the initial lexicon can be classified just by using the structural information of the taxonomy. That is why we introduce the following corpus-based learning approach to enhance the lexicon to enable a correct sentence classification and alignment.

5 Methods

5.1 Conclusions from the corpus and initial lexicon analysis

When comparing German and English reports, one can observe two characteristics in both languages: syntactic shortness and reduced semantic complexity. Based on this observation, (Friedman et. al., 1994; Friedman et. al., 2002; Sager et. al., 1994) successfully created semantic grammars for medical text parsing. We conclude, that this is also possible for German reports.

We use a semantic grammar for sentence classification, thus, we conduct that the learning of classified vocabulary from pre-annotated sentences is possible. The insights gained from the *statistical analysis* simplify the grammar creation: For deriving additional vocabulary from the reports, the short length of the sentences is of advantage. The short structure allows for derivation of knowledge with high certainty. Even if only little amount of seed vocabulary is available, the unknown vocabulary can be classified easily and with high reliability.

5.2 Derive grammar

The grammar rules are derived from the sentences in the development set. First, the semantic classes are defined and finally they are combined into valid grammar rules. The semantic classes are initially adapted from (Friedman et. al., 2002), but then reduced to 32 classes which either

1. are necessary for classification (distinguish between words containing pathological or non-pathological semantics),

2. carry special semantic properties (e.g. anatomical entities),

3. or carry linguistic features (negations, prepositions, enumerations, etc.).

The classes are combined into 238 grammar rules. The grammar follows the same intention as the grammars developed by (Friedman et. al., 1994; Sager et. al., 1994): to model the structure of the reports' sentences. But it pursues a different goal: The grammar is used to classify the sentences as either 'pathological' or 'non-pathological'.

The top-most non-terminals designate the classification: A sentence can be reduced to a PATH or NOPATH non-terminal. All subsequent grammar rules are hierarchially embedded into these non-terminals and form the semantic structure of sentences. Sample rules and sentences are listed below:

- PATH → DISEASE
  Tracheostoma$_{[DISEASE]}$.

- PATH → DISEASE MOD_PATH
  Nierenzyste$_{[DISEASE]}$ *rechts*$_{[MOD\_PATH]}$. [Kidney cyst right.]

- NOPATH → NEGATION DISEASE
  Kein$_{[NEGATION]}$ *Ödem*$_{[DISEASE]}$. [No edema.]

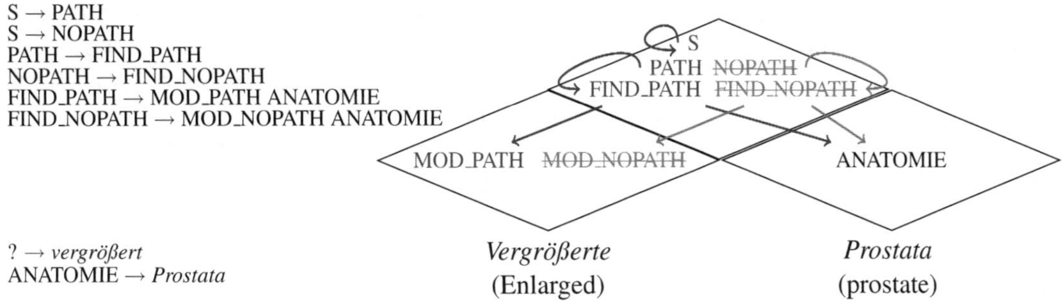

Figure 2: Learning lexical knowledge from sentence *Vergrößerte Prostata* (Enlarged prostate)

- NOPATH → ANATOMY MOD_NOPATH KOMMA NEGATION MOD_PATH *Milz*$_{[ANATOMY]}$ *homogen*$_{[MOD\_NOPATH]}$,$_{[KOMMA]}$ *nicht*$_{[NEGATION]}$ *vergrößert*$_{[MOD\_PATH]}$. [Spleen homogeneous, nor enlarged.]

As observed in the corpus analysis, the sentences describing pathological findings are longer, and thus, more complex in syntax compared to sentences describing non-pathological findings. This requires a higher amount of grammar rules for the description of the structure of pathological sentences. We manage this requirement by defining a set of rules of which the majority of 52% define the structures of sentences to be classified as pathological.

5.3 Learn from the development set

Rationale for learning method Our learning algorithm models the process medical students undergo when learning medical terms directly from texts. To align this model with our approach, we assume that the students know whether a sentence describes pathological or non-pathological findings. In addition, they have (basic) medical knowledge, which they can apply, e.g. about anatomical entities. When learning new vocabulary and its correlating pathology classification, they use this as seed knowledge. To validate their knowledge and derive new words with high certainty, they start with the shortest sentences. Proceeding with the sentences length-wise, they re-validate their knowledge and continue learning. The reliability of newly learned knowledge and classification decreases with the sentence length.

Learning process Our approach follows the same steps:

- We apply initial medical knowledge (in the form of pathology classification) from the lexicon.
- Knowledge about possible syntactic constructs is given with the grammar rules.
- Each sentence to learn from has information annotated about the correct pathology classification.
- We start with the shortest sentences to derive new vocabulary and pathology classification from. This is done, because learned knowledge from shorter sentences (with limited syntactic diversity) is correct with higher certainty.
- We apply the existing and learned knowledge in the following iterations to derive additional vocabulary and pathology classification.

Learning method We apply a semi-supervised learning algorithm: Each of the sentences to learn from is annotated with the target classification. But actually, we learn on the word level, where no annotations are available. Applying the rules of the semantic grammar, we derive the word-level semantic classification (which includes both the non-terminal assignment and the pathology classification) from the overall sentence classification.

Input for each parsing iteration is the sentence as an ordered list of words and the attached pathology classification. Starting with the shortest sentences, we can derive new vocabulary with high reliability, as those sentences are low in syntactic diversity. Additionally, the information about the target pathology classification reduces the rules that can be applied during the parsing process.

For learning, we adapt the standard probabilistic CKY parsing algorithm. How the algorithm operates in detail is illustrated in Figure 2. The goal is to learn the pathology classification of the word *vergößert* [enlarged], which is currently not available.

The initial step of non-terminal assignment is mainly based on the lexical resource. If terms are contained in the lexicon, their non-terminal assignment can be derived from the semantic classification. (As the non-terminal for *Prostata* [prostate] is ANATOMIE.) If a term is not contained in the lexicon, we assign a number of possible non-terminals. Those non-terminals include one symbol that presumes that the terms describe a pathological state and one that presumes the opposite. (I.e., vergrößert is initially assigned the non-terminals MOD_PATH and MOD_NOPATH)

The disambiguation of the non-terminal assignment is resolved during the parsing process: On the one hand, the probabilistic nature of the grammar rules enable a disambiguation of the most probable constituent structures. On the other hand, the target pathology classification excludes invalid rules. (Which is in case of the example, the sentence is annotated as PATH, so any subsequent rule for this non-terminal is not considered; struck-through in the figure.) In the end, the non-terminals assigned to existing or unknown vocabulary is used to enhance the lexicon. (Finally, we can derive that *vergößert*, assigned MOD_PATH, describes a pathology.)

Results of the learning process After the learning step, the lexicon is extended to 10344 vocabulary terms (before 9479). But even more important, the overall amount of lexicon entries classified as 'pathological' increased by 18.8 % to now 2036 entries (before 1714). We consider this a key success of the learning, as our classification depends on this encoded knowledge.

6 Evaluation of the classification results

We evaluate the system using 40 randomly-chosen radiology reports containing 1294 sentences. We compare results of the sentence classification using the initial linguistic resource and the extended one. Table 3 shows the classification results for the two evaluated cases.

The learning resulted in an increase of vocabulary by 9.1%. At the same time, the pathology classification could be increased overproportionally by 18.8%. While the learning increased recall (from 45.4% with initial lexicon to 74.3% with additional, learned vocabulary), precision decreased.

Higher recall importance Before discussion these numbers, the higher importance of the recall value for our use case of aligning radiology text and images has to be underlined:

Only for sentences correctly classified as 'pathological', the contained anatomical entities are extracted and anatomical annotations are created. If sentences are misclassified as 'pathological' (although they describe non-pathological findings), this is a minor issue. As a result of this misclassification, anatomical entities in the sentence are extracted and links to the image annotations are created, although the images do not show any pathologies. We accept those additional, but not intended links.

In the workflow, links from textual findings to image positions for non-pathological findings are no problem compared to non-existing ones for pathological findings. In case links from text to images cannot be created because a sentence was misclassified as non-pathological, the radiologist still has to link the textual findings to the correlating image position manually. This should be avoided.

We conclude, that the true classification of pathological sentence is more important for the alignment, hence, the recall value indicating this case has higher weight for us.

Discussion But still the quality of the learning step can be improved: While the sentences correctly classified as 'pathological' increase using the learned vocabulary, the sentences correctly classified as 'non-pathological' decrease at the same time. The latter is indicated by the increasing 'false positive' (FP) value. This is the main reason for decreasing precision.

We see that the learned vocabulary contains several entries misclassified as 'pathological' **(Error type 1).** The consequence of this misclassification are more sentences classified as 'pathological' although they describe non-pathological findings.

Examples can be identified both from FP and FN cases in the test set: Terms that do not describe pathological properties such as *Voraufnahme* [previous examination] or *Lymphknoten* [lymph node] were classified as pathological. Even very obvious pathological findings such as *Läsion* [lesion] or *Infiltrat* [infiltrate] are not classified correctly. Because of their high usage frequency, these four terms are accountable for 169 of the misclassified sentences in the test set.

	vocabulary	PATH class	FP	TN	P	R
baseline	9,479	1,714	149	682	0.585	0.455
extended lexicon	10,344	2,036	288	543	0.544	0.743

Table 3: Classification results with initial lexicon

The application of a semi-supervised learning approach with sentence-level annotations for word-level vocabulary acquisition is obviously point for improvement. We will include a probabilistic feature in the learning process that takes into account all occurrences of a vocabulary term to be learn in order to increase the leaning certainty.

The second major issue for correct pathological classification is the lack of grammar rules for long sentence structures. Since those sentences are more likely describing pathological findings and they cannot be considered in the learning process, the contained pathology descriptions are missing in the lexicon **(Error type 2)**. A more sophisticated grammar engineering can help to bridge this gap.

Two further, but minor error types remain. **Error type 3** describe incorrectly resolved non-terminal matches because of not considered linguistic details:

- **Failed subtoken matching in composita** E.g. the term *Nasennebenhöhle* does not match the subtoken *Nase* as expected because the token itself was learnt before as new, non-anatomical lexicon entry.
- **Naming mismatch between lexicon and text** E.g. *Lebersegment II nach Couinaud* (RID62) is expected to match, but in the text it is only refered to as *Segment 2*. This can be resolved detecting synonyms.
- **Mismatch of (distant) multi-token matches** This is of special importance as 72 % of the lexicon entries are multi-token entries. Their individual components can be distributed within a sentence. E.g. The multi-token text *Lymphknoten im oberen Mediastinum* does not match the lexicon entry *Oberer mediastinaler Lymphknoten* (RID7739).

The failure of the type 3 errors can be solved by introducing more elaborated linguistic techniques.

And finally, **Error type 4** indicates the still missing amount of vocabulary not available for classification. Even though, we tried to extend the development corpus to a maximum, it is not possible to cover all possible description applied in radiology. For a higher learning rate, the development corpus has to be extended significantly.

The extension of the lexicon has a significant impact on the classification results. Comparing the results of the classification using the initial lexicon and using an extended lexicon, the impact of a complete controlled vocabulary becomes apparent. In particular, the completeness of the lexicon contributes to the correct classification of sentences describing pathological findings.

7 Conclusion

For implemented a system that aligns findings in radiology reports with findings in images based on semantic annotations, the incomplete linguistic resource has to be extended with vocabulary. We overcome this issue by introducing a semi-supervised learning approach that adapts the existing grammar rules to learn new and classified vocabulary. Incorporating this learned vocabulary, the grammar-based classification delivers a recall value of 74.3%.

The issue we are dealing with is relevant for further work on German clinical texts: Still, the coverage of controlled vocabularies and ontologies for medical texts written in languages other than English include a large gap. We believe that lexicons are the most crucial resources for language processing in the medical domain. That is why we will focus our future work on extending and enriching existing lexicons and establishing new resources for linguistic analysis.

Acknowledgments

This work was partially supported by EIT ICT Labs (in the Medical CPS activity).

This research has been supported in part by the THESEUS Program in the MEDICO Project, which is funded by the German Federal Ministry of Economics and Technology under grant number 01MQ07016. The responsibility for this publication lies with the authors.

References

D. A. Campbell, S. B. Johnson. 1999. A technique for semantic classification of unknown words using UMLS resources.. *Proc AMIA Symp*, 716–20.

J. W. Fan and C. Friedman. 2011. Deriving a probabilistic syntacto-semantic grammar for biomedicine based on domain-specific terminologies.. *J Biomed Inform.*, 44(5):805-14.

Carol Friedman, Philip O. Alderson, John H. M. Austin, James J. Cimino, and Stephen B. Johnson. 1994. A General Natural-Language Text Processor for Clinical Radiology. *Journal of the American Medical Informatics Association*, 1:161–174.

Carol Friedman, Pauline Kra, and Andrey Rzhetksy. 2002. Two biomedical sublanguages: a description based on the theories of Zellig Harris. *Journal of Biomedical Informatics*, 35:222–235.

S. B. Johnson. 1999. A semantic lexicon for medical language processing.. *J Am Med Inform Assoc*, 6(3):205-18.

T. Kasami. 1965. An efficient recognition and syntax-analysis algorithm for context-free languages. *Scientific Report AFCRL-65-758*, Air Force Cambridge Research Lab.

H. Liu, S. T. Wu, D. Li, S. Jonnalagadda, S. Sohn, K. Wagholikar, P. J. Haug, S. M. Huff, and C. G. Chute. 2012. Towards a semantic lexicon for clinical natural language processing.. *AMIA Annu Symp Proc*, 568-576.

D. Marwede, P. Daumke, K. Marko, D. Lobsien, S. Schulz, and T. Kahn. 2009. RadLex - German version: a radiological lexicon for indexing image and report information. *Fortschr Röntgenstr*, 181(1): 38–44.

Stephane M. Meystre, Guergana K. Savova, Karin C. Kipper-Schuler, and John F. Hurdle. 2008. Extracting Information from Textual Documents in the Electronic Health Record: A Review of Recent Research. *Yearbook of Medical Informatics*, 24(11):128–144.

Radiological Society of North America. 2012. RadLex. `http://rsna.org/RadLex.aspx`.

Naomi Sager, Margaret Lyman, Christine Bucknall, Ngo Nhan, and Leo J. Tick. 1994. Natural Language Processing and the Representation of Clinical Data. *Journal of the American Medical Informatics Association*, 1:142–160.

G. K. Savova, J. J. Masanz, P. V. Ogren, J. Zheng, S. Sohn, K. C. Kipper-Schuler, and C. G. Chute. 2010. Mayo clinical Text Analysis and Knowledge Extraction System (cTAKES): architecture, component evaluation and applications.. *J Am Med Inform Assoc.*, 17(5):507-13.

Sascha Seifert. 2010. THESEUS-Anwendungsszenario MEDICO. `http://www.joint-research.org/das-theseus-forschungsprogramm/medico/`.

S. Seifert, A. Barbu, K. Zhou, D. Liu, J. Feulner, M. Huber, M. Suehling, A. Cavallaro, and D. Comaniciu. 2009. Hierarchical Parsing and Semantic Navigation of Full Body CT Data. *SPIE Medical Imaging*.

S. T. Wu, H. Liu, D. Li, C. Tao, M. A. Musen, C. G. Chute, N. H. Shah. 2012. Unified Medical Language System term occurrences in clinical notes: a large-scale corpus analysis.. *J Am Med Inform Assoc*, 19(1):149–56.

P. Zweigenbaum, R. Baud, A. Burgun, F. Namer, E. Jarrousse N. Grabar, P. Ruch, F. Le Duff, B. Thirion, and S. Darmoni. 2003. UMLF: a Unified Medical Lexicon for French. *AMIA Annu Symp Proc*, 1062.

Recognising and Interpreting Named Temporal Expressions

Matteo Brucato
University of Bologna
matteo.brucato@studio.unibo.it

Leon Derczynski
University of Sheffield
leon@dcs.shef.ac.uk

Hector Llorens
Nuance Communications
hector.llorens@nuance.com

Kalina Bontcheva
University of Sheffield
kalina@dcs.shef.ac.uk

Christian S. Jensen
Aarhus University
csj@cs.au.dk

Abstract

This paper introduces a new class of temporal expression – named temporal expressions – and methods for recognising and interpreting its members. The commonest temporal expressions typically contain date and time words, like *April* or *hours*. Research into recognising and interpreting these typical expressions is mature in many languages. However, there is a class of expressions that are less typical, very varied, and difficult to automatically interpret. These indicate dates and times, but are harder to detect because they often do not contain time words and are not used frequently enough to appear in conventional temporally-annotated corpora – for example *Michaelmas* or *Vasant Panchami*.

Using Wikipedia and linked data, we automatically construct a resource of English named temporal expressions, and use it to extract training examples from a large corpus. These examples are then used to train and evaluate a named temporal expression recogniser. We also introduce and evaluate rules for automatically interpreting these expressions, and we observe that use of the rules improves temporal annotation performance over existing corpora.

1 Introduction

The ability to express time in language is critical. We require this ability in order to communicate plans, to tell stories, and to describe change in the world around us.

Phrases that explicitly describe certain periods of time, or **temporal expressions**, are particularly useful. They may be calendar dates, mentions of months, relative expressions like *"tomorrow"*, and so on. In-depth accounts of temporal expressions – **timexes** – are given by Ferro et al. (2005) and Llorens et al. (2012a).

In this paper, we discuss a new class of timexes that signify a date or range of dates, but that do not explicitly include information about which dates these are (e.g., *October 31* vs. *Halloween*). Following the description of expressions that clearly identify one entity from a set of others by use of a proper noun as named entities, we call these **named temporal expressions** (or **NTE**s).

As with many linguistic phenomena, the phrases used as timexes have a power law-like frequency distribution in text. A few forms of expression make up for the bulk of occurrences of temporal expressions. However, existing research has been typically evaluated on only a small corpus of hand-annotated temporal expressions. With such resources, it is difficult to build or evaluate tools for recognising or interpreting the less-frequent temporal expressions, and this is reflected in the performance plateau of recent TempEval exercises (Verhagen et al., 2010; UzZaman et al., 2013).

Existing temporal expression recognition tools are typically rule-based (Strötgen and Gertz, 2010). These perform reasonably well on existing datasets, achieving F-scores of around 0.90, and improving them is an active area of research. However, as temporal annotation is expensive, existing datasets are not particularly large, and therefore do not contain as challenging a variety of forms of expression as general, unannotated text. Therefore, evaluations using these resources are unlikely to indicate the true variety of forms of temporal expression. This leaves us poorly equipped to handle the long tail of temporal expressions, which is likely to be very long (Steedman, 2011), in terms of both tools and resources.

As the most common temporal expressions can be recognised automatically with reasonable accuracy, we propose methods for attacking the long tail of temporal expressions. We address the following questions:

- What share of all temporal expressions is accounted for by existing tools and corpora?
- How can we recognise previously unseen named temporal expressions?
- Having found a named temporal expression, how can we anchor it to a calendar date?

The remainder of this paper discusses the most closely related work, examines variety in temporal expressions in the available corpora, introduces our approach for named timex recognition, briefly examines their role in information seeking, and discusses the problem of interpreting these unusal temporal expressions.

2 Related Work

There is a reasonable amount of prior work on general-purpose timex recognition. The state of the art in temporal expression recognition is extended regularly with TempEval exercises (UzZaman et al., 2013). Currently, HeidelTime (Strötgen and Gertz, 2010) offers strong temporal expression recognition performance, though as it is rule-engineered, it is likely to perform poorly at recognising unseen named timexes. TIPSem (Llorens et al., 2012b) is based on machine learning and, given appropriate training data, has the potential to recognise named timexes. ANNIE (Cunningham et al., 2002) adopts a finite state approach to recognising a commonly-occurring but constrained set of temporal expressions. Han et al. (2006) propose interpreting temporal expressions through iterative constraint satisfaction, which yields some ability to interpret previously unseen timexes. Finally, as opposed to timexes, Shaw et al. (2009) used linked data to aid in event entity recognition. The distinguishing features of our approach are that we concentrate on temporal expressions that do not follow a general, structured format, and that instead of addressing the general timex recognition problem (which has been covered repeatedly in the

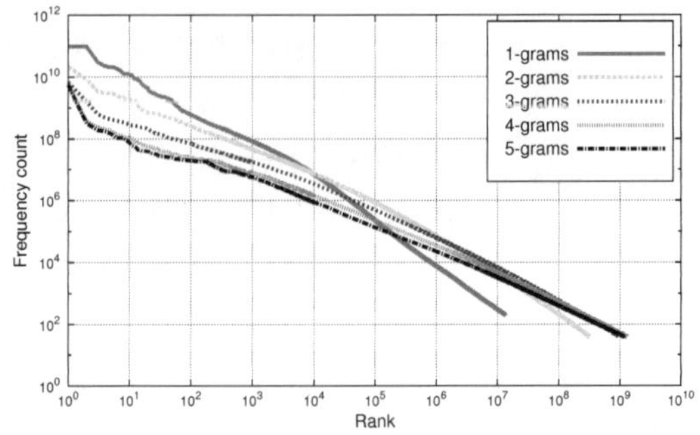

Figure 1: Frequency distribution of general terms

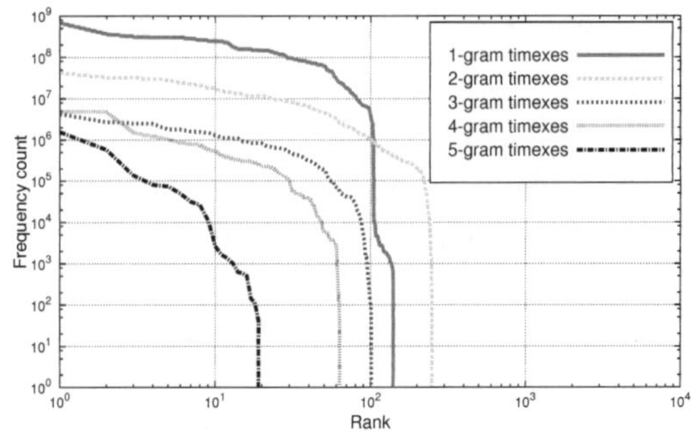

Figure 2: Frequency distribution of terms used as timexes in TimeBank and AQUAINT

literature, often from scratch), we address unusual expressions which are typically ignored by general purpose approaches.

3 Variety in Temporal Expressions

Our goal is to be able to recognise temporal expressions beyond the scope of current temporal annotation systems, thus extending timex recognition. In order to measure the scope of existing systems, we need to estimate the scale of variety in temporal expressions.

Using Google's Web1T n-gram corpus (Brants and Franz, 2006), we drew the shape of the timex distribution curve. Firstly, we extracted the shape of the general term distribution curve; see Figure 1. Note the characteristic "knee" in the curve, after which terms become rarer than a plain Zipf-Mandelbrot distribution would suggest, as per Montemurro (2001). For timexes, we counted n-grams based on timex strings found in two temporally-annotated corpora; TimeBank (Pustejovsky et al., 2003), and the AQUAINT TimeML corpus. The resulting curve is shown in Figure 2.

The sharp falloff of this timex curve is what

Date	English name
21 February	Language Martyrs' Day
17 March	Father of the Nation's birth anniversary
26 March	Independence Day
1 May	May Day
15 August	National Mourning Day
16 December	Victory Day
25 December	Christmas Day

Figure 3: Holidays from a country (Bangladesh), as shown on a Wikipedia page

```
en.wikipedia.org/wiki/...
  Federal_holidays_in_the_United_States
  Public_and_Bank_holidays_in_Scotland
  Public_holidays_in_Australia
  Public_holidays_in_Canada
  Public_holidays_in_Denmark
  Public_holidays_in_France
  Public_holidays_in_Germany
  Public_holidays_in_Hong_Kong
  Public_holidays_in_India
  Public_holidays_in_Italy
  Public_holidays_in_Malaysia
  Public_holidays_in_South_Africa
  Public_holidays_in_the_European_Union
  Public_holidays_in_the_United_Kingdom
  Public_holidays_in_the_United_States
```

Figure 4: URLs from which source NTE descriptions were extracted

Official name	Date
Columbus Day	Second Monday in October
Veterans Day	November 11
Thanksgiving Day	Fourth Thursday in November
Christmas	December 25

Table 1: Sample Wikipedia events and interpretations

one might expect to see from a very small corpus. Namely, some of the more common expressions are found, in relatively high frequency (the initial shallow curve). The remaining expressions found in the small sample that this corpus represents are much rarer, as shown by the sharp drop at the low-frequency end of the curve.

This suggests that existing TimeML corpora are so small that they do not include a sufficiently diverse selection of these terms. Indeed, TimeBank has only around 65K tokens. To build and evaluate approaches for recognising NTEs, a new source of data is required.

4 Automatic Named Timex Recognition

Having described named timexes, we build a named timex resource taking a re-usable, low-supervision approach, and then construct a tool for automatic named timex discovery.

4.1 Mining Existing Named Timexes

Current TIMEX3-annotated resources do not account for a representatively broad set of temporal expressions (Figure 2). To supplement these resources, we automatically mined named temporal expressions from Wikipedia.

We started by identifying collections of these terms, for example on pages listing public holidays. The selection criterion was that the page be in English and have a reasonable number of NTE descriptions, marked up in a wiki table (e.g., Figure 3). The pages used are listed in Figure 4. We then automatically extracted the terms and their textual descriptions from these collections. An example extract is given in Table 1.

This data was supplemented using the holiday terms given in JollyDay, a Java date-handling library.[1] In total, we found 247 unique terms from 15 manually-selected Wikipedia pages, and 239 from JollyDay (containing an overlap of 54), for a total of 432 named timexes.

The resulting list of candidate named temporal expressions contained two types of anomaly. It contained some conventional temporal expressions (e.g., *August*) which should be removed; these were filtered out using HeidelTime, a rule-engineered timex system. It also contained polysemous named timexes, that were not only used in a temporal sense. For example, *Carnival* is both a specific festival, a tour operator, and a polysemous common noun indicating a period of revelry or an exciting mixture of something.

4.2 Disambiguating NTEs with Linked Data

Following Shaw et al. (2009), we used linked open data to handle ambiguous temporal entities. We discriminated monosemous timexes (e.g., *Reformation Day*) from polysemous ones (e.g., *Easter*,

[1] See http://jollyday.sourceforge.net/

which may be both a holiday and part of a compound noun referring to e.g. a chocolate egg) via DBpedia (Bizer et al., 2009), looking for entities with matching names.

After discarding URIs of media that were in film and song titles, NTEs that still had more than one remaining corresponding entity URI were identified as polysemous. The final set comprised 424 expressions, of which 342 were monosemous and 82 were polysemous.

4.3 Recognising Named Timexes in Text

Having built a collection of named temporal expressions, we moved on to the task of NTE discovery. Our approach was to first develop a statistical tagger adapted to NTE recognition, and then apply it to new data, to observe what expressions it annotates beyond those in the collection extracted from Wikipedia.

The collection was used to construct a corpus and then a statistical named temporal expression recogniser. The corpus was constructed as follows. Using our list of monosemous named timexes, we searched the Gigaword corpus to retrieve paragraphs containing the timexes. These paragraphs were split into sentences (Kiss and Strunk, 2006), and the sentences matching any NTE were extracted; the sentences were then broken down into lists of tokens. We marked all monosemous named timexes in the sentences as target entities.

Some NTEs are polysemous, having both temporal and non-temporal sense. Observation of a small part of the corpus suggested that these polysemous NTEs generally occurred in a temporal sense when in the same sentence as other temporal phrases. Rather than excluding any sentence containing a polysemous NTE from the corpus on grounds of ambiguity, based on this observation, we adopted a simple heuristic: polysemous NTEs are included if they are collocated with a monosemous NTE. This reduced the considered set of polysemous NTEs by 22 to 60, for a total of 402 unique expressions.

Tokens in each sentence were then labelled according to a simple in-entity/out-of-entity binary format. The sentences were then split into training and evaluation sets, with no named temporal expressions found in both groups, i.e., every NTE is exclusively in either one or the other set.

In total, 3 861 sentences (117 060 tokens) were

System	Recall	Precision	F1
	strict		
Gazetteer baseline	5.6%	15.2%	8.2%
TIPSem	56.5%	71.7%	63.2%
TIPSem-B	56.6%	**75.5%**	**64.7%**
Stanford NER	**56.7%**	74.2%	64.3%
	lenient		
Gazetteer baseline	6.8%	19.4%	10.1%
TIPSem	**75.8%**	**97.3%**	**85.9%**
TIPSem-B	71.4%	95.0%	81.5%
Stanford NER	73.7%	97.2%	83.8%

Table 2: Sample Wikipedia events and interpretations. Lenient matches includes annotations that at least overlap with the reference.

extracted from English Gigaword v5 (Graff et al., 2003), containing 4 180 named timex annotations. The training split contained 1 053 of these sentences. The entire corpus construction method requires no human intervention aside from supplying source Wikipedia pages.

Regarding the NTE recognisers, we adapted three entity recognition approaches to the task by discarding their default models and rebuilding new models based solely on this NTE corpus. The recognition tools were CRF-based: a multipurpose system incorporating non-local information, Stanford NER (Finkel et al., 2005); one for temporal entity recognition that uses semantic role information, TIPSem (Llorens et al., 2012b); and TIPSem-B, a baseline temporal entity recognition variant of TIPSem.

Recognisers were learned from the training split and evaluated on the test split. As we are attempting to recognise named timexes only, we do not do comparison against tools designed for standard timex recognition, as these are designed for a different task.

A naïve gazetteer-matching baseline was used, based on timex strings found in existing resources (TimeBank and the AQUAINT TimeML annotations). This behaved exactly as a direct case-insensitive word look-up, matching any whole phrases found within the corpus. Its recall should tell us how broad the range of temporal expressions found in prior TimeML resources is. Evaluation was performed using GATE (Cunningham et al., 2013); results are reported in Table 2.

Precision was generally higher than recall, with both at reasonable levels for a first attempt at this new class of entities. This indicates that while our

Recogniser	% of query texts	% of queries
HeidelTime	2.90	1.97
NTE gazetteer	0.06	0.14

Table 3: Temporal intent indicator prevalence in a web search query log

approaches do not identify too many non-timexes as being timexes, further work is called for at improving the range of named timexes they recognise. In particular, the temporal expressions used in the TimeBank and AQUAINT corpora have a very small overlap with the named temporal expressions we identified.

4.4 Finding New NTEs

With a system that is capable of recognising named temporal expressions in our test data, which contains previously-unseen NTEs, it may be possible to discover new NTEs. Unlabelled text can be labelled using statistical NTE recognisers. One may have concerns over using a system with strict recognition precision in the 70s for this purpose; however, lenient recognition precision is in the mid- to high-90s, which indicates that the negative impact of spurious annotations will be low.

We attempted to find new NTEs by applying the TIPSem model to another portion of the Gigaword text. Sample results include phrases such as:

- *European Cup*
- *Hamlet Cup*
- *bank holiday*
- *Dayton peace agreement*

Although these are difficult to evaluate directly, they can readily applied in semi-supervised approaches to temporal annotation, e.g., in part of a bootstrapping approach to NTE recognition and general timex recognition.

5 Temporal Intent Queries

This section contains a brief investigation of named temporal expressions (and general temporal expression recognition) in information retrieval query interpretation.

In classical information retrieval with a textual query over a document collection, the query represents the lexicalisation of a searcher's information need. To identify a *temporal* information need, one must recognise signals in the query that reflect this (Jones and Diaz, 2007; Metzler et al., 2009). Detecting temporal intent in queries may benefit from linguistic approaches to query understanding and decomposition (Campos et al., 2012).

Beyond common formulations of timexes, this is a challenging problem in two regards. As we have already explained, certain forms of temporal expression are not recognised by existing tools. Also, event-related queries (e.g., *"stock market reaction to michael jackson's death"*) signify temporal intent but may not contain any temporal expressions at all. While the second class is not covered here, we do address the first.

We are interested in the proportion of temporal intent search queries that can be captured with awareness of named temporal expressions. Our method is to examine existing records of text questions and search engine queries, similar to the approach of Nunes et al. (2008). We used 1 200 000 randomly sampled query strings from the AOL search log (Pass et al., 2006) as a corpus. This corpus comprises 167 794 unique terse query strings.

We ran HeidelTime (Strötgen and Gertz, 2010) over this corpus. We also computed the intersection of query texts with our mined named timexes. Results are given in Table 3.

While temporal expressions in general are notably frequent in the data, it can be seen that only a relatively small proportion of queries contain named temporal expressions (0.14%). Named temporal expressions are not dominant in queries from this corpus. Indeed, while the data suggests that general temporal expressions are in the long tail (as the proportion of timexes recognised in unique queries is greater than that in all queries), the inverse is true for named temporal expressions. Examining the data, only a few variants of NTE occur in the query log.

6 Temporal Expression Interpretation

Once one has recognised that a particular expression is used in a temporal sense, the next step is to interpret the expression. This may entail anchoring it to a calendar or other formal representation.

We consider the task of interpreting timexes to the TimeML/TIMEX3 standard (Ferro et al., 2005). This produces normalised values from timexes, as shown below.

(1) *January 2nd, 1980* → 1980-01-02
Summer 2012 → 2012-SU
now → PRESENT_REF

```
id      expression        interpretation
--      ----------        --------------
92      Autumn_Holiday    DATE_WEEK_WEEKNUM(DCT, -1, Monday ,TO_MONTH("September"))
178     Liberation_Day    DATE_MONTH_DAY(DCT, TO_MONTH("April"), TO_DAY("25"))
179     Republic_Day      DATE_MONTH_DAY(DCT, TO_MONTH("June"), TO_DAY("2"))
180     Ferragosto        DATE_MONTH_DAY(DCT, TO_MONTH("August"), TO_DAY("15"))
```

Figure 5: Example named timex rules in TIMEN

Discovering such interpretations is a difficult task. For example, based on text, it is difficult to automatically learn or infer the link between *"New Year's Day"* and 1st January, or the associations between north/south hemisphere and which months fall in summer, especially given the cost of temporal annotation and resulting scarcity of annotated resources. This often leaves the task of developing such interpretations to human computation (Sabou et al., 2012). The closest computational method for solving this problem uses a more flexible compositional approach to timex interpretation (Angeli et al., 2012), though it is prone to floundering and failing on completely new expressions, such as named timexes.

As the named timexes mined from Wikipedia were generally accompanied by a textual description of the time (e.g., as in Figure 3), we used these descriptions to work out how to interpret the expression. We created a custom parser that worked well with the majority of uncurated, natural language descriptions of named timex dates. Having gathered information from Wikipedia, we then encoded it as rules in a popular timex interpretation system, TIMEN (Llorens et al., 2012a).

TIMEN operates using expression capture rules over a language-specific knowledge base that contains information on temporal primitives such as weekday and month names. Rules chosen for normalisation are those that match the timex's pattern, in order of priority, highest first. If a rule has conditions, it can only be applied if the timex satisfies them. Matched rules operate on a priority and constraint-satisfaction basis.

The rules in TIMEN allow the linking of contextual temporal information not explicit in the expression (such as document creation year) with time information in the expression. This expression-based information is often qualitative (i.e., text), and so TIMEN also includes rules for rendering it quantitative. For example, there are built-in functions that convert language-specific terms such as *Monday*, *lunes* or *the second* into quantitative offsets that operate over an internal knowledge base provided for that language. The result is a numeric representation of the temporal expression. This representation can be underspecified. For example, in the scope of NTEs, often the year is not mentioned, as it is document-dependent. As a result, the TIMEN rules for handling NTEs often do not declare any information about years, leaving this to TIMEN's management of reference time (Reichenbach, 1947).

Corpus	TIMEN	Augmented	ER
TempEval-3	69.6%	**69.8%**	0.7%
TimenEval	68.0%	**69.4%**	4.3%

Table 4: Timex interpretation accuracy with and without rules mined from Wikipedia. ER is Error Reduction

Example rules for NTEs are shown in Figure 5. In total, we successfully extracted interpretation rules for 298 of the previously-identified named timexes (70.3% of the NTEs in our inventory).

To evaluate this approach, we did timex interpretation only, using reference annotations of timex bounds. We ran the standard and augmented TIMEN over recent existing corpora (the TempEval-3 corpus and the TIMEN test data);results are in Table 4. The additional rules improved TIMEN's ability to interpret named timexes. The error reduction figures demonstrate that improvements can be achieved by accounting for these timexes.

Note the small improvement over the small TempEval-3 corpus (0.7%); upon examination, we found that this newswire corpus' content not only contained few named timexes, but in fact seemed to take pains to avoid mentioning festivals, possibly as part of areligious journalist guidelines.

In any event, the indication is that newswire is a poor genre for the evaluation of timex annotation systems, due to its limited forms of expression. The TimenEval corpus was designed to be difficult to process, and it is over this data that we see the greatest improvement. The real contribution here is increasing the range of expressions that can be recognised and interpreted.

7 Discussion

While recognising and interpreting named timexes is useful in many scenarios, and while it is possible to perform this task automatically, we encountered some interesting problems during our work.

Spatial Variations: Many expressions are interpreted differently depending on the locale. For example, *Labor Day* is May 1 in much of the world, but is the first Monday in May in parts of Australia (Queensland and the Northern Territories) and the first Monday in September in the USA. While TIMEN can process variations in named timex interpretation over time (e.g., *Washington Day* is February 22 until 1971, after which it falls on the third Monday in February), this locale-based information is not always available and is not considered for the interpretation task. This may be possible as a future extension: separate modules can assess the origin or subject locale of the input text (based on, e.g., newswire lead-in, spelling variation, or location mentions, the last of which also requires spatial grounding or entity disambiguation) and pass this region information to rules for normalising, e.g., *Summer*.

Easter: Easter is difficult to interpret.[2] Its time is based on locale, year, which equinox is to be used (astronomical vs. religious), and many other factors. Also, many other named timexes depend on Easter, such as Pentecost, Lent, and Pancake Day. Being able to use Easter as an offset in date calculus will improve the coverage of named timex interpretation. The liturgical origins of the named timexes associated with the date provide some indication of the frequency of texts associated with named temporal expressions.

Multiple Calendars: Not all named timexes can be calculated with one calendar. When building interpretation rules, demand for, e.g., lunar, astronomical, and Hebrew calendars emerges quickly. Even conventional dates require different calendars when one goes far back enough. A comprehensive timex interpretation tool must account for multiple calendars (Urgun et al., 2007).

Forms of Expression: Finally, diversity of expression may impair named timex recognition. The NTE *Martin Luther King day*, for example, may also be expressed as *MLK day*. In a sufficiently long text, one may use co-reference resolution to link and resolve the two. A statistical approach like our named timex recogniser (Section 4.3) may help here.

[2]See https://en.wikipedia.org/wiki/Computus

8 Conclusion

In this paper, we have introduced a new class of entities: named temporal expressions. These are hard to deal with because they do not resemble conventional temporal expressions, they can be expressed in a wide range of ways, they occur infrequently, and they cannot readily be interpreted to calendar dates.

8.1 Summary

We developed an approach for automatically extracting these named temporal expressions from Wikipedia, and we developed a named temporal expression corpus using linked data. This then helped train classifiers for automatically recognising (and thus discovering) named temporal expressions, with reasonable success (64.7% F1 measure). We also extracted interpretation rules for these expressions, allowing them to be converted to calendar dates, and used these to extend an existing state-of-the-art system. This augmented system had improved performance on existing temporally-annotated corpora.

8.2 Resources

The mined expressions and the annotated sentences extracted from Gigaword are made available via an author's website.[3] Further, the TIMEN rules for normalising named timexes are also released, to be included in TIMEN.

8.3 Future Work

Building basic approaches to timex normalisation is no longer an interesting or useful task. Multiple actively-maintained, state-of-the art tools address this problem, achieving good performance. However, as with many natural language processing problems, diminishing returns are being seen in the field. Therefore, next efforts must address the temporal expressions that we cannot yet already detect and interpret.

It is of interest to consider the automatic extraction of named timex resolution rules, perhaps using the most important timexes (Strötgen et al., 2012) from articles describing the corresponding occasion. It is also relevant to merge our named timex corpus with existing timex corpora

[3]See http://derczynski.com/sheffield/

(e.g. Derczynski et al. (2012)), after annotating the conventional timexes in our named timex training data. Such a corpus could be extended by extracting sentences that cite the Wikipedia or DBpedia entries corresponding to named timexes. Evaluation against such a resource is less likely to over-report the variety of expressions recognised by timex annotation systems, and can provide a solid base for future wide-coverage approaches to temporal expression recognition.

Decomposing the complex temporal annotation task so that it can be reliably crowdsourced would enable the construction of more resources. Using human computation like this is also likely to be useful in named timex sense disambiguation and interpretation, making it a promising source of more and better data.

Acknowledgments

This work was partially supported by funding from CHIST-ERA grant No. EP/K017896/1, uComp (www.ucomp.eu). The authors thank Barry Norton of Ontotext for helpful discussions on resolving events on the semantic web. The first two authors would also like to thank Aarhus University for their support.

References

G. Angeli, C. D. Manning, and D. Jurafsky. 2012. Parsing time: Learning to interpret time expressions. In *Proceedings of the Conference of the North American Chapter of the Association for Computational Linguistics: Human Language Technologies*, pages 446–455. Association for Computational Linguistics.

C. Bizer, J. Lehmann, G. Kobilarov, S. Auer, C. Becker, R. Cyganiak, and S. Hellmann. 2009. DBpedia-A crystallization point for the Web of Data. *Web Semantics: Science, Services and Agents on the World Wide Web*, 7(3):154–165.

T. Brants and A. Franz. 2006. The Google Web 1T 5-gram corpus version 1.1. *LDC2006T13*.

R. Campos, G. Dias, A. M. Jorge, and C. Nunes. 2012. Enriching temporal query understanding through date identification: how to tag implicit temporal queries? In *Proceedings of the 2nd Temporal Web Analytics Workshop*, pages 41–48. ACM.

H. Cunningham, D. Maynard, K. Bontcheva, and V. Tablan. 2002. GATE: A Framework and Graphical Development Environment for Robust NLP Tools and Applications. In *Proceedings of the Annual Meeting of the Association for Computational Linguistics*. Association for Computational Linguistics.

H. Cunningham, V. Tablan, A. Roberts, and K. Bontcheva. 2013. Getting More Out of Biomedical Documents with GATE's Full Lifecycle Open Source Text Analytics. *PLoS computational biology*, 9(2):e1002854.

L. Derczynski, H. Llorens, and E. Saquete. 2012. Massively Increasing TIMEX3 Resources: A Transduction Approach. In *Proceedings of the international Conference on Language Resources and Evaluation*, pages 3754–3761.

L. Ferro, L. Gerber, I. Mani, B. Sundheim, and G. Wilson. 2005. TIDES 2005 standard for the annotation of temporal expressions.

J. R. Finkel, T. Grenager, and C. Manning. 2005. Incorporating non-local information into information extraction systems by Gibbs sampling. In *Proceedings of the 43rd Annual Meeting on Association for Computational Linguistics*, pages 363–370. Association for Computational Linguistics.

D. Graff, J. Kong, K. Chen, and K. Maeda. 2003. English Gigaword. *Linguistic Data Consortium, Philadelphia*.

B. Han, D. Gates, and L. Levin. 2006. From language to time: A temporal expression anchorer. In *Temporal Representation and Reasoning, 2006. TIME 2006. Thirteenth International Symposium on*, pages 196–203. IEEE.

R. Jones and F. Diaz. 2007. Temporal profiles of queries. *ACM Transactions on Information Systems (TOIS)*, 25(3):14.

T. Kiss and J. Strunk. 2006. Unsupervised multilingual sentence boundary detection. *Computational Linguistics*, 32(4):485–525.

H. Llorens, L. Derczynski, R. Gaizauskas, and E. Saquete. 2012a. TIMEN: An Open Temporal Expression Normalisation Resource. In *Proceedings of the 7th International Conference on Language Resources and Evaluation*.

H. Llorens, E. Saquete, and B. Navarro-Colorado. 2012b. Applying semantic knowledge to the automatic processing of temporal expressions and events in natural language. *Information Processing & Management*.

D. Metzler, R. Jones, F. Peng, and R. Zhang. 2009. Improving search relevance for implicitly temporal queries. In *Proceedings of the 32nd international ACM SIGIR conference on Research and development in information retrieval*, pages 700–701. ACM.

M. A. Montemurro. 2001. Beyond the Zipf–Mandelbrot law in quantitative linguistics. *Physica A: Statistical Mechanics and its Applications*, 300(3):567–578.

S. Nunes, C. Ribeiro, and G. David. 2008. Use of temporal expressions in web search. In *Advances in Information Retrieval*, pages 580–584. Springer.

G. Pass, A. Chowdhury, and C. Torgeson. 2006. A picture of search. In *Proceedings of the 1st International Conference on Scalable Information Systems*.

J. Pustejovsky, J. Castano, R. Ingria, R. Sauri, R. Gaizauskas, A. Setzer, G. Katz, and D. Radev. 2003. TimeML: Robust specification of event and temporal expressions in text. *New directions in question answering*, 3:28–34.

H. Reichenbach. 1947. The tenses of verbs. In *Elements of Symbolic Logic*. Dover Publications.

M. Sabou, K. Bontcheva, and A. Scharl. 2012. Crowdsourcing research opportunities: lessons from natural language processing. In *Proceedings of the 12th International Conference on Knowledge Management and Knowledge Technologies*, page 17. ACM.

R. Shaw, R. Troncy, and L. Hardman. 2009. LODE: Linking Open Descriptions of Events. In *Proceedings of the Asian Semantic Web Conference*, volume LNCS 5926, pages 153–167. Springer.

M. Steedman. 2011. Romantics and revolutionaries. *Linguistic Issues in Language Technology*, 6(11).

J. Strötgen and M. Gertz. 2010. HeidelTime: High quality rule-based extraction and normalization of temporal expressions. In *Proceedings of the 5th International Workshop on Semantic Evaluation*, pages 321–324. Association for Computational Linguistics.

J. Strötgen, O. Alonso, and M. Gertz. 2012. Identification of top relevant temporal expressions in documents. In *Proceedings of the 2nd Temporal Web Analytics Workshop*, pages 33–40. ACM.

B. Urgun, C. E. Dyreson, R. T. Snodgrass, J. K. Miller, N. Kline, M. D. Soo, and C. S. Jensen. 2007. Integrating multiple calendars using τ ZAMAN. *Software: Practice and Experience*, 37(3):267–308.

N. UzZaman, H. Llorens, L. Derczynski, M. Verhagen, J. F. Allen, and J. Pustejovsky. 2013. SemEval-2013 Task 1: TempEval-3: Evaluating Time Expressions, Events, and Temporal Relations. In *Proceedings of the 7th International Workshop on Semantic Evaluations*.

M. Verhagen, R. Saurí, T. Caselli, and J. Pustejovsky. 2010. SemEval-2010 task 13: TempEval-2. In *Proceedings of the 5th International Workshop on Semantic Evaluation*, pages 57–62. Association for Computational Linguistics.

Unsupervised Improving of Sentiment Analysis Using Global Target Context

Tomáš Brychcín **Ivan Habernal**
NTIS – New Technologies for the Information Society, and
Department of Computer Science and Engineering,
Faculty of Applied Sciences, University of West Bohemia,
Univerzitní 8, 306 14 Plzeň, Czech Republic
{brychcin,habernal}@kiv.zcu.cz

Abstract

Current approaches to document-level sentiment analysis rely on local information, e.g., the words within the given document. We try to achieve better performance by incorporating global context of the sentiment target (e.g., a movie or a product). We assume that sentiment labels of reviews about the same target are often consistent in some way. We model this consistency by Dirichlet distribution over sentiment labels and use it together with Maximum entropy classifier to gain significant improvement. This unsupervised extension increases the classification F-measure by almost 3% absolute on both Czech and English movie review datasets and outperforms the current state of the art.

1 Introduction

Sentiment analysis on the document level has been one of the most targeted research topic in the past decade (Liu and Zhang, 2012). Given a document (e.g. a review, a blog post, or a tweet), the goal is to automatically obtain its sentiment which is mostly considered as a binary value (positive and negative) or is more granular (e.g. positive, negative, and neutral or a number on the pre-defined scale).

Since the pioneering research by Pang et al. (2002), movie reviews have represented a very popular domain for evaluating sentiment analysis systems, mainly because of abundance of labeled data from existing on-line movie databases.[1] Large datasets are crucial for employing machine learning approaches.

Both approaches to sentiment analysis (machine learning-based and vocabulary-based) attempt to estimate the polarity of the document taking into account only its content (e.g. words, morphology patterns, syntax, and other features). Other external information, such as the sentiment target, the author, and others, are mostly ignored in the polarity estimation step. This means that the distribution of sentiment for each target is considered as random.

We assume that sentiment labels for each target are not independent of each other. This means that given a movie with the majority of positive reviews, there is a chance that the next unknown review will be positive as well. We model this assumption as a Dirichlet distribution over sentiment labels for each target. In summary, our approach to sentiment analysis consists of two steps. In the first step, we employ a supervised Maximum entropy classifier in order to estimate sentiment label probabilities for each review. In the second (unsupervised) step, these labels are iteratively updated using Gibbs sampling in order to maximize the probability of sentiments of each target.[2]

A big challenge in the sentiment analysis task are non-mainstream languages,[3] mostly because of the lack of precise polarity lexicons, annotated datasets, and other resources. Morphologically rich languages may also require different treatment than English, because of their rich vocabulary. Therefore, we report our result on two movie review datasets in two languages — the English IMDB and Czech CSFD datasets.

[1] One might argue that if movie or product databases already contain reviews labeled with e.g. number of stars, it is useless to try to estimate it automatically; however, not all databases are alike, e.g., the Polish movie database has no such star rating and contains only pure text reviews.

[2] Through the rest of the paper, we will use *target* and *movie* interchangeably.

[3] Majority of research in sentiment analysis focuses on English or Chinese.

2 Related work

An up-to-date survey of the entire sentiment analysis field can be found in (Liu and Zhang, 2012). Recently, there has been a shift to semi-supervised or unsupervised methods. Many of them build on graphical models, mostly adapting the topic model idea from LDA (Blei et al., 2003), such as Joint ST (Lin and He, 2009), ARO (Zhang et al., 2011), Twofold-LDA (Burns et al., 2011), NB-LDA (Zhang et al., 2013), ME-LDA (Zhao et al., 2012), and others (Li et al., 2010; Maas et al., 2011). Most of these approaches try to identify the polarity of words on the first place. Furthermore, they treat each document or target entity separately in the sentiment identification phase. The global context of documents is taken into account in cases where sentiment is conditioned on the user or topics. Some of these approaches still require a seed of sentiment-bearing words, however, they do not require large sets of labeled data as in supervised machine learning approaches (Liu and Zhang, 2012).

In Czech, sentiment analysis has gained attention only very recently. In their first attempt, Steinberger et al. (2011) used machine translation and vocabulary triangulation to obtain the Czech sentiment lexicon for entity-level analysis. They reported results on the news domain. Veselovská (2012) tested Naive Bayes classifier on two small sentence-level corpora that were manually annotated; however, the results were described only as preliminary by the author. Habernal et al. (2013) created three large labeled corpora (10k, 90k, and 130k reviews/posts) and tested various preprocessing techniques suitable for Czech, as well as various features and classifiers. They further employed semantic spaces as a mean for reducing data sparsity in morphologically rich languages (Habernal and Brychcín, 2013) and achieved state-of-the-art performance in Czech.

Although an exhaustive amount of research is devoted to semi-supervised methods, to the best of our knowledge, no related work tried to combine a supervised approach to document-level sentiment analysis with modeling dependencies of sentiment according to their targets in an unsupervised manner.

3 Baseline

Let the data are divided into M review targets, where each target contains N_m reviews. In the following text, we will use T_{mn} for denoting the review at the position n in the m-th target.

As a baseline we used the Maximum entropy classifier (Berger et al., 1996)

$$P^{\mathrm{ME}}(S_{mn} = s|T_{mn}) = \frac{1}{Z(T_{mn})} \prod_{i=1}^{I} e^{\lambda_i f_i(T_{mn},s)}, \tag{1}$$

where s is a sentiment label (a member from a finite set $\mathfrak{S}$) for a review, T_{mn} is our knowledge about review (the review itself at n-th position in m-th target), $f_i(T_{mn}, s)$ is an i-th feature function, λ_i is corresponding weight and $Z(T_{mn})$ is a normalization factor. For estimating parameters of Maximum entropy model we used limited memory BFGS (L-BFGS) method (Nocedal, 1980).

In the baseline classifier, we rely on two kinds of binary features, namely the presence of word unigrams and bigrams in the review text (the same baseline that was used in (Habernal et al., 2013)). This model is denoted as *ME* in following text.

We also extend the feature set by presence of word clusters (derived from semantic spaces) in the same way as in (Habernal and Brychcín, 2013). We refer to this model as *ME+sspace*.

4 Global context extension

Our idea is that the final label decision would take into account both the score from Maximum entropy classifier as well as the likelihood of appropriate sentiment label in whole context of a review target (global context). Each sentiment label classification S_{mn} on each position n affects the probability of the sentiment labels of all other reviews in target $\boldsymbol{T}_m$. The selection of the most probable sequence of sentiment labels leads to exponential complexity.

We provide approximation of this problem by Gibbs sampling in the generative model defined bellow. The complete overview of our approach is depicted in Figure 1. The generative process for sentiment labels sequence is as follows:

1. For each target $\boldsymbol{T}_m \in \boldsymbol{T}$ sample a distribution $\boldsymbol{\theta}_m \sim Dirichlet(\boldsymbol{\alpha})$ over all sentiment labels $s \in \mathfrak{S}$, where $\boldsymbol{\alpha}$ is a vector of hyper-parameters of Dirichlet distribution.

2. For each review $T_{mn} \in \boldsymbol{T}_m$, where $1 \leq n \leq N_m$ sample a sentiment label S_{mn} according to

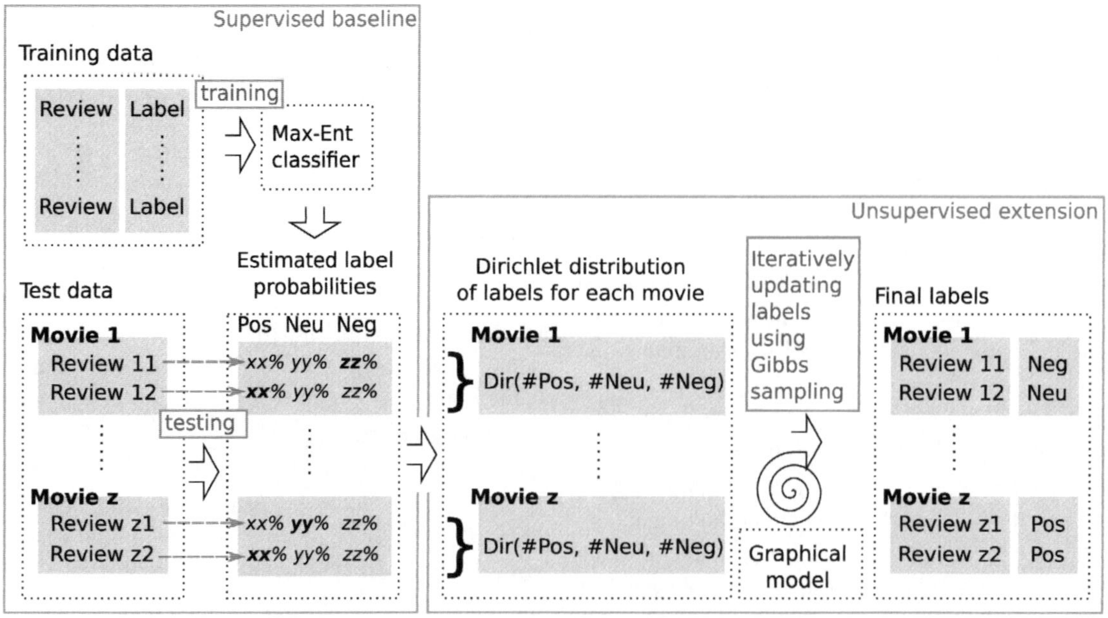

Figure 1: Diagram describing our sentiment model.

$$S_{mn} \sim \frac{\theta_m^{(s)} P^{\mathrm{ME}}\left(S_{mn} = s | T_{mn}\right)}{\sum\limits_{i \in \mathfrak{S}} \theta_m^{(i)} P^{\mathrm{ME}}\left(S_{mn} = i | T_{mn}\right)}, \quad (2)$$

where $\theta_m^{(s)}$ is the probability of sentiment label s in target $\boldsymbol{T}_m$ and $P^{\mathrm{ME}}(s|T_{mn})$ is the label probability of the current review given by Maximum entropy model. The probability distribution, from which the labels S_{mn} are sampled, is given by probability $\theta_m^{(s)}$ rescaled by the score from Maximum entropy classifier.

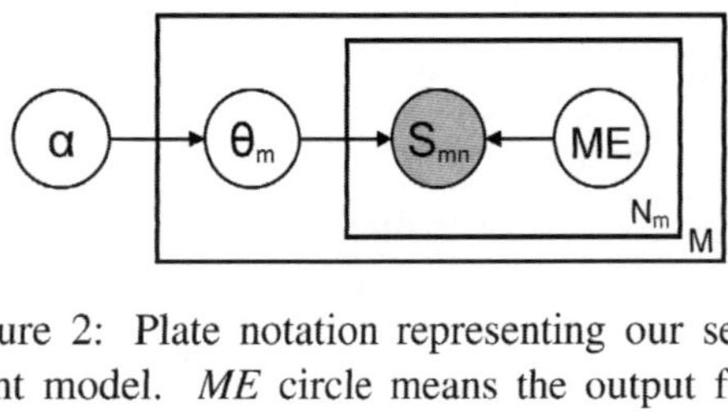

Figure 2: Plate notation representing our sentiment model. *ME* circle means the output from Maximum entropy classifier.

Plate representation of our generative model is shown in figure 2.

The Gibbs sampler needs to compute $P(S_{mn}|\boldsymbol{S}_{\neg mn}, T_{mn}, \boldsymbol{\alpha})$, the probability of a sentiment label S_{mn} that is being assigned to a review T_{mn}, given all other labels assignments to all other reviews in appropriate review target $\boldsymbol{T}_m$.

Gibbs sampling of the Dirichlet-multinomial distribution, already derived for LDA by Griffiths and Steyvers (2004), results in simple formula

$$P\left(S_{mn} = s | \boldsymbol{S}_{\neg mn}, \boldsymbol{\alpha}\right) = \frac{c_{\neg mn}^{(s)} + \alpha_s}{\sum\limits_{i \in \mathfrak{S}} c_{\neg mn}^{(i)} + \alpha_i} \propto c_{\neg mn}^{(s)} + \alpha_s, \quad (3)$$

where $\boldsymbol{S}_{\neg mn}$ means all sentiment labels except the one at position n in m-th review target. The $c_{\neg mn}^{(s)}$ denotes the number of times that the sentiment label s was assigned to the review in m-th target except the position n.

We use Maximum entropy classifier to rescale these probabilities. Final formula for sampling sentiment labels combines the information from particular review as well as contextual information about other reviews in appropriate review target

$$\begin{aligned} &P\left(S_{mn} = s | \boldsymbol{S}_{\neg mn}, T_{mn}, \boldsymbol{\alpha}\right) \\ &\propto \frac{\left(c_{\neg mn}^{(s)} + \alpha_s\right) P^{\mathrm{ME}}\left(s | T_{mn}\right)}{\sum\limits_{i \in \mathfrak{S}} \left(c_{\neg mn}^{(i)} + \alpha_i\right) P^{\mathrm{ME}}\left(i | T_{mn}\right)} \\ &\propto \left(c_{\neg mn}^{(s)} + \alpha_s\right) P^{\mathrm{ME}}\left(s | T_{mn}\right). \quad (4) \end{aligned}$$

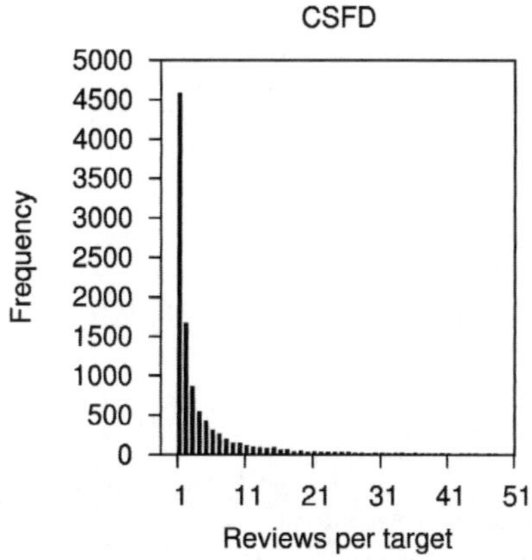

Figure 3: Histogram of reviews per target on CSFD dataset. Frequency (y axis) means how many targets have the given number of reviews (x axis).

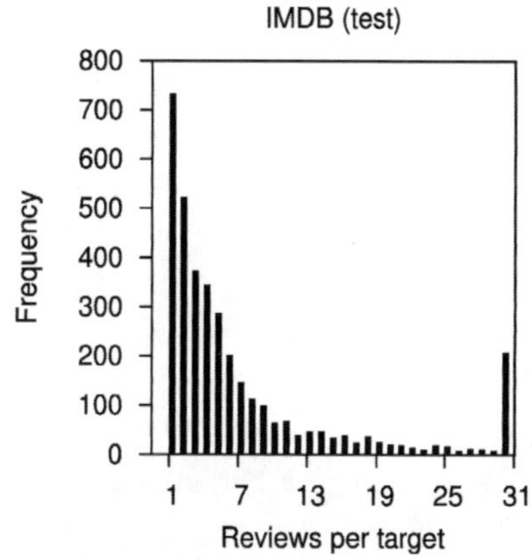

Figure 4: Histogram of reviews per target on IMDB test dataset.

5 Datasets

We perform our experiments on two datasets in the movie review domain. An English dataset from the Internet Movie Database (IMDB), provided by (Maas et al., 2011), contains 25k training and 25k test examples labeled with either positive or negative sentiment. There are also another 50k additional unlabeled reviews. All reviews are accompanied with their corresponding movies' URLs.

A Czech dataset from the Czech Movie Database (CSFD), provided by (Habernal et al., 2013), consists of $\approx$ 90k reviews equally split into positive, negative, and neutral ones. As the provided dataset did not contain information about the target movies, we tried to match the reviews and movies automatically. Unfortunately, in few cases we were not able to find the appropriate movie given the review, thus the resulting dataset slightly differs from the one from (Habernal et al., 2013). However, we report all results on the new dataset (where the reviews are paired with their movies) and also provide it for any further research.[4]

5.1 Data statistics

Figures 3 and 4 display statistics for the CSFD and IMDB test datasets, respectively, in terms of the frequency of targets with a particular number of reviews. In both datasets, the overall trend is that most of the movies have 1–10 reviews. The mean is 8.6 reviews per movie in CSFD and 7.0 in IMDB, respectively. The reason of the large peak at 30 in IMDB is the restriction of maximum reviews per movie to 30 by Maas et al. (2011).

To support our idea of some consistency in sentiment related to one target, we captured the percentage of the major sentiment label for each target, as shown in Figure 5. Each 'bin' on the Y axis deals with targets having a certain number of reviews, i.e., 1–10, 11–20, etc. For each bin, we compute the ratio of the major sentiment (i.e., if a movie has 7 positive, 2 neutral, and 1 negative review, the ratio is 0.7) and plot it as a probability distribution. It actually corresponds to consistency of reviews per target. Obviously, for targets with 1–5 or 1–10 reviews (the first Y axis bin), the graph is skewed towards 1.0. This is caused by targets with only a single review, thus the probability of major sentiment for these targets is always 1.0. With increasing number of reviews per target, the sentiment becomes a mixture where the prevalence of the major sentiment declines, yet it remains dominant (as can be seen in Figure 5).

Note that we show these statistics only on test data in the IMDB dataset, as our extension does not involve the training data.

6 Results and discussion

We perform our experiments in 10-fold cross validation manner on the CSFD dataset. For the IMDB dataset, the training and test data are already separated.

In our experiment we used symmetric Dirichlet distribution, which do not favor any sentiment label over another. Results obtained by 100 iterations of Gibbs sampling and hyper-parameters $\alpha_s = 0.0001$ are shown in Table 1.

[4]http://liks.fav.zcu.cz/sentiment

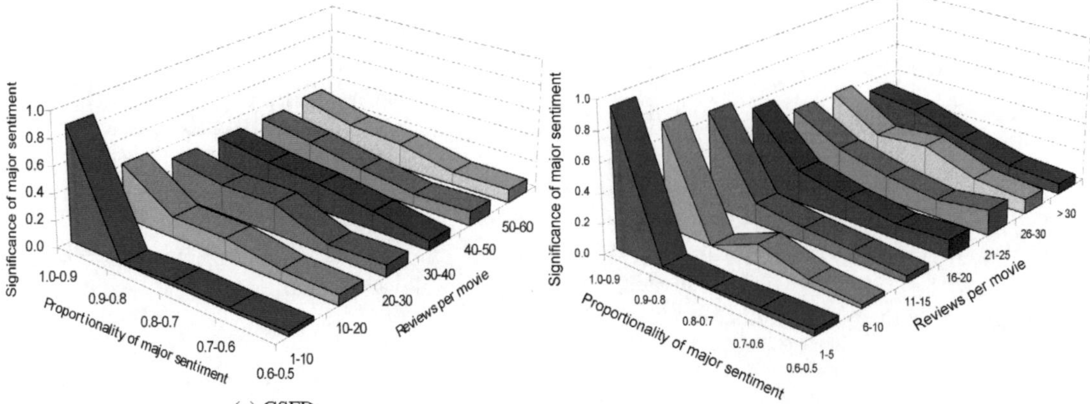

(a) CSFD

(b) IMDB

Figure 5: Proportionality of major sentiments for various numbers of reviews per target.

model \ dataset	CSFD	IMDB
(Maas et al., 2011)		88.89
(Habernal and Brychcín, 2013)	78.92	89.46
(Trivedi and Eisenstein, 2013)		91.36
ME baseline	77.58	89.34
ME + sspace	78.72 (+1.14)	89.46 (+0.12)
ME + Dir	80.57 (+2.99)	92.09 (+2.75)
ME + sspace + Dir	**81.53** (+3.95)	**92.24** (+2.90)

95% confidence interval for CZ = ± 0.3.
95% confidence interval for EN = ± 0.4.

Table 1: F-measure achieved on both datasets. The improvements are measured against baseline. Note that improvement given by semantic spaces extension on English dataset is not statistically significant.

We also experimented with the number of iterations needed for sufficient inference (Figure 6) and concluded that 100 iterations is far enough. Note that the improvements in Figures 6 and 7 are always taken against the same model without global context, i.e. *ME+sspace+Dir* is compared to the *ME+sspace*, not to the *ME*.

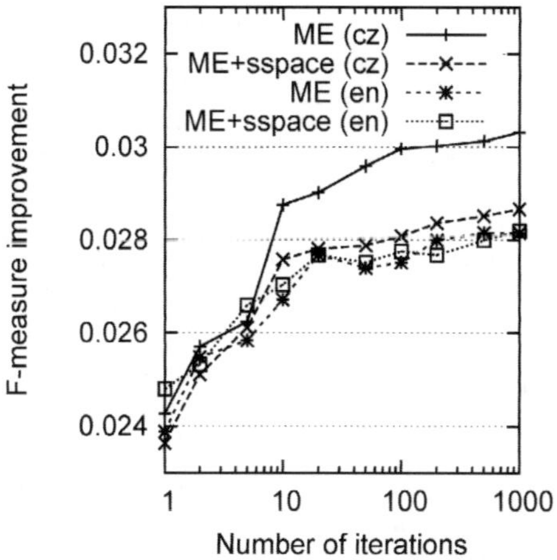

Figure 6: Improvement in F-measure depending on number of iterations of Gibbs sampling.

The selection of appropriate hyper-parameters of Dirichlet distribution can be important for such a task. The improvements in F-measure depending on different α_s are shown in figure 7. Lower α_s achieves higher improvement in performance. With lower α_s, the Dirichlet distribution is sharper and also the more consistent the review labels are expected to be in average.

We suppose this is caused mainly by the fact that many review targets have only one review (100% consistency). See Figures 3 and 4 for detailed statistics on datasets. Thus the global context should help in widely reviewed targets. In cases where the target has only one review, our extension has no effect on the final sentiment label (the label is only determined by Maximum entropy classifier).

7 Summary

7.1 Future work

In future work we would like to investigate another combinations of document level information together with global context information. We expect that linear interpolation with weights tuned on held-out data would be an efficient combination of such sources of information.

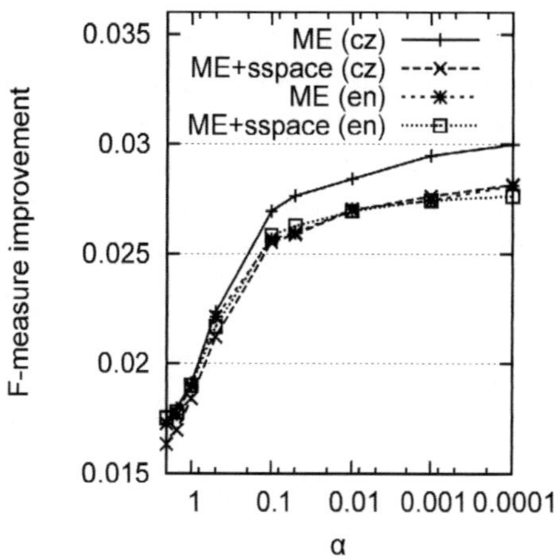

Figure 7: Improvement in F-measure depending on the parameter of Dirichlet distribution.

Another interesting idea is to use Dirichlet distribution with different hyper-parameters for targets with different number of reviews, as the Dirichlet distribution is supposed to have different shape for sparsely reviewed targets, compared to the targets with many reviews.

7.2 Conclusion

In this work we investigated global target context as a new source of information for sentiment analysis. We placed the Dirichlet distribution on sentiment labels belonging to the same review target. We combined the global target context information together with the document level classification (Maximum entropy classifier) and used Gibbs sampling for inference the sentiment labels. Our extension satisfies the unsupervised fashion and significantly improves classification F-measure by almost 3% which yields new state-of-the-art results.

Acknowledgments

This work was supported by grant no. SGS-2013-029 Advanced computing and information systems, by the POSTDOC grant from University of West Bohemia, and by the European Regional Development Fund (ERDF), project "NTIS – New Technologies for Information Society", European Center of Excellence, CZ.1.05/1.1.00/02.0090. Access to the MetaCentrum computing facilities provided under the program "Projects of Large Infrastructure for Research, Development, and Innovations" LM2010005, funded by the Ministry of Education, Youth, and Sports of the Czech Republic, is highly appreciated. The access to the CERIT-SC computing and storage facilities provided under the programme Center CERIT Scientific Cloud, part of the Operational Program Research and Development for Innovations, reg. no. CZ. 1.05/3.2.00/08.0144 is acknowledged. We also thank the reviewers for their detailed and insightful comments.

References

A. L. Berger, V. J. D. Pietra, and S. A. D. Pietra. 1996. A maximum entropy approach to natural language processing. *Computational Linguistics*, 22:39–71, March.

David M. Blei, Andrew Y. Ng, and Michael I. Jordan. 2003. Latent dirichlet allocation. *J. Mach. Learn. Res.*, 3:993–1022, March.

Nicola Burns, Yaxin Bi, Hui Wang, and Terry Anderson. 2011. A twofold-lda model for customer review analysis. In *Proceedings of the 2011 IEEE/WIC/ACM International Conferences on Web Intelligence and Intelligent Agent Technology - Volume 01*, WI-IAT '11, pages 253–256, Washington, DC, USA. IEEE Computer Society.

Thomas L. Griffiths and Mark Steyvers. 2004. Finding scientific topics. *Proceedings of the National Academy of Sciences of the United States of America*, 101(Suppl 1):5228–5235, April.

Ivan Habernal and Tomáš Brychcín. 2013. Semantic spaces for sentiment analysis. In *Text, Speech and Dialogue*, volume 8082 of *Lecture Notes in Computer Science*, pages 482–489, Berlin Heidelberg. Springer.

Ivan Habernal, Tomáš Ptáček, and Josef Steinberger. 2013. Sentiment analysis in czech social media using supervised machine learning. In *Proceedings of the 4th Workshop on Computational Approaches to Subjectivity, Sentiment and Social Media Analysis*, pages 65–74, Atlanta, Georgia, June. Association for Computational Linguistics.

Fangtao Li, Minlie Huang, and Xiaoyan Zhu. 2010. Sentiment analysis with global topics and local dependency. In Maria Fox and David Poole, editors, *Proceedings of the Twenty-Fourth AAAI Conference on Artificial Intelligence, AAAI 2010, Atlanta, Georgia, USA*. AAAI Press.

Chenghua Lin and Yulan He. 2009. Joint sentiment/topic model for sentiment analysis. In *Proceedings of the 18th ACM conference on Information and knowledge management*, CIKM '09, pages 375–384, New York, NY, USA. ACM.

Bing Liu and Lei Zhang. 2012. A survey of opinion mining and sentiment analysis. In *Mining Text Data*, pages 415–463. Springer.

Andrew L. Maas, Raymond E. Daly, Peter T. Pham, Dan Huang, Andrew Y. Ng, and Christopher Potts. 2011. Learning word vectors for sentiment analysis. In *Proceedings of the 49th Annual Meeting of the Association for Com putational Linguistics: Human Language Technologies*, pages 142–150, Portland, Oregon, USA, June. Association for Computational Linguistics.

Jorge Nocedal. 1980. Updating Quasi-Newton Matrices with Limited Storage. *Mathematics of Computation*, 35(151):773–782.

Bo Pang, Lillian Lee, and Shivakumar Vaithyanathan. 2002. Thumbs up?: sentiment classification using machine learning techniques. In *Proceedings of the ACL-02 conference on Empirical methods in natural language processing - Volume 10*, EMNLP '02, pages 79–86, Stroudsburg, PA, USA. Association for Computational Linguistics.

Josef Steinberger, Polina Lenkova, Mijail Alexandrov Kabadjov, Ralf Steinberger, and Erik Van der Goot. 2011. Multilingual entity-centered sentiment analysis evaluated by parallel corpora. In *Proceedings of the 8th International Conference on Recent Advances in Natural Language Processing*, RANLP'11, pages 770–775.

Rakshit Trivedi and Jacob Eisenstein. 2013. Discourse connectors for latent subjectivity in sentiment analysis. In *Proceedings of the 2013 Conference of the North American Chapter of the Association for Computational Linguistics: Human Language Technologies*, pages 808–813, Atlanta, Georgia, June. Association for Computational Linguistics.

Kateřina Veselovská. 2012. Sentence-level sentiment analysis in czech. In *Proceedings of the 2nd International Conference on Web Intelligence, Mining and Semantics*, WIMS '12, pages 65:1–65:4, New York, NY, USA. ACM.

Yong Zhang, Dong-Hong Ji, Ying Su, and Cheng Sun. 2011. Sentiment analysis for online reviews using an author-review-object model. In *Proceedings of the 7th Asia conference on Information Retrieval Technology*, AIRS'11, pages 362–371, Berlin, Heidelberg. Springer-Verlag.

Yong Zhang, Dong-Hong Ji, Ying Su, and Hongmiao Wu. 2013. Joint naive bayes and lda for unsupervised sentiment analysis. In Jian Pei, VincentS. Tseng, Longbing Cao, Hiroshi Motoda, and Guandong Xu, editors, *Advances in Knowledge Discovery and Data Mining*, volume 7818 of *Lecture Notes in Computer Science*, pages 402–413. Springer Berlin Heidelberg.

Tong Zhao, Chunping Li, Qiang Ding, and Li Li. 2012. User-sentiment topic model: refining user's topics with sentiment information. In *Proceedings of the ACM SIGKDD Workshop on Mining Data Semantics*, MDS '12, pages 10:1–10:9, New York, NY, USA. ACM.

An Agglomerative Hierarchical Clustering Algorithm for Labelling Morphs

Burcu Can
Department of Computer Engineering
Hacettepe University
Beytepe, Ankara 06800 Turkey
burcu.can@hacettepe.edu.tr

Suresh Manandhar
Department of Computer Science
University of York
Heslington, York, YO10 5GH, UK
suresh.manandhar@york.ac.uk

Abstract

In this paper, we present an agglomerative hierarchical clustering algorithm for labelling morphs. The algorithm aims to capture allomorphs and homophonous morphemes for a deeper analysis of segmentation results of a morphological segmentation system. Most morphological segmentation systems focus only on segmentation rather than labelling morphs according to their roles in words, i.e. inflectional (cases, tenses etc.) vs. derivational. Nevertheless, it is helpful to have a better understanding of the roles of morphs in a word to be able to judge the grammatical function of that word in a sentence; i.e. the syntactic category. We believe that a good morph labelling system can also help part-of-speech tagging. The proposed clustering algorithm can capture allomorphs in Turkish successfully. We obtain a recall of 86.34% for Turkish and 84.79% for English.

1 Introduction

Most morphological segmentation systems (Creutz and Lagus (2002; Creutz and Lagus (2004; Goldsmith (2001)) perform only the segmentation of words and do not label morphs according to how they function in a word. As a rule, some morphemes function as inflective, whereas some morphemes function as derivative. However, we do not aim to distinguish inflection or derivation within a word, but we aim to distinguish between various types of morphs which are either inflective or derivative, e.g. allomorphs, homophonous morphemes. Labelling morphs not only helps with analysing the segmentation of a word, but can also help other natural language problems, i.e. part-of-speech tagging.

The main purpose of this paper is to serve as a post-processing tool to label morphs that have been discovered by a morphological segmentation system. Our main aim is directed towards the Morpho Challenge competition (Mikko Kurimo (2011)), which provides a platform to compare participant morphological segmentation systems. In Morpho Challenge, morph labels in a segmented word and the respective morph labels in its gold standard are compared.

Example 1.1 *For example, the gold standard analyses of 'arrangements' and 'standardizes' in Morpho Challenge are given as:*

arrangements	*arrange_V*	*ment_s*	*+PL*
standardizes	*standard_A*	*ize_s*	*+3SG*

Although in both analyses -s occurs, their labels are different; +PL (plural) and +3SG (third person singular).

There is not much work done in morpheme labelling. Spiegler (Spiegler, 2011) presents two algorithms for morpheme labelling: one of them learns morpheme labels once morphological segmentation is completed and the other finds morpheme labels during morphological segmentation. Both algorithms work in a supervised setting in which ground truth morphemes are provided. Bernhard (Bernhard, 2008) suggests another morpheme labelling algorithm which labels morphemes as a stem, suffix, base, or prefix. Therefore, the proposed labelling method does not consider any allomorphs or homophonous morphemes.

The paper is organised as follows: section 2 gives the intuition behind this work, section 3 describes our clustering algorithm, section 4 presents our experiment results, and finally section 5 and section 6 conclude the paper with a discussion on the obtained results.

2 Intuition

Most morphological segmentation algorithms consider only segmenting words into its morphs and ignore labelling morphs. However, morph labels are not only useful for other NLP problems (e.g. PoS tagging), but also they give a better understanding on the morphological analysis of words. There are different types of morphs having different grammatical functions. The algorithm presented in this paper aims to group morphs according to their functions within a word. This grouping is accomplished by considering two types of distinction among morphemes: allomorphs and homophonous morphemes.

2.1 Allomorphs

Morphs may differ in shape but still can carry out the same function in words, such as the plural morpheme *-s* and *-ies* in English. Allomorphs are also seen quite often in some languages where vowel harmony[1] takes place, such as in Turkish, Hungarian, Finnish, etc. Some examples in Turkish are given below:

- The plural form (i.e. *-lar, -ler*): e.g. *elma**lar*** (apples), *ev**ler*** (houses).
- The possessive case (i.e. *-in, -un, -ün*): e.g. *Ali'**nin*** (Ali's), *Banu'**nun*** (Banu's), *Üstün'**ün*** (Üstün's).
- The present tense (i.e. *-ar, -ir*): e.g. *yap**ar*** (he does), *gel**ir*** (he comes).
- The prepositional case (i.e. *-de, -da*): e.g. *ev**de*** (at home), *okul**da*** (in the school).

Vowel harmony is not the only phonological change which causes allomorphs in Turkish. Furthermore, morphs that are attached to an unvoiced consonant ending word are also harmonised and the first morph letters become also an unvoiced consonant (i.e. *p*, *ç*, *t*, *k*, *s*, *ş*, and *h*):

- The ablative case (i.e. *-den, -ten*): e.g. *ülke**den*** (from the country), *sepet**ten*** (from the basket).
- The locative case (i.e. *-de, -te*): e.g. *şehir**de*** (in the city), *ken**tte*** (in the town).
- The third person singular (i.e. *-dir, -tir*): e.g. *nefis**tir*** (it is delicious), *zeki**dir*** (she is clever).

Due to vowel and consonant harmonies, Turkish comprises of many examples of morphs that have the same function but that are phonological variants of each other. It would be beneficial to group the allomorphs in the same cluster by assigning the same morpheme label as described before.

2.2 Homophonous morphemes

In contrast to allomorphs, some morphemes might sound the same phonetically; however, they might function differently. These morphemes are called homophonous morphemes (i.e. homophones). Homophonous morphemes belong to different clusters, due to the difference in their meanings. Some examples of homophonous morphemes in Turkish are given below:

- *kalemi*: *-i* might correspond to either an accusative form (e.g. *his/her pen*) or a possessive form (e.g. *give me the pen*) which can be determined from the context.
- *yapın* and *kapının*: *-ın* corresponds to an imperative form in the first example, whereas it corresponds to a possessive form in the latter.
- *geliyor**lar*** and *yatak**lar***: *-lar* corresponds to 3rd person plural in the first example, whereas it corresponds to plural in the latter.

Although homophonous morphemes do not occur as often as allomorphs, it is crucial to determine homophony in order to be able to distinguish morphemes which have different functions and thereby meanings. Homophonous morphemes should be grouped in different clusters; however, allomorphs should be grouped in the same cluster.

3 The Algorithm for Clustering Morphemes

For morph labelling, we propose a bottom-up agglomerative hierarchical clustering algorithm in which morphs showing functional similarities are clustered together. The functional similarities of the morphs are defined by a set of features as an input to the algorithm. Therefore, a feature vector is constructed to represent each morph by a feature vector. Each feature vector consists of a sequence of features which are given below:

- Current morph to be clustered.

[1] Vowel harmony involves rules on vowels that follow each other within a word.

- Previous morph that precedes the current morph in the analysis of the same word.
- Following morph that follows the current morph in the same word.
- Stem of the word.
- The last morph of the preceding word.
- The last morph of the following word.
- Morph position in the word (i.e. if the morph comes just after the stem, then it is 0. If the morph is the last morph of the word, then it is 2, and if it is surrounded by other morphs, this value is 1.)
- Morph length in letters.

Example 3.1 *In Turkish, the morph -ıl that occurs in the analysed sentence "O+n+lar ceza+lan+dır+**ıl**+acak+lar." (i.e. they will be punished) has got the features given below:*

- *Current morph: -ıl*
- *Previous morph: -dır*
- *Following morph: -acak*
- *Stem of the word: ceza*
- *The last morph of the preceding word: -lar*
- *The last morph of the following word: -*
- *Morph position in the word: 1*
- *Morph length: 2*

Constructing the feature vector of each morph initially, morph are placed in distinct clusters. In each iteration of the clustering algorithm, the two clusters having the minimum distance are merged. The distance between two clusters is measured by Kullback-Leibler (KL) divergence through all features in their feature vectors. Recall that KL divergence is not a distance metric, since it is not symmetric:

$$KL(p \parallel q) = \sum_i p(i) log \frac{p(i)}{q(i)} \quad (1)$$

KL divergence can be formed into a symmetric measure $D(p \parallel q)$ as follows:

$$D(p \parallel q) = KL(p \parallel q) + KL(q \parallel p) \quad (2)$$

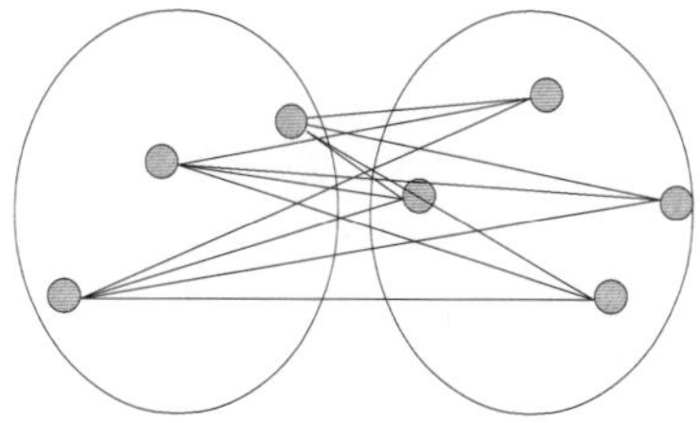

Figure 1: Average linkage clustering.

We use average linkage clustering, an instance of agglomerative clustering, for clustering morphs. In average linkage agglomerative clustering, the distance between two clusters is the average distance which is calculated through all pairs of data points in the clusters (see Figure 1):

$$D(R, S) = \frac{1}{N_R \times N_S} \sum_{i=1}^{N_R} \sum_{j=1}^{N_S} d(r_i, s_i) \quad (3)$$

where the total distance between two clusters R and S with sizes N_R and N_S respectively is the summation of distances between each data pair in the clusters. The distance is normalised with the number of pairs. The cluster pair having the minimum distance is merged in each iteration.

In contrast to single-linkage and complete-linkage clustering, average-linkage clustering takes each data member into account; thereby leads to a more realistic measurement.

Using average linkage clustering, each cluster is defined by a feature vector which keeps all the information that comes from each morph in the cluster. For example, the previous morph in a cluster is a combination of all previous morphs that are owned by each morph in the cluster. While qualitative features are combined, quantitative features, such as morph position and morph length, are averaged for the feature vector of the cluster. Having a feature vector for each cluster, the similarity between two clusters, c_1 and c_2, is measured as follows:

$$\begin{aligned} Sim(c_1, c_2) &= \alpha D(CurMor_{c_1} \parallel CurMor_{c_2}) \\ &+ \beta D(PreMor_{c_1} \parallel PreMor_{c_2}) \\ &+ \delta D(FolMor_{c_1} \parallel FolMor_{c_2}) \\ &+ \gamma D(Stem_{c_1} \parallel Stem_{c_2}) \\ &+ \pi D(PreWMor_{c_1} \parallel PreWMor_{c_2}) \\ &+ \kappa D(FolWMor_{c_1} \parallel FolWMor_{c_2}) \\ &+ x|pos_{c_1} - pos_{c_2}| \\ &+ y|len_{c_1} - len_{c_2}| \end{aligned} \quad (4)$$

where $CurMor_{c_1}$ denotes the set of current morphs $PreMor_{c_1}$ denotes the set of previous morphs, $FolMor_{c_1}$ denotes the set of following morphs, $Stem_{c_1}$ denotes the set of stems, $PreWMor_{c_1}$ is the set of last morphs of previous words and $FolWMor_{c_1}$ is the set of last morphs of following words in c_1. In addition to the qualitative features, quantitative features pos_{c_1} and len_{c_1} refer to the average position and the average length of the morphs belonging to the cluster c_1. Here, the quantitative features (i.e. pos_{c_i},len_{c_i}) are simply subtracted to find the distance between them. The weights of each feature are denoted by $alpha$, β, δ, γ, π, κ, x, and y.

Imagine that we have two clusters and let the current morphs be: c1: {*-i,-u*} and c2: {*-i,-ü*}. In order to compute $D(CurMor_{c_1} \parallel CurMor_{c_2})$, we use Equation 2 over each morph in the combination of two sets; c1+c2: {*-i,-u,-ü*}. We apply add-n smoothing to eliminate counts having a zero value in the vectors (e.g. the probability of *-u* would be zero for c_2 otherwise).

The algorithm starts with N morphs, each belonging to a distinct cluster. In each iteration, the two clusters with the minimum KL divergence are merged until all the morphs are merged in one cluster. The final cluster will be the root node in the hierarchical tree.

4 Experiments & Results

We used the gold standard analyses of words in Turkish and English for all of our experiments, which are provided by the Morpho Challenge (Mikko Kurimo, 2011). The word lists contain 552 English words and 783 Turkish words. Words are segmented and the morphemes are labelled in the gold standard, such that:

abacuses	*abacus*	N	PL
abstained	*abstain*	V	PAST

We modified the analyses manually, by replacing morpheme labels with actual morphs, such as:

abacuses	*abacus*	es
abstained	*abstain*	ed

As an input to the clustering algorithm, we extracted all morphs in the lists. The final lists contain 567 morphs in English and 1749 morphs in Turkish. We constructed the feature vectors of all morphs and applied the hierarchical clustering algorithm as described before. Once the trees were constructed, we cut the trees at different levels to retrieve the final clusters. Some resulting clusters in English are given in Table 1.

Morphemes	Words
-ism, -ion,	*hero**ism**, deduc**tion** etc.*
-ed, -ing	*insert**ed**, roof**ed**, leak**ed**, aris**ing**, puls**ing**, rat**ing** etc.*
-ness, -ity	*extensive**ness**, commun**ity**, earthi**ness** etc.*
-s	*town**s**man, yacht**s**, yacht**s**man etc.*
-er	*baby-sitt**er**s, plann**er**s, match-mak**er**s etc.*
-s'	*humaniti**es'**, protestant**s'**, swimmer**s'**, reduction**s'** etc.*

Table 1: Some morph clusters in English.

Since English is not a morphologically rich language, no homophonous morphemes or allomorphs could be captured. The reason for this is that morphs do not have sufficient contextual information. Nevertheless, morphs that show similar functional properties (i.e. tenses, derivative morphemes) are captured by the clustering algorithm. For example, both *-ism* and *-ion* are derivative morphemes that make the word a noun; *-ed* and *-ing* are inflectional morphemes that define the tense of a verb and *-ness* and *-ity* are derivative morphemes. There are many redundant clusters that have only one type of morpheme, such as plural morpheme *-s*, possessive morpheme *-s'* etc.

Experiments in Turkish provide a better understanding of what type of clusters are obtained from the clustering algorithm. Some resulting clusters in Turkish are given in Table 2. It is easier to see from the results that a good number of allomorphs are captured in Turkish due to the widely used vowel harmony. For example, allomorphs *-i* and *ı*; *-dır* and *-dir*, and *-nı* and *-ni* are captured. In addition to allomorphs, functionally similar morphemes *-a*, *-e*, *-i* and *-ı*, *-in* that refer to dative, accusative and genitive case respectively are also captured.

In order to evaluate our results, we again replaced the morphs in the gold standard with the obtained cluster labels, such that:

Morphemes	Words
-a, -e, -i, ı, -in	*faturalar**ını**, kongreler**i**, bilinmeler**ine**, bağışıklığ**ın**, mağazalar**ına** etc.*
-dır, -dir	*almakta**dır**, ödeyecekler**dir**, değinilmeli**dir** etc.*
-let, -t	*iş**let**ecek, kuru**t**urken, uza**t**abilir etc.*
-lığ, -liğ, -yış	*başarısız**lığ**ı, başla**yış**ını, isteksiz**liğ**inin etc.*
-nı, -ni, -ne, -na	*bırakabileceği**ni**, yakalandığı**nı**, düzeyleri**ne**, mağazaları**na** etc.*

Table 2: Some morph clusters in Turkish.

commutation	Cluster50	*mutate*	+Cluster34
contradiction	*contradict*	+Cluster34	
decoded	Cluster50	*code*	+Cluster43
knifed	*knife*	+Cluster43	

Suffixes were inserted with a plus sign, whereas the other morphs were inserted with their labels. This provides a more comprehensive analysis on affixes and non-affixes separately.

We applied the evaluation method that Morpho Challenge (see Mikko Kurimo (2011)) follows. In the Morpho Challenge evaluation method, segmentations are evaluated through word pairs that have common morphemes. For example, in order to decide whether *book-s* is segmented correctly, another word in the results having the morph *-s* is found. Let's imagine we find *pen-s* in the results to make a word pair with *book-s*. In order to decide whether *book-s* is segmented correctly, we find the two words in the gold standard segmentations and check whether they really share a common morph. In that case, it does not matter whether the morphs or morph labels are used.

We tested our algorithm with different combinations of features. The results for Turkish by using the features, previous morph, following morph, current morph, stem and morph position are given in Table 3. The results consist of 162 clusters. The number of clusters is chosen in accordance with the highest evaluation score obtained.

Here, two types of analyses are presented: non-affixes and affixes. As mentioned above, the evaluation with non-affixes considers only non-affixes; whereas the evaluation with affixes considers the rest of the morphemes (i.e. stems and prefixes). Scores show that the algorithm is better at labelling suffixes than prefixes.

	Non-affixes	Affixes	Total
Precision	84.53	62.14	68.02
Recall	77.62	28.40	42.86
F-measure	80.93	38.98	52.58

Table 3: Evaluation results according to 162 clusters in Turkish by employing previous morph, following morph, current morph, stem and morph position as features.

	Non-affixes	Affixes	Total
Precision	87.15	57.45	65.04
Recall	79.51	31.76	45.79
F-measure	83.15	40.91	53.74

Table 4: Evaluation results according to 162 clusters in Turkish by employing previous morph, following morph, current morph, stem, morph position and morph length as features.

Results from another experiment that employs previous morph, following morph, current morph, stem, morph position and morph length are given in Table 4 for Turkish. The results are analysed according to the same number of clusters in order to investigate the impact of using different features. Here we can observe that using morph length as a feature improves the results.

The third experiment explores the impact of using the last morph of the previous word and the following word. The results of the experiment that uses previous morph, following morph, current morph, stem, the last morph of the previous word and the last morph of the following word are given in Table 5 for Turkish. The results show that using the last morph of the previous and following word does not improve the scores, but reduces contrarily.

All experiments that are presented above use equal weights for the features. We carried out another experiment by assigning weights to the features according to their importance. We set the weights manually, such that:

$$\begin{aligned} Sim(c_1, c_2) &= 0.3D(CurMor_{c_1} \parallel CurMor_{c_2}) \\ &+ 0.2D(PreMor_{c_1} \parallel PreMor_{c_2}) \\ &+ 0.2D(FolMor_{c_1} \parallel FolMor_{c_2}) \\ &+ 0.2D(Stem_{c_1} \parallel Stem_{c_2}) \\ &+ 0.1|pos_{c_1} - pos_{c_2}| \end{aligned} \quad (5)$$

The results of the weighted clustering algo-

	Non-affixes	Affixes	Total
Precision	87.93	46.95	61.06
Recall	73.05	12.03	29.96
F-measure	79.80	19.15	40.20

Table 5: Evaluation results according to 162 clusters in Turkish by employing previous morph, following morph, current morph, stem, morph position, the last morph of the previous word and following word as features.

	Non-affixes	Affixes	Total
Precision	93.82	69.64	80.23
Recall	86.34	44.08	74.41
F-measure	89.92	53.98	77.21

Table 6: Evaluation results by employing weighted features, which are previous morph, following morph, current morph, stem and morph position in Turkish.

rithm that employs the previous morph, following morph, current morph, stem and morph position are given in Table 6 for Turkish.

We also evaluated the algorithm for English by employing previous morph, following morph, current morph, stem, morph position and morph length as features. We obtained the results according to 100 clusters. The results are given in Table 7. In the experiment, the features were also weighted the same as the previous experiment.

5 Discussion

We tested the proposed clustering algorithm with various combinations of features. It should be noted that using previous and following morphs in English is not very beneficial due to the simple morphology of the language. However, we used these two features because of a number of words having more than one morph. Since Turkish is richer in morphology compared to English, previous and following morphs are more beneficial in clustering of Turkish morphs.

Another issue in Turkish morphology that needs to be noted that is the ambiguity of morphs. Words can be segmented in different ways depending on the meaning of the word, which can be discovered by looking at the context of the word. Hence, it also makes sense to employ the context of a morph in clustering. We employ the last morphs of the previous and following words to make use of

	Non-affixes	Affixes	Total
Precision	95.60	90.72	92.93
Recall	84.79	34.46	70.59
F-measure	89.87	49.95	80.24

Table 7: Evaluation results according to 100 clusters in English by weighting features, which are previous morph, following morph, current morph, stem, morph position, the last morph of the previous word and the last morph of the following word.

the context in clustering. This makes a considerable amount of improvement in the results because Turkish grammar has noun phrases, subject-verb agreement etc.

In all experiments we manually assign weights to the features. Weighting features improves results since the features are not equally important in clustering. We leave the issue of estimating weights to be explored in the future.

6 Conclusion & Future Work

In this paper, an agglomerative hierarchical clustering algorithm is presented for labelling morphs. The algorithm aims to capture allomorphs and homophonous morphemes for a deeper analysis of morphological segmentation results. Most morphological segmentation systems focus only on segmentation, rather than labelling morphs. Nevertheless, it is helpful to label morphs in order to have an idea about the grammatical function of the word in a sentence; i.e. the syntactic category. We believe that a good morph labelling system will help PoS tagging, as well.

The presented algorithm can find allomorphs in Turkish by clustering them together. However, as far as we could observe from the results, it cannot show the same accuracy for homophonous morphemes.

We aim to improve the proposed approach by adopting mixture components for each morph label in a nonparametric Bayesian framework. We aim to handle the sparsity in the data with a nonparametric approach. Even with an infinite mixture model, it is possible to make the number of morph labels infinitely defined.

References

Delphine Bernhard, 2008. *Simple Morpheme Labelling in Unsupervised Morpheme Analysis*, pages 873–880. Springer-Verlag, Berlin, Heidelberg.

Mathias Creutz and Krista Lagus. 2002. Unsupervised discovery of morphemes. In *Proceedings of the ACL-02 workshop on Morphological and phonological learning - Volume 6*, MPL '02, pages 21–30, Stroudsburg, PA, USA. Association for Computational Linguistics.

Mathias Creutz and Krista Lagus. 2004. Induction of a simple morphology for highly-inflecting languages. In *Proceedings of the 7th Meeting of the ACL Special Interest Group in Computational Phonology: Current Themes in Computational Phonology and Morphology*, SIGMorPhon '04, pages 43–51, Stroudsburg, PA, USA. Association for Computational Linguistics.

John Goldsmith. 2001. Unsupervised learning of the morphology of a natural language. *Computational Linguistics*, 27(2):153–198.

Sami Virpioja Ville Turunen Mikko Kurimo, Krista Lagus. 2011. Morpho challenge 2010. `http://research.ics.tkk.fi/events/morphochallenge2010/`, June.

Sebastian Spiegler. 2011. *Machine Learning For The Analysis Of Morphologically Complex Languages*. Ph.D. thesis, Merchant Venturers School of Engineering, University of Bristol, April.

Temporal Text Classification for Romanian Novels Set in the Past

Alina Maria Ciobanu
Liviu P. Dinu
Octavia-Maria Şulea
Faculty of Mathematics and Computer Science
Center for Computational Linguistics
University of Bucharest
alinamaria.ciobanu@yahoo.com
ldinu@fmi.unibuc.ro
mary.octavia@gmail.com

Anca Dinu
Faculty of Foreign Languages
University of Bucharest
anca_d_dinu@yahoo.com

Vlad Niculae
University of Wolverhampton
vlad@vene.ro

Abstract

In this paper we look at a task in historical linguistics and the study of language development, namely that of identifying the time when a text was written. The novelty is that we evaluate our classifier and our selected features on literary texts having their action placed in the past and written so as to give off the impression of the respective epoch. We investigate several types of features and ultimately go with a very simple set of 10 features which very accurately classifies the texts based on the century they were actually written in. We use random forests to obtain high performance.

1 Introduction and Motivation

Determining the time when a document was written is a task not only with implications in cultural heritage but one which proves important to many other domains such as historical and literary criticism, diachronic linguistics, manuscript phylogeny and stemmatics, and the elaboration of critical theories about the author of the texts in question. A more practical, coarser grained approach is to classify according to the century in which a text was written, approach that we take in this paper.

Within many instances of this task, disputes between linguists and historians appear. For example, among the first texts written in Romania there are four religious texts, *Codicele Voroneţean*, *Psaltirea Scheiană*, *Psaltirea Voroneţeană* and *Psaltirea Hurmuzachi*, for which the dating is disputed between the 15th century (idea promoted by historians such as Nicolae Iorga) and the end of the 16th century (idea maintained by linguists such as Rosetti) (Tagliavini, 1972). Often times, the texts present characteristics of a translation, yet they are not original translations but modern copies of lost originals.

For Romanian, the 16th century represents the beginning of Romanian writing. In (Dimitrescu, 1994, p. 13) the author states that the modern Romanian vocabulary cannot be completely understood without a thorough study of the texts written in this period, which should be considered the source of the literary language used today. In the 17th century, some of the most important cultural events took place, such as the improvement of the education system and the establishing of several printing houses, and this led to a new development of the Romanian language (Dimitrescu, 1994, p.75). Then, in the 18th century, a diversification of the philological interests in Romania took place through writing the first Romanian-Latin bilingual lexicons, the draft of the first monolingual dictionary, the first Romanian grammar, and the earliest translations from French (Lupu, 1999, p. 29).

The transition to the Latin alphabet, which was a significant cultural achievement, is completed in the 19th century. The Cyrillic alphabet is maintained in Romanian writing until around 1850, afterwards being gradually replaced with the Latin alphabet (Dimitrescu, 1994, p. 270). The 19th century is marked by the conflict (and eventually the compromise) between etymologism and phonetism in Romanian orthography. In (Maiorescu, 1866) the author argues for applying the phonetic principle and several reforms are enforced for this purpose. In the 20th century, some variations regarding the usage of diacritics in Romanian orthography are noticed.

In this paper we approach an interesting version of the epoch disambiguation task, successfully disambiguating the century in which Romanian novels with the action set in the past and written so as to simulate the action's epoch *appear* have been written in. We used novels of Romanian writers Mihail Sadoveanu and Ştefan Agopian with the action developing in different time periods between the 16th to the 20th century. For training and evaluation we used a multitude of texts written in either one of the 5 centuries.

2 Related Work

The influence of the temporal effects in automatic document classification is analyzed in (Mourão et al., 2008; Salles et al., 2010). The authors state that a major challenge in building text classification models may be the change which occurs in the characteristics of the documents and their classes over time (Mourão et al., 2008). Therefore, in order to overcome the difficulties which arise in automatic classification when dealing with documents dating from different epochs, identifying and accounting for document characteristics changing over time (such as class frequency, relationships between terms and classes and the similarity among classes over time (Mourão et al., 2008)) is essential and can lead to a more accurate discrimination between classes.

Dalli and Wilks (2006) successfully apply a method for classification of texts and documents based on their predicted time of creation, proving that accounting for word frequencies and their variation over time is accurate. Kumar et al. (2012) argue as well for the capability of this method, of using words alone, to determine the epoch in which a text was written or the time period a document refers to.

The effectiveness of using models for individual partitions in a timeline with the purpose of predicting probabilities over the timeline for new documents is investigated in (Kumar et al., 2011; Kanhabua and Nørvåg, 2009). This approach, based on the divergence between the language model of the test document and those of the timeline partitions, was successfully employed in predicting publication dates and in searching for web pages and web documents.

In (de Jong et al., 2005) the authors raise the problem of access to historical collections of documents, which may be difficult due to the different historical and modern variants of the text, the less standardized spelling, words ambiguities and other language changes. Thus, the linking of current word forms with their historical equivalents and accurate dating of texts can help reduce the temporal effects in this regard.

Chambers (2012) states that applying timestamps to documents is, to some extent, similar to topic classification, focusing on choosing a time period instead of a topic, but also relating to temporal words and phrases which describe the time period to be determined and are often comprised in the investigated documents. Therefore, he argues for the inclusion of these temporal expressions into the learning system for automatic document dating and proposes such a model which obtains better results than previous generative models.

In (Mihalcea and Nastase, 2012) the authors introduced the task of identifying changes in word usage over time, disambiguating the epoch at word-level.

Recently, Stajner and Zampieri (2013) used stylistic features, such as lexical richness, to predict the century of historical Portuguese texts.

3 Approach

3.1 Datasets used

In order to investigate the diachronic changes and variations in the Romanian lexicon over time, we used a corpus containing texts ranging from the 16th to the 20th century, representing the five different stages in the evolution of the Romanian language, as discussed in the introduction. We used this corpus for feature selection, model training and evaluation, following the methodology described in Section 3.2.

We used this model to classify 20th century novels with action set in the past. The novels we used are shown in Table 2 along with the century in which the action takes place.

For preprocessing, we removed words that are irrelevant for our investigation, such as dates and numbers and non-textual annotations marked by non alphanumeric characters. We performed basic word segmentation, using whitespace and punctuation marks as delimiters and we lower-cased all words.

Century	Title
16	Codicele Todorescu Codicele Martian Coresi, Evanghelia cu învăţătură Coresi, Lucrul apostolesc Coresi, Psaltirea slavo-română Coresi, Târgul evangheliilor Coresi, Tetraevanghelul Manuscrisul de la Ieud Palia de la Orăştie Psaltirea Hurmuzaki
17	The Bible Miron Costin, Letopiseţul Ţării Moldovei Miron Costin, De neamul moldovenilor Grigore Ureche, Letopiseţul Ţării Moldovei Dosoftei, Viaţa si petreacerea sfinţilor Varlaam Motoc, Cazania Varlaam Motoc, Răspunsul împotriva Catehismului calvinesc
18	Antim Ivireanul, Opere Axinte Uricariul, Letopiseţul Ţării Romănesti şi al Ţării Moldovei Ioan Canta, Letopiseţul Ţării Moldovei Dimitrie Cantemir, Istoria ieroglifică Dimitrie Eustatievici Braşoveanul, Gramatica românească Ion Neculce, O samă de cuvinte
19	Mihai Eminescu, Opere, v. IX Mihai Eminescu, Opere, v. X Mihai Eminescu, Opere, v. XI Mihai Eminescu, Opere, v. XII Mihai Eminescu, Opere, v. XIII
20	Eugen Barbu, Groapa Mircea Cartarescu, Orbitor Marin Preda, Cel mai iubit dintre pământeni

Table 1: Historical Romanian dataset, used for training and evaluation

3.2 Classifiers and features

The texts in the corpus (in Table 1) were split into chunks of 500 sentences in order to increase the number of sample entries and have a more robust evaluation. A quarter of the chunks were held out as a test set. On the training set, we experimented with several intuitive engineered features based on dictionaries, sentence length, stop word frequencies, and on word endings, but the most effective feature set turns out to be extremely simple.

We represented the texts using a simple bag-of-words model, applying *tf* re-weighting, and performed χ^2 feature selection. The ten best features turn out to classify both the training set and the test set without error. The classifier used is a random forest ensemble with 20 trees. The tree parameter `max_features`, the maximum number of features to consider in a split, is left at the default value of $\sqrt{d}$, where $d = 10$ is the number of features. There is no need for further search since the accuracy is perfect.

For comparison, a multinomial Naive Bayes classifier on the same feature set obtains 90.1% accuracy. To check whether the random forest actually learns to identify parts of the same document, we trained the same model using the document name as label. In this case, the accuracy with which the system assigned to a chunk the name of the document from which it was extracted was only 72.1%. However, the misclassifications happen mostly within century level. A chunk was assigned to a document from the correct century

Author	Title	Century
Agopian	Tobit	17
	Sara	17
	Tache de Catifea	19
	Manualul Întamplărilor	19
	Ziua Mâniei	20
Sadoveanu	Fraţii Jderi	16
	Neamul Şoimareştilor	17
	Baltagul	19
	Hanu Ancuţei	19
	Păuna Mică	20
	Nicoară Potcoavă	20

Table 2: Literary texts written in the 20th century used in our evaluation.

with 98.1% accuracy.

For understanding this phenomenon more clearly, we plotted the mean and standard deviation of each feature across the five centuries investigated in Figure 1.

The system was put together using the *scikit-learn* machine learning library for Python, version 0.14 (Pedregosa et al., 2011).

4 Results

On the held-out test set, our system obtains a perfect accuracy of 100%, as discussed in Section 3.2. We classified, using this system, the texts from Table 2. Because the interest is at document level, we did not split into chunks of 500 sentences, but because of *tf* normalization, this does not affect the results.

We examined the confidence (estimated class probability score) of the classification, which is the average of the probabilities given by the 20 trees in the randomized forest. Classification is very confident and places all texts in the century when they were actually written in, namely the 20th. From Agopian's texts, only *Ziua Mâniei* is not classified with 100% confidence, getting a 5% chance of being from the 19th century. Mihail Sadoveanu's text *Hanu Ancuței* is also given a 5% confidence for the 19th century, while *Nicoară Potcoavă* gets 5% for the 18th century, 10% for the 19th, leaving still a high confidence of 85% for the true class, 20th century.

5 Conclusions

Our results exhibit good performance. Despite the fact that the problem is simple, overfitting is effectively prevented by extreme feature selection and the features used promise to be useful in determining the period of some disputed writings from Romanian literature. It is interesting to see that the features contain pairs of old and new variants of the same word (*cari/ care*, *pre/ pe*), as well as only old variants of a word (*amu* for *acum*, *derept* for *drept*), and are mostly functional words.

It is possible that a justification similar to the one encountered in authorship attribution holds: authors can try to mimic the lexicon of the century where they are setting the action, and use rare, loaded words that set the frame for readers. But by counting very frequent functional words in temporal variations, such as the 10 best features extracted by our pipeline, we can find the signal of the contemporary language of the author, one difficult to fake.

In this paper we focused on temporal classification which can be a first step in many applications such as building a system for automatically translating between language stages. An interesting next step would be to extend the study at a lexical level and identify all forms of a word in order to create a map of its historical development, something also useful in the task mentioned above.

Acknowledgements

The contribution of the authors to this paper is equal. Research supported by a grant of the Romanian National Authority for Scientific Research, CNCS – UEFISCDI, project number PN-II-ID-PCE-2011-3-0959.

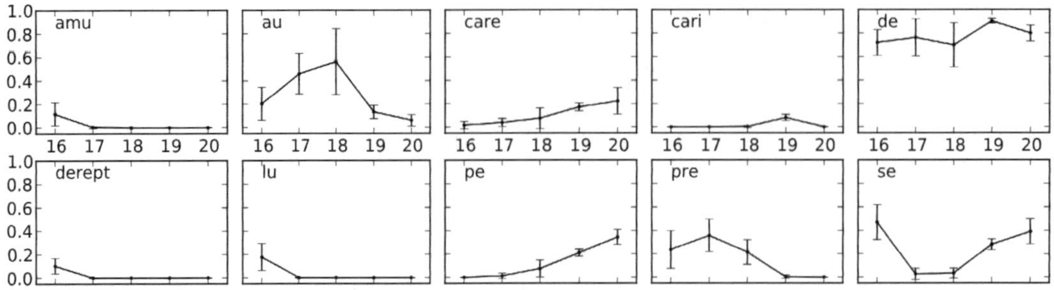

Figure 1: Mean and standard deviation of the keyword frequencies (y axis) for the 16-20 centuries (x axis). The translation of the feature words, from top to bottom and from left to right, are: old form of *now*, *(they) have*, modern form of *which*, old form of *which*, *of*, old form of *fair*, old form of *on*, modern form of *on*, reflexive form of the third person pronoun

References

Nathanael Chambers. 2012. Labeling documents with timestamps: learning from their time expressions. In *Proceedings of the 50th Annual Meeting of the Association for Computational Linguistics: Long Papers - Volume 1*, ACL '12, pages 98–106, Stroudsburg, PA, USA. Association for Computational Linguistics.

Angelo Dalli and Yorick Wilks. 2006. Automatic dating of documents and temporal text classification. In *Proceedings of the Workshop on Annotating and Reasoning about Time and Events, Sydney,*, pages 17—-22.

Franciska de Jong, Henning Rode, and Djoerd Hiemstra. 2005. Temporal language models for the disclosure of historical text. In *Humanities, computers and cultural heritage: Proceedings of the XVIth International Conference of the Association for History and Computing.*

Florica Dimitrescu. 1994. *Dinamica lexicului românesc - ieri şi azi*. Editura Logos. In Romanian.

Nattiya Kanhabua and Kjetil Nørvåg. 2009. Using temporal language models for document dating. In *ECML/PKDD (2)*, pages 738–741.

Abhimanu Kumar, Matthew Lease, and Jason Baldridge. 2011. Supervised language modeling for temporal resolution of texts. In *CIKM*, pages 2069–2072.

Abhimanu Kumar, Jason Baldridge, Matthew Lease, and Joydeep Ghosh. 2012. Dating texts without explicit temporal cues. *CoRR*, abs/1211.2290.

Coman Lupu. 1999. *Lexicografia românească în procesul de occidentalizare latino-romanică a limbii române moderne*. Editura Logos. In Romanian.

Titu Maiorescu. 1866. Despre scrierea limbei rumăne. *Ediţiunea şi Imprimeria Societăţei Junimea*. In Romanian.

Rada Mihalcea and Vivi Nastase. 2012. Word epoch disambiguation: Finding how words change over time. In *ACL (2)*, pages 259–263. The Association for Computer Linguistics.

Fernando Mourão, Leonardo Rocha, Renata Araújo, Thierson Couto, Marcos Gonçalves, and Wagner Meira Jr. 2008. Understanding temporal aspects in document classification. In *WSDM '08 Proceedings of the 2008 International Conference on Web Search and Data Mining*, pages 159–170.

F. Pedregosa, G. Varoquaux, A. Gramfort, V. Michel, B. Thirion, O. Grisel, M. Blondel, P. Prettenhofer, R. Weiss, V. Dubourg, J. Vanderplas, A. Passos, D. Cournapeau, M. Brucher, M. Perrot, and E. Duchesnay. 2011. Scikit-learn: Machine learning in Python. *Journal of Machine Learning Research*, 12:2825–2830, Oct.

Thiago Salles, Leonardo Rocha, Fernando Mourão, Gisele L. Pappa, Lucas Cunha, Marcos Gonçalves, and Wagner Meira Jr. 2010. Automatic document classification temporally robust. *Journal of Information and Data Management*, 1:199–211, June.

Sanja Stajner and Marcos Zampieri. 2013. Stylistic changes for temporal text classification. In *Proceedings of the 16th International Conference on Text Speech and Dialogue (TSD2013), Lecture Notes in Artificial Intelligence (LNAI 8082)*, pages 519–526, Pilsen, Czech Republic. Springer.

Carlo Tagliavini. 1972. *Le origini delle lingue neolatine*. Casa editrice Patron. In Italian.

A Dictionary-Based Approach for Evaluating Orthographic Methods in Cognates Identification

Alina Maria Ciobanu
Faculty of Mathematics
and Computer Science
University of Bucharest
alina.ciobanu@my.fmi.unibuc.ro

Liviu P. Dinu
Faculty of Mathematics
and Computer Science
Center for Computational Linguistics
University of Bucharest
ldinu@fmi.unibuc.ro

Abstract

In this paper we propose a method for identifying cognates based on etymology and etymons. We employ this approach to evaluate the extent to which lexical similarity can be used for automatic detection of cognate pairs. We investigate some orthographic approaches widely used in this research area and some original metrics as well. We apply this procedure for Romanian and its most closely related languages, French and Italian, but our method is applicable to any languages.

1 Introduction and Related Work

Cognates are words in different languages having the same etymology and a common ancestor. The task of cognates identification is widely used in historical and comparative linguistics, in the study of languages relatedness (Chin et al, 2010), phylogenetic inference (Atkinson et al, 2005) and in identifying how and to what extent languages changed over time. Besides these research areas, in which the genetic relationships between words are extremely relevant, cognates have been successfully used in other fields, such as language acquisition, bilingual word recognition (Dijkstra et al, 2012), corpus linguistics (Simard et al, 1992), cross-lingual information retrieval (Buckley et al, 1998) and machine translation (Knight et al, 2003). In these domains, the term "cognates" is usually used with a somewhat different meaning, denoting words with high orthographic/phonetic and cross-lingual meaning similarity, the condition of common etymology being left aside. Kondrak (2001) makes the distinction between the different interpretations of the notion and Inkpen et al (2005) present the definition of "genetic cognates".

In this paper we focus on genetic relationships between words and we use the term "cognates" in a broader meaning, counting as cognates the word-etymon pairs as well. Our motivation is that these pairs of words also share a common ancestor, thus complying with the cognates' definition. For example, the Romanian word *campion* (meaning *champion*) has Italian etymology and the etymon *campione*, which has Latin etymology and the etymon *campione(m)*. Thus, the Romanian word *campion* and the Italian word *campione* are cognates, as they share a common Latin ancestor.

The paper is organized as follows: we introduce our approach to cognates identification in Section 2. We describe the corpus used for our research in Section 3. We present several orthographic approaches used for cognates identification in Section 4. We evaluate these metrics and analyse the results of our experiments in Section 5. Finally, we draw some conclusion regarding our research in Section 6.

2 Our Approach

We focus on the Romanian language and we investigate its cognate pairs with two other Romance languages, French and Italian. We believe this comparison is interesting for the following reason: the two related languages differ significantly with respect to their orthographic depth: the mapping rules between graphemes and phonemes are more complex for French, which has a deep orthography, than for Italian, which has a highly phonemic orthography.

We identify the etymologies and etymons of the Romanian words using *dexonline* [1] machine-readable dictionary, which is an aggregator for over 30 Romanian dictionaries. By parsing its definitions, we are able to automatically extract information regarding words' etymologies and etymons. The most frequently used pattern is shown below.

[1] http://dexonline.ro

```
<abbr class="abbrev"
title="limba language_name">
language_abbreviation </abbr>
<b> etymon </b>
```

As an example, we provide below an excerpt from a *dexonline* entry which uses this pattern to specify the etymology of the Romanian word *capitol* (which means *chapter*). When more options are possible for explaining a word's etymology, *dexonline* provides multiple etymologies. We account for all the given alternatives, enabling our method to provide more accurate results. In our example, the word *capitol* has double etymology: Latin (with the etymon *capitulum*) and Italian (with the etymon *capitolo*).

```
<b> CAPÍTOL </b>
<abbr class="abbrev"
title="limba italiana"> it. </abbr>
<b> capitolo </b>
<abbr class="abbrev"
title="limba latina"> lat. </abbr>
<b> capitulum </b>
```

After determining the etymologies of the Romanian words, we translate in French all words without French etymology and in Italian all words without Italian etymology using *Google Translate* [2]. We consider cognate candidates pairs formed of Romanian words and their translations. Using French[3] and Italian[4] dictionaries, we extract etymology-related information for French and Italian words. To identify cognates we compare, for each pair of candidates, the etymologies and the etymons. If they match, we identify the words as being cognates. Our solution for addressing cognates identification answers Swadesh's question, as cited in (Campbell, 2003): "Given a small collection of likely-looking cognates, how can one definitely determine whether they are really the residue of common origin and not the workings of pure chance or some other factor?", as we limit the analysis only to words that share a common etymology, i.e. words that are known to be related.

For example, for the Romanian word *victorie*, *dexonline* reports Latin etymology and the etymon *victoria*. Because this word does not have Italian etymology, we assume it might have a cognate pair in Italian. Consequently, we translate it in Italian, obtaining the word *vittoria*. We consider the words *victorie* and *vittoria* cognate candidates. Using the Italian dictionary we identify, for this word, Latin etymology and the etymon *victoria*. We compare etymologies and etymons for the Romanian word and its translation in Italian and, as they match, having a common ancestor (Latin) and the same etymon (*victoria*), we identify them as a cognate pair.

3 The Corpus

We apply our method on a high-quality Romanian corpus comprising of the transcription of the parliamentary debates held between 1996 and 2007 in the Romanian Parliament, recently proposed in (Grozea, 2012). The sessions deal with a wide variety of topics regarding the political, social and economic fields. In this paper we decided to run our experiments using words extracted from a large corpus of transcribed spoken language, in order to investigate the cognates that are most frequently used in Romanian. This dataset covers particular cases in the task of cognates identification, such as cognates between which the degree of orthographic similarity is low (for example the Romanian word *atotputernicie*, which means *almightiness*, and its French cognate pair *omnipotence*, both sharing the Latin etymon *omnipotentia*) and vice versa, non-cognates that resemble one another (for example the Romanian word *mănăstire*, meaning *monastery* and having the Old Slavic etymon *monastyrí*, and its Italian translation *monastero*, having the Latin etymon *monasteriu(m)*).

Many words have undergone transformations by the augmentation of language-specific diacritics when entering a new language. From an orthographic perspective, the resemblance of words is higher between words without diacritics than between words with diacritics. For example, the similarity seems lower for the Romanian word *amiciţie* (which means *friendship*) and its French cognate pair *amitié* than for their corresponding forms without diacritics, *amicitie* and *amitie*. For this reason, we investigate the performances of the orthographic approaches to the task of cognates identification using two versions of the corpus: with and without diacritics included.

For preprocessing this corpus, we removed words that are irrelevant for our investigation, such

[2] http://translate.google.com
[3] http://www.cnrtl.fr/etymologie
[4] http://www.sapere.it/sapere/dizionari.html

as dates and numbers and all the transcribers' descriptions of the parliamentary sessions (such as *"The session began at 8:40."*), as we focus on the spoken language. We performed word segmentation, using whitespace and punctuation marks as delimiters, we lower-cased all words and we removed stop words, using a list of Romanian stop words provided by *Apache Lucene* [5] text search engine library . We lemmatized the words using *dexonline*, which provides information regarding the words' inflected forms and enables us to correctly identify lemmas where no part-of-speech or semantic ambiguities arise (in this case we consider the first occurred lemma).

4 Orthographic Approaches

Various word distances have been used in the task of string similarity computation. They have been applied in many different research areas, besides cognates identification, such as sentence alignment (Brew and McKelvie, 1996), record linkage (Jaro, 1989), stemming (Dalbelo and Snajder, 2009) and bioinformatics (Dinu and Sgarro, 2006). In (Kondrak, 2001) some of the most widely used measures are analysed, and their flaws and the differences between them are emphasized.

The approaches used to evaluate cognate pairs are divided in two groups: phonetic and orthographic. The orthographic approaches are usually used in corpus linguistics (Kondrak, 2001). We employ our method of identifying cognates to evaluate the extent to which lexical similarity can be used for automatic detection of cognates. We investigate some orthographic approaches widely used in this research area and some original metrics as well.

In (Inkpen et al, 2005) several orthographic similarity measures are used for the classification of pairs of words as cognates or false friends. For our investigation we chose some of the distances used in this paper, another distance that was successfully employed for record linkage and also an original metric in the field of cognates identification, rank distance.

- Levenshtein distance (Levenshtein, 1965), also named the edit distance, counts the minimum number of operations (insertion, deletion and substitution) required to transform one string into another. We use a normalized Levenshtein distance computed as:

[5] http://lucene.apache.org

$$EDIT(w_i, w_j) = \frac{LD(w_i, w_j)}{max(|w_i|, |w_j|)}$$

where $LD(w_i, w_j)$ is the Levenshtein distance for words w_i and w_j.

E.g. $\Delta(langue, lingua) = \frac{2}{6} = 0.33$

- Rank distance (Dinu and Dinu, 2005) is used to measure the similarity between two rank lists. A ranking of a set of n objects can be represented as a permutation of the integers $1, 2, ..., n$. S is a set of ranking results. $\sigma \in S$. $\sigma(i)$ represents the rank of object i in the ranking result σ. The rank distance is computed as:

$$RD(\sigma, \tau) = \sum_{i=1}^{i=n} |\sigma(i) - \tau(i)|$$

The ranks of the elements are given from bottom up, i.e. from n to 1, in a Borda order. The elements which do not occur in one of the rankings receive the rank 0. To extend the rank distance to strings, we index each occurence of a given letter a with a_k, where k is the number of its previous occurences, and then compute the rank distance for the new indexed strings which become in this situation rankings. In order to normalize it, we divide the obtained value by the maximum possible distance between two strings u and v, which is:

$$\frac{|u|(|u|+1)}{2} + \frac{|v|(|v|+1)}{2}$$

E.g. $\Delta(langue, lingua) = \frac{10}{42} = 0.23$

- Longest common subsequence ratio (Melamed, 1995) computes the similarity between two words dividing the length of the longest common subsequence of the two words by the length of the longer word:

$$LCSR(w_i, w_j) = \frac{LCS(w_i, w_j)}{max(|w_i|, |w_j|)}$$

where $LCS(w_i, w_j)$ is the longest common subsequence of w_i and w_j. We subtract this value from 1, in order to obtain the distance between two words.

E.g. $\Delta(langue, lingua) = 1 - \frac{4}{6} = 0.33$

- XDice (Brew and McKelvie, 1996) is a version of Dice's coefficient (Adamson and Boreham, 1972) which counts the number of shared character bigrams between two words and divides it by the number of bigrams in both words, allowing also extended bigrams (formed by the first and third letter of trigrams):

$$XDICE(w_i, w_j) = \frac{2 * |xbi(w_i) \cap xbi(w_j)|}{|xbi(w_i) + xbi(w_j)|}$$

where $xbi(w)$ is a function which determines the multi-set of character bigrams and extended bigrams in w. As XDice computes similarity between words, we subtract its value from 1 to obtain distances.

E.g. $\Delta(langue, lingua) = 1 - \frac{2*4}{18} = 0.55$

- Jaro distance (Jaro, 1989) and its version, Jaro-Winkler distance (Winkler, 1990), are measures which account for the number and position of common characters between words. These metrics are described in (Delmestri and Dinu, 2012). Given two strings $w_i = (w_{i1}, ..., w_{im})$ and $w_j = (w_{j1}, ..., w_{jn})$, the number of common characters for w_i and w_j is the number of charachters w_{ik} in w_i which satisfy the condition:

$$\exists w_{jl} \text{ in } w_j : w_{ik} = w_{jl}, |k - l| \leq \frac{max(m, n)}{2} - 1$$

Let c be the number of common characters in w_i and w_j and t the number of character transpositions (i.e. the number of common characters in w_i and w_j in different positions, divided by 2). Jaro distance is defined as follows:

$$J(w_i, w_j) = \frac{1}{3} * \left(\frac{c}{m} + \frac{c}{n} + \frac{c - t}{c}\right)$$

As both Jaro and Jaro-Winkler metrics are string similarity measures, we subtract these values from 1 to obtain distances between words.

E.g. $\Delta(langue, lingua) = 1 - \frac{1}{3} * (\frac{4}{6} + \frac{4}{6} + \frac{4-0}{4}) = 0.22$

Jaro-Winkler distance accounts also for the length l of the common preffix of w_i and w_j ($l \leq 4$) and considers a scaling factor $p = 0.1$.

$$JW(w_i, w_j) = J(w_i, w_j) + p * l * (1 - J(w_i, w_j))$$

where $J(w_i, w_j)$ is the Jaro distance for words w_i and w_j.

E.g. $\Delta(langue, lingua) = 1 - (0.77 + 0.1 * 1 * (1 - 0.77)) = 0.20$

5 Evaluation and Results Analysis

In order to evaluate the performances of these orthographic approaches to the task of cognates identification, we apply the method presented in Section 2 for determining cognate pairs in Italian and French for each word in the preprocessed corpus. The statistics for this phase of our procedure are listed in Table 1.

	Nwords	**Ncognates**	
		French	**Italian**
Type	162,399	77,029	35,581
Token	22,469,290	15,858,140	10,895,298
Lemmas	40,065	17,929	6,768

Table 1: Statistics for the Romanian corpus: the total number of type words, token words and lemmas (in column 1) and the number of type words, token words and lemmas having an etymon or a cognate pair in French (column 2) or in Italian (column 3). It can be noticed that the sum of token words with cognate pairs or etymons in French and Italian is higher than the total number of token words after preprocessing the corpus, due to the fact that many of these words have cognate pairs or etymons in both languages

Further, we excerpt from the corpus, for each of the two languages, random samples of 5,000 words which have a cognate pair in the related language and 5,000 which do not have such matching pair. We match these latter words with their translations. Thus, we obtain a sample of 10,000 pairs of words for Romanian and Italian, 5,000 pairs of cognates and 5,000 pairs of non-cognates. We obtain a similar set for Romanian and French. For each dataset we also consider the version without diacritics. We compute the lexical distances for each pair of words, setting various thresholds

French

th	EDIT				LCSR				RD				JW				XDICE			
	R	P	A	F	R	P	A	F	R	P	A	F	R	P	A	F	R	P	A	F
0.0	06.4	100.0	53.2	12.0	06.4	100.0	53.2	12.0	06.4	100.0	53.2	12.0	06.4	100.0	53.2	12.0	06.4	100.0	53.2	12.0
0.1	08.9	94.3	54.2	16.3	09.3	93.8	54.4	17.0	15.2	87.6	56.5	26.0	41.9	81.1	66.1	55.3	09.4	92.5	54.3	17.0
0.2	24.9	83.2	60.0	38.4	26.4	82.5	60.4	40.0	40.6	83.4	66.3	54.7	71.8	78.6	76.1	75.1	18.1	83.1	57.2	29.8
0.3	47.6	83.1	68.9	60.5	50.3	82.3	69.7	62.4	63.3	81.1	74.3	71.1	88.2	75.9	**80.1**	81.6	34.0	81.8	63.2	48.0
0.4	68.7	80.6	76.1	74.2	71.8	79.4	76.6	75.4	79.7	78.5	78.9	79.1	95.6	71.1	78.3	81.5	49.1	80.6	68.7	61.0
0.5	84.9	78.2	80.6	81.4	87.1	76.4	**80.1**	81.4	89.9	75.5	**80.3**	82.0	98.2	62.7	69.8	76.5	65.4	79.5	74.3	71.8
0.6	91.3	76.0	**81.3**	83.0	93.2	73.1	79.4	81.9	94.4	71.3	78.2	81.2	99.4	54.3	57.9	70.2	74.7	78.4	77.1	76.5
0.7	94.8	72.9	79.8	82.4	96.4	67.4	74.9	79.3	97.2	65.3	72.7	78.1	99.4	53.3	56.1	69.4	81.8	77.1	78.8	79.4
0.8	98.2	65.1	72.8	78.3	98.8	57.5	63.0	72.7	98.5	58.7	64.6	73.6	99.4	53.2	56.1	69.3	89.9	74.3	**79.4**	81.4
0.9	99.4	57.1	62.4	72.6	99.7	52.2	54.1	68.5	99.5	54.0	57.3	70.0	99.4	53.2	56.1	69.3	94.5	69.2	76.3	79.9
1.0	100.0	50.0	50.0	66.7	100.0	50.0	50.0	66.7	100.0	50.0	50.0	66.7	100.0	50.0	50.0	66.7	100.0	50.0	50.0	66.7

Italian

th	EDIT				LCSR				RD				JW				XDICE			
	R	P	A	F	R	P	A	F	R	P	A	F	R	P	A	F	R	P	A	F
0.0	03.8	100.0	51.9	07.2	03.8	100.0	51.9	07.2	03.8	100.0	51.9	07.2	03.8	100.0	51.9	07.2	03.8	100.0	51.9	07.2
0.1	08.5	71.3	52.5	15.3	08.6	70.0	52.5	15.4	15.7	72.7	54.9	25.9	58.3	70.8	67.1	64.0	15.4	72.4	54.8	25.4
0.2	35.7	70.6	60.4	47.4	36.3	69.1	60.0	47.6	40.8	68.9	61.2	51.2	80.5	67.8	71.1	73.6	33.4	72.9	60.5	45.8
0.3	60.3	70.6	67.6	65.0	61.9	69.7	67.5	65.6	64.1	68.0	67.0	66.0	91.5	66.4	**72.6**	77.0	47.8	70.6	64.0	57.0
0.4	76.0	68.5	70.6	72.1	77.7	67.6	70.2	72.3	79.6	66.8	70.0	72.6	96.7	63.5	70.5	76.7	61.1	69.2	66.9	64.9
0.5	88.5	67.4	**72.8**	76.5	90.1	66.1	**72.0**	76.3	88.5	65.1	**70.6**	75.0	99.4	58.2	64.0	73.4	72.6	67.7	69.0	70.1
0.6	93.1	66.0	72.6	77.3	94.6	64.0	70.7	76.4	94.2	63.0	69.5	75.5	99.8	52.5	54.7	68.8	80.0	66.9	70.2	72.9
0.7	96.5	64.4	71.6	77.3	97.7	61.0	67.7	75.1	98.0	59.7	66.0	74.2	99.8	51.8	53.4	68.2	85.8	65.9	**70.7**	74.5
0.8	99.1	59.4	65.7	74.3	99.7	54.4	58.1	70.4	99.3	55.5	59.8	71.2	99.8	51.7	53.3	68.1	92.6	64.4	70.6	76.0
0.9	99.8	54.5	58.2	70.5	99.9	51.3	52.6	67.8	99.7	52.3	54.4	68.6	99.8	51.7	53.3	68.1	96.5	61.5	68.0	75.1
1.0	100.0	50.0	50.0	66.7	100.0	50.0	50.0	66.7	100.0	50.0	50.0	66.7	100.0	50.0	50.0	66.7	100.0	50.0	50.0	66.7

Table 2: Recall (R), precision (P), accuracy (A) and f-score (F) values (computed as percentages) for orthographic measures in the task of cognates identification when diacritics are accounted for

for identifying cognates. The lists of cognates and non-cognates and the values computed by the orthographic distances for all the words in the Romanian-French and Romanian-Italian datasets are available from the authors on request. We count the occurences of each possible outcome: true positive (TP), true negative (TN), false positive (FP) and false negative (FN). In order to analyse and compare the relevance of these metrics, we further use these results to compute the values for recall, precision, accuracy and f-score using the formulas shown below, as presented in (Manning et al, 2008).

$$recall = \frac{TP}{TP + FN}$$

$$precision = \frac{TP}{TP + FP}$$

$$accuracy = \frac{TP + TN}{TP + TN + FP + FN}$$

$$f - score = 2 * \frac{precision * recall}{precision + recall}$$

The results of our research are listed in Table 2 for the corpus with diacritics and in Table 3 for the corpus without diacritics. We highlighted the maximum accuracy obtained by each metric for thresholds between 0 and 1. Between Jaro and Jaro-Winkler distances, we decided to use only the latter metric in our analysis, as they are similar to a certain extent and we noticed that Jaro-Winkler distance provides better results.

According to the outcome of our investigation, the edit distance identifies Romanian-French and Romanian-Italian cognates with the highest degree of accuracy, reaching its maximum for a threshold value of 0.5 (and 0.6 for French, when diacritics are accounted for), followed closely by Jaro-Winkler distance and the longest common subsequence ratio. An interesting situation can be observed for Jaro-Winkler distance, whose accuracy decreses dramatically starting with 0.5 threshold, especially when diacritics are not taken into consideration. As expected, for each orthographic method the accuracy increases, reaches a maximum and then decreases, due to the precision-recall tradeoff. However, it is interesting to observe the similarity for the longest common subsequence ratio, rank distance and edit distance with regard to their accuracy curves when diacritics are accounted for. XDice and Jaro-Winkler distances exhibit different behaviours, in that Jaro-Winkler reaches its maximum accuracy for a threshold value lower than the average, while XDice has maximum accuracy for a higher threshold value. This behaviour stands for both languages.

It can be noticed that the orthographic approaches we used obtain higher degrees of accuracy for French than for Italian, which implies the fact that the orthographic changes undergone in the process of adapting to the Romanian language are a better indicator of cognacy for words with

French

th	EDIT				LCSR				RD				JW				XDICE			
	R	P	A	F	R	P	A	F	R	P	A	F	R	P	A	F	R	P	A	F
0.0	08.9	100.0	54.4	16.3	08.9	100.0	54.4	16.3	08.9	100.0	54.4	16.3	08.9	100.0	54.4	16.3	08.9	100.0	54.4	16.3
0.1	12.3	94.0	55.8	21.7	12.9	93.2	56.0	22.6	21.4	87.7	59.2	34.4	58.1	80.6	72.0	67.5	13.4	90.3	56.0	23.3
0.2	34.1	81.2	63.1	48.0	35.9	80.6	63.6	49.7	54.6	82.5	71.5	65.7	82.6	77.9	79.6	80.2	28.3	81.8	61.0	42.1
0.3	60.5	82.0	73.6	69.6	62.9	81.0	74.1	70.8	73.4	79.9	77.4	76.5	92.5	74.5	**80.4**	82.5	48.8	80.6	68.5	60.8
0.4	77.1	79.8	78.8	78.4	79.3	78.2	78.6	78.8	85.4	77.1	**80.0**	81.1	96.7	69.4	77.0	80.8	63.8	79.5	73.7	70.8
0.5	89.1	77.1	**81.4**	82.7	90.9	75.0	**80.3**	82.2	92.3	73.4	79.4	81.8	98.8	60.6	67.3	75.1	76.4	78.5	77.7	77.4
0.6	93.9	74.8	81.1	83.3	95.3	71.2	78.4	81.5	95.5	68.9	76.2	80.0	99.5	53.6	56.7	69.7	82.5	77.3	79.1	79.8
0.7	96.5	71.4	78.9	82.1	97.6	65.3	72.9	78.3	97.8	62.7	69.9	76.4	99.6	52.6	55.0	68.9	87.5	75.6	**79.6**	81.1
0.8	98.5	63.1	70.5	76.9	99.1	55.8	60.3	71.4	98.9	56.7	61.8	72.1	99.6	52.6	54.9	68.8	93.0	72.2	78.6	81.3
0.9	99.6	55.6	60.0	71.3	99.8	51.6	53.0	68.0	99.7	52.9	55.4	69.1	99.6	52.6	54.9	68.8	96.7	66.6	74.1	78.9
1.0	100.0	50.0	50.0	66.7	100.0	50.0	50.0	66.7	100.0	50.0	50.0	66.7	100.0	50.0	50.0	66.7	100.0	50.0	50.0	66.7

Italian

th	EDIT				LCSR				RD				JW				XDICE			
	R	P	A	F	R	P	A	F	R	P	A	F	R	P	A	F	R	P	A	F
0.0	06.7	100.0	53.4	12.6	06.7	100.0	53.4	12.6	06.7	100.0	53.4	12.6	06.7	100.0	53.4	12.6	06.7	100.0	53.4	12.6
0.1	12.2	77.0	54.3	21.0	12.3	75.7	54.2	21.2	17.5	73.8	55.7	28.3	63.8	70.9	68.8	67.1	19.1	74.4	56.2	30.4
0.2	41.4	70.9	62.2	52.3	42.3	69.5	61.9	52.6	43.5	68.6	61.8	53.2	84.9	68.0	72.5	75.5	38.6	72.8	62.1	50.5
0.3	64.6	70.3	68.6	67.3	66.3	69.4	68.6	67.9	66.8	67.9	67.6	67.4	94.0	66.2	**73.0**	77.7	52.6	70.6	65.3	60.2
0.4	80.1	68.9	72.0	74.1	82.0	67.8	71.5	74.2	82.9	66.7	70.8	74.0	97.7	62.7	69.8	76.4	65.9	69.4	68.4	67.6
0.5	91.8	67.5	**73.8**	77.8	93.3	66.1	**72.7**	77.4	91.3	64.9	**70.9**	75.8	99.6	57.1	62.3	72.6	76.9	68.1	70.4	72.2
0.6	95.4	65.7	72.9	77.8	96.7	63.4	70.5	76.6	95.9	62.2	68.8	75.5	99.9	52.0	53.9	68.4	84.1	67.2	71.6	74.7
0.7	97.8	63.7	71.0	77.1	98.6	59.8	66.2	74.5	98.5	58.5	64.3	73.4	99.9	51.4	52.6	67.8	90.0	66.0	**71.9**	76.2
0.8	99.4	58.1	63.9	73.4	99.7	53.3	56.2	69.5	99.3	54.2	57.7	70.2	99.9	51.3	52.6	67.8	95.1	63.9	70.7	76.4
0.9	99.9	53.6	56.7	69.7	99.9	50.8	51.6	67.4	99.8	51.7	53.4	68.1	99.9	51.3	52.6	67.8	97.7	60.4	66.8	74.6
1.0	100.0	50.0	50.0	66.7	100.0	50.0	50.0	66.7	100.0	50.0	50.0	66.7	100.0	50.0	50.0	66.7	100.0	50.0	50.0	66.7

Table 3: Recall (R), precision (P), accuracy (A) and f-score (F) values (computed as percentages) for orthographic measures in the task of cognates identification when diacritics are not accounted for

French etymons or cognate pairs than for words with Italian etymons or cognate pairs. A possible explanation is that starting with the 19th century numerous words were imported from French. That period represents a stage in the Romanian's language evolution in which norms for the vocabulary of the literary language were defined, including patterns for adapting neologisms to Romanian, and probably many of the French words which entered the language in the 19th century are in this situation.

6 Conclusion and Future Work

In this paper we proposed a dictionary-based approach to identifying cognate pairs. We extracted etymology-related information from online dictionaries and we accounted for etymologies and etymons to detect cognates. We applied our method on a high-volume Romanian corpus and we focused on detecting cognate pairs between Romanian and its most closely related languages, Italian and French. We used this method to investigate to which extent the lexical similarity can be used for automatic detection of cognates, analysing the performances obtained by various orthographic approaches: edit distance, rank distance, longest common subsequence ratio, XDice distance and Jaro-Winkler distance. Our results show that the edit distance classifies pairs of words as cognates or non-cognates with the highest degree of accuracy, obtaining better results for French than for Italian, with some improvements when diacritics are not accounted for.

A possible application for cognates identification is native language detection (Popescu and Ionescu, 2013). We believe that accounting for genetic relationships between words could prove useful for this task. In our future work we intend to further investigate the performances of the orthographic approaches to the task of cognates identification by introducing an additional step of parameter tuning for the threshold value in our procedure. We plan to apply this method of identifying cognates on the entire *dexonline* dictionary. In this paper we focused on the cognates that are most frequently used in Romanian, but we believe that obtaining an almost exhaustive dataset of Romanian-French and Romanian-Italian cognate pairs would be an important achievement.

Acknowledgements

The authors thank the anonymous reviewers for their helpful and constructive comments. The contribution of the authors to this paper is equal. Research supported by a grant of the Romanian National Authority for Scientific Research, CNCS – UEFISCDI, project number PN-II-ID-PCE-2011-3-0959.

References

George.W. Adamson and Jillian Boreham. 1974. The use of an association measure based on character structure to identify semantically related pairs of words and document titles. *Information Storage and Retrieval*, 10: 253–260.

Quentin D. Atkinson, Russell D. Gray and Geoff K. Nicholls, David J. Welch. 2005. From words to dates: water into wine, mathemagic or phylogenetic inference? *Transactions of the Philological Society*, 103: 193–219.

Chris Brew and David McKelvie. 1998. Word-pair extraction for lexicography. *Proceedings of the 2nd International Conference on New Methods in Language Processing, Ankara, Turkey*, 45–55.

Chris Buckley, Claire Cardie, Mandar Mitra and Janet Walz 1998. Using Clustering and SuperConcepts within SMART: TREC 6. *Proceedings of the Sixth Text Retrieval Conference (TREC-6).*

Lyle Campbell. 2003. How to Show Languages are Related: Methods for Distant Genetic Relationship. In Joseph, Brian D. and Richard W. Janda (eds.). *The Handbook of Historical Linguistics. Blackwell.*

Beatrice Chin, Bali Ranaivo-Malançon, Ee-Lee Ng and Alvin W. Yeo. 2010. Identification of Closely-Related Indigenous Languages: An Orthographic Approach. *International Journal of Asian Language Processing*, 20(2): 43–62.

Bojana Dalbelo Bašic and Jan Šnajder. 2009. String distance-based stemming of the highly inflected Croatian language. *Proceedings of the International Conference RANLP-2009. Borovets, Bulgaria*, 411–415.

Antonella Delmestri and Liviu P. Dinu. 2012. An Assessment of String Similarity Methods for Cognate Identification *In Methods and Applications of Quantitative Linguistics: Selected papers of the VIIth International Conference on Quantitative Linguistics (QUALICO), Belgrade, Serbia, April, Editors: Ivan Obradović, Emmerich Kelih, Reinhard Köhler*, 16–19.

Ton Dijkstra, Franc Grootjen and Job Schepens. 2012. Distributions of cognates in Europe as based on Levenshtein distance. *Bilingualism: Language and Cognition*, 15: 157–166.

Anca Dinu and Liviu P. Dinu. 2005. On the Syllabic Similarities of Romance Languages. *A. Gelbukh (ed.): CICLing 2005, Lecture Notes in Computer Science*, 3406: 785–789.

Liviu P. Dinu and Andrea Sgarro. 2006. A Low-complexity Distance for DNA Strings. *Fundam. Inform.*, 73(3): 361–372.

Diana Inkpen, Oana Frunza and Grzegorz Kondrak. 2005. Automatic Identification of Cognates and False Friends in French and English *RANLP-2005, Bulgaria*, 251–257.

Cristian Grozea. 2012. Experiments and Results with Diacritics Restoration in Romanian. *TSD 2012*, 199–206.

Matthew A. Jaro. 1989. Advances in record linkage methodology as applied to the 1985 census of Tampa Florida. *Journal of the American Statistical Society*, 84(406): 414--20.

Kevin Knight, Grzegorz Kondrak and Daniel Marcu. 2003. Cognates Can Improve Statistical Translation Models. *Proceedings of the Human Language Technology Conference of the North American Chapter of the Association for Computational Linguistics, Companion volume of the Proceedings of HLT-NAACL 2003*, 46–48.

Grzegorz Kondrak. 2001. Identifying cognates by phonetic and semantic similarity. *NAACL '01 Proceedings of the second meeting of the North American Chapter of the Association for Computational Linguistics on Language technologies*, 1–8.

Vladimir I. Levenshtein. 1965. Binary Codes Capable of Correcting Deletions, Insertions, and Reversals. *Soviet Physics Doklady*, 10: 707–710.

Christopher D. Manning, Prabhakar Raghavan and Hinrich Schütze. 2008. *Introduction to Information Retrieval.* Cambridge University Press, Cambridge, UK.

Dan Melamed. 1995. Automatic Evaluation and Uniform Filter Cascades for Inducing N-Best Translation Lexicons. *In Proceedings of the Third Workshop on Very Large Corpora.*

Marius Popescu and Radu Tudor Ionescu. 2013. The Story of the Characters, the DNA, and the Native Language. *In Proceedings of the BEA-8 Workshop of NAACL.*

Michel Simard, George F. Foster and Pierre Isabelle. 1992. Using Cognates to Align Sentences in Bilingual Corpora. *In Proceedings of the Fourth International Conference on Theoretical and Methodological Issues in Machine Translation.*

William E. Winkler. 1990. String Comparator Metrics and Enhanced Decision Rules in the Fellegi-Sunter Model of Record Linkage. *Proceedings of the Section on Survey Research Methods (American Statistical Association)*, 354—359.

A Pilot Study on the Semantic Classification of Two German Prepositions: Combining Monolingual and Multilingual Evidence

Simon Clematide
Computational Linguistics
University of Zurich
simon.clematide@cl.uzh.ch

Manfred Klenner
Computational Linguistics
University of Zurich
klenner@cl.uzh.ch

Abstract

This paper reports on the annotation and maximum-entropy modeling of the semantics of two German prepositions, *mit* ('with') and *auf* ('on'). 500 occurrences of each preposition were sampled from a treebank and annotated with syntacto-semantic classes by two annotators. The classification is guided by a perspective of information extraction, relies on linguistic tests and aims at the separation of semantically transparent and opaque meanings (that is of collocational constructions). Apart from descriptive statistical material, we present results of experiments using monolingual and multilingual evidence (the latter from informative English and Spanish translations) in order to predict the semantic classes.

1 Introduction

In linguistics, scientific grammars (Zifonun et al., 1997) as well as grammars for language learners (Helbig and Buscha, 2001) follow a long-standing tradition of semantic classification of prepositional phrases. However, it is less well-known which classification schemes can be used for automatic sense disambiguation, supporting for instance applications of information extraction and knowledge discovery.

In this pilot study, we want to gain experience of how to classify the semantic contributions of various prepositions from a multilingual perspective. Our main goal is to distinguish between semantically transparent contributions that prepositions can provide in a general or productive manner and the less transparent contributions in collocational constructions. Many prepositions are subcategorized by verbs (or adjectives) and the semantic contribution of a selected preposition is weak or unspecific—a fact that is often revealed by cross-lingual comparisons of subcategorization frames. In this study we want to assess the influence of syntactic dependencies and subcategorization on semantic classification. Therefore, we chose to take our material from a syntactically annotated treebank.

The rest of this paper is organized as follows. Section 2 presents related work and approaches. In Section 3, we describe our syntacto-semantic classification system used in the annotation of prepositions sampled from a German treebank. We also present the types of evidence used in the machine learning experiments for the automatic prediction of the classes. Section 4 contains a systematic evaluation of the performance of the different evidence that we have integrated in our approach.

2 Related Work

As Baldwin et al. (2009, p.134) have put it in their introduction to a special issue on that topic in the *Computational Linguistics Journal*: "Information extraction is one application where prepositions are uncontroversially crucial to system accuracy". The underlying task can be cast as preposition (word) sense disambiguation (WSD). It also has been recognized in the machine translation community that "prepositions are hard to translate" (Shilon et al., 2012, p.106). Although semantic information helps to tackle the translation task, the semantic class of a preposition does not perfectly determine the correct translation. As a consequence, these approaches do not strive to carry out preposition WSD, but to use semantic features in order to more directly map source prepositions to target prepositions (Li et al., 2005), be it rule-based (Agirre et al., 2009) or with machine learning given aligned bilingual data (Gustavii, 2005).

A great deal of work on preposition classification and WSD has been carried out on the English language. Most prominent the *Preposition*

Project (Litkowski and Hargraves, 2006) that uses a fine-grained classification scheme derived from the *Oxford Dictionary* (see also the *SemEval* Task on WSD of prepositions, Litkowski (2007)). Other elaborated classification schemes can be found as part of *VerbNet* (Kipper et al., 2004) and *PrepNet* (Saint-Dizier, 2008).

Annotated data is available from the *Penn Treebank* II (Marcus et al., 1994), where thematic roles occurring with prepositional phrases are marked, and *FrameNet* (Baker et al., 1998), which was annotated as part of the *Preposition Project*. There have been a couple of ACL-SIGSEM workshops on prepositions (the last one in 2007) covering all aspects of preposition processing (not only the semantics).

On the methodological side, preposition disambiguation sometimes is coupled with semantic role resources, e.g. O'Hara and Wiebe (2009). There, traditional features for WSD (e.g. the preposition, stem of embedded noun, POS and stem of words in a fixed window around the preposition) are augmented with semantic features stemming from knowledge resources such as FrameNet and *WordNet* (Fellbaum, 1998). In O'Hara and Wiebe (2009), a new feature, hypernym collocation (the WordNet hypernym of the embedded noun), is used to carry out disambiguation relative to either coarse-grained Penn treebank functional roles or more sophisticated FrameNet roles. Syntactic information, e.g. the syntactic function of the PP, is ignored in their system (in contrast to our approach).

As can be seen from the discussion above, there is no canonical classification scheme for preposition disambiguation. Furthermore, the semantic class that a preposition can take is language specific. For German, there are but a few approaches (Hartrumpf et al., 2006; Müller et al., 2011). Müller et al. (2011) rely on an annotation scheme derived from various traditional linguistic theories. 22 prepositions are modeled on the basis of 27 top-level senses. A sense hierarchy is defined (especially for temporal and spatial senses) in order to allow for a more flexible and fine-grained classification. Manually specified decision trees are then used to produce the gold standard classifications.

This scheme is, for our purposes, far too fine-grained and also hard to automatically model by machine learning. However, if their resources were available, we could probably map their scheme to our scheme. No attempt was made by Müller et al. (2011) to learn a model for preposition classification based on their semantic classes. Their approach based on logistic regression as described in Kiss et al. (2010) focuses on determiner omission in PPs.

The work of Hartrumpf et al. (2006) is geared towards a semantic formalism called *MultiNet* (Helbig, 2006), it fully relies on this proprietary resource.

sem\syn	opp	mod	vmod	?mod	–	p	$\sum$
verbal	131	2	3		3		139
nominal	2	120	2	2	3		129
coll	42	3	8			2	55
TEM			6				6
MOD	3		8	4	1		16
LOC	8	10	77	8	5	2	110
DIR	16		7				23
TLOC			9				9
CAU			3	3	1		7
?		1	2		2	1	6
$\sum$	202	136	125	17	15	5	500

Table 1: Distribution of semantic functions of *auf* (*on*) in relation to the syntactic function. The syntactic function "predicative" is labelled as "p".

sem\syn	vmod	mod	opp	?mod	–	$\sum$
verbal	16	8	107	2	1	134
nominal	4	53	7			64
coll	3		1			4
TEM	4			1		5
MOD	46	2	2	6	4	60
INS	75	3	4	1	1	84
ORN	5	56		4	1	66
COM	30	10	3	2	1	46
IDE	8	1		7		16
SIZ	4	6	1	1		12
?	1	3		1	3	8
$\sum$	196	142	125	25	11	499

Table 2: Distribution of the semantic function of *mit* in relation to the syntactic function. The syntactic function predicative is not shown in the table because it appeared only once.

3 Methods

3.1 Resources

As mentioned in Section 2, the Penn Treebank comprises shallow semantic annotations to prepositional phrases (PP). There, a distinction is made between six semantic classes of PPs (and, thus, prepositions): locative, direction, manner, purpose, temporal, and extent. Unfortunately, none of the large German treebanks (TIGER (Brants and Hansen, 2002), Tüba-D/Z (Telljohann et al., 2004)) provide such a comparable rudimentary scheme that could be a starting point for our pilot study. There is no resource, we could use, although one is currently being developed by another group (Müller et al., 2011), but it is not yet released. Since we believe that treebanks could benefit from such an additional annotation layer, we decided to work with a German treebank, the *Tübinger Baumbank* Tüba-D/Z 7.0. It comprises about 65,000 annotated sentences, besides phrase structure, also topological fields and grammatical functions are specified. PPs can act as obligatory or optional (opp) complements of verbs, or as adjuncts (vmod). In the current study, we mainly focus on PPs acting as verb complements (opp) or adjuncts (vmod).

From the ten most frequent prepositions in the Tüba-D/Z we have chosen one with a predominant local and temporal meaning (*auf* 'on') and one with more broader meaning spectrum (*mit* 'with'). We randomly sampled 500 occurrences of each preposition from the Tüba-D/Z and annotated each preposition according to our classification scheme described below.

3.1.1 Semantics of *auf* and *mit*

The intended application is information extraction and question answering. Accordingly, our semantic classes had to be tightly coupled with question words. That is, the way users may ask, determines the granularity of the classification scheme. Typical interrogative words and phrases are *how* (modal), *how long* (temporal, duration), *when* (temporal, time point), *where* (locative).

In the case of *auf* (cf. Table 1), we distinguish between locative (LOC *where*), directional (DIR *where to*), temporal (TEM *when*, *how long*), modal (MOD *how*), and causal (CAUS *why*) PPs. If in a temporal PP the noun is an event (e.g. *party*), then often a locative or a temporal reading is possible (e.g. *when or where did he laugh? - at his party*). We use TLOC to refer to this usage. If the PP acts as a modifier of an adjective or noun, it is annotated with "nominal" (e.g. 'the cup *on the table*'). For the preposition *auf*, we have annotated currently only adjuncts and verb complements with their semantic classes. In case that the verb governs an otherwise semantically vacuous preposition (*warten auf* 'to wait for'), the preposition is marked with "verbal". Finally, any idiomatic expression comprising a PP having a non-compositional meaning like *auf den Putz hauen*, 'to kick up one's heels' is annotated as collocational ("coll"). The preposition does not contribute any semantics in these cases. Sometimes no decision was possible (e.g. given sentence fragments, missing global context, unclear semantics), we used "?" to annotate these cases.

Table 1 shows the distribution of these classes and their syntactic realization. Verb/preposition collocations form the largest class (139), followed by nominal modification (129) and locatives (110). Syntactically, there are three groups to be distinguished: PP complements (opp, 202), NP and PP modification (mod, 136) and adjuncts (vmod, 125). The table reveals a moderate number of interpretation divergences between the Tüba-D/Z annotators and us. Some stem from structural ambiguity (e.g. "?mod" denotes PP attachment ambiguities), and are to be expected. Ideally, however, if a PP bears the functional label "mod", it should be classified as "nominal" in our scheme. Also, a "vmod" should not be annotated as "verbal", since "verbal" means that the preposition is vacuous, while "vmod" means that it acts as an adjunct. For instance, we disagreed with 3 "vmod" (adjuncts) and interpreted them as verb-preposition collocations, also 2 "vmod" are better classified as "nominal" in our view. However, the majority of decisions does not contradict or even is in line with the functional assignments of the Tüba-D/Z. For example, of the 136 "mod" (NP or PP modifications), we placed 120 in our corresponding class "nominal".

In the case of *mit* (cf. Table 2), the syntactic classification labels "verb", "nominal" and "coll" are used as introduced above for *auf*. The prepositions *auf* and *mit* also share two core semantic classes, namely TEM (temporal) and MOD (modal). The other semantic classes of *mit* are: COM for comitative use (*to watch a movie with a friend*), ORN for ornative use (*to tell with humor*), SIZ indicating size or extent (*to demonstrate with 100 people against*), INS for the instrument reading which is a subclass of MOD (modal) (*to break with a hammer*), and IDE for identity (*with him, hope enters the room* meaning: *he represents/is identical with hope*).

As with *auf*, there are some divergences between the functional annotations of the Tüba-D/Z and our annotation decisions, especially concerning “vmod” and “mod”. We have not fully traced these divergences back to their origins, but see the previous discussion in the context of *auf*.

3.1.2 Inter-Annotator Agreement

We have measured inter-annotator agreement in two stages: after our initial annotation round, and after some discussion and refinements of our annotation scheme in a second step on a harmonized version of the data. One reason for disagreement concerning *mit* was the annotation with "ornative": a rather sophisticated annotation scheme would allow the use of ORN even in cases where it is modal, but also implicitely qualifies the subject of the sentence (*he says it with a gentle voice*). In these cases, however, it is more natural to ask *how* (*has he said it*), so we disallowed ORN in such examples.

We report the annotator agreement as percentage of agreeing pairs and as Cohen's κ. The initial inter-annotator agreement for *mit* was 85% (κ = .82), while after harmonization it was 91.8% (κ = .90) and 92% (κ = .90) between the harmonized version and the separately created initial annotations of the two annotators, respectively. With *auf* the agreement was lower, namely initially 74% (κ = .67). After harmonization is was 84.8% (κ = .81) and 86.2% (κ = .83), respectively. The main source of confusion here was the annotation scheme of PPs in the context of local verbs (LOC and DIR). The question was whether to treat these roles as adjuncts or as verb complements. Also the decision when to treat a verb-preposition combination as a collocation or not, was not sufficiently well described and operationalized in the guidelines.

The rationale behind our two-stage procedure was to first independently create annotation strategies based on existing classes from the literature and to later refine them to valid annotation guidelines based on the evidence found in the data.

3.1.3 Multilingual Evidence

As already mentioned, prepositional semantics is language-specific: The semantic classes a preposition might express do vary between languages, the semantic contributions given by a preposition in one language are often realized by different prepositions in different languages. Moreover, the semantic functions a preposition (e.g. *mit*) and its direct translation ('with') can bear, might differ. The identity reading of German *mit* is not possible for English 'with'.

The question is, whether a multilingual perspective (for instance in the form of Statistical Machine Translation (SMT)) helps determining the semantic class of a given preposition in the source language. Tables 3 and 4 give a detailed overview of how the prepositions *mit* and *auf* are translated into English and Spanish by *Google Translate*.[1] For instance, *mit* is translated into English as *with*, *of*, *to*, *by*, *in*, or not at all ("0"). Of course, there are predominant translations, for instance *mit* was translated 372 times by *with* and *con*. There is also a tendency to choose equivalent prepositions across languages, e.g. *a* and *to* (Table 4: 71 cases), but quite often different prepositions are selected. Since we use imperfect translations from SMT we cannot be sure whether the aforementioned differences stem from mistranslations or whether they reveal a true difference. In order to clarify this question one could exploit parallel treebanks. However, currently available resources covering German such as SMULTRON (Volk et al., 2010) still have a limited size (approx. 2500 sentences).

The question is whether inter-language divergence of preposition usage helps to determine the semantic class of a preposition in the source language. Or more technically, whether there is a correlation between semantic classes of the source language preposition and a translation made by SMT. Even if such a correlation turns out not to be a strong one, it might nevertheless help as a feature in a machine learning model.

3.1.4 Annotation and Translation: Examples

For illustration purposes, we give two examples of semantic annotations of PPs and the mapping of the German prepositions therein to English prepositions via automatic translation with Google translate.

In the first case, *auf* does not carry any semantics, it is part of the verb (*warten auf*). Accordingly, it is annotated as "verbal". In English, the corresponding verb construction is 'to listen to',

[1]For this experiment, we manually mapped the prepositions from the translated sentences using the phrase alignment visualization of `http://translate.google.com`. English and Spanish was chosen since according to `http://matrix.statmt.org/matrix` the translation quality of German to English and Spanish is best and at the same time both target languages belong to different language families.

es\en	*with*	0	*by*	*to*	*of*	*in*	*on*	*about*	*as*	*from*	∑
con	372	7	1	6	1			1			388
0	3	48		2	1	1	1		1		57
de	10	5	1		6					1	23
a	7	5	1			1					14
por	1	1	6								8
en	1					2	2				5
como		2									2
y		2									2
para				1							1
∑	394	70	9	9	8	4	3	1	1	1	500

Table 3: Translations (Google Translate) of German *mit* in English and Spanish. Columns and rows are ordered by margin frequencies.

es\en	*on*	*to*	0	*in*	*at*	*of*	*for*	*about*	*by*	*with*	*around*	∑
en	182	7	7	27	17		1		1		2	244
a	8	71	6	2	10	2	2			1		102
0	7	7	33			3	6	1				57
de	9	10	2	5	1	17	3					47
sobre	15	2						1				18
para		8					4					12
por	5		1				1		1			8
con	1	2			1					1		5
contra	2											2
∑	229	107	49	34	29	22	17	2	2	2	2	495

Table 4: Translations of German *auf* in English and Spanish. Translations appearing only once are not shown.

which is correctly identified by Google Translate. The sentence pairs are: *Man muss auf diesen Aufschrei hören* and 'You have to listen to this outcry'.

The second examples illustrates that the same semantic class, LOC (local), might be realized by two different prepositions in German and in English. The preposition *auf* in German can be used to indicate the 'place of living' of a person, if it is a small island (like Sardinia). This is not possible in English. The sentence pairs are: *Selbst wenn sie in entlegenen Städtchen auf Sardinien leben* and 'Even if they live in remote town in Sardinia'.

Note that in these examples *auf* was not mapped to its direct translation which is 'on'.

3.2 Supervised Machine Learning Approach

In order to measure the difficulty of an automatic classification of the syntacto-semantic classes expressed by *auf* and *mit* we conducted several experiments with the Maximum-Entropy Modeling tool MegaM (Daumé III, 2008).[2] For this pilot study, we focused on simple features gained from the syntactical configuration (perfect data from the Tüba-D/Z), textual data from the context, and multilingual evidence from Spanish and English translations (imperfect Google translations).

In Section 4 we present and analyze the contribution of the following feature sets:

head Word, part of speech (POS), and lemma of the head word (typically a noun) of the dependent phrase of the preposition, for instance, the head of *mit Sorgfalt* is *Sorgfalt* 'care'. In case of coordinated PPs and multi-word heads, the first token was selected.
syntax The syntactic function of the PP taken from the TübaD/Z.
neighbor Word, POS, and lemma of the preceding and following token.
context Word, POS, and lemma in a window of 5 preceding and following tokens (taken as a bag of words, lemmas and POS).
en English translation of the preposition produced by the Google translation of the German sentence.
es Spanish Google translation of the preposition.

[2]Maximum-Entropy modeling is also known as logistic regression. In our experiments, we used the default regularization parameter $\lambda = 1$ of MegaM.

4 Results and Discussion

The evaluations described below assess the performance improvement for the multi-class predictions of our annotated prepositions (500 occurrences each) by using different sets of features as evidence. We evaluate against a baseline system which basically predicts the majority class given the lack of any additional evidence. All results are reported as mean accuracy computed by cross-validation. No stratification of class labels has been applied to the folds of the cross-validation. Accuracy is the proportion of true classifications delivered by the system.

4.1 Syntacto-Semantic Classification

We performed a 10-fold cross-validation evaluation for the scenario of predicting the full set of all syntactic and semantic classes (cf. Table1 and 2).

The evaluation results of *auf* are shown in Table 5. The best system uses the feature sets "head", "neighbor" and "syntax", however, "syntax" is by far the strongest feature. If perfect syntactic analyses are not available, "head" and "neighbor" information can compensate for more than 2/3 of the performance gain. The effect of "syntax" is especially strong for *auf* because the nominal modifiers are classified according to syntactic criteria only. A future, more semantically oriented classification of noun modifiers will probably weaken this effect. Multilingual evidence from informative Google translations improves considerably over the (weak) baseline. Combining the evidence from Spanish and English performs slightly better than each language separately does. Therefore, translations into multiple languages are useful for the case of *auf*. However, the best systems are those without any translation evidence from Spanish or English.

Table 6 shows the corresponding results for *mit*. The overall performance is lower but the feature sets have a very similar ranking of predictive power. The lower performance stems from the fact that *mit* has 11 syntacto-semantic classes with a more uniform distribution than *auf* (10 classes). The best system without the feature "syntax" involves 3 different feature sets, "context", "neighbor" and "en". However, these feature sets can only compensate for less than half of the performance gain of the feature set "syntax" derived from the treebank syntax structure. The best system performance is reached if either English or Spanish evidence is added. However, the improvement given by multilingual evidence is rather small.

Evidence	Mean	SD	$_\triangle abs_{bs}$	$_\triangle rel_{bs}$
baseline	25.4	7.5		
head	27.2	7.8	+1.8	+7.1
en	38.6	10.5	+13.2	+52.0
es	39.0	8.7	+13.6	+53.5
context	45.4	9.9	+20.0	+78.7
neighbor	53.4	7.6	+28.0	+110.2
syntax	68.6	7.2	+43.2	+170.1
en/es	39.4	8.3	+14.0	+55.1
head/neighbor	58.2	6.4	+32.8	+129.1
head/syntax/neigh.	**71.0**	6.6	+45.6	+179.5

Table 5: Performance of feature sets for syntacto-semantic classification accuracy: *auf* ($N = 500$). The column "Mean" contains the average accuracy computed from the cross-validation sets. The column $_\triangle abs_{bs}$ contains the absolute performance gain with respect to the baseline. $_\triangle rel_{bs}$ expresses the relative performance gain. The last row contains the feature set with the best performance.

Evidence	Mean	SD	$_\triangle abs_{bs}$	$_\triangle rel_{bs}$
baseline	26.8	7.1		
head	28.8	7.1	+2.0	+7.5
context	34.6	5.8	+7.8	+29.1
neighbor	36.2	4.0	+9.4	+35.1
syntax	46.4	8.4	+19.6	+73.1
neighbor/context/en	40.4	6.7	+13.6	+50.7
head/syn./neigh.	57.2	7.5	+30.4	+113.4
head/syn./neigh./en	**57.4**	8.2	+30.6	+114.2
syn./neigh./cont./es	**57.4**	7.9	+30.6	+114.2

Table 6: Performance of feature sets for syntacto-semantic classification accuracy: *mit* ($N = 500$).

4.2 Semantic Classification

In a further evaluation, we measured how well the purely semantic classes (i.e. those without "nominal", "verb" and "coll") can be predicted. For *auf* we have 171 cases with a defined semantic classification, for *mit* 290. Due to the smaller training sizes we performed 5-fold cross-validation.

Table 7 illustrates the problems from the skewed distribution of semantic classes in the case of *auf*: Just guessing the largest class LOC represents a baseline decision which is hard to beat. Only the feature set "head" can improve over this baseline, all other features either deteriorate the system performance or do not improve it. Interestingly, the best system combines the translation evidence from Spanish with the feature set "head". Adding

Evidence	Mean	SD	$\triangle abs_{bs}$	$\triangle rel_{bs}$
baseline	72.9	6.7		
head	75.3	6.4	+2.4	+3.2
head/syntax/neigh./es	**77.6**	7.7	+4.7	+6.5
head/es	**77.6**	7.7	+4.7	+6.5

Table 7: Performance of feature sets for semantic classification accuracy: *auf* ($N = 171$). The following classes are considered: LOC, DIR, MOD, TLOC, CAU, TEM.

Evidence	Mean	SD	$\triangle abs_{bs}$	$\triangle rel_{bs}$
baseline	26.2	9.9		
head	27.6	8.8	+1.4	+5.3
context	36.6	12.3	+10.3	+39.5
neighbor	39.3	13.7	+13.1	+50.0
syntax	42.1	4.5	+15.9	+60.5
head/neigh./en/es	40.7	11.3	+14.5	+55.3
head/syntax/neigh.	**52.4**	5.7	+26.2	+100.0

Table 8: Performance of feature sets for semantic classification accuracy: *mit* ($N = 290$). The following classes are considered: TEM, MOD, INS, ORN, COM, IDE, SIZ.

more feature sets does not improve the results (see Table 7 second last row).

The less skewed distribution of semantic classes in the case of *mit* allows for a significant improvement over the baseline system. Table 8 shows that most feature sets have a beneficial effect, and therefore, classification performance is almost doubled by the best system. In contrast to the syntacto-semantic classification, multilingual evidence does not contribute to the best system. The only configuration where multilingual evidence improves performance appears if the syntactic dependency information from the treebank is dropped. The best system without the feature set "syntax" relies on English and Spanish evidence.

The results of our experiments in using multilingual evidence for the syntacto-semantic and semantic classification of prepositions are mixed. The syntactico-semantic classification of *auf* works best without multilingual evidence although there is a weak correlation between the feature sets "en" and "es" and the syntacto-semantic classes. However, the best system of the syntactico-semantic classification of *mit* profits from added multilingual evidence although this evidence taken as a single feature set cannot beat the baseline.

For the purely semantic classification, no improvement over the baseline can be found by the multilingual evidence for both prepositions. Still, multilingual evidence helps in these cases where syntactic information is not valuable (in the case of *auf*), or if we mute this feature (in the case of *mit*).

5 Conclusion

Our annotation and modeling experiments illustrate the different semantic and distributional characteristics of the considered German prepositions *auf* and *mit*. The skewed distribution of the semantic classes of *auf* represent a challenge for any classifier. If small semantic classes should be detected, more training material is needed for these cases. The application of Active Learning techniques (Settles, 2012) might help to efficiently collect such data.

Our experiments with maximum entropy modeling indicate that informative Google translations of prepositions do not lead to a significant performance improvement in semantic classification. Simple monolingual contextual features generally perform better. The inclusion of perfect (i.e. treebank-derived) syntactic dependency information generally performs best. However, for practical systems only imperfect syntax analyses from error-producing parsers are available. Future research is needed to assess the performance decrease if parser output is provided instead of handcrafted manual annotation.

Another topic for future work is the integration of further language resources. Bilingual lexicons such as dict.cc[3] contain information about semantically void subcategorized prepositions, for instance *auf jdn warten* is linked to *to wait for sb.* Statistical collocation analyses derived from large German corpora are provided by services such as "Wortschatz Leipzig"[4] or "Digitales Wörterbuch der Deutschen Sprache"[5].

Given the available amount of electronic texts, the application of distributional semantics for preposition disambiguation and for modeling of the semantic fingerprint of prepositions also seems promising (cf. (de Cruys and Apidianaki, 2011)).

Finally, contextual features might profit from synonym expansion or synonym set classification, a technique also used by Kiss et al. (2010).

[3]See `http://www.dict.cc`

[4]See `http://wortschatz.uni-leipzig.de`

[5]See `http://dwds.de`

References

Eneko Agirre, Aitziber Atutxa, Gorka Labak, Mikel Lersundi, Aingeru Mayor, and Kepa Sarasola. 2009. Use of rich linguistic information to translate prepositions and grammar cases to Basque. In *Proceedings of the XIII Conference of the European Association for Machine Translation (EAMT)*, pages 58–65.

Collin F. Baker, Charles J. Fillmore, and John B. Lowe. 1998. The Berkeley FrameNet project. In Christian Boitet and Pete Whitelock, editors, *COLING-ACL*, pages 86–90. Morgan Kaufmann Publishers / ACL.

Timothy Baldwin, Valia Kordoni, and Aline Villavicencio. 2009. Prepositions in applications: A survey and introduction to the special issue. *Computational Linguistics*, 35(2):119–149.

Sabine Brants and Silvia Hansen. 2002. Developments in the TIGER annotation scheme and their realization in the corpus. In *Proceedings of the Third Conference on Language Resources and Evaluation (LREC 2002)*, pages 1643–1649, Las Palmas.

Hal Daumé III. 2008. MegaM: Maximum entropy model optimization package. ACL Data and Code Repository, ADCR2008C003.

Tim Van de Cruys and Marianna Apidianaki. 2011. Latent semantic word sense induction and disambiguation. In Dekang Lin, Yuji Matsumoto, and Rada Mihalcea, editors, *ACL*, pages 1476–1485. The Association for Computer Linguistics.

Christiane Fellbaum. 1998. *WordNet: An Electronic Lexical Database*. Bradford Books.

Ebba Gustavii. 2005. Target language preposition selection – an experiment with transformation-based learning and aligned bilingual data. In *Proceedings of the XIII Conference of the European Association for Machine Translation (EAMT)*, pages 112–118.

Sven Hartrumpf, Hermann Helbig, and Rainer Osswald. 2006. Semantic interpretation of prepositions for NLP applications. In *Proceedings of the Third ACL-SIGSEM Workshop on Prepositions*, pages 29–36.

Gerhard Helbig and Joachim Buscha. 2001. *Deutsche Grammatik: Ein Handbuch für den Ausländerunterricht*. Langenscheidt.

Hermann Helbig. 2006. *Knowledge Representation and the Semantics of Natural Language*. Cognitive Technologies. Springer.

Karin Kipper, Benjamin Snyder, and Martha Palmer. 2004. Using prepositions to extend a verb lexicon. In *Proceedings of the HLT/NAACL Workshop on Computational Lexical Semantics*, pages 23–29.

Tibor Kiss, Katja Keßelmeier, Antje Müller, Claudia Roch, Tobias Stadtfeld, and Jan Strunk. 2010. A logistic regression model of determiner omission in PPs. In Chu-Ren Huang and Dan Jurafsky, editors, *COLING (Posters)*, pages 561–569. Chinese Information Processing Society of China.

Hui Li, Nathalie Japkowicz, and Caroline Barrière. 2005. English to Chinese translation of prepositions. In *Canadian Conference on AI*, volume 3501 of *Lecture Notes in Computer Science*, pages 412–416. Springer.

Kenneth C. Litkowski and Orin Hargraves. 2006. Coverage and inheritance in The Preposition Project. In *Third ACL-SIGSEM Workshop on Prepositions*, pages 37–44.

Kenneth C. Litkowski. 2007. CLR: Integration of FrameNet in a text representation system. In *Proceedings of the Fourth International Workshop on Semantic Evaluations (SemEval-2007)*, pages 113–116, Prague, Czech Republic, June. ACL.

Mitchell P. Marcus, Grace Kim, Mary Ann Marcinkiewicz, Robert MacIntyre, Ann Bies, Mark Ferguson, Karen Katz, and Britta Schasberger. 1994. The Penn treebank: Annotating predicate argument structure. In *HLT*, pages 114–119. Morgan Kaufmann.

Antje Müller, Claudia Roch, Tobias Stadtfeld, and Tibor Kiss. 2011. Annotating spatial interpretations of German prepositions. In *ICSC*, pages 459–466. IEEE.

Tom O'Hara and Janyce Wiebe. 2009. Exploiting semantic role resources for preposition disambiguation. *Computational Linguistics*, 35(2):151–184.

Patrick Saint-Dizier. 2008. Syntactic and semantic frames in PrepNet. In *IJCNLP*, pages 763–768. ACL.

Burr Settles. 2012. *Active Learning*, volume 6 of *Synthesis Lectures on Artificial Intelligence and Machine Learning*. Morgan & Claypool.

Reshef Shilon, Hanna Fadida, and Shuly Wintner. 2012. Incorporating linguistic knowledge in statistical machine translation: Translating prepositions. In *Proceedings of the EACL-2012 Workshop on Innovative Hybrid Approaches to the Processing of Textual Data*, pages 106–114.

Heike Telljohann, Erhard W. Hinrichs, and Sandra Kübler. 2004. The Tüba-D/Z Treebank: Annotating German with a Context-Free Backbone. In *LREC*, pages 2229–2232. European Language Resources Association.

Martin Volk, Anne Göhring, Torsten Marek, and Yvonne Samuelsson. 2010. SMULTRON (version 3.0) — The Stockholm MULtilingual parallel TReebank. electronic.

Gisela Zifonun, Ludger Hoffmann, and Bruno Strecker. 1997. *Grammatik der deutschen Sprache*. Schriften des Instituts für deutsche Sprache; 7.1-3. de Gruyter, Berlin; New York.

Semantic Relations between Events and their Time, Locations and Participants for Event Coreference Resolution

Agata Cybulska
VU University Amsterdam
De Boelelaan 1105
1081HV Amsterdam
a.k.cybulska@vu.nl

Piek Vossen
VU University Amsterdam
De Boelelaan 1105
1081HV Amsterdam
piek.vossen@vu.nl

Abstract

In this study, we measure the contribution of different event components and particular semantic relations to the task of event coreference resolution. First we calculate what event times, locations and participants add to event coreference resolution. Secondly, we analyze the contribution by hyponymy and granularity within the participant component. Coreference of events is then calculated from the coreference match scores of each event component. Coreferent action candidates are accordingly filtered based on compatibility of their time, locations, or participants. We report the success rates of our experiments on a corpus annotated with coreferent events.

1 Introduction

In this paper, we present an approach to event coreference resolution that employs the importance of full and partial linguistic coreference between events and their participants, times and locations. The goal of this work is to measure the contribution of different components of event descriptions to the task of event coreference resolution. Another goal is to calculate what semantic relations add to event coreference. Considering the goals, we deliberately do not use machine learning as we want to have a clear picture of what the contributions are by different factors. Having an idea of how various event components influence event coreference, will guide the feature choice for machine learning.

Descriptions of one and the same event can differ in specificity and granularity (compare: *two students taken hostage in Beslanian school* vs. *two people taken hostage in a classroom in Beslan Russia*). High level events, as *war*, are more general and abstract with longer time span and group participants; low level events, e.g. a *shooting* event, are rather specific with shorter duration, and individual participants (Cybulska, Vossen, 2010). To capture differences between event representations and to identify relations between events, we applied an event model that consists of 4 components: a location, time, participant and an action slot (see Van Hage et al., 2011 for the formal SEM model along the same lines). In our previous work we extracted conflict-related actions (e.g. *war, genocide, shooting* or *fighting*) and their participants, locations and times from text. Next, we determine relations between event mentions, starting with getting some insights into event coreference.

2 Related Work

One of the recent approaches to event coreference resolution was proposed by Bejan and Harabagiu (2010), who experimented with nonparametric Bayesian models. Another one, by Chen et al. (2011) employs support vector machines with tree kernels and spectral graph partitioning. These approaches do not explicitly account for partial coreference of events, where some of the event components are related through hyponymy or part-of relationship, which is the focus of our work. Bejan and Harabagiu noted in their paper that not accounting for partial coreference is the reason for one of the common errors in their output. The approach of Chen et al. accounts for synonymy between mentions but not for meronymy or hyponymy.

Soft matching was successfully used for entity coreference resolution. Taxonomy based semantic similarity and semantic relatedness (Wikipedia based) were used as features in a machine learning approach to entity coreference by

Ponzetto and Strube (2006). Some semantic features based on synset relations in WordNet are used by Ng and Cardie (2002) and Ng (2005), while Harabagiu et al. (2001) use hyponymy, meronymy and other semantic relations from WordNet for NP coreference. They employ WordNet to distinguish between individuals and groups amongst entities of category PERSON.

Entity coreference has been used explicitly for event coreference resolution in the experiments by Lee et al. (2012); where entities and event clusters are merged by means of linear regression. Partial coreference is incorporated by using distributional similarity as one of features for cluster comparison. Other approaches use entities for event coreference in a more indirect way e.g. Bejan and Harabagiu (2008 and 2010) by using semantic roles as features for their SVM classifiers. Bejan and Harabagiu (2010) account only for synonymy amongst heads of semantic roles. Chen and Ji (2009) check for verbal argument compatibility for *Time-Within* and *Place* roles. Their results indicate that features related to event arguments only slightly (ca. +1% MUC and B3) improve event coreference, possibly due to wrong argument labeling. In this work, we measure the influence of time, place and participants on the task of event coreference resolution.

A theory-oriented discussion about the nature of full-, near- and non-identity and a continuum approach to entity coreference is presented in Recasens et al. (2011a). A discussion of full and quasi identity of events, pointing out the significance of partial coreference for coreference resolution, is held in Hovy et al. (2013).

Semantic shifts have been used before in NLP applications. Mulkar-Mehta et al. (2011a) investigated granularity shifts and structures in natural language. They focused on modeling part-whole relations between entities and events and causal relations between coarse and fine granularities. In their follow-up work (2011b), they described an algorithm for extracting causal granularity structures from text and its possible applications. Howard and Abramson (2012) use granularity types for prediction of rhetorical relations. Their results show that granularity types significantly improve prediction of rhetorical relations amongst clauses. In our work, we measure the contribution of shifts in granularity and abstraction to the task of event coreference resolution.

3 Approach to Coreference Resolution

Our approach to event coreference makes two crucial assumptions. First of all, we assume that solving coreference between actions is not enough to solve event coreference. If one only considers the action component it is impossible to determine whether two action mentions refer to the same event in reality, compare: *car bombing in Madrid in 1995* with *car bombing in Spain in 2009*. This is why, to solve event coreference we employ an event model which consists of 4 components: action, (human) participant(-s), location, and time. In accordance with the Quinean theory (1985), we assume that coreference between elements of the contextual setting of events is crucial for solving event coreference. Time and place in which an event happened form the starting point for event coreference resolution, compare: *genocide in Srebrenica* with *genocide in Rwanda*. Without time and place information event actions are just denotations of abstract classes of concepts. They need to be anchored in time and space to become instantiated.[1] Coreference thus only makes sense for events within the same time and place. Hence for each event mention in text, one should first define time and place and after that, for events occurring within a compatible time and space, search for linguistic coreference clues. From a practical point of view, determining event time and place should limit the number of candidates for coreferent events and improve the precision of event coreference resolution.

Secondly, we make the assumption that (linguistic) coreference is not an absolute notion. For example, *shooting* and *several shots* can refer to the same event and people may have different or vague intuitions about their identity (for a discussion of full and partial coreference see also Hovy et al. 2013). This approach employs a gradable notion of confidence in coreference with a continuum of non-disjoint events on which coreference of events (*bombing* vs. *bombing attack*) gradually transitions into other event relations as scriptal (event vs. its subevent e.g. *explosion* as a step in the script of a *bombing attack*), is-a (*bombing* being a kind of *attack*) and membership relations (*attack* being a member of *series of attacks*). The gradual notion of confidence in coreference inversely correlates with semantic distance between two instances. Semantic distance between instances of an event component can be determined by the kind of se-

[1] An interesting exception are event descriptions that depict instances of events that over time have become proper names as *World War II, 9/11, Srebrenica massacre*.

Event Components	Is-a: *Class>Subclass*	Inclusion: *Part-of, Member*
Location	*city>capital*	*Bosnia>Srebrenica*
Participants	*officer>colonel*	*army>soldier*
Time	*weekday>Friday*	*week>Monday*
Action	*attack>bombing*	*series of attacks>attack*

Table 1. Examples of event components related through hyponymy and meronymy.

mantic relation between them. In text one comes across specific and general actions, participants, time expressions and locations; compare e.g. *shooting, fighting, genocide* and *war,* or participants: *soldier* vs. (multiple) *soldiers* vs. *troops* and *multiple troops*. The same holds for time markers as *day, week* and *year* and for locations: *city* vs. *region* vs. *continent.* Table 1 exemplifies instances of event components related through hyponymy and meronymy. Mentions of event components are either (partially) overlapping or disjoint. Next to rather clear indicators typically used in coreference resolution as repetition, synonymy, anaphora and disjunction (negative indicator), significant relations between event components are along a hyponymy axis: class vs. its subclass such as *officer* being a subclass of the class *person*, instance-of a class such as *Bosnia* being an instance of the class *country*; and along a meronymy axis: member vs. group i.e. *Colonel Karremans* being a member of the group of *Dutch UN soldiers* or part vs. whole relation as *Srebrenica* being a part of *Bosnia*. For a thorough description of the model that captures the relationship between different semantic relations and coreference on one end of the spectrum and (if not disjoint) other event relations on the other, see our previous work (Cybulska, Vossen, 2012).

Within this approach, we analyze semantic relations and semantic distance between two instances of each event component, to obtain a coreference score per component. We do not only take exact lemma-based matches of event mentions into account but we allow for soft matching based on shifts in levels of granularity and abstraction. Our intuition is that shifts vs. agreement in the level of granularity and in the level of abstraction play a crucial role in establishing coreference relations; obviously together with other coreference indicators such as lemma repetition, anaphora, synonymy and disjunction. Once semantic distance and granularity agreement is calculated for every component of an event pair, the separate scores are combined into a single score for an event pair indicating the likelihood of real world coreference as a whole. Through empirical testing, we determine thresholds for establishing optimal coreference relations across events and their components.

4 Experiments

For the experiments we used the stand-off annotation of events (Lee et al. 2012) on top of the EventCorefBank (ECB) corpus[2], annotated with cross - document coreference between event mentions. The corpus contains 482 texts from Google News (selected based on inclusion of keywords such as *commercial transaction, attack, death* or *sports*) and grouped into 43 topics.

To measure the influence of time, location and participants on event coreference resolution, we first extract the set of events from the evaluation data. The ECB texts were processed by means of tools developed within the KYOTO project[3]. First, the corpus was lemmatized and tagged with PoS and syntactic information (Stanford Parser[4]). Next, word sense disambiguation was performed and the corpus was annotated with synsets from the English Wordnet (version 3.0) and with predefined ontology classes. The event ontology was manually assigned to 266 hypernyms in WordNet. It consists of four main semantic classes of concepts – one for each event component – location, time, participant and action which altogether cover 53964 synsets. All manually annotated actions from the corpus were used as input in the experiments. To extract participants, locations and times newly created extraction rules for English were used, based on manual annotation of event components in 5 independent texts. By means of the Kybot module of KYOTO, event times, participants and locations were extracted through rules employing some syntactic clues, PoS and combinatory information together with semantic class definition and exclusion by means of WordNet (Cybulska, Vossen, 2011).

There are two main stages to this experiment. First we generate preliminary chains of

[2] http://faculty.washington.edu/bejan/data/ECB1.0.tar.gz, Bejan and Harabagiu, 2010
[3] The ECB corpus texts after processing with the KYOTO tools (a pipeline of linguistic processors) are available at http://www.newsreader-project.eu/results/data/.
[4] http://www-nlp.stanford.edu/software/lex-parser.shtml

coreferring actions within a topic based on semantic similarity with the objective to ensure maximal recall. Similarity between mentions can be calculated by means of different techniques. We employed a taxonomy based edge counting technique of Leacock and Chodorow (1998) [5], which considers the closest hyponymy path in WordNet between two synsets scaled by the overall depth of the taxonomy:

*(Si,j)=log(M(Di,j)/(2*Avg(Ddepth)))*

where *Si,j* is the similarity between mentions *i* and *j* from *M* (total set of mentions in a topic); where *M(Di,j)* is the minimal distance between two concepts and *Avg(Ddepth)* is the average depth in WordNet for all meanings of all candidates in the topic. Mentions with relatively short semantic distance between their heads, constitute candidates for coreference chains. For mentions that use the same word, we ignore the synset but consider distance of 1. For synonyms, we use distance of 2. In all other cases, we add the hypernym distance to the initial value of 2. After obtaining the similarity scores for all mentions in a topic we normalize the scores. We created a matrix between all mentions in a topic and calculated the Leacock and Chodorow similarity (from now on also referred to as L&C) scores. A maximum recall was obtained if we keep equivalence relations for similarity scores of 20% or more of the highest score within a topic (usually the lemma). For each event mention, we thus keep candidate coreference relations to other mentions if the score is 0.2 or higher.

In our previous work, coreference of event actions was based solely on action similarity. In this part of the research, a second step was added to the process namely additional filtering of semantically similar actions based on compatibility of their participants, times and locations.

To experiment with semantic relations we use two different heuristics to determine participant compatibility: hyponymy and granularity. Note that this participant compatibility is not limited to full identity of participants. Soft matching of participants is more appropriate for the purpose of this task to account for cases of metonymy, e.g. *US aircrafts* instead of *US army.*

To generate chains of coreferent participants based on hyponymy, again we use the L&C (the same procedure as in case of action similarity). We determined the optimal coreference threshold for participant mentions on 0.7 normalized L&C score.

Our second heuristic calculates distance in granularity. Coreference chains are created in case of small distance in granularity levels between mentions. To determine granularity levels, we defined two semantic classes over synsets in WordNet: *gran_person* (e.g. *soldier, doctor)* denoting individual participants and *gran_group* referring to multiple participants (e.g. *army* or *hospital*). These two classes cover 36 WordNet hypernyms which map to 9922 synsets. On top of agreement in granularity levels, we also account for lexical granularity clues within a level such as number and multiplications. At this point we make a rough distinction between one and multiple items within a concept type (e.g. *gran_person*). Difference in granularity level or number is treated as indication of a granularity shift and is turned into a distance measure. To better handle 43415 [6] participant mentions that were POS - tagged as named entities, we decided to add an intermediate *gran_instance* class (for named entity participants that have no synsets such as person or organization names as *John,* or *Doctors Without Borders*) so that we can encourage number matching for our measurements of what granularity exclusively can contribute to event coreference. For agreement in semantic class level, two participant instances can maximally get 3 points. If there is 1 level difference between them (*gran_person* > *gran_instance* or *gran_instance* > *gran_group*) distance of 2 is determined. In case of participant pairs with *gran_person* and *gran_group* we have distance of 1. For number agreement we can maximally assign 2 points. If there is number disagreement – we assign 1 point. If there is both – level type agreement as well as number agreement a participant pair is given the maximum of 5 points.

As this paper aims at measuring the influence of different event components on event coreference, in the evaluation we filter our action chains based on location and time compatibility. In line with our theoretical approach, we see filtering on disjoint time and locations as crucial for event coreference resolution. For locations and time expressions, very strict thresholds were used, to avoid matches as *Monday* and *Tuesday*, sharing a short path in the taxonomy and consequently a high L&C score. The same holds for the granularity and domain heuristics. This is why, for the time being, only lemma and synonym matches are used. In the future we will look into treating proper names differently, and apply

[5] In the future we will also experiment with other methods.

[6] Out of the total of 54236 extracted participant mentions.

Heuristic	Event Slot	MUC			B3			CEAF	BLANC			CoNLL
		R	P	F	R	P	F	R/P/F	R	P	F	F
LmB	**All N&V**	63.8	82.8	71.2	65.3	90.6	75.0	65.9	68.0	84.1	71.1	70.7
L&C	**Action**	69.4	72.4	69.5	69.4	73.3	68.9	58.7	68.6	71.8	67.5	65.2
Action L&C, Time Lm	**Action Time**	66.0	77.7	70.6	66.9	84.2	73.6	63.9	68.4	78.1	70.1	69.4
Action L&C, Location Lm	**Action Location**	66.3	77.4	70.6	67.4	83.0	73.4	64.1	68.6	77.3	70.0	69.3
Action L&C, Participant Lm	**Action Participant**	66.0	78.4	70.8	67.0	84.9	73.9	64.5	68.6	79.0	70.4	69.7
Action L&C, ParticipantL&C	**Action Participant**	65.2	79.4	70.7	66.8	85.7	74.1	64.9	68.5	79.7	70.4	69.8
Action L&C, Part.granularity	**Action Participant**	66.5	0,7 7.8	70.4	67.6	81.7	72.2	62.5	68.3	77.9	69.4	68.2

Table 2. Coreference Evaluation in MUC, B3, CEAFm, BLANC and CoNLL F (macro averages).

similarity and granularity measurements to time expressions and locations that are not proper names. We will also consider employing geo and temporal ontologies containing proper names.

Our current approach boosts the score of action coreference for each participant, time and location coreference chain they share, taking the coreference score of each chain as a weight for sharing. We used a formula in which membership to a coreference set of an event is initially based on the coreference score of the action mention but it is strengthened by the proportion that participants, time references or locations are shared with other mentions:

$Coref(m,E)=MAXLC(m,E) + P(p) \vee P(t) \vee P(l)$

where E is the set of mentions in action coreference set, $MAXLC$ is the highest similarity score for the mention m in the set E. The coreference score of action mention m equals the sum of the maximum coreference score $MAXLC$, and proportion P of overlapping participants p (of m with the other members of the set) or times t or locations l, with other members of the set.

5 Evaluation Results

For the evaluation, the manual annotations of actions from the ECB corpus were used as key chains and were compared with the response chains generated for each topic by means of the above described heuristics. Since our goal was to evaluate the importance of coreference between other event components (than actions) for the task of event coreference resolution, we compare our evaluation results with system results based on action similarity only, i.e. when disregarding other event components. We also aimed at getting some insights into the contribution by shifts in hyponymy and granularity (soft matching). This is why we use a lemma baseline *(LmB)* that assigns coreference relation to all nouns and verbs that belong to the same lemma (strict matching). Table 2 presents coreference evaluation results achieved by means of the different heuristics: the L&C measure, granularity agreement as well as lemma match *(Lm)* in comparison to the baseline results *(LmB)* in terms of recall *(R)*, precision *(P)* and F-score *(F)*, employing the commonly used coreference evaluation metrics: MUC (Vilain, 1995), B3 (Bagga, Baldwin, 1998), mention-based CEAF (Luo, 2005), BLANC (Recasens, Hovy, 2011b), and CoNLL F1 (Pradhan et al., 2011).

Compared to the lemma baseline, our approach using similarity of event actions only (second row in table 2), across majority of the evaluation metrics improves *R* with up to 6% while loses (2-17%) *P*, what is expected. It is worth noticing, that the baseline achieves remarkably good results, what could be caused by the fact that the annotators are drawn to pick up on the most obvious coreference cases. Within narrowly defined topics, such as news articles of the same day on a specific event, these are usually expressed by the same lemma.

When comparing the contribution of participants, times and locations (all lemma matches for the sake of comparison) with the approach using exclusively action similarity, we see that the approach combining action and participant components achieved slightly better results (ca. 1% higher precision scores) than the two other approaches employing time and location slots. Altogether, the differences between the scores are in this case rather subtle. When analyzing these results one must keep in mind that these evaluation scores are conditioned by the fact that participant descriptions occur much more frequently in event descriptions than time and place markers.[7]

Out of the two different heuristics used in participant approaches; ca. 1% higher F-scores (a 2-4% improvement of precision) on most evaluation metrics were obtained with L&C similarity. Both participant approaches in most metrics improve the F-scores achieved by the action similarity heuristic; the granularity approach with ca. 1-4% and participant similarity with ca. 1-6%.

Compared to the lemma baseline *(LmB)*, our best scoring approach of all, that is action similarity with participant similarity, on most metrics loses ca. 1% on the F-scores. It gains up to 2 points in recall, while generating output with ca. 4% lower precision. This small decline in F measure can be motivated by the fact that we are dealing here with within topic coreference (although cross – document). Also, evaluation data seem to be biased towards coreference chains around smaller events. Corpora, even those annotated with cross-document coreference of events, (intentionally) tend to be composed around specific real world events, such as attacks or earthquakes, so that coreference chains are captured in a rather small time frame. The diversity of event instances from the same type of event class that happened in different time frames, places and with different participants is much lower in such a corpus than in the real world, e.g. realistic daily news streams. The relatively high scores achieved by the lemma baseline show the need for different event coreference datasets, where cross-document coreference is marked in text across different instances of particular event classes, e.g. describing two different *wars* that take place over longer stretches of time and include similar types of events. Only then the data will become more representative of the sampled population.

Compared to evaluation results achieved in related work:

- Bejan and Harabagiu, 2010: 83.8% B3 F, 76.7% CEAF F on the ACE (2005) data set and on the ECB corpus 90% B3 F, 86.5% CEAF F-score
- Lee et al., 2012: 62.7% MUC, 67.7% B3 F, 33.9% (entity based) CEAF,71.7% BLANC F-score on the ECB corpus
- Chen et al., 2011: 46.91% B3 F on the OntoNotes 2.0 corpus

by means of our best scoring approach, using action and participant similarity, coreference between actions was solved with an F-score of 70.7% MUC, 74.1% B3, 64.9% CEAFm, 70.4% BLANC F and 69.8 CoNLL F1. Considered that our approach neither considers anaphora resolution nor syntactic features, there is definitely room for improvement of event coreference resolution for an approach that combines these with semantic matches of event components.

6 Conclusion and Future Work

In this paper, we presented our approach to event coreference that employs the importance of coreference (also partial linguistic coreference) between participants, locations and times for the task of event coreference resolution. Our results show that filtering coreferent action candidates based on compatibility of their participants (our best scoring approach) in comparison to the baseline slightly improves precision of the resolution of coreference between events. The results are especially promising given the limitations of the approach, such as not performing anaphora resolution. In the future, we will further experiment with coreference resolution, amongst others by applying our method to cross – topic coreference of events, to find out whether there is more variation in structural properties if one considers not only different texts, but also various topics. If that is the case, semantic matches should turn out to be even more important.

Furthermore, we will experiment with clustering techniques as a heuristic to identify coreference sets, where different event components as well as hyponymy and meronymy agreement, are used as features.

Acknowledgments

This study is part of the Semantics of History research project at the VU University Amsterdam and the European FP7 project NewsReader (316404). The authors are grateful to the anonymous reviewers as well as the generous support of the Network Institute of the VU University Amsterdam. All errors are our own.

[7] From the ECB corpus we extracted 54236 participant, 5728 location and 3435 time mentions.

References

ACE-Event. 2005. ACE English Annotation Guidelines for Events, ver. 5.4.3 2005.07.01.

Bagga, Amit and Breck Baldwin, "Algorithms for Scoring Coreference Chains", in Proceedings of LREC 1998

Bejan, Cosmin Adrian and Sanda Harabagiu, "A Linguistic Resource for Discovering Event Structures and Resolving Event Coreference", in Proceedings of the 6th International Conference on Language Resources and Evaluation (LREC), Marrakech, Morocco, 2008

Bejan, Cosmin Adrian and Sanda Harabagiu, "Unsupervised Event Coreference Resolution with Rich Linguistic Features", in Proceedings of the 48th Annual Meeting of the Association for Computational Linguistics, Uppsala, Sweden, 2010

Chalupsky, Hans et al., "The RACR Machine Reading System", in prep. 2013

Chen, Zheng and Heng Ji, "Event Coreference Resolution: Algorithm, Feature Impact and Evaluation", in Proceedings of Events in Emerging Text Types (eETTs) Workshop, in conjunction with RANLP, Bulgaria, 2009

Chen, Bin, Su, Jian, Pan, Sinno Jialin and Chew Lim Tan, "A Unified Event Coreference Resolution by Integrating Multiple Resolvers", in Proceedings of the 5th International Joint Conference on Natural Language Processing, Chiang Mai, Thailand, November, 2011

Cybulska, Agata and Piek Vossen, "Event models for Historical Perspectives: Determining Relations between High and Low Level Events in Text, Based on the Classification of Time, Location and Participants", in Proceedings of LREC 2010, Valletta, Malta, May 17-23, 2010

Cybulska, Agata and Piek Vossen, "Historical Event Extraction from Text", in Proceedings of ACL LaTeCH, Portland, US, June 2011

Cybulska, Agata, and Piek Vossen, "Using Semantic Relations to Solve Event Coreference in Text", in Proceedings of the Workshop: Semantic Relations-II. Enhancing Resources and Applications (SemRel2012), Istanbul, Turkey, May 2012

van Hage, Willem Robert, Malaisé, Véronique, Segers, Roxane, Hollink, Laura and Guus Schreiber, "Design and use of the Simple Event Model (SEM)", in Journal of Web Semantics 9(2):128-136, July 2011.

Harabagiu, Sanda M., Bunescu, Razvan C. and Steven J. Maiorano, "Text and Knowledge Mining for Coreference Resolution", in Proceedings of the second meeting of the North American Chapter of the Association for Computational Linguistics on Language technologies, 2001

Howald, Blake Stephen and Martha Abramson, "The Use of Granularity in Rhetorical prediction", in Proceedings of the First Joint Conference on Lexical and Computational Semantics (*SEM), pages 44-48, Montreal, Canada, 2012

Hovy, Eduard, Mitamura, Teruko, Verdejo, Felisa and Philpot, Andrew, "Identity and Quasi-Identity Relations for Event Coreference", in prep.2013

Ide, Nancy and David Woolner, 2007, "Historical Ontologies", in: Ahmad, Khurshid, Brewster, Christopher, and Mark Stevenson (eds.), Words and Intelligence II: Essays in Honor of Yorick Wilks, Springer, 137-152.

Kuebler, Sandra and Denislava Zhekova, "Singletons and Coreference Resolution Evaluation", in Proceedings of Recent Advances in NLP, Hissar, Bulgaria, September, 2011

Leacock, Claudia and Martin Chodorow, "Combining local context with WordNet similarity for word sense identification", in Christiane Fellbaum (ed.), WordNet: A lexical Reference System and its Application, MIT Press, Cambridge, MA.

Lee, Heeyoung, Recasens, Marta, Chang, Angel, Surdeanu, Mihai and Dan Jurafsky, "Joint Entity and Event Coreference Resolution across Documents", Proceedings of the 2012 Conference on Empirical Methods in Natural Language Processing and Natural Language Learning (EMNLP-CoNLL), 2012

Luo, Xiaoqiang, "On coreference resolution performance metrics", in *Proceedings of the Human Language Technology Conference and Conference on Empirical Methods in Natural Language Processing (EMNLP-2005)*, 2005

Mulkar-Mehta, Rutu, Hobbs, Jerry R. and Eduard Hovy,"Granularity in Natural Language Discourse",in Proceedings of International Conference on Computational Semantics, 2011a

Mulkar-Mehta, Rutu, Hobbs, Jerry R. and Eduard Hovy, "Applications and Discovery of Granularity Structures in Natural Language Discourse", in Proceedings of The Tenth International Symposium on Logical Formalizations of Commonsense Reasoning at the AAAI Spring Symposium, Palo Alto, 2011b

Ng, Vincent, "Machine Learning for Coreference Resolution: From Local Classification to Global Ranking", in *Proceedings of the 43rd Annual Meeting of the Association for Computational Linguistics (ACL)*, 2005

Ng, Vincent and Claire Cardie, "Improving Machine Learning Approaches to Coreference Resolution", in *Proceedings of the 40th Annual Meeting of the*

Association for Computational Linguistics (ACL), Philadelphia, 2002

Ponzetto, Simone Paolo and Michael Strube, "Exploiting Semantic Role Labeling, WordNet and Wikipedia for Coreference Resolution", in Proceedings of the Human Language Technology Conference of the North American Chapter of the ACL, pages 192-199, New York, 2006

Pradhan, Sameer, Ramshaw, Lance, Marcus, Mitchell, Palmer, Martha, Weischedel, Ralph and Nianwen Xue, "CoNLL-2011 shared task: Modeling unrestricted coreference in OntoNotes", in *Proceedings of CoNLL 2011: Shared Task,* 2011.

Quine, Willard V., "Events and Reification" in E. LePore and B.P. McLaughlin (eds.), Action and Events, Basil Blackwell, New York, 1985

Recasens, Marta, Hovy, Eduard and M. Antònia Martí, "Identity, non-identity, and near-identity: Addressing the complexity of coreference", Lingua, 121(6):1138-1152, 2011a

Recasens, Marta and Eduard Hovy, "BLANC: Implementing the Rand index for coreference evaluation", *Natural Language Engineering*, 17(4):485–510, 2011b

Vilain, Marc, Burger, John, Aberdeen, John, Connolly Dennis and Lynette Hirschman, "A model theoretic coreference scoring scheme", in *Proceedings of MUC-6*, 1995

Sense Clustering Using Wikipedia

Bharath Dandala, Chris Hokamp and Rada Mihalcea
University of North Texas
bharathdandala@gmail.com
chris.hokamp@gmail.com
rada@cs.unt.edu

Razvan C. Bunescu
Ohio University
bunescu@ohio.edu

Abstract

In this paper, we propose a novel method for generating a coarse-grained sense inventory from Wikipedia using a machine learning framework. Structural and content-based features are employed to induce clusters of articles representative of a word sense. Additionally, multilingual features are shown to improve the clustering accuracy, especially for languages that are less comprehensive than English. We show the effectiveness of our clustering methodology by testing it against both manually and automatically annotated datasets.

1 Introduction

The granularity of word sense repositories has been recognized as an important factor in the development of annotated datasets for Word Sense Disambiguation (WSD) (Snow et al., 2007), with significant impacts upon both the performance of automatic WSD systems and their utility for downstream applications. Previous work on manual sense annotations with respect to WordNet has revealed low levels of agreement between human annotators, ranging between 65% (Chklovski and Mihalcea, 2002) and 72% (Snyder and Palmer, 2004), which is a clear indicator of very fine-grained word senses that are difficult to differentiate, even for humans.

To achieve the sense granularity appropriate for WSD, word senses that are closely related in meaning are grouped together in a sense clustering step. While this task was originally defined in relation to more traditional sense inventories, such as WordNet (Hovy et al., 2006; Mihalcea and Moldovan, 2001) or the Oxford dictionary (Navigli, 2006), newer user-contributed sense inventories such as Wikipedia or Wiktionary are also quickly expanding and refining the senses defined for a word, thus pointing to the need of sense clustering for coarser word sense distinctions.

In this paper, we specifically focus on the task of sense clustering over Wikipedia senses. Wikipedia has been recently recognized as a rich resource for WSD (Bunescu and Pasca, 2006; Mihalcea, 2007; Mihalcea and Csomai, 2007; Milne and Witten, 2008), offering a significantly increased coverage of word meanings relative to established repositories such as WordNet or Roget. At the same time, WSD systems using Wikipedia have been shown to obtain comparable or even increased disambiguation precision. While earlier work on WSD using the 2007 version of Wikipedia reported an average of three senses per word for a dataset of 30 nouns (Mihalcea, 2007), more recent work on the same dataset using the 2012 version of Wikipedia has shown a significant increase to an average of nine senses per word (Dandala et al., 2012). For instance, the noun "paper", which used to have five different senses, now has ten senses; similarly, the noun "bar", which previously had ten senses, now has 23 senses. The accuracy of a WSD system on the same set of 30 nouns dropped from an average of 85% when using Wikipedia 2007 to 62% when using Wikipedia 2012 (Dandala et al., 2012). Thus, the rapid growth of Wikipedia over the recent years has brought benefits, such as increased word and sense coverage, but it has also led to complications, such as finer sense granularity, resulting in a markedly reduced performance of WSD systems.

Related work on lexical resources, such as WordNet, has demonstrated the benefit of sense clustering. For example, work on mapping WordNet senses to the coarser Oxford dictionary (Navigli, 2006; Navigli et al., 2007) has resulted in improved WSD performance. The OntoNotes project, a large-scale effort to cluster and supplement word senses in WordNet in order to produce a high-quality dataset for automatic WSD (Hovy et al., 2006), has also been beneficial for other language processing tasks such as discourse analysis, coreference resolution, and semantic parsing. Coarser sense inventories also make it easier to identify synonyms or translations of selected words in context, which can lead to improvements in information retrieval (Zhong and Ng, 2012), semantic indexing (Gonzalo et al., 1998), and machine translation (Chan et al., 2007).

In this paper, we address two main research questions. First, can we build an accurate method to automatically cluster the fine-grained senses in Wikipedia? We describe a set of structural and content features that are integrated in a machine learning framework in order to automatically predict when two Wikipedia senses are close in meaning and should be clustered together. Second, can we use the multilingual links in Wikipedia to derive additional multilingual features to enhance this clustering? We rely upon the interlingua links in Wikipedia, and upon features that can be obtained from sense representations in other languages, in order to enrich the feature space and improve clustering accuracy.

In the following sections, we first briefly review Wikipedia as a large encyclopedic resource, focusing on the specific representation of word senses and groups of related word senses. We then introduce several novel datasets for sense clustering, which we use in our evaluations. Several structural and content features are described next, followed by a description of the experiments that we ran in order to evaluate the utility of these features. We conclude the paper with a discussion of the results and a presentation of related work.

2 Senses and Sense Clusters in Wikipedia

The basic entry in Wikipedia is an *article* (or, for the purpose of this paper, *word sense*[1]), which defines and describes a concept, an entity, or an event, and consists of a hypertext document with hyperlinks to other pages within or outside Wikipedia. The role of the hyperlinks is to guide the reader to pages that provide additional information about the entities or events mentioned in an article. Articles are organized into *categories*, which in turn are organized into category hierarchies. For instance, the article on ALAN TURING is included in the category BRITISH CRYPTOGRAPHERS, which in turn has a parent category named BRITISH SCIENTISTS, and so forth.

Each article in Wikipedia is uniquely referenced by an identifier, consisting of one or more words separated by spaces or underscores, and occasionally a parenthetical explanation. For example, the article for the entity Turing that refers to the *"English computer scientist"* has the unique identifier ALAN TURING, whereas the article on Turing with the *"stream cipher"* meaning has the unique identifier TURING (CIPHER).

The disambiguation pages and the internal link graph of Wikipedia are a source of metadata, which can be exploited to transform the flat encyclopaedic format of Wikipedia into a rich Ontology. A structure that is particularly relevant to the work described in this paper is that of the *disambiguation pages*, which are specifically created for ambiguous entities, and consist of links to articles defining the different meanings of the entity. The unique identifier for a disambiguation page typically consists of the parenthetical explanation (DISAMBIGUATION) attached to the name of the ambiguous entity, as in e.g. SENSE_(DISAMBIGUATION), which is the unique identifier for the disambiguation page of the noun "sense". Disambiguation pages, if well-curated, can provide good clues about the set of senses defined in Wikipedia for a word, as well as the possible clusters over these senses, through the headings that group articles along named semantic axes generally corresponding to mid-level nodes in the Wikipedia category hierarchy.

Finally, also relevant for the work described in this paper are the *interlingual links*, which explicitly connect articles in different languages. For instance, the English article for the noun SENSE is connected, among others, to the Spanish article SENTIDO (PERCEPCIÓN) and the Latin article SENSUS (BIOLOGIA). On average, about half of the articles in any Wikipedia version include interlingual links to articles in other languages. The number of interlingual links per article varies

[1]The terms "article" and "word sense" are interchangeably used in this paper. Note that we are excluding articles that refer to named entities.

from an average of 5 in the English Wikipedia, to 10 in the Spanish Wikipedia, to 23 in the Arabic Wikipedia. Wikipedia editions are available for more than 280 languages, which vary widely in size. We use four of these Wikipedias in this work, namely the English, Spanish, German, and Italian versions.

3 Datasets for Sense Clustering

To evaluate our automatic sense clustering method, we build four datasets: two that are generated automatically through a set of heuristics applied on clusters extracted from existing disambiguation pages in English or Spanish, and two that are obtained through manual annotations. Additionally, we create a dataset obtained from clustering a set of Semeval word senses. All datasets follow the same format, and consist of pairs of articles annotated as either positive or negative, depending on whether they should be grouped together under one sense or not.

3.1 Automatically Extracted Datasets

We first create two large datasets using the clusters already available in some of the disambiguation pages in Wikipedia. We specifically selected only disambiguation pages that have at least five subheadings, a requirement that ensures that the word is polysemous and that also indicates that the disambiguation page is well-curated and likely to be trustworthy. After resolving redirects, we removed any duplicate senses. We then removed those senses that have less than three mentions in Wikipedia. Finally, since one of our goals is to experiment with multilingual features, we also removed senses that do not exist in all four target languages.

From the set of disambiguation pages obtained after applying all of these heuristics, we generate a dataset as follows: all of the senses that are listed under the same subheading (except for the OTHER, SEE ALSO, and MISCELLANEOUS headings) are used to create pairs of senses that are labeled as positive (i.e., they should be clustered together). All of the senses that are listed under different headings, while still on the same disambiguation page, are used to create pairs of senses that are labeled as negative (i.e., they should not be clustered). From the resulting list of pairs, we first exclude all named entities, since our work is primarily concerned with word sense clustering rather than named entity clustering. Additionally, the groupings of the named entities in the Wikipedia disambiguation pages are too coarse; for instance, in the disambiguation page for "Newton," the articles "Isaac Newton" and "Newton (surname)" are listed under the same heading "People." As mentioned above, we exclude those senses that do not have interlingua links with the other three languages of interest (i.e., a word sense in our dataset has to be represented in all languages English, Spanish, German, Italian). This constraint is applied so that we have a complete multilingual representation for our dataset, which allows us to test our hypothesis concerning the usefulness of multilingual features.

Using this approach, we automatically create two datasets, one for English and one for Spanish. Starting with the English Wikipedia disambiguation pages, from all the sense pairs obtained using the heuristics above, we randomly select a set of 3,000 positive examples and their corresponding 3,106 negative examples extracted from the same disambiguation pages, for a total of 6,106 examples.

We then use the same strategy to automatically extract a Spanish sense clustering dataset, this time starting with the Spanish Wikipedia disambiguation pages. Here, we obtain 3,270 positive examples and their corresponding 1,730 negative examples, for a total of 5,000 examples. Our goal with this second dataset is to determine to what extent the sense clustering method can be effectively applied to a language that has fewer articles and contributors than to the English Wikipedia.

3.2 Manually Annotated Datasets

We also create two smaller datasets of 500 examples each, again for English and Spanish, which were manually annotated. The sense pairs (250 positive and 250 negative pairs) were uniformly sampled from sense clusters obtained using the same automatic method described above, excluding the sense pairs that were included in the automatically created datasets. In other words, there is no overlap between the 500 sense pairs in the manually annotated datasets, and the 6,106 (5,000) sense pairs in the automatically created datasets. Annotators were asked to determine whether each pair used the same sense of the target word, or different senses. To help them in this task, an interface was created so that annotators could view each pair of pages side-by-side, in order to decide whether the pair was a positive or a negative example of senses that could be clustered together. Annotators were also given an unknown option to use in cases where they were unsure whether to label a pair as positive or negative.

Two annotators independently labeled the 500 pairs in each of the datasets. The pairwise Pearson correlation between the two annotators was measured at 0.77 and 0.83 for English and Spanish respectively, which represents a high agreement. All disagreements between annotators were resolved through adjudication by a third annotator. The final label distribution was 254 positive pairs and 246 negative pairs in the English dataset, and 212 positive pairs and 288 negative pairs in the Spanish dataset.

3.3 Semeval Dataset

Finally, we also create a dataset using a set of highly ambiguous nouns drawn from the Semeval evaluations, which was previously used in WSD experiments on Wikipedia (Mihalcea, 2007). As before, the sense pairs were labeled as either positive or negative, which resulted in 763 sense pairs marked as negative and 162 sense pairs labeled as positive, for a total of 925 examples. This dataset is built to test our system in a more realistic setting that does not follow all the constraints that we used during the construction of the manually annotated datasets. The only constraint that we placed on this dataset is the removal of named entities, for the reasons outlined above.

4 Structural and Content Features for Sense Clustering

To characterize the similarity of two word senses, we extract two types of features: *structural features*, which exploit the link structure of Wikipedia articles, and *content features* that capture vector space similarities between articles or lexical contexts. We obtain a total of 13 features for each pair of articles in each language.

4.1 Structural Features

Two well-established metrics are used to measure the similarity between the link structures of the senses in each pair. For each pair of articles, we derive four graph-based similarity features using Pointwise Mutual Information (PMI) and Google Similarity Distance (GSD) (Cilibrasi and Vitanyi, 2007). PMI and GSD features are calculated between the sets of outgoing links and between the sets of incoming links. Thus, there are four features that indicate the similarity between the sets of pages that link to the articles, and the sets of pages that are linked to by the articles. These features exploit the link structure of Wikipedia to measure the pages' relative positions in the link graph.

Two features are added to indicate whether the articles have direct links to each other. The first takes a value of 1 if both articles have a link to each other in the first paragraph, and a value of 0.5 if one of the articles links to the other in the first paragraph (0 otherwise). The second feature extends the context to the entire articles, using the same values to indicate whether one or both of the articles contain a direct link to the other anywhere on the page.

One feature is also included to indicate whether an article's template uses the {{main * <other_article>}} syntax to point to the other article in the pair. The weighting of this feature is the same as that of the direct link features.[2]

Since links between pages are very common in Wikipedia, structural features can provide a good measure of the semantic closeness of two articles, and since our data only contains pairs of articles that are potential disambiguations of a certain word, two articles that have similar link structures are likely to be good candidates for clustering.

4.2 Content Features

The ubiquitous *tf.idf* method for measuring content similarity is used to obtain four additional features. For each article in each language, we created two tf.idf indexes: one for the actual content, and one for the aggregated context of all the inlinks to the page. To construct the aggregated inlink context, the sentences containing a link to the article are globbed into one index, representative of the contexts in which this sense is used across the encyclopedia. Obtaining tf.idf scores for the articles required construction of a global Inverse Document Frequency (idf) index for each language, which was accomplished using Hadoop[3] and Apache Pig.[4] For each pair of senses, we generate four tf.idf features using each possible com-

[2]Note that it is unlikely, though not impossible, that each article could point to the other as its main article

[3]http://hadoop.apache.org/

[4]http://pig.apache.org/

bination of the indexes.

We also use the Stanford Dependency Parser(De Marneffe et al.,) to extract the head noun from each article's title, adding a binary feature that indicates whether the article titles share the same head noun.

Finally, we add a feature for the cosine similarity between the labels for each page. The set of labels for a page is obtained from the anchor text of all inlinks to the page across Wikipedia versions. We remove all occurrences of the target word from the list of labels to prevent unintended bias. For example, if the word in question is "bar" we remove the label "bar". When we move across languages to calculate this feature, the target word is obtained using Google Translate.[5] This set of keywords represents all possible labels for the particular article, and forms a "bag of labels" for that article, to be used in the calculation of the cosine similarity.

4.3 Multilingual Features

The intuition that multilingual features may improve the accuracy of sense clustering is a major inspiration for this work. With this in mind, we calculate the same set of features for the parallel sense pairs in all four languages. This allows evaluation of each language's contribution to the result of sense clustering in a particular language. We do not average the features across languages by creating a centroid vector, preferring instead to append features as languages are added.

5 Experiments and Evaluations

The WEKA toolkit (Witten and Frank, 2005) was used for all experiments. The classifiers were trained using the SMO implementation of Support Vector Machines provided by WEKA, with a quadratic kernel.

5.1 Evaluation on the Automatically Extracted Datasets

In the first experiment, we use the automatically extracted datasets to evaluate the accuracy of the sense clustering classifier, as well as the role of the multilingual features in this classification. We perform cross-validation on the automatically extracted datasets. We use the English and Spanish datasets described in Section 3.1, which include positive and negative examples of sense

[5]http://translate.google.com/

Language(s)	Acc.	Avg. Acc.
Monolingual(English)	84.5%	
English+German	92.0%	
English+Italian	**93.2%**	92.5%
English+Spanish	92.3%	
English+Spanish+German	**93.8%**	
English+Spanish+Italian	93.2%	93.03%
English+German+Italian	92.1%	
English+Spanish+German+Italian	93.6%	**93.6%**

Table 1: Classification accuracy on the automatically extracted English dataset.

pairs along with their corresponding senses in three other languages. For each sense pair, and for each language, we generate the structural and content features described above.

Tables 1 and 2 show the results obtained during these experiments, using one, two, three, or four languages at a time. The results indicate that sense clustering can be effectively performed, and the performance improves consistently as more languages are added. The overall improvements are significant over the most frequent class baseline of 50.8% for English and 65.4% for Spanish.

Language(s)	Acc.	Avg. Acc.
Monolingual (Spanish)	68.3%	
Spanish+English	**74.0%**	
Spanish+German	73.8%	73.0%
Spanish+Italian	71.1%	
Spanish+German+Italian	**75.7%**	
Spanish+Italian+English	75.5%	75.5%
Spanish+German+English	75.4%	
Spanish+English+German+Italian	**76.2%**	**76.2%**

Table 2: Classification accuracy on the automatically generated Spanish dataset.

5.2 Evaluation on Manually Created Datasets

We also perform evaluations on the English and Spanish manually annotated datasets, described in Section 3.2. Here, we use the automatically generated datasets to train the sense clustering classifiers, which we then test on the manually labeled data. Tables 3 and 4 show the results obtained in these experiments, again for one, two, three, and four languages at a time.

As before, the sense clustering classifiers improve over the most frequent class baseline of

Language(s)	Acc.	Avg. Acc.
Monolingual(English)	77.4%	
English+Spanish	85.6%	
English+German	84.8%	85.1%
Spanish+Italian	**85.4%**	
English+German+Italian	**86.0%**	
English+Italian+Spanish	84.4%	85.2%
English+German+Spanish	85.4%	
Spanish+English+German+Italian	**84.4%**	**84.4%**

Table 3: Classification accuracy on manually annotated English dataset.

Language(s)	Acc.	Avg. Acc.
Monolingual(Spanish)	83.7%	
Spanish+English	88.4%	
Spanish+German	87.1%	88.7%
Spanish+Italian	**90.5%**	
Spanish+German+Italian	89.6%	
Spanish+Italian+English	**92.2%**	90.9%
Spanish+German+English	90.9%	
Spanish+English+German+Italian	**95.6%**	**95.6%**

Table 4: Classification accuracy on manually annotated Spanish dataset.

50.8% on the English dataset and 57.6% on the Spanish dataset,[6] and the inclusion of features drawn from additional languages improves the performance of the monolingual classifier significantly.

5.3 Evaluation on Semeval Dataset

The final evaluation is performed on the sense clusters derived from the set of 30 Semeval nouns, as described in Section 3.3. The most frequent class baseline for this dataset is 82.5%, obtained by assigning by default a negative label to all the sense pairs in the dataset. Using the automatically labeled data for training, the monolingual classifier yields an accuracy of 83.5%, and improves to 85.5% when the multilingual features are added. For this dataset, which includes highly ambiguous words and follows a more realistic distribution of positive versus negative sense pairs, the distribution is very skewed, so we also calculate the ROC area, measured at 76.6 for the monolingual classifier, and 79.1 for the multilingual classifier.

[6]These baselines are obtained from the distribution of positive and negative examples in the manual annotation of these datasets.

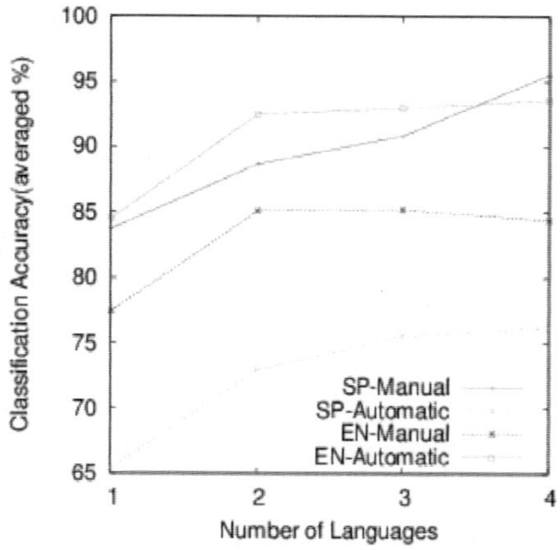

Figure 1: Using automatically and manually created English and Spanish datasets, how the sense clusters benefit from incorporating more languages

6 Discussion

The monolingual sense clustering algorithm leads to significant improvements over the most frequent class baseline, with error rate reductions of 68.5% and 8.3% obtained in the evaluations on the automatically created datasets for English and Spanish respectively, and 54.8% and 67.4%, obtained from the evaluations on the manually-created English and Spanish datasets. On the Semeval dataset, we obtained an error rate reduction of 5.7%.

An even more important result is the role played by the multilingual features in improving the sense clustering method. The incremental addition of new languages leads to steady increases in clustering accuracy. The highest accuracy is obtained when features drawn from all four languages are used, with the following error rate reductions from with the multilingual classifier relative to the monolingual classifier: 58.7% for the English automatic dataset; 24.9% for the Spanish automatic dataset; 30.9% for the English manual dataset; 73.0% for the Spanish manual dataset; and 12.1% for the Semeval dataset. To illustrate the effect of adding more languages graphically, Figure 1 shows how the performance of the Spanish sense clustering benefits from the addition of multilingual features.

The improved performance observed for all possible language groupings is good evidence that the clustering improves consistently as features from a language are supplemented with features from other languages. Even for English, which is a major language with significant resources, we observe improvements when multilingual features are added.These results support our hypothesis that multilingual features can improve the accuracy of sense clustering, even in a more realistic setting where we do not have corresponding sense pairs in all languages. In such cases, when trying to cluster a sense pair from e.g. Spanish, even if features from a more resourceful language such as English are not available, the feature space can still be adjusted with sense pairs from other languages such as German or Italian.

7 Related Work

A large number of techniques have been proposed for clustering the collection of fine-grained senses available in WordNet. One of the early approaches was the automatic system of (Peters et al., 1998), in which two senses are clustered together based on a set of relational cues extracted from WordNet. (Mihalcea and Moldovan, 2001) extend the collection of WordNet relational features and propose a set of semantic and probabilistic rules for either collapsing synsets very similar in meaning or removing synsets that are very rarely used. (McCarthy, 2006) defines vector profiles for WordNet senses based on *neighboring words*, where the distributional similarity between neighbors is computed from statistics over grammatical relations extracted from the British National Corpus corpus. Similarity between two senses is then computed as the Spearman rank correlation of their corresponding vector profiles. The OntoNotes project (Hovy et al., 2006) uses a corpus-based iterative approach for sense clustering in which a sample of 50 sentences is annotated with a preliminary set of coarse senses. If the inter-annotator agreement is too low, the sense clusters are revised, and the annotation process is repeated until the agreement passes 90%. Also related is the work of (Navigli, 2006), who generates coarse senses over WordNet by mapping the WordNet senses into the more coarse-grained Oxford dictionary.

Similar to our approach, (Snow et al., 2007) train an SVM classifier to make binary "merge" vs. "not-merge" decisions. Their WordNet sense pairs are represented using a diverse set of features derived from WordNet structure, corpus-based evidence, and other lexical resources. Furthermore, the binary sense merging classifier is integrated into a model for sense clustering that takes into account taxonomic constraints that arise when merging senses in a hierarchical structures.

Another closely related work is that of (Pedersen et al., 2005), which describes an unsupervised method for discriminating ambiguous names by clustering contexts, and relies upon features found in corpora obtained for a language with more resources.

The major aim of the coarse-grained all-words WSD task at Semeval-2007 was to determine whether a more accurate WSD system can enable sense-aware applications, such as information retrieval, question answering, or machine translation.

Finally, in recent work, Erk and McCarthy (Erk and McCarthy, 2009) also considered the sense granularity issue, and introduced the idea of graded WSD, in which they relax the single sense assignment and allow for multiple sense assignments for a particular target word.

8 Conclusion

Wikipedia's sense inventory is constantly growing, and the sense distinctions in this inventory are becoming finer-grained, which means that robust methods for sense clustering are needed in order to maintain its usefulness for WSD. In this paper, we described an approach to automatically cluster senses in Wikipedia using data obtained from disambiguation pages, utilizing the multilingual data available in Wikipedia to create a rich feature space for sense clustering.

The automatic sense clustering method significantly outperforms the most frequent baseline, and these results are consistent for several datasets and several languages. Moreover, the integration of multilingual information into the clustering method was found to improve significantly over the monolingual models, with consistent improvements as features from new languages are added. Wikipedia editions are available for a large number of languages, which means that this method can be used to generate sense hierarchies and build accurate word sense clustering classifiers for many languages, even in cases where the disambiguation pages for a particular language are not well-curated.

The sense clustering datasets created during this work are publicly available at http://lit.csci.unt.edu

Acknowledgments

This material is based in part upon work supported by the National Science Foundation IIS awards #1018613 and #1018590 and CAREER award #0747340. Any opinions, findings, and conclusions or recommendations expressed in this material are those of the authors and do not necessarily reflect the views of the National Science Foundation.

References

R. Bunescu and M. Pasca. 2006. Using encyclopedic knowledge for named entity disambiguation. In *Proceedings of the European Conference of the Association for Computational Linguistics*, Italy.

Y.S. Chan, H.T. Ng, and D. Chiang. 2007. Word sense disambiguation improves statistical machine translation. In *Proceedings of the Association for Computational Linguistics*, Prague, Czech Republic.

T. Chklovski and R. Mihalcea. 2002. Building a sense tagged corpus with Open Mind Word Expert. In *Proceedings of the ACL 2002 Workshop on "Word Sense Disambiguation: Recent Successes and Future Directions"*, Philadelphia, July.

Rudi L Cilibrasi and Paul MB Vitanyi. 2007. The google similarity distance. *Knowledge and Data Engineering, IEEE Transactions on*, 19(3):370–383.

B. Dandala, R. Mihalcea, and R. Bunescu. 2012. Towards building a multilingual semantic network: Identifying interlingual links in wikipedia. In *Proceedings of the First Joint Conference on Lexical and Computational Semantics (*SEM 2012)*, Montreal, Canada.

Marie-Catherine De Marneffe, Bill MacCartney, Christopher D Manning, et al. Generating typed dependency parses from phrase structure parses.

K. Erk and D. McCarthy. 2009. Graded word sense assignment. In *Proceedings of the Conference on Empirical Methods in Natural Language Processing*.

J. Gonzalo, F. Verdejo, I. Chugur, and J. Cigarran. 1998. Indexing with WordNet synsets can improve text retrieval. In *Proceedings of COLING-ACL '98 Workshop on Usage of WordNet in Natural Language Processing Systems*, Montreal, Canada, August.

E. Hovy, M. Marcus, M. Palmer, L. Ramshaw, and R. Weischedel. 2006. Ontonotes: The 90% solution. In *Proceedings of the Human Language Technology Conference of the NAACL, Companion Volume: Short Papers*, New York City.

D. McCarthy. 2006. Relating wordnet senses for word sense disambiguation. In *Proceedings of ACL Workshop on Making Sense of Sense*.

R. Mihalcea and A. Csomai. 2007. Wikify!: linking documents to encyclopedic knowledge. In *Proceedings of the Sixteenth ACM Conference on Information and Knowledge Management*, Lisbon, Portugal.

R. Mihalcea and D. Moldovan. 2001. Automatic generation of a coarse grained wordnet. In *NAACL 2001 Workshop on WordNet and Other Lexical Resources: applications, extensions and customizations*, pages 35–41, Pittsburgh, June.

R. Mihalcea. 2007. Using Wikipedia for automatic word sense disambiguation. In *Human Language Technologies 2007: The Conference of the North American Chapter of the Association for Computational Linguistics*, Rochester, New York, April.

D. Milne and I. Witten. 2008. Learning to link with Wikipedia. In *Proceedings of the Seventeenth ACM Conference on Information and Knowledge Management*.

R. Navigli, K. Litkowski, and O. Hargraves. 2007. Semeval-2007 task 07: Coarse-grained english all-words task. In *Proceedings of the Fourth International Workshop on Semantic Evaluations (SemEval-2007)*, Prague, Czech Republic, June.

R. Navigli. 2006. Meaningful clustering of senses helps boost word sense disambiguation performance. In *Proceedings of the Annual Meeting of the Association for Computational Linguistics*, Sydney, Australia.

T. Pedersen, A. Purandare, and A. Kulkarni. 2005. Name discrimination by clustering similar contexts. In *Proceedings of the Conference on Computational Linguistics and Intelligent Text Processing*. Springer.

W. Peters, I. Peters, and P. Vossen. 1998. Automatic sense clustering in EuroWordNet. In *Proceedings of the First International Conference on Language Resources and Evaluation*, pages 409–416, Granada.

R. Snow, S. Prakash, D. Jurafsky, and A. Ng. 2007. Learning to merge word senses. In *Proceedings of the Joint Conference on Empirical Methods in Natural Language Processing and Computational Natural Language Learning (EMNLP-CoNLL)*, Czech Republic.

B. Snyder and M. Palmer. 2004. The English all-words task. In *Proceedings of ACL/SIGLEX Senseval-3*, Spain.

I. Witten and E. Frank. 2005. *Data Mining: Practical Machine Learning Tools and Techniques*. Morgan Kaufmann.

Z. Zhong and H. T. Ng. 2012. Word sense disambiguation improves information retrieval. In *Proceedings of the Association for Computational Linguistics*, Jeju Island, Korea.

Effective Spell Checking Methods Using Clustering Algorithms

Renato Cordeiro de Amorim
Glyndŵr University, UK
r.amorim@glyndwr.ac.uk

Marcos Zampieri
University of Cologne, Germany
mzampier@uni-koeln.de

Abstract

This paper presents a novel approach to spell checking using dictionary clustering. The main goal is to reduce the number of times distances have to be calculated when finding target words for misspellings. The method is unsupervised and combines the application of anomalous pattern initialization and partition around medoids (PAM). To evaluate the method, we used an English misspelling list compiled using real examples extracted from the Birkbeck spelling error corpus.

1 Introduction

Spell checking is a well-known task in computational linguistics, dating back to the 1960s, most notably to the work of Damerau (1964). Nowadays, spell checkers are an important component of a number of computer software such as web browsers, text processors and others.

In recent years, spell checking has become a very important application to search engines (Martins and Silva, 2004). Companies like *Google* or *Yahoo!* use log files of all users' queries to map the relation between misspellings and the intended spelling reaching very high accuracy. The language of queries, however, is typically shorter than naturally occurring text, making this application of spell checking very specific (Whitelaw et al., 2009).

Spell checking methods have two main functions. The first one is to identify possible misspellings that a user may commit. As described by Mitton (1996), misspellings can be related to the writer's (poor) writing and spelling competence, to learning disabilities such as dyslexia, and also to simple performance errors, known as *typos*. The written production of non-native speakers also plays an important role in spell checking as they are, on average, more prone to errors than native speakers. These phenomena generate a wide range of different spelling possibilities that a spell checker should be trained to recognize.

The second function of spell checkers is to suggest the users' intended spelling of a misspelled word or at least to suggest a list of candidates in which the target word appears. This is often done by calculating the distance between the misspelled word and a set of potential candidates. As will be discussed in this paper, this is by no means trivial and several methods have been proposed to address this task.

This paper presents a novel unsupervised spell checking method combining anomalous pattern initialization and partition around medoids (PAM). To the best of our knowledge this is the first attempt to apply these methods for spell checking. The approach described here aims to improve spell checking' speed and performance.

2 Related Work

Spell checking techniques have been substantially studied over the years. Mitton (2010) points out that the first attempt to solve the problem can be traced back to the work of Blair (1960) and later more attention was given to the work of Damerau (1964). Most spell checking methods described in the literature, including this one, use dictionaries as a list of correct spellings that help algorithms to find target words. Only a few attempts try to address this problem without the use of dictionaries (Morris and Cherry, 1975).

Morris and Cherry use the frequency of character trigrams to calculate an 'index of peculiarity'. This coefficient estimates the probability of a given trigram occurring in English words. If a trigram is rare in English, the algorithm flags the word containing this trigram as a misspelled one. For example, *wha* is a frequent trigram in English whereas *wah* is not, therefore the word *waht* is very likely to be assigned as a misspelling by the system.

In the 1970s, the main issue with dictionary-based approaches was computing power. The small size of computer memories was a bottleneck for this kind of approach, as systems should ideally hold all entries of the dictionary in memory. The solution was to keep the dictionary on disk and retrieve small portions of it, storing them in the main memory when required. This was extremely time consuming. One technique used to minimize this limitation was to use affix-stripping (McIlroy, 1982). The basic idea is to store a stem word, e.g. *read*, instead of all its possible derivations: *reading, readable, reads, etc.* and apply a set of rules to handle affixes and adjust the stems if necessary. The method proved to be effective in identifying misspellings but it failed to suggest suitable target words, as in this process non-existent words were often generated such as *unreading* or *readation*.

In the present day, the challenge of coping with short memory size no longer exists. It is possible to store large-sized dictionaries in memory for immediate processing without using the disk to store data. However, dictionary-based techniques (de Amorim, 2009), still have a performance limitation due to their intrinsic architecture. State-of-the-art spell checking techniques often apply similarity metrics to calculate the distance between the target word and possible candidates in the dictionary. The bigger the dictionary, the greater the number of calculations, making the algorithms' performance slower. One common alternative to this performance limitation is the use of dictionaries organized as Finite State Automata (FSA) such as in Pirinen and Linden (2010b). These techniques will be better explained in section 2.1.

2.1 State-of-the-art Approaches

A known shortcoming of dictionary-based systems is handling so-called *real-word errors*. This kind of error is difficult to identify using these methods because the misspelled word exists in the dictionary. It is only by taking context into account that these misspellings become recognizable, such as in *better then me* or *were the winners*. The use of confusion sets (Golding and Roth, 1999; Carlson et al., 2001) is a solution to this problem. Confusion sets are a small group of words that are likely to be confused with one another, e.g. *(there, their, theyre)* or *(we're, were)* or *(than, then, them)*. The use of confusion sets in spell checking approaches takes syntax and semantics into account.

A number of confusion sets are provided to the spell checker, so that the context (words in window size n) in which a given target word occurs can be used to assess if the target word was correctly written or not. Carlson et al. (2001) uses 265 confusion sets and later Pedler and Mitton (2010) increases this number to 6,000 confusion sets reporting around 70% of real-word errors detected. Another approach to tackle *real-word errors* is the one by Verberne (2002) which proposed a context-sensitive word trigram-based method calculated using probability. The method works under the assumption that the misspelling of a word often results in an unlikely sequence of (three) words. To calculate this probability, the method uses the British National Corpus (BNC) as training corpus.

Other spell checking methods developed to address the question of real-word errors include the one by Islam and Inkpen (2009). This method uses the Google Web IT 3-gram dataset and aims to improve recall rather than precision. It reports 0.89 recall for detection and 0.76 recall for correction outperforming two other methods for the same task. More recently, Xue et al. (2011) address this problem using syntactic and distributional information.

The vast majority of state-of-the-art spell checking systems use similarity measures to compare the distance between two strings (Damerau, 1964; Levenshtein, 1966). Algorithms consider words that are not found in the dictionary as misspelling candidates. The distance between the candidates or target words to all words in the dictionary is then calculated and the words with the smallest distance are presented as suggestions. Using these techniques, spell checkers have become very effective at offering the top candidates of these suggestions lists as the correct spelling, creating what is described in the literature as the Cupertino Effect[1].

Another important aspect of state-of-the-art spell checkers is the aforementioned organization

[1]The Cupertino Effect was named after an anecdotal yet representative spell checking problem of the 1990s. Microsoft Word did not have the spelling *cooperation* in its dictionary, but the hyphenated one: *co-operation*. When someone typed *cooperation*, the system would offer *Cupertino* as its first suggestion.

of dictionaries as Finite State Automata (FSA). FSA-based methods use techniques from finite state morphology (Beesley and Karttunen, 2003) where the finite set of states of a given automaton correspond to characters of the words in the dictionary. FSA are particularly interesting for morphologically rich languages such as Finnish, Hungarian and Turkish. One example of a resource for spell checking that organizes the dictionary as FSA is Hunspell[2] originally developed for Hungarian, but adapted to several other languages (Pirinen and Linden, 2010a).

The technique presented in this paper serves as an alternative to the FSA-based dictionaries that reduce the number of distances that have to be calculated for each misspelling and therefore improving processing speed. Hulden (2009) observes that the calculation of distances is time consuming and investigates techniques to find approximate string matches in FSA faster. He defines the problem as 'a single word w and a large set of words W, quickly deciding which of the words in W most closely resembles w measured by some metric of similarity, such as minimum edit distance' and points out that finding the closest match between w and a large list of words, is an extremely demanding task.

3 Anomalous Pattern Initialization and PAM

The partition around medoids (PAM) algorithm (Kaufman and Rousseeuw, 1990) divides a dataset Y into K clusters $S = \{S_1, S_2, ..., S_K\}$. Each cluster S_k is represented by a medoid m_k. The latter is the entity $y_i \in S_k$ with the smallest distance to all other entities assigned to the same cluster. PAM creates compact clusters by iteratively minimising the criterion below.

$$W(S, M) = \sum_{k=1}^{K} \sum_{i \in S_k} \sum_{v \in V} (y_{iv} - m_{kv})^2, \quad (1)$$

where V represents the features of the dataset, and M the returned set of medoids $\{m_1, m_2, ..., m_K\}$. This criterion represents the sum of distances between each medoid m_k and each entity $y_i \in S_k$. The minimisation of (1) follows the algorithm below.

1. Select K medoids at random from Y, $M = \{m_1, m_2, ..., m_K\}$, $S \leftarrow \emptyset$.

2. Update S by assigning each entity $y_i \in Y$ to the cluster S_k represented by the closest medoid to y_i. If this update does not generate any changes in S, stop, output S and M.

3. Update each medoid m_k to the entity $y_i \in S_k$ that has the smallest sum of distances to all other entities in the same cluster. Go back to Step 2.

PAM is a very popular clustering algorithm and it has been used in various scenarios. However, it does have known weaknesses, for instance: (i) its final clustering depends heavily on the initial medoids used, and these are normally found at random; (ii) it requires the user to know how many clusters there are in the dataset; (iii) because of its iterative nature, it may get trapped in local optima; (iv) it does not take into account different features that may have varying degrees of relevance.

Weakness (iv) has been the subject of our previous research in feature weighting using cluster dependent weights and the L_p norm (de Amorim and Fenner, 2012). We do not deal with this nor weakness (iii) in this paper, leaving them for future research in our particular scenario. Here we do address the intrinsically-related weaknesses (i) and (ii). It is impossible to define good initial medoids for PAM without knowing how many of these should be used.

The above has lead to a considerable amount of research addressing the quantity and initial position of medoids. Such effort generated a number of algorithms addressing one or both sides of the problem, such as Build (Kaufman and Rousseeuw, 1990), anomalous pattern initialization (Mirkin, 2005), the Hartigan index (Hartigan and Wong, 1979) and other initializations based on hierarchical clustering (Milligan and Isaac, 1980).

There have been numerous comparisons of various initializations on different scenarios (Chiang and Mirkin, 2010; Emre Celebi et al., 2013; de Amorim, 2012; de Amorim and Komisarczuk, 2012), leading us to conclude that it is difficult to appoint a single initialization that would always work. However, we do see the anomalous pattern initialization introduced by Mirkin (2005) favourably. His initialization addresses both sides of the problem and researchers observed previous success using it (Chiang and Mirkin, 2010; de Amorim, 2012; de Amorim and Komisarczuk, 2012).

[2]http://hunspell.sf.net

This initialization was originally designed for K-Means, taking the name intelligent K-Means. Below we present our medoid version of the anomalous pattern initialization, which we have used in our experiments.

1. Set m_c as the entity with the smallest sum of distances to all other entities in the dataset Y.
2. Set m_t to the entity farthest away from m_c.
3. Apply PAM to Y using m_c and m_t as initial medoids, m_c should remain unchanged during the clustering.
4. Add m_t to M.
5. Remove m_t and its cluster from Y. If there are still entities to be clustered go to Step 2.
6. Apply PAM to the original dataset Y initialized by the medoids in M and $K = |M|$.

Based on the above we have developed a method used to find the target words of misspellings. Our method is open to the use of virtually any distance measure valid for strings. Our main aim with this method is to reduce the number of times distances have to be calculated. To do this we apply the anomalous pattern initialization and PAM, as per below.

1. Apply the anomalous pattern initialization to the dictionary, finding the number of clusters K and a set of initial medoids M_{init}
2. Using the medoids in M_{init}, apply PAM to the dictionary to find K clusters. This should output a final set of medoids $M = \{m_1, m_2, ..., m_K\}$.
3. Given a misspelling w, calculate its distance to each medoid $m_k \in M$. Save in M_* the medoids that have the distance to w equal to the minimum found plus a constant c.
4. Calculate the distance between w and each word in the clusters represented by the medoids in M_*, outputting the words whose distance is the minimum possible to w.
5. Should there be any more misspellings, go back to Step 3.

We have added a constant c to increase the chances of the algorithm finding the target word. Clearly a large c will mean more distance calculations. In our experiments with the Levenshtein distance (Levenshtein, 1966) we have used $c = 1$.

4 Setting of the Experiment

For our experiments we first acquired an English dictionary containing 57,046 words, and a corpus consisting of a list of 36,133 misspellings together with its 6,136 target words[3]. This misspelling list was previously used by Mitton (2009) and it was extracted from the Birkbeck spelling error corpus. The corpus includes misspellings from young children as well as extremely poor spellers subject to spelling tests way beyond their ability. For this reason, some of the misspellings are very different from their target words. As stated in the guidelines of the corpus, the misspellings compiled were often very distant from the target words, examples of these include the misspellings o, a, $cart$ and $sutl$ for the targets $accordingly$, $above$, $sure$ and $suitable$, respectively.

As a second step, we removed from our corpus all misspellings whose targets were not present in the dictionary. This reduced the corpus to 34,956 misspellings, just under 97% of the original dataset. Dictionaries tend to be large, making their clustering time consuming. In order to reduce this processing time we segmented the dictionary in 26 sub-datasets, based on the first letter of each word. We have then applied the first and second steps of our method to each of these 26 sub-datasets. This segmentation, however, does not mean that our method will not find the target word when the misspelling happens in the first letter. The clustering of a large dictionary can be time consuming. However, this needs to be done only once.

We took Peter Norvig's (2009) spell checker[4] as our baseline performance. This spell checker is a simplified adaptation of the methods used in *Google* and is being frequently used as baseline for state-of-the-art experiments in spell checking. For our method, Norvig's experiments are particularly interesting because it uses the same dataset, the Birkbeck Spelling Error Corpus. The author reports performance of 74% for a development dataset and 67% for a test dataset. To use as baseline we consider Norvig's best result, 74% success rate, plus 3.24%, which is the percentage of

[3]http://www.dcs.bbk.ac.uk/ roger/corpora.html

[4]http://norvig.com/spell-correct.html

the dataset that we did not consider in our experiments. This results in a baseline performance of 77.24%.

The use of Norvig's method in this paper is exclusive to serve as a baseline performance and not an attempt to compare both methods. As it will be discussed next section, the two methods are conceptually different, making it very difficult to stablish a fair-ground comparison between them. We see Norvig's simplistic adaptation of *Google*'s algorithm for spell checking the same way as, for example, the majority class baseline is used in text classification. In other words, the minimum expectable performance that an algorithm should achieve.

5 Results

The main aim of our method is to reduce the number of times distances are calculated. Should one measure the distance between a misspelling and each word in our dictionary, this distance function would be called 57,046 times, the size of the dictionary. By applying our method to each of the 34,956 misspelling in the corpus we previously described, the distance measure was calculated on average 3,251.4 times for each misspelling. We find this is an important result from a computational point of view, as we are reducing considerably the number of calculations.

Regarding the recovery of the target words, it depends very much on the distance measure in use. We have experimented with the popular Levenshtein distance (Levenshtein, 1966). In 88.42% of cases our method returned a cluster containing the target word or a word with a smaller distance to the misspelling than the target. We attribute some of the latter to misspellings that are actual words (real-word errors), an issue that we do not address in this paper. Results are summarized in table number 1:

Total Misspellings	34,956 words
Success Rate (%)	88.42%
Success Rate (Nominal)	30,908 words
Baseline Gain (pp)	+ 11.18
Total Number of Clusters	1,570 clusters
Average Cluster Length	3.78 words
Average Distance Calculations	3,251.4

Table 1: Results

The cardinality of the clusters returned by our method is also of interest. Ideally the clusters should be rather small, so that users can easily identify the target word in the cluster. In our experiments with the corpus, the average cluster contained 3.78 words, with a median of 2. However, in 7.98% of cases the cluster had over 10 words.

We find the results obtained quite promising as the method outperforms the baseline in 11.18 percentage points[5] using the same dataset (this number takes into account that we had to reduce ours in just over 3%, as described in Section 4). As mentioned in section 4, the corpus contains many misspellings whose target we find impossible to identify.

As previously mentioned, there are a few factors we should take into account when considering Norvig's (2009) method as baseline. His method is based on supervised learning, requiring a rather large sample of misspellings and their corresponding targets - our method has no such requirement and it is open to the use of various distance measures. As an example, he states that his method achieves better performance when 'pretending that we have seen the correctly spelled word 1, 10, or more times'. Another different aspect of both methods is that his method returns a single suggested target, while ours returns a cluster of suggested target words.

6 Conclusion

The method we introduced in this paper reduces the number of distances to be calculated without removing a single word from the dictionary. This makes the algorithm faster than other approaches and presents a satisfactory success rate of 88.42% in a challenging dataset. The success rate is 11.18% higher than the baseline for this task. The question of using a supervised method as a baseline performance have also been discussed in this paper.

We decided to work with a large complete dictionary, in contrast to a number of studies that discard rare words to decrease the number of instances in the dictionary. This decision was based on previous studies (Damerau and Mays, 1989). As stated by Mitton (Mitton, 2010): 'when people use a rare word, it is very likely to be a correct spelling and not a real-word error'. Therefore, a spell checker with a small dictionary would

[5] As discussed in section 4, Norvig's method returns a candidate to the target word, while ours return a cluster. We consider the success rate score of 88.42% and this does not correspond to accuracy or precision.

be very likely to raise false alarms over correctly spelt rare words.

As previously mentioned, the corpus contained the attempts of very poor spellers and therefore misspelled words were often very far from their targets. Another shortcoming of the corpus is the fact that it is organized as a simple list of words without context, making it difficult to refine calculations specifically for real-word errors.

6.1 Future Work

We are continuing the experiments described here and taking them in a couple of directions. First we aim to experiment by reducing the cardinality of clusters and by ranking words in these clusters. In so doing, suggestions presented by the algorithm would be even more accurate and suitable for real-world applications. Another aspect we would like to explore is the use of measures that learn from a corpus of misspellings, such as the one presented by de Amorim (2009).

As previously mentioned, in terms of processing speed, we see our method as an alternative to FSA-based methods. We are at the moment comparing the performance of our algorithm to state-of-the-art FSA-based methods, trying to stablish fair metrics to compare our cluster-based unsupervised method to supervised FSA methods. Methods are conceptually different in their architectures and establishing a fair ground for comparison is by no means trivial.

We would also like to investigate the possibility of reducing the number of distance calculations even further by merging our method with finite state automata, using a dictionary containing solely stem words. Under this approach we would have a smaller amount of medoids, however, this could have a considerable impact on accuracy.

Finally, we aim to replicate these experiments to a corpus in which misspellings are present in running text. This would make it possible to use context to improve the calculation of distances with features commonly used in other NLP problems such as word sense disambiguation (Zampieri, 2012). In so doing, we believe the results obtained by our method would be improved.

Acknowledgments

We would like to thank the anonymous reviewers for their valuable suggestions to increase the quality of this paper.

References

K. Beesley and L. Karttunen. 2003. Finite-state morphology. *CSLI*.

C. Blair. 1960. A program for correcting spelling errors. *Information and Control*, 3:60–67.

A.J. Carlson, J. Rosen, and D. Roth. 2001. Scaling up context-sensitive text correction. In *Proceedings of the 13th Innovative Applications of Artificial Intelligence Conference*, pages 45–50. AAAI Press.

M.M.T. Chiang and B. Mirkin. 2010. Intelligent choice of the number of clusters in k-means clustering: an experimental study with different cluster spreads. *Journal of classification*, 27(1):3–40.

F. Damerau and E. Mays. 1989. An examination of undetected typing errors. *Information Processing & Management*, 25(6):659–664.

F. Damerau. 1964. A technique for computer detection and correction of spelling errors. *Communications of the ACM*, 7:171–176.

R.C. de Amorim and T. Fenner. 2012. Weighting features for partition around medoids using the minkowski metric. *Lecture Notes in Computer Science*, 7619:35–44.

R.C. de Amorim and P. Komisarczuk. 2012. On initializations for the minkowski weighted k-means. *Lecture Notes in Computer Science*, 7619:45–55.

R.C. de Amorim. 2009. An adaptive spell checker based on ps3m: Improving the clusters of replacement words. *Computer Recognition Systems 3*, pages 519–526.

R.C. de Amorim. 2012. An empirical evaluation of different initializations on the number of k-means iterations. *Lecture Notes in Computer Science*, 7629:15–26.

M. Emre Celebi, H.A. Kingravi, and P.A. Vela. 2013. A comparative study of efficient initialization methods for the k-means clustering algorithm. *Expert Systems with Applications*, 40(1):200–210.

A. Golding and D. Roth. 1999. A winnow-based approach to context-sensitive spelling correction. *Machine Learning*, 34(1-3):107–130.

J.A. Hartigan and M.A. Wong. 1979. Algorithm as 136: A k-means clustering algorithm. *Journal of the Royal Statistical Society. Series C (Applied Statistics)*, 28(1):100–108.

M. Hulden. 2009. Fast approximate string matching with finite automata. *Procesamiento del Lenguaje Natural*, 43:57–64.

A. Islam and D. Inkpen. 2009. Real-word spelling correction using googleweb 1t 3-grams. In *Proceedings of Empirical Methods in Natural Language Processing (EMNLP2009)*, pages 1241–1249, Singapore.

L. Kaufman and P.J. Rousseeuw. 1990. *Finding groups in data: an introduction to cluster analysis*, volume 39. Wiley Online Library.

V. Levenshtein. 1966. Binary codes capable of correcting deletions, insertions and reversals. *Soviet Physics Doklady*.

Bruno Martins and Mário J Silva. 2004. Spelling correction for search engine queries. In *Advances in Natural Language Processing*, pages 372–383. Springer.

M. McIlroy. 1982. Development of a spelling list. *IEEE Transactions on Communications*, 1:91–99.

G.W. Milligan and P.D. Isaac. 1980. The validation of four ultrametric clustering algorithms. *Pattern Recognition*, 12(2):41–50.

B. Mirkin. 2005. *Clustering for data mining: a data recovery approach*, volume 3. CRC Press.

R. Mitton. 1996. *English spelling and the computer*. Longman.

R. Mitton. 2009. Ordering the suggestions of a spellchecker without using context. *Natural Language Engineering*, 15(2):173–192.

R. Mitton. 2010. Fifty years of spellchecking. *Writing Systems Research*, 2(1):1–7.

R. Morris and L. Cherry. 1975. Computer detection of typographical errors. *IEEE Transactions on Professional Communication*, 18:54–64.

P. Norvig. 2009. Natural language corpus data. In *Beautiful Data*, pages 219–249. O'Reilly.

J. Pedler and R. Mitton. 2010. A large list of confusion sets for spellchecking assessed against a corpus of real-word errors. In *Proceedings of LREC 2010*, Malta.

T. Pirinen and K. Linden. 2010a. Creating and weighting hunspell dictionaries as finite-state automata. *Investigationes Linguisticae*, 21.

T. Pirinen and K. Linden. 2010b. Finite-state spellchecking with weighted language and error models. In *Proceedings of the Seventh SaLTMiL workshop on creation and use of basic lexical resources for less-resourced languages*, Malta.

S. Verberne. 2002. Context-sensitive spell checking based on word trigram probabilities. Master's thesis, University of Nijmegen.

C. Whitelaw, B. Hutchinson, G. Chung, and G. Ellis. 2009. Using the web for language independent spellchecking and autocorrection. In *Proceedings of Empirical Methods in Natural Language Processing (EMNLP2009)*, pages 890–899, Singapore.

W. Xu, J. Tetreault, M. Chodorow, R. Grishman, and L. Zhao. 2011. Exploiting syntactic and distributional information for spelling correction withweb-scale n-gram models. In *Proceedings of Empirical Methods in Natural Language Processing (EMNLP2011)*, pages 1291–1300, Edinburgh, Scotland.

M. Zampieri. 2012. Evaluating knowledge-rich and knowledge-poor features in automatic classification: A case study in WSD. In *Proceedings of the 13th IEEE International Symposium on Computational Intelligence and Informatics (CINTI2012)*, pages 359–363, Budapest, Hungary.

Normalization of Dutch User-Generated Content

Orphée De Clercq[1,2], **Sarah Schulz**[3], **Bart Desmet**[1,2], **Els Lefever**[1,2] **and Véronique Hoste**[1,3]

[1] LT[3], Language and Translation Technology Team – University College Ghent
Groot-Brittanniëlaan 45, 9000 Ghent, Belgium
[2] Department of Applied Mathematics and Computer Science – Ghent University
Krijgslaan 281 (S9), 9000 Ghent, Belgium
[3] Department of Lingusitics – Ghent University
Blandijnberg 1, 9000 Ghent, Belgium

`Firstname.Lastname@UGent.be`

Abstract

This paper describes a phrase-based machine translation approach to normalize Dutch user-generated content (UGC). We compiled a corpus of three different social media genres (text messages, message board posts and tweets) to have a sample of this recent domain. We describe the various characteristics of this noisy text material and explain how it has been manually normalized using newly developed guidelines. For the automatic normalization task we focus on text messages, and find that a cascaded SMT system where a token-based module is followed by a translation at the character level gives the best word error rate reduction. After these initial experiments, we investigate the system's robustness on the complete domain of UGC by testing it on the other two social media genres, and find that the cascaded approach performs best on these genres as well. To our knowledge, we deliver the first proof-of-concept system for Dutch UGC normalization, which can serve as a baseline for future work.

1 Introduction

In the past two decades, many resources have been invested to develop state-of-the-art text processing tools for Dutch[1]. Similar to other reported languages, these tools, which have all been developed with standard text in mind, show a significant drop in performance when applied to user-generated content (UGC). This is for example the case when applying parsing (Foster et al., 2011) or named entity recognition (Liu et al., 2011b; Ritter et al., 2011) to Twitter data. Typical problems that hinder automatic text processing include the use and productivity of abbreviations, deliberate misspellings, phonetic text, colloquial and ungrammatical language use, lack of punctuation and inconsistent capitalization.

No systems currently exist to automatically normalize Dutch noisy text into its standard equivalent. In order to develop a system which can handle different types of user-generated content, we collected and studied three social media genres: text messages, message board posts and tweets. In this paper, we investigate the viability of adopting a character-based machine translation approach to the normalization task. This is different from previous research investigating MT approaches for normalization, which has mainly focused on token-based translation (Aw et al., 2006; Kobus et al., 2008).

For our experiments we first focus on the genre that poses the largest number of normalization challenges in our corpus, namely text messages, in order to have a proof of concept. We will show that a cascaded SMT system with a token-based module followed by a transliteration at the character level yields the best results, i.e. a 63% drop in word error rate. In this cascade, the first module aims at obtaining high precision, thus presenting high-confidence translations. The second module further improves this output by generalizing over character mappings.

To conclude, we applied this proof-of-concept system tuned for text messages to the other genres and observed similar improvements.

The paper is structured as follows. After the literature overview (Section 2) we discuss the social

[1] Among others, in the framework of the STEVIN programme, see Spijns and Odijk (2013) for an overview.

media genres used, their characteristics and how these have been normalized in Section 3. The setup and experiments are presented in Section 4. We examine the results in Section 5, perform a qualitative error analysis in Section 6 to end with some conclusions and prospects for future work in Section 7.

2 Related Work

Traditionally, the task of text normalization is a crucial first step for every text-to-speech system, in which specific numbers and digit sequences, acronyms, etc. need to be rewritten in order to have them pronounced correctly. A thorough overview of the main characteristics and bottlenecks can be found in Sproat et al. (2001).

More recently, however, the surge of user-generated content has introduced new problems such as non-existent abbreviations and deliberate misspellings. This reality combined with the need to process UGC data has revived the interest in normalization techniques. In this regard, we can define three dominant approaches to transfer noisy into standard text. These are referred to as the spell-checking, machine translation and speech recognition metaphors (Kobus et al., 2008).

The most intuitive way of normalizing text would be to approach the problem as a spell-checking one where noisy text has to be transformed to standard text using noisy channel models. Choudhury et al. (2007), for example, proposed a supervised noisy channel model using Hidden Markov Models to calculate the probability of less frequent words. Extensions to this approach were made by studying word processes (Cook and Stevenson, 2009), adapting weighted finite-state machines and rewrite rules (Beaufort et al., 2010) or by adding other elements such as orthographic, phonetic and contextual factors (Xue et al., 2011).

Another approach is using statistical machine translation (SMT) techniques for text normalization. Previous work in this field has mostly focused on phrase-based machine translation at the word level. Aw et al. (2006) were the first to compare dictionary substitution using frequencies with phrase-based machine translation. They revealed that SMT improves BLEU scores for English SMS translation. Also working on English text, Raghunathan et al. (2009) confirmed that using an SMT system outperforms a dictionary look-up, most notably when used on an out-of-domain test set.

Kobus et al. (2008) followed the same approach but combined the machine translation features with a speech recognition approach using HMMs on a French corpus. They concluded that the two systems perform better on different aspects of the task and that combining these two modules works best.

A different way of approaching normalization is the work by Liu et al. (2011a; 2012). They propose a cognition-driven text normalization system using an unsupervised approach. By observing and simulating human techniques for the normalization task, they avoid dependence on human annotations. They construct a broad-coverage system to enable better word-coverage, using three key components: enhanced letter transformation, visual priming and string/phonetic similarity.

If we consider normalization, the task intuitively has a lot in common with transliteration tasks for which character-based SMT systems have proven adequate (Vilar et al., 2007). Pennell and Liu (2011) were the first to study character-based normalization. They, however, limited their approach by only focusing on abbreviations.

In this paper, we propose a cascaded model that follows a machine translation approach and tries to tackle the full range of normalization problems.

3 Three Genres of UGC

In order to normalize using a machine translation system, and to evaluate the performance, it is essential to build a gold standard data set that can serve as training and test material. As far as we know, no such data set is currently available for Dutch.

3.1 Corpus Compilation

To ensure that our corpus is representative of the domain of user-generated content (UGC), we decided to include three different social media genres: text messages (SMS), message board posts from a social networking site (SNS) and tweets (TWE). As text messages, we sampled 1,000 messages from the Flemish part of the SoNaR corpus (Treurniet et al., 2012), aimed at a balanced spread of two characteristics: age and region. In order to also include longer streams of UGC, 1,505 message board posts were randomly selected from the social networking site Netlog, which is popular amongst Belgian teenagers. In order to take into

	ORIGINAL	NORMALIZED	TRANSLATED
SMS	Oguz ! Edde me Jana gesproke ? En ze flipt lyk omdak ghsmoord heb .. !	Oh gods ! Heb je met Jana gesproken ? En ze flipt gelijk omdat ik gesmoord heb ... !	Oh god ! Did you speak to Jana ? And she's flipping because I smoked ... !
SNS	schaaaat , Je komt wel boven die Blo , je et em nii nodig wie jou laat gaan is gwn DOM :p Iloveyouuuu hvj	schat , Je komt wel boven die Blo , je hebt hem niet nodig wie jou laat gaan is gewoon dom :p I love you hou van je	honey, You'll get over that Blo, you don't need him whoever lets you go is just stupid :p I love you I love you
TWE	@minnebelle top ! Tis voor m'n daddy !	@minnebelle top ! Het is voor m'n daddy !	@minnebelle great ! It is for my daddy !

Table 1: Examples of UGC from the three social media genres representing the original utterance, its normalized version and an English translation

account the vast amount of normalization research done on Twitter data, we also included 246 randomly selected tweets. It is to be noted, however, that average Twitter content in Belgium differs from that in English-speaking countries or The Netherlands, because Twitter has mainly been adopted amongst professionals. An example of each genre can be found in the left column of Table 1.

These examples clearly illustrate the main characteristics of Dutch UGC, most of which are similar to previously reported problems in other languages (Baron, 2003; Beaufort et al., 2010).

Some of the more well-known problems include the omission of words or characters, e.g. the omission of the final *n* in *gesproke* (Eng: *spoke* versus *spoken*). The frequent use of abbreviations and acronyms, such as *gwn, hvj* (Eng: *LOL*), which are highly productive. Moreover, many utterances deviate from the standard spelling at the lexical level, such as *lyk* instead of *gelijk* (Eng: *luv* versus *love*) or by writing colloquially, e.g. *et em* instead of *hebt hem* (Eng: *you iz* vs *you are*). In UGC, emotions are also expressed by using flooding (repetition of the same character or sequence, *baaaaaaby*), emoticons (*:p*) and capitalized letters (*STUPID*).

More specific to the Dutch language is the concatenation of tokens which leads to the elimination of clitics and pronouns (*Edde* instead of *Heb je, khou* instead *ik hou, Tis* instead of *Het is*). Moreover, the influence of the English-speaking world on Belgium and the fact that it is a trilingual country often leads to various languages within a single utterance, which are often adapted to Dutch aspects (*Oguz, daddy, we are forever*).

3.2 Corpus Annotation

All text material was annotated by two annotators, independently of each other using newly developed normalization guidelines. These guidelines, tailored for Dutch, have been drawn up in close collaboration with the developers of the Chatty Corpus (Kestemont et al., 2012).

The guidelines can be roughly divided into two parts. The first part consists of the actual text normalization and comprises three steps: clearing all obvious tokenization problems, stating the different normalization operations and writing down the full normalized version. We allow four different operations: insertions, deletions, substitutions and transpositions; examples of tokens requiring these operations are given below (in English).

- INS: spoke (spoken), sis (sister)
- DEL: baaaaabyyyy (baby)
- SUB: iz (is), stoopid (stupid)
- TRANS: liek (like)

Insertions allow to indicate missing characters in a string. Deletions are used when characters should be deleted from a certain string. Substitutions are used when a character has been replaced with another similar one. Finally, transpositions are used when a combination of characters should be switched within one string.

The second part consists of flagging additional information that might be useful for automatic processing purposes. Within each utterance the

Genre	#	Before	After	%	#INS	#DEL	#SUB	#TRANS
SMS	1000	16630	17194	3.39	3622	338	547	57
SNS	1505	31513	32221	2.25	4165	1500	1692	57
TWE	246	3276	3357	2.47	923	67	127	4

Table 2: Data statistics of the three genres of UGC. The left-hand side shows the number of tokens before and after normalization and the increase in %. The right-hand side visualizes the actual normalization effort expressed in the number of operations.

annotators were asked to indicate the end of a thought (to account for missing punctuation), regional words, foreign words and named entities. They could also flag words that are ungrammatical, stressed, part of a compound, used as interjections or words that require consecutive normalization operations.

To check the reliability of our annotation guidelines, the two annotators each normalized the 1,000 text messages. We estimated the inter-annotator reliability by computing the word error rate (cf. infra) between the two fully normalized versions. The WER was 0.048, which indicates near-perfect overlap.

In order to give an idea of the normalization effort required, we present some data statistics for each genre in Table 2. The left-hand side visualizes the increase in the number of tokens before and after normalization in absolute numbers and percentage-wise. On the right one can see the actual normalization effort, which is expressed by the number of individual operations. The normalized versions of the previously mentioned examples can be found in the middle column of Table 1 and their translation to English in the right column.

For the experiments presented in this paper we work with the first part of the manual normalization (ignoring flagging information such as ends of thought). We chose to focus on SMS, because it was the noisiest data in our corpus, with a token increase of 3.39% (see Table 2).

4 System Architecture

Using SMT for noisy text normalization can be done at various levels of granularity. The advantage of working at the token level is that the high-frequency words and abbreviations can be translated in context, which outperforms a simple dictionary look-up (Raghunathan and Krawczyk, 2009). However, working at the character level allows one to generalize over character mappings which makes the system more robust (Pennell and Liu, 2011).

Prior to any sort of learning, we adapted our tokenizer to be able to handle emoticons, hyperlinks, hashtags and at-replies. Similar to Beaufort et al. (2010), we devised some rewrite rules: we decided to tackle the flooding of characters before translating in order to avoid too many confounding factors. Characters and character sequences were allowed to occur twice consecutively, at maximum. A higher number of repetitions was reduced to two. The validity of this approach was checked by running the rewrite module on the CELEX database (Baayen et al., 1995), which contains 381,292 valid Dutch words, including inflections. Only two (highly infrequent) entries were changed by the module, which confirms that it virtually does not overnormalize.

After this preliminary preprocessing, the noisy text is processed by two modules. First, the standard phrase-based SMT approach at the token level is used to ensure the translation of the more frequently used abbreviations (such as *fb* for *facebook* and other highly frequent normalization problems, e.g. *tht* for *that*). Afterwards, the translated text is split into characters and a translation at the character level takes place. This intuitively makes sense, because transformations at the character level are more likely to be reproduced than a combination of possible transformations at the word level. Trying to generalize such character transformations at the word level would probably fail due to data sparseness. We worked with both character unigram and bigram translation models. Bigrams supposedly have the advantage that one character of context across phrase boundaries is used in the selection of translation alternatives from the phrase table (Tiedemann, 2012). This means that more precise translations will be suggested.

For our experiments we first focus on the individual performance we can achieve within the

SMS genre, after which we test this approach on the other genres to see whether it is possible to create a robust system that can process all three UGC genres.

To evaluate our approach, both the Word Error Rate (WER) and BLEU scores were calculated. WER, an evaluation metric that is based on edit distance at the word level, is very well suited for the evaluation of NLP tasks where the input and output strings are closely related. As a consequence, the metric is used for the evaluation of optical character recognition (Kolak et al., 2003), grapheme-to-phoneme conversion (Demberg et al., 2007), diacritization (Schlippe et al., 2008) and vocalization of Arabic (Kübler and Mohamed, 2008). The BLEU metric, which has been specifically designed for measuring machine translation quality, measures the n-gram overlap between the translation being evaluated and a set of target translations. We therefore believe that BLEU is less appropriate for evaluation in the current set-up, but we include it for comparison's sake (as other systems mention it such as Aw et al. (2006), Kobus et al. (2008), etc.).

5 Experimental Set-up and Results

For all experiments, we used the Moses SMT system (Koehn et al., 2007). As a target corpus for our language model, we used the Spoken Dutch Corpus (Corpus Gesproken Nederlands, CGN (Oostdijk, 2000)) since spoken language could better reflect the language used in UGC. The target training data was also added to the model. All language models were built using the SRILM toolkit (Stolcke, 2002) with Witten-Bell discounting which has been proven to work well on small data sets (Tiedemann, 2012)

We experimented with different translation models. The token-level translation model was each time built using Moses with standard settings and a 5-gram language model. For the character-level model the same Moses setting was used. For the language model we experimented with different sizes of n on our training data, 5 - 7 - 10 - 15, and found that a 10-gram language model gave the best results.

For the first set of experiments (Section 5.1), training was performed on the SMS data, which was divided into three data sets: 625 messages for training, 125 for development and 125 for testing. In order to estimate the system's robustness to unseen genres, the SMS-tuned system was tested on the other two genres, 125 SNS posts and 125 tweets (Section 5.2).

5.1 Results on SMS

This is, to our knowledge, the first study on Dutch text normalization, so there is no basis for comparison to other systems. Figure 1 present a visual overview of the different set-ups' performance on the Dutch SMS data. We start by reporting the difference between the original source and target text (A) as well as a baseline where only the rewrite rules have been applied (B). We see that a moderate improvement in WER, from 21.70 to 21.47%, already occurs by eliminating flooding.

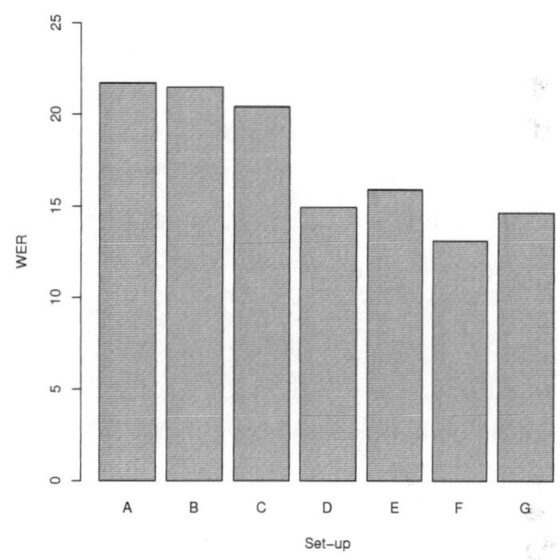

Figure 1: Visualisation of the WER reduction on the SMS data set using our seven different set-ups

In the next step, the various translation models were trained and tested and we clearly see that all the following results outperform the baseline. The token-based model (C) accounts for a moderate improvement but clearly the character-based models, both with unigrams (D) and bigrams (E), perform much better. Introducing the unigram and bigram cascaded models leads to the best results (F and G). The best result is reached by the cascaded unigram model (F). This model has a WER of 13.11 which is a 63% drop in word error rate over the baseline and 56% over the non-cascaded word level SMT.

If we perform the same analysis on the BLEU results (Figure 2), we observe a different tendency. Clearly, the token-based model (C) accounts here for the best performance whereas the cascaded un-

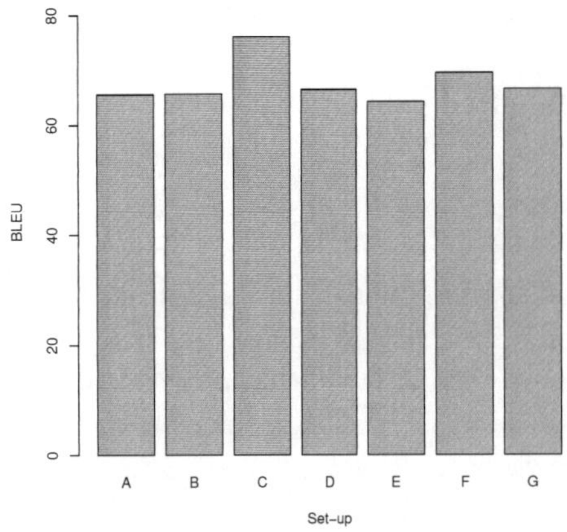

Figure 2: Visualisation of BLEU on the SMS data set using our seven different set-ups

igram model (F) only achieves the second best result. This could be explained by the inherent differences between the metrics. WER is based on the edit distance whereas BLEU measures n-gram overlap. This means that the output of the unigram cascaded model can be closer - but not perfect - to the reference than the output from the token model. If we consider the example below from our data we see that the token model was not able to find the correct version, whereas the cascaded unigram output is already a bit closer. If we would then feed this closer version back into our token model it should be able to resolve it correctly[2]. This insight could be used to improve our system by extending the cascaded unigram module with another run of the token-based system in future work.

- original: *laatk* – target: *laat ik*
- output C: *laatk* – output F: *laat k* – output C based on output F: *laat ik*

All experimental results on the SMS data, expressed both in WER and BLEU, can be found in Table 3.

5.2 Results on three genres of UGC

By testing our translation models tuned for text messages on the other two genres, we aim to verify the robustness of our approach. These results can be found in Table 3.

Applying the baseline system with rewrite rules gives the same minor positive effect for SNS as for SMS, compared to the original source and target text. For tweets, on the other hand, no improvement is noted. Upon closer inspection of the Twitter data, not a single instance of flooding was found, which explains this status quo.

When comparing the other models, the same evolution in word error rate can be observed. For each genre, the best WER reduction over the baseline is reached with the cascaded unigram model, namely 63% for SMS, 39% for SNS and 28% for TWE. For the SNS data, the cascaded unigram and bigram translation models give an equal performance.

6 Error Analysis

We performed a qualitative error analysis of our best performing set-up, i.e. the cascaded unigram approach (F). After close inspection of the output on the SMS test data we learned that the system was able to locate and resolve 172 of the 320 words requiring normalization. Besides this, the system also generated 51 false positives, which leads to a precision of 77.13%, a recall of 55.66% and thus an overall F-measure of 64.66%.

In order to gain more insights, the instances our system missed were classified in two ways. We first inspected which types of operations seem most difficult to resolve (cf. Section 3.2).

Operations	Total required	Absolute # missed	Relative # missed
INS	549	270	49%
DEL	28	20	71%
SUB	55	30	54%
TRANS	11	6	54%

Table 4: Absolute number of the operations missed at the character-level together with the relative number when compared to the total number of operations

Since one word may need multiple or different operations[3], this was calculated at the character level. Table 4 presents the number of operations missed by our system both in absolute and relative numbers.

At first sight, especially the deletions seem hard to resolve, followed by the substitutions and trans-

[2]Proof of this was found in the output of our token-based system.

[3]For example *sis* requires three insertions and *luv* requires both a substitution and an insertion.

Training Set-ups	Testing					
	SMS		SNS		TWE	
	WER	BLEU	WER	BLEU	WER	BLEU
A. Original	21.70	65.54	20.41	66.03	13.26	76.10
B. Baseline	21.47	65.64	20.36	65.93	13.26	76.10
C. Token-level only	20.41	76.04	25.03	73.26	19.03	78.32
D. Unigram only	14.93	66.45	15.41	64.02	13.52	66.29
E. Bigram only	15.90	64.26	15.17	63.94	14.08	65.50
F. Cascaded unigram	**13.11**	69.48	**14.59**	65.17	**10.35**	72.25
G. Cascaded bigram	14.65	66.55	**14.59**	64.79	10.36	72.25

Table 3: Results of the different set-ups on the SMS genre

positions. When taking the absolute numbers into account, however, proportionally these classes are much less frequent than the total number of insertions needed (549 to be exact). Apparently our system is able to resolve most of these insertions (i.e. 51%). On closer inspection, however, we found that the system is especially good in normalizing shorter words requiring only one or two insertions, such as *eb* for *heb*, *nie* for *niet*, and not in building longer words such as *gr* for *groetjes*. If we extrapolate this finding to the number of insertions needed at the word level, we indeed discovered that at the word level 60% gets successfully resolved. Another observation at the word level is that words requiring different types of operations are difficult for our system: only 44% is successfully replaced.

The second error classification consists of a more linguistically motivated subdivision. Inspired by the work of Androutsopoulos (2007), we defined three categories: abbreviation (ABBR), phonetic (PHON) and orthographic (ORTH) issues. Examples of some instances our system missed following this classification are presented in Table 5.

Classes	Output	Correct
ABBR	aug	augustus
PHON	hebk	heb ik
ORTH	uan	van

Table 5: Missed instances according to error classification 2

This classification is visualized in Figure 3, where we see that especially resolving phonetic problems seems difficult for our system, i.e. 103 instances. In order to better grasp this we had a closer look at the various phonetic issues and

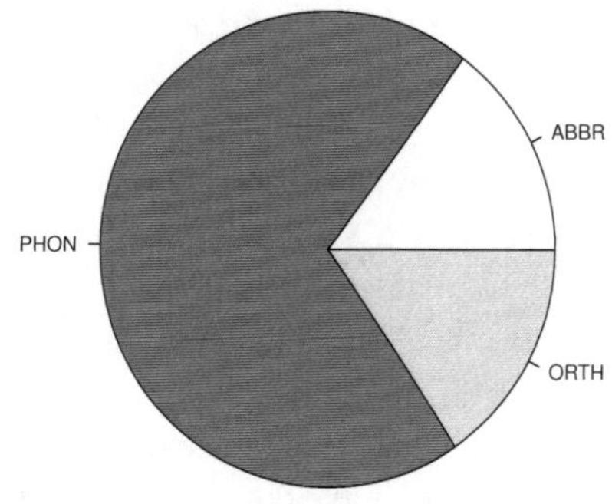

Figure 3: Pie chart visualizing the number of missed instances according to the second error classification

further classified these into fusions (concatenations of words, 25%), omissions (missing characters, 43%), equivalents (characters referring to the same sound, 26%) and onomatopoeias (sounds like, 6%). Especially the omission of characters seems problematic, which is consistent with the high number of missed insertions (i.e. 270 characters).

This error analysis indicates that our system might benefit from including other modules besides machine translation. The orthographic issues might probably be resolved using a spell checker, whereas the phonetic ones, especially the equivalents, might benefit from grapheme-to-phoneme conversion.

As far as the hypercorrections are concerned

(our system generated 51 false positives), we found that 15 of these are actually named entities or foreign words which should not be normalized at all. This is why we are also thinking of expanding our preprocessing module so that these words can be filtered out before processing them with the other modules.

7 Conclusion and Future Work

In this paper, we have discussed a cascaded machine translation approach to normalize Dutch user-generated content (UGC). Three social media genres have been collected and normalized using newly developed guidelines. After a short description of the main normalization errors and characteristics of this particular domain, we investigated the viability of an SMT approach at the character level.

Experiments on text messages, the genre requiring most normalization, revealed that a cascaded model where a token-based module is followed by a translation at the character level yields the best results. Testing this model on two other genres revealed the same trend, which indicates that this approach is robust across genres. To our knowledge, we have developed the first proof-of-concept system for Dutch UGC normalization, which can serve as a baseline for future work. A first error analysis revealed that our best system already reaches an F-measure of 64.66%. Looking at the different operations, insertions occur most frequently. Moreover, it appears that our system is best at resolving smaller words requiring only one or two insertions. When we analyzed the output in a different way, especially the high number of phonetic alternations remaining unresolved drew our attention.

For future work we believe that incorporating other modules into our system will further increase the overall performance. Considering the error analysis, we feel that a combination of the three metaphors (machine translation, spell checking and speech recognition) might produce an optimal combination of various features. Moreover, sometimes we would like to introduce a second round through some modules to tackle module-specific problems. In order to really evaluate the ability to generalize over multiple genres we are currently training and testing our system on the individual text genres. Since we aim to make a system that can handle UGC, we also envisage to combine our three genres and thus experiment on the full set. First experiments have revealed that this does indeed increase overall performance. For now, we have only focused on normalization at the lexical level, so colloquial and ungrammatical language usage also presents an interesting alley for future work. Since previous work on English text normalization using MT approaches at the character-level has only focussed on abbreviations (Pennell and Liu, 2011), we would also like to investigate whether our methodology can be applied to English noisy text as well.

We are looking for ways to make our data sets publicly available.

Acknowledgments

We would like to thank our annotators for their hard work. and the reviewers for their valuable comments. This work was funded by three projects: PARIS[4], SUBTLE[5] and AMiCA[6].

References

Jannis Androutsopoulos. 2007. Neue Medien neue Schriftlichkeit? *Mitteilungen des Deutschen Germanistenverbandes*, 1(7):72–97.

AiTi Aw, Zhang Min, Xiao Juan, and Su Jian. 2006. A Phrase-based Statistical Model for SMS Text Normalization. In *Proceedings of the COLING/ACL 2006 Main Conference Poster Sessions*, pages 33–40, Sydney, Australia.

Harald R. Baayen, Richard Piepenbrock, and Leon Gulikers. 1995. The CELEX Lexical Database. Linguistic Data Consortium. CD-ROM.

Naomi S. Baron. 2003. Language of the internet. *The Stanford Handbook for Language Engineers*, pages 59–127.

Richard Beaufort, Sophie Roekhaut, Louise-Amélie Cougnon, and Cédrick Fairon. 2010. A hybrid rule/model-based finite-state framework for normalizing sms messages. In *Proceedings of ACL*, pages 770–779.

Paul Cook and Suzanne Stevenson. 2009. An unsupervised model for text message normalization. In *Proceedings of the NAACL HLT Workshop on Computational Approaches to Linguistic Creativity*.

Vera Demberg, Helmut Schmid, and Gregor Möhler. 2007. Phonological Constraints and Morphological Preprocessing for Grapheme-to-Phoneme Conversion. In *45th Annual Meeting of the Association for Computational Linguistics (ACL 2007)*,

[4]www.parisproject.be

[5]http://lt3.hogent.be/en/projects/subtle/

[6]http://www.amicaproject.be/

Prague, Czech Republic. Association for Computational Linguistics.

Jennifer Foster, Ozlem Cetinoglu, Joachim Wagner, Joseph Le Roux, Stephen Hogan, Joakim Nivre, Deirdre Hogan, and Josef van Genabith. 2011. #hard-toparse: POS tagging and parsing the twitterverse. In *Proceedings of the AAAI workshop on Analyzing Microtext*, pages 20–25.

Mike Kestemont, Claudia Peersman, Benny De Decker, Guy De Pauw, Kim Luyckx, Roser Morante, Frederik Vaassen, Janneke van de Loo, and Walter Daelemans. 2012. The netlog corpus. a resource for the study of flemish dutch internet language. In *Proceedings of the Eight International Conference on Language Resources and Evaluation (LREC'12)*, Istanbul, Turkey, may.

Catherine Kobus, Yvon François, and Damnati Géraldine. 2008. Normalizing SMS: are two metaphors better than one? In *Proceedings of the 22nd International Conference on Computational Linguistics (Coling 2008)*, pages 441–448, Manchester, UK.

Philipp Koehn, Hieu Hoang, Alexandra Birch, Chris Callison-Burch, Marcello Federico, Nicola Bertoldi, Brooke Cowan, Wade Shen, Christine Moran, Richard Zens, Chris Dyer, Ondrej Bojar, Alexandra Constantin, and Evan Herbst. 2007. Moses: Open Source Toolkit for Statistical Machine Translation. In *Proceedings of the ACL 2007 Demo and Poster Sessions*, pages 177–180, Prague, Czech Republic.

Okan Kolak, William J. Byrne, and Philip Resnik. 2003. A Generative Probabilistic OCR Model for NLP Applications. In *HLT-NAACL 2003: conference combining Human Language Technology conference series and the North American Chapter of the Association for Computational Linguistics conference series*, Edmonton, Canada.

Sandra Kübler and Emad Mohamed. 2008. Memory-based vocalization of Arabic. In *Proceedings of the LREC Workshop on HLT and NLP within the Arabic World.*, Marrakech, Morocco.

Fei Liu, Fuliang Weng, Bingqing Wang, and Yang Liu. 2011a. Insertion, deletion or substitution? Normalizing text messages without pre-categorization nor supervision. In *Proceedings of the Annual Meeting of the Association for Computational Linguistics (ACL)*, pages 71–76.

Xiaohua Liu, Furu Wei Shaodian Zhang, and Ming Zhou. 2011b. Recognizing named entities in tweets. In *Proceedings of the Annual Meeting of the Association for Computational Linguistics (ACL)*, pages 359–367.

Fei Liu, Fuliang Weng, and Xiao Jiang. 2012. A broad-coverage normalization system for social media language. In *Proceedings of the Annual Meeting of the Association for Computational Linguistics (ACL)*, pages 1035–1044.

Nelleke Oostdijk. 2000. The spoken dutch corpus. Outline and rst evaluation. In *Proceedings of the Second International Conference on Language Resources and Evaluation*, pages 887–894.

Deana L. Pennell and Yang Liu. 2011. A character-level machine translation approach for normalization of SMS abbreviations. In *Proceedings of 5th International Joint Conference on Natural Language Processing*, Chiang Mai, Thailand. Asian Federation of Natural Language Processing.

Karthik Raghunathan and Stefan Krawczyk. 2009. CS224N: Investigating SMS Text Normalization using Statistical Machine Translation. Technical report, Stanford University: Department of Computer Science.

Alan Ritter, Sam Clark, Mausam, and Oren Etzioni. 2011. Named entity recognition in tweets: An experimental study. In *Proceedings of Empirical Methods for Natural Language Processing EMNLP*, pages 1524–1534.

Monojit Choudhury Rahul Saraf, Vijit Jain, Animesh Mukherjee, Sudeshna Sarkar, and Anupan Basu. 2007. Investigating and modeling the structure of texting language. *International Journal on Document Analysis and Recognition*, 10(3):157–174.

Tim Schlippe, ThuyLinh Nguyen, and Stephan Vogel. 2008. Diacritization as a machine translation problem and as a sequence labeling problem. In *MT at work: Proceedings of the Eighth Conference of the Association for Machine Translation in the Americas (AMTA-2008)*, pages 270–278, Waikiki, Hawai'i.

Richard Sproat, Alan W. Black, Stanley Chen, Shankar Kumar, Mari Ostendorf, and Christopher Richards. 2001. Normalization of non-standard words. *Computer, Speech and Language*, 15(3):287–333.

Peter Spyns and Jan Odijk. 2013. *Essential Speech and Language Technology for Dutch, Theory and Applications of Natural Language Processing*. Springer, Berlin.

Andreas Stolcke. 2002. Srilm - an extensible language modeling toolkit. In *Proceedings of the 7th International Conference on Spoken Language Processing (ICSLP 2002*, pages 901–904.

Jörg Tiedemann. 2012. Character-based pivot translation for under-resourced languages and domains. In *Proceedings of the 13th Conference of the European Chapter of the Association for Computational Linguistics*, pages 141–151, Avignon, France.

Maaske Treurniet, Orphée De Clercq, Henk van den Heuvel, and Nelleke Oostdijk. 2012. Collection of a Corpus of Dutch SMS. In *Proceedings of the 8th Language Resources and Evaluation Conference (LREC'12)*, pages 2268–2273, Istanbul, Turkey.

David Vilar, Jan-Thorsten Peter, and Herman Ney. 2007. Can we translate letters? In *Proceedings of the Second Workshop on Statistical Machine Translation*, pages 33–39, Prague, Czech Republic.

Zhenzhen Xue, Dawei Yin, and Brian D. Davison. 2011. Normalizing microtext. In *Proceedings of the AAAI Workshop on Analyzing Microtext*, pages 74–79.

Linguistic Profiling of Texts Across Textual Genres and Readability Levels. An Exploratory Study on Italian Fictional Prose

Felice Dell'Orletta, Simonetta Montemagni, Giulia Venturi
Istituto di Linguistica Computazionale "Antonio Zampolli" (ILC–CNR)
ItaliaNLP Lab - *www.italianlp.it*
Via G. Moruzzi, 1 – Pisa (Italy)
{felice.dellorletta,simonetta.montemagni,giulia.venturi}@ilc.cnr.it

Abstract

In this paper we present a case study focusing on the literature genre, in particular on Italian fictional prose, aimed at identifying the features characterizing this text type. Identified features were tested in two classification tasks, i.e. by genre and by readability, with promising results. Interestingly, the same multi–level set of linguistic features turned out to reliably capture variation within and across textual genres.

1 Introduction

Over the last ten years, Natural Language Processing (NLP) techniques combined with machine learning algorithms started being used to investigate the "form" of a text rather than its content. The range of tasks sharing this approach to the analysis of texts is wide, ranging e.g. from native language identification (see among the others Koppel et al. (2005) and Wong and Dras (2009)), author recognition and verification (see e.g. van Halteren (2004), authorship attribution (see Juola (2008) for a survey), genre identification (Mehler et al., 2011) to readability assessment (see Dell'Orletta et al. (2011a) for an updated survey). Besides obvious differences at the level of selected linguistic features and learning techniques, which are also motivated by the language varieties targeted by the different tasks, they share a common approach: they succeed in determining the language variety, the author, the text genre or the level of readability of a text by exploiting the distribution of features automatically extracted from texts. The issues typically dealt with in this type of studies can be summarised in two main research questions aimed at investigating 1) which linguistic features work best for a given task, and 2) which type of machine learning algorithms are best suited for a given task.

In this paper, we focus on the first issue, i.e. on the typology of linguistic features which could be reliably extracted from automatically analysed texts with particular attention to the potential impact of achieved results on two classification tasks. In particular, we identified the set of linguistic features characterizing classes of documents, based on their textual genre or the type of audience they target: to put it in van Halteren words (van Halteren, 2004), we carried out "linguistic profiling" of texts selected as representative of different genres and/or readability levels. Achieved theoretical results were tested in two text classification tasks, aimed at classifying texts by genre or readability level. This goal was pursued in a case study focusing on the literature genre, in particular on Italian fictional prose. First, we studied variation within and across genres, by carrying out a contrastive linguistic analysis a) of a corpus of literature texts with respect to corpora representative of other textual genres, and b) within the class of literary texts based on the expected target audience (adult vs children). Second, identified features were exploited as a proof of concept in two classification tasks, aimed at automatically discriminating literature texts from texts belonging to other genres, and literature texts targeting adults vs children. A qualifying feature of our approach to the problem consists in the fact that the set of linguistic features explored to capture variation within and across textual genres is wide and, thanks to the most recent developments of NLP technologies, covers different levels of linguistic description, including syntax. The selection of features was not driven by the specific task we had in mind: we show that the same set of features turned out to be appropriate for two different and quite unrelated tasks such as genre classification and readability assessment. According to the most recent literature on readability, the degree of readability appears to be, at least to some extent, connected to the textual genre of the document under evaluation (Kate, 2010; Štajner, 2012; Dell'Orletta et al., 2012): linguistic features correlated with readability are also genre dependent. In particular, the results achieved in this case study are in line with those obtained by (Sheehan, 2013) who demonstrated that, when genre effects are ignored, readability scores for informational texts (e.g. newspaper texts) tend to be overestimated, while those for literary texts (e.g. short stories, novels) tend to be underestimated, and that the accuracy of readability predictions can be improved by using genre-specific models (this is also claimed by (Dell'Orletta et al., 2012)).

2 Linguistic Features

As Biber and Conrad (2009) put it, linguistic varieties – which they qualify as "registers" from a functional perspective – differ "in their characteristic distributions of pervasive linguistic features, not the single occurrence of an individual feature". This is to say that by carrying out the linguistic analysis of a variety, e.g. a textual genre, we need to quantify the extent to which a given feature occurs. Differences lie at the level of the distribution of linguistic features, which can be common and pervasive in some varieties but comparatively rare in others: e.g. the relative distribution of nouns and pronouns differs greatly between texbooks and literature (the former have fewer pronouns and more repetitions of nouns, while fiction shows a greater use of pronouns). For the specific concerns of this study, we focused on a wide set of features ranging across different linguistic description levels which are typically used in studies focusing on the "form" of a text, e.g. on issues of genre, style, authorship or readability. This represents a peculiarity of our approach: we resort to general features qualifying the lexical and grammatical characteristics of a text, rather than ad hoc features, specifically selected for a given text type or task. This choice makes the selected features highly domain–independent and portable across different tasks (see Section 5).

The set of selected features is described below, organised into four main categories defined on the basis of the different levels of linguistic analysis automatically carried out (tokenization, lemmatization, morpho–syntactic tagging and dependency parsing): i.e. raw text features, lexical features as well as morpho-syntactic and syntactic features.

Raw Text Features

They include *Sentence Length*, calculated as the average number of words per sentence, and *Word Length*, calculated as the average number of characters per word.

Lexical Features

Basic Italian Vocabulary rate features: they refer to the internal composition of the vocabulary of the text. As a reference resource we took the *Basic Italian Vocabulary* by De Mauro (2000), including a list of 7000 words highly familiar to native speakers of Italian. In particular, we calculated two different features corresponding to: *i)* the percentage of all unique words (types) on this reference list (calculated on a per–lemma basis); *ii)* the internal distribution of the occurring basic Italian vocabulary words into the usage classification classes of 'fundamental words' (very frequent words), 'high usage words' (frequent words) and 'high availability words' (relatively lower frequency words referring to everyday life).

Type/Token Ratio: the Type/Token Ratio (TTR) is a measure of vocabulary variation which has shown to be helpful for measuring lexical variety within a text. Due to its sensitivity to sample size, TTR has been computed for text samples of equivalent length (the first 1000 tokens).

Morpho–syntactic Features

Distribution of Part-Of-Speech unigrams: this feature is based on a unigram language model assuming that the probability of a token is independent of its context. The model is simply defined by a list of types (POS) and their individual probabilities.

Lexical density: it refers to the ratio of content words (verbs, nouns, adjectives and adverbs) to the total number of lexical tokens in a text.

Mood, tense and person of verbs: this complex feature refers to the distribution of verbs according to their mood, tense and person. It is a central feature in a language like Italian, characterized by a rich verbal morphology.

Syntactic Features

Distribution of dependency types: this feature refers to the distribution of different types of syntactic dependencies (e.g. subject, direct object, modifier, etc.).

Parse tree depth features: tree depth is indicative of sentence complexity as stated by, among others, Yngve (1960), Frazier (1985) and Gibson (1998). This set of features includes the following measures: a) the *depth of the whole parse tree*, calculated in terms of the longest path from the root of the dependency tree to some leaf; b) the *average depth of embedded complement 'chains'* governed by a nominal head and including either prepositional complements or nominal and adjectival modifiers; c) the *the distribution of embedded complement 'chains' by depth*.

Verbal predicates features: these features capture different aspects of the behaviour of verbal predicates and include a) the *number of verbal roots* with respect to number of all sentence roots occurring in a text, b) their arity calculated as the number of instantiated dependency links sharing the same verbal head (covering both arguments and modifiers), c) the *distribution of verbal predicates by arity* and d) the *percentage of verbal predicates with elliptical subject* (Italian is a pro–drop language). Concerning b), we believe that both a low and a high number of dependents can represent peculiar features of a given linguistic variety, corresponding to elliptical constructions in the former case and to a high number of modifiers (locative, temporal, manner, etc.) in the latter.

Subordination features: Features in this class include: a) the *distribution of subordinate vs main clauses*; b) the *relative ordering of subordinates with respect to the main clause* (according to Miller and Weinert (1998) sentences containing subordinate clauses in post–verbal rather than in pre–verbal position are easier to process); c) the *average depth of 'chains' of embedded subordinate clauses*; and d) the *the distribution of embedded subordinate clauses 'chains' by depth*.

Length of dependency links: Lin (1996) and Gibson (1998) showed that the syntactic complexity of sentences can be predicted with measures based on the length of dependency links. We measure the dependency length in terms of the words occurring between the head and the dependent.

3 Corpora and Pre–processing Tools

Four corpora representative of traditional textual genres, i.e. Literature, Journalism, Educational writing and Scientific prose, are considered. These corpora (detailed in Table 1) are internally subdivided into two different sets, according to the expected target audience. In particular, the journalistic corpus is articulated into a newspaper corpus, *La Repubblica*, and an easy–to–read newspaper corpus, *Due Parole*, which was specifically written by linguists expert in text simplification using a controlled language for an audience of adults with a rudimentary literacy level or with mild intellectual disabilities (Piemontese, 1996). The Educational corpus is partitioned into two subclasses, including texts targeting primary school vs high school. The scientific prose corpus includes articles from Wikipedia as opposed to scientific articles. For what concerns the Literature genre, we focused on one of the three major literary genres, namely fictional prose. In particular, the corpus of Italian literary texts explored here is subdivided into two different sub–corpora, constituted by adult and children literature respectively. The adult literature corpus is part of the Italian PAROLE Corpus (Marinelli et al., 2003) and includes 44 novels, either written by Italian writers or Italian translations of foreign novels (very few cases), published between 1974 and 1989. The children literature corpus is part of the wider corpus used for building a statistically–based children's lexicon (Marconi et al., 1994) and includes novels whose target are children of the primary school.

All corpora were automatically morpho-syntactically tagged by the POS tagger described in Dell'Orletta (2009) and dependency–parsed by the DeSR parser (Attardi, 2006) using Support Vector Machine as learning algorithm. DeSR, trained on the ISST–TANL treebank consisting of articles from newspapers and periodicals, achieves a performance of 83.38% and 87.71% in terms of LAS and UAS respectively when tested on texts of the same type (Attardi et al., 2009). However, since Gildea (2001) it is widely acknowledged that parsers have a drop of accuracy when tested against corpora differing from the typology of texts on which they were trained. Therefore, we can assume that the performance of DeSR is probably worse when parsing texts belonging to a different textual genre, such as literature or scientific writing. Despite this fact, we expect that useful information can be extracted from the linguistically annotated text, especially for what concerns the way lexical and grammatical patterns instantiating the features described in Section 2 recur across different text types.

Genre	Corpus	N.documents	N.words
Literature	*Children Literature* (Marconi et al., 1994)	101	19,370
	Adult Literature (Marinelli et al., 2003)	327	471,421
		Total: 428	**Total: 490,791**
Journalism	*La Repubblica* (Marinelli et al., 2003), Italian newspaper	321	232,908
	Due Parole, easy–to–read Italian newspaper (Piemontese, 1996)	322	73,314
		Total: 643	**Total: 306,222**
Educational	*Educational Materials* for Primary School (Dell'Orletta et al., 2011b)	127	48,036
	Educational Materials for High School (Dell'Orletta et al., 2011b)	70	48,103
		Total: 197	**Total: 96,139**
Scientific prose	*Wikipedia* articles from the Italian Portal "Ecology and Environment"	293	205,071
	Scientific articles on different topics (e.g. climate changes and linguistics)	84	471,969
		Total: 377	**Total: 677,040**

Table 1: Corpora.

4 Linguistic Profiling Results

4.1 Linguistic Profiling across Genres

In this section, we discuss a selection of linguistic profiling results corresponding to some of the features which turned out to strongly characterize the Literature genre with respect to the other textual genres taken into account. Starting from raw textual features, it can be noticed (see Table 2) that both average sentence length and average word length show much lower values if compared with the other corpora: this is in line with the Biber and Conrad (2009)'s claim that words and sentences in scientific writing as well as in other types of highly informative texts are much longer than fictional prose where short and simple words are typically used instead of long technical terms. Among the lexical features, the Literature genre appears to record the higher TTR value, meaning that this text type is characterized by a greater lexical variety. For what concerns morpho–syntactic features such as Part–of–Speech distribution, literary texts show a higher occurrence of pronouns and verbs, two features which are more common in conversation than in written language varieties (Biber and Conrad, 2009). On the other hand, quite a low frequency of occurrence of nouns can be observed, giving rise to a much lower noun/verb ratio. Following Voghera (2005) this can be explained in different ways: first, differently from informative texts fictional prose can have dialogical parts, which presumably present a distribution of nouns and verbs closer to that of spoken language; secondly, novels have long narrative parts in which the progression of the text leads to chains of verbal clauses, and this is crucial to determine a higher frequency of verbs. Other important features of fictional prose concern the use of subordinating constructions. This tendency comes out clearly from the different linguistic annotation layers: at the level of morpho–syntax we can observe a higher occurrence of subordinative conjunctions (as opposed to coordinative conjunctions) with respect to the other genres; at the dependency annotation level a higher percentage of subordinate clauses (as opposed to main clauses) is registered, which is also confirmed by the highest average depth of embedded subordinated constructions associated with the literature genre. This strong tendency towards the use of subordination is reminiscent of spoken language which commonly relies on dependent clauses embedded in higher level clauses: e.g. *that* complement clauses controlled by a verb and finite adverbial clauses (e.g. *because*– or *if*–clauses) which are actually much more common in conversation than in informative writing (Biber and Conrad, 2009). Other features which fictional prose shares with spoken language but make it differ from other genres are concerned with the use of ellipsis (see the lower percentage of verbal roots with explicit subject) and of verbal tense (see the lower occurrence of present tense verbs and the high frequency of past tense verbs).

4.2 Linguistic Profiling of Child vs Adult Literature Corpora

In spite of the fact that when compared with other textual genres the Literature corpus taken

Features	*Lit*	*Jour*	*ScientArt*	*Edu*
Average sentence length	17.99	22.90	27.19	28.15
Average word length	4.91	5.09	5.57	5.00
Type/token ratio (first 100,000 tokens)	0.71	0.63	0.66	0.69
Distribution of Parts–Of–Speech:				
– nouns	23.63	28.29	28.53	23.25
– verbs	15.20	13.30	10.67	13.87
– pronouns	6.32	3.05	3.12	5.42
Noun/verb ratio	1.55	2.13	2.67	1.68
Internal distribution of conjunctions:				
– subordinating	29.80	21.60	16.21	21.71
– coordinating	70.20	78.40	83.79	78.29
Distribution of verb tense:				
– simple present	36.26	55.63	54.33	40.67
– simple past	9.79	1.02	1.40	7.27
– imperfect	17.01	4.68	1.27	15.32
Average length of the longest dependency link	7.26	9.11	10.37	10.91
Average parse tree depth	4.57	5.91	6.74	6.57
Average depth of embedded complement 'chains'	1.17	1.30	1.38	1.22
Main vs subordinate clauses distribution:				
– main clauses	66.53	70.55	72.26	67.01
– subordinate clauses	33.23	29.30	27.47	32.23
Average depth of 'chains' of embedded subordinate clauses	1.14	1.09	0.96	1.09
Distribution of verbal roots with explicit subject	48.79	69.70	76.60	66.90

Table 2: An excerpt of linguistic profiling results.

as a whole has a peculiar linguistic profile which makes it significantly different from the other genres, the genre–internal analysis of children vs adult literary texts shows systematic differences. For illustrative purposes, the results of this genre–internal analysis have been compared with a corpus representative of another genre in order to show that in spite of the recorded differences the peculiarities of the literature genre are still clear and visible. We selected to this end Scientific prose, which turned out to be the most distant genre from Literature. Starting from the analysis of the lexical features, it can be noticed that the corpus of texts targeting children (henceforth, *ChildLit*) differs from the collection of texts addressing adults (henceforth, *AduLit*). As Table 3 shows, the *ChildLit* corpus contains a higher percentage of lemmas (types) belonging to the "Basic Italian Vocabulary" (BIV in the table) with respect to the *AduLit* corpus. This is in line with the outcomes of the studies on the discriminative power of vocabulary clues in a readability assessment task (see, among others, Petersen and Ostendorf (2009)): it witnesses the efforts of the authors of children books towards the use of a simple and comprehensible vocabulary. In spite of these differences, a more extended use of basic vocabulary is observed in the literature as a whole with respect to the *ScientArt* corpus characterized by a much lower percentage of BIV words. At the syntactic level, the *ChidLit* and *AduLit* corpora are characterized by different complexity levels. *AduLit* contains *i)* sentences longer than those occurring in the books for children, *ii)* the highest percentage of long dependency links as well as the deepest syntactic trees, and *iii)* the highest percentage of complex nominal constructions with deep sequences of embedded complements. Conversely, for what concerns *iii)*, *ChidLit* is characterized by: a higher percentage of short sequences, i.e. with depth=1 (83.18%) with respect to *AduLit* (77.16%); a lower percentage of sequences of embedded complement chains with depth=≥ 3, covering only 1.73% of all 'chains' as opposed to 2.64% in *AduLit*. Despite these genre–internal differences, the lower syntactic complexity level of the literature with

Features	*ChildLit*	*AduLit*	*ScientArt*
Average sentence length	16.96	18.25	27.19
% of lemmas (types) in BIV	73.95	69.57	58.54
% of lemmas (types) NOT in BIV	26.05	30.43	41.46
Distribution of Parts–Of–Speech:			
– nouns	21.96	24.08	28.53
– verbs	15.83	14.96	10.67
– pronouns	6.88	6.13	3.12
Average length of the longest dependency link	6.63	7.43	10.37
Average parse tree depth	4.51	4.57	6.74
Distribution of 'chains' by depth:			
– 1 embedded complement	83.18	77.16	69.77
– 2 embedded complements	14.11	15.61	22.66
$\geq$ 3 embedded complements	1.73	2.64	7.05
Main vs subordinate clauses distribution:			
– main clauses	68.32	65.77	72.26
– subordinate clauses	30.69	33.92	22.47
Distribution of post–verbal subordinate clauses	88.54	81.16	78.55
Distribution of verbal roots with explicit subject	52.33	47.54	76.60

Table 3: An excerpt of features discriminating adult from children literature corpora.

respect to the scientific prose genre is still visible: *ScientArt* contains longer dependency links, higher syntactic trees and deeper sequences of embedded complements. As seen in Section 4.1, a further qualifying feature of the literary genre is the recurrent use of subordination, which occurs much less frequently in the *ScientArt* corpus. In *ChildLit* subordinate clauses represent the 30.69% of the total amount of clauses occurring in the corpus and they mostly follow the main clause, i.e. 88.54% of the subordinate clauses occur in post–verbal position, while subordinated clauses represent 33.92% of the clauses in the *AduLit* corpus and occur less frequently (81.16%) in post–verbal position. This can be taken as a further proof of the higher syntactic complexity of the *AduLit* corpus. According to the literature, the use of parataxis is preferable to a hypotactic structure since a coordinated construction is in principle more easy–to–read and comprehensible than a subordinate one (Beaman, 1984; Piemontese, 1996). The higher number of post–verbal subordinates in *ChildLit* is in line with Miller and Weinert (1998) claim that subordinate clauses occurring in post–verbal rather than in pre–verbal position are easier to process. Among the features concerning verbal predicates, the distribution of verbal roots with explicit subject, 52.33% in *ChildLit* and 47.54% in *AduLit*, can be indicative of a greater occurrence of elliptical constructions in the adult literature: this represents a peculiarity of literary texts which show a stronger tendency towards the ellipsis of grammatical elements.

5 Two Classification Tasks

5.1 Automatic Textual Genre Assessment

In order to explore whether and to what extent the features illustrated in Section 2 can be successfully exploited in an automatic genre classification task, the four corpora were randomly split into training and test sets. For each corpus, the test sets consist of 30 documents while the training sets include the following numbers of documents: 368 (Literature), 583 (Journalistic), 137 (Educational writing), 317 (Scientific prose). We built a classifier based on Support Vector Machines using LIBSVM (Chang and Lin, 2001) and we used two different models of features: a **Lexical Model**, using a combination of *raw text* and *lexical* features and a **Syntax Model**, combining all feature types. Achieved results have been evaluated in terms of *i)* overall Accuracy of the system and *ii)* Precision, Recall and F–measure. Table 4 reports the results achieved with the two models. The *Syntax Model* shows a significant improvement at the level of the accuracy score with respect to the

	Lexical model (**Accuracy: 62.18**)			Syntax model (**Accuracy: 76.47**)		
Genre	Prec	Rec	F–measure	Prec	Rec	F–measure
Journalism	44.64	83.33	58.14	61.63	88.33	72.60
Literature	77.59	76.27	76.92	85.71	91.52	88.52
Educational	80	6.77	12.5	92.59	42.37	58.14
Scientific prose	77.78	81.67	79.67	80.64	83.33	81.97

Table 4: Genre classification results.

Lexical Model, demonstrating that when the aim is capturing the "form" of a text a crucial role is played by morpho–syntactic and syntactic features, which also play a significant role in the linguistic profiling of texts. It can be noted that, using the *Syntax Model*, the classification of the documents in the class *Literature* achieves a higher F–measure (88.52%) with respect to the *Educational* class which shows the lowest F–measure value (58.14%). We can hypothesize that, as reported in Table 2, the *Literature* genre is strongly characterized with respect to the other textual genres considered here. The fictional prose documents show a strong tendency towards, for example, short dependency links, shallow syntactic trees as well as towards a low percentage of verbal roots with explicit subjects. On the contrary, the results achieved with respect to the *Educational* texts can follow from the internal composition of this corpus gathing a heterogeneous collection of documents (such as textbooks, anthologies, exercises, etc.): this fact may have negatively affected the classification accuracy of the *Educational* texts.

5.2 Automatic Readability Assessment

Starting from the assumption that the expected target audiences of *ChildLit* and *AduLit* texts can be taken as indicative of their accessibility level, we modeled the task of automatically discriminating between children and adult literature as a genre–specific automatic readability assessment task. For this purpose, we used READ–IT (Dell'Orletta et al., 2011a), the only available NLP–based readability assessment tool for Italian. READ–IT exploits the wide typology of lexical, morpho–syntactic and syntactic features illustrated in Section 2. As in the previous case, the classifier is based on SVM that, given a set of features and a training corpus, creates a statistical model which is used for assessing the readability of unseen documents. In this experiment, the *ChildLit* and *AduLit* corpora were split into training and test sets. For each of them, the test sets consist of 30 documents, whereas the training sets include respectively 71 and 297 documents. Achieved results are evaluated in terms of overall Accuracy, Precision, Recall and F–measure. As shown in Table 5, READ–IT performs better at the level of F–measure in the classification of *AduLit* rather than of *ChildLit* texts. As discussed in (Dell'Orletta et al., 2012), this may follow from the small amount of training data available for the children literature class. However, interestingly enough, even if the *AduLit* and *ChildLit* training sets have quite different sizes, the variation internal to the genre was successfully captured by the classifier which achieves an overall Accuracy of 80%. Achieved results show that the set of selected features is also able to reliably capture genre–internal variation.

	Prec	Rec	F–measure
ChildLit	84.61	73.33	78.57
AdLit	76.47	86.67	81.25
	Accuracy: 80		

Table 5: Readability assessment results.

6 Conclusion

In this paper we reported the results of a case study focusing on the literature genre and aimed at carrying out "linguistic profiling" of literary texts as opposed to other textual genres such as Journalism, Educational writing and Scientific prose. Achieved theoretical results concerning the linguistic characterization of the genre represented by Italian fictional prose are nicely complemented by applicative results showing that the features identified can be reliably put at work in two text classification tasks, i.e. the automatic assessment of textual genre and readability level. Interestingly, the same multi–level set of linguistic features was used to capture variation within and across textual genres, without any ad hoc selection of features. Current developments include feature selection and ranking for both genre classification and readability assessment tasks.

References

Giuseppe Attardi. 2006. Experiments with a multilanguage non-projective dependency parser. In *Proceedings of the Tenth Conference on Computational Natural Language Learning (CoNLL-X '06)*, New York City, New York, 166–170.

Giuseppe Attardi, Felice Dell'Orletta, Maria Simi, Joseph Turian. 2009. Accurate Dependency Parsing with a Stacked Multilayer Perceptron. In: Proceedings of Evalita'09.

Douglas Biber. 1993. Using Register–diversified Corpora for General Language Studies. *Computational Linguistics Journal*, 19(2): 219–241.

Douglas Biber and Susan Conrad. 2009. Genre, Register, Style. Cambridge: CUP.

Karen Beaman. 1984. Coordination and Subordination Revisited: Syntactic Complexity in Spoken and Written Narrative Discourse. In Tannen D. and Freedle R. (eds), *Coherence in Spoken and Written Discourse*, 45–80.

Chih-Chung Chang and Chih-Jen Lin. 2001. LIBSVM: a library for support vector machines. *Software available at http://www.csie.ntu.edu.tw/ cjlin/libsvm*

Jeanne S. Chall and Edgar Dale. 1995. *Readability Revisited: The New Dale–Chall Readability Formula.* Brookline Books, Cambridge, MA.

Felice Dell'Orletta. 2009. Ensemble system for Part-of-Speech tagging. In *Proceedings of Evalita'09, Evaluation of NLP and Speech Tools for Italian*, Reggio Emilia, December.

Felice Dell'Orletta, Simonetta Montemagni, Eva Maria Vecchi and Giulia Venturi. 2011b. Tecnologie linguistico–computazionali per il monitoraggio della competenza linguistica italiana degli alunni stranieri nella scuola primaria e secondaria. In G. C. Bruno, I. Caruso, M. Sanna, I. Vellecco (eds.), *Percorsi migranti: uomini, diritto, lavoro, linguaggi*, McGraw–Hill, 319–336.

Felice Dell'Orletta, Simonetta Montemagni and Giulia Venturi. 2011a. READ-IT: Assessing Readability of Italian Texts with a View to Text Simplification. In *Proceedings of the Workshop on "Speech and Language Processing for Assistive Technologies" (SLPAT 2011)*, Edinburgh, July 30, 73–83.

Felice Dell'Orletta, Simonetta Montemagni and Giulia Venturi. 2012. Genre–oriented Readability Assessment: a Case Study. In *Proceedings of the Workshop on Speech and Language Processing Tools in Education (SLP-TED)*, 91–98.

Tullio De Mauro. 2000. *Il dizionario della lingua italiana.* Torino, Paravia.

David Elson, Anna Kazantseva, Rada Mihalcea and Stan Szpakowicz (eds.). 2012. Proceedings of the NAACL-HLT 2012 Workshop on Computational Linguistics for Literature. Montréal, Canada, June 2012, Association for Computational Linguistics, http://www.aclweb.org/anthology/W12-25.

Lyn Frazier. 1985. Syntactic complexity. In D.R. Dowty, L. Karttunen and A.M. Zwicky (eds.), *Natural Language Parsing*, Cambridge University Press, Cambridge, UK.

Edward Gibson. 1998. Linguistic complexity: Locality of syntactic dependencies. In *Cognition*, 68(1), pp. 1–76.

Daniel Gildea. 2001. Corpus variation and parser performance. In *Proceedings of Empirical Methods in Natural Language Processing (EMNLP 2001)*, 167–202.

Patrick Juola. 2008. *Authorship Attribution.* Now Publishers Inc.

Rohit J. Kate, Xiaoqiang Luo, Siddharth Patwardhan, Martin Franz, Radu Florian, Raymond J. Mooney, Salim Roukos and Chris Welty. 2010. Learning to Predict Readability using Diverse Linguistic Features. In *Proceedings of the 23rd International Conference on Computational Linguistics (COLING 2010)*, 546–554.

Moshe Koppel, Jonathan Schler and Kfir Zigdon. 2005. 2005. Automatically determining an anonymous author's native language. In *Intelligence and Security Informatics*, vol. 3495, LNCS, Springer–Verlag, 209–217.

Dekan Lin. 1996. On the structural complexity of natural language sentences. In *Proceedings of COLING 1996*, 729–733.

Lucia Marconi, Michela Ott, Elia Pesenti, Daniela Ratti and Mauro Tavella. 1994. *Lessico Elementare.* Zanichelli, Bologna.

R. Marinelli, L. Biagini, R. Bindi, S. Goggi, M. Monachini, P. Orsolini, E. Picchi, S. Rossi, N. Calzolari, A. Zampolli. 2003. The Italian PAROLE corpus: an overview. In Zampolli A. et al. (eds.), *Computational Linguistics in Pisa*, Special Issue, XVI–XVII, Pisa-Roma, IEPI. Tomo I, 401–421.

Ryan McDonald and Joakim Nivre. 2007. Characterizing the Errors of Data-Driven Dependency Parsing Models. In *Proceedings of EMNLP-CoNLL, 2007*, 122–131.

Alexander Mehler, Serge Sharoff and Marina Santini (Eds.). 2011. *Genres on the Web. Computational Models and Empirical Studies.* Springer Series: Text, Speech and Language Technology.

Jim Miller and Regina Weinert. 1998. *Spontaneous spoken language. Syntax and discourse.* Oxford, Clarendon Press.

Sarah E. Petersen and Mari Ostendorf. 2009. A machine learning approach to reading level assessment. In *Computer Speech and Language (23)*, 89–106.

Maria Emanuela Piemontese. 1996. *Capire e farsi capire. Teorie e tecniche della scrittura controllata* Napoli, Tecnodid.

Sze–Meng Jojo Wong and Mark Dras. 2009. Contrastive Analysis and Native Language Identification. In *Proceedings of the Australasian Language Technology Association Workshop*.

Kathleen M. Sheehan, Michael Flor and Diane Napolitano. 2013. A Two-Stage Approach for Generating Unbiased Estimates of Text Complexity. In *Proceedings of the Workshop on Natural Language Processing for Improving Textual Accessibility*, 49-58.

Sanja Štajner, Richard Evans, Constantin Orasan and Ruslan Mitkov. 2012. What can readability measures really tell us about text complexity?. In *Proceedings of the the Workshop on Natural Language Processing for Improving Textual Accessibility (NLP4ITA)*.

Hans van Halteren. 2004. Linguistic profiling for author recognition and verification. In *Proceedings of the Association for Computational Linguistics (ACL04)*, 200–207.

Miriam Voghera. 2005. Nouns and Verbs in Speaking and Writing. In E. Burr (eds.), *Tradizione e innovazione. Il parlato: teoria - corpora- linguistica dei corpora*, Firenze, Cesati, 2005, 485–498.

Victor H.A. Yngve. 1960. A model and an hypothesis for language structure. In *Proceedings of the American Philosophical Society*, 444–466.

Twitter Part-of-Speech Tagging for All: Overcoming Sparse and Noisy Data

Leon Derczynski
University of Sheffield
leon@dcs.shef.ac.uk

Alan Ritter
University of Washington
aritter@cs.washington.edu

Sam Clark
University of Washington
ssclark@cs.washington.edu

Kalina Bontcheva
University of Sheffield
kalina@dcs.shef.ac.uk

Abstract

Part-of-speech information is a pre-requisite in many NLP algorithms. However, Twitter text is difficult to part-of-speech tag: it is noisy, with linguistic errors and idiosyncratic style. We present a detailed error analysis of existing taggers, motivating a series of tagger augmentations which are demonstrated to improve performance. We identify and evaluate techniques for improving English part-of-speech tagging performance in this genre.

Further, we present a novel approach to system combination for the case where available taggers use different tagsets, based on vote-constrained bootstrapping with unlabeled data. Coupled with assigning prior probabilities to some tokens and handling of unknown words and slang, we reach 88.7% tagging accuracy (90.5% on development data). This is a new high in PTB-compatible tweet part-of-speech tagging, reducing token error by 26.8% and sentence error by 12.2%. The model, training data and tools are made available.

1 Introduction

Twitter provides a wealth of uncurated text. The site has over 200 million users active each month (O'Carroll, 2012) generating messages at a peak rate over 230 000 per minute (Ashtari, 2013). Information found on Twitter has already been shown to be useful for a variety of applications (e.g. monitoring earthquakes (Sakaki et al., 2010) and predicting flu (Culotta, 2010)). However, the lack of quality part-of-speech taggers tailored specifically to this emerging genre impairs the accuracy of key downstream NLP techniques (e.g. named entity recognition, term extraction), and by extension, overall application results.

Microblog text (from e.g. Twitter) is characterised by: short messages; inclusion of URIs; username mentions; topic markers; and threaded conversations. It often presents colloquial content containing abbreviations and errors. Some of these phenomena comprise linguistic noise, which when coupled with message brevity (140 characters for "tweets") and the lack of labeled corpora, make microblog part-of-speech tagging very challenging. Alongside the genre's informal nature, such limits encourage "compressed" utterances, with authors omitting not only needless words but also those with grammatical or contextualising function.

Part-of-speech tagging is a central problem in natural language processing, and a key step early in manly NLP pipelines. Machine learning-based part-of-speech (PoS) taggers can exploit labeled training data to adapt to new genres or even languages, through supervised learning. Algorithm sophistication apart, the performance of these taggers is reliant upon the quantity and quality of available training data. Consequently, lacking large PoS-annotated resources and faced with prevalent noise, state-of-the-art PoS taggers perform poorly on microblog text (Derczynski et al., 2013), with error rates up to ten times higher than on newswire (see Section 3).

To address these issues, we propose a data-intensive approach to microblog part-of-speech tagging for English, which overcomes data sparsity by using the thousands of unlabeled tweets created every minute, coupled with techniques to smooth out genre-specific noise. To reduce the impact of data sparsity, we introduce a new method for *vote-constrained* bootstrapping, evaluated in the context of PoS tagging. Further, we introduce methods for handling the genre's characteristic errors and slang, and evaluate the performance impact of adjusting prior tag probabilities of unambiguous tokens.

1. A comprehensive comparative evaluation of existing POS taggers on tweet datasets is carried out (Section 3), followed by a detailed analysis and classification of common errors (Section 4), including errors due to tokenisation, slang, out-of-vocabulary, and spelling.
2. Address tweet noisiness through handling of rare words (Section 5.1) and adjusting prior tag probabilities of unambiguous tokens, using external knowledge (Section 5.2).
3. Investigate vote-constrained bootstrapping on a large corpus of unlabeled tweets, to create needed tweet-genre training data (Section 5.3).
4. Demonstrate that these techniques reduce token-level error by 26.8% and sentence-level error by 12.2% (Section 6).

Tagger	Known	Unknown	Overall	Sentence
TnT	96.76%	85.86%	96.46%	-
SVMTool	97.39%	89.01%	97.16%	-
TBL	-	-	93.67%	-
Stanford	-	90.46%	**97.28%**	56.79%

Table 1: Token-level labeling accuracy for four off-the-shelf PoS taggers on newswire. Not all these performance measures are supplied in the literature.

Tagger	T-dev		D-dev	
	Token	Sentence	Token	Sentence
TnT	71.50%	1.69%	77.52%	14.87%
SVMTool	**74.84%**	**4.24%**	82.92%	**22.68%**
TBL	70.52%	2.54%	76.22%	11.52%
Stanford	73.37%	1.67%	**83.29%**	22.22%

Table 2: Token tagging performance of WSJ-trained taggers (sections 0-18) on Twitter data. Figures listed are the proportion of tokens labeled with the correct part-of-speech tag, and the proportion of sentences in which all tokens were correctly labeled.

2 Related Work

Regarding Twitter part-of-speech tagging, the two most similar earlier papers introduce the ARK tagger (Gimpel et al., 2011) and T-Pos (Ritter et al., 2011). Both these approaches adopt clustering to handle linguistic noise, and train from a mixture of hand-annotated tweets and existing PoS-labeled data. The ARK tagger[1] reaches 92.8% accuracy at token level but uses a coarser, custom tagset. T-Pos[2] is based on the Penn Treebank set and, in its evaluation, achieves an 88.4% token tagging accuracy. Neither report sentence/whole-tweet accuracy rates. Foster et al. (2011) introduce results for both PoS tagging and parsing, but do not present a tool, and focus more on the parsing aspect.

Previous work on part-of-speech tagging in noisy environments has focused on either dealing with noisy tokens either by using a lexicon that can handle partial matches through e.g. topic models (Darling et al., 2012) or Brown clustering (Clark, 2003), or by applying extra processing steps to correct/bias tagger performance, e.g., post-/pre-processing respectively (Gadde et al., 2011). Finally, classic work on bootstrapped PoS tagging is that of Clark et al. (2003), who use a co-training approach to improve tagger performance using unlabeled data.

3 Comparing taggers on Twitter data

In order to evaluate a new tagging approach, we must first have a good idea of the current performance of state-of-the art tools, and a common basis (e.g. corpus and tagset) for comparison.

3.1 Conventional Part-of-speech Taggers

To quantify the disadvantage conventional PoS taggers have when faced with microblog text, we evaluate state-of-the-art taggers against Twitter data. We used the same training and evaluation data for each tagger, re-training taggers where required.

When measuring the performance of taggers, as per popular convention we report the overall proportion of tags that are accurately assigned. Where possible we report performance on "unknown" words – those that do not occur in the training data. Further, as per Manning (2011) we report the rate of getting whole sentences right, since "a single bad mistake in a sentence can greatly throw off the usefulness of a tagger to downstream tasks".[3]

We evaluated four state-of-the-art trainable and publicly available PoS taggers that used the Penn Treebank tagsettrereetagger: SVMTool (Giménez and Marquez, 2004), the Stanford Tagger (Toutanova et al., 2003), TnT (Brants, 2000) and a transformation-based learning (TBL) tagger (Brill, 1995) supported by sequential n-gram backoff. The NLTK implementations of TnT and TBL were used (Bird et al., 2009). The 'left3words' model was used with the Stanford tagger, and 'M0' with SVMTool. For initial comparison, taggers were tested on standard newswire text from the Penn Treebank (Marcus et al., 1993),[4] training with Wall Street Journal (WSJ) sections 0-18 and evaluating on sections 19-21. The base performance for each tagger is given in Table 1.

3.2 Labeled Tweet Corpora

Three PoS-labeled microblog datasets are currently available. The T-Pos corpus of 15K tokens introduced by Ritter et al. (2011) uses a tagset based on the Penn Treebank tagset,plus four new tags for URLs (`URL`), hashtags (`HT`), username mentions (`USR`) and retweet signifiers (`RT`). The DCU dataset of 14K tokens (Foster et al., 2011) is also based on the Penn Treebank (**PTB**) set, but does not have the same new tags as T-Pos, and uses slightly different tokenisation. The ARK corpus of 39K tokens (Gimpel et al., 2011) uses a novel tagset, which, while suitable for the microblog genre, is somewhat less descriptive than the PTB sets on many points. For example, its `V` tag corresponds to any verb, conflating PTB's `VB`, `VBD`, `VBG`, `VBN`, `VBP`, `VBZ`, and `MD` tags. Intuitively, this seems to be a simpler tagging task, and performance using it reaches 92.8% (Owoputi et al., 2012).

[1] http://www.ark.cs.cmu.edu/TweetNLP/

[2] https://github.com/aritter/twitter_nlp

[3] In fact, as sentence boundaries are at best unclear in many tweets, we use a slightly stricter interpretation of "sentence" and only count entire tweets that are labeled correctly.

[4] LDC corpus reference LDC99T42

Tagger	T-dev		D-dev	
	Token	Sentence	Token	Sentence
TnT	79.17%	5.08%	80.05%	16.73%
SVMTool	77.70%	4.24%	78.22%	11.15%
TBL	78.64%	**8.47%**	79.02%	13.75%
Stanford	**83.14%**	6.78%	**84.19%**	**24.07%**
T-Pos	83.85%	10.17%	84.96%	27.88%

Table 3: Performance of taggers trained on a WSJ/IRC/Twitter (T-train) corpus. T-Pos is the only tagger with Twitter-specific customisations.

Although it is possible to transduce data labeled using the T-Pos or PTB tagsets to the ARK tagset, the reverse is not true. We built a tagger using the T-Pos tagset. This choice was motivated by the tagset's PTB compatibility, the volume of existing tools which rely on a PTB-like tagging schema, and the fact that labeling microtext using this more complex tagset is not vastly more difficult than with the ARK tagset (e.g. Ritter et al. (2011))

The following datasets were used in our study. We shuffled and then split the T-Pos data 70:15:15 into training, development and evaluation sets named T-train, T-dev and T-eval. Splits are made at whole-tweet level. For comparability, we mapped the DCU development and evaluation datasets (D-dev and D-eval) into the T-Pos tokenisation and tagset schema.

Some near-genre corpora are available. For example, resources are available of IRCtext and SMS text (Almeida et al., 2011). Of these, only one is annotated for part-of-speech tags – the NPS IRC corpus (Forsyth and Martell, 2007) – which we use.

3.3 Performance Comparison

For training data composition, we approximate Ritter's approach. We use 50K tokens from the Wall Street Journal part of the Penn Treebank (**WSJ**), 32K tokens from the NPS IRC corpus, and T-train (2.3K tokens). We vary in that we have a fixed split of Twitter data, where earlier work did four-way cross-validation.

The first experiment was to evaluate the performance of the news-trained taggers described in Section 3.1 on two tweet corpora: T-dev and D-dev. As shown in Table 2, performance on tweets is poor and, in some cases, absolute token accuracy is 20% lower than with newswire (Table 1). This comparison is somewhat unfair as not all labels in the test set are seen in the training data. Combining training data of 10K tokens of tweets, 10K tokens of a genre similar to tweets (IRC) and 50K tokens of non-tweets (newswire) is fairer; performance of taggers trained on this dataset is given in Table 3. All taggers performed better against T-dev after having T-train and the IRC data included in their training data (e.g. from 73.37% to 83.14% for the Stanford tagger), showing the impact of tweet-genre training data.

However, the improvements are much less impressive on D-dev, which is a completely different corpus. There, e.g. Stanford improves only from 83.29% on WSJ to 84.19%. Candid analysis suggests that the DCU corpus contains less noisy utterances, with better grammatical consistency and fewer orthographic errors.

Training data	Token	Sentence	No. tokens
WSJ	73.37%	1.67%	50K
IRC	70.03%	2.54%	36K
WSJ+IRC	78.37%	5.08%	86K
Twitter (T-train)	78.19%	6.78%	10K
IRC+Twitter	79.75%	**8.47%**	46K
WSJ+Twitter	82.11%	**8.47%**	60K
All three	**83.14%**	6.78%	96K

Table 4: Performance of Stanford tagger over the development dataset T-dev using a combination of three genres of training data.

Category	Count	Proportion
GS error	6	6.7%
IV	24	27.0%
Pre-taggable	7	9.0%
Proper noun	10	11.2%
Slang	24	27.0%
Tokenisation	8	9.0%
Twitter-specific	2	2.2%
Typo	7	7.9%
Total Result	89	

Table 5: Categorisation of mis-tagged unknown words.

Based on its strong performance, we concentrate on the Stanford tagger for the remainder of this paper. Using this, we measured the impact that tweet and tweet-like training data have on PoS tagging accuracy. As shown in Table 4, the newswire-only trained Stanford tagger performed worst, with IRC (a tweet-like genre) training data yielding some improvement and tweet-genre data having greatest effect.

4 Error analysis

We investigated errors made on words not in the training lexicon (**unknown** words). For the basic Stanford tagger model trained using WSJ+IRC+Twitter (T-train), the tagging accuracy on known tokens (e.g. those in the training lexicon) is 83.14%, and 38.56% on unknown words. One approach for improving overall accuracy is to better handle unknown words.

Tagging of unknown words forces the tagger to rely on contextual clues. Errors on these words make up a large part of the mis-tagged tokens. One can see the effect that improving accuracy on unknown words has on overall performance by comparing, for example, the Stanford tagger when trained on non-tweet vs. tweet data in Table 4. We identified the unknown words that were tagged incorrectly and categorised them into eight groups.

Gold standard error – Where the ground truth data is wrong. For example, the Dutch *dank je* should in an English corpus be tagged as foreign words (`FW`), but in our dataset is marked *dank/URL je/IN*. These are not tagger errors but rather evaluation errors, avoided by

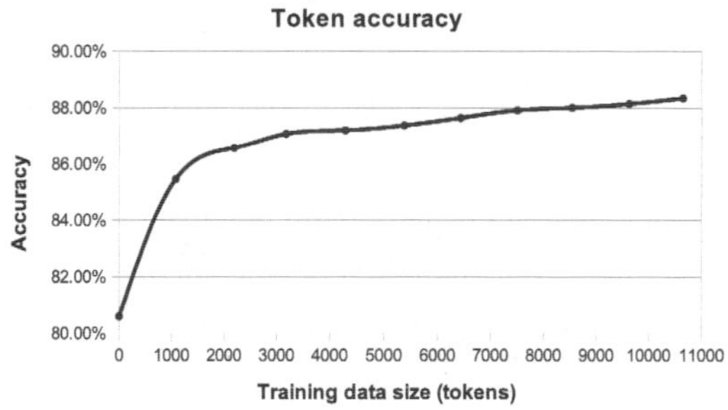

Figure 1: Stanford tagger token-level accuracy on T-dev with increasing amounts of microblog training text.

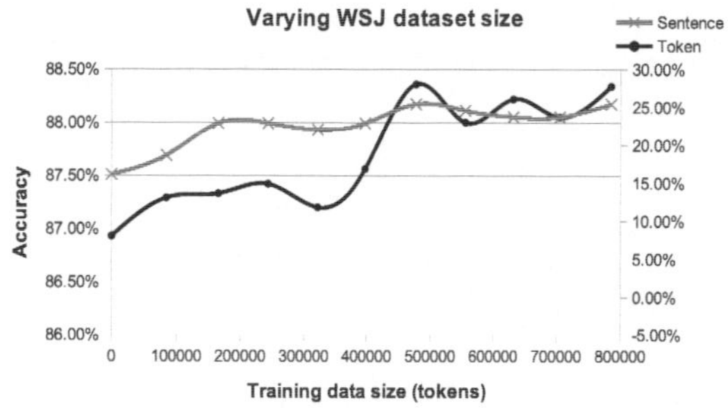

Figure 2: Token-level performance on T-dev with varying amounts of WSJ text, in addition to T-train and IRC data.

repairing the ground truth.

In-vocabulary – Tokens that are common in general, but do not occur in the training data. For example, *Internet* and *bake* are unknown words and mis-tagged in the evaluation corpus. This kind of error may be fixed by a larger training set or the use of a lexicon, especially for monosemous words.

Pre-taggable – Words to which a label may be reliably assigned automatically. This group includes well-formed URLs, hash tags and smileys.

Proper noun – Proper nouns not in the training data. Most of these should be tagged NNP, and are often useful for later named entity recognition. Incorrectly tagged proper nouns often had incorrect capitalisation; for example, *derek* and *birmingham*. Gazetteer approaches may help annotate these, in cases of words that can only occur as proper nouns.

Slang – An abundance of slang is a characteristic feature of microblog text, and these words are often incorrectly tagged, as well as being rarely seen due to a proliferation of spelling variations (all incorrect). Examples include *LUVZ*, *HELLA* and *2night*. Some kind of automatic correction or expanded lexicon could be employed to either map these back to dictionary words or to include previously-seen spelling variations.

Tokenisation error – Occasionally the tokeniser or original author makes tokenisation errors. Examples include *ass**sneezes*, which should have been split into more than one token as indicated by special/punctuation characters, and *eventhough*, where the author has missed a space. These are hard to correct. Specific subtypes of error, such as the joined words in the example, could be checked for and forcibly fixed, though this requires distinguishing intentional from unintentional word usage.

Genre-specific – Words that are unique to specific sites, often created for microblog usage, such as *unfollowing*. Extra tweet-genre-specific training data may to reduce genre-specific word errors.

Orthographic error – Finally, although it is difficult to detect the intent of the user, some content seems likely to have been accidentally mis-spelled. Examples include *Handle]* and *suprising*. Automatic spelling correction may improve performance in these cases.

We also examined the impact the volume of training data had on performance. Figure 1 shows a continuing performance increase as ground-truth tweets are added, suggesting more tweet-genre training data will yield improvements. Conversely, there is already enough newswire-type training data and adding more is unlikely to greatly increase performance (Figure 2). Consequently, subsequent experiments do not include more newswire beyond the 50K-token WSJ corpus excerpt also used in T-Pos.

5 Addressing Noise and Data Sparseness

Our examination of frequent PoS tagging errors identified some readily rectifiable classes of problem. These were: slang, jargon and common mis-spellings; genre-related phrases; smileys; and unambiguous named entities. In addition, observations suggested that more tweet training data would help. Thus, we augmented our approach in three ways: improved handling of unknown and slang words; conversion of unambiguous tags into token prior probabilities; and addition of semi-supervised training data.

5.1 Normalisation for Unknown Words

Tagging accuracy on tokens not seen in the training data (out-of-vocabulary, or **OOV** tokens) is lower than that on those previously encountered (see Table 1). Consequently, reducing the proportion of unknown words is likely to improve performance. Informal error analysis suggested that slang makes up a notable proportion of the unknown word set. To provide in-vocabulary (**IV**) versions of slang words (i.e. to normalise them), we created a set of mappings from OOV words to their IV equivalents, using slang dictionaries and manual examination of the training data. The mapping is applied to text before it is tagged, and the original token is labeled with a PoS tag based on the mapped (normalised) word.

Many texts contain erroneous or slang tokens, which can be mapped to in-lexicon versions of themselves via *normalisation*. A critical normalisation subtask is

Features	Token	Sent.
Baseline[7]	83.14%	6.78%
Word shape features[8]	87.91%	22.88%
As above, excl. company suffixes	88.34%	**25.42%**
Low common word threshold[9]	88.36%	**25.42%**
Low common & rare word thresh.[10]	**88.49%**	**25.42%**

Table 6: Impact of introduction of word shape features, as token accuracy on T-dev.

distinguishing previously-unseen but correctly spelled words (such as proper nouns) from those with orthographic anomalies. Anomalous tokens are those with unusual orthography, either intentional (e.g. slang) or unintentional (e.g. typos). Slang words account for a large proportion of mislabeled unknowns (Table 5).

Normalisation is a difficult task and current approaches are complex (Kaufmann and Kalita, 2010; Han and Baldwin, 2011; Liu et al., 2012). Rather than apply sophisticated word clustering or multi-stage normalisation, we took a data-driven approach to investigating and then handling problematic tokens.

Setup In our data, a small subset of orthographic errors and otherwise-unusual words account for a large part of the total anomalous words. We use a lookup list (derived from unknown words in the training corpus) to map these to more common forms, e.g. *luv*→*love* and *hella*→*very*.[5] This lookup list is based upon both external slang gazetteers and observations over T-train.

To supplement this knowledge-based approach, we enable and fine-tune unknown-word handling features of the Stanford tagger. The tagger contains highly-configurable feature generation options for handling unknown words. These extra **rare word features** accounted for information such as word shape, word length and so on.[6] Their inclusion should increase the amount of unknown word handling information in the final model. Results are given in Table 6.

We also tuned the rare word thresholds for our corpus, changing the threshold for inclusion of a token's rare word features. We tried values from zero to 20 in steps of 1; per-token performance peaked at 88.49% for $rarewordthreshold = 3$. It slowly declined for higher values up to 700 (tested in larger steps). This modest improvement indicates value in optimising the rare word threshold.

Unknown Handling Results Thus, we were able to increase part-of-speech tagging performance in three ways: by adapting the idea of normalisation and implementing it with both fixed word-lists (repairing all but 20% of problem tokens), with extra features encoding word shapes to handle OOV terms, and with a more sensitive threshold to inclusion of rare words in the model.

Entity pre-labeled	Token
Baseline	88.49%
Slang	88.76%
Named Entities	88.71%
Smileys	88.54%
Genre-specific	88.58%
All	**89.07%**
Error reduction	5.03%

Table 7: Impact of prior labeling and mapping slang to IV terms on T-dev; rare word threshold is 3.

5.2 Tagging from External Knowledge

It is possible to constrain the possible set of sentence labelings by pre-assigning probability distributions to tokens for which there is an unambiguous tag. In these cases, the distribution is just $P(t_{correct}) = 1.0$. This strategy not only improves accuracy on these tokens, but also reduces uncertainty regarding the set of potential sentence taggings.

For example, in a simplified HMM bigram tagging scenario, one has a sequence of words $w_0, w_1..w_n$ having corresponding tags $t_0, t_1..t_n$, and is concerned with emission distributions $P(w_i|t_i)$ and tag transition probabilities $P(t_i|t_{i-1})$. Knowing $P(t_i)$ for one word affects all subsequent tag distributions. As the tagger is typically used in a bidirectional mode (effectively adding reverse transition probabilities $P(t_i|t_{i+1})$), using prior knowledge to inform labels reduces tagging uncertainty over the whole sentence.

Setup In the above error analysis, off-the-shelf taggers made errors on some Twitter-specific phenomena. Some errors on tokens where the four tweet-specific labels `URL`, `USR`, `RT` and `HT` apply can be reliably and automatically prevented by using regular expression patterns to detect pertinent tokens.

A second category of mistakes was smileys (aka emoticons), of which the most frequent can be labeled `UH` unambiguously using a look-up list. Some flexibility is required to capture smiley variations, e.g. -__- vs. -____- (Park et al., 2013), which was implemented again with high-accuracy regular expressions.

Proper noun errors (`NN`/`NNP`) were relatively common – an observation also made by Ritter et al. (2011). It is possible to recognise unambiguous named entities (i.e. words that only ever occur as `NNP`) using external knowledge sources, such as a gazetteer list or an entity database. In this case, we used GATE's ANNIE gazetteer lists of personal first-names and cities (Cunningham et al., 2002) and, in addition, a manually constructed list of corporation and website names frequently mentioned in the training data (e.g. *YouTube*, *Toyota*). Terms were excluded from the latter list if their PoS tag is ambiguous (e.g. *google* may occur as a proper noun or verb and so is not included).

[5]An intensifier, from the original *"one hell of a ..."*.

[6]http://nlp.stanford.edu/nlp/javadoc/javanlp/edu/stanford/nlp/tagger/maxent/ExtractorFramesRare.html

[8]The tagger's `naacl2003unk` feature set

[9]veryCommonWordThresh = 40

[10]veryCommonWordThresh = 40, rarewordthreshold = 3

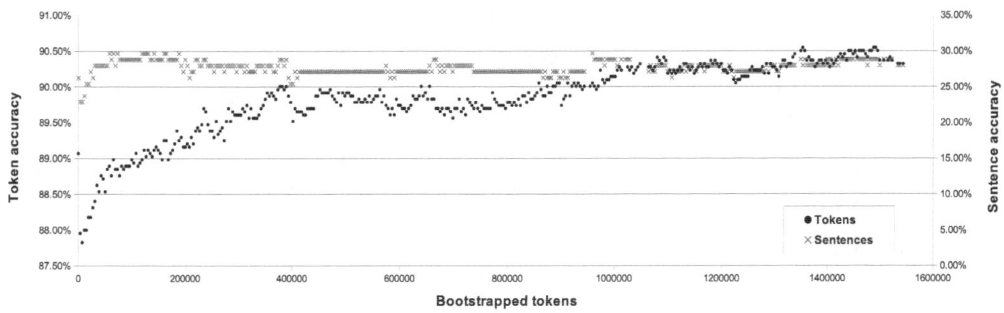

Figure 3: Bootstrapping the tagger using data with vote-constrained labelings.

Tagging with Priors Results In our experiments, the tagger was adapted to take prior probabilities into account, and experiments run using a model trained on WSJ+IRC+T-train that includes the noise-handling augmentations described in Section 5.1. Table 7 shows the performance difference on each of the four categories of token discussed above. Each has an effect, combining to yield a 5.0% error reduction (P<0.005, McNemar's test). When the original model detailed in Table 3 is used, token performance improves from 83.14% accuracy to 86.93%. Assignment of priors affords 22.5% error reduction in this scenario. We compare fixing the tag *before* tagging the rest of the sentence, with tagging the whole sentence and overwriting such tokens' tags. While the latter only affects unambiguous tokens, the former affects the other tags in the sentence during tagging, via e.g. transmission probabilities and window features. This is a novel adaptation of this tagger. To compare, when correcting this model's labels *post*-tagging, error reduction is only 19.0% (to 86.34%).

5.3 Vote-constrained Bootstrapping

Having seen the impact that tweet data has on performance, one choice is to increase the amount of labeled training tweets. We have only a small amount of ground-truth, labeled data. However, large amounts of unlabeled data are readily accessible; a day's discourse on Twitter comprises 500 million tweets of unlabeled data (Terdiman, 2012). In this scenario, one option is bootstrapping (Goldman and Zhou, 2000; Cucerzan and Yarowsky, 2002).

In bootstrapping, the training data is bolstered using semi-supervised data, a "pool" of examples not human curated but labeled automatically. To maintain high data quality, one should only admit to the pool instances in which there is a high confidence. We propose vote-constrained bootstrapping as bootstrapping where not all participating systems (or classifiers) use the same class label inventory. This allows different approaches to the same task to be combined into an ensemble. It is less strict than classic voting, because although both approaches constrain the set of labels that are seen in agreement with each other, classic voting constrains this maximally, to a 1:1 mapping.

In this scenario, equivalence classes are determined for class labels assigned by systems. Matches occur when all outputs are in the same class, thus only constraining the set of agreeing votes. This permits the constraint of valid responses through voting. The caveat is that at least one voting classifier must use the same class inventory as the eventual trained classifier. Given unlabeled data, the method is for each system to perform feature extraction and then classifications of instances. For instances where all classifiers assign a label in the same equivalence class, the instance may be admitted to the pool, using whichever class label is that belonging to the eventual output system.

In this instances, our approach is to use T-Pos and the ARK tagger to create semi-supervised data. We used a single tokeniser based on the T-Pos tokenisation scheme (PTB but catering for Twitter specific phenomena such as hashtags). To label the unlabeled data with maximum accuracy, we combined the two taggers, which are trained on different data with different features and different tagsets. The ARK tagger uses a tagset that is generally more coarse-grained than that of T-Pos, and so instead of requiring direct matches between the two taggers' output, the ARK labelings *constrain* the set of tags that could be considered a match.

To increase fidelity of data added to the pool, for PoS-tagging, we add a further criterion to the vote-constraint requirement. We define high-confidence instances as those from the tweets where the T-Pos labelings fit within the ARK tagger output's constraints on every token.

Setup We gathered unlabeled data directly from Twitter using the "garden hose" (a streaming 10% sample of global messages). Tweets were collected, automatically filtered to remove non-English tweets using the language identification of Preotiuc-Pietro et al. (2012), tokenised, and then labeled using both taggers. The labelings were compared using manually-predefined equivalence classes, and if consistent for the whole tweet, the tweet-specific tags re-labeled using regular expressions (see Section 5.2) and the T-Pos tagset labeled tweet added to the pool.

Tagger	T-eval		D-eval	
	Token	**Sentence**	**Token**	**Sentence**
T-Pos (Ritter et al., 2011)	84.55%	9.32%	84.83%	28.00%
Our Augmented tagger	**88.69%**	**20.34%**	**89.37%**	**36.80%**
Error reduction	26.80%	12.15%	29.93%	12.22%

Table 8: Performance of our augmented tagger on the held-out evaluation data. ER is error reduction.

Vote-constraint results We set out to From our unlabeled data, taggers reached agreement on 19.2% of tweets. This reduced an initial capture of 832 135 English tweets (9 523 514 tokens) to 159 492 tweets with agreed PoS labelings (1 542 942 tokens). To see how confident we can be in taggings generated with this method, we checked accuracy of agreed tweets on T-dev. When tested on the T-dev dataset, the taggers agreed on 17.8% of tweets (accounting for 15.2% of tokens). Of the labelings agreed upon over T-dev, these were correct for 97.4% of tokens (71.3% of sentences).

After an initial dip, adding bootstrapped training data gave a performance increase. Figure 3 shows the benefit of using vote-constrained bootsrapping, giving **90.54% token accuracy** (28.81% for sentences) on T-dev after seeing 1.5M training tokens. The shape of the curve suggests potential benefit from even more bootstrapping data.

6 Results

We set out to improve part-of-speech tagging on tweets, using the full, rich Penn Treebank set. We made a series of improvements based on observed difficulties with microblog tagging, including the introduction of a bootstrapping technique using labelers that have different tag sets.

Based on our augmentations, we evaluated against the held-out evaluation sets T-eval and D-eval. Results are in Table 8, comparing with T-Pos (the other taggers are far behind as to not warrant direct comparison). Significance is at P<0.01 using the McNemar (1947) test with Yates' continuity correction.

Note that we use different evaluation splits in this paper compared to that used in the original T-Pos work. In this paper, training data and evaluation data are always the same across compared systems.

The augmentations offered significant improvements, which can be both extended (in terms of bootstrapping data, prior-probability lists and slang lists) as well as readily distributed independent of platform. The performance on the development set is even higher, reaching over 90.5% tagging accuracy. Both these tagging accuracies are significantly above anything previously reached on the Penn Treebank tagset. Critically, the large gains in sentence-level accuracy offer significant improvements for real world applications.

Regarding limits to this particular approach, the technique is likely sensitive to annotator errors given the size of the initial data, and probably limited by inter-annotator agreement. We have partially quantified the linguistic noise this genre presents, but it is still a significant problem – unknown word tagging does not reach nearly as high performance as on e.g. newswire. Finally, the wide variation in forms of expression (possibly encouraged by message length limits) may reduce the frequency of otherwise common phrases, making data harder to generalise over.

7 Conclusion

Twitter is a text source that offers much, but is difficult to process, partially due to linguistic noise. Additionally, existing approaches suffer from insufficient labeled training data. We introduced approaches for overcoming this noise, for taking advantage of genre-specific structure in tweets, and for generating data through heterogeneous taggers. These combined to provide a readily-distributable and improved part of speech tagger for twitter. Our techniques led to significant reductions in error rate, not only at the token but also at sentence level, and the creation of a 1.5 million token corpus of high-confidence PoS-labeled tweets.

Resources Presented – Our twitter part-of-speech tagger is available in four forms. First, as a standalone Java program, including handling of slang and prior probabilities. Second, a plugin for the popular language processing framework, GATE (Cunningham et al., 2013). Third, a model for the Stanford tagger, distributed as a single file, for use in existing applications. Finally, a high-speed model that trades about 2% accuracy for doubled pace. We also provide the bootstrapped corpus and its vote-constraint based creation tool, allowing replication of our results and the construction of new taggers with this large, high-confidence dataset.

This tagger is now part of the GATE TwitIE toolkit for processing social media text (Bontcheva et al., 2013). The tagger and datasets are also distributed via the GATE wiki, at:

`http://gate.ac.uk/wiki/twitter-postagger.html`

Acknowledgments

This work was partially supported by funding from UK EPSRC grants EP/K017896/1 the CHIST-ERA uComp project (www.ucomp.eu) and EP/I004327/1. The authors would also like to thank John Bauer of Stanford University for his kind assistance with the Stanford Tagger, and Jennifer Foster of Dublin City University for her generous help with extra labeled data. Finally, the first author thanks Aarhus University for their facilities support.

References

T. Almeida, J. Hidalgo, and A. Yamakami. 2011. Contributions to the study of SMS spam filtering: new collection and results. *Proceedings of the 11th ACM symposium on Document engineering*, pages 259–62.

O. Ashtari. 2013. The super tweets of #sb47. http://blog.twitter.com/2013/02/the-super-tweets-of-sb47.html.

S. Bird, E. Loper, and E. Klein. 2009. *Natural Language Processing with Python*. O'Reilly Media Inc.

K. Bontcheva, L. Derczynski, A. Funk, M. A. Greenwood, D. Maynard, and N. Aswani. 2013. TwitIE: A Fully-featured Information Extraction Pipeline for Microblog Text. In *Proceedings of the International Conference on Recent Advances in Natural Language Processing*. Association for Computational Linguistics.

T. Brants. 2000. TnT: a statistical part-of-speech tagger. In *Proceedings of the sixth conference on Applied Natural Language Processing*, pages 224–231. ACL.

E. Brill. 1995. Transformation-based error-driven learning and natural language processing: A case study in part-of-speech tagging. *Computational Linguistics*, 21(4):543–565.

S. Clark, J. Curran, and M. Osborne. 2003. Bootstrapping PoS taggers using unlabelled data. In *Proceedings of the seventh Conference on Natural Language Learning*, pages 49–55. ACL.

A. Clark. 2003. Combining distributional and morphological information for part of speech induction. In *Proceedings of the tenth conference of the European chapter of the Association for Computational Linguistics*, pages 59–66. ACL.

S. Cucerzan and D. Yarowsky. 2002. Bootstrapping a multilingual part-of-speech tagger in one person-day. In *Proceedings of the 6th Conference on Natural Language Learning*, pages 1–7. ACL.

A. Culotta. 2010. Towards detecting influenza epidemics by analyzing twitter messages. In *Proceedings of the First Workshop on Social Media Analytics*, pages 115–122. ACM.

H. Cunningham, D. Maynard, K. Bontcheva, and V. Tablan. 2002. GATE: an Architecture for Development of Robust HLT Applications. In *Proceedings of the 40th Anniversary Meeting of the Association for Computational Linguistics*. ACL.

H. Cunningham, V. Tablan, A. Roberts, and K. Bontcheva. 2013. Getting more out of biomedical documents with gate's full lifecycle open source text analytics. *PLoS Computational Biology*, 9(2):e1002854, 02.

W. Darling, M. Paul, and F. Song. 2012. Unsupervised part-of-speech tagging in noisy and esoteric domains with a syntactic-semantic Bayesian HMM. In *Proceedings of the conference of the European chapter of the Association for Computational Linguistics*, pages 1–9. ACL.

L. Derczynski, D. Maynard, N. Aswani, and K. Bontcheva. 2013. Microblog-Genre Noise and Impact on Semantic Annotation Accuracy. In *Proceedings of the 24th ACM Conference on Hypertext and Social Media*. ACM.

E. Forsyth and C. Martell. 2007. Lexical and discourse analysis of online chat dialog. In *International Conference on Semantic Computing*, pages 19–26. IEEE.

J. Foster, O. Cetinoglu, J. Wagner, J. Le Roux, S. Hogan, J. Nivre, D. Hogan, and J. van Genabith. 2011. #hardtoparse: POS Tagging and Parsing the Twitterverse. In *Proceedings of the AAAI Workshop on Analyzing Microtext*.

P. Gadde, L. Subramaniam, and T. Faruquie. 2011. Adapting a wsj trained part-of-speech tagger to noisy text: preliminary results. In *Proceedings of the Joint Workshop on Multilingual OCR and Analytics for Noisy Unstructured Text Data*, pages 5:1–5:8. ACM.

J. Giménez and L. Marquez. 2004. SVMTool: A general POS tagger generator based on Support Vector Machines. In *Proceedings of the 4th International Conference on Language Resources and Evaluation*.

K. Gimpel, N. Schneider, B. O'Connor, D. Das, D. Mills, J. Eisenstein, M. Heilman, D. Yogatama, J. Flanigan, and N. Smith. 2011. Part-of-speech tagging for twitter: annotation, features, and experiments. In *Proceedings of the 49th Annual Meeting of the Association for Computational Linguistics: Human Language Technologies*, pages 42–47. ACL.

S. Goldman and Y. Zhou. 2000. Enhancing supervised learning with unlabeled data. In *Proceedings of the International Conference on Machine Learning*, pages 327–334.

B. Han and T. Baldwin. 2011. Lexical normalisation of short text messages: Makn sens a# twitter. In *Proceedings of the 49th Annual Meeting of the Association for Computational Linguistics: Human Language Technologies*, volume 1, pages 368–378.

M. Kaufmann and J. Kalita. 2010. Syntactic normalization of twitter messages. In *International Conference on Natural Language Processing*.

F. Liu, F. Weng, and X. Jiang. 2012. A broadcoverage normalization system for social media language. In *Proceedings of the 50th Annual Meeting of the Association for Computational Linguistics*.

C. Manning. 2011. Part-of-speech tagging from 97% to 100%: is it time for some linguistics? *Computational Linguistics and Intelligent Text Processing*, pages 171–189.

M. Marcus, M. Marcinkiewicz, and B. Santorini. 1993. Building a large annotated corpus of English: The Penn Treebank. *Computational Linguistics*, 19(2):313–330.

Q. McNemar. 1947. Note on the sampling error of the difference between correlated proportions or percentages. *Psychometrika*, 12(2):153–157.

L. O'Carroll. 2012. Twitter active users pass 200 million. http://www.guardian.co.uk/technology/2012/dec/18/twitter-users-pass-200-million.

O. Owoputi, B. O'Connor, C. Dyer, K. Gimpel, and N. Schneider. 2012. Part-of-Speech Tagging for Twitter: Word Clusters and Other Advances. Technical Report CMU-ML-12-107, Machine Learning Department, Carnegie Mellon University.

J. Park, V. Barash, C. Fink, and M. Cha. 2013. Emoticon Style: Interpreting Differences in Emoticons Across Cultures. In *Proceedings of the Seventh International AAAI Conference on Weblogs and Social Media*, pages 466–475. AAAI Press.

D. Preotiuc-Pietro, S. Samangooei, T. Cohn, N. Gibbins, and M. Niranjan. 2012. Trendminer: An architecture for real time analysis of social media text. In *Proceedings of the workshop on Real-Time Analysis and Mining of Social Streams*.

A. Ritter, S. Clark, O. Etzioni, et al. 2011. Named entity recognition in tweets: an experimental study. In *Proceedings of the Conference on Empirical Methods in Natural Language Processing*, pages 1524–1534. ACL.

T. Sakaki, M. Okazaki, and Y. Matsuo. 2010. Earthquake shakes Twitter users: real-time event detection by social sensors. In *Proceedings of the 19th international conference on World Wide Web (WWW)*, pages 851–860. ACM.

D. Terdiman. 2012. Report: Twitter hits half a billion tweets a day. http://news.cnet.com/8301-1023_3-57541566-93/report-twitter-hits-half-a-billion-tweets-a-day/.

K. Toutanova, D. Klein, C. Manning, and Y. Singer. 2003. Feature-rich part-of-speech tagging with a cyclic dependency network. In *Proceedings of the Conference of the North American Chapter of the Association for Computational Linguistics on Human Language Technology*, pages 173–180. ACL.

Weighted maximum likelihood as a convenient shortcut to optimize the F-measure of maximum entropy classifiers

Georgi Dimitroff, Laura Toloşi, Borislav Popov and Georgi Georgiev
Ontotext AD, Sofia, Bulgaria
georgi.dimitrov, laura.tolosi, borislav.popov, georgi.georgiev@ontotext.com

Abstract

We link the weighted maximum entropy and the optimization of the expected F_β-measure, by viewing them in the framework of a general common multi-criteria optimization problem. As a result, each solution of the expected F_β-measure maximization can be realized as a weighted maximum likelihood solution - a well understood and behaved problem. The specific structure of maximum entropy models allows us to approximate this characterization via the much simpler class-wise weighted maximum likelihood. Our approach reveals any probabilistic learning scheme as a specific trade-off between different objectives and provides the framework to link it to the expected F_β-measure.

1 Introduction

In many NLP classification applications, the classes are not symmetric and the user has some preference towards a high Precision or Recall of a particular target class. Thus, appropriate tuning of the model is often necessary, depending on the particular tolerance of the application to false positive or false negative results. This preference can be expressed by requiring a large F_β measure for a particular β describing the desired Precision/Recall trade-off. Ideally, the parameters of the linear model should be estimated such that a desired F_β measure is maximized. However, directly maximizing F_β is hard, due to its non-concave shape.

Maximum likelihood-based classifiers such as the maximum entropy are relatively easy to fit, but they are rigid and cannot be tuned to a desired Precision and Recall trade-off. In this article, we consider a more flexible maximum entropy model, which optimizes a *weighted* likelihood function. If appropriate weights are chosen, then the maximum weighted likelihood model coincides with the optimal F_β model. The advantage of the weighted likelihood as a loss function is that it is concave and standard gradient methods can be used for its optimization. In fact an existing maximum entropy implementation can be easily generalized to the weighted case.

To the best of our knowledge, such a link between the maximum likelihood and the F_β has not been established before. The article is focused on the intuition of the relation and the sketch of the proof of the main result. We also present numerical experiment supporting the theoretical findings. Additional value of our theoretical observation is that it establishes the methodology of viewing a particular probabilistic model as a specific solution of a common multi-criteria optimization problem.

This article is organized as follows. In Section 2 we present related work, Sections 3 to 6 present the theoretical aspects of link between the weighted maxent and F measure. Section 7 introduces the algorithm, Section 8 explains the steps for evaluation of the algorithm, Section 9 presents the datasets. Sections 10 and 11 present aspects of performance of our method on the datasets and Section 12 concludes the paper.

2 Related work

The most popular heuristic for Precision-Recall trade-off is based on adjusting the acceptance threshold given by maximum entropy models (or any learning framework). However, this procedure amounts to a simple translation of the maximum likelihood hyperplane towards or away from the target class and does not fit the model anew.

The expected F measure $\tilde{F}$ is also considered in (Nan et al., 2012), where also its consistency is studied and even a Hoeffding bound for the convergence is given. However, the authors there mainly concentrate on the acceptance threshold to optimize the F-measure.

(Dembczyn'ski et al., 2011) gave a general algorithm for F measure optimization for a particular parametrization involving $m^2 + 1$ parameters where m is the number of examples in the binary classification case. Determining the parameters of the models however can be very hard. A very interesting result in (Dembczyn'ski et al., 2011) is that in the worst case there is a lower bound on the discrepancy between the optimal solution and the solution obtained by means of optimal acceptance threshold, which further motivates our approach. In our approach we directly find the parameters of the model that maximize the expected F measure using the link to the weighted maximum likelihood.

(Jansche, 2005) describe a maximum entropy model that optimizes directly an expected F_β-based loss. However the expected F_β is not concave and is rather cumbersome to deal with. Therefore the standard gradient methods do not guarantee optimality of the solution.

(Minkov et al., 2006) introduce another heuristics, which is based on changing the weight of a special feature, which indicates if a sample is in the complementary class or not.

The weighted logistic regression is well known, see for example (Vandev and Neykov, 1998), and the corresponding estimation is barely harder than in the standard case without weights. See also (Simecková, 2005) for an interesting discussion.

3 The Maximum Entropy Model

The maximum entropy modeling framework as introduced in the NLP domain by (Berger et al., 1996) has become the standard for various NLP tasks. To fix notations consider a training set of m samples $\{(x(i), y(i)) : i \in 1, \dots m\}$ where $x(i)$ is a sample with class $y(i)$, where $y(i)$ takes values in some finite set $\mathcal{Y}$. In this paper we aim at explaining the main idea of the link between the weighted maximum entropy and the expected F_β; to keep things technically simple we restrict to the case $|\mathcal{Y}| = 2$. Each observation is represented by a set of features $\{f_j(x(i), y(i)) : j \in 1, \dots, N\}$.

The maximum entropy principle forces the model conditional probabilities $p(y|x, \lambda)$ to have the form:

$$p(y|x, \lambda) = \frac{1}{Z_\lambda(x)} \exp \sum_j \lambda_j \cdot f_j(x, y),$$

where $\lambda \in \mathbb{R}^N$ are the model parameters and $Z_\lambda(x)$ is a normalization constant. The calibration of the model amounts to (see (Berger et al., 1996)) maximizing the log-likelihood

$$l(\lambda : x, y) = \sum_{i=1}^{m} \log p(y(i)|x(i), \lambda).$$

In the following for a weight vector $w \in \mathbb{R}^m$ we will make use of the weighted log-likelihood function

$$l^W(\lambda : w, x, y) = \sum_{i=1}^{m} w(i) \log p(y(i)|x(i), \lambda).$$

In our case the weights will be defined mostly class-wise, i.e. examples from the same class will always have the same weights.

4 Precision/Recall trade off. Expected F_β-measure.

The performance of a classifier is typically measured using the Precision and Recall metrics, and in particular their tradeoff described by a constant $\beta \in [0, 1]$ and expressed as the β-weighted harmonic mean called F_β-measure:

$$F_\beta := \left(\frac{\beta}{P} + \frac{1-\beta}{R} \right)^{-1}.$$

The larger the β the greater the influence of the Precision as compared to the Recall on the F_β-measure. The Precision and Recall are defined in terms of the true/false positive/negative counts.

For a given example with attributes x the maximum entropy model will produce the conditional probabilities $p(y|x, \lambda)$ of the example being into one of the classes $y \in \mathcal{Y}$. When used for classification however, one would typically choose the class $y(x)$ having the largest probability i.e.

$$y(x) = \text{argmax}_y p(y|x, \lambda).$$

This means that we would completely disregard the additional information incorporated into the model. A more probabilistic approach would be to draw the class $y(x)$ randomly out of the model distribution given by the probability weights $\{p(y|x, \lambda) : y \in \mathcal{Y}\}$. This way the classes $y(x)$ as well as the true/false positive/negative counts would be random variables. However if we perform this sampling many times and take the average we will end up having the expected true/false positive/negative counts. For example the expected true positive and true negative counts are given by

$$\begin{aligned} \tilde{A}_u &= \mathbb{E}\#\text{true pos} = \sum_{i:y(i)=1} p(1|x(i), \lambda); \\ \tilde{D}_u &= \mathbb{E}\#\text{true neg} = \sum_{i:y(i)=0} p(0|x(i), \lambda) \end{aligned} \quad (1)$$

Using the expected counts instead of the realized ones we can define the mean field approximation $\tilde{P}$ and $\tilde{R}$ of the precision and recall metrics and consequently define the mean field approximation $\tilde{F}_\beta$ of the standard F_β measure

$$\tilde{F}_\beta := \left(\frac{\beta}{\tilde{P}} + \frac{1-\beta}{\tilde{R}} \right)^{-1}.$$

As in (Jansche, 2005) with a slight abuse of notation we will call $\tilde{F}_\beta$ the expected F_β measure. For a large training set and a good model the expected F_β measure on the training set will be close to the standard one since the model probabilities $p(y(i)|x(i), \lambda)$ will be close to one for the training examples.

5 Weighted maximum likelihood vs. expected F_β-measure maximization.

Clearly the log-likelihood and the expected F_β measure are two different, however one would hope, not orthogonal objectives.

Intuitively every reasonable machine learning model would try to set the model parameters λ in such a manner that for all training examples the model conditional probabilities of the observed classes $y(i)$ given the example's attributes $x(i)$, namely $p(y(i)|x(i), \lambda)$, are as large as possible. In general if the used model is not overfitting it would not be possible for all conditional probabilities to be close to one simultaneously, and implicitly every particular model would handle the trade-offs in its own manner. In this sense the important difference between the log-likelihood and the expected F_β measure seen as objective functions is that, while the log-likelihood approach gives equal importance to all training examples on the logarithmic scale the (expected) F_β measure has a parameter controlling this trade-off on a class-wise level. On the other hand, as noted in (Jansche, 2005) the flexibility in $\tilde{F}_\beta$ comes at a price - the $\tilde{F}_\beta$ is by far not that nice function to optimize as the log-likelihood is. The next proposition gives a useful link between the $\tilde{F}_\beta$ and the weighted log-likelihood enabling us to find $\tilde{F}_\beta$ optimizers by solving the very well behaved and understood weighted maximum likelihood problem.

Proposition 1. *Let $\hat{\lambda}_\beta$ be the maximizer of the expected F_β measure $\tilde{F}_\beta$. Then there exists a vector of weights $w(\beta) \in \mathbb{R}^m$ such that $\hat{\lambda}_\beta$ coincides with the weighted maximum likelihood estimator*

$$\hat{\lambda}_{ML}^{w(\beta)} = arg\max l^W(\lambda : w(\beta), x, y)$$

Moreover, we can approximate the β-implied weights $w(\beta)$ with a class-wise weight vector $\bar{w}(\beta)$ (i.e., the weights of training examples from the same class have the same weights), that is

$$\hat{\lambda}_\beta = \hat{\lambda}_{ML}^{w(\beta)} \quad \textit{and} \quad \hat{\lambda}_\beta \approx \hat{\lambda}_{ML}^{\bar{w}(\beta)}$$

Below we give the intuition of the proof and some formal arguments, without presenting all technical details, due to lack of space.

Sketch of proof:

The proof makes use of multicriteria optimization techniques (Ehrgott, 2005), which are typically applied when two or more conflicting objectives need to be optimized simultaneously. In our case, the number of true positives and the number of true negatives need to be maximized at the same time, but most classifiers (at least those that do not overfit badly) trade-off between them. The solutions of multicriteria optimization problem are called Pareto optimal solutions. A solution is Pareto optimal if none of the objectives can be improved without deteriorating at least one of the other objectives.

Intuitively, the maximum likelihood optimizes simultaneously the conditional probabilities $p(y(i)|x(i), \lambda)$ via implicitly setting some trade-offs between them. Therefore our idea is to adjust these trade-offs using the weights in such a manner that the $\tilde{F}_\beta$ is optimized rather than the likelihood. The most natural and general way to look at these trade-offs is to consider the multicriteria optimization problem (MOP) $\max\{\log p(y(1)|x(1),\lambda),...,\log p(y(m)|x(m),\lambda)\}$. It turns out that both the max likelihood and the $\tilde{F}_\beta$ optimizer are particular solutions of the MOP. On the other hand all solutions of the MOP can be obtained by maximizing nonnegative linear combinations of the objectives (Ehrgott, 2005). However a nonnegative combination of the objectives $\{\log p(y(1)|x(1),\lambda),...,\log p(y(m)|x(m),\lambda\}$ is precisely the weighted maximum entropy objective function.

Technically, for each β the $\tilde{F}_\beta$ maximizer $\hat{\lambda}_\beta$ can actually be seen as an element of the Pareto optimal set of the multi-criteria optimization problem

$$\max_\lambda\{\tilde{A}(\lambda),\tilde{D}(\lambda)\}, \tag{2}$$

where $\tilde{A}(\lambda)$ and $\tilde{D}(\lambda)$ are the model expected true positive and true negative counts on the training set. This follows from the fact that we can rewrite $\tilde{F}_\beta$ as follows:

$$\tilde{F}_\beta(\lambda)=\frac{\tilde{A}(\lambda)}{\beta(\tilde{A}(\lambda)-\tilde{D}(\lambda))+(1-\beta)m_1+\beta m_0},$$

where m_1 is the total number of positive examples and m_0 the number of negative ones. Furthermore the Pareto optimal set of (2) is a subset of the Pareto optimal set of the finer granularity multi-criteria optimization problem

$$\max_\lambda\{p(y(1)|x(1),\lambda),...,p(y(m)|x(m),\lambda)\}.$$

Clearly, because of the strict monotonicity of the logarithm the above optimization problem is equivalent to

$$\max_\lambda\{\log p(y(1)|x(1),\lambda),...,\log p(y(m)|x(m),\lambda)\}. \tag{3}$$

On the other hand each element of the Pareto optimal set of (3) can be realized as a weighted maximum likelihood estimator associated to some weight vector $w \in R^m$, which concludes the proof. The pass to approximate class-wise weights is achieved using a linearization of the log-conditional probabilities of the training examples. □

6 Interpretation of the weights

Apart from the obvious technical generalization of the likelihood function the weights could on average be interpreted as a modification of the training set by adding new examples with intensity $w(i)$ while keeping the attributes and the classes $(x(i),y(i))$. In particular for $w(i)<1$ the ith example is deleted with probability $1-w(i)$. If $w(i)>1$, say $w(i)=q+w_f(i)$ for some integer $q\geq 1$ and $0\leq w_f(i)<1$ then generate q identical training examples $(x(i),y(i))$ and additionally clone it with probability $w_f(i)$.

This view highlights yet another interpretation of the weights: an asymmetric regularization. Removing some examples when the weight is smaller than 1 is a well known regularization technique called drop-out. When it is applied to features involving only a subset of the classes then obviously it is an asymmetric regularization. The case of weights larger than 1 can be viewed in the same light by simple renormalization. If we have an exogenous L^2 regularization, adding class-wise weights would alter the influence of the regularization on the parameters corresponding to different classes, yet again we achieve an asymmetric regularization.

7 The algorithm

We search for a value w in a predefined interval $[w_{min},w_{max}]$ which gives maximum $F_\beta(w)$. Our experiments on artificial and real data suggest that the expected $F_\beta(w)$ is unimodal on intervals like $[\varepsilon,w_{max}]$, for a small ε close to zero. This suggests that a golden section search algorithm (Kiefer, 1953) can find the maximum efficiently, i.e. with a minimum number of trained weighted likelihood models.

In practice however the estimate of $F_\beta(w)$ may not be unimodal, because numerical methods are used for training weighted maximum entropy models and the optimal model is only approximately identified. It is safe to assume however that deviation from unimodality is not considerable, for example, we can accept that the function $F_\beta(w)$ is δ - unimodal (as defined in (Brent, 1973)) for some δ. Then, (Brent, 1973) show that the golden section search approximates the location of the maximum with a tolerance of 5.236δ.

Below we describe the steps of the algorithm:

8 Evaluation of the algorithm

In order to demonstrate that our algorithm is an efficient tool for optimizing the F_β measure, we performed the following tests, the results of which

Algorithm 1 Golden Section Search

Require: Unimodal function f, interval $[a, b]$
Ensure: $x^* = \arg\max_x f(x)$

```
φ ← (1+√5)/2
function GSS(f, a, b, p1, p2)
    if |b − a| < ε then
        return a
    else
        if f(p1) > f(p2) then
            b ← p2
            p2 ← p1
            p1 ← (2 − φ)(b − a)
        else
            a ← p1
            p1 ← p2
            p2 ← (2 − φ)(b − a)
        end if
        return GSS(f, a, b, p1, p2)
    end if
end function
p1 ← a + (2 − φ)(b − a)
p2 ← b − (2 − φ)(b − a)
x* ← GSS(f, a, b, p1, p2)
```

are described in the Results section.

First, we evaluated Precision and Recall at different values of the class weight w in the interval $[0.1, 5]$ and show that they are antagonistic, which demonstrates that weighted maxent can trade-off Precision and Recall.

Second, we show that our golden section search algorithm finds a good approximation of the optimum class-weight w, necessary for maximizing a specific $F_\beta(w)$, despite the violation of the unimodality of $F_\beta(w)$. We can identify the optimum weights by means of a *brute-force* approach, by which we try a large number of values for the weight of the target class (in practice, 50 values evenly distributed in $[0.1, 5]$). The *brute-force* is infeasible practical applications, because it requires training a large number of weighted maxent models. The comparison to the *brute-force* method is carried on the training set, because finding the appropriate class weight w is part of model fitting, together with the estimation of the model weights λ.

Third, we demonstrate that the models that we fit are superior (i.e. yield better test F_β) than the maxent model. To this end, we compute F_β for a range of values of $\beta \in [0, 1]$. We compare these results with the test F_β that our algorithm delivers. For a reliable comparison, we also estimate the variance of the F_β values – both for our method and for the baseline – by training on 20 bootstrap samples of the training set instead of the original train set.

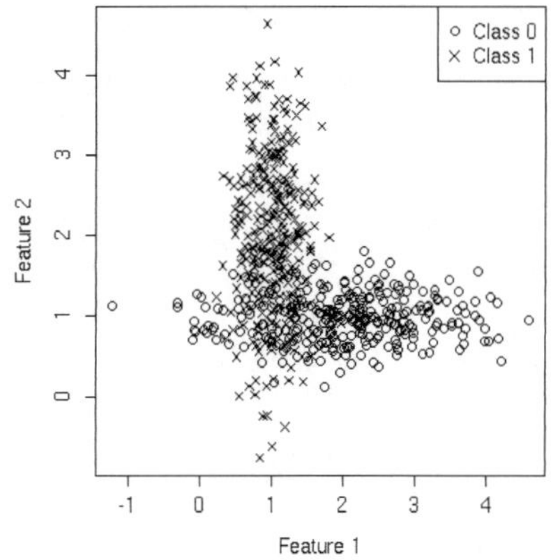

(a)

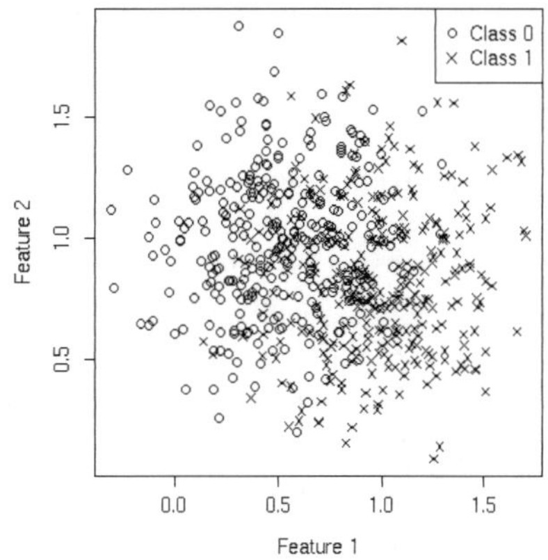

(b)

Figure 1: Distribution of the samples in the space of features for the synthetic datasets: a) dataset A ; b) dataset B

9 Datasets

9.1 Synthetic datasets

We simulated two datasets, A and B, of 600 samples each of them with two equally populated classes and only two features. In dataset A the samples from class 0 are distributed as $\mathcal{N}(\mu_0^A, \Sigma_0^A)$, with $\mu_0^A = (2, 1)$ and $\Sigma_0^A = (1, 0.3)^\top I_2$. Class 1 is generated by $\mathcal{N}(\mu_1^A, \Sigma_1^A)$, with $\mu_1^A = (1, 2)$ and $\Sigma_1^A = (0.3, 1)^\top I_2$.

Dataset B consists of two symmetric spherical Gaussians - $\mathcal{N}(\mu_0^B, \Sigma_0^B)$ and $\mathcal{N}(\mu_1^B, \Sigma_1^B)$ with $\mu_0^B = (0.5, 1)$, $\Sigma_0^B = (0.3, 0.3)^\top I_2$, $\mu_1^B = (1, 0.8)$ and $\Sigma_1^B = (0.3, 0.3)^\top I_2$.

In Figure 1 we visualize both synthetic datasets. We used 400 of the samples for training and 200 for testing.

9.2 Twitter sentiment corpus

We used the Sanders Twitter Sentiment Corpus (http://www.sananalytics.com/lab/twitter-sentiment/), from which we filtered 3425 tweets, labeled as either *positive*, *negative* or *neutral*. We classified tweets that expressed a sentiment (either positive or negative), versus neutral tweets. The neutral tweets are about twice more than the positive and negative tweets together. For the experiments, we used 3081(90%) tweets for training and 343 (10%) for testing. We processed the tweets and obtained about 6095 features. In order to avoid overfitting and speed up computations, we used a filter method based on Information Gain to remove uninformative features. We kept 60 (10%) of the features for our experiments.

10 Experiments and results

By varying the weight of the target class, the weighted maximum entropy achieves Precision-Recall trade-off. Figure 2 clearly illustrates the trade-off, for the synthetic data A and the twitter sentiment data. Additionally, note that Precision and Recall are in equilibrium for a a weight that reflects the ratio of the class cardinalities, namely $w = 1$ for the balanced synthetic dataset A and $w = 2$, for the twitter corpus.

The *brute force* method reveals the shape of the $F_\beta(w)$, as a function of β and w (see Figure 4 a) and c)). Both of our datasets suggest that there is a critical value of w which marks a switch point in the monotony of the $F_\beta(w)$ (regarded as a function of β). For w smaller than the critical switch, $F_\beta(w)$ increases with β, and for w larger than the switch, $F_\beta(w)$ decreases with β. This switch is probably directly related to the ratio of the class cardinalities and deserves further theoretical investigation.

Figures 4 a) and c) show also the 'path' that marks the maximum F_β achievable for each β, in solid black line. The path corresponding to our golden search algorithm falls fairly close to that of the *brute force*, as shown by the dotted lines (marking the mean and one standard deviation to each side). Even if sometimes the optimal w is not found exactly by the golden search, the F_β is still very close to the optimum, as shown in Figures 4 b) and d). In fact, the optimum F_β is always within one standard deviation from the expected value of our golden search algorithm.

Finally, we demonstrate that our method performs very well on the test set, compared to the simple maxent baseline. Figure 3 a) and b) show that the test F_β is superior to the baseline, due to its ability to adapt the fitted model to the specific Precision - Recall trade-off, expressed by a value of β.

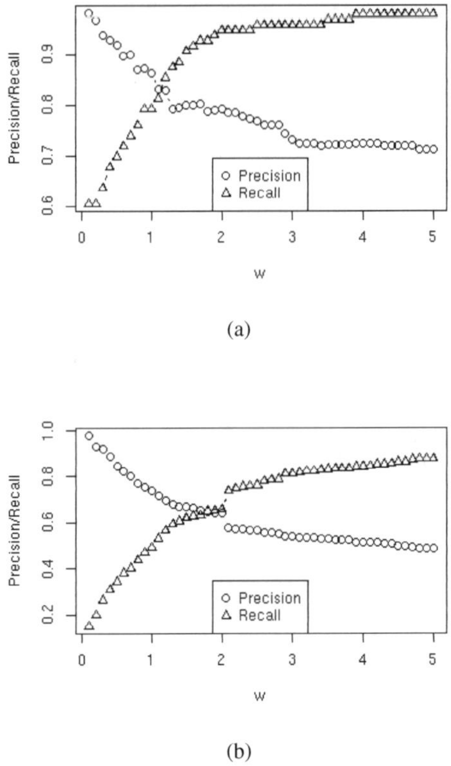

Figure 2: Precision-Recall trade-off on the train set by changing class-weights: a) synthetic dataset A; b) sentiment tweeter dataset.

11 Limits and merits of the weighted maximum entropy

In this section we compare the weighted maximum entropy and the acceptance threshold method with the help of the two artificial data sets A and B shown on Figure 1. The acceptance threshold corresponds to a translation of the separating hyperplane obtained by the standard maximum entropy model. We show that acceptance threshold fails to fit the data well for most values of β, if the data resemble more dataset A than dataset B. In contrast, the weighted maxent is more adaptive, fitting nicely both datasets for all values of β.

It is rather clear that with translation we can achieve an optimal Precision/Recall trade-off for

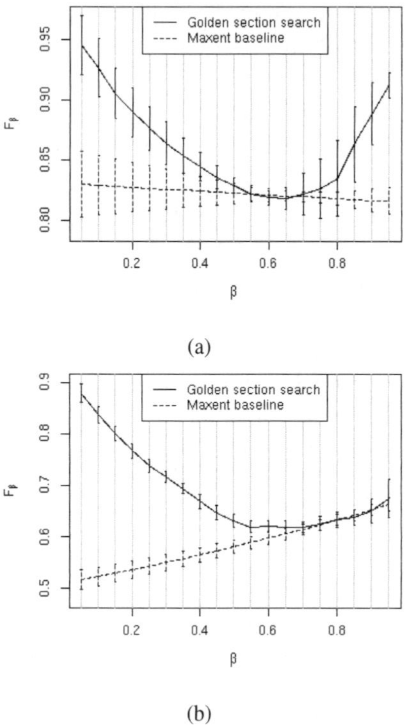

Figure 3: Test F_β for our method, compared to the maxent baseline. One standard deviation bars are added. a) synthetic data; b) twitter corpus.

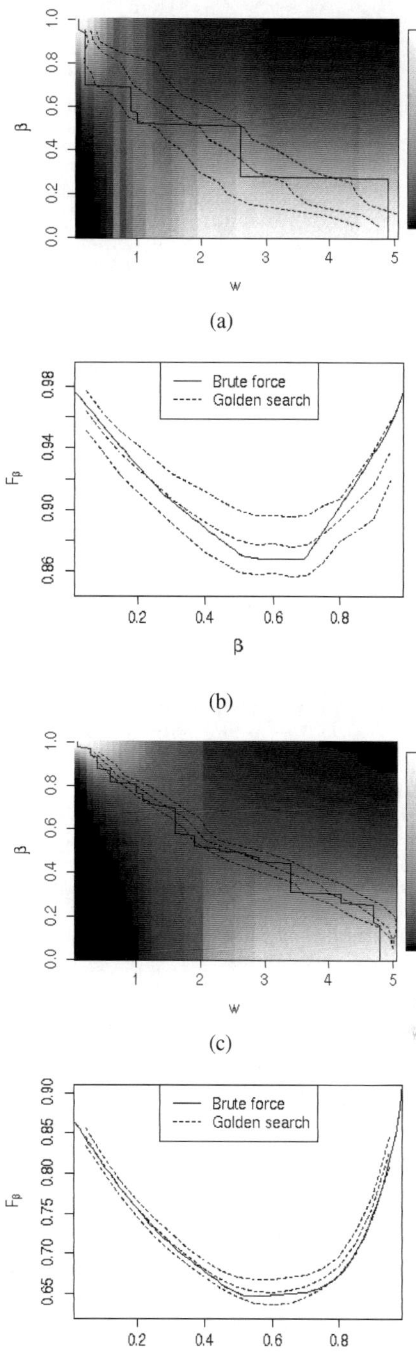

Figure 4: Heatmap showing in grayscale the $F_\beta(w)$ values obtained by the *brute force* method. The solid black line shows the optimal models for each beta. The dotted lines show the estimates given by the golden search: a) synthetic data; c) sentiment corpus. Comparison of the train F_β obtained with the *brute force* (solid line) and with the golden section search (dotted line, with standard deviation): b) synthetic data; d) sentiment corpus.

the synthetic data set B. Indeed, Figure 5 b) shows that the acceptance threshold and the weighted maximum entropy do result in virtually the same optimal F_β values.

The optimal Precision/Recall trade-off for dataset A however requires additional rotation/tilting of the separating hyperplane that cannot be produced by adjusting the acceptance threshold. In line with this intuition Figure 5 a) demonstrates that the weighted likelihood settles at a better Precision-Recall pairs and consequently results in larger F_β values.

Clearly, in the general case the optimal shift of the separating plane is expected to have a rotation component that is unaccessible by simply adjusting the acceptance threshold.

12 Conclusion and future work

The main result of the paper is that the weighted maximum likelihood and the expected F_β measure are simply two different ways to specify a particular trade-off between the objectives of the same multi-criteria optimization problem. Technically we unify these two approaches by viewing them as methods to pick a particular point from

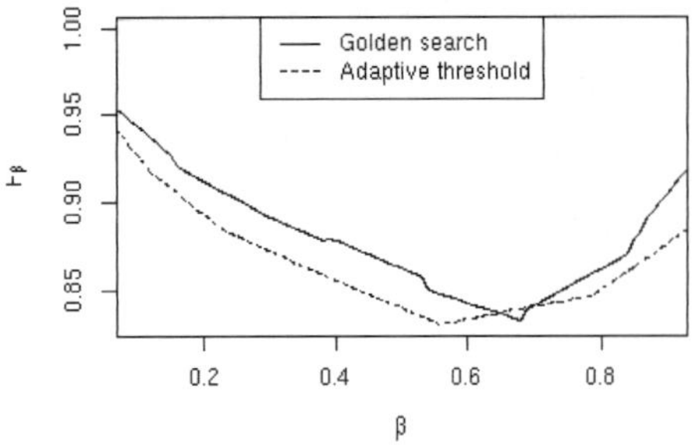

(a)

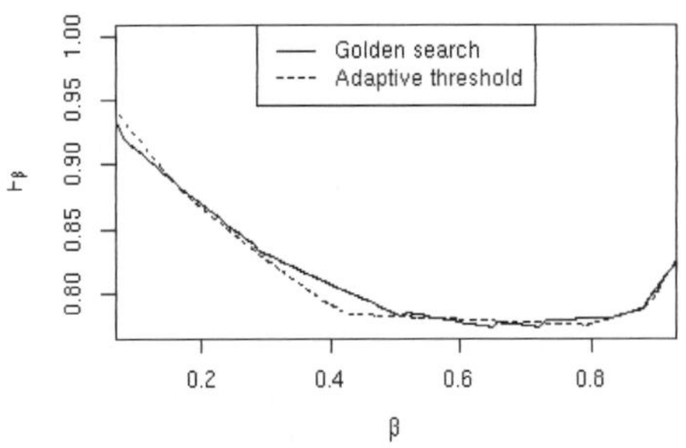

(b)

Figure 5: Comparison of the acceptance threshold versus the weighted maximum likelihood on the stylized synthetic data: a) dataset A ; b) dataset B

the Pareto optimal set associated with a common multi-criteria optimization problem.

As a consequence each expected F_β maximizer can be realized as a weighted maximum likelihood estimator and approximated via a class-wise weighted maximum likelihood estimator.

The presented results can be generalized to the regularized and multi-class case which is a subject for future work.

Furthermore, the proposed approach to view any probabilistic learning scheme as a specific trade-off between different objectives and thus to link it to the expected F_β measure is general and can be applied beyond the maximum entropy framework.

The difficulty in exploiting the statement of Proposition 1 lies in the fact that it is not apriori clear how to choose the weights $w(\beta)$ for a given β. In a larger paper the authors will present algorithms maximizing the $\tilde{F}_\beta$ measure exploiting the theoretical results from this paper via adaptively finding the right weights. Even without a precise estimate for the weights the presented results give the qualitative connection between the Precision/Recall trade-off and the weights: if one aims at higher Precision then smaller weights are appropriate and conversely larger Recall is achieved via larger weights.

We showed with experiments on artificial and real data that using weighted maximum entropy we can achieve a desired Precision - Recall trade-off. We also presented an efficient algorithm based on golden section search, that approximates well the class weights at which the maximum F_β is attained. We showed that on the test set, we achieve larger F_β than the simple maximum entropy baseline.

References

A.L. Berger, V.J. Della Pietra, and S.A. Della Pietra. 1996. A maximum entropy approach to natural language processing. *Comput. Linguist.*, 22(1):39–71.

R. P. Brent. 1973. *Algorithms for Minimization Without Derivatives*. Prentice-Hall, Inc., Englewood Cliffs, New Jersery.

Krzysztof Dembczyn'ski, Willem Waegeman, Weiwei Cheng, and Eyke Hü llermeier. 2011. An exact algorithm for f-measure maximization. In *Neural information processing systems : 2011 conference book*. Neural Information Processing Systems Foundation.

Matthias Ehrgott. 2005. *Multi Criteria Optimization*. Springer, Englewood Cliffs, New Jersery.

M. Jansche. 2005. Maximum expected F-measure training of logistic regression models. In *HLT '05*, pages 692–699, Morristown, NJ, USA. Association for Computational Linguistics.

J. Kiefer. 1953. Sequential minimax search for a maximum. *Proceedings of the American Mathematical Society*, 4(3):502–506.

E. Minkov, R.C. Wang, A. Tomasic, and W.W. Cohen. 2006. NER systems that suit user's preferences: adjusting the recall-precision trade-off for entity extraction. In *Proceedings of NAACL*, pages 93–96.

Ye Nan, Kian Ming Adam Chai, Wee Sun Lee, and Hai Leong Chieu. 2012. Optimizing f-measure: A tale of two approaches. In *ICML*.

M. Simecková. 2005. Maximum weighted likelihood estimator in logistic regression.

D. L. Vandev and N. M. Neykov. 1998. About regression estimators with high breakdown point. *Statistics*, 32:111–129.

Sequence Tagging for Verb Conjugation in Romanian

Liviu P. Dinu and **Octavia-Maria Şulea**
Faculty of Mathematics and Computer Science
Center for Computational Linguistics
University of Bucharest
ldinu@fmi.unibuc.ro
mary.octavia@gmail.com

Vlad Niculae
University of Wolverhampton
vlad@vene.ro

Abstract

Verbs in Romanian sometimes manifest local irregularities in the form of alternating letters. We present a sequence tagging based method for learning stem alternations and ending sequences. Supervised training is based on a morphological dictionary, with a few regular expression paradigms encoded by hand. Our best model improves upon previous machine learning approaches to Romanian verb conjugation, and can generalize to unseen paradigms that can be constructed as variations of the ones in the training set.

1 Introduction

Romanian has a rich inflectional morphology which, in the verbal domain, manifests through complex conjugational patterns. In Table 1, we give an example comparing from left to right: a regular verb, which exhibits an invariable stem, another regular verb, which also exhibits an invariable stem but receives an additional infix *-ez*, a partially irregular verb, which exhibits stem alternation, and a completely irregular verb, which exhibits stem suppletion. The example also shows different syncretism patterns between different conjugated forms. Namely, the 1st and 4th verbs (*a merge* and *a fi*) exhibit 1sg and 3pl syncretism, the 2nd and 3rd verbs (*a dansa* and *a purta*) exhibit 3sg and 3pl syncretism.

Given the richness in ending sequences, stem alternations, and syncretisms, many attempts have been made throughout Romanian linguistics to give conjugational classifications with stronger predictive power than the traditional, Latin-inspired one introduced by Tiktin (1905) which divided verbs into four conjugation classes based on the theme vowel surfacing as the ending in the infinitive form (Costanzo, 2011) and attributed to each of these classes only one general conjugational ending sequence.

The traditional analysis was followed by structuralist ones: Lombard (1955) arrived at 6 classes investigating 667 verbs, Felix (1964) proposed 12 classes, Guţu-Romalo (1968) investigated over 400 verbs and proposed 38 *ending sequences*, which she reduced to 10 verb classes by employing specifically designed homonymy argued against, however, by Avram (1969). When attempting to combine the information gathered about stress shift, ending sequences, and stem alternations, Guțu-Romalo unfortunately ended up with a very extensive classification mirroring a near-exhaustive enumeration of the verbs employed.

More recently, Barbu (2007) distinguished 41 conjugational classes for all tenses and 30 for the indicative present, covering 7,295 contemporary Romanian verbs. Her classes did not take into account stem alternations but only ending sequences, making her classification similar to Guțu-Romalo's 38 ending sequences. On the opposite end, new studies like (Feldstein, 2004) and (Şulea, 2012) take a unifying approach to Romanian conjugation that is elegant in theory but, like

a merge	a dansa	a purta	a fi
to walk	*to dance*	*to wear*	*to be*
merg-λ	dans-ez-λ	port-λ	sunt-λ
merg-i	dans-ez-i	porț-i	eș-ti
merg-e	dans-eaz-ă	poart-ă	est-e
merg-em	dans-ăm	purt-ăm	sunt-em
merg-eți	dans-ați	purt-ați	sunt-eți
merg-λ	dans-eaz-ă	poart-ă	sunt-λ

Table 1: Indicative present conjugation of some Romanian verbs. The first is regular without *-ez*, the next is regular with *-ez*, the next is partially irregular, and the last is fully irregular. We denote the null suffix with λ.

many previous approaches, does not lend itself very useful to computational applications.

2 Related work

The first to attempt a computational approach to Romanian morphology was Moisil (1960) who proposed five regrouped classes of verbs, with numerous subgroups. To model stem alternation, he introduced the concept of variable letters, which were letters that changed their value for different forms of the same verb. Following Moisil, Dinu et al. (2011) first implemented a context-free grammar based on alternation rules, using the idea of variable letters. Ultimately, an implementation based on regular expression was used to label the infinitives from a dataset of Romanian verbs conjugated in the indicative present. This was fed into a classifier that attains 90.64% accuracy rate and 89.89% paradigm F_1 score. (Dinu et al., 2012), but in section 3, we point out significant improvements that can be made to this method.

A dictionary-based morphological generator for Romanian was developed by Irimia (2009), based on paradigmatic theory that aims to model roots and suffixes. Access to the resource is restricted. In this paper we attempt a more flexible modelling that covers, in the same way, suffixes and generic variation within the root.

Goldsmith and O'Brien (2006) use neural networks and word-level encodings similar to (Dinu et al., 2011) for learning inflectional classes, but only on highly regular, predictable patterns, with the goal of learning hidden representations, meaningful for psycholinguistic arguments of language acquisition.

Sequence tagging has been successfully used for other morphological applications in recent years. Closest to our application is the application of mined morphological paradigms in (Durrett and DeNero, 2013), the morphological unit segmentation in (Chang and Chang, 2012) and the Finnish morphological generation for machine translation in (Clifton and Sarkar, 2010). A long standing application of such models is the analysis of unsegmented languages, particularly east Asian languages such as Thai (Kruengkrai et al., 2006), Chinese, and Japanese (Nakagawa, 2004).

3 Paradigm overlap and variable letters

In previous work (Dinu et al., 2011; Dinu et al., 2012), we proposed a labelling system that was learned by a linear SVM with 90.64% leave-one-out accuracy. However, when taking a closer look at the labelling rules described, a considerable amount of overlap can be spotted, in terms of what alternations the rules model. Namely, we saw that some rules ended up corresponding to the same variable letter which, however, varied in a different pattern relative to the person and number verb forms. Table 2 illustrates this situation.

rule 10 a cânta	rule 12 a deștepta	rule 13 a deșerta
to sing	*to rise*	*to empty*
^(. *)t$	^(. *)e(. *)t$	^(. *)e(. *)t$
^(. *)ți$	^(. *)e(. *)ți$	^(. *)e(. *)ți$
^(. *)tă$	^(. *)ea(. *)tă$	^(. *)a(. *)tă$
^(. *)tăm$	^(. *)e(. *)tăm$	^(. *)e(. *)tăm$
^(. *)tați$	^(. *)e(. *)tați$	^(. *)e(. *)tați$
^(. *)tă$	^(. *)ea(. *)tă$	^(. *)a(. *)tă$

Table 2: Example of rule overlap in the unstructured system (Dinu et al., 2012)

We noticed that we can treat each word-level paradigm as a set of local variation patterns. These patterns are equivalent to the variable letters introduced by Moisil (1960). Through this reorganisation, several problems with the system from (Dinu et al., 2012) can be alleviated:

- **Class sparsity:** Certain cooccurrences of variable letters are very rare in the dataset, but the individual variable letters may appear more frequently. The global class corresponding to the joint paradigm is difficult to learn due to lack of data. An example is that of the verb *a putea* (to be able to), whose stem vowel *u* transforms into *o* and *oa*, forming a singleton alternation pattern. However, the specific alternation *o-oa* appears in other patterns (*dormi-doarme*).

- **Class interaction:** Word-level classes that include the same variable letters see each other's instances as negative cases and cannot therefore benefit from what they share. By learning each variable letter separately, all occurrences are used as positive cases.

4 Approach

4.1 Available data

Our labelled data is generated from *RoMorphoDict*, an electronic morphological dictionary for Ro-

	T_1	T_2	T_5	T_6	T_{10}	T_{11}	T_{12}	T_{13}
1sg	$	u$	ez$	ez$	$	i$	esc$	iesc$
2sg	i$	i$	ezi$	ezi$	i$	i$	ești$	iești$
3sg	ă$	ă$	ează	ază$	e$	ie$	este$	ieste$
1pl	ăm$	ăm$	ăm$	em$	im$	im$	im$	im$
2pl	ați$	ați$	ați$	ați$	iți$	iți$	iți$	iți$
3pl	ă$	ă$	ează$	ază$	$	ie$	esc$	iesc$

Table 3: A few of the main ending patterns

manian. The resource is divided according to parts of speech. The subset describing verbs has the following structure for each verb form:

- form
- infinitive
- morphosyntactic description

In (Dinu et al., 2012), we grouped verb forms by their infinitive. We identified, for each of them, six distinct forms covering the two numbers and three persons that are typical of most verbs in Romanian. We wrote sets of six regular expressions that matched paradigms including alternations in the root and could therefore unambiguously describe the conjugation. This is the only place where the morphosyntactic description is used. The matching rules were used as target classes in a one-vs-all multiclass SVM classifier whose input was a bag of all the n-grams within the infinitive, effectively learning to predict the full conjugation paradigm of a verb given its infinitive.

As a follow-up, we propose a finer-grained labelling based on the literature on Romanian conjugation discussed in Section 1. We divided the word-level patterns from in (Dinu et al., 2012) into character-level ones: 16 ending patterns and 17 alternating letters. We used the same regular expressions to identify the verbs that exhibit each combination of patterns and generate labelled instances.

4.2 Sequence tagging

In order to account for multiple interacting variable letters within each verb, we pose verb conjugation as a sequence tagging problem. Each letter in the infinitive is tagged with the particular alternation pattern the verb exhibits for that infinitive letter, or with 0 if the verb exhibits no alternation in that letter during conjugation. Thus, the verb *a tresălta* (to quiver) is labelled as follows:

t	r	e	s	ă	l	t	a
0	0	0	0	a_1	0	t_0	T_1

Here, T_1 encodes the ending pattern received by the class of verbs to which *a tresălta* belongs, as presented in Table 3 along with a few other ending patterns.

4.3 Models and software

The probabilistic model we applied to the verb conjugation problem is a linear-chain conditional random field (CRF). Such models have been often used in NLP because of the linear nature of text: part-of-speech tagging and chunking are important examples of problems that can be successfully solved by sequential prediction models. In the current case, the prediction occurs at the character level, offering a significant computational advantage. The length of a word in letters is usually less than the length of a sentence in words, and the space of possible feature values is also considerably restricted.

Our feature mapping consists of character n-grams to each side of the current letter, up to a fixed window size n, as well as the current letter. The current letter does not form n-grams with the letters around it. For example, the instance of the letter u in *triumfa*, with $n = 2$, would be encoded as:

```
c[-2]=r c[-1]=i c[-2-1]=ri
c[0]=u c[1]=m c[2]=f c[12]=mf
```

The feature names could just as well be arbitrary, as long as they stay consistent over instances.

The usual way of training CRFs is the maximum likelihood (ML) method (Lafferty et al., 2001). Implementations typically maximize the regularized conditional log likelihood of the data.

Recently, online discriminative methods have been shown to be effective for non-probabilistic training of CRF parameters.

						Cross-validation accuracy			Test accuracy		
method	*ps*	*pt*	n	Θ	N	word	char	char′	word	char	char′
SVM				—		0.886	—	—	0.896	—	—
ML	1	1	4	$\alpha = 0.1$	—	0.924	0.987	0.913	0.914	0.985	0.900
AP	0	1	4	—	10	0.923	0.987	0.917	0.912	0.985	0.900
PA	1	0	4	$C = 1$	10	0.925	0.987	0.917	0.912	0.984	0.900
AROW	1	1	4	$r = 100$	100	0.916	0.986	0.912	0.908	0.984	0.895

Table 4: Results obtained by the best hyperparameter set for each training method. 'word' and 'char' are word-level and character-level scores, respectively. The 'char′' column is the character-level accuracy excluding the '0' class.

The structured averaged perceptron (Collins, 2002) is a simple, fast and effective iterative algorithm. It comes from the even simpler structured perceptron learning algorithm, where at each iteration, a data point (x_i, y_i) is chosen and the model prediction $\hat{y}_i$ is computed. If the prediction is wrong, the model parameters are updated in the direction of the current feature vector.

The averaged perceptron approach takes, instead of the final value of the parameter vector θ, its average $\bar{\theta}$ over all the iterations.

The passive aggressive (PA) algorithm (Crammer et al., 2006) is similar to the averaged perceptron: instead of updating when classification is incorrect, it updates when the margin of the misclassification is more than 1, i.e. when the multiclass structured hinge loss ℓ_t is positive. The update is aggressive in the sense that it forces the new parameter vector to correctly classify the input point with margin of at least 1. Finally, averaging is applied in the same fashion.

The AROW algorithm (Mejer and Crammer, 2010) maintains normal distributions over the parameters of the model and updates their parameters in a way that generalizes PA.

We used *CRFsuite* v0.12 (Okazaki, 2007) for implementation of the learning methods listed above. *CRFsuite* can expand the feature expansion implemented by us at character-level to a vector that optionally includes all possible states (*ps*), all possible transitions (*pt*), or both. These flags, along with the window length n that we have searched for in $\{2, 3, 4, 5, 6\}$, control the feature expansion $f(x, y)$. Apart from this, each algorithm has its own hyperparameters. For ML, we used limited-memory BFGS training with ℓ_2 regularization controlled by α. For AP, we varied the number of iterations N. For PA, we varied N and the aggressiveness parameter C. For AROW, we varied N and the trade-off parameter r. We searched for α, C, r (denoted generally as Θ) over $\{0.01, 0.1, 1, 10, 100\}$ and for N over $\{1, 5, 10, 25, 100\}$. The notations given in parantheses in this paragraph correspond to columns of Table 4.

For more appropriate comparison, we reproduced the word-level SVM results from our previous work (Dinu et al., 2011) but with a held-out test set of a quarter of the labelled data. The best parameters chosen for the linear SVM by 3-fold cross validation on the training set are $n = 8$, $C = 0.15$, *tf-idf* normalization, squared hinge loss and ℓ_2 regularization. The labelling used was the same as in the previous work, with the very small classes discarded, making the problem slightly simpler for the SVM.

5 Results

5.1 Automatic evaluation

We optimized the system hyperparameters using grid search over the parameter spaces described above. The collection of $7,295$ infinitive forms was split into a training set of size $4,699$, a held-out test set of size $2,257$[1], and 339 instances that are still left unlabelled by the identified paradigms.

The validation scores are computed using tenfold cross-validation over the training set, and the best hyperparameters, in terms of word-level accuracy, for each learning method, are presented in Table 4.

5.2 Manual evaluation

While the previous method verifies that a sequence model benefits from the extra informa-

[1]The split is ad hoc: the first occurrence of any label gets put into the test set, and subsequent occurrences are put into the test set with probability $1/3$. By making sure that all labels are represented in the test set we avoid underestimating the test error.

tion and more accurately reconstructs the conjugation classes for which Dinu et al. (2011) proposed regular expressions, we anticipate that because of higher granularity, a sequence model can give useful results on verbs whose conjugation does not match the predefined patterns. Out of the total of 339 verbs that did not fit into the variable letter and termination patterns that we enumerated, we manually checked the tags given by PA to the first 105 verbs against their actual conjugations (as given in RoMorphoDict). Out of these, 30 had at least one non-null tag correct, demonstrating our method's ability to generalize. The overall tag predictions fell into these categories:

1. completely wrong: neither ending nor alternations (if any) were correctly tagged

2. correct ending, wrong alternations

3. correct alternations, wrong ending.

In terms of wrong endings, the most common mistakes were those when T_1, which represents the tag for the regular conjugational pattern of verbs ending in *-a*, was confused with T_5, the tag corresponding to the standard conjugational pattern of the special class of verbs ending in *-a* which also receive the infix *-ez*. It is likely that the features correlated with these tags are similar, and the tagger thus finds it difficult to choose between the two. We see the same confusion between T_2 and T_6, which are both variations of T_1 and T_5, respectively. And, for the case of verbs with infinitives ending in *-i*, the second largest traditional conjugational class after the first and one which has the *-esc* infix subclass, we see the same type of confusion between T_{10}, T_{12}, T_{11}, and T_{13}. The reason is the same: new verbs, when entering the language, are assigned to either the *-ez* subclass (corresponding to ending tags T_5, T_6) or to the *-esc* subclass (T_{12}, T_{13}) so these classes are the largest in our dataset and, since etymological information is not available, the system cannot tell the difference between these classes.

In terms of alternations, there were 3 verbs which received a correct alternation tag: two which received t_0 and one which received d_0. Both alternations refer to the shift in the 2nd person singular of the letter *t*, respectively *d*, into *ț*, respectively *z*, due to palatalization.

6 Conclusions and future work

We have found that sequential modelling with variable letters is effective for verb conjugation in Romanian. Our system, evaluated on a held-out test set, attains better scores than the leave-one-out results from (Dinu et al., 2011), and furthermore offers greater potential for extensibility to other tenses and modes, through reuse of character-level variations.

After comparing multiple discriminative training methods for CRFs, we have not observed significant variation between their results in terms of accuracy. This is not unexpected, given the small size of the dataset. However, online algorithms lead to much sparser weight vectors: the PA model is almost 40 times smaller than the ML one, and the others are even smaller. Sparse solutions are desired for better interpretability, faster tagging and less overfitting.

A multi-target CRF implementation would permit even more granularity in terms of letter variation, and therefore would be able to learn shared patterns within the same paradigm (i.e. how the variable letter's behaviour in the first person singular influences its behaviour in the first person plural) as well as across tenses and modes. Such models are not readily available in structured learning libraries at the moment since inference in them is costly. For this task, because of the way word lengths are distributed, we expect the problem to be tractable.

Acknowledgements

The contribution of the authors to this paper is equal. Research supported by a grant of the Romanian National Authority for Scientific Research, CNCS – UEFISCDI, project number PN-II-ID-PCE-2011-3-0959.

References

Andrei Avram. 1969. Pe marginea unei morfologii structurale a limbii române ii. *Studii și cercetări lingvistice*, XX(5):557–577. (In Romanian).

Ana-Maria Barbu. 2007. *Conjugarea verbelor românești. Dicționar: 7500 de verbe românești grupate pe clase de conjugare.* Bucharest: Coresi. 4th edition, revised. (In Romanian.) (263 pp.).

Joseph Z. Chang and Jason S. Chang. 2012. Word root finder: a morphological segmentor based on CRF.

In Martin Kay and Christian Boitet, editors, *COLING (Demos)*, pages 51–58. Indian Institute of Technology Bombay.

Ann Clifton and Anoop Sarkar. 2010. Morphology generation for statistical machine translation. In *The Pacific Northwest Regional NLP Workshop (NW-NLP)*.

Michael Collins. 2002. Discriminative training methods for Hidden Markov models: theory and experiments with perceptron algorithms. In *Proceedings of the ACL-02 conference on Empirical methods in natural language processing - Volume 10*, EMNLP '02, pages 1–8, Stroudsburg, PA, USA. Association for Computational Linguistics.

Angelo Roth Costanzo. 2011. *Romance Conjugational Classes: Learning from the Peripheries*. Ph.D. thesis, Ohio State University.

Koby Crammer, Ofer Dekel, Joseph Keshet, Shai Shalev-Shwartz, and Yoram Singer. 2006. Online passive-aggressive algorithms. *Journal of Machine Learning Research*, 7:551–585.

Liviu P. Dinu, Emil Ionescu, Vlad Niculae, and Octavia-Maria Șulea. 2011. Can alternations be learned? A machine learning approach to Romanian verb conjugation. In *Recent Advances in Natural Language Processing*, pages 539–544.

Liviu P. Dinu, Vlad Niculae, and Octavia-Maria Şulea. 2012. Learning how to conjugate the Romanian verb. Rules for regular and partially irregular verbs. In *European Chapter of the Association for Computational Linguistics 2012*, pages 524–528, April.

Greg Durrett and John DeNero. 2013. Supervised learning of complete morphological paradigms. In *Proceedings of the North American Association for Computational Linguistics*, NAACL '13, Stroudsburg, PA, USA. Association for Computational Linguistics.

Ronald F. Feldstein. 2004. On the structure of syncretism in Romanian conjugation. In J. Auger, J. C. Clements, and B. Vance, editors, *Selected Papers from the 33rd linguistic symposium on Romance Languages*, pages 177–195. John Benjamins.

Jiři Felix. 1964. *Classification des verbes roumains*, volume VII. Philosophica Pragensia. In French.

John Goldsmith and Jeremy O'Brien. 2006. Learning inflectional classes. *Language Learning and Development*, 2(4):219–250.

Valeria Guţu-Romalo. 1968. *Morfologie Structurală a limbii române*. Editura Academiei Republicii Socialiste România. In Romanian.

Elena Irimia. 2009. Rog – a paradigmatic morphological generator for Romanian. In Zygmunt Vetulani and Hans Uszkoreit, editors, *Human Language Technology. Challenges of the Information Society*, volume 5603 of *Lecture Notes in Computer Science*, pages 74–84. Springer Berlin Heidelberg.

Canasai Kruengkrai, Virach Sornlertlamvanich, and Hitoshi Isahara. 2006. A conditional random field framework for Thai morphological analysis. In *Proceedings of LREC*.

John D. Lafferty, Andrew McCallum, and Fernando C. N. Pereira. 2001. Conditional random fields: Probabilistic models for segmenting and labeling sequence data. In *Proceedings of the Eighteenth International Conference on Machine Learning*, ICML '01, pages 282–289, San Francisco, CA, USA. Morgan Kaufmann Publishers Inc.

Alf Lombard. 1955. *Le verbe roumain. Etude morphologique*, volume 1. Lund, C. W. K. Gleerup. In French.

Avihai Mejer and Koby Crammer. 2010. Confidence in structured-prediction using confidence-weighted models. In *EMNLP*, pages 971–981. ACL.

Grigore C. Moisil. 1960. Probleme puse de traducerea automată. Conjugarea verbelor în limba română. *Studii si cercetări lingvistice*, XI(1):7–29. In Romanian.

Tetsuji Nakagawa. 2004. Chinese and Japanese word segmentation using word-level and character-level information. In *Proceedings of the 20th international conference on Computational Linguistics*, page 466. Association for Computational Linguistics.

Naoaki Okazaki. 2007. CRFsuite: a fast implementation of Conditional Random Fields (CRFs).

H. Tiktin. 1905. *Rumänisches Elementarbuch*. Heidelberg: C. Winter. In German.

Octavia-Maria Şulea. 2012. Alternations in the Romanian verb paradigm. Analyzing the indicative present. Master's thesis, Faculty of Foreing Languages and Literatures, University of Bucharest. Available at http://ling.auf.net/lingbuzz/001562.

A Tagging Approach to Identify Complex Constituents for Text Simplification

Iustin Dornescu **Richard Evans** **Constantin Orăsan**
Research Institute in Information and Language Processing
University of Wolverhampton
United Kingdom
{I.Dornescu2, R.J.Evans, C.Orasan}@wlv.ac.uk

Abstract

The occurrence of syntactic phenomena such as coordination and subordination is characteristic of long, complex sentences. Text simplification systems need to detect and categorise constituents in order to generate simpler sentences. These constituents are typically bounded or linked by *signs of syntactic complexity*, which include conjunctions, complementisers, wh-words, and punctuation marks. This paper proposes a supervised tagging approach to classify these signs in accordance with their linking and bounding functions. The performance of the approach is evaluated both intrinsically, using an annotated corpus covering three different genres, and extrinsically, by evaluating the impact of classification errors on an automatic text simplification system. The results are encouraging.

1 Introduction

This paper presents an automatic method to determine the specific coordinating and bounding functions of several reliable signs of syntactic complexity in natural language. This method can be useful for automatic text simplification. The syntactic complexity of input text can be reduced by the application of rules triggered by patterns expressed in terms of the parts of speech of words and the syntactic linking and bounding functions of signs of syntactic complexity occurring within it (Evans, 2011). Previous work indicates that syntactic simplification can improve text accessibility (Just et al., 1996) and the reliability of NLP applications such as information extraction (Agarwal and Boggess, 1992; Rindflesch et al., 2000), machine translation (Gerber and Hovy, 1998), and syntactic parsing (Tomita, 1985; McDonald and Nivre, 2011). The research described in the current paper is part of the FIRST project[1] which aims to automatically convert documents into a more accessible form for people with autistic spectrum disorders (ASD). Many of the decisions taken in the research presented in this paper were informed by the psycholinguistic experiments carried out in the FIRST project and summarised in Martos et al. (2013).

The remainder of this paper is structured as follows. Section 2 provides background information about the context of this work, Section 3 presents the annotation scheme, Section 4 describes the approach and the main objectives of this study. The results and the main findings are presented in Section 5. Section 6 provides an overview of previous related work. In Section 7, conclusions are drawn.

2 Syntactic Simplification in the FIRST Project

Research carried out in the FIRST project and investigation of related work revealed that certain types of syntactic complexity adversely affect the reading comprehension of people with ASD (Martos et al., 2013). This section presents a brief overview of the context in which this research is carried out. It builds on the approach proposed by Evans (2011) who presented a rule-based method to simplify sentences containing coordinated constituents to facilitate information extraction. In that work, punctuation marks and conjunctions were considered to be reliable signs of syntactic complexity in English. These signs were automatically classified in accordance with a scheme indicating their specific syntactic linking function. They then serve as triggers for the application of distinct sets of simplification rules. Their accurate labelling is thus a prerequisite for

[1] http://www.first-asd.eu

the simplification process.

In that work, signs of syntactic complexity were considered to belong to one of two broad classes, denoted as *coordinators* and *subordinators*. These groups were subcategorised according to class labels specifying the syntactic projection level of conjoins[2] and of subordinated constituents, and the grammatical category of those phrases. Manual annotation of a limited set of signs was exploited to develop a memory-based learning classifier that was used in combination with a part-of-speech tagger and a set of rules to rewrite complex sentences as sequences of simpler sentences. Extrinsic evaluation showed that the simplification process evoked improvements in information extraction from clinical documents.

One weakness of the approach presented by Evans (2011) is that the set of functions of signs of syntactic complexity was derived by empirical analysis of rather homogeneous documents from a specialised source (a collection of clinical assessment items). The restricted range of linguistic phenomena encountered in the texts makes the annotation applicable only to that particular genre/category. The scheme is incapable of encoding the full range of syntactic complexity encountered in texts of different genres.

In more recent work, Evans and Orăsan (2013) addressed these weaknesses by considering three broad classes of signs: *left subordination boundaries*, *right subordination boundaries* and *coordinators*. The classification scheme was also extended to enable the encoding of links and boundaries between a wider range of syntactic constituents to cover more syntactic phenomena. The current paper presents a method to classify signs of syntactic complexity using the annotated dataset they developed.

3 Annotation Scheme

The annotated signs comprise three conjunctions ([*and*], [*but*], [*or*]), one complementiser ([*that*]), six wh-words ([*what*], [*when*], [*where*], [*which*], [*while*], [*who*]), three punctuation marks ([,], [;], [:]), and 30 compound signs consisting of one of these lexical items immediately preceded by a punctuation mark (e.g. [, *and*]). In this paper, signs of coordination are referred to as *coordinators* whereas signs of subordination are referred to as *subordination boundaries*. In the annotation scheme, the class labels, also called sign tags, are acronyms expressing four types of information:

1. $\{C|SS|ES\}$, the generic function as a coordinator (C), the left boundary of a subordinate constituent (SS), or the right boundary of a subordinate constituent (ES).

2. $\{P|L|I|M|E\}$, the syntactic projection level of the constituent(s): prefix (P), lexical (L), intermediate (I), maximal (M), or extended/clausal (E).

3. $\{A|Adv|N|P|Q|V\}$, the grammatical category of the constituent(s): adjectival (A), adverbial (Adv), nominal (N), prepositional (P), quantificational (Q), and verbal (V).

4. $\{1|2\}$, used to further differentiate sub-classes on the basis of some other label-specific criterion.

The annotation scheme also includes classes which bound interjections, tag questions, and reported speech and a class denoting false signs of syntactic complexity, such as use of the word *that* as a specifier or anaphor.

Collection	Genre	Signs
1. METER corpus	News	12718
2. *www.patient.co.uk*	Healthcare	10796
3. Gutenberg	Literature	11204

Table 1: Characteristics of the annotated dataset.

Signs of syntactic complexity occurring in texts belonging to three categories/genres were annotated in accordance with this scheme[3]. Their characteristics are summarised in Table 1. Absolute and cumulative frequencies of signs and tags reveal a skewed distribution in each genre, e.g. in the news corpus 15 of 40 tags and 11 of 29 signs account for more than 90% of total occurrences.

In the context of information extraction, Evans (2011) showed that automatic syntactic simplification can be performed by annotating input sentences with information on the parts of speech of words and the syntactic functions of coordinators. These annotated sentences can then be simplified according to an iterative algorithm which aggregates several methods to identify specific

[2]Conjoins are the elements linked in coordination.

[3]The annotated dataset and a description of each sign is available at `http://clg.wlv.ac.uk/resources/SignsOfSyntacticComplexity/`

syntactic patterns and then transform the input sentence into several simpler sentences. Each pattern is recognised on the basis of the class assigned to the sign which triggers it and the words surrounding the sign, and is rewritten according to manually created rules.

When a particular syntactic pattern is recognised, a rewriting rule is activated which identifies coordinated structures, the conjoins linked in coordination, and subordinated constituents. Each sign triggers the activation of a simplification rule. The rule applied varies according to the specific class to which the sign belongs.

One advantage of this general approach to syntactic simplification is that it does not depend on syntactic parsing, a process whose reliability depends both on the characteristics of the treebank exploited in training and on the length and complexity of the sentences being processed (McDonald and Nivre, 2011). Another advantage is its flexibility: subsets of rewriting operations can be activated in accordance with user requirements.

4 Tagging Signs of Syntactic Complexity

4.1 Approach

The automatic classification of signs of syntactic complexity is challenging because of the skewed nature of the dataset. As mentioned in Section 2, Evans (2011) proposed a supervised approach to distinguish different types of coordinators in order improve relation extraction from biomedical texts. For each occurrence of a coordinator, a separate training instance was created to describe the surrounding context and then a statistical classifier was built for each coordinator. In that work, experiments were carried out with different classification models such as decision trees, SVM, and naïve Bayes. The best results were obtained by a memory-based learning (MBL) classifier.

In addition to the approach proposed by Evans (2011), we also built and evaluated CRF tagging models (Lafferty et al., 2001; Sutton and McCallum, 2010). These models perform joint inference which can better exploit interactions between different signs present in one sentence, and leads to better performance than is possible when each sign is classified independently. CRF models also achieve state of the art performance in many sequence tagging tasks such as named entity recognition (Tjong Kim Sang and De Meulder, 2003; McCallum and Li, 2003; Settles, 2004), biomedical information extraction (Settles, 2005) or shallow parsing (Sha and Pereira, 2003).

In the annotated dataset, signs of syntactic complexity typically delimit syntactic constituents. Each sign has a tag which reflects the types of constituent it links or bounds. For coordinators, the tag reflects the syntactic category of its conjoins. For subordination boundaries, the tag reflects the syntactic category or type of the bound constituent. This annotation is sign-centric, meaning that the actual extent and type of constituents is not explicitly annotated. To employ a tagging approach, the dataset needs to be converted to a suitable format.

4.2 Tagging Modes

A straightforward way to convert the annotated corpus into a sequence tagging dataset is to consider each sign as a single token chunk whose tag encodes specific information about its syntactic linking or bounding function (Section 2). All the other words are considered as being external to these chunks (tagged as NA). The weakness of this approach is that a baseline predicting the tag NA for every token, providing no useful information, achieves an overall token accuracy greater than 90% because less than 10% of tokens are signs. This can have negative implications for the convergence of the model.

Another mode, inspired by the BIO model adopted in NLP tasks such as named entity recognition (Nadeau and Sekine, 2007) or shallow parsing (Sha and Pereira, 2003), assigns each token the tag of the nearest preceding sign. This amounts to considering the sentence to be split into a set of non-overlapping chunks, each starting with a sign of syntactic complexity. A baseline applying the most common tag (SSEV[4]) to every token achieves an accuracy of 26%, much lower than in the previous setting. The two modes use equivalent information, but in the second mode both signs and words influence the overall tagging of the sentence, which can sometimes lead to different predictions than those made by the first tagging mode. The accuracy of the two modes is compared in Section 5. To have a more informative estimation of performance, only tags assigned to signs are considered for evaluation, while the tags predicted for other tokens are ignored.

[4]Denoting the left boundary of a subordinate clause.

4.3 Tag Sets

As noted in Section 2, the simplification algorithm processes syntactic complexity by iterative application of simplification rules that are specific to signs with particular tags. Given that, when simplifying a specific phenomenon not all tags are necessarily relevant, one research question is whether it is better to use a single CRF model, trained using the complete tagset, or to train a more specialised CRF model instead, using a reduced tagset in which tags irrelevant for the simplification process are combined into a few generic tags. This issue is also investigated in Section 5.

4.4 Feature Sets

The features proposed by Evans (2011) included information about each potential coordinator and its surrounding context (a window of 10 tokens and their POS tags), together with information on the distance of the potential coordinator to other instances in the same sentence and the types of these potential coordinators. This is called the *extended* feature set.

A statistical significance analysis of the extended features showed that most features have very low χ^2 score and that supervised classifiers achieve similar performance when only the features of surrounding tokens are used, i.e. word form and POS tag. This is called the *core* feature set. We investigate whether this finding is observed for the CRF models in Section 5.

5 Evaluation and Discussion

5.1 Setting of the Experiment

Table 1 gives an overview of the size of the annotated corpus described in (Evans and Orăsan, 2013). Sentences from this dataset which contain annotated signs of syntactic complexity were extracted, tokenised and POS-tagged using GATE (Cunningham, 2002). For each genre, sentences were shuffled and split into 10 folds to carry out experiments using cross validation.

Both signs and tags have a skewed distribution. More than 90% of occurrences consist of less than half of the set of tags. A similar observation can be made for the different signs. This makes it difficult to build accurate models for infrequent tags which together comprise less than 10% of occurrences.

An objective of this study is to determine the set of features that are most effective for tagging signs of syntactic complexity. The core feature set is based on word forms and POS tags which are generic features which can be easily and reliably extracted. Evans (2011) uses a more comprehensive set of features. We have employed that system to extract additional features for the annotated signs, the extended set. This also affords an indirect comparison between the classification approach and the sequence labelling approach. Since that system creates a classification instance for each sign independently, in order to use the additional features in a sequence labelling model, an additional unigram CRF template was created for each feature to condition the tag of a sign. As these features are only computed for signs, no templates were used to link the feature values to those of neighbouring tokens. The approach of Evans (2011) was also employed as a baseline (i.e. training supervised classification models which predict a label for each sign independently using the extended set of features) to compare the performance of the CRF model on this dataset. Table 2 shows that the extended feature set (CRF-extended) improves results of the simple tagging on the news genre by 2 points compared to the model using just words and their POS (CRF-core). The table also shows the performance of the baseline approach, when training standard classifiers from Weka (Hall et al., 2009). Regardless of the classifier model used, the baseline approach performs substantially worse than the sequence tagging models. In the following sections all experiments are carried out using CRFs.

	Correct	Accuracy
CRF-extended	10248	80.58%
CRF-core	9979	78.46%
SMO	7213	56.71%
NB	6712	52.78%
J48	6742	53.01%
IB7	6662	52.38%

Table 2: Performance on news corpus using the extended features proposed by Evans (2011)

5.2 Results on the Whole Corpus

Table 3 shows the results achieved for each of the three genres when using two tagging modes, simple and BIO, and two different tag sets, complete and reduced. Results were computed using 10-fold cross-validation. For both news and literature corpora, using the BIO tagging mode leads to better

Genre	tagging	tagset	**P**	**R**	**F1**	Signs	Correct	Incorrect
news	simple	complete	0.7971	0.7846	0.7894	12718	9979	2739
news	BIO	complete	0.8157	0.7991	**0.8053**	12718	10163	2555
literature	simple	complete	0.8414	0.8267	0.8326	11204	9262	1942
literature	BIO	complete	0.8597	**0.8383**	0.8468	11204	9392	1812
healthcare	simple	complete	0.8422	0.8323	**0.8358**	10796	8985	1811
healthcare	BIO	complete	0.8406	0.8244	0.8300	10796	8900	1896
news	simple	reduced	0.8206	0.8161	0.8176	12718	10379	2339
news	BIO	reduced	0.8382	0.8328	**0.8348**	12718	10592	2126
literature	simple	reduced	0.8698	0.8595	0.8639	11204	9630	1574
literature	BIO	reduced	0.8840	**0.8680**	0.8746	11204	9725	1479
healthcare	simple	reduced	0.8636	0.8567	**0.8593**	10796	9249	1547
healthcare	BIO	reduced	0.8602	0.8510	0.8544	10796	9187	1609

Table 3: Overall performance using 10-fold cross validation on the three genres, using two tagging modes (simple and BIO) and two tagsets (complete and reduced)

performance than using simple tagging, while the opposite is true for the health corpus.

One of the objectives of these experiments is to establish whether using a reduced tag set offers performance benefits. When tackling a specific syntactic phenomenon, only a subset of signs and tags may be involved. For example, a set of 11 tags were identified which are relevant for detecting appositions and other noun post-modifiers. The remainder were combined into three coarse grained tags indicating the generic function of the sign as the start (SS) or end (ES) of a subordinated constituent or as coordinator (C) of two constituents. These correspond to the first level used for the class labels in the annotated dataset. Performance achieved with the full and the reduced tag set is listed in Table 3. For all genres and irrespective of tagging mode, using the reduced tag set leads to a performance increase of 2-3 percentiles. A more detailed analysis however reveals that this performance increase is not linked to the relevant 11 original tags, but to the 3 coarse tags.

For example, in the news dataset, the three coarse tags account for 35.84% of all signs. Although the reduced tag set demonstrates a 50% error reduction for two signs (*and*, *or*), the performance for the other signs is largely unchanged. The performance on the 11 tags of interest is also unchanged. This result suggests that using a reduced tag set yields a more informative performance estimation for some specific task because irrelevant tagging errors are not taken into account, but it does not necessarily lead to increased performance for the relevant original tags. Therefore there is no real benefit in training multiple tagging models with reduced tag sets.

	Test genre		
Train genre	news	healthcare	literature
news	**78.46%**	63.96%	69.98%
healthcare	44.95%	**83.23%**	48.74%
literature	62.59%	58.53%	**82.67%**

(a) Simple tagging mode

	Test genre		
Train genre	news	healthcare	literature
news	**79.91%**	61.29%	71.48%
healthcare	48.75%	**82.44%**	51.95%
literature	64.03%	56.44%	**83.83%**

(b) BIO tagging mode

Table 4: Cross-genre F_1 performance of the tagging models; main diagonal represents performance using 10-fold cross-validation

A relevant issue in the context of text simplification is robustness. To gain insights into the strengths and weaknesses of CRF models we measure the impact on performance when models trained on each genre are applied to the other two genres. In this experiment the complete tag set was used. Table 4a) shows the results using simple tagging, while Table 4b) shows the results when using BIO tagging. In both cases, the main diagonal shows within-genre F_1 performance measured using 10-fold cross-validation; the other entries show cross-genre performance. For all

Genre	Signs	Correct	**Accuracy**
merged	34718	28297	81.51%
merged-bio	34718	28642	82.50%
combined	34718	28226	81.30%
combined-bio	34718	28455	81.96%

Table 5: Joint training performance using 10-fold cross validation: merging data from the three genres leads to better performance than that achieved by the best individual models.

models a considerable performance drop can be observed. The news models are the ones that have the best cross-domain performance, while the healthcare models perform worst. This impact on performance is not unexpected, but rather a proof that the three genres differ from a syntactic perspective. In addition, although all genres have a skewed distribution of signs and tags, the actual rankings differ.

To tackle this issue, a supervised genre classifier can be used to detect the genre of a text to select the best model for the genre, however this approach is limited to genres for which annotated data is available. An alternative approach to minimise the effect of over-fitting is to train models using data from all genres. Table 5 compares these two approaches. In the first two runs (merged), 10-fold cross-validation was performed using stratified sampling; each fold in the merged dataset consists of 3 folds, one from each genre. The last two runs (combined), demonstrate the performance achievable when an oracle selects the correct cross-validated model for each prediction. This represents a performance upper-bound since in practice an actual classifier will be used which would introduce additional errors. The experiment indicates that training a single model on the entire dataset (all three genres) yields better results than using the best models for each genre. Although the differences are not large, merging all available data produces a model with superior tagging performance which should also generalise better to new genres.

5.3 Results on the News Corpus

To better understand the nature of the dataset and the performance of the approach, this section presents more in-depth results for the news genre. Although some differences exist, the other two genres are similar (analysis of them is omitted due to space constraints). Tables 6 and 7 show the CRF model's performance on the news genre using 10-fold cross-validation for the most frequent tags and signs, respectively. In terms of micro-averaged statistics the predictions have a good balance between precision and recall. There is more variance when looking at performance of specific tags or signs. For example, some tags such as SSEV, SSCM, SSMA and ESCM have very good performance ($F_1 > 90\%$); most of these tags mark the start of a constituent (the left boundary). Other tags, despite having comparable frequencies are more difficult to identify and only reach substantially lower levels of performance ($F_1 < 70\%$), e.g. CMN_1, ESEV, ESMP, ESMN, ESMA. Most of these signs mark the right boundary of a constituent, which suggests that identifying the end of a constituent is more difficult than identifying the start. This could be caused by multiple embedded constituents, in which the same sign marks the right boundary of several constituents. In such cases, several tags could be considered correct, but in the annotated dataset only the type of the longest constituent was considered: a sign can only have one tag.

A similar situation occurs when looking at the performance achieved per sign in Table 7. Excellent performance ($F_1 > 95\%$) is noted for the complementiser *that* and *wh-* signs such as *who*, *when* or *which*. Due to the skewed distribution, more than 83% of all errors are linked to the two most frequent signs [,] and [and], which only reach F_1 of 75%.

Table 8 shows the feature templates used to train CRF models in these experiments. To evaluate the impact of each feature template, a simple feature selection methodology was employed: a CRF++ model (Kudo, 2005) was trained on the news corpus using a single template and its performance was ranked and compared with a baseline. For this dataset the baseline was considered using the word form of the current token as the single feature, which achieves 40% accuracy. The best templates, reaching 58% accuracy, used part-of-speech trigrams. When used together, the templates in Table 8 achieve 79.91% accuracy when using the simple tagging mode on the news corpus.

5.4 Extrinsic Evaluation

To determine the extrinsic impact of the errors made by the sign classifier, two rule-based syntactic

	Tag	**P**	**R**	**F_1**	Support	Cumulative	True-pos	False-pos	False-neg
1	SSEV	0.9642	0.9298	**0.9467**	3275	26%	3045	113	230
2	CMV_1	0.8618	0.8083	0.8342	1111	34%	898	144	213
3	CMN_1	0.7381	0.6601	*0.6969*	1059	43%	699	248	360
4	CEV	0.8071	0.7795	0.7931	907	50%	707	169	200
5	SSMN	0.8865	0.8384	**0.8618**	885	57%	742	95	143
6	ESEV	0.6383	0.5631	*0.5984*	586	62%	330	187	256
7	SSCM	0.9659	0.9759	**0.9708**	580	66%	566	20	14
8	SSMA	0.9303	0.9574	**0.9437**	516	70%	494	37	22
9	ESMP	0.5858	0.5611	*0.5732*	499	74%	280	198	219
10	CLN	0.7535	0.6918	0.7214	464	78%	321	105	143
11	SSMP	0.8469	0.8167	0.8315	420	81%	343	62	77
12	ESMN	0.5972	0.6101	0.6036	418	84%	255	172	163
13	SSMV	0.8418	0.8103	0.8258	348	87%	282	53	66
14	ESCM	0.9207	0.9379	**0.9292**	322	90%	302	26	20
15	ESMA	0.6457	0.7049	0.6740	305	92%	215	118	90
	avg/total	0.8157	0.7991	0.8053	12718	100%	10163		

Table 6: Per tag performance on the 15 most frequent types of complexity signs in the news corpus using BIO style CRF mode (covering > 90% of occurrences); the last row shows the weighted average performance (for P, R and F1) and counts (total signs and correct predictions)

	Sign	**P**	**R**	**F_1**	Support	Cumulative	Correct	Incorrect
1	,	0.7488	0.7312	0.7377	5443	43%	3980	1463
2	and	0.7778	0.7430	0.7562	2564	63%	1905	659
3	that	0.9608	0.9589	**0.9594**	1313	73%	1259	54
4	who	0.9952	0.9928	**0.9940**	418	77%	415	3
5	,and	0.8089	0.7253	0.7585	324	79%	235	89
6	but	0.8921	0.8658	0.8761	313	82%	271	42
7	when	0.9872	0.9840	**0.9856**	312	84%	307	5
8	or	0.6597	0.5961	*0.6146*	255	86%	152	103
9	,who	1.0000	0.9715	**0.9856**	246	88%	239	7
10	which	1.0000	0.9888	**0.9944**	178	89%	176	2
11	what	0.9867	0.9605	**0.9734**	152	91%	146	6
	Overall	0.8157	0.7991	0.8053	12718	100%	10163	2555

Table 7: Per tag performance on the most frequent signs in the news corpus using BIO style CRF mode (covering > 90% of occurrences); for each sign micro-averaged P, R and F1, as well as total number of signs and of correct predictions

Template	**Accuracy**	Form	Description
b94	58.13%	%x[0,1]/%x[1,1]	CRF++ Bigram Feature POS-bigram(0,1)
u51	58.29%	%x[-1,1]/%x[0,1]/%x[1,1]	POS-trigram(-1,0,1)
u52	55.20%	%x[0,1]/%x[1,1]/%x[2,1]	POS-trigram(0,1,2)
u47	55.90%	%x[0,1]/%x[1,1]	POS-bigram(0,1)
u32	47.11%	%x[0,0]/%x[1,0]	sign(token and POS)
u00	40.40%	%x[0,0]	sign(token)

Table 8: CRF feature templates which outperform the baseline feature template u00

simplification methods were employed which rely on annotated signs. Each method uses a set of rules to identify certain syntactic structures which are then simplified and was developed using the gold standard annotations. The first method addresses noun post-modifiers, such as appositions, adjectival phrases and relative clauses. When the method is run on the gold standard dataset, 1910 sentences containing noun post-modifiers were identified and simplified. When sign annotations produced using 10-fold cross-validation are used instead, due to classification errors 6.91% fewer sentences are automatically simplified, while the remaining 1778 (93.09%) sentences are still simplified accurately, suggesting that the tagging errors have less impact on this particular method.

The second text simplification method addresses a wider range of syntactic phenomena including coordination. It identifies conjoins and subordinate constituents in complex sentences and re-writes them as sequences of shorter, simpler sentences. When this method is applied on automatic annotations, 22.42% of sentences are no longer simplified by the method, suggesting that the method is more sensitive to tagging errors. These results demonstrate that the automatic sign classifier can usefully be exploited in text simplification applications, especially when addressing specific syntactic phenomena.

6 Related Work

There are two major areas of previous work of relevance to the research described in the current paper. They comprise methods for the automatic classification of signs of syntactic complexity and annotated resources that may be exploited for the development of such approaches.

In closely-related work, van Delden and Gomez (2002) present a system to assign syntactic roles to commas. The classification scheme uses 30 class labels to denote coordinating functions (series commas), boundaries of subordinate constituents (enclosing commas), functions linking and bounding clauses and verb phrases (clausal commas), and bounding direct and indirect speech. There is considerable overlap between their scheme and the dataset used in this paper.

Adopting a two phase approach, van Delden and Gomez (2002) apply 38 finite state automata to part of speech tagged data to derive an initial tagging of commas. After this, information from a tag co-occurrence matrix derived from hand annotated training data is used to improve the initial tagging. The system achieved accuracy of 91-95% in identifying the syntactic function of commas in a collection of encyclopaedia and news articles. This is more accurate than the results reported in the current paper (79-87%), which predicts class labels from a wider selection of classes (44 vs. 30) of a wider variety of signs of syntactic complexity (29 vs. one) in documents from three genres: news, patient healthcare, and literature.

In related work, Maier et al. (2012) proposed the addition of a new annotation layer to disambiguate the role of punctuation in the Penn Treebank. They present a detailed scheme to ensure consistent and reliable manual annotation of commas and semicolons with information to indicate their coordinating function. Compared to the dataset used in this paper, their scheme only encodes coarse-grained information with no discrimination between subclasses of coordinating and non-coordinating functions. The task addressed in the current paper is to tag coordinators and subordination boundaries with more detailed syntactic information about the constituents that they link or bound, the first step in a text simplification application.

7 Conclusions

The decision to tag signs of syntactic complexity with information about pairs of single conjoins or single bound constituents means that in many cases, subordination boundaries and coordinators lack information on the full set of constituents bounded or linked by them. As a result, signs bounding subordinate constituents are often not matched pairs. A second limitation of the scheme is the fact that syntactic complexity not signalled by the signs specified in Section 2 of the current paper cannot be identified. These characteristics of the training data (embedded constituents and missing boundaries) exert a negative influence on tagging right subordination boundaries.

Acknowledgments

The research described in this paper was partially funded by the European Commission under the Seventh (FP7-2007-2013) Framework Programme for Research and Technological Development (FP7-ICT-2011.5.5 FIRST 287607).

References

Rajeev Agarwal and Lois Boggess. 1992. A simple but useful approach to conjunct identification. In *Proceedings of the 30th annual meeting for Computational Linguistics*, pages 15–21, Newark, Delaware. Association for Computational Linguistics.

Hamish Cunningham. 2002. GATE, a general architecture for text engineering. *Computers and the Humanities*, 36(2):223–254.

Richard Evans and Constantin Orăsan. 2013. Annotating signs of syntactic complexity to support sentence simplification. In Ivan Habernal and Vaclav Matousek, editors, *Text, Speech and Dialogue. Proceedings of the 16th International Conference TSD 2013*, Lecture Notes in Computer Science, Plzen, Czech Republic, September. Springer.

Richard Evans. 2011. Comparing methods for the syntactic simplification of sentences in information extraction. *Literary and Linguistic Computing*, 26 (4):371–388.

Laurie Gerber and Eduard H. Hovy. 1998. Improving translation quality by manipulating sentence length. In David Farwell, Laurie Gerber, and Eduard H. Hovy, editors, *AMTA*, volume 1529 of *Lecture Notes in Computer Science*, pages 448–460. Springer.

Mark Hall, Eibe Frank, Geoffrey Holmes, Bernhard Pfahringer, Peter Reutemann, and Ian H. Witten. 2009. The WEKA data mining software: an update. *ACM SIGKDD Explorations Newsletter*, 11(1):10–18.

Marcel Adam Just, Patricia A. Carpenter, Timothy A. Keller, William F. Eddy, and Keith R. Thulborn. 1996. Brain activation modulated by sentence comprehension. *Science*, 274:114–116.

Taku Kudo. 2005. CRF++: Yet another CRF toolkit. *Software available at http://crfpp. sourceforge. net.*

John Lafferty, Andrew McCallum, and Fernando CN Pereira. 2001. Conditional random fields: Probabilistic models for segmenting and labeling sequence data. In *Proc. 18th International Conf. on Machine Learning*, pages 282–289. Morgan Kaufmann.

Wolfgang Maier, Sandra Kübler, Erhard Hinrichs, and Julia Kriwanek. 2012. Annotating Coordination in the Penn Treebank. In *Proceedings of the Sixth Linguistic Annotation Workshop*, pages 166–174, Jeju, Republic of Korea, July. Association for Computational Linguistics.

Juan Martos, Sandra Freire, Ana Gonzalez, and David Gil. 2013. D2.2 user preferences: updated report. Technical report. Also available as `http://www.first-asd.eu/D2.2`.

Andrew McCallum and Wei Li. 2003. Early results for named entity recognition with conditional random fields, feature induction and web-enhanced lexicons. In *Proceedings of the seventh conference on Natural language learning at HLT-NAACL 2003-Volume 4*, pages 188–191. Association for Computational Linguistics.

Ryan T. McDonald and Joakim Nivre. 2011. Analyzing and integrating dependency parsers. *Computational Linguistics*, 37(1):197–230.

David Nadeau and Satoshi Sekine. 2007. A survey of named entity recognition and classification. *Lingvisticae Investigationes*, 30(1):3–26.

Thomas C. Rindflesch, Jayant V. Rajan, and Lawrence Hunter. 2000. Extracting molecular binding relationships from biomedical text. In *Proceedings of the sixth conference on Applied natural language processing*, pages 188–195, Seattle, Washington. Association of Computational Linguistics.

Burr Settles. 2004. Biomedical named entity recognition using conditional random fields and rich feature sets. In *Proceedings of the International Joint Workshop on Natural Language Processing in Biomedicine and its Applications*, pages 104–107. Association for Computational Linguistics.

Burr Settles. 2005. ABNER: an open source tool for automatically tagging genes, proteins and other entity names in text. *Bioinformatics*, 21(14):3191–3192.

Fei Sha and Fernando Pereira. 2003. Shallow parsing with conditional random fields. In *Proceedings of the 2003 Conference of the North American Chapter of the Association for Computational Linguistics on Human Language Technology-Volume 1*, pages 134–141. Association for Computational Linguistics.

Charles Sutton and Andrew McCallum. 2010. An introduction to conditional random fields. *arXiv preprint arXiv:1011.4088.*

Erik F. Tjong Kim Sang and Fien De Meulder. 2003. Introduction to the CoNLL-2003 shared task: Language-independent named entity recognition. In *Proceedings of the seventh conference on Natural language learning at HLT-NAACL 2003-Volume 4*, pages 142–147. Association for Computational Linguistics.

Masaru Tomita. 1985. *Efficient Parsing for Natural Language: A Fast Algorithm for Practical Systems.* Kluwer Academic Publishers, Norwell, MA, USA.

Sebastian van Delden and Fernando Gomez. 2002. Combining finite state automata and a greedy learning algorithm to determine the syntactic roles of commas. In *Proceedings of the 14th IEEE International Conference on Tools with Artificial Intelligence*, ICTAI '02, pages 293–, Washington, DC, USA. IEEE Computer Society.

Automatic Evaluation Metric for Machine Translation that is Independent of Sentence Length

Hiroshi Echizen'ya
Hokkai-Gakuen University
S26-Jo, W11-Chome, Chuo-ku,
Sapporo 064-0926 Japan
echi@lst.hokkai-s-u.ac.jp

Kenji Araki
Hokkaido University
N 14-Jo, W 9-Chome, Kita-ku,
Sapporo 060-0814 Japan
araki@media.eng.hokudai.ac.jp

Eduard Hovy
Carnegie Mellon University
5000 Forbes Avenue
Pittsburgh, PA 15213 USA
hovy@cmu.edu

Abstract

We propose new automatic evaluation metric to evaluate machine translation. Different from most similar metrics, our proposed metric does not depend heavily on sentence length. In most metrics based on f-measure comparisons of reference and candidate translations, the relative weight of each mismatched word in short sentences is larger than it in long sentences. Therefore, the evaluation score becomes disproportionally low in short sentences even when only one non-matching word exists. In our metric, the weight of each mismatched word is kept small even in short sentences. We designate our metric as **A**utomatic Evaluation Metric that is **I**ndependent of Sentence **Le**ngth (AILE). Experimental results indicate that AILE has the highest correlation with human judgments among some leading metrics.

1 Introduction

Various automatic evaluation metrics for machine translation have been proposed through the metrics task on the Workshop on statistical Machine Translation (WMT). One can identify three kinds of automatic evaluation metrics (C. Liu et al., 2010): the heavyweight linguistic approach, which corresponds to RTE (S. Padó et al., 2009) and ULC (J. Giménez and L. Márquez, 2007); the lightweight linguistic approach, which corresponds to METEOR (A. Lavie and A. Agarwal, 2007) and MaxSim (Y. Seng Chan and H. Tou Ng, 2008) and the non-linguistic approach, which includes BLEU (K. Papineni et al., 2002), TER (M. Snover et al., 2006), RIBES (H. Isozaki et al., 2010) and IMPACT (H. Echizen-ya and K. Araki, 2007)(H. Echizen-ya et al., 2012). In this paper, we specifically examine a metric that corresponds to the lightweight linguistic and non-linguistic approaches because they are useful and are very easily built.

Among these metrics, METEOR and IMPACT are based on the f-measure, which combines precision and recall between the reference and candidate texts. The metrics' simple f-measure (P. Koehn, 2010) obtains precision and recall using Eqs. (1)–(3):

$$precision = \frac{matching\ words}{length\ of\ candidate} \quad (1)$$

$$recall = \frac{matching\ words}{length\ of\ reference} \quad (2)$$

Then f-measure is calculated using Eq. (3):

$$f\text{-}measure = \frac{2 \times precision \times recall}{precision + recall} \quad (3)$$

For example, in the reference "doctor cured a patient" and candidate "doctor treated a patient", the precision and the recall are respectively 0.75 ($=\frac{3}{4}$). Therefore, the f-measure is 0.75 ($=\frac{2\times0.75\times0.75}{0.75+0.75}$), even though there is only one non-matching word. This is because the denominator is so small, since the sentences are short: the weight of each non-matched word is 0.25 ($=\frac{1}{4}$) in this example. In general, the relative influence of each non-matching word increases when sentences are short, distorting the overall score. This problem is especially serious in short sentences. On the other hand, the weight of each mismatched word is small when the number of words is large. For example, the weight of each word is 0.05 ($=\frac{1}{20}$) when the sentence length is 20. Therefore, an automatic evaluation metric in which the weight of each mismatched word does not depend heavily on sentence length would be highly desirable.

In this paper, we propose a new automatic evaluation metric in which the weight of each mismatched word does not depend heavily on sentence length. In our metric, the weight of each mismatched word is kept small even in short sentences. Therefore, our metric can obtain a stable evaluation score without regard to sentence length. We designate the metric as **A**utomatic Evaluation Metric that is **I**ndependent of Sentence **Le**ngth (AILE). Through experimentally obtained results, we confirmed that AILE indicates the highest correlation with human judgment among several leading metrics.

2 AILE: Automatic Evaluation Metric Independent of Sentence Length

In AILE, a chunk sequence is decided using **L**ongest **C**ommon **S**ubsequence (LCS) between the reference and candidate. A chunk is a string of consecutive words. In "doctor cured a patient" and "doctor treated a patient", the value of LCS is 3 because the matching words are "doctor", "a" and "patient". Therefore, the chunks are "doctor" and "a patient".

Moreover, AILE obtains $AILEscore$ as the evaluation score using the following Eqs. (4)–(8).

$$P = \left(\frac{\sum_{i=0}^{RN-1} (\alpha^i \times C\_score) + weight}{m^\beta + weight} \right)^{\frac{1}{\beta}} \quad (4)$$

$$R = \left(\frac{\sum_{i=0}^{RN-1} (\alpha^i \times C\_score) + weight}{n^\beta + weight} \right)^{\frac{1}{\beta}} \quad (5)$$

$$C\_score = \sum_{c \in c\_num} length(c)^\beta \quad (6)$$

$$weight = \begin{cases} \left(\frac{\delta}{log(m+n)}\right)^\beta, & C\_score > 0.0 \\ 0.0, & C\_score = 0.0 \end{cases} \quad (7)$$

$$AILE\ \ score = \frac{(1+\gamma^2)RP}{R+\gamma^2 P} \quad (8)$$

In Eq. (6), c and c_num mean each chunk and the number of chunks, respectively. Moreover, $length(c)$ means the number of words in each chunk and β is a parameter for the weight of chunk length. In "doctor cured a patient" and "doctor treated a patient", two chunks (*i.e.*, "doctor" and "a patient") exist. Therefore, C_score is 5.0 ($=1^{2.0}+2^{2.0}$) when β is 2.0. The $weight$ of Eq. (7) controls the weight of each matching word according to the sentence length. The m and n mean respectively the candidate length and reference length. The δ and β are parameters. The value of $weight$ is 0.0 when C_score is 0.0 because it means that the matching words between the reference and candidate do not exist. In "doctor cured a patient" and "doctor treated a patient", the value of $weight$ in Eq. (7) is 1.2261 ($=(\frac{1.0}{log(4+4)})^{2.0}$) when δ and β are respectively 1.0 and 2.0.

In Eqs. (4) and (5), P and R respectively indicate precision and recall. Moreover, RN means the repetition number for the decision of C_score. For example, in "doctor cured a patient" and "A patient helped doctor", the appearance order of chunks (*i.e.*, "doctor" and "a patient") between two sentences is different. In this case, $RN-1$ is 1 because $\alpha^0 \times C\_score$ for the chunk "a patient" is firstly calculated and $\alpha^1 \times C\_score$ for the chunk "doctor" is secondly calculated. That is, α is used as the parameter for the penalty when the appearance order of chunks between reference and candidate is different. In "doctor cured a patient" and "doctor treated a patient", the value of $\sum_{i=0}^{RN-1} (\alpha^i \times C\_score)$ is

Table 1: Spearman's rank correlation coefficient of system-level in AILE using NTCIR-7.

Parameters	Adequacy (14 systems)	Fluency (14 systems)	Avg.
$\alpha = 0.1, \beta = 1.2, \delta = 2.0$	0.9912	0.9253	**0.9583**
$\alpha = 0.3, \beta = 1.2, \delta = 2.0$	0.9868	0.9297	**0.9583**
$\alpha = 0.5, \beta = 1.2, \delta = 2.0$	0.9780	0.9253	0.9517
$\alpha = 0.7, \beta = 1.2, \delta = 2.0$	0.9560	0.9033	0.9297
$\alpha = 0.9, \beta = 1.2, \delta = 2.0$	0.9473	0.8945	0.9209
$\alpha = 0.1, \beta = 1.0, \delta = 2.0$	0.9912	0.9253	**0.9583**
$\alpha = 0.1, \beta = 1.4, \delta = 2.0$	0.9780	0.9165	0.9473
$\alpha = 0.1, \beta = 1.6, \delta = 2.0$	0.9780	0.9165	0.9473
$\alpha = 0.1, \beta = 1.8, \delta = 2.0$	0.9780	0.9165	0.9473
$\alpha = 0.1, \beta = 2.0, \delta = 2.0$	0.9736	0.9121	0.9429
$\alpha = 0.1, \beta = 1.2, \delta = 1.0$	0.9780	0.9253	0.9517
$\alpha = 0.1, \beta = 1.2, \delta = 3.0$	0.9868	0.9297	**0.9583**
$\alpha = 0.1, \beta = 1.2, \delta = 4.0$	0.9768	0.9297	**0.9583**
$\alpha = 0.1, \beta = 1.2, \delta = 5.0$	0.9834	0.9241	0.9538
$\alpha = 0.1, \beta = 1.2, \delta = 6.0$	0.9780	0.9165	0.9473
square root	0.9780	0.9253	0.9517
arctangent	0.9912	0.9253	**0.9583**

5.0 ($=0.5^0 \times 5.0$) when α is 0.5 because $RN-1$ is 0. The value of P and R in Eqs. (4) and (5) is respectively 0.6012 ($=\sqrt{\frac{5.0+1.2261}{4^{2.0}+1.2261}}$). Eq. (8) indicates f-measure using P and R. The γ is obtained as P/R. In "doctor cured a patient" and "doctor treated a patient", the value of $AILEscore$ is 0.6012 ($=\frac{(1+1.0^2)\times 0.6012\times 0.6012}{0.6012+1.0^2\times 0.6012}$) because the value of γ is 1.0 ($=\frac{0.6012}{0.6012}$).

The evaluation score increases from 0.5590 to 0.6012 using *weight* in Eq. (7). The $AILEscore$ without *weight* is 0.5590 because the value of P and R is respectively 0.5590 ($=\sqrt{\frac{5.0}{4^{2.0}}}$). This means that AILE can increase the evaluation score in short sentences using *weight* in Eq. (7). The value of *weight* is 1.2261 ($=(\frac{1.0}{log(4+4)})^{2.0}$) when m and n are respectively 4. The value of *weight* is 0.3896 ($=(\frac{1.0}{log(20+20)})^{2.0}$) when m and n are respectively 20. That is, the weight of non-matched words decreases in short sentences adding the large value (*e.g.*, 1.2261) of *weight* to the matching words (*i.e.*, $\sum_{i=0}^{RN-1}(\alpha^i \times C\_score)$ in Eqs. (4) and (5)). On the other hand, the weight of non-matched words does not change in long sentences, adding only the small value (*e.g.*, 0.3869) of *weight* to the matching words (*i.e.*, $\sum_{i=0}^{RN-1}(\alpha^i \times C\_score)$ in Eqs. (4) and (5)). Therefore, AILE can obtain a stable evaluation score without depending on sentence length.

3 Experiments

3.1 Experimental Procedure

We performed experiments to confirm the effectiveness of AILE. The correlations between the scores by automatic evaluation and the scores by human judgments are calculated, respectively, at the system level and the sentence level. Spearman's rank correlation coefficient is used at the system level and the Kendall tau rank correlation coefficient is used in the sentence level. In the first experiment, the references and candidates were obtained from patent data in NTCIR-7 (A. Fujii et al., 2008). We used as candidates the machine translation system's translation of Japanese sentences into English sentences. In NTCIR-7 data, 14 machine translation systems were used and each machine translation system translated 100 Japanese sentences into 100 English sentences. Therefore, we obtained 1,400 candidates. We used single references. The median value in the evaluation results of three human judges was used as the scores of 1–5. The experiments determined suitable values for the three parameters α, β and δ. Moreover, the

Table 2: Kendall tau rank correlation coefficient of sentence-level in AILE using NTCIR-7.

Parameters	Adequacy (1,400 sentences)	Fluency (1,400 sentences)	Avg.	Total Avg.
$\alpha = 0.1, \beta = 1.2, \delta = 2.0$	0.4304	0.3627	0.3965	**0.6774**
$\alpha = 0.3, \beta = 1.2, \delta = 2.0$	0.4231	0.3596	0.3914	0.6749
$\alpha = 0.5, \beta = 1.2, \delta = 2.0$	0.4095	0.3533	0.3814	0.6666
$\alpha = 0.7, \beta = 1.2, \delta = 2.0$	0.3862	0.3414	0.3638	0.6468
$\alpha = 0.9, \beta = 1.2, \delta = 2.0$	0.3449	0.3156	0.3303	0.6256
$\alpha = 0.1, \beta = 1.0, \delta = 2.0$	0.4058	0.3400	0.3729	0.6656
$\alpha = 0.1, \beta = 1.4, \delta = 2.0$	0.4300	0.3645	0.3973	0.6723
$\alpha = 0.1, \beta = 1.6, \delta = 2.0$	0.4211	0.3605	0.3908	0.6691
$\alpha = 0.1, \beta = 1.8, \delta = 2.0$	0.4116	0.3550	0.3833	0.6653
$\alpha = 0.1, \beta = 2.0, \delta = 2.0$	0.4040	0.3503	0.3772	0.6601
$\alpha = 0.1, \beta = 1.2, \delta = 1.0$	0.3993	0.3467	0.3730	0.6624
$\alpha = 0.1, \beta = 1.2, \delta = 3.0$	0.4178	0.3588	0.3883	0.6733
$\alpha = 0.1, \beta = 1.2, \delta = 4.0$	0.4239	0.3624	0.3932	0.6758
$\alpha = 0.1, \beta = 1.2, \delta = 5.0$	0.4278	0.3647	0.3963	0.6751
$\alpha = 0.1, \beta = 1.2, \delta = 6.0$	0.4303	0.3457	**0.3980**	0.6727
square root	0.4182	0.3537	0.3860	0.6689
arctangent	0.4288	0.3617	0.3953	0.6768

Table 3: Spearman's rank correlation coefficient of system-level in NTCIR-7.

Metrics	Adequacy (14 systems)	Fluency (14 systems)	Avg.
AILE	0.9912	0.9253	**0.9582**
BLEU	0.8505	0.8242	0.8374
IMPACT	0.9912	0.9253	**0.9582**
METEOR	0.8022	0.7538	0.7780
RIBES	0.9121	0.8374	0.8747
TER	-0.9473	-0.8769	-0.9121

correlations in both system-level and sentence-level were obtained using AILE. In the second and third experiments, the references and candidates were respectively obtained from WMT10 (C. Callison-Burch et al., 2010) and WMT11 (C. Callison-Burch et al., 2011). In these experiments, as candidate we used the machine translation system's translations of European (*i.e.*, Czech, German, Spanish and French) sentences into English sentences, compared to a single reference. The correlations with system-level translations were obtained using AILE in these experiments.

Moreover, we used the following automatic evaluation metrics: BLEU (ver. 12), METEOR (ver. 1.4), RIBES (ver. 1.02.3), TER (tercom ver. 0.7.25), and IMPACT (ver. 4.0.2) to compare with AILE. In all experiments, the software "tokenizer.perl" and "lowercase.perl" (P. Koehn, 2011) were used for all references and candidates before the evaluation scores were calculated using the metrics.

3.2 Experimental Results

Tables 1 and 2 respectively provide Spearman's rank correlation coefficients of system-level and Kendall tau rank correlation coefficients of sentence-level in AILE based on the various values of parameters. In Table 2, "Total Avg." indicates the average value between "Avg." in Table 1 and "Avg." in Table 2. Moreover, "square root" and "arctangent" respectively indicate the correlation coefficients obtained by replacing $log(m + n)$ in Eq. (7)

Table 4: Kendall tau rank correlation coefficient of sentence-level in NTCIR-7.

Metrics	Adequacy (1,400 sentences)	Fluency (1,400 sentences)	Avg.
AILE	0.4304	0.3627	**0.3965**
BLEU	0.1146	0.1491	0.1319
IMPACT	0.4138	0.3503	0.3820
METEOR	0.1838	0.2060	0.1949
RIBES	0.3558	0.2950	0.3254
TER	-0.2664	-0.2605	-0.2635

Table 5: Spearman's rank correlation coefficient of system-level in WMT10.

Metrics	cz-en (12 systems)	de-en (25 systems)	es-en (14 systems)	fr-en (24 systems)	Avg.
AILE	0.6573	0.6769	0.6029	0.5878	0.6312
BLEU	0.7203	0.7885	0.3890	0.6862	**0.6460**
IMPACT	0.6643	0.7115	0.6381	0.5635	0.6443
METEOR	0.5594	0.8538	0.4330	0.4957	0.5855
RIBES	0.4895	0.5423	0.6615	0.5200	0.5533
TER	-0.8042	-0.3700	-0.5429	-0.3983	-0.5288

with $\sqrt{m+n}$ and $\arctan(x+y)$. In these case, 0.1, 1.2 and 2.0 were respectively used as the values of parameters α, β and δ.

Tables 3 and 4 respectively provide Spearman's rank correlation coefficients of system-level and Kendall tau rank correlation coefficients of sentence-level in NTCIR-7(A. Fujii et al., 2008). Table 5 provides the Spearman's rank correlation coefficient of system-level in WMT10 (C. Callison-Burch et al., 2010). Table 6 provides the Spearman's rank correlation coefficient of system-level in WMT11(C. Callison-Burch et al., 2011). In Table 6, "indiv" and "comb" respectively indicate a single machine translation system and the combination of two machine translation systems.

3.3 Discussion

Through Table 2, the value 0.6774 was the highest value in "Total Avg.". Therefore, 0.1, 1.2, and 2.0 were determined as the most suitable values of parameters α, β and δ respectively. In AILE of Tables 3-6, their values were used as the values.

AILE provided the highest correlation with human judgments, except for Table 5. These results show the effectiveness of AILE. Moreover, we investigated the effectiveness of AILE in short sentences and long sentences. The AILE can obtain a high correlation by decreasing the weight of mismatched words in short sentences. We performed the experiments using two data sets in which the numbers of word in the pairs of the reference and candidate are respectively small and large. In NTCIR-7 data, the average of word number in all pairs of the reference and candidate is 61.59. Therefore, we divided all pairs in two kinds of data. One is the pairs of short sentences (numbers of words in reference and candidate under 60). Another is the pairs of long sentences (numbers of words in reference and candidate over 61). The number of short sentence pairs is 763 and the number of long sentence pairs is 637. Moreover, we used AILE with *weight* and AILE without *weight* to confirm the effectiveness of *weight* in Eq. (7). Tables 7 and 8 provide Kendall tau rank correlation coefficients of sentence-level using short sentences and long sentences. In system-level, the Spearman's rank correlation coefficients of AILE using *weight* are the same as those of AILE without *weight*.

Through Table 7, the correlation coefficients of AILE using *weight* are higher them of AILE without *weight*. The value of "Avg." improved 0.0043 (from 0.3729 to 0.3772) using *weight* of Eq. (7) in long sentences. On the

Table 6: Spearman's rank correlation coefficient of system-level in WMT11.

Metrics	cz-en indiv (8 systems)	de-en indiv (20 systems)	es-en indiv (15 systems)	es-en comb (6 systems)
AILE	0.9048	0.1729	0.7571	-0.0857
BLEU	0.8333	0.2309	0.8204	-0.1739
IMPACT	0.9048	0.1722	0.7857	-0.3714
METEOR	0.9286	0.5308	0.8321	-0.6000
RIBES	0.8333	0.0406	0.5393	-0.0667
TER	-0.9524	-0.1985	-0.7250	0.8286

Metrics	fr-en indiv (18 systems)	fr-en comb (6 systems)	Avg.
AILE	0.7503	0.7714	**0.5451**
BLEU	0.7730	-0.1449	0.3898
IMPACT	0.7750	0.6377	0.4840
METEOR	0.7998	0.0857	0.4295
RIBES	0.7337	-0.0857	0.3324
TER	-0.7564	0.0286	-0.2959

Table 7: Kendall tau rank correlation coefficient of sentence-level in long sentences.

Metrics	Adequacy (637 sentences)	Fluency (637 sentences)	Avg.
AILE using *weight*	0.4011	0.3532	0.3772
AILE without *weight*	0.3975	0.3482	0.3729

other hand, in Table 8, the value of "Avg." improved 0.0096 (from 0.3461 to 0.3557) using *weight* of Eq. (7) in short sentences. These results indicate the effectiveness of the use of *weight* in Eq. (7). Especially, *weight* is effective in short sentences described in Section 2. The improved value 0.0096 in short sentences is higher than 0.0043 in long sentences. Therefore, we confirmed that *weight* of Eq. (7) is especially effective in short sentences. As a result, AILE can obtain stable evaluation scores without depending on sentence length.

4 Conclusion

In this paper, we proposed a new automatic evaluation metric, in which the weight of each mismatched word does not depend heavily on sentence length. Our metric can obtain stable evaluation scores that are not distorted by sentence length. Our experimental results indicated that the correlation coefficient of our metric is the highest among some leading metrics. Therefore, we confirmed the effectiveness of our metric.

Future studies will work to increase the correlation coefficients. Moreover, we will use our metric as tuning in SMT. The AILE software will be released as IMPACT version 4.0.3 by `http://www.lst.hokkai-s-u.ac.jp/~echi/impact.html`.

Acknowledgments

This work was done as research under the AAMT/JAPIO Special Interest Group on Patent Translation. The Japan Patent Information Organization (JAPIO) and the National Institute of Information (NII) provided corpora used in this work. The author gratefully acknowledges support from JAPIO and NII.

References

C. Liu, D. Dahlmeier and H. Tou Ng. 2010. TESLA: Translation Evaluation of Sentences with Linear-programming-based Analysis. Proceedings of the Joint Fifth Workshop on Statistical Machine Translation and Metrics MATR. pp.354–359.

S. Padó, M. Galley, D. Jurafsky and C. D. Manning. 2009. Textual Entailment Features for

Table 8: Kendall tau rank correlation coefficient of sentence-level in short sentences.

Metrics	Adequacy (763 sentences)	Fluency (763 sentences)	Avg.
AILE using *weight*	0.3897	0.3217	0.3557
AILE without *weight*	0.3774	0.3147	0.3461

Machine Translation Evaluation. Proceedings of the Fourth Workshop on Statistical Machine Translation.

J. Giménez and L. Márquez. Heterogeneous Automatic MT Evaluation Through Non-Parametric Metric Combinations. 2007. Proceedings of IJCNLP. pp.319–326.

A. Lavie and A. Agarwal. 2007. Meteor: An Automatic Metric for MT Evaluation with High Levels of Correlation with Human Judgments. Proceedings of the Second Workshop on Statistical Machine Translation. pp.228–231.

Y. Seng Chan and H. Tou Ng. 2008. MAXSIM: An Automatic Metric for Machine Translation Evaluation Based on Maximum Similarity. Proceedings of the Metrics-MATR Workshop of AMTA-2008. pp.319–326.

K. Papineni, S. Roukos, T. Ward, and Wei-Jing Zhu. 2002. BLEU: a Method for Automatic Evaluation of Machine Translation. Proceedings of the 40th Annual Meeting of the Association for Computational Linguistics (ACL). pp.311–318.

M. Snover, B. Dorr, R. Schwartz, L. Micciulla and J. Makhoul. 2006. A Study of Translation Edit Rate with Targeted Human Annotation. Proceedings of the Seventh Conference of the Association for Machine Translation in the Americas (AMTA). pp.223–231.

H. Isozaki, T. Hirao, K. Duh, K. Sudoh and H. Tsukada. 2010. Automatic Evaluation of Translation Quality for Distant Language Pairs. Proceedings of the 2010 Conference on Empirical Methods in Natural Language Processing. pp.944–952.

H. Echizen-ya and K. Araki. 2007. Automatic Evaluation of Machine Translation based on Recursive Acquisition of an Intuitive Common Parts Continuum. Proceedings of the Eleventh Machine Translation Summit. pp.151–158.

H. Echizen'ya, K. Araki and H. Hovy. 2012. Optimization for Efficient Determination of Chunk in Automatic Evaluation for Machine Translation. Proceedings of the First International Workshop on Optimization Techniques for Human Language Technology. pp.17–30.

P. Koehn. 2010. *Statistical Machine Translation*. Cambridge University Press, Cambridge, UK.

H. Echizen-ya, T. Ehara, S. Shimohata, A. Fujii, M. Utiyama, M. Yamamoto, T. Utsuro, N. Kando. 2009. Meta-Evaluation of Automatic Evaluation Methods for Machine Translation using Patent Translation Data in NTCIR-7. Proceedings of the Third Workshop on Patent Translation. pp.9–16.

A. Fujii, M. Utiyama, M. Yamamoto and T. Utsuro. 2008. Overview of the Patent Translation Task at the NTCIR-7 Workshop. Proceedings of the Seventh NTCIR Workshop Meeting on Evaluation of Information Access Technologies: Information Retrieval, Question Answering and Cross-lingual Information Access. pp.389–400.

C. Callison-Burch, P. Koehn, C. Monz, K. Peterson, M. Przybocki and O. F. Zaidan. 2010. Findings of the 2010 Joint Workshop on Statistical Machine Translation and Metrics for Machine Translation. Proceedings of the Join Fifth Workshop on Statistical Machine Translation and Metrics MATR. pp.17–53.

C. Callison-Burch, P. Koehn, C. Monz and O. F. Zaidan. 2011. Findings of the 2011 Workshop on Statistical Machine Translation, Proceedings of the Sixth Workshop on Statistical Machine Translation. Proceedings of the Sixth Workshop on Statistical Machine Translation. pp.22–64.

H. Schmid. 1994. Probabilistic Part-of-Speech Tagging Using Decision Trees. Proceedings of the International Conference on New Methods in Language Processing. pp.389–400.

P. Koehn. 2011. `http://www.statmt.org/wmt11/translation-task.html`.

Acronym Recognition and Processing in 22 Languages

Maud Ehrmann
Department of Computer Science
Sapienza University of Rome
ehrmann@di.uniroma1.it

Leonida Della Rocca
European Commission
Joint Research Centre
IPSC-GlobeSec
leonida.della-rocca@ext.jrc.ec.europa.eu

Ralf Steinberger
European Commission
Joint Research Centre
IPSC-GlobeSec
ralf.steinberger@jrc.ec.europa.eu

Hristo Tannev
European Commission
Joint Research Centre
IPSC-GlobeSec
hristo.tannev@jrc.ec.europa.eu

Abstract

We are presenting work on recognising acronyms of the form *Long-Form (Short-Form)* such as "*International Monetary Fund (IMF)*" in millions of news articles in twenty-two languages, as part of our more general effort to recognise *entities* and their variants in news text and to use them for the automatic analysis of the news, including the linking of related news across languages. We show how the acronym recognition patterns, initially developed for medical terms, needed to be adapted to the more general news domain and we present evaluation results. We describe our effort to automatically merge the numerous long-form variants referring to the same short-form, while keeping non-related long-forms separate. Finally, we provide extensive statistics on the frequency and the distribution of short-form/long-form pairs across languages.

1 Introduction and Motivation

An acronym is an abbreviation formed from the initial letters of the various word elements and read as a single word.[1] Acronyms are formed to speed up and ease communication, mainly to create *words* for concepts frequently used or difficult to describe. Like entities, acronyms have a high reference value, in the sense that they most of the time act as reference anchors of textual content. However, they are not always explicitly defined, which can cause comprehension problems, both for humans and machines. In addition, due to the large number of acronyms – we found over one million when analysing our news data set – the same short-form (SF) can have several conceptually different long-forms (LF) (see Table 1). Even for the same SF-LF pair, many LF variants may exist. In addition to simple wording differences, there can be grammatical inflection forms and cross-lingual variants.

Acronyms are productive words, i.e. new acronyms are created every day, requiring frequent updating of any acronym database. In the first month of applying the tool to our large throughput of multilingual news articles, we identified 66,000 acronyms (before merging variants, i.e. unique SF-LF pairs). After only five months of analysis, the monthly number of newly identified acronym pairs has halved and the number of newly found acronyms seems to be stabilising around this value. We are adding these new acronyms to our multilingual dataset every day and we plan to publicly release the more frequently occurring ones in regular intervals as part of the multilingual name variant resource JRC-Names (Steinberger et al. 2011), which currently predominantly contains person names. This dataset

[1] See http://dictionary.reference.com/help/faq/language/t08.html to distinguish acronyms from related concepts such as *initials* and *contractions*.

Found in English text
capital adequacy ratio
Capital Adequate Ratio
Capital Adequacy Ration
Capital Adequacy Returns
Center for Autism Research
central African Republic
Certified Automotive Recycler Program
Commission for Aviation Regulation
Confederations of Africa Rugby
Cordilleral Administrative Region

Found in French text
Caisse Autonome des Retraites
capacité africaine contre les risques
Cellule d'Action Routière
Collectif d'artistes de reggae
Collectivité d'accueil régionale
Comité d'Action pour le Renouveau
Communauté d'agglomération de Rufisque

Found in German text
Centers for Automotive Research
Central African Republic
chimären Antigenrezeptoren
Computer Assisted Reporting

Found in Italian text
Cogenerazione ad Alto Rendimento
Computer Assisted Reporting
consumo annuo di riferimento

Table 1. Multilingual examples of acronym long forms for the short form CAR

can be used for named entity recognition and other natural language processing tasks, including information retrieval, question answering, summarisation and machine translation.

For acronym recognition, we use the simple and efficient algorithm which was initially developed by Schwartz & Hearst (2003) for the recognition of biomedical abbreviations in English text, but we adapted it for our purposes.

Our contributions are (a) the adaptation of the method to another text type (news); (b) the application to over twenty languages; (c) the generation of highly multilingual statistics on acronym use and on (d) acronym SF ambiguity; and (e) the automatic grouping of LF variant forms.

We first present related work (Section 2), then present our adaptation of the original algorithm, together with recognition statistics and evaluation results (3). We then describe our method to group LF variants (4). We finish by summarising and by pointing to future work (5).

2 Related Work

Since the pioneering achievement of Taghva and Gilbreth (1999), a significant amount of work has been completed in the domain of abbreviation processing. Focusing almost exclusively on the bio-medical domain and on the English language, research has developed into three main directions: acronym extraction and mapping to their full forms; acronym variant clustering; and, more recently, acronym disambiguation. We report here on the first two.

With regard to acronym extraction, existing approaches can be divided into four main categories, as suggested by Torii et al. (2007) in their comparative study: *alignment-based* approaches, which exploit the fact that SF and LF show letter or string ordered similarities; *collocation-based* approaches, which exploit the fact that SF and LF frequently occur together and can be considered as collocations; *pattern/rule-based* approaches, which explore regularities of abbreviation conventions; and, finally, *machine-learning* approaches, most of which supervised. Major representatives of these approaches are, respectively: Schwartz and Hearst (2003), whose letter matching algorithm proved to be, despite its simplicity, very efficient; Okazaki and Ananiadou (2006), who address the problem as a term recognition task and perform acronym extraction using statistical co-occurrence evidence in large text collections; Pustejovsky *et al.* (2001), Wren and Garber (2002) and Adar (2004), who look at regular patterns in occurrences of acronyms and manually design templates for their extraction; and Chang *et al.* (2002) and Nadeau and Turney (2005) who apply supervised machine learning algorithms after pre-selection of acronym candidates through the use of Longest Common Subsequence for the former, the use of heuristics for the latter. Although not comparable because focusing on different acronym sub-types (showing different levels of difficulty), these methods perform overall quite well and one can consider the extraction-recognition step a mature technology in the domain of English biomedical literature.

However, not much work exists for languages other than English. Kompara (2010) describes some preliminary work on Slovene, English, French and Italian, while Kokkinakis and Dannélls (2006) investigate the specificity of Swedish – a compounding language – with regard to acronym extraction and present good results obtained thanks to an approach similar to that of Nadeau and Turney (2005). The work showing most similarity with ours is that by Hanh *et al.* (2005). Applying Schwartz and Hearst's algorithm on textual data retrieved from the web in English, German, Portuguese and Spanish, they present a method to align acronyms and their definitions across languages, thanks to an interlingual representation layer. They explore interlingua phenomena and report statistics on the four languages they consider. As opposed to this work, we consider a wider range of languages and we do not intend to use any interlingua.

Finally, it is worth mentioning work on acronym variant clustering: Okazaki *et al.* (2010) present a method to gather similar English acronym expansions based on hierarchical clustering applied over a *pseudo* distance metric. This distance corresponds to a conditional probability, itself computed through binary classification based on various string similarity metric features. Combining all features, they obtain an F-measure of 0.89, noticing that the n-gram similarity was contributing most to the efficiency of the conditional probability. Looking at the same problem, Adar (2004) applies a variant of k-means clustering using the cosine similarity measure over acronym expansion trigrams, and then refined the obtained results taking into account the MeSH category available for each initial n-gram cluster, eventually reaching very good results.

3 Multilingual Acronym Extraction

3.1 Recognition Algorithm

We use the algorithm presented by Schwartz & Hearst (2003), with minor modifications, mostly consisting of post-processing and filtering the results. In simple words, the algorithm recognises short uppercase expressions between brackets (the SF) and searches in the left-hand-side con-text for the letters used in the SF. At least the first letter must be word-initial. Unlike Schwartz & Hearst, we do not currently recognise acronym pairs of the format SF (LF) as these are much rarer (in our dataset, less than 10% of all occurrences) and we achieve high recall due to the sheer size of our dataset.

Here are some more details about the algorithm proposed by Ariel & Schwartz: SFs are valid candidates only if they consist of at most two words and if they are between 2 and 10 characters long. If the expression in parentheses is longer, they assume the pattern SF (LF). LF candidates must appear in the same sentence and they must be adjacent to the SF. Regarding their length (the search window), they must not be longer than (a) twice as many words as there are characters in the SF, or (b) the number of characters in the SF plus five words, whichever is the smaller (i.e. $min(|A|+5,|A|*2)$ words, with $|A|$ being the number of characters of the SF).

After applying this pattern to text, we filter the resulting acronym pairs to reduce noise and to avoid unwanted acronym pairs, eliminating cases where either the SF or the LF satisfies any of the following conditions:

a) SFs with currency symbols;
b) SFs with punctuation marks other than hyphens, with quotation marks and word-final apostrophes;
c) SFs starting with a single letter followed by a space;
d) SFs having no uppercase letters.

We additionally eliminate acronyms with LFs satisfying any of the following conditions:

e) LFs excluding white spaces (one-word LFs).

Furthermore, SFs must not:

f) be part of a multilingual stop word list consisting of closed class words (mostly determiners), days of the week or the month and individual words like *north*. Our mixed language stop word list contains about 300 words.

These rules are being applied continuously to large numbers of news texts in the 22 languages of the Europe Media Monitor (EMM) which use the Latin alphabet. EMM processes a current average of 175,000 news articles per day in 70 languages (Steinberger et al. 2009). All acronym pairs are stored, together with meta-information such as date, language, news source and news category, allowing the preparation of detailed statistics.

3.2 Multilingual Evaluation

We manually annotated acronyms in 400 articles each in the seven languages Czech, English, French, German, Hungarian, Romanian and Spanish. 200 of these articles were selected randomly (spread over time). The other 200 were selected if our patterns matched at least one acronym pair, to ensure that there is a reasonable number of acronym occurrences to evaluate. The evaluation results in Table 2 show that the performance across languages is rather good and consistent. In comparison, Schwartz & Hearst (2003) report a precision of 0.95 and a Recall of 0.82 when applying their algorithm to the biomedical domain. We conclude that the algorithm works well for a variety of languages, and presumably for all languages using an alphabetic writing system distinguishing lower and upper-case letters.

ISO	Language	N°	Prec.	Rec.	F1
Cs	Czech	267	.96	.90	.93
De	German	274	.94	.92	.93
En	English	404	.97	.91	.93
Es	Spanish	339	.93	.88	.90
Fr	French	371	.87	.83	.85
Hu	Hungarian	318	.98	.96	.92
Ro	Romanian	277	.93	.91	.92

Table 2: Acronym recognition performance results for seven languages (Language ISO code; Number of acronyms evaluated; Precision; Recall; F1 measure).

The major reason for *non-recognition* (lowering Recall) are cases where the acronym's SF is in a different language from the LF, such as in the German *Vereinigte Nationen (UNO)*, where the German LF is followed by the English SF. However, there is a non-negligible number of cases where such cases get coincidentally recognised correctly. Such a lucky case is *Namibische Rundfunkanstalt (NBC)*, where *NBC* stands for the English equivalent *Namibian Broadcasting Corporation*.

The major source of *wrongly recognised* acronym pairs, across all languages, are generic SFs

ISO	Language	AA distrib.	AS/AA	AA/ PU	PO/AA *100	PO/PU	PU f=1/PU	PU f≥10/PU	PU f≥100/PU	Avg. LF/SF
Ca	Catalan	0.2%	16.5%	**22**	21.2	4.66	61.4%	6.03%	0.63%	**1.75**
Cs	Czech	1.5%	7.5%	101	8.9	8.95	49.6%	10.55%	1.40%	2.26
Da	Danish	3.3%	2.8%	**330**	3.0	9.92	55.2%	**13.99%**	1.16%	1.81
De	German	12.7%	10.6%	69	13.3	9.09	56.4%	8.33%	0.99%	3.52
En	English	**25.1%**	16.4%	29	26.2	7.51	58.8%	7.55%	0.90%	3.75
Es	Spanish	11.9%	**21.8%**	38	30.7	11.64	58.2%	8.92%	1.26%	3.31
Et	Estonian	0.9%	3.5%	96	3.9	3.76	62.7%	5.35%	0.40%	2.31
Eu	Basque	**0.0%**	2.6%	69	2.9	**1.98**	68.9%	**2.20%**	**0.00%**	1.82
Fi	Finnish	2.2%	**1.3%**	320	**1.4**	4.33	64.8%	6.87%	0.45%	2.36
Fr	French	8.8%	19.3%	23	28.8	6.59	61.5%	6.86%	0.71%	3.89
Hu	Hungarian	2.7%	7.7%	93	9.5	8.79	56.5%	8.48%	1.12%	2.43
It	Italian	4.8%	2.8%	76	3.2	2.48	71.3%	3.02%	0.12%	2.98
Lt	Lithuanian	1.0%	16.5%	47	22.3	10.43	52.7%	10.48%	1.40%	2.73
Lv	Latvian	0.9%	21.4%	45	**32.4**	**14.67**	54.1%	11.48%	**2.33%**	3.18
Nl	Dutch	4.2%	6.9%	90	8.0	7.25	59.6%	7.54%	0.74%	2.06
No	Norwegian	1.4%	5.5%	87	6.2	5.41	61.2%	6.90%	0.64%	2.03
Pl	Polish	2.5%	3.3%	118	3.9	4.65	55.7%	7.36%	0.49%	2.27
Pt	Portuguese	4.9%	20.4%	47	27.9	13.13	**46.3%**	11.08%	1.52%	2.91
Ro	Romanian	5.7%	10.4%	60	13.5	8.11	59.2%	7.86%	1.15%	**4.32**
Sl	Slovene	1.1%	7.6%	67	9.2	6.16	55.3%	8.91%	0.80%	2.62
Sv	Swedish	4.0%	2.2%	289	2.4	6.96	58.7%	10.60%	0.85%	1.89
Sw	Swahili	0.1%	13.6%	26	16.6	4.32	**77.2%**	3.21%	0.52%	1.94
TOTAL		**100%**	**13.0%**	**44**	**18.6**		**58.7%**	**7.85%**	**0.95%**	**3.40**

Table 3: Statistics on acronym recognition in 22 languages, showing the distribution of articles per language (AA distrib.); the percentage of articles containing at least one acronym (AS/AA); the n° of articles that needs to be parsed to find a new unique acronym (AA/PU); the n° of acronym occurrences per 100 articles (PO/AA*100); the average n° of times a (unique) acronym was reused (PO/PU); the percentage of acronyms that were found only once (PU f=1/PU), at least 10 times (PU f≥10/PU), at least 100 times (PU f≥100/PU); the average number of LFs per SF.

such as the title *CEO* (Chief Executive Officer) or party acronyms such as *PS* (Parti Socialiste) following person names, leading to the erroneous recognition of the acronym pairs like the following: *Stephan Dorgerloh (SPD)*; *Charles Otieno (CEO)*; *consists of Pieter van Oord (CEO)*. Some of these cases are hard to avoid. It might therefore be useful to produce lists of such SFs and to filter them additionally, e.g. by combining the recognition patterns with a named entity recognition tool or by training classifiers to get rid of unwanted LFs. It might also be possible to exploit the fact that these SFs occur with unusually high numbers of different LFs, but care must be taken not to also exclude the good LFs. In our evaluation, we came across small numbers of such SFs, leading however to many wrongly recognised acronym pairs.

3.3 Multilingual Recognition Statistics

We applied the method described in Section 3.1 to many million news articles in 22 languages and produced various types of statistics. These are shown in Table 3. When looking at statistics on, for instance, how many acronyms are used in the different languages, we have to bear in mind that these statistics are biased to some extent by the choices we have made. For instance, we only identify acronym pairs of the form LF (SF), while some languages may more frequently use the inverse order SF (LF) or other alternatives such as *LF, SF* (i.e. the short form is shown inside the text, separated by a comma) or *SF, acronym for LF* (i.e. explicitly mentioning in the text that SF is the acronym for LF). All the numbers in Table 3 refer to successfully recognised acronyms, i.e. after the filtering process described in Section 3.1. When counting unique acronym pairs (PU – pairs unique) or unique SFs, we strictly distinguish case and we consider space and punctuation. For instance, *UNO*, *Uno* and *U.N.O.* are three different SFs. Acronym pair *occurrences* without distinguishing uniqueness are referred to as PO (pairs occurrences). We furthermore use the abbreviations AA for *all articles* analysed and AS for *selected articles*, i.e. only those in which we found acronyms. The highest and the lowest value in each of the columns in Table 3 is written in boldface to give an idea of the range of values.

The first column with numerical contents gives an indication on the relative amount of news text we have analysed. The next column shows that the ratio of news articles AS in which good acronyms (acronyms passing the filtering process) were found, compared to all news articles analysed (AA), is 13%. However, there are enormous differences from one language to the other, with Spanish, Latvian and Portuguese having the highest density of acronyms and Finnish, Swedish and Basque having the lowest.

The third column summarises how many news articles need to be analysed to find a new (i.e. unique) acronym. The fourth column shows how many acronym pair *occurrences* (i.e. non-unique) there are per 100 articles analysed. The fifth column depicts the ratio between unique acronyms PU compared to all acronyms found (PO), thus giving an indication of the number of repetitions of acronyms in the corpus. The sixth column presents the ratio of acronym pairs that have been found exactly once in the corpus (almost 60%), while the next two columns give an indication of how many acronyms have been found at least 10 times or at least 100 times in the corpus. Note that the numbers in Table 3 refer to acronym pairs *before* the merging of acronym variants (described in Section 4). The last column provides the ratio between the number of LFs for the same SF, considering *all* SFs. We thus see that there is an average of 3.4 LFs for each SF. When considering only those SFs that are ambiguous at all (i.e. ignoring SFs that are found with only one LF), the ratio is 6.87.

The statistics on the average number of different SFs for the same unique LF (i.e. the inverse ratio) is less interesting as there are only 1.08 different SFs for the same LF. When considering only the *ambiguous* LFs, the ratio is 2.23, i.e. there are just over two SFs for the same LF. The two different SFs are typically due to varying case, due to plural formation (*ROV* and *ROVs* for *Remotely Operated Vehicles*) or due to punctuation (e.g. *UP* and *U.P.* for *Uttar Pradesh*). However, occasionally, there are also more fundamental differences in the LFs. For instance, in Italian texts, we found the following three acronyms *AUSTRADE*, *Austrade* and *ATC*, all representing the same LF *Australian Trade Commission*.

4 Merging related acronym variants

Having identified hundreds of thousands distinct acronym pairs, it is necessary to structure this dataset. We do this by grouping together conceptually related variant LFs belonging to the same SF.

		N° unique LFs	N° unique SFs	N° LF clusters	N° LF clusters ≥ 2	Precision	Recogn. Error	Border error
DE	German	947	57	402	110	0.99	0.07	0.09
En	English	955	26	411	144	1.00	0.03	0.08
Fr	French	662	21	276	89	0.99	0.05	0.03
It	Italian	576	34	142	55	1.00	0.05	0.09

Table 4: Evaluation results for the clustering (separately for each language) of all LFs having the same SF.

4.1 Clustering of acronym variants

Given that there are many SFs for which a variety of (relevant and conceptually related) LFs exist, we cluster – separately for each language – all LFs having the same SF. By setting an empirically determined threshold for intra-cluster similarity (or cluster homogeneity), we can group related LFs while keeping unrelated ones separate. We apply binary (hierarchical) group-average clustering. The clustering is based on a pair-wise string similarity for each LF pair in the set. This string similarity is a normalised Levenshtein edit distance where the number of required insertions, deletions and substitutions is divided by the number of characters of the longer LF, yielding a distance value D between 0 and 1. The string similarity S is then the inverse value 1/D. The intra-cluster similarity threshold is set empirically, separately for each language, by optimising it on a development set. For each acronym pair cluster, we choose the most frequently found LF as the representative acronym name.

4.2 Evaluation of the clustering

For the evaluation, we manually selected a small number of widely known acronym SFs, for which we could expect that they would be present in each of the languages. Examples are IAEA (International Atomic Energy Agency), IMF (International Monetary Fund), CAR (Central African Republic), ECB (European Central Bank) and FIFA (Fédération Internationale de Football Association), and their respective translations in the four languages (e.g. German EZB and IAEO). This was to make the results comparable across languages. For the rest (the majority), we selected SFs that existed in each of the languages, without knowing whether they would be related across languages and whether the LFs would be similar. This selection was made in preparation of our future work on clustering LF variants *across* languages if they have the same SF.

Table 4 summarises the evaluation results for the acronym LF clustering step for English, French, German and Italian (languages for which we had evaluation volunteers). The first three columns show the number of SF clusters evaluated (unique SF), the number of LFs that had been found and evaluated for these SFs (unique LFs), as well as the number of distinct clusters

Agenzia internazionale per l'energia atomica (AIEA)
agenzia delle Nazioni Unite per l'energia atomica
Agenzia di controllo sul nucleare delle Nazioni Unite
Agenzia internazionale energia atomica
Agenzia Internazionale delEnergia Atomica
Agenzia internazionale dell'Onu per l'energia atomica
Agenzia internazionale delOnu per energia atomica
Agenzia internazionale Energia atomica
Agenzia Internazionale Onu per l'Energia Atomica
agenzia Internazionale per Energia Atomica
Agenzia internazionale per il nucleare
Agenzia Internazionale per la Sicurezza Nucleare
Agenzia internazionale per l'energia atomica Onu
Agenzia nucleare delOnu
Agenzia Onu per il Nucleare
Agenzia Onu sul nucleare
Agenzia per l'Energia atomica
Agenzia per l'energia nucleare Onu
all'Agenzia internazionale dell'energia atomica
all'Organizzazione iraniana dell'energia atomica
Atomic Energy Agency
Atomica delle Nazioni Unite
dell'Agenzia dell'Onu sul nucleare
dell'Agenzia delle Nazioni Unite per l'energia atomica
dell'Agenzia di controllo sul nucleare delle Nazioni Unite
dell'agenzia nazionale per l'energia atomica

Table 5. Subset of LF variants for the Italian SF AIEA, equivalent to English IAEA – International Atomic Energy Agency. All forms were found in real-life news texts.

identified by the clustering algorithm and evaluated (LF clusters). Comparing the third column with the fourth column (clusters ≥ 2) shows that about two thirds of the acronym pairs were not clustered at all and remained single acronyms.

The precision was evaluated keeping an application-centred approach in mind. Within the framework of ENM, the purpose of the acronym recognition and of the long-form clustering is (a) to display to the users name-like entities as meta-information to news articles and (b) to use these extracted 'entities' as anchors to establish links between related documents (eventually also across languages). For that purpose, we evaluated the precision generously, accepting acronym pairs as rightfully belonging to the same cluster if the intention of the journalist seems to have been to refer to the same entity, even if the acronym LF was not perfectly captured. For that reason, we show recognition error rates separately in Table 4: The column *Recognition Error* describes cases where the system captured non-acronyms or the LFs did not belong to the SF. The column *Border Error* reflects cases where the acronym was detected, but the border of the LF was identified wrongly (e.g. recognising the string *assisted by the International Energy Atomic Agency* for the SF *IAEA*. In such a case, if the erroneous LF was placed in the correct cluster, it was annotated as being correct for clustering, but it was also marked as a *border error*. Journalists are sometimes very lax in their usage of names (see Table 5). It is our intention to capture these references even if the naming may in itself be wrong.

In summary, we find that the clustering process works surprisingly well and that it manages to group LF variants with the same SF, while only rarely excluding LFs that should also be grouped with the cluster. The cases where LFs that refer to the same real-world entity are excluded from a cluster are usually those where the LF differs substantially from those of the entries in the cluster, making it almost impossible to automatically merge the variants. For instance, the German equivalences for *Common Agricultural Policy (CAP)*: *gemeinsame Landwirtschaftspolitik* and *Gemeinsamen Europäischen Agrarpolitik* (GAP) are so different that we do not expect these variants to be recognised automatically without making use of the context of the acronym.

5 Conclusion and future work

Acronyms are important referential text elements with high information content that are useful for a whole range of text processing applications. We have shown that an existing English language acronym recognition pattern from the biomedical domain can be adapted successfully to the news domain and to 22 languages from different language families, yielding over one million acronym short-form/long-form pairs. The method works well, for all languages using an alphabetic writing system and distinguishing case. Case is important (a) to select the more promising acronym pairs, thus excluding possible false positives, and also (b) to detect the beginning of the LF string. While we suspect that the method will work well with languages using for instance the Cyrillic or Greek alphabets, it will probably not work well for languages using the Arabic or Hebrew scripts because these do not distinguish case. Clustering turned out to be an efficient method to group acronym spelling variants and separating non-related acronym long-forms coincidentally having the same short-form.

We are interested in categorising the multilingual acronym collection into acronym subtypes such as organisations, programmes (e.g. FP7), stock exchange terminology (e.g. DOW), etc. As our biggest interest are organisation names, we have built a rule-based categoriser using dictionaries with organisation name parts (e.g. *bank, organisation, international, club*, etc.). We believe that, in order to categorise strings in 22 different languages, it is faster to establish and apply such dictionaries than it would be to annotate data in each of the languages and to train a machine learning classifier, but future experiments will show.

The acronym dataset we have created opens up further research avenues. The most interesting challenge probably is how to automatically link acronym long forms across languages. We have several fundamentally different solutions in mind on how to achieve this and we will tackle this task next.

Regarding the recognition of acronyms, it would be interesting to improve the acronym extraction by merging our current method with co-occurrence statistics, which would mostly benefit the recognition of cross-language SF-LF pairs.

Finally, we are interested in recognising and disambiguating acronym SFs that are not accompanied by their LFs, using the local context.

Acknowledgments

The authors gratefully acknowledge the support of the ERC Starting Grant MultiJEDI No. 259234.

References

Adar Eytan. 2004. SaRAD: a Simple and Robust Abbreviation Dictionary. BioInformatics 20:527-533.

Chang Jeffrey T., Hinrich Schütze & Russ B. Altman. 2002. Creating an Online Dictionary of Abbreviations from MEDLINE. Journal of the American Medical Informatics Associations 9:262-272.

Hahn Udo, Philipp Daumke, Stefan Schulz & Kornél Markó. 2005. Cross-language mining for acronyms and their completions from the web. Discovery Science, Springer Berlin Heidelberg. 113-123.

Hiroko Ao & Toshihisa Takagi. 2005. ALICE: an algorithm to extract abbreviations from MEDLINE. Journal of the American Medical Informatics Association 12(.5):576-586.

Karipis George. 2005. Cluto: Software for clustering high dimensional datasets. Internet website (last accessed, June 2008), http://glaros.dtc.umn.edu/gkhome/cluto/cluto/overview (2005).

Kompara Mojca. 2010. Automatic recognition of abbreviations and abbreviations' expansions in multilingual electronic texts. Proceedings of CAMLing. 82-91.

Kokkinakis Dimitrios & Dana Dannélls. 2006. Recognizing acronyms and their definitions in Swedish medical texts. Proceedings of the 5th Conference on Language Resources and Evaluation (LREC). Genoa, Italy.

Okazaki Naoaki & Sophia Ananiadou. 2006. Building an abbreviation dictionary using a term recognition approach. Bioinformatics 22(24):3089-3095.

Okazaki Naoaki, Sophia Ananiadou & Jun'ichi Tsujii. 2010. Building a high-quality sense inventory for improved abbreviation disambiguation. Bioinformatics 26(9):1246-1253.

Park Youngja and Roy J. Byrd. 2001. Hybrid text mining for finding abbreviations and their definitions. Proceedings of the 2001 conference on empirical methods in natural language processing, 126-133.

Pustejovsky James, José Castano, Brent Cochran, Maciej Kotecki & Michael Morrell. 2001. Automatic extraction of acronym-meaning pairs from MEDLINE databases. Studies in health technology and informatics 1:371-375.

Nadeau David & Peter Turney. 2005. A supervised learning approach to acronym identification. Proceedings of the Canadian Conference on Artificial Intelligence. 319-329.

Schwartz Ariel S. & Marti A. Hearst. 2003. A simple algorithm for identifying abbreviation definitions in biomedical text. Proceedings of the PAC on Biocomputing, 451-462.

Steinberger Ralf, Bruno Pouliquen & Erik van der Goot (2009). An Introduction to the Europe Media Monitor Family of Applications. In: Fredric Gey, Noriko Kando & Jussi Karlgren (eds.): Information Access in a Multilingual World - Proceedings of the SIGIR 2009 Workshop (SIGIR-CLIR'2009), pp. 1-8. Boston, USA. 23 July 2009.

Steinberger Ralf, Bruno Pouliquen, Mijail Kabadjov & Erik van der Goot (2011). JRC-Names: A freely available, highly multilingual named entity resource. Proceedings of the 8th International Conference Recent Advances in Natural Language Processing (RANLP'2011), pp. 104-110. Hissar, Bulgaria, 12-14 September 2011.Taghva Kazem & Jeff Gilbreth. 1999. Recognizing acronyms and their definitions. International Journal on Document Analysis and Recognition, 1(4):191-198.

Torii Manabu, Zhang-zhi Hu, Min Song, Cathy H Wu & Hongfang Liu. 2007. A comparison study on algorithms of detecting long forms for short forms in biomedical text. BMC Bioinformatics, 8 (suppl. 9):S5.

Wren J. D. & H. R. Garner. 2002. Heuristics for Identification of Acronym-Definition Patterns within Text: Towards an Automated Construction of Comprehensive Acronym-Definition Dictionaries. Methods of Information in Medicine 41(5):426-434.

An Evaluation Summary Method Based on a Combination of Content and Linguistic Metrics

Samira Ellouze	Maher Jaoua	Lamia Hadrich Belguith
University of Sfax	University of Sfax	University of Sfax
ANLP Research Group, MIRACL Laboratory, Sfax, Tunisia	ANLP Research Group, MIRACL Laboratory, Sfax, Tunisia	ANLP Research Group, MIRACL Laboratory, Sfax, Tunisia
ellouze.samira@gmail.com	Maher.Jaoua@fsegs.rnu.tn	l.belguith@fsegs.rnu.tn

Abstract

This paper presents a new automated method for evaluating the content of a text summary. The proposed method is based on a combination of features encompassing scores of content and others of linguistic quality. This method relies on a learning technique called linear regression. The objective of this combination is to predict the PYRAMID score from the features used. In order to evaluate the presented method, we are interested in two levels of granularity evaluation: the first is named Micro-evaluation and proposes an evaluation of each summary while the second is called Macro-evaluation and it is applied at the level of each system. The resulting metric shows an improvement upon standard metrics by increasing the correlation with the PYRAMID metric.

1 Introduction

The evaluation of a summary is an important and necessary task. It quantifies the informativeness and linguistic quality of a summary and it can be of two types: extrinsic or intrinsic (Jing et al., 1998). Extrinsic evaluation measures the impact of using a summary in the place of the source document(s) on tasks such as document classification and indexing while intrinsic evaluation assesses the overall quality of the summary either manually or automatically. It should be noted that the manual evaluation is a difficult and expensive task because it requires a lot of time and expertise in the field of the source text topic. For this reason, several automatic evaluation metrics have been developed such as ROUGE (Lin, 2004), BE (Hovy et al., 2006), BEwTE (Tratz and Hovy, 2008), AutoSummENG (Giannakopoulos et al., 2008), etc. The advent of automatic evaluation metrics generates in its turn a new step: meta-evaluation i.e. the evaluation of evaluation metrics. We perform this meta-evaluation by making a comparison between these metrics and manual metrics. To achieve this comparison, the TAC[1] conference proposed various metrics of correlations (i.e. Pearson, Spearman, Kandall). Most of the evaluation metrics assessed by the TAC conference are based on the evaluation of the relevance of a summary content. However, a summary with relevant content may be unreadable. To encourage researchers to evaluate the readability of a summary, the TAC 2011 session added a new goal to the task of automatic evaluation of summaries consisting in evaluating the readability of summaries. In this context, we suggest in this paper an evaluation method based on the combination of several evaluation metrics (i.e. content metrics and linguistic quality metrics). This paper is organized as follows: in section 2, we give a brief historical overview on the evolution of the evaluation of intrinsic methods used in the field of automatic summarization; section 3 describes the proposed method, which operates by the linear combination of content and linguistic features. We define content and linguistic quality features in section 4. Finally, the final section presents the results of our experiments.

[1] Text Analysis Conference http://www.nist.gov/tac

2 Overview of intrinsic metrics

Initial assessments in the field of automatic summarization are made by human judges. Judges evaluate a summary by answering questions about coherence, coverage, relevance, etc. This evaluation procedure is expensive because it requires significant human resources and a huge time. Besides, it is subjective since it varies from one assessor to another. In fact, it can vary for the same assessor at two separate times. Despite all these disadvantages the evaluation by human judges is used by several evaluation metrics. Prior to 2005, the DUC[2] conference evaluated summaries using the Summary Evaluation Environment (SEE) interface (Lin, 2001). This interface helps assessors in the evaluation of the content and the linguistic quality of a candidate summary. In 2006, DUC added the Overall Responsiveness metric (Dang and Owczarzak, 2008) to evaluate a candidate summary. This metric is a combination of content and linguistic quality. It differs from other metrics of summary evaluation in that it doesn't compare a candidate summary against a model summary. Since the 2005 DUC, the PYRAMID metric (Nenkova and Passonneau, 2004) has been added as an optional manual evaluation metric. This metric, which is based on the identification of minimal semantic units called SCUs (Summary Content Units), has become one of the principal manual metrics for evaluating summaries in the TAC conference.

Because of the difficulties encountered during the manual evaluation, more research has focused on automatic evaluation. ROUGE (Lin, 2004) is one of the first automatic metrics for the intrinsic evaluation of automatic summaries. This metric is based on the overlap of N-grams between a candidate summary and one or more reference summaries. (Hovy et al., 2006) introduced the BE metric, which allows the correspondence between syntactic units called BEs. A BE is composed of a head representing one element (noun, verb, etc.) or a dependency relationship between a head and its modifier. In a more recent work (Giannakopoulos et al., 2008) introduced the metric AutoSummENG allowing the representation of a candidate summary and a reference summary each as a graph of n-grams. Then, it makes a comparison between these two graphs. Other evaluation metrics which do not use reference summaries have also been proposed by (Louis and Nenkova, 2009) and (Torres-Moreno et al., 2010). These metrics are used to compare each candidate summary to source documents using the Jensen-Shannon divergence measure.

New metrics such as ROSE (Conroy and Dang, 2008) and Nouveau-ROUGE (Conroy et al., 2011) have involved a combination of ROUGE variants to predict PYRAMID or the Overall Responsiveness score. Other works have focused on metrics of linguistic quality evaluation. In this context, (Pilter et al., 2010) evaluated the five linguistic properties used in TAC by combining different types of features such as entity grid (Barzilay and Lapata, 2008), modeling language, etc. The most recent work, namely that of (Conroy et al, 2010), assessed content and linguistic quality using a combination of features. Concerning content features, (Conroy et al, 2010) use ROUGE scores for initial summaries and Nouveau-ROUGE scores for update summaries. In a later work (Conroy et al., 2011) and (Rankel et al., 2012) combined features of content (six variations of bigram scores) and others of linguistic quality. In contrast to Conroy, (Lin et al., 2012) combined a machine translation metric adapted to summary evaluation with a coherence metric based on an entity grid to predict the Overall Responsiveness metric.

3 Proposed method

Most single automatic metrics use one level of evaluation (i.e. lexical, syntactic or semantic) while the metric based on machine learning techniques can combine multiple levels of evaluation into one model. For this reason, we proposed a method based on a machine learning technique to predict the PYRAMID metric. We performed a linear combination of content metrics (i.e. ROUGE, BE and AutoSummENG) and linguistic metrics (i.e. part-of-speech features, traditional readability metrics features, shallow features). Thus, the equation used to estimate the PYRAMID score is written:

$$\hat{y} = w_0 + w_1 x_1 + w_2 x_2 + \cdots + w_n x_n$$

where $\hat{y}$ is the predictive value, n is the number of features, $x_1 \ldots x_n$ are the feature values and $w_0 \ldots w_n$ are the feature weights.

[2] Document Understanding Conference http://duc.nist.gov/

We used a linear regression to find the linear combination that maximizes the correlation between the used features and PYRAMID. So the problem of linear regression is expressed as a set of features and their corresponding PYRAMID scores. Subsequently, we determined a vector X of length $n+1$ maximizing the correlation as:

$$w = argmax\ \rho(w_0 + \sum_{j=1}^{n} a_{ij}w_j, b_i)$$

where a_{ij} is the value of the jth feature for System i (respectively for a summary i) at the macro-evaluation (respectively at the micro-evaluation) with i varying from 1 to m and j varying from 1 to n; b_i is the PYRAMID score for system i (respectively summary i) at the macro-evaluation (respectively at the micro-evaluation); and ρ is the Pearson correlation.

We used the least squares method to minimize the sum of squared deviations between the PYRAMID score (y_i) and the predicted PYRAMID score ($\hat{y}_i$). Then, the equation of minimization is:

$$min \sum_{i=1}^{m} (y_i - \hat{y}_i)^2$$

4 Features

The features used by our method are chosen in such a way that their combination correlates the maximum with the PYRAMID score.

4.1 Content features

From the correlation results obtained in the 2008 TAC (Dang and Owczarzak, 2008), we noted that the standard metrics ROUGE-2 (R2), ROUGE-SU4 (R-SU4) and BE-HM[3] (BE) and the candidate AutoSummENG metric have a high correlation with the PYRAMID metric. For this reason, we used principally these four metrics as features to evaluate the summary. We also added, on the one hand, ROUGE-3 (R3) and ROUGE-4 (R4) as they take into account large contexts that capture the linguistic characteristics of the summary such as some grammatical phenomena and, on the other hand, ROUGE-1 (R1) because it provides a good indicator of the relevance of the contents of a given summary.

4.2 Linguistic features

PYRAMID is a manual method based on the extraction of SCUs representing minimal semantic units. A human judge cannot identify the SCUs in a summary that does not have a good linguistic quality. Therefore, a summary with a poor linguistic quality cannot have a good PYRAMID score. Thus, to ensure a better prediction of the PYRAMID score, it is interesting to include linguistic metrics in addition to content metrics. In the next subsection, we mention multiple linguistic features which influence the quality of the summary.

Traditional readability measure features

The readability analysis allows us to determine whether a text is easy to understand or not; in other words, it can indicate the complexity of the text. However, a candidate summary must be easy to understand as well as relevant. For this reason, we use traditional readability measures which are based on the number of sentences, words, characters, syllables and / or complex words in a summary. These measures are:

- The Gunning Fog Index (GFI) measure (Gunning, 1968): it indicates the readability of an English text. More precisely, it is an index for specifying the years of education needed to understand the text at first reading. This measure uses the average sentence length and the percentage of complex words (i.e. words with three or more syllables).

- The Flesch Reading Ease (FRE) measure (Flesch, 1951): it predicts the difficulty of reading documents for adults. This is specific to English texts and uses a score from 0 to 100. It is based on the average sentence length and the average number of syllables per word.

- The Flesch-Kincaid Index (FKI) measure (Kincaid, 1975): it can judge the level of readability of texts and books in English; that is to say, it indicates the difficulty of understanding when reading these texts and these books. This measure is widely used in the field of education; this is why the formula

[3] BE-HM uses only the head and the modifier.

translates a score between 0 and 100 into an American grade level. It is based on the average sentence length and the average number of syllables per word.

- The Automated Readability Index (ARI) was designed by (Smith and Senter, 1967). Like the previously described measure of readability, the score approximates the grade level needed to understand the text. This measure uses the average number of characters per word and the average number of words per sentence.

Shallow features

Shallow features are limited to the surface structure of the text. Many of these features are used by traditional readability measures. In our work, we used four shallow features: the Average number of syllables per word (ASW), the average number of characters per word (ACW), the average number of words per sentence (AWS) and the number of sentences (NbPh) which was used by (Rankel et al., 2012) and which is equal to log (Number of sentences)).

Language modeling features

Several recent works have used the language model to assess some aspects of the linguistic quality. (Pilter et al., 2010) is one of those works. They trained three language models (uni-grams, bi-grams and tri-grams) over the New York Times corpus. In our work, we also trained three language models (unigram, bi-grams and trigrams) over the Open American National Corpus. We used the SRI language modeling toolkit (Stolcke, 2002) to calculate the log probability (log_prob) and two measures of perplexity.

Part-of-speech features

(Feng et al., 2010) show that the Part-of-speech features are helpful in the prediction of the linguistic quality. So, we calculated the density of a variety of function words and content words. The density of various categories of function words can tell us about the cohesion of a text. In fact, according to (Halliday and Hasan, 1976), the concept of cohesion includes phenomena which allow a link between sentences or phrases. They identified five types of cohesion: reference, substitution, ellipsis, conjunction and lexical cohesion. For example, discourse connectives (e.g. "and", "while") are used to connect sentences. Since many functional words represent reference devices or discourse connectives, we decided to calculate the density of the four categories of function words: determinants (DET), conjunctions (CC), prepositions and subordinating conjunctions (PSC), and personal pronouns (PRP). In addition to the density of function words, we calculated the density of content words which is used in many works such as (To et al, 2013) and (Feng et al, 2010) to predict the readability of a text. So, we calculated the density of four categories of content words: adjectives (ADJ), nouns (N), verbs (V) and adverbs (ADV). The density of each of the above categories is the ratio between the number of words presenting one of the categories and the total number of words in the summary.

To detect function words and content words, we used the morphological tagger "Stanford Postagger[4]", which provides the grammatical category of words.

5 Evaluation

We used the corpus of the 2008 TAC conference to evaluate our metric. This corpus consists of 48 topics and 58 systems. For each topic, there are 20 documents sorted in chronological order. Each system produces an initial summary constructed using only the first 10 documents and an update summary built from the following 10 documents. An update summary describes the new events introduced by the last 10 documents compared to the events described in the first 10 documents. In total, each system produced 96 summaries (48 initial summaries (A) and 48 update summaries (B)).

The evaluation of the new metric is based on the study of its correlation with PYRAMID. In order to measure the correlation, we used Pearson's rho, Spearman's rho and Kendall's tau which are employed by the TAC conference in meta-evaluation (evaluation of evaluation metrics). All correlation measures gave a value between -1 and 1. A value of 1 or -1 indicates a strength relationship between the two measures.

[4] This labeler provides bidirectional inference. (http://www.nlp.stanford.edu/software/tagger.shtml)

The closer the value of the correlation to 0, the weaker the relation between the two measures is. We remind that Pearson's rho uses the values that each metric (PYRAMID, predicted PYRAMID) takes while Spearman's rho and Kendall's tau use the ranks of values for each metric. We examined the predictive power of our features on two evaluation levels: the summary level (Micro-evaluation) and the system level (Macro-evaluation). In both levels, we performed a 10-fold cross validation on our training data.

5.1 Micro-evaluation

In this section, we investigate the predictive power of the features used in a micro-evaluation level. In other words, we make a summary level evaluation in which we take each summary score in a separate entry. We conducted an experiment for each assessment task (initial summary, update summary).

Features	A	B
R1	0.6708	0.8929
R2	0.9955	-0.1767
R3	-1.49	0.6069
R4		-0.6058
R-SU4	-0.2474	-0.6044
BE	0.2954	0.6605
AutoSummENG	1.6692	1.7244
NbPh	0.0175	0.0157
GFI	-0.0162	-0.005
FKI	0.017	0.0017
FRE		-0.0008
Density(DET)	-0.3765	-0.1275
Density(PRP)		0.5527
log_prob		0.0002
Density(V)		0.1984
Density(N)	0.0761	0.1836
Density(ADV)	-0.4586	
ASW		0.043
ACW		-0.0236
AWS		-0.001
w_0	-0.0902	-0.0737

Table 1 : Features used in initial (A) and update (B) summary tasks at the Micro-Evaluation level

The weight of each feature is shown in table 1. As can be seen in Table 1, our experiment in both assessment tasks shows that AutoSummENG has the best weight. The lowest weights are obtained by the traditional readability measure features, the shallow features and the language modeling features. Typically, the weights of content features are better than the weights of linguistic quality features. This is due to the nature of the PYRAMID metric, which measures the content of the summary.

To measure the effectiveness of our experiments in the micro-level, we calculated the correlation between our experiments and PYRAMID. Then, we compared this correlation with the correlation between PYRAMID and ROUGE-1[5], the standard metrics used by the TAC (ROUGE-2, ROUGE-SU4, BE). As seen in Table 2 and in the two tasks of evaluation, we found that the correlation of our experimentation with PYRAMID is not high enough, although it is greater than the correlation of PYRAMID with standard metrics or with ROUGE-1.

	Pearson	Spearman	Kendall
Initial summary			
ROUGE-1	0.5452	0.5372	0.3764
ROUGE-2	0.4646	0.4855	0.3361
ROUGE-SU4	0.4942	0.5070	0.3531
BE	0.3796	0.4122	0.2831
Our experimentation	**0.6048**	**0.5943**	**0.4224**
Update summary			
ROUGE-1	0.6060	0.6303	0.4484
ROUGE-2	0.5645	0.6033	0.4252
ROUGE-SU4	0.6013	0.6359	0.4505
BE	0.5391	0.5968	0.4213
Our experimentation	**0.6628**	**0.6807**	**0.4911**

Table 2: Correlation with PYRAMID in initial and update summaries evaluation tasks, micro-evaluation level (p-value <2.2 e-16)

5.2 Macro-evaluation

In this section, we make a macro-evaluation, that is to say, a system-level evaluation. In this type of evaluation, we measure the average quality of a summarizing system by computing the average score for a system over the entire set of produced summaries. For each evaluation task, we conducted an experiment. Table 3 gives an overview of the features used in each task as well as their weights.

As shown in table 3, ROUGE-2 has the best weight in the initial summary evaluation. Also,

[5] We calculated the correlation between ROUGE-1 and PYRAMID because (Nenkova and Passonneau, 2004) show a high correlation between those two metrics.

ROUGE-1 and Density of determinants have good weights. In the update summary evaluation, ROUGE-4 has the best weight. The lowest weight is obtained by the density of noun. In the system level, some linguistic features have a good weight. Hence, the role of linguistic features is more important in the system level than in the summary level.

Features	A	B
R1	0.9959	
R2	1.5019	
R4		3.8316
BE		2.0254
AutoSummENG		0.9983
Density(DET)	-1.0099	
Density(N)	0.3478	0.3659
w_0	-0.2269	-0.1826

Table 3: Features used in initial and updated summary tasks at the Macro-Evaluation level

	Pearson	**Spearman**	**Kendall**
Initial summary			
ROUGE-1	0.8764	0.8655	0.7089
ROUGE-2	0.8981	0.9095	0.7611
ROUGE-SU4	0.8780	0.8859	0.7340
BE	0.9045	0.9022	0.7319
Our experimentation	**0.9578**	**0.9576**	**0.8350**
Update summary			
ROUGE-1	0.8768	0.9149	0.7453
ROUGE-2	0.9366	0.9415	0.8000
ROUGE-SU4	0.9174	0.9310	0.7842
BE	0.9398	0.9376	0.7951
N-ROUGE-2	0.9525	0.9434	0.8085
N-ROUGE-SU4	0.9359	0.9339	0.7908
Our experimentation	**0.9569**	**0.9616**	**0.8352**

Table 4: Correlation with PYRAMID in the initial summary and update summary evaluation tasks, macro-evaluation level (p-value <2.2 e-16)

We measured the effectiveness of our experiments in the macro-level, as we did in the micro-level. Table 4 shows the correlation coefficients of the PYRAMID score with:

- standard metrics (ROUGE-2, ROUGE-SU4 and BE) and ROUGE-1,
- the experiments described in Table 3 and
- the Nouveau-ROUGE-2 (N-ROUGE-2) and the Nouveau-ROUGE-SU4 (N-ROUGE-SU4) metrics which are performed by (Conroy et al., 2011) to evaluate update summaries only at the macro-evaluation level.

By examining Table 4, we see that our experiments give a good correlation with PYRAMID. We also note that our experiment is better than the standard metrics used by the TAC, ROUGE-1 and the two variants of Nouveau-ROUGE metric which were intended to evaluate update summaries.

6 Conclusion

In this article, we presented a method to evaluate the contents and the linguistic quality of a summary using a combination of linguistic and content features. The combination of these features is performed using a linear regression method.

In examining the results, we find that the correlation of our experiments with PYRAMID, at the micro-evaluation level, is not high enough; in spite of this, it is greater than standard metrics and ROUGE-1. However, our experiments give a good correlation with PYRAMID at the macro-evaluation level. In addition, we notice that the weights of the content features are higher than the weights of the linguistic quality features. This is due to the nature of the PYRAMID metric which measures the content of a summary. Also, in observing the weights of the linguistic features, we note that the weights of traditional readability measures, language modeling features and shallow features are very low.

As perspectives, we may use other linguistic features such as the grid of entity used by (Barzilay and Lapata, 2008) to measure the coherence of the summary. Also, we can add syntactic and semantic features to our model.

References

Barzilay R. and Lapata M. 2008. Modeling Local Coherence: An Entity-based Approach. *Computational Linguistics Journal*, Volume 34 No: 1, pages 1-34.

Conroy, J. M., Schlesinger, J. D. and O'LEARY, D. P. 2011. Nouveau-ROUGE: A Novelty Metric for Update Summarization. *In Computational Linguistics journal*, Volume 37 No: 1, pages 1-8.

Conroy J. M., Schlesinger J. D., Rankel P. A., and O'Leary D. P. 2010. Guiding CLASSY toward More Responsive Summaries. *In proceedings of the Text Analysis Conference*.

Conroy J. M. and Dang H. T. 2008. Mind the Gap: Dangers of Divorcing Evaluations of Summary

Content from Linguistic Quality. *In proceedings of COLING 2008*, pages 145-152.

Dang H. T. and Owczarzak K. 2009. Overview of TAC 2009 summarization track. *In proceedings of the Text Analysis Conference*.

Dang H. T. and Owczarzak K. 2008. Overview of the TAC 2008 Update Summarization Task. *In proceedings of the Text Analysis Conference*.

Feng L., Jansche M. and Huenerfauth M. 2010. A comparison of features for automatic readability assessment, *In Proceedings of the 23rd International Conference on Computational Linguistics (COLING 2010)*, pages 276-284.

Flesch R. F. 1951. *How to test readability*. Harper & Brothers, New York.

Giannakopoulos G. and Karkaletsis V. 2010. Summarization system evaluation variations based on n-gram graphs. *In the proceedings of TAC 2010 Workshop*.

Giannakopoulos G., Karkaletsis V., Vouros G. A. and Stamatopoulos P. 2008. Summarization system evaluation revisited: N-gram graphs. *TSLP journal*, Vol: 5 No: 3.

Gunning R. 1968. *The techniques of clear writing, (Rev. ed.)*. New York: McGraw-Hill.

Halliday M. A. K. and Hasan R. 1976. *Cohesion in English*. Longman (Londres).

Harnly A., Nenkova A., Passonneau R. and Rambow, O. 2005. Automation of Summary Evaluation by the Pyramid Method. *In proceedings of RANLP*, pages 226-233.

Hovy E., Lin C., Zhou L. and Fukumoto J. 2006. Automated Summarization Evaluation with Basic Elements. *In proceedings of the 5th Conference on Language Resources and Evaluation*.

Kincaid J.P., Fishburne Jr. R.P., Rodgers R.L., and Chisson B.S. 1975. *Derivation of new readability formulas for Navy enlisted personnel*. Research Branch Report 8-75, U.S. Naval Air Station, Memphis.

Lin C. 2001. Summary Evaluation Environment. http://www.isi.edu/~cyl/SEE.

Lin C. 2004. ROUGE: a package for automatic evaluation of summaries. *In proceedings of the ACL 2004 Workshop on Text Summarization Branches Out (WAS 2004)*, pages 74–81.

Lin Z., Liu C., Ng H. T. and Kan M. 2012. Combining Coherence Models and Machine Translation Evaluation Metrics for Summarization Evaluation. *In proceedings of ACL (1)*, pages 1006-1014.

Lin Z., Ng H. T. and Kan M. 2011. Automatically Evaluating Text Coherence Using Discourse Relations. *In proceedings of ACL 2011*, pages 997-1006.

Louis A. and Nenkova A. 2009. Automatically Evaluating Content Selection in Summarization without Human Models. *In proceedings of EMNLP 2009*, pages 306-314.

Nenkova A. and Passonneau R. 2004. Evaluating Content Selection in Summarization: The Pyramid Method. *In proceedings of HLT-NAACL 2004*, pages 145-152.

Owczarzak K. and Dang H. T. 2011. Overview of the TAC 2011 summarization track: Guided task and AESOP task. *In proceedings of the Text Analysis Conference*.

Pitler E., Louis A. and Nenkova A. 2010. Automatic Evaluation of Linguistic Quality in Multi-Document Summarization. *In proceedings of ACL 2010*, pages 544-554.

Rankel P. A., Conroy J. M. and Schlesinger J. D. 2012. Better Metrics to Automatically Predict the Quality of a Text Summary. *Algorithms journal*, No: 4, pages 398-420.

Smith E. and Senter R. 1967. Automated readability index. AMRL-TR. *Aerospace Medical Research Laboratories (6570th)*, page 1.

Stolcke A. 2002. SRILM – an extensible language modeling toolkit. *In Proceedings of International Conference on Spoken Language Processing*, vol 2, pages 901–904.

To, V., Fan, S. and Thomas, DP. 2013. Lexical density and Readability: A case study of English Textbooks. *The International Journal of Language, Society and Culture*, vol 37, No 7, pages 61-71.

Torres-Moreno J. M., Saggion H., da Cunha I., San-Juan E. and Velazquez-Morales P. 2010. Summary Evaluation With and Without References. *Polibits ISSN1870-9044*, pages 13-19.

Tratz S. and Hovy E. 2008. BEwTE: basic elements with transformations for evaluation. *In TAC 2008 Workshop*.

Hierarchy Identification for Automatically Generating Table-of-Contents

Nicolai Erbs[α] **Iryna Gurevych**[α,β] **Torsten Zesch**[γ]

[α]Ubiquitous Knowledge Processing Lab
Department of Computer Science, Technische Universität Darmstadt

[β]Information Center for Education
German Institute for Educational Research and Educational Information

[γ]Language Technology
University of Duisburg-Essen

Abstract

A table-of-contents (TOC) provides a quick reference to a document's content and structure. We present the first study on identifying the hierarchical structure for automatically generating a TOC using only textual features instead of structural hints e.g. from HTML-tags. We create two new datasets to evaluate our approaches for hierarchy identification. We find that our algorithm performs on a level that is sufficient for a fully automated system. For documents without given segment titles, we extend our work by automatically generating segment titles.

We make the datasets and our experimental framework publicly available in order to foster future research in TOC generation.

1 Introduction

A table-of-contents (TOC) provides an easy way to gain an overview about a document as a TOC presents the document's content and structure. At the same time, a TOC captures the relative importance of document topics by arranging the topic titles in a hierarchical manner. Thus, TOCs might be used as a short document summary that provides more information about search results in a search engine. Figure 1 provides a sketch of such a search interface. Instead of a thumbnail of the document like most search engines, or a clustering of search results (Carpineto et al., 2009), we propose to use an automatically extracted TOC.

The task of automatically generating a table-of-contents can be tackled with the subtasks document segmentation, segment title generation, and hierarchy identification. The first step splits the document into topical parts, the second step generates an informative title for each segment, and the third step decides whether a segment is on a higher, equal, or lower level than the previous segment. This paper presents novel approaches for the third subtask: hierarchy identification. Additionally, it presents a detailed analysis of results for segment title generation on the presented datasets.

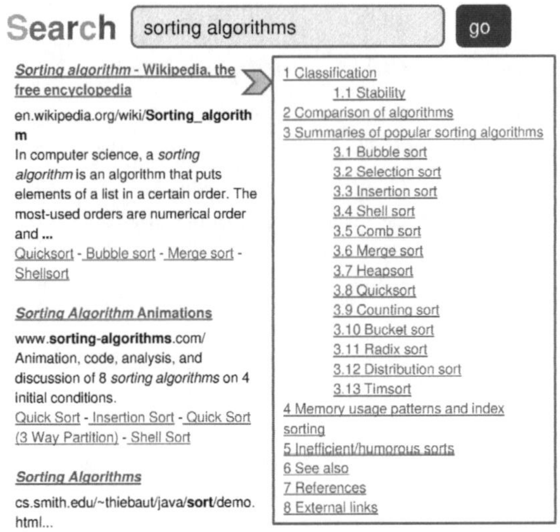

Figure 1: Search user interface showing a TOC along with the search results.

Many documents are already segmented but only few documents already contain an explicit hierarchical TOC (e.g. Wikipedia articles), while for most documents it needs to be automatically identified. For some documents, identification is straight-forward, e.g. if an HTML document already contains hierarchically structured headlines (`<h1>`, `<h2>`, etc). We focus on the most challenging case in which only the textual content of the documents' segments are available and the hierarchy needs to be inferred using Natural Language Processing.

We present a framework for automatically identifying the hierarchy of two segments based on semantic and lexical features. We perform linguistic

Contents

Figure 2: TOC of this paper

preprocessing including named entity recognition (Finkel et al., 2005), keyphrase extraction (Mihalcea and Tarau, 2004), and chunking (Schmid, 1994) which are then used as features for machine learning.

To foster future research, we present two new datasets and compare results on these datasets and the one presented by Branavan et al. (2007).

Our research contribution is to develop new algorithms for segment hierarchy identification, to present new evaluation datasets for all subtasks, and to compare our newly developed methods with the state of the art. We also provide a comprehensive analysis of the benefits and shortcomings of the applied methods. Figure 2 gives an overview of the paper's organization (and at the same time highlights the usefulness of a TOC for the reader). Thus, we may safely skip the enumeration of paper sections and their content that usually concludes the introduction.

2 Related Work

For some documents, the hierarchy of segments can be induced using HTML-based features. Pembe and Güngör (2010) focus on DOM tree and formatting features, but also use occurrences of manually crafted cue phrases such as *back to top*. However, most features are only applicable in very few cases where HTML markup directly provides a hierarchy. In order to provide a uniform user experience, a TOC also needs to be generated for documents where HTML-based methods fail or when only the textual content is available.

Feng et al. (2005) train a classifier to detect semantically coherent areas on a page. However, they make use of the existing HTML markup and return areas of the document instead of identifying hierarchical structures for segments. Besides markup and position features, they use features based on unigrams and bigrams for classifying a segment into one of 12 categories.

For segment title generation we divide related work into the following classes:

Text-based approaches make use of only the text in the corresponding segment. Therefore, titles are limited to words appearing in the text. They can be applied in all situations, but will often create trivial or even wrong titles.

Supervised approaches learn a model of which document segments usually have a certain title. They are highly precise, but require training data and are limited to an *a priori* determined set of titles for which the model is trained.

In the following, we organize the few available previous papers on this topic according to these two classes. The text-based approach by Lopez et al. (2011) uses a position heuristic. Each noun phrase in a segment is given a score depending on its position and its tf.idf value.

The supervised approach by Branavan et al. (2007) trains an incremental perceptron algorithm (Collins and Roark, 2004; Daumé and Marcu, 2005) to predict titles. It uses rules based on the hierarchical structure of the document[1] to rerank the candidates towards the best global solution. Nguyen and Shimazu (2009) expand the supervised approach by Branavan et al. (2007) using word clusters as additional features. Both approaches are trained and tested on the Cormen dataset. The book is split into a set of 39 independent documents at boundaries of segments of the second level. The newly created documents are randomly selected for training (80%) and testing (20%). Such an approach is not suited for our scenario of end-to-end TOC creation, as we want to generate a TOC for a whole document and cannot train on parts of it. Besides, this tunes the system towards special characteristics of the book instead of having a domain-independent system.

Keyphrase extraction methods (Frank et al., 1999; Turney, 2000) may also be used for segment title generation if a reader prefers even shorter headlines. These methods can be either text-based or supervised.

[1] E.g. neighboring segments must not have the same title.

3 Experimental Setup

Our system tackles the problem using a supervised classifier predicting the relation between the segments. Two segments can be on the *same*, *higher*, or *lower* level. Formally, the difference of a segment with level l_0 and a following segment with level l_1 is any integer n $\in [-\infty..\infty]$ for which n$= l_1 - l_0$. However, our analysis on the development data has shown that n typically is in the range of $\in [-2..2]$ which means that a following segment is at most 2 levels higher or lower than the previous segment.

We identified the following categories of features that solely make use of the text in each segment (we refer to these features as in-document features):

N-gram features We identify the top-500 n-grams in the collection and use them as Boolean features for each segment. The feature value is set to `true` if the n-gram appears, `false` otherwise. These features reflect reoccurring cue phrases and generic terms for fixed segments like the introduction.

Length-based We compute the number of characters (including whitespaces) for both segments and use their difference as feature value. We apply the same procedure for the number of tokens and sentences. A higher-level segment might be shorter because it provides a summary of the following more detailed segments.

Entity-based We identify all named entities in each segment and return a Boolean feature if they share at least one entity. This feature is based on the assumption that two segments having the same entities are related. Two related segments are more likely on the same level or the second segment is a lower-level segment.

Noun chunk features All noun chunks in both segments are identified using the TreeTagger (Schmid, 1994) and then the average number of tokens for each of the segments is computed. The feature value is the difference of the average phrase length. Phrases in lower-level segments are longer because they are more detailed. In the example from Figure 1, the term *bubble sort algorithm* is longer than the frequently occurring upper level phrase *sorting algorithm*.

Additionally, the number of chunks that appear in both segments is divided by the number of chunks that appear in the second segment. If a term like *sorting algorithm* is the only shared term in both segments and the second segment contains in total ten phrases, then the noun chunk overlap is 10%. This feature is based on the assumption that lower-level segments mostly mention noun chunks that have been already introduced earlier.

Keyphrase-based We apply the state-of-the-art keyphrase extraction approach TextRank (Mihalcea and Tarau, 2004) and identify a ranked list of keyphrases in each segment. We compare the top-k (k $\in [1, 2, 3, 4, 5, 10, 20]$) keyphrases of each segment pair and return `true` if at least one keyphrase appears in both segments. These features also reflect topically related segments.

Frequency We apply another feature set which uses a background corpus in addition to the text of the segments. We use the Google Web1T corpus (Brants and Franz, 2006) to retrieve the frequency of a term. The average frequency of the top-k (k $\in [5, 10]$) keyphrases in a segment is calculated and the difference between two segments is the feature value. We expect lower-level segments to contain keyphrases that are less frequently used.

We use WEKA (Hall et al., 2009) to train the classifier and report results obtained with SVM, which performed best on the development set.[2] We evaluate all approaches by computing the accuracy as the fraction of correctly identified hierarchy relations. As a baseline, we consider all segments to be on the same level.

3.1 Datasets

Branavan et al. (2007) extracted a single TOC from an algorithms textbook (Cormen et al., 2001) and split it into a training and a test set. We use the complete TOC as a test set and refer to it as *Cormen*. As a single TOC is a shallow basis for experimental results, we create two additional datasets

[2]We experimented with Naïve Bayes and J48 but results were significantly lower.

Name	*doc*	*seg*	$\varnothing\frac{tok}{seg}$
Cormen	1	607	733
Gutenberg	18	1,312	1927
Wikipedia	277	3,680	399

Table 1: Characteristics of evaluation datasets. Showing the total number of documents (*doc*), segments (*seg*) and average number of tokens in each segment ($\varnothing\frac{tok}{seg}$).

	Hierarchy level				
Name	1	2	3	4	5
Cormen	.00	.02	.08	.41	.48
Wikipedia	.07	.48	.41	.04	.00
Gutenberg	.01	.35	.49	.12	.03

Table 2: Distribution of segments over levels of the evaluation corpora.

containing real-world tables of contents, allowing us to evaluate on different domains and styles of hierarchies.

We create the first dataset from randomly selected featured articles in Wikipedia. They have been shown to be of high quality (Stein and Hess, 2007) and are complex enough to contain hierarchical TOCs. We create a second dataset using 55 books from the project Gutenberg.[3] We refer to these datasets as *Wikipedia* and *Gutenberg*. We annotated these datasets with the hierarchy level of each segment, ranging from 1 (top-level segment) to the lowest-level segment found in the datasets.

Table 1 gives an overview of the datasets regarding the segment structure. Although the Cormen dataset consists of one book only, it contains more segments than an average document in any other dataset and thus is a valuable evaluation resource. The Wikipedia dataset contains on average the fewest tokens in each segment, in other words – the most fine-grained TOC. The Wikipedia and Gutenberg dataset cover a broad spectrum of topics while the Cormen dataset is focused on computational algorithms.

Table 2 shows the distribution of levels in the datasets. The *Cormen* dataset has a much deeper structure compared to the other two datasets. The fraction of segments on the first level is below 1% because a single document may have only one top-level segment and this document contains far more

[3]The same collection of books was used by Csomai and Mihalcea (2006) for experiments on back-of-the-book indexing. They mostly cover the domains humanities, science, and technology.

	Pairwise hierarchy relation				
Name	n= 2	n= 1	n= 0	n= −1	n= −2
Cormen	.00	.20	.60	.16	.03
Wikipedia	.00	.15	.71	.13	.01
Gutenberg	.00	.10	.80	.09	.01

Table 3: Distribution of pairwise level difference of segments of the evaluation corpora.

than 100 segments. This is a special characteristic of this book: since it is often used to quickly look up specific topics, the authors provide a very fine-grained table-of-contents. In *Wikipedia*, most of the segments are on the second level. Articles in Wikipedia are rather short, because according to the Wikipedia author guidelines a segment of a Wikipedia article is moved into an independent article if it gets too long. The *Gutenberg* dataset is more balanced as it contains documents from different authors. Similar to the Wikipedia dataset, most segments are on the second and third level.

We focus on the pairwise classification in this paper and investigate the pairwise relation of neighboring segments. Two segments on the same level have a hierarchy relation of n=0, a segment that is one level lower has a hierarchy relation of n=1. Table 3 shows that for all datasets most of the segment pairs (neighboring segments) are on the same level. Although there are segments which are two level higher or three levels higher than the previous segment, this is the case for no more than 1% of all segment pairs. The Cormen has the highest deviation of level relation. This is due to the fact that its segments have a broad distribution of levels (see Table 2). Segments in the Gutenberg dataset, on the other hand, are in 80% of all cases on the same level as the previous segment. The case that the next segment is two level lower, i.e. n=2, is very unlikely. This is in line with our expectations that a writer does not skip levels when starting a lower level segment.

4 Experiments and Results

We evaluate performance of our system using 10-fold cross-validation on previously unseen data using The Lab as experimental framework (Eckart de Castilho and Gurevych, 2011). Performance is measured in terms of accuracy and is defined as the ratio of correctly identified relations.

Table 4 shows our results on each dataset. Always predicting two segments to be on the same level is a strong baseline, as this is the case for

	Cormen	WP	Gutenb.
Baseline (*always equal)*	.60	.71	.80
(1) N-gram features	**.86**	.64	.86
(2) Length features	.62	.76	.80
(3) Entity features	.60	.71	.80
(4) Noun chunk features	.83	**.86**	**.91**
(5) Keyphrase features	.60	.71	.80
(6) Frequency features	.60	.71	.80
All features	.86	.77	.86
All features w/o (1)	.83	**.86**	**.91**
All features w/o (3) & (5)	**.87**	.77	.86

Table 4: Accuracy of approaches for hierarchy identification. Best results of feature groups and combinations are marked bold.

Actual \ Predicted	2	1	0	−1	−2
2	**-**	4	-	-	-
1	-	**567**	-	-	-
0	-	-	**2,585**	-	-
−1	-	-	478	**-**	-
−2	-	-	24	-	**-**

Table 5: Confusion matrix for best system (all features w/o n-gram features) on Wikipedia dataset. Correctly identified segments are marked bold.

60.2% of cases in the Cormen and 79.8% of cased in the Gutenberg dataset. The table shows results for each of the feature groups defined in Section 3 numbered from (1) to (6). N-gram features perform best on the Cormen dataset while they perform worse than the baseline on the Wikipedia (WP) dataset. This difference might be due to the topic diversity in the Wikipedia and Cormen datasets. Wikipedia covers many topics, while Cormen is focused on a single topic (algorithms) and thus containing reappearing n-grams.

Noun chunk features are the best-performing group of features on the Wikipedia and Gutenberg and second best on the Cormen dataset. Entity, keyphrase, and frequency features do not improve the baseline in any of the presented datasets. Apparently, they are no good indicator for the hierarchical structure of document segments.

Combining all features further improves results on the Cormen dataset. However, the best results are obtained by combining all besides entity and keyphrase features. On the other two datasets (Wikipedia and Gutenberg), a combination of all features decreases accuracy compared to a supervised system using only noun chunk features. The highest accuracy is obtained by using all features besides n-gram features.

Based on our observation that a combination of all features performs worse than a selection of features, we analyzed the confusion matrix of the corresponding systems. Table 5 shows the confusion matrix for the best performing system from Table 4 on the Wikipedia dataset using selected features (all w/o n-gram features). The system is optimized towards accuracy and trained on unbalanced training data. This leads to a system returning either n= 1 (next level is one level lower) or n= 0 (same level). There are no cases where a lower-level segment is incorrectly classified as a higher-level segment but all cases with $|n| \geq 2$ are incorrectly classified as having a level difference of one.

Actual \ Predicted	2	1	0	−1	−2
2	**-**	4	-	-	-
1	-	**539**	17	11	-
0	-	14	**2,115**	455	1
−1	-	1	323	**154**	-
−2	-	-	12	12	**-**

Table 6: Confusion matrix for a system using all features on Wikipedia dataset. Correctly identified segments are marked bold.

Table 6 shows the confusion matrix for a system using all features on the same dataset as before (Wikipedia). The system also covers the case n= −1 (next level is one level higher), thus creating more realistic TOCs. In contrast to the previous system (see Table 5), some higher-level segment relations (n<0) are incorrectly classified as lower-level segment relations (n>0). Although the system using all features returns a lower precision than the one using selected features, it better captures the way writers construct documents (also having segments on a higher level than previous segments).

Overall, results show that automatic hierarchy identification provides a TOC with a sufficient quality. To support this observation, Figure 3 shows the correct and predicted TOCs for the article about *Apollo 8* from the Wikipedia dataset. The correct TOC is on the left and the predicted TOC is on the right.

Section 1.3 (*Mission control*) was erroneously identified as being on a higher level than the previous section. The system fails to identify that both segments are about the crew (backup and mission control crew). The section *Planning* is correctly identified as having a higher level than the previous segment but leading to a different numbering

Correct TOC	Predicted TOC
1 Crew	1 Crew
1.1 Backup crew	1.1 Backup crew
1.2 Mission control	2 Mission control
1.3 Mission insignia	2.1 Mission insignia
2 Planning	3 Planning
3 Saturn V	4 Saturn V
4 Mission	5 Mission
4.1 Parameter summary	5.1 Parameter summary
4.2 Launch and trans-lunar injection	5.2 Launch and trans-lunar injection
4.3 Lunar trajectory	5.3 Lunar trajectory
4.4 Lunar sphere of influence	5.4 Lunar sphere of influence
4.5 Lunar orbit	5.5 Lunar orbit
4.5.1 Earthrise	5.5.1 Earthrise
4.6 Unplanned manual re-alignment	5.5.2 Unplanned manual re-alignment
4.7 Cruise back to Earth and re-entry	5.6 Cruise back to Earth and re-entry
5 Historical importance	6 Historical importance
6 Spacecraft location	7 Spacecraft location
7 In film	8 In film

Figure 3: Correct and predicted TOCs of article about Apollo 8 from the Wikipedia dataset.

(5 instead of 4 due to earlier errors). Not all of the remaining segment relations are correctly identified but the overall TOC still provides a quick reference of the article's content. It allows a reader to quickly decide whether the article about *Apollo 8* fulfills his information need.

5 Segment Title Generation

So far, we have shown that our system is able to automatically predict a TOC for documents segment boundaries. In order to extend our system to documents that do not have titles for segments, we add a segment title generation step. News documents are very often segmented into smaller parts, but usually do not contain segment titles.[4]

We decided not to reuse existing datasets from summarization or keyphrase extraction tasks, as they are only focused on one possible style of titles (i.e. summaries or keyphrases). Instead, we apply our algorithms to the previously presented datasets for hierarchy identification (see Section 3.1) and analyze their characteristics with respect to their segment titles. The percentage of titles that actually appear in the corresponding segments is lowest for the Wikipedia dataset (18%) while it is highest on the Cormen dataset (27%). In the Gutenberg dataset 23% of all titles appear in the text. The high value for the Cormen dataset is due to the specific characteristic that segment titles are repeated very often at the beginning of a segment.[5]

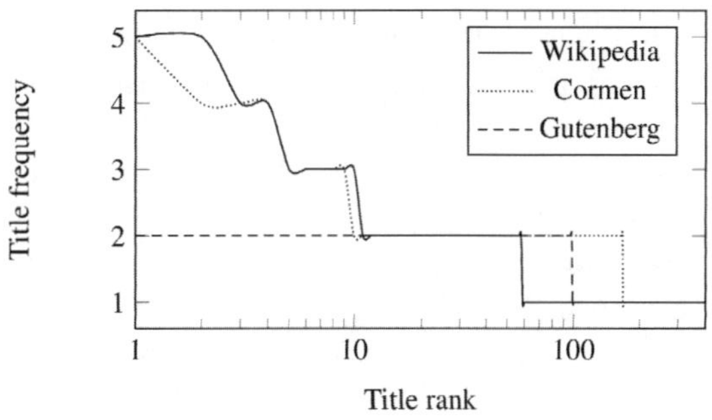

Figure 4: Frequency distribution of a random sample of 607 titles on log-log-scale: it follows a power-law distribution.

Frequency Distribution of Titles We further analyze the datasets in terms of segment counts for each title. Figure 4 shows the frequency of titles in the evaluation set on a logarithmic scale. We choose a random sample of 607 titles, which is the lowest number of titles in all three corpora, to allow a fair comparison across corpora. For all three datasets, most titles are used for few segments. For the datasets Wikipedia and Cormen some titles are used more frequently. In comparison to that, the most-frequent title of the Gutenberg dataset appears twice, only. Thus, we expect the supervised approaches to be most beneficial on the Wikipedia dataset. On the Cormen dataset we cannot apply any supervised approaches due to the lack of training data.

5.1 Experimental Setup

Text-based approaches As simple baselines, we use the first token and the first noun phrase occurring in each segment. As a more sophisticated baseline, we rank tokens according to their tf–idf scores. Additionally, we use TextRank (Mihalcea and Tarau, 2004) to rank noun phrases according to their co-occurrence frequencies.

As named entities from a segment are often used as titles, we extract them using the Stanford Named Entity Tagger (Finkel et al., 2005) and take the first one as the segment title.[6]

Supervised approaches We train a text classification model based on character 6-grams.[7] for

[4]For example, cnn.com uses *story paragraphs*.

[5]For example, the segment *Quicksort* begins with: *Quicksort is a sorting algorithm ...*

[6]We also experimented using the most frequent entity but achieved lower results.

[7]A previous evaluation has shown that 6-grams yield the best results for this task on all development sets. We used LingPipe: http://alias-i.com/lingpipe for classification.

each of the most frequent titles in each dataset. In Wikipedia, most articles have sections like *See also*, *References*, or *External links*, while books usually start with a chapter *Preface*. We restrict the list of title candidates to those appearing at least twice in the training data. We use a statistical model for predicting the title of a segment

In contrast to previous approaches (Branavan et al., 2007; Nguyen and Shimazu, 2009; Jin and Hauptmann, 2001), we do not train on parts of the same document for which we want to predict titles, but rather on full documents of the same type (Wikipedia articles and books). This is an important difference, as in our usage scenario we need to generate full TOCs for previously unseen documents. On the Cormen dataset we cannot perform a trainings phase as it consists of one book.

Evaluation Metrics We evaluated all approaches using two evaluation metrics. We propose **accuracy** as evaluation metric. A generated title is counted as correct only if it exactly matches the correct title. Hence, methods that generate long titles by adding many important phrases are penalized.

The **Rouge** evaluation metric is commonly used for evaluating summarization systems. It is based on n-gram overlap, where —in our case— the generated title is compared to the gold title. We use Rouge-L which is based on the longest common subsequence. This metric is frequently used in previous work for evaluating supervised approaches to generating TOCs because it considers near misses. We believe that it is not well suited for evaluating title generation, however, we use it for the sake of comparison with related work.

5.2 Experiments and Results

Table 7 shows the results of title generation approaches on the three datasets. On the Cormen dataset, we compare our approaches with two state-of-the-art methods. For the newly created datasets no previous results are available.

Using the first noun phrase returns the best titles on the Cormen dataset, which is in agreement with our observation from Section 5.1 that many segments repeat their title in the beginning. This also explains the high performance of the state-of-the-art approaches which are also taking the position and part of speech of candidates into account. Branavan et al. (2007) report about a feature for the supervised systems eliminating generic phrases without giving example of these phrases.

Supervised text classification approach works quite well in case of the Wikipedia dataset with its frequently appearing titles. The approach does not work well on the Gutenberg dataset, as segments such as *Preface* treat different topics in most Gutenberg books. Consequently, the text classifier is not able to learn the specific properties of that segment. In future work, it will be necessary to adapt the classifier in order to focus on non-standard features that better grasp the function of a segment inside a document. For example, the introduction of a scientific paper always reads "introduction-like" while the covered topic changes from paper to paper. This is in line with research concerning topic bias (Mikros and Argiri, 2007; Brooke and Hirst, 2011) in which topic-independent features are applied.

The overall level of performance in terms of accuracy and Rouge seems rather low. However, accuracy is only a rough estimate of the real performance, as many good titles might not be represented in the gold standard and Rouge is higher when comparing longer texts. Besides, a user might be interested in a specialized table-of-contents, such as one consisting only of named entities. For example, in a document about US presidential elections, a TOC consisting only of the names of presidents might be more informative than one consisting of the dates of the four-year periods. A flexible system for generating segment titles enables the user to decide on which titles are more interesting and thus increasing the user's benefit.

Combination of approaches As we have discussed, the usage of titles highly depends on the domain of the document and the expectations of the reader. We aim to overcome the limitations of single approaches by combining multiple approaches and integrating the reader's choice to improve the overall acceptance of a title generation system. It is essential that a combination reflects different styles of titles to cover most of the reader's preferences.

We combine complementary approaches based on three baseline systems (first NP, tf–idf, and named entities) and additionally the supervised approach (text classification). We expect the three text-based features to provide a stable performance, while the supervised approach may boost

Approach	Type	Wikipedia Acc.	Wikipedia Rouge-L	Gutenberg Acc.	Gutenberg Rouge-L	Cormen Acc.	Cormen Rouge-L
(Branavan et al., 2007)	*Supervised*	-	-	-	-	-	*.249*
(Nguyen and Shimazu, 2009)		-	-	-	-	-	*.281*
First token	Baselines	.007	.034	.004	.078	.010	.137
First NP		.012	.112	.037	**.180**	**.061**	**.364**
tf–idf		.017	.057	**.042**	.094	.020	.206
TextRank	Text	.014	.058	.011	.060	.012	.195
Named entity		.006	.046	.011	.065	.000	.037
Text classification	Supervised	**.133**	**.169**	.004	.008	*	*
First NP, tf–idf, named entity	Combination	.034	n/a	.069	n/a	.076	n/a
+ Text classification		.168	n/a	.072	n/a	.077	n/a

Table 7: Title generation results. No results for supervised text classification on the Cormen dataset are shown since no training data is available.

the performance on some datasets. As these approaches typically use an independent set of title candidates, they can potentially achieve a higher performance. Commonly used combination strategies like *voting* or complex strategies (Chen, 2011) can only be applied within approaches from the same class, as different classes will output different titles. Besides, it is desirable to create a diversity of candidates without ignoring titles generated by only one approach.

Results in Table 7 reveals that a combination of approaches provides the highest accuracy of all approaches. We cannot compare a list of generated titles to a gold title with Rouge, thus not presenting any numbers (n/a). We utilize the benefit of accuracy allowing to compare a set of generated titles to a gold title. In a real-world setting, a user selects the best title from the list which means that only one suggestion has to match the gold standard. Although providing a larger result set increases accuracy, results are stable for all datasets.

6 Conclusions and Future Work

We presented the first study on automatically identifying the hierarchical structure of a table-of-contents for different kinds of text (articles and books from different domains). The task of *segment hierarchy identification* is a new task which has not been investigated for non-HTML text. We created two new evaluation datasets for this task, and used a supervised approach based on textual features and a background corpus and significantly improved results over a strong baseline. For documents with missing segment titles, *generating segment titles* is an interesting use case for keyphrase extraction and text classification techniques. We applied approaches from both tasks the existing and two new evaluation datasets and show that the performance of approaches is still quite low. Overall, we have shown that for most documents a TOC can be generated by detecting the hierarchical relations if the documents already contain segments with corresponding titles. In the other cases, one can use segment title generation, but additional research based on our newly created datasets will be necessary to further improve the task performance.

In future work, we want to develop a prototype of our search interface and perform user acceptance tests. Furthermore, we want to continue develop better features for the task of hierarchy identification, and want to create methods for post-processing a TOC in order to generate a coherent table-of-contents.

We made the newly created evaluation datasets and our experimental framework publicly available in order to foster future research in table-of-contents generation.[8]

Acknowledgements

This work has been supported by the Volkswagen Foundation as part of the Lichtenberg-Professorship Program under grant No. I/82806, by the Klaus Tschira Foundation under project No. 00.133.2008, and by the German Federal Ministry of Education and Research (BMBF) within the context of the Software Campus project *open window* under grant No. 01IS12054. The authors assume responsibility for the content. We thank Tri Duc Nghiem and Marko Martin for their valuable contributions and the we thank the anonymous reviewers for their helpful comments.

[8]Available at `http://www.ukp.tu-darmstadt.de/data/table-of-contents-generation/`

References

S.R.K. Branavan, P. Deshpande, and R. Barzilay. 2007. Generating a Table-of-Contents. In *Annual Meeting of Association for Computational Linguistics*, volume 45, pages 544–551.

T. Brants and A. Franz. 2006. Web 1T 5-gram Corpus version 1.1. Technical report, Google Inc., Philadelphia, USA.

J. Brooke and G. Hirst. 2011. Native Language Detection with 'cheap' Learner Corpora. In *Learner Corpus Research 2011 (LCR 2011)*.

C. Carpineto, S. Osiński, G. Romano, and D. Weiss. 2009. A Survey of Web Clustering Engines. *ACM Computing Surveys (CSUR)*, 41(3):17.

Z. Chen. 2011. Collaborative Ranking: A Case Study on Entity Linking. pages 771–781.

M. Collins and B. Roark. 2004. Incremental Parsing with the Perceptron Algorithm. In *Proceedings of the 42nd Meeting of the Association for Computational Linguistics*, pages 111–118.

T.H. Cormen, C.E. Leiserson, R.L. Rivest, and C. Stein. 2001. *Introduction to Algorithms*. The MIT press, Cambridge, MA, USA, 2nd edition.

A. Csomai and R. Mihalcea. 2006. Creating a Testbed for the Evaluation of Automatically Generated Back-of-the-book Indexes. In *Computational Linguistics and Intelligent Text Processing*, pages 429–440.

H. Daumé and D. Marcu. 2005. Learning as Search Optimization: Approximate Large Margin Methods for Structured Prediction. *Proceedings of the 22nd International Conference on Machine Learning*, (1):169–176.

R. Eckart de Castilho and I. Gurevych. 2011. A Lightweight Framework for Reproducible Parameter Sweeping in Information Retrieval. In *Proceedings of the 2011 workshop on Data infrastructures for supporting information retrieval evaluation*, DESIRE '11, pages 7–10, New York, NY, USA.

J. Feng, P. Haffner, and M. Gilbert. 2005. A Learning Approach to Discovering Web Page Semantic Structures. In *Eighth International Conference on Document Analysis and Recognition (ICDAR'05)*, pages 1055–1059. Ieee.

J.R. Finkel, T. Grenager, and C. Manning. 2005. Incorporating non-local Information into Information Extraction Systems by Gibbs Sampling. In *Proceedings of the 43rd Annual Meeting on Association for Computational Linguistics*, pages 363–370.

E. Frank, G.W. Paynter, and I.H. Witten. 1999. Domain-specific Keyphrase Extraction. In *Proceedings of 16th International Joint Conference on Artificial Intelligence*, pages 668–673.

M. Hall, E. Frank, G. Holmes, B. Pfahringer, P. Reutemann, and I.H. Witten. 2009. The WEKA Data Mining Software: an Update. *SIGKDD Explorations*, 11(1):10–18.

R. Jin and A.G. Hauptmann. 2001. Automatic Title Generation for Spoken Broadcast News. In *Proceedings of the first international conference on Human language technology research*, pages 1–3. Association for Computational Linguistics.

C. Lopez, V. Prince, and M. Roche. 2011. Automatic Titling of Articles using Position and Statistical Information. *Proceedings of the International Conference on Recent Advances in Natural Language*, pages 727–732.

R. Mihalcea and P. Tarau. 2004. TextRank: Bringing Order into Text. In *Proceedings of the 2004 Conference on Empirical Methods in Natural Language Processing*, pages 404–411.

G. Mikros and E.K. Argiri. 2007. Investigating Topic Influence in Authorship Attribution. In *Proceedings of the SIGIR 2007 International Work- shop on Plagiarism Analysis, Authorship Identifica- tion, and Near-Duplicate Detection, PAN 2007*.

L.M. Nguyen and A. Shimazu. 2009. A Semi-supervised Approach for Generating a Table-of-Contents. In *Proceedings of the International Conference RANLP-2009*, number 1, pages 312–317.

F.C. Pembe and T. Güngör. 2010. A Tree Learning Approach to Web Document Sectional Hierarchy Extraction. In *Proceedings of 2nd International Conference on Agents and Artificial Intelligence*.

H. Schmid. 1994. Probabilistic Part-of-Speech Tagging using Decision Trees. In *Proceedings of International Conference on new Methods in Language Processing*, volume 12, pages 44–49.

K. Stein and C. Hess. 2007. Does It Matter Who Contributes? - A Study on Featured Articles in the German Wikipedia. In *HT '07: Proceedings of the eighteenth conference on Hypertext and hypermedia*, pages 171–174, New York, NY, USA.

P.D. Turney. 2000. Learning Algorithms for Keyphrase Extraction. *Information Retrieval*, 2(4):303–336.

Temporal Relation Classification in Persian and English Contexts

Mahbaneh Eshaghzadeh Torbati
Department of Computer Engineering,
Sharif University of Technology,
Tehran, Iran
Mahbaneh.eshaghzadeh@gmail.com

Gholamreza Ghassem-sani
Department of Computer Engineering,
Sharif University of Technology,
Tehran, Iran
sani@sharif.edu

Seyed Abolghasem Mirroshandel
Faculty of Engineering,
University of Guilan,
Rasht, Iran
mirroshandel@guilan.ac.ir

Yadollah Yaghoobzadeh
Department of Computer Engineering,
Sharif University of Technology, Tehran, Iran
yaghoobzadeh@ce.sharif.edu

Negin Karimi Hosseini
School of Computer Science,
Faculty of Information Science & Technology, Universiti Kebangsaan Malaysia
Negin62_k@yahoo.com

Abstract

This paper introduces the first pattern-based Persian Temporal Relation Classifier (PTRC) that finds the type of temporal relations between pairs of events in the Persian texts. The proposed system uses support vector machines (SVMs) equipped by combinations of simple, convolution tree, and string subsequence kernels (SSK). In order to evaluate the algorithm, we have developed a Persian TimeBank (PTB) corpus. PTRC not only increases the performance of the classification by applying new features and SSK, but also alleviates the probable adverse effects of the Free Word Orderness (FWO) of Persian on temporal relation classification. We have also applied our proposed algorithm to two standard corpora on English (i.e., TimeBank and TempEval-2) to measure the efficiency of the new features and SSK. The experiments show the accuracies of 65.6%, 59.53%, 50.2%, and 62.17% on an augmented version of PTB, TimeBank, tasks E and F of TempEval-2, respectively. Consequently, we have achieved the third best result on TimeBank, and the second best result on the task F of TempEval-2.

1 Introduction

The goal in temporal relation classification is to find the temporal ordering between temporal entities of the input text. As a result, these relations can be used in applications such as question answering and summarization systems.

In general, temporal relation classification is the task of determining when an event/time expression has taken place with respect to some other event/time expressions. In this study, we only try to find these relations between events, not between events and time expressions.

In temporal corpora that have been created so far, different temporal relation classes have been considered. In TimeBank (Pustejovsky et al., 2003), the first corpus that has changed the research trend towards machine learning methods, there are six different temporal relations, namely SIMULTANEOUS, INCLUDES, BEFORE, IBEFORE, BEGINS, and ENDS. On the other hand, in TempEval-1 (Verhagen et al., 2007) and TempEval-2 (Verhagen et al., 2010), the temporal relations are BEFORE, OVERLAP, AFTER, BEFORE-OR-OVERLAP, OVERLAP-OR-AFTER, and VAGUE.

Despite the multitude of speakers of Persian (Bateni, 1995), there has not existed any corpus tagged with temporal relations in Persian yet. Thus, as the first step, events and its attributes were tagged in the PTB corpus (Yaghoobzadeh et al., 2012). We have continued their work by annotating temporal relations between tagged events and Signals, manually and based on an adapted version of the ISO-TimeML guideline (Pustejovsky et al., 2010).

In the second step, our goal has been designing a system that classifies temporal relations in Persian texts. Considering that Free Word Orderness (FWO) could have a negative impact on classification, we have aimed to design our Persian Temporal Relation Classifier (PTRC) in a way that prevents side-effects as much as possible. Thus, a simple kernel was applied to a group of lexical and semantic features that were inherently resistant against FWO. Then, according to the efficiency of dependency relations in temporal classification, as well as their robustness and stability in dealing with FWO, for each sentence two dependency-based tree structures were built. In addition, two different convolution tree kernels with various weighting methods were applied to them subsequently. Finally, a novel FWO-resistant kernel named string subsequent kernel (SSK) was applied to aforementioned structures.

In the third step, in order to further evaluate the efficiency of the new features and SSK in temporal classification, PTRC was applied to TimeBank and tasks E and F of TempEval-2.

The remainder of this paper is as follows: Section 2 is about temporal classification methods. Section 3 explains some challenges in Persian, and accordingly Section 4 represents the solution for tackling such difficulties. Section 5 includes the explanation of proposed system. Finally, in Sections 6 and 7, the results of the experiments and our conclusion are reported.

2 Related work

One of the most widely used temporal logics, which is the foundation of the most existing achievements related to temporal relation classification, was proposed by Allen (1984). Various rule-based studies were conducted based on 13 temporal relations defined between intervals in this logic. By creation of different temporal corpora, the research trend turned into machine learning methods, which so far achieved the best results in this regard.

Among the outstanding methods performed on TimeBank, we can report four researches by (Lapata and Lascarides, 2006), (Chambers et al., 2007), and (Mirroshandel et al., 2011a, b). The first method extracts novel syntactic features in an ensemble classification method (Lapata and Lascarides, 2006). They have simplified the problem by restricting the diversity of temporal classes. In the second method, a two-stage SVM-based classification technique was proposed, in which event and attribute extraction in addition to temporal relation classification were executed (Chambers et al., 2007). Mirroshandel et al. (2011a, b) showed that the parse tree structures can be used as informative features in the temporal classification process. By applying convolution tree kernels to constituent and dependency parse trees, they developed two separated systems. Moreover, Mirroshandel and Ghassem-Sani (2010) have applied a bootstrapping method to their system and outperformed all related works.

In TempEval workshops, systems with more innovative classifiers were presented. For instance, a classifier named Conditional Random Field (CRF) algorithm was applied in both (Kolya et al., 2010) and (Llorens et al., 2010). The system presented in (Yoshikawa et al., 2009) can be considered as the first advent of Markov Logic Network (MLN) in temporal classification participated in the TempEval-1 competition. Ha et al. (2010) also achieved the best accuracy for Task F in TempEval-2 by use of MLN.

3 Persian Language Challenges

3.1 Compound Verbs and Free Word Orderness

Persian compound verbs are a kind of multiword light verb construction that still has remained as one of Persian challenges in NLP tasks (Rasooli et al., 2011). The complexity is due to the variety in count and type of nonverbal elements, in addition to syntactic flexibility such as unlimited word distance between the light verb and its components. *Delxor kardan* (to annoy), *talâq dâdan* (to divorce), and *pas dâdan* (to return) are some examples of compound verbs in Persian.

Although formal sentences in Persian have the SOV structure, it is also a free word order language, in which the sentential constituents can be arbitrarily moved around in the sentence.

3.2 Tackling Persian Challenges

The task of temporal relation classification in Persian is more complicated than in other languages such as English. High Frequency of compound verbs and their by-product noun and adjective phrases in Persian, makes the feature extraction more complex. Fortunately, by the multiword annotation method that has been performed on PTB, feature extraction and dependency tree pruning (to be discussed in Section 5) have become straightforward. Furthermore, the syntactic feature efficiency can be devalued, due to the existence of FWO in sentence structures. Hence, in order to alleviate the adverse impact of FWO, a combination of three FWO-resistant kernels has been employed in the SVM classifier.

The first kernel, named K_{simple}, is a linear kernel that neutralizes the FWO side-effects by exploiting a collection of lexical and semantic features. These features are inherently stable against FWO. The second group of kernels consists of two weighted convolution tree kernels applied to two tree structures constructed and valued based on dependency relations and POS tags of sentence elements. These kernels take advantage of both dependency structures and a bi-gram estimation of tree-constructing features. By utilization of dependency relations and a tree sorting method, the FWO side-effects can be eliminated from these kernels. The third kernel is known as a string subsequence kernel (SSK) that evaluates the identical sub-strings of the tree paths joining the events involved in temporal relations. This kernel is being used in temporal classification for the first time and since it is operated on a dependency-based path, it is independent of sentence structure and FWO problem. In the following section, each kernel group will be discussed in more detail.

4 Proposed Features and Kernels

4.1 K_{Simple} kernel and relevant features

In this section the FWO-resistant feature set for both Persian and English systems as well as the K_{Simple} kernel are discussed.

Features: We divided features into three categories of Event-based, Temporal-Relation (TR)-based, and governing-based features. All new features are marked by * in this section.

Event-based features: These features are determined for each event involved in a temporal relation. *Tense*, *Mood*, *Aspect*, *Modality*, *Polarity*, and *Class* are human annotated features extracted from related Persian and English corpora. The others, consist of Lemma, Voice* and Synset, are extracted automatically.

Voice*: It is a binary feature, based on verb transitivity status, assigned to verbal events.

Synset: WordNet and FarsNet (Shamsfard et al., 2010) synsets are categorized based on their part of speech tags. Hence, the synset feature is partly evaluated incorrectly due to the probable dissimilarity of POS tags of events, although they are semantically related. Temporal pair of (*Announced*, *Denote*), which involves adjectival and verbal event respectively, is a constructive example in this respect. As a solution, we have developed this feature and estimate it based on all event derivations that exist in WordNet. Comparing with Wordnet, there still exist some deficiencies in Farsnet. Therefore in Persian synset extraction process, words have been initially mapped to their English peers in Wordnet, and then the required information has been extracted from Wordnet database.

TR-based: These features are defined for each temporal relation listed as follows:

Text order: This feature refers to the event appearance orders in the context.

Inter/Intra relation: This feature defines whether the events are within the same sentence or not.

Be numerical*: It defines whether the nominal events have numerical essence or not.

Be aspectual*: It defines whether the events have a triggering or terminating essence.

Context topic*: This feature categorizes each context in one of the narrative, financial, biography, or accidental fields.

Classified distance*: It classifies the eventual distance in the adjacent, near, or far classes.

Signal lemma*: It contains the lemma of involved signal in a temporal relation.

Signal class*: It classifies the signals into temporal classes based on (Mortazavinia, 2010).

Governing-based features: Clearly, features such as *Tense, Aspect, Voice*, and *Mood* are verb-specific and also crucial to temporal classification. Therefore, based on "NONE" values allocated to their mentioned features, non-verbal events may be devalued in the classification process. In order to alleviate this probable impact, these feature values owned by governing verb of non-verbal events have been selected as substitute for the former ones. The governing verbs have been distinguished based on dependency relations.

K_{Simple} kernel: By utilization of this kernel, we try to calculate the temporal relation similarity in features in section 5.1. By defining K_S, TR, E, f, Tf, n, and C as K_{Simple} kernel, temporal relation, event, event-based feature, TR-based feature, the feature count, and function of counting the number of common features of events involved in a temporal relation respectively, the K_{Simple} kernel can be introduced as follows:

$$K_S(TR_1,TR_2)=\sum_{i=1,2}K_E(TR_1.E_i,TR_2.E_i) + C(TR_1.Tf,TR_2.Tf) \quad (1)$$

$$K_E(E_1,E_2)=\sum_{i=1}^{n}C(E_1.f_i,E_2.f_i) \quad (2)$$

It should be noted that equation (1) is the manipulated version of the kernel introduced in (Mirroshandel et al., 2011b) utilized for the involving TR-based features in kernel evaluation.

4.2 Tree kernels and syntactic feature

Dependency relation transformation: The dependency relation contributes to utilize a mostly FWO-resistant version of sentence structure, in temporal classification. In order to construct dependency trees, two structures named $Trans_1$ and $Trans_2$ proposed in (Mirroshandel and Ghassem-Sani, 2011a) have been implemented. Afterwards, a minor manipulation for applying tree kernels to inter-sentence relations has been exerted on the parse trees. This process includes combining tree structures of each sentence by selecting them as children to arbitrary augmented node. The tree constructions are shown in figure 1 and 2.

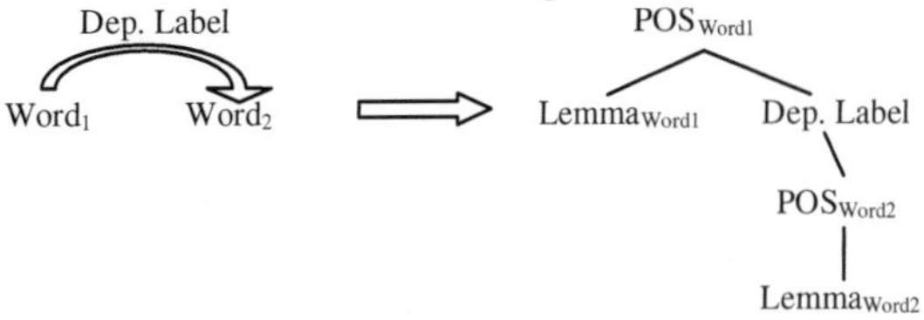

Figure 1: *$Trans_1$* transformation. (Mirroshandel and Ghassem-Sani, 2011a)

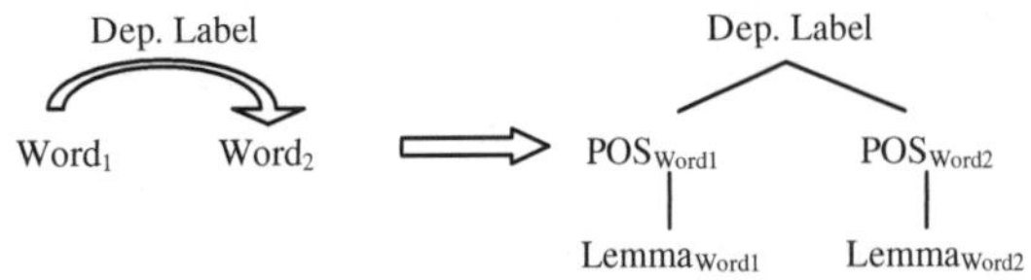

Figure 2: *$Trans_2$* transformation. (Mirroshandel and Ghassem-Sani, 2011a)

$Trans_2$ transformation is partially similar to constituent parse tree. As a result, it can be substituted for the original one in the proposed system. However, this structure would partly be FWO-affected. In other words, the priority of node appearance in a tree is dependent on their orders in the sentence. In *$Trans_1$*, just children priority is manipulated by FWO, therefore a sorting method, based on ordered list of whole tree node values, has solved the problem and finally made *$Trans_1$* completely FWO-resistant. In *$Trans_2$*, both dependency relation and sentence element order assign children of nodes, therefore this manipulation has been too complicated to be solved by a simple sorting method. Based on these explanations, *$Trans_2$* still remains FWO-affected and would be just efficient for English temporal classifier. As we will see in Section 6, this structure will be automatically omitted among best Persian classifiers.

Tree pruning and weighting methods: It has been shown that tree kernels operate more efficiently by being applied to pruned trees (Zhang et. al., 2006). Based on this observation, the path enclosed tree (PET) method has been exerted on the desired dependency trees. In this method, all the nodes of the path (the path from event nodes to their common parent) and the ones among this path would be designated as the desired portion of tree.

In the next stage, three various weighting methods, inspired by (Mirroshandel et al., 2011b), are applied to the pruned trees. The first method, named Argument Ancestor Path (AAP), just considers the nodes on the path enclosed by the event nodes, as well as their immediate descendants. The second one, named Argument Ancestor Path Distance (AAPD), allocates weights to all pruned tree nodes based on their distance from the nearest ancestor of one of the events in the path. The third method, known as Argument Distance Kernel (AD) is very similar to AAPD except that weights are evaluated based on the distance from the nearest event.

Convolution tree kernels: Sentence structure can be referenced as one of the invaluable knowledge sources in the NLP applications. Convolution tree kernels compute the similarity between two trees by counting the number of common sub-trees. In our method, among various tree kernels, both subset tree (SST) (Collins and Duffy, 2001) and partial tree (PT) kernels (Moschitti, 2006b) have been applied to pruned and weighted tree structures. SST and PT have been reported to result more efficiently on constituent and dependency parse trees respectively (Moschitti, 2006b). SST sub-trees are restricted by the rule that states all nodes of sub-tree must appear with either all or none of its children. In contrast, PT sub-trees have no limitation on their structures and can have any arbitrary construction.

4.3 Dependency path in SSK kernel

Dependency path: The dependency path is a sequence of nodes enclosed between *$Trans_1$* event nodes. Based on the *$Trans_1$* design, this path contains the dependency relations among the components of the dependents of the root of each sentence that contains temporal related events. Considering that FWO just changes the children orders of *$Trans_1$*, the path will be FWO-resistant. Consequently, no extra method is required for tackling the probable side-effects.

SSK Kernel: SSK was initially proposed for estimating a similarity measure between sequences (Lodhi et. al., 2002). This similarity measure is based on the number of weighted sub-string matches that occur among sequences. The length of a sub-string, *K*, can be initialized manually based on the problem definition. In this method, both kinds of continuous and discrete matches are acceptable. For instance, both pairs of (*car*, *card*) and (*car*, *custard*) have the matches with the sub-string length of three as continuous and discrete matches, respectively.

SSK adaptation process: Benefiting from discrete match recognition, SSK contributes to compare extracted paths according to various sub-strings of POS and/or dependency tags, which is not possible by the aid of tree kernels. In order to take advantage of this capability, at first, a simple adaptation process needs to be executed on SSK. In original SSK, an alphabet letter is assumed as a comparing unit that can be expanded to sub-string by increasing the *K* value. On the other hand, in this study the comparing unit has been changed to POS and/or dependency labels. Therefore, a simple mapping method that relates a node label to an individual ASCII character can be used for the SSK adaptation.

4.4 Kernel normalization and composition

Normalization: The process of normalization is achieved by performing the equation $\frac{K(TR_1,TR_2)}{\sqrt{K(TR_1,TR_1).K(TR_2,TR_2)}}$ on kernel value.

Composition: The proposed kernels have been combined in two types of linear (K_L) and polynomial (K_P) forms. Considering α as an adapted parameter, the definitions of these compositions are as follows:

$$K_L(TR_1,TR_2)=\alpha K_1(TR_1,TR_2)+(1-\alpha)K_2(TR_1,TR_2) \quad (3)$$

$$K_P(TR_1,TR_2)=\alpha K_1(TR_1,TR_2)+(1-\alpha)K_2^P(TR_1,TR_2) \quad (4)$$

$$K_2^P=(1+K_2)^2 \quad (5)$$

5 Evaluation

5.1 Characteristic of the Persian corpus

Since there has not been created any temporal corpus in Persian yet, signals (as temporal entities) and event-event temporal relations were tagged in PTB (augmented PTB). For the evaluation purpose, PTRC in addition to English-adapted version of this system were implemented and evaluated over various corpora such as augmented PTB, TimeBank and TempEval-2. The annotation process was performed according to the ISO-TimeML guideline. 401 signals and 1,613 temporal relations were extracted within 72 texts selected from PTB. The statistics of temporal relation classes are reported in Table 1.

5.2 Feature selection

In feature selection, we performed a two-stage analysis on the feature set by measuring the accuracies of both *single-feature-included* and *single-feature-excluded* models for each feature. In other words, two K_{Simple} kernels were trained on two feature sets. In the *single-feature-included* kernel, feature set just includes a target feature. On the other hand, in the *single-feature-excluded* kernel, the feature set comprises all the features except the target feature. The final judgment about feature efficiency was made based on two measures named IncEva and ExcEva. The IncEva measure is based on *single-feature-included* model and presents the accuracy in sole presence of the feature. The ExcEva is based on *single-feature-excluded* model and presents the accuracy decrement encountering the feature omission.

Relation Type	Frequency	Frequency(%)
BEFORE	807	50
IBEFORE	83	5.15
Begins	72	4.46
Ends	47	2.91
SIMULTENOUS	461	28.58
INCLUDES	143	8.87
TOTAL	1613	100

Table 1: Temporal relation statistics in PTB.

Features	ExcEva (%)	G-ExcEva (%)	G-IncEva (%)
Lemma	0.31	0.49	55.26
Class	0.49	0.80	50.22
POS	0.19	0.31	51.45
Tense	-0.18	0.43	50.28
Mood*	-0.12	0.43	49.91
Aspect	-0.18	0.12	49.29
Voice*	0	0.31	49.91
Synset	0.43	0.62	45.42
Signal class*	0.92	1.23	2.89
Signal lemma*	0.12	0.49	2.89
Be numerical*	0	0.06	49.60
Be Aspectual*	0.43	0.8	51.63
Text order	0.19	0.25	49.91
Inter/Intra Relation	0.12	0.12	49.91
Context Subject*	0	0.06	49.91
Classified Distance*	0	0.12	49.91
Tree	1.11	1.48	52.86
K_{Simple} Accuracy	-	-	61.6

Table 2: Feature selection evaluations on PTB.

Persian feature selection: Table 2 shows the feature selection results on the feature set explained in Section 5, as well as $Trans_1$ that is a tree feature extracted from augmented PTB.

The table has been designed in a way that features were separated into two event-based and TR-based parts. Governing-based evaluations have been specified by the "G" prefix and governing features have been highlighted. In addition, the new features have been marked by *. The highlighted features contribute more efficiently than the simple event-based ones. Furthermore, as the number of signal-involved temporal relations is insignificant (about 199 relations), the unsatisfactory G-IncEva value is justifiable. In fact, the signal-based features have been designed in a way to improve the classification accuracy in cooperation with other features. High G-ExcEva of the signal class is an evidence of this improvement. All features in Table 2, except $Trans_1$, are exploited by the K_{Simple} kernel. The last row shows the accuracy obtained by K_{Simple} kernel on the standard test set.

Features	TE2-E	TE2-F	TimeBank
Lemma	✓	✓	✓
Class	✓	✓	✓
POS	✓	✓	✓
Tense	G[1]	✓	✓
Aspect	G	✓	✓
Polarity	✓	✓	-
Modality	✓	✓	-
Synset	✓	-	✓
Signal class	-	-	✓
Signal lemma	-	-	✓
Be numerical	-	-	✓
Be Aspectual	✓	✓	-
Text order	✓	✓	-
Inter/Intra Relation	✓	✓	✓
Context Subject	-	-	✓
Classified Distance	✓	-	✓
K_{simple} Accuracy	49%	58.2%	57.98%

Table 3. Selected features for TimeBank and TempEval-2 task E and F.

English feature selection: Table 3 contains the designated features through the feature selection process on TimeBank (TB), the task E of TempEval-2 (TE2-E) and the task F of TempEval-2 (TE2-F). Signals are not annotated in the TempEval-2 database. As a result, the Signal-based features are ignored in the TempEval tasks. Similar to Table 2, the last row includes the K_{Simple}-trained SVM results based on the marked features in the table.

Table 4 contains the ExcEva evaluations of the novel features extracted from the English corpora. Despite the negative ExcEva value of the *Classified Distance* feature, its acceptable IncEva value, 50.2%, can justify the selection of this feature. It can be inferred from this table that the new features are also beneficial in English temporal classification.

Features	TE2-E (%)	TE2-F (%)	TB (%)
Signal class	-	-	0.29
Signal lemma	-	-	0.15
Be numerical	-	-	0.50
Be Aspectual	0.39	0.33	-
Context Topic	-	-	0.32
Classified Distance	0.39	-	-0.32

Table 4. Feature selection measures on TimeBank and TempEval-2 task E and F.

5.3 Experimental Results

We made use of LIBSVM Matlab source (Chang and Lin, 2001) for SVM classification, the MateParser (Bohnet, 2010) for dependency parsing, and JAWS (Spell, 2008) for retrieving information from WordNet. The implemented systems were applied to augmented PTB, TimeBank, tasks E and F of TempEval-2. We applied the five-fold cross validations method to PTB and TimeBank as well as simple classification to TempEval tasks. The evaluated accuracies are reported in tables 5, 6, 7, and 8. For more clarity, kernel compositions are formulated. In formulation method, names related to kernel compositions and either of tree and sequential kernels are subscripted by weighting and kernel methods, respectively. Moreover, "1" and "2" postfixes are added to the tree and sequential kernel names to indicate $Trans_1$ and $Trans_2$ structures.

Experiments on PTB: In order to measure the effectiveness of PTRC kernel, a variety of linear and polynomial kernel compositions and different weighting methods have been implemented and evaluated. Among these compositions, the most efficient ones, based on three weighting methods, are reported in a two-stage process in Table 5. In the first stage (SSK-excluded), various tree kernels and K_{Simple} compositions are examined. In the second stage

[1] Governing version of selected feature.

(SSK-included), the former compositions include the SSK to utilize its efficiency. Finally, Sorted-PK_{AAPD}, a sorted version of PK_{AAPD}, is selected as the PTRC kernel. As it is shown in Table 5, the last kernel outperforms the other compositions. The definitions of these compositions are as follows (PK_{AAPD} and Sorted-PK_{AAPD} exclude the $Trans_2$ structure):

$$PK_{AAP} = \alpha(K_{simple}) + (1-\alpha)(1+K1_{SST}+K2_{SST}+K1_{SSK})^2 \quad (6)$$

$$PK_{AD} = \alpha(K_{simple}) + (1-\alpha)(1+K1_{SST}+K1_{SSK})^2 \quad (7)$$

$$PK_{AAPD} = \alpha(K_{simple}) + (1-\alpha)(1+K1_{SST}+K1_{PT}+K1_{SSK})^2 \quad (8)$$

Methods	SSK-excluded (%)	SSK-included (%)
Baseline[2]	50	50
PK_{AAP}	64.43	65.17
PK_{AD}	63.63	65.17
PK_{AAPD}	**64.68**	65.30
Sorted-PK_{AAPD}	64.55	**<u>65.60</u>**

Table 5. The accuracy of PTRC on PTB.

Experiments on TimeBank: Various compositions have been tested on AAPD weighted trees. Comparing to both supervised and semi-supervised methods, our system has gained the third best accuracy that have been achieved so far. Although, by excluding the state-of-the-art method, Mir-semi-supervised (Mirroshandel and Ghassem-Sani, 2010), which profits from external sources, the proposed system has gained second best place inferior to Chambers (Chambers et al., 2007). However, our method has outperformed the equivalent method, Mir-supervised (Mirroshandel et al., 2011b), which benefits from both constituent and dependency parse trees. The TB-K_{AAPD} definition is as follow and the mentioned accuracies are reported in Table 6.

$$TB - K_{AAPD} = \alpha(Ksimple) + (1-\alpha)(K1_{PT} + K2_{SST} + K_{SSK} + 1)^2 \quad (9)$$

Methods	Accuracy (%)
Mir-semi-supervised	**66.18**
Chambers	60.45
TB-K_{AAPD}	59.53
Mir-supervised	58.76

Table 6. Accuracy of methods on TimeBank.

[2] The Baseline is the majority class for relations.

Experiments on TempEval tasks: Both tasks E and F are discussed in this section. As it is reported in Table 7, we have surpassed Mir-semi-supervised system (Mirroshandel, Ghassem-sani, 2012) with notable improvement, although the acquired accuracy is still far from the state-of-the-art system named TRIPS (UzZaman and Allen, 2010). However, the result in task E is more promising, as we have achieved the second best result after NCSU (Ha et al., 2010). Obviously our method has outperformed Mir-semi-supervised (Mirroshandel and Ghassem-sani, 2012) in this task, too. The definitions of tasks E and F are as follows:

Task E:

$$TE - K_{AAPD} = \alpha(K_{simple}) + (1-\alpha)(1+K2_{SST}+K1_{SSK})^2 \quad (10)$$

Task F:

$$TE - K_{AAPD} = \alpha(K_{simple}) + (1-\alpha)(1+K1_{SST}+K2_{PT}+K1_{SSK})^2 \quad (11)$$

Methods	Task E (%)	Task F (%)
TRIPS|NCSU-indi	**58**	**66**
TE-K_{AAPD}	50.20	62.17
Mir-semi-Supervised	45.62	50.41

Table 7. Accuracy of system on TempEval.

Tree and SSK efficiency: The accuracy increases caused by applying tree and string subsequence kernels to both English and Persian corpora are more observable in Table 7, 8.

Methods	SSK-excluded (%)	SSK-included (%)
Sorted-PK_{AAPD}	64.55	65.60
TB-K_{AAPD}	58.76	59.53
TE-K_{AAPD}	49.80	50.20
TE-K_{AAPD}	60.85	62.17

Table 8. Results of all implemented systems on Persian and English corpora.

6 Conclusion

In this paper, we have addressed the problem of temporal relation classification in Persian and English and SSK kernel applicable to both languages. As the first Persian temporal corpus, signals and event-event temporal relations have been annotated in PTB. Variety of compositions including tree structures, various kernels and several weighting methods were examined and consequently the best compositions were selected as kernels in SVM. The experiments show notable improvement in both languages.

References

James F. Allen. 1984. *Towards a general theory of action and time.* Articial intelligence, 23(2):123-154.

Mohammadreza Bateni. 1995. Tosif-e Sakhtari Zaban-e Farsi (Describing the Persian Structure). Amir-Kabir Press, Tehran, Iran (in Persian).

Bernd Bohent. 2010. *Top accuracy and Fast Dependency Parsing is not a Contradiction.* In Proceedings of Coling 2010, pp. 89-7.

Nathanael Chambers, Shan Wang and Dan Jurafsky. 2007. *Classifying temporal relations between events.* In Proceedings of the 45th Annual Meeting of the ACL on Interactive Poster and Demonstration Sessions, pp. 173-176. Association for Computational Linguistics.

Chih C. Chang and Chih J. Lin. 2001. *Libsvm: a library for support vector machines.* ACM Transactions on Intelligent Systems and Technology (TIST), 2(3).

Michael Collins and Nigel Duffy. 2001. *Convolution kernels for natural language.* In Proceedings of NIPS, Vol. 14, pp. 625-632.

Christiane Fellbaum. 1998. *WordNet: An Electronic Lexical Database.* MIT Press.

Eun Y. Ha, Alok Baikadi, Carlyle Licata and James C. Lester. 2010. *Ncsu: Modeling temporal relations with markov logic and lexical ontology.* In Proceedings of the 5th International Workshop on Semantic Evaluation, pp. 341-344. Association for Computational Linguistics.

Anup K. Kolya, Asif Ekbal and Sivaji Bandyopadhyay. 2010. *Ju-cse-temp: A first step towards evaluating events, time expressions and temporal relations.* In Proceedings of the 5th International Workshop on Semantic Evaluation, pp. 345-350. Association for Computational Linguistics.

Mirella Lapata and Allex Lascarides. 2006. *Learning sentence-internal temporal relations.* Journal of Articial Intelligence Research, 27(1): 85-117.

Hector Llorens, Estela Saquete and Borja Navarro. 2010. *Tipsem (english and spanish): Evaluating crfs and semantic roles in tempeval-2.* In Proceedings of the 5th International Workshop on Semantic Evaluation, pp. 284-291. Association for Computational Linguistics.

Huma Lodhi, Craig Saunders, John Shawe-Taylor, Nello Cristianini and Chris Watkins. 2010. *Text Classification using String Kernels.* In Proceedings of Neural Information Processing Systems, NIPS'00. , MIT Press, pp. 563-569.

Ryan McDonald, Koby Crammer and Fernando Pereira. 2005. *Online large-margin training of dependency parsers.* In Proceedings of the 43rd Annual Meeting on Association for Computational Linguistics, pp. 91-98.

S. Abolghasem Mirroshandel and Gholamreza Ghassem-Sani. 2010. *Temporal Relations Learning with a Bootstrapped Crossdocument Classifier.* In Proceeding of the 2010 conference on ECAI 2010: 19th European Conference on Artificial Intelligence, pp. 829–834. IOS Press.

S. Abolghasem Mirroshandel, and Gholamreza Ghassem-Sani. 2011a. *Temporal Relation Classification Using Dependency Convolution Tree Kernels.* In Proceedings of the 5th Language & Technology Conference: Human Language Technologies as a Challenge for Computer Science and Linguistics, pp. 146-150.

S. Abolghasem Mirroshandel and Gholamreza Ghassem-Sani. 2012. *Towards Unsupervised Learning of Temporal Relations between Events.* Journal of Artificial Intelligence Research 45:125-163. DOI:10.1613/jair.3693.

S. Abolghasem Mirroshandel, Gholamreza Ghassem-Sani and Mahdy Khayyamian. 2011b. *Using syntactic-based kernels for classifying temporal relations.* Journal of Computer Science and Technology, 26(1):68-80.

Marzieh Mortazavinia. 2010. *A rule-based event detection System.* (Unpublished Persian Master degree Thesis). University of Tehran, Tehran, Iran.

Alessandro Moschitti. 2006a. *Efficient convolution tree kernels for dependency and constituent syntactic trees,* In Proceedings of the 17th European Conference on Machine Learning, pp. 318-329.

Alessandro Moschitti. 2006b. *Making tree kernels practical for natural language learning,* In Proceedings of EACL, pp. 113-120.

James Pustejovsky, Kiyong Lee, Harry Bunt and Laurent Romary. 2010. *ISO-TimeML: An International Standard for Semantic Annotation.* In Proceedings of the Seventh conference on International Language Resources and Evaluation (LREC'10).

James Pustejovsky, Patrick Hanks, Roser Sauri, Andrew See, Robert Gaizauskas, Andrea Setzer, Dragomir Radev, Beth Sundheim, David Day, Lisa Ferro and Marcia Lazo. 2003. *The timebank corpus.* In Corpus Linguistics, Vol. 2003, pp. 40.

Mohammad S. Rasooli, Heshaam Faili, Behruz Minaei-Bidgoli, 2011. *Unsupervised identication of Persian compound verbs.* In Proceedings of the Mexican international conference on arti-cial intelligence (MICAI), pp. 394-406

Mehrnoush Shamsfard, Akbar Hesabi, Hakimeh Fadaei, Niloofar Mansoory, Ali Famian, Somayeh Bagherbeigi, Elham Fekri, Maliheh Monshizadeh, and S. Mostafa Assi. 2010. *Semi-automatic development of FarsNet; the Persian wordnet.* In Proceedings of 5th Global WordNet Conference (GWA2010).

Brett Spell. 2010. *Java API for WordNet Searching (JAWS)*, lyle.smu.edu/~tspell/jaws/index.html.

Naushad UzZaman and James F. Allen. 2010. *Trips and trios system for tempeval-2: Extracting temporal information from text.* In Proceedings of the 5th International Workshop on Semantic Evaluation, pp. 276-283. Association for Computational Linguistics.

Mark Verhagen, Robert Gaizauskas, Frank Schilder, Mark Hepple, Graham Katz and James Pustejovsky. 2007. *Semeval-2007 task 15: Tempeval temporal relation identification.* In Proceedings of the 4th International Workshop on Semantic Evaluations, pp. 75-80. Association for Computational Linguistics.

Mark Verhagen, Roser Sauri, Tommaso Caselli and James Pustejovsky. 2010. *Semeval-2010 task 13: Tempeval-2.* In Proceedings of the 5th International Workshop on Semantic Evaluation, pp. 57-62. Association for Computational Linguistics.

Yadollah Yaghoobzadeh, Gholamreza Ghassem-Sani, S. Abolghasem Mirroshandel, and Mahbaneh Eshaghzadeh. 2012. *ISO-TimeML Event Extraction in Persian Text.* In Proceedings of the 24th International Conference on Computational Linguistics (COLING), Mumbai, India, December 2012.

Katsumasa Yoshikawa, Sebastian Riedel, Masayuki Asahara and Yuji Matsumoto. 2009. *Jointly identifying temporal relations with markov logic.* In Proceedings of the Joint Conference of the 47th Annual Meeting of the ACL and the 4th International Joint Conference on Natural Language Processing of the AFNLP: Vol. 1, pp. 405-413. Association for Computational Linguistics.

Min Zhang, Jie Zhang, Jian Su and Guodong Zhou. 2006. *A composite kernel to extract relations between entities with both flat and structured features.* In Proceedings of the 21st International Conference on Computational Linguistics and the 44th annual meeting of the Association for Computational Linguistics, pp. 825-832. Association for Com-putational Linguistics.

The Extended Lexicon: Language Processing as Lexical Description

Roger Evans
Natural Language Technology Group
Computing Engineering and Mathematics
University of Brighton, UK
R.P.Evans@brighton.ac.uk

Abstract

In this paper we introduce an approach to lexical description which is sufficiently powerful to support language processing tasks such as part-of-speech tagging or sentence recognition, traditionally considered the province of external algorithmic components. We show how this approach can be implemented in the lexical description language, DATR, and provide examples of modelling extended lexical phenomena. We argue that applying a modelling approach originally designed for lexicons to a wider range of language phenomena brings a new perspective to the relationship between theory-based and empirically-based approaches to language processing.

1 The Extended Lexicon

A lexicon is essentially a structured description of a set of lexical entries. One of the first tasks when developing a lexicon is to decide what the lexical entries are. This task has two dimensions: what kind of linguistic object does a lexical entry describe, and what does it say about it. So for example, one might decide to produce a lexicon which describes individual word instances, and provides the orthographic form and part-of-speech tag for each form. It is the first of these dimensions that is most relevant to the idea of the Extended Lexicon. Conventionally, there are two main candidates for the type of linguistic object described by a lexicon: word forms (such as ***sings***, ***singing***, ***sang***[1]), corresponding to actual words in a text and lexemes (such as **SING**, **WALK**, **MAN**), describing abstract words, from which word forms are somehow derived. Choosing between these two candidates might be a matter of theoretical disposition, or a practical consideration of how the lexicon is populated or used.

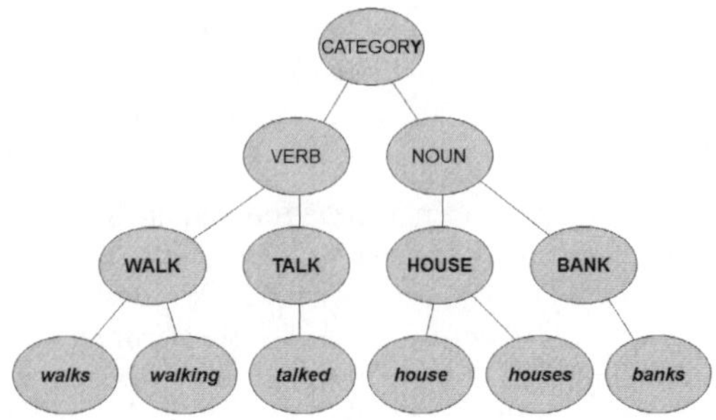

Figure 1: A simple inheritance-based lexicon

In the Extended Lexicon, we introduce a third kind of linguistic object, called word instances (or just instances), consisting of word forms as they occur in strings (sequences of words, typically sentences). For example, a string such as *the cats sat on the mat* contains two distinct instances of the word *the*. *the cats slept* contains further (distinct) instances of *the* and *cats*. However the instances in a repetition of *the cats sat on the mat* are the same as those in the original (because instances are defined relative to strings, that is, string types not string tokens).

So in an extended lexicon, the lexical entries are word instances, and the lexicon itself is a structured description of a set of word instances. In order to explore this notion in more detail, it is helpful to introduce a more specific notion of a 'structured description'. We shall use an inheritance-based lexicon, in which there are internal abstract 'nodes' representing information that is shared by several lexical entries and inherited by them. Figure 1 shows the structure of a simple inheritance-based lexicon with some abstract high-level structure (CATEGORY, VERB, NOUN), then a layer of lexemes (**WALK**, **TALK**, **HOUSE**, **BANK**), and below that a layer of word forms (***walks***, ***walking***,

[1]Typographical conventions for object types: ABSTRACT, **LEXEME**, ***wordform***, *instance*, `code`.

talked, ***house***, ***houses***, ***banks***, as well as many more). Thus the word form ***walks*** inherits information from the lexeme **WALK**, which inherits from abstract node VERB and then abstract node CATEGORY.

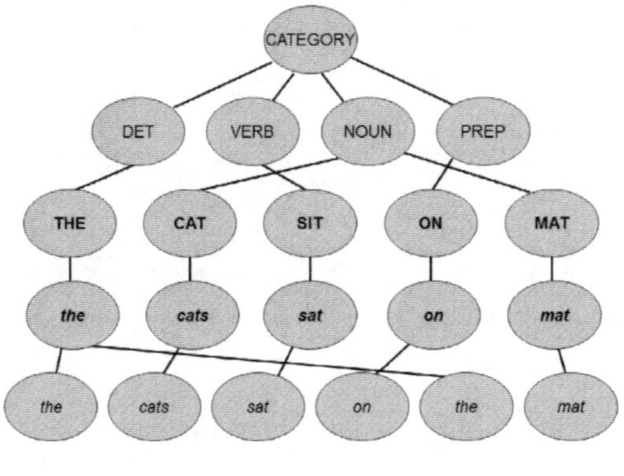

Figure 2: A lexicon with instance nodes

Adding instances to this model is in principle very easy: one just creates a further layer of nodes below the word forms. The word instances are now the lexical entries, and the word form nodes are abstractions, representing information shared by all instances of the form. Figure 2 shows a first pass at adding an instance layer to a lexicon supporting the string *the cats sat on the mat*, by adding new nodes for each instance in the string. However, what is missing from this figure is any representation of the string as a whole – nothing distinguishes the two instance nodes *the* from each other, or indeed from their parent word form node ***the***, and nothing identifies them as members of a specific string. One way this information could be added is simply by stipulating it: each instance node could have a feature whose value is the string, and another whose value is the index in the string of the current instance. However, in the Extended Lexicon, we adopt a structural solution, by linking the instance nodes of a string together into a chain, using inheritance links `prev` ('previous') and `next` to inherit information from this instance's neighbours in the string. Diagrammatically, we represent this as in figure 3.

To summarise, in the Extended Lexicon model, a lexicon is an inheritance-based structured description of a set of word instances. This notion simultaneously captures and combines two important modelling properties: first, that instances of the same word share properties via an abstract word form node, and second that the lexicon explicitly encodes word strings, as maximal chains of linked instances.

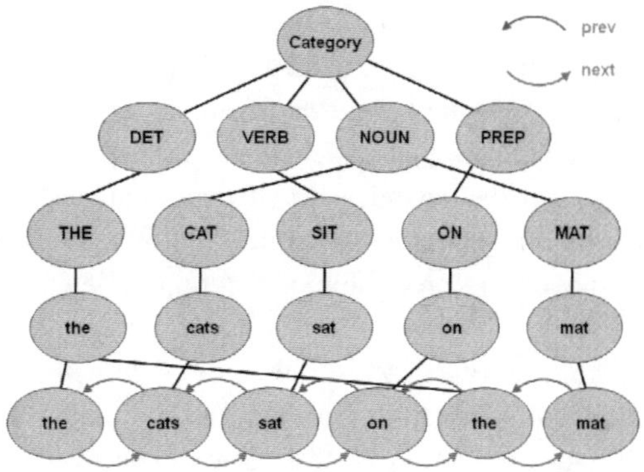

Figure 3: A simple Extended Lexcion, with instance nodes linked into a chain

2 The Extended Lexicon in DATR

2.1 DATR in brief

DATR (Evans and Gazdar, 1996) is a lexical description language originally designed to model the structure of lexicons using default inheritance. The core descriptive unit in DATR is called a node, which has a unique node name (capitalised) and has associated with it a set of definitional path equations mapping paths (sequences of features) onto value definitions.

```
DOG:
  <cat> == noun
  <form> == dog.
```

Figure 4: DATR description – version 1

Figure 4 is a simple example of DATR code. This fragment defines a node called `DOG` with two path equations, specifying that the (syntactic) category is `noun`, and the (morphological) form is `dog`.

```
NOUN:
  <cat> == noun
  <form> == "<root>".
DOG:
  <> == NOUN:<>
  <root> ==  dog.
```

Figure 5: DATR description – version 2

Figure 5 provides a slightly more complex definition. In this version, there is an abstract node, `NOUN`, capturing information shared between all nouns and a new definition for `<form>` which is defined to be the same as the path `<root>`. `DOG` now specifies a value for `<root>`, and inherits everything else from `NOUN`.

Inheritance in DATR operates as follows: to determine the value associated with a path at a particular node, use the definition from the equation for the longest path that matches a leading (leftmost) subpath of the desired path (if none matches, the value is undefined). The definition might give you a value, or a redirection to a different node and/or path, or a combination of these. If the definition contains path values, extend those paths with the portion of the desired path that did not match the left-hand-side and seek the value of the resulting expression.

So in this example, the path `<root>` at `DOG` matches a definition equation path exactly, and so has value `dog`. The path `<cat>` is not defined at `DOG` and the longest defined subpath is `<>`, so this definition is used. It specifies a value `NOUN:<>`, but the path is extended with the unmatched part of the original path, so the definition becomes `NOUN:<cat>`. This has the value `noun`, so this is the value for `DOG:<cat>` as well. Finally, the path `<form>` at `DOG` similarly matches the `<>` path and is rewritten to `NOUN:<form>`. This matches the definition in NOUN which specifies `"<root>"`. The quotes here specify this is evaluated as `DOG:<root>` (without the quotes it would be interpreted locally as `NOUN:<root>`), and because the entire path matched, there is nothing further to add to the path here, so the value is `DOG:<root>`, that is, `dog`.

```
NOUN:
  <cat> == noun
  <num> == sing
  <form> == "<table "<num>" >"
  <table> == "<root>"
  <table plur> == "<root>" s.
DOG:
  <> == NOUN:<>
  <root> ==  dog.
Dog:
  <> == DOG:<>.
Dogs:
  <> == DOG:<>
  <num> == plur.
```

Figure 6: DATR description – version 3

Finally, the version in figure 6 extends the definition of `NOUN` in several ways: the path `<num>` defines morphological number (`sing` or `plur`); the path `<form>` now defines the morphological form in terms of a table of forms indexed by the number feature[2]; finally the definition for

```
Word1:
  <> == The:<>
  <next> == "Word2:<>".
Word2:
  <> == Dogs:<>
  <prev> == "Word1:<>"
  <next> == "Word3:<>".
Word3:
  <> == Slept:<>
  <prev> == "Word2:<>".
```

Figure 7: Instance node for *the dogs slept*

`<table>` has a default value which is just the root, and a plural value which appends an `s` to the morphological root. Two word form nodes have also been added, `Dog` whose `form` will be `dog`, and `Dogs` whose `form` will be `dog s`.

2.2 Modelling the Extended Lexicon

Figure 6 provides an example of DATR code to represent lexeme and word form nodes. Extending this to represent instance nodes as well is quite straightforward. The instance nodes themselves inherit directly from the corresponding word form nodes. The `prev` and `next` links map between the instance nodes, as shown in figure 7, for the word string *the dogs slept*.

As a first simple example of the Extended Lexicon approach, figure 8 provides a definition for the lexeme A which varies the actual form according to whether the next word starts with a vowel or not. This definition presupposes a feature `<vstart>` which returns true for words that start with a vowel, false otherwise[3]. `A` evaluates `vstart` not on itself, but on the word instance that follows it (signified by `<next vstart>`) to determine whether its own form is `a` or `an`.

```
A:
  <> == DET
  <form> == <table "<next vstart>">
  <table> == a
  <table true> == an.
```

Figure 8: Word form definition for ***A***

This example illustrates some important features of the approach. First, lexeme (or word form) nodes can make assertions about instance nodes which do not hold for the abstract nodes themselves – **A** contains no definition for `<next>`, so evaluation of `<form>` is undefined, but an instance node inheriting from it will define `<next>`

[2]Note the use of embedded path expressions here: the inner expression is evaluated first and the result spliced into the outer expression

[3]We do not define `<vstart>` here – its default definition would be at the topmost abstract node, but some lexemes could override it, for example **HISTORIC** in some dialects would set it true (as in *an historic event*).

and hence <form>. Second, these assertions do not need to make direct reference to other lexical definitions – they are entirely local to **A**. Finally, these assertions do not alter the definition of the instance nodes – the only properties unique to an instance node are its parent node and its previous and next instance nodes.

This last point has considerable practical importance. In the Extended Lexicon the number of lexical entries (instances) is unbounded, since the number of possible word strings is unbounded. This is not significant problem as long as it is possible to provide an effective procedure for specifying instance definitions for any desired string dynamically. But this is straightforward: for each string create instance nodes such as shown in figure 7 with unique (but arbitrary) names for each node. The definition of each of these nodes requires only the names of the previous and next instance nodes and the name of the parent word form node. The former are known to the specification algorithm, and various conventions are possible for locating the word form node; in figure 7 we assume the word form itself, capitalised, is the name of the node.

3 Examples

3.1 Part of speech tagging

A more challenging task is part-of-speech (POS) tagging. Conventionally, POS taggers are configured as applications which are applied to texts and use either rule-based algorithms (eg (Brill, 1992)) or statistical algorithms (eg (Garside, 1987)) to provide POS tags for each word in the text. In the Extended Lexicon approach, POS tagging is conceived as a sequence of inferences required to determine the value of the feature path <pos> for a given instance node. As before, the definition is provided entirely by abstract nodes. Figure 9 presents a simple abstract lexicon with five word form nodes and one common root node. Each node is annotated with DATR code to support simple POS tagging.

The definition of the <pos> path is provided at the root node, WORDFORM, and inherited by all other nodes. It defines <pos> to be the value "<table "<prev pos>" "<prev prev pos>" >". In other words, to determine pos use the lookup table table, indexed with the pos of the previous two words. The lookup tables are defined on a per-word form basis, but inherit

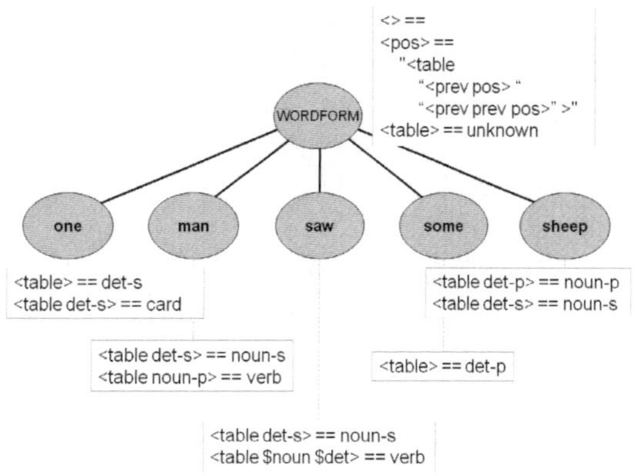

Figure 9: POS tagging

the default definition (the value unknown) from the root when not specified. Finally the root node also specifies a catch-all empty value (<> ==) for unspecified paths (including <prev> paths from Word1).

With just these definitions, the lexicon defines <pos> values for the word form nodes without access to any context (so the <prev paths return nothing). The <pos> for ***one*** is det-s (singular determiner), for ***man***, ***saw***, and ***sheep***, it is unknown (inherited from WORDFORM), and for ***some***, it is det-p. The tables vary this behaviour for instances according to previous context: ***one*** becomes a card if preceded by a det-s, ***man*** is a noun-s if preceded by a det-s, and a verb if preceded by a noun-p. ***saw*** makes use of the full context: if preceded by det-s it is a noun, but it is a verb if preceded by a noun and before that a determiner[4]. ***some*** is always a plural determiner, and ***sheep*** takes its number from the preceding determiner.

Figures 10 and 11 show what happens when we add word instances, linked together into strings. The two strings, *one man saw some sheep* and *some sheep man one saw*, use exactly the same abstract definitions, but derive different POS values for each word.

In this example, it is interesting to note that the POS inference model is specified in one place. It could easily be changed, for example to index on the previous three parts-of-speech, or to use word forms instead of parts-of-speech etc., and could be overridden with a specialised definition for subclasses of words (for example, open class versus

[4]Here DATR variables are used to range over all possible POS tags associated with nouns and variables.

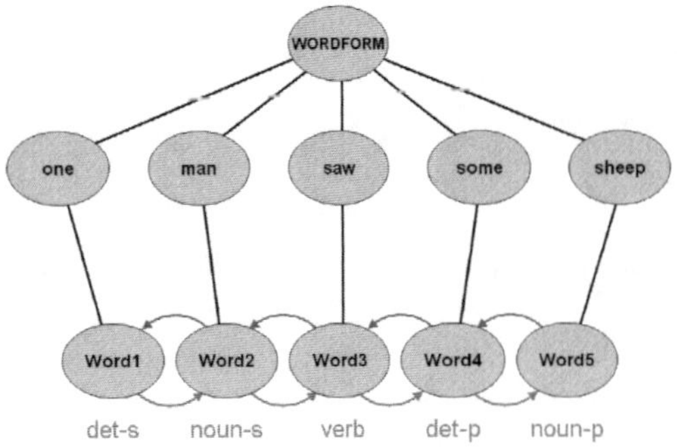

Figure 10: POS mapping for *one man saw some sheep*

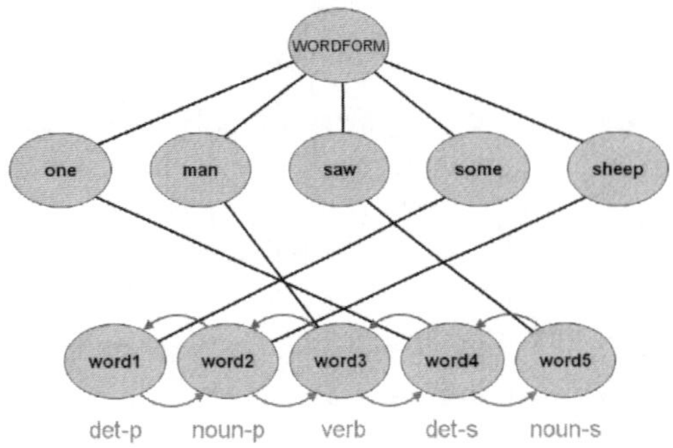

Figure 11: POS mapping for *some sheep man one saw*

closed class words). In addition the table definitions can take advantage of both the longest subpath principle (ignoring previous context they do not care about), and the inheritance hierarchy to produce compact yet highly detailed POS mappings.

3.2 Syntactic recognition

Similar techniques can also be applied to the task of syntactic recognition, which we exemplify for the case of regular languages (Hopcroft and Ullman, 1979)[5]. A simple approach is to take a context-free grammar for a regular language and transform it into left-regular form, where every rule has a rightmost lexical daughter and at most one other non-lexical daughter. Figure 12 illustrates the process for a simple context-free grammar. The key steps are expanding any non-lexical final daughters, introducing new non-terminals to make rules binary, and weeding out redundant productions.

In this form, the grammar rules can be transformed into lexical features. For example, the rule `S → NP VI` can be interpreted as "VI completes an S if the previous word completes an NP". This can be captured by introducing a path `<completes $cat>` (for any non-terminal category `$cat`), which is true for an instance node if that instance is the final lexical item of the corresponding non-terminal. Then the feature definitions in figure 13 correspond to the application of the rules. The root node specifies that by default all `<completes>` paths are `false`. The word form nodes have two kinds of definitions: for lexical categories or unary productions, simply set the corresponding `<completes>` path `true`. For binary productions, this instance completes the parent category if the previous instance completes the left daughter.

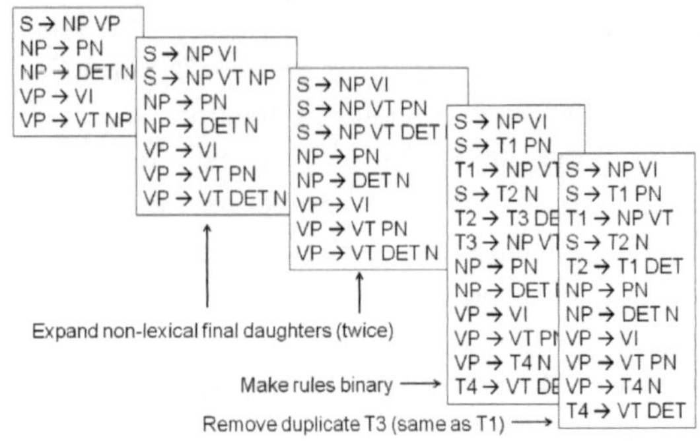

Figure 12: Transforming a grammar into left-regular form

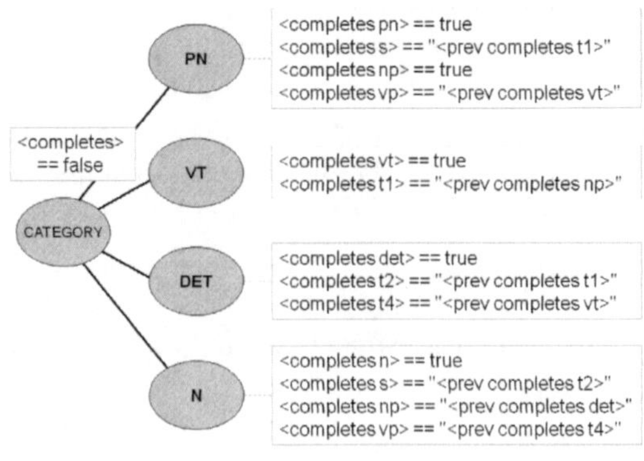

Figure 13: The grammar implemented as recognition features

Finally figure 14 shows the effect of these rules in a simple sentence *john saw the man*. Each instance now has binary features corresponding to all the categories recognised as terminating at that instance.

[5]The techniques described in this paper are at least powerful enough to recognise $a^n b^n$, a non-regular language.

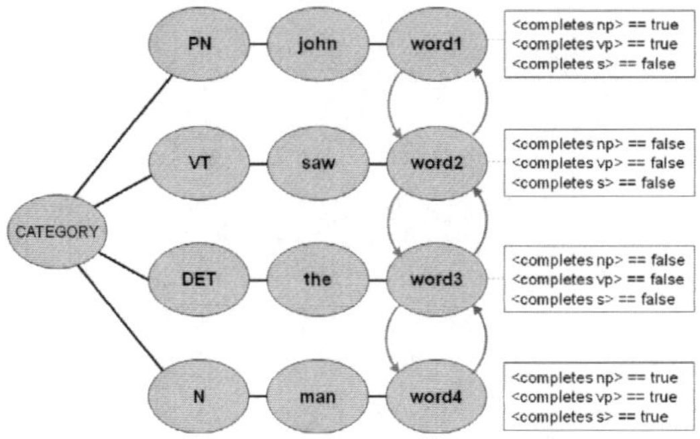

Figure 14: Recognising phrases in *john saw the man*

4 Discussion

The examples above show some of the potential for the Extended Lexicon approach: with a quite small change to the notion of a lexical entry, substantive language processing tasks can be construed as lexical description. Lexical description languages like DATR were designed to bring order to a domain, the lexicon, which exhibits quite a lot of apparent disorder – many regularities, but also sub-regularities, irregularities, strange corner-cases etc..[6] In the Extended Lexicon we bring those descriptive techniques to bear on language processing tasks more broadly, implicitly claiming that grammar is less orderly than grammarians sometimes suggest. Of course, statistical approaches to language processing have similar goals: statistical techniques are a powerful tool for modelling 'messy' systems. And indeed many properties of our model have statistical echoes: inheritance relations which provide symbolic analogues of backing off or smoothing etc. In the POS example above, the processing task was mapped to a table lookup distributed across a lexical hierarchy. An interesting next step would be to learn that table from corpus data, identifying how much context was required for different situations, how to generalise effectively from individual cases etc. This would be empirically-based but purely symbolic NLP.

The approach taken here has some similarities to various forms of Dependency Grammar (Mel'cuk, 1988), in particular because it does not include an explicit notion of phrase structure, in the grammatical sense. However, the Extended Lexicon is intended as a modelling tool, rather than a linguistic theory, and it has no explicit notion of dependency, or any kind of relationship beyond word adjacency.

Construction Grammar is a family of linguistic theories with a common theme that they do not make a sharp distinction between lexicon and grammar. Instead, they have a single framework which can represent words, phrases and sentences and can easily combine idiosyncratic phenomena with regular compositional processes. A recent manifestation of Construction Grammar, Sign-Based Construction Grammar, or SBCG (Boas and Sag, 2012), uses the unification-based type-theoretic framework of HPSG (Pollard and Sag, 1994) to provide a formal foundation for Construction Grammar. Although this framework is essentially monostratal in a similar way to the Extended Lexicon, it is far from lexically-oriented, making use of a considerable range of grammatical description mechanisms to constrain the overall behaviour of the system, in the same way that HPSG does. In essence it has absorbed the lexicon back into the grammar, rather than vice versa.

5 Future directions

The examples presented here are hugely simplified. In current work the Extended Lexicon approach is being applied to Text Mining and Sentiment Analysis, with a more sophisticated layered treatment of the relationships between instances. The core principle remains the same: that language can be described in terms of the behaviour of word instances and word adjacency relations, out of which the behaviour of whole sentences emerges.

Future directions for this work include exploring the use of corpora to build empirically-based Extended Lexicon systems; introducing non-deterministic and statistical processing into the system; and exploring the use of other 'topologies' for word instances – the word-string-based topology described here is appropriate for text processing, but other topologies, such as a lattice topology for speech recognition, or a bag-of-words topology for generation, are also possible.

[6]More recent work on lexical description, such as LMF (Francopoulo et al, 2006) and *lemon* (McCrae et al, 2012), is more concerned with representation and standardisation of surface lexical entries rather than deeper lexical generalisations, and uses less powerful inference mechanisms such as description logics.

References

Hans Boas and Ivan A. Sag (eds.). 2012. *Sign-Based Construction Grammar*. CSLI Publications, Stanford.

Eric Brill. 1992. "A simple rule-based part of speech tagger". In *Proceedings of the third conference on Applied Natural Language Processing (ANLC '92)*. Association for Computational Linguistics, Stroudsburg, PA, USA,

Roger Evans and Gerald Gazdar. 1996 "DATR: a Language for Lexical Knowledge Representation." *Computational Linguistics* , 22(2), pp. 167–216.

Gil Francopoulo, Monte George, Nicoletta Calzolari, Monica Monachini, Nuria Bel, Mandy Pet, and Claudia Soria 2006 "Lexical markup framework (LMF)." *International Conference on Language Resources and Evaluation – LREC 2006* Genoa

Roger Garside. 1987. "The CLAWS Word-tagging System." In: R. Garside, G. Leech and G. Sampson (eds), *The Computational Analysis of English: A Corpus-based Approach*. Longman, London.

John E. Hopcroft and Jeffrey D. Ullman. 1979. *Introduction to Automata Theory, Languages, and Computation*. Addison-Wesley.

John McCrae, Guadalupe Aguado-de-Cea, Paul Buitelaar, Philipp Cimiano, Thierry Declerck, Asunción Gómez-Pérez, Jorge Gracia, Laura Hollink, Elena Montiel-Ponsoda, Dennis Spohr and Tobias Wunner, 2012. "Interchanging lexical resources on the semantic web." *Language Resources and Evaluation*, 46(4). pp. 701–719 Springer

Igor A. Mel'cuk. 1988. *Dependency Syntax: Theory and Practice*. State University of New York Pres, Albany, NY.

Carl J. Pollard and Ivan A. Sag. 1994. *Head-Driven Phrase Structure Grammar*. University of Chicago Press, Chicago.

Did I really mean that?
Applying automatic summarisation techniques to formative feedback

Debora Field, Stephen Pulman
University of Oxford, Oxford, UK
`debora, stephen.pulman@cs.ox.ac.uk`
Nicolas Van Labeke, Denise Whitelock, John T.E. Richardson
The Open University, Milton Keynes, UK
`Nicolas.Vanlabeke, Denise.Whitelock, John.T.E.Richardson@open.ac.uk`

Abstract

(2)This paper reports on an application that delivers automated formative feedback designed to help university students improve their assignments. (3)The aim of the system is to improve the confidence and skills of the user by promoting self-directed learning through metacognition. (4)The system focuses on the content of an essay by using automatic summarisation techniques, automatic structure recognition, diagrams, animations, and interactive exercises that promote reflection. (15)The system is currently undergoing initial exploratory rounds of testing by ex-student volunteers and will be the subject of two full-scale empirical evaluations starting in September 2013. (1)The main claims of this paper are the application and adaptation of graph-based key word and key sentence ranking methods for a novel purpose, and ensuing observations concerning the suitability of two different centrality algorithms for the purposes of key word extraction.

1 Introduction

A fundamental problem in distance education is student attrition, particularly during the early months of enrolment, which appears to be largely due to low morale. Graduation rates at distance-learning institutions are often less than 20% (Simpson, 2012). Poor retention is evident at the level of individual modules or course units, where completion rates may be as low as 60–70%, or even lower for particular groups of students, such as those from ethnic minorities (Richardson, 2012). Some students who have dropped out of Open University courses have reported that the reason they left was a conviction of their own inadequacy when faced with completing course assignments. These reports are backed up by the drop-out rate that occurs just before the first assignment is due, which, for some courses, is typically as high as 30%.

It appears, then, that there is a need for strategies that increase students' confidence and skills during the early weeks of enrolment. The ideal strategy would be to provide frequent consultations with human tutors, but resource implications dictate that this is not a viable solution. (10)We therefore decided to build an automated formative feedback system that could provide students with immediate feedback on the quality of their draft assignment essays and reports.

(11)The purpose and design of our system are very different from existing automated assessment systems. (6)The system is primarily focused on user understanding and self-directed learning, rather than on essay improvement, and it engages the user on matters of content, rather than pointing out failings in grammar, style, and structure.

(18)An early prototype of the system (called 'openEssayist') is implemented, and is currently undergoing first rounds of user testing. (17)Results from the user testing will inform improvements to the system, which is to be used this September by real university students taking a real Master's degree module.

2 Background

(20)A number of 'automated essay scoring' (AES) or 'automated writing evaluation' (AWE) systems exist and some are commercially available (including Criterion (Burstein et al., 2003), Pearson's WriteToLearn (based on Landauer's Intelligent Essay Assessor (Landauer et al., 2003) and Summary Street (Franzke and Streeter, 2006)), IntelliMetric (Rudner et al., 2006), and LightSIDE (Mayfield and Rosé, 2013)). All these systems now include feedback functionality, though they have their roots in systems designed to attribute a grade to a piece of work. The primary concern of these systems is to help the user make step-wise improvements to a piece of writing. In contrast, the primary concern of our system is to promote self-regulated learning, self-knowledge, and metacognition. (13)Rather than telling the user in detail how to fix the incorrect and poor attributes of her essay, openEssayist encourages the user to reflect on the *content* of her essay. (16)It uses linguistic technologies, graphics, animations, and interactive exercises to enable the user to comprehend the content of his/her essay more objectively, and to reflect on whether the essay adequately conveys his/her intended meanings. Writing-Pal (Dai et al., 2011; McNamara et al., 2011) is the system that is most similar to ours in that it aims to improve the user's skills. Like openEssayist, Writing-Pal also uses interactive exercises to promote understanding. Writing-Pal is very different from openEssayist in terms of its underlying linguistic technologies and the design of its exercises.

The empirical evaluations of openEssayist will focus on users' perceptions and observations about the system (its usability and its effectiveness), and tutors' opinions of same (*cf* (Chen and Cheng, 2008)), rather than on how human-like its marking strategies are (it has none), and we will be carrying out controlled experiments to assess the effectiveness of the system in improving students' writing proficiency.

There is educational research that argues that using summaries in formative feedback on essays is very helpful for students (Nelson and Schunn, 2009). *Ibid* concluded that summaries make effective feedback because they are associated with understanding. They found that understanding of the *problem* concerning some aspect of an essay was the only significant mediator of feedback implementation, whereas understanding of the *solution* was not (*ibid*, p. 389). By 'summaries' the authors meant both the traditional notion of a short précis, and also some simpler representations, such as lists of key topics. As generating simple summaries falls within the scope of natural language processing (NLP), we decided to use automatic summarisation techniques as the foundation of the linguistic analysis module in the first prototype of the system.

A consequence of the choice to focus on summarisation techniques is that openEssayist is domain-independent, which characteristic also sets openEssayist apart from existing AES/AWEs. This means that it will be possible to quickly apply the system to new domains without the need for manual annotation and machine training of a mass of data from the new domain.

3 Linguistic engine

(5)Our initial approach to producing essay summaries uses two simple extractive summarisation techniques: *key phrase extraction* and *key sentence extraction*. Key phrases (as defined in, for example, (Witten et al., 1998)) are individual words and short phrases that are the most suggestive of the content of a discourse. (9)Similarly, key sentences are the *sentences* that are most suggestive of a text's content. (7)To identify the key phrases and key sentences of a text, we use unsupervised graph-based ranking methods to calculate the relative importance of words and sentences (following TextRank (Mihalcea and Tarau, 2004) and LexRank (Erkan and Dragomir, 2004)) and select a proportion of the top-ranking items. Before extracting key terms and sentences from the text, the text is automatically pre-processed using four tokenisers, a part-of-speech tagger, and a lemmatiser from the Natural Language Processing Toolkit (NLTK) (Bird et al., 2009). We also remove stop words (articles, prepositions, auxiliary verbs, pronouns, *etc.*), which are the most frequently occurring in natural language but for our purposes the least interesting.[1] The system also attempts to recognise some structural components.

3.1 Automatic structure recognition

(12)Automatic structure recognition is carried out to ensure that the key word and key sentence analyses are performed on the appropriate data, and to facilitate observations about structure to be used in feedback. Only student-authored sentences are included in the derivation of key phrases and sentences. Non-sentential components like tables of contents, headings, table entries, and captions are also excluded from the calculations, because they are not true sentences and are unsuitable for inclusion in the extractive summary. (8)Some observations about the structure of the essay are used in the feedback, for example, how many of the key

[1]The stop words are removed prior to the construction of the key word and key sentence graphs, but when the key sentences are presented to the student, they look exactly as they appear in the original text.

sentences are in the introduction and conclusion sections, and how the key words are distributed across the different sections of the essay.

Previous work on automatic essay structure recognition includes by Burstein and Marcu (2003) and Crossley et al. (2011). The former work was concerned with recognising 'initial', 'middle', and 'final' paragraphs, and found that these types of paragraph can be recognised from their linguistic features as automatically identified by Coh-Metrix (Graesser et al., 2004). The latter concerns identifying thesis and conclusion statements in essays using Bayesian classification.

Our own structure recognition is currently achieved through manually-crafted inference rules that have been developed through experimentation with a corpus of 135 university student essays.[2] Each sentence of the essay is labelled according to its role in the essay's structure. The structural components that the system currently attempts to recognise include the following: title, introduction, discussion, conclusion, heading, figure, bibliography, preface, summary, table of contents, quoted word count, afterword, appendices, sentences quoted from the assignment question.

3.2 Key word extraction

(19)Once each sentence of the essay has been labelled with its structural role, the key words are extracted. The 'key-ness' of key words can be thought of as 'importance' or 'significance'. Formally, key-ness aligns with centrality, as in the centrality of a node in a graph. The centrality of a node tells you, roughly speaking, how strongly connected a particular node is to the whole graph—here, how strongly connected a word is to the whole text. Top-scoring words ranked in this way turn out to be highly suggestive of a text's content. This has been verified by a formal evaluation carried out by Mihalcea & Tarau (2004).

To compute the words' key-ness values, each lemma as derived from the essay's surface form is represented by a node in a graph, co-occurrence relations (specifically, within-sentence word adjacency) are represented by edges in the graph, and a centrality algorithm is used to calculate the key-ness (centrality) score of each lemma. We have experimented with betweenness centrality (Freeman, 1977) and PageRank (Brin and Page, 1998) (see section 5.2).

[2]These essays were submitted for the same module that will be targeted for a full empirical evaluation of openEssayist in September 2013.

essay,	word,	use,	key,
system,	sentence,	lemma,	student,
summary,	user,	score,	pagerank,
feedback,	openessayist,	betweenness,	

Table 1: This paper's ranked key lemmas

(key, lemmas, 17),	(key, words, 15),
(key, word, 10),	(key, sentences, 9),
(key, sentence, 4),	(betweenness, scores, 2),
(key, lemma, 2),	(using, betweenness, 1),
(betweenness, lemmas, 1),	(student, using, 1),
(student, essays, 1),	(essays, using, 1),
(using, summaries, 1),	(feedback, system, 1)

Table 2: This paper's bigrams

Since a centrality score is attributed to every lemma in the essay, a decision needs to be made as to what proportion of the essay's lemmas qualify as *key* lemmas. (14)Using manual observations of the distribution of key lemma scores for all essays, we currently define key lemmas as those in the top 20% of the ranked nodes that have a centrality score of .03 or more. Table 1 shows the key lemmas extracted by the program from the final draft of this paper in descending rank order of centrality (reading from left to right).

After the key lemmas have been calculated, key *phrases* are derived by finding within-sentence sequences of key *words* occurring in the original text. The essay's key *words* are the inflections and base forms of the key lemmas, as found in the original surface form. Table 2 shows the bigrams from this paper in descending order of frequency.

3.3 Key sentence extraction

A graph-based ranking method is also used to derive key-ness scores for entire sentences. First, every true sentence (not headings, not captions, not references...) is represented by a node in the graph. Each sentence is then compared to every other sentence and a value is derived representing the semantic similarity of each pair of sentences. The similarity measure we are currently using is cosine similarity, which is a vector space model much used for measuring the similarity of a pair of terms since (Salton et al., 1975). For sentences whose similarity value is greater than 0, the similarity value becomes a weight that attaches to the edge that links the corresponding nodes in the key sentence graph. These 'edge weights', are then used in the TextRank algorithm to rank the sentences according to key-ness.

As with key words, no threshold is set by the ranking algorithm to define where in the ranking key-ness ends. Currently we set the number of key sentences to be the top 17 ranked sentences. This value takes into account the mean average number of sentences in the essays in our corpus (65) and the fact that summaries are by definition short.

To illustrate, the top twenty key sentences of this paper as identified by the system have been labelled with sentence-initial superscript numbers (signifying the rank) in parentheses.[3]

4 Front end

At the front end of the openEssayist system (see (Labeke et al., 2013)), the student pastes her essay into an online form, and a UTF-8-encoded version of the essay is passed to the linguistic engine. This version of the essay preserves the words and the sentence and paragraph structure of the text, but all formatting and graphics are lost. openEssayist analyses the submitted text and presents key words and phrases to the student using different external representations, including a list, a word cloud (see Figure 1[4]), and a diagram showing their distribution across the essay. Students are invited by the system orchestration to reflect on whether they agree that the key lemmas are representative of the messages they intended their essay to convey, and they are invited to explore the key words by grouping them into themes (using drag-and-drop), and adding new key words. The student's key sentences are presented to the student in a list. The system orchestration asks whether the student thinks the extracted sentences constitute a good summary of the essay, whether important ideas are missing from the summary, and other questions. A 'mash-up' is also presented, in which the student can opt to view key words or key sentences highlighted in context.

[3]The actual input .txt file used (converted from the .pdf) and fuller output from the program will be viewable at conference time at:
http://www.cs.ox.ac.uk/people/debora.field/did_i_really_mean_that.txt

[4]The size of the words and phrases is proportional to their frequency.

Figure 1: Key word cloud

5 Informal Evaluation

We have carried out three informal evaluations of the linguistic engine with respect to key word extraction, as follows.

5.1 Predict abstract's terms from a paper

We evaluated the system on 33 journal papers copied and pasted from an online science journal. We used *Journal of the Royal Society Interface* and took the January and February 2012 issues, which at the time happened to be the most recent free full issues that could be downloaded.[5] We deliberately chose a very different domain from that of our essay corpus so as to emphasise the non-reliance of the linguistic analysis on any domain-specific information. We used the program exactly as described in this paper, and derived the percentage of an article's identified key lemmas that also occurred in the lemmas of the same article's abstract. (The abstract and the journal-assigned key words for each article were excluded from the derivation of key lemmas.) The range was 31.8% to 82.6%, with a median average of 57.2% and 0.25, 0.5 and .75 quantiles of 50.0%, 59.2% and 65.4% respectively. We were encouraged to find that what we deemed to be good proportions of the identified key lemmas appeared in the abstracts.

5.2 Comparison of centrality algorithms

In a second evaluation, we applied the abstracts evaluation described above to comparing the betweenness and PageRank centrality algorithms.

[5] http://rsif.royalsocietypublishing.org/content/by/year/2012

No. key lemmas	5	10	20
Betweenness mean	82.558	71.913	60.281
PageRank mean	77.394	69.648	58.832
Betweenness median	70.000	70.000	57.500
PageRank median	70.000	70.000	54.850

Table 3: Key word algorithm scores comparison

model,	epidemic,	parameter,	disease,
cholera,	network,	value,	node,
case,	individual,	mobility,	figure,
rate,	water,	condition,	assume,
pattern,	outbreak,	use,	thus

Table 4: Cholera paper: PageRank key lemmas

We ran the program on the same set of journal papers, and looked at the results for the top 5, 10 and 20 key lemmas (see Table 3). We observed that betweenness outperformed PageRank, in that it was better at predicting which lemmas would be in a paper's abstract in all these three cases.

The difference in the scores is small, but its significance becomes clearer when the data is qualitatively examined. Consider, for example, the top 20 PageRank key lemmas (see Table 4) for a paper about cholera and the corresponding betweenness key lemmas (Table 5). The lemma 'pattern' occurs in the PageRank top 20 lemmas, but not in the betweenness top 20. In the surface text, 'pattern' frequently occurs immediately following 'mobility' (8 times). Notably, 'mobility' is also a key lemma for both algorithms. Pagerank has promoted 'pattern', because 'mobility', which is frequently adjacent to 'pattern' in the paper, has a high centrality score. In contrast, betweenness does not promote a node's score if it has a high-scoring neighbour. 'Pattern' ranks 16th in the PageRank scores and 32nd in the betweenness scores.

We first noted this promotion in the ranking of a word by its adjacent word in an essay about the Open University. PageRank returned 'open' ranked 7th, and betweenness ranked it 26th. In the essay, 'open' appeared preceding 'university' 22 out of 25 times (88%), Whereas 'university' appeared immediately following 'open' 15 times out of 24 (62.5%). 'Open' has been promoted by the high score of its neighbour 'university'.

model,	cholera,	epidemic,	parameter,
disease,	node,	network,	use,
water,	local,	human,	mobility,
kzn,	figure,	value,	case,
assume,	individual,	condition,	epidemiological,
thus,	community		

Table 5: Cholera paper: betweenness key lemmas

One might think these observations suggest that PageRank would be a better algorithm for identifying key n-grams, whereas betweenness might be better for identifying individual key words. However, the most frequent key bigram according to betweenness is 'human mobility' (19 occurrences), which does not appear at all in the PageRank bigrams, owing to the absence of 'human' from the PageRank key lemmas. 'Human' ranks 34th in the PageRank lemmas, whereas it ranks 10th in the betweenness lemmas.

5.3 Comparison with the null model of random word order

We further examined the difference between Pagerank and betweenness scores by comparing, for one essay, each word's scores with a null model distribution of scores generated from multiple 'bootstrapped' randomised word order versions of the essay. We reasoned, since the key word algorithms rely on word adjacency relations, the randomisations should provide us with an expected distribution of scores independent of word ordering with which to compare key word results. We obtained *expected* centrality scores for 200 randomised versions, and for the *real* essay; to determine differences, significance was set at 95%.

In the betweenness results, six of the 30 top-scoring key words had real scores significantly greater than the null model, and none of the real scores was significantly less than the null model. In the PageRank results, three of the 30 top-scoring key words had real scores significantly greater than the null model, but four of the real scores were significantly less. Three of those words occurred in the text adjacent to a word which received a higher PageRank score, and the fourth also had an adjacent key word, though slightly lower-ranking. This experiment, therefore, illustrated by a different method the influence of neighbouring nodes in the PageRank algorithm, and it also raised further suspicions that PageRank might not be the most appropriate centrality algorithm for key word and key phrase extraction.

6 General conclusions

Supervised user testing of the system has recently begun. One user was surprised at the first eight key lemmas identified by the system, saying, “it's only when we get to ‘education’, [the ninth key lemma] ‘learning’, [tenth...] ‘experience’, ‘user’, those are the things that seem a bit more like what I thought it was about”. Key lemma results that surprise the user are invaluable for reflection purposes, as they strongly suggest that the main themes of the text are not the ones the student intended. The same user was also surprised at the system's decision concerning where the introduction ended. The user was encouraged to reflect on why the system might have misidentified his introduction. He said, “erm, arguably there's not a very good introduction, maybe it would be the first, erm, like, three paragraphs. It's certainly not this one here [pointing to the part identified by the system as the introduction]”. He was beginning to consider that a human might also have difficulty recognising his introduction. The user also thought that the 15 key sentences were not representative of his intended messages, and he was disarmed to find only one of the key sentences in the conclusion, explaining that his conclusion expressed the main messages of his essay, and everything that preceded it was building up to a “crescendo” at the end. Clearly the system was provoking the user to reflect on essay characteristics in general, and those of his own essay.

It was clear to observers of the session that using the system helped the student to see what his essay's main messages were, and to see that his essay was perhaps not conveying the message that he intended. The user reflected more deeply and carefully on the essay as the session progressed. At the end of the session, this user reported that he enjoyed using the system, and said he thought it would be a valuable tool for essay drafting. This user's reactions were echoed by other users from the testing sessions.

7 Future work

It may be that a different method of key phrase extraction, such as RAKE (Rose et al., 2010), would produce more appropriate results for key n-grams. Roughly speaking, RAKE uses stop words as phrase delimiters, and whole phrases are treated as nodes in the graph, which is quite a different approach from TextRank. In RAKE, however, the score of a node depends on its degree (its immediately neighbouring nodes), so it is more similar to PageRank than betweenness.

We will therefore shortly be carrying out a formal evaluation comparing the performance of betweenness, PageRank, and RAKE with regard to key lemmas, key words, and n-grams of different lengths. As there is a very strong relationship between word frequency and word centrality, we will also be comparing the results with straight frequency counts. The results will inform the design of our prototype. For now, we are using betweenness for key word extraction.

An adaptation we are considering in the key word analysis is to merge key phrases in which the head words are semantically related, *e.g.*, by hyponymy, using WordNet or similar.

We are intending to experiment with alternative sentence similarity measures, including vector space measures of word similarity originally described in (Schütze, 1998).

We intend to add a second dimension to the linguistic engine's capabilities: to train a classifier to recognise each place in an essay where feedback that falls into a particular category (as proposed by (Nelson and Schunn, 2009)) might be helpful for the student. Then we will employ natural language generation technology informed by research into formative feedback to generate an appropriate feedback comment wherever in-line opportunities for feedback are identified by the system.

We are planning two empirical educational evaluations of openEssayist, which will take place in September 2013 and February 2014, targeting two different Master's degree modules. The participants will be asked to work on two essays within the openEssayist environment. A third and final essay will be used as a reference point to see if the grades of the students who used openEssayist are higher than for their earlier two essays. Participants will also be encouraged to submit multiple pre-final drafts to the system. We will interview selected participants about their learning experience with openEssayist and we will also obtain judgements from experienced tutors as to the quality of the different essays submitted.

Acknowledgments

This work was supported by the Engineering and Physical Sciences Research Council (grant numbers EP/J005959/1 and EP/J005231/1).

References

Steven Bird, Ewan Klein, and Edward Loper. 2009. *Natural Language Processing with Python: Analyzing Text with the Natural Language Toolkit*. O'Reilly, Beijing.

Sergey Brin and Lawrence Page. 1998. The anatomy of a large-scale hypertextual web search engine. In *Seventh InternationalWorld-WideWeb Conference (WWW 1998)*, Brisbane, Australia, April.

Jill Burstein and Daniel Marcu. 2003. A machine learning approach for identification of thesis and conclusion statements in student essays. *Computers and the Humanities*, 37(4):455–467.

Jill Burstein, Martin Chodorow, and Claudia Leacock. 2003. CriterionSM online essay evaluation: An application for automated evaluation of student essays. In J. Riedl and R. Hill, editors, *Proceedings of the Fifteenth Conference on Innovative Applications of Artificial Intelligence*, pages 3–10, Cambridge, MA. MIT Press.

Chi-Fen Emily Chen and Wei-Yuan Eugene Cheng. 2008. Beyond the design of automated writing evaluation: Pedagogical practices and perceived learning effectiveness in EFL writing classes. *Language Learning and Technology*, 12(2):94–112.

Scott A. Crossley, Kyle Dempsey, and Danielle S. McNamara. 2011. Classifying paragraph types using linguistic features: Is paragraph positioning important? *Journal of Writing Research*, 3(2):119–143.

Jianmin Dai, Roxanne B. Raine, Rod D. Roscoe, Zhiqiang Cai, and Danielle S. McNamara. 2011. The Writing-Pal tutoring system: Development and design. *Journal of Engineering and Computer Innovations*, 2(1):1–11. ISSN 2141-6508 2011 Academic Journals.

Güneş Erkan and R. Radev Dragomir. 2004. LexRank: Graph-based lexical centrality as salience in text summarization. *Journal of Artificial Intelligence Research*, 22(1):457–479.

Marita Franzke and Lynn A. Streeter. 2006. Building student summarization, writing and reading comprehension skills with guided practice and automated feedback. White paper, Pearson Knowledge Technologies. Accessed: 14 May, 2013.

Linton C. Freeman. 1977. A set of measures of centrality based on betweenness. *Sociometry*, 40:35–41.

Arthur C. Graesser, Danielle S. McNamara, Max Louwerse, and Zhiqiang Cai. 2004. Coh-Metrix: Analysis of text on cohesion and language. *Behavior Research Methods, Instruments, and Computers*, 36:193–202.

Nicolas Van Labeke, Denise Whitelock, Debora Field, Stephen Pulman, and John T. Richardson. 2013. What is my essay really saying? Using extractive summarization to motivate reflection and redrafting. In *Proceedings of Formative Feedback in Interactive Learning Environments: A Workshop at the 16th International Conference on Artificial Intelligence in Education (AIED 2013)*, Memphis, Tennessee, USA, July. To appear.

Thomas K. Landauer, Darrell Laham, and Peter W. Foltz. 2003. Automatic essay assessment. *Assessment in Education: Principles, Policy and Practice*, 10(3):295–308.

Elijah Mayfield and Carolyn Penstein Rosé. 2013. LightSIDE: Open source machine learning for text. In Mark D. Shermis and Jill Burstein, editors, *Handbook of Automated Essay Assessment Evaluation*, pages 124–135. Taylor and Francis.

Danielle S. McNamara, Roxanne Raine, Rod Roscoe, Scott Crossley, G. Tanner Jackson, Jianmin Dai, Zhiqiang Cai, Adam Renner, Russell Brandon, Jennifer Weston, Kyle Dempsey, Diana Lam, Susan Sullivan, Loel Kim, Vasile Rus, Randy Floyd, Philip McCarthy, and Art Graesser. 2011. The Writing-Pal: Natural language algorithms to support intelligent tutoring on writing strategies. In P.M. McCarthy and Chutima Boonthum-Denecke, editors, *Applied Natural Language Processing and Content Analysis: Advances in Identification, Investigation and Resolution*, pages 298–311. IGI Global, Hershey, PA.

Rada Mihalcea and Paul Tarau. 2004. TextRank: Bringing order into texts. In Dekang Lin and Dekai Wu, editors, *Proceedings of Empirical Methods in Natural Language Processing (EMNLP) 2004*, pages 404–411, Barcelona, Spain, July. Association for Computational Linguistics.

Melissa M. Nelson and Christian D. Schunn. 2009. The nature of feedback: how different types of peer feedback affect writing performance. *Instructional Science*, 37:375–401.

John T.E. Richardson. 2012. The attainment of white and ethnic minority students in distance education. *Assessment and Evaluation in Higher Education*, 37:393–408.

Stuart Rose, Dave Engel, Nick Cramer, and Wendy Cowley. 2010. Automatic keyword extraction from individual documents. In M.W. Berry and J. Kogan, editors, *Text Mining: Applications and Theory*, pages 1–20, Chichester. John Wiley and Sons, Ltd. doi: 10.1002/9780470689646.ch1.

Lawrence M. Rudner, Veronica Garcia, and Catherine Welch. 2006. An evaluation of the IntelliMetricSM essay scoring system. *The Journal of Technology, Learning, and Assessment*, 4(4).

Gerard M. Salton, Andrew K. C. Wong, and Chung-Shu Yang. 1975. A vector space model for automatic indexing. *Communications of the ACM*, 18(11):613–620.

Hinrich Schütze. 1998. Automatic word sense discrimination. *Computational Linguistics*, 24(1):97–123.

Ormond Simpson. 2012. *Supporting students for success in online and distance education.* Routledge, London, third edition.

Ian H. Witten, Gordon W. Paynter, Eibe Frank, Carl Gutwin, and Craig G. Nevill-Manning. 1998. Kea: Practical automatic keyphrase extraction. In *Proceedings of the 4Th ACM Conference on Digital Libraries*, pages 254–255.

Matching sets of parse trees for answering multi-sentence questions

Boris Galitsky
Knowledge Trail Inc. San Jose
USA
bgalitsky@hotmail.com

Dmitry Ilvovsky, Sergey Kuznetsov, Fedor Strok
Higher School of Economics, Moscow Russia
dilv_ru@yahoo.com;
skuznetsov@hse.ru;
fdr.strok@gmail.com

Abstract

The problem of answering multi-sentence questions is addressed in a number of products and services-related domains. A candidate set of answers, obtained by a keyword search, is re-ranked by matching the set of parse trees of an answer with that of the question. To do that, a graph representation and learning technique for parse structures for paragraphs of text have been developed. Parse Thicket (PT) as a set of syntactic parse trees augmented by a number of arcs for inter-sentence word-word relations such as co-reference and taxonomic relations is introduced. These arcs are also derived from other sources, including Speech Act and Rhetoric Structure theories. The proposed approach is subject to evaluation in the product search and recommendation domain, where search queries include multiple sentences. An open source plugin for SOLR is developed so that the proposed technology can be easily integrated with industrial search engines.

1 Introduction

Modern search engines are not very good at tackling queries consisting of multiple sentences. They either find very similar documents, if they are available, or very dissimilar ones, so that search results are not very useful to the user. This is due to the fact that for multi-sentences queries it is rather hard to learn ranking based on user clicks, since the number of longer queries is practically unlimited. Hence we need a linguistic technology, which would rank candidate answers based on structural similarity between the question and the answer. In this study we build a graph-based representation for a paragraph of text so that we can track the structural difference between these paragraphs, taking into account not only parse trees, but the whole discourse as well.

Paragraphs of text as queries appear in the search-based recommendation domains (Montaner et al., 2003; Bhasker and Srikumar 2010; Thorsten, 2012). Recommendation agents track user chats, user postings on blogs and forums, user comments on shopping sites, and suggest web documents and their snippets, relevant to a purchase decisions. To do that, these recommendation agents need to take portions of text, produce a search engine query, run it against a search engine API such as Bing or Yahoo, and filter out the search results which are determined to be irrelevant to a purchase decision. The last step is critical for a sensible functionality of a recommendation agent, and poor relevance would lead to a lost trust in the recommendation engine. Hence an accurate assessment of similarity between two portions of text is critical to a successful use of recommendation agents.

Parse trees have become a standard form of representing the syntactic structures of sentences (Abney, 1991; Punyakanok *et al.*, 2005; Domingos and Poon, 2009). In this study we will attempt to represent a linguistic structure of a paragraph of text based on parse trees for each sentence of this paragraph. We will refer to the set of parse trees plus a number of arcs for inter-sentence relations between nodes for words as *Parse Thicket* (PT). A PT is a graph, which includes parse trees for each sentence, as well as additional arcs for inter-sentence relationship between parse tree nodes for words.

We define the operation of generalization of text paragraphs via generalization of respective PTṡ to assess similarity between them. The use of generalization for similarity assessment is inspired by structural approaches to machine learning (Mill, 1843; Mitchell, 1997; Furukawa 1998; Finn, 1999) versus statistical alternatives where similarity is measured by a distance in feature space (Fukunaga, 1990; Manning and

Schütze, 1999; Byun and Lee, 2002; Jurafsky and Martin, 2008). Our intention is to extend the operation of least general generalization (e.g., the antiunification of logical formulas (Robinson, 1965; Plotkin, 1970)) towards structural representations of paragraph of texts to compute similarity between multi-sentence questions and answers. Hence we define the operation of generalization on a pair of PT as finding the maximal common sub-thickets based on generalizing phrases from two paragraphs of text.

Generalization of text paragraphs is based on the operation of generalization of two sentences, explored in a few studies (Galitsky *et al.*, 2008; Galitsky, 2012). In addition to learning generalizations of individual sentences, we learn how the links between words in sentences other than syntactic ones can be used to compute similarity between texts. We rely on our formalizations of the theories of textual discourse such as *Rhetoric Structure Theory* (Mann et al., 1992) to improve the ranking of paragraph-based question answering.

Whereas machine learning of syntactic parse trees for individual sentences is an established area of research, the contribution of this paper is a structural approach to learning syntactic information at the level of paragraphs. A number of studies applied machine learning techniques to syntactic parse trees (Collins and Duffy, 2002), convolution kernels (Haussler, 1999) being the most popular approach (Lodhi *et al.*, 2002; Moschitti, 2006; Zhang *et al.*, 2008, Zhang *et al.*, 2008, Sun *et al.*, 2010).

2 Parse Thickets for matching questions and answers

Once we have a sequence of parse trees for a question, and that of an answer, how can we match these sequences? A number of studies compute pair-wise similarity between parse trees (Collins and Duffy, 2002; Punyakanok *et al.*, 2003; Moschitti, 2006). However, to rely upon discourse structure of paragraphs, and to avoid dependence of how content is distributed through sentences, we represent the whole paragraphs of questions and answers as a single graph and call it Parse Thicket (PT). To determine how good is an answer for a question, we match their respective PTs.

We extend the syntactic relations between the nodes of the syntactic dependency parse trees towards more general text discourse relations. Once we have such relations as "the same entity", "sub-entity", "super-entity" and anaphora, we can extend the notion of phrase to be matched between texts. In case of single sentences, we match noun, verb, and other types of phrases in questions and answers. In case of multiple sentences in each, we extend the notion of phrases so that they are independent of how information being communicated is split into sentences. Relations between the nodes of parse trees (which are other than syntactic) can merge phrases from different sentences or from a single sentence, which are not syntactically connected. We will refer to such extended phrases as thicket phrases.

We will consider two cases for text indexing, where establishing proper coreferences inside and between sentences connects entities in an index for proper match with a question:

Text for indexing 1: … *Tuberculosis is usually a lung disease. It is cured by doctors specializing in pulmonology.*

Text for indexing 2: … *Tuberculosis is a lung disease… Pulmonology specialist Jones was awarded a prize for curing a special form of disease.*

Question: *Which specialist doctor should treat my tuberculosis?*

In the first case, establishing coreference link *Tuberculosis* → *disease* → *is cured by doctors pulmonologists* helps to match these entities with the ones from the question. In the second case this portion of text does not serve as a relevant answer to the question, although it includes keywords from this question. Hence at indexing time, keywords should be chained not just by their occurrence in individual sentences, but additionally on the basis of coreferences. If words X and Y are connected by a coreference relation, an index needs to include the chain of words $X_0, X_1 \ldots X, Y_0, Y_1 \ldots Y$, where chains $X_0, X_1 \ldots X$ and $Y_0, Y_1 \ldots Y$ are already indexed (phrases including X and Y). Hence establishing coreferences is important to extend index in a way to improve search recall. Usually, keywords from different sentences can only be matched with query keywords with a low score (high score is delivered by inter-sentence match).

If we have two parse trees P_1 and P_2 of text T_1, and an arc for a relation $r: P_{1j} \rightarrow P_{2j}$ between the nodes P_{1j} and P_{2j}, we can now match $\ldots, P_{1i-2}, P_{1i-1}, P_{1i}, P_{2j}, P_{2j+1}, P_{2j+2}, \ldots$ of T_1 against a phrase of a single sentence or a merged phrases of multiple sentences from T_2.

2.1 Finding similarity between a question and an answer

We will compare the following approaches to assessing the similarity of questions and answers as paragraphs:

- Baseline: bag-of-words approach, which computes the set of common keywords/n-grams and their frequencies.
- Pair-wise matching: we will apply syntactic generalization to each pair of sentences, and sum up the resultant commonalities. This technique has been developed by Galitsky (2013).
- Paragraph-paragraph matching.

The first approach is most typical for industrial NLP applications today, and the second one was used in (Galitsky *et al.*, 2012). The kernel-based approach to parse tree similarities (Zhang *et al.*, 2008), as well as tree sequence kernel (Sun *et al.*, 2011), being tuned to parse trees of individual sentences, also belongs to the second approach.

We intend to demonstrate the richness of the approach being proposed, and in the consecutive sections we will provide a step-by-step explanation. We will introduce a pair of short texts (articles) and compare the above three approaches. The first paragraph can be viewed as a search query, and the second paragraph can be viewed as a candidate answer. A relevant answer should be a closely related text, which is not a piece of duplicate information.

"Iran refuses to accept the UN proposal to end the dispute over work on nuclear weapons",
"UN nuclear watchdog passes a resolution condemning Iran for developing a second uranium enrichment site in secret",
"A recent IAEA report presented diagrams that suggested Iran was secretly working on nuclear weapons",
"Iran envoy says its nuclear development is for peaceful purpose, and the material evidence against it has been fabricated by the US",
^
"UN passes a resolution condemning the work of Iran on nuclear weapons, in spite of Iran claims that its nuclear research is for peaceful purpose",
"Envoy of Iran to IAEA proceeds with the dispute over its nuclear program and develops an enrichment site in secret",
"Iran confirms that the evidence of its nuclear weapons program is fabricated by the US and proceeds with the second uranium enrichment site"

The list of common keywords gives a hint that both documents are on nuclear program of Iran, however it is hard to get more specific details.

Iran, UN, proposal, dispute, nuclear, weapons, passes, resolution, developing, enrichment, site, secret, condemning, second, uranium

Pair-wise generalization gives a more accurate account on what is common between these texts.

[NN-work IN-* IN-on JJ-nuclear NNS-weapons], [DT-the NN-dispute IN-over JJ-nuclear NNS-*], [VBZ-passes DT-a NN-resolution],
[VBG-condemning NNP-iran IN-*],
[VBG-developing DT-* NN-enrichment NN-site IN-in NN-secret]],
[DT-* JJ-second NN-uranium NN-enrichment NN-site]],
[VBZ-is IN-for JJ-peaceful NN-purpose],
[DT-the NN-evidence IN-* PRP-it], [VBN-* VBN-fabricated IN-by DT-the NNP-us]

Parse Thicket generalization gives the detailed similarity picture which looks more complete than the pair-wise sentence generalization result above. Please see also Fig. 3.

[NN-Iran VBG-developing DT-* NN-enrichment NN-site IN-in NN-secret]
[NN-generalization-<UN/nuclear watchdog> * VB-pass NN-resolution VBG condemning NN- Iran]
[NN-generalization-<Iran/envoy of Iran> Communicative_action DT-the NN-dispute IN-over JJ-nuclear NNS-*
[Communicative_action - NN-work IN-of NN-Iran IN-on JJ-nuclear NNS-weapons]
[NN-generalization <Iran/envoy to UN> Communicative_action NN-Iran NN-nuclear NN-* VBZ-is IN-for JJ-peaceful NN-purpose],
Communicative_action - NN-generalize <work/develop> IN-of NN-Iran IN-on JJ-nuclear NNS-weapons]*
[NN-generalization <Iran/envoy to UN> Communicative_action NN-evidence IN-against NN Iran NN-nuclear VBN-fabricated IN-by DT-the NNP-us]
condemn^proceed [enrichment site] <leads to> suggest^condemn [work Iran nuclear weapon]

"^" in the following example and through all the paper means *generalization* operation. Describing parse trees we use standard notation for constituency trees: **[...]** represents subphraze, **NN**, **JJ**, **NP** etc. denote parts-of-speech and types of subphrases, ***** is used to denote random tree node.

One can feel that PT-based generalization almost as complete as human would do in terms of similarity between texts. To obtain these results, we need to be capable of maintaining connections between sentences such as coreferences, and also of apply the relationships between entities to our analysis (entities, sub-entities, super-entities) obtained from WordNet or via web mining (Galitsky et al 2013). We also need to be able to identify communicative actions and generalize them together with their subjects according to the specific patterns of speech act theory, if a text describes an interaction between people. Moreover, we need to maintain rhetoric structure relationship between sentences, to generalize at a higher level above sentences irrespectively of how information is distributed through sentences. We define Parse Thicket as a set of parse trees for sentences with arcs for links between the words of different sentences. These arcs are for coreferences, entity-entity and rhetoric relations, and communicative actions.

The focus of this paper is to apply parse thickets and their generalization to search relevance where a query is a paragraph of text.

2.2 From phrase to paragraph-level generalization

Although the generalization is defined as the set of maximal common sub-graphs, its computation in this study is based on matching phrases. To generalize a pair of sentences, we perform chunking and extract all noun, verb, prepositional and other types of phrases from each sentence. Then we perform generalization for each type of phrases, attempting to find a maximal common sub-phrase for each pair of phrases of the same type. The resultant phrase-level generalization can then be interpreted as a set of paths in resultant common sub-trees (Galitsky *et al.*, 2012).

Thicket phrases are the regular phrases extended by the words from other sentences linked by inter-sentence arcs. The algorithm of forming thicket phrases is as follows. Most types of thicket arcs will be illustrated below. Please refer to (Galitsky *et al.*, 2012) for further details.

For each sentence S in a paragraph P:

1 Form a list of previous sentences in a paragraph S_{prev}

2 For each word in the current sentence:

2.1 If this word is a *pronoun*: find all nouns or noun phrases in the S_{prev} which are:

- The same entities (via anaphora resolution)

2.2 If this word is a *noun*: find all nouns or noun phrases in the S_{prev} which are:

- The same entities (via anaphora resolution)
- Synonymous entity
- Super entities
- Sub and sibling entities

2.3 If this word is a *verb*:

2.3.1 If it is a *communicative action*:

2.3.1.1 Form the phrase for its subject $VBCA_{phrase}$, including its verb phrase VB_{phrase}

2.3.1.2 Find a preceding communicative action $VBCA_{phrase0}$ from S_{prev} with its subject

2.3.1.3 Form a thicket phrase [$VBCA_{phrase}$, $VBCA_{phrase0}$]

2.3.2 If it indicates *RST relation*:

2.3.2.1 Form the phrase for the pair of phrases which are the subjects [VBRSTphrase1, VBRSTphrase2], of this RST relation, VBRSTphrase1 belongs to S_{prev}.

3 Arcs of parse thicket based on theories of discourse

We treat computationally the following approaches to textual discourse:

- Rhetoric structure theory (RST) (Mann *et al.*, 1992);
- Speech Act theory or shortly SpActT (Searle, 1969).

Although both these theories have psychological observation as foundations and are mostly of a non-computational nature, a specific computational framework need to be built for them (Galitsky *et al.*, 2010; 2013a). We use these sources to find links between sentences to enhance indexing for search. For RST, we attempt to extract an RST relation and form a thicket phrase around it, including a placeholder for RST relation itself. For SpActT, we use a vocabulary of *communicative actions* to find their subjects (Galitsky and Kuznetsov, 2008), add respective arcs to PT and form the respective set of thicket phrases.

RST example

Fig.1 shows the generalization instance based on RST relation "RCT-evidence" (Marcu, 1997). This relation occurs between the phrases *evidence-for-what [Iran's nuclear weapon program]* and *what-happens-with-evidence [Fabricated by USA]*
and *evidence-for-what [against Iran's nuclear development]* and *what-happens-with-evidence [Fabricated by the USA]*.

Notice that in the latter case we need to merge (perform anaphora substitution) the phrase *' its nuclear development'* with *'evidence against it'* to obtain *'evidence against its nuclear development'*. Notice the arc *it - development*, according to which this anaphora substitution occurred. *Evidence* is removed from the phrase because it is the indicator of RST relation, and we form the subject of this relation to match. Furthermore, we need another anaphora substitution *its* - *Iran* to obtain the final phrase.

As a result of generalizations of two RST relations of the same sort (evidence) we obtain *Iran nuclear NNP – RST-evidence – fabricate by USA*.

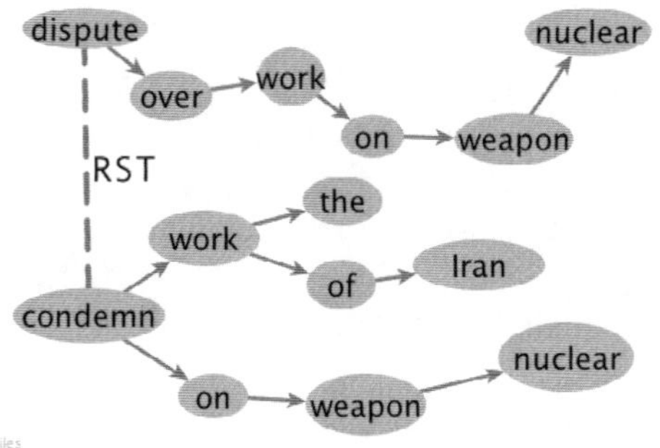

Fig.1: An example of the mapping for the rhetoric structures

Notice that we could not obtain this similarity expression by using sentence-level generalization.

Communicative actions example

Communicative actions are used by text authors to indicate the structure of a dialogue or a conflict (Searle, 1969). Hence analyzing the communicative actions' arcs of PT, one can find implicit similarities between texts. We can generalize:

- one communicative actions with its subject from T_1 against another communicative action with its subject from T_2 (communicative action arc is not used) ;
- a pair of communicative actions with their subjects from T_1 against another pair of communicative actions from T_2 (communicative action arcs are used).

In our example, we have the same communicative actions with subjects with low similarity:

condemn ['Iran for developing second enrichment site in secret'] vs condemn ['the work of Iran on nuclear weapon']

or different communicative actions with similar subjects.

The two distinct communicative actions dispute and condemn have rather similar subjects: 'work on nuclear weapon'. Generalizing two communicative actions with their subjects follows the rule: generalize communicative actions themselves, and 'attach' the result to generalization of their subjects as regular sub-tree generalization. Two communicative actions can always be generalized, which is not the case for their subjects: if their generalization result is empty, the generalization result of communicative actions with these subjects is empty too. The generalization result here for the case 1 above is:

condemn^dispute [work-Iran-on-nuclear-weapon].

Generalizing two different communicative actions is based on their attributes and is presented in (Galitsky *et al.*, 2013).

T_1 T_2

condemn [second uranium enrichment site] ↔ proceed [develop an enrichment site in secret]
↓ *communicative action arcs* ↓
suggest [Iran is secretly working on nuclear weapon] ↔ condemn [the work of Iran on nuclear weapon]

which results in *condemn^proceed [enrichment site] <leads to> suggest^condemn [work Iran nuclear weapon]*.

Notice that generalization

condemn [second uranium enrichment site] ↔ condemn [the work of Iran on nuclear weapon]
↓ *communicative action arcs* ↓
suggest [Iran is secretly working on nuclear weapon] ↔ proceed [develop an enrichment site in secret]

gives zero result because the arguments of *condemn* from T_1 and T_2 are not very similar. Hence we generalize the subjects of communicative actions first before we generalize communicative actions themselves.

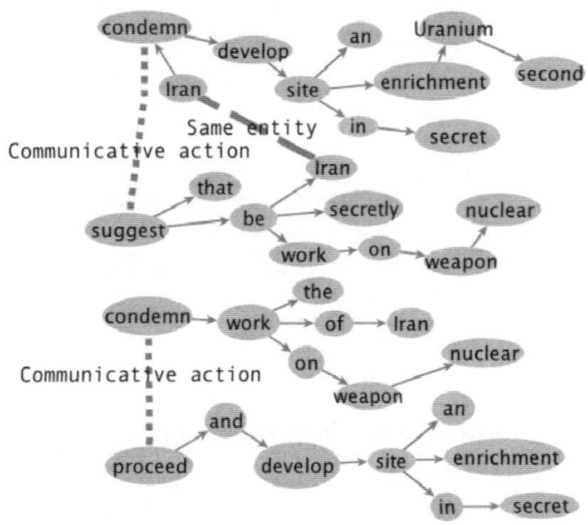

Fig. 2: A fragment of PT showing the mapping for the pairs of communicative actions.

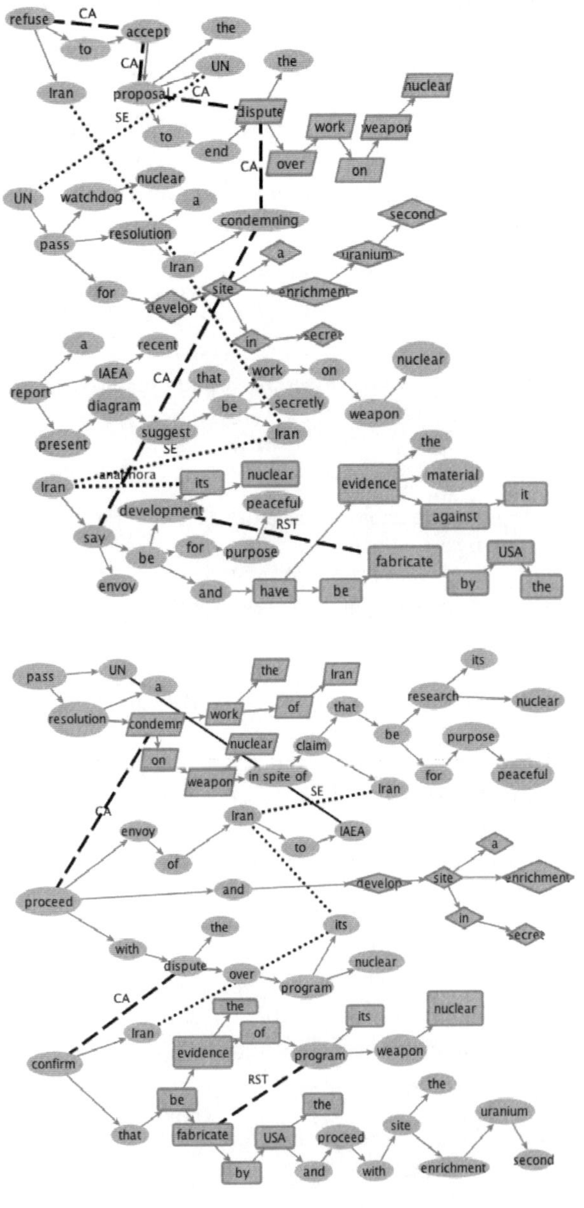

Fig.3: Finding similarity between two parse thickets. Groups of vertices with the same shape and dark-gray border show the maximum common sub-thickets, where the number of vertexes serves as a score for similarity between a question and answer.

3 Evaluation of multi-sentence question answering

We proceed to evaluation of how generalization of PTs can improve multi-sentence search, where one needs to compare a query as a paragraph of text against a candidate answer as a paragraph of text (search result snippet).

Evaluation is based on a re-ranking search results obtained by Bing search engine API, relying on the PT similarity score. The similarity score is defined as a total number of vertexes in a common maximum subgraph. We approximate this estimate by calculating the number of words in maximal common sub-phrases, taking into account weight for parts of speech (Galitsky et al 2012).

Evaluation results are shown in Table 1. Three domains are used in evaluation:

- Product recommendation, where an agent reads chats about products and finds relevant information on the web about a particular product.
- Travel recommendation, where an agent reads chats about travel and finds relevant information on the travel websites about a hotel or an activity.
- Facebook recommendation, where an agent reads wall postings and chats, and finds a piece of relevant information for friends on the web.

In each of these domains we selected a portion of text on the web to form a query, and then filtered search results delivered by Bing search engine API. One can observe that unfiltered precision is 58.2%, whereas improvement by pair-wise sentence generalization is 11%, thicket phrases/snippets – additional 6%, and thicket phrases for original sentences in the documents – additional 1.5%.

One can also see that the higher the complexity of sentence, the higher the contribution of generalization technology, from sentence level to thicket phrases.

4 Algorithms and scalability of the approach

The generalization operation on parse trees for sentences and parse thickets for paragraphs is defined as finding a set of maximum common sub-trees and sub parse thickets respectively. Although for the trees this problem is $O(n)$, for the general case of graphs finding maximal common sub-graphs is NP-complete (Kann, 1992).

To estimate the complexity of generalization of two PT, let us consider an average case with five sentences in each paragraph and 15 words in each sentence. Such thickets have on average 10 phrases per sentence, 10 inter-sentence arcs, which give us up to 40 thicket phrases each.

Query type	Query complexity	Relevance of baseline Bing search, %,	Relevance single-sentence phrase-based generalization search, %,	Relevance of thicket-based phrase generalization search, %, **using snippets**	Relevance of parse thicket-based phrase generalization search, %, **using original sentences**
Product recommendation search	1compound sent	62.3	69.1	72.4	72.9
	2 sent	61.5	70.5	71.9	72.8
	3 sent	59.9	66.2	72.0	73.4
	4 sent	60.4	66	68.5	69.2
Travel recommendation search	1compound	64.8	68	72.6	74.7
	2 sent	60.6	65.8	73.1	76.9
	3 sent	62.3	66.1	70.9	70.8
	4 sent	58.7	65.9	72.5	73.9
Facebo-ok friend agent support search	1compound	54.5	63.2	65.3	68.1
	2 sent	52.3	60.9	62.1	63.7
	3 sent	49.7	57	61.7	63.0
	4 sent	50.9	58.3	62.0	64.6
Avg		58.15	64.75	68.75	70.33

Table 1: Evaluation results

Hence for such parse thickets we have to generalize up to 50 linguistic phrases and 40 thicket phrases of the first thicket against the set of similar size for the second thicket. Taking into account a separate generalization of noun and verb phrases, this average case consists of 2* 45*45 generalizations, followed by the subsumption checks. Each phrase generalization is based on up to 12 string comparisons, taking an average size of phrase as 5 words. Hence on average the PT generalization includes 2*45*45*12*5 operations. Since a string comparison takes a few microseconds, thicket generalization takes on average 100 milliseconds without use of index. However, in an industrial search application where phrases are stored in an inverse index, the generalization operation can be completed in constant time, irrespectively of the size of index (Lin, 2013).

5 Conclusions

In this work we build the framework for generalizing PTs as sets of phrases to re-rank search results obtained via keyword search.

The operation of generalization to learn from parse trees for a pair of sentences turned out to be important for text relevance tasks. Once we extended it to learning parse thickets for two paragraphs, we observed that the relevance is further increased compared to the baseline (Bing search engine API), which relies on keyword statistics in the case of multi-sentence query.

We considered the following sources of relations between words in sentences: coreferences, taxonomic relations such as sub-entity, partial case, predicate for subject etc., rhetoric structure relation and speech acts. We demonstrated that search relevance can be improved if search results are subject to confirmation by parse thicket generalization, when answers occur in multiple sentences.

The system architecture serves as a basis of OpenNLP – similarity component, which is a separate Apache Software foundation project, accepting input from either OpenNLP or Stanford NLP. Code and libraries described here are available at http://code.google.com/p/relevance-based-on-parse-trees and http://svn.apache.org/repos/asf/opennlp/sandbox/opennlp-similarity/.

The system is ready to be plugged into Lucene library to improve search relevance. Also, a SOLR request handler is provided so that search engineers can switch to a PT-based multi-sentence search to quickly verify if relevance is improved. The system is designed for search engineers not familiar with linguistic technologies, who can plug in the richness of linguistic features of OpenNLP and Stanford NLP to work for them in a search application.

References

Galitsky, B. *Natural Language Question Answering System: Technique of Semantic Headers*. Advanced Knowledge International, Australia (2003).

Galitsky, B., Josep Lluis de la Rosa, Gábor Dobrocsi. *Inferring the semantic properties of sentences by mining syntactic parse trees*. Data & Knowledge Engineering. Volume 81-82, November (2012) 21-45.

Galitsky, B., Daniel Usikov, Sergei O. Kuznetsov: *Parse Thicket Representations for Answering Multi-sentence questions*. 20th International Conference on Conceptual Structures, ICCS 2013 (2013).

Galitsky, B., Kuznetsov S.O., *Learning communicative actions of conflicting human agents*. J. Exp. Theor. Artif. Intell. 20(4): 277-317 (2008).

Galitsky, B., Machine Learning of Syntactic Parse Trees for Search and Classification of Text. *Engineering Application of AI*, http://dx.doi.org/10.1016/j.engappai.2012.09.017, (2012).

Jiangning Wu, Zhaoguo Xuan and Donghua Pan, *Enhancing text representation for classification tasks with semantic graph structures*, International Journal of Innovative Computing, Information and Control (ICIC), Volume 7, Number 5(B).

Haussler, D. *Convolution kernels on discrete structures*, 1999.

Moschitti, A. *Efficient Convolution Kernels for Dependency and Constituent Syntactic Trees*. In Proceedings of the 17th European Conference on Machine Learning, Berlin, Germany, 2006.

Mann, William C., Christian M. I. M. Matthiessen and Sandra A. Thompson (1992). *Rhetorical Structure Theory and Text Analysis*. Discourse Description: Diverse linguistic analyses of a fund-raising text. ed. by W. C. Mann and S. A. Thompson. Amsterdam, John Benjamins: 39-78.

Searle, John. 1969. *Speech acts: An essay in the philosophy of language*. Cambridge, England: Cambridge University.

Sun, J., Min Zhang, Chew Lim Tan. *Tree Sequence Kernel for Natural Language*. AAAI-25, 2011.

Zhang, M.; Che, W.; Zhou, G.; Aw, A.; Tan, C.; Liu, T.; and Li, S. 2008. *Semantic role labeling using a grammar-driven convolution tree kernel*. IEEE transactions on audio, speech, and language processing 16(7):1315–1329.

Montaner, M.; Lopez, B.; de la Rosa, J. L. (June 2003). *A Taxonomy of Recommender Agents on the Internet*. Artificial Intelligence Review 19 (4): 285–330.

Collins, M., and Duffy, N. 2002. *Convolution kernels for natural language*. In Proceedings of NIPS, 625–632.

Heeyoung Lee, Angel Chang, Yves Peirsman, Nathanael Chambers, Mihai Surdeanu and Dan Jurafsky. *Deterministic coreference resolution based on entity-centric, precision-ranked rules. Computational Linguistics* 39(4), 2013.

Plotkin, G.D. *A note on inductive generalization*. In B. Meltzer and D. Michie, editors, Machine Intelligence, volume 5, pages 153-163. Elsevier North-Holland, New York, 1970.

Lin, Jimmy. *Data-Intensive Text Processing with MapReduce*. intool.github.io/MapReduceAlgorithms/MapReduce-book-final.pdf , 2013.

Cascading en.wikipedia.org/wiki/Cascading. http://www.cascading.org/ 2013.

Dean, Jeff. *Challenges in Building Large-Scale Information Retrieval Systems*. research.google.com/people/jeff/WSDM09-keynote.pdf 2009.

Viggo Kann. 1992. *On the Approximability of the Maximum Common Subgraph Problem*. In (STACS '92), Alain Finkel and Matthias Jantzen (Eds.). Springer-Verlag, London, UK, UK, 377-388.

Lodhi, H.; Saunders, C.; Shawe-Taylor, J.; Cristianini, N.; and Watkins, C. 2002. *Text classification using string kernels*. The Journal of Machine Learning Research 2:419–444.

Moschitti, A. 2004. *A study on convolution kernels for shallow semantic parsing*. In Proceedings of ACL, 335–342.

Sun, J.; Zhang, M.; and Tan, C. 2010. *Exploring syntactic structural features for sub-tree alignment using bilingual tree kernels*. In Proceedings of ACL, 306–315.

Zhang, M.; Che, W.; Zhou, G.; Aw, A.; Tan, C.; Liu, T.; and Li, S. 2008. *Semantic role labeling using a grammar-driven convolution tree kernel. IEEE transactions on audio, speech,and language processing*. 16(7):1315–1329.

Zhang, M.; Zhou, G.; and Aw, A. 2008. *Exploring syntactic structured features over parse trees for relation extraction using kernel methods*. Information Processing & Management 44(2):687–701.

Byun, H. and Seong-Whan Lee. 2002. *Applications of Support Vector Machines for Pattern Recognition: A Survey*. In Proceedings of the First International Workshop on Pattern Recognition with Support Vector Machines (SVM '02), Seong-Whan Lee and Alessandro Verri (Eds.). Springer-Verlag, London, UK, UK, 213-236.

Manning, C. and Hinrich Schütze, *Foundations of Statistical Natural Language Processing*, MIT Press. Cambridge, MA: May 1999.

Daniel Jurafsky and James H. Martin. *Speech and Language Processing. An Introduction to Natural*

Language Processing, Computational Linguistics, and Speech Recognition. 2008.

OpenNLP http://incubator.apache.org/opennlp/documentation/manual/opennlp.htm (2012).

Robinson J.A. *A machine-oriented logic based on the resolution principle*. Journal of the Association for Computing Machinery, 12:23-41, 1965.

Mill, J.S. (1843) *A system of logic, ratiocinative and inductive*. London.

Fukunaga, K. *Introduction to statistical pattern recognition* (2nd ed.), Academic Press Professional, Inc., San Diego, CA, 1990.

Finn, V.K. (1999) *On the synthesis of cognitive procedures and the problem of induction.* NTI Series 2, N1-2 pp. 8-45.

Mitchell, T. (1997) *Machine Learning*. McGraw Hill.

Furukawa, K. (1998) *From Deduction to Induction: Logical Perspective. The Logic Programming Paradigm.* In Apt, K.R., Marek V.W., Truszczynski, M., Warren, D.S., Eds. Springer.

Bharat Bhasker; K. Srikumar (2010). *Recommender Systems in E-Commerce.* CUP. ISBN 978-0-07-068067-8.

Hennig-Thurau, Thorsten, André Marchand, and Paul Marx. (2012), *Can Automated Group Recommender Systems Help Consumers Make Better Choices?* Journal of Marketing, 76 (5), 89-109.

Punyakanok, V.,Roth, D. and Yih, W. *The Necessity of Syntactic Parsing for Semantic Role Labeling.* IJCAI-05.

Domingos P. and Poon, H. *Unsupervised Semantic Parsing*, In: Proceedings of the 2009 Conference on Empirical Methods in Natural Language Processing, 2009. Singapore: ACL.

Marcu, D. (1997) *From Discourse Structures to Text Summaries*, in I. Mani and M.Maybury (eds) Proceedings of ACL Workshop on Intelligent Scalable Text Summarization, pp. 82–8, Madrid, Spain.

Abney, S. *Parsing by Chunks*, Principle-Based Parsing, Kluwer Academic Publishers, 1991, pp. 257-278.

Realization of Common Statistical Methods in Computational Linguistics with Functional Automata

Stefan Gerdjikov
Faculty of Mathematics and Informatics,
Sofia University
5 James Bourchier blvd.,
1164 Sofia, Bulgaria
st_gerdjikov@abv.bg

Petar Mitankin
Faculty of Mathematics and Informatics,
Sofia University
5 James Bourchier blvd.,
1164 Sofia, Bulgaria
pmitankin@fmi.uni-sofia.bg

Vladislav Nenchev
Faculty of Mathematics and Informatics,
Sofia University
5 James Bourchier blvd.,
1164 Sofia, Bulgaria
lucifer.dev.0@gmail.com

Abstract

In this paper we present the *functional automata* as a general framework for representation, training and exploring of various statistical models as LLM's, HMM's, CRF's, etc.

Our contribution is a new construction that allows the representation of the derivatives of a function given by a functional automaton. It preserves the natural representation of the functions and the standard product and sum operations of real numbers. In the same time it requires no additional overhead for the standard dynamic programming techniques that yield the computation of a functional value.

1 Introduction

Statistical models such as n-gram language models (Chen and Goodman, 1996), hidden Markov models (Rabiner, 1989), conditional random fields (Lafferty et al., 2001), log-linear models (Darroch and Ratcliff, 1972) are widely applied in the natural language processing in order to approach various problems, e.g. parsing (Sha and Pereira, 2003), speech recognition (Juang and Rabiner, 1991), statistical machine translation (Brown et al., 1993). Different statistical models perform differently on different tasks. Thus in order to find the best practical solution one might need to try several approaches before getting the desired effect. Disposing on a general framework that allows the flexibility to change the statistical model or/and training scheme would spend much efforts and time.

Focusing on this pragmatical problem, we propose the *functional automata* as a possible solution. The basic idea is to consider the mathematical expressions of sums and products arising in the statistical models as regular expressions. Thus regarding the functions in these expressions as individual characters, the sums as unions and the products as concatenation, we get the desired correspondence. The relation between a particular statistical model and a functional automaton for its representation is then rather straightforward.

The training of the statistical models is in a way more involved. Most of the approaches require a gradient method that estimates the best model parameters. To this end one needs to have an efficient representation not only of the function used by the model but also of its (partial) derivatives.

To solve similar problem Eisner and Li introduce first-order and second-order expectation semirings. In (Jason Eisner, 2002; Zhifei Li and Jason Eisner, 2009) it is shown how derivatives of functions arising in statistical models can be represented. This is achieved by the means of an algebraic construction that: (i) considers pairs of functions (first-order expectation semiring) and quadruples of functions (second-order expectation semiring); (ii) introduces an operation on pairs and quadruples, respectively, of functions that replaces the multiplication and is used to simulate the multiplication of first- and second-order derivatives, respectively. Thus the higher the order of the derivatives in interest, the more complex would be the necessary expectation semiring and the operations that it would require.

In the current paper we propose an alternative approach. It is based on a combinatorial construction that allows preserving both: (i) manipulation with single functions and (ii) the usage of the standard multiplication and addition of real numbers. Thus we get a uniform representation of functions, their first- and higher order derivatives. Our approach requires the same storage as the approach in (Jason Eisner, 2002; Zhifei Li and Jason Eisner, 2009) and enables the same efficiency for the traversal procedures described in (Zhifei Li and Jason Eisner, 2009).

In Section 3 we show that the values of a function represented by an acyclic functional automaton can be efficiently computed by the means of a standard dynamic programming technique. We further describe how to construct functional automata for the partial derivatives of F by given functional automaton representing F. We show in Sections 2 and 6 that such automata can be used for training log-linear models, hidden Markov models and conditional random fields. We only require that the objective function is represented via functional automata. In Section 5 we present a construction of functional automaton for a log-linear model where one of the feature functions uses an n-gram language model (Chen and Goodman, 1996).

In Section 7 we present evaluation of a developed system, based on functional automata, on the tasks of (i) noisy historical text normalization and (ii) OCR postcorrection.

2 Log-linear models

We consider the task of automatic normalization of Early Modern English texts. In the next two paragraphs we define some notions related to this task. We use them afterwards to formulate typical problems of training and search that can be effectively solved by functional automata.

Given a *source* text s, say s = *theldest sonn hath bin kild*, and the goal is to find the most relevant modern English equivalent of s. A *candidate generator* is an algorithm that for a fixed source word or sequence of words, say $s_i s_{i+1} \dots s_{i+k}$, generates finite number of *normalization candidates* and supplies each normalization candidate, c, with a conditional probability, $p_{cg}(c \mid s_i s_{i+1} \dots s_{i+k})$. Hence we can assume that the candidate generator provides the information in the form of Table 1. In this sense the candidate generator corresponds to the word-to-word or phrase-to-phrase translation tables in statistical machine translation systems (Koehn et al., 2003). From the candidates we construct possible normalization *targets*: *eldest sun hat been kid, the eldest soon has bean killed, the eldest son has been killed* etc. For normalization of texts produced by OCR system from noisy

source word	set of target candidates
$theldest$	$\{\langle the\ eldest, 0.75\rangle, \langle eldest, 0.25\rangle\}$
$sonn$	$\{\langle son, 0.92593\rangle, \langle soon, 0.03704\rangle, \langle sun, 0.03704\rangle\}$
$hath$	$\{\langle hat, 0.0088\rangle, \langle hats, 0.0044\rangle, \langle has, 0.9868\rangle\}$
bin	$\{\langle bin, 0.1\rangle, \langle been, 0.8\rangle, \langle bean, 0.1\rangle\}$
$kild$	$\{\langle kid, 0.01\rangle, \langle killed, 0.99\rangle\}$

Table 1: Source words and their corresponding set of candidates provided by the candidate generator. Each target candidate c for the source word s_i is associated with a probability $p_{cg}(c \mid s_i)$.

historical documents the candidate generator could take into account both typical OCR errors and historical spelling variations, (Reffle, 2011) or can use directly automatically extracted spelling variations, for example (Gerdjikov et al., 2013).

A *normalization pair* is a pair $p = \langle w, c\rangle$ such that the sequence of target words c is a normalization candidate for the sequence of source words w. We call w *left side* and c *right side* of the normalization pair p. The left and the right sides of p are denoted $l(p)$ and $r(p)$ respectively. In our example some of the normalization pairs are $\langle theldest, eldest\rangle$, $\langle theldest, theeldest\rangle$, $\langle kild, killed\rangle$, etc. A *normalization alignment* from s to t, denoted $s \to t$, is a sequence of normalization pairs $p_1 p_2 \dots p_k$ such that $s = l(p_1)l(p_2)\dots l(p_k)$ and $t = r(p_1)r(p_2)\dots r(p_k)$. The i-th normalization pair p_i of the alignment $s \to t$ is denoted $(s \to t)_i$. The length k of the alignment is denoted $|s \to t|$. Thus a possible normalization alignment in our example, from s = *theldest sonn hath bin kild* to t = *eldest sun hat been kid* is ⟨*theldest, eldest*⟩ ⟨*sonn, sun*⟩⟨*hath, hat*⟩⟨*bin, been*⟩⟨*kild, kid*⟩. We denote with A_s the set of all normalization alignments from s. Note that A_s is always finite, because the number of normalization candidates for each sequence $s_i s_{i+1} \dots s_{i+k}$ of source words is finite.

Problem. Given a training corpus of normalization alignments *train* a log-linear model that combines the candidate generator with an n-gram statistical language model. Once the model is trained, *find* a best normalization alignment $s \to t$ for a given source s.

Firstly, we consider the case where $n = 1$, i.e. we have a monogram language model which assigns a nonzero probability $p_{lm}(t_i)$ to each target word t_i. The general case of arbitrary n-gram language model is postponed to Section 5. There are two feature functions: $h_{lm}(s \to t) = \log \prod_{i=1}^{|t|} p_{lm}(t_i)$ and $h_{cg}(s \to t) = \log \prod_{i=1}^{|s \to t|} p_{cg}[r((s \to t)_i) \mid l((s \to t)_i)]$. The probability of a normalization alignment $s \to t$ given s is $p_\lambda(s \to t \mid s) =$

$$\frac{\exp[\lambda_{lm} h_{lm}(s \to t) + \lambda_{cg} h_{cg}(s \to t)]}{\sum_{s \to t' \in A_s} \exp[\lambda_{lm} h_{lm}(s \to t') + \lambda_{cg} h_{cg}(s \to t')]},$$

where $\lambda = \langle \lambda_{lm}, \lambda_{cg} \rangle$ are the parameters of the model.

Training. Assume that we have a training corpus T of N normalization alignments, $T = \langle s^{(1)} \to t^{(1)}, s^{(2)} \to t^{(2)}, \ldots, s^{(N)} \to t^{(N)} \rangle$. The training task is to find parameters $\hat{\lambda}$ that optimize the joint probability over the training corpus, $\hat{\lambda} = argmax_\lambda \prod_{n=1}^{N} p_\lambda(s^{(n)} \to t^{(n)} \mid s^{(n)})$.

Search. Once the parameters $\hat{\lambda}$ are fixed, the problem is to find a best normalization alignment $s \to t = argmax_{s \to t' \in A_s} p_{\hat{\lambda}}(s \to t')$ for a given input s.

Introducing $e_{s \to t}(\lambda) = \exp[\lambda_{lm} h_{lm}(s \to t) + \lambda_{cg} h_{cg}(s \to t)]$ and

$$Z_s(\lambda) = \sum_{s \to t' \in A_s} e_{s \to t'}(\lambda), \quad (1)$$

we obtain $\hat{\lambda} = argmax_\lambda L(\lambda)$, where

$$L(\lambda) = \sum_{n=1}^{N} [\lambda_{lm} h_{lm}(s^{(n)} \to t^{(n)}) + \lambda_{cg} h_{cg}(s^{(n)} \to t^{(n)}) - \log Z_{s^{(n)}}(\lambda)]. \quad (2)$$

To optimize $L(\lambda)$ we use a gradient method that requires the computation of $L(\lambda)$, $\frac{\partial L}{\partial \lambda_{cg}}(\lambda)$ and $\frac{\partial L}{\partial \lambda_{lm}}(\lambda)$ by given λ. For $i = lm, cg$ we obtain

$$\frac{\partial L}{\partial \lambda_i}(\lambda) = \sum_{n=1}^{N} [h_i(s^{(n)} \to t^{(n)}) - \frac{\frac{\partial Z_{s^{(n)}}}{\partial \lambda_i}(\lambda)}{Z_{s^{(n)}}(\lambda)}]. \quad (3)$$

One possible choice of first order gradient method for the optimization of L is a variant of the conjugate gradient method that converges to the unique maximum of L for each starting point $\lambda_0 = \langle \lambda_{lm0}, \lambda_{cg0} \rangle$, (Gilbert and Nocedal, 1992).

3 Functional automata

The problem we faced in the previous Section is how to compute $L(\lambda)$ and $\frac{\partial L}{\partial \lambda_i}(\lambda)$ at a given point λ. The computation of the terms $\lambda_i h_i(s^{(n)} \to t^{(n)})$ for $i = cg$ (or $i = lm$) is easy since it requires a single multiplication and $|s^{(n)} \to t^{(n)}|$ (or $|t^{(n)}|$) additions. However the

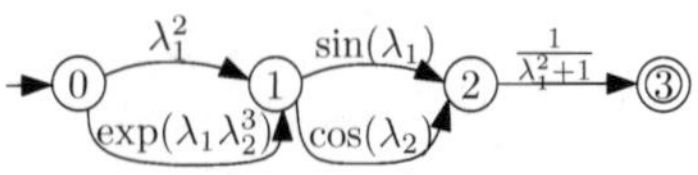

Figure 1: Functional automaton representing the function $F(\lambda_1, \lambda_2) = \lambda_1^2 \sin(\lambda_1)\frac{1}{\lambda_1^2+1} + \lambda_1^2 \cos(\lambda_2)\frac{1}{\lambda_1^2+1} + \exp(\lambda_1\lambda_2^3)\sin(\lambda_1)\frac{1}{\lambda_1^2+1} + \exp(\lambda_1\lambda_2^3)\cos(\lambda_2)\frac{1}{\lambda_1^2+1}$

term $Z_s(\lambda)$ may require much more efforts. It suffices that each source word s_i generates two candidates for the expression in Equation 1 to explode in exponential number of summation terms. Computing the derivatives then becomes even harder. In this Section we present a novel efficient solution to these problems. It is based on a compact representation of the mathematical expressions via *functional automata*.

Imagine, that we have the function $F(\lambda_1, \lambda_2)$ given as an expression: $\lambda_1^2 \sin(\lambda_1)\frac{1}{\lambda_1^2+1} + \lambda_1^2 \cos(\lambda_2)\frac{1}{\lambda_1^2+1} + \exp(\lambda_1\lambda_2^3)\sin(\lambda_1)\frac{1}{\lambda_1^2+1} + \exp(\lambda_1\lambda_2^3)\cos(\lambda_2)\frac{1}{\lambda_1^2+1}$. Let us further assume that we interpret the individual functions λ_1^2, $\cos(\lambda_2)$, $\frac{1}{\lambda_1^2+1}$, etc, as single symbols. If we further interpret the multiplication of functions as concatenation and the addition as union, then the expression for $F(\lambda_1, \lambda_2)$ given above can be viewed as a regular expression for which a finite state automaton can be compiled, see Figure 1. This is the motivation for the following two definitions:

Definition 3.1 Let d be a positive natural number. *Functional automaton* is a quadruple $\mathcal{A} = \langle Q, q_0, \Delta, T \rangle$, where Q is a finite set of states, $q_0 \in Q$ is a start state, Δ is a finite multiset of transitions of the form $q \xrightarrow{W} p$ where $p, q \in Q$ are states and $W : \mathbb{R}^d \to \mathbb{R}$ is a function and $T \subseteq Q$ is a set of final states.

Definition 3.2 Let $\mathcal{A} = \langle Q, q_0, \Delta, T \rangle$ be an acyclic functional automaton (AFA). A *path* π *from* p_0 *to* p_k *in* $\mathcal{A}$ is a sequence of $k \geq 0$ transitions $\pi = p_0 \xrightarrow{W_1} p_1 \xrightarrow{W_2} p_2 \ldots p_{k-1} \xrightarrow{W_k} p_k$. *The label of* π is defined as $l_\pi = \prod_{j=1}^{k} W_j$. If π is empty ($k = 0$), then $l_\pi = 1$. A *successful path* is a path from q_0 to a final state $q \in T$. *The function* $F_\mathcal{A} : \mathbb{R}^d \to \mathbb{R}$ *represented by* $\mathcal{A}$ is defined as $F_\mathcal{A} = \sum_{\pi \text{ is a successful path in } \mathcal{A}} l_\pi$.

Since $\mathcal{A}$ is acyclic, the number of successful paths is finite and $F_\mathcal{A}$ is well defined.

target word	*the*	*eldest*	*son*	*soon*	*sun*
probability	0.017	0.00002	0.0003	0.0005	0.0002

target word	*hat*	*hats*	*has*	*bin*
probability	0.0001	0.00002	0.002	0.000005

target word	*been*	*bean*	*kid*	*killed*
probability	0.003	0.000005	0.00002	0.0001

Table 2: Target words and their language model probabilities.

Classical constructions for *union* and *concatenation* of automata (Hopcroft and Ullman, 1979) can be adapted for functional automata. If $\mathcal{A}$ is the result of the union (concatenation) of $\mathcal{A}_1$ and $\mathcal{A}_2$, then $F_{\mathcal{A}} = F_{\mathcal{A}_1} + F_{\mathcal{A}_2}$ ($F_{\mathcal{A}} = F_{\mathcal{A}_1} \cdot F_{\mathcal{A}_2}$).

3.1 Computation of a function $F_{\mathcal{A}}$ represented by an AFA $\mathcal{A}$

In order to efficiently compute $F_{\mathcal{A}}(\lambda)$ for a given $\lambda = \langle \lambda_1, \lambda_2, \ldots, \lambda_n \rangle$, we use standard dynamic programming. Without loss of generality we assume that $\mathcal{A} = \langle Q, q_0, \Delta, T \rangle$ has only one final state and each transition in A belongs to some successful path. Firstly, we sort topologically the states of the automaton $\mathcal{A}$ in decreasing order. Let $p_1, p_2, \ldots, p_{|Q|}$ be one such order of the states, i.e. (i) $p_1 \in T$ is the only one final state, (ii) $p_{|Q|} = q_0$ is the start state and (iii) if there is a transition from p_i to p_j then $j < i$. For example for the automaton on Figure 1 we obtain $3, 2, 1, 0$. Afterwards for each state p_j we compute a value v_j in the following way: $v_1 = 1$ and $v_{j+1} = \sum_{p_{j+1} \xrightarrow{W(\lambda)} p_k} W(\lambda) \cdot v_k$. Eventually $F_{\mathcal{A}}(\lambda) = v_{|Q|}$. If the computation of $W(\lambda)$ by given λ takes time $O(1)$ for all label functions W, then the time for the computation of $F_{\mathcal{A}}(\lambda)$ is $O(|\Delta|)$.

Now we focus on the problem how to compute $Z_s(\lambda)$ at a given point λ, see Equation 1. We illustrate how $Z_s(\lambda)$ can be represented by an AFA, $\mathcal{A}_s$, on the example from Section 2, $s =$ *theldest sonn hath bin kild*. Table 1 lists the sets of candidates in modern English for each source word s_i. Table 2 presents the language model probabilities for each target word. Given this data we represent the possible normalization alignments via an acyclic two-tape automaton, see Figure 2. This automaton can be considered as a string-to-weight transducer (Mohri, 1997) parameterized with λ_{lm} and λ_{cg}. Specifically, each path from state $i-1$ to state i, $1 \leq i \leq |s|$, corresponds to a target candidate c for the i-th source word s_i and has a label $exp[\lambda_{cg} log(p_{cg}(c \mid s_i)) + \lambda_{lm} log(p_{lm}(c))]$. On our example, for $i \geq 2$ each such path consists of a single transition, because the candidates are single words. In order to represent the candidate $the\ eldest$ we use the additional state 6. The transition from 0 to 6 corresponds to the first word the of the candidate and accumulates the whole probability $p_{cg}(the\ eldest \mid theldest) = 0.75$. The transition from 6 to 1 corresponds to the second word $eldest$ of the candidate. It should be clear that removing the target words from the transitions, we obtain the AFA $\mathcal{A}_s$ representing $Z_s(\lambda)$. For each alignment $s^{(n)} \to t^{(n)}$ from the training corpus we build a separate functional automaton, like the one on Figure 2, representing $Z_{s^{(n)}}(\lambda)$. Thus we have N automata that we use to compute $L(\lambda)$ via Equation (2).

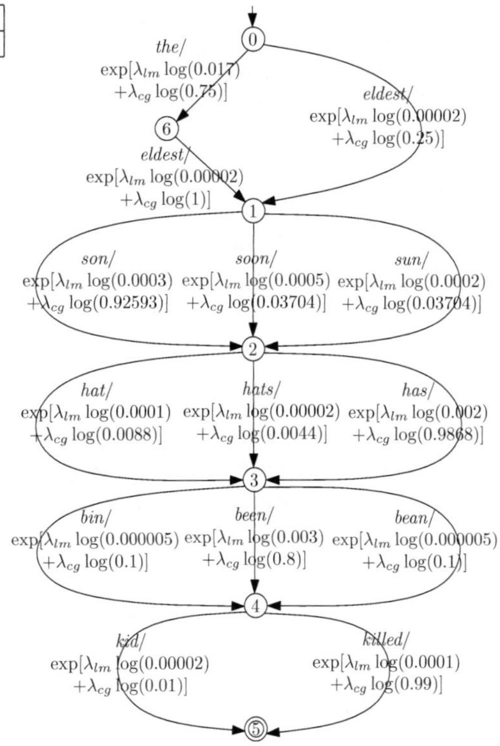

Figure 2: The functional automaton $\mathcal{A}_{theldest\ sonn\ hath\ bin\ kild}$ is obtained by removing the words from the transition labels.

3.2 Computation of partial derivates via AFA

Our next goal is to compute the partial derivates $\frac{\partial L}{\partial \lambda_i}(\lambda)$. Let us turn back to the function $F(\lambda_1, \lambda_2)$ represented by the automaton on Figure 1. We show how to construct a functional automaton for

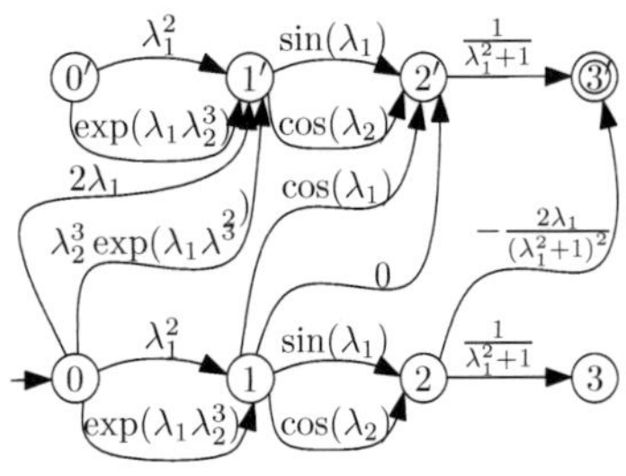

Figure 3: A functional automaton for the partial derivative of $F(\lambda_1, \lambda_2)$.

$\frac{\partial F}{\partial \lambda_1}(\lambda_1, \lambda_2)$. Let $G(\lambda_1, \lambda_2) = \lambda_1^2 \sin(\lambda_1)\frac{1}{\lambda_1^2+1}$ be the first of the four summation terms of F. The partial derivative $\frac{\partial G}{\partial \lambda_1}$ can be written as a sum of three terms: $\frac{\partial(\lambda_1^2)}{\partial \lambda_1}\sin(\lambda_1)\frac{1}{\lambda_1^2+1}$, $\lambda_1^2\frac{\partial(\sin(\lambda_1))}{\partial \lambda_1}\frac{1}{\lambda_1^2+1}$ and $\lambda_1^2\sin(\lambda_1)\frac{\partial(\frac{1}{\lambda_1^2+1})}{\partial \lambda_1}$. Each of the summation terms differs from the original expression for $G(\lambda_1, \lambda_2)$ in exactly one multiplier whose partial derivative with respect to λ_1 is computed. Thus in order to construct a functional automaton for $\frac{\partial F}{\partial \lambda_1}$ we can take two disjoint copies of the original functional automaton, see Figure 3, and set transitions between them in order to reflect the partial derivatives with respect to λ_1 of the single multipliers. The general result is presented in the following Proposition:

Proposition 3.3 *Let $\mathcal{A}$ be an AFA with k states and t transitions and let $\mathcal{A}' = \langle Q', q_0', \Delta', T'\rangle$ be a disjoint copy of $\mathcal{A}$. If the partial derivatives $\frac{\partial W}{\partial \lambda_i}$ exist for each transition $q \overset{W(\lambda_1,\lambda_2,\dots,\lambda_d)}{\longrightarrow} p$ in $\mathcal{A}$, then $\mathcal{B} = \langle Q \cup Q', q_0, \Delta \cup \Delta' \cup \{q \overset{\frac{\partial W}{\partial \lambda_i}}{\to} p' \mid q \overset{W}{\to} p \in \Delta\}, T'\rangle$ is an AFA with $2k$ states, $3t$ transitions and $F_{\mathcal{B}} = \frac{\partial F_{\mathcal{A}}}{\partial \lambda_i}$.*

Sketch of proof. We have $\frac{\partial F_{\mathcal{A}}}{\partial \lambda_i} = \sum_{\pi \text{ is a successful path in } \mathcal{A}} \frac{\partial l_\pi}{\partial \lambda_i} = \sum_{\substack{\pi = q_0 \overset{W_1}{\longrightarrow} q_1 \dots q_{m-1} \overset{W_m}{\longrightarrow} q_m \\ \text{is a successful path in } \mathcal{A}}} \sum_j \pi_{(j,i)}$, where $\pi_{(j,i)} = W_1 \dots W_{j-1}\frac{\partial W_j}{\partial \lambda_i}W_{j+1}\dots W_m$. There is a one-to-one correspondence between the successful paths in $\mathcal{B}$ and the terms $\pi_{(j,i)}$ in the above summation. □

Let us note that the construction presented in Proposition 3.3 can be iterated i times in order to build a functional automaton with $2^i k$ states and $3^i t$ transitions for each i-th order partial derivate of $F_{\mathcal{A}}$. Thus we can build functional automata with $4k$ states and $9t$ transitions for $\frac{\partial^2 F_{\mathcal{A}}}{\partial \lambda_i \lambda_j}$. This gives the possibility to use some second order gradient method in the training procedure. Note that if the computation of $W(\lambda)$ for a given λ and all label functions, W, takes constant time, then using functional automata we achieve an $O(t)$-time computation of both $\frac{\partial F_{\mathcal{A}}}{\partial \lambda_i}(\lambda)$ and $\frac{\partial^2 F_{\mathcal{A}}}{\partial \lambda_i \lambda_j}(\lambda)$.

4 Search procedure

By given source sequence s we want to find best alignment $s \to t = argmax_{s\to t' \in A_s}\, p_{\hat{\lambda}}(s \to t') = argmax_{s\to t' \in A_s}\, e_{s\to t'}(\hat{\lambda})$. For this purpose we use again a standard dynamic programming procedure on the automaton $\mathcal{A}_s$ representing the function $Z_s(\lambda)$, Figure 2. The only difference with the procedure described in Subsection 3.1 is that instead of summation over all transtions from the current state we need to take maximum and to mark a transition that gives the maximum. Finally the successful path of marked transitions represents a best alignment. Actually this procedure corresponds to the backward version of the Viterbi decoding algorithm (Omura, 1967). If the computation of $W(\lambda)$ by given λ takes time $O(1)$ for all label functions W, then the search procedure is linear in the number of the transitions in the functional automaton.

5 n-gram language models

In this Section we generalize the constructions of the automaton $\mathcal{A}_s$ from Section 3 and 4 to the case of an arbitrary n-gram language model, $n > 1$. In this case $h_{lm}(s \to t) = \log\prod_{i=1}^{|t|} p_{lm}(t_i \mid t_{i-n+1}t_{i-n+2}\dots t_{i-1})$. We construct an automaton representing $Z_s(\lambda)$ as follows. Firstly, we build automaton $\mathcal{A}_1$ that represents the function $Z_s(\langle 0, \lambda_{cg}\rangle) = \sum_{s\to t' \in A_s} \exp[\lambda_{cg} h_{cg}(s \to t')]$. Each transition in $\mathcal{A}_1$ is associated with a target word, see Figure 2. Now we would like to add $\exp[\lambda_{lm}\log(p_{lm}(t_i \mid t_{i-n+1}t_{i-n+2}\dots t_{i-1}))]$ to the label of each transition associated with t_i. However the problem is that there may be multiple sequences of preceding words $t_{i-n+1}t_{i-n+2}\dots t_{i-1}$ for one and the same transition. For example for $n = 3$ on Figure 2 for the transition associated with $t_i =$ *has* from state 2 to state 3 there are three different possible pairs of preceding words $t_{i-2}t_{i-1}$: *eldest son*, *eldest soon* and *eldest sun*. We overcome this problem of ambiguity by extending $\mathcal{A}_1 = \langle Q_1, q_1, \Delta_1, T_1\rangle$ to equivalent automaton $\mathcal{A}_2$ in which for each state the sequence of $n-1$ preceding words is uniquely determined. The set of states of $\mathcal{A}_2$ is $Q_2 = \{\langle w_1 w_2 \dots w_{n-1}, q\rangle \mid q \in Q_1$ and $w_1 w_2 \dots w_{n-1}$ is a sequence of preceding words for q in $\mathcal{A}_1\}$. The set of transitions of $\mathcal{A}_2$ is $\Delta_2 = \{\langle w_1 w_2 \dots w_{n-1}, q'\rangle \xrightarrow{W} \langle w_2 \dots w_{n-1} w_n, q''\rangle \mid$ transition $q' \xrightarrow{W} q'' \in \Delta_1$ is associated with $w_n\}$. In $\mathcal{A}_2$ the transition $\langle w_1 w_2 \dots w_{n-1}, q'\rangle \xrightarrow{W} \langle w_2 \dots w_{n-1} w_n, q''\rangle$ is associated with the word w_n. Finally, from $\mathcal{A}_2$ we construct functional automaton $\mathcal{A}_3$ that represents $Z_s(\langle\lambda_{lm}, \lambda_{cg}\rangle)$ by adding $\exp[\lambda_{lm} \log(p_{lm}(w_n \mid w_1 w_2 \dots w_{n-1}))]$ to the label of each transition t where w_n is the word associated with t.

If m is an upper bound for the number of correction candidates for every sequence $s_i s_{i+1} \dots s_{i+k}$, then $|Q_2| \leq m^{n-1}|Q_1|$ and $|\Delta_2| \leq m^{n-1}|\Delta_1|$.

6 Other statistical models

In this section we apply the technique developed in Sections 3 and 4 to other statistical models.

Conditional random fields. A linear-chain CRF serves to assign a label y_i to each the observation x_i of a given observation sequence x. We assume that the observations x_i belong to a set X and the labels y_i belong to a finite set Y. We shall further consider that the probability measure of a linear-chain CRF with $|x|$ states is

$$p_\lambda(y \mid x) = \frac{\exp[\sum_{i=2}^{|x|}\sum_{j=1}^{K} \alpha_j f_j(y_{i-1}, y_i, x, i) + \sum_{i=1}^{|x|}\sum_{j=1}^{K} \beta_j g_j(y_i, x, i)]}{Z_x(\lambda)}$$

where $|x| = |y|$, $f_j : Y \times Y \times X^* \times \mathbb{N} \to \mathbb{R}$ and $g_j : X^* \times \mathbb{N} \to \mathbb{R}$ are predefined feature functions, $\lambda = \langle \alpha_1, \alpha_2, \dots, \alpha_K, \beta_1, \beta_2, \dots, \beta_K\rangle$ are parameters and $Z_x(\lambda) = \sum_{y \in Y^{|x|}} \exp[\sum_{i=2}^{|x|}\sum_{j=1}^{K} \alpha_j f_j(y_{i-1}, y_i, x, i) + \sum_{i=1}^{|x|}\sum_{j=1}^{K} \beta_j g_j(y_i, x, i)]$. The training task is similar to the one described in Section 2. We have a training corpus of N pairs $\langle x^{(1)}, y^{(1)}\rangle, \langle x^{(2)}, y^{(2)}\rangle, \dots, \langle x^{(N)}, y^{(N)}\rangle$ and we need to find the parameters $\hat{\lambda} = argmax_\lambda \prod_{n=1}^{N} p_\lambda(y^{(n)} \mid x^{(n)})$. Formulae very similar to (2) and (3) can be derived. Thus the main problem is again in the computation of the term $Z_x(\lambda)$. In (Lafferty et al., 2001) $Z_x(\lambda)$ is represented as an entity of a special matrix which is obtained as a product of $|x|+1$ matrices of size $(|Y|+2) \times (|Y|+2)$. The states of an AFA $\mathcal{A}_x$ representing $Z_x(\lambda)$ are as follows: a start state s, a final state f and $|x| \cdot |Y|$ "intermediate" states $q_{i,\gamma}$, $1 \leq i \leq |x|, \gamma \in Y$. The transitions are $s \xrightarrow{G} q_{1,\gamma}$ for $G = \exp\sum_{j=1}^{K} \beta_j g_j(\gamma, x, 1)$, $q_{i,\gamma'} \xrightarrow{F} q_{i+1,\gamma''}$ for $F = \exp\sum_{j=1}^{K}[\alpha_j f_j(\gamma', \gamma'', x, i+1) + \beta_j g_j(\gamma'', x, i+1)]$ and $q_{|x|,\gamma} \xrightarrow{1} f$. Transitions with label 0 can be removed from the automaton. If there are many such transitions this could significantly reduce the time for training.

Hidden Markov models. We adapt the notations and the definitions from (Rabiner, 1989). Let $\lambda = \langle A, B, \pi\rangle$ be the parameters of a HMM with R states $S = \{S_1, S_2, \dots, S_R\}$ and M distinct observation symbols $V = \{v_1, v_2, \dots, v_M\}$, where $A = \{a_{S_i S_j}\}$ is a $R \times R$ matrix of transition probabilities, $B = \{b_{S_j}(v_k)\}$ are the observation symbol probability distributions and $\pi = \{\pi_{S_j}\}$ is the initial state distribution. The probability of $O_1 O_2 \dots O_T$ is $p_\lambda(O_1 O_2 \dots O_T) = \sum_{q_1 q_2 \dots q_T \in S^T} c(q_1 q_2 \dots q_T)$, where $c(q_1 q_2 \dots q_T) = \pi_{q_1} b_{q_1}(O_1) a_{q_1 q_2} b_{q_2}(O_2) \dots a_{q_{T-1} q_T} b_{q_T}(O_T)$.

Given a training set of N observations $O^{(1)}, O^{(2)}, \dots, O^{(N)}$ the optimal parameters $\hat{\lambda} = argmax_\lambda \prod_{n=1}^{N} p_\lambda(O^{(n)})$ have to be determined under the stohastic constraints $\sum_j a_{S_i S_j} = 1$, $\sum_k b_{S_j}(v_k) = 1$ and $\sum_j \pi_{S_j} = 1$. Applying the method of Lagrange multipliers we obtain a new function $F(\lambda, \alpha, \beta, \gamma) = \prod_{n=1}^{N} p_\lambda(O^{(n)}) + \sum_i \alpha_i[(\sum_j a_{S_i S_j}) - 1] + \sum_i \beta_i[(\sum_k b_{S_j}(v_k)) - 1] + \gamma[(\sum_j \pi_{S_j}) - 1]$. For each training observation sequence $O^{(n)}$ with $T^{(n)}$ symbols the function $p_\lambda(O^{(n)})$ can be represented by an AFA $\mathcal{A}_{O^{(n)}}$ with $RT^{(n)}+2$ states, $R(T^{(n)}+1)$ transitions and a single final state as follows. We have the start state s, the final state f and $RT^{(n)}$ "intermediate" states q_{t,S_i}, $1 \leq t \leq T^{(n)}$, $1 \leq i \leq R$. The transitions are $s \xrightarrow{\pi_{S_i} b_{S_i}(O_1^{(n)})} q_{1,S_i}$, $q_{t,S_i} \xrightarrow{a_{S_i S_j} b_{S_j}(O_{t+1}^{(n)})} q_{t+1,S_j}$ and $q_{T^{(n)},S_i} \xrightarrow{1} f$. The concatenation of all N automata $\mathcal{A}_{O^{(n)}}$ gives one automaton representing $\prod_{n=1}^{N} p_\lambda(O^{(n)})$. The union of two automata representing functions F_1 and F_2 gives an automaton for the function $F_1 + F_2$. So using unions and concatenations we obtain one AFA (with a single final state) representing the function $F(\lambda, \alpha, \beta, \gamma)$. We can directly construct functional automata for the partial derivatives of F (first order and if needed second order), see Proposition 3.3. Thus we can use a gradient method to find a local extremum of F.

7 Evaluation

In this section we evaluate the quality of a noisy text normalization system that uses the log-linear model presented in Section 2. The system uses a globally convergent variant of the conjugate gradient method, (Gilbert and Nocedal, 1992). The computation of the gradient and the values of the objective function is implemented with functional automata. We test the system on two tasks: (i) OCR-postcorrection of the TREC-5 Confusion Track corpus[1] and (ii) normalization of the 1641 Depositions[2] - a collection of highly non-standard 17th century documents in Early Modern English, (Sweetnam, 2011), digitized at the Trinity College Dublin.

For the task (i) we use a parallel corpus of 30000 training pairs (s, t), where s is a document produced by an OCR system and t is the corrected variant of s. The 30000 pairs were randomly selected from the TREC-5 corpus that has about 5% error on character level. We use 25000 pairs as a training set and the remaining 5000 pairs serve as a test set. With a heruistic dynamic programming algorithm we automatically converted all these 25000 pairs (s, t) into normalization alignments $s \to t$, see Section 2. We use these alignments to train (a) a candidate generator, (b) smoothed 2-gram language model, to find (c) statistics for the length of the left side of a normalization pair and (d) statistics for normalization pairs with equal left and right sides. Our log-linear model has four feature functions induced by (a), (b), (c) and (d). As a candidate generator we use a variant of the algorithm presented in (Gerdjikov et al., 2013). The word error (WER) rate between s and t in the test set of 5000 pairs is 22.10% and the BLEU (Papineni et al., 2002) is 58.44%. In Table 3 we compare the performace of our log-linear model with four feature functions against a baseline where we use only one feature function, which encodes the candidate generator. Table 3 shows that the combination of the four features reduces more than twice the WER. Precision and recall, obtained on the TREC 5 dataset, for different candidate generators can be found in (Mihov et al., 2007; Schulz et al., 2007; Gerdjikov et al., 2013). To test our system on the task of normalization of the 1641 Depositions, we use a corpus of 500 manually created normalization alignments $s \to t$, where s is a document in Early Modern English from the 1641 Depositions and t is the normalization of s in contemporary English. We train our system on 450 documents and test it on the other 50. We use five feature functions: (b), (c) and (d) as above and two language models: (a1) one 2-gram language model trained on part of the normalized training documents and (a2) another 2-gram language model trained on large corpus of documents extracted from the entire Gutenberg English language corpus[3]. We obtain WER 5.37% and BLEU 89.34%.

Log-linear model	WER	BLEU
only candidate generator	6.81%	85.24%
candidate generator + language model + other features	3.27%	92.82%

Table 3: Only candidate generator vs. candidate generator + other features. OCR-postcorrection of the TREC-5 corpus.

8 Conclusion

In this paper we considered a general framework for the realization of statistical models. We showed a novel construction proving that the class of functional automata is closed under taking partial derivatives. Thus the functional automata yield efficient training and search procedures using only the usual sum and product operations on real numbers.

We illustrated the power of this mechanism in the cases of CRF's and HMM's, LLM's and n-gram language models. Similar constructions can be applied for the realization of other methods, for example MERT (Och, 2003).

We presented a noisy text normalization system based on functional automata and evaluated its quality.

Acknowledgments

The research work reported in the paper is supported by the CULTURA project, grant 269973, funded by the FP7 Programme (STReP) and Project BG051PO001-3.3.06-0022/19.03.2012.

[1] http://trec.nist.gov/pubs/trec5/t5_proceedings.html

[2] http://1641.tcd.ie

[3] http://www.gutenberg.org

References

Peter F. Brown, Vincent J. Della Pietra, Stephen A. Della Pietra, and Robert L. Mercer, 1993. The mathematics of statistical machine translation: parameter estimation. *Computational Linguistics*, 19(2):263–311.

Stanley F. Chen and Joshua Goodman. 1996. An empirical study of smoothing techniques for language modeling. *Proceedings of the 34th annual meeting on Association for Computational Linguistics*, ACL '96, 310–318.

J. N. Darroch and D. Ratcliff. 1972. Generalized iterative scaling for log-linear models. *The Annals of Mathematical Statistics*, 43:1470–1480.

Jason Eisner. 2002. Parameter Estimation for Probabilistic Finite-State Transducers. *Proceedings of the 40th annual meeting on Association for Computational Linguistics* ACL '02, 1–8.

Stefan Gerdjikov, Stoyan Mihov, and Vladislav Nenchev. 2013. Extraction of spelling variations from language structure for noisy text correction. *Proceedings of the International Conference on Document Analysis and Recognition*

Jean Charles Gilbert and Jorge Nocedal. 1992. Global Convergence Properties of Conjugate Gradient Methods for Optimization. *SIAM Journal on Optimization*, 2(1):21–42.

John E. Hopcroft and Jeffrey D. Ullman. 1979. *Introduction to Automata Theory, Languages, and Computation*. Addison-Wesley Publishing Company.

B. H. Juang and L. R. Rabiner. 1991. Hidden Markov Models for Speech Recognition. *Technometrics*, 33(3):251–272.

Philipp Koehn, Franz Josef Och, and Daniel Marcu. 2003. Statistical phrase-based translation. *Proceedings of the 2003 Conference of the North American Chapter of the Association for Computational Linguistics on Human Language Technology - Volume 1*, 48–54

John D. Lafferty, Andrew McCallum, and Fernando C. N. Pereira. 2001. Conditional Random Fields: Probabilistic Models for Segmenting and Labeling Sequence Data. *Proceedings of the Eighteenth International Conference on Machine Learning*, ICML '01, 282–289.

Zhifei Li and Jason Eisner 2009. First- and second-order expectation semirings with applications to minimum-risk training on translation forests. *Proceedings of the 2009 Conference on Empirical Methods in Natural Language Processing: Volume 1 - Volume 1*, EMNLP '09, 40–51.

S. Mihov, P. Mitankin, A. Gotscharek, U. Reffle, C. Schulz, and K. U. Ringlstetter. 2007. Using automated error profiling of texts for improved selection of correction candidates for garbled tokens. *AI 2007: Advances in Artificial Intelligence*, 456-465.

Mehryar Mohri. 1997. Finite-state transducers in language and speech processing. *Computational Linguistics*, 23(2): 269–311.

Franz Josef Och. 2003. Minimum error rate training in statistical machine translation. *Proceedings of the 41st Annual Meeting on Association for Computational Linguistics - Volume 1*, 160–167.

J. Omura. 1967. On the Viterbi decoding algorithm. *IEEE Transactions on Information Theory*, 13(2):260–269.

Kishore Papineni, Salim Roukos, Todd Ward, and Wei-Jing Zhu. 2002. BLEU: a Method for Automatic Evaluation of Machine Translation. *Proceedings of the 40th Annual Meeting of the Association for Computational Linguistics*, 311–318.

Lawrence Rabiner. 1989. A tutorial on HMM and selected applications in speech recognition. *Proceedings of the IEEE*, 77(2):257–286.

Ulrich Reffle. 2011. Efficiently generating correction suggestions for garbled tokens of historical language. *Natural Language Engineering*, 17(02):265–282.

K. U. Schulz, S. Mihov, and P. Mitankin, 2007. Fast selection of small and precise candidate sets from dictionaries for text correction tasks, *Proceedings of the International Conference on Document Analysis and Recognition* 471-475.

Fei Sha and Fernando Pereira, 2003. Shallow parsing with conditional random fields, *Proceedings of the 2003 Conference of the North American Chapter of the Association for Computational Linguistics on Human Language Technology - Volume 1*, 134–141.

Mark S. Sweetnam and Barbara A. Fennell. 2011. Natural language processing and early-modern dirty data: applying IBM Languageware to the 1641 depositions. *Literary and Linguistic Computing*, 27(1):39–54

Mining Fine-grained Opinion Expressions with Shallow Parsing

Sucheta Ghosh
CLCS, Trinity College Dublin
ghoshs@tcd.ie

Sara Tonelli
FBK, Trento, Italy
satonelli@fbk.eu

Richard Johansson
University of Gothenberg, Sweden
richard.johansson@svenska.gu.se

Abstract

Opinion analysis deals with public opinions and trends, but subjective language is highly ambiguous. In this paper, we follow a simple data-driven technique to learn fine-grained opinions. We select an intersection set of Wall Street Journal documents that is included both in the Penn Discourse Tree Bank (PDTB) and in the Multi-Perspective Question Answering (MPQA) corpus. This is done in order to explore the usefulness of discourse-level structure to facilitate the extraction of fine-grained opinion expressions. Here we perform shallow parsing of MPQA expressions with connective based discourse structure, and then also with Named Entities (NE) and some syntax features using conditional random fields; the latter feature set is basically a collection of NEs and a bundle of features that is proved to be useful in a shallow discourse parsing task. We found that both of the feature-sets are useful to improve our baseline at different levels of this fine-grained opinion expression mining task.

1 Introduction

The explosion of data in all forms from blogs, online forums, Facebook, Twitter and other social media channels has given an opportunity of unprecedented reach to publicly sharing thoughts on events, products and services. However, there are some open issues related to this research area, commonly known as *Opinion Mining*, which can be summarized as follows: *(1)* Opinions are potentially ambiguous, and *(2)* Contextual interpretation of polarity is hard to achieve. Subsidiary important problem is the non-availability of large corpora with good annotation quality.

Fine-grained opinion analysis is a different task from the *coarse-grained* one (e.g. document level analysis), in that it classifies opinion phrases, chunks or expressions from a given text. In this work, we perform fine-grained analysis by focusing on higher-level linguistic structure like discourse, without rich linguistic or knowledge-intensive features, to classify subjective opinion expressions using the Multi-Perspective Question Answering corpus (MPQA) scheme Wiebe et al. (2005).

We perform two different experiments sets. We first exploit gold features based on shallow discourse structure[1] to classify fine-grained opinion expressions. In a second experiment, we use some syntax based features, those are found useful on a shallow discourse structure classification task, along with the named entities. Both of the experiments are found to be useful at different levels of fine-grained opinion expression mining. We use conditional random fields for this entire shallow parsing task. A set of documents from the Wall Street Journal (WSJ) corpus Marcus et al. (1993) annotated both in the Penn Discourse Treebank Prasad et al. (2008) and MPQA corpus is used. We also take advantage of the availability of several robust natural language processing tools pretrained on WSJ data.

2 Related Work

Fine-grained sentiment analysis methods have been developed by Hatzivassiloglou and McKeown (1997), Hu and Liu (2004) and Popescu and Etzioni (2007), among others. The first approach focuses on conjoined adjectives (i.e. the adjectives which are joined with discourse connectives) within the WSJ corpus. While the second one operates at the sentence level, the third one extracts

[1] By *shallow discourse structure* we mean the explicit discourse connective sense and its two argument spans Ghosh (2012).

opinion phrases at the subsentence level for product features. Rich sets of linguistic features are used in the works of Choi et al. (2005), Wilson et al. (2005a), Breck et al. (2007). The first use conditional random models with information extraction patterns; the second is more focused on the classification of opinion phrases using contextual polarity; the third approach improved the performance of Wilson et al. (2005a), using conditional random fields and external knowledge sources.

Johansson and Moschitti (2013) developed a joint model-based sequence labeler for fine-grained opinion expression using relational features except discourse-level features, beside a set of classifier to determine opinion holder and also a multi-class classifier that assigns polarity to a given opinion expression. These classifiers were further used to generate the hypothesis sets for a re-ranking system that further improved the performance of the classification. Täckström and McDonald (2011) combine fully and partially supervised structured conditional models for a joint classification of the polarity of whole reviews and review sentences.

The impact of discourse relations for sentiment analysis is investigated in Asher et al. (2009). The authors conduct a manual study in which they represent opinions in text as shallow semantic feature structures. These are combined with overall opinion using hand-written rules based on manually annotated discourse relations. An interdependent classification scenario to determine polarity as well as discourse relations is presented in Somasundaran and Wiebe (2009). In their approach, text is modeled as opinion graphs including discourse information. In Somasundaran and Wiebe (2009) the authors try alternative machine learning approaches with combinations of supervised and unsupervised methods for the same task. However, they do not automatically identify discourse relations, but used task-specific manual annotations.

Polanyi and Zaenen (2006) investigate the usage of contextual valence shifters and discourse connectives inside a text. In the approach of Kim and Hovy (2006) the system makes use of conjunctions like "and" to infer polarities and applies a specific rule to sentences including the word "but": if no polarity can be identified for the clause containing "but", the polarity of the previous phrase is negated. In a more recent system, Zirn et al. (2011) incorporated this information using discourse relations. Zirn et al. (2011) studied a fully automatic framework for fine-grained sentiment analysis at sub-sentence level, combining multiple sentiment lexicons and neighbourhood as well as discourse relations. They used Markov logic to integrate polarity scores from different sentiment lexicons with information about relations between neighbouring segments, and evaluate the approach on product reviews. The authors used only contrast and no contrast discourse relations to achieve their results, conducting a survey on a small amount of data that showed that the contrast relation was the most frequent one. However, the survey presented in Hatzivassiloglou and McKeown (1997) on the WSJ corpus showed that contrast is actually the third most important relation in the corpus. Therefore the hypothesis made by Zirn et al. (2011) may be data specific.

The framework of Heerschop et al. (2011) achieved even better results than Zirn et al. (2011). The system uses deep discourse structure as well as SentiWordNet and WordNet in order to disambiguate words.

Kim and Hovy (2004) define opinion as a quadruple composed by topic, holder, claim and sentiment. The authors use a Named Entity tagger to identify the potential holder of the opinion. Later Stoyanov and Cardie (2008) argue that in fine grained subjectivity analysis, topic identification is very relevant, and treat the task from the perspective of topic coreference resolution. The authors use named entities beside other topic based features to represent the topical structure of text.

3 Data Resources

In order to test our hypothesis we used 80 Wall Street Journal documents Marcus et al. (1993) that are part both of the Penn Discourse TreeBank (PDTB) and of the Multi-Perspective Question-Answer (MPQA) bank.

3.1 Penn Discourse TreeBank (PDTB) 2.0

The Penn Discourse Treebank (PDTB) is a resource containing one million words from the Wall Street Journal corpus Marcus et al. (1993) annotated with discourse relations.

Connectives in the PTDB are treated as discourse predicates taking two text spans as arguments (Arg), i.e. parts of the text that describe events, propositions, facts, situations. Such two arguments in the PDTB are called Arg1 and Arg2, with the numbering not necessarily corresponding to their order in text. Indeed, Arg2 is the argument syntactically bound to the connective, while Arg1 is the other one.

In the PDTB, discourse relations can be either overtly or implicitly expressed. However, we focus here exclusively on explicit connectives and the identification of their arguments, including the exact spans. This kind of classification is very complex, since Arg1 and Arg2 can occur in many different configurations (see Table).

In PDTB the senses are assigned according to a three-layered hierarchy: the top-level classes are the most generic ones and include TEMPORAL, CONTINGENCY, COMPARISON and EXPANSION labels. We used these four surface senses only in our task.

We define our discourse structure as shallow since it includes only the discourse connective senses and its two argument spans, excluding other types of hierarchical annotation.

3.2 Multi-Perspective Question Answering (MPQA)

We use the version 2.0 of the MPQA corpus, whose central building block is opinion expression. Opinion expressions belong to two categories: Direct subjective expressions (DSEs) are explicit mentions of opinion, whereas expressive subjective elements (ESEs) signal the attitude of the speaker by the choice of words, other than these there are Objective Speech Events (OSEs). Opinions have two features: polarity and intensity, and most expressions are also associated with a holder, also called source. In this work, we only consider polarities, not intensities or holders. Polarity can be POSITIVE, NEUTRAL, NEGATIVE, and BOTH; for compatibility with Choi and Cardie (2010), we mapped BOTH to NEUTRAL.

4 Our Approach

The goal of our first experiment is to observe the effect of a limited number of gold label features from PDTB. Since no previous work documented the effect of PDTB senses on the task of opinion expression mining using MPQA, we use four PDTB surface senses (described in the Subsection 3.1) as one of the features in this experiment. We then run the second experiment in order to observe the effect of named entities with the mentioned feature bundle. This set of features encoding some syntactic-level information may improve the overall classification performance like the same features facilitated a shallow discourse parsing task by Ghosh et al. (2011); in addition to the feature bundle, the named entities might reflect some information about distribution of discourse entities.

5 Experiments

We perform our experiments at two different stages: (1) we first draw a baseline using basic features from the previous work and a standard sentiment lexicon by Wilson et al. (2005b), then (2) we run further experiments to improve the baseline with additional features. Our goal is to investigate possible improvements using discourse features or some other features that may encode discourse information via shallow parsing.

The experiments are entirely run using conditional random fields, keeping the same settings for the three experiments. We used standard training technique for conditional random fields, as provided by the tool developers in the instruction manual. We use the CRF++ tool [2] for sequence labeling classification by Lafferty et al. (2001), with second-order Markov dependency between tags. Beside the individual specification of a feature in the feature description template, the features in various combinations are also represented. We used this tool because the output of CRF++ is compatible with CoNLL 2000 chunking shared task, and we view our task as an opinion expression chunking task. On the other hand, linear-chain CRFs for sequence labeling offer advantages over both generative models like HMMs and classifiers applied at each sequence position. Also Sha and Pereira (2003) claim that, as a single model, CRFs outperform other models for shallow parsing. We use conditional random fields to classify subjective (any of direct or expressive) and objective expressions. We encode the opinion expression spans by means of the IOB2 scheme Sang et al. (1999). In order to represent MPQA opinion expressions with IOB2 tags, we remove the expressions where the expression spans are overlapping expressions (i.e. an opinion expression span can be overlapped by another opinion expression span), though overlapping expressions are rare in MPQA [Johansson and Moschitti (2013)].

[2](http://crfpp.sourceforge.net/)

Since the dataset is fairly small, we perform a 5-fold cross validation over the dataset to have a rough estimation of how accurately the predictive model will perform in practice. One round of cross-validation involves random multiple rounds to partition data into complementary subsets: the training set (75%), the validation set (10%) and the test set (15%). The results are averaged over the rounds. This multiple round partition is kept the same for all the experiments in this paper in order to make results comparable. Our training, validation and test sets are different from the respective sets used by Breck et al. (2007) and Johansson and Moschitti (2013).

5.1 Evaluation

We present all results using precision, recall and F1 measures. To compute precision and recall, we used two scoring schemes: exact and overlap-based scoring. A span is counted as exact-correct if its extent exactly coincides with one in the gold standard, whereas in overlap-based measures, a span is counted as correctly detected if it overlaps with a span in the gold standard. Note that all the partial measures are bounded below by the exact measures and above by the overlap-based measures. Further details on these scoring techniques are given in Johansson and Moschitti (2013).

The results are primarily compared using two metrics: micro-averages and macro-averages of precision, recall and F1 measures. In order to facilitate comparison between baseline and other experiments results we compute macro and micro averages of results from the 5-fold cross validation for each experiments.

5.2 Baseline

We construct our baseline with four features. three of them are linguistic features, viz. the current token, the lemma and the part-of-speech (PoS) tag of the token. The fourth one is the polarity value of the current token taken from a standard subjectivity lexicon maintained by Wilson et al. (2005b). The selection of baseline features is motivated by the work of Breck et al. (2007). The features are listed in the Table 1.

Features used to prepare the baseline.	
BF1.	Token (T)
BF2.	Lemma (L)
BF3.	PoS tag
BF4.	Polarity Values (POLV)

Table 1: Baseline Feature sets opinion expression labeling.

5.3 Experiment with Discourse Connectives & Arguments

In order to observe the effect of (explicit) discourse connective senses and their argument spans, we use conditional random fields with an extended set of features from shallow discourse structure by Ghosh (2012) on the top of the baseline features. In particular, we use one of the four explicit discourse connective senses (viz. Expansion, Contingency, Comparison and Temporal) and its two arguments with spans. We also use IOB2 tags with argument spans. In order to reduce the complexity of the classification, overlapping argument span tags are removed, which however are fairly small in amount. We illustrate the features used in this experiment in Table 2. The features viz. CONN, ARG1 and ARG2 are gold-labeled features, i.e. they are directly extracted from available PDTB annotation.

Features used to perform Expt. with discourse structure.	
E1F1.	Sense of Connective (CONN)
E1F2.	Arg1 Span (ARG1)
E1F3.	Arg2 Span (ARG2)
Additional features used	
BF1-BF4.	All baseline features

Table 2: Feature sets for opinion expression labeling with Shallow Discourse Structure Features.

5.4 Experiment with Named Entities (NEs) and syntax based features

In this experiment we used four new features on the top of baseline features, which are listed in Table 3. Apart from Named Entities (NE), a bundle of other features are used (IOB, L+I, BMV), which were previously used in a shallow discourse parsing task Ghosh et al. (2011). No member of this bundle feature-set from the shallow discourse parsing task directly provides information about discourse, but when used altogether these may reflect some discourse information. Among the bundle of features, IOB chain and Inflection provide morpho-syntactic information, whereas the lemma and boolean value of the main verb of the main clause provide lexical information.

We use the scripts provided for the CoNLL chunking shared task 2000 [3] to extract IOB chains. Besides, we use the Morpha tool by Minnen et al. (2001) to extract lemma and inflection for the tokens. The main verb of the main clause is extracted following the head rules by Yamada and

[3](http://ilk.uvt.nl/team/sabine/homepage/software.html)

Matsumoto[4]. We used the Stanford Named Entity tagger by Finkel et al. (2005) to tag the named entities. This tagger is a three-class (viz. PERSON, ORGANISATION, LOCATION) tagger for English. The pre-trained models are trained both on CoNLL 2003 and MUC data, for the intersection of those class sets. NEs are included as a feature following the previous work by Stoyanov and Cardie (2008), where the authors show that information from NEs contribute to the entity relation structure in a discourse.

Features used to perform Expt. with NE & other features.	
E2F1.	Named Entities (NE)
E2F2.	IOB chain (IOB)
E2F3.	Lemma+Inflection (L+I)
E2F4.	Boolean feature for main verb of main clause (BMV)
Additional features used	
BF1-BF4.	All baseline features

Table 3: Feature sets for opinion expression labeling with NE & other features.

6 Results

We present the results obtained at different levels of fine-grained opinion mining. We attempt to compare some of the results with the respective results from Johansson and Moschitti (2013) in order to understand the trend of improvement of results over our baseline. The explored levels of fine-grained mining is demonstrated in the Table 4. We report here the interesting findings and comparisons from this level-wise studies.

All the systems (i.e. baseline, discourse-structure based and NE-syntax based systems) perform the worst for the polarity detection. This trend is the same with the system of Johansson and Moschitti (2013) (J&M). In the Table 5 we compare the macro-averages of our system to the system of J&M, in the case of polarity tagged expression classification, where the OSEs are removed, and the DSEs and ESEs are included but not distinguished. In this case NE and syntax based system performs better than the baseline and discourse structure based system, because may be NEs are better feature for polarity extraction than surface senses of discourse connectives. The recall of the J&M's system is balanced with precision therefore it performs better than the other systems.

[4]The software can be downloaded from `http://www.jaist.ac.jp/\~h-yamada/`

L1. With Not Distinguished DSE+ESE+OSE+Polarity		
L2.Without OSE+Polarity	1.	ND(DSE+ESE)
	2.	(DSE+ESE)
L3. Without Polarity	1.	ND(DSE+ESE)+OSE
	2.	DSE+ESE+OSE
L4. Without OSE	1.	ND(DSE+ESE)+Polarity
	2.	(DSE+ESE)+Polarity
L5. With DSE+ESE+OSE+Polarity		

Table 4: The Explored Levels of Opinion Mining Results (ND: Not Distinguished).

Partial Metric			
Metrics	P	R	F1
J&M	0.547	0.456	0.497
Baseline	0.628	0.208	0.313
Discourse based	0.596	0.127	0.209
NE&Syntax based	0.658	0.228	0.339

Table 5: Results for identifying Polarity expressions without OSEs and with not distinguished DSEs and ESEs (Ref. level L4.1 in Tab. 4).

Overlap Metric			
Metrics	P	R	F1
J&M	0.834	0.75	0.79
Baseline	0.768	0.411	0.536
Discourse based	0.772	0.425	0.548
NE&Syntax based	0.733	0.321	0.447

Table 6: Results for identifying Subjective expressions without OSEs and polarity tags (Ref. level L3.2 in Fig. 4).

In the Table 6 we also compare another most relevant result by J&M with our macro average results at corresponding level, where the OSEs removed, the DSEs and ESEs included but not distinguished, and there is no polarity values. We observe that the system of J&M outperforms our systems. In this case the results of J&M's system is computed using 10-fold cross validation, whereas we used 5-fold cross validation, in addition to this the test data of J&M is not the same with our system. This comparisons make it clear that all the systems perform well with no polarity tags and perform worse for polarity tagged expression classification. J&M's system has a balanced precision and recall score wheres our systems suffer from low recall.

We view the experiment results with no distinguished DSEs, ESEs, OSEs and polarities (Level: L1 Fig. 4). The best results obtained with NEs and syntax-based feature set is highlighted in the Table 7. We observe that the exact macro-average scores obtained with shallow discourse structure feature classification outperforms our own baseline; NEs and syntax based feature fails to outperform that baseline, this is may be due to the fact that at this level the discourse structure provide more information than the NEs.

Table 10 shows that shallow discourse structure features do not provide any improvement to our baseline results at the level of L5 (Table 4). The

Experiments	Averages	Exact Measures		
		P	R	F1
Baseline	macro avg	0.826	0.442	0.576
	micro avg	0.819	0.417	0.553
Expt with discourse struct.	macro avg	**0.833**	**0.459**	**0.592**
	micro avg	**0.830**	**0.425**	**0.562**
Expt with NE based features	macro avg	0.849	0.372	0.517
	micro avg	0.856	0.338	0.484

Table 7: Baseline & Other Experiment Results with not distinguished DSE+ESE+OSE+Polarities (L1).

NE & Syntax based Feature			
Metrics	P	R	F1
Before Feature optimisation	0.816	0.477	0.602
After Feature optimisation	0.886	0.477	0.620

Table 8: Exact Score comparison for identifying subjective expressions with NE based features with the best performing split before and after feature optimisation with test split.

Features	P	R	F1
Features in Isolation			
Baseline (B)	0.765	0.433	0.553
Named Entity (NE)	0.500	0.122	0.196
IOB_Chain (IOB)	0.428	0.100	0.162
Morph(L+INFL)	0.044	0.067	0.053
Hill-Climbing Feature Analysis			
B+NE	0.794	0.467	0.588
B+NE+IOB	0.824	0.467	0.596
B+NE+IOB+Morph	**0.816**	**0.477**	**0.602**
B+NE+IOB+Morph+BMV	0.875	0.431	0.577
Feature Ablation			
B+NE+IOB	0.824	0.467	0.596
B+NE+Morph	0.794	0.467	0.588
IOB+NE+Morph	0.285	0.067	0.108
B+IOB+Morph	0.750	0.400	0.522

Table 9: Feature Analysis Results with Single and Combined Features for the `Expt` with NE and syntax based feature set

reason behind this may be that the information provided by the current shallow discourse structure is falling short to achieve an improvement, whereas at this level the NE and syntax-based feature-set is useful to achieve better performance over the baseline scores. Results reported in Table 8 show a considerable improvement in the results over best performing split after the optimisation.

6.0.1 Feature Analysis

Our baseline feature set includes a small set of lexical and syntactic features, which convey the essential information needed to classify opinion expressions. We enrich this baseline set with some additional features, which better represent the position of opinion expressions and the respective boundaries, as well as the internal clause structure. Then, we carry out a selection step in order to identify only the feature combination that performs best in our parsing task.

We follow the hill-climbing (greedy) feature selection technique proposed by Caruana and Freitag (1994). In this optimization scheme, the best-performing set of features is selected on the basis of the best F1 "exact" score. Therefore, we increase the number of features at each step, and report the corresponding performance. In order to understand better the contribution of each feature and also to avoid sub-optimal solutions, we also run an ablation test by leaving out one feature in turn from the best-performing set. We use the development split to generate results for the feature analysis to find the best performing feature set, whereas the train split is used to build the model. Final results are generated using only the test split.

We run the hill climbing feature analysis on the best performing partition among the five partitions prepared for cross-validation. The results of our feature analysis are reported in Table 9. We do not report the scores having zero as F1-measure. We also run backward hill climbing technique, and the result is the same with forward hill climbing, because our feature set is fairly small in size. Therefore we do not report it in Table 9.

Both the feature-in-isolation procedure and the ablation test show that the bundle of baseline features is the best performing because it conveys the most essential information to classify any opinion expression. Apart from that, the named entity feature is the next most relevant feature, which carries the sufficient information on the position of a opinion expression, because an opinion expression starts frequently just after a NE occurrence. The named entity feature is more effective when integrated with information from the IOB chain, because the IOB chain feature conveys information on the span. The boolean value of the main verb in the main clause is not an important feature, probably because it conveys redundant information, therefore we do not use it any more.

We observe that the performance of the lemma increases if integrated with the inflection feature, while inflection in isolation scores a null Precision, Recall and F1. Therefore, we consider lemma and inflection together as a single feature (we call it Morph in Table 9). The best performing set includes three new features: named entities and the two features used in shallow discourse parsing, namely IOB chain and Morph.

Finally we compute the results with the test split

Experiments	Averages	Exact Measures		
		P	R	F1
Baseline	macro avg	0.671	0.361	0.468
	micro avg	0.659	0.337	0.446
Expt with discourse struct.	macro avg	0.656	0.330	0.436
	micro avg	0.638	0.317	0.423
Expt with NE based features	macro avg	**0.793**	**0.376**	**0.510**
	micro avg	**0.772**	**0.356**	**0.487**

Table 10: Baseline & Other Experiment Results with DSE+ESE+OSE+Polarities (L5).

given in Table 10. The best results obtained with NEs and syntax-based feature set is highlighted in the Table 10. We observe that the exact macro-average scores obtained with NE and syntax-based feature classification outperforms our own baseline.

7 Discussion

The classification result suffers from low recall values whereas the precision is considerably high. This is because the CRF classifier is being too conservative to tag subjectivity labels. We also analyze the result outputs from the experiment described in Section 5.4. We present here some interesting representative examples of mistakes done by the classifier.

The classifier is not able to tag a long opinion span like "*Neither Equus nor Tony Lama gave a reason* for the changed offer and Tony Lama couldn't be reached for comment". This may depend on the fact that the classifier may not get enough clue from the features on how many tokens to tag.

The use of shallow discourse structure was meant to facilitate the classification of opinion expression boundaries by exploiting information on argument spans. Some interesting cases observed while manually inspecting the problematic cases are the following (the italics strings in the examples are argument 1, while the bold parts mark argument 2, and the underlined tokens are discourse connectives according to PDTB annotations):

(a) an example with intra-sentential explicit relation:

(eg1) The White House said *Mr. Bush decided to grant duty-free status for 18 categories,* <u>but</u> **turned down such treatment for other types of watches, " because of the potential for material injury to watch producers located in the U.S. and the Virgin Islands.** [COMPARISON]

This sentence is annotated in both schemes, wholly in PDTB and partly in MPQA. There are MPQA expressions annotated both in Arg1 and in Arg2, as MPQA annotation implicitly makes use of the contrastive sense of "but". Our classifier performs well with these kind of sentences, where the relation is straightforward because no other deeper sense of the relations is implied. Problems arise when there is no MPQA annotation in one of the two arguments (i.e. the next example).

(b) an example with inter-sentential explicit relation:

(eg2) The White House said *President Bush has approved duty-free treatment for imports of certain types of watches that are n't produced in "significant quantities" in the U.S., the Virgin Islands and other U.S. possessions.* The action came in response to a petition filed by Timex Inc. for changes in the U.S. Generalised System of Preferences for imports from developing nations. <u>Previously,</u> **watch imports were denied such duty-free treatments.** [TEMPORAL]

In this case, only part of argument 1 (i.e. *has approved*) is annotated as subjective opinion expression, whereas no MPQA annotation is present in argument 2. Therefore in this case the features based on the discourse relation are not helpful. On the other hand, in this example the NE tags play a significant role in correctly locating the opinion expressions.

8 Conclusion

In this paper we investigated whether shallow discourse-level information improves the classification of subjective opinions. We chose two standard annotation schemes, viz. PDTB and MPQA, to analyze the interoperability of these schemes. Primarily we used a baseline using few linguistic features and polarity feature from a standard subjectivity lexicon by Wilson et al. (2005b). Then we performed another experiment using a set of syntax-based features from Ghosh et al. (2011) and named entities.

We found that both of the feature-sets succeed to improve the baseline considerably at various levels of fine-grained opinion mining. This is probably because the named entities tend to express the information on the opinion holder usually preceding an opinion expression. Also discourse-based features are useful, because they provide the meaning structural information on the text.

As a future work, we plan to enrich the feature-set with additional discourse level information. A constraint based approach could also be chosen to balance precision and recall.

References

Nicholas Asher, Farah Benamara, and Yannick Mathieu. 2009. Appraisal of opinion expressions in discourse. In *Lingvisticae Investigations*, volume 31(2), pages 279–292.

Eric Breck, Yejin Choi, and Claire Cardie. 2007. Identifying expressions of opinion in context. In *the 20th international joint conference on Artifical intelligence.* Morgan Kaufmann Publishers Inc.

R. Caruana and D. Freitag. 1994. Greedy attribute selection. In *11th International Conference in Machine Learning.* Morgan Kaufmann.

Yejin Choi and Claire Cardie. 2010. Hierarchical sequential learning for extracting opinions and their attributes. In *Proceedings of the 48th Annual Meeting of the Association for Computational Linguistics*, pages 269–274.

Yejin Choi, Claire Cardie, Ellen Riloff, and Siddharth Patwardhan. 2005. Identifying sources of opinions with conditional random fields and extraction patterns. In Association for Computational Linguistics, editor, *Human Language Technology and Empirical Methods in Natural Language Processing.*

Jenny Rose Finkel, Trond Grenager, and Christopher Manning. 2005. Incorporating non-local information into information extraction systems by gibbs sampling. In *Proceedings of the 43nd Annual Meeting of the Association for Computational Linguistics (ACL 2005)*, pages 363–370.

Sucheta Ghosh, Richard Johansson, Giuseppe Riccardi, and Sara Tonelli. 2011. Shallow discourse parsing with conditional random fields. In *Proceedings of the 5th International Joint Conference on Natural Language Processing (IJCNLP)*, Chiang Mai, Thailand.

Sucheta Ghosh. 2012. *End to End Discourse Parsing with Cascaded Structured Prediction.* Ph.D. thesis, University of Trento.

Vasileios Hatzivassiloglou and Kathleen R. McKeown. 1997. Predicting the semantic orientation of adjectives. In *eighth conference on European chapter of the Association for Computational Linguistics.*

B. Heerschop, Goossen F., Hogenboom A., Frasincar F., Kaymak U., and F. de Jong. 2011. Polarity analysis of texts using discourse structure. In ACM, editor, *20th ACM international conference on Information and knowledge management*, pages 1061–1070.

Minqing Hu and Bing Liu. 2004. Mining and summarizing customer reviews. In ACM, editor, *the tenth ACM SIGKDD international conference on Knowledge discovery and data mining.*

Richard Johansson and Alessandro Moschitti. 2013. Relational features in fine-grained opinion analysis. *Computational Linguistics.*

Soo-Min Kim and Eduard Hovy. 2004. Determining the sentiment of opinions. In ACL, editor, *the 20th international conference on Computational Linguistics.*

Soo-Min Kim and Eduard Hovy. 2006. Automatic identification of pro and con reasons in online reviews. In *COLING-ACL-06 Poster Session*, pages 483–490.

John Lafferty, Andrew McCallum, and Fernando Pereira. 2001. Conditional random fields: Probabilistic models for segmenting and labeling sequence data. In *Proceeding of the 18th International Conf. on Machine Learning.* Morgan Kaufmann.

Mitchell P. Marcus, Beatrice Santorini, and Mary Ann Marcinkiewicz. 1993. Building a Large Annotated Corpus of English: the Penn Treebank. *Computational Linguistics*, 19(2):313–330.

G. Minnen, J. Carroll, and D. Pearce. 2001. Applied morphological processing of english. *Natural Language Engineering*, 7(3):207–223.

Livia Polanyi and Annie Zaenen. 2006. Contextual valence shifters. In Springer Netherlands, editor, *Computing attitude and affect in text: Theory and applications.*, pages 1–10.

Ana-Maria Popescu and Orena Etzioni. 2007. Extracting product features and opinions from reviews. In Springer London, editor, *Natural language processing and text mining.*

Rashmi Prasad, Nikhil Dinesh, Alan Lee, Eleni Miltsakaki, Livio Robaldo, Aravind Joshi, and Bonnie Webber. 2008. The Penn Discourse Treebank 2.0. In *Proceedings of the 6th International Conference on Languages Resources and Evaluations (LREC 2008)*, Marrakech, Morocco.

Tjong Kim Sang, F. Erik, and Jorn Veenstra. 1999. Representing text chunks. In *In Proceedings of the Ninth Conference of the European Chapter of the Association for Computational Linguistics*, pages 173–179.

Fei Sha and Fernando Pereira. 2003. Shallow parsing with conditional random fields. In *Proceedings of HLT/NAACL*, pages 213–220.

Swapna Somasundaran and Janyce Wiebe. 2009. Recognizing stances in online debates. In *Proc. of ACL-IJCNLP-09*, pages 226–234.

Veselin Stoyanov and Claire Cardie. 2008. Topic identification for fine-grained opinion analysis. In Association for Computational Linguistics, editor, *22nd International Conference on Computational Linguistics*, volume 1.

Oscar Täckström and Ryan McDonald. 2011. Semi-supervised latent variable models for sentence-level sentiment analysis. In *ACL-11*, pages 569– 574.

Janyce Wiebe, Theresa Wilson, and Claire Cardie. 2005. Annotating expressions of opinions and emotions in language. In *Language Resources and Evaluation*, volume 39, pages 165–210.

Theresa Wilson, Janyce Wiebe, and Paul Hoffmann. 2005a. Recognizing contextual polarity in phrase-level sentiment analysis. In Association for Computational Linguistics, editor, *Human Language Technology and Empirical Methods in Natural Language Processing*.

Theresa Wilson, Janyce Wiebe, and Paul Hoffmann. 2005b. Recognizing contextual polarity in phrase-level sentiment analysis. In *Proceedings of Human Language Technology Conference and Conference on Empirical Methods in Natural Language Processing*, pages 347–354.

Cäcilia Zirn, Mathias Niepert, Heiner Stuckenschmidt, and Michael Strube. 2011. Fine-grained sentiment analysis with structural features. In *Proceedings of 5th International Joint Conference on Natural Language Processing*, pages 336–344, Chiang Mai, Thailand, November. Asian Federation of Natural Language Processing.

Justifying Corpus-Based Choices in Referring Expression Generation

Helmut Horacek
German Research Center for Artificial Intelligence (DFKI)
Saarbrücken, GERMANY
helmut.horacek@dfki.de

Abstract

Most empirically-based approaches to NL generation elaborate on co-occurrences and frequencies observed over a corpus, which are then accommodated by learning algorithms. This method fails to capture generalities in generation subtasks, such as generating referring expressions, so that results obtained for some corpus cannot be transferred with confidence to similar environments or even to other domains. In order to obtain a more general basis for choices in referring expression generation, we formulate situational and task-specific properties, and we test to what degree they hold in a specific corpus. As a novelty, we incorporate features of the role of the underlying task, object identification, into these property specifications; these features are inherently domain-independent. Our method has the potential to enable the development of a repertoire of regularities that express generalities and differences across situations and domains, which supports the development of generic algorithms and also leads to a better understanding of underlying dependencies.

1 Introduction

Choices in NL generation, as geared by examples taken from a corpus, are essentially driven by observed frequencies of partial surface expressions and their co-occurrences in this corpus. Generating referring expressions (GRE) aiming at the identification of an entity or a set of entities in a situational context is the subtask addressed by most approaches in this fashion: corpora are created for the purpose of analyzing human preferences, and several GRE challenges have been conducted over some corpora and are still under way (e.g., (Gatt and Belz 2008)). By and large, this strategy leads to quite good results, the best systems performing very accurately. However, this approach has an essential drawback: it fails to capture regularities that underly the choices observed, so that they can be expressed in a somehow general form that abstracts from details of the domain and ideosyncracies of the corpus. Abstractions of this kind are a prerequisite to transfer the results obtained in the context of a corpus to similar environments or even to other domains with reasonable confidence, which is an essential goal of empirically-based approaches.

In this paper, we attempt to find out relations between task-relevant situational properties and components of the referring expressions that subjects produced for a given corpus. We formulate situational and task-specific properties, and we test to what degree they hold in a specific corpus. As a novelty, we incorporate features of the role of the task, object identification, into these property specifications; these features are inherently domain-independent. We are convinced that the resulting regularities capture facets of principled preferences in a mildly abstracted form so that they allow a reasonable transfer to other domains. Ultimately, this techniques is intended to provide an improved basis for choices in GRE.

This paper is organized as follows. We first discuss previous work, then we motivate our approach. In the main sections, we describe the ingredients in building hypothesized regularities, and we define this method in formal terms. Then we give some preliminary results. Finally, we discuss our achievements and possible impacts, and we sketch extensions and future developments.

2 Previous Work

The task of generating referring expressions is a subtask in the traditional NL generation pipeline, the most intensively addressed one in the past decade (see (Krahmer, van Deemter 2012) for a recent overview). For a long time, there was a debate about algorithmic solutions that adequately combine computational issues with human preferences in the selection of attributes. Earlier work was characterized by featuring computational issues, such as full brevity versus the greedy heuristic (Dale, 1989), which models task properties in the search process in terms of the discriminatory power of attributes. These approaches were challenged by psychological insights, such as the role of salience (e.g., color can be perceived much quicker than other properties) and the use of redundant attributes (Pechmann 1989), a crucial issue in the GRE task. Ultimately, the dabate has been settled in favor of the incremental algorithm (Dale and Reiter 1995), which is intended to reflect these insights. The algorithms proposed have been compared in terms of their searching techniques (Bohnet and Dale 2005). The incremental algorithm contains a parameter for expressing domain-specific preferences among attributes – its instantiation has significant impact on results and quality of the expressions generated. However, the motivated specification of preferences and the attitude towards the use of redundant attributes still remain open questions.

In order to address this issue, corpora are built to examine human preferences in detail. These corpora must be the product of controled experiments, since precise evidence is needed about the situational context in which a corpus has been created. A prominent example is the TUNA corpus (Gatt, v. d. Sluis, and Deemter 2007, van Deemter et al. 2012). It comprises referring expressions from two domains: the identification of a piece of furniture resp. a person out of a set of such items, presented in a small grid. An even bigger corpus is (Guhe and Bard 2008), and two corpora based on more realistic situational 3D scenes underlying the experiments are GRE3D3 (Viethen and Dale 2008), and the bigger follow-up corpus GRE3D7 (Viethen and Dale 2011)[1] .

[1] The corpus is available for download online at www.clt.mq.edu.au/research/projects/gre3d7.

These corpora served then for the investigation of more data-oriented approaches to GRE so that they could be evaluated (Gupta and Stent 2005). Some of these corpora have been used or they are built through challenges, such as (Koller et al. 2010); competing systems try to approximate unseen examples on the basis of a corpus subset. A challenge based on the TUNA corpus is the shared task of GRE (Gatt and Belz 2008, Gatt and Belz 2010). Most participants used an adaptation of the *Incremental Algorithm*, the domain-specific parameter being modified by corpus frequencies that are accommodated by some learning algorithm. Further elements to drive choices are hard-coded rules (Kelleher and McNamee 2008), and personalized preferences (Bohnet 2008) – trials contain labels to identify the subject who produced the expression. The best systems, which used suitable learning algorithms, performed very well (see the summaries in (Belz and Gatt 2007, Gatt, Belz, and Kow 2008, Gatt, Belz, and Kow 2009)).

Apart from these challenges, a number of approaches have tried to find principles or generalities on the basis of observed data. Jordan and Walker (2005) have encapsulated the ingredients of choices in GRE in terms of rules, Viethen et al. (2010) and Viethen, Dale and Guhe (2011a) have examined the role of visual context. Finally, Viethen, Dale and Guhe (2011b) have attempted to characterize the behavior of humans in GRE: they found that the view of accommodating previous references is generally more appropriate than a purely constructive view, which is a little surprising for the first reference to an object.

3 Motivation

While the results in the TUNA challenge (and also in some other less extensive challenges) were quite satisfactory, these systems have the essential drawback of being dependent on that corpus. Similarly, this assessment also holds for the principled approaches referrred to in the last paragraph of the previous section, since they do not attempt to generalize over the corpus examined, which is even the case for the study by Viethen, Dale and Guhe (2011b). Altogether, abstracting from some given corpus is crucial, since it is unrealistic to make a new corpus evaluation for each application, corpora being rare and typically small, if available at all. In order to increase the generality of the corpus interpretation, the results must be lifted to more general grounds, so that they can be transferred to other, somehow similar domains.

Unfortunately, learning algorithms and the structure of their results are hardly useful for this purpose – they are widely human-inaccessible, without connection to easily understandable conceptions, and a comparison of results across corpora and domains is hard to imagine. In order to enable reasonable comparisons, we attempt to formulate regularities over attributes of objects and situational properties that can be tested against a corpus. In order for a regularity to qualify for this purpose, we require that it must be

- expressed in cognitive meaningful terms,
- as domain-independent as possible, and
- hold over the entire corpus to a significant degree.

The hope is that these regularities can reasonably be transferred to related domains by accommodating the domain- and corpus-dependent parts, since these regularities contain a reasonable share of domain-independent factors that can be transferred with little adaptation. Since regularities of this kind always contain some degree of domain- and/or corpus dependency, abstraction is a crucial conponent in the formulation of the regularity or in expressing the transfer method.

A major source for our motivation is the observation that previous approaches do not take the proper task, which is *identification* of objects, into account. Their corpus analyses would also work if the purpose of the expressions in the corpus would be descriptions of properties that the subjects like or dislike or have some other attitude against. We are convinced that the task to accomplish, identification, has some, possibly an essential influence on the choice of attributes. It must make a difference whether the task is even easier than average – e.g., if one salient attribute is sufficient for achieving identification – or whether producing an identifying description is really challenging – e.g., if several attributes are needed for obtaining identification, including some less salient ones.

4 Hypothesizing Regularities

Our basic idea is to establish relations between the properties of the situation in which the subjects have chosen some expressions and properties of these expressions, and to aggregate over these relations for similar situations, to find commonalities among the association between given situations and expressions chosen. There are two crucial assumptions behind our approach:

- The choices made by the subjects in the creation of the corpus can be conceived in terms of components, typically by a systematic abstraction from surface expressions (this is shared by the GRE challenges).
- There are properties of the underlying situation which capture essentials in driving the subjects' choices – hence, the selection process is to a certain extent oriented on the task to be accomplished, with some personal preferences (this is not shared by systems in the GRE challenges, at least not explicitly).

Thus, we assume that people not only choose attributes on the basis of some intrinsic properties, such as salience, but also on the basis of their contribution to the identification of the intended referent. In particular, an attribute is more likely to be chosen if it alone allows the identification rather than in a situation where several objects share the value of this attribute. Depending on the contribution of attributes to the preferred expressions, the use of an attribute may be essential or of minor relevance. Also taking into account some degree of influence between attributes, we distinguish the following basic categories:

1. *obligatory* elements, that is, attributes that must be chosen in some sort of situation
2. *exclusive* alternatives, that is, two attributes where one of them but not the other must be chosen in some sort of situation
3. *optional* elements that is, attributes that may be chosen in some sort of situation
4. *contextual* factors leading to preferences in choosing among exclusive alternatives

or distinguishing situations from others where optional elements are chosen or not

In order to test whether some attribute belongs to one of these categories, aggregations over a set of situations are made; if the test is positive, then a regularity has been found which categorizes an attribute in the context of a set of situations. The set of situations which become subject to these tests are built on the basis of conceptual commonalities. This is where we incorporate properties of the task at hand: sets of situations are built in such a way that their commonality lies in how identification can be achieved. For example, in one set of situations identification may be possible by a single attribute, in another set of situations, a pair of attributes is required. A further distinction is whether the attribute to be examined belongs to a set of attributes that represents a minimally distinguishing description, or whether it is some extra, typically salient attribute.

We do not expect to find regularities that provide one hundred percent agreement about the use of some element in preferred expressions. Moreover, corpus data can be noisy, since humans are inherently fallible. We do, however, expect sets of observations that qualify as regularities to hold over a significantly large subset.

These regularities are interpreted as a set of rules, which are intended as a backbone of a procedure that performs the same task as the subjects in the controled experiments. It is hoped that these rules capture essentials of the rationale underlying the choices made in a better way than mere surface frequencies. Then the rules can be used in principled selection procedures, hopefully even beyond the scope of the given corpus. The success of our method depends on two crucial factors:

- the identification of properties which have a chance of leading to useful discriminations
- carefully selecting and efficiently organizing the aggregation over sets of situations that enables one to test whether or not the properties suspected to lead to good discriminations indeed do so

In what follows, we present the formalization of these issues.

5 Formalization

In formal terms, a situation is conceived as a set of properties expressed as attribute value pairs, $S = \{(a_1,v_1),\ldots,(a_n,v_n)\}$, and the result as a set of components $R = \{e_1,\ldots,e_n\}$. In a pair (a,v), a is an attribute or a predicate about the attribute's contribution to the identification (prototypically, *distinguishing*), and v is a value resp. a subset of attributes of the intended referent. e is either an attribute (implicitly including all values), or a specific attribute-value pair. A trial, that is, an individually identifiable piece in the corpus, is then an association between a situation S (only with the attribute-value pair variant) and a result R, represented as $T = (S,R)$.

Aggregations of trials are formed over common properties of the situations in these trials (with a predicate about the contribution to identification), so that a set of trials $ST = \{(S_1,R_1),\ldots,(S_n,R_n)\}$ such that a set of attribute value pairs $CP=\{(a_1,v_1), \ldots,(a_n,v_n)\}$ is common to all situations: $\forall i=1,n$: $S_i \supset CP$.

In order for a regularity to fulfil the requirements of a conceptual relation stated above, the following constraints must hold, correspondingly:

1. *obligatory elements* e_{obl}

   e_{obl} must occur in the results of ST in most cases, at least as often as $thresh_{obl}$

   $e_{obl} \in R_i$ for some i: $|(S_i,R_i)| \,/\, |ST| > thresh_{obl}$

2. *exclusive alternatives* e_{alt1}, e_{alt2}

   either e_{alt1} or e_{alt2} must occur in most of the results of ST, at least as often as $thresh_{alt1}$, each of them in several, at least as often as $thresh_{alt2}$, while they generally do not co-occur, with exceptions less than $thresh_{alt3}$

   $e_{alt1} \in R_i$ for some i, $e_{alt2} \in R_j$ for some j: $|(S_i,R_i) \cup (S_j,R_j)| \,/\, |ST| > thresh_{alt1}$ ^
   $|(S_i,R_i)| \,/\, |ST|$, $|(S_j,R_j)| \,/\, |ST| > thresh_{alt2}$ ^
   $|(S_i,R_i) \cap (S_j,R_j)| \,/\, |ST| < thresh_{alt3}$

3. *optional elements* e_{opt}

   e_{opt} must occur in the results of ST in some cases, at least as frequent as $thresh_{opt}$, but it must not be obligatory and it must also not appear in a pair of exclusive alternatives (second part omitted in the formalization)

   $e_{opt} \in R_i$ for some i: $|(S_i,R_i)| \,/\, |ST| > thresh_{opt}$

Situations S_1		*Results*	*Situations* S_2		*Results*
(a_1,v_1)	(a_2,v_3)	$\{e_1,e_2\}$	(a_1,v_2)	(a_2,v_3)	$\{e_1,e_2,e_4\}$
(a_1,v_1)	(a_2,v_3)	$\{e_1,e_3\}$	(a_1,v_2)	(a_2,v_3)	$\{e_1,e_2\}$
(a_1,v_1)	(a_2,v_3)	$\{e_1,e_2,e_4\}$	(a_1,v_2)	(a_2,v_3)	$\{e_1,e_2\}$
(a_1,v_1)	(a_2,v_3)	$\{e_1,e_3\}$	(a_1,v_2)	(a_2,v_3)	$\{e_1,e_2\}$
(a_1,v_1)	(a_2,v_3)	$\{e_1,e_2\}$	(a_1,v_2)	(a_2,v_3)	$\{e_1,e_2,e_4\}$
(a_1,v_1)	(a_2,v_4)	$\{e_1,e_2,e_4\}$	(a_1,v_2)	(a_2,v_4)	$\{e_1,e_3\}$
(a_1,v_1)	(a_2,v_4)	$\{e_1,e_3,e_4\}$	(a_1,v_2)	(a_2,v_4)	$\{e_1,e_3\}$
(a_1,v_1)	(a_2,v_4)	$\{e_1,e_2\}$	(a_1,v_2)	(a_2,v_4)	$\{e_1,e_3,e_4\}$
(a_1,v_1)	(a_2,v_4)	$\{e_1,e_3\}$	(a_1,v_2)	(a_2,v_4)	$\{e_1,e_3\}$
(a_1,v_1)	(a_2,v_4)	$\{e_2,e_3\}$	(a_1,v_2)	(a_2,v_4)	$\{e_2,e_3\}$

Table 1. Illustrating categories of components

4. *contextual factors* (a_{cf},v_{cf})
   A contextual factor (a_{cf},v_{cf}) that is considered the driving force behind the choice among exclusive alternatives e_{alt1} and e_{alt2}, in the sense that it appears in the situations where one of the exclusive alternatives is part of the chosen expression, while it does not appear in the situations where the other exclusive alternative is part of the chosen expression, with exceptions less than $thresh_{cf}$

   $e_{alt1} \in R_i$ for some i, $e_{alt2} \in R_j$ for some j:
   $\forall k: (a_{cf},v_{cf}) \in S_k: |S_k \cap S_i| > thresh_{cf} \wedge$
   $|S_k \cap S_j| < (1 - thresh_{cf})$

Table 1 illustrates these categories of elements. There are two sets of situations, S_1 on the left half, and S_2 on the right, with their associated results. (a_1,v_1) is the property common to S_1, (a_1,v_2) the one common to S_2. e_1 is an obligatory element in S_1 and S_2 with $thresh_{obl} \leq 0.9$. e_2 and e_3 are exclusive alternatives in S_1 and S_2 ($thresh_{alt1} \leq 1.0$, $thresh_{alt2} \leq 0.4$, $thresh_{alt3} \geq 0.1$), even combined with a contextual factor in S_2 ($thresh_{obl} \leq 0.9$). e_4 is an optional element ($thresh_{opt} \leq 0.3$).

The thresholds in this example are purely the result of calculations based on the data, that is, they correspond precisely to the number of cases that fulfil the respective predicates – we have chosen ten instances to make the computations simple. An independent question is, how reasonable thresholds can be nailed down in numerical values. We think that the values in the example are plausible ones, but it is not clear how much weaker they may get – for example, a threshold of around 0.6 may build a transition between an obligatory and an optional element. More practical corpus examinations are needed.

6 Preliminary Results

We have applied our method to the publically available segment of the TUNA corpus. The corpus comprises referring expressions from two domains: the identification of a piece of furniture resp. a person out of a set of such items, presented in a small grid (v. d. Sluis, Gatt, and van Deemter 2006). In the furniture domain, attributes include the type of the object, its color, size, and orientedness. In the people domain, attributes most used are beardedness, wearing glasses, age, hair, and its color. In both domains, the positions on the grid are attributes. The result is simply the subset of attribute-value pairs attributed to the intended referent in the referring expression chosen by the subjects.

In addition to that, we have enhanced the representation of situations by several attributes that we thought might be driving forces in the selection of attributes for the referring expression. The ones we have built and tested so far are essentially based on two concepts:

1) subcategories of attributes (an example of linguistic evidence), and
2) contribution to identification of an object (an example of a task-specific property).

Subcategorization comprises
1) the type,
2) most salient attributes (here: color, beardedness, wearing glasses),
3) location, and
4) remaining attributes.

Concerning the contribution to identification, we distinguish for an attribute whether
1) it allows identification by itself,
2) does so together with the type attribute,
3) does so in connection with the type and a most salient attribute, and
4) neither of these.

Hence, these distinctions allow one to discriminate between varying complexities of the underlying identification task.

Based on these attributes, we have selectively tested a number of aggregations, the set of similar trials presented to subjects, which differ only in the positions of the items on the grid, and some further aggregations, combining sets of trials with comparable task complexity according to the measure introduced above. Within these aggregations, we have examined several attribute-value pairs in the set of results, as to whether their uses qualify for one of the regularities as defined in the previous section. Specifically, we have tested the role of the most salient attributes color, wearing glasses, and beardedness, we have made a comparison between size and orientation of pieces of furniture, and we have tested the role of some values of a person's hair (color, no hair).

The results are listed in Table 2. This Table contains the attributes that categorize the set of situations aggregated and the regularity derived for each set of situations. In the furniture domain, color was always used very often (regularity 1). If orientation resp. size gives a distinguishing description together with type and color, orientation resp. size and location are conceived as alternatives (regularities 2 and 3). Having a beard is at least optional (regularity 4), but obligatory if it is distinguishing (regularity 5). Similar regularities are derived for wearing glasses and hair color. Finally, hair color, if distinguishing, is conceived as an alternative to location (regularity 6). All thresholds involved are at least .75 ($thresh_{oblig}$), resp. .33 ($thresh_{alt2}$ and $thresh_{aalt}$). We did not discover any contextual factors; preferences for the use of position attributes can be grounded in personal choices (Bohnet 2008), but we did not model this aspect. Our major findings include the better effectiveness of color of pieces of furniture (*obligatory*) than color of hair (only *exclusive* alternative), and more frequent uses of position with increasing task complexity.

Set of situations	*Regularity*
1. furniture domain	obligatory (color)
2. distinguishing (type+color+orientation)	alternatives (position,orientation)
3. distinguishing (type+color+size)	alternatives (position,size)
4. applicable (beardedness)	optional (beardedness)
5. distinguishing (beardedness)	obligatory (beardedness)
6. distinguishing (hair color)	alternatives (hair color,position)

Table 2. Regularities found for the GRE task

6 Discussion

The regularities found can form the backbone of a choice mechanism in an NL generation component – obligatory elements are collected, one out of each set of the exclusive alternatives is taken, and optional elements are added until a distinguishing description is obtained. Choices in this procedure can be made more specific by the corpus frequencies, thus incorporating some element of the majority of approaches to the GRE challenge (such as (Bohnet 2008) and (Kelleher, McNamee 2008)). In contrast to these approaches, which are strictly performance-oriented, we envision a distribution of forces between human modeling of linguistically motivated and task-relevant factors and computation of the role of these factors regarding the choice among alternatives. In addition, some representation elements, notably aggregations and exclusive alternatives, give us more expressiveness than mere frequencies. As a result, we obtain a set of pieces of symbolic knowledge, which increase understanding of the task and are likely to pertain beyond the given corpus to some extent.

The regularities found constitute a set of crisp and cognitively meaningful rules; to some extent, they encapsulate particularities of the corpus against which they were tested. In terms of specificity, they are more concrete and detailed than principles tested on the basis of controled experiments. Conversely, these regularities are less specific than results obtained by learning methods.

A crucial question is to what extent our results can be accommodated for transferring regularities to related domains, and what data is missing for that purpose. The two domains examined, people and furniture, are significantly different from one another to discuss possible cross-relations, with the only commonality in terms of the grid, that is, location attributes. A comparison of regularities between the two domains shows that impacts of the domain-independent factors, that is, the cardinality of a minimally identifying expression, and the domain-specific properties, that is, the attributes, are interwoven. For example, *color*, a seamingly salient attribute in the furniture domain, is *obligatory* over the whole corpus, while a salient attribute in the people domain, *beardedness*, is only *optional*, unless it is *distinguishing* by itself. May be, this is an impact of the presence of another very salient attribute, *wearing glasses*; in the furniture domain, *color* stands out in terms of salience. Moreover, the role of *hair color*, which might be considered as ontologically related to *color* in the furniture domain, is much less prominent than *color*: even in cases where it is *distinguishing* by itself, it is only *alternative* to *location*. However, this result may be an impact of the pictures used in the experiments: they all showed scientists, and one might suspect that the role of hair color would be more prominent in other kinds of situations, e.g., for identifying attractive women.

These observations suggest a number of extensions and further uses. First of all, applying our method to a larger set of corpora would not only extent the coverage beyond people and pieces of furniture, but it would also enable different views on these kind of entities in varying situations and salience. For example, a significantly increased examination of the role of attributes and their combinations might then be possible, which is inhibited by data sparseness in the TUNA corpus and also by the fact that the corpus appears to be biased in some ways. For example, there are plenty of instances where beardedness or wearing glasses are distinguishing attributes by themselves, but this is not the case for most other attributes (e.g., wearing a tie). In addition to the increased quantity of data, it is necessary to make more fine-grained distinctions of salience categories than we did so far. In particular, a context-dependent aspect appears to be useful, which would allow one to distinguish attributes that stand out in terms of salience (such as color in the furniture domain) from similarly salient attributes – there exist several in the TUNA corpus (such as wearing glasses and beardedness). As a consequence, the number and complexity of regularities would increase.

Our general idea is that a transfer to other domains looks promising on the level of some sort of salience categories; the success of this method relies on the following assumptions:

1) people behave similarly in comparable situations (easy or difficult identification task)
2) people behave similarly in comparable perception circumstances (attribute salience)
3) salience can be reasonably generalized across situations and domains

Provided these assumptions hold, a big gain can be achieved, since assessing salience categories in some other domain appears to be much less costly than creating a corpus; moreover, such assessments may serve also other purposes than GRE. Furthermore, regularities with references to attributes abstracted into salience categories are entirely domain-independent and ready for transfer, that is, to be instantiated by attributes of suitable salience categories in the target domain.

Altogether, the results are unlikely to get as accurate as this can be done by the use of learning procedures. However, if transferring is working reasonably well to domains where learning methods are not applicable - due to lack of corpora, we can potentially achieve a big gain: decision criteria are grounded in abstractions from empirical data, which is superior to using hand-crafted rules.

7 Conclusion and Further Work

In this paper, we have presented a method for finding out relations between task-relevant situational properties and components of the expressions used in a corpus that features human preferences in the GRE subtask. We have described an application to the TUNA corpus, which uncovered some yet unobserved regularities of language use in this corpus. Since the criteria used in our method are reasonably general, we believe that some of our findings also pertain beyond the TUNA corpus and even beyond its domains.

There are at least three directions for further extensions of our approach. An obvious one is the application to other corpora in the GRE task. Another direction concerns methodological improvements – so far, choosing and testing suitable aggregations has been done semi-automatically; in the long run, this should be done by a fully automated procedure. Finally, we expect that these directions of extensions will suggest refinements in the description of regularities, e.g., more than two exclusive alternatives, and some more complex dependencies may need to be modeled, especially more fine-grained situational contexts for *optionals*.

References

Belz, A., and Gatt, A. 2007. The Attribute Selection for GRE Challenge: Overview and Evaluation Results. In Proceedings of the *Workshop on Using Corpora for NLG: Language Generation and Machine Translation (UCNLG+MT)*, pp. 75–83, Copenhagen, Denmark.

Bohnet, B. 2008. The Fingerprint of Human Referring Expressions and their Surface Realization with Graph Transducers (IS-FP, IS-GT, IS-FP-GT). In Proceedings of the *5th International Natural Language Generation Conference (INLG'08)*, pp.104-112, Salt Fork OH, USA.

Bohnet, B., and Dale, R. 2005. Viewing Referring Expression Generation as a Search Problem. In Proceedings of the *19th International Joint Conference on Artificial Intelligence (IJCAI-2005)*, pp. 1004-1009, Edinburgh, Scotland.

Dale, R. 1989. Cooking up Referring Expressions. In Proceedings of the *27th Annual Meeting of the ACL*, pp. 68-75.

Dale, R., and Reiter, E. 1995. Computational Interpretations of the Gricean Maxims in the Generation of Referring Expressions. *Cognitive Science* 18, pp. 233-263.

Gatt, A., and Belz, A. 2008. Attribute Selection for Referring Expression Generation: New Algorithms and Evaluation Methods. In Proceedings of the *5th International Natural Language Generation Conference (INLG'08)*, pp. 50-58, Salt Fork OH, USA.

Gatt, A. and Belz, A. 2010. Introducing shared task evaluation to NLG: The TUNA shared task evaluation challenges. In Emiel Krahmer and Mariet Theune, editors, Empirical Methods in Natural Language Generation. Springer Verlag, Berlin, pp. 264–293.

Gatt, A., Belz, A., and Kow, E. 2008. The TUNA Challenge 2008: Overview and Evaluation Results. In Proceedings of the *5th International Conference on Natural Language Generation (INLG'08)*, pp. 198–206, Salt Fork OH, USA.

Gatt, A., Belz, A., and Kow, E. 2009. The TUNA–REG Challenge 2009: Overview and Evaluation Results. In Proceedings of the *12th European Workshop on Natural Language Generation (ENLG-09)*, pp. 174–182, Athens, Greece.

Gatt, A, van der Sluis, I., and van Deemter, K. 2007. Evaluating algorithms for the generation of referring expressions using a balanced corpus. In Proceedings of the *11th European Workshop on Natural Language Generation (ENLG-07)*, pp. 49–56, Schloss Dagstuhl, Germany.

Guhe, M. and Bard, E. 2008. Adapting referring expressions to the task environment. In Proceedings of the *30th Annual Conference of the Cognitive Science Society (CogSci)*, pages 2404–2409, Austin, TX.

Gupta, S., and Stent, A. 2005. Automatic evaluation of referring expression generation using corpora. In Proceedings of the *Workshop on Using Corpora for Natural Language Generation*, pp. 1–6, Brighton, UK.

Jordan, P., and Walker, M. 2005. Learning content selection rules for generating object descriptions in dialogue. *Journal of Artificial Intelligence Research*, 24, pp. 157–194.

Kelleher, J., and MacNamee, B. 2008. Referring Expression Generation Challenge 2008 DIT System Descriptions (DIT-FBI, DIT-TVAS, DIT-CBSR, DIT-RBR, DIT-FBI-CBSR, DIT-TVAS-RBR). In Proceedings of the *5th International Natural Language Generation Conference (INLG'08)*, Salt Fork OH, USA.

Koller, A., Striegnitz, K., Byron, D., Cassell, J., Dale, R., Moore, J., and Oberlander, J. 2010. The first challenge on generating instructions in virtual environments. In Emiel Krahmer and Mariet Theune, editors, Empirical Methods in Natural Language Generation. Springer Verlag, Berlin, pp. 328–352.

Krahmer, E. and van Deemter, K. 2012. Computational Generation of Referring Expressions: A Survey. *Computational Linguistics* 38(1), pp. 173-218.

Pechmann, T. 1989. Incremental speech production and referential overspecification. *Linguistics* 27, pp. 98–110.

van Deemter, K., Gatt, A., van der Sluis, I., and Power, R. 2012. Generation of referring expressions: Assessing the Incremental Algorithm. *Cognitive Science*, 36(5) pp. 799-836.

van der Sluis, I., Gatt, A. and van Deemter, K. 2006. Manual for the TUNA Corpus: Referring expressions in two domains. Technical Report AUCS/ TR0705, University of Aberdeen.

Viethen, J., and Dale, R. 2008. The use of spatial relations in referring expression generation. In Proceedings of the *5th International Conference on Natural Language Generation (INLG'08)*, pp. 59–67, Salt Fork OH, USA.

Viethen, J., and Dale, R. 2011. GRE3D7: A Corpus of Distinguishing Descriptions for Objects in Visual Scenes In Proceedings of the *UCNLG+ Eval: Language Generation and Evaluation Workshop*, pp. 12–22, Edinburgh, Scotland, UK.

Viethen, J., Dale, R., and Guhe, M. 2011a. The Impact of Visual Context on the Content of Referring Expressions. In Proceedings of the *13th European Workshop on Natural Language Generation (ENLG-11)*, pp. 44–52, Nancy, France.

Viethen, J., Dale, R., and Guhe, M. 2011b. Generating subsequent reference in shared visual scenes: Computation vs. re-use. In Proceeding of the *2011 Conference on Empirical Methods in Natural Language Processing (EMNLP)*, pp. 1-9, Edinburgh, UK.

Viethen, J., Zwarts, S., Dale, R., and Guhe, M. 2010. Dialogue reference in a visual domain. In Proceedings of the *7th International Conference on Language Resources and Evaluation (LREC)*, pp. 1-1, Valetta, Malta.

A Boosting-based Algorithm for Classification of Semi-Structured Text using Frequency of Substructures

Tomoya Iwakura
Fujitsu Laboratories Ltd
iwakura.tomoya@jp.fujitsu.com

Abstract

Research in text classification currently focuses on challenging tasks such as sentiment classification, modality identification, and so on. In these tasks, approaches that use a structural representation, like a tree, have shown better performance rather than a bag-of-words representation. In this paper, we propose a boosting algorithm for classifying a text that is a set of sentences represented by tree. The algorithm learns rules represented by subtrees with their frequency information. Existing boosting-based algorithms use subtrees as features without considering their frequency because the existing algorithms targeted a sentence rather than a text. In contrast, our algorithm learns how the occurrence frequency of each subtree is important for classification. Experiments on topic identification of Japanese news articles and English sentiment classification shows the effectiveness of subtree features with their frequency.

1 Introduction

Text classification is used to classify texts such as news articles, E-mails, social media posts, and so on. A number of machine learning algorithms have been applied to text classification successfully. Text classification handles not only tasks to identify topics, such as politics, finance, sports or entertainment, but also challenging tasks such as categorization of customer E-mails and reviews by types of claims, subjectivity or sentiment (Wiebe, 2000; Banea et al., 2010; Bandyopadhyay and Okumura, 2011). To identify difficult categories on challenging tasks, a traditional bag-of-words representation may not be sufficient. Therefore, a richer, structural representation is used rather than the traditional bag-of-words. A straightforward way to extend the traditional bag-of-words representation is to heuristically add new types of features such as fixed-length n-grams such as word bi-gram or tri-gram, or fixed-length syntactic relations. Instead of such approaches, learning algorithms that handle semi-structured data have become increasingly popular (Kudo and Matsumoto, 2004; Kudo et al., 2005; Ifrim et al., 2008; Okanohara and Tsujii, 2009). This is due to the fact that these algorithms can learn better substructures for each task from semi-structured texts annotated with parts-of-speech, base-phrase information or syntactic relations.

Among such learning algorithms, boosting-based algorithms have the following advantages: Boosting-based learning algorithms have been applied to Natural Language Processing problems successfully, including text classification (Kudo and Matsumoto, 2004), English syntactic chunking (Kudo et al., 2005), zero-anaphora resolution (Iida et al., 2006), and so on. Furthermore, classifiers trained with boosting-based learners have shown faster classification speed (Kudo and Matsumoto, 2004) than Support Vector Machines with a tree kernel (Collins and Duffy, 2002).

However, existing boosting-based algorithms for semi-structured data, boosting algorithms for classification (Kudo and Matsumoto, 2004) and for ranking (Kudo et al., 2005), have the following point that can be improved. The weak learners used in these algorithms learn classifiers which do not consider frequency of substructures. This is because these algorithms targeted a sentence as their input rather than a document or text consisting of two or more sentences. Therefore, even if crucial substructures appear several times in their target texts, these algorithms cannot reflect such frequency. For example, on sentiment classification, different types of negative expressions may be preferred to a positive expression which appears several times. As a result, it may happen that a positive text using the same positive expression several times with some types of negative expressions is classified as a negative text because consideration of frequency is lacking.

This paper proposes a boosting-based algorithm for semi-structured data that considers the occurrence frequency of substructures. To simplify the problem, we first assume that a text to be classified is represented as a set of sentences represented by labeled ordered trees (Abe et al., 2002). Word sequence, base-phrase annotation, dependency tree and an XML document can be modeled as a labeled ordered tree. Experiments on topic identification of news articles and sentiment classification confirm the effectiveness of subtree features with their frequency.

2 Related Works

Prior boosting-based algorithms for semi-structured data, such as boosting algorithms for classification (Kudo and Matsumoto, 2004) and for ranking (Kudo et al., 2005), learns classifiers which do not consider frequency of substructures. Ifrim et. al (Ifrim et al., 2008) proposed a logistic regression model with variable-length N-gram features. The logistic regression learns the weights of N-gram features. Compared with these two algorithms, our algorithm learns frequency thresholds to consider occurrence frequency of each subtree.

Okanohara and Tsujii (Okanohara and Tsujii, 2009) proposed a document classification method using all substrings as features. The method uses Suffix arraies (Manber and Myers, 1990) for efficiently using all substrings. Therefore, the trees used in our method are not handled. Their method uses feature types of N-grams features, such as term frequency, inverted document frequency, and so on, in a logistic regression. In contrast, our algorithm differs in the learning of a threshold for feature values. Tree kernel (Collins and Duffy, 2002; Kashima and Koyanagi, 2002) implicitly maps the example represented in a labeled ordered tree into all subtree spaces, and Tree kernel can consider the frequency of subtrees. However, as discussed in the paper (Kudo and Matsumoto, 2004), when Tree kernel is applied to sparse data, kernel dot products between similar instances become much larger than those between different instances. As a result, this sometimes leads to overfitting in training. In contrast, our boosting algorithm considers the frequency of subtrees by learning the frequency thresholds of subtrees. Therefore, we think the problems caused by Tree kernel do not tend to take place because of the difference presented in the boosting algorithm (Kudo and Matsumoto, 2004).

3 A Boosting-based Learning Algorithm for Classifying Trees

3.1 Preliminaries

We describe the problem treated by our boosting-based learner as follows. Let $\mathcal{X}$ be all labeled ordered trees, or simply trees, and $\mathcal{Y}$ be a set of labels $\{-1, +1\}$. A labeled ordered tree is a tree where each node is associated with a label. Each node is also ordered among its siblings. Therefore, there are a first child, second child, third child, and so on (Abe et al., 2002).

Let S be a set of training samples $\{(\mathbf{x}_1, y_1), ..., (\mathbf{x}_m, y_m)\}$, where each example $\mathbf{x}_i \in \mathcal{X}$ is a set of labeled ordered trees, and $y_i \in \mathcal{Y}$ is a class label.

The goal is to induce a mapping

$$F : \mathcal{X} \rightarrow \mathcal{Y}$$

from S.

Then, we define subtrees (Abe et al., 2002).

Definition 1 *Subtree*

Let $\mathbf{u}$ *and* $\mathbf{t}$ *be labeled ordered trees. We call* $\mathbf{t}$ *a subtree of* $\mathbf{u}$*, if there exists a one-to-one mapping* φ *between nodes in* $\mathbf{t}$ *to* $\mathbf{u}$*, satisfying the conditions: (1)* φ *preserves the parent relation, (2)* φ *preserves the sibling relation, and (3)* φ *preserves the labels. We denote* $\mathbf{t}$ *as a subtree of* $\mathbf{u}$ *as*

$$\mathbf{t} \subseteq \mathbf{u}.$$

If a tree $\mathbf{t}$ is not a sbutree of $\mathbf{u}$, we denote it as

$$\mathbf{t} \nsubseteq \mathbf{u}.$$

We define the frequency of the subtree $\mathbf{t}$ in $\mathbf{u}$ as the number of times $\mathbf{t}$ occurs in $\mathbf{u}$ and denoted as

$$|\mathbf{t} \subseteq \mathbf{u}|.$$

The number of nodes in a tree $\mathbf{t}$ is referred as the size of the tree $\mathbf{t}$ and denote it as

$$|\mathbf{t}|.$$

To represent a set of labeled ordered trees, we use a single tree created by connecting the trees with the root node of the single tree in this paper. Figure 1 is an example of subtrees of a tree consisting of two sentences "a b c" and "a b" connected with the root node Ⓡ. The trees in the right box are a portion of subtrees of the left tree. Let $\mathbf{u}$ be

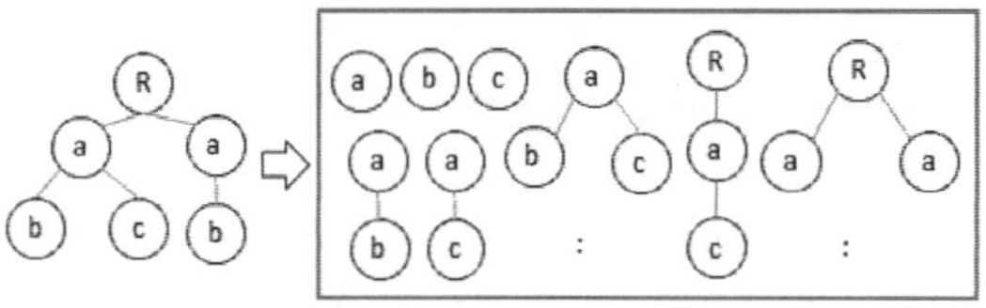

Figure 1: A labeled ordered tree and its subtrees.

the tree in the left side. For example, the size of the subtree ⓐ-ⓑ (i.e. |ⓐ-ⓑ|) is 2 and the frequency |ⓐ-ⓑ $\in$ **u**| is also 2. For the subtree ⓐ-ⓒ, the size |ⓐ-ⓒ| is also 2, however, the frequency |ⓐ-ⓒ $\in$ **u** | is 1.

3.2 A Classifier for Trees with the Occurrence Frequency of a Subtree

We define a classifier for trees - that is used as weak hypothesis in this paper. A boosting algorithm for classifying trees uses subtree-based decision stumps, and each decision stump learned by the boosting algorithm classifies trees whether a tree is a subtree of trees to be classified or not (Kudo and Matsumoto, 2004). To consider the frequency of a subtree, we define the following decision stump.

Definition 2 *Classifier for trees*

Let $\mathbf{t}$ *and* $\mathbf{u}$ *be trees,* z *be a positive integer, called frequency threshold, and* a *and* b *be a real number, called a confidence value, then a classifier for trees is defined as*

$$h_{\langle \mathbf{t},z,a,b\rangle}(\mathbf{u}) = \begin{cases} a & \mathbf{t} \subseteq \mathbf{u} \wedge z \leq |\mathbf{t} \subseteq \mathbf{u}| \\ -a & \mathbf{t} \subseteq \mathbf{u} \wedge |\mathbf{t} \subseteq \mathbf{u}| < z \\ b & otherwise \end{cases}.$$

Each decision stump has a subtree $\mathbf{t}$ and its frequency threshold z as a condition of classification, and two scores, a and b. If $\mathbf{t}$ is a subtree of $\mathbf{u}$ (i.e. $\mathbf{t} \subseteq \mathbf{u}$), and the frequency of the subtree $|\mathbf{t} \subseteq \mathbf{u}|$ is greater than or equal to the frequency threshold z, the score a is assigned to the tree. If $\mathbf{u}$ satisfies $\mathbf{t} \subseteq \mathbf{u}$ and $|\mathbf{t} \subseteq \mathbf{u}|$ is less than z, the score - a is assigned to the tree. If $\mathbf{t}$ is not a subtree of $\mathbf{u}$ (i.e. $\mathbf{t} \not\subseteq \mathbf{u}$), the score b is assigned to the tree.

This classifier is an extension of decision trees learned by learning algorithms like C4.5 (Quinlan, 1993) for classifying trees. For example, C4.5 learns the thresholds for features that have continuous values, and C4.5 uses the thresholds for classifying samples including continuous values. In a similar way, each decision stump for trees uses a frequency threshold for classifying samples with a frequency of a subtree.

3.3 A Boosting-based Rule Learning for Classifying Trees

To induce accurate classifiers, a boosting algorithm is applied. Boosting is a method to create a final hypothesis by repeatedly generating a weak hypothesis in each training iteration with a given weak learner. These weak hypotheses are combined as the final hypothesis. We use real AdaBoost used in BoosTexter (Schapire and Singer, 2000) since real AdaBoost-based text classifiers show better performance than other algorithms, such as discrete AdaBoost (Freund and Schapire, 1997).

Our boosting-based learner selects R types of rules for creating a final hypothesis F on several training iterations. The F is defined as

$$F(\mathbf{u}) = sign(\textstyle\sum_{r=1}^{R} h_{\langle \mathbf{t}_r,z_r a_r,b_r\rangle}(\mathbf{u})).$$

We use a learning algorithm that learns a subtree and its frequency threshold as a rule from given training samples $S = \{(\mathbf{x}_i, y_i)\}_{i=1}^{m}$ and weights over samples $\{w_{r,1}, ..., w_{r,m}\}$ as a weak learner. By training the learning algorithm R times with different weights of samples, we obtain R types of rules.

$w_{r,i}$ is the weight of sample number i after selecting $r-1$ types of rules, where $0 < w_{r,i}$, $1 \leq i \leq m$ and $1 \leq r \leq R$. We set $w_{1,i}$ to $1/m$.

Let $W_{r\langle y,\leq,z\rangle}(\mathbf{t})$ be the sum of the weights of samples that satisfy $\mathbf{t} \subseteq \mathbf{x}_i$ $(1 \leq i \leq m)$, $z \leq |\mathbf{t} \subseteq \mathbf{x}_i|$ and $y_i = y$ $(y \in \{\pm 1\})$,

$$W_{r\langle y,\leq,z\rangle}(\mathbf{t}) = \sum_{i \in \{i' | \mathbf{t} \subseteq \mathbf{x}_{i'}\}} w_{r,i}[[C_{\leq}(\mathbf{x}_i, \mathbf{t}, y, z)]],$$

where $[[C_{\leq}(\mathbf{x}, \mathbf{t}, y, z)]]$ is

$$[[y_i = y \wedge z \leq |\mathbf{t} \subseteq \mathbf{x}|]]$$

and $[[\pi]]$ is 1 if a proposition π holds and 0 otherwise. Similarly, let $W_{r\langle y,<,z\rangle}(\mathbf{t})$ be the sum of the weights of samples that satisfy $\mathbf{t} \subseteq \mathbf{x}_i$, $|\mathbf{t} \subseteq \mathbf{x}_i| < z$ and $y_i = y$,

$$W_{r\langle y,<,z\rangle}(\mathbf{t}) = \sum_{i \in \{i' | \mathbf{t} \subseteq \mathbf{x}_{i'}\}} [[C_{\leq}(\mathbf{x}_i, \mathbf{t}, y, z)]],$$

where $[[C_{<}(\mathbf{x}, \mathbf{t}, y, z)]]$ is

$$[[y_i = y \wedge |\mathbf{t} \subseteq \mathbf{x}| < z]].$$

$W_{r\langle y,z\rangle}(\mathbf{t})$ is the sum of $W_{r\langle y,\leq,z\rangle}(\mathbf{t})$ and $W_{r\langle -y,<,z\rangle}(\mathbf{t})$,

$$W_{r\langle y,z\rangle}(\mathbf{t}) = W_{r\langle y,\leq,z\rangle}(\mathbf{t}) + W_{r\langle -y,<,z\rangle}(\mathbf{t}).$$

$W_{r\langle y,z\rangle}(\mathbf{t})$ means the sum of the weights of samples that are classified correctly or incorrectly with a rule, $\mathbf{t}$ and z. For example, if a confidence value of the rule is positive, $W_{r\langle +1,\leq,z\rangle}(\mathbf{t})$ is the weight of correctly classified samples that have +1 as their labels, and $W_{r\langle -1,<,z\rangle}(\mathbf{t})$ is the weight of correctly classified samples that have -1 as their labels.

$W^{\neg}_{r\langle y\rangle}(\mathbf{t})$ is the sum of the weights of samples that a rule is not applied to (i.e. $\mathbf{t} \not\subseteq \mathbf{x}_i$) and $y_i = y$,

$$W^{\neg}_{r\langle y\rangle}(\mathbf{t}) = \sum_{i \in \{i' | \mathbf{t} \not\subseteq \mathbf{x}_{i'} \wedge y_i = y\}} w_{r,i}.$$

To select a tree $\mathbf{t}$ and a frequency threshold z the following $gain$ is used as the criterion:

$$gain(\mathbf{t}, z) \stackrel{\text{def}}{=} |\sqrt{W_{r\langle +1,z\rangle}(\mathbf{t})} - \sqrt{W_{r\langle -1,z\rangle}(\mathbf{t})}| + |\sqrt{W^{\neg}_{r\langle +1\rangle}(\mathbf{t})} - \sqrt{W^{\neg}_{r\langle -1\rangle}(\mathbf{t})}|.$$

To find the decision stump that maximizes $gain$ is the equivalent of finding the decision stump that minimizes the upper bound of the training error for real AdaBoost (Schapire and Singer, 2000; Collins and Koo, 2005). At boosting round r, a weak learner selects a subtree $\mathbf{t}_r$ ($\mathbf{t}_r \in \mathcal{X}$) and a frequency threshold z_r that maximizes $gain$ as a rule from training samples S with the weights of training samples $\{w_{r,1}, ..., w_{r,m}\}$:

$$(\mathbf{t}_r, z_r) = \underset{(\mathbf{t}',z')\in \mathbf{ZT}}{\arg\max}\ gain(\mathbf{t}', z'),$$

where $\mathbf{ZT}$ is

$$\{(\mathbf{t}, z) \mid \mathbf{t} \in \cup_{i=1}^{m}\{\mathbf{t}|\mathbf{t} \subseteq \mathbf{x}_i\} \wedge 1 \leq z \leq \max_{1\leq i\leq m} |\mathbf{t} \subseteq \mathbf{x}_i|\}.$$

Then the boosting-based learner calculates the confidence value of $\mathbf{t}_r$ and updates the weight of each sample. The confidence values a_r and b_r are defined as follows:

$$a_r = \tfrac{1}{2}\log(\tfrac{W_{r\langle +1,z\rangle}(\mathbf{t}_r)}{W_{r\langle -1,z\rangle}(\mathbf{t}_r)}), \text{ and}$$

$$b_r = \tfrac{1}{2}\log(\tfrac{W^{\neg}_{r\langle +1\rangle}(\mathbf{t}_r)}{W^{\neg}_{r\langle -1\rangle}(\mathbf{t}_r)}).$$

After the calculation of the confidence values for $\mathbf{t}_r$ and z, the learner updates the weight of each sample with

$$w_{r+1,i} = w_{r,i} \exp(-y_i h_{\langle \mathbf{t}_r, z_r a_r, b_r\rangle}(\mathbf{x}_i))/Z_r, \quad (1)$$

where Z_r is a normalization factor for $\sum_{i=1}^{m} w_{r+1,i} = 1$. Then the learner adds $\mathbf{t}_r$, $z_r a_r$, and b_r, to F as the r-th rule and its confidence values. The learner continues training until the algorithm obtains R rules.

3.4 Learning Rules Efficiently

We use an efficient method, rightmost-extension, to enumerate all subtrees from a given tree without duplication (Abe et al., 2002; Zaki, 2002) as

```
## S = {(x_i, y_i)}_{i=1}^m : x_i ⊆ X, y_i ∈ {±1}
## W_r = {w_{r,i}}_{i=1}^m: Weights of samples after
## learning r types of rules. w_{1,i} = 1/m
## r : The current rule number.
## The initial value of r is 1.
## T_l: A set of subtrees of size l.
## T_1 is a set of all nodes.
procedure BoostingForClassifyingTree()
While (r ≤ R)
 ## Learning a rule with the weak-learner
 {t_r, z_r} = weak-learner(T_1, S, W_r);
 ## Update weights with {t_r, z_r}
 a_r = 1/2 log(W_{r<+1,≤,z_r>}(t_r) / W_{r<-1,≤,z_r>}(t_r))
 b_r = 1/2 log(W¬_{r<+1>}(t_r) / W¬_{r<-1>}(t_r))
 ## Update weights. Z_r is a normalization
 ## factor for Σ_{i=1}^m w_{r+1,i} = 1.
 For i=1,..,m
  w_{r+1,i} = w_{r,i} exp(-y_i h_{<t_r,z_r a_r,b_r>}(x_i))/Z_r
 r++;
end While
return F(u) = sign(Σ_{r=1}^R h_{<t_r,z_r a_r,b_r>}(u)).

## learning a rule
procedure weak-learner(T_l, S, W_r)
 ## Select the best rule from
 ## subtrees of size l in T_l.
 (t_l, z_l) = selectRule(T_l, S, W_r)
 ## If the selected (t_l, z_l) is better than
 ## current optimal rule (t_o, z_o),
 ## the (t_o, z_o) is replaced with (t_l, z_l).
 If ( gain(t_o, z_o) < gain(t_l, z_l) )
  (t_o, z_o) = (t_l, z_l);
 ## The gain of current optimal rule τ.
 τ = gain(t_o, z_o);
 ## Size constraint pruning
 If (ζ ≤ l) return (t_o, z_o);
 ## Generate trees that size is l + 1.
 Foreach ( t ∈ T_l)
  ## The bound of gain
  If ( u(t) < τ) continue;
  ## Generate trees of size l + 1 by rightmost
  ## extension of a tree t of size of l.
  T_{l+1} = T_{l+1} ∪ RME(t, S);
 end Foreach
 return weak-learner(T_{l+1}, S, W_r);
end procedure
```

Figure 2: A pseudo code of the training of a boosting algorithm for classifying trees.

in (Kudo and Matsumoto, 2004). The rightmost-extension starts with a set of trees consisting of single nodes, and then expands a given tree of size $k-1$ by attaching a new node to this tree to obtain trees of size k. The rightmost extension enumerates trees by restricting the position of attachment of new nodes. A new node is added to a node existing on the unique path from the root to the rightmost leaf in a tree, and the new node is added as the rightmost sibling. The details of this method can be found in the papers (Abe et al., 2002; Zaki, 2002).

In addition, the following pruning techniques are applied.

Size constraint: We examine subtrees whose size is no greater than a size threshold ζ.

A bound of gain: We use a bound of gain u($\mathbf{t}$):

$$u(\mathbf{t}) \stackrel{\text{def}}{=} \max_{y\in\{\pm1\},\ 1\leq z\leq \max_{1\leq i\leq m}|\mathbf{t}\subseteq\mathbf{x}_i|} \sqrt{W_{r\langle y,z\rangle}(\mathbf{t})} + \max_{u\in\{\pm1\}} U_{r\langle u\rangle}(\mathbf{t}),$$

where

$$U_{r\langle u\rangle}(\mathbf{t}) = |\sqrt{\textstyle\sum_{i=1}^{m} w_{r,i}[[y_i = u]]} - \sqrt{W^{\neg}_{r\langle -u\rangle}(\mathbf{t})}|.$$

For any tree $\mathbf{t}' \in \mathcal{X}$ that has $\mathbf{t}$ as a subtree (i.e. $\mathbf{t} \subseteq \mathbf{t}'$), the $gain(\mathbf{t}', z)$ for any frequency thresholds z' of $\mathbf{t}'$, is bounded under $u(\mathbf{t})$, since, for $y \in \{\pm1\}$,

$$|\sqrt{W_{r\langle +1,z'\rangle}(\mathbf{t}')} - \sqrt{W_{r\langle -1,z'\rangle}(\mathbf{t}')}| \leq \max(\sqrt{W_{r\langle +1,z'\rangle}(\mathbf{t})}, \sqrt{W_{r\langle -1,z'\rangle}(\mathbf{t})}) \leq \sqrt{W_{r\langle y,z\rangle}(\mathbf{t})},$$ [1]

and

$$|\sqrt{W^{\neg}_{r\langle +1\rangle}(\mathbf{t}')} - \sqrt{W^{\neg}_{r\langle -1\rangle}(\mathbf{t}')}| \leq U_{r\langle u\rangle}(\mathbf{t}),$$ [2]

where z, y and u maximize $u(\mathbf{t})$.

Thus, if $u(\mathbf{t})$ is less than or equal to the $gain$ of the current N-th optimal rule τ, candidates containing $\mathbf{t}$ are safely pruned.

Figure 2 is a pseudo code representation of our boosting-based algorithm for classifying trees. First, the algorithm sets the initial weights of samples. Then, the algorithm repeats the rule learning procedure until it obtains R rules. At each boosting round, a rule is selected by the weak-learner. The weak-learner starts to select a rule from subtrees of size 1 and the new candidates are generated by rightmost extension. After a rule is selected, the weights are updated with the rule.

4 Data Set

We used the following two data sets.

- Japanese news articles: We used Japanese news articles from the collection of news articles of Mainichi Shimbun 2010 which have at least one paragraph[3] and one of the following five categories: business, entertainment, international, sports, and technology. Table 1 shows the statistics of the Mainichi Shimbun data set. The training data is 80% of the selected news articles and test and development data are 10%. We used the text data represented by bag-of-words as well as text data represented by trees in this experiment. To convert sentences in Japanese news articles to trees, we used CaboCha (Kudo and Matsumoto, 2002), a Japanese dependency parser. [4] Parameters are decided in terms of F-measure on positive samples of the development data, and we evaluate F-measure obtained with the decided parameters. F-measure is calculated as $\frac{2\times r\times p}{p+r}$, where r and p are recall and precision.

- English Amazon review data: This is a data set from (Blitzer et al., 2007) that contains product reviews from Amazon domains. The 5 most frequent categories, book, dvd, electronics, music, and video, are used in this experiment. The goal is to classify a product review as either positive or negative. We used the file, all.review, for each domain in the data set for this evaluation. By following the paper (Blitzer et al., 2007), review texts that have ratings more than three are used as positive reviews, and review texts that have ratings less than three are used as negative reviews. We used only the text data represented by word sequences in this experiment because a parser could not parse all the text data due to either the lack of memory or the parsing speed. Even if we ran the parser for two weeks, parsing on a data set

[1]We see it from $W_{r\langle y,z'\rangle}(\mathbf{t}') \leq W_{r\langle y,z'\rangle}(\mathbf{t})$ for $\mathbf{t} \subseteq \mathbf{t}'$ and $y \in \{\pm1\}$.

[2]We see it from $W^{\neg}_{r\langle y\rangle}(\mathbf{t}) = \sum_{i\in\{i'|\mathbf{t}\not\subseteq\mathbf{x}_{i'}\wedge y_i=y\}} w_{r,i} \leq \sum_{i\in\{i'|\mathbf{t}'\not\subseteq\mathbf{x}_{i'}\wedge y_i=y\}} w_{r,i} \leq \sum_{1\leq i\leq m} w_{r,i}[[y_i = y]]$ for $\mathbf{t} \subseteq \mathbf{t}'$ and $y \in \{\pm1\}$.

[3]There are articles that do not have body text due to copyright.

[4]http://code.google.com/p/cabocha/

Table 1: Statistics of Mainichi Shimbun data set. #P, #N and #W relate to the number of positive samples, the number of negative samples, and the number of distinct words, respectively.

Mainichi Shimbun									
Category	Training			Development			Test		
	#P	#N	#W	#P	#N	#W	#P	#N	#W
business	4,782	18,790	67,452	597	2,348	29,023	597	2,348	29,372
entertainment	938	22,632	67,682	117	2,829	29,330	117	2,829	28,939
international	4,693	18,879	67,705	586	2,359	28,534	586	2,359	29,315
sports	12,687	10,884	67,592	1,586	1,360	28,658	1,585	1,360	29,024
technology	473	23,097	67,516	59	2,887	29,337	59	2,887	28,571

Table 2: Statistics of Amazon data set. #N, #P and #W relate to the number of negative reviews, the number of positive reviews, and the number of distinct words, respectively.

Amazon review data									
Category	Training			Development			Test		
	#N	#P	#W	#N	#P	#W	#N	#P	#W
books	357,319	2,324,575	1,327,312	44,664	290,571	496,453	44,664	290,571	496,412
dvd	52,674	352,213	446,628	6,584	44,026	157,495	6,584	44,026	155,468
electronics	12,047	40,584	85,543	1,506	5,073	26,945	1,505	5,073	26,914
music	35,050	423,654	571,399	4,381	52,956	180,213	4,381	52,956	179,787
video	13,479	88,189	161,920	1,685	11,023	61,379	1,684	11,023	61,958

would not finish. Table 2 shows the statistics of the Amazon data set. Each training data is 80% of samples in all.review of each category, and test and development data are 10%. Parameters are decided in terms of F-measure on negative reviews of the development data, and we evaluate F-measure obtained with the decided parameters. The number of positive reviews in the data set is much larger than negative reviews. Therefore, we evaluated the F-measure of the negative reviews.

To represent a set of sentences represented by labeled ordered trees, we use a single tree created by connecting the sentences with the root node of the single tree.

5 Experiments

5.1 Experimental Results

To evaluate our classifier, we compare our learning algorithm with an algorithm that does not learn frequency thresholds. For experiments on Mainichi Shimbun, the following two data representations are used: Bag Of Words (BOW) (i.e. $\zeta = 1$), and trees (Tree). For the representations of texts of Amazon data set, BOW and N-gram are used. The parameters, R and ζ, are $R = 10,000$ and $\zeta = \{2, 3, 4, 5\}$.

Table 3 and Table 4 show the experimental results on the Mainichi Shimbun and on the Amazon data set. +FQ suggests the algorithms learn frequency thresholds, and -FQ suggests the algorithms do not. A McNemars paired test is employed on the labeling disagreements. If there is a statistical difference ($p < 0.01$) between a boosting (+FQ) and a boosting (-FQ) with the same feature representation, better results are asterisked (*).

The experimental results showed that classifiers that consider frequency of subtrees attained better performance. For example, Tree(+FQ) showed better accuracy than Tree(-FQ) on three categories on the Mainichi Shimbun data set. Compared with BOW(+FQ), Tree(+FQ) also showed better performance on four categories.

On the Amazon data set, N-gram(+FQ) also had better performance than BOW and N-gram(-FQ). N-gram(+FQ) performed better performances than BOW on all five categories, while performing better than N-gram(-FQ) on four categories. These results show that our proposed methods contributed to improved accuracy.

5.2 Examples of Learned Rules

By learning frequency thresholds, classifiers learned by our boosting algorithm can distinguish subtle differences of meanings. The following are some examples observed in rules learned from the book category training data. For example, three types of thresholds for "great" were learned. This seems to capture more occurrences of "great" indicated positive meaning. For classifying texts as positive, "I won't read" with $2 \leq$, which means

Table 3: Experimental Results of the training on the Mainichi Shinbun. Results in bold show the best accuracy, and while an underline means the accuracy of a boosting is better than the booting algorithm with the same feature representation (e.g. Tree(-FQ) for Tree(+FQ)) on each category.

	BOW		Tree	
Category	+FQ	-FQ	**+FQ**	-FQ
business	88.79	88.87*	**91.45***	90.89
entertaiment	95.07*	94.27	**95.11***	94.64
international	85.25	85.99*	87.91	**88.28***
sports	98.17	98.52*	**98.70***	98.64
technology	**83.02***	78.50	79.21	80.77*

Table 4: Experimental Results of the training on the Amazon data set. The meaning of results in bold and each underline are the same as Figure 3.

	BOW		N-gram	
Category	+FQ	-FQ	**+FQ**	-FQ
books	74.35*	74.13	**87.33***	87.20
dvd	83.18*	82.96	93.35	**93.66***
electronics	89.39*	89.06	93.36	**93.57***
music	77.85*	77.57	**91.65***	91.30
video	95.09*	95.04	**97.10***	96.86

more than once, was learned. Generally, "I won't read" seems to be used in negative reviews. However, reviews in training data include "I wont' read" more than once is positive reviews. In a similar way, "some useful" and "some good" with < 2, which means less than 2 times, were learned for classifying as negative. These two expression can be used in both meanings like "some good ideas in the book." or "... some good ideas, but for ... ". The learner seems to judge only one time occurrences as a clue for classifying texts as negative.

6 Conclusion

We have proposed a boosting algorithm that learns rules represented by subtrees with their frequency information. Our algorithm learns how the occurrence frequency of each subtree in texts is important for classification. Experiments with the tasks of sentiment classification and topic identification of new articles showed the effectiveness of subtree features with their frequency.

References

Kenji Abe, Shinji Kawasoe, Tatsuya Asai, Hiroki Arimura, and Setsuo Arikawa. 2002. Optimized substructure discovery for semi-structured data. In *PKDD'02*, pages 1–14.

Sivaji Bandyopadhyay and Manabu Okumura, editors. 2011. *Sentiment Analysis where AI meets Psychology*. Asian Federation of Natural Language Processing, Chiang Mai, Thailand, November.

Carmen Banea, Rada Mihalcea, and Janyce Wiebe. 2010. Multilingual subjectivity: are more languages better? In *Proc. of COLING '10*, pages 28–36.

John Blitzer, Mark Dredze, and Fernando Pereira. 2007. Biographies, bollywood, boom-boxes and blenders: Domain adaptation for sentiment classification. In *Proc. of ACL'07*, pages 440–447.

Michael Collins and Nigel Duffy. 2002. New ranking algorithms for parsing and tagging: Kernels over discrete structures, and the voted perceptron. In *Proc. of ACL'02*, pages 263–270.

Michael Collins and Terry Koo. 2005. Discriminative reranking for natural language parsing. *Computational Linguistics*, 31(1):25–70.

Yoav Freund and Robert E. Schapire. 1997. A decision-theoretic generalization of on-line learning and an application to boosting. *Journal of computer and system sciences 55(1)*.

Georgiana Ifrim, Gökhan Bakir, and Gerhard Weikum. 2008. Fast logistic regression for text categorization with variable-length n-grams. In *Proc. of KDD'08*, pages 354–362.

Ryu Iida, Kentaro Inui, and Yuji Matsumoto. 2006. Exploiting syntactic patterns as clues in zero-anaphora resolution. In *Proc. of Meeting of Association for Computational Linguistics*.

Hisashi Kashima and Teruo Koyanagi. 2002. Kernels for semi-structured data. In *ICML'02*, pages 291–298.

Taku Kudo and Yuji Matsumoto. 2002. Japanese dependency analysis using cascaded chunking. In *Proc. of CoNLL'02*, pages 1–7.

Taku Kudo and Yuji Matsumoto. 2004. A boosting algorithm for classification of semi-structured text. In *Proc. of EMNLP'04*, pages 301–308, July.

Taku Kudo, Jun Suzuki, and Hideki Isozaki. 2005. Boosting-based parse reranking with subtree features. In *Proc. of ACL'05*, pages 189–196.

Udi Manber and Gene Myers. 1990. Suffix arrays: a new method for on-line string searches. In *Proceedings of the first annual ACM-SIAM symposium on Discrete algorithms*, SODA '90, pages 319–327.

Daisuke Okanohara and Jun'ichi Tsujii. 2009. Text categorization with all substring features. In *SDM*, pages 838–846.

J. R. Quinlan. 1993. *C4.5: Programs for Machine Learning*. Morgan Kaufmann.

Robert E. Schapire and Yoram Singer. 2000. Boostexter: A boosting-based system for text categorization. *Machine Learning*, 39(2/3):135–168.

Janyce Wiebe. 2000. Learning subjective adjectives from corpora. In *Proceedings of the Seventeenth National Conference on Artificial Intelligence and Twelfth Conference on Innovative Applications of Artificial Intelligence*, pages 735–740. AAAI Press.

Mohammed Javeed Zaki. 2002. Efficiently mining frequent trees in a forest. In *Proc. of KDD'02*, pages 71–80.

Headerless, Quoteless, but not Hopeless? Using Pairwise Email Classification to Disentangle Email Threads

Emily K. Jamison [‡] **and Iryna Gurevych** [†‡]
† Ubiquitous Knowledge Processing Lab (UKP-DIPF),
German Institute for Educational Research and Educational Information
Schloßstr. 29, 60486 Frankfurt, Germany
‡Ubiquitous Knowledge Processing Lab (UKP-TUDA),
Department of Computer Science, Technische Universität Darmstadt
Hochschulstr. 10, 64289 Darmstadt, Germany
`http://www.ukp.tu-darmstadt.de`

Abstract

Thread disentanglement is the task of separating out conversations whose thread structure is implicit, distorted, or lost. In this paper, we perform email thread disentanglement through pairwise classification, using text similarity measures on non-quoted texts in emails. We show that i) content text similarity metrics outperform style and structure text similarity metrics in both a class-balanced and class-imbalanced setting, and ii) although feature performance is dependent on the semantic similarity of the corpus, content features are still effective even when controlling for semantic similarity. We make available the Enron Threads Corpus, a newly-extracted corpus of 70,178 multi-email threads with emails from the Enron Email Corpus.

1 Introduction

Law enforcement agencies frequently obtain large amounts of electronic messages, such as emails, which they must search for evidence. However, individual messages may be useless without the conversational context they occur in. Most modern emails contain useful metadata such as the MIME header `In-Reply-To`, which marks relations between emails in a thread and can be used to disentangle threads. However, there are easy methods of obfuscating email threads: opening an email account for a single purpose; using multiple email accounts for one person; sharing one email account among multiple persons; changing the `Subject` header; and removing quoted material from earlier in the thread.

How can emails be organized by thread without metadata such as their MIME headers?

We propose to use text similarity metrics to identify emails belonging to the same thread. In this paper, as a first step for temporal thread disentanglement, we perform pairwise classification experiments on texts in emails using no MIME headers or quoted previous emails. We have found that content-based text similarity metrics outperform a Dice baseline, and that structural and style text similarity features do not; adding these latter feature groups does not significantly improve total performance. We also found that content-based features continue to outperform the others in both a class-balanced and class-imbalanced setting, as well as with semantically controlled or non-controlled negative instances.

In NLP, Elsner and Charniak (2010) described the task of *thread disentanglement* as "the clustering task of dividing a transcript into a set of distinct conversations," in which extrinsic thread delimitation is unavailable and the threads must be disentangled using only intrinsic information. In addition to emails with missing or incorrect MIME headers, entangled electronic conversations occur in environments such as interspersed Internet Relay Chat conversations, web 2.0 article response conversations that do not have a hierarchical display order, and misplaced comments in Wiki Talk discussions.

Research on disentanglement of conversation threads has been done on internet relay chats (Elsner and Charniak, 2010), audio chats (Aoki et al., 2003), and emails *with* headers and quoted material (Yeh, 2006; Erera and Carmel, 2008). However, to the best of our knowledge, no work has investigated reassembling email threads *without* the help of MIME headers or quoted previous emails.

Previous researchers have used a number of email corpora with high-precision (non-Subject-clustered) thread marking. Joti et al. (2010) used the BC3 corpus of 40 email threads and 3222 emails for topic segmentation. Carenini et al. (2008) annotated 39 email "conversations" from the Enron Email Corpus for email summariation. Wan and McKeown (2004) used a privately-available corpus of 300 threads for summary generation. Rambow et al. (2004) used a privately-available corpus of 96 email threads for thread summarization.

2 Data

The Enron Email Corpus (EEC)[1] consists of the 517,424 emails (159 users' accounts and 19,675 total senders) that existed on the Enron Corporation's email server (i.e., other emails had been previously deleted, etc) when it was made public .

2.1 Gold Standard Thread Extraction from the Enron Email Corpus

We define an email thread as a directed graph of emails connected by *Reply* and *Forward* relations. In this way, we attempt to identify email discussions between users. However, the precise definition of an email thread actually depends on the implementation that we, or any other researchers, used to identify the thread.

Previous researchers have derived email thread structure from a variety of sources. Wu and Oard (2005), and Zhu et al. (2005) auto-threaded all messages with identical, non-trivial, `Fwd:` and `Re:`-stripped `Subject` headers. Klimt and Yang (2004) auto-threaded messages that had stripped `Subject` headers and were among the same users (addresses). Lewis and Knowles (1997) assigned emails to threads by matching quotation structures between emails. Wan and McKeown (2004) reconstructed threads by header Message-ID information. Rambow et al. (2004) used a privately-available corpus of 96 email threads, but did not specify how they determined the threads.

As the emails in the EEC do not contain any inherent thread structure, it was necessary for us to create email threads. First, we implemented Klimt and Yang (2004)'s technique of clustering the emails into threads that have the same `Subject` header (after it has been stripped of prefixes such as `Re:` and `Fwd:`) and shared participants. To determine whether emails were among the same users, we split a `Subject`-created email proto-thread apart into any necessary threads, such that the split threads had no senders or recipients (including `To`, `CC`, and `BCC`) in common.

The resulting email clusters had a number of problems. Clusters tended to over-group, because a single user included as a recipient for two different threads with the `Subject` "Monday Meeting" would cause the threads to be merged into a single cluster. In addition, many clusters consisted of all of the issues of a monthly subscription newsletter, or nearly identical petitions (see Klimt and Yang (2004)'s description of the "Demand Ken Lay Donate Proceeds from Enron Stock Sales" thread), or an auto-generated log of Enron computer network problems auto-emailed to the Enron employees in charge of the network. Such clusters of "broadcast" emails do not satisfy our goal of identifying email discussions between users.

Many email discussions between users exist in previously quoted emails auto-copied at the bottom of latter emails of the thread. A single-annotator hand-investigation of 465 previously quoted emails from 20 threads showed that none of them had interspersed comments or had otherwise been altered by more recent thread contributors. Threads in the EEC are quoted multiple times at various points in the conversation in multiple surviving emails. In order to avoid creating redundant threads, which would be an information leak risk during evaluation, we selected as the thread source the email from each Klimt and Yang (2004) cluster with the most quoted emails, and discarded all other emails in the cluster. We used the quote-identifying regular expressions from Yeh (2006) (see Table 1) to identify quoted previous emails.[2]

There are two important benefits to the creation methodology of the Enron Threads Corpus[3]. First, since the emails were extracted from the same document, and the emails would only have been included in the same document by the email client if one was a `Reply` or `Forward` of the other, precision is very high (approaching 100%).[4] This is

[1]The EEC is in the public domain: `http://www.cs.cmu.edu/~enron/`

[2]The variety of email clients used at the time of these emails results in a variety of headers available in the EEC. Also, some emails have no sender, etc., because they were only saved as incomplete drafts.

[3]We have made the Enron Threads Corpus available online at `www.ukp.tu-darmstadt.de/data/text-similarity/email-disentanglement`

[4]In a handcount of 465 emails and 20 email threads, our

[-]+ Auto forwarded by <anything>[-]+
[-]+ Begin forwarded message [-]+
[-]+ cc:Mail Forwarded [-]+
[-]+ Forwarded by <person>on <datetime>[-]+
[_]+ Forward Header [_]+
[-]+ Forwarded Letter [-]+
[-]+ Forwarded Message: [-]+
"<person>" wrote:
Starts with To:
Starts with <
... and more ...

Table 1: Representative examples of Yeh (2006) regular expressions for identifying quoted emails.

Thread Size	Num threads
2	40,492
3	15,337
4	6,934
5	3,176
6	1,639
7	845
8	503
9	318
10	186
11-20	567
21+	181

Table 2: Thread sizes in the Enron Threads Corpus.

better precision than threads clustered from separate email documents, which may have the same `Subject`, etc. generating false positives. Some emails will inevitably be left out of the thread, reducing recall, because they were not part of the thread branch that was eventually used to represent the thread, or simply because they were not quoted. Our pairwise classification experiments, described in Section 4, are unaffected by this reduced recall, because each experimental instance includes only a pair of emails, and not the entire thread.

Second, because the thread source did not require human annotation, using quoted emails gives us an unprecedented number of threads as data: 209,063 emails in 70,178 threads of two emails or larger. The sizes of email threads in the Enron Threads Corpus is shown in Table 2. Emails have an average of 80.0$\pm$201.2 tokens, and an average count of 4.4$\pm$9.3 sentences. Many of the emails are quite short: 18% are under 10 tokens, 19% are 10-20 tokens, and 13% are 20-30 tokens.

3 Text Similarity Features

We cast email thread disentanglement as a text similarity problem. Ideally, there exists a text similarity measure that marks pairs of emails from the same thread as *more similar* than pairs of emails from different threads. We evaluate a number of text similarity measures, divided according to Bär et al. (2011)'s three groups: Content Similarity, Structural Similarity, Style Similarity. Each set of features investigates a different manner in which email pairs from the same thread may be identified. In our experiments, all features are derived from the body of the email, while all headers such as `Recipients`, `Subject`, and `Timestamp` are ignored.

Content features. Content similarity metrics capture the string overlap between emails with similar content. A pair of emails with a high content overlap is shown below.

The *Longest Common Substring measure* (Gusfield, 1997) identifies uninterrupted common strings, while the *Longest Common Subsequence measure* (Allison and Dix, 1986) and the single-text-length-normalized *Longest Common Subsequence Norm measure* identify common strings containing interruptions and text replacements and *Greedy String Tiling measure* (Wise, 1996) allows reordering of the subsequences. Other measures which treat texts as sequences of characters and compute similarities with various metrics include *Levenshtein* (1966), *Monge Elkan Second String measure* (Monge and Elkan, 1997), *Jaro Second String* measure (Jaro, 1989), and *Jaro Winkler Second String* measure (Winkler, 1990). A *Cosine Similarity-type measure* was used, based on term frequency within the document. Sets of n-grams from the two emails are compared using the Jaccard coefficient (from Lyon et al. (2004)) and Broder's (1997) *Containment* measure.

Structural features. Structural features attempt to identify similar syntactic patterns between the two texts, while overlooking topic-specific vocabulary. We propose that sturctural features, as well as style features below, may help in classification by means of communication accommodation theory (Giles and Ogay, 2007).

Stamatatos's *Stopword n-grams* (2011) capture syntactic similarities, by identifying text reuse where just the content words have been replaced and the stopwords remain the same. We measured the stopword n-gram overlap with Broder's (1997) *Containment* measure and four different stopword lists. We also tried the *Containment* measure and an *NGram Jaccard measure* with *part-of-speech* tags. *Token Pair Order* (Hatzivassiloglou et al.

system misidentified about 1% of emails from regular expression error.

1999) uses pairs of words occurring in the same order for the two emails; *Token Pair Distance* (Hatzivassiloglou et al., 1999) measures the distance between pairs of words. Both measures use computed feature vectors for both emails along all shared word pairs, and the vectors are compared with Pearson correlation.

Style features. Style similarity reflects authorship attribution and surface-level statistical properties of texts.

Type Token Ratio (TTR) measure calculates text-length-sensitive and text-homogeneity-sensitive vocabulary richness (Templin, 1957). However, as this measure is sensitive to differences in document length between the pair of documents (documents become less lexically diverse as length and token count increases but type count levels off), and fluctuating lexical diversity as rhetorical strategies shift within a single document, we also used *Sequential TTR* (McCarthy and Jarvis, 2010), which corrects for these problems. *Sentence Length* and *Token Length* (inspired by (Yule, 1939)) measure the average number of tokens per sentence and characters per token, respectively. *Sentence Ratio* and *Token Ratio* compare *Sentence Length* and *Token Length* between the two emails (Bär et al., 2011). *Function Word Frequencies* is a Pearson's correlation between feature vectors of the frequencies of 70 pre-identified function words from Mosteller and Wallace (1964) across the two emails. We also compute *Case Combined Ratio*, showing the percentage of UPPERCASE characters in both emails combined ($\frac{UPPERCASE_{e1}+UPPERCASE_{e2}}{ALLCHARS_{e1}+ALLCHARS_{e2}}$), and *Case Document similarity*, showing the similarity between the percentage of UPPERCASE characters in one email versus the other email.

4 Evaluation

In this series of experiments, we evaluate the effectiveness of different feature groups to classify pairs of emails as being from the same thread (*positive*) or not (*negative*). Each instance to be classified is represented by the features from a pair of emails and the instance classification, positive or negative.

We used a variation of K-fold cross-validation for evaluation. The 10 folds contained carefully distributed email pairs such that email pairs with emails from the same thread were never used in pairs of training, development, and testing sets, to avoid information leakage. All instances were at one point in a test set. Instance division was roughly 80% training, 10% development, and 10% test data. Reported results are the weighted averages across all folds.

The evaluation used logistic regression, as implemented in Weka (Hall et al., 2009). Default parameters were used. We use a baseline algorithm of Dice Similarity between the texts of the two emails as a simple measure of set similarity. We created an upper bound by annotating 100 positive and 100 negative instances. A single native English speaker annotator answered the question, "Are these emails from the same thread?"

4.1 Data Sampling

Although we had 413,814 positive instances available in the Enron Threads Corpus, we found that classifier performance was unaffected by the amount of training data, down to very low levels (see Figure 1). However, because the standard deviation in the data did not level out until around 1,200 class-balanced training instances[5], we used this number of positive instances (600) in each of our experiments.

In order to estimate effectiveness of features for different data distributions, we used three different subsampled datasets.

Random Balanced (RB) Dataset. The first dataset is class-balanced and uses 1200 training instances. Minimum email length is one word. For every positive instance we used, we created a negative email pair by taking the first email from the positive pair and pseudo-randomly pairing it with another email from a different thread that was assigned to the same training, development, or test set.

However, the probability of semantic similarity between two emails in a positive instance is much greater than the probability of semantic similarity between two emails in a randomly-created negative instance. The results of experiments on our first dataset reflect both the success of our text similarity metrics and the semantic similarity (i.e., topical distribution) within our dataset. The topical distribution will vary immensely between different email corpora. To investigate the performance of our features in a more generaliable environment, we created a subsample dataset that con-

[5]Each fold used 1,200 training instances and 150 test instances.

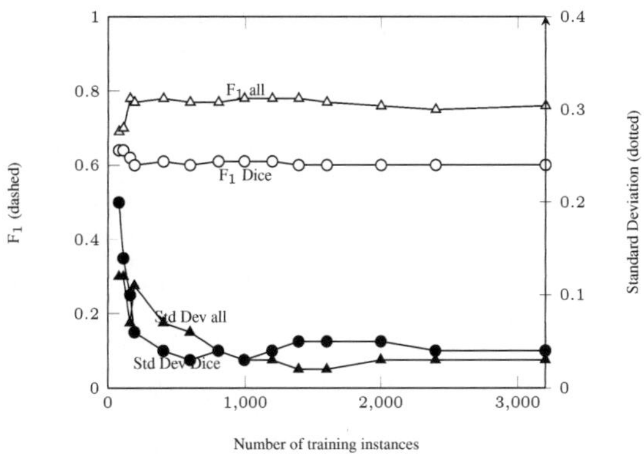

Figure 1: Training data sizes and corresponding F_1 and standard deviation.

trolls for semantic similarity within and outside of the email thread.

Semantically Balanced (SB) Dataset. The second dataset combines the same positive instances as the first set with an equal number of semantically-matched negative instances for a training size of 1200 instances, and a minimum email length of one word. For each positive instance, we measured the semantic similarity within the email pair using Cosine Similarity and then created a negative instance with the same ($\pm$.005) similarity. Emails had an average of 96$\pm$287 tokens and 5$\pm$11sentences, and a similar token size distribution as SB.

Random Imbalanced (RI) Dataset. However, both the RB and SB datasets use a class-balanced distribution. To see if our features are still effective in a class-imbalanced environment, we created a third dataset with a 90% negative, 10% positive distribution for both the training and test sets[6]. Specifically, we used the first dataset and then added an extra 8 negative instances for each positive instance. Experiments with this dataset use 10-fold cross validation, where each fold has 6000 training and 750 test instances. No minimum email length was used, similar to a more natural distribution.

4.2 Results

Our results are shown in Table 3. Since we aim to detect pairs of emails belonging to the same thread rather than unrelated emails, we measure the system performance on the positive class. We use the standard F-measure of $F_1=\frac{2\times P(pos)\times R(pos)}{P(pos)+R(pos)}$. As a measure to show performance on both positive and negative classes, we provide a standard accuracy measure of $Acc=\frac{TP+TN}{TP+FN+TN+FP}$. Feature groups are shown in isolation as well as the complete set of features minus one group. [7]

With the RB corpus, the best performing single feature configuration, content features group (P=.83 $\pm$.04), matches the human upper bound precision(P=.84). The benefit of content features is confirmed by the reductions in complete feature set performance when they are left out. The content features group was the only group to perform significantly above the Dice baseline. Adding the other feature groups does not significantly improve the overall results. Further leave-one-out experiments revealed no single high performing feature within the content features group.

Structural features produced low performance, failing to beat the Chance baseline. Structural similarity from rhetorical strategy is rare in an email conversational setting. Any structural benefits are likely to come from sources unavailable in a disguised email situation, such as auto-signatures identifying senders as the same person. The low results on structural features show that we are not relying on such artifacts for classification.

Style features were also unhelpful, failing to significantly beat the Dice baseline. The features failed to identify communication accomodation within the thread.

Results on the SB dataset show that there is a noticeable drop in classification for all feature groups when negative instances have a similar semantic similarity as positive instances. The configuration with all features showed a 15 percentage point drop in precision, and a 12 percentage point drop in accuracy. However, content features continues to be the best performing feature group with semantically similar negative instances, as with random negative instances, and outperformed the Dice baseline. Adding the additional feature groups does not significantly improve overall performance.

The results on the RI corpus mirror results from the balanced (RB) corpus. The best-performing

[6]This class imbalance is still artificially lower than a more natural 99.99+% negative natural class imbalance.

[7]Additionally, we tried a semantic similarity measures features group. We used Gabrilovich & Markovitch's (2007) Explicit Semantic Analysis (ESA) vector space model, with three different lexical-semantic resources: WordNet, Wikipedia, and Wiktionary. The performance of this feature group (P=.50) was not good enough to include in Table 3.

Feature	RB F_1	SB F_1	RI F_1	RB Acc	SB Acc	RI Acc
Chance	.50	.50	.90	.50	.50	.90
Dice Baseline	.61 $\pm$.04	.56 $\pm$.04	.09 $\pm$.04	.63 $\pm$.03	.58 $\pm$.03	.9 $\pm$.0
Upper Bound	.89	-	-	.89	-	-
Just content	.78 $\pm$.03	.65 $\pm$.04	.38 $\pm$.06	.79 $\pm$.03	.67 $\pm$.03	.92 $\pm$.01
Just struct	.42 $\pm$.05	.33 $\pm$.04	.06 $\pm$.05	.55 $\pm$.03	.52 $\pm$.03	.90 $\pm$.00
Just style	.60 $\pm$.05	.57 $\pm$.03	.00 $\pm$.00	.60 $\pm$.04	.56 $\pm$.03	.90 $\pm$.00
No content	.60 $\pm$.03	.55 $\pm$.03	.08 $\pm$.05	.62 $\pm$.03	.57 $\pm$.02	.90 $\pm$.00
No struct	.78 $\pm$.03	.66 $\pm$.03	.41 $\pm$.06	.79 $\pm$.02	.67 $\pm$.02	.92 $\pm$.01
No style	.78 $\pm$.03	.63 $\pm$.04	.38 $\pm$.06	.79 $\pm$.03	.65 $\pm$.03	.92 $\pm$.00
Everything	.78 $\pm$.02	.65 $\pm$.03	.40 $\pm$.05	.79 $\pm$.02	.67 $\pm$.03	.92 $\pm$.00

Table 3: Email pair classification results, with random negative instances.

Text	Freq in Corpus
FYI	48
FYI <*name* >	23
one person's autosignature	7
Thanks!	5
Please print.	5
yes	4
FYI, Kim.	3
ok	3
please handle	3

Table 4: Common texts and their frequencies in the corpus.

individual feature group in both experiments was the content feature group; in the class-imbalanced experiments the group alone beats the Dice baseline in F_1 by 29 percentage points and reduces accuracy error by about 20%.

Elsner and Charniak (2011) use coherence models to disentangle chat, using some features (entity grid, topical entity grid) which correspond to the information in our content features group. They also found these content-based features to be helpful.

4.3 Inherent limitations

Certain limitations are inherent in email thread disentanglement. Some email thread relations cannot be detected with text similarity metrics, and require extensive discourse knowledge, such as the emails below.

> **Email1:** *Can you attend the Directors Fund Equity Board Meeting next Wednesday, Nov 5, at 3pm?*
>
> **Email2:** *Yes, I will be there.*

Several other problems in email thread disentanglement cannot be solved with any discourse knowledge. One problem is that some emails are identical or near-identical; there is no way to choose between textually identical emails. Table 4 shows some of the most common email texts in our corpus, based on a <.05 similarity value from Jaro Second String similarity, as described in Section 3.

However, near identical texts make up only a small portion of the emails in our corpus. In a sample of 5,296 emails, only 3.6% of email texts were within a .05 Jaro Second String similarity value of another text.

Another problem is that some emails are impossible to distinguish without world and domain knowledge. Consider a building with two meeting rooms: *A101* and *A201*. Sometimes *A101* is used, and sometimes *A201* is used. In response to the question, *Which room is Monday's meeting in?*, there may be no way to choose between *A101* and *A201* without further world knowledge.

Another problem is topic overlap. For example, in a business email corpus such as the EEC, there are numerous threads discussing Monday morning 9am meetings. The more similar the language used between threads, the more difficult the disentanglement becomes, using text similarity. This issue is addressed with the SB dataset.

Finally, our classifier cannot out-perform humans on the same task, so it is important to note human limitations in email disentanglement. Our human upper bound is shown in Table 3. We will further address this issue in Sections 4.4.

4.4 Error Analysis

We inspected 50 email pairs each of true positives, false positives, false negatives, and true negatives from our RB experiments[8] . We inspected for both technical details likely to affect classification, and for linguistic features to guide future research. Technical details included small and large text errors (such as unidentified email headers or incorrect email segmentation), custom and non-custom email signatures, and the presense of large signatures likely to affect classification. Linguistic features included an appearance of consecutivity (emails appear in a Q/A relation, or one is informative and one is 'please print', etc.), similarity of social style ("Language vocab level, professionalism, and social address are a reasonable match"), and the annotator's perception that the emails could be from the same thread.

An example of a text error is shown below.

> **Sample text error:**
>
> *Craig Young*
>
> *09/08/2000 01:06 PM*

[8]Despite the semantic similarity control, an error analysis of our SB experiments showed no particularly different results.

Names and dates occur frequently in legitimate email text, such as meeting attendance lists, etc., which makes them difficult to screen out. Emails from false positives were less likely to contain these small errors (3% versus 14%), which implies that the noise introduced from the extra text has more impact than the false similarity potentially generated by similar text errors. Large text errors (such as 2 emails labelled as one) occurred in only 1% of emails and were too rare to correlate with results.

Autosignatures, such as the examples below, mildly impacted classification.

> **Custom Autosignature:**
> *Carolyn M. Campbell*
> *713-276-7307 (phone)*
>
> **Non-custom Autosignature:**
> *Get your FREE download of MSN Explorer at http://explorer.msn.com*

Instances classified as negative (both FN and TN) were marginally more likely to have had one email with a non-customized autosignature (3% versus 1.5%) or a customized auto-signature (6.5% versus 3.5%). Autosignatures were also judged likely to affect similarity values more often on instances classified as negative (20% of instances). The presence of the autosignature may have introduced enough noise for the classifier to decide the emails were not similar enough to be from the same thread. We define a non-custom auto-signature as any automatically-added text at the bottom of the email. We did not see enough instances where both emails had an autosignature to evaluate whether similarities in autosignatures (such as a common area code) impacted results.

Some email pair similarities, observable by humans, are not being captured by our text similarity features. Nearly all (98%) positive instances were recognized by the annotator as potential consecutive emails within a thread, or non-consecutive emails but still from the same thread, whereas only 46% of negative instances were similarly (falsely) noted. Only 2% of negative instances were judged to look like they were consecutive emails within the same thread.

The following TP instance shows emails that look like they could be from the same thread but do not look consecutive.

> **Email1:** *give me the explanations and i will think about it*
> **Email2:** *what do you mean, you are worth it for one day*

Below is a TN instance with emails that look like they could be from the same thread but do not look consecutive.

> **Email1:** *i do but i havent heard from you either, how are things with wade*
> **Email2:** *rumor has it that a press conference will take place at 4:00 - more money in, lower conversion rate.*

The level of professionalism ("Language vocab level, professionalism, and social address are a reasonable match") was also notable between class categories. All TP instances were judged to have a professionalism match, as well as 94% of FN's. However, only 64% of FP's and 56% of TN's were judged to have a professionalism match. Based on a review of our misclassified instances, we are surprised that our classifier did not learn a better model based on style features (F_1=.60). Participants in an email thread appear to echo the style of emails they reply to. For instance, short, casual, all-lowercase emails are frequently responded to in a similar manner.

5 Conclusion

In this paper, we have described the creation of the Enron Threads Corpus, which we made available online. We have investigated the use of text similarity features for the pairwise classification of emails for thread disentanglement. We have found that content similarity features are more effective than style or structural features across class-balanced and class-imbalanced environments. There appear to be more stylistic features uncaptured by our similarity metrics, which humans access for performing the same task. We have shown that semantic differences between corpora will impact the general effectiveness of text similarity features, but that content features remain effective.

In future work, we will investigate discourse knowledge, highly-tuned stylistic features, and other email-specific features to improve headerless, quoteless email thread disentanglement.

Acknowledgments

This work has been supported by the Volkswagen Foundation as part of the Lichtenberg-Professorship Program under grant No. I/82806, and by the Center for Advanced Security Research (`www.cased.de`).

References

Allison, L. and Dix, T. I. (1986). A bit-string longest-common-subsequence algorithm. *Information Processing Letters*, 23:305–310.

Aoki, Paul M. and Romaine, Matthew and Szymanski, Margaret H. and Thornton, James D. and Wilson, Daniel and Woodruff, Allison. 2003. The mad hatter's cocktail party: a social mobile audio space supporting multiple simultaneous conversations. In Gilbert Cockton and Panu Korhonen, editors, *CHI*, pages 425–432. ACM.

Bär, Daniel and Zesch, Torsten and Gurevych, Iryna. 2011. A reflective view on text similarity. In *Proceedings of the International Conference on Recent Advances in Natural Language Processing*, pages 515–520, Sep.

Broder, A. Z. (1997). On the resemblance and containment of documents. *Proceedings of Compression and Complexity of Sequences*, pages 21–29.

Carenini, Giuseppe and Ng, Raymond T. and Zhou, Xiaodong (1997). Summarizing Emails with Conversational Cohesion and Subjectivity. *Proceedings of the 46th Annual Meeting of the Association for Computational Linguistics, June 15-20, 2008, Columbus, Ohio, USA*, pages 353–361.

Elsner, Micha and Charniak, Eugene. 2010. Disentangling chat. *Comput. Linguist.*, 36(3):389–409, September.

Elsner, Micha and Charniak, Eugene. 2011. Disentangling Chat with Local Coherence Models *Proceedings of the 49th Annual Meeting of the Association for Computational Linguistics, June, 2011, Portland, Oregon, USA*, pages 1179–1189.

Erera, Shai and Carmel, David. 2008. Conversation detection in email systems. In *Proceedings of the IR research, 30th European conference on Advances in information retrieval*, ECIR'08, pages 498–505, Berlin, Heidelberg. Springer-Verlag.

Gabrilovich, E. and Markovitch, S. (2007). Computing Semantic Relatedness using Wikipedia-based Explicit Semantic Analysis. In *Proceedings of the 20th International Joint Conference on Artificial Intelligence*, pages 1606–1611, Hyderabad, India.

Giles, Howard and Ogay, Tania (2007). Communication Accommodation Theory. In Bryan B. Whaley and Wendy Samter, editors. *Explaining Communication: Contemporary Theories and Exemplars*, Mahwah, NJ. Lawrence Erlbaum.

Gusfield, D. (1997). *Algorithms on Strings, Trees and Sequences: Computer Science and Computational Biology.* Cambridge University Press.

Hall, Mark and Frank, Eibe and Holmes, Geoffrey and Pfahringer, Bernhard and Reutemann, Peter and Witten, Ian H. (2010). The WEKA data mining software: an update. In *SIGKDD Explor. Newsl.*, 11(1):10–18.

Hatzivassiloglou, V., Klavans, J. L., and Eskin, E. (1999). Detecting text similarity over short passages: Exploring linguistic feature combinations via machine learning. In *Proceedings of the Joint SIGDAT Conference on Empirical Methods in Natural Language Processing and Very Large Corpora*, pages 203–212, College Park, MD, USA.

Jaro, M. A. (1989). Advances in record linkage methodology as applied to the 1985 census of Tampa Florida. *Journal of the American Statistical Association*, 84(406):414–420.

Joty, Shafiq and Carenini, Giuseppe and Murray, Gabriel and Ng, Raymond T. (2010). Exploiting conversation structure in unsupervised topic segmentation for emails. *Proceedings of the 2010 Conference on Empirical Methods in Natural Language Processing.*

Klimt, Bryan and Yang, Yiming. 2004. Introducing the enron corpus. In *CEAS*.

Levenshtein, V. I. (1966). Binary codes capable of correcting deletions, insertions, and reversals. *Soviet Physics Doklady*, 10(8):707–710.

Lewis, D. D. (1966). Threading electronic mail: a preliminary study . In *Information Processing and Management* 33(2):209–217.

Lyon, C., Barrett, R., and Malcolm, J. (2004). A theoretical basis to the automated detection of copying between texts, and its practical implementation in the Ferret plagiarism and collusion detector. In *In Plagiarism: Prevention, Practice and Policies Conference.*

McCarthy, P. M. and Jarvis, S. (2010). MTLD, vocd-D, and HD-D: A validation study of sophisticated approaches to lexical diversity assessment. *Behavior research methods*, 42(2):381–392.

Monge, A. and Elkan, C. (1997). An efficient domain-independent algorithm for detecting approximately duplicate database records. In *Proceedings of the SIGMOD Workshop on Data Mining and Knowledge Discovery*, pages 23–29, Tucson, AZ, USA.

Mosteller, F. and Wallace, D. L. (1964). *Inference and disputed authorship: The Federalist.* Addison-Wesley.

Rambow, Owen and Lokesh, Shrestha and Chen, John and Lauridsen, Chirsty. (2004). Summarizing email threads. In *Proceedings of the Conference of the North American Chapter of the Association for Computational Linguistics (NAACL) Short Paper Section.*

Stamatatos, E. (2011). Plagiarism detection using stopword n-grams. *Journal of the American Society for Information Science and Technology*, 62(12):2512–2527.

Templin, M. C. (1957). *Certain language skills in children.* University of Minnesota Press.

Wan, Stephen and McKeown, Kathy. (2004). Generating overview summaries of ongoing email thread discussions. In *Proceedings of COLING 2004.*

Weizhong Zhu, Robert B. Allen, and Min Song. 2005. Trec 2005 enterprise track results from drexel. In Ellen M. Voorhees and Lori P. Buckland, editors, *Proceedings of the Fourteenth Text REtrieval Conference, TREC 2005, Gaithersburg, Maryland, November 15-18, 2005*, volume Special Publication 500-266. National Institute of Standards and Technology (NIST).

Winkler, W. E. (1990). String Comparator Metrics and Enhanced Decision Rules in the Fellegi-Sunter Model of Record Linkage. In *Proceedings of the Section on Survey Research Methods*, pages 354–359.

Wise, M. J. (1996). YAP3: Improved detection of similarities in computer program and other texts. In *Proceedings of the 27th SIGCSE technical symposium on Computer science education*, pages 130–134, Philadelphia, PA, USA.

Wu, Yejun and Oard, Douglas W. 2005. Indexing emails and email threads for retrieval. In *Proceedings of the 28th annual international ACM SIGIR conference on Research and development in information retrieval*, SIGIR '05, pages 665–666, New York, NY, USA. ACM.

Yeh, Jen-Yuan. 2006. Email thread reassembly using similarity matching. In *CEAS 2006 - The Third Conference on Email and Anti-Spam, July 27-28, 2006, Mountain View, California, USA*.

Yule, G. U. (1939). On sentence-length as a statistical characteristic of style in prose: With application to two cases of disputed authorship. *Biometrika*, 30(3/4):363–390.

Using Parallel Corpora for Word Sense Disambiguation

Ahmad R. Shahid[1,2]
[1]Department of Computer Science
COMSATS Institute of IT
Islamabad, Pakistan
ahmadrshahid@comsats.edu.pk

Dimitar Kazakov[2]
[2]Department of Computer Science
University of York
York, United Kingdom
dimitar.kazakov@york.ac.uk

Abstract

This paper presents a method of lexical semantic disambiguation in multilingual corpora and describes the construction of an artificial word-aligned and lexically disambiguated gold-standard corpus from an existing multilingual resource. The suggested approach uses sets of aligned words and phrases across languages as unique semantic tags similar to WordNet synsets that can be used as a part of unsupervised natural language processing and information retrieval tasks. The approach goes beyond one-to-one word alignment, and uses an algorithm for the aggregation of results of pair-wise word alignment when the corpus contains several languages. When applied to the new corpus, this methodology has proven capable of reducing the ambiguity of a polysemous word by one third on average.

1 Introduction

This is a study of the specific potential that parallel corpora provide for word and phrase sense disambiguation (WPSD). We do not discuss any of the methods that can be applied to monolingual texts, as these can be considered complementary approaches that are not mutually exclusive, but, rather, can always be combined together. We focus instead on the specific contribution that the availability of multiple translations of the same text can make towards rejecting some of the alternative senses of the words and phrases in the corpus for any of the individual languages represented in it. We describe an approach in which the N translations in a parallel corpus are word-aligned, and the result used to group words and phrases that are translations of each other into N-tuples that can be seen as multilingual synsets akin to the sets of synonyms used in WordNet (Fellbaum, 1998). These synsets can then be used as semantic tags for word and phrase sense disambiguation. The approach was applied to a large, real-world parallel corpus, namely, Europarl (Koehn, 2005).

In this setting the full potential of the idea can be obscured by errors introduced by one pre-processing step, such as imperfect word alignment, or the lack of another, e.g., morpholexical analysis. We therefore use an existing multilingual lexical resource (Lefever, 2009) to develop a large, artificial parallel corpus containing semantically disambiguated polysemous words, and use it to calculate the maximum contribution that parallel corpora can make towards WPSD under ideal conditions, when all other processing steps are 100% accurate and therefore do not introduce any noise to the process. This result gauges the potential contribution of multiple translations to WPSD, providing its upper limit for the data studied.

The multilingual synsets produced in this framework represent a potentially valuable resource on its own, which could be used (as is, or after filtering out the errors) as a translation memory or as a lexicographer's resource. The unedited multilingual synsets from the experiments with Europarl have been made available online.[1] The Web interface includes search for words and phrases in the four languages used, and also displays all the contexts in which the word or phrase in question appears in the corpus.

[1]http://www.goodwithlanguages.com

2 Background

Dagan *et al* (1991) first noted the usefulness of two corpora (one for each language) for lexical semantic disambiguation in the context of machine translation. Binary syntactic relations are identified in the source language and all of their possible translations are initially produced, and then gradually pruned based on the observed likelihood of these pairs of words in the target language corpus. It is noted that the target language word choice can indicate the sense of ambiguous words in the source language.

Gale *et al* (1992) used a parallel corpus to label ambiguous source words (along with their context) with the target language word translation. One could then learn from the labelled examples using the source context words as features to distinguish between the senses of unseen examples of the ambiguous word in the source language. All this of course assumed different target words were used for different senses of the source word.

More recently, parallel corpora have been used to create new linguistic resources, such as lexicons and WordNet-like resources (Fišer, 2007; Sagot, 2008; Shahid, 2009; Shahid, 2010; Lefever, 2009; Lefever, 2010a; Lefever, 2010b).

Fišer (2007) word aligned the translations of Orwell's *1984* (Dimitrova et al., 1998) in five languages: English, Czech, Romanian, Bulgarian and Slovene. She carried out pair-wise word alignment of nouns, verbs, adjectives, and adverbs using GIZA++ (Och, 2003). Only 1:1 alignments between words of the same part of speech were considered and alignments occurring only once were discarded. The bilingual word alignments (lexicons) thus generated were used to create a multilingual lexicon with 1500 entries. The multilingual lexicon was then compared against the existing WordNets: PWN (Fellbaum, 1998) for English; BalkaNet (Tufis, 2000) for Czech, Romanian and Bulgarian. If all the translations in a particular entry in the lexicon shared the synset ID, the same synset ID was assigned to the Slovene translation. Slovene words that shared the same synset ID were then grouped into synsets.

Sagot (2008) created WOLF, a freely available French WordNet. They used the *extend approach* (Vossen, 1998) whereby a subset of synsets was taken from the PWN and translated into the target language, preserving the structure of the PWN. 82% of the entries in the PWN are monosemous and only require a bilingual lexicon. For the polysemous words they pair-wise word aligned the subcorpus of the JRC-Acquis (Steinberger et al., 2006) in five languages, that is, English, Romanian, Czech, Bulgarian, and French. The bilingual lexicons thus created were used to create the multilingual lexicons. Translations in the multilingual lexicon were then compared against the corresponding WordNet in BalkaNet (Tufis, 2000). If all translations shared the same synset ID, the corresponding French translation was also assigned the same synset ID.

Shahid and Kazakov (2009; 2010) have used the notion of synsets in a multilingual context (cf. (Lavric, 2008)), defined as translation equivalences. They used the Europarl parallel corpus and word-aligned a subset of it for four languages, English, German, French and Greek, using an off-the-shelf tool (GIZA++ (Och, 2003)). English was used as the pivotal language. The resulting $1:1$ and $1:N$ mappings between words in each pair of languages were then grouped into 4-tuples of synonymous words, resp. phrases, using an in-house algorithm (Algorithm 1, (Shahid, 2010)). The resulting sets of translations are referred to as multilingual proto-synsets, to highlight the fact that they can be further improved, e.g., by merging those showing morphological variants of the same lexical entry. Similarly, one could consider merging multilingual proto-synsets if they only contained pairs of synonyms for each language.

It is also of relevance that Lefever and Hoste (2009; 2010a; 2010b) proposed an unsupervised multilingual Word Sense Disambiguation (WSD) task for polysemous English nouns. Rather than manually sense tagging individual occurrences of the nouns in the example sentences, they built a gold standard sense inventory using the Europarl parallel corpus in six languages: English, German, French, Spanish, Italian, and Dutch. The parallel corpus was word aligned using GIZA++. The word alignments were then manually verified by certified translators who were also asked to annotate 20 sentences per trial target word giving at most 3 suggested meanings at a time. These sense annotated sentences can also be treated as gold standard data.

3 Design

We have built here on Shahid and Kazakov's approach (Shahid, 2010) to use the multilingual proto-synsets they propose for word and phrase sense disambiguation, as described in the introduction.

The words were collated into phrases in the following way. Initially, each word in each language in the word-aligned parallel corpus is given a separate, unique identifier. Two data structures, an 'open' and a 'closed' list are created. Initially, all words are placed in the open list, and the closed list is empty. A simple recursive procedure, `fanout/1`, is used to extract all phrases. It takes a word from the open list, and gradually spread its ID to all words it is aligned with. Each processed word is transferred on to the closed list, which in the end, when the open list is empty, contains all words. All words that could be connected through one or more pair-wise alignments, now have the same ID. In other terms, all words forming a phrase and its translation into each language, are now indexed with the same ID. Each phrase and the corresponding translations form a multilingual proto-synset.

Algorithm 1 Multilingual Synset Construction

```
main(){
foreach Word in OpenList
  fanout(Word)
}

fanout(Word) {
  move Word from OpenList to ClosedList
  foreach W in OpenList that is aligned with Word
    W.ID=Word.ID
    fanout(W)
}
```

The process is deterministic and is not prone to introducing errors on its own. However, the errors introduced in the preceding steps are carried over to subsequent steps after phrase formation. In other words, the quality of proto-synsets is only as good as the quality of word alignment, not worse. Table 1 shows a larger sample of the results

3.1 Using Phrases in the Multilingual Synsets

In the word alignments generated by GIZA++ there are many words in a non-pivotal language that are aligned with N words in the pivotal language, or in other words they have $1 : N$ word mapping. Earlier research did not use this information to generate phrases from words (Fišer, 2007; Sagot, 2008). Our experiments with the parts of the Europarl corpus produced phrase alignments rather than $1 : 1$ word mapping in 28% of all cases. This is a substantial figure which shows that phrase alignment can have a substantial impact on the overall result. The quality of this alignment however cannot be tested without an appropriate annotated resource.

3.2 SemEval Parallel Corpora

We have have therefore set off to create a large, artificial parallel corpus where the semantics of selected key words (in their canonical lexical entry form) has been disambiguated. The result was to be used to evaluate the maximum contribution of multilingual synsets to the WSD process.

We made use of a resource which was part of the SemEval-2010 Task 3 on Cross-Lingual Word Sense Disambiguation (Lefever, 2009; Lefever, 2010a; Lefever, 2010b). This data is in six languages, namely, English, French, German, Dutch, Italian and Spanish.

Lefever and Hoste used the parallel corpus in all six languages to generate a gold standard data set and a sense inventory. They provided five target nouns to be disambiguated, namely, *bank*, *movement*, *occupation*, *passage*, and *plant* (Lefever, 2010b). They also provided a sense inventory for each of the target nouns.

The sense inventory defined meanings in which a target word could be used. It also contained combinations of words/phrases in all the six languages with semantics related to a particular meaning of the target word. For instance, the word *bank* had five different meanings: *Financial Institution*, *Supply/Stock*, *Sloping land beside water*, *Cisjordan*, and *group of similar objects (row/tiers)*. Further sub-meanings were also defined but for the purposes of this exercise we assumed them to be part of the main meanings.

The sense inventory was used by annotators to annotate 20 sentences per target word. They were asked to provide contextually relevant translations for each of the languages considered. The sentences were extracted from JRC-ACQUIS[2] and the British National Corpus (BNC)[3].

[2]http://langtech.jrc.it/JRC-Acquis.html

[3]http://www.natcorp.ox.ac.uk/

English	German	French	Greek
resumption of session	wiederaufnahme sitzungsperiode	reprise de session	επανάληψη της συνοδου
adjourned on friday	erkläre am freitag	interrompue vendredi	διακοπεί παρασκευή
thank you	vielen dank	merci	ευχαριστώ
shall do so gladly	will tun gerne	ferai volontiers	πράξω ευχαρίστως

Table 1: Sample multilingual synsets

There were 20 English sentences per each target word provided. Multiple translators were asked to translate the target words into 5 other languages, and a gold inventory of the possible translations of each word in each of its meanings was compiled. Annotators were asked to provide 3 or fewer relevant translations from the sense inventory. The proposed translations were stored with their frequency counts, of how many times a word/phrase from the sense inventory was used to translate a target word for a given language.

Given below is the list of possible translations of the word 'bank' to German for different senses with the frequency of its usage by a translator.

bank.n.de 1 :: bank 4;bankengesellschaft 1;kreditinstitut 1;zentralbank 1;finanzinstitut 1;
bank.n.de 2 :: bank 4;zentralbank 3;finanzinstitut 1;notenbank 1;kreditinstitut 1;nationalbank 1;
bank.n.de 3 :: westjordanufer 3;westufer 2;westjordanland 2;westjordanien 2;westbank 2;west-bank 1;

This data can be the basis for a gold standard corpus: the translations of the words in question are perfectly aligned, and the words themselves are in their lexical entry form, that is, not needing any morphological analysis. Therefore, any experiments with this data will eliminate the errors introduced by GIZA++ and the lack of morphological analysis.

We used this data set to theoretically gauge the maximum by which the polysemy of an ambiguous word could be reduced by translations of a word across different languages. For the said purpose, we generated all possible multilingual synsets (combinations of possible translations) from the gold standard data and checked in the sense inventory to find all meanings to which this combination of translations across the six languages could possibly correspond. For instance, any combination of the words (bank:EN, westjordanien:GE...) could only correspond to the third and last meaning of the English word 'bank', that of a bank of a river.

On occasions, a combination of translations would correspond to more than one sense of the word. These combinations of translations (aka synsets) were weighted with the frequency with which its constituent words were proposed by the individual translators. We calculated polysemy (number of senses) for each word and synset, and the ratio by which such a synset would reduce the polysemy of the original English word.

Table 2 gives a summary of the results. It can be seen that polysemy is reduced by over 36% on average when translations of a word are used as sense tags. This is a significant result, which suggests that the previous negative results are due to other factors, some of which were already mentioned; however, the idea of using multilingual synsets for WSD is viable, and can be used when the other techniques needed reach a more mature stage of development.

3.3 Further Evaluation

For an evaluation of the synsets thus generated, we annotated the 5 target English words in the 20 trial sentences using the senses in the sense inventory. Two native speakers and one speaker with near-native proficiency were asked to annotate the target words. To generate consensus, only those senses were considered for evaluation where at least two annotators agreed. The annotated sentences were taken as gold standard (GS), against which the senses proposed by our synsets generated from the SemEval data were compared.

We used the Most Frequent Sense (MFS) as the first baseline for this comparison. Thus, among all the sense annotations for a target word the most fre-

Word	# of synsets	Before WSD	After WSD	Reduction [%]
bank	17,873	5	2.7	46%
movement	230,061	3	2.51	16%
occupation	81,706	4	3.39	15%
passage	95,363	7	3.71	47%
plant	91,830	3	1.67	44%
Total	516,833	4.4	2.796	36.45%

Table 2: Lexical ambiguity (polysemy) of English words before and after the use of multilingual synsets for disambiguation.

quent was taken and it was assumed that all the occurrences of the target word bore the same sense, referred to as 'GS-MFS.' We also took the top sense for a target word from PWN (Fellbaum, 1998), which orders them by frequency, and assumed that all the occurrences of the same target word bore the same meaning. It can be called as PWN-MFS. We compared the GS-MFS, PWN-MFS and senses proposed by our synsets for each occurrence of the target word against the GS. The results indicate that the accuracy of senses proposed by the multilingual synsets is 86%, 52% for PWN-MFS, and 59% for GS-MFS. This clearly shows the benefits of our approach.

4 Conclusion

We have demonstrated how a parallel corpus can be used for word (and phrase) sense disambiguation for each of its languages. The described approach also produces a new lexical resources as a side effect, which can be independently used for a variety of purposes. We demonstrated the viability and the upper limit of the potential of multilingual synsets for WSD on a novel data set specifically constructed for the purpose. There is a pleasing feeling about the fact that such an upper bound can be measured at all with rigor.

We have shown at the same time that the idea still has its limitations in practice due to the imperfections of other preprocessing techniques, such as word alignment, on which it is based.

5 Future Work

Rather than using existing resources to carry out morpholexical analysis in order to improve the results, we have considered the possibility of first learning such resources in the form of word paradigms from the parallel corpus. Once word paradigms are learned, they can be used for the above mentioned purpose of merging multilingual synsets, as the ambiguity such variant synsets indicate is spurious. We have chosen to frame these experiments as an unsupervised learning task, where the only resource available is the corpus. A comparison of the results to an existing gold standard and to another, monolingual unsupervised morphology learning approach have shown the clear potential of this approach, which will be the subject of a separate publication.

References

Leo Breiman, Jerome Friedman, Charles J. Stone, and R. A. Olshen. 1984. *Classification and Regression Trees*. Chapman and Hall/CRC, Florida, USA.

Ashok K. Chandra, Dexter C. Kozen, and Larry J. Stockmeyer. 1981. Alternation. *Journal of the Association for Computing Machinery*, 28(1):114–133.

Ido Dagan, Alon Itai, and Ulrike Schwall. 1991. *Two languages are more informative than one. ACL-91 Proceedings of the 29th annual meeting on Association for Computational Linguistics*, 114–133. Stroudsburg, PA, USA.

Ludmila Dimitrova, Nancy Ide, Vladimir Petkevic, Tomaz Erjavec, Heiki Jaan Kaalep, and Dan Tufis. 1998. *Multext-East: Parallel and Comparable Corpora and Lexicons for Six Central and Eastern European Languages*. Proceedings of the 17th International Conference on Computational Linguistics - Volume 1 (COLING 98). Stroudsburg, PA, USA.

Christiane Fellbaum. 1998. *WordNet An Electronic Lexical Database*. MIT Press, Cambridge, MA.

Darja Fišer. 2007. *Leveraging parallel corpora and exisitng wordnets for automatic construction of the Slovene Wordnet*. Proceedings of L&TC 2007. Poznań, Poland.

William A. Gale, Kenneth W. Church and David Yarowsky. 1992. *Using bilingual materials to develop word sense disambiguation methods. TMI*. Montreal.

Philipp Koehn. 2005. *Europarl: A Parallel Corpus for Statistical Machine Translation* Proceedings of the MT summit 2005.

Eva Lavric, Gerhard Pisek, Andrew Skinner, and Wolfgang Stadler (Eds). 2008. *The Linguistics of Football*. Narr Francke Attempto Verlag.

Els Lefever and Véronique Hoste. June 2009. *SemEval-2010 Task 3: Cross-lingualWord Sense Disambiguation*. Proceedings of the NAACL HLT Workshop on Semantic Evaluations: Recent Achievements and Future Directions. pp. 82-87. Boulder, Colorado.

Els Lefever and Véronique Hoste. 2010. *Construction of a Benchmark Data Set for Cross-Lingual Word Sense Disambiguation*. Proceedings of the Seventh International Conference on Language Resources and Evaluation. Malta.

Els Lefever and Véronique Hoste. July 2010. *SemEval-2010 Task 3: Cross-Lingual Word Sense Disambiguation*. Proceedings of the 5th International Workshop on Semantic Evaluation, ACL 2010. pp. 15-20. Uppsala, Sweden.

Franz J. Och and Hermann Ney. 2003. A Systematic Comparison of Various Statistical Alignment Models. *Computational Linguistics*, 29(1):19-51.

Benoît Sagot and Darja Fišer. 2008. *Building a free French wordnet from multilingual resources*. Proceedings of OntoLex 2008. Marrakesh.

Ahmad Shahid and Dimitar Kazakov. 2009. Unsupervised Construction of a Multilingual WordNet from Parallel Corpora. Proc. of the RANLP Workshop on NLP methods and Corpora in Translation, Lexicography, and Language Learning. Borovets, Bulgaria.

Ahmad Shahid and Dimitar Kazakov. 2010. Retrieving Lexical Semantics from Multilingual Corpora. *Polibits* 5:25–28.

Steinberger Ralf, Bruno Pouliquen, Anna Widiger, Camelia Ignat, Tomaž Erjavec, Dan Tufis, and Dániel Varga. 24-26 May 2006. *The JRC-Acquis: A multilingual aligned parallel corpus with 20+ languages*. Proceedings of the 5th International Conference on Language Resources and Evaluation. Genoa, Italy.

Dan Tufis. 2000. Design and Development of a Multilingual Balkan WordNet. *Romanian Journal of Information Science and Technology Special Issue*, 7:1-2.

Piek Vossen. 1998. *EuroWordNet: a multilingual database with lexical semantic networks for European Languages*. Kluwer, Dordrecht.

R Wagner and M Fischer. 1974. The String-to-String Correction Problem. *Journal of the Association for Computing Machinery*, 21(1):168-173.

Semantic relation recognition within Polish noun phrase: A rule-based approach

Paweł Kędzia
Institute of Informatics
Wrocław University of Technology
pawel.kedzia@pwr.wroc.pl

Marek Maziarz
Institute of Informatics
Wrocław University of Technology
marek.maziarz@pwr.wroc.pl

Abstract

The paper[1] presents a rule-based approach to semantic relation recognition within the Polish noun phrase. A set of semantic relations, including some thematic relations, has been determined for the need of experiments. The method consists in two steps: first the system recognizes word pairs and triples, and then it classifies the relations. Evaluation was performed on random samples from two balanced Polish corpora.

1 Introduction

Semantic relation recognition is a well-known task in natural language processing. Although the relation recognition within noun phrase and between nominals was studied intensely, the task is still challenge for semantic analysis of Polish. We are aware of few papers and projects dealing with Semantic Role Labelling between predicates and their arguments, cf. (Gołuchowski and Przepiórkowski, 2012) or (Lun, 2009), but of none concerning semantic relation recognition inside Polish noun phrase.

2 Related work

In (Nastase et al., 2006) authors classify semantic relations between a head and a modifier of a noun phrase. Number of all relation types was equal to 30. These relations were grouped into 5 more general groups. The authors experimented with decision trees, instance-based learning and Support Vector Machines. For each relation they learnt the binary classifier; as the baseline for F-measure they used the model with all of examples classified as positive and recall being equal to 100%. With regard to the semantic relation the baseline ranged between 17.78% and 60.35%.

Identifying the semantic relations inside compound nouns was presented in (Uchiyama et al., 2008). The authors used SVM classifier and in the best configuration of features, they achieved accuracy of about 84%.

In (Rosario and Hearst, 2001) authors used neural networks to determine 20 semantic relations – similarily to (Nastase et al., 2006) – between a head and a modifier of noun phrase. They used a domain-specific lexical hierarchy of medicine. The authors achieved accuracy of about 60%.

The workshop SemEval-2010 (task 8) concerned the recognition of semantic relations between nominals. In (Tratz and Hovy, 2010) the authors developed a system based on the Maximum Entropy classifier, able to detect 10 bidirectional semantic relations Achieved F-measures depended on the system configuration and lay between 66, 68% and 77, 75%. The same set of semantic relations was used in (Rink and Harabagiu, 2010). The authors used Support Vector Machines classifier and a very rich set of features (i.e., part of speech for all constituents of a semantic relation pair, number of words between the nominals, features based on paths in the dependency tree from Stanford dependency parser). F-measure of this approach was 82.19%.

Authors in (Tymoshenko and Giuliano, 2010) used shallow syntactic parsing and semantic information from ResearchCyc (Lenat, 1995) in the same task of recognizing semantic relations. They used liner combination of kernels (semantic and syntactic) using Support Vector Machines classifier. For the best combination of kernels, they obtained F-measure equal to 77.62%.

There are some works, where rule-based approaches were used. In (Huang, 2009) there has been proposed an approach for automatic construction of rules identifying ten types of seman-

[1]Work financed by The National Centre for Research and Development project SP/I/1/77065/10.

tic relations, using five types of input informations. The relation instances were extracted from Modern Chinese Standard Dictionary. The authors achieved very high precision (range from $0,81$ to 0.99), but recall was low - about $0,2$. In (Hearst, 1992) authors used set of manually written rules for identification of hyperonymy relations. (Ben Abacha and Zweigenbaum, 2011) used linguistic patterns (built semi-automatically from corpora) to identify semantic relatios in medical texts. In this domain-specific task they achieved 75.72% precision and $60,46\%$ recall.

3 Recognized semantic relation types

We seek for semantic relations within nominal phrases. The relation set consists of 12 semantic relations, of which 5 are thematic (semantic) roles[2]. Definitions of our semantic relations are based on works of (Kearns, 2011), (Palmer et al., 2010), (Van Valin, 2004), (Larson, 1996), (Dowty, 1991), (Jędrzejko, 1993), (Laskowski and Wróbel, 1997). We tried to select relations that are very frequent or frequent in Polish texts.[3] The relation set is following (thematic roles are marked with *theta*, other relations – with *rho*):

Proto-Agent$_\theta$ – it is an instigator of an action or an entity that is in a particular state, it may undergoe change of state not caused by another participant; for predicates denoting relations – it is the first element of the relation: (człowiek) wykształcony przez Jana$_\theta$ '(man) educated by John$_\theta$', wyjący wilk$_\theta$ 'howling wolf$_\theta$'. The Proto-Agent macrorole covers subroles of Agent, Causer and nonagentive non-causative Actor (cf. *Actor* macrorole in (Kearns, 2011)).

Proto-Patient$_\theta$ is the second macrorole – it is an entity undergoing action, event or change of state caused by another participant; for predicates denoting relations – it is the second element of a given relation: wykształcenie kogoś$_\theta$ 'educating someone$_\theta$', (Jan) posiadający majątek$_\theta$ '(John) possessing an estate$_\theta$'. According to (Dowty, 1991) many thematic roles come down to the macroroles of Proto-Patient and Proto-Agent.

Instrument$_\theta$ is a tool, a device or means used by someone in order to cause something, it is sometimes regarded as a secondary cause of situation or change of state: przeszyty włócznią 'speared with a spear', lina$_\theta$ cumownicza$_{adjective}$ 'a hawser, lit. mooring rope$_\theta$'.

Material$_\theta$ is an entity that is used by someone to produce something from it, material undergoes change of state resulting in its disappearance and emerging of a result: zrobiony z mosiądzu$_\theta$ 'made out of brass$_\theta$', mosiężna$_\theta$ figurka 'brass$_\theta$ statuette'.

Purpose$_\theta$ – an entity or a situation toward which the event is directed or an individual which benefits from the event (purpose combines goal, beneficiary and recipient roles): wręczenie (medali) olimpijczykom 'giving (medals) to Olympians$_\theta$, sala koncertowa$_\theta$ 'a concert$_\theta$ hall'.

Location is a physical place at which a given event is localised, a place being destination of an event, a path or a source of motion, or simply a place at which a particular individual is situated: wręczenie (medali) w auli$_\varrho$ 'giving (medals) at the lecture theatre$_\varrho$', przedzieranie się przez moczary$_\varrho$ 'struggling through the swamp$_\varrho$'.

Time is a particular moment or a duration of an event – it localises a situation within the flow of events or gives its duration: przedzieranie się przez godzinę$_\varrho$/w środę$_\varrho$ 'struggling for an hour$_\varrho$/on Wednesday$_\varrho$'.

Temporal/spatial meronymy – these relations point onto a spatial or temporal part of a place/location/time/period): poniedziałkowy poranek$_\varrho$ 'Monday morning$_\varrho$', środek$_\varrho$ zimy 'middle$_\varrho$ of the winter', koniec$_\varrho$ drogi 'end$_\varrho$ of the road', stolica$_\varrho$ kraju 'capital$_\varrho$ of the country'.

Attribute is a property of an individual or an event, such as colour, size, weigth, intensity, duration etc., which might be expressed with a qualitative adjective: czerwony$_\varrho$ samochód 'red$_\varrho$ car', głośna$_\varrho$ muzyka 'loud$_\varrho$ music'.

Family (member) is a relative or an in-law to someone, the relation is bidirectional and reflexive: syn$_\varrho$ króla$_\varrho$ 'king's$_\varrho$ son$_\varrho$', moja$_\varrho$ żona$_\varrho$ 'my$_\varrho$ wife$_\varrho$' (I am a relative to my wife).

Order gives a position of an entity or an event in an ordered sequence/chain: druga$_\varrho$ odpowiedź '2nd answer', lata 80$_\varrho$. 'eighties, lit. eightieth$_\varrho$ years'.

Quantity is an amount of something or a cardinality of a given set: pięciu$_\varrho$ panów 'five$_\varrho$ men',

[2]In Polish, as in other Indo-European languages, verbs could be nominalized during a process of syntactic transformation (Jędrzejko, 1993), (Kolln, 1990). Such nominalized predicates could be linked with nouns by thematic relations.

[3]Rationale for selection of the presented semantic relation types was their frequencies in a four-text sample taken from a Polish corpus *KPWr*. Together chosen relations account for ca 80% of all semantic relation occurrences in these texts. Most of our relation types could be found on the list of the most frequent relation types in the English noun phrase (Moldovan et al., 2004, Tab. 1).

kieliszek$_{\varrho}$ wina 'glass$_{\varrho}$ of wine'.

4 Semantic relation recognition rule-based algorithm

Our rule-based system proceeds in two steps[4]: first it recognizes word pairs and triples, then operators classifying relations enter.

4.1 Recognizing word pairs and triples

Since we consider relations within noun phrases, we must identify them correctly. We made use of a CRF shallow parser (Radziszewski and Pawlaczek, 2012) trained on an annotated corpus of Polish (KPWr) (Broda et al., 2012) which comprises shallow syntactic annotation level (Radziszewski et al., 2012).

KPWr contains 326 annotated text samples representing different genres and styles: blogs, press articles, official and legal texts and Polish Wikipedia articles, it comprises 106358 annotations (phrases and phrase heads, and predicate-argument relations).

Noun and preposition phrases (NPs/PPs) from the corpus correspond to arguments of predicate-argument structure. Each such NP/PP constists of one or several smaller phrases based on agreement (*AgPs*, for details, please look at cited works). Here is an example NP from the corpus (a head of the phrase is boldfaced, AgP heads are underlined):

> [[**samolot** wyprodukowany]$_{AgP}$ [przez PZL]$_{AgP}$ [w roku 1938]$_{AgP}$ [w Łodzi]$_{AgP}$]$_{NP}$
>
> 'aircraft made by PZL in (year) 1938 in Łódź (city)'

There is no reliable deep parser for Polish (Gołuchowski and Przepiórkowski, 2012), thus we decided to construct a simple rule-based algorithm for deepened shallow parsing of Polish NPs/PPs. The algorithm works on tagged texts – we used (Radziszewski, 2013) tagger. Parsing rules make use of an output from the CRF shallow parser (Radziszewski and Pawlaczek, 2012), in particular: borders of whole NPs/PPs, and of their constituents (i.e., phrases based on agreement, *AgPs*). Found pairs and triples are directly connected within a syntactic structure.

Hand-written rules act like a partial dependency parser. The pairs consist of one subordinate and one superordinate token, the triples comprise one superordinate token and a subordinate preposition phrase (preposition + governed nominal head of a subordinate noun phrase).

The whole algorithm runs in a main loop which iterates AgP$_i$ heads. We start from the first AgP$_0$ head to the left, then we proceed to the right, jumping from AgP$_i$ head to the closest AgP$_{i+1}$ head to the right. For every AgP$_i$ head we run a cascade-like chain of rules (numbered from 1 to 7) for genetives, nominatives, small preposition phrases (being a part of larger NPs or PPs), coordination, other known to the tagger tokens, other unknown to the tagger tokens and for modifiers. The algorithm in pseudocode was shown in Algorithm 1

The algorithm gives following description for just analysed phrase, "R + number" denotes the number of a rule in the Algorithm 1 activated on the word pair or triple (for instance, *R3* means that the rule number 3 was activated): *R7*: samolot ← wyprodukowany 'plane made', *R3*: wyprodukowany ← przez PZL 'by PZL',*R3*: wyprodukowany ← w roku 'in year', *R3*: wyprodukowany ← w Łodzi 'in Łódź' .

Such simple shallow parsing algorithm operates quite well on an annotated part of KPWr with F-measure equal to 84%, P = 88%, R = 80%.[5]

4.2 Applying WCCL operators

Having identified pairs and triples we run on them operators written in a constraint language WCCL (Radziszewski et al., 2011). The operators are language-specific and utilize morphosyntactic features (POS, case, number and gender), domains of Polish WordNet lexical units (word-sense pairs (Maziarz et al., 2012)), thousands of derivational relation instances between nouns, adjectives and verbs from the wordnet[6] and information about syntactic frames of nominalized predicates, taken from Polish valence dictionary (Dębowski and Woliński, 2007).

Each of written operators refers to one semantic relation. In other words, each semantic relation is described by one or by many WCCL operators. If an operator is successfully applied to a pair (or a

[4] Similarly to system presented in (Gamallo et al., 2002).

[5] Random sample of 200 NPs/PPs taken from KPWr, 331 relation instances, bootstrap confidence intervals are following P = 83÷91%, R = 76÷84%, F = 79÷87%, $\alpha = 0.05$. The corpus was divided by us into two parts: one working set for testing and preparing parsing rules and semantic operators - consisting of 300 texts, and a smaller evaluation part of 26 texts.

[6] Since we do not use any word sense disambiguation system, we simply take the first sense of every given word.

Algorithm 1 Rule-based algorithm for the recognition of word pairs and triples

1. **genetive attachment** – link AgP_i head in genetive to the closest AgP_{i-1} head to the left or to the closest nominalized predicate to the left:
   - if there is none - link it to the closest predicate to the right;
   - if there is none - link the considered AgP_i head to the head of the whole NP/PP;
2. **nominative attachment** – link AgP_i head in nominative to the closest AgP_{i-1} head to the left or to the closest nominalized predicate to the left:
   - if there is none - link it to the closest AgP_{i+1} head to the right or to the closest nominalized predicate to the right;
   - if there is none - link the considered AgP_i head to the head of the whole NP/PP;
3. **small PP attachment** – link a head of AgP_i containing a small PP to the closest nominalized predicate to the left:
   - if there is none - to the closest nominalized predicate to the right such that it is not an element of $\text{AgP}_{j>i}$ containing a preposition;
   - if there is none - to the closest AgP_{i-1} head to the left;
   - if there is none - link AgP_i with our whole NP/PP head;
4. **coordinated syntactic groups** – look for such AgP_i that is preceded by a coordination conjunction (i.e., *i* 'and', *oraz* 'and', *lub* 'or') or by coordinating comma ('coordinating comma' is such a comma that is placed between two AgPs whose heads are agreed on case), such coordination marker cannot be an element of any AgP:
   - if there is such a marker, look to the left in order to find such $\text{AgP}_{j<i}$ head which is agreed on case with our AgP_i head – then create a new relation instance by copying the link $\text{AgP}_j \rightarrow X$ and replacing AgP_j head by the AgP_i head in that copied linkage, i.e., create the relation instance $\text{AgP}_i \rightarrow X$;
   - if it is not possible – do not introduce any relation;
5. head token provided with **POS known to the CRF tagger** – link the AgP_i head to the closest nominalized predicate to the left:
   - if there is none - to the closest nominalized predicate to the right such that it is not an element of $\text{AgP}_{j>i}$ containing a preposition;
   - if there is none - link AgP_i head to the closest $\text{AgP}_{j<i}$ head to the left such that $\text{AgP}_{j<i}$ does not contain any preposition;
   - if there is none such $\text{AgP}_{j<i}$ – connect AgP_i to the whole NP/PP head;
6. **other cases** (the AgP_i head was not provided any known POS by the CRF tagger) – in such cases link AgP_i head to the closest $\text{AgP}_{j<i}$ head to the left; if there is none – do not make any decision;
7. **relations inside AgPs** – link adjectival and participial modifiers to the head of AgP_i.

triple), then we know what semantic relation between the pair (or triple) occurs. Otherwise, we assume that the semantic relation does not occur.

For example, our `Proto-Patient` relation was described by the 6 WCCL operators. One of them is presented in Listing 1. This operator uses two dictionaries with valence frames (`acc` - a list of verbs possessing any accusative frame, `frames` - a list of verbs described in the Polish valence dictionary (Dębowski, 2013)) and morphosyntactic information about part of speech (`class`) and `case`.

This operator `PROTO-PATIENT-acc` captures pairs like $\textit{dręczący}_{pact}$ $\textit{Janka}_{noun.acc-\theta}$ 'tormenting John_θ' with a noun playing a Proto-Patient role of the predicate *dręczący*. The operator first checks whether a predicate (active participle) has an accusative frame or is outside the dictionary of Dębowski (`"frames"`). Since *dręczyć* 'to torment' is in `acc` dictionary and since *Janek* 'John' has `subst` class and `acc` case - the boolean operator returns 'true'.

Let us present another example: the Proto-Agent macrorole is recognized by 5 operators, in Listing 2 was shown one of them. The `PROTO-AGENT-ger-przez-acc` operator is written for triples, i.e., for a triple $\textit{wydanie}_{pact}$ $\textit{przez}_{pron}$ $\textit{wydawcę}_{noun.acc-\theta}$ 'publishing by the publisher$_{\theta}$'. The first element in the triple is a gerund form of verb *wydać* 'to publish'. The operator checks whether the verb *wydać* has in its frame accusative/genetive or whether it cannot be found in Dębowski's dictionary (position 0 in the triple, `frames`).

Listing 1: One of the WCCL operators describing Proto-Patient relation. Language details has been described in (Radziszewski et al., 2011), abbreviations for grammatical categories has been explained in (Przepiórkowski et al., 2012)

```
@b:"PROTO-PATIENT-acc" (
 and(
  // 0 - accusative frame
  equal(class[0], pact),
  or(
   equal(lex(base[0], "acc"), ["1"]),
   not(equal(
   lex(base[0], "frames"), ["1"]))
  ),
  // 1 - noun or adj. & accusative
  in(class[1], {subst,depr,ger,adj}),
  equal(cas[1],acc)
 )
)
```

Next the operator seeks for the preposition *przez* 'by' at position 1. Then it tests if the first meaning of the lemma *wydawca* 'publisher' does not belong to the domain 'time' (= Polish `czas`) in Polish WordNet (position 2). Indeed, the first meaning of *wydawca* is in the domain 'person' (that iformation is avaiable in the dictionary `noun_domain`). At the end, we check whether the last token of our triple is in accusative. Because all of these conditions are fulfilled, the operator returns 'true', and we may assume that the last token takes the role of Proto-Agent.

Listing 2: A WCCL operator for the Proto-Agent relation

```
@b:"PROTO-AGENT-ger-przez-acc" (
 and(
  // 0 - gerund
  equal(class[0],{ger}),
  or(
   equal(lex(base[0], "acc"), ["1"]),
   equal(lex(base[0], "gen"), ["1"]),
   not(equal(
    lex(base[0], "frames"), ["1"]))
  ),
  // 1 - preposition "przez"
  equal(orth[1],"przez"),
  // 2 - not 'time' & accusative
  equal(cas[2], acc),
  not(
   equal(lex(if(
    equal(class[2], {ger}),
    lex(base[2], "ger_base"), base[2]),
   "noun_domain"), ["czas"]))
 )
)
```

In Listing 3 one operator for family ralation was shown. `FAMILY-agpp` used to recognize this relation for word pairs. The operator, inter alia, uses semantic dictionary of kinship names built on the basis of Polish WordNet (the dictionary `kinship`), lammas of possessive pronouns (e.g., `mój` 'my', `twój` 'yours').

Listing 3: Two WCCL operators describing Family relation

```
@b:"FAMILY-agpp" (
 and(
  // agreement
  agrpp(0,1, {nmb, gen, cas}),
  // position 0
  in(base[0], ["moj", "twoj",
   "swoj", "nasz", "wasz"])
  // position 1
  equal(lex(base[1], "kinship"), ["1"]),
  equal(lex(
   base[1], "noun_domain"), ["os"]),
  in(class[1], {ger, subst, depr}),
 )
)
```

5 Results and conclusions

Evaluation of the presented semantic relation recognition algorithm was performed in three steps. First experiment (labelled `kpwr`) was performed on a random sample of the KPWr corpus (26 out of 326 texts, aproximately one thirteenth of the corpus). In this experiment we made use of syntactic annotations from KPWr (cf. Tab. 1). Second experiment was performed on a random sample of 100 texts taken from yet another Polish corpus, called *NKJP* (Przepiórkowski et al., 2012, `nkjp`, approximately one tenth of the corpus)[7]. Since NKJP lacked syntactic annotations of KPWr style, we were forced to run on it the CRF shallow parser (described in Sec. 4.1). This experiment gave us information about performance of our algorithm on a 'bare' text (see Tab. 2). Evaluation in the experiments was done by a professional linguist.

At last, four baseline models were constructed and evaluated on the two corpora (Tab. 3). We created baselines similar to that presented in (Uchiyama et al., 2008), which was majority model. We chose the most frequent relation, which in the sample from KPWr was Proto-Patient (with the number of 113 instances out of 268 relation instances), this relation type was also the most frequent in the sample of NKJP (411 out of 1950 relation instances). For each corpora two baselines

[7]We focused on one-million balanced version of the much bigger corpus.

Relation	TP/FP/FN	P [%]	R [%]	F1 [%]
Proto-Agent	7/5/16	58.3	30.4	40.0
Proto-Patient	45/8/68	84.9	39.8	54.2
Instrument	0/0/7	—	0.0	—
Material	0/0/3	—	0.0	—
Purpose	1/7/30	12.5	3.2	5.1
location	3/9/25	25.0	10.7	15.0
sp. meronymy	0/3/2	0.0	0.0	—
time	2/2/3	50.0	40.0	44.4
t. meronymy	1/0/1	—	—	—
attribute	14/18/10	43.8	58.3	50.0
family	0/0/2	—	—	—
order	5/0/5	100.0	50.0	66.7
quantity	10/2/8	83.3	55.6	66.7
All	88/54/186	53.8-70.1	*26.8-38.0	*36.2-48.3

Table 1: Results of the algorithm on a sample from KPWr: P = Precision, R = recall, F1 = F-measure, TP = true positives, FP = false positives, FN = false negatives, sp. = spatial, t. = temporal. Percentile bootstrap confidence intervals are calculated at $\alpha = 0.05$. Asterisks denote significant differences between `kpwr` and `nkjp` in one-tailed tests, $\alpha = 0.05$

Relation	TP/FP/FN	P [%]	R [%]	F1 [%]
Proto-Agent	75/7/143	91.5	34.4	50.0
Proto-Patient	181/17/230	91.4	44.0	59.4
Instrument	2/1/8	66.7	20.0	30.8
Material	3/4/36	42.9	7.7	13.0
Purpose	13/7/94	65.0	12.2	20.5
location	90/75/202	54.6	30.8	39.4
sp. meronymy	12/11/25	52.2	32.4	40.0
time	25/16/75	61.0	25.0	35.5
t. meronymy	2/0/66	100	2.9	57.1
attribute	200/248/64	44.6	75.8	56.2
family	18/0/6	100.0	60.0	85.7
order	33/0/100	100.0	24.8	39.8
quantity	113/68/146	62.4	43.6	51.4
All	767/454/1195	60.1-65.6	*36.9-41.2	*46.0-50.3

Table 2: Results of the algorithm on a sample from NKJP, labels as in the previous table. Percentile bootstrap confidence intervals are calculated at $\alpha = 0.05$. Asterisks denote significant differences between `kpwr` and `nkjp` in one-tailed tests, $\alpha = 0.05$

were calculated: in Baseline #1 we assumed that we had perfectly recognized all occurences of semantic relations (of any type), in Baseline #2 we simply signed with 'Proto-Patient' label every recognized by our system semantic relation instance. Baseline #2 is realistic, while #1 is idealistic, since to obtain #1 we should be able to recognize every single relation instance within a corpus. Baselines #1 are upper limits for all majority models (including #2). Our two idealistic baselines are higher than the realistic baselines (see Tab. 3).

Percentile bootstrap methods (DiCiccio and Efron, 1996), (DiCiccio and Romano, 1988) were applied to statistical significance and confidence interval (*CI*) analysis of the data.[8] We took 10000

`kpwr`	P	R	F1
Baseline #1	*42.2%	***42.2%**	**42.2%**
Baseline #2	*26.2%	*20.0%	*22.7%
Experiment	**62.0%**	32.8%	**42.9%**
`nkjp`	P	R	F1
Baseline #1	*21.1%	*21.0%	*21.0%
Baseline #2	*14.9%	*9.2%	*11.4%
Experiment	**62.5%**	**38.9%**	**47.9%**

Table 3: Precision, recall and F1 for baselines (#1 & #2) and experiments (`kpwr`, `nkjp`). Asterisks denote significant differences between an experiment and a baseline in one-tailed test at $\alpha = 0.05$

bootstrap resamplings for each measure (P, R, F1), α was equal to 0.05 for each one-tailed test and CI (a percentile CI need not be symmetrical).

In `nkjp` we have beaten both idealistic and realistic baselines. Precision, recall and F1 for `kpwr` are higher than Baseline #2. Only idealistic Baseline #1 for the KPWr corpus has overtaken our rule-based algorithm with regard to recall (42.2% vs. 32.8%), while its precision is lower and F1's are statistically indistinguishable.

Results are promising, precisions go above 50% (the lower endpoint for the `kpwr` confidence intervel), for `nkjp` we may assess it even more precisely as 60%-65%. Some semantic relations are recognized with higher precision: Proto-Agent (`nkjp`: 89-100%, `kpwr`: 90-100%, $\alpha = 0.05$), Proto-Patient (`nkjp`: 88-95%, `kpwr`: 83%-98%), family (`nkjp`: 90-100%) and order (`nkjp`: 91-100%). Our system is thus comparable in this aspect to the systems described in Sec. 2.[9]

Overall recall is low, but higher than realistic baselines. In `kpwr` we obtained R = 27-38%, while for `nkjp` we got statistically higher interval of 37-41%. It seems that recall was not affected by lack of marked NP/PP borders in the corpus (these should have been brought out by the CRF shallow parser). F-measures calculated on our both corpora are also much higher than realistic baselines #2.

We can already conclude that our preliminary experiments turned successful. Now we are aiming at improving our operators to raise their recall and at expanding the semantic role set (e.g., for Agent, Causer, Experiencer, Possessor or Result). Parallel, we start work on construction of automatic algorithms for relation recognition.

[8] Our data for NKJP were merged, so cross-validation was not avaiable.

[9] Not directly, of course.

References

Asma Ben Abacha and Pierre Zweigenbaum. 2011. Automatic extraction of semantic relations between medical entities: a rule based approach. *Journal of Biomedical Semantics*, 2(5):1–11.

Bartosz Broda, Michał Marcińczuk, Marek Maziarz, Adam Radziszewski, and Adam Wardyński. 2012. KPWr: Towards a Free Corpus of Polish. In Nicoletta Calzolari, Khalid Choukri, Thierry Declerck, Mehmet Uğur Doğan, Bente Maegaard, Joseph Mariani, Jan Odijk, and Stelios Piperidis, editors, *Proceedings of LREC'12*, Istanbul, Turkey. ELRA.

Thomas J. DiCiccio and Bradley Efron. 1996. Bootstrap confidence intervals. *Statistical Science*, 11(3):189–212.

Thomas J. DiCiccio and Joseph P. Romano. 1988. A review of bootstrap confidence intervals. *Journal of the Royal Statistical Society. Series B (Methodological)*, 50(3):338–354.

David Dowty. 1991. Thematic proto-roles and argument selection. *Language*, 67(3):547–619.

Łukasz Dębowski and Marcin Woliński. 2007. Argument co-occurrence matrix as a description of verb valence. In *Proc. of the 3rd Language & Technology Conference*, volume 3, pages 260–264, Poznań, Poland.

Łukasz Dębowski. 2013. Polish valence dictionary (http://nlp.ipipan.waw.pl/ppjp/ slownik/swigra/koncowy.txt).

Pablo Gamallo, Marco Gonzalez, Alexandre Agustini, Gabriel Lopes, and Vera S. De Lima. 2002. Mapping syntactic dependencies onto semantic relations. In *ECAI Workshop on Machine Learning and Natural Language Processing for Ontology Engineering*.

Konrad Gołuchowski and Adam Przepiórkowski. 2012. Semantic role labelling without deep syntactic parsing. In Hitoshi Isahara and Kyoko Kanzaki, editors, *Advances in Natural Language Processing*, volume 7614 of *Lecture Notes in Computer Science*, pages 192–197. Springer Berlin Heidelberg.

Marti A. Hearst. 1992. Automatic acquisition of hyponyms from large text corpora. In *Proceedings of the 14th conference on Computational linguistics - Volume 2*, COLING '92, pages 539–545, Stroudsburg, PA, USA. Association for Computational Linguistics.

Rongfeng Huang. 2009. Semantic relation extraction by automatically constructed rules. In *Proceedings of the International Conference on Artificial Intelligence and Computational Intelligence*, AICI '09, pages 425–434, Berlin, Heidelberg. Springer-Verlag.

Ewa Jędrzejko. 1993. *Nominalizacje w systemie i tekstach współczesnej polszczyzny*. Uniwersytet Śląski, Katowice.

Kate Kearns. 2011. *Semantics*. Palgrave.

Martha J. Kolln. 1990. *WordNet: Understanding English Grammar*. Macmillan.

Gabriel Larson, Richard & Segal. 1996. *Knowledge of Meaning: An Introduction to Semantic Theory*. The MIT Press.

Roman Laskowski and Henryk Wróbel, editors. 1997. *Gramatyka współczesnego języka polskiego. Morfologia [Grammar of contemporary Polish: Morphology]*. PWN.

Douglas B. Lenat. 1995. Cyc: a large-scale investment in knowledge infrastructure. *Commun. ACM*, 38(11):33–38, November.

2009. Luna project: Spoken language understanding in multilingual communication systems (http://zil.ipipan.waw.pl/luna).

Marek Maziarz, Adam Radziszewski, and Jan Wieczorek. 2011. Chunking of Polish: guidelines, discussion and experiments with Machine Learning. In *Proc. of the LTC*.

Marek Maziarz, Maciej Piasecki, and Stanisław Szpakowicz. 2012. Approaching plWordNet 2.0. In *Proceedings of the 6th Global Wordnet Conference*, Matsue, Japan, January.

Dan Moldovan, Adriana Badulescu, Marta Tatu, Daniel Antohe, and Roxana Girju. 2004. Models for the semantic classification of noun phrases. In *Proceedings of the HLT-NAACL Workshop on Computational Lexical Semantics*, CLS '04, pages 60–67, Stroudsburg, PA, USA. Association for Computational Linguistics.

Vivi Nastase, Jelber Sayyad Shirabad, Marina Sokolova, and Stan Szpakowicz. 2006. Learning noun-modifier semantic relations with corpus-based and wordnet-based features. In *Proceedings of the 21st National Conference on Artificial Intelligence*.

Palmer, Martha & Gilldea, Daniel & Xue, and Nianwen. 2010. *Semantic Role Labeling*. Morgan & Claypool Publishers.

Adam Przepiórkowski, Miroslaw Banko, Rafal Górski, and Barbara Lewandowska-Tomaszczyk, editors. 2012. *Narodowy Korpus Jezyka Polskiego*. Wydawnictwo Naukowe PWN.

Adam Radziszewski and Adam Pawlaczek. 2012. Large-scale experiments with NP chunking of Polish. In *Proceedings of TSD 2012*, Brno, Czech Republic. Springer.

Adam Radziszewski, Adam Wardyński, and Tomasz Śniatowski. 2011. WCCL: A Morpho-syntactic Feature Toolkit. In *Proceedings of the Balto-Slavonic Natural Language Processing Workshop*. Springer.

Adam Radziszewski, Marek Maziarz, and Jan Wieczorek. 2012. Shallow syntactic annotation in the Corpus of Wrocław University of Technolog. *Cognitive Studies*, 12.

Adam Radziszewski. 2013. A tiered CRF tagger for Polish. In R. Bembenik, Ł. Skonieczny, H. Rybiński, M. Kryszkiewicz, and M. Niezgódka, editors, *Intelligent Tools for Building a Scientific Information Platform: Advanced Architectures and Solutions*.

Bryan Rink and Sanda Harabagiu. 2010. Utd: Classifying semantic relations by combining lexical and semantic resources. In *Proceedings of the 5th International Workshop on Semantic Evaluation*, SemEval '10, pages 256–259, Stroudsburg, PA, USA. Association for Computational Linguistics.

Barbara Rosario and Marti Hearst. 2001. Classifying the semantic relations in noun compounds via a domain-specific lexical hierarchy. In *Proceedings of the 2001 Conference on Empirical Methods in Natural Language Processing (EMNLP-01)*, pages 82–90.

Stephen Tratz and Eduard Hovy. 2010. Isi: Automatic classification of relations between nominals using a maximum entropy classifier. In *Proc. of the 5th Intern. Workshop on Semantic Evaluation*, Sweden. Association for Computational Linguistics.

Kateryna Tymoshenko and Claudio Giuliano. 2010. Fbk-irst: Semantic relation extraction using cyc. In *Proceedings of the 5th International Workshop on Semantic Evaluation*, pages 214–217, Uppsala, Sweden, July. Association for Computational Linguistics.

Kiyoko Uchiyama, Shunsuke Aihara, and Shun Ishizaki. 2008. Identifying semantic relations in japanese compound nouns for patent documents analysis. In *Proceedings of the 3rd international conference on Large-scale knowledge resources: construction and application*, LKR'08, pages 75–81, Berlin, Heidelberg. Springer-Verlag.

Robert D. Van Valin. 2004. Semantic macroroles in role and reference grammar. In Rolf Kailuweit and Martin Hummel, editors, *Semantische Rollen*, pages 62–82. Tuebingen Narr.

Unsupervised Induction of Arabic Root and Pattern Lexicons using Machine Learning

Bilal Khaliq
Dept. of Informatics
University of Sussex
bk54@sussex.ac.uk

John Carroll
Dept. of Informatics
University of Sussex
johnca@sussex.ac.uk

Abstract

We describe an approach to building a morphological analyser of Arabic by inducing a lexicon of root and pattern templates from an unannotated corpus. Using maximum entropy modelling, we capture orthographic features from surface words, and cluster the words based on the similarity of their possible roots or patterns. From these clusters, we extract root and pattern lexicons, which allows us to morphologically analyse words. Further enhancements are applied, adjusting for morpheme length and structure. Final root extraction accuracy of 87.2% is achieved. In contrast to previous work on unsupervised learning of Arabic morphology, our approach is applicable to naturally-written, unvowelled Arabic text.

1 Introduction

The number and diversity of human languages makes it impractical to manually craft lexicons and morphological processors for more than a very small proportion of them. Further challenges are posed by the need to deal with dialects and colloquial forms of languages. This has motivated recent increased interest in approaches to morphological analysis based on unsupervised learning. Inspired by competitions such as the Morpho Challenge, many techniques have been proposed for unsupervised morphology learning.

Although these techniques are often intended to be language independent, they are often directed to a specific group of languages. Most work has aimed at sequential separation or segmentation of morphemes concatenated together in a surface word form. This type of analysis, outputting stems and appended morphemes aims to identify some kind of border between the different morphemes. However, another type of word formation consists of the interdigitation of a root morpheme with an affix or pattern template; in this case there is no boundary between morphemes, since they are rather intercalated with each other. This type of non-concatenative morphology, which is characteristic of the Semitic group of languages, has attracted far less interest for unsupervised learning.

In this paper we present an approach to unsupervised learning of non-concatenative morphology, applying it to Arabic. We describe an approach to learning tri-literal roots and affix template of Arabic by first inducing root and affix lexicons. Our approach uses Maximum Entropy modelling to obtain clusters[1] of words based on concatenative and non-concatenative orthographic features, and induces the lexicons from these clusters.

Our data is an undiacritized version of the Quranic Arabic Corpus since we assume a realistic setting of unvowelled text, as most Arabic text is written without vowels; we chose this corpus since correct roots of each word are available, facilitating the evaluation process. The fact that the corpus contains a relatively small vocabulary of around 7000 words also simulates the scenario for most of the world's languages of scarcity of linguistic resources and data.

This paper is structured as follows: Section 2 surveys previous related work. Section 3 provides an introduction to Arabic root and pattern morphology. Our approach to unsupervised lexicon induction based on Maximum Entropy (ME) modelling is explained in section 4. Section 5 describes the procedure for performing morphological analysis of words, followed by evaluation in section 6 and conclusions in section 7.

2 Related Work

An active current area of natural language processing research is applying statistical and information-theoretic approaches to unsupervised learning of morphology and grammar. A common starting point is raw (unannotated) text corpora, inducing the target knowledge from word forms and their patterns of usage.

Information theoretic approaches, particularly Minimum Description Length (MDL) as investigated by Goldsmith (2000, 2006) and others

[1] Cluster here refers to a collection of words related in terms of morpheme types, without referring to application of any clustering algorithm.

(Cruetz and Lagus, 2005, 2007), have brought a theoretical perspective considering input data to be 'compressed' into a morphologically analysed representation. This optimization scheme has achieved good results, and is amongst the most effective approaches for unsupervised morphological analysis.

Most work on unsupervised learning of morphology has focused on concatenative morphology (De Pauw and Wagacha 2007; Hammarström and Borin 2011). Another perspective adopted by Schone and Jurafsky (2001) incorporates orthographic and phonological features, and induces semantic relatedness between word pairs using Latent Semantic Indexing. Their work shows comparable performance to Goldsmith's (2000) Linguistica system. Yarowsky and Wicentowski (2000) experiment with learning irregular mnaturaorphology using a lightly supervised technique to align irregular words to their lemmas by estimating the distribution of ratios over part-of-speech classes of inflected words to lemmas.

More recently, researchers have addressed non-concatenative morphology, such as for Semitic languages, using a variety of empirical approaches. Daya et al. (2008) learn Semitic roots using supervised learning, building a multi-class classifier for individual root radicals. Clark (2007) uses Arabic as a test-bed to study semi-supervised learning of complex broken plural structure modelled using memory-based algorithms, with the aim of gaining insights into human language acquisition.

Most work on unsupervised learning of morphology has focused on concatenative morphology (Hammarström and Borin 2011). The few studies that have focussed on non-concatenative morphology, such as for Semitic languages, have not used naturally written text. For example, Rodriguez and Ćavar (2005) learn roots using a number of orthographic heuristics and then apply constraint-based learning to improve the quality of roots. Xanthos (2008) works on phonetic transcriptions of Arabic text to decipher roots and patterns. The approach is to initially create crude Root and Pattern (RP) transcriptions from words based on vowel-consonant distinctions, and then to apply an MDL approach similar to Goldsmith's (2006) in order to refine the RP structures.

In contrast to previous work, we learn intercalated morphology, identifying the root and transfixes/ incomplete pattern for words from 'natural' text without short vowels or diacritical markers.

3 Root and Pattern Morphology

Words in Arabic are formed through three morphological processes. The first (i) is the fusion of a root form and pattern template to derive a base word, which can be a noun, verb or adjective, all of which are semantically related to the root. The second (ii) is affixation, by means of prefixes, suffixes or infixes, including inflectional morphemes marking gender, plurality and/or tense, resulting in a stem. Thirdly (iii) a final layer of clitics may be attached to a word, including a subset of prepositions, conjunctions, determiners and pronouns; these appear at the beginning (proclitics) or end (enclitics) of a word but never in the middle.

Since techniques for concatenative morphology learning are fairly advanced we have focused on using stemmed words, computable through such approaches. We used the QAC stem vocabulary where appended morphemes of type (iii) are mostly absent[2] and hence ignored from analysis. Most of type (ii) are present as part of the stem. In the case of (i), most derived forms consist of short vowels and occasional long vowels or a consonant interdigitated with the root. In unvowelled text the short vowels are ignored, so derived words have at most single letter affixation.

Table 1 shows two example words with their roots and affix pattern templates. The 'y' and 't' in the respective words are clitic/inflectional markers, which are part of the affix template. 'A' is the derivational infix marker for nouns.

Word	Root	Pattern
ktAby	Ktb	--A-y
tEArf	Erf	t-A--

Table 1: Example words with their roots and affix pattern templates.

For analysis, each word, w, is decomposed, using a decomposition function, into a set of tuples encoding all n possible combinations of a root (of at least 3 letters) and associated pattern:

$$d(w) \rightarrow \{\langle r^x, p^x \rangle\} \quad \text{(Eq. 1)}$$

where x ranges from 1 to n. For example, the decomposition of the word 'yErf', is shown in Figure 1.

[2] Stems in QAC include the attached pronoun clitics

$$yErf \rightarrow \left\{ \begin{array}{ll} \langle y\,E\,r, & ---f\,\rangle, \\ \langle y\,E\,f, & --r\,-\rangle, \\ \langle y\,r\,f, & -E\,--\rangle, \\ \langle E\,r\,f, & y\,---\rangle, \\ \langle y\,E\,r\,f, & ----\rangle \end{array} \right\}$$

Figure 1: Decomposition of a word into all possible combinations of roots and patterns.

4 Using Maximum Entropy Modelling for Unsupervised Learning

In this study we apply an supervised machine learning technique, Maximum Entropy (ME) modelling, in a completely unsupervised way, taking our inspiration from the work of De Pauw and Wagacha (2007), who applied the approach for extracting prefixes in an African language.

Unlike for supervised learning, no annotated text is used. Instead we simply derive features automatically from the vocabulary words of the dataset. Each word is represented as an output class mapped to by the corresponding features of the words. These word-features are used to train a classifier. Rather than applying the classifier to classify unseen data, we apply the model back to the 'training data' to obtain, not the classification but the proximities of each word/class with every other word/class. These proximities are then utilized to derive root and pattern lexicons.

The advantage of this approach to gauge relatedness of words over other approaches, such as minimum edit distance, is the ability to better capture morpheme dependencies between words with common roots which may be orthographically quite different due to substantial affixing.

4.1 Building the Lexicons

We derive two lexicons: a root lexicon and an affix or pattern lexicon. We do this by training ME classifiers on orthographic features computed from each word in the corpus dataset. The classifiers are then applied to the same data to obtain word clusters relating each word to every other word with respect to either common roots or common patterns. Thus, for the root lexicon we obtain neighbours of words that have the same or similar patterns. Conversely, for the pattern lexicon we obtain neighbours of words that have common root radicals.

4.2 Modelling Orthographic Features

We first extract orthographic features for obtaining word clusters with similar roots (i.e. for pattern lexicon acquisition). We then construct the inverse of these features for obtaining word clusters with similar patterns (i.e. for root lexicon acquisition).

In the former case, feature extraction proceeds as follows: we first enclose each word with beginning and end boundary markers, '@' and '#' respectively. (This is in order to provide context information for the first and last characters of a word). We next compute the power-set of all the character combinations in a word, and then exclude features where the first and last letter of the word appear without the boundary markers (to give emphasis to word boundary features). The final set of these features for the word 'yErf' is shown in the first column of Table 2.

In the latter case, pattern features are obtained such that corresponding to each root feature, we replace root radicals with a placeholder; characters between root radicals that are omitted from the root features appear as potential affix characters in the pattern template. These inverse features are shown in the second column of Table 2.

Root Features (for Pattern Lexicon)		**Pattern features (for Root Lexicon)**	
@y,	@yE,	@-,	@--,
@yEr,	@yErf#,	@---,	@----#,
@yEr#,	@yEf#,	@---f#,	@--r-#,
@yE#,	@yr,	@--rf#,	@-E-,
@yrf#,	@yr#,	@-E--#,	@-E-f#,
@yf#,	@y#,	@-Er-#,	@-Erf#,
@E,	@Er,	@y-,	@y--,
@Erf#,	Er#,	@y---#,	@y--f#,
@Ef#,	@E#,	@y-r-#,	@y-rf#,
@r,	@rf#,	@yE-,	@yE--#,
@r#,	@f#,	@yE-f#,	@yEr-#,
E,	Er,	-,	--,
Erf#,	Er#,	---#,	--f#,
Ef#,	E#,	-r-#,	-rf#,
r,	rf#,	-,	--#,
r#,	f#	-f#,	-#

Table 2: Features for the word 'yErf'.

4.3 Word Nearest Neighbors

The classifier is trained using Limited Variable LBFGS optimization method. The number of iterations for training is stopped automatically when 100% accuracy on the training data is achieved. Each trained classifier is reapplied to its respective training data features to get proximity values between each word and every other word. Sorting the list gives us the most related word in terms of root based or pattern based proximity values, with the highest value (≈ 1) for the headword, *h*, i.e. the word's own features. Table 3 shows an example of the closest neighbours in a cluster, along with their headword.

Using these words and proximity measures we next apply a strategy to induce the morpheme. Not all words in the list of N elements for each word are relevant to us since the proximity value starts to drop rapidly towards zero as we go down the ranked list. With each headword we choose a 500 nearest neighbours cluster for each type of morpheme as a sufficient number beyond which we expect no gain in efficiency is expected.

Head-Word, *h*	**Proximity for Root Cluster** *k*	*P(k)*	**Proximity for Pattern Cluster** *k*	*P(k)*
yErf	*yErf*	0.9897420	*yErf*	0.99999
	Erf	0.0023982	*yHrf*	2.59E-07
	yEf	0.0022552	*ysrf*	2.58E-07
	tErf	0.0015299	*ySrf*	2.32E-07
	yErD	0.0014147	*yEkf*	2.31E-07
	yEr$	0.0011525	*tErf*	1.10E-09
	yErj	0.0009722	*yErj*	4.24E-10
	Ef	0.0001968	*yErD*	3.29E-10
	yr	0.0001052	*yEr$*	2.36E-10
	'Etrf	2.5629E-05	*msrf*	2.14E-12
	yrd	8.6797E-06	*zxrf*	1.51E-12
	…	…	…	…

Table 3: ME values for the word *yErf*.

4.4 Dictionary Induction

Using the respective word clusters we create dictionaries for two types of morphemes, roots and patterns, such that we score the morphemes thus: Higher scoring morphemes are more plausible and ranked higher in the lexical list than lower ones. The procedure for scoring is adapted and amended from the work of De Pauw and Wagacha (2007).

For the pattern lexicon, we score each pattern in the following manner: for each headword, h_i (having probability value ≈ 1) in cluster c_i (with each of the $i = 1,2,\ldots N$ words in the vocabulary), we obtain all possible decompositins(equation 1) into template patterns p_h^x (shown in column 1 of Table 4) and roots, r_h^x (column 2 of Table 4) with respect to the headword, h_i. Each pattern is scored with a function $S(p_h^x)$ (equation 2) which aggregates the Logarithmically Scaled (LS) probability value, P_{kj} of words k_j ($j = 1,2,\ldots 500$ words in each cluster), such that r_h^x matches any of the roots in word k, r_k^y ($y=1,2,\ldots m$ root combinations in k). This aggregation is not only local to each cluster but covers all occurrences of the pattern in each of the N clusters.

$$S(p_h^x) = \sum_{i=1}^{N}\sum_{j=1}^{500}\left(LS(P_{kj}) \times LA(|p_h^x|)\middle| r_{h_i}^x = r_{kj}^y\right)$$

(Eq. 2)

Logarithmic scaling is necessary since the probability drops too rapidly and too low in order to provide a feasible ratio between words. After taking the log of the probability the resulting ratios are negative which are then adjusted by subtracting the log of a base probability value, P_0, thus linearly inverting the ratios (equation 3). P_0 is hence chosen to be small enough to ensure the resulting logarithmic score is positive. We chose the smallest occurring probability value in our clusters as the value for P_0.

$$LS(P_{kj}) = \log P(k_j) - \log P_0$$

(Eq. 3)

The score is also exponentially Length Adjusted (LA) for each pattern, p, according to the length of the pattern, $|p|$, in terms of the number of affix charaters in p. This boosts the score for lengthier morphemes which are relatively infrequent. The intuition for adjustment formula comes from the work of (Chung and Gildea, 2009) and (Liang and Klein, 2009), who use a exponential Length Penalty measure to adjust their model for morpheme length.

$$LA(|p|) = e^{|p|}$$

(Eq. 4)

Thus the pattern is scored according to the score of words containing plausible roots. Commonly occurring patterns such as '*y---*' gather weight and ascend the list of the most frequent (and hence potentially sound) affix templates. Table 4 shows how each pattern for the headword '*yErf*' is scored, aggregating the logarithmic score over words (in column 4 of Table 4) containing the roots in column 2 of Table 4.

Pattern	**Root**	**Word, *k*, with Root**	**Pattern Weight**
y---	*Erf*	*Erf, tErf, 'Etrf*	19.97328
-E--	*Yrf*	–	0.0
--r-	*yEf*	*yEf*	7.353
---f	*yEr*	*yErD,yEr$, yErj*	21.200

Table 4: Example pattern candidate scoring.

Similarly, we score the root, $S(r_h^x)$, with respect to the pattern occurrence in each word k of cluster c_i:

$$S(r_h^x) = \sum_{i=1}^{N} \sum_{j=1}^{500} \left(LS(P_{kj}) \middle| p_{h_i}^x = p_{kj}^y \right)$$

(Eq. 5)

The scoring aggregates over the log scaled probability of words in the affix-based clusters having pattern occurrences in a word in each cluster. There is no need for length adjustment to these ratios since we are considering only three letter roots. Table 5 exemplifies this for scoring roots with words (in column 3 of Table 5) that have corresponding patterns (in column 2 of Table 5).

Root	Pattern	Word, *k*, with Pattern	Pattern weight
Erf	*y---*	*yHrf, ysrf, ySrf, ...*	25.190
Yrf	*-E--*	*yEkf, tErf, yErj, ...*	20.032
yEf	*--r-*	*yHrf, ysrf, ySrf,...*	54.259
yEr	*---f*	*yHrf, ysrf, ySrf,...*	46.104

Table 5: Example pattern candidate scoring.

Table 6 shows the top lexicon entries for roots and patterns along with their respective scores. The top entries in the lexicon would plausibly be correct morphemes while lower entries would be not so plausible.

Root Lexicon	
'mn	49067.2
Sdq	44801.4
xlf	42768.4
$hd	42607.8
xrj	40872.8
nSr	40111.4
k*b	37881.9
HfZ	37784.5
Elm	35639.1
kfr	35585.5
...	

Pattern Lexicon	
y---	62987.8
'---	61905.4
t---	54634.3
---A	51777.1
n---	44257
--y-	31058.9
---t	30770
m---	29784.2
--A-	28105.6
-A--	24129.8
...	

Table 6: Top Entries in Root and Pattern Lexicons

5 Morphological Analysis

A word is analysed into its root and pattern template by considering every possible combination of trilateral root and corresponding pattern pairs, $\langle r^x, p^x \rangle$, as defined in equation 1 for the word, w_i, in the vocabulary, scoring each analysis with the sum of the scores for the root, r^x, and pattern, p^x, in the root lexicon and pattern lexicon, respectively. Due to the different ranges of scores for root and pattern, the score for the former is scaled with respect to the latter, as in equation 6, in order to guarantee equal contributions.

$$SS(r) = S(r) \times \frac{\max(S(p))}{\max(S(r))}$$

(Eq. 6)

The analysis, x, with the highest score is selected as the output, as illustrated in equation 7.

$$\max_{x=1..n} \left(S(r_w^x) + SS(p_w^x) \right)$$

(Eq. 7)

Since we are considering text without diacritics, due to absence of short vowels, we only expect words to contain single letter infixes. Hence we experiment with an alternative configuration of the word decomposition, $\langle r^z, p^z \rangle$: non-contiguous root radicals formed with more than one intervening character are dropped; correspondingly patterns with more than one consecutive character between radical place holder markers are dropped.

6 Evaluation

We carry out our evaluation using the Quranic Arabic Corpus (QAC)[3], since it identifies the root of each word, facilitating the evaluation.

In this section, we first detail some information about our dataset before going onto evaluation of the analyses for correct root extraction.

6.1 Data

The QAC consists of approximately 77,900 word tokens, with a total of around 19,000 unique tokens. Since we are interested in investigating learning from undiacritized text, we removed all short vowels and diacritical markers. The size of the resulting vocabulary, after removal of vowels, is approximately 14,850.

We take as input lightly stemmed text, with clitics removed, but with most inflectional markers attached. We assume that stemmed words are obtainable using existing tools for unsupervised concatenative morphology learning. For example, the technique of Poon et al (2009) could be used to obtain accurate stems for each word. The stemmed unvowelled vocabulary size is around 7370.

The original corpus is annotated with roots for all derived and inflected words. More than 95% of words are tagged with their root forms since the

[3] http://corpus.quran.com/

Quran consists mostly of words of derivable forms, with very few proper nouns. There are 7192 stemmed words with available roots.

In Arabic, sometimes alterations in root radicals take place; for example, in hollow roots, when moving from a root containing a long vowel to the surface word, the long vowel might change its form to another type or get dropped. Such words with hollow roots or reduplicated radicals, whose characters do not match every radical of the root, were removed from the evaluation as they are beyond the scope of the learning algorithm to identify. Leaving aside these word and root evaluation pairs we evaluated with 5468 stemmed types.

6.2 Baseline

As a baseline for evaluation, we derived lexicons in a similar manner to procedure for derivation from clusters (section 5.3). Instead of using clusters we simply scored patterns that matched the largest number of vocabulary words having corresponding roots. Likewise, the root score was obtained by counting the number of words with corresponding patterns.

Comparing our system to the baseline is meant to elucidate the advantage of using the machine learning technique to enhance our lexicons. In the baseline we do not have the ME based word clusters with proximities to the target word; only one cluster exist: the vocabulary set with unit promitiy of 1.

6.3 Evaluation of Lexicons

In this section we compare our lexicons, built using maximum entropy modeling approach, (ME), to the baseline(BL).

We evaluated the effect of logarithmic scaling (ME_LS) comparing it to using raw probability values(ME_RW). Also we gauged the performance improvement with Length Adjustment (ME_LS_LA) for morphemes.

Finally, we evaluated morphological analysis restricted to patterns with single affixes which correspond to roots with single non-contiguous characters from words (ME_NC1).

We evaluate morphological analysis through correct identification of the root. The accuracy is measured in terms of percentage of the roots that are correctly identified. As stated above, we evaluate on a total of 5468 words. The results for the different configuration evaluations is given in table 7.

Configuration	Total Correct	Percentage Correct
Baseline	4055	74.16
ME_RW	3597	65.78
ME_LS	4415	80.74
ME_LS_LA	4700	85.95
ME_LS_LA_NC1	4768	87.20

Table 7: Evaluation of System Configurations

The accuracy of 74% shows a sound and competitive baseline. The low results for ME_RW highlights the weakness of considering raw probability values which are too low to provide adequate weightage to morphemes. Hence the dismal performace. The true value for the ME based processing is realized in ME_LS, where the probabilities have been logarithmically scaled be summing. We see an accuracy gain of 6% over the baseline which is quite significant and encouraging. Further improvements can be seen when the score has been adjusted for morpheme length, ME_LS_LA, with performance increase by further 5%. Still more improvement is seen using knowledge of word structure of undiacritized text, ME_LS_LS_NC1, with further accuracy gain of 2.25 %. The final result for ME based analysis with further enhancements gives an promising accuracy result of 87.20%.

7 Conclusion and Future directions

In this paper we have presented an approach to solve the problem of learning intercalated morphology in an unsupervised manner with no parameter settings and minimal linguistic knowledge. We applied the machine learning based techniques to learn clusters of words related on basis of either root or pattern morpheme. Thereafter, plausible morphemes are extracted using a scoring method which takes advantage of knowledge of word proximities from clusters built using a maximum entropy classifier. We further apply enhancements to the procedure by accommodating for length and structure of morphemes. The finalized procedure offers significant boost in performance.

The dynamicity of the technique allows its applicability to other types of morphological structures. Also, the system can easily be extended to cater to roots beyond tri-literals by adapting the soring function to accommodate for morpheme length.

References

Alexander Clark. 2007. Supervised and unsupervised learning of Arabic morphology. *Arabic Computational Morphology*, volume 38 of *Text, Speech and Language Technology*, pages 181-200.

Tagyoung Chung and Daniel Gildea. 2009. Unsupervised tokenization for machine translation. In Conference on *Empirical Methods in Natural Language Processing (EMNLP).*

Mathias Creutz and Krista Lagus. 2005. Inducing the morphological lexicon of a natural language from unannotated text. In *Proceedings of the International and Interdisciplinary Conference on Adaptive Knowledge Representation and Reasoning* (AKRR '05), 106-113.

Mathias Creutz and Krista Lagus. 2007. Unsupervised models for morpheme segmentation and morphology learning. *ACM Transactions on Speech and Language Processing*, 4(1-3):1-33.

Ezra Daya, Dan Roth, and Shuly Wintner. 2008. Identifying Semitic roots: Machine learning with linguistic constraints. *Computational Linguistics*, 34:429-448.

Percy Liang and Dan Klein. 2009. Online EM for unsupervised models. In *North American Association for Computational Linguistics (NAACL).*

Guy De Pauw and Peter Wagacha. 2007. Bootstrapping morphological analysis of Gikuyu using unsupervised maximum entropy learning. In *Proceedings of the Eighth Annual Conference of the International Speech Communication Association.* Antwerp, Belgium.

John Goldsmith. 2000. Linguistica: An automatic morphological analyser. In *Proceedings of the 36th Meeting of the Chicago Linguistic Society.* 125-139.

John Goldsmith. 2006. An algorithm for the unsupervised learning of morphology. *Natural Language Engineering*, 12(4):353-371.

Margaret A. Hafer and Stephen F. Weiss. 1974. Word segmentation by letter successor varieties. *Information Storage and Retrieval*, 10(11-12):371-385.

Harold Hammarström and Lars Borin. 2011. Unsupervised learning of morphology. *Computational Linguistics* 37 (2): 309-350.

Hoifung Poon, Colin Cherry, and Kristina Toutanova. 2009. Unsupervised morphological segmentation with log-linear models. *Proceedings of NAACL '09: The 2009 Annual Conference of the North American Association for Computational Linguistics*, pages 209–217, Morristown, NJ.

Paul Rodrigues and Damir Ćavar. 2005. Learning Arabic morphology using information theory. In *Proceedings of the Chicago Linguistics Society. Vol 41*. Chicago: University of Chicago. 49-58.

Patrick Schone and Daniel Jurafsky. 2001. Knowledge-free induction of inflectional morphologies. In *Proceedings of the Conference of the North American Chapter of the Association for Computational Linguistics*, Pittsburgh, PA, 183-191.

Aris Xanthos. 2008. *Apprentissage automatique de la morphologie: Le cas des structures racine-schème.* Berne, Switzerland: Peter Lang.

David Yarowsky and Richard Wicentowski. 2000. Minimally supervised morphological analysis by multimodal alignment. In *Proceedings of the 38th Annual Meeting of the Association for Computational Linguistics*, 207-216.

Towards Domain Adaptation for Parsing Web Data

Mohammad Khan
Indiana University
Bloomington, IN USA
khanms@indiana.edu

Markus Dickinson
Indiana University
Bloomington, IN USA
md7@indiana.edu

Sandra Kübler
Indiana University
Bloomington, IN USA
skuebler@indiana.edu

Abstract

We improve upon a previous line of work for parsing web data, by exploring the impact of different decisions regarding the training data. First, we compare training on automatically POS-tagged data vs. gold POS data. Secondly, we compare the effect of training and testing within sub-genres, i.e., whether a close match of the genre is more important than training set size. Finally, we examine different ways to select out-of-domain parsed data to add to training, attempting to match the in-domain data in different shallow ways (sentence length, perplexity). In general, we find that approximating the in-domain data has a positive impact on parsing.

1 Introduction and Motivation

Parsing data from the web is notoriously difficult, as parsers are generally trained on news data (Petrov and McDonald, 2012). The problem, however, varies greatly depending upon the particular piece of web data: what is often termed web data is generally a combination of different sub-genres, such as Facebook posts, Twitter feeds, YouTube comments, discussion forums, blogs, etc. The language used in such data does not follow standard conventions in various respects (see Herring, 2011): 1) The data is edited to varying degrees, with Twitter on the lower end and professional emails and blog on the upper end of the scale. 2) The sub-genres often display characteristics of spoken language, including sentence fragments and colloquialisms. 3) Some web data, especially social media data, typically contains a high number of emoticons and acronyms such as *LOL*.

At the same time, there is a clear need to develop basic NLP technology for a variety of types of web data. To perform tasks such as sentiment analysis (Nakagawa et al., 2010) or information extraction (McClosky et al., 2011), it helps to part-of-speech (POS) tag and parse the data, as a step towards providing a shallow semantic analysis.

We continue our work (Khan et al., 2013) on dependency parsing web data from the English Web Treebank (Bies et al., 2012). We previously showed that text normalization has a beneficial effect on the quality of a parser on web data, that we can further improve the parser's accuracy by a simple, n-gram-based parse revision method, and that having a balanced training set of out-of-domain and in-domain data provides the best results when parsing web data. The current work extends this previous work by more closely examining the data given as input for training the parser. Specifically, we take the following directions:

1. All previous experiments were carried out on gold part of speech (POS) tags. Here, we investigate using a POS tagger trained on out-of-domain data, thus providing a more realistic setting for parsing web data. We specifically test the impact of training the parser on automatic POS tags (section 4).

2. The web data provided in the English Web Treebank (EWT) is divided into five different sub-genres: 1) answers to questions, 2) emails, 3) newsgroups, 4) reviews, and 5) weblogs. Figure 1 shows examples from the different sub-genres. So far, we used the whole set across these genres, which raises questions about whether a closer match of the genre is more important than the data size, and we thus investigate parsing results within

1. **Answer:** where can I get morcillas in tampa bay , I will like the argentinian type , but I will try anothers please ?
2. **Email:** Michael : <s> Thanks for putting the paperwork together . <s> I would have interest in meeting if you can present unique investment opportunities that I do n't have access to now .
3. **News:** complete with original Magnavox tubes - all tubes have been tested they are all good - stereo amp
4. **Review:** Buyer Beware !! <s> Rusted out and unsafe cars sold here !
5. **Blog:** The Supreme Court announced its ruling today in Hamdan v. Rumsfeld divided along ideological lines with John Roberts abstaining due to his involvement at the D.C. Circuit level and Anthony Kennedy joining the liberals in a 5 - 3 decision that is 185 pages long .

Figure 1: Example sentences from each sub-genre (<s> = sentence boundary)

each sub-genre, and whether adding easy-to-parse data to training improves performance for the difficult sub-genres (section 5).

3. Finally, from our previous work, we know that combining the EWT training set with sentences from the Penn Treebank is beneficial. However, we do not know how to best select the out-of-domain sentences. Should they be drawn randomly; should they match in size; should the sentences match in terms of parsing difficulty (cf. perplexity)? We explore different ways to match the in-domain data (section 6).

2 Related Work

There is a growing body of work on parsing web data, as evidenced by the 2012 Shared Task on Parsing the Web (Petrov and McDonald, 2012). There have been many techniques employed for improving parsing models, including normalizing the potentially ill-formed text (Foster, 2010; Gadde et al., 2011; Øvrelid and Skjærholt, 2012) and training parsers on unannotated or reannotated data, e.g., self-training or uptraining, (e.g., Seddah et al., 2012; Roux et al., 2012; Foster et al., 2011b,a). Less work has gone into investigating the impact of different genres or on specific details of the sentences given to the parser.

Indeed, Petrov and McDonald (2012) mention that for the shared task, "[t]he goal was to build a single system that can robustly parse all domains, rather than to build several domain-specific systems." Thus, parsing results were not obtained by genre. However, Roux et al. (2012) demonstrated that using a genre classifier, in order to employ specific sub-grammars, helped improve parsing performance. Indeed, the quality and fit of data has been shown for in-domain parsing (e.g. Hwa, 2001), as well as for other genres, such as questions (Dima and Hinrichs, 2011).

One common, well-documented ailment of web parsers is the effect of erroneous tags on POS accuracy. Foster et al. (2011a,b), e.g., note that propagation of POS errors is a serious problem, especially for Twitter data. Researchers have thus worked on improving POS tagging for web data, whether by tagger voting (Zhang et al., 2012) or word clustering (Owoputi et al., 2012; Seddah et al., 2012). There are no reports about the impact of the quality of POS tags for training—i.e., whether worse, automatically-derived tags might be an improvement over gold tags—though Søgaard and Plank (2012) note that training with predicted POS tags improves performance.

Researchers have trained parsers using additional data which generally fits the testing domain, as mentioned above. There has been less work, however, on extracting specific types of sentences which fit the domain well. Bohnet et al. (2012) noticed a problem with parsing fragments and so extracted longer NPs to include in training as stand-alone sentences. From a different perspective, Søgaard and Plank (2012) weight sentences in the training data rather than selecting a subset, to better match the distribution of the target domain. In general, identifying sentences which are similar to a particular domain is a concept familiar in active learning (e.g., Mirroshandel and Nasr, 2011; Sassano and Kurohashi, 2010), where dissimilar sentences are selected for hand-annotation to improve parsing.

3 Experimental Setup

3.1 Data

For our experiments, we use two main resources, the Wall Street Journal (WSJ) portion of the Penn Treebank (PTB) (Marcus et al., 1993) and the English Web Treebank (EWT) (Bies et al., 2012). The EWT is comprised of approx. 16 000 sentences from weblogs, newsgroups, emails, reviews, and question-answers. Note that our data sets are different from the ones in Khan et al. (2013) since in the previous work we had removed sentences with POS labels AFX and GW.

To create training and test sets, we broke the data into the following sets:

- WSJ training: sections 02-22 (42 009 sent.)
- WSJ testing: section 23 (2 416 sent.)
- EWT training: 80% of the data, taking the first four out of every five sentences (13 298 sent.)
- EWT testing: 20% of the data, taking every fifth sentence (3 324 sent.)
- EWT sub-genre training and test data: here, we create individual training and test sets for the 5 genres: EWT_{blog}, EWT_{news}, EWT_{email}, EWT_{review}, and EWT_{answer}, using the same sampling described above

The two corpora were converted from PTB constituency trees into dependency trees using the Stanford dependency converter (de Marneffe and Manning, 2008).[1] Since the EWT uses data that shows many of the characteristics of non-standard language, we decided to normalize the spelling of the EWT training and the test set.

For the normalization, we reduce all web URLs to a single token, i.e., each web URL is replaced with the place-holder URL. Similarly, all emoticons are replaced by a single marker EMO. Repeated use of punctuation, e.g., *!!!*, is reduced to a single punctuation token.

3.2 POS Tagger

We use TnT (Brants, 2000), a Markov model POS tagger using a trigram model. It it is fast to train and has a state-of-the-art model for unknown words, using a suffix trie of hapax legomena.

3.3 Parser

We use MSTParser (McDonald and Pereira, 2006),[2] a freely-available parser that reaches state-of-the-art accuracy in dependency parsing for English. MST is a graph-based parser which optimizes its parse tree globally (McDonald et al., 2005), using a variety of feature sets, i.e., edge, sibling, context, and non-local features, employing information from words and POS tags. We use its default settings for all experiments.

Train	Test	POS acc.
WSJ	WSJ	96.73%
EWT	EWT	**94.28%**
WSJ	EWT	88.73%
WSJ+EWT (balanced)	EWT	93.48%

Table 1: Results of using TnT in and out of domain

3.4 Evaluation

For parser evaluation, we report unlabeled attachment scores (UAS) and labeled attachment scores (LAS), the percentage of dependencies which are attached correctly or attached and labeled correctly (Kübler et al., 2009). Parser evaluation is carried out with MSTParser's evaluation module. For POS tagger evaluation, we report accuracy based on TnT's evaluation script. Significance testing was performed using the CoNLL 2007 shared task evaluation using Dan Bikel's Randomized Parsing Evaluation Comparator.[3]

4 The effect of POS tagging

We here explore the effect of POS tagging on parsing web data, to see how closely the conditions for training should match the conditions for testing.

However, first we need to gauge the effect of using the TnT POS tagger out of domain. For this reason, we conducted a set of experiments, training and testing TnT in different conditions. The results are shown in table 1. They show that TnT reaches an accuracy of 96.7% when trained and tested on the WSJ. This corroborates findings by Brants (2000). When we train TnT on EWT training data, running it on the EWT testing data delivers an accuracy of 94.28%, already 2–3% below performance on news data. However, note that the EWT is much smaller than the full WSJ. In contrast, if we train TnT on WSJ and then use it for POS tagging EWT data, we only reach an accuracy of 88.73%. Even if we balance the source and target domain data, which proved beneficial in our previous experiments on parsing (Khan et al., 2013), we reach an accuracy of 93.48%, well below the in-domain tagging result for the EWT. This means that in contrast to parsing, the POS tagger requires less training data and profits more

[1] http://nlp.stanford.edu/software/stanford-dependencies.shtml

[2] http://sourceforge.net/projects/mstparser/

[3] http://nextens.uvt.nl/depparse-wiki/SoftwarePage

Train	Test	POS acc.	UAS	LAS
Gold	Gold	100%	85.78%	83.14%
Gold	TnT	94.28%	81.89%	77.69%
TnT	TnT	94.28%	***82.52%**	***78.54%**

Table 2: The effect of POS tagging on parser performance, using the base EWT data split (*=sig. at the 0.01 level, as compared to Train=Gold/ Test=TnT)

from the small target domain training set than from a larger training set with out-of-domain data.

Given this degree of error in tagging, a parser trained with similar noise in POS tags may outperform one which is trained on gold tags. Thus, we run TnT on the training data, using a 10-fold split of the training set: each tenth of the training corpus is tagged using a POS tagger trained on the other 9 folds. Then we use the combination of all the automatically POS tagged folds and insert those POS tags into the gold standard dependency trees before we train the parser.

The three conditions for POS tagging are shown in table 2. The first point to note is the impact of switching from gold to automatic POS tags: testing on TnT tags results in a degradation of about 4.5–5.5% in LAS, as compared to gold standard POS tags in the test set, consistent with typical drops in performance (e.g., Rehbein et al., 2012).

More to the point for our purposes, we see in table 2 that training a parser on automatically-assigned POS tags outperforms a parser trained on gold POS tags. LAS increases from 77.69% to 78.54%. This supports the notion that training data should match testing closely. However, it also shows that we need to investigate methods for improving POS tagger accuracy.

5 The effect of domain

As mentioned, the EWT contains subcorpora from five different genres, and, while they share many common features (misspellings, unknown words), they have many unique properties, as illustrated in the examples in figure 1. In terms of sentence length, domains such as weblogs lend themselves more easily to longer, more well-edited sentences, matching news data better. Reviews, on the other hand, often have shorter sentences—similar to, e.g., email greetings. Run-ons are common across genres, but we see them here in the answer and news sub-genres. The example for the answer sub-corpus shows some of the difficult challenges faced by a parser, as it contains a declarative sentence embedded within the question, where the final word (*please*) attaches back to the question.

To gauge the effect of different sub-genres, we trained and tested the parser within each sub-genre. In order to concentrate on the differences in parsing, we used gold POS tags for these experiments. Results for the five individual sub-corpora are given in the first five rows of table 3. It is noteworthy that there is nearly a 5% difference in LAS between the best sub-genre (EWT_{email}) and the worst (EWT_{answer}). We also show various properties of the sub-corpora, including number of tokens (*Tokens*), the average sentence length (*SenLen*), and the number of finite verbal roots (*FinRoot*)[4] in training; and also the percentage of unknown word tokens in the test corpus, as compared to the training corpus (*Unk.*)

In general, emails and reviews fare the best, likely due to a combination of shorter sentences (11.84 and 14.58, respectively) and text that tends to follow grammatical conventions. Blogs and newsgroups are in the middle, with longer, harder-to-parse sentences (18.17 and 22.07, respectively) and higher levels of unknown words in testing (12.2% and 10.2%), but being consistently fairly well-edited. While it might be surprising that the results for these two sub-genres are lower than emails and reviews, note that the training for both domains is significantly lower, on the order of 10,000 words less than the other corpora. It is possible that with more data, these well-edited domains would see improved parser performance.

On the lower end of the parsing spectrum is the domain of answers, which is a curious trend. There is nearly as much training data as with emails and reviews, and the average sentence length is comparable. If we look at the number of non-finite sentence roots—as a way to approximate the number of non-fragment sentences—it is nearly identical to the email sub-genre. We suspect that the fragments are not as systematic as greetings and that users may post replies quickly, leading to less well-formed text, but this deserves future consideration.

Given the poor performance on the answer domain and the higher performance of the parser on

[4]The Stanford converter treats the predicate as the head of copular sentences, e.g., a noun or adjective; thus, the number of finite roots does not correspond directly to the number of non-fragmentary sentences.

Train	Tokens	Sen-Len	Fin-Root	Test	Unk.	UAS	LAS
EWT_{answer}	43 173	15.47	767	EWT_{answer}	8.2%	81.25%	78.03%
EWT_{email}	46 473	11.85	765	EWT_{email}	8.0%	85.04%	82.82%
EWT_{news}	34 762	18.17	558	EWT_{news}	12.2%	81.65%	79.12%
EWT_{review}	44 483	14.58	1 048	EWT_{review}	8.5%	82.92%	79.64%
EWT_{blog}	35 868	22.07	635	EWT_{blog}	10.2%	81.68%	79.00%
EWT_{answer}+EWT_{email}	89 646	13.36	1 532	EWT_{answer}	6.5%	**82.16%	**79.05%
EWT_{answer}+EWT_{news}	77 935	16.57	4571	EWT_{answer}	6.3%	**82.84%	**79.59%
EWT_{answer}+EWT_{blog}	79 041	17.90	4874	EWT_{answer}	6.5%	**82.53%	**79.43%
EWT_{answer}+$EWT_{balanced}$	102 717	19.13	1 482	EWT_{answer}	5.7%	**83.07%	**79.74%
EWT_{answer}+EWT_{rest}	204 759	19.24	12 312	EWT_{answer}	4.4%	****84.01%**	****80.97%**

Table 3: The effect of domain on parser performance, using gold POS tags (** = sig. at the 0.01 level, testing all conditions below the line, as compared to the first row Train=EWT_{answer})

emails, we decided to see whether parsing could be improved by adding data to the small answer training set 1) from the domain that is easiest to parse: emails, 2) from the news domain because of its similar average sentence length, and 3) from the blog domain because it has the longest sentences. We compare these configurations with one where we add the same number of sentences, but sampled from all four remaining domains (*balanced*) and one where we add all the training data from all other genres (*rest*). We see a clear improvement for all settings, in comparison with using only the answer data for training. The best results are obtained by using all other genres as additional training data, showing that the size of the training set is the most important variable.

The results also show that the sampling from all remaining sub-genres results in higher parsing accuracy than just using the easiest to parse data set, illustrating that we should not look for data which is generally easy to parse, but data which is the best fit for the test data.

6 The effect of sentence selection

In our previous work (Khan et al., 2013), we showed that we obtain the best results when we use a balanced training corpus with the same number of sentences from the EWT and the WSJ. On the one hand, these results show that in-domain data is critical for the success of the parser; on the other hand, out-of-domain data is important to increase the size of the training set. It is thus important to find a good balance between using more training data and not overpowering the in-domain data. This leads to the question of whether it is possible to choose sentences from an out-of-domain data set that are similar to the sentences in the target domain rather than just selecting a portion of consecutive sentences. In other words, can we identify sentences from the WSJ that will have the best impact on a parser for web data?

Train	Tokens	UAS	LAS
EWT+WSJ	1 205 621	85.73%	83.12%
EWT+WSJSent	524 236	**86.34%**	**83.83%**
EWT+WSJToken	399 915	86.26%	83.69%
EWT+WSJDist	424 297	**86.34%**	83.73%
EWT+LowP	619 591	***86.68%**	****84.20%**
EWT+AllLowP	819 856	*86.64%	*84.08%
EWT+MedLowP	568 666	86.41%	83.85%
EWT+MidP	529 936	86.13%	*83.54%

Table 4: The effect of selection on parser performance: all experiments on EWT testing data with gold POS tags; WSJ data defined in the text (*/** = sig. at the 0.05/0.01 level, testing the 4 perplexity models as compared to EWT+WSJSent)

In the first set of experiments, we investigate simple heuristics to choose a good set of training sentences from the WSJ: In the first experiment, we use the full WSJ (*EWT+WSJ*). Then we restrict the WSJ part to match the number of sentences from the EWT (*EWT+WSJSent*). However, since WSJ sentences are longer on average than EWT sentences, we repeat the experiment but choose the WSJ subset so that it matches the number of words in the EWT training set (*EWT+WSJToken*). Finally, we choose the WSJ sentences so that they match the distribution of sentence lengths in EWT (*EWT+WSJDist*). For example, if EWT has 100 sentences with 10 words, we select 100 sentences of length 10 from the WSJ. All of these experiments are again carried out with gold POS tags.

The results of these experiments are shown in the first two parts of table 4. The results for the selection methods show that selecting the WSJ part based on the number of words results in the lowest parsing accuracy. Choosing the WSJ part based on the number of sentences or the distribution of sentence length results in the same unlabeled accuracy (UAS) of 86.34%, as compared to 86.26% for the word based selection. However, the selection based on the number of sentences results in a higher labeled accuracy of 83.83%, as opposed to 83.73% for the distribution of sentence length. We suspect that the random selection of sentences gives more variety, which is beneficial for training. However, note that the difference in the number of words in the training set across these three methods is minimal: they vary only by 41 words.

In a second set of experiments, we decided to use a more informed method for choosing similar sentences: perplexity. Thus, we trained a language model on the (stemmed) words of the test set based on a 5-gram word model, and then calculated perplexity for each sentence in the WSJ, normalized by the length of the sentence. We used the *CMU-Cambridge Statistical Language Modeling Toolkit*[5] for calculating perplexity. Perplexity should give an approximation of distance between sentences in the two corpora. We experimented with different selection strategies:

1. Low Perplexity (*LowP*): We select the sentences with the lowest perplexity, i.e., the most similar ones to the test set; we restricted the number of sentences from the WSJ to match the size of the EWT training set.
2. All Low Perplexity (*AllLowP*): Here, we also selected sentences with low perplexity, but this time used all sentences below the median, i.e. half the WSJ sentences.
3. Low Perplexity close to the median (*MedLowP*): Here, we investigate the effect of choosing sentences that are less similar to the test sentences: we select the same number of sentences as with LowP, but this time from the median down. In other words, the sentences with the lowest perplexity, i.e., the most similar sentences, are excluded. This is based on the assumption that if the chosen sentences are too similar, it will not have much effect on the trained model.
4. Mid-range Perplexity (*MidP*): In this set, we choose sentences that are even less similar to the test sentences. We again choose the same number of sentences as in the EWT training set, but half of them from the median and down and half from the median up.

[5] http://www.speech.cs.cmu.edu/SLM_info.html

The results are in the final four rows of table 4. Interestingly, the best-performing method adds low-perplexity data to training. Thus, selecting data which is more similar to the domain helps the most. Furthermore, once the data is farther away, it starts to harm parsing performance, as can be seen in the (albeit minimal) difference between the EWT+LowP and EWT+AllLowP models.

7 Summary and Outlook

Exploring the parsing of web data, we have investigated different decisions that go into the training data, demonstrating how the better the fit of the training data to the testing data—in properties ranging from the nature of the POS tags to which sentences go into the data—the better performance the parser will have. We first compared training on automatically POS-tagged data vs. gold POS tag data, showing that performance improves by automatically tagging the training data. Next, we compared the effect of training and testing within sub-genres and saw that features such as sentence length have a strong effect. Finally, we examined ways to select out-of-domain parsed data to add to training, attempting to match the in-domain data in different shallow ways, and we found that matching training sentences to a language model improves parsing. In short, fitting the training data to the in-domain data, in even fairly superficial ways, has a positive impact on parsing results.

There are several directions to take this work. First, the sentence selection methods, for example, can be combined with self-training techniques to not only increase the training data size, but to only add sentences which fit the test domain well. Secondly, the work on understanding sub-genres of web parsing deserves more thorough treatment in the future to tease apart which components are most problematic (e.g., sentence fragments), how they can be automatically identified, and how the parser can be adjusted to accommodate them.

References

Ann Bies, Justin Mott, Colin Warner, and Seth Kulick. 2012. English Web Treebank. Linguistic Data Consortium, Philadelphia, PA.

Bernd Bohnet, Richard Farkas, and Ozlem Cetinoglu. 2012. SANCL 2012 shared task: The IMS system description. In *Workshop on the Syntactic Analysis of Non-Canonical Language (SANCL 2012)*. Montreal, Canada.

Thorsten Brants. 2000. TnT – a statistical part-of-speech tagger. In *Proceedings of the Sixth Applied Natural Language Processing Conference (ANLP)*, pages 224–231. Seattle, WA.

Marie-Catherine de Marneffe and Christopher D. Manning. 2008. The Stanford typed dependencies representation. In *COLING 2008 Workshop on Cross-framework and Cross-domain Parser Evaluation*. Manchester, England.

Corina Dima and Erhard Hinrichs. 2011. A semi-automatic, iterative method for creating a domain-specific treebank. In *Proceedings of the International Conference Recent Advances in Natural Language Processing (RANLP)*, pages 413–419. Hissar, Bulgaria.

Jennifer Foster. 2010. "cba to check the spelling": Investigating parser performance on discussion forum posts. In *Proceedings of NAACL-HLT 2010*, pages 381–384. Los Angeles, CA.

Jennifer Foster, Ozlem Cetinoglu, Joachim Wagner, Joseph Le Roux, Stephen Hogan, Joakim Nivre, Deirdre Hogan, and Josef van Genabith. 2011a. #hardtoparse: POS tagging and parsing the twitterverse. In *The AAAI-11 Workshop on Analyzing Microtext*. San Francisco.

Jennifer Foster, Ozlem Cetinoglu, Joachim Wagner, Joseph Le Roux, Joakim Nivre, Deirdre Hogan, and Josef van Genabith. 2011b. From news to comment: Resources and benchmarks for parsing the language of Web 2.0. In *Proceedings of IJCNLP-11*, pages 893–901. Chiang Mai, Thailand.

Phani Gadde, L. V. Subramaniam, and Tanveer A. Faruquie. 2011. Adapting a WSJ trained part-of-speech tagger to noisy text: Preliminary results. In *Proceedings of Joint Workshop on Multilingual OCR and Analytics for Noisy Unstructured Text Data*. Beijing, China.

Susan Herring. 2011. Discourse in Web 2.0: Familiar, reconfigured, and emergent. In *Georgetown University Round Table on Languages and Linguistics 2011: Discourse 2.0: Language and New Media*. Washington, DC.

Rebecca Hwa. 2001. On minimizing training corpus for parser acquisition. In *Proceedings of the Workshop on Computational Natural Language Learning (CoNLL)*. Toulouse, France.

Mohammad Khan, Markus Dickinson, and Sandra Kübler. 2013. Does size matter? Text and grammar revision for parsing social media data. In *Proceedings of the NAACL Workshop on Language Analysis in Social Media*. Atlanta, GA.

Sandra Kübler, Ryan McDonald, and Joakim Nivre. 2009. *Dependency Parsing*. Morgan & Claypool Publishers.

Mitchell Marcus, Beatrice Santorini, and Mary Ann Marcinkiewicz. 1993. Building a large annotated corpus of English: The Penn Treebank. *Computational Linguistics*, 19(2):313–330.

David McClosky, Mihai Surdeanu, and Christopher Manning. 2011. Event extraction as dependency parsing. In *Proceedings of ACL-HLT-11*, pages 1626–1635. Portland, OR.

Ryan McDonald, Koby Crammer, and Fernando Pereira. 2005. Online large-margin training of dependency parsers. In *Proceedings of ACL-05*, pages 91–98. Ann Arbor, MI.

Ryan McDonald and Fernando Pereira. 2006. Online learning of approximate dependency parsing algorithms. In *Proceedings of EACL-06*. Trento, Italy.

Seyed Abolghasem Mirroshandel and Alexis Nasr. 2011. Active learning for dependency parsing using partially annotated sentences. In *Proceedings of the 12th International Conference on Parsing Technologies*, pages 140–149. Dublin, Ireland.

Tetsuji Nakagawa, Kentaro Inui, and Sadao Kurohashi. 2010. Dependency tree-based sentiment classification using CRFs with hidden variables. In *Proceedings of NAACL-HLT 2010*, pages 786–794. Los Angeles, CA.

Lilja Øvrelid and Arne Skjærholt. 2012. Lexical categories for improved parsing of web data. In *Proceedings of the 24th International Conference on Computational Linguistics (COLING 2012)*, pages 903–912. Mumbai, India.

Olutobi Owoputi, Brendan O'Connor, Chris Dyer, Kevin Gimpel, Nathan Schneider, and Noah A. Smith. 2012. Improved part-of-speech tagging for online conversational text with word clusters. In *Proceedings of NAACL 2013*. Atlanta, GA.

Slav Petrov and Ryan McDonald. 2012. Overview of the 2012 shared task on parsing the web. In *Workshop on the Syntactic Analysis of Non-Canonical Language (SANCL 2012)*. Montreal, Canada.

Ines Rehbein, Hagen Hirschmann, Anke Lüdeling, and Marc Reznicek. 2012. Better tags give better trees - or do they? *Linguistic Issues in Language Technology (LiLT)*, 7(10).

Joseph Le Roux, Jennifer Foster, Joachim Wagner, Rasul Samad Zadeh Kaljahi, and Anton Bryl. 2012. DCU-Paris13 systems for the SANCL 2012 shared task. In *Workshop on the Syntactic Analysis of Non-Canonical Language (SANCL 2012)*. Montreal, Canada.

Manabu Sassano and Sadao Kurohashi. 2010. Using smaller constituents rather than sentences in active learning for Japanese dependency parsing. In *Proceedings of the 48th Annual Meeting of the Association for Computational Linguistics*, pages 356–365. Uppsala, Sweden.

Djamé Seddah, Benoit Sagot, and Marie Candito. 2012. The alpage architecture at the sancl 2012 shared task: Robust pre-processing and lexical bridging for user-generated content parsing. In *Workshop on the Syntactic Analysis of Non-Canonical Language (SANCL 2012)*. Montreal, Canada.

Anders Søgaard and Barbara Plank. 2012. Parsing the web as covariate shift. In *Workshop on the Syntactic Analysis of Non-Canonical Language (SANCL 2012)*. Montreal, Canada.

Meishan Zhang, Wanxiang Che, Yijia Liu, Zhenghua Li, and Ting Liu. 2012. Hit dependency parsing: Bootstrap aggregating heterogeneous parsers. In *Workshop on the Syntactic Analysis of Non-Canonical Language (SANCL 2012)*. Montreal, Canada.

Capturing Anomalies in the Choice of Content Words in Compositional Distributional Semantic Space

Ekaterina Kochmar
Computer Laboratory
University of Cambridge
ek358@cl.cam.ac.uk

Ted Briscoe
Computer Laboratory
University of Cambridge
ejb@cl.cam.ac.uk

Abstract

In this work, we present a new task for testing compositional distributional semantic models. Recently, there has been a spate of research into how distributional representations of individual words can be combined to represent the meaning of phrases. Vecchi *et al.* (2011) have shown that some compositional models, including the additive and multiplicative models of Mitchell and Lapata (2008; 2010) and the linear map-based model of Baroni and Zamparelli (2010), can be applied to detect semantically anomalous adjective–noun combinations. We extend their experiments and apply these models to the combinations extracted from texts written by learners of English.

Our work contributes to the field of compositional distributional semantics by introducing a new test paradigm for semantic models and shows how these models can be used for error detection in language learners' content word combinations.

1 Introduction

Vector-based (*distributional*) models are widely used for representing the meaning of single words. They rely on the assumption that word meaning can be learned from the linguistic environment and can be approximated by a word's *distribution* across contexts. Words are represented as vectors in a high-dimensional space, with vector dimensions encoding word co-occurrence with contextual elements – other words within a local window, words linked by specific dependencies to the target word, and so forth. Distributional models provide a clear basis for interpreting word meaning, as well as a simple means for measuring semantic similarity. These properties have been exploited in many NLP tasks, including automatic thesaurus extraction (Grefenstette, 1994), word sense induction (Schütze, 1998) and disambiguation (McCarthy et al., 2004), collocation extraction (Schone and Jurafsky, 2001) and others.

In contrast to single words, the distribution of phrases cannot be used as a reliable approximation of their meaning, as phrase vectors are much sparser. Irrespective of the size of the corpus considered, some content word combinations will remain unattested as a consequence of their Zipf-like distributions. For example, Vecchi *et al.* (2011) have shown that both semantically acceptable and semantically deviant word combinations will be absent from large English corpora. A promising alternative is to use *compositional* models which combine distributional vectors for the component words in some way, for example, using a direct vector combination function (Kintsch, 2001; Mitchell and Lapata, 2008; Erk and Padó, 2008; Thater et al., 2010) or linear transformations on vectors (Baroni and Zamparelli, 2010).

In spite of the spate of recent work in this area, the question of how to combine word representations is far from answered. Compositional models can be assessed by their ability both to provide a solid theoretical basis for meaning composition and to represent composite meaning for relevant practical tasks. Promising results have been shown with such models on similarity detection and paraphrase ranking (Mitchell and Lapata, 2008; Erk and Padó, 2008; Thater et al., 2010), adjective–noun vector prediction (Baroni and Zamparelli, 2010) and semantic anomaly detection (Vecchi et al., 2011). Of these tasks, the latter appears to be particularly challenging since it addresses the ability of compositional models to account for linguistic productivity.

No corpus can effectively sample all possible content word combinations. On the other hand, some corpus-attested word combinations may appear semantically deviant when considered out of context (for example, when they are used metaphorically). Vecchi *et al.* (2011) have focused on unattested adjective–noun (AN) combinations and noted that if a combination does not occur in a corpus, it may be due to various reasons including data sparsity as well as nonsensicality. The task of distinguishing between the two cases is challenging. Vecchi *et al.* use the following examples:

(1) a. *blue rose*
b. *residential steak*

Whereas both may well be unattested in a corpus, the concept of *blue rose* is perfectly conceivable while that of *residential steak* is nonsensical and only interpretable in specifically-constructed discourse contexts. Vecchi *et al.* argue that there should be a detectable difference between the model-generated representations for the semantically deviant combinations and those for the acceptable ones, and assess compositional models by their ability to capture this difference. Vecchi *et al.* have created a set of corpus-unattested AN combinations, annotated them as semantically acceptable or deviant, and applied the *additive (add)* and *multiplicative (mult)* models of Mitchell and Lapata (2008) and *adjective-specific linear maps (alm)* of Baroni and Zamparelli (2010).

Given that promising results have been obtained in their experiments, we propose that a useful extension of this task is to test the compositional models on errors in content word combinations extracted from texts written by learners of English. This task provides a natural setting for testing semantic models on genuine examples and is a potential practical application for such models.

Language learners' errors are diverse, but many of them can naturally be explained in terms of non-productive, semantically anomalous combination of content words (Leacock et al., 2010). Learners may lack robust intuitions about words' selectional preferences and subtle differences in meaning, so they may confuse near-synonyms, overuse words with broad meaning, and otherwise choose words inappropriately. Consider the following examples extracted from our data:

(2) a. **big importance* vs *great importance*
b. **economical crisis* vs *economic crisis*
c. **deep regards* vs *kind regards*
d. *best moment* vs *best time*

These examples illustrate that learner errors can often be explained by confusions stemming from similar meaning (*2a*) or form (*2b*). When a word combination appears to be nonsensical as in *2c*, the words chosen might still be related to the appropriate ones in the learner's mental lexicon. We recognise that although error detection in learners' content word combinations is a natural extension to semantic anomaly detection, it also poses additional difficulties that semantic models might not be able to deal with. For example, some erroneous word combinations may not be completely devoid of compositional meaning, while violating language conventions. However, semantic models might still be able to capture some of these conventions. Another challenge is that some expressions cannot be unambiguously classified as either correct or incorrect, as their interpretation depends on the context of use: *best moment* (*2d*) is appropriate when used to denote a short period of time, but it is often incorrectly used by learners instead of *best time*.

To make our work comparable with previous work on semantic anomaly, we investigate AN combinations extracted from texts written by non-native speakers of English, and apply the *add*, *mult* and *alm* models of semantic composition. The main contributions of this work are to show that error detection in content word combinations provides a natural testbed and useful application for the compositional distributional models, and that the results obtained on this task provide a more natural estimate of the models' performance than ones based on artificially constructed examples. If the compositional distributional models can distinguish between correct and incorrect content word combinations, these models can then be used for writing or pedagogical assistance. To the best of our knowledge, this is the first attempt to handle learner errors in the choice of content words using compositional distributional semantics.

Plan of the paper. We overview related work on error detection and discuss the three models of semantic composition in Section 2. Section 3 presents the data and experimental setup. We discuss the results of our experiments in Section 4 and conclude in Section 5.

2 Related Work

2.1 Error Detection in Content Words

Research on error detection has mostly been concerned with function words, such as determiners and prepositions (Leacock et al., 2010; Dale et al.,

2012). Such errors are more frequent, but they are also more systematic which makes them easier to detect. Function words constitute a closed class, so the set of possible corrections is also limited. By comparison, errors in content word combinations pose a bigger challenge. Since content words primarily express meaning rather than encode syntax, detection and correction of such errors depend on a system's ability, in the limit, to recognise the communicative intent of the writer. Moreover, the set of possible corrections is much larger than for function words.

Previous work has either focused on correction alone assuming that errors are already detected (Liu et al., 2009; Dahlmeier and Ng, 2011), or has reformulated the task as *writing improvement* (Shei and Pain, 2000; Wible et al., 2003; Chang et al., 2008; Futagi et al., 2008; Park et al., 2008; Yi et al., 2008). In the former case error detection, which is a difficult task in itself, is not addressed, while in the latter case it is integrated into that of suggesting alternatives according to some metric (for example, frequency or mutual information). In some cases, a database of typical errors in word combinations is collected from learner texts and suggestions are only made for these error-prone combinations. Otherwise suggestions will be made for many acceptable phrases.

In this work, we treat error detection in the choice of content words as an independent task and assess the ability of compositional distributional models to discriminate incorrect from correct AN combinations – a frequent source of error in learner texts.

2.2 Composition by Component-wise Operations

In the *additive* and *multiplicative* compositional models of Mitchell and Lapata (2008; 2010), the components of the composite vector are obtained by component-wise operations applied to the word vectors. If **c** is a word combination vector and **a** and **b** are word vectors, then **c**'s i-th component is the sum of the i-th components of **a** and **b** for the *add* model:

$$c_i = a_i + b_i \quad (1)$$

and the product of the corresponding components for the *mult* model:

$$c_i = a_i b_i \quad (2)$$

An advantage of using these models is that they provide a clear and simple interpretation of vector composition, requiring no training or tuning. They have also been shown to be promising models of composition in a number of NLP tasks, including semantic anomaly detection (Vecchi et al., 2011). However, the principal weakness of these models is that they use commutative operations, and therefore fail to represent the difference in the grammatical function of the component words, their order, and "headedness". For example, these models would produce the same composite vectors for *component vector* and *vector component*.

In addition, the *add* model does not take "incompatibility" of constituent vectors along individual dimensions into account. If one vector has a high value in its i-th dimension while another vector has 0, the composed vector will receive the high value from the first input vector, even though, intuitively, this dimension should get 0 or near-0 value. This problem does not arise with the *mult* model. On the other hand, the *mult* model is heavily biased towards dimensions with high values in both input vectors (Baroni et al., 2012).

2.3 Distributional Functions and Linear Maps

The *adjective-specific linear maps* of Baroni and Zamparelli (2010) take the grammatical functions of the words within a combination into account. Focusing on AN combinations, they try to model the fact that adjectives modify nouns and the resulting combination is nominal. They note that the meaning of nouns can be represented with their distributional vectors, but the meaning of attributive adjectives cannot be fully captured by their distribution alone: for example, *new* in *new friend* is not the same as *new* in *new shoes*. The meaning of the adjective *new* is defined through its application to the denotations of the nouns. Therefore, Baroni and Zamparelli (2010) suggest treating adjectives as *distributional functions* that map between semantic vectors representing nouns to ones representing AN combinations.

Within this approach, adjectives are represented with weight matrices. The composition is defined by matrix-by-vector multiplication as follows:

$$f(noun) =_{def} \mathbf{F} \times \mathbf{a} = \mathbf{b} \quad (3)$$

where **F** is the matrix representing an adjective and encoding function *f*, which maps the input noun vector **a** to the output AN vector **b**. The ij-th cell of the matrix contains the weight determining how much the component corresponding to the j-th context element in the noun vector contributes to the value assigned to the i-th context element in the AN vector (Baroni et al., 2012). These weights are estimated separately for each adjective from all corpus-observed noun–AN vector pairs using (multivariate) partial least squares regression.

3 Experimental Setup

3.1 Test Data

We have extracted a set of AN combinations from the publicly available CLC-FCE dataset (Yannakoudakis et al., 2011), a subset of the Cambridge Learner Corpus (CLC),[1] which is a large corpus of texts produced by English language learners sitting Cambridge Assessment's examinations.[2]

These texts have been manually error-coded (Nicholls, 2003). Using the error annotation, we have divided extracted ANs into two subsets – correctly used ANs and those that are annotated with error codes due to inappropriate choice of an adjective or/and noun.[3] For the ANs that are used correctly in some contexts and incorrectly in others we use the most frequent annotation from the data.

Our test set contains 4681 correct and 530 incorrect combinations. In contrast to Vecchi *et al.* (2011), who have used a limited set of constituent adjectives and nouns and an approximately equal number of semantically acceptable and deviant combinations, our test set is more skewed towards correct combinations and consists of a wider range of constituent words. It also includes ANs occurring in the BNC[4] – 3294 of the correct test ANs and 256 of the incorrect ones are corpus-attested. The set of corpus-attested ANs annotated as incorrect in our data includes low-frequency combinations from the BNC, as well as combinations whose error-annotation depends on context. We believe that this test set reflects practical applications of semantic anomaly detection more closely.[5]

3.2 Semantic Space Construction

In constructing the *semantic space* we follow the procedure outlined in Vecchi *et al.* (2011). We populate the semantic space with a large number of distributional vectors for the *target elements* – constituent nouns and adjectives from the test ANs, and the most frequent nouns and adjectives from a corpus of English as well as AN combinations of these words. To estimate the frequency rankings, we use a concatenation of two well-formed English corpora – the 100M word BNC and the Web-derived 2B word ukWaC corpus.[6]

The semantic space is represented by a matrix encoding word co-occurrences, with the rows representing the target elements and the columns representing a set of 10K *context words* consisting of 6,590 nouns, 1,550 adjectives and 1,860 verbs most frequent in the combined corpus. The ij-th cell of the original matrix contains a sentence-internal co-occurrence count of the i-th target element with the j-th context word. The raw sentence-internal co-occurrence counts from the original matrix have been transformed into Local Mutual Information scores (Baroni and Zamparelli, 2010; Evert, 2005).

An interesting research question is how much data are needed to obtain reliable word co-occurrence counts. We estimate the word co-occurrence statistics using the BNC only, and leave it for future research to explore the impact of estimating them from larger corpora, for example, the ukWaC or the concatenated corpus mentioned above. We lemmatise, tag and parse the data with the RASP system (Briscoe et al., 2006; Andersen et al., 2008), and extract all statistics at the lemma level.

The target elements are selected as follows: we first select the 4K adjectives and 8K nouns which are most frequent in the concatenated corpus. In each case, we exclude the top 50 most frequent words since those may have too general meanings.

Next, we extract the constituent adjectives and nouns from our test data and populate the semantic space with the words not yet contained in it. As a result, our semantic space contains 8,364 nouns.

Since we aim at investigating AN behaviour in a highly-populated semantic space, we add more AN combinations to that. We select 218 very frequent adjectives (occurring more than 100K but

[1]http://www.cup.cam.ac.uk/gb/elt/catalogue/subject/custom/item3646603/Cambridge-International-Corpus-Cambridge-Learner-Corpus/

[2]http://www.cambridgeenglish.org

[3]The corresponding error codes are `RJ` and `RN`.

[4]http://www.natcorp.ox.ac.uk/

[5]The examples extracted for our experiments are publicly available at http://www.cl.cam.ac.uk/~ek358/.

[6]http://wacky.sslmit.unibo.it/

less than 740K times) and merge them with the adjectives from the test ANs. We generate all possible AN combinations by crossing this combined set of adjectives and the set of 8,364 nouns. This results in a set of ANs of which 1,6M combinations are corpus-attested. From these we randomly choose 62,205 ANs that occur more than 100 times in the corpus. As a result, we populate our semantic space with ANs with the number of unique corpus-attested combinations per adjective ranging from 1 to 1,226 and being 84.52 on average. Since we apply our approach to real data, we cannot avoid having a different number of training examples for different adjectives. It is worth exploring how many training examples are needed for a single adjective, since some highly frequent adjectives may have more training examples in the data, while some adjectives may require more training examples than others due to polysemy or lack of strong selectional preferences.

Finally, we check our test set against the combined corpus and add 1,131 test ANs which are corpus-attested but not yet contained in the semantic space. Our final semantic space consists of 8,364 nouns, 4,353 adjectives and 63,336 corpus-attested ANs.

We perform all operations on vectors in the full semantic space, using a 76,053 $\times$ 10K matrix. We leave it for future research to perform dimensionality reduction (for example, using Singular Value Decomposition) and to compare the results with the ones reported here.

3.3 Composition Methods

For the *add* and *mult* models, the AN vectors are obtained by component-wise addition and multiplication without normalisation. For the *alm* model, the weight coefficients are estimated with multivariate partial least squares regression using the R `pls` package (Mevik and Wehrens, 2007), using the leave-one-out training regime. This model is computationally expensive since a separate weight matrix must be learned for each adjective and since we use the non-reduced semantic space. Therefore, for the experiments presented here we limit the number of test adjectives to 38. The selected adjectives are, on the one hand, frequently misused by language learners, and, on the other, have a manageable number of training examples. The reduced set of test ANs consists of 347 combinations.

The number of latent variables used by the training algorithm depends on the number of available noun–AN training pairs. We have gradually changed this number from 3 to 20 depending on the adjective and the number of available training pairs with the aim of keeping the independent-variable-to-training-item ratio stable. However, we have not optimised this number and leave it for future research.

3.4 Measures of Semantic Anomaly

Once the composite vectors are obtained, the next question is how to distinguish between the vectors for correct and anomalous combinations. Vecchi *et al.* (2011) propose three simple measures for distinguishing between the two sets of vectors:

1. **Vector Length (VLen)**: they hypothesise that vectors for anomalous ANs are shorter than those for acceptable ones. Since the distributional vectors encode word occurrence, words that do not "match" semantically should have their co-occurrence counts distributed differently along the dimensions, and their composition is expected to have many near-0 values.

2. **Cosine with the Noun Vector (CosN)**: they hypothesise that in nonsensical ANs the meaning of the input nouns is degraded and their model-generated vectors are situated further away from the original noun vectors. For example, since a *big dog* is still a *dog* and an **extensive dog* is less clearly so, in the semantic space the vector for *big dog* would be closer to that of *dog* than the vector for **extensive dog* to *dog*. Semantically deviant ANs are expected to have lower cosine between their vectors and the original noun vectors.

3. **Density of the AN Neighbourhood (Dens)**: it is hypothesised that deviant ANs will have fewer close neighbours and be more "isolated" in the semantic space. This is measured by the average cosine with the top 10 nearest neighbours, which is assumed to be lower for anomalous ANs.

We hypothesise that some cues alternative to the ones already proposed may also be effective:

1. **Cosine with the Adjective Vector (CosA)**: since both *add* and *mult* models are symmetric and both input vectors contribute to the

Measure	*all*	*attest*	*unattest*
VLen	0.1992	0.6226	0.1840
CosN	0.0797	0.1538	$0.00001^{(*)}$
Dens	0.9792	0.3921	0.5589
CosA	0.6867	0.3790	$0.0026^{(*)}$
RDens	0.6915	0.7493	0.1414
Num	0.8756	0.5753	0.1050
COver	0.6028	0.2126	0.1200

Table 1: p values for the *add* model

Measure	*all*	*attest*	*unattest*
VLen	$0.0033^{(*)}$	0.1549	$0.0004^{(*)}$
CosN	$0.0017^{(*)}$	$0.0182^{(*)}$	$0.0083^{(*)}$
Dens	0.3531	0.6656	0.2703
CosA	$0.00002^{(*)}$	$0.0144^{(*)}$	0.3352
RDens	$0.0002^{(*)}$	$0.0300^{(*)}$	$0.0001^{(*)}$
Num	$0.0001^{(*)}$	$0.0091^{(*)}$	$0.0001^{(*)}$
COver	$0.0041^{(*)}$	$0.0096^{(*)}$	0.7317

Table 2: p values for the *mult* model

output combination equally, we also measure the distance to the original adjective vector.

2. **Ranked Density (RDens)**: we define *close proximity* to the model-generated AN vector as the neighbourhood populated with vectors for which the cosine to the AN vector is higher than 0.8. Since the number of close neighbours is different for different ANs, we measure *ranked density* as $\sum_{i=1}^{N} rank_i\, distance_i$, where N is the number of neighbours.

3. **Number of Neighbours within Close Proximity (Num)**: the number of close neighbours itself can be used as a measure.

4. **Component Overlap (COver)**: we assume that AN combinations, unless they are idiomatic, are similar to the constituent words or combinations with the same constituents. The models can be assessed by their ability to place the AN vector in the neighbourhood populated by similar words and combinations. We measure this as the proportion of nearest neighbours containing same constituent words as in the tested ANs.

4 Results

We use the measures described above and compute the difference between the mean values for the correct and incorrect model-generated ANs. We apply the unpaired t-test, assuming a two-tailed distribution, to assess the statistical significance of the difference between these values. In Tables 1 to 3 we report p values estimating statistical significance at the 0.05 level, and statistical significance is marked with an asterisk $(*)$.

We assume that there might be a difference between the corpus-attested and corpus-unattested test ANs, with each of the subgroups being more homogeneous than the entire test set. Our corpus-unattested examples are more similar to the ANs considered by Vecchi *et al.* (2011). We report the results on the full set of test ANs, as well as on each of the two subgroups separately.

Our goals are to:

- comparatively evaluate performance of the three composition models;
- assess the appropriateness of the proposed metrics;
- investigate models' performance on the corpus-attested and corpus-unattested combinations.

4.1 Comparative Performance of the Models

Of the three composition models, the *mult* model (Table 2) shows the best results overall.

The *alm* model (Table 3) shows statistically significant difference between the model-generated vectors for the correct and incorrect combinations with the cosines and component overlap, but it does not detect the difference on the corpus-unattested subset with any of the metrics.

The *add* model (Table 1) shows statistically significant differences only with the cosine measures on the corpus-unattested subset. The poor performance of this model may be due to its weaknesses outlined in Section 2.2. Also, Baroni and Zamparelli (2010) note that normalisation may help improving its performance.

4.2 Appropriateness of the Metrics

Cosines to the original input vectors show promising results with all three models. In contrast to the results reported by Vecchi *et al.* (2011), the density of the semantic neighbourhood does not differ significantly with any of the models, but since

Measure	*all*	*attest*	*unattest*
VLen	0.6537	0.2840	0.5557
CosN	$0.00003^{(*)}$	$0.0003^{(*)}$	0.1555
Dens	0.8160	0.4902	0.1799
CosA	$0.0188^{(*)}$	$0.0070^{(*)}$	0.8440
RDens	0.9106	0.6804	0.8588
Num	0.5959	0.9619	0.1402
COver	$0.00001^{(*)}$	$0.0004^{(*)}$	0.1484

Table 3: p values for the *alm* model

AN	bad intention	*bad information
add	***bad***, ***bad*** *company*, ***bad*** *image*	***information***, *other* ***information***, *real* ***information***
mult	*uncomplicated*, *improbable*, *suggestive*	*uncomplicated*, *improbable*, *humane*
alm	***intention***, *main* ***intention***, *real* ***intention***	*people*, *blind people*, *like-minded*

Table 4: Top 3 neighbours for each model

many of the combinations tested in our experiments are not genuinely anomalous, the fact that they are situated in densely populated semantic neighbourhoods is not surprising. Measures based on close proximity neighbourhood – RDens and Num – show statistical difference when applied to the *mult*-generated vectors only.

With COver, the *alm* model, followed by the *mult* model, produce sensible results. Table 4 shows the top 3 nearest neighbours found by the models for the correct AN *bad intention* and the incorrect **bad information*. The latter is annotated as incorrect since its meaning is quite vague and a possible correction is *inaccurate information*. Note that only the *alm* model is able to discriminate between the correct and the incorrect word combinations suggesting sensible nearest neighbours for *bad intention* and less sensible ones for **bad information*.

4.3 Attested vs Unattested Combinations

Our results show that the models perform differently on the two subsets and somewhat better on corpus-attested ANs. However, the results also confirm that appropriate models and metrics can be found to distinguish between correct and incorrect ANs in both subsets.

5 Conclusion

In this paper we have introduced a new task on which compositional distributional semantic models can be tested. Our results support the hypothesis that semantic models can be applied to detect errors in the choice of content words by English language learners. The original contribution of our paper is to show how compositional and distributional semantics can be linked to error detection to provide a solution to a practical task.

Our results suggest that with the metrics considered it is easier to detect the difference between the model-generated vectors for the correct and incorrect word combinations with the *multiplicative* model. On the other hand, qualitative analysis suggests that the *adjective-specific linear maps* of Baroni and Zamparelli (2010) are superior, since they place the model-generated vectors in semantically sensible neighbourhoods.

We plan to investigate further whether the use of a bigger corpus for collecting word co-occurrence statistics provides more reliable counts, and whether dimensionality reduction and/or normalisation of the models improves the results. We also plan to apply the *alm* model to a larger number of examples. Some other models such as the ones by Erk and Padó (2008) and Thater *et al.* (2010) which take selectional preferences and context into account may yield better results on this task, and we plan to test this experimentally in the future. Finally, since these models can discriminate between correct and anomalous combinations, the next step is to incorporate them into an error detection classifier.

Acknowledgments

We are grateful to Cambridge ESOL, a division of Cambridge Assessment, and Cambridge University Press for supporting this research and for granting us access to the CLC for research purposes. We would like to thank Helen Yannakoudakis, Øistein Andersen and the anonymous reviewers for their valuable comments.

References

Andersen Ø., Nioche J., Briscoe T. and Carroll J. 2008. *The BNC parsed with RASP4UIMA*. In Proceedings of the 6th International Conference on Language Resources and Evaluation (LREC).

Baroni M., Bernardi R. and Zamparelli R. 2012. *Frege in Space: A Program for Compositional Distributional Semantics.* http://clic.cimec.unitn.it/composes/materials/frege-in-space.pdf

Baroni M. and Zamparelli R. 2010. *Nouns are vectors, adjectives are matrices: Representing adjective–noun constructions in semantic space.* In Proceedings of the EMNLP-2010, pp. 1183–1193.

Briscoe E., Carroll J., and Watson R. 2006. *The Second Release of the RASP System.* In Proceedings of the COLING/ACL-2006 Interactive Presentation Sessions, pp. 59–68.

Chang Y.C., Chang J.S., Chen H.J., and Liou H.C. 2012. *An automatic collocation writing assistant for Taiwanese EFL learners: A case of corpus-based NLP technology.* Computer Assisted Language Learning, 21(3):283–299.

Dahlmeier D. and Ng H.T. 2011. *Correcting Semantic Collocation Errors with L1-induced Paraphrases.* In Proceedings of the EMNLP-2011, pp. 107–117.

Dale R., Anisimoff I., and Narroway G. 2012. *HOO 2012: A Report on the Preposition and Determiner Error Correction Shared Task.* In Proceedings of the 7th Workshop on Innovative Use of NLP for Building Educational Applications, pp. 54–62.

Erk K. and Padó S. 2008. *A Structured Vector Space Model for Word Meaning in Context.* In Proceedings of the EMNLP-2008, pp. 897–906.

Evert S. 2005. *The Statistics of Word Cooccurrences.* Dissertation, Stuttgart University.

Futagi Y., Deane P., Chodorow M., and Tetreault J. 2009. *A computational approach to detecting collocation errors in the writing of non-native speakers of English.* Computer Assisted Language Learning, 21(4):353–367.

Grefenstette G. 1994. *Explorations in Automatic Thesaurus Discovery.* Kluwer Academic Publishers.

Kintsch W. 2001. *Predication.* Cognitive Science, 25:173–202.

Leacock C., Chodorow M., Gamon M. and Tetreault J. 2010. *Automated Grammatical Error Detection for Language Learners.* Morgan and Claypool Publishers.

Liu A. L.-E., Wible D., and Tsao N.-L. 2009. *Automated suggestions for miscollocations.* In Proceedings of the 4th Workshop on Innovative Use of NLP for Building Educational Applications, pp. 47–50.

McCarthy D., Koeling R., Weeds J. and Carroll J. 2004. *Finding predominant word senses in untagged text.* In Proceedings of the 42nd Annual Meeting on Association for Computational Linguistics, pp. 280–287.

Mevik B. and Wehrens R. 2007. *The pls package: Principal component and partial least squares regression in R.* Journal of Statistical Software, 18(2).

Mitchell J. and Lapata M. 2008. *Vector-based models of semantic composition.* In Proceedings of ACL, pp. 236–244.

Mitchell J. and Lapata M. 2010. *Composition in distributional models of semantics.* Cognitive Science, 34:1388–1429.

Nicholls D. 2003. *The Cambridge Learner Corpus: Error coding and analysis for lexicography and ELT.* In Proceedings of the Corpus Linguistics conference, pp. 572–581.

Park T., Lank E., Poupart P., and Terry M. 2008. *Is the sky pure today? AwkChecker: an assistive tool for detecting and correcting collocation errors.* In Proceedings of the 21st annual ACM symposium on User interface software and technology, pp. 121–130.

Schone P. and Jurafsky D. 2001. *Is Knowledge-Free Induction of Multiword Unit Dictionary Headwords a Solved Problem?.* Pittsburg, PA, pp. 100–108.

Schütze H. 1998. *Automatic word sense discrimination.* Computational Linguistics, 24(1):97–123.

Shei C.C. and Pain H. 2000. *An ESL Writer's Collocation Aid.* Computer Assisted Language Learning, 13(2):167–182.

Thater S., Fürstenau, H., and Pinkal M. 2010. *Contextualizing Semantic Representations Using Syntactically Enriched Vector Models.* In Proceedings of the 48th Annual Meeting of the Association for Computational Linguistics, pp. 948–957.

Vecchi E., Baroni M. and Zamparelli R. 2011. *(Linear) maps of the impossible: Capturing semantic anomalies in distributional space.* In Proceedings of the DISCO Workshop at ACL-2011, pp. 1–9.

Wible H., Kwo C.-H., Tsao N.-L., Liu A., and Lin H.-L. 2003. *Bootstrapping in a language-learning environment.* Journal of Computer Assisted Learning, 19(4):90–102.

Yannakoudakis H., Briscoe T. and Medlock B. 2011. *A New Dataset and Method for Automatically Grading ESOL Texts.* In Proceedings of the 49th Annual Meeting of the Association for Computational Linguistics: Human Language Technologies, 1:180–189.

Yi X., Gao J., and Dolan W.B. 2008. *A Web-based English Proofing System for English as a Second Language Users.* In Proceedings of the third International Joint Conference on Natural Language Processing (IJCNLP), pp. 619–624.

Incremental and Predictive Dependency Parsing under Real-Time Conditions

Arne Köhn and Wolfgang Menzel
Fachbereich Informatik
Universität Hamburg
{koehn, menzel}@informatik.uni-hamburg.de

Abstract

We present an incremental dependency parser which derives predictions about the upcoming structure in a parse-as-you-type mode. Drawing on the inherent strong anytime property of the underlying transformation-based approach, an existing system, jwcdg, has been modified to make it truly interruptible. A speed-up was achieved by means of parallel processing. In addition, MaltParser is used to bootstrap the search which increases accuracy under tight time constraints. With these changes, jwcdg can effectively utilize the full time span until the next word becomes available which results in an optimal quality-time trade-off.

1 Introduction

Users prefer incremental dialogue systems to their non-incremental counterparts (Aist et al., 2007). For a syntactic parser to contribute to an incremental dialogue system or any other incremental NLP application, it also needs to work incrementally. However, parsers usually operate on whole sentences only and few parsers exist that are capable of incremental parsing or are even optimized for it.

This paper focuses on using a parser as part of an incremental pipeline that requires timely response to natural language input. In such a scenario, delay imposed by a parser's lookahead is more severe than delay caused by parsing speed since the parsing speed is capped by the user's input speed. Depending on the input method, the maximum typing speed varies between 0.75 seconds per word (qwerty keyboard) and 6 seconds per word (mobile 12-key multi-tap) (Arif and Stuerzlinger, 2009) and is usually lower if the sentence has to be phrased while typing.

In such a scenario, the objective of the parser is to yield high quality results and produce them as soon as they are needed by a subsequent component. It is rarely known beforehand when the next word will be available for processing. Therefore, in an incremental pipeline a) computation should continue until the next word occurs if this might contribute to a better result, and b) a new word should be included immediately to avoid delays. A parser which works pull-based, i.e. processes one prefix until it is deemed finished and then pulls the next word, is insufficient under conditions, since it would require to determine the time used for processing before the processing can even start. Either the estimated processing time will be too short, violating a), or it will be too long, violating b). In contrast, push-based architectures can meet both requirements since the processing of the prefix can be interrupted when new input is available.

Beuck et al. (2011) showed that Weighted Constraint Dependency Grammar-based parsers are capable of producing high-quality incremental results but neglected the processing time needed for each increment. In this paper, we will use jwcdg[1], a reimplementation of the WCDG parser written in Java. jwcdg uses a transformation-based algorithm. It comes equipped with a strong anytime capability, causing the quality of the results to depend on the processing time jwcdg is allowed to consume. We will show that jwcdg can produce high quality results even if only granted fairly low amounts of processing time.

1.1 Incremental Predictive Dependency Parsing

Dependency parsing assigns every word to another word or NIL as its regent and the resulting edges are annotated with a label. If dependency analyses

[1] `http://nats-www.informatik.uni-hamburg.de/CDG/`; detailed resources for the experiments in this paper can be found there as well.

are used to describe the syntactic structure of sentence prefixes, different amounts of prediction can be provided. The interesting cases are those where either the regent or a dependent is not yet part of the sentence prefix.

If the regent of a word w is not yet available, the parser can make a prediction about where and how w should be attached. One possibility is to simply state that the regent of w lies somewhere in the future without giving any additional information. This can be modelled by attaching w to a generic *nonspec* node (Daum, 2004). Beuck et al. (2011) call this *minimal prediction*.

However, it is usually possible to predict more: The existence of upcoming words can be anticipated and w can then be attached to one of these words. Of course, most of the time it will not be possible to predict exact words but abstract pseudo-words can be used instead that stand for a certain type such as nouns or verbs. Beuck et al. (2011) call these pseudo-words *virtual nodes* and the approach of using virtual nodes *structural prediction* (because the virtual nodes accommodate crucial aspects of the upcoming structure of the sentence). A virtual node can be included into an analysis to represent words that are expected to appear in later increments.

As an example, "Peter drives a red" can be analyzed as

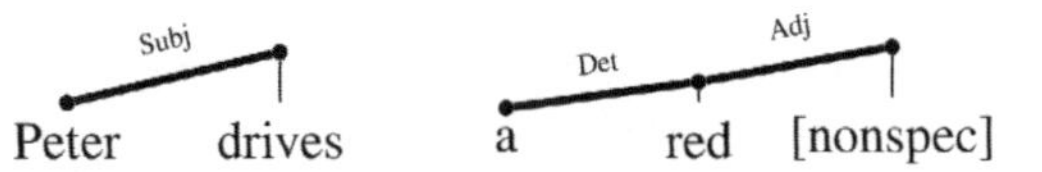

using minimal prediction or as

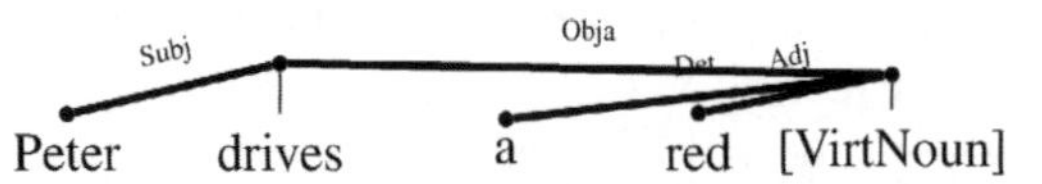

using structural prediction. Minimal prediction leads to disconnected analyses while structural prediction allows for connected analyses which resemble the structure of whole sentences. Tn this case, the analysis includes the information that the regent of "red" is the object of "drives", which is missing in the analysis using minimal prediction.

1.2 Challenges in Incremental Predictive Parsing

The key difference between non-incremental and incremental parsing is the uncertainty about the continuation of the sentence. If a prediction about upcoming structure is being made, there is no guarantee that this prediction will be accurate.

Using a beam of possible prefixes, as done in Demberg-Winterfors (2010), is a strategy to deal with this uncertainty. It guarantees that each new analysis is an extension of an old one. With this approach, the whole beam becomes incompatible with the observed sentence continuation if no fitting prediction is contained in the beam. Thus, such sentences can not be parsed.

Minimal prediction, as another option, largely abstains from prediction. This allows for monotonous extensions even without a beam since the analysis of a prefix will not be incompatible with the continuation of the sentence. This approach is used by MaltParser (Nivre et al., 2007).

A transformation-based parser, finally, can also deal with non-monotonic extensions. In contrast to beam search, only a single analysis is generated for each prefix and there is no guarantee that the analysis of a prefix p_n is a monotonic extension of p_{n-1}. Because the analysis of p_{n-1} is only used to initialize the transformation process, the search space is not restricted by the results that were obtained in former prefixes although they still guide the analysis.

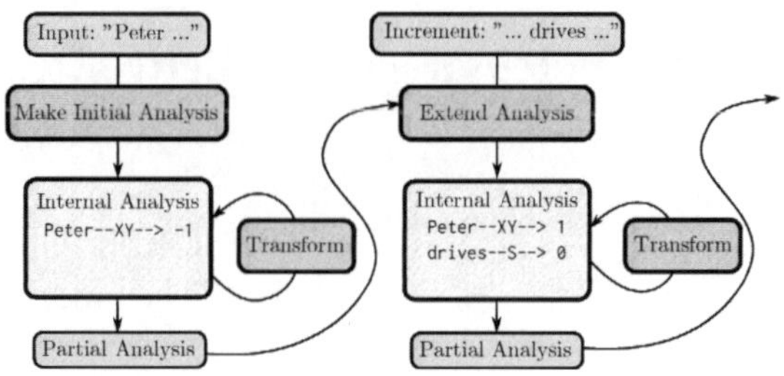

Figure 1: Incremental Parsing with jwcdg

2 WCDG Parsing

In the Weighted Constraint Dependency Grammar formalism, a grammar is used to judge the quality of analyses. The grammar consists of constraints that are evaluated on one or more edges of an analysis. If a constraint is violated, a penalty is computed. Constraints can incorporate more edges into their computation than the edges they are evaluated on (McCrae et al., 2008). They can traverse the current analysis by using special predicates. This way, a constraint evaluated on one edge could, for example, check if that edge is adjacent to an edge with certain properties. If a constraint uses such predicates, it is considered *context sensitive*.

In the WCDG formalism, the best analysis of a

sentence is defined by

$$ba = \mathop{\arg\max}_{a \in Analyses} \prod_{c \in Conflicts(a)} penalty(c)$$

where the *conflicts* are the parts of an analysis that stand in conflict with the grammar and $penalty(c)$ is the penalty that the grammar assigns to the conflict c.

2.1 The Frobbing Algorithm

jwcdg tries to find an analysis by transforming a given one until it cannot be improved further. The algorithm employed for this purpose is called frobbing (Foth et al., 2000).

Frobbing consists of two phases: first, the problem is initialized. In this phase, all possible edges are constructed and the constraints defined for a single edge are evaluated on them. An initial analysis is constructed using the best-scored edge for every word, which is repeatedly transformed in the second phase. Frobbing is described as pseudocode in Algorithm 1. A set of conflicts (constraints that are violated on specific edges) is computed and the most severe of them is attacked by transforming the analysis (attackConflict, line 7). This either results in a (not necessarily better) analysis that does not have this conflict or in the insight that the conflict cannot be removed (line 12). The algorithm repeatedly tries to remove the most severe conflict. If in this process a new best analysis is found, it is marked as the new starting point. If the conflict can not be removed, the algorithm tracks back to the starting point. The procedure can be interrupted at any time and the best analysis that was found up to that point will be returned.

In its incremental mode, jwcdg works as depicted in Figure 1. The new word is added to the previous analysis using the best edge. The frobbing algorithm is then run until no better result can be found or the parser is interrupted. To allow for prediction, either a *nonspec* node (Daum, 2004) or a set of virtual nodes (Beuck et al., 2011) is added to the set of words. This way, all changes regarding incrementality are completely transparent to the frobbing algorithm, only the constraints in the grammar need to be aware of virtual nodes and `nonspec`.

```
   Data: sentence S
   Result: Analysis of S
1  List removedConflicts ← [ ];
2  Analysis best ← makeInitialAnalysis(S);
3  Analysis current ← best;
4  Conflict initialConflict ←
   getHardestSolvableConflict(current);
5  while solvable conflicts remain do
6  |  Conflict c ←
   |  getHardestSolvableConflict(current);
7  |  current ← attackConflict(c, current,
   |  removedConflicts);
8  |  if score(current) > score(best) then
9  |  |  best ← current;
10 |  |  reset();
11 |  |  initialConflict ←
   |  |  getHardestSolvableConflict(current);
12 |  else if current == null then
13 |  |  setUnresolvable(initialConflict);
14 |  |  current ← best;
15 |  |  removedConflicts ← [ ];
16 |  end
17 end
18 return best;
```

Algorithm 1: `frobbing`

3 Related Work

One of the few broad-coverage parsers that are capable of incremental processing is PLTAG, a Tree Adjoining Grammar parser that tries to model psycholinguistic phenomena such as surprisal, paying less attention to high parsing accuracy or fast parsing speed. It works incrementally and provides predictions for upcoming structure. Since PLTAG uses beams that get expanded, it needs a lookahead of one word to reduce ambiguity (Demberg-Winterfors, 2010, p. 217). Even with this lookahead, some sentences can not be parsed: PLTAG has a coverage of 93.8% on sentences of the Penn Treebank with less than 40 words.

MaltParser is a shift-reduce based parser. It uses a classifier to determine locally optimal actions from a set of possible actions of a parsing algorithm. The classifier is trained using manually annotated sentences. MaltParser can use several different parsing algorithms. In this paper, the *2planar* algorithm described in Gómez-Rodríguez and Nivre (2010) will be used, which is able to produce non-projective analyses.

While MaltParser's processing is fast compared to jwcdg, a lookahead of one word already translates into a delay of one to three seconds, depending on the input speed of the user. Beuck et al. (2011) showed that, at least for German, Malt-

input:	The	fox	jumped	over
tagger:	The/DT	fox/NN	jumped/VBD	
parser:	stack: [The]			
output:	[none]			

Figure 2: Effect of lookahead for MaltParser

Parser suffers from a fairly small decrease in accuracy if only features from the next two words instead of three are used. However, since the PoS tags are needed and a PoS tagger needs lookahead as well to achieve good accuracy, a lookahead of at least three words is needed for the whole tagger-parser pipeline to achieve a high accuracy. The effect of this delay is illustrated in Figure 2. In addition, MaltParser is not capable of producing structural predictions.

4 Parallelizing jwcdg

Among the two phases of frobbing, only the second one can be interrupted. Therefore, initialization needs to be faster than the shortest time limit we would like to impose. Initialization is mostly concerned with evaluating constraints on all edges that come from or point towards the new word. To make this judgement faster, the code has been changed so that it can be done in parallel, using worker threads instead of a sequential constraint evaluation.

Table 1 shows the time needed to construct new edges and judge them while parsing a subset of the NEGRA corpus (Brants et al., 2003).[2] Although the median time is already relatively good in the non-parallelized case, its maximum amounts to almost two seconds. Parallelization brings most benefits for the more complex initializations: the time needed for the 3rd quartile scales nearly linear up to eight cores. More than sixteen cores yield no further improvement.

With the parallelized initialization, jwcdg can spend more time on transforming analyses. In addition, it is able to perform anytime parsing with a lower bound of about 200 ms per word on current hardware.

The heart of the frobbing algorithm is the attackConflict method which, given an analysis a and a conflict c, systematically tries all changes of edges that are part of c. It then returns the best resulting analysis that does not violate the constraints $constr(c)$. Since these transformations all work independently, they have been parallelized in the same manner as the initialization. The result can be seen in Table 2. While the introduction of parallelized code causes a small overhead, using two cores already provides a noticeable benefit. The parallelized code can benefit from up to 32 cores, yet the overhead of managing more cores results in a sub-linear speedup.

These optimizations have a noticeable impact on parsing performance under time pressure: With a time limit of two seconds per word, jwcdg$_{base}$ scores an unlabeled accuracy of 72.54% for the final analyses, while jwcdg$_{parallel}$ scores 76.29%. jwcdg$_{base}$ only reaches this accuracy with a time limit of four seconds. Unless otherwise noted, all evaluations have been carried out on sentences 18602 to 19601 of the NEGRA corpus.

5 MaltParser as a Predictor for jwcdg

When facing a tight time limit, jwcdg has only very little time to improve an analysis by transforming it. Therefore, with tighter time limits a good initial attachment becomes more important and a method which provides frobbing with a good initial analysis could help to achieve drastically better results.

Foth and Menzel (2006) showed that WCDG can be augmented by trainable components to raise the accuracy of WCDG. The output of these predictors was converted into constraints to help WCDG finding a good analysis. One of the components was a shift-reduce parser modeled after Nivre (2003), which was the first description of the MaltParser architecture. Although the shift-reduce parser was relatively simple compared to MaltParser and had a labeled accuracy of only 80.7 percent, it helped to raise the accuracy of WCDG from 87.5 to 89.8 percent. This approach has later been used by Khmylko et al. (2009) to integrate MST-Parser (McDonald et al., 2006) (which does not work incrementally) as an external data source for WCDG. We integrated MaltParser in a similar way.

MaltParser consumes the input from left to right and, if using the 2planar algorithm, constructs edges as soon as possible: An edge can only be created between the word on top of the stack and the current input word. This means that every edge has to be constructed as soon as the second word

[2] All experiments have been carried out on a 48-core machine with four AMD Opteron 6168 processors.

	number of threads used							
	np	1	2	4	8	16	32	48
1st Qu.	43	45	23	13	9	8	8	9
Median	86	91	46	26	17	14	14	15
Mean	161	170	86	47	30	25	24	27
3rd Qu.	186	197	100	56	36	31	31	34
Max.	1940	2049	1029	553	433	200	197	555

Table 1: Timing requirements in ms of the initialization phase for different thread numbers; np = not parallelized (time limit per word = 16 seconds)

	number of threads used							
	np	1	2	4	8	16	32	48
1st Qu.	19	20	14	10	8	7	6	6
Median	62	64	48	36	28	24	22	22
Mean	181	190	141	110	92	81	76	79
3rd Qu.	193	199	153	117	95	84	76	77
Max.	12112	13611	8033	8734	8469	6376	8554	6297

Table 2: Timing requirements in ms of attacking conflicts (Algorithm 1, Line 7) for different thread numbers; np = not parallelized (time limit per word = 16 seconds)

of the edge is the current input word. As soon as that word gets shifted onto the stack, the creation of the edge would no longer be possible.

The parser works monotonically since edges are only added to but never removed from the set of edges. This means that all decisions by the parser are final; if word a is not attached to word b, we can be sure that a will never be attached to b in subsequent analyses. As a corollary, if MaltParser has an accuracy of X percent on whole sentences, the probability that a newly created edge is correct will also be X percent.

As a delay is not acceptable for our application scenario, we will use MaltParser and the TnT tagger (Brants, 2000) without lookahead despite their inferior accuracy in that mode[3].

5.1 An Interface Between MaltParser and jwcdg

A predictor (MaltPredictor) for jwcdg has been implemented that uses a newly written incremental interface for MaltParser so that the regents and labels predicted by MaltParser can be accessed by constraints as soon as they become available. MaltPredictor uses the PoS-tags that are provided by the tagger predictor. Each time a new word w is pushed to jwcdg, MaltPredictor forwards w together with its PoS-tag onto MaltParsers input queue and runs MaltParser's algorithm until a shift operations occurs. With this shift operation, w is consumed from the input queue. If the sentence is marked as being finished, MaltParser is run until it has fully parsed the sentence. MaltPredictor then reads the state of MaltParser and stores for each word the regent it has been assigned to by MaltParser. If Maltparser did not assign a regent to a word, this fact is also stored. Since – as already mentioned – MaltParser works eagerly (i. e. constructs every edge as soon as possible), the regent of such a word must either lie in the future or be the root node.

The three constraints that are used for accessing MaltParser's analyses are depicted as pseudocode in Figure 3. If only these constraints and the tagger constraint (which selects the PoS-tag for every word) are used as a grammar, jwcdg will parse sentences exactly as MaltParser does. This way, jwcdg acts as an incremental interface to MaltParser.

The first two constraints are only applicable if MaltPredictor has made a prediction for the word in question. The first constraint checks whether

[3]both were trained on sentences 1000 to 18000 of the negra corpus

```
prediction_exists(word)
 -> regent_of(word) =
     predicted_regent(word)

prediction_exists(word)
 -> label_of(word) =
     predicted_label(word)

not prediction_exists(word)
 -> (regent(word) is virtual or
     regent(word) is nonspec or
     regent(word) is NIL or
     word is virtual)
```

Figure 3: Constraints for incorporating MaltParser's results into jwcdg

the regent of a word is the one that has been selected by MaltParser. The second constraint checks that the predicted label matches the label of the edge in the analysis given that a label has been predicted. The third constraint is not as straightforward as the other two: Since we know that MaltParser creates edges as soon as possible and we know that MaltParser has not created an edge with this word as dependent, either the regent lies in the future (i. e. it should be a virtual node in jwcdg's analysis) or the regent is NIL (as MaltParser does not explicitly create edges to NIL while parsing). In the other possible case, the dependent of the current edge is a virtual node. In this case MaltParser cannot possibly predict an attachment. A parameter tuning on sentences 501 to 1000 of the NEGRA corpus has shown that a penalty of 0.9 works best for these constraints.

When the input sentence is going to be extended, the new word is attached using the edge that violates the least unary, non context-sensitive constraints. The MaltParser constraints are unary and not context sensitive and therefore jwcdg will use the edge predicted by MaltParser if no other constraints prevent it from doing so.

5.2 Comparison of MaltParser and jwcdg

To compare MaltParser and jwcdg, the richer prediction of jwcdg has to be transformed into minimal prediction. In this mode, every attachment of a word to a virtual node is considered correct if the word is attached to an upcoming word in the gold standard. The two accuracies that are used for evaluation are *initial attachment* accuracy (how often is the newest word attached correctly?) and the *final accuracy* (how many attachments are correct in the parse trees for the whole sentences?).

Figure 4 shows the accuracy for initial attachment and final accuracy as a function of a given time limit. Since MaltParser does not use an anytime algorithm, its results are the same for all time limits[4]. Note that the labeled initial attachment score is fairly low because MaltParser can not predict labels for edges that have `nonspec` as the regent. When ignoring labels, Maltparser's initial attachment accuracy is higher than its final accuracy since it does not change edges it has created (therefore the accuracy cannot rise) and words can be counted as correct initially but wrong in the final analysis: If the correct regent of a word lies somewhere in the future, the initial decision to not attach it is counted as correct. If it is later attached to a wrong word, it will be counted as wrong in the final accuracy.

As can be seen, jwcdg outperforms MaltParser in most aspects when given enough time. The only exception is the unlabeled attachment score for the initial attachment. Here, however, one has to keep in mind that jwcdg produces more informative predictions with virtual nodes, which is not honored in this evaluation.

5.3 Enhancing jwcdg with MaltParser

jwcdg$_{malt}$ has been derived from jwcdg$_{parallel}$ by adding the MaltParser constraints discussed before to the grammar.

The results (Figure 4) show that jwcdg$_{malt}$ has a considerably higher initial accuracy than jwcdg$_{parallel}$, more than ten percentage points for a time limit of one second. The final accuracy is noticeably better as well. This shows that MaltParser's output helps jwcdg find a good initial analysis which can then be optimized by jwcdg.

6 Evaluation on Additional Corpora

The evaluations discussed so far have been carried out on the NEGRA corpus. NEGRA consists of newspaper texts and thus represents a very specific kind of text. However, most sentences from other text types (e.g. chat) are shorter and have a lower structural complexity. This section tries to measure the impact of these differences between different data sources.

[4]MaltParser parses fast enough to never violate the time limit of one second per word.

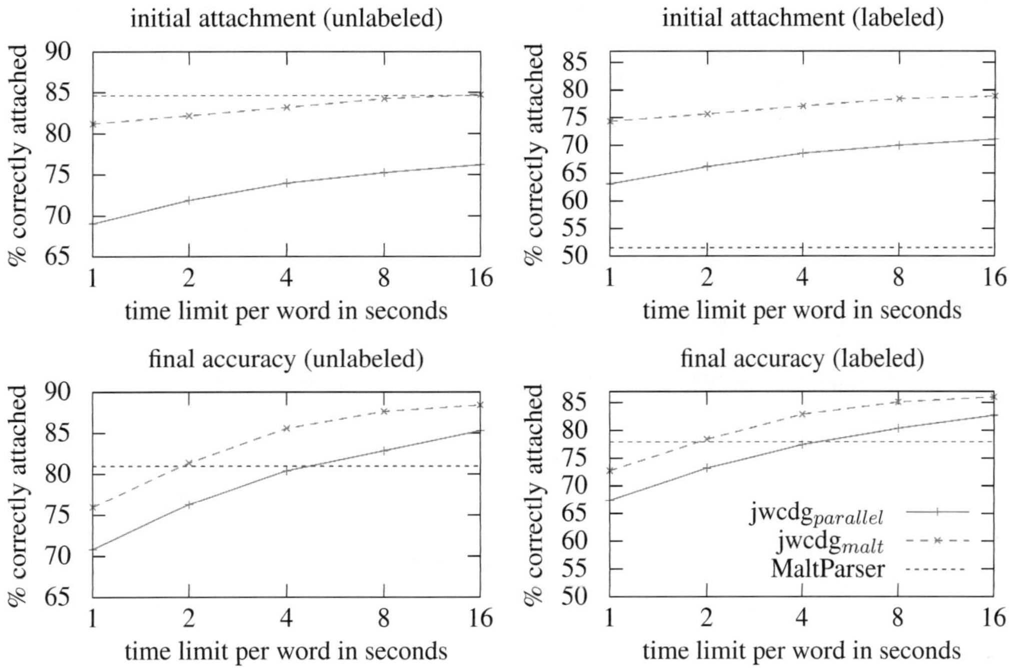

Figure 4: Comparison of jwcdg and MaltParser using minimal prediction

6.1 Evaluation on Subsets of NEGRA

To evaluate how sentence length influences the parsing results, jwcdg has been evaluated on a subset of the NEGRA corpus. Sentences with a length of less than three have been excluded. In addition, sentences longer than twenty have been excluded. The resulting subset NEGRA-3-20 contains 57.8% of the sentences of the original NEGRA test set.

The results shown in Figure 5 confirm the assumption that jwcdg's accuracy increases when being evaluated only on short sentences. This difference could be due to the syntactic simplicity of short sentences and the shorter initialization time needed for short increments leaving more time for the transformation. In addition, jwcdg$_{malt}$ already approaches its best result with a time limit of four seconds.

6.2 Evaluation on the creg-109 Corpus

Since interactive Computer-Assisted Language Learning could be an interesting application domain for an incremental parser, an additional evaluation has been conducted on the creg-109 corpus, a set of 109 sentences of the corpus described in Meurers et al. (2010). The creg-109 corpus "consists of answers to German reading comprehension questions written by American college students learning German" (Meurers et al., 2010).

Figure 6 shows the accuracy of the different parser versions on this corpus. The results have a different pattern than the ones for the NEGRA corpus: jwcdg$_{parallel}$ has nearly the same initial attachment accuracy as jwcdg$_{malt}$ and even slightly outperforms it in the final score. In addition to that, the result does not improve much with a time limit of more than two seconds. Both phenomena could be due to the lesser syntactic complexity of the sentences so that the MaltParser's analyses are not so beneficial for guiding jwcdg.

7 Conclusion

We have shown that it is possible to gain parse-as-you-type speed with good accuracy using a combination of different incremental approaches to dependency parsing. Our solution based on a parallelized version of jwcdg benefits from using up to 32 cores. In contrast to other approaches, which have to make algorithmic refinements, jwcdg can take advantage from the advances in processing speed due to its anytime property. MaltParser turned out to be a good predictor that helps jwcdg to produce good analyses earlier.

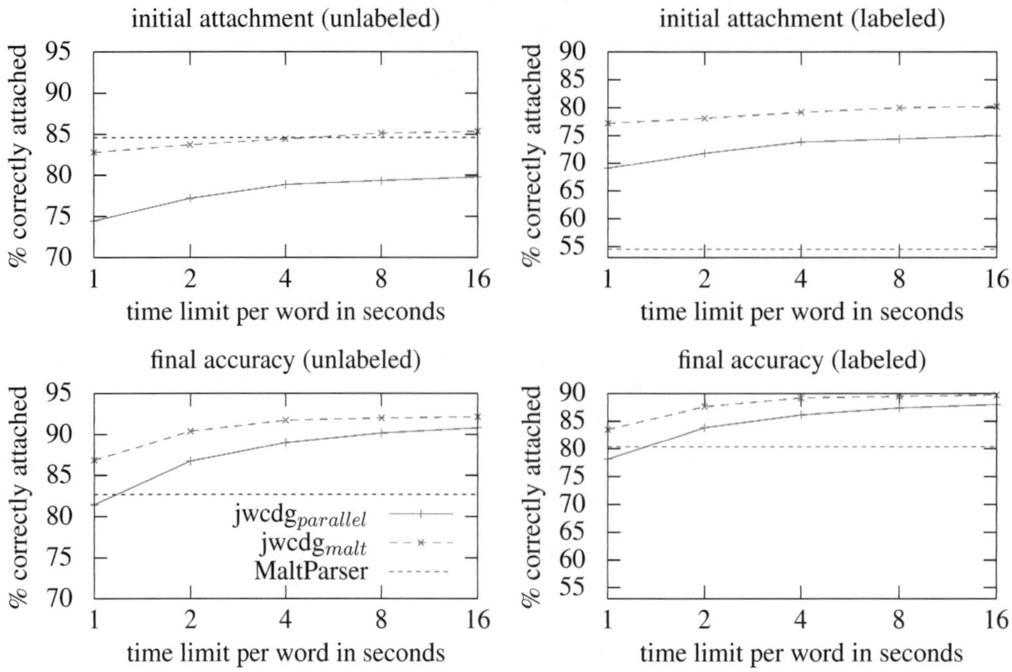

Figure 5: Comparison on NEGRA-3-20 using minimal prediction

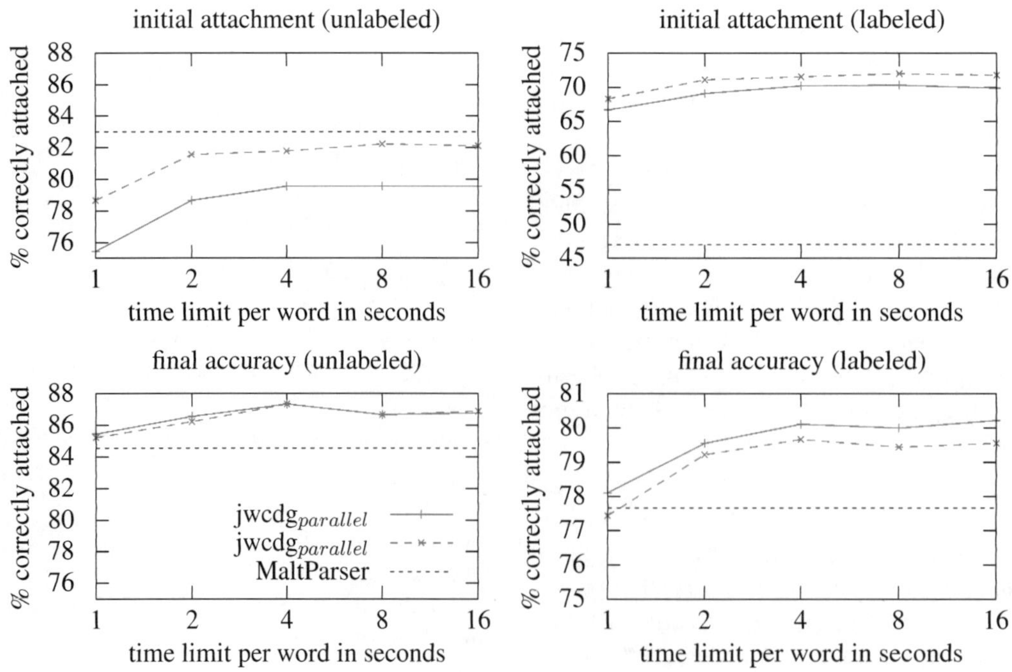

Figure 6: Comparison on creg-109 using minimal prediction

References

Gregory Aist, James Allen, Ellen Campana, Carlos Gomez Gallo, Scott Stoness, Mary Swift, and Michael K. Tanenhaus. 2007. Incremental dialogue system faster than and preferred to its nonincremental counterpart. In *Proceedings of the 29th Annual Meeting of the Cognitive Science Society*, pages 761–766.

A.S. Arif and W. Stuerzlinger. 2009. Analysis of text entry performance metrics. In *Science and Technology for Humanity (TIC-STH), 2009 IEEE Toronto International Conference*, pages 100–105.

Niels Beuck, Arne Köhn, and Wolfgang Menzel. 2011. Incremental parsing and the evaluation of partial dependency analyses. In *Proceedings of the 1st International Conference on Dependency Linguistics*. Depling 2011.

Thorsten Brants, Wojciech Skut, and Hans Uszkoreit. 2003. Syntactic annotation of a german newspaper corpus. In Anne Abeillé and Nancy Ide, editors, *Treebanks*, volume 20 of *Text, Speech and Language Technology*, pages 73–87. Springer Netherlands.

Thorsten Brants. 2000. TnT: a statistical part-of-speech tagger. In *Proceedings of the sixth conference on Applied natural language processing*, pages 224–231, Stroudsburg, PA, USA. Association for Computational Linguistics.

Michael Daum. 2004. Dynamic dependency parsing. In *Proceedings of the Workshop on Incremental Parsing: Bringing Engineering and Cognition Together*, IncrementParsing '04, pages 67–73, Stroudsburg, PA, USA. Association for Computational Linguistics.

Vera Demberg-Winterfors. 2010. *A Broad-Coverage Model of Prediction in Human Sentence Processing*. Ph.D. thesis, University of Edinburgh.

Kilian A. Foth and Wolfgang Menzel. 2006. Hybrid parsing: Using probabilistic models as predictors for a symbolic parser. In *Proceedings of the 21st International Conference on Computational Linguistics and 44th Annual Meeting of the ACL*, pages 321–328, Sydney, Australia. Association for Computational Linguistics.

Kilian A. Foth, Wolfgang Menzel, and Ingo Schröder. 2000. A transformation-based parsing technique with anytime properties. In *4th Int. Workshop on Parsing Technologies, IWPT-2000*, pages 89 – 100, Trento, Italy.

Carlos Gómez-Rodríguez and Joakim Nivre. 2010. A transition-based parser for 2-planar dependency structures. In *Proceedings of the 48th Annual Meeting of the Association for Computational Linguistics*, pages 1492–1501, Uppsala, Sweden. Association for Computational Linguistics.

Lidia Khmylko, Kilian A. Foth, and Wolfgang Menzel. 2009. Co-parsing with competitive models. In *Proceedings of the International Conference RANLP-2009*, pages 173–179, Borovets, Bulgaria. Association for Computational Linguistics.

Patrick McCrae, Kilian A. Foth, and Wolfgang Menzel. 2008. Modelling global phenomena with extended local constraints. In Jørgen Villadsen and Henning Christiansen, editors, *Proceedings of the 5th International Workshop on Constraints and Language Processing (CSLP 2008, Hamburg, Germany)*, pages 48–60. Roskilde University.

Ryan McDonald, Kevin Lerman, and Fernando Pereira. 2006. Multilingual dependency analysis with a two-stage discriminative parser. In *Proceedings of the Tenth Conference on Computational Natural Language Learning*, CoNLL-X '06, pages 216–220, Stroudsburg, PA, USA. Association for Computational Linguistics.

Detmar Meurers, Niels Ott, and Ramon Ziai. 2010. Compiling a task-based corpus for the analysis of learner language in context. In *Pre-Proceedings of Linguistic Evidence 2010*, pages 214–217, Tübingen.

Joakim Nivre, Johan Hall, Jens Nilsson, Atanas Chanev, Gülsen Eryigit, Sandra Kübler, Svetoslav Marinov, and Erwin Marsi. 2007. Maltparser: A language-independent system for data-driven dependency parsing. *Natural Language Engineering*, 13(2):95–135.

Joakim Nivre. 2003. An efficient algorithm for projective dependency parsing. In *Proceedings of the 8th International Workshop on Parsing Technologies (IWPT*, pages 149–160.

Rationale, Concepts, and Current Outcome of the Unit Graphs Framework

Maxime Lefrançois and **Fabien Gandon**
Wimmics, Inria, I3S, CNRS, UNSA
2004 rte des Lucioles, BP. 93, 06902 Sophia Antipolis, France
{maxime.lefrancois,fabien.gandon}@inria.fr

Abstract

The Unit Graphs (UGs) framework is a graph-based knowledge representation (KR) formalism that is designed to allow for the representation, manipulation, query, and reasoning over linguistic knowledge of the Explanatory Combinatorial Dictionary of the Meaning-Text Theory (MTT). This paper introduces the UGs framework, and overviews current published outcomes. It first introduces rationale of this new formalism: neither semantic web formalisms nor Conceptual Graphs can represent linguistic predicates. It then overviews the foundational concepts of this framework: the UGs are defined over a UG-support that contains: i) a hierarchy of unit types which is strongly driven by the actantial structure of unit types, ii) a hierarchy of circumstantial symbols, and iii) a set of unit identifiers. On these foundational concepts and on the definition of UGs, this paper finally overviews current outcomes of the UGs framework: the definition of a deep-semantic representation level for the MTT, representation of lexicographic definitions of lexical units in the form of semantic graphs, and two formal semantics: one based on UGs closure and homomorphism, and one based on model semantics.

1 Introduction

The Meaning-Text Theory (MTT) is a theoretical dependency linguistics framework for the construction of models of natural language. As such, its goal is to write systems of explicit rules that express the correspondence between meanings and texts (or sounds) in various languages (Kahane, 2003). From semantic representations to surface phonologic representations, seven different levels of linguistic representation are supposed for each set of synonymous utterances. Thus, two times six modules containing transformation rules are used to transcribe representations of a level into representations of an adjacent level. The main constituent of the MTT is the dictionary model where lexical units are described, which is called the Explanatory Combinatorial Dictionary (ECD) (Mel'čuk, 2006).

As for any community of interest, linguists and lexicographers of the MTT framework produce knowledge. Knowledge Representation (KR) is an area of artificial intelligence that deals with recurrent needs that emerge with such knowledge production.

The aim of this paper is to introduce the Unit Graphs KR formalism that is designed to allow for the representation, manipulation, query, and reasoning over dependency structures, rules and lexicographic knowledge of the ECD.

The rest of this paper is organized as follows. We will first introduce rationale of this new KR formalism (§2), then the fundamental concepts of the UGs framework (§3), implications for the MTT, lexicographic definitions and application to a specific MTT lexicographic edition project (§4), and finally two approaches to assign UGs with logical semantics, so as to enable reasoning in the UGs framework (§5).

2 Rationale: Representation of Valency-based Predicates

Most past or current projects that aimed at implementing the ECD did so in a lexicographic perspective. One important example is the RELIEF project (Lux-Pogodalla and Polguère, 2011), which aims at representing a lexical system graph named RLF (Polguère, 2009), where lexical units are interlinked by paradigmatic and syntagmatic links of lexical functions (Mel'čuk, 1996). In the RELIEF project, the description of Lexical Functions is based on a formalization proposed by Kahane and Polguère (2001). Moreover, lexicographic definitions start to be partially formalized in the RELIEF project using the markup type that has been developed in the Definiens project (Barque and Polguère, 2008; Barque et al., 2010).

One exception is the proprietary linguistic processor ETAP-3 that implements a variety of ECD for Natural Language Processing (Apresian et al., 2003; Boguslavsky et al., 2004). Linguistic knowledge are asserted, and transformation rules are directly formalized in first order logic.

Adding to these formalization works, our goal is to propose a formalization from a knowledge engineering perspective, compatible with standard KR formalisms. The term *formalization* here means not only *make non-ambiguous*, but also *make operational*, i.e., *such that it supports logical operations* (e.g., knowledge manipulation, query, reasoning). We thus adopt a knowledge engineering approach applied to the domain of the MTT.

At first sight, two existing KR formalisms seem interesting for this job: semantic web formalisms (e.g., RDF[1], RDFS[2], OWL[3], SPARQL[4]), and Conceptual Graphs (CGs) (Sowa, 1984; Chein and Mugnier, 2008). Both of them are based on directed labelled graph structures, and some research has been done towards using them to represent dependency structures and knowledge of the ECD (OWL in (Lefrançois and Gandon, 2011; Boguslavsky, 2011), CGs at the conceptual level in (Bohnet and Wanner, 2010)). Yet Lefrançois (2013) showed that neither of these KR formalisms can represent valency-based predicates, therefore lexicographic definitions. One crucial issue is the following: in RDFS, OWL and the CGs, there is a strong distinction between concept types and relations. Yet, a linguistic predicate may be considered both as a concept type as it is instantiated in dependency structures, and as a relation as its instances may link other instances. The simple semantic representation illustrated on figure 1 thus cannot be represented with these formalisms unless we use reification of n-ary relations. But then these formalisms lack logical semantics to reason with such relations.

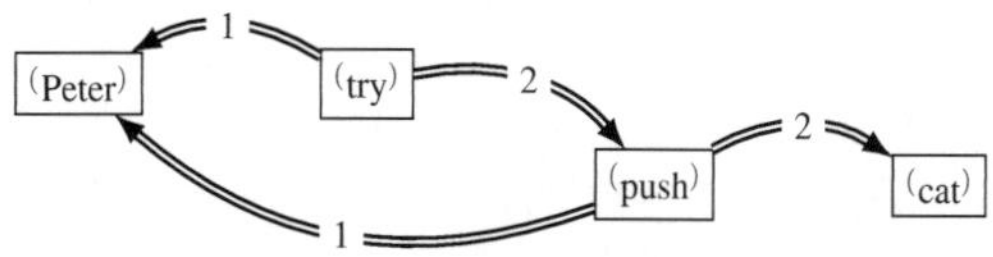

Figure 1: Semantic representation of sentence *Peter tries to push the cat.*

As the CGs formalism is the closest to the semantic networks, the following choice has been made to overcome these issues: *Modify the CGs formalism basis, and define transformations to syntaxes of Semantic Web formalisms for sharing and querying knowledge.* As we are to represent linguistic units of different nature (e.g., semantic units, lexical units, grammatical units, words), term *unit* has been chosen to be used in a generic manner, and the result of this adaptation is thus *the Unit Graphs (UGs) framework.*

3 Fundamental Concepts of the UGs Framework

First, for a specific Lexical Unit L, Mel'čuk (2004, p.5) distinguishes considering L in language (i.e., in the lexicon), or in speech (i.e., in an utterance). KR formalisms and the UGs formalism also do this distinction using types. In this paper and in the UGs formalism, there is thus a clear distinction between *units* (e.g., semantic unit, lexical unit), which will be represented in the UGs, and their *types* (e.g., semantic unit type, lexical unit type), which are roughly classes of units that share specific features. It is those types that will specify through their so-called actancial structure (Mel'čuk, 2004) how their instances (i.e., units) are to be linked to other units in a UG.

3.1 Hierarchy of Unit Types

The core of the UGs framework is a structure called *hierarchy of unit types* and noted $\mathcal{T}$, where unit types and their actantial structure are described. This structure is thoroughly described in (Lefrançois, 2013; Lefrançois and Gandon, 2013b) and studied in (Lefrançois and Gandon, 2013d).

Whether they are semantic, lexical or grammatical, unit types are assigned a set of *Actant Slots (ASlots)*, and every ASlot has a so-called *Actant*

[1]RDF - Resource Description Framework, c.f., `http://w3.org/RDF/`

[2]RDFS - RDF Schema, c.f., `http://www.w3.org/TR/rdf-schema/`

[3]OWL - Web Ontology Language, c.f., `http://www.w3.org/TR/owl2-overview/`

[4]SPARQL, c.f., `http://www.w3.org/TR/sparql11-overview/`

Symbol (ASymbol) which is chosen in a set denoted $S_{\mathcal{T}}$. $S_{\mathcal{T}}$ contains numbers for the semantic unit types, and other "classical" symbols for the other levels under consideration (e.g, roman numerals **I** to **VI** for the Deep Syntactic actants). The set of ASlots of a unit type t is represented by the set $\boldsymbol{\alpha}(t)$ of ASymbols these ASlots have. Moreover,

- some ASlots are obligatory, they form the set $\boldsymbol{\alpha_1}(t)$ of *Obligatory Actant Slots (OblASlots)*;
- other are prohibited, they form the set $\boldsymbol{\alpha_0}(t)$ of *Prohibited Actant Slots (ProASlots)*;
- the ASlots that are neither obligatory nor prohibited are said to be optional, they form the set $\boldsymbol{\alpha_?}(t)$ of *Optional Actant Slots (OptASlots)*.

Finally, every unit type t has a signature function ς_t that assigns to every ASlot of t a unit type, which characterises units that fill such a slot.

The set of unit types is then pre-ordered[5] by a specialization relation $\lesssim$, and for mathematical reasons as one goes down the hierarchy of unit types the actantial structure of unit types may only become more and more specific: (i) some ASlot may appear, be optional a moment, and at some points become obligatory or prohibited; (ii) the signatures may only become more specific.

3.2 Hierarchy of Circumstantial Symbols

UGs include actantial relations, which are considered of type predicate-argument and are described in the hierarchy of unit types. Now UGs also include circumstantial relations which are considered of type instance-instance. Example of such relations are the deep syntactic representation relations **ATTR**, **COORD**, **APPEND** of the MTT, but we may also use such relations to represent the link between a lexical unit and its associated surface semantic unit for instance. Circumstantial relations are labelled by symbols chosen in a set of so-called *Circumstantial Symbols (CSymbols)*, denoted $S_{\mathcal{C}}$, and their categories and usage are described in a hierarchy denoted $\mathcal{C}$, that has been formally defined in (Lefrançois and Gandon, 2013a).

3.3 Unit Graphs

UGs are defined over a so-called support, $\mathcal{S} \stackrel{\text{def}}{=} (\mathcal{T}, \mathcal{C}, \boldsymbol{M})$ where $\mathcal{T}$ is a hierarchy of unit types, $\mathcal{C}$ is a hierarchy of CSymbols, and $\boldsymbol{M}$ is a set of *unit identifiers*.

A UG G defined over a support $\mathcal{S}$ is a tuple denoted $G \stackrel{\text{def}}{=} (U, \boldsymbol{l}, A, C, Eq)$, where U is the set of unit nodes, $\boldsymbol{l}$ is a labelling mapping over U that associate every unit node with a unit type and one or more unit identifiers, A and C are respectively actantial and circumstantial triples, and Eq is a set of asserted unit node equivalences. Unit nodes are illustrated by rectangles with their label written inside, actantial triples are illustrated by double arrows, circumstantial triples are illustrated by simple arrows, and asserted unit node equivalences are illustrated by dashed arrows.

For instance, figure 1 is a semantic representation of sentence *Peter tries to push the cat.* in which units are typed by singletons and ASymbols are numbers, in accordance with the MTT. Figure 2 is a simplified deep syntactic representation of *Peter is gently pushing the cat.* In this figure unit nodes u_2 and u_4 are typed by singletons, and only unit node u_2 is not generic and has a marker: $\{Peter\}$. P is composed of $(u_1, \mathbf{I}, u_2)$ and $(u_1, \mathbf{II}, u_3)$, where **I** and **II** are ASymbols. C is composed of $(u_1, \mathbf{ATTR}, u_4)$ where **ATTR** is a CSymbol. In the relation Eq there is (u_1, u_1), (u_2, u_2), and (u_3, u_3).

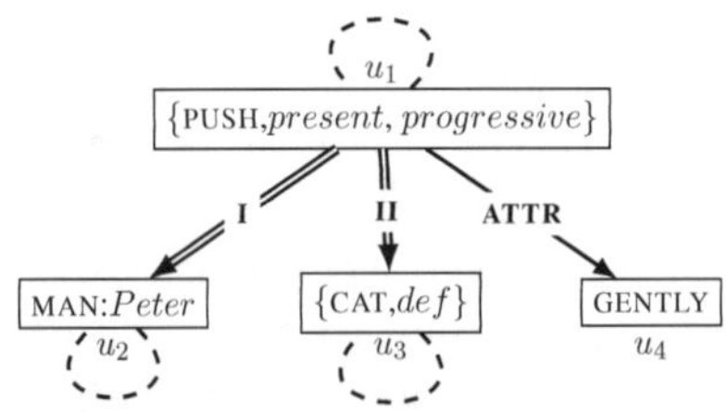

Figure 2: Deep syntactic representation of sentence *Peter is gently pushing the cat.*

UGs so defined are the core dependency structures of the UGs mathematical framework.

4 Unit Graphs and the Meaning-Text Theory

4.1 A Deep-Semantic Representation Level

As the unit types hierarchy $\mathcal{T}$ is driven by the actantial structure of unit types, and as semantic ASymbols are numbers, the pre-order over unit types at the semantic level represents a specialization of the actantial structure, and not of meanings. For instance, the french lexical unit INSTRUMENT

[5]A pre-order is a reflexive and transitive binary relation.

(en: instrument) has a Semantic ASlot 1 that corresponds to the activity for which the instrument is designed. Now PEIGNE (en: comb) has a stricter meaning than INSTRUMENT, and also two Semantic ASlots: 1 correspond to the person that uses the comb, and 2 is a split variable[6] that corresponds either to the hair or to the person that is to be combed. Then semantic unit type $^{(}\text{peigne}^{)}$ cannot be more specific than $^{(}\text{instrument}^{)}$ in the hierarchy of unit types because the signature of its ASlot 1 is not more specific than the signature of the ASlot 1 of $^{(}\text{instrument}^{)}$, i.e., $\varsigma_{(\text{peigne})}(1) = {}^{(}\text{person}^{)} \not\lesssim {}^{(}\text{activity}^{)} = \varsigma_{(\text{instrument})}(1)$. In fact, the meaning of ASlot 1 is not the same for $^{(}\text{instrument}^{)}$ and $^{(}\text{peigne}^{)}$.

Lefrançois and Gandon (2013b) therefore introduced a deeper level of representation to describe meanings: the *deep semantic level*, and defined the deep and surface semantic unit types and their actantial structure. The Deep Semantic Unit Type (DSemUT) associated with a Lexical Unit Type (LexUT) L is denoted $^{/}\text{L}^{\backslash}$. So that the ASlots of deep semantic unit types convey meanings, the set of ASsymbols that is used to symbolize ASlots at this level is a set of lexicalized semantic roles (e.g., $agent$, $combedhair$, $combedperson$). For instance the DSemUT $^{/}\text{instrument}^{\backslash}$ associated with the LexUT INSTRUMENT may have an ASlot arbitrarily symbolized $activity$, which would be inherited by the DSemUT $^{/}\text{peigne}^{\backslash}$. Then $^{/}\text{peigne}^{\backslash}$ also introduces three new ASlots: one arbitrarily symbolized $possessor$ that corresponds to the ASlot 1 of $^{(}\text{peigne}^{)}$, and two arbitrarily symbolized $combedhair$, and $combedperson$ that correspond to the ASlot 2 of $^{(}\text{peigne}^{)}$.

Actually, one may need to introduce a new ASymbol every time a Semantic ASlot that conveys a new meaning is introduced. The set of semantic roles thus cannot be bound to a small set of universal semantic roles.

4.2 Lexicographic Definitions

It is at the deep semantic representation level that one may represent the actual meaning of a LexUT L. The lexicographic definition of L corresponds to the definition of its associated DSemUT $^{/}\text{L}^{\backslash}$, which is roughly an equivalence between two deep semantic UGs. Unit type definitions have been formally defined in (Lefrançois and Gandon, 2013a), and the definition of $^{/}\text{L}^{\backslash}$ is a triple $D_{/\text{L}\backslash} \stackrel{\text{def}}{=} (D^{-}_{/\text{L}\backslash}, D^{+}_{/\text{L}\backslash}, \kappa)$, where (roughly):

- $D^{-}_{/\text{L}\backslash}$ represents only a central unit node typed with $^{/}\text{L}^{\backslash}$, and some other unit nodes that fill some of the ASlots of $^{/}\text{L}^{\backslash}$;
- $D^{+}_{/\text{L}\backslash}$ is a UG called the *expansion* of $^{/}\text{L}^{\backslash}$,
- there is no circumstantial triple in these two UGs because circumstantials must not be part of the lexicographic definition of a LexUT.
- κ is a mapping from the unit nodes of $D^{-}_{/\text{L}\backslash}$ to some unit nodes of $D^{+}_{/\text{L}\backslash}$.

Figure 3 is an example of lexicographic definition of PEIGNE: an instrument that a person X uses to untangle the hair Y_1 of a person Y_2.

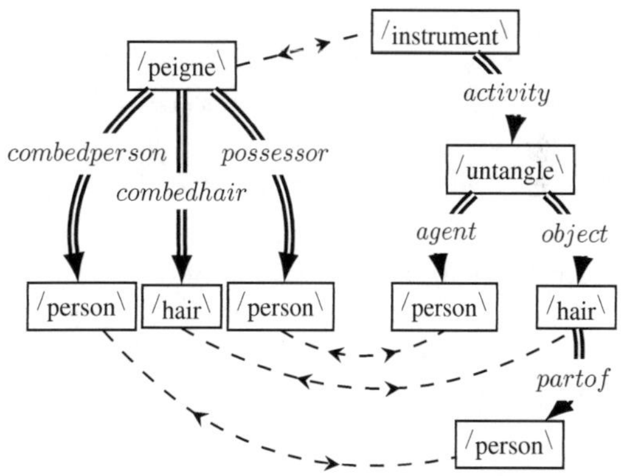

Figure 3: Lexicographic definition of PEIGNE.

Intuitively, a definition corresponds to two reciprocal rules. If there is the defined PUT in a UG then one may infer its definition, and vice versa. A set of unit type definitions $\mathcal{D}$ may thus be added to the unit types hierarchy.

Lefrançois et al. (2013) illustrated how the UGs framework may be used to edit lexicographic definitions in the RELIEF lexicographic edition project (Lux-Pogodalla and Polguère, 2011). Lexical Units are assigned a semantic label that may be considered as a deep semantic unit type and to which one may assign an actantial structure. A lexicographer may then manipulate nodes in a graphical user interface so as to little by little construct a deep semantic UG that represents the decomposition of the DSemUT associated with the defined LexUT. A prototype web application has been developed, and a demonstration is available online: `http://wimmics.inria.fr/doc/video/UnitGraphs/editor1.html`. We currently lead an ergonomic study in partnership

[6]For details about split Semantic ASlots, see (Mel'čuk, 2004, p.43)

with actors of the RELIEF project in order to enhance the workflow of this prototype.

5 Reasoning in the Unit Graphs Framework

The prime decision problem of the UGs framework is the following: *Considering two UGs G and H defined over the same support $\mathcal{S}$, does the knowledge of G entails the knowledge of H ?*

5.1 Reasoning with UGs-Homomorphisms

Lefrançois and Gandon (2013a) proposed to use the notion of UGs homomorphism to define this entailment problem. There is a homomorphism from a UG H to a UG G if and only if there is a homomorphism from the underlying oriented labelled graphs of H to that of G.

Now one need to define the notion of knowledge of a UG. In fact, the UGs framework makes the open-world assumption, which means that a UG along with the support on which it is defined represents explicit knowledge, and that additional knowledge may be inferred. Consider the UG $G = (U, \boldsymbol{l}, A, C, Eq)$ defined over the support $\mathcal{S}$ illustrated in figure 4a. Some knowledge in G is implicit:

1. two unit nodes u_1 and u_2 share a common unit marker $Mary$, so one may infer that they represent the same unit. (u_1, u_2) may be added to Eq.
2. every unit type is a subtype of the prime universal unit type $\top$, so one could add $\top$ to all the types of unit nodes in G.
3. there are two unit nodes v_1 and v_2 that fill the same ASlot $activity$ of the unit node typed /instrument\. So one may infer that v_1 and v_2 represent the same unit. Said otherwise, (v_1, v_2) may be added to Eq.
4. one may recognize the expansion of /peigne\ as defined in figure 3, so this type may be made explicit in the unit node typed /instrument\.

Each of the rules behind these cases explicit knowledge in G. More generally, Lefrançois and Gandon (2013a) listed a set of rules which defines the axiomatization of the UGs semantics. The process of applying this set of rules on a UG G until none of them has any effect is called closing G. Figure 4b illustrates the closure of G, where all of the inferable knowledge has been made explicit.

The notion of *entailment* may hence be defined as follows: G entails H, noted $G \vDash_{\mathrm{h}} H$, if and only if there is a homomorphism from H to the closure of G. Lefrançois and Gandon (2013a) illustrated problematic cases where the closure is infinite for finite UGs. If that occurs it makes the closure undecidable, along with the entailment problem. We are currently working of the definition of restrictions of the unit types hierarchy and the set of definitions in order to ensure that any UG has a finite closure.

5.2 Model Semantics for the UGs framework

Another approach to defining the entailment problem has been presented in (Lefrançois and Gandon, 2013c), using model semantics based on relational algebra. The model of a support $\mathcal{S} = (\mathcal{T}, \mathcal{C}, \boldsymbol{M})$ is a couple $M = (D, \delta)$, where D is a set called the domain of M, and δ is denoted the *interpretation function*. In order to deal with the problem of prohibited and optional ASlots, D contains a special element denoted $\bullet$ that represents *nothing*, plus at least one other element, and must be such that:

- M is a model of $\mathcal{T}$;
- M is a model of $\mathcal{C}$;
- for all unit identifier $m \in \boldsymbol{M}$, the interpretation of m is an object of the domain D except for the special *nothing* element;

Lefrançois and Gandon (2013c) listed the different equations that the interpretation function must satisfy so that a model is a model of a unit types hierarchy and of a CSymbols hierarchy.

A model of a UG G is a model of the support on which it is defined, augmented with an assignment function β, which is a mapping from the set of unit nodes of G to the domain D. Such a model needs to satisfy a list of equations so that it may be said to satisfy the unit graph G.

Then the notion of entailment is defined as classically done with model semantics: Let H and G be two UGs defined over a support $\mathcal{S}$. G *entails* H, or H is a *semantic consequence* of G, noted $G \vDash_{\mathrm{m}} H$, if and only if for any model (D, δ) of $\mathcal{S}$ and for any assignment β_G such that (D, δ, β_G) satisfies G, then there exists an assignment β_H of the unit nodes in H such that (D, δ, β_H) satisfies H.

There are multiple directions of research for the reasoning problem.

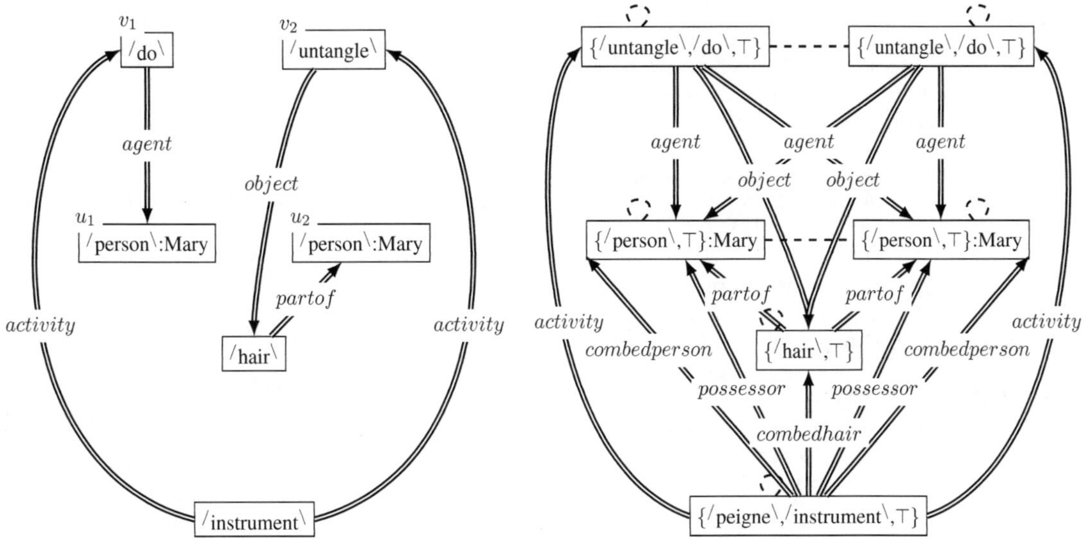

(a) Incomplete deep semantic representation G (b) Closure of the unit graph G

Figure 4: Closure of a UG.

- the definition of the model semantics of the UGs shall be completed so as to take lexicographic definitions into account.
- one need to define algorithms to construct a model that satisfy a UG, and to check the entailment of a UG by another.
- such algorithms may lead to an infinite domain. A condition over the unit types hierarchy and the lexicographic definitions must be found so as to ensure that the model is decidable for a finite UG.
- are the two entailment relations $\models_{\mathrm{h}}$ and $\models_{\mathrm{m}}$ equivalent ?

6 Conclusion

We thus introduced rationale of the new Unit Graphs Knowledge Representation formalism that is designed to formalize, in a knowledge engineering perspective, the dependency structures, the valency-based predicates, and lexicographic definitions in the ECD.

The strong coherence in the unit types hierarchy justifies the introduction of a deep semantic representation level that is deeper than the MTT semantic level, and in which one may represent the lexicographic definitions.

Finally, two different logical semantics have been provided for UGs and the prime entailment decision problem has been defined in two ways. More research is needed to determine if these two decision problems are equivalent, and what their complexity is.

There are other longer-term directions of research for the Unit Graphs framework:

We are working on a syntax based on semantic web standards for the different objects of the framework. Like WordNet today, the linguistic knowledge written with that syntax could be shared and queried on the web of linked data[7]. This would support their use as a highly structured lexical resource by consumers of the linked data cloud.

Rules have already been defined in the UGs framework. Let G_{DSem} be a deep semantic UG, we need algorithms to select and apply correspondence rules to transcribe G_{DSem} to a surface semantic UG G_{SSem} for instance.

We are working on defining generic rules to formally represent semantic derivations. This is a first step towards representing Lexical Functions that play a very important role in the MTT.

Finally, the design of the Unit Graphs framework is a first step towards Natural Language Processing applications. Future work include (semi-automatically) populating this model with linguistic data, and formulating classical NLP tasks in terms of UGs, such as machine translation, question answering, text summarization, and so on.

[7]The web of data is a W3C initiative, highly active today, `http://linkeddata.org`

References

Juri Apresian, Igor Boguslavsky, Leonid Iomdin, Alexander Lazursky, Vladimir Sannikov, Victor Sizov, and Leonid Tsinman. 2003. ETAP-3 linguistic processor: A full-fledged NLP implementation of the MTT. In *First International Conference on Meaning–Text Theory (MTT'2003)*, pages 279–288.

Lucie Barque and Alain Polguère. 2008. Enrichissement formel des définitions du Trésor de la Langue Française informatisé (TLFi) dans une perspective lexicographique. *Lexique*, 22.

Lucie Barque, Alexis Nasr, and Alain Polguère. 2010. From the Definitions of the 'Trésor de la Langue Française' To a Semantic Database of the French Language. In Fryske Akademy, editor, *Proceedings of the XIV Euralex International Congress*, Fryske Akademy, pages 245–252, Leeuwarden, Pays-Bas. Anne Dykstra et Tanneke Schoonheim, dir.

Igor Boguslavsky, Leonid Iomdin, and Viktor Sizov. 2004. Multilinguality in ETAP-3: reuse of lexical resources. In Gilles Sérasset, editor, *Proc. COLING 2004 Multilingual Linguistic Ressources*, pages 1–8, Geneva, Switzerland. COLING.

Igor Boguslavsky. 2011. Semantic Analysis Based on Linguistic and Ontological Resources. In Igor Boguslavsky and Leo Wanner, editors, *Proceedings of the 5th International Conference on Meaning-Text Theory (MTT'2011)*, pages 25–36, Barcelona, Spain. INALCO.

Bernd Bohnet and Leo Wanner. 2010. Open source graph transducer interpreter and grammar development environment. In *Proceedings of the Seventh International Conference on Language Resources and Evaluation (LREC'10)*, pages 19–21, Valletta, Malta. European Language Resources Association (ELRA).

Michel Chein and Marie-Laure Mugnier. 2008. *Graph-based Knowledge Representation: Computational Foundations of Conceptual Graphs*. Springer-Verlag New York Incorporated.

Sylvain Kahane and Alain Polguère. 2001. Formal foundation of lexical functions. In *Proceedings of ACL/EACL 2001 Workshop on Collocation*, pages 8–15.

Sylvain Kahane. 2003. The Meaning-Text Theory. *Dependency and Valency, An International Handbooks of Contemporary Research*, 25(1):546–569.

Maxime Lefrançois and Fabien Gandon. 2011. ILexicOn: Toward an ECD-Compliant Interlingual Lexical Ontology Described with Semantic Web Formalisms. In Igor Boguslavsky and Leo Wanner, editors, *Proceedings of the 5th International Conference on Meaning-Text Theory (MTT'2011)*, pages 155–164, Barcelona, Spain. INALCO.

Maxime Lefrançois and Fabien Gandon. 2013a. Reasoning with Dependency Structures and Lexicographic Definitions using Unit Graphs. In *Proc. of the 2nd International Conference on Dependency Linguistics (Depling'2013)*, Prague, Czech Republic. ACL Anthology.

Maxime Lefrançois and Fabien Gandon. 2013b. The Unit Graphs Framework: A graph-based Knowledge Representation Formalism designed for the Meaning-Text Theory. In *Proceedings of the 6th International Conference on Meaning-Text Theory (MTT'2013)*, Prague, Czech Republic.

Maxime Lefrançois and Fabien Gandon. 2013c. The Unit Graphs Framework: Foundational Concepts and Semantic Consequence. In *Proceedings of the 9th International Conference on Recent Advances in Natural Language Processing (RANLP'2013)*, Hissar, Bulgaria. ACL Anthology.

Maxime Lefrançois and Fabien Gandon. 2013d. The Unit Graphs Mathematical Framework. Research Report RR-8212, Inria.

Maxime Lefrançois, Romain Gugert, Fabien Gandon, and Alain Giboin. 2013. Application of the Unit Graphs Framework to Lexicographic Definitions in the RELIEF project. In *Proceedings of the 6th International Conference on Meaning-Text Theory (MTT'2013)*, Prague, Czech Republic.

Maxime Lefrançois. 2013. Représentation des connaissances du DEC: Concepts fondamentaux du formalisme des Graphes d'Unités. In *Actes de la 15ème Rencontre des Étudiants Chercheurs en Informatique pour le Traitement Automatique des Langues (RECITAL'2013)*, pages 164–177, Les Sables d'Olonne, France.

Veronika Lux-Pogodalla and Alain Polguère. 2011. Construction of a French Lexical Network: Methodological Issues. In *Proceedings of the International Workshop on Lexical Resources*, Ljubljana.

Igor Mel'čuk. 1996. Lexical Functions: A Tool for the Description of Lexical Relations in a Lexicon. In Leo Wanner, editor, *Lexical Functions in Lexicography and Natural Language Processing*, pages 37–102. Benjamins Academic Publishers, Amsterdam/Philadelphia.

Igor Mel'čuk. 2004. Actants in Semantics and Syntax I: Actants in Semantics. *Linguistics*, 42(1):247–291.

Igor Mel'čuk. 2006. Explanatory combinatorial dictionary. *Open Problems in Linguistics and Lexicography*, pages 225–355.

Alain Polguère. 2009. Lexical systems: graph models of natural language lexicons. *Language resources and evaluation*, 43(1):41–55.

John F Sowa. 1984. *Conceptual structures: information processing in mind and machine*. System programming series. Addison-Wesley Pub., Reading, MA.

The Unit Graphs Framework: Foundational Concepts and Semantic Consequence

Maxime Lefrançois and **Fabien Gandon**
Wimmics, Inria, I3S, CNRS, UNSA
2004 rte des Lucioles, BP. 93, 06902 Sophia Antipolis, France
{maxime.lefrancois,fabien.gandon}@inria.fr

Abstract

We are interested in a graph-based Knowledge Representation formalism that would allow for the representation, manipulation, query, and reasoning over dependency structures, and linguistic knowledge of the Explanatory and Combinatorial Dictionary in the Meaning-Text Theory framework. Neither the semantic web formalisms nor the conceptual graphs appear to be suitable for this task, and this led to the introduction of the new Unit Graphs framework. This paper first introduces the foundational concepts of this framework: Unit Graphs are defined over a support that contains: i) a hierarchy of unit types which is strongly driven by their actantial structure, ii) a hierarchy of circumstantial symbols, and iii) a set of unit identifiers. Then, this paper provides all of these objects with a model semantics that enables to define the notion of semantic consequence between Unit Graphs.

1 Introduction

We are interested in the ability to reason over dependency structures and linguistic knowledge of the Explanatory and Combinatorial Dictionary (ECD), which is the lexicon at the core of the Meaning-Text Theory (MTT) (Mel'čuk, 2006).

Some formalisation works have been led on the ECD. For instance Kahane and Polguère, 2001) proposed a formalization of Lexical Functions, and the Definiens project (Barque and Polguère, 2008; Barque et al., 2010) aims at formalizing lexicographic definitions with genus and specific differences for the TLFi[1]. Adding to these formalization works, the goal of the Unit Graphs formalism is to propose a formalization from a knowledge engineering perspective, compatible with standard Knowledge Representation (KR) formalisms. The term *formalization* here means not only *make non-ambiguous*, but also *make operational*, i.e., *such that it supports logical operations* (e.g., knowledge manipulation, query, reasoning). We thus adopt a knowledge engineering approach applied to the domain of the MTT.

At first sight, two existing KR formalisms seemed interesting for representing dependency structures: semantic web formalisms (RDF/S, OWL, SPARQL), and Conceptual Graphs (CGs) (Sowa, 1984; Chein and Mugnier, 2008). Both formalisms are based on directed labelled graph structures, and some research has been done towards using them to represent dependency structures and knowledge of the lexicon (OWL in (Lefrançois and Gandon, 2011; Boguslavsky, 2011), CGs at the conceptual level in (Bohnet and Wanner, 2010)). Yet Lefrançois, 2013) showed that neither of these KR formalisms can represent linguistic predicates. As the CG formalism is the closest to the semantic networks, the following choice has been made (Lefrançois, 2013): *Modify the CGs formalism basis, and define transformations to the RDF syntax for sharing, and querying knowledge.* As we are to represents linguistic units of different nature (e.g., semantic units, lexical units, grammatical units, words), term *unit* has been chosen to be used in a generic manner, and the result of this adaptation is thus *the Unit Graphs (UGs) framework.* The valency-based predicates are represented by unit types, and are described in a structure called the unit types hierarchy. Unit types specify through actant slots and signatures how their instances (i.e., units) may be linked to other units in a UG. Unit Graphs are then defined over a support that contains: i) a hierarchy of unit types which is strongly driven by their actantial structure, ii) a hierarchy of circumstantial sym-

[1]Trésor de la Langue Française informatisé, http://atilf.atilf.fr

bols, and iii) a set of unit identifiers.

Apart from giving an overview foundational concepts of the UGs framework, the main goal of this paper is to answer the following research question: *What semantics can be attributed to UGs, and how can we define the entailment problem for UGs ?*

The rest of this paper is organized as follows. Section 2 overviews the UGs framework: the hierarchy of unit types (§2.1), the hierarchy of circumstantial symbols (§2.2), and the Unit Graphs (§2.3). Then, section 3 provides all of these mathematical objects with a model, and finally the notion of semantic consequence between UGs is introduced (§3.4).

2 Background: overview of the Unit Graphs Framework

For a specific Lexical Unit L, (Mel'čuk, 2004, p.5) distinguishes considering L in language (i.e., in the lexicon), or in speech (i.e., in an utterance). KR formalisms and the UGs formalism also make this distinction using types. In this paper and in the UGs formalism, there is thus a clear distinction between *units* (e.g., semantic unit, lexical unit), which will be represented in the UGs, and their *types* (e.g., semantic unit type, lexical unit type), which are roughly classes of units for which specific features are shared. It is those types that specify through actant slots and signatures how their instances (i.e., units) are to be linked to other units in a UG.

2.1 Hierarchy of Unit Types

Unit types and their actantial structure are described in a structure called *hierarchy*, that specifies how units may, must, or must not be interlinked in a UG.

Definition 2.1. A hierarchy of unit types is denoted $\mathcal{T}$ and is defined by a tuple:

$$\mathcal{T} \stackrel{\text{def}}{=} (T_D, \boldsymbol{S}_\mathcal{T}, \boldsymbol{\gamma}, \boldsymbol{\gamma_1}, \boldsymbol{\gamma_0}, C_A, \perp_A^\sqcap, \{\varsigma_t\}_{t\in \boldsymbol{T}})$$

This structure has been thoroughly described in (Lefrançois and Gandon, 2013a; Lefrançois, 2013). Let us overview its components.

T_D is a set of *declared Primitive Unit Types (PUTs)*. This set is partitioned into linguistic PUTs of different nature (e.g., deep semantic, semantic, lexical). $\boldsymbol{S}_\mathcal{T}$ is a set of Actant Symbols (ASymbols). $\boldsymbol{\gamma}$ (resp1. $\boldsymbol{\gamma_1}$, resp2. $\boldsymbol{\gamma_0}$) assigns to every $s \in \boldsymbol{S}_\mathcal{T}$ its radix[2] (resp1. obligat[3], resp2. prohibet[4]) unit type $\boldsymbol{\gamma}(s)$ (resp1. $\boldsymbol{\gamma_1}(s)$, resp2. $\boldsymbol{\gamma_0}(s)$) that introduces (resp1. makes obligatory, resp2. makes prohibited) an Actant Slot (ASlot) of symbol s. The set of PUTs is denoted $\boldsymbol{T}$ and defined as the disjoint union of T_D, the ranges of $\boldsymbol{\gamma}$, $\boldsymbol{\gamma_1}$ and $\boldsymbol{\gamma_0}$, plus the *prime universal PUT* $\top$ and the *prime absurd PUT* $\perp$ (eq. 1).

$$\boldsymbol{T} \stackrel{\text{def}}{=} T_D \uplus \boldsymbol{\gamma}(\boldsymbol{S}_\mathcal{T}) \uplus \boldsymbol{\gamma_1}(\boldsymbol{S}_\mathcal{T}) \uplus \boldsymbol{\gamma_0}(\boldsymbol{S}_\mathcal{T}) \uplus \{\perp, \top\} \quad (1)$$

$\boldsymbol{T}$ is then pre-ordered by a relation $\lesssim$ which is computed from the set $C_A \subseteq \boldsymbol{T}^2$ of asserted PUTs comparisons. $t_1 \lesssim t_2$ models the fact that the PUT t_1 is more specific than the PUT t_2. Then a unit type has a set (that may be empty) of ASlots, whose symbols are chosen in the set $\boldsymbol{S}_\mathcal{T}$. Moreover, ASlots may be obligatory, prohibited, or optional. The set of ASlots (resp1. obligatory ASlots, resp2. prohibited ASlots, resp3. optional ASlots) of a PUT is thus defined as the set of their symbols $\boldsymbol{\alpha}(t) \subseteq \boldsymbol{S}_\mathcal{T}$ (resp1. $\boldsymbol{\alpha_1}(t)$, resp2. $\boldsymbol{\alpha_0}(t)$, resp3. $\boldsymbol{\alpha_?}(t)$).

The set of ASlots (resp1. obligatory ASlots, resp2. prohibited ASlots) of a PUT $t \in \boldsymbol{T}$ is defined as the set of ASymbol whose radix (resp1. obligat, resp2. prohibet) is more general or equivalent to t, and the set of optional ASlots of a PUT t is the set of ASlots that are neither obligatory nor prohibited. The number of ASlots of a PUT is denoted its *valency*. $\{\varsigma_t\}_{t\in\boldsymbol{T}}$, the set of signatures of PUTs, is a set of functions. For all PUT t, ς_t is a function that associates to every ASlot s of t a set of PUT $\varsigma_t(s)$ that characterises the type of the unit that fills this slot. Signatures participate in the specialization of the actantial structure of PUTs, which means that if $t_1 \lesssim t_2$ and s is a common ASlot of t_1 and t_2, the signature of t_1 for s must be more specific or equivalent than that of t_2. Hence $t_1 \lesssim t_2$ implies that the actancial structure of t_1 is more specific than the actantial structure of t_2.

Now a unit type may consist of several conjoint PUTs. We introduce the set $\boldsymbol{T}^\sqcap$ of possible *Conjunctive Unit Types (CUTs)* over $\boldsymbol{T}$ as the power-

[2] radix is a latin word that means ⟨root⟩.

[3] obligat is the conjugated form of the latin verb obligo, 3p sing. indic., ⟨it makes mandatory⟩.

[4] prohibet is the conjugated form of the latin verb prohibeo, 3p sing. indic., ⟨it prohibits⟩.

set[5] of $\boldsymbol{T}$. The set $\bot^{\cap}_{A}$ is the set of declared absurd CUTs that can not be instantiated. The definition of the actancial structure of PUTs is naturally extended to CUTs as follows:

$$\boldsymbol{\alpha}^{\cap}(t^{\cap}) \stackrel{\text{def}}{=} \bigcup_{t \in t^{\cap}} \boldsymbol{\alpha}(t) \quad (2)$$

$$\boldsymbol{\alpha_1}^{\cap}(t^{\cap}) \stackrel{\text{def}}{=} \bigcup_{t \in t^{\cap}} \boldsymbol{\alpha_1}(t) \quad (3)$$

$$\boldsymbol{\alpha_0}^{\cap}(t^{\cap}) \stackrel{\text{def}}{=} \bigcup_{t \in t^{\cap}} \boldsymbol{\alpha_0}(t) \quad (4)$$

$$\boldsymbol{\alpha_?}^{\cap}(t^{\cap}) \stackrel{\text{def}}{=} \boldsymbol{\alpha}^{\cap}(t^{\cap}) - \boldsymbol{\alpha_1}^{\cap}(t^{\cap}) - \boldsymbol{\alpha_0}^{\cap}(t^{\cap}) \quad (5)$$

$$\varsigma^{\cap}_{t^{\cap}}(s) \stackrel{\text{def}}{=} \bigcup_{t \in t^{\cap} | s \in \boldsymbol{\alpha}(t)} \varsigma_t(s) \quad (6)$$

Finally the pre-order $\lesssim$ over $\boldsymbol{T}$ is extended to a pre-order $\stackrel{\cap}{\lesssim}$ over $\boldsymbol{T}^{\cap}$ as defined by Lefrançois and Gandon, 2013a). Lefrançois and Gandon, 2013b) proved that in the hierarchy of unit types, if $t_1^{\cap} \stackrel{\cap}{\lesssim} t_2^{\cap}$ then the actantial structure of $t_1^{\cap}$ is more specific than that of $t_2^{\cap}$, except for some degenerated cases. Thus as one goes down the hierarchy of unit types, an ASlot with symbol s is introduced by the radix $\{\boldsymbol{\gamma}(s)\}$ and first defines an optional ASlot for any unit type $t^{\cap}$ more specific than $\{\boldsymbol{\gamma}(s)\}$, as long as $t^{\cap}$ is not more specific than the obligat $\{\boldsymbol{\gamma_1}(s)\}$ (resp. the prohibet $\{\boldsymbol{\gamma_0}(s)\}$) of s. If that happens, the ASlot becomes obligatory (resp. prohibited). Moreover, the signature of an ASlot may only become more specific.

2.2 Hierarchy of Circumstantial Symbols

Unit types specify how unit nodes are linked to other unit nodes in the UGs. As for any slot in a predicate, one ASlot of a unit may be filled by only one unit at a time. Now, one may also encounter dependencies of another type in some dependency structures: circumstantial dependencies (Mel'čuk, 2004). Circumstantial relations are considered of type instance-instance contrary to actantial relations. Example of such relations are the deep syntactic representation relations **ATTR**, **COORD**, **APPEND** of the MTT, but we may also define other such relations to represent the link between a lexical unit and its sense for instance.

We thus introduce a finite set of so-called Circumstantial Symbols (CSymbols) $\boldsymbol{S_{\mathcal{C}}}$ which is a set of binary relation symbols. In order to classify $\boldsymbol{S_{\mathcal{C}}}$ in sets and subsets, we introduce a partial order $\stackrel{\mathcal{C}}{\lesssim}$ over $\boldsymbol{S_{\mathcal{C}}}$. $\stackrel{\mathcal{C}}{\lesssim}$ is the reflexo-transitive closure of a set of *asserted comparisons* $\boldsymbol{C_{S_{\mathcal{C}}}} \subseteq \boldsymbol{T}^2$.

[5]The powerset of X is the set of all subsets of X: 2^X

Finally, to each CSymbol is assigned a signature that specifies the type of units that are linked through a relation having this symbol. The set of signatures of CSymbol $\{\boldsymbol{\sigma}_s\}_{s \in \boldsymbol{S_{\mathcal{C}}}}$ is a set of couples of CUTs: $\{(domain(s), range(s))\}_{s \in \boldsymbol{S_{\mathcal{C}}}}$. As one goes down the hierarchy of PUTs, we impose that the signature of a CSymbol may only become more specific (eq. 7).

$$s_1 \lesssim s_2 \Rightarrow \boldsymbol{\sigma}(s_1) \stackrel{\cap}{\lesssim} \boldsymbol{\sigma}(s_2) \quad (7)$$

We may hence introduce the hierarchy of CSymbols:

Definition 2.2. The hierarchy of CSymbols, denoted $\mathcal{C} \stackrel{\text{def}}{=} (\boldsymbol{S_{\mathcal{C}}}, \boldsymbol{C_{S_{\mathcal{C}}}}, \mathcal{T}, \{\boldsymbol{\sigma}_s\}_{s \in \boldsymbol{S_{\mathcal{C}}}})$, is composed of a finite set of CSymbols $\boldsymbol{S_{\mathcal{C}}}$, a set of declared comparisons of CSymbol $\boldsymbol{C_{S_{\mathcal{C}}}}$, a hierarchy of CUTs $\mathcal{T}$, and a set of signatures of the CSymbols $\{\boldsymbol{\sigma}_s\}_{s \in \boldsymbol{S_{\mathcal{C}}}}$.

2.3 Definition of Unit Graphs (UGs)

The UGs represent different types of dependency structures. Parallel with the Conceptual Graphs, UGs are defined over a so-called *support*.

Definition 2.3. A UGs *support* is denoted $\mathcal{S} \stackrel{\text{def}}{=} (\mathcal{T}, \mathcal{C}, \boldsymbol{M})$ and is composed of a hierarchy of unit types $\mathcal{T}$, a hierarchy of circumstantial symbols $\mathcal{C}$, and a set of unit identifiers $\boldsymbol{M}$. Every element of $\boldsymbol{M}$ identifies a specific unit, but multiple elements of $\boldsymbol{M}$ may identify the same unit.

In a UG, unit nodes that are typed and marked are interlinked by dependency relations that are either actantial or circumstantial.

Definition 2.4. A UG G defined over a UG-support $\mathcal{S}$ is a tuple denoted $G \stackrel{\text{def}}{=} (U, \boldsymbol{l}, A, C, Eq)$ where U is the set of unit nodes, $\boldsymbol{l}$ is a labelling mapping over U, A and C are respectively actantial and circumstantial triples, and Eq is a set of asserted unit node equivalences.

Let us detail the components of G.

U is the set of *unit nodes*. Every unit node represents a specific unit, but multiple unit nodes may represent the same unit. Unit nodes are typed and marked so as to respectively specify what CUT they have and what unit they represent. The marker of a unit node is a set of unit identifiers for mathematical reasons. The set of *unit node markers* is denoted $\boldsymbol{M}^{\cap}$ and is the powerset[5] of $\boldsymbol{M}$. If a unit node is marked by $\varnothing$, it is said to be *generic*, and the represented unit is unknown. On the other hand, if a unit node is marked $\{m_1, m_2\}$, then the unit identifiers m_1 and m_2 actually identify the same unit. $\boldsymbol{l}$ is thus a labelling mapping over U that assigns to each unit node $u \in U$ a couple $\boldsymbol{l}(u) = (t^\cap, m^\cap) \in \boldsymbol{T}^\cap \times \boldsymbol{M}^\cap$ of a CUT and a unit node marker. We denote $t^\cap = type(u)$ and $m^\cap = marker(u)$.

A is the set of *actantial triples* $(u, s, v) \in U \times \boldsymbol{S_T} \times U$. For all $a = (u, s, v) \in A$, the unit represented by v fills the ASlot s of the unit represented by u. We denote $u = governor(a)$, $s = symbol(a)$ and $v = actant(a)$. We also denote $arc(a) = (u, v)$.

C is the set of *circumstantial triples* $(u, s, v) \in U \times \boldsymbol{S_C} \times U$. For all $c = (u, s, v) \in C$, the unit represented by u governs the unit represented by v with respect to s. We denote $u = governor(c)$, $s = symbol(c)$ and $v = circumstantial(c)$. We also denote $arc(c) = (u, v)$.

$Eq \subseteq U^2$ is the set of so-called *asserted unit node equivalences*. For all $(u_1, u_2) \in U^2$, $(u_1, u_2) \in Eq$ means that u_1 and u_2 represent the same unit. The Eq relation is not an equivalence relation over unit nodes[6]. We thus distinguish explicit and implicit knowledge.

UGs so defined are the core dependency structures of the UGs mathematical framework. On top of these basic structures, one may define for instance rules and lexicographic definitions. Due to space limitation we will not introduce such advanced aspects of the UGs formalism, and we will provide a model to UGs defined over a support that does not contain definitions of PUTs.

3 Model Semantic for UGs

3.1 Model of a Support

In this section we will provide the UGs framework with a model semantic based on a relational algebra. Let us first introduce the definition of the model of a support.

Definition 3.1 (Model of a support). Let $\mathcal{S} = (\mathcal{T}, \mathcal{C}, \boldsymbol{M})$ be a support. A model of $\mathcal{S}$ is a couple $M = (D, \delta)$. D is a set called the domain of M that contains a special element denoted $\bullet$ that represents *nothing*, plus at least one other element. δ is denoted the *interpretation function* and must be such that:

- M is a model of $\mathcal{T}$;
- M is a model of $\mathcal{C}$;
- $\forall m \in \boldsymbol{M}, \delta(m) \in D \setminus \bullet$;

This definition requires the notion of model of a unit types hierarchy, and model of a CSymbols hierarchy. We will sequentially introduce these notions in the following sections.

3.2 Model of a Hierarchy of Unit Types

The interpretation function δ associates with any PUT $t \in \boldsymbol{T}$ a relation $\delta(\{t\})$ of arity $1 + valency(t)$ with the following set of attributes (eq. 8):

- a primary attribute denoted 0 ($0 \notin \boldsymbol{S_T}$) that provides $\{t\}$ with the semantics of a class;
- an attribute for each of its ASlot in $\boldsymbol{\alpha}(t)$ that provides $\{t\}$ with the dual semantics of a relation.

$$\forall t \in \boldsymbol{T}, \delta(\{t\}) \subseteq D^{1+valency(t)} \text{ with attributes } \{0\} \cup \boldsymbol{\alpha}(t) \tag{8}$$

Every tuple r of $\delta(\{t\})$ can be identified to a mapping, still denoted r, from the attribute set $\{0\} \cup \boldsymbol{\alpha}(t)$ to the universe D. r describes how a unit of type $\{t\}$ is linked to its actants. $r(0)$ is the unit itself, and for all $s \in \boldsymbol{\alpha}(t)$, $r(s)$ is the unit that fills ASlot s of $r(0)$. If $r(s) = \bullet$, then *there is no unit* that fills ASlot s of $r(0)$. A given unit may be described at most once in $\delta(\{t\})$, so 0 is a unique key in the interpretation of every PUT:

$$\forall t \in \boldsymbol{T}, \forall r_1, r_2 \in \delta(\{t\}), \quad r_1(0) = r_2(0) \Rightarrow r_1 = r_2 \tag{9}$$

$\top$ must be the type of every unit, except for the special *nothing* element $\bullet$, and $\bot$ must be the type of no unit. As the projection $\pi_0\delta(\{t\})$ on the main attribute 0 represents the set of units having type $\{t\}$, equations 10 and 11 model these restrictions.

$$\pi_0\delta(\{\top\}) = D \setminus \bullet; \tag{10}$$
$$\delta(\{\bot\}) = \varnothing \tag{11}$$

The ASlot s of the obligat $\boldsymbol{\gamma_1}(s)$ must be filled by some unit, but no unit may fill ASlot s of the prohibet $\boldsymbol{\gamma_0}(s)$. As for every $s \in \boldsymbol{\alpha}(t)$, the projection $\pi_s\delta(\{t\})$ represents the set of units that fill the ASlot s of some unit that has type t, equations 12 and 13 model these restrictions.

[6]An equivalent relation is a reflexive, symmetric, and transitive relation.

$$\forall s \in \boldsymbol{S}_{\mathcal{T}}, \bullet \notin \pi_s\delta(\{\boldsymbol{\gamma_1}(s)\}); \quad (12)$$

$$\forall s \in \boldsymbol{S}_{\mathcal{T}}, \pi_s\delta(\{\boldsymbol{\gamma_0}(s)\}) = \{\bullet\}; \quad (13)$$

Now if a unit $i \in D$ is of type $\{t_1\}$ and t_1 is more specific than t_2, then the unit is also of type $\{t_2\}$, and the description of i in $\delta(\{t_2\})$ must correspond to the description of i in $\delta(\{t_1\})$. Equivalently, the projection of $\delta(\{t_1\})$ on the attributes of $\delta(\{t_2\})$ must be a sub-relation of $\delta(\{t_2\})$:

$$\forall t_1 \lesssim t_2, \quad \pi_{\{0\}\cup\boldsymbol{\alpha}(t_2)}\delta(\{t_1\}) \subseteq \delta(\{t_2\}) \quad (14)$$

The interpretation of a CUT is the join of the interpretation of its constituting PUTs, except for $\varnothing$ which has the same interpretation as $\{\top\}$, and asserted absurd CUTs $t^\cap \in \perp^\sqcap_A$ that contain no unit.

$$\forall t^\cap \in \boldsymbol{T}^\cap \setminus \varnothing - \perp^\sqcap_A, \quad \delta(t^\cap) = \bowtie_{t \in t^\cap} \delta(\{t\}) \quad (15)$$

$$\delta(\varnothing) = \delta(\{\top\}) \quad (16)$$

$$\forall t^\cap \in \perp^\sqcap_A, \delta(t^\cap) = \varnothing \quad (17)$$

Finally, for every unit of type $\{t\}$ and for every ASlot of t, the unit that fills ASlot s must be either *nothing*, or a unit of type $\boldsymbol{\varsigma}_t(s)$:

$$\forall t \in \boldsymbol{T}, \forall s \in \boldsymbol{\alpha}(t), \quad \pi_s\delta(\{t\}) \setminus \bullet \subseteq \pi_0\delta(\boldsymbol{\varsigma}_t(s)) \quad (18)$$

We may now define the model of a unit type hierarchy.

Definition 3.2. Let be a unit types hierarchy $\mathcal{T} = (T_D, \boldsymbol{S}_{\mathcal{T}}, \boldsymbol{\gamma}, \boldsymbol{\gamma_1}, \boldsymbol{\gamma_0}, C_A, \perp^\sqcap_A, \{\boldsymbol{\varsigma}_t\}_{t\in\boldsymbol{T}})$. A model of $\mathcal{T}$ is a couple $M = (D, \delta)$ such that the interpretation function δ satisfies equations 8 to 18.

3.3 Model of a Hierarchy of Circumstantial Symbols

So as to be also a model of a CSymbols hierarchy, the interpretation function δ must be extended and further restricted as follows.

The interpretation function δ associates with every CSymbol $s \in \boldsymbol{S}_{\mathcal{C}}$ a binary relation $\delta(s)$ with two attributes : gov which stands for governor, and $circ$ which stands for circumstantial.

$$\forall s \in \boldsymbol{S}_{\mathcal{C}}, \delta(s) \subseteq (D \setminus \bullet)^2, \quad \text{a relation with attributes } \{gov, circ\}; \quad (19)$$

Parallel with binary relations in the semantic model of the CGs formalism, if a CSymbol s_1 is more specific than another CSymbol s_2, then the interpretation of s_1 must be included in the interpretation of s_2.

$$\forall s_1, s_2 \in \boldsymbol{S}_{\mathcal{C}}, s_1 \overset{\mathcal{C}}{\lesssim} s_2 \Rightarrow \delta(s_1) \subseteq \delta(s_2) \quad (20)$$

Finally, the type of the units that are linked through a CSymbol s must correspond to the signature of s.

$$\forall s \in \boldsymbol{S}_{\mathcal{C}}, \pi_{gov}\delta(s) \subseteq \pi_0\delta(domain(s)); \quad (21)$$

$$\forall s \in \boldsymbol{S}_{\mathcal{C}}, \pi_{circ}\delta(s) \subseteq \pi_0\delta(range(s)); \quad (22)$$

We may thus define the model of a CSymbols hierarchy.

Definition 3.3 (Model of a Circumstantial Dependency Symbols Hierarchy)**.** Let be a CSymbols hierarchy $\mathcal{C} = (\boldsymbol{S}_{\mathcal{C}}, \boldsymbol{C}_{\boldsymbol{S}_{\mathcal{C}}}, \mathcal{T}, \{\boldsymbol{\sigma}_s\}_{s\in\boldsymbol{S}_{\mathcal{C}}})$. A model of $\mathcal{C}$ is a model $M = (D, \delta)$ of $\mathcal{T}$ such that the interpretation function δ satisfies equations 19 to 22.

3.4 Model Satisfying a UG and Semantic Consequence

Now that the model of a support is fully defined, we may define the model of a UG. A model of a UG is a model of the support on which it is defined, augmented with an *assignment* mapping over unit nodes that assigns to every unit node an element of D.

Definition 3.4 (Model of a UG)**.** Let $G = (U, \boldsymbol{l}, A, C, Eq)$ be a UG defined over a support $\mathcal{S}$. A model of G is a triple (D, δ, β) where:

- (D, δ) is a model of $\mathcal{S}$;
- β, called an *assignment*, is a mapping from U to D.

So as to satisfy the UG, the assignment β must satisfy a set of requirements. First, if a unit node $u \in U$ has a marker $m \in marker(u)$, then the assignment of u must correspond to the interpretation of m.

$$\forall u \in U, \forall m \in marker(u), \beta(u) = \delta(m) \quad (23)$$

Then, the assignment of any unit node u must belong to the set of units that have type $type(u)$.

$$\forall u \in U, \beta(u) \in \pi_0\delta(type(u)) \quad (24)$$

For every actantial triple $(u, s, v) \in A$, and as $\{\boldsymbol{\gamma}(s)\}$ is the CUT that introduces a ASlot s, the interpretation $\delta(\{\boldsymbol{\gamma}(s)\})$ must reflect the fact that the unit represented by v fills the actant slot s of the unit represented by u.

$$\begin{aligned}&\forall(u, s, v) \in A,\\ &\quad \pi_{0,s}\delta(\{\boldsymbol{\gamma}(s)\}) = \{(\beta(u), \beta(v))\}\end{aligned} \quad (25)$$

Similarly, for every circumstantial triple $(u, s, v) \in C$, the interpretation of s must reveal the fact that the unit represented by v depends on the unit represented by u with respect to s.

$$\forall(u, s, v) \in C, (\beta(u), \beta(v)) \in \delta(s) \quad (26)$$

Finally, if two unit nodes are asserted to be equivalent, then the unit they represent are the same and their assignment must be the same.

$$\forall(u_1, u_2) \in Eq, \beta(u_1) = \beta(u_2) \quad (27)$$

We may now define the notion of satisfaction of a UG by a model.

Definition 3.5 (Model satisfying a UG)**.** Let $G = (U, \boldsymbol{l}, A, C, Eq)$ be a UG defined over a support $\mathcal{S}$, and (D, δ, β) be a model of G. (D, δ, β) is a *model satisfying* G, noted $(D, \delta, \beta) \models_{\mathrm{m}} G$, if β is an assignment that satisfies equations 23 to 27.

Using the notion of a support model and a UG model it is possible to define an entailment relation between UGs as follows.

Definition 3.6 (Entailment and equivalence)**.** Let H and G be two UGs defined over a support $\mathcal{S}$.

- G *entails* H, or H is a *semantic consequence* of G, noted $G \models_{\mathrm{m}} H$, if and only if for any model (D, δ) of $\mathcal{S}$ and for any assignment β_G such that $(D, \delta, \beta_G) \models_{\mathrm{m}} G$, then there exists an assignment β_H of the unit nodes in H such that $(D, \delta, \beta_H) \models_{\mathrm{m}} H$.
- H and G are *model-equivalent*, noted $H \equiv_{\mathrm{m}} G$, if and only if $H \models_{\mathrm{m}} G$ and $G \models_{\mathrm{m}} H$.

4 Conclusion

We thus studied how to formalize, in a knowledge engineering perspective, the dependency structures and the valency-based predicates. We gave an overview of the foundational concepts of the new graph-based Unit Graphs KR formalism. The valency-based predicates are represented by unit types, and are described in a unit types hierarchy. Circumstantial relations are another kind of dependency relation that are described in a hierarchy, and along with a set of unit identifiers these two structures form a UGs support on which UGs may be defined.

We then provided these foundational structures with a model, in the logical sense, using a relational algebra. We dealt with the problem of prohibited and optional actant slots by adding a special *nothing* element • in the domain of the model, and listed the different equations that the interpretation function must satisfy so that a model satisfies a UG. We finally introduced the notion of semantic consequence, which is a first step towards reasoning with dependency structure in the UGs framework.

We identify three future directions of research.

- We did not introduce the definition of PUTs that are to model lexicographic definitions in the ECD and shall be included to the support. The definition of the model semantics of the UGs shall be completed so as to take these into account.
- A UG represents explicit knowledge that only partially define the interpretations of unit types, CSymbols, and unit identifiers. One need to define algorithms to complete the model, so as to check the entailment of a UG by another.
- We know from ongoing works that such an algorithm may lead to an infinite domain. A condition over the unit types hierarchy must be found so as to ensure that the model is decidable for a finite UG.

References

Barque, L., Nasr, A., and Polguère, A. (2010). From the Definitions of the 'Trésor de la Langue Française' To a Semantic Database of the French Language. In Fryske Akademy, editor, *Proceedings of the XIV Euralex International Congress*, Fryske Akademy, pages 245–252, Leeuwarden, Pays-Bas. Anne Dykstra et Tanneke Schoonheim, dir.

Barque, L. and Polguère, A. (2008). Enrichissement formel des définitions du Trésor de la Langue Française informatisé (TLFi) dans une perspective lexicographique. *Lexique*, 22.

Boguslavsky, I. (2011). Semantic Analysis Based on Linguistic and Ontological Resources. In Boguslavsky, I. and Wanner, L., editors, *Proceedings of the 5th International Conference on Meaning-Text Theory (MTT'2011)*, pages 25–36, Barcelona, Spain. INALCO.

Bohnet, B. and Wanner, L. (2010). Open source graph transducer interpreter and grammar development environment. In *Proceedings of the Seventh International Conference on Language Resources and Evaluation (LREC'10)*, pages 19–21, Valletta, Malta. European Language Resources Association (ELRA).

Chein, M. and Mugnier, M.-L. (2008). *Graph-based Knowledge Representation: Computational Foundations of Conceptual Graphs*. Springer-Verlag New York Incorporated.

Kahane, S. and Polguère, A. (2001). Formal foundation of lexical functions. In *Proceedings of ACL/EACL 2001 Workshop on Collocation*, pages 8–15.

Lefrançois, M. (2013). Représentation des connaissances du DEC: Concepts fondamentaux du formalisme des Graphes d'Unités. In *Actes de la 15ème Rencontre des Étudiants Chercheurs en Informatique pour le Traitement Automatique des Langues (RECITAL'2013)*, pages 164–177, Les Sables d'Olonne, France.

Lefrançois, M. and Gandon, F. (2011). ILexicOn: Toward an ECD-Compliant Interlingual Lexical Ontology Described with Semantic Web Formalisms. In Boguslavsky, I. and Wanner, L., editors, *Proceedings of the 5th International Conference on Meaning-Text Theory (MTT'2011)*, pages 155–164, Barcelona, Spain. INALCO.

Lefrançois, M. and Gandon, F. (2013a). The Unit Graphs Framework: A graph-based Knowledge Representation Formalism designed for the Meaning-Text Theory. In *Proceedings of the 6th International Conference on Meaning-Text Theory (MTT'2013)*, Prague, Czech Republic.

Lefrançois, M. and Gandon, F. (2013b). The Unit Graphs Mathematical Framework. Research Report RR-8212, Inria.

Mel'čuk, I. (2004). Actants in Semantics and Syntax I: Actants in Semantics. *Linguistics*, 42(1):247–291.

Mel'čuk, I. (2006). Explanatory combinatorial dictionary. *Open Problems in Linguistics and Lexicography*, pages 225–355.

Sowa, J. F. (1984). *Conceptual structures: information processing in mind and machine*. System programming series. Addison-Wesley Pub., Reading, MA.

Confidence Estimation for Knowledge Base Population

Xiang Li
Computer Science Department
New York University
xiangli@cs.nyu.edu

Ralph Grishman
Computer Science Department
New York University
grishman@cs.nyu.edu

Abstract

Information extraction systems automatically extract structured information from machine-readable documents, such as newswire, web, and multimedia. Despite significant improvement, the performance is far from perfect. Hence, it is useful to accurately estimate confidence in the correctness of the extracted information. Using the Knowledge Base Population Slot Filling task as a case study, we propose a confidence estimation model based on the Maximum Entropy framework, obtaining an average precision of 83.5%, Pearson coefficient of 54.2%, and 2.3% absolute improvement in F-measure score through a weighted voting strategy.

1 Introduction

Despite significant progress in recent years, Information Extraction (IE) technologies are still far from completely reliable. Errors result from the fact that language itself is ambiguous as well as methodological and technical limitations (Gandrabur et al., 2006). Therefore, evaluating the probability that the extracted information is correct can contribute to improve IE system performance. Confidence Estimation (CE) is a generic machine learning rescoring approach for measuring the probability of correctness of the outputs, and usually adds a layer on top of the baseline system to analyze the outputs using additional information or models (Gandrabur et al., 2006). There is previous work in IE using probabilistic and heuristic methods to estimate confidence for extracting fields using a sequential model, but to the best of our knowledge, this work is the first probabilistic CE model for the multi-stage systems employed for the Knowledge Base Population (KBP) Slot Filling task (Section 2).

The goal of Slot Filling (SF) is to collect information from a corpus of news and web documents to determine a set of predefined attributes ("slots") for given person and organization entities (Ji et al., 2011a) (Section 3). Many existing methodologies have been used to address the SF task, such as Distant Supervision (Min et al., 2012) and Question Answering (Chen et al., 2010), and each method has its own strengths and weaknesses. Many current KBP SF systems actually consist of several independent SF pipelines. The system combines intermediate responses generated from different pipelines into final slot fills. Since these intermediate outputs may be highly redundant, if confidence values can be associated, it will definitely help re-ranking and aggregation. For this purpose, we require comparable confidence values from disparate machine learning models or different slot filling strategies.

Robust probabilistic machine learning models are capable of accurate confidence estimation because of their intelligent handling of uncertainty information. In this paper, we use the Maximum Entropy (MaxEnt) framework (Berger et al., 1996) to automatically predict the correctness of KBP SF intermediate responses (Section 4). Results achieve an average precision of 83.5%, Pearson's r of 54.2%, and 2.3% absolute improvement in final F-measure score through a weighted voting system (Section 5).

2 Related Work

Confidence estimation is a generic machine learning approach for measuring confidence of a given output, and many different CE methods have been used extensively in various Natural Language Processing (NLP) fields (Gandrabur et al., 2006). Gandrabur and Foster (2003) and Nguyen et al. (2011) investigated the use of machine learning approaches for confidence estimation in machine translation. Agichtein (2006) showed

Expectation-Maximization algorithms to estimate the confidence for partially supervised relation extraction. White et al. (2007) described how a maximum entropy model can be used to generate confidence scores for a speech recognition engine. Louis and Nenkova (2009) presented a study of predicting the confidence of automatic summarization outputs. Many approaches for confidence estimation have also been explored and implemented in other NLP research areas.

There are also many previous confidence estimation studies in IE, and most of these have been in the Active Learning literature. Thompson et al. (1999) proposed a rule-based extraction method to compute confidence. Scheffer et al. (2001) utilized hidden Markov models to measure the confidence in an IE system, but they only estimated the confidence of singleton tokens. Culotta and McCallum (2004)'s work is the most relevant to our work, since they also utilized a machine learning model to estimate the confidence values for IE outputs. They estimated the confidence of both extracted fields and entire multi-field records mainly through a linear-chain Conditional Random Field (CRF) model, but their case studies are not as complicated and challenging as slot filling, since SF systems need to handle difficult cross-document coreference resolution, sophisticated inference, and also other challenges (Min and Grishman, 2012). Furthermore, to the best of our knowledge, there is no previous work in confidence estimation for the KBP slot filling task.

3 KBP Slot Filling

3.1 Task Definition

The Knowledge Base Population (KBP) track, organized by U.S. National Institute of Standards and Technology (NIST)'s Text Analysis Conference (TAC), aims to promote research in discovering information about entities and augmenting a Knowledge Base (KB) with this information (Ji et al., 2010). KBP mainly consists of two tasks: Entity Linking, linking names in a provided document to entities in the KB or NIL; and Slot Filling (SF), extracting information about an entity in the KB to automatically populate a new or existing KB. As a new but influential IE evaluation, Slot Filling is a challenging and practical task (Min and Grishman, 2012).

The Slot Filling task at *KBP2012* provides a large collection of 3.7 million newswire articles and web texts as the source corpus, and an initial KB derived from the Wikipedia infoboxes. In such a large corpus, some information can be highly redundant. Given a list of person (PER) and organization (ORG) entity names ("queries"), SF systems retrieve the documents about these entities in the corpus and then fill the required slots with correct, non-redundant values. Each query consists of the name of the entity, its type (PER or ORG), a document (from the corpus) in which the name appears, its node ID if the entity appears in the provided KB, and the slots which need not be filled. Along with each slot fill, the system should also provide the ID of the document that justifies this fill. If the system does not extract any information for a given slot, the system just outputs "NIL" without any document ID. The task defines a total of 42 slots, 26 for person entities and 16 for organization entities. Some slots are single-valued, like "per:date_of_birth", which can only accept at most a single value, while the other slots, for example "org:subsidiaries", are list-valued, which can take a list of values. Since the overall goal is to augment an existing KB, the redundancy in list-valued slots must be detected and avoided, requiring a system to identify different but equivalent strings. Such as, both "United States" and "U.S." refer to the same country. More information can be found in the task definition (Ji et al., 2010).

3.2 Baseline System Description

We use a slot filling system that has achieved highly competitive results (ranked top 2) at the *KBP2012* evaluation as our baseline. Like most SF systems, our system has three basic components: Document Retrieval, Answer Extraction, and Response Combination. Our SF system starts by retrieving relevant documents based on a match to the query name or the results of query expansion. Then our system applies a two-stage process to generate final slot fills: Answer Extraction, which produces intermediate responses from different pipelines, and Response Combination, which merges all intermediate responses into final slot fills. Answer extraction begins with document pre-processing, such as part-of-speech tagging, name tagging, and coreference resolution. Then it uses a set of 6 SF pipelines operating in parallel on the retrieved documents to extract answers. Our pipelines consist of two that use hand-coded

	PER#	ORG#	Total#	Response#
KBP2010	50	50	100	7917
KBP2011	50	50	100	14976
KBP2012	40	40	80	8989
total	140	140	280	31878

Table 1: Number of Queries and Number of Intermediate Responses from Each Year Data

patterns, two pattern-based slot fillers in which the patterns are generated semi-automatically from a bootstrapping procedure, one based on name coreference, and one distant-supervision based pipeline. The result of this stage is a set of intermediate slot responses, potentially highly redundant. Next, Response Combination validates answers and eliminates redundant answers to aggregate all intermediate responses into final slot fills, where the best answer is selected for each single-valued slot and non-redundant fills are generated for list-valued slots. More details about our KBP Slot Filling system can be found in the system description paper (Min et al., 2012).

4 Confidence Estimation Model

Our confidence estimation model is based on the Maximum Entropy (MaxEnt) framework, a probabilistic model able to incorporate all features into a uniform model by assigning weights automatically. We implement a mix of binary and real-valued features from different aspects to estimate confidence of each intermediate slot filling response under a consistent and uniform standard, incorporating four categories of features: **Response Features** extract features from the slot and the *Response* context; **Pipeline Features** indicate how well each pipeline performed previously; **Local Features** explore how *Query* and *Response* are correlated in the supporting context *Sentence*; **Global Features** detect how closely *Query* correlates with *Response* in the global context. Each specific feature in the above categories is listed in Table 2, where *Q* refers to a person or organization *Query*; *R* indicates the pipeline-generated *Response* for a particular slot of a query; and *S* represents the *Sentence* that supports the correctness of the *Response*.

5 Experiments

We have collected and merged the previous three years' KBP SF evaluation data, which consists of a total of 280 queries, and Table 1 lists the number of person and organization queries as well as the number of intermediate responses from each year. There are in total 31878 intermediate responses generated by 6 different pipelines from our SF system. We trained our CE model and measured the confidence values through a 10-fold cross-validation, so that each fold randomly contains 14 person queries and 14 organization queries with their associated intermediate responses. Then for each iteration, the CE model is trained on 9 folds and approximates the confidence values in the remaining fold, and it assigns the probability of each intermediate response being correct as confidence.

5.1 Voting Systems

To evaluate the reliability of confidence values generated by this model, we used the weighted voting method to investigate the relationship between the confidence values and the performance.

5.1.1 Baseline Voting System

Our baseline SF system applies a basic plurality voting to combine all intermediate responses to generate the final response submission. This voting system simply counts the frequencies of each response entity, which is a unique response tuple in the form <Query_ID, Slot_Name, Response_Fill>. For a single-valued slot of a query, the response with the highest count is returned as the final response fill. For the list-valued slots, all non-redundant responses are returned as the final response fills. In this basic voting system, each intermediate response contributes equally.

5.1.2 Weighted Voting System

Weighted voting is based on the idea that not all the voters contribute equally. Instead, voters have different weights concerning the outcome of an election. In our experiment, voters are all of intermediate responses generated by all pipelines, and the voters' weights are their confidence values. We set a threshold τ in this weighted voting system, where those intermediate responses with

Category	Feature	Description
Response Features	slot_name	The slot name
	slot_response_length	The conjunction of the length of R and the slot name
	name_response_slot	The slot requires a name as the response
Pipeline Features	pipeline_name	The name of pipeline which generates R
	pipeline_precision	The Precision of the pipeline which generates R
	pipeline_recall	The Recall of the pipeline which generates R
	pipeline_fmeasure	The F-measure of the pipeline which generates R
Local Features	sent_contain_QR	S contains both original Q and R
	sent_contain_ExQR	S contains both co-referred Q or expanded Q and R
	dpath_length	The length of shortest dependency path between Q and R in S
	shortest_dpath	The shortest dependency path between Q and R in S
	NE_boolean	R is a person or organization name in S
	NE_margin	The difference between the log probabilities of this name R and the second most likely name
	n-gram	Tri-gram context window associated with part-of-speech tags containing Q or R
	genre	The supporting document is a newswire or web document
Global Features	query_doc_num	The number of documents retrieved by Q
	response_doc_num	The number of documents retrieved by R
	co-occur_doc_num	The number of documents retrieved by the co-occurrences of Q and R
	cond_prob_givenQ	The conditional probability of R given Q
	cond_prob_givenR	The conditional probability of Q given R
	mutual_info	The Point-wise Mutual Information (PMI) of Q and R

Table 2: Features of Confidence Estimation Model

confidences that are lower than τ would be eliminated. For each response entity, this weighted voting system simply sums all the weights of the intermediate responses that support this response entity as its weight. Then for a single-valued slot of a query, it returns the response with the highest weight as the final slot fill, while it returns all non-redundant responses as the final slot fills for the list-valued slots. The maximum confidence ψ of supporting intermediate responses is used as the final confidence for that slot fill. We also set a threshold η (optimized on a validation data set), where the final slot fills with confidence ψ lower than η would not be submitted finally.

5.1.3 Results

Table 3 compares the results of this weighted voting system (with $\tau = 0$, $\eta = 0.17$) and the baseline voting system, where the responses were judged based only on the answer string, ignoring the document ID. As we can see, the weighted voting system achieves 2.3% absolute improvement in F-measure over the baseline, at a 99.8% confidence level according to the Wilcoxon Matched-Pairs Signed-Ranks Significance Test. Precision obtains 9.0% absolute improvement with only a small loss of 0.5% in Recall.

	Precision	Recall	F-measure
Baseline	0.351	**0.246**	0.289
Weighted	**0.441**	0.241	**0.312**

Table 3: Results Comparison between Baseline Voting System and Weighted Voting System

Figure 1 summarizes the results of this weighted voting system with different threshold τ settings. When τ is raised, Precision continuously increases to around 1, while Recall gradually decreases to 0.

In addition to improving overall performance, the confidence estimates can be used to convey to the user of slot filling output our confidence in individual slot fills. After the intermediate responses are combined by the above weighted voting system (setting τ and η as 0), we divide the range of confidence values (0 to 1) into 10 equal intervals (0 to 0.1, 0.1 to 0.2, and so on) and categorize these

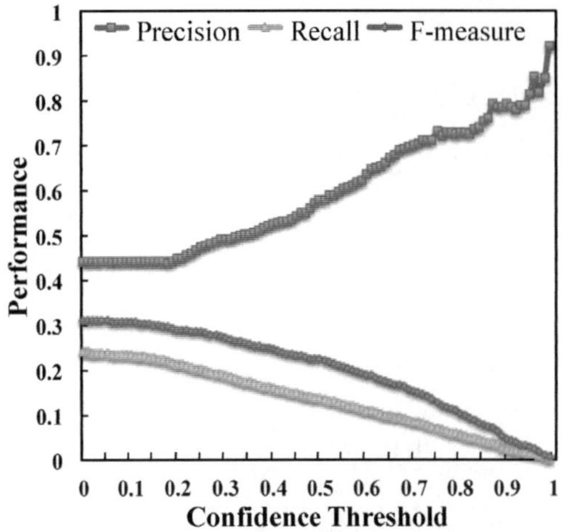

Figure 1: Impact of Threshold Settings

final slot fills by their confidence values. Then for each category, the final slot fills are scored in Precision. Figure 2 strongly demonstrates that the slot fills with higher confidence consistently generate more precise answers, indirectly validating the reliability of the confidence estimates.

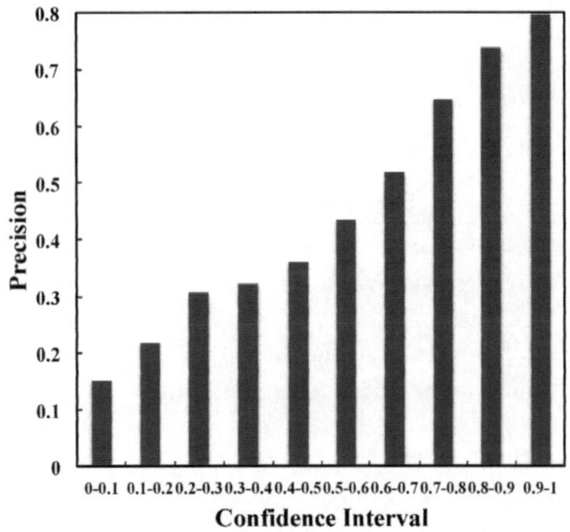

Figure 2: Performance of Confidence Intervals

5.2 Evaluation

We use another two different methods to evaluate the quality of confidence estimation in a more direct way. The first method is *Pearson's r*, a correlation coefficient ranging from -1 to 1 that measures the correlation between a confidence value and whether or not the instance is correct. It is widely used in the sciences as a measure of linear dependence between two variables. The second method is *average precision*, used in the Information Retrieval community to evaluate a ranked list. It calculates the precision at each point in the ranked list where a relevant document is found and then averages these values. Instead of ranking documents by their relevance scores, the intermediate responses are ranked by their confidence values.

	Avg. Prec	Pearson's r
RANKED	**0.835**	**0.542**
RANDOM	0.525	0.001
WORSTCASE	0.330	-

Table 4: Evaluation of Confidence Estimates

Table 4 shows the Pearson's r and average precision results for all intermediate responses, where RANKED ranks the responses based on their confidence values; RANDOM assigns confidence values uniformly at random between 0 and 1; WORSTCASE ranks all incorrect responses above all correct ones.

Applying the features separately, we find that *slot_response_length* and *response_doc_num* are the best predictors of correctness. *dpath_length* (the length of the shortest dependency path between query and response) is also a significant contributor. Among the features, only *NE_margin* seeks to directly estimate the confidence of a pipeline component, and it makes only a minimal contribution to the result. Overall this shows that confidence can be predicted quite well from features of the query and response, their appearance in the corpus, and prior IE system performance, without modeling the confidence of individual pipeline components.

6 Conclusion

We have presented our Maximum Entropy based confidence estimation model for information extraction systems. The effectiveness of this model has been demonstrated in the challenging Knowledge Base Population Slot Filling task, where a weighted voting system achieves 2.3% absolute improvement in F-measure score based on the confidence estimates. A strong correlation between the confidence estimates in KBP slot fills and the correctness has also been proved by obtaining an average precision of 83.5% and Pearson's r of 54.2%. In the future, further experiments are planned to investigate more elaborate models, explore more interesting feature sets, and study the contribution of each feature through a more detailed and thorough analysis.

References

Eugene Agichtein. 2006. *Confidence Estimation Methods for Partially Supervised Relation Extraction.* In Proceedings of SDM 2006.

Adam Berger, Vincent Della Pietra, and Stephen Della Pietra. 1996. *A Maximum Entropy Approach to Natural Language Processing.* Computational Linguistics, Volume 22 Issue 1, March 1996, Pages 39-71, MIT Press Cambridge, MA, USA.

Zheng Chen, Suzanne Tamang, Adam Lee, Xiang Li, Wen-Pin Lin, Javier Artiles, Matthew Snover, Marissa Passantino, and Heng Ji. 2010. *CUNY-BLENDER TAC-KBP2010 Entity Linking and Slot Filling System Description.* In Proceedings of Text Analytics Conference (TAC) 2010.

Aron Culotta and Andrew McCallum. 2004. *Confidence Estimation for Information Extraction.* In Proceedings of HLT-NAACL 2004.

Simona Gandrabur, George Foster, and Guy Lapalme. 2006. *Condence Estimation for NLP Applications.* In ACM Transactions on Speech and Language Processing, Vol. 3, No. 3, October 2006, Pages 129.

Simona Gandrabur and George Foster. 2003. *Confidence Estimation for Translation Prediction.* In Proceedings of CoNLL 2003.

Heng Ji, Ralph Grishman, Hoa Trang Dang, Kira Griffitt, and Joe Ellis. 2010. *Overview of the TAC2010 Knowledge Base Population Track.* In Proceedings of Text Analytics Conference (TAC) 2010.

Heng Ji, Ralph Grishman, and Hoa Trang Dang. 2011. *Overview of the TAC2011 Knowledge Base Population Track.* In Proceedings of Text Analytics Conference (TAC) 2011.

Heng Ji and Ralph Grishman. 2011. *Knowledge Base Population: Successful Approaches and Challenges.* In Proceedings of ACL 2011.

Annie Louis and Ani Nenkova. 2009. *Performance Confidence Estimation for Automatic Summarization.* In Proceedings of ACL 2009.

Bonan Min, Xiang Li, Ralph Grishman, and Ang Sun. 2012. *New York University 2012 System for KBP Slot Filling.* In Proceedings of Text Analytics Conference (TAC) 2012.

Bonan Min and Ralph Grishman. 2012. *Challenges in the TAC-KBP Slot Filling Task.* In Proceedings of LREC 2012.

Bach Nguyen, Fei Huang, and Yaser Al-Onaizan. 2011. *Goodness: A Method for Measuring Machine Translation Confidence.* In Proceedings of ACL 2011.

Tobias Scheffer, Christian Decomain, and Stefan Wrobel. 2001. *Active Hidden Markov Models for Information Extraction.* In Proceedings of IDA 2001.

Ang Sun, Ralph Grishman, Wei Xu, and Bonan Min. 2011. *New York University 2011 System for KBP Slot Filling.* In Proceedings of Text Analytics Conference (TAC) 2011.

Cynthia Thompson, Mary Califf, and Raymond Mooney. 1999. *Active Learning for Natural Language Parsing and Information Extraction.* In Proceedings of 16th International Conference on Machine Learning.

Christopher White, Alex Acero, and Julian Odell. 2007. *Maximum Entropy Confidence Estimation For Speech Recognition.* In Proceedings of ICASSP 2007.

Towards Fine-grained Citation Function Classification

Xiang Li Yifan He Adam Meyers Ralph Grishman
Computer Science Department
New York University
{xiangli, yhe, meyers, grishman}@cs.nyu.edu

Abstract

We look into the problem of recognizing citation functions in scientific literature, trying to reveal authors' rationale for citing a particular article. We introduce an annotation scheme to annotate citation functions in scientific papers with coarse-to-fine-grained categories, where the coarse-grained annotation roughly corresponds to citation sentiment and the fine-grained annotation reveals more about citation functions. We implement a Maximum Entropy-based system trained on annotated data under this scheme to automatically classify citation functions in scientific literature. Using combined lexical and syntactic features, our system achieves the F-measure of 67%.

1 Introduction

Citations in scientific papers serve different purposes, from comparing one work to another to acknowledging the inventor of certain concepts. Recognizing citation functions is important for understanding the structure of a single scientific document as well as mining citation graphs within a document collection. Therefore, this task has attracted researchers from the fields of discourse analysis, sociology of science, and information sciences for decades (Teufel et al., 2006a).

Most of the existing research in this area focused on the analysis of citation sentiment, which has achieved good accuracy (see, e.g., (Teufel et al., 2006a)). Citation sentiment analysis systems are usually able to identify positive, neutral, or negative opinions, but if we want to better understand the exact function of a citation, we need to know not only whether the authors like the citation, but also how the citation is used in a given context (Section 2).

In this paper, we try to reveal citation functions more accurately than simply classifying citation sentiment. We first create a two level coarse-to-fine grained annotation scheme (Section 3). The coarse-level annotation corresponds roughly to sentiment categories, including `POSITIVE`, `NEGATIVE`, and `NEUTRAL`. The fine-grained annotation scheme provides a more detailed description of citation functions, such as `Significant`, which asserts the importance of an article or a work, and `Discover`, which acknowledges the original discoverer/inventor of a method or material.

Using data annotated under this scheme, we train classifiers to determine citation functions, and experiment with features from lexical to syntactic levels (Section 4). We predict the fine-grained citation function at 67% in F-measure in our experiments, which is at the same level as the coarse-grained citation sentiment classification (Section 5).

2 Related Work

The background for our work is in citation analysis. Applications of citation analysis include evaluating the impact of a published literature through a measurable bibliometric (Garfield, 1972; Luukkonen, 1992; Borgman and Furner, 2002), analyzing bibliometric networks (Radev et al., 2009), summarizing scientific papers (Qazvinian and Radev, 2008; Abu-Jbara and Radev, 2011), generating surveys of scientific paradigms (Mohammad et al., 2009), among others. Correctly and accurately recognizing citation functions is a cornerstone for these tasks.

Citation Function	Description
Based_on$^+$	A work is based on the cited work
Corroboration$^+$	Two works corroborate each other
Discover$^+$	Acknowledge the invention of a technique
Positive$^+$	The cited work is successful
Practical$^+$	The cited work has a practical use
Significant$^+$	The cited work is important
Standard$^+$	The cited work is a standard
Supply$^+$	Acknowledge the supplier of a material
Contrast$^=$	Compares two works in a neutral way
Co-citation$^=$	Citations that appear closely
Neutral$^=$	The cited work not belonging to other functions
Negative$^-$	The weakness of the cited work is discussed

Table 1: Annotation Scheme for Citation Function: $^+$ represents POSITIVE sentiment, $^=$ represents NEUTRAL sentiment, and $^-$ represents negative sentiment

Researchers have introduced several annotation schemes for citation analysis. The work of Teufel et al. (2006b) is the most related to ours. They proposed an annotation scheme for citation functions based on why authors cite a particular paper, following Spiegel-Rüsing (1977). This scheme provides clear definition for some of the basic citation functions, such as Contrast, but mainly concerns the citations that authors compare to or build upon, ignoring the relationship between two cited works. Sometimes the relationship between two cited works is also meaningful and important, from which we can know more about the functions and influences of one cited work on other works. For example, the cited work may be utilized or applied by another cited work, which would be captured by Practical in our annotation scheme but considered as neutral under their scheme. In addition, their annotation scheme does not explicitly recognize milestone or standard work in a particular research field, while our annotation scheme does through the Significant function. We continue to use these basic functions, but try to expand their scheme by incorporating more functions, such as acknowledgement and corroboration, which reflects the attitude of the research community towards a citation.

Regarding the automatic recognition of citation functions or citation categories, Teufel et al. (2006a) presented a supervised learning framework to classify citation functions mainly utilizing features from cue phrases. Athar (2011) explored the effectiveness of sentence structure-based features to identify sentiment polarity of citations. Dong and Schäfer (2011) proposed a four-category definition of citation functions following Moravcsik and Murugesan (1975) and a self-training-based classification model. Different from previous work that mainly classified citations into sentiment categories or coarse-grained functions, our scheme, we believe, is more fine-grained. It is also worth noting that Teufel et al. (2006a), Athar (2011), and Dong and Schäfer (2011) all worked on citations in computational linguistics papers, but we investigate citations in biomedical articles.

3 Annotation

Our annotation scheme contains three general citation function categories POSITIVE, NEUTRAL, and NEGATIVE: POSITIVE citations reflect agreement, usage, or compatibility with cited work; NEUTRAL citations refer to related knowledge or background in cited work; and NEGATIVE citations show weakness of cited work. These three general categories are often used as citation sentiments in previous citation sentiment analysis work. We extend these categories by sorting them into smaller subcategories that reflect the functions of citations. POSITIVE (see $^+$ in Table 1), for example, shows a general sentiment of agreement. We divide POSITIVE into Based_on, Corroboration, Discover, Positive, Practical, Significant, Standard, and Supply in order to more accurately describe how a citation is used. The details about each citation function are summarized in Table 1. We provide

Citation Function	Example
Based_on$^+$	*Results* ***based on*** *the Comparative Toxicogenomics Database (CTD)* ***[14]****, we constructed a human P-PAN.*
Corroboration$^+$	*This observation is* ***in accordance with*** *previously published data* ***[39]****.*
Discover$^+$	*The core of our procedure is derived from the "target hopping" concept* ***defined*** *previously* ***[3]****.*
Positive$^+$	*Therefore, a systems biology approach, such as the one that* ***was successfully employed*** *by Chen and colleagues* ***[1]****, is an effective alternative for analyzing complex diseases.*
Practical$^+$	*Molecular Modeling and Docking Genetic algorithm GOLD (Genetic Optimization for Ligand Docking), a docking program based on genetic algorithm* ***[39][42] was used to*** *dock the ligands to the protein active sites.*
Significant$^+$	*In addition to nanomaterial composition, size and concentration, the influence of cell type* ***is of paramount importance*** *in nanomaterial toxicity as highlighted in other recent investigations in cell vs. cell comparisons* ***[49]****.*
Standard$^+$	*A* ***standard*** *genetic algorithm* ***[31]*** *was used to select the final physicochemical properties of Pafig with population size of 10, crossover probability of 0.8, mutation probability of 0.01 and predetermined number of 200 generations.*
Supply$^+$	*The rate constants* ***obtained directly from*** *the ultrafast, time-resolved optical spectroscopic experiments carried out* ***(Polivka et al. 2005)*** *are shown in Table.*
Contrast$^=$	***In contrast to Rodgers et al., [34]*** *who targeted planktonic species in AMD solutions and sediments,* ***Bond et al.*** *[37] primarily sampled biofilms.*
Co-Citation$^=$	*They bear specific regulatory properties and mechanisms* ***(Babu et al, 2004; Wang and Purisima, 2005)****.*
Neutral$^=$	***Lage and collaborators [12]*** *predicted 113 new disease-candidate genes by comparing their protein-interaction* neighborhood with associated phenotypes.
Negative$^-$	*A range of methods have been applied to S. mutans typing, one of the earliest of which was based on susceptibilite to bacteriocins* ***[14], [15]*** *but was found to* ***lack reproducibility and was not readily transferred between laboratories****.*

Table 2: Citation Function Examples

an example for each function in Table 2 to illustrate how it is defined.

Two annotators are trained to perform the annotation. The articles we work on are from the open access subset of PubMed, which consists of articles from the biomedical domain. We require the annotators to mark citation functions, and point to textual evidence for assigning a particular function.

4 Recognizing Citation Functions

We use the Maximum Entropy (MaxEnt) model to classify all citations into the above citation function categories. We experiment with both surface and syntactic features. When parsing the context sentence, we replace each citation content with a <CITATION> symbol, in order to remove the contextual bias.

4.1 Surface Features

We capture n-grams, signal words collected by system developers, pronouns, negation words, and words related to formulae, graphs, or tables in the context sentence as surface level features.

- **N-Gram Features** use both uni-grams of the context sentence and the tri-gram context window that contains the citation.

- **Signal Word Features** check whether the text signals for a citation function (151 words/phrases in total, collected by system developers from dictionaries) appear in the context sentence.

- **Pronoun Features** look for third-person pronouns and their positions in the context sentence.

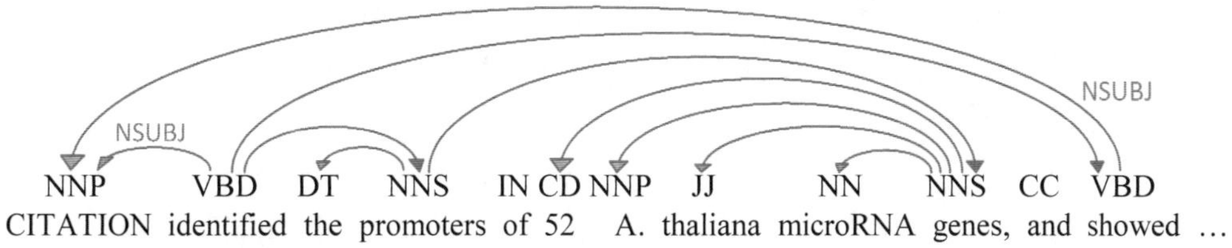

Figure 1: POS and Dependency Features

- **Negation Features** fire if negation words (135 words in total) appear in the context sentence with its scope.

- **FGT Features** fire if words or structures like formula, graph, or table appear in the context sentence.

4.2 Syntactic Features

We capture more generalized or long-distance information by taking advantages of syntactic features.

The Part-of-Speech Features use Part-of-Speech (POS) tags adds generalizability to surface level signals, e.g., "VERB with" covers signals like "experiment with" and "solve with", which might indicate a `Practical` function. We use a combination of POS tags and words in a two-word context window around the <CITATION> as features. In Figure 1, "VBD_DT", "identified_DT", and "VBD_the" would be extracted.

The Dependency Features use the dependency structure of the context sentence to capture grammatical relationships between a citation and its signal words regardless of the distance between them. We extract both dependency triples and dependency labels as features. In Figure 1, if we extract dependency relations and labels attached to a <CITATION>, we would obtain "NSUBJ_identified_CITATION", "NSUBJ", and "NSUBJ_showed_CITATION" as dependency features. "NSUBJ_showed_CITATION" captures the long-distance relation between <CITATION> and a signal word "showed", which other features miss.

5 Experiments

From 91 annotated articles with total 6,355 citation instances, we train our model and test the performance through a 10-fold cross-validation procedure, so that each fold randomly contains 9 (or 10) articles with their associated citation instances.

Features	P	R	F1
baseline	0.67	0.44	0.53
baseline + fgt	0.67	0.44	0.53
baseline + sig	0.67	0.44	0.53
baseline + neg	0.68	0.44	0.54
baseline + pron	0.68	0.44	0.54
baseline + dep	0.72	0.54	0.62
baseline + pos	**0.75**	0.58	0.65
baseline + pos + dep	0.74	**0.61**	**0.67**

Table 3: Overall Performance Using Different Features: n-gram features (baseline), FGT features (fgt), signal word features (sig), negation features (neg), pronoun features (pron), dependency structure features (dep), and Part-of-Speech features (pos).

Table 3 shows the overall performance in Precision (P), Recall (R), and F-measure (F1) by incorporating different feature sets, at a 99.8% confidence level according to the Wilcoxon Matched-Pairs Signed-Ranks Significance Test. If we randomly assign one of the citation function classes to each citation instance, the performance is only 3.8% in F-measure. In addition, a simple majority classifier assigns each citation with whichever class that is in the majority in the training set, also only obtaining F-measure of 42.2%. Our results clearly show that our MaxEnt system easily outperforms these two simple baseline classifiers.

We report macro-average numbers over all citation functions, except for `NEUTRAL:Neutral`, which simply reflects that a work is cited without any particular information. We observe that surface features do not work well enough alone, as they cannot generalize beyond the signal knowledge observed in a relatively small training set. Syntactic features, on the other hand, can utilize linguistic knowledge to solve the problem, and lead to better results.

We compare F-measure of coarse-grained sentiment classification and fine-grained citation func-

Function Class	P	R	F1	Distribution
Based_on$^+$	0.250	0.029	0.051	0.028
Corroboration$^+$	**1.000**	0.022	0.043	0.036
Discover$^+$	0.861	0.750	**0.802**	0.123
Positive$^+$	N/A	0.000	N/A	0.001
Practical$^+$	N/A	0.000	N/A	0.010
Significant$^+$	N/A	0.000	N/A	0.006
Standard$^+$	0.500	0.333	0.400	0.002
Supply$^+$	0.000	0.000	N/A	0.012
Contrast$^=$	0.667	0.250	0.364	0.006
Co-Citation$^=$	0.721	**0.792**	0.755	0.333

Table 4: Performance and Distribution of Citation Function Classes

Citation Sentiment	P	R	F1
coarse-grained POSITIVE	0.93	0.45	0.60
fine-grained POSITIVE	0.82	0.43	0.57

Table 5: Comparison of Coarse- and Fine-grained Citation Function Classification on POSITIVE

tion prediction on more interesting POSITIVE functions in Table 5. We see that coarse-grained classification performs only slightly better. We suspect that each citation function in the POSITIVE category needs different signal information to identify, so a more fine-grained annotation scheme could lead to a stronger correlation between a class label and its signals. This can explain the close performance between these two paradigms, although citation function prediction is more informative and harder.

We report performance and distribution in annotated data for each citation function in Table 4. Note that the numbers in the "Distribution" column does not sum to 1, because we omit the NEUTRAL:Neutral category that does not carry information and some categories (e.g., Negative) that are too few (e.g., less than 5) in the corpus. We see that some of the functions (such as Discover) can perform much better than others. The major reason for the difference in performance is the imbalance distribution of citation functions in the annotated corpus, which, in turn, results in the difference in prediction ability of our classifier. In the extreme case, our system fails to find any positive instance for some of the categories because of the scarcity of training examples. In order to mitigate this problem, we plan to perform more function-specific annotation to obtain more data on current scarce functions.

6 Conclusion

In this paper, we introduced the task of citation sentiment analysis and citation function classification, which aims to analyze the fine-grained utility of citations in scientific documents. We described an annotation scheme to annotate citation functions in scientific papers into fine-grained categories. We presented our Maximum Entropy-based system to automatically classify the citation functions, explored the advantages of different feature sets, and confirmed the necessity of using syntactic features in our task, obtaining 67% of final F-measure score.

For future work, we plan to explore more features and perform more citation function-specific annotation for scarce functions in the current annotated corpus. Furthermore, we will also apply our annotation scheme and classification method in scientific literature from different domains, as well as investigate more elaborate machine learning models and techniques.

Acknowledgement

Supported by the Intelligence Advanced Research Projects Activity (IARPA) via Department of Interior National Business Center contract number D11PC20154. The U.S. Government is authorized to reproduce and distribute reprints for Governmental purposes notwithstanding any copyright annotation thereon. Disclaimer: The views and conclusions contained herein are those of the authors and should not be interpreted as necessarily representing the official policies or endorsements, either expressed or implied, of IARPA, DoI/NBC, or the U.S. Government. Approved for Public Release; Distribution Unlimited.

References

Amjad Abu-Jbara and Dragomir Radev. 2011. *Coherent Citation-Based Summarization of Scientific Papers.* In Proceedings of ACL 2011, Portland, Oregon, USA.

Awais Athar. 2012. *Sentiment Analysis of Citations using Sentence Structure-Based Features.* In Proceedings of ACL-HLT 2011 Student Session, Portland, Oregon, USA.

Awais Athar and Simone Teufel. 2012. *Detection of Implicit Citations for Sentiment Detection.* In Proceedings of ACL 2012 Workshop on Discovering Structure in Scholarly Discourse, Jeju Island, South Korea.

Awais Athar and Simone Teufel. 2012. *Context-Enhanced Citation Sentiment Detection.* In Proceedings of NAACL-HLT 2012, Montreal, Canada.

Christine Borgman and Jonathan Furner. 2002. *Scholarly Communication and Bibliometrics.* Annual Review of Information Science and Technology: Vol. 36.

Jean Carletta. 1996. *Assessing Agreement on Classification Tasks: The Kappa Statistic.* Computational Linguistics, 22(2):249254.

Cailing Dong and Ulrich Schäfer. 2011. *Ensemble-style Self-training on Citation Classification.* In Proceedings of IJCNLP 2011, Chiang Mai, Thailand.

Eugene Garfield. 1955. *Citation Indexes for Science - A New Dimension in Documentation through Association of Ideas.* Science, July 15, 1955: 108-111.

Eugene Garfield. 1965. *Can Citation Indexing Be Automated?.* Statistical Association Methods for Mechanized Documentation, Symposium Proceedings, Washington.

Eugene Garfield. 1972. *Citation Analysis as a Tool in Journal Evaluation.* Essays of an Information Scienties, Vol 1, p.527-544.

Terttu Luukkonen. 1992. *Is Scientists' Publishing Behaviour Reward-seeking?.* Scientometrics, 24: 297319.

Saif Mohammad, Boonie Dorr, Melissa Egan, Ahmed Hassan, Pradeep Muthukrishan, Vahed Qazvinian, Dragomir Radev, and David Zajic. 2009. *Using citations to generate surveys of scientific paradigms* In Proceedings of NAACL-HLT 2009, Boulder, Colorado, USA.

Michael J. Moravcsik and Poovanalingam Murugesan. 1975. *Some Results on the Function and Quality of Citations.* Social Studies of Science, 5:8692.

Vahed Qazvinian and Dragomir R. Radev. 2008. *Scientific Paper Summarization Using Citation Summary Networks.* In Proceedings of Coling 2008, Manchester, UK.

Dragomir R. Radev, Mark Thomas Joseph, Bryan Gibson, and Pradeep Muthukrishnan. 2009. *A Bibliometric and Network Analysis of the field of Computational Linguistics.* Journal of the American Society for Information Science and Technology.

Ina Spiegel-Rüsing. 1977. *Bibliometric and Content Analysis.* Social Studies of Science, 7:97113.

Simone Teufel, Advaith Siddharthan, and Dan Tidhar. 2006. *Automatic classification of citation function.* In Proceedings of EMNLP 2006, Sydney, Australia.

Simone Teufel, Advaith Siddharthan, and Dan Tidhar. 2006. *An annotation scheme for citation function.* In Proceedings of Sigdial 2006, Sydney, Australia.

Supervised Morphology Generation Using Parallel Corpus

Alireza Mahmoudi, Mohsen Arabsorkhi[†] and **Heshaam Faili**
School of Electrical and Computer Engineering
College of Engineering
University of Tehran, Tehran, Iran
{ali.mahmoudi,hfaili}@ut.ac.ir
[†]marabsorkhi@ece.ut.ac.ir

Abstract

Translating from English, a morphologically poor language, into morphologically rich languages such as Persian comes with many challenges. In this paper, we present an approach to rich morphology prediction using a parallel corpus. We focus on the verb conjugation as the most important and problematic phenomenon in the context of morphology in Persian. We define a set of linguistic features using both English and Persian linguistic information, and use an English-Persian parallel corpus to train our model. Then, we predict six morphological features of the verb and generate inflected verb form using its lemma. In our experiments, we generate verb form with the most common feature values as a baseline. The results of our experiments show an improvement of almost 2.1% absolute BLEU score on a test set containing 16K sentences.

1 Introduction

One of the main limitations of statistical machine translation (SMT) is the sensitivity to data sparseness, due to the word-based or phrased-based approach incorporated in SMT (Koehn et al., 2003). This problem becomes severe in the translation from or into a morphologically rich language, where a word stem appears in many completely different surface forms. Therefore, morphological analysis is an important phase in the translation from or into such languages, because it reduces the sparseness of model. So, modeling rich morphology in machine translations (MT) has received a lot of research interest in several studies.

In this paper, we present a novel approach to rich morphology prediction for Persian as target language. We focus on the verb conjugation as a highly inflecting class of words and an important part of morphological processing in Persian. Our model incorporates decision tree classifier (DTC) (Quinlan, 1986), which is an approach to multistage decision making. In order to train DTC, we use both English and Persian linguistic information such as syntactic parse tree and dependency relations obtained from an English-Persian parallel corpus. Morphological features which we predict and use to generate the inflected form of verb are voice (VOC), mood (MOD), number (NUM), tense (TEN), negation (NEG) and person (PER). Our proposed model can be used as a component to generate rich morphology for any kind of languages and MTs.

The reminder of the paper is organized as follows: Section 2 briefly reviews some challenges in Persian verb conjugation, Section 3 presents our proposed approach to generate rich morphology, in Section 4 our experiments and results are presented, in Section 5 we cover conclusions and future work, and finally, in Section 6 we describe related works.

2 Morphology Challenges of the Persian Verbs

Verbs in Persian have a complex inflectional system (Megerdoomian, 2004). This complexity appears in the following aspects:

- Different verb forms
- Different verb stems
- Affixes marking inflections
- Auxiliaries used in certain tenses

Simple form and *compound* form are two forms used in Persian verbal system. Simple form is broken into two categories according to the stem used in its formation. Compound form refers to those that require an auxiliary to form a correct verb.

Two stems are used to construct a verb: present stem and past stem. Each of which is used in creating of specific tenses.

We cannot derive the two stems from each other due to different surface forms they usually have. Therefore, they treated as distinct characteristics of verbs. Several affixes are combined with stems to mark MOD, NUM, NEG and PER inflections. Auxiliaries are used to make a compound form in certain tenses to indicate VOC and TEN inflections, similar to HAVE and BE in English. Two examples are given in Table 1 for نمیفروشیم /nmyfrvŝym[1] /nemiforushim (we are not selling) and فروخته شده است /frvxth ŝdh ast/ forukhte shode ast (it has been sold), which both of them have the same infinitive form.

feature	nmyfrvŝym	frvxth ŝdh ast
verb form	simple	compound
stem	frvŝ(present)	frvxt(past)
prefix	n, my	-
suffix	ym	h
auxiliary	-	ŝdh, ast
VOC	active	passive
MOD	subjunctive	indicative
NUM	plural	singular
TEN	simple present	present perfect
NEG	negative	positive
PER	first	third

Table 1: Inflections and morphological features of ن+ می+ فروش+ یم /n+my+frvŝ+ym (we are not selling) and فروخت+ ه+ شده+ است /frvxt+h+ŝdh+ast (it has been sold).

3 Approach

Our proposed approach is broken into two main steps: DTC training and Morphology prediction. Then we can generate a verb form using a finite state automaton (Megerdoomian, 2004), if we are given the six morphological features of the verb. In the next subsections we describe these steps more precisely.

3.1 DTC Training

To make train and test set, we use an English-Persian parallel corpus containing 399K sentences (367K to train,16K to validate and 16K to test). More details about this corpus, which is used by Mansouri and Faili (2012) to build an SMT, are presented in Table 2. Giza++ (Och and Ney, 2003) is used to word alignment. We only select such an alignment that is most probable to translate both from English to Persian and Persian to English among those assigned to each verb. With this heuristic we ignore a lot of alignments to produce a high quality data set. We selected 100 sentences randomly and evaluated the alignments manually, so that 27% recall and 93% precision were obtained.

	English	Persian
Sentences	399,000	399,000
Tokens	6,528,241	6,074,550
Unique tokens	65,123	101,114
Stems	40,261	91,329

Table 2: Some statistics about the English-Persian parallel corpus (Mansouri and Faili, 2012).

Then, we define a set of syntactic features on English side as DTC learning features. These features consist of several language-specific features such as English part-of-speech tag (POS) of the verb, dependency relationships of the verb and POS of subject of the verb. English is parsed using Stanford Parser (Klein and Manning, 2003). After that, we can produce training data set by analyzing the Persian verb aligned to each English verb using (Rasooli et al., 2011), in which two unsupervised learning methods have been proposed to identify compound verbs with their corresponding morphological features. The first one which is extending the concept of pointwise mutual information, uses a bootstraping method and the second one uses K-means clustering algorithm to detect compound verbs. However, as we have the verb, we only use their proposed method to determine VOC, MOD, NUM, TEN, NEG and PER for a given verb as our class labels. Also, we use their tool to extract the lemma of the verb (in Figure 1 "Verb lemmatizer" refers to this tool in which there is a lookup table to find the lemma of a verb). This lemma is used to generate an inflected verb form using FSA.

3.2 Morphology Prediction

Toutanova et al. (2008) predict fully inflected word form and Clifton and Sarkar (2011) predict mor-

[1]The short vowels such as *o, a, e* are not generally transcribed in Persian.

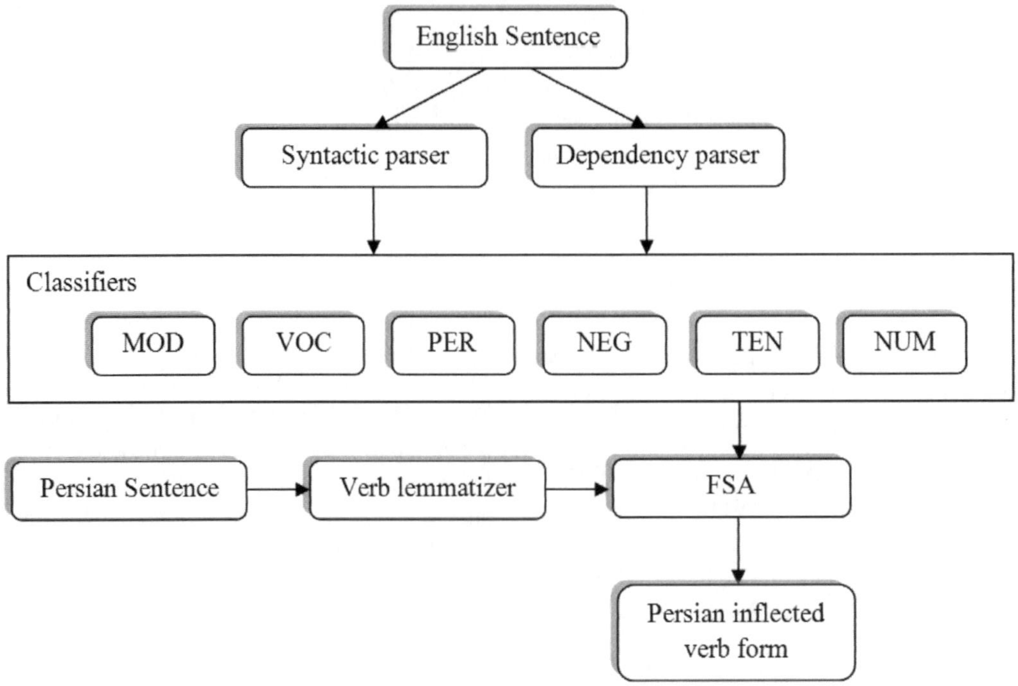

Figure 1: General schema of the verb generation process.

phemes. Unlike these approaches, we predict morphological features like El Kholy and Habash (2012a and b). Using our training data set, we build six language specific DTCs to predict each of the morphological features. Each DTC uses a subset of our feature set and predicts corresponding morphology feature independently. Then, we use a FSA to generate an inflected verb form using these six morphological features. Figure 1, shows the general schema of verb generation process.

Table 3 shows Correct Classification Ratio (CCR) of each DTC learned on our train data containing 178782 entries and evaluated on a test set containing more than 20k verbs. The most common feature value is used as our baseline for each classifier. The most improvement is achieved in the prediction of MOD and NUM. Others have high CCR but they also have very high baselines.

Predicted Feature	**Baseline CCR %**	**Prediction CCR %**	**Improv-ement**
MOD	61.12	79.63	**18.51**
NUM	68.58	83.60	15.02
VOC	85.32	87.98	2.66
TEN	85.06	88.10	3.4
PER	93.66	96.00	2.44
NEG	**95.91**	**97.13**	1.22

Table 3: CCR (%) of six DTCs and corresponding improvements.

4 Experiments

In this section, we present the results of our experiments on a test set containing 16K sentences selected from an English-Persian parallel corpus. As the main goals of our experiments, we are interested in knowing the effectiveness of our approach to rich morphology prediction and the contribution each feature has. To do so, like Minkov et al. (2007) and El Kholy and Habash (2012), who use aligned sentence pair of reference translations (reference experiments) instead of the output of an MT system as input, we also perform reference experiments because they are golden in terms of word order, lemma choice and morphological features. Table 4 shows detailed n-gram BLEU (Papineni et al., 2002) precision (for n=1,2,3,4), BLEU and TER (Snover et al., 2006) scores for morphology generation using gold lemma with the most common feature values (LEM) as a baseline and other gold morphological features and their combinations as our reference experiments.

In this experiment, we replace each sentence

Generation Input	BLEU-1	BLEU-2	BLEU-3	BLEU-4	BLEU	TER
Baseline	96.8	93.4	91.7	89.9	91.46	0.0473
RB	95.8	92.7	90.7	88.8	91.99	0.0474
LEM+MOD	97.0	94.0	92.4	90.8	93.60	0.0370
LEM+NUM	97.3	94.4	92.9	91.3	92.48	0.0420
LEM+VOC	97.1	93.9	92.2	90.5	92.06	0.0434
LEM+TEN	96.9	93.9	92.0	90.3	92.44	0.0400
LEM+PER	96.9	93.9	91.8	90.0	91.59	0.0460
LEM+NEG	96.9	93.6	91.8	90.1	91.60	0.0460
LEM+MOD+NUM	97.9	95.9	94.7	93.60	95.03	0.0280
++VOC	98.3	96.6	95.5	94.5	95.88	0.0234
++TEN	98.5	97.2	96.3	95.6	96.92	0.0156
++PER	98.8	97.8	97.1	96.5	97.54	0.0130
++NEG	**98.9**	**98.1**	**97.5**	**97.0**	**97.9**	**0.0114**

Table 4: Morphology generation results using gold Persian lemma plus different set of gold morphological features. When we add a feature to the previous feature set we use "++" notation. RB refers to the results of verb generation using rule-based approach.

verb with predicted verb generated by FSA using gold lemma plus the most common feature values as a baseline. In comparison with the baseline used by El Kholy and Habash (2012), this baseline is more stringent. As another baseline we have used a rule-based morphological analyzer which determines morphological features of the verb grammatically and generates inflected verb form (this rule-based morphological analyzer uses syntactic parse, POS tags and dependency relationships of English sentence). We use each gold feature separately to investigate the contribution each feature has. Finally, we combine gold features incrementally based on their CCR. Adding more features improve BLEU and TER scores. Since, there are some cases in which with the same morphological features it is possible to generate different but correct verb forms, the maximum BLEU score of 100 is hard to be reached even if we are given the gold features. So, the best result (97.90 of BLEU and 0.0114 of TER) could be considered as an upper bound for proposed approach. Note that, these results are obtained from our reference experiments in which a reference is duplicated and modified by our approach. In fact, there is no translation task here and a reference is evaluated by its modified version.

We perform the same reference experiments on the same data using predicted features instead of the gold features. Table 5 reports the results of detailed n-gram BLEU precision, BLUE and TER scores. According to the results, our approach outperforms the baselines in all configurations. The best configuration uses all predicted features and shows an improvement of about 2.1% absolute BLEU score and 0.102% absolute TER against our first baseline. Also, in comparison with our second baseline, rule-based approach, we achieve improvements of about 1.6% absolute BLEU score and 0.103% absolute TER.

5 Conclusions and Future Work

In this paper we present a supervised approach to rich morphology prediction. We focus on verb inflections as a highly inflecting class of words in Persian, a morphologically rich language. Using different combination of morphological features to generate inflected verb form, we evaluate our approach on a test set containing 16K sentences and obtain better BLEU and TER scores compared with our baseline, morphology generation with lemma plus the most common feature values.

Our proposed approach predicts each morphological feature independently. In the future, we plan to investigate how the features affect each other to present an order in which a predicted morphological feature is used as a learning feature for the next one. Furthermore, we also plan to use our approach as a post processing morphology generation to improve machine translation output.

Generation Input	BLEU-1	BLEU-2	BLEU-3	BLEU-4	BLEU	TER
Baseline	96.8	93.4	91.7	89.9	91.46	0.0473
RB	95.8	92.7	90.7	88.8	91.99	0.0474
LEM+MOD	96.5	93.3	91.5	89.7	92.45	0.043
LEM+NUM	**96.9**	93.6	91.8	90.1	91.63	0.0457
LEM+VOC	96.8	93.5	91.7	89.9	91.60	0.0462
LEM+TEN	96.8	93.5	91.7	89.9	91.64	0.0455
LEM+PER	**96.9**	93.5	91.7	89.9	91.51	0.0464
LEM+NEG	**96.9**	93.5	91.7	89.9	91.51	0.0464
LEM+MOD+NUM	96.8	93.9	92.2	90.5	93.05	0.0398
++VOC	96.8	93.9	92.2	90.5	93.14	0.0396
++TEN	96.8	94.0	92.3	90.7	93.39	0.0381
++PER	**96.9**	**94.2**	**92.5**	90.9	93.56	0.0373
++NEG	**96.9**	**94.2**	**92.5**	**91.0**	**93.60**	**0.0371**

Table 5: Morphology generation results using gold Persian lemma plus different set of predicted morphological features. When we add a feature to the previous feature set we use "++" notation. RB refers to the results of verb generation using rule-based approach.

6 Related Work

In this section we introduce the main approaches to morphology generation. The first approach is based on factored models, an extension of phrased-based SMT model (Koehn and Hoang, 2007). In this approach each word is annotated using morphology tags on morphologically rich side. Then, morphology generation is done based on the word level instead of phrase level, which is also the limitation of this approach. A similar approach is used by Avramidis and Koehn (2008) to translate from English into Greek and Czech. They especially focus on noun cases and verb persons. Mapping from syntax to morphology in factored model is used by Yeniterzi and Oflazer (2010) to improve English-Turkish SMT. Hierarchical phrase-based translation, an extension of factored translation model, proposed by Subotin (2011) to generate complex morphology using a discriminative model for Czech as the target laguage.

Maximum entropy model is another approach used by Minkov et al. (2007) for English-Arabic and English-Russian MT. They proposed a post-processing probabilistic framework for morphology generation utilizing a rich set of morphological knowledge sources. There are some similar approaches used by Toutanova et al. (2008) for Arabic and Russian as the target languages and by Clifton and Sarkar (2011) for English-Finnish SMT. In these approaches, the model of morphology prediction is an independent process of the SMT system.

Segmentation is another approach that improves MT by reducing the data sparseness of translation model and increasing the similarity between two sides (Goldwater and McClosky, 2005; Luong et al., 2010; Oflazer, 2008). This method analyzes morphologically rich side and unpacks inflected word forms into simpler components. Goldwater and McClosky (2005) showed that modifying Czech as the input language using 'pseudowords' improves the Czech-English machine translation system. Similar approaches are used by Oflazer (2008) for English to Turkish SMT, Luong et al. (2010) for translating from English into Finnish and Namdar et al. (2013) to improve Persian-English SMT.

Recently, a novel approach to generate rich morphology is proposed by El Kholy and Habash (2012). They use SMT to generate inflected Arabic tokens from a given sequence of lemmas and any subset of morphological features. They also have used their proposed method to model rich morphology in SMT (El Kholy and Habash, 2012). Since we use lemma and the most common feature values as our baseline, the results of their experiments is somewhat comparable to ours. However, they use only lemma with no prediction as their baseline. So, our baseline is more stringent than the baseline used by El Kholy and Habash (2012).

Our work is conceptually similar to that of de Gispert and Marino (2008), in which they incorporate a morphological classifier for Spanish verbs and define a collection of context dependent linguistic features (CDLFs), and predict each morphology feature such as PER or NUM. However, we use a different set of CDLFs and incorporate DTC to predict the morphology features of Persian verbs.

Acknowledgment

This work has been partially funded by Iran Telecom Research Center (ITRC) under contract number 9513/500.

References

Eleftherios Avramidis and Philipp Koehn. 2008. Enriching morphologically poor languages for statistical machine translation. *Proceedings of ACL-08: HLT*, pages 763–770.

Ann Clifton and Anoop Sarkar. 2011. Combining morpheme-based machine translation with postprocessing morpheme prediction. In *Proceedings of the 49th Annual Meeting of the Association for Computational Linguistics: Human Language Technologies*, volume 1, pages 32–42. Association for Computational Linguistics.

Adri de Gispert and JB Marino. 2008. On the impact of morphology in english to spanish statistical mt. *Speech Communication*, 50(11):1034–1046.

Ahmed El Kholy and Nizar Habash. 2012. Translate, predict or generate: Modeling rich morphology in statistical machine translation. In *Proc. of EAMT*, volume 12.

Sharon Goldwater and David McClosky. 2005. Improving statistical mt through morphological analysis. In *Proceedings of the conference on Human Language Technology and Empirical Methods in Natural Language Processing*, pages 676–683. Association for Computational Linguistics.

Ahmed El Kholy and Nizar Habash. 2012. Rich morphology generation using statistical machine translation. In *Proceedings of the Seventh International Natural Language Generation Conference*, pages 90–94. Association for Computational Linguistics.

Dan Klein and Christopher D Manning. 2003. Accurate unlexicalized parsing. In *Proceedings of the 41st Annual Meeting on Association for Computational Linguistics-Volume 1*, pages 423–430. Association for Computational Linguistics.

Philipp Koehn and Hieu Hoang. 2007. Factored translation models. In *Proceedings of the 2007 joint conference on empirical methods in natural language processing and computational natural language learning (EMNLP-CoNLL)*, volume 868, page 876. Prague.

Philipp Koehn, Franz Josef Och, and Daniel Marcu. 2003. Statistical phrase-based translation. In *Proceedings of the 2003 Conference of the North American Chapter of the Association for Computational Linguistics on Human Language Technology-Volume 1*, pages 48–54. Association for Computational Linguistics.

Minh-Thang Luong, Preslav Nakov, and Min-Yen Kan. 2010. A hybrid morpheme-word representation for machine translation of morphologically rich languages. In *Proceedings of the 2010 Conference on Empirical Methods in Natural Language Processing*, pages 148–157. Association for Computational Linguistics.

Amin Mansouri and Heshaam Faili. 2012. State-of-the-art english to persian statistical machine translation system. In *Artificial Intelligence and Signal Processing (AISP), 2012 16th CSI International Symposium on*, pages 174–179. IEEE.

Karine Megerdoomian. 2004. Finite-state morphological analysis of persian. In *Proceedings of the Workshop on Computational Approaches to Arabic Script-based Languages*, pages 35–41. Association for Computational Linguistics.

Einat Minkov, Kristina Toutanova, and Hisami Suzuki. 2007. Generating complex morphology for machine translation. In *ANNUAL MEETING-ASSOCIATION FOR COMPUTATIONAL LINGUISTICS*, volume 45, page 128.

Saman Namdar, Heshaam Faili, and Sahram Khadivi. 2013. Using inflected word form to improve persian to english statistical machine translation. In *Proceedings of the 18th National CSI (Computer Society of Iran) Computer Conference*.

Franz Josef Och and Hermann Ney. 2003. A systematic comparison of various statistical alignment models. *Computational linguistics*, 29(1):19–51.

Kemal Oflazer. 2008. Statistical machine translation into a morphologically complex language. In *Computational linguistics and intelligent text processing*, pages 376–387. Springer.

Kishore Papineni, Salim Roukos, Todd Ward, and Wei-Jing Zhu. 2002. Bleu: a method for automatic evaluation of machine translation. In *Proceedings of the 40th annual meeting on association for computational linguistics*, pages 311–318. Association for Computational Linguistics.

J. Ross Quinlan. 1986. Induction of decision trees. *Machine learning*, 1(1):81–106.

Mohammad Sadegh Rasooli, Heshaam Faili, and Behrouz Minaei-Bidgoli. 2011. Unsupervised identification of persian compound verbs. In *Advances in Artificial Intelligence*, pages 394–406. Springer.

Matthew Snover, Bonnie Dorr, Richard Schwartz, Linnea Micciulla, and John Makhoul. 2006. A study of translation edit rate with targeted human annotation. In *Proceedings of association for machine translation in the Americas*, pages 223–231.

Michael Subotin. 2011. An exponential translation model for target language morphology. In *Proc. ACL*.

Kristina Toutanova, Hisami Suzuki, and Achim Ruopp. 2008. Applying morphology generation models to machine translation. pages 514–522.

Reyyan Yeniterzi and Kemal Oflazer. 2010. Syntax-to-morphology mapping in factored phrase-based statistical machine translation from english to turkish. In *Proceedings of the 48th Annual Meeting of the Association for Computational Linguistics*, pages 454–464. Association for Computational Linguistics.

Sentiment Analysis of Reviews:
Should we analyze writer intentions or reader perceptions?

Isa Maks and Piek Vossen
Vu University, Faculty of Arts
De Boelelaan 1105, 1081 HV Amsterdam
e.maks@vu.nl, p.vossen@vu.nl

Abstract

Many sentiment-analysis methods for the classification of reviews use training and test-data based on star ratings provided by reviewers. However, when reading reviews it appears that the reviewers' ratings do not always give an accurate measure of the sentiment of the review. We performed an annotation study which showed that reader perceptions can also be expressed in ratings in a reliable way and that they are closer to the text than the reviewer ratings. Moreover, we applied two common sentiment-analysis techniques and evaluated them on both reader and reviewer ratings. We come to the conclusion that it would be better to train models on reader ratings, rather than on reviewer ratings (as is usually done).

1 Introduction

There is a growing volume of product reviews on the web which help customers to make decisions when planning to travel or buying a product. Sentiment-analysis tools try to discover user opinions in these reviews by converting the text to numerical ratings. Building these tools requires a large set of annotated data to train the classifiers. Most developers compile a training and test corpus by collecting reviews from web sites on which customers post their reviews and give a star rating. They test and train their tools against these reviewer ratings assuming that they are an accurate measure of the sentiment of the review.

However, when reading reviews and comparing them with the reviewer ratings there does not always seem to be a clear and consistent relation between these ratings and the text (cf. also Carrillo de Albornoz et al., 2011). That is, from a reader's perspective, there is a discrepancy between what the reviewer expresses with the numerical rating and what is expressed in text. For example, the following hotel review was rated '7' (weakly positive), whereas possible guests probably would not go to the hotel after having read the review.

The hotel seems rather outdated. The breakfast room is just not big enough to cope with the Sunday-morning crowds.

This mismatch between the reviewer's rating and the review's sentiment may lead to problems. For example, reviews are often ranked according to their reviewer's ratings from highly positive to highly negative. If the review text is not in accordance with its ranking, the rankings may become ineffective. In the area of sentiment analysis and opinion mining the mismatch may lead to methodological problems. Testing and training of sentiment-analysis tools on reviewer ratings may lead to the wrong results if the mismatch between the ratings and the text proves to be a common phenomenon.

We assume that one of the most important sources of this mismatch is the fact that the reviewer writes the review and, separately, rates the experience (i.e., with the book he read, with the hotel he stayed at, with a product he bought). Of course, both text and rating are based on the same experience but they do not

necessarily express the same aspects of it. If we have a closer look at the hotel review above, the reviewer probably rates the hotel with a '7', because there may be some positive aspects which he does not mention in his review.
We hypothesize that reader ratings which express the reader's perceptions of the sentiment of a text are a good alternative. As the reader's judgment is based solely on the text of the review, we assume that its rating is closer to the sentiment of the text than the reviewer's rating.

In this study we investigate whether the observed mismatch between reviewer rating and the sentiment of the review is a common phenomenon and whether reader ratings could be a more reliable measure of this sentiment than reviewer ratings.

The next section presents related work. In section 3, the reliability of reviewer and reader ratings as a measure of a review's sentiment is further investigated by performing an annotation study. In section 4, we study the effect of the different types of ratings on the performance of two widely used sentiment-analysis techniques. Finally, we conclude with a discussion of our findings.

2 Related Work

There is a large body of work concerning sentiment analysis of customer reviews (Liu, 2012). Most of these studies regard sentiment analysis as a classification problem and apply supervised learning methods where the positive and negative classes are determined by reviewer ratings. Studies propose additional annotations only when focusing on novel information which is not reflected in the user ratings (Toprak et al., 2010, Ando and Ishizaki, 2012). The issue of a possible mismatch between reviewer ratings and review text is usually not addressed.

Much attention is paid to the customer's (or reader's) perspective in studies in the area of business and social science. Mahony et al. (2010) and Ghose et al. (2012) study product reviews in relation to customer behavior. Their aim is to identify reviews which are considered helpful to customers and to know what kind of reviews affect sales. Their work is similar to ours because of the focus on the effect of the review text on the customer/reader, but they also include other types of information such as transaction data, consumer browser behavior and customer preferences. However, none of these studies focus on the relationship between reviewer rating and review text.

As far as we know, Carrillo de Albornoz et al. (2011) is the only study which mentions the mismatch between rating and text. They ignore reviewer ratings and employ a new set of ratings for the training and testing of their system. From their work, however, it is neither clear to what extent the new ratings differ from the user ratings as they do not report inter-annotator agreement scores nor what the effect is of the different ratings on classifier performance.

3 Reviewer and reader annotations

To get a better understanding of the relationship between reviewer ratings, review text and reader ratings, we perform an annotation study which allows us to answer the following research questions: (1) To what extent are mismatches between reviewers' ratings and sentiments common? And (2) Can reader ratings be employed to measure review sentiment more reliably?

3.1 Hotel review corpus

For the annotation study we compiled a corpus of Dutch hotel reviews. The corpus consists of 1,171 reviews extracted from four different booking sites during the period 2010-2012. The reviews have been collected in such a way that they are evenly distributed among the following categories:

- They are collected from different booking site like Tripadvisor.com, zoover.com, hotelnl.com and booking.com
- They include most frequent text formats: pro-con (where boxes are provided for positive and negative remarks) and free text.

- They include reviews on hotels from all over the world (although the majority is Dutch).
- They include reviewer's ratings ranging from strong negative to strong positive

Each review contains the following information:

- Reviewer rating: a user rating given by the reviewer translated to a scale ranging from 0 to 10 (very negative to very positive) describing the overall opinion of the hotel customer.
- Review text: a brief text describing the reviewer's opinion of the hotel.
- Reader ratings: ratings of two readers on a scale ranging from 0 to 10. These ratings are described in more detail in the next section.

3.2 Reader ratings and agreement scores

Two annotators (R1 and R2), both native speakers of Dutch and with no linguistic background, added a reader rating to each review. They were asked to read the review and rate the text on a scale from 1-10 (very negative to very positive), answering the question whether the reviewer would advise them to choose the hotel, or not. They were asked to ignore their own preferences as much as possible.

We measured the Pearson Correlation Coefficient (r) between the 10-point numerical rating scales of each annotator pair (R1, R2 and reviewer), regarding the reviewer (REV) also as an annotator. As correlation can be high without necessarily high agreement on absolute values, we also performed evaluations on categorical values. A 2-class evaluation was performed by translating 1 to 5 ratings to 'positive' and 6 to10 ratings to 'negative'; a 4-class evaluation is performed by translating 1-3 ratings to 'strong negative', 4 to 5 ratings to 'weak negative', 6 to 7 ratings to 'weak positive' and 8 to 10 to 'strong positive'. Agreement was measured between each annotator pair in terms of percentage of agreement (%) and kappa agreement (κ).

raters	1/10	2-class		4-class	
REV-R1	0.82 r	0.81 κ	0.90%	0.51 κ	0.63%
REV-R2	0.83 r	0.82 κ	0.91%	0.53 κ	0.65%
R1-R2	0.92 r	0.92 κ	0.96%	0.71 κ	0.78%

Table 1. Inter-annotator agreement.

Table (1) shows that inter-annotator agreement is quite high between all raters, both when correlation is measured on the 10-point-scale (r >= 0.82) and when agreement is measured with the 2-class annotation sets (κ >= 0.81). Agreement on the 4 class annotations is much lower (κ >= 0.51) showing that polarity strength is difficult to annotate. However, given the purpose of this study, we are not interested in agreement as such. Our focus is on the differences in agreement between readers and reviewers. From that perspective it is interesting to note that, according to all measures, the reviewer is an outlier. Agreement between each individual reader and the reviewer (REV-R1 and REV-R2, respectively) is consistently lower than agreement between both readers (R1-R2). The differences already become important when measuring agreement on 2-class annotations, but even more prominent when measuring agreement on 4-class annotations. All observed differences ranging from 5 up to 15%, are statistically significant ($p < 0.01$).

On the basis of these results, we can answer our research questions (cf. section 3). We infer that the observed mismatch between the sentiment of the review and reviewer rating is a relatively common phenomenon. With respect to at least 10% (cf. table 1, row 2, column 4) of the reviews (when reviews are categorized in 2 categories) up to approx. 37% (cf. table 1, row 1, column 6) of the reviews (when reviews are categorized in more fine-grained categories) readers do not agree with the reviewer. Secondly, the fact that readers have higher agreement with each other than with the reviewer confirms our hypothesis that reader ratings are a more accurate measure of the review's sentiment than reviewer ratings.

4 Implications for sentiment analysis

We investigated how automated sentiment analysis methods perform with the different sets of annotations by applying two widely used approaches to document-level sentiment classification. Classifier accuracy is measured against the three sets of ratings (R1, R2 and REV) we described in the previous section.

4.1 The lexicon-based approach

The first method is a lexicon-based approach which starts from a text which is lemmatized with the Dutch Alpino-parser[1].The approach is similar to the "vote-flip-algorithm" proposed by Choi and Cardie (2008). The intuition about this algorithm is simple: for each review the number of matched positive and negative words from the sentiment lexicon are counted. If polar words are preceded by a negator, their polarity is flipped; if polar words are preceded by an intensifier, their polarity is doubled. We then assign the majority polarity to the review. In the case of a tie (being zero or higher than zero), we assign neutral polarity. The sentiment lexicon used in this approach is an automatically derived general language sentiment lexicon obtained by WordNet propagation (Maks and Vossen, 2011).

4.2 The machine-learning approach

The second method is a machine learning approach that also starts from a text that is lemmatized by the Dutch Alpino-parser. After lemmatization the text is transformed to a word-vector representation by applying Weka's StringToWord Vector with frequency representation (instead of binary). We used Weka's NaiveBayesMultinominal (NBM) classifier to classify the reviews. The NBM was chosen because our review texts are rather short (with an average of 68 words) and, according to Wang and Manning (2012), NBM classifiers perform well on short snippets of text. Results reported are average of ten-fold-cross-validation-accuracies using R1, R2 and REV ratings as training and test data.

4.3 Results on different types of ratings

Results are evaluated against the whole set of 1,172 reviews (cf. table 2 'all'). As many approaches to sentiment analysis do not use the class of weak sentiment (Liu, 2012), we also evaluated against a subset of strong negative (ratings 1 to 3) and strong positive (ratings 8 to 10) reviews (cf. table 2, 'strong'). Table (2) shows the classification results in terms of accuracy, obtained by the lexicon-based approach (LBA, row 1, 2, 3) and the machine-learning approach (NBM, row 4, 5, 6).

	name	ratings	all	strong
1	LBA	REV	78.3	85.0
2	LBA	R1	80.5	88.1
3	LBA	R2	80.7	88.1
4	NBM	REV	83.6	86.4
5	NBM	R1	86.9	92.2
6	NBM	R2	86.7	92.2

Table 2. Results of sentiment analysis.

The results show that both approaches perform well against all ratings. Classification of the strong sentiment reviews seems considerably easier than classification of the whole review set. Interestingly, both sentiment analysis approaches appear to perform better on reader ratings than on reviewer ratings. The better performance holds across both selections of reviews and with both approaches. Differences are statistically significant (chi-square test, $p<0.05$) in all cases but the LBA approach on the whole dataset which is almost statistically significant.

5 Discussion and Conclusions

We performed an annotation study that showed that the observed mismatch between reviewer ratings and review's sentiment is a rather frequent phenomenon. Considerable part of the reviews (ranging from 9 to 37% depending on the granularity of the classification) is classi-

[1] http://www.let.rug.nl/ vannoord/alp/Alpino/

fied by the reviewer in the wrong sentiment class.

The annotation study also showed that reader ratings are a more accurate measure. We already expected reader ratings to be closer to the text because they are exclusively based on it. In addition, the annotation study shows that readers agree in their ratings and that the review's sentiment can be reliably annotated by readers.

Our experiments in section 4 show that sentiment-analysis tools perform better with reader ratings than with reviewer ratings. This should probably not surprise us as sentiment analysis behaves like a reader whose only source of information is the review text. As such, this is a promising result. However, since reviewer ratings are widely available and come for free with the text, they will often be used to evaluate the tools. Likewise, training and fine-tuning will be done with reviewer ratings rather than with reader ratings.

We think that researchers and system developers should be aware of the differences between reviewer and reader ratings and their effects on the system they develop. Recently, many sentiment analysis tools perform a more in-depth analysis identifying aspects of products (and services) and their sentiments (Liu, 2012). Again, reviewer ratings are used to train and test these systems. In view of our findings, it seems advisable that researchers and system developers make the effort to collect a set of reader ratings and train and test their tools with them. The additional value of sentiment analysis should be sought in finding the sentiment of the text rather than in finding the sentiment of its writer.

Acknowledgements

This research is supported by the European Unions 7th Framework Programme via the OpeNER (Open polarity enhanced Named Entity Recognition) Project (ICT-296451).

References

Ando, M. and S. Ishizaki (2012) Analysis of travel review data from Reader's point of View. In *Proceedings of WASSA-2012*. Jeju, South-Korea.

Carrillo de Albornoz, J., L. Plaza, P. Gervás and A. Diaz (2011). A joint model for feature mining and sentiment analysis for product review rating. In *Proceedings of ECIR-2011*. Dublin, Ireland.

Choi, Y. and C. Cardie (2008). Learning with Compositional Semantics as Structural Inference for Subsentential Sentiment Analysis. In *Proceedings of EMNLP '08*. Hawaii, USA.

Ghose, A., G. Ipeirotis and B. Li (2012). Designing Ranking Systems for Hotels on Travel Search Engines by Mining User-Generated and Crowdsourced Content. *Marketing Science*, Vol. 31.

Liu, B. (2012). *Sentiment Analysis and Opinion Mining*.
Morgan & Claypool Publishers, USA.

Mahony, M., P. Cunningham and B. Smyth (2010). An
assessment of machine learning techniques for review recommendation. In *Proceedings of AICS*.

Maks, I., and P. Vossen (2011) Different Approaches to Automatic Polarity Annotation at Synset Level. In: *Proceedings of the First International Workshop on Lexical Resources*, WoLeR 2011, Ljubljana.

Toprak, C., N. Jakob and I. Gurevych. (2010) Sentence and Expression Level Annotation of Opinions in User-Generated Discourse. In *ACL 2010*. Uppsala, Sweden.

Wang, S. and C. Manning. (2012). Baselines and Bigrams: Simple, Good Sentiment and Topic Classification. In *Proceedings of ACL-2012*.

Revisiting The Old Kitchen Sink: Do We Need Sentiment Domain Adaptation?

Riham Hassan Mansour[1]
rihamma@microsoft.com

Nesma Refaei[3]
nesma.a.refaei@eng.cu.edu.eg

Michael Gamon[2]
mgamon@microsoft.com

Khaled Sami[1]
t-ksami@microsoft.com

Ahmed Abdel-Hamid[1]
ahmedab@microsoft.com

[1]Microsoft Research, 306 Maadi Courniche, Basatin, Cairo, Egypt
[2]Microsoft Research, One Microsoft Way, Redmond, WA 98051, USA
[3]Computer Engineering, Cairo University/ Gamaet El Qahera St., Giza, Egypt

Abstract

In this paper we undertake a large cross-domain investigation of sentiment domain adaptation, challenging the practical necessity of sentiment domain adaptation algorithms. We first show that across a wide set of domains, a simple "all-in-one" classifier that utilizes all available training data from all but the target domain tends to outperform published domain adaptation methods. A very simple ensemble classifier also performs well in these scenarios. Combined with the fact that labeled data nowadays is inexpensive to come by, the "kitchen sink" approach, while technically non-glamorous, might be perfectly adequate in practice. We also show that the common anecdotal evidence for sentiment terms that "flip" polarity across domains is not borne out empirically.

1 Introduction

Automatic detection and analysis of sentiment around products, brands, political issues etc. has triggered a large amount of research in the past 15 – 20 years (for a recent overview see Pang & Lee 2008 and Liu 2012). Early work focused on algorithms for mining sentiment dictionaries (Hatzivassiloglou and McKeown 1997, Turney 2002); this was followed by the exploration of supervised techniques (Pang et al. 2002) and, somewhat more recently, by investigations of domain adaptation techniques. Also more recently, the focus has broadened from the detection of polarity (negative/positive sentiment) to more nuanced approaches that try to identify targets and holders of sentiment, sentiment strength, or finer-grained mood distinctions (e.g. Wilson et al. 2006, Kim and Hovy 2006). Within the polarity detection paradigm, a number of common assumptions have been shared in the community and are frequently repeated in the literature. Two of these fundamental assumptions are:

1. Obtaining sufficient labeled data for supervised training is expensive
2. Sentiment models trained on one domain tend to perform poorly on new, unseen domains

A conclusion that is often drawn from these assumptions is that domain adaptation of sentiment models from a domain with sufficient labeled data to a new domain with little labeled data is an important problem and requires new and sophisticated algorithms.

In this paper, we empirically re-examine the assumptions above. Based on a wide range of experiments on 27 different domains, we challenge the conclusion that domain adaptation for polarity detection necessarily requires novel and sophisticated machinery. It is important to keep in mind, however, that our claims are strictly limited to the problem under investigation, namely polarity detection. We do not make any claims whatsoever about domain adaptation for other sentiment-related problems or general problems in machine learning. Based on readily available data from 27 domains, we show that a "kitchen sink" approach where all source domain data are combined to train a single classifier sets a surprisingly high baseline for polarity identification accuracy across domains. We also show on a previously released data set of four domains that the result is competitive with a state-of-the-art domain adaptation approach using Structural

Correspondence Learning. We then show that a straightforward ensemble learner can, for some domains, improve results further, without any need for specialized learning algorithms. Since most work in domain-adaptation only provides published results on pairwise adaptation between domains and not on multi-domain adaptation, we hope to establish a new baseline for future adaptation techniques to compare against.

2 Related Work

Of direct importance to the discussion in this paper are results from domain adaptation in polarity detection. One of the earlier successful approaches (Blitzer et al. 2006, 2007) involved Structural Correspondence Learning (SCL). SCL identifies "pivot" features that are both highly discriminative in the labeled source domain data and also frequent in the unlabeled target domain data. In a subsequent step, linear predictors for the pivot terms are learned from the unlabeled target data and from the source data.

Daumé (2007) approached domain adaptation from a fully labeled source domain to a partially labeled target domain by augmenting the feature space. Instead of using a single, general, feature set for source and target, three distinct feature sets are created: the general set of features, a source-domain specific version of the feature set, and a target-specific version of the feature set.

Li and Zong (NLP-KE 2008) explore a classifier combination technique they call "Multiple-Label Consensus Training" which results in better accuracy than non-adapted models on the data sets used in Blitzer et al. (2007). They also addressed the multi-domain sentiment analysis problem using feature –level fusion and classifier-level fusion approaches in Li and Zong (ACL 2008).

Dredze and Crammer (2008) have proposed a multi-domain online learning framework based on parameter combination from multiple Confidence Weighted (CW) classifiers. Their Multi-Domain Regularization (MDR) framework seeks to learn domain specific parameters guided by the shared parameter across domains.

Samdani and Yih (2011) propose an ensemble learner that consists of classifiers trained on different feature groups. The feature groups are identified based on how stable the feature distribution is across domains, which can either be estimated from the data directly or can be hypothesized based on domain knowledge.

Chen et al. (2011) use a specific co-training algorithm for domain adaptation on the Blitzer et al. (2007) data set. In averaged pair-wise comparisons they establish gains over a source-plus-target logistic regression baseline.

Glorot et al. (2011) investigate a deep learning approach to domain adaptation and report increased accuracy across domains both on the Blitzer et al. (2007) 4-domain data set and the larger Amazon review data set (25 domains) also made available in that release. They also introduce a new metric for transfer learning: *Transfer Ratio*.

3 Datasets & Experimental Setup

This section illustrates the datasets, the methods and the setup of our experiments.

3.1 Datasets

The datasets we used in our experiments have been obtained from three sources:

1. Amazon reviews[1]: this dataset contains more than 5.8 million reviews. It has been used in previous work on sentiment analysis (see Glorot et al. (2011)). The Amazon reviews include 25 domains as shown in Table 1.
2. Hotel reviews[2]: this dataset includes full reviews of hotels in 10 different cities (Dubai, Beijing, London, New York City, New Delhi, San Francisco, Shanghai, Montreal, Las Vegas, Chicago). There are about 80-700 hotels in each city. The extracted fields include date, review title and the full review. The total number of reviews is 259,000.
3. Twitter: this dataset has been obtained and annotated in Choudhury et al. (AAAI 2012) over a 1 year period of time from Nov. 1, 2010 to Oct. 31, 2011. The dataset has been originally annotated for affects. We mapped the positive affects "joviality" and "serenity" to positive sentiment and the negative affects "fatigue", "hostility", and "sadness" to negative sentiment. We selected a balanced dataset of 2,000 tweets from the various months of the collected tweets.

The average review length for the Amazon and hotel reviews is 437 characters and 97 words. In total, we used 27 domains namely the

---

1 Amazon reviews could be obtained at http://liu.cs.uic.edu/download/data/

2 Hotel reviews could be obtained at http://mlr.cs.umass.edu/ml/datasets/OpinRank+Review+Dataset

25 Amazon domains, the hotel domain and the Twitter domain. We considered Twitter as a domain though the content of tweets spans multiple domains since it has different characteristics from the product reviews. Tweets are constrained to 140 characters each and lack context.

Domain	Dataset Size	Labeled Data Size	Domain	Dataset Size	Labeled Data Size	Domain	Dataset Size	Labeled Data Size
Apparel	9252	2000	Kitchen & housewares	19856	2000	Electronics	23009	2000
Automotive	736	304	Magazines	4191	1940	Gourmet food	1575	416
Baby	4256	1800	Music	174180	2000	Grocery	2632	704
Beauty	2884	986	Musical instruments	332	96	Health & personal care	7225	2000
Books	975194	2000	Office products	431	128	Jewelry & watches	1981	584
Camera & photo	7408	1998	Outdoor living	1599	654	Toys & games	13147	2000
Cell phones & service	1023	768	Software	2390	1830	Video	36180	2000
Computer & video games	2771	916	Sports & outdoors	5728	2000	Hotel	259,000	2000
Dvd	124438	2000	Tools & hardware	112	28	Tweets	1,107,282	2000

Table 1: Dataset sizes of the 27 Domains.

The Amazon reviews and the hotel reviews are rated between 1 and 5 on a 5 point scale where 1 is the most negative and 5 is the most positive. We have extracted only the reviews that are rated 5 and 1 to represent the positive and negative reviews respectively. Further, we ensured that the datasets we extracted and used for training are balanced between positive and negative reviews. Table 1 summarizes the 27 domains and their dataset sizes including the balanced datasets we used for training.

3.2 Experimental Setup

In our experiments, we employed the datasets of the 27 domains mentioned in section 3.1. In each experiment, we have employed one domain for testing while the other 26 domains have been used for training. We compared four domain adaptation techniques:

1. One classifier trained in all source domains.
2. An ensemble of classifiers, each trained on a source domain, combined into an ensemble.
3. The domain adaptation approach proposed in Daumé (2007).
4. We also compared the results of approaches 1 and 2 to published results on Structural Correspondence Learning (SCL) by using the same datasets as in Blitzer et al. (2007).

In all our experiments, we employed Maximum Entropy-based classification with vanilla parameter settings and feature reduction using log-likelihood ratio (LLR). Further, we used the accuracy metric to indicate the performance of each of the above four domain adaptation techniques. We also employed the Transfer Ratio metric proposed by Glorot et al. (2011) to measure the performance of the all-in-one and ensemble classifiers. The rest of the subsection illustrates the experimental setup for each of the above four approaches.

In-domain Classifiers

To establish a "ceiling" performance we built an in-domain classifier for each of the 27 domains. The in-domain classifier is trained with a dataset of that one domain and tested on the same domain (using cross-validation). This standard in-domain supervised setup establishes an upper bound for classification performance (although in some cases we will see that other techniques can outperform this upper bound). Features consist of binary unigram and bigram features. On average, the total number of features in each domain is 52,039. Feature reduction was performed using LLR, retaining only the top 20,000 most predictive features as established on the training set.

We compare the results obtained from testing each domain with the three approaches to its in-domain classifier results.

All-in-one Classifier

The all-in-one classifier is a maximum entropy classifier trained with the source domain datasets merged together. In this setting, the classifier is trained with data from multiple domains, which exposes it to multiple sentiment vocabularies at training time, creating a somewhat domain-independent and general model. The all-in-one classifier is trained with 26 domains datasets while being tested on the held-out 27th domain.

Ensemble Classifiers

One approach to address the problem of domain adaptation is to construct an ensemble of classifiers, all of which contribute partially to the final result (see Dietterich (1997) for an overview). We constructed an ensemble of in-domain sentiment classifiers, one for each source domain. There are various techniques to combine the contribution of each classifier in the ensemble. We employed three techniques in our experiment settings:

1. Majority vote: the results are obtained by taking the majority of votes from the multiple classifiers in the ensemble. For example, if 20 classifiers vote positive and only 6 classifiers vote negative, the final result is positive
2. Sum of weights: the results are obtained by summing up the class probabilities from each classifier.
3. Meta-classification: the results are obtained by combining the weight of each classifier's vote in a meta-classifier. The meta-classifier weights are learned through a machine learning model trained on a small labeled set of data from the target domain. We used both logistic regression and SVM to train the meta-classifier. We have experimented with multiple sizes of labeled target data ranging from 5 positive and 5 negative meta-training examples to 50 positive and 50 negative examples. The following steps are used to train the meta-classifier.
    a) For each review *r* in the set of labeled data in target domain D that is used to train the meta-classifier; we create a vector V consisting of the vote of each source-domain classifier on *r* and the label of r.
    b) We construct a matrix M of the set of vectors Vs created in step 1.
    c) We employ either logistic regression or SVM. We have used SVM^{light} implementation[3] to train the ensemble using SVM with the matrix M and a radial basis kernel function.

Hal Daumé's Domain-Adaptation Approach

Daumé (2007) addresses domain adaptation where a large, annotated corpus of data from the source domain is available with only a small, annotated corpus of the target domain. Daumé's work leverages both annotated datasets to obtain a model that performs well on the target domain. For K source domains, the augmented feature space consists of K+1 copies of the original feature space. However, creating three versions of each feature in both the source and the target domains grows the feature space exponentially, which is prohibitive in a many-domain adaptation scenario such as ours which consists of a total of 27 domains.

We addressed this challenge by considering the 26 source domains as a single source domain being adapted to the target domain. This setup along with feature reduction enabled us to apply Daumé's approach without too much of an inflation of the feature space. However, we also recognize that this likely compromises the power of the feature augmentation approach.

Blitzer's Structural Correspondence Learning

Blitzer et al. (2007) employ the Structural Correspondence Learning (SCL) algorithm for sentiment domain adaptation. Blitzer et al. evaluate the SCL domain adaptation on four publicly released datasets from Amazon product reviews: books, DVDs, electronics and kitchen appliances. In these four datasets, reviews with rating > 3 were labeled positive, those with rating < 3 were labeled negative, and the rest discarded because their polarity was ambiguous. 1000 positive and 1000 negative labeled examples were used for each domain. Some unlabeled data were additionally used including 3685 (DVDs) and 5945 (kitchen). Each labeled dataset was split into 1600 instances for training and 400 instances for testing. The baseline in Blitzer et al. (2007) is a linear classifier trained without adaptation, while their ceiling reference is the same as ours, which is the in-domain classifier trained and tested on the same domain.

We conducted a set of experiments employing the four datasets used for SCL domain adaptation. In these experiments, we compare the results of our all-in-one classifier and the ensemble classifier trained and tested on the four datasets to the results of SCL and its variation SCL-MI domain adaptation as reported by Blitzer et al. (2007) on the same datasets. We employ the same training and test split size for cross-validation of the SCL domain adaptation approach. Further, we replicated both the approach

[3] Implementation of SVM^{light} : http://svmlight.joachims.org/

baseline and ceiling in-domain classifiers for the four domains.

4 Results & Discussion

This section summarizes the results of the experiments described in section 3.2 while further scrutinizing the comparison between the four domain adaptation sentiment analysis techniques. We also report the Transfer Ratio results of the all-in-one and ensemble classifiers. Generally, the all-in-one classifier is closely comparable to the in-domain classifier of each domain

4.1 Results

In this section, we summarize the various results obtained from the set of experiments described in section 3.2. In the summary of each experiment results, we also plot the in-domain classifier results of each domain as the ceiling of comparison.

All-in-one Classifier Experiments

In the all-in-one classifier experiments, the sentiment classifier is trained with 26 domain datasets while testing it with the 27th domain. Table 3 summarizes the results. The results of the all-in-one classifier are very close to the in-domain classifiers in most domains except for the apparel, beauty, magazines, outdoor living, office products and software.

Ensemble Classifier Experiments

We produced the results of the ensemble of classifiers using the three settings: majority votes, sum of weights, and meta-classification using both logistic regression and SVM. Table 3 summarizes the results of the three settings used in the ensemble.

Table 3 shows that the ensembles with sum of weights and meta-training (SVM sigmoid kernel) are the most comparable to the in-domain classifier of each domain. We also experimented with variations of logistic regression and SVM for meta-training. The non-linear (RBF kernel) SVM meta-classifier outperforms the linear logistic regression model. We have employed two variations of SVM, namely, a radial basis function with gamma 0.01 and sigmoid kernel. In most domains, the SVM model trained with 50 positive and 50 negative feedback examples is not far off the one trained with 5 positive and 5 negative feedback examples. This shows that even with little labeled data in the target domain, the ensemble could effectively combine the weights of the classifier votes. We expect the ensemble to achieve steady but slow performance gains over time while collecting more feedback examples.

Hal Daumé's Domain-Adaptation Approach

We compared the performance of the all-in-one and ensemble classifiers to Daumé's feature augmentation algorithm. Table 3 shows that the all-in-one classifier exceeds Daumé's approach in all 27 domains given our current implementation of Daumé's approach. The ensemble exceeds Daumé's approach on all domains except office, kitchen & housewares, magazines, office products, and tweets.

Structural Correspondence Learning (SCL)

We employed the four domains datasets used in Blitzer et al. (2007) to train and test the all-in one and the ensemble classifiers. We also replicated the in-domain results of these four datasets using our maximum entropy classifier. We compare the results of the all-in-one and the ensemble classifier to the SCL and its variation SCL-MI adaptation techniques using the four datasets used to evaluate SCL and SCL-MI in Blitzer et al. (2007).

Note that the results published in Blitzer's work represent pairwise domain-adaptation, while our ensemble and all-in-one results are based on training on three of Blitzer's domains and testing on the held-out fourth domain. This makes it impossible to draw a direct comparison, but we can still observe that in general, it is best to simply combine as many domains as possible in an all-in-one or ensemble approach as compared to carefully adapting a single domain. Table 2 summarizes the results of the comparison.

Classifier	Books	DVD	Electronics	Kitchen
In-Domain	81.50%	83.00%	84.50%	83.50%
SCL Adaptation	72.80%	74.60%	78.40%	80.80%
SCL-MI Adaptation	74.60%	76.30%	78.90%	82.10%
All-in-one Classifier	79.00%	82.50%	79.50%	80.00%
Ensemble	79.00%	77.50%	80.00%	85.50%

Table2: Comparison of SCL, All-in-one, and Ensemble Classifiers

Reporting Transfer Ratio

Glorot et al. (2011) introduced a definition for the *transfer loss* t for a source domain S and a target domain T. It represents loss of accuracy using a transfer model compared to an in-domain model:

Where is the transfer error defined as the test error obtained by a method trained on the source domain S and tested on the target domain T. is the test error obtained by the base-line method.

The *transfer ratio* Q also characterizes the transfer but is defined by replacing the difference by a quotient in t:

Domain	In-Domain	All-in-one	Ensemble-sum of weights	Ensemble-majority votes	Ensemble (logistic re-gression)	Ensemble (sigmoid kernel)	Hal-Daume
Apparel	90.87%	92.81%	96.40%	90.30%	90.65%	97.12%	92.09%
Automotive	83.85%	92.31%	92.31%	86.76%	96.15%	96.15%	76.92%
Baby	91.94%	89.15%	89.15%	89.72%	77.52%	83.72%	82.95%
Beauty	90.00%	89.87%	84.81%	87.88%	87.34%	83.54%	75.95%
Books	87.19%	87.50%	82.03%	83.16%	74.22%	80.47%	75.78%
Camera & photo	94.33%	94.03%	92.54%	90.35%	89.55%	88.81%	87.31%
Cell-phones & service	93.13%	95.31%	89.06%	90.45%	95.31%	95.31%	75.00%
Computer & video-games	95.77%	90.14%	87.32%	87.87%	80.28%	77.46%	71.83%
DVD	91.11%	89.68%	85.71%	83.65%	78.57%	86.51%	82.54%
Electronics	92.35%	92.65%	90.44%	87.22%	91.91%	85.29%	80.15%
Gourmet-food	89.68%	94.12%	82.35%	83.89%	82.35%	85.29%	79.41%
Grocery	92.41%	90.74%	92.59%	88.18%	85.19%	88.89%	79.63%
Health & personal-care	93.55%	95.65%	92.75%	89.78%	83.33%	87.68%	86.23%
Hotel	95.15%	96.00%	93.00%	90.36%	87.50%	88.50%	85.00%
Jewelry & watches	94.78%	97.83%	97.83%	89.90%	93.48%	93.48%	80.43%
Kitchen & housewares	93.33%	92.03%	92.03%	90.30%	86.23%	89.86%	93.07%
Magazines	96.38%	90.58%	89.86%	83.81%	76.81%	85.51%	89.13%
Music	90.39%	89.15%	88.37%	81.61%	79.07%	80.62%	72.87%
Musical instruments	95.71%	100.00%	100.00%	91.18%	100.00%	100.00%	85.71%
Office products	95.56%	100.00%	100.00%	92.00%	100.00%	88.89%	100.00%
Outdoor living	97.27%	89.09%	90.91%	89.37%	85.45%	89.09%	83.64%
Software	94.81%	90.70%	94.57%	89.08%	93.80%	89.92%	87.60%
Sports & outdoors	94.62%	89.23%	88.46%	88.76%	83.08%	86.92%	86.15%
Tools & hardware	100.00%	100.00%	100.00%	92.86%	100.00%	100.00%	100.00%
Toys & games	93.80%	96.27%	94.78%	89.47%	91.79%	94.03%	91.79%
Video	91.93%	90.30%	81.34%	85.22%	73.13%	82.09%	80.60%
Tweets	72.82%	68.50%	63.50%	62.82%	60.00%	57.50%	61.50%

Table 3: Performance of the All-in-One, Ensemble and Hal Daume's Classifiers

$$- \; Q = \frac{1}{n}\sum\nolimits_{(S,T)S\neq T} \frac{e(S,T)}{e_b(T,T)}$$

Where n is the number of couples (S, T) with S≠T.

The all-in-one classifier had a 1.12 transfer ratio across domains, which is very close to the best result of ~1.07 in Glorot et al. The ensemble with Sigmoid kernel of SVM trained on 50 positive and 50 negative feedback examples from the target domain had 1.81 transfer ratio. The ensemble with radial basis function (gamma=0.01) trained on 5 positive and 5 negative feedback examples from the target domain had 1.85 transfer ratio. Note that the transfer ratio of the in-domain classifier, which is used a base-line for calculating the transfer ratio is 1. The transfer ratio of the all-in-one classifier is better than the transfer ratio of the ensemble with its two variations.

4.2 Discussion

The results in the previous section indicate that both the all-in-one and the ensemble approaches exceed both Daumé's domain adaptation technique on the 27 datasets (given our current implementation of Daumé's approach) and SCL on the four datasets in Blitzer et al. (2007) and that the all-in-one approach achieves comparable results in terms of transfer ratio to Glorot et al. (2011).

The ensemble approach exceeds the all-in-one in some domains like apparel and automotive. They both are very close in some domains like cell phones & services, musical instruments, tools & hardware and outdoor living. For the rest of the 27 domains, the all-in-one exceeds the ensemble classifier. The all-in-one classifier exceeds the ensemble in using the transfer ratio metric.

When comparing the all-in-one and the ensemble approaches on the four datasets in Blitzer et al. (2007), the all-in-one exceeds the ensemble only in the DVD domain. The ensemble exceeds the all-in-one in electronics and kitchen & housewares. They both perform at the same accuracy level on the books domain.

We have also employed NcNemar significance test between pairs of the all-in-one, the ensemble and Daumé's approaches on the 27 domains. Table 4 shows the significance difference between the approaches' combinations.

Pair of Approaches	Average NcNemar Test	p-value
All-in-one & In-domain	2.066976595	No significant difference p = 0.20
All-in-one & Ensemble	2.736901971	No significant difference p = 0.10
All-in-one & Daumé's	8.976122	Significant at p = 0.01
Ensemble & In-domain	4.077642586	Significant at p = 0.05
Ensemble & Daumé's	11.47808047	Significant at p = 0.001
Daumé's & In-domain	10.46852763	Significant at p = 0.01

Table 4: NcNemar Significance Test Results

Finally, we would like to do some initial exploration of the role of features across domains. The commonly held belief is that sentiment indicators such as "hot" can change their polarity from domain to domain (e.g. it is positive in the food domain while it is negative in the negative domain), contributing to the need for domain adaptation. On the other hand, the success of the all-in-one classifier indicates that a greater number of observed sentiment features and more solid statistics on those features are more important than capturing domain-specific polarity changes.

In order to gather evidence for or against these hypotheses, we first calculated the number of overlapping features between each pair of domains within the 27 domains. The average percentage of features that overlap between pairs of domain is only 12.48%. Furthermore, only a very small set of the highly sentiment-correlated features overlap. 16 features overlap among the 27 domains which accounts for only 0.08% of the features. Examples of positive overlapping feature are "highly", "excellent", and "great". Negative overlapping features are "waste", "terrible", and "worst". This low feature overlap of sentiment-bearing features lends some support to the hypothesis that in order to capture a general, large-scale sentiment vocabulary nothing beats diverse and plentiful training data. The low feature overlap also justifies why the all-in-one classifier exceeds the ensemble though the latter has access to some labeled data in the target

Second, we examined the question of polarity-changing sentiment features. Among the top 1000 features in each domain ranked by LLR, we counted the common features among multiple domains. The number of common features among 15 domains is 42 features. Only 13 features are common among 20 domains while there are no common features from the highest 1000 likelihood ratio features among the 27 domains. Most features do not flip polarity across domains. For example the word "waste" is common among 20 domains and maintains a negative polarity across the domains. Very few features flip polarity across domains. The word "highly" is shared across 23 domains. It maintains a positive polarity in all domains while it flips in Tools & Hardware. The word "refund" is shared in 20 domains. It maintains a negative polarity in almost all domains except Gourmet Food.

5 Conclusion

In this paper, we empirically re-examine the assumption that adapting one or multiple domains with plenty of labeled sentiment polarity data to one domain with little labeled data requires new and sophisticated algorithms. We evaluate four domain adaptation techniques on a wide variety of domains in two major groups of state-of-the-art datasets. Our experiments show that overall, simple domain adaptation techniques like the all-in-one classifier do comparably well if not better than more sophisticated domain adaptation techniques. Combined with the fact that labeled sentiment data tends to be cheap to come by through either the collection of product reviews from the web or inexpensive crowd-sourced labeling, this indicates that in practice, domain-adaptation for sentiment detection might be of less importance than previously claimed.

We also show that the often anecdotally observed "polarity-flip" of sentiment terms from one domain to another in practice is a rather rare occurrence and might not be as detrimental to sentiment domain adaptation as assumed in much of the literature.

References

John Blitzer, Ryan McDonald and Fernando Pereira. 2006. Domain Adaptation with Structural Correspondence Learning. In *Proceedings of EMNLP*.

John Blitzer, Mark Dredze and Fernando Pereira. 2007. Biographies, Bollywood, Boom-boxes and Blenders: Domain-Adaptation for Sentiment Classification. In *Proceedings of ACL.*

Minmin Chen, Kilian Q. Weinberger and John C. Blitzer. 2011. Co-Training for Domain Adaptation. In *Proceedings of Advances in Neural Information Processing (NIPS).*

Hal Daumé III. 2007. Frustratingly Easy Domain Adaptation. In *Proceedings of ACL.*

Thomas G. Dietterich.1997. Machine Learning Research: Four Current Directions. *In: AI Magazine. 18 (4), 97-136.*

Xavier Glorot, Antoine Bordes and Yoshua Bengio. 2011. Domain-Adaptation for Large-Scale Sentiment Classification: A Deep Learning Approach. In *Proceedings of ICML.*

Soo-Min Kim and Edward Hovy. 2006. Extracting Opinions, Opinion Holders, and Topics Expressed in Online News Media Text. In: *Proceedings of the ACL Workshop on Sentiment and Subjectivity in Text, 1-8.*

Shoushan Li and Chengqing Zong. 2008. Multi-Domain Adaptation for Sentiment Classification: Using Multiple Classifier Combining Methods. In *Proceedings of Natural Language Processing and Knowledge Engineering.*

Shoushan Li and Chengqing Zong. 2008. Multi-Domain Sentiment Classification. In *Proceedings of Association of Computing Linguistics..*

Mark Dredze and Koby Crammer. 208. Online Methods for Multi-Domain Learning and Adaptation. In *proceedings of the 2008 Conference on Empirical Methods in Natural Language Processing.*

Bo Pang and Lilian Lee. 2008. Opinion Mining and Sentiment Analysis. *Foundations and Trends® in Information Retrieval*: Vol. 2: No 1–2, pp 1-135.

Bo Pang, Lillian Lee, and Shivakumar Vaithyanathan. 2002. Thumbs up?: sentiment classification using machine learning techniques. In *Proceedings of Conference on Empirical Methods in Natural Language Processing (EMNLP-2002).*

Bing Liu. 2012. Sentiment Analysis and Opinion Mining. Morgan & Claypool Publishers.

Vasileios Hatzivassiloglou and Kathleen R. McKeown. 1997. Predicting the semantic orientation of adjectives. In *Proceedings of Annual Meeting of the Association for Computational Linguistics (ACL-1997).*

Rajhans Samdani and Wen-Tau Yih. 2011. Domain Adaptation with Ensemble of Feature Groups. In *Proceedings of the 22nd International Joint Conference on Artificial Intelligence.*

Peter D. Turney. 2002. Thumbs up or thumbs down?: semantic orientation applied to unsupervised classification of reviews. In *Proceedings of Annual Meeting of the Association for Computational Linguistics (ACL-2002).*

Theresa Wilson , Janyce Wiebe, & Rebecca Hwa. 2006. Recognizing strong and weak opinion clauses. *Computational Intelligence 22 (2)*: 73-99.

Munmun De Choudhury, Michael Gamon, and Scott Counts. Happy, Nervous or Surprised? Classification of Human Affective States in Social Media, *Association for the Advancement of Artificial Intelligence, June 2012*

Munmun De Choudhury, Scott Counts, and Michael Gamon. Not All Moods are Created Equal! Exploring Human Emotional States in Social Media. *Association for the Advancement of Artificial Intelligence, June 2012*

Evaluation of a Baseline Information Retrieval for a Polish Open-domain Question Answering System

Michał Marcińczuk and **Adam Radziszewski** and **Maciej Piasecki**
Dominik Piasecki and **Marcin Ptak**
Wrocław University of Technology
{michal.marcinczuk,adam.radziszewski,maciej.piasecki}@pwr.wroc.pl
{dominik.piasecki,mp.marcin.ptak}@gmail.com

Abstract

We report on our efforts aimed at building an Open Domain Question Answering system for Polish. Our contribution is twofold: we gathered a set of question–answer pairs from various Polish sources and we performed an empirical evaluation of two re-ranking methods. The gathered collection contains factoid, list, non-factoid and yes-no questions, which makes a challenging material for experiments. We show that using two re-ranking methods based on term proximity allows to obtain significant improvement on simple information retrieval baseline. The improvement is observed as finding more answer-bearing documents among the top n search results.

1 Background

Question Answering (QA) is an information retrieval task in which the user information need is expressed in terms of a natural language question. As this way of expressing information needs is very flexible, QA systems are mostly constructed as Open Domain QA systems (ODQA), not limited to any particular text collection or narrow domain (Paşca, 2003). An ODQA system can deliver an answer, as a text of a data record, but mostly it is required that it returns passages extracted from a collection of documents that are supposed to include an answer to the user's question. The goal of ODQA is to answer questions not restricted to any pre-defined domain (Paşca, 2003).

Most ODQA systems process user questions in four steps, cf (Paşca, 2003; Monz, 2003; Ferrucci, 2012): question analysis, document retrieval, document analysis and answer selection. In addition to this general scheme, we can distinguish several typical substeps or tasks: question classification (Lally et al., 2012), query selection and expansion (Paşca, 2003), passage retrieval and ranking (Paşca, 2003), candidate answer identification (Chu-Carroll et al., 2012), answer extraction and ranking (Gondek et al., 2012), etc., but the core is shared among systems.

There are only a few known works on ODQA (working on text collections) for Polish, e.g. Walas and Jassem (2011), Walas (2012), and two systems publicly available: `Hipisek.pl` and `KtoCo.pl`. The latter is a commercial system and little is known about its structure. *Hipisek* implements the ODQA blueprint described above (Walas and Jassem, 2011), but was focused on processing *yes-no* questions about time and location. The system depends on a dedicated rule-based parser (Walas and Jassem, 2011), and was extended with a knowledge base for spatial relations (Walas, 2012).

Our long-term goal is large-scale, broad-application ODQA with respect to different types of questions and documents indexed. We utilize the following architecture of QA system:

- **query analysis** — query processing by language tools and rules, and generation of the search query,
- **search engine** — fetches the N most relevant documents from a large collection of documents,
- **module for document ranking** — the set of documents returned by the search engine is re-ranked using medium time-consuming techniques. The M top documents are selected, where $M \ll N$,
- **module for extracting candidate answers** — the most time-consuming operations are performed on the reduced set of documents,
- **module for answer ranking** — the list of candidate answers with their context are

ranked and best items are presented to user.

In this paper we focus on the first three elements of QA system with the special focus on search engine and document re-ranking.

2 QA dataset for Polish

Most works performed for English rely upon the TREC datasets (Voorhees, 2001). No such dataset was available for Polish, so we started construction of a set of question-answer pairs for Polish. We surveyed several possible ways of collecting questions and answers for Polish from the available resources.

Our first idea was to crawl Internet QA communities such as `zapytaj.onet.pl`, `pytki.pl`, `pytano.pl` (Polish counterparts of `ask.com`) and grab both questions and answers. We anticipated the need for substantial manual work needed to select and curate the data, but the actual scale of the problem was quite overwhelming: while it is already not easy to find suitable questions there, finding a number of suitable answers in reasonable time was practically infeasible. The main problem was that if the answers would serve as a testing material for a system based on document retrieval, the answers should mimic normal documents. The answers posted by users of such sites are usually very short and devoid of the necessary context to understand them — they make sense only when paired with the corresponding questions (those that make sense at all). The same problem turned out to apply for FAQ sites, even official ones. This way we faced the necessity to divide the process into two separate phases: gathering questions and then finding documents that provide answers to them.

2.1 Gathering questions

We developed simple guidelines that help to recognise acceptable questions. A question must have syntactic structure of a question (rather than a string of query terms), be simple (one question per a sentence), not requiring any additional context for its interpretation. We did not accept questions referring to the person asked (*'What bands do you like?'*). Questions about opinions were discouraged unless could be conceived as addressed to a domain expert (e.g. *'Which wines go well with fish?'*). We did not exclude questions which were vulgar or asked just for fun as long as they satisfied all other requirements.

We considered four sources of candidate questions which we hope to reflect the actual information need of the Internet users. First, thanks to the courtesy of Marcin Walas we were given access to user query logs of `Hipisek.pl`. The second source was 'manual crawling' around the QA communities. Similarly, we considered FAQ sites of several Inland Revenue offices. Lastly, we decided to abuse the auto-complete feature of Google and Bing search engines to gain insight into the questions that have actually been posed (it turns out that a number of users indeed ask natural language questions as search engine queries). The task was to enter word/words that typical questions start with and copy the suggestions. This could have led to some bias concerning the selection of the question-initial words. On the other hand, the mechanism seems to work surprisingly well and it is sufficient to give two words to obtain a lot of sensible questions. All of the questions that were decided as appropriate were subjected to orthographical and grammatical correction.

We considered manual translation of the TREC questions, as was done, e.g., in (Lombarović et al., 2011). We decided against this solution, since the TREC questions seem too much oriented on the American culture and geography for our purposes. Also the TREC datasets cotains mainly factoid questions while we wanted to create a balanced dataset containing both factoid and non-factoid questions.

2.2 Finding answers

We required from the answer documents to have included at least one passage (a couple of consecutive sentences) that contained the answer, i.e. that there was no necessity to construct an answer from information scattered across the document. This is because we assume the final version of the system will present such a passage to the user. We also required the answer-bearing passage to be comprehensive even when not paired with the question, e.g. if the question was about Linux, this name or its equivalent should appear in the passage rather than only general terms such as *'the system'*.

The set of candidate questions was given to linguists, which were asked to devote a couple of minutes per each question and try to find a satisfactory answer using search engines. They were asked to avoid typing the whole question as a query to prevent from favouring those documents that contain questions.

For each candidate at most one answer document was found. Each answer document (a website) was downloaded as HTML files. We used the *Web As Corpus Toolkit* (Ziai and Ott, 2005) to clean up the files and remove boilerplate elements. The final output contained no mark-up and its structure was limited to plain text divided into paragraphs. Note that only those questions that the linguists were able to find an answer for have made their way to the final dataset.

2.3 Final collection

Ultimately, the set of questions paired with answers contains 598 entries. The statistics regarding source distribution is given as Table 1.

Source	Questions	Percentage
Hipisek.pl	236	39%
QA communities	98	16%
Search engines	244	41%
Revenue FAQ	20	3%
Overall	598	100%

Table 1: Distribution of sources in our dataset.

The collection contains the following types of questions (according to the expected answer type):

1. Factoid and list questions (Voorhees, 2004; Voorhees and Dang, 2005):
   - **person** — individual, group; *Who killed Osama bin Laden?*,
   - **location** — city, country, location-other; *In what city is the UAM located?*,
   - **organization** — band, company, institution, media, political-party; *What companies are listed within the WIG20?*,
   - **temporal** — date, period; *When was Albert Einstein born?*
   - **numerical** — count, money, numeric-other, size, temperature; *How many legs does a caterpillar have?*,
   - **other** — action, animal, artifact, band, color, disease, entity-other, expression, food, intellect-other, lake, language, plant, river, software, substance, vehicle, web-page; *Which dogs are aggressive?*, *What software can read epub files?*,
2. Non-factoid quesetions (Mizuno et al., 2007; Fukumoto, 2007):
   - **definition** — *What is X?*, *What does X mean?*, *Who is X?*,
   - **description** — *What powers does the president have?*,
   - **manner** — *how* questions; *How to start a business?*, *How to make a frappe coffe?*,
   - **reason** — *why* questions; *Why do cats purr?*, *How do I catch a cold?*.
3. Yes-no questions (Walas, 2012; Kanayama et al., 2012); *Is Lisbon in Europe?*.

Table 2 presents the number and the percentage of question types and subtypes in the the gathered collection.

Type	Count	Percent
Factoid and list questions	**267**	**44.65%**
– person	29	4.85%
– location	66	11.04%
– organization	15	2.51%
– temporal	37	6.19%
– numerical	45	7.53%
– other	75	12.54%
Non-factoid questions	**274**	**45.82%**
– definition	59	9.87%
– description	88	14.71%
– manner	68	11.36%
– reason	59	9.87%
Yes-no questions	**57**	**9.53%**

Table 2: Types of questions.

To perform a reliable evaluation of the system, we had to index a lot more data than just the answers to our 598 test questions. We acquired also several collections to serve as 'distractors' and a source of possible answers, namely:

- Polish Wikipedia (using dump from 22 January 2013) — 956 000 documents.
- A collection of press articles from *Rzeczpospolita* (Weiss, 2008) — 180 000 documents.
- Three smaller corpora: KPWr (Broda et al., 2012), CSEN and CSER (Marcińczuk and Piasecki, 2011) — 3 000 documents.

3 Evaluation metrics

The evaluation was based on the following metrics:

- **answers at n-th cutoff** (a@n) (Monz, 2003) — *relevant documents recall*; a fraction of questions for which the relevant document was present in the first n documents returned by the search engine;

- **mean reciprocal rank** (MRR) — an average of the query reciprocal ranks[1] MRR is used to compare re-ranking algorithms. The higher MRR is, the higher in the ranking the relevant documents are.

4 Baseline information retrieval

As a basis for search engine we selected an open source search platform called *Solr* (The Apache Software Foundation, 2013a). *Solr* indexes large collection of documents and provides: full-text search, rich query syntax, document ranking, custom document fields and terms weighting. It was also shown that Lucene (the retrieval system underlying Solr) performs no worse for QA than other modern Information Retrieval systems (Tellex et al., 2003).

In the baseline approach we used an existing tool called *Web as Corpus ToolKit* (Adam Kilgarriff and Ramon Ziai and Niels Ott, 2013) to extracted plain text from the collection of HTML documents. Then, the text was tagged using WCRFT tagger (Radziszewski, 2013) and their base forms were indexed in the Solr.

To fetch a ranked list of documents for a query we used a default search ranking algorithm implemented in the *Lucene* that is a combination of Boolean Model (BM) with refined Vector Space Model (VSM). BM is used to fetch all documents matching the boolean query. Then, VSM is applied to rank the answer documents. The detailed formula used to compute the ranking score is presented in (The Apache Software Foundation, 2013b). The formula includes following factors:

- fraction of query terms present in the document — documents containing more query terms are scored higher than those with fewer,

- query normalizing factor — to make the score comparable between queries,

- document term frequency — documents containing more occurrences of query terms receive higher scores,

- inverse document frequency — common terms (present in many documents) have lower impact on the score,

- term boosting factor — weight specified in the query can be used to increase importance of selected terms (not used in our approach),

- field boosting factor — some fields might be more important than others (not used by us),

- field length normalization factor — shorter fields obtain higher scores.

Figure 1 presents all steps of *question analysis*. First, a question is tagged with WCRFT tagger. All punctuation marks and words from a stoplist (including 145 prepositions) are discarded. We assumed that in most cases the answer have a form of a statement and does not mimic question structure. The remaining words are used in a query, formed as a boolean disjunction of the base forms.

The a@n and MRR values for the baseline configuration are presented in Table 3. We measured the a@n for several distinct values of n between 1 and 200 (this is an estimated maximum number of documents which can be effectively processed during re-ranking). The a@n ranges from 26% for $n = 1$ to 87% for $n = 200$. This means than only for 26% questions the relevant document was on the first position in the ranking. In the reported tests all non-stop words from the question were used to form a query. We tested also several modification of the heuristic for query term selection proposed in (Paşca, 2003), but the results were lower.

5 Proximity-based re-ranking

Lucene default ranking algorithm does not take into consideration proximity of query terms in the documents. This leads to favouring longer documents as they are more likely to contain more query terms. However such documents can describe several different topics not related to the question. Ranking of longer documents cannot be decreased by default, as they might contain an answer. A possible solution is to analyse query term

[1] A reciprocal rank for a query is equal to $\frac{1}{K}$, where K is the position of first relevant document in the ranking.

1.	**Input:**	*Co można odliczyć od podatku?* ("What can be deducted from tax?")
2.	**Tagging:**	*co można odliczyć od podatek ?* (base forms)
3.	**Filtering:**	*można odliczyć od podatek* ("can", "deduct", "tax")
4.	**Query:**	`base:mozna OR base:odliczyć OR case:od OR base:podatek`

Figure 1: Steps of processing for a sample question.

	a@n
n	**baseline**
1	26.09%
5	52.17%
10	62.04%
20	70.57%
50	76.76%
100	82.61%
200	87.29%
MRR	0.3860

Table 3: a@n and MRR for baseline configuration of information retrieval.

proximity inside the documents. We have evaluated two approaches to utilising term proximity in re-ranking.

5.1 Maximum Cosine Similarity Weighting

Maximum Cosine Similarity Weighting (MCSW) is based on the idea of using the same ranking scheme as in the retrieval component, but applied to short passages, not whole documents. Every document is divided into continuous blocks of k sentences. For every block we compute the cosine similarity between a vector representing the block and a vector representing a query. Standard *tf-idf weighting* (Manning et al., 2008) and cosine measure are used. A document is assigned the maximum per-block cosine similarity that was encountered. Several block sizes (k from 1 to 5) were tested producing very similar results, thus we report results only for $k = 1$. The final document score is computed as follows:

$$score'(d) = \frac{score(d)}{\arg\max_{d \in D} score(d)} \cdot \frac{mcs(d)}{\arg\max_{d \in D} mcs(d)} \qquad (1)$$

where:

- D, ordered list od documents returned from search engine for a query,
- $score(d)$, score for document d returned by *Solr*,
- $mcs(d)$, maximum cosine similarity for document d.

5.2 Minimal Span Weighting

Monz (2003) presented a simple method for weighting based on a minimal text span containing all terms from a query that occur in the document. The re-ranking score combines the original score with MSW score and is computed as follows:

$$score''(d) = score(d) * \lambda + (1 - \lambda) \cdot \left(\frac{|q \cap d|}{|s|}\right)^{\alpha} \cdot \left(\frac{|q \cap d|}{|q|}\right)^{\beta} \qquad (2)$$

where:

- q, set of query terms,
- s, the shortest text fragment containing all query terms occurring in the document,
- λ, α, β, significance weights for the respective factors (we used default values (Monz, 2003), i.e. $\lambda = 0.4$, $\alpha = 0.125$, $\beta = 1$)

5.3 Evaluation

The a@n and MRR values for MCSW and MSW are presented in Table 4. For both methods we noticed a small improvement. The increase of MRR values for both methods indicates that the average position of the relevant documents in the ranking was improved. The a@n was improved by up to 12 percentage points for MCSW and $n = 1$. The lower improvement for MSW might be caused by the assumption that the minimal span must contain all query terms occurring in the document.

This may result in very long spans covering almost complete documents. In the case of MCSW we force the sentence-based segmentation and mostly only fractions of the covered query terms influence MCSW score.

	a@n		
n	**baseline**	**MCSW** ($k = 1$)	**MSW**
1	26.09%	38.63%	33.95%
5	52.17%	63.04%	58.36%
10	62.04%	71.24%	68.73%
20	70.57%	78.43%	74.58%
50	76.76%	83.95%	79.93%
100	82.61%	86.45%	84.11%
200	87.29%	87.29%	87.29%
MRR	0.3860	0.5007	0.4555

Table 4: a@n and MRR for baseline information retrieval with reranking.

In addition, the proximity-based ranking algorithms can be used to extract the most relevant document fragments as answers instead of presenting the whole document. According to (Lin et al., 2003), users prefer paragraph-level chunks of text with appropriate answer highlighting.

Despite the observed improvements, the results are still below our expectations. If we assume that user reads up to 10 answers for a question (a typical number of results displayed on a single page in many web search engines), the top a@n will be about 70%. This means that we will not provide any relevant answer for 3 out of 10 questions. According to (Monz, 2003), results for English reported for TREC sets are between 73% and 86% for a@10. Thus, further improvement in reranking is necessary.

6 Conclusion

We presented a preliminary results for a baseline information retrieval system and the simple proximity-based re-ranking methods in the context of a Open Domain Question Answering task for Polish. The evaluation was performed on a corpus of 598 questions and answers, collected from a wide range of questions asked by Internet users (i.e. search engines, `Hipisek.pl`, QA communities and Revenue FAQ). The collection covers major types of questions including: factoid, list, non-factoid and yes-no questions.

The a@n of the baseline IR system (*Solr*) configuration ranges from 26% for $n = 1$ to 87% for $n = 200$ top documents considered. Our queries consisted of base forms of all question words except words from a stoplist. Several heuristics for query term selection inspired by the one proposed in (Monz, 2003) produced lower results. This can be explained by the properties of the ranking algorithm used in *Solr* — the number of terms covered and their total frequency in a document are important factors. For $n = 10$ (a typical single page in a Web search) we obtained 62% a@n. Two re-ranking methods based on query term proximity were applied. For both methods we obtained a noticeable improvement up to 12 percentage points of a@n for $n = 1$ and 9 percentage points for $n = 10$. Nevertheless, the results are still slightly lower than in the case of systems built for English, e.g., (Monz, 2003). However, results reported by Monz were obtained on the TREC datasets, which contain mostly factoid and list questions. Our datasets includes also non-factoid and yes-no questions which are more difficult to deal with. The comparison with *Hipisek* is difficult as no results concerning ranking precision were not reported. Moreover, *Hipisek* was focused on selected subclasses of questions.

We plan to extend the information retrieval model on the level of document fetching and re-ranking. We want to utilize plWordNet 2.0 (the Polish wordnet)[2] (Maziarz et al., 2012), tools for proper names (Marcińczuk et al., 2013) and semantic relations recognition (Marcińczuk and Ptak, 2012), dependency[3] and shallow syntactic parsers. More advanced but also more time-consuming tools will be used to select relevant passages in the documents fetched by the presented information retrieval module.

Acknowledgements The work was funded by the European Union Innovative Economy Programme project NEKST, No POIG.01.01.02-14-013/09.

We would like to thank Marcin Walas for sharing the collection of historic questions that have been posed to the Hipisek system.

[2] `http://www.nlp.pwr.wroc.pl/plwordnet/`

[3] `http://zil.ipipan.waw.pl/PolishDependencyParser`

References

Adam Kilgarriff and Ramon Ziai and Niels Ott. 2013. Web as Corpus ToolKit. March.

Bartosz Broda, Michał Marcińczuk, Marek Maziarz, Adam Radziszewski, and Adam Wardyński. 2012. KPWr: Towards a Free Corpus of Polish. In Nicoletta Calzolari, Khalid Choukri, Thierry Declerck, Mehmet Uğur Doğan, Bente Maegaard, Joseph Mariani, Jan Odijk, and Stelios Piperidis, editors, *Proceedings of LREC'12*, Istanbul, Turkey. ELRA.

Jennifer Chu-Carroll, James Fan, Branimir Boguraev, David Carmel, Dafna Sheinwald, and Chris Welty. 2012. Finding needles in the haystack: Search and candidate generation. *IBM Journal of Research and Development*, 56(3):6.

David A. Ferrucci. 2012. Introduction to "This is Watson". *IBM Journal of Research and Development*, 56(3):1.

Junichi Fukumoto. 2007. Question Answering System for Non-factoid Type Questions and Automatic Evaluation based on BE Method. In Kando and Evans (Kando and Evans, 2007), pages 441–447.

David Gondek, Adam Lally, Aditya Kalyanpur, J. William Murdock, Pablo Ariel Duboué, Lei Zhang, Yue Pan, Zhaoming Qiu, and Chris Welty. 2012. A framework for merging and ranking of answers in DeepQA. *IBM Journal of Research and Development*, 56(3):14.

Hiroshi Kanayama, Yusuke Miyao, and John Prager. 2012. Answering Yes/No Questions via Question Inversion. In *COLING*, pages 1377–1392.

Noriko Kando and David Kirk Evans, editors. 2007. *Proceedings of the Sixth NTCIR Workshop Meeting on Evaluation of Information Access Technologies: Information Retrieval, Question Answering, and Cross-Lingual Information Access*, 2-1-2 Hitotsubashi, Chiyoda-ku, Tokyo 101-8430, Japan, May. National Institute of Informatics.

Adam Lally, John M. Prager, Michael C. McCord, Branimir Boguraev, Siddharth Patwardhan, James Fan, Paul Fodor, and Jennifer Chu-Carroll. 2012. Question analysis: How Watson reads a clue. *IBM Journal of Research and Development*, 56(3):2.

Jimmy J. Lin, Dennis Quan, Vineet Sinha, Karun Bakshi, David Huynh, Boris Katz, and David R. Karger. 2003. What Makes a Good Answer? The Role of Context in Question Answering. In *Human-Computer Interaction INTERACT '03: IFIP TC13 International Conference on Human-Computer Interaction, 1st–5th September 2003, Zurich, Switzerland*. IOS Press.

Tomislav Lombarović, Jan Šnajder, and Bojana Dalbelo Bašić. 2011. Question classification for a Croatian QA system. In *Proceedings of the 14th international conference on Text, speech and dialogue*, TSD'11, pages 403–410, Berlin, Heidelberg. Springer-Verlag.

Christopher D. Manning, Prabhakar Raghavan, and Hinrich Schütze. 2008. *Introduction to Information Retrieval*. Cambridge University Press, New York, NY, USA.

Michał Marcińczuk and Maciej Piasecki. 2011. Statistical Proper Name Recognition in Polish Economic Texts. *Control and Cybernetics*, 40(2).

Michał Marcińczuk and Marcin Ptak. 2012. Preliminary Study on Automatic Induction of Rules for Recognition of Semantic Relations between Proper Names in Polish Texts. In Petr Sojka, Aleš Horák, Ivan Kopecek, and Karel Pala, editors, *Text, Speech and Dialogue*, volume 7499 of *Lecture Notes in Computer Science*, pages 264–271. Springer Berlin / Heidelberg. 10.1007/978-3-642-32790-2_32.

Michał Marcińczuk, Jan Kocoń, and Maciej Janicki. 2013. Liner2 – A Customizable Framework for Proper Names Recognition for Polish. In Robert Bembenik, Lukasz Skonieczny, Henryk Rybinski, Marzena Kryszkiewicz, and Marek Niezgodka, editors, *Intelligent Tools for Building a Scientific Information Platform*, volume 467 of *Studies in Computational Intelligence*, pages 231–253. Springer Berlin Heidelberg.

Marek Maziarz, Maciej Piasecki, and Stanisław Szpakowicz. 2012. Approaching plWordNet 2.0, January.

Junta Mizuno, Tomoyosi Akiba, Atsushi Fujii, and Katunobu Itou. 2007. Non-factoid Question Answering Experiments at NTCIR-6: Towards Answer Type Detection for Realworld Questions. In Kando and Evans (Kando and Evans, 2007), pages 487–492.

Christof Monz. 2003. *From Document Retrieval to Question Answering*. Phd thesis, Universiteit van Amsterdam.

Marius Paşca. 2003. *Open-Domain Question Answering from Large Text Collections*. University of Chicago Press.

Adam Radziszewski. 2013. A Tiered CRF Tagger for Polish. In Robert Bembenik, Łukasz Skonieczny, Henryk Rybiński, Marzena Kryszkiewicz, and Marek Niezgódka, editors, *Intelligent Tools for Building a Scientific Information Platform*, volume 467 of *Studies in Computational Intelligence*, pages 215–230. Springer Berlin Heidelberg.

Stefanie Tellex, Boris Katz, Jimmy Lin, Aaron Fernandes, and Gregory Marton. 2003. Quantitative evaluation of passage retrieval algorithms for question answering. In *Proceedings of the 26th annual international ACM SIGIR conference on Research and development in informaion retrieval*, SIGIR '03, pages 41–47, New York, USA. ACM.

The Apache Software Foundation. 2013a. Apache Solr. March.

The Apache Software Foundation. 2013b. Implementation of Lucene default search and ranking algorithm. March.

Ellen M. Voorhees and Hoa Trang Dang. 2005. Overview of the TREC 2005 Question Answering Track. In Ellen M. Voorhees and Lori P. Buckland, editors, *TREC*, volume Special Publication 500-266. National Institute of Standards and Technology (NIST).

Ellen M. Voorhees. 2001. The TREC question answering track. volume 7, pages 361–378, New York, USA, December. Cambridge University Press.

E. Voorhees. 2004. Overview of the TREC 2004 Question Answering Track. In Ellen M. Voorhees and Lori P. Buckland, editors, *Proceedings of the 13th Text Retrieval Conference (TREC)*, volume Special Publication 500-261, pages 52–62. National Institute of Standards and Technology (NIST).

Marcin Walas and Krzysztof Jassem. 2011. Named Entity Recognition in a Polish Question Answering System. In *Proceedings of Intelligent Information Systems*, pages 181–191.

Marcin Walas. 2012. How to Answer Yes/No Spatial Questions Using Qualitative Reasoning? In Alexander F. Gelbukh, editor, *CICLing (2)*, volume 7182 of *Lecture Notes in Computer Science*, pages 330–341. Springer.

Dawid Weiss. 2008. Korpus Rzeczpospolitej. [on-line] `http://www.cs.put.poznan.pl/dweiss/rzeczpospolita`. Corpus of text from the online edtion of Rzeczypospolita.

Ramon Ziai and Niels Ott, 2005. *Web as Corpus Toolkit: User's and Hacker's Manual.* Lexical Computing Ltd., Brighton, UK. Manual for version pre3.

WCCL Relation — a Toolset for Rule-based Recognition of Semantic Relations Between Named Entities

Michał Marcińczuk
Wrocław University of Technology
michal.marcinczuk@pwr.wroc.pl

Abstract

In this paper we cover the problem of recognition of semantic relations between proper names (PNs) in running text. We focus on the manual rule creation approach and discuss to what extent the existing tools can be used for this task. As a result of our initial research we developed a rule-based toolset for recognition of relations between PNs called WCCL Relation. The toolset is built on the top of WCCL Match — a language for text annotation, which is a part of a WCCL framework (an open source, released under the GNU LGPL 3.0). The WCCL Relation toolset is language independent and can be used for almost any natural language and language tagset. We present several use cases and sample rules for recognition of semantic relations in Polish texts.

1 Introduction

Recognition of semantic relations between named entities is one of the information extraction major tasks. Its goal is to identify pairs of named entities (text fragments) connected other by a semantic relation on the basis of their context. In the majority of approaches the named entities are recognised beforehand and the task is limited to discovering and categorising connections between those entities. The list of possible relation categories is unbounded and it depends on the desired application, the scope of the named entities and the available resources. For example Marcińczuk and Ptak (2012) defined 8 coarse-grained categories of semantic relations (location, origin, nationality, affiliation, neighbourhood, creator, composition and alias). In turn Linguistic Data Consortium (2008) defined a set of 8 general relations (i.e., physical, part-whole, personal-social, organization-affiliation, agent-artifact and general-affiliation) with several subcategories. In the bioinformatic domain there are two common categories of relations between genes, proteins and associated entities — *protein-component* and *subunit-complex* (Pyysalo et al., 2011).

There are two main approaches to relation recognition — construction of human-readable rules and construction of statistical models (machine learning). According to Jiang (2012) the most common approach is the one based on the statistical models. There are also several rule-based approaches, like manual rule creation (Marciniak and Mykowiecka, 2007; Santos et al., 2010; Abacha and Zweigenbaum, 2011) and rule induction (Feldman et al., 2006; Brun and Hagège, 2009). The low interest in developing rule-based systems might be caused by a lack of robust and accessible tools for rule construction and execution. For example, the well-known general framework GATE (Cunningham et al., 2011) does not support relation recognition within its rule formalism JAPE (Cunningham et al., 2000).

Despite the manual rule creation is less popular than the statistical approaches in the task of relation recognition, the rule-based approaches have several advantages over statistical-based approaches. The first one is the traceability and full control on decisions made by the system. The other one is the ease in manual tuning for new types of text. The last but not least it does not require annotated data.

In this paper we investigate the problem of rule creation for recognition of semantic relations between proper names. We present a language independent formalism for rule creation and execution called *WCCL Relation*. The language is built on top of an open-source framework WCCL (Radziszewski et al., 2011). We present several use cases of the language applications in the context of recognition of semantic relations between proper names for Polish.

2 Related works

Before we decided to create the WCCL Relation toolset we had considered several existing approaches described in the literature. Abacha and Zweigenbaum (2011) used a custom rule notion and a software to develop a set of rules for their task. However, the main emphasis was put on the task definition and discussion of its difficulties. Less effort was made to create a general solution that would result in an universal system or formalism for rule creation and execution.

There is another group of works utilizing the Xerox Incremental Parser (XIP). According to Aït-Mokhtar et al. (2002), XIP is a formalism which allows to recognise n-ary linguistic relations between words or constituents on the basis of global or local structural, topological and/or lexical conditions. Brun and Hagège (2009) used the formalism in semi-supervised rule creation (the rules were used to recognise Olympic games events). Santos et al. (2010) used XIP to create rules for recognition of family relations between people. Despite the formalism looks very promising the distribution and licensing is not clear and the XIP implementation is not freely available.

There is also another system called TEG (Feldman et al., 2006) which offers a stochastic context-free grammar (SCFG) to write rules for recognition of relations between named entities. The system offers a semi-supervised method for rule creation. Unfortunately, according to our best knowledge the system is not publicly accessible.

An open-source Python platform for text processing called NLTK[1] (Bird et al., 2009) provides a simple tool to relation recognition based on regex patterns. The patterns are tested against a plain text enriched with part of speech tags. This approach can be suitable for many simple uses cases but it is troublesome to use for languages with rich morphology (each word is described by a set of morphological attributes, not only by the part of speech tag). It also does not support multi-layered semantic annotations.

Taking into consideration the above solutions we decided to construct a customized toolset for the rule-based relation recognition utilizing an existing open-source framework for text matching and annotation. The following section presents the current version of WCCL Relation toolset.

[1] `http://nltk.org`

3 WCCL Relation

WCCL Relation is a toolset designed for a rule-based recognition of relations between pairs of annotations within a sentence in a morphologically tagged and semantically annotated texts. Its grammar is based on the WCCL Match[2] (Marcińczuk and Radziszewski, 2013) and extends it by a new operator for relation creation. A WCCL Relation rule consists of three sections. The first section (`match`) contains a set of operators used to match a sequence of tokens and annotations (named entities, chunks, etc.). The second section (`cond`) is optional and contains a set of additional conditions which must be satisfied by the matched elements. The last section (`actions`) contains a set of operators to be performed on the matched elements. Comparing to the original WCCL Match grammar, the WCCL Relation grammar contains an additional operator called `link` which allows to create a connection of given category between two matched elements. Below is a sample rule which matches a sequence "PERSON born in CITY" and creates a connection between the PERSON and the CITY names of type *origin*.

```
apply(
  match(
    // match annotation of type person_nam
    is("person_nam"),                 // group 1
    // match word with base form 'born'
    equal( base[0], "urodzić"),       // group 2
    equal( base[0], "się"),           // group 3
    // match word with base form 'in'
    equal( base[0], "w"),             // group 4
    // match annotation of type city_nam
    is("city_nam"),                   // group 5
  ),
  actions(
    link(1, "person_nam", 5, "city_nam", "origin")
))
```

WCCL Match offers a set of operators for matching a sequence of elements. Below is a list of operators used in the examples presented in the article[3]:

- `is(type)` — matches an annotation of given type,
- `equal(base[0], value)` — matches a token with a base form equal to *value*,
- `inter(base[0], values)` — matches a token with a base form present in the array of values,

[2] Part of WCCL framework (Radziszewski et al., 2011)

[3] The complete list of the WCCL Match operators can be found in Marcińczuk and Radziszewski (2013).

- `repeat(op)` — matches a sequence of elements matching the *op* operator,
- `not(op)` — matches a token not matching the *op* operator,
- `isannpart(0, type)` — matches a token that is a part of an annotation of given type,
- `and(op1,op2,..,opn)` — matches a token if all operators are valid,
- `oneof(variant1,...,variant2)` — matches a sequence of elements for the first valid variant,
- `annsub(token, type)` — test if given token is part of an annotation of given type,
- `agrpp(word1, word2)` — test agreement of two given words,
- `outside(index)` — test if given token index is inside sentence boundary, can be used to test if given token is the first or the last token in the sentence,

The execution of a WCCL Relation rule consists of three steps (all of them are transparent to user). In the first step, the WCCL Relation rule is transformed into a WCCL Match rule. In this step all the additional operators are transformed to operators valid for WCCL Match. In the second step, the WCCL Match rule is run on a given text. In the last step, the result of matching (set of annotations) is interpreted and transformed into a set of relations.

Below is the result of transformation the WCCL Relation rule to the WCCL Match rule. Here, the `link` operator was replaced with a set of three `match` operators.

```
apply(
  match(
    // match annotation of type person_nam
    is("person_nam"),
    // match word with base form 'born'
    equal( base[0], "urodzić"),
    equal( base[0], "się"),
    // match word with base form 'in'
    equal( base[0], "w"),
    // match annotation of type city_nam
    is("city_nam"),
  ),
  actions(
    mark(:1, :5, "relation.origin.r1"),
    mark(:1, "relation.origin.r1.person_nam"),
    mark(:5, "relation.target.r1.city_nam")
))
```

4 Case studies

In this section we present several use cases already covered by the WCCL Relation toolset. We assumed that the proper names were recognised beforehand using an external tool. For Polish we used a tool called Liner2[4] (Marcińczuk et al., 2013) with a model for 56 categories of proper names.

4.1 Auxiliary annotations

The standard WCCL Match operator `mark` can be used to introduce the auxiliary annotations which can be referenced by other rules. This simplifies the final rules recognising the relations. For example, a common action is to ignore phrases in parentheses which can separate two named entities. This can be done using the following rule. The rule matches a text that is delimited by a pair of elements: "(" and ")" or "[" and "]".

```
apply(
  match(
    oneof(
      variant(
        in("(", base[0]),
        repeat(not(inter(base[0], [")", "("]))),
        in(")", base[0])
      ),
      variant(
        in("[", base[0]),
        repeat(not(inter(base[0], ["]", "["]))),
        in("]", base[0])
      )
    )
  ),
  actions(
    mark(M, "parentheses")
))
```

The following rule extends the previous rule recognising the *origin* relation between a person name and a city name by including an optional phrase in parentheses after the person name.

```
apply(
  match(
    // match annotation of type person_nam
    is("person_nam"),              // group 1
    // match optional phrase in parentheses
    optional(is("parentheses"))    // group 2
    // match word with base form 'born'
    equal( base[0], "urodzić"),    // group 3
    equal( base[0], "się"),        // group 4
    // match word with base form 'in'
    equal( base[0], "w"),          // group 5
    // match annotation of type city_nam
    is("city_nam"),                // group 6
  ),
  actions(
    link(1, "person_nam", 6, "city_nam", "origin")
))
```

4.2 Possessive named entities

The following rule is a naïve rule for recognition of a *location* relation between a person name and

[4] http://nlp.pwr.wroc.pl/liner2

a city name (i.e. a person is in a city).

```
apply(
  match(
    is("person_nam"),              // group 1
    // match word with base form 'in'
    in("w", base[0]),              // group 2
    is("city_nam")                 // group 3
  ),
  actions(
    link(1, "person_nam", 3, "city_nam", "location")
))
```

However this rule is not always true. For example when the person name is an possessive argument of an other subject then the relation does not occur between the person name and the city name but between the possessive phrase and the city name. Consider the following sentence: *Pomnik Wojtyły w Krakowie* (eng. *Wojtyła monument in Kraków*). In the sentence it is stated that the *monument* is located in Kraków and it does not mean that *Wojtyła* is also in Kraków. In order to handle properly such situations we must recognise the possessive nouns. This can be done with the following rule. This rule test a person name preceded by a noun. If the person name and the noun do not agree in case then the person name is being recognised as possessive phrase.

```
apply(
  match(
    in(subst, class[0]),
    is("person_nam")
  ),
  cond(
    in(subst, class[first(:2)]),
    not(agrpp(first(:1), first(:2), {cas}))
  ),
  actions(
    mark(M, "possessive")
))
```

Now we can add a condition in the `cond` section to ignore the person names which are part of a possessive phrase. Below is the original rule with the mentioned condition.

```
apply(
  match(
    is("person_nam"),          // group 1
    in("w", base[0]),          // group 2, eng. "in"
    is("city_nam")             // group 3
  ),
  cond(
    not(annsub(:1, "possessive"))
  ),
  actions(
    link(1, "person_nam", 3, "city_nam", "location")
))
```

4.3 Multiple relations

The other common situation is recognition of multiple relations within a single matched sequence. Below is a sample rule which matches the sequence "COUNTRY (CITY and CITY)" and creates two links: both city names are connected with the country name as separate relations.

```
apply(
  match(
    is("country_nam"),          // group 1
    inter(base[0], "("),        // group 2
    is("city_nam"),             // group 3
    inter(base[0], "i"),        // group 4
    is("city_nam"),             // group 5
    inter(base[0], ")"),        // group 6
  ),
  actions(
    link(1,"country_nam",3,"city_nam","location"),
    link(1,"country_nam",5,"city_nam","location")
))
```

4.4 Detecting sentences containing only two annotations

In some cases when there are only two proper names of given categories in a sentence, the proper names can be connected with a certain relation category no matter of their context. For example, in most case a road name and a city name preceded by a preposition *in* are connected with a *location* relation. Below is an auxiliary rule that matches the text fragments not annotated with a road name nor a city name.

```
apply(
  match(
    repeat(
      and(
        not(isannpart(0,"road_nam")),
        not(isannpart(0,"city_nam"))
      )
    )
  ),
  actions(
    mark(M, "not_road_city")
))
```

Using the above auxiliary annotation `not_road_city` we can construct the following rule (the `cond` is used to check if the matched sequence spans over a whole sentence).

```
apply(
  match(
    is("not_road_city"),        // group 1
    is("road_nam"),             // group 2
    is("not_road_city"),        // group 3
    in("w", base[0]),           // group 4, eng. ''in''
    is("city_nam"),             // group 5
    is("not_road_city")         // group 6
  ),
  cond(
    outside(first(M) - 1), outside(last(M) + 1)
  ),
  actions(
    link(2, "road_nam", 4, "city_nam", "location")
))
```

5 Evaluation

In the evaluation we used the KPWr corpus (Broda et al., 2012)[5], which is the only available corpus annotated with semantic relations between proper names for Polish. We followed the evaluation procedure presented by Marcińczuk and Ptak (2012),

[5] `http://nlp.pwr.wroc.pl/kpwr`.

where the corpus was divided into three parts: train, tune and test. The train and tune parts were used for the rule development and the test part for the final performance comparison.

As the work is still in progress we started from the most numerous relation category in KPWr that is *location* (about 800 relations). The current set contains 34 rules (6 of them are auxiliary rules). It took about 6 hours to develop the rules. The set covers almost 40% of *location* relations in the train part, 30% in the tune part and 22% in the test part with the precision between 87–90%. The recall is low but in terms of F-measure the results are comparable with the results obtained for the statistical methods presented by Marcińczuk and Ptak (2012). On the test part the statistical model obtained 36.09% F-measure with 31.20% precision, while the manually crafted rules obtained already 34.97% F-measure with 87.18% precision. Higher precision is more useful for processing large volumes of texts where recall is not an issue. Our final goal is to construct a set of rules covering all categories of semantic relations present in the KPWr corpus.

6 WCCL Relation is language independent

Since the WCCL framework is language independent, also WCCL Relation is language independent. Note, that the rules written for one language are not directly usable for other languages. They can be adopted to another language or tagset but they have to be anywise translated.

WCCL Relation can be used to process any language which tagset conforms the following requirements:

- the tagset defines a non-empty set of grammatical classes and possibly empty set of attributes;
- each grammatical class is assigned a set of attributes that are required for the class and a set of optional attributes;
- each attribute is assigned a set of its possible values;
- mnemonics used for grammatical classes and attribute values are unique;
- and the tags are represented as a string of comma-separated mnemonics.

7 Input/output format

The WCCL Relation rules can be executed in two ways: in a console to process an XML file in the CCL format or in a code using the API.

7.1 Processing CCL files

Below is a sample XML in the CCL format for a sentence "Eiffel Tower is located in Paris". The file contains morphological tags for each word and semantic annotations (`facility_nam` for *Eiffel Tower* and `city_nam` for *Paris*).

```
<?xml version="1.0" encoding="UTF-8"?>
<!DOCTYPE chunkList SYSTEM "ccl.dtd">
<chunkList>
 <chunk type="p" id="ch1">
  <sentence id="s1">
   <tok>
    <orth>Wieża</orth> <!-- Tower : facility_nam -->
    <lex disamb="1"><base>wieża</base>
      <ctag>subst:sg:nom:f</ctag></lex>
    <ann chan="city_nam">0</ann>
    <ann chan="facility_nam">1</ann>
   </tok>
   <tok>
    <orth>Eiffla</orth> <!-- Eiffel : facility_nam-->
    <lex disamb="1"><base>Eiffel</base>
      <ctag>subst:sg:gen:m1</ctag></lex>
    <ann chan="city_nam">0</ann>
    <ann chan="facility_nam">1</ann>
   </tok>
   <tok>
    <orth>znajduje</orth> <!-- is located -->
    <lex disamb="1"><base>znajdować</base>
      <ctag>fin:sg:ter:imperf</ctag></lex>
    <lex disamb="1"><base>znajdywać</base>
      <ctag>fin:sg:ter:imperf</ctag></lex>
    <ann chan="city_nam">0</ann>
    <ann chan="facility_nam">0</ann>
   </tok>
   <tok>
    <orth>się</orth>
    <lex disamb="1"><base>się</base>
      <ctag>qub</ctag></lex>
    <ann chan="city_nam">0</ann>
    <ann chan="facility_nam">0</ann>
   </tok>
   <tok>
    <orth>w</orth> <!-- in -->
    <lex disamb="1"><base>w</base>
      <ctag>prep:loc:nwok</ctag></lex>
    <ann chan="city_nam">0</ann>
    <ann chan="facility_nam">0</ann>
   </tok>
   <tok>
    <orth>Paryżu</orth> <!-- Paris : city_nam -->
    <lex disamb="1"><base>Paryż</base>
      <ctag>subst:sg:loc:m3</ctag></lex>
    <ann chan="city_nam">1</ann>
    <ann chan="facility_nam">0</ann>
   </tok>
  </sentence>
 </chunk>
</chunkList>
```

Below is an XML output generated by the tool containing a single semantic relation of type *location* between *Eiffel Tower* and *Paris*.

```
<?xml version="1.0" encoding="UTF-8"?>
<!DOCTYPE chunkList SYSTEM "ccl.dtd">
<relations>
 <rel name="location" set="Syntactic relations">
  <from sent="s1" chan="facility_nam">1</to>
  <to sent="s1" chan="city_nam">1</from>
 </rel>
</relations>
```

7.2 Using API

The WCCL Relation tool provides set of API functions in Python to execute the rules directly in the code. Below we present a very brief description of the API. More information and examples can be found on the following page: `http://nlp.pwr.wroc.pl/wccl-relation`. The API provides the following functions:

- `process_file(filepath)` — process a single CCL file,
- `process_files(filepaths)` — process a set of CCL files,
- `process_sentence(sentence)` — process a single sentence represented as an object of class `corpus2.AnnotatedSentence`[6],
- `process_document(document)` — process a single document represented as on object of class `corpus2.DocumentPtr`[6].

All the presented functions return a set of objects of class `corpus2.Relation`[6] representing the recognised relations.

8 Conclusion and future work

In the paper we presented a result of ongoing work on creation a language independent rule-based toolset for recognition of relations between named entities, called WCCL Relation. The toolset is build on the top of an open-source framework called WCCL. A set of use cases for recognition of semantic relations between proper names for Polish was presented.

WCCL Relation is build on the top of an open-source framework called WCCL which is implemented in C++ and its source code is released under GNU LGPL 3.0[7]. WCCL Relation has a form of a Python script that is also released under the same license[8].

The described work is still in progress. On one hand we are still working on a set of rules for recognition of 8 categories of semantic relations between PNs for Polish. On the other hand we are still extending the WCCL Relation toolset with new features. One of the planned features is a support for names enumerations. The other are access to word dependency features, tests on distance between matched elements and support for relations between nested annotations.

[6] `http://nlp.pwr.wroc.pl/redmine/projects/corpus2/wiki`

[7] `http://www.nlp.pwr.wroc.pl/wccl.`

[8] `http://nlp.pwr.wroc.pl/wccl-relation.`

Acknowledgments

The work was funded by the NCBiR NrU.: SP/I/1/77065/10.

References

Asma Ben Abacha and Pierre Zweigenbaum. 2011. Medical entity recognition: a comparison of semantic and statistical methods. In *Proceedings of BioNLP 2011 Workshop*, BioNLP '11, pages 56–64, Stroudsburg, PA, USA. Association for Computational Linguistics.

S. Aït-Mokhtar, J.-P. Chanod, and C. Roux. 2002. Robustness beyond shallowness: incremental deep parsing. *Natural Language Engineering*, 8(3):121–144, June.

Steven Bird, Ewan Klein, and Edward Loper. 2009. *Natural Language Processing with Python*. O'Reilly Media, Inc., 1st edition.

Bartosz Broda, Michał Marcińczuk, Marek Maziarz, Adam Radziszewski, and Adam Wardyński. 2012. KPWr: Towards a Free Corpus of Polish. In Nicoletta Calzolari, Khalid Choukri, Thierry Declerck, Mehmet Uğur Doğan, Bente Maegaard, Joseph Mariani, Jan Odijk, and Stelios Piperidis, editors, *Proceedings of the Eight International Conference on Language Resources and Evaluation (LREC'12)*, Istanbul, Turkey, may. European Language Resources Association (ELRA).

Caroline Brun and Caroline Hagège. 2009. Semantically-Driven Extraction of Relations between Named Entities. *Research in Computing Science*, 41:35–46.

Hamish Cunningham, Diana Maynard, and Valentin Tablan. 2000. JAPE: a Java Annotation Patterns Engine. Technical Report CS—00—10, University of Sheffield, Department of Computer Science.

Hamish Cunningham, Diana Maynard, Kalina Bontcheva, Valentin Tablan, Niraj Aswani, Ian Roberts, Genevieve Gorrell, Adam Funk, Angus Roberts, Danica Damljanovic, Thomas Heitz, Mark A. Greenwood, Horacio Saggion, Johann Petrak, Yaoyong Li, and Wim Peters. 2011. *Text Processing with GATE (Version 6)*. University of Sheffield Department of Computer Science.

Ronen Feldman, Benjamin Rosenfeld, and Moshe Fresko. 2006. TEG — a hybrid approach to information extraction. *Knowledge and Information Systems*, 9(1):1–18, January.

Jing Jiang. 2012. Information Extraction from Text. In Charu C. Aggarwal and Cheng Xiang Zhai, editors, *Mining Text Data*, pages 11–41. Springer.

Linguistic Data Consortium. 2008. ACE (Automatic Content Extraction) English Annotation Guidelines for Relations (Version 6.2).

Michał Marcińczuk and Marcin Ptak. 2012. Preliminary Study on Automatic Induction of Rules for Recognition of Semantic Relations between Proper Names in Polish Texts. In Petr Sojka, Aleš Horák, Ivan Kopecek, and Karel Pala, editors, *Text, Speech and Dialogue, 15th International Conference, TSD 2012, Brno, Czech Republic, September 3-7, 2012. Proceedings*, volume 7499 of *Lecture Notes in Computer Science*, pages 264–271. Springer Berlin Heidelberg.

Małgorzata Marciniak and Agnieszka Mykowiecka. 2007. Automatic processing of diabetic patients' hospital documentation. *Annual Meeting of the ACL*, pages 35–42.

Michał Marcińczuk and Adam Radziszewski. 2013. Wccl match – a language for text annotation. In MieczysławA. Kłopotek, Jacek Koronacki, Małgorzata Marciniak, Agnieszka Mykowiecka, and SławomirT. Wierzchoń, editors, *Language Processing and Intelligent Information Systems*, volume 7912 of *Lecture Notes in Computer Science*, pages 131–144. Springer Berlin Heidelberg.

Michał Marcińczuk, Jan Kocoń, and Maciej Janicki. 2013. Liner2 – a customizable framework for proper names recognition for polish. In Robert Bembenik, Lukasz Skonieczny, Henryk Rybinski, Marzena Kryszkiewicz, and Marek Niezgodka, editors, *Intelligent Tools for Building a Scientific Information Platform*, volume 467 of *Studies in Computational Intelligence*, pages 231–253. Springer Berlin Heidelberg.

Sampo Pyysalo, Tomoko Ohta, and Jun'ichi Tsujii. 2011. Overview of the Entity Relations (REL) supporting task of BioNLP Shared Task 2011. In *Proceedings of BioNLP Shared Task 2011 Workshop*, pages 83–88, Portland, Oregon, USA. Association for Computational Linguistics.

Adam Radziszewski, Adam Wardyński, and Tomasz Śniatowski. 2011. WCCL: A Morpho-syntactic Feature Toolkit. In Ivan Habernal and Václav Matoušek, editors, *Text, Speech and Dialogue, 14th International Conference, TSD 2011, Pilsen, Czech Republic, September 1-5, 2011. Proceedings*, volume 6836 of *Lecture Notes in Computer Science*, pages 434–441. Springer Berlin Heidelberg.

Daniel Santos, Nuno Mamede, and Jorge Baptista. 2010. Extraction of Family Relations between Entities. In Luıs S. Barbosa and Miguel P. Correia, editors, *Proceedings of INForum 2010 - II Simposio de Informatica*, pages 549–560.

Beyond the Transfer-and-Merge Wordnet Construction: plWordNet and a Comparison with WordNet

Marek Maziarz & Maciej Piasecki & Ewa Rudnicka
Institute of Informatics
Wrocław University of Technology
Poland
mawroc@gmail.com
maciej.piasecki@pwr.wroc.pl
ewa.rudnicka78@gmail.com

Stan Szpakowicz
Institute of Computer Science
Polish Academy of Sciences, Poland
&
School of Electrical Engineering
and Computer Science
University of Ottawa, Canada
szpak@eecs.uottawa.ca

Abstract

Wordnets are lexico-semantic resources essential in many NLP tasks. Princeton WordNet is the most widely known, and the most influential, among them. Wordnets for languages other than English tend to adopt unquestioningly WordNet's structure and its net of lexicalised concepts. We discuss a large wordnet constructed independently of WordNet, upon a model with a small yet significant difference. A mapping onto WordNet is under way; the large portions already linked open up a unique perspective on the comparison of similar but not fully compatible lexical resources. We also try to characterise numerically a wordnet's aptitude for NLP applications.

1 Introduction

It is hard to imagine NLP without lexico-semantic resources. The Princeton WordNet (PWN) is a powerful case in point: we have come to rely on it even in "hard-core" statistical methods of processing English texts. Wordnets for other languages, which soon followed PWN,[1] have usually been built by the transfer-and-merge method: the structure of PWN is copied over to the target language, the lexical material is translated, and the inevitable differences in language typology and cultural background are a matter of post-processing.[2]

The transfer-and-merge construction allows high compatibility between PWN and the target wordnet, so also between any wordnets built in the same way. Multi-lingual NLP work benefits from dependable interlingual relations – ensured if one uses a wordnet with PWN's structure. PWN's semantic relations are undoubtedly of general utility, but they do exhibit certain "English bias", and that – combined with the anglocentric network of concept underlying PWN's synsets – is a downside of the translation method of building a new wordnet.[3] The result need not be an accurate reflection of the lexico-semantic system of the target language.

The translation method has another advantage: it is rather affordable, because PWN is now very complete and quite stable. To start the construction of a wordnet without looking to PWN may seem a little foolhardy, but it offers certain intriguing benefits. This paper looks at one of such independent projects, a wordnet for Polish.

The plWordNet project aims to construct a large lexical resource (comparable in size to the largest existing wordnets, including PWN), based on few but precise principles and definitions. The goal is to achieve a faithful description of Polish while enabling compatibility with PWN (and by corollary with many wordnets), and yet avoid any semantic influences due to the transfer of the net of lexicalised concepts from PWN.[4] The work is semi-automatic and corpus-based. Linguists make final decisions, but supporting tools supply most of the raw material for those decisions, and naturally

[1] See www.globalwordnet.org/gwa/wordnet_table.html for an up-to-date list.

[2] Such differences are non-trivial even within the same language family – for example, Germanic, Romance or Slavic – and become highly significant as one moves further away from Indo-European languages.

[3] The term "concept" in this paper denotes objects which can be expressed by words. This deliberately skirts all the philosophical, cognitive and semantic issues, better left for another occasion.

[4] It would be impossible to avoid PWN's architectural influences. It is a model all wordnet creators aspire to.

keep track of all aspects of the growing network.

No appropriately large machine-tractable thesaurus of Polish was available to jump-start the project. The construction has been based predominantly on the exploration of large corpora, with some help from traditional dictionaries. This required precise guidelines for linguists to facilitate the consistency of decisions and definitions – focused on linguistic data analysis and well anchored in the linguistic tradition. All information was fed into a steadily growing wordnet.

Today, plWordNet is large and mature enough to allow a wide-ranging observations. We analyse the consequences of the underlying wordnet model, the principles adopted, and the construction process. We take a varied perspective, including a multi-faceted comparison with PWN.

2 The structure of plWordNet

2.1 Constitutive relations

"A wordnet is a collection of synsets linked by semantic relations." This must be the most common quick take on wordnets in the literature. A synset is a set of synonyms which represent the same lexicalised concept, while synonyms are members of the same synset: this introduces a troubling circularity. An elaborate theory of synonymy could be a way of breaking the circle, but no such theory is operational enough in the sense of allowing precise guidelines for wordnet editors. This problem was discussed in (Derwojedowa et al., 2008; Piasecki et al., 2009; Maziarz et al., 2013).

Relations between synsets are often assumed to link concepts, and are fittingly described as conceptual relations. Their names, however, come up mainly in lexical semantics, where one considers hypernymy, meronymy etc. not between concepts but rather between words or lexical units (LUs).[5] Substitution tests usually proposed for synset relations refer to pairs of LUs (Vossen, 2002). Relations between LUs are relatively rare in PWN and in wordnets based on it, but antonymy, for example, never holds between synsets.

Neither concepts nor synsets occur directly in texts. LUs and their contexts of use *do* – and thus can be recognised, analysed and compared in corpora. This observation had led to a model of plWordNet different from that adopted by PWN: the basic building block is the LU, and semantic relations hold between LUs. A definition of a lexico-semantic relation includes a substitution test obligatorily applied by wordnet editors whenever a relation instance is added.[6]

The synset is a *secondary* notion. Synsets certainly appear in plWordNet, but they are defined via LUs. The cornerstone of this definitional machinery is a set of lexico-semantic *constitutive relations*, which contains in particular hypernymy, hyponymy, holonymy and meronymy. A relation is considered constitutive if its instances are frequent enough and frequently shared by groups of LUs.[7] It is also important that constitutive relations be established in linguistics (so wordnet builders feel comfortable around them) and accepted in the wordnet tradition (so compatibility among wordnets is easy to accomplish).

A synset is a group of LUs which share all constitutive relations; plWordNet software determines such groupings automatically. Thus, if relation R is noted as linking synsets S_1 and S_2, it links every pair of LUs $s_1 \in S_1$ and $s_2 \in S_2$. An instance of a synset relation is naturally interpreted as an abbreviation for a set of LU relation instances.

It seems harder to recognise synonymy than LU pairs linked by constitutive relations. Relation instances are identified primarily via language data analysis (section 2.2). Avoiding the often troublesome synonymy is one of the facets of the *minimal commitment* principle which underlies the construction of plWordNet: make as few assumptions as possible. If no theory of meaning needs to be constantly invoked, and few intuitions about meaning variations are necessary, the construction process becomes "agnostic" about schools of linguistic thought. That is perhaps an opportunity: more applications are possible if fewer theoretical restrictions are imposed on a wordnet.

The relation set in plWordNet (Maziarz et al., 2011a; Maziarz et al., 2011b; Maziarz et al., 2012) elaborates on relations in PWN, EuroWordNet (Vossen, 2002) and GermaNet.[8] In addition to the expected (hyponymy, meronymy, antonymy, cause, instance for proper names, entailment – all adjusted to the reality of Polish), some relations account for the rich inflection and highly productive derivation of Polish. Assorted examples:

[5]A lexical unit is a lemma *and* its sense.

[6]An instantiated test is automatically presented by the editor-supporting software. As a tiny example, the test «if X is a Y, then "X" is a hyponym of "Y"» can be used to determine that in PWN *tiger 2* is a hyponym of *big cat 1*.

[7]As an example, antonymy is seldom shared, while it is common for several LUs to share a hypernym.

[8]`www.sfs.uni-tuebingen.de/GermaNet/`

INHABITANT (*góral* 'highlander' – *góry* 'highlands'); INCHOATIVITY (*zapalić się*$_{perf}$ 'ignite' – *palić się*$_{imperf}$ 'burn'); GRADATION (*gorący* 'hot' – *ciepły* 'warm' – *ciepławy* 'warmish', *letni* 'lukewarm' etc.); MODIFIER (*piwny* 'hazel' – *oko* 'eye'); PROCESS (*chamieć* 'roughen' – *cham* 'boor'); STATE (*panować* 'rule' – *władca* 'ruler'); AGENT (*spawacz* 'welder' – *spawać* 'weld'); INSTRUMENT (*nadajnik* 'transmitter' – *nadawać* 'transmit'); DIMINUTIVE (*córeczka* 'little daughter' – *córka* 'daughter').[9]

2.2 The construction process

Wordnet construction is rather like writing a dictionary (Fellbaum, 1998; Broda et al., 2012b). Lexicography distinguishes four phases: data collection, selection, analysis and presentation (Svensén, 2009). In the plWordNet project, language technologies support all four phases. Professional linguists under the supervision of senior coordinators work with *WordnetLoom*, a Web application. This graph-based wordnet editor allows visual browsing and concurrent editing. Many semi-automatic tools are integrated into *WordnetLoom*.

In the data collection phase, a large corpus is essential (Wynne, 2005). A multi-source corpus with 1.8 billion tokens, the foundation of plWordNet's systematic growth, supports the other phases of plWordNet's construction. The collected texts have been tagged by the morphological analyser *Morfeusz* (Woliński, 2006) and the TaKIPI tagger (Piasecki, 2007).[10]

In the data selection phase, the most frequent lemmas are chosen (plWordNet, 2012) and presented to the editors by *WordnetLoom*. The editors can also browse the plWordNet corpus using the Poliqarp interface (Janus and Przepiórkowski, 2005). To avoid time-consuming queries on the corpus, the process employs a word-sense disambiguation algorithm (Broda et al., 2010); it selects up to 10 examples of word usage, representing different meanings.[11] Finally, editing is supported by *WordnetWeaver* (Piasecki et al., 2009), a system which suggests several places where best to link a given lemma in the lexico-semantic net. Its hints usually yield new distinguished senses. The corpus browser, usage examples and *WordnetWeaver* enable increasingly complex language processing: from simple queries in the plWordNet corpus, through the presentation of a small list of disambiguated usage examples, to highly sophisticated lemma-placement suggestions.

In the data analysis phase, the editors answer a few central questions:

- whether a given lemma is correct in Polish (e.g., tagger mistakes are weeded out);
- how many LUs should be distinguished – whether all existing senses appear in usage examples or *WordnetWeaver*'s suggestions;
- how to describe a given LU by plWordNet relations – what relation types should be used.

Apart from primary sources and automated tools, the editors are encouraged to look up words and their descriptions in the available Polish dictionaries, thesauri, encyclopaedias, lexicons, and on the Web. At the end, the new lemma and all its LUs, or senses, are integrated with plWordNet and displayed in *WordnetLoom*.

Intuition matters despite even the strictest definitions and tests, so one cannot expect two linguists to come up with the same wordnet structure. In corpus-building it is feasible to have two people edit the same portion and adjudicate the effect, but wordnet development is a more complicated matter. That is why we have a three-step procedure: (i) wordnet editing by a linguist, (ii) wordnet verification by a coordinator (a senior linguist), and (iii) wordnet revision, again by a linguist. Full verification would be too costly, so it is done on (large) samples of the editors' work. A coordinator corrects errors, adjust the wordnet editor's guidelines,[12] and initiates revision during which systematic errors are corrected and the wordnet undergoes synset-specific modification.[13]

There also is a unique opportunity to verify the content of plWordNet meticulously: a mapping of its synsets onto PWN. That process sees every LU in plWordNet re-examined by a separate team of linguists. Section 4 explains in detail.

[9] MODIFIER is a syntagmatic relation. Its inclusion in plWordNet (rather like in Mel'čuk's Sense-Text Model) can add a lot of links, but we apply it in moderation.

[10] The corpus consists of 250 million tokens in the ICS PAS Corpus (Przepiórkowski, 2004); 113m tokens of news items (Weiss, 2008); ≈80m tokens in a corpus made of Polish *Wikipedia* (Wikipedia, 2010); an annotated corpus KPWr with ≈0.5m tokens (Broda et al., 2012a); ≈60m tokens of shorthand notes from the Polish parliament; and ≈1.2 billion tokens collected from the Internet.

[11] Usage examples, welcome by the editors, help them distinguish senses (Broda et al., 2012b).

[12] That is a 120-page document at present.

[13] All in all, an experienced editor, assisted by *WordnetLoom*, can increase plWordNet by up to 2000 LUs a month.

wordnet	synsets	lemmas	LUs	avs
PWN	117659	155593	206978	1.76
plWN	116323	106438	160100	1.37
GermaNet	74612	89819	99523	1.33

Table 1: The count of synsets, lemmas and LUs, and average synset size **avs**, in PWN 3.1, plWordNet 2.0 (*plWN*) and GermaNet 8.0.

POS	synsets	lemmas	LUs	avs
N-PWN	82115	117798	146347	1.78
N-*plWN*	80037	77662	109967	1.37
V-PWN	13767	11529	25047	1.81
V-*plWN*	21726	17486	31980	1.47
A-PWN	18156	21785	30004	1.65
A-*plWN*	14560	11290	18153	1.25

Table 2: The count of Noun/Verb/Adjective synsets, lemmas and LUs, and average synset size **avs**, in PWN 3.1 and plWordNet 2.0 (*plWN*).

2.3 The effects

A wordnet ought to be large to be really useful. Its coverage matters a lot to potential applications. Intuitively, the higher the coverage, the more information can be acquired from the resource. The size of plWordNet approaches that of PWN, a first for a resource not built by the transfer method. A comparison may not be foolproof given the different language typologies and plWordNet's choice of the lexical unit as a basic element, but it is quite instructive nonetheless.

2.3.1 Size in numbers

Tables 1-2 present the statistics of the three largest manually constructed wordnets: Princeton WordNet 3.1, plWordNet 2.0 and GermaNet. PWN outstrips plWordNet when it comes to the number of lemmas and lexical units (word-sense pairs). Table 2 gives the precise counts of nouns, verbs and adjectives in PWN and plWordNet. The latter has more verbs, but fewer nouns and adjectives.

2.3.2 Lexical coverage

The size of a wordnet can be contrasted with a frequency list from a large corpus. Such a measure of coverage sheds a light on the usability of a resource. A count was made of how many PWN lemmas appear in the text of English Wikipedia and how many plWordNet lemmas show up in the corpus described in section 2.2. The corpus sizes are comparable: *Wikipedia.en* has ≈1.2 billion words, the plWordNet corpus ≈1.4 billion words.[14] Table 3 shows percentages of wordnet noun lemmas by frequency bins (≥ 1000, 500, 200, 100, 50 occurrences). List of lemmas within particular frequencies are created from corpora, and then the presence of each of those lemmas in plWordNet or PWN is checked. The fast decreasing tails suggest that both wordnets more willingly absorb frequent lemmas than lemmas with lower frequencies. The plWordNet counts are higher simply because the same corpus underlies the frequency list and the vocabulary of plWordNet. The highest coverage ratio (≥ 1000) is much less than 100% because plWordNet contains almost no proper names.[15]

FRC	≥1000	≥500	≥200	≥100	≥50
PWN	0.383	0.280	0.170	0.107	0.064
plWN	0.535	0.456	0.350	0.277	0.210

Table 3: Percentage of PWN noun lemmas in *Wikipedia.en* and plWordNet (*plWN*) lemmas in the plWordNet corpus. FRC is lemma frequency in the reference corpus.

2.3.3 Polysemy

Table 4 shows the statistics of polysemy. Average polysemy is calculated by dividing the count of LUs by the count of lemmas. The column 'poly.' lists average polysemy for polysemous lemmas, the column '+mono.' gives the polysemy statistics for polysemous and monosemous lemmas together, the last column presents the ratio of polysemous lemmas to all lemmas. Nouns and adjectives are more polysemous in plWordNet than in PWN, verbs – conversely. This ought to be considered in the light of the part-of-speech statistics in Table 2 and the measure of corpus coverage in Table 3.

There are more nouns and adjectives in PWN, and since both wordnets tend to absorb high-frequency lemmas first, the polysemy in PWN must be lower. The paradox can be explained thus: the larger a wordnet, the higher the number of monosemous lemmas it contains, because more frequent lemmas are more polysemous. On the other hand, there are more monose-

[14]The corpus, with different genres and styles, is large enough to draw conclusions about coverage in applications.

[15]A large gazetteer with many semantic categories is ready to be incorporated into the wordnet (NELexicon, 2013).

polysemy	poly.	+mono.	ratio
PWN - nouns	2.38	1.24	0.18
plWN - nouns	2.57	1.42	0.26
PWN - verbs	2.93	2.17	0.60
plWN - verbs	3.00	1.83	0.41
PWN - adjectives	2.14	1.38	0.32
plWN - adjectives	2.59	1.61	0.38

Table 4: Average polysemy in PWN 3.1 and plWordNet 2.0 (*plWN*); poly. = only polysemous lemmas, +mono. = all lemmas, ratio = % of polysemous lemmas).

mous verb lemmas in plWordNet than in PWN. This puzzling difference between the ratio for polysemous verbs (2.93 vs. 3.00) and for all verb lemmas (2.17 vs. 1.83) can be explained if one assumes that in plWordNet polysemous verbs have statistically more fine-grained distinctions.

3 Indicators for WordNet 3.1 and plWordNet 2.0

3.1 Synset size

A relatively strict definition of synonymy and synsets adopted in plWordNet may be expected to lead to fewer lexical units per synset than in PWN. Column **avs** in Table 1 confirms: the average synset size in LUs is 1.37 and 1.76 respectively. Table 2 shows the averages per part of speech – the same overall effect. In general, plWordNet synsets are around 0.4 LU smaller than those in PWN. Statistics per domain, not shown here, also support this finding. The only larger difference occurs in the domain *animal*, probably because PWN synsets systematically include Latin names of species. For example, PWN has {dog 1, domestic dog 1, Canis familiaris 1} 'a member of the genus Canis (probably descended from the common wolf) that has been domesticated by man since prehistoric times; occurs in many breeds'. The equivalent plWordNet synset, linked by inter-lingual synonymy, is {pies 2} – just one common noun.

3.2 Relation density

Relation density comparison for PWN 3.1 and plWordNet 2.0 in Table 5 shows the average number of relations per synset.[16] The density is higher in plWordNet for nouns and verbs (+0.5 and +0.8 relation, respectively), lower for adjectives (-0.9). The total density is higher in plWordNet: on average, every other Polish synset has one synset relation instance more than PWN. The net is denser, a fact which can be explained like this: plWordNet has a stricter definition of synonymy, so there are more smaller synsets and thus the system needs more differentiating relations (and having more relations creates a feedback loop with a magnifying effect).

POS	PWN	plWordNet
nouns	3.54	3.99
verbs	2.21	3.06
adjectives	2.43	1.56
total	3.11*	3.51

Table 5: Synset relation density in PWN 3.1 and in plWordNet 2.0 with regard to part of speech [*adverbs included].

The mapping of plWordNet onto PWN, described in detail in section 4, makes it possible to collate synsets from both wordnets linked by inter-lingual synonymy. It is interesting to see how relation density looks for corresponding synsets. Calculations have been run for all domains selected for mapping and described in Section 4 – see Table 6. For every plWordNet synset with inter-lingual synonymy, the count includes all relation instances to and from that synset, except obligatory inverse relations. The only outliers are the domains *body* and *location*: PWN has a higher density, even though Polish noun synsets have on average more relations than English noun synsets.

Now, locations and body parts are special vocabulary with many instances of meronymy. In plWordNet, meronymy suffices to link a new LUs to the net. In PWN, the most welcome relation for nouns is hyponymy. For example, {dłoń 1, ręka 3} 'hand' is a meronym of {ręka 1} 'arm', while its English I-synonym {hand 1, manus 1, mitt 1, paw 2} 'the (prehensile) extremity of the superior limb' is not only a meronym of {arm 1} 'a human limb', but also a hyponym of {extremity 5} 'that part of a limb that is farthest from the torso'. Hyponymy is absent from plWordNet for synsets defined more naturally by part/whole semantics.[17]

[16]The count excludes obligatory inverse relations, usually counted in other publications (Tenenbaum, 2005, Table 2).

[17]Our policy is to avoid redundancy as much as possible.

POS	PWN	plWordNet
noun domains	**PWN**	**plWordNet**
artifact	3.90	4.83
body	8.06	6.70
communication	4.15	4.33
food	4.70	4.49
location	14.70	5.71
person	3.94	3.94
time	6.39	6.59

Table 6: Synset relation density in PWN 3.1 and in plWordNet 2.0 in selected domains.

path	avg.	std.	q1	q2	q3	max
PWN *up*	7.76	2.42	7	8	9	18
plWN up	5.71	3.33	4	6	8	21
PWN *down*	0.57	1.25	0	0	1	14
plWNdown	0.60	1.15	0	0	1	23

Table 7: Hypernymy path length for nouns in PWN 3.1 and plWordNet 2.0 (*plWN*). The headings: avg. = average, std. = standard deviation, q1, q2, 3 = quartiles; the minimum values are 0.

3.3 Hypernymy depth

A comparison of the average hypernymy depth in plWordNet and in PWN concerned noun synsets linked via inter-lingual synonymy and presumably located at the same or a very close level in the taxonomy. Next, the number of their intra-lingual relations *up* and *down* has been checked. The average hypernymy depth *up* is longer in PWN (7.76 relation) than in plWordNet (5.71). This is expected in view of the fact that PWN has a complex hyponymy structure above unique beginners and many of top synsets map straight to SUMO categories. plWordNet is mainly linguistically oriented, so there are very few SUMO categories in the hyponymy hierarchy (see Table 7).

The average hypernymy depth *down* is comparable: PWN 0.57, plWordNet 0.60. This is explained by the fact that the inter-lingual mapping was constructed bottom-up, thus at least half of the I-synonyms in both wordnets are leaves – the lowest nodes in the hierarchy.

4 Linking differently structured wordnets

A partial mapping of plWordNet onto PWN is ready (Rudnicka et al., 2012). A hierarchically arranged set of inter-lingual relations (I-relations) and a unique mapping procedure have been defined. The set was inspired by equivalence relations in EuroWordNet (Vossen, 2002) and by intra-lingual relations in plWordNet (Maziarz et al., 2011a). I-relations, complete with effective substitution tests, are considered in a strict order: I-synonymy, I-inter-register synonymy,[18] I-near-synonymy, I-hyponymy, I-hypernymy, I-meronymy, I-holonymy. The mapping procedure, working at the level of synsets, is based on a correspondence in meaning and position in the two wordnets' structures. There are three stages: recognize the sense of a source-language synset, find a target-language synset, and link the two synsets with one of the I-relations. Editors are supported by *WordnetLoom* (section 2.2) and by an automatic prompt system. They can also consult mono- and bilingual dictionaries.

The mapping is systematically verified. For the majority of the inter-lingual links entered thus far, a coordinator examines the source and target synsets' LUs and the type of the I-relation. The coordinator reviews any questionable link in *WordnetLoom* and either repairs it immediately or consults the editor in order to reach a consensus.

Besides the obvious advantage of building a bilingual wordnet, the mapping process enabled additional verification for plWordNet itself. The semantic domains selected for mapping were shared in such a way that one linguist constructed a particular plWordNet hypernymy branch and another linguist performed its mapping. This allowed re-editing the structure and content of plWordNet in case of mistakes. Linguists who did the mapping were encouraged to review critically the plWordNet side and introduce changes when they felt them necessary. The whole process was, naturally, regularly monitored by coordinators.

Table 8 shows the number of instances of I-relations in plWordNet 2.0 and in GermaNet 8.0, another partially manually constructed and mapped wordnet.[19] I-synonymy, a primary relation in both wordnets has a comparable number of instances. It is the most frequent relation in GermaNet, while in plWordNet it has been overtaken by I-hyponymy. The latter statistic can be explained by profound differences in the struc-

[18]Two LUs mean roughly the same but belong to different stylistic registers.

[19]We thank Verena Henrich for providing us with the relevant GermaNet data.

Relation type	plWordNet 2.0	GermaNet 8.0
I-synonymy	14240	15259
I-hyponymy	22873	1397
I-hypernymy	3329	760
I-meronymy	1732	126
I-holonymy	394	52
I-near synonymy	923	3389
I-inter-register synonymy	522	—

Table 8: Inter-lingual relation count (instances) in plWordNet and in GermaNet.

ture and content of plWordNet and PWN, discovered during mapping and discussed below. In GermaNet, I-hyponymy has quite few instances. On the other hand, the second largest relation in GermaNet is I-near synonymy.

There are lexico-semantic and lexico-grammatical differences between English and Polish: lexical and cultural gaps as well as different structuring of information, differences in the degree of gender lexicalisation and the frequency of marked forms such as diminutive or augmentative. Another type of contrasts is to do with the concept of synonymy and synsets, due mainly to the existence of "mixed" PWN synsets made up of neutral and marked, feminine and masculine, singular and plural, mass and count, and even hypernym and hyponym forms in the same synset. Additionally, hypernymy in plWordNet is strictly conjunctive (the meaning of a hyponym must comprise the meaning components of all its hypernyms), while PWN also allows disjunctive hypernymy (easily found in the glosses describing the meaning contribution of a given synset).[20] There are also differences in the use of more than one intra-lingual relation to code the same conceptual dependencies, various granularity of meaning description, and dictionary content mismatches.

Most, but not all, of these contrasts were accounted for by I-hyponymy: there were usually more lexically marked forms on the plWordNet side, while the larger, more general synsets were usually on the PWN side. It is another factor contributing to high hyponymy count in the overall statistics of relations.

Semantic domains selected for the first stage of mapping included *person*, *artefact*, *location*, *time*, *food* and *communication*. On average, the coverage of PWN domains amounts to approximately 50% of the respective plWordNet domain coverage, except for *location* where it is about 25%. That is mainly because the mapping went from plWordNet to PWN, but also because of the percentages of proper-name synsets. Proper-name synsets are rare in plWordNet – it was a deliberate decision – while they have a considerable share in PWN domains such as *person* and *location*.

The distribution of specific inter-lingual relations within the selected domains is as follows. For the most mapped domains – *person* and *location* – it mirrors the general distribution of I-relations (I-hyponymy slightly overtakes I-synonymy). For *artefact* and *communication* they are similar, while for *food* and *time* I-synonymy decidedly overtakes I-hyponymy. The high percentage of I-hyponymy in the *person* domain can be explained by the existence of many lexical and cultural gaps such as, for example, names of aristocratic titles or administrative functions, specific or even limited to one language community.

All in all, the set of inter-lingual relations and the mapping procedure developed for the purpose of mapping plWordNet, and the strategies of handling different types of mapping dilemmas, appear perfectly usable in linking other wordnets. The I-hyponymy links are now a clear sign of gaps which can be repaired in the further stages of the development of the networks. Mapping plWordNet to PWN also opens up the possibility of establishing links to other wordnets already linked to PWN.

5 Applications

Freely available for any purpose on a licence identical to the PWN licence, plWordNet has already proven its value in at least 16 research applications and in many publication which cite it.

The verb portion of plWordNet was used in semantic annotation in a corpus of referential gestures (Lis, 2012) and in a lexicon of semantic valency frames (Hajnicz, 2011; Hajnicz, 2012). In the latter, plWordNet domains were also used in algorithms of verb classification. In (Maciołek, 2010; Maciołek and Dobrowolski, 2013) plWordNet is used to extend a set of features for text mining from Web pages. In (Wróblewska et al., 2013)

[20]Glosses for all synsets are a relatively late addition to PWN. We have only recently begun to introduce them into plWordNet.

plWordNet was the basis for building a mapping between a lexicon and an ontology. Miłkowski (2010) included plWordNet in a set of dictionaries in his proofreading tool. There are applications of plWordNet in word-to-word similarity measures utilised in research on ontologies (Lula and Paliwoda-Pękosz, 2009) or in calculating text similarity (Siemiński, 2012). As a semantic lexicon, plWordNet has been useful in text classification (Maciołek, 2010), terminology extraction and clustering (Mykowiecka and Marciniak, 2012), automated extraction of opinion attribute lexicons from product descriptions (Wawer and Gołuchowski, 2012), named entity recognition, word-sense disambiguation, extraction of semantic relations (Gołuchowski and Przepiórkowski, 2012), temporal information (Jarzębowski and Przepiórkowski, 2012) and anaphora resolution.

Open Multilingual Wordnet (Bond, 2013) now includes plWordNet. It is referred to in other work on wordnets and semantic lexicons (Pedersen et al., 2009; Lindén and Carlson, 2010; Borin and Forsberg, 2010; Mititelu, 2012; Zafar et al., 2012; Šojat et al., 2012).

The resource has attracted about 450 registered individual and institutional users (registration upon download is not mandatory). The plWordNet Web page and Web service have had tens of thousands of visitors (hundreds of thousands of searches). The intended use includes 70 commercial applications, and 50 scientific and educational applications (at all levels: university, high school and primary school). The declared topics of scientific applications include semantic word similarity calculation, multilingual word-sense disambiguation, text classification, knowledge base for recommender systems and information retrieval (e.g., wordnet-based query expansion, user modelling, personalisation and user profile), Question Answering, Information Extraction systems (including automated event extraction), Text Mining, Opinion Mining, parsing disambiguation, ontology-based systems (ontology construction, integration and mapping to a lexicon), comparative research on languages and wordnets, chatbot systems (as a lexicon), text similarity in processing legal texts, anti-plagiarism, contrastive/comparative studies (e.g., "Comparison of Polish, English and Swedish terms of motion and emotion, including analysis of metaphorical expressions." or "Conducting a cross-linguistic study on phonesthemes."), Affect Analysis (multilingual systems), humour analysis, development of Polish Link Grammar, and plWordNet as an object of analysis of complex networks.

Companies downloaded plWordNet for knowledge base management systems (e.g., automated conversion of text documents into a knowledge base), Business Intelligence, document similarity calculation, Polish website mapping and keyword tracking, online multilingual dictionary, search engine component development, translation inference support, analysis of public discourse, use as an additional bilingual dictionary in translation practice, Question Answering, text verification during editing, meta-data for publications, Polish dictionary and a basis for the development of bilingual dictionaries.

In education, plWordNet was named in many student projects in NLP, lectures on NLP, a course on Text mining for sociologists. It has been also utilised in teaching linguistics and even as an illustration of linguistic notions in education in primary and secondary schools.

6 Conclusions

The paper has discussed the construction of plWordNet, a national wordnet not adapted from Princeton WordNet by the transfer-and-merge method. The present contents of plWordNet are comparable in size to "The Mother of All WordNets", as well as in lexical coverage, hypernymy depth and relation density. The treatment of synonymy and synsets is an alternative to the usual model adopted in PWN and numerous other wordnets: synset membership depends only on constitutive relations between lexical units.

In its current mature stage of development, plWordNet is being mapped onto PWN. A unique mapping strategy aims at linking synsets based on the correspondence of meaning and position in the wordnet structure. The mapping process has revealed a number of contrasts between the two networks. They can be explained by lexico-grammatical differences between English and Polish, and the subtly different methodologies behind the construction of the two networks.

Acknowledgment

Work financed by the European Union, Project POIG.01.01.02-14-013/09 in the European Innovative Economy Programme.

References

Francis Bond. 2013. Open multilingual wordnet. Web page of the resource and project: `http://casta-net.jp/~kuribayashi/multi/`, May.

Lars Borin and Markus Forsberg. 2010. From the people's synonym dictionary to fuzzy synsets – first step. In *Proceedings of LREC 2010*.

Bartosz Broda, Marek Maziarz, and Maciej Piasecki. 2010. Evaluating LexCSD — a Weakly-Supervised Method on Improved Semantically Annotated Corpus in a Large Scale Experiment. In S. T. Wierzchoń M. A. Kłopotek, A. Przepiórkowski and K. Trojanowski, editors, *Proceedings of a Conference on Intelligent Information Systems*.

Bartosz Broda, Michał Marcińczuk, Marek Maziarz, Adam Radziszewski, and Adam Wardyński. 2012a. KPWr: Towards a Free Corpus of Polish.

Bartosz Broda, Marek Maziarz, and Maciej Piasecki. 2012b. Tools for plWordNet Development. Presentation and Perspectives. In Nicoletta Calzolari, Khalid Choukri, Thierry Declerck, Mehmet Uğur Doğan, Bente Maegaard, Joseph Mariani, Jan Odijk, and Stelios Piperidis, editors, *Proceedings of the Eight International Conference on Language Resources and Evaluation (LREC'12)*, pages 3647–3652, Istanbul, Turkey, may. European Language Resources Association (ELRA).

Nicoletta Calzolari, Khalid Choukri, Thierry Declerck, Mehmet Ugur Dogan, Bente Maegaard, Joseph Mariani, Jan Odijk, and Stelios Piperidis, editors. 2012. *Proceedings of the Eighth International Conference on Language Resources and Evaluation (LREC-2012), Istanbul, Turkey, May 23-25, 2012*. European Language Resources Association (ELRA).

Magdalena Derwojedowa, Stanisław Szpakowicz, Magdalena Zawisławska, and Maciej Piasecki. 2008. Lexical Units as the Centrepiece of a Wordnet. In Mieczysław A. Kłopotek, Adam Przepiórkowski, Sławomir T. Wierzchoń, and Krzysztof Trojanowski, editors, *Proceedings of the 16th International Conference Intelligent Information Systems*, Advances in Soft Computing, pages 351–358, Warsaw. Academic Publishing House EXIT.

Christiane Fellbaum. 1998. A Semantic Network of English: The Mother of All WordNets. *Computers and the Humanities*, 32:209–220.

Konrad Gołuchowski and Adam Przepiórkowski. 2012. Semantic role labelling without deep syntactic parsing. In Isahara and Kanzaki (Isahara and Kanzaki, 2012), pages 192–197.

Elżbieta Hajnicz. 2011. Grouping alternating schemata in semantic valence dictionary of polish verbs. In *Proceedings of Text, Speech and Dialogue*, volume 6836 of *Lecture Notes in Computer Science*, pages 155–162. Springer.

Elżbieta Hajnicz. 2012. Similarity-based method of detecting diathesis alternations in semantic valence dictionary of polish verbs. In *Proceedings of Security and Intelligent Information Systems*, volume 7053 of *Lecture Notes in Computer Science*, pages 345–358.

Hitoshi Isahara and Kyoko Kanzaki, editors. 2012. *Advances in Natural Language Processing: Proceedings of the 8th International Conference on NLP, JapTAL 2012, Kanazawa, Japan, October 22-24, 2012*, volume 7614 of *Lecture Notes in Artificial Intelligence*. Springer-Verlag, Heidelberg.

Daniel Janus and Adam Przepiórkowski. 2005. Poliqarp 1.0: Some technical aspects of a linguistic search engine for large corpora. In *The proceedings of Practical Applications of Linguistic Corpora*.

Przemysław Jarzębowski and Adam Przepiórkowski. 2012. Temporal information extraction with cross-language projected data. In Isahara and Kanzaki (Isahara and Kanzaki, 2012), pages 198–209.

Krister Lindén and Lauri Carlson. 2010. Finnwordnet – wordnet på finska via översättning. *LexicoNorcdica*, 17.

Magdalena Lis. 2012. Polish multimodal corpus - a collection of referential gestures. In Calzolari et al. (Calzolari et al., 2012), pages 1108–1113.

Paweł Lula and Grażyna Paliwoda-Pękosz. 2009. PodobieŃstwo semantyczne w analizie danych przekrojowych. In Krzysztof Jajuga and Marek Walesiak, editors, *Taksonomia 16 Klasyfikacja i analiza danych — teoria i zastosowania*, Prace naukowe Uniwersytetu Ekonomicznego we Wrocławiu, pages 104–112. Uniwersytet Ekonomiczny we Wrocławiu.

Przemysław Maciołek and Grzegorz Dobrowolski. 2013. Cluo: Web-scale text mining system for open source intelligence purposes. *Computer Science*, 14(1):45–62.

Przemysław Maciołek. 2010. Is shallow semantic analysis really that shallow? a study on improving text classification performance. In *Proceedings of the 2010 International Multiconference on Computer Science and Information Technology (IMCSIT)*.

Marek Maziarz, Maciej Piasecki, Stan Szpakowicz, and Joanna Rabiega-Wiśniewska. 2011a. Semantic Relations among Nouns in Polish WordNet Grounded in Lexicographic and Semantic Tradition. *Cognitive Studies*, 11:161–181.

Marek Maziarz, Maciej Piasecki, Stan Szpakowicz, Joanna Rabiega-Wiśniewska, and Bożena Hojka. 2011b. Semantic Relations Between Verbs in Polish Wordnet 2.0. *Cognitive Studies*, 11:183–200.

Marek Maziarz, Stan Szpakowicz, and Maciej Piasecki. 2012. Semantic Relations among Adjectives in Polish WordNet 2.0: A New Relation Set, Discussion and Evaluation. *Cognitive Studies*, 12:149–179.

Marek Maziarz, Maciej Piasecki, and Stanisław Szpakowicz. 2013. The chicken-and-egg problem in wordnet design: synonymy, synsets and constitutive relations. *Language Resources and Evaluation*. DOI 10.1007/s10579-012-9209-9, 28 pages.

Verginica Barbu Mititelu. 2012. Adding morpho-semantic relations to the romanian wordnet. In *Proceedings of LREC 2012*.

Marcin Miłkowski. 2010. Developing an open-source, rule-based proofreading tool. *Software – Practice and Experience*.

Agnieszka Mykowiecka and Małgorzata Marciniak. 2012. Combining wordnet and morphosyntactic information in terminology clustering. In *Proceedings of COLING 2012: Technical Papers COLING 2012, Mumbai, December 2012.*, pages 1951–1962.

NELexicon. 2013. NELexicon: a gazetteer of proper names for Polish. www.nlp.pwr.wroc.pl/en/tools-and-resources/nelexicon.

Bolette Sandford Pedersen, Sanni Nimb, Jørg Asmussen, Nicolai Hartvig Sørensen, Lars Trap-Jensen, and Henrik Lorentzen. 2009. Dannet: the challenge of compiling a wordnet for danish by reusing a monolingual dictionary. *Language Resources and Evaluation*.

Maciej Piasecki, Stanisław Szpakowicz, and Bartosz Broda. 2009. *A Wordnet from the Ground Up*. Oficyna Wydawnicza Politechniki Wrocławskiej. www.plwordnet.pwr.wroc.pl/main/content/files/publications/A_Wordnet_from_the_Ground_Up.pdf.

M. Piasecki. 2007. Polish Tagger TaKIPI: Rule Based Construction and Optimisation. *Task Quarterly*, 11(1–2):151–167.

plWordNet. 2012. Frequency List from plWorNet Corpus. www.nlp.pwr.wroc.pl/pl/narzedzia-i-zasoby/lista-frekwencyjna.

Adam Przepiórkowski. 2004. *The IPI PAN Corpus, Preliminary Version*. Institute of Computer Science PAS.

Ewa Rudnicka, Marek Maziarz, Maciej Piasecki, and Stanisław Szpakowicz Szpakowicz. 2012. A strategy of Mapping Polish WordNet onto Princeton WordNet. In *Proceedings of COLING 2012*. ACL.

Andrzej Siemiński. 2012. Fast algorithm for assessing semantic similarity of texts. *International Journal of Intelligent Information and Database Systems*, 6(5):495–512.

Bo Svensén. 2009. *A Handbook of Lexicography. The Theory and Practice of Dictionary-Making*. Cambridge University Press.

Mark Steyvers & Joshua B. Tenenbaum. 2005. The large-scale structure of semantic networks: Statistical analyses and a model of semantic growth. *Cognitive Science*, 29:41–78.

Piek Vossen. 2002. EuroWordNet General Document Version 3. Technical report, Univ. of Amsterdam.

Aleksander Wawer and Konrad Gołuchowski. 2012. Expanding opinion attribute lexicons. In *Proceedings of Text, Speech and Dialogue, Brno 2012*, volume 7499 of *Lecture Notes in Computer Science*, pages 72–80. Springer.

Dawid Weiss. 2008. Korpus Rzeczpospolitej. [on-line] www.cs.put.poznan.pl/dweiss/rzeczpospolita. Corpus of text from the online edtion of Rzeczypospolita.

Wikipedia. 2010. Polish Wikipedia. online. pl.wikipedia.org, accessed in 2010.

Marcin Woliński. 2006. Morfeusz – a practical tool for the morphological analysis of Polish. In M.A. Kłopotek, S.T. Wierzchoń, and K. Trojanowski, editors, *Intelligent Information Processing and Web Mining: Proceedings of the International Conference IIS: IIPWM'06*, Advances in Soft Computing, pages 511–520, Berlin. Springer.

Anna Wróblewska, Grzegorz Protaziuk, Robert Bembenik, and Teresa Podsiadły-Marczykowska. 2013. Associations between texts and ontology. In *Intelligent Tools for Building a Scientific Information Platform*, volume 467 of *Studies in Computational Intelligence*, pages 305–321. Springer.

M. Wynne, editor. 2005. *Developing Linguistic Corpora: a Guide to Good Practice*. Oxbow Books, Oxford.

Ayesha Zafar, Afia Mahmood, Farhat Abdullah, Saira Zahid, Sarmad Hussain, and Asad Mustafa. 2012. Developing urdu wordnet using the merge approach. In *Proceedings of the Conference on Language and Technology*, pages 55–59.

Krešimir Šojat, Matea Srebačić, and Marko Tadić. 2012. Derivational and semantic relations of croatian verbs. *Journal of Language Modelling*, 0(1):111–142.

History Based Unsupervised Data Oriented Parsing

Mohsen Mesgar
Department of Computer Engineering,
Sharif University of technology,
Tehran, Iran
mmesgar@ce.sharif.ir

Gholamreza Ghasem-Sani
Department of Computer Engineering,
Sharif University of technology,
Tehran, Iran
sani@sharif.edu

Abstract

Grammar induction is a basic step in natural language processing. Based on the volume of information that is used by different methods, we can distinguish three types of grammar induction method: supervised, unsupervised, and semi-supervised. Supervised and semi-supervised methods require large tree banks, which may not currently exist for many languages. Accordingly, many researchers have focused on unsupervised methods. Unsupervised Data Oriented Parsing (UDOP) is currently the state of the art in unsupervised grammar induction. In this paper, we show that the performance of UDOP in free word order languages such as Persian is inferior to that of fixed order languages such as English. We also introduce a novel approach called History-based unsupervised data oriented Parsing, and show that the performance of UDOP can be significantly improved by using some history information, especially in dealing with free word order languages.

1 Introduction

Statistical methods of natural language processing have shown to be very successful in corpus based linguistics. One reason is that electronic based texts are now available more than ever (Charniak, 1997; Church, 1998). The success of statistical Part Of Speech (POS) tagger systems has caused the trend of research in lexical analysis, language modeling, and machine translation to be changed towards using various statistical methods (Feili and Ghassem-Sani, 2004; Charniak, 1996).

Grammar is an essential tool in many applications of natural language processing (Feili and Ghassem-Sani, 2004). Writing a natural language grammar by hand is not only a time-consuming and difficult task, but also it needs a large amount of skilled efforts. Availability of large parsed corpus such as Penn Treebank (Marcus et al., 1993) has facilitated the development of automatic methods of grammar induction.

Based on the level of supervision information that is used by the different grammar induction methods, they are divided in to three major groups (i.e., supervised, semi-supervised, and unsupervised).

Supervised and semi-supervised methods require large treebanks, which may not exist for many languages. Therefore, many researchers have focused on unsupervised methods. Unsupervised Data Oriented Parsing (UDOP) is currently the state of the art in unsupervised grammar induction. But in the case of free word order languages such as Persian, its performance is inferior to that of fixed order languages like English.

In this paper, we present a novel unsupervised algorithm, named History-Based Unsupervised Data Oriented Parsing (HUDOP), and show, how to improve the performance of UDOP by using history information.

In section 2, we discuss about different methods of grammar induction. In section 3, UDOP is explained. In section 4, the details of HUDOP are introduced. Section 5 presents our experimental results on English and Persian. Finally, we conclude the paper in section 6.

2 Grammar induction methods

As it was mentioned above, based on the level of information, there are three types of grammar inductions: supervised, semi-supervised and unsupervised.

Supervised methods need fully-parsed and tagged corpora such as Penn Treebank (Marcus et al., 1993; Charniak, 1997; Collins, 1997; Charniak, 2000; Magerman, 1995; BoonkWan and Steedman, 2011). There are also some semi-supervised methods (Pereira and Schabes, 1992; Schabes et al., 1993; Koo et al., 2008), which use less information than their supervised counterparts. Also, semi-supervised methods need a rich corpus that for some natural language (e.g., Persian) does not currently exist. Thus, we have focused our attention on unsupervised methods. Unsupervised methods do not need to pars tree of sentences in training corpus.

Inside-Outside (IO) was introduced by Baker (1979) as an unsupervised algorithm. IO uses Expectation-Maximization (EM) to construct a grammar based on an un-bracketed corpus. The algorithm re-estimates rule probabilities toward some maximization on the training corpus. The algorithm may converge to local optima in different runs. This method is regarded as one of the basic algorithms of unsupervised grammar induction (Pereira and Schabes, 1992; Amaya et al., 1999; Casacuberta, 1996).

Alignment based Learning (ABL) is a learning method based on a linguistic principle: two constituents that belong to one family can be used instead of each other (Van Zaanen, 2000; Van Zaanen, 2002; Van Zaanen and Adriaans, 2001). EMILE, another grammar induction system based on this principle, initially used some levels of supervision, but later was modified to be a completely unsupervised system (Adriaans, 2001).

Another important category of unsupervised induction method is based on the distribution of words in sentences. It usually uses some distributional evidence to identify the constituents' structures (Klein and Manning, 2001). The main idea is that "the same constituents appear in the same contexts" (Clark, 2001; Klein and Manning, 2005). The so-called Context-Constituent Model (CCM) is based on this idea and works on the basis of a weakened version of the classic linguistic constituency test (Radford, 1988): constituents occur in their contexts.

The independence of the input sentence and its surrounding context are usually assumed in parsing. For instance in a Probabilistic Context Free Grammar (PCFG) model, each constituent is assumed to be independent of its surrounding constituents (Charniak, 1997). Such assumptions are not in fact valid in many cases. For instance, in English a noun phrase is more likely to be a pronoun when it is a subject of the sentence than when the noun phrase is in an object position (Allen, 1995). Similar condition exists in Persian, too. For instance, in Persian a pronoun subject can be dropped whereas pronouns in object positions cannot be dropped (Bijankhan, 2003; Bateni, 1995).

We can reduce the impact of this invalid independence assumption by using some form of history in parsing. For instance, the information about parent non-terminals can be utilized as a history of parsing. More specifically, $P(NP \rightarrow Pronoun | Parent=SUBJ)$ is higher than $P(NP \rightarrow Pronoun | Parent = VP)$. Therefore, some of the parsing dependencies between constituents can be modeled by history based parsing. History based models were initially developed at IBM (Black et al., 1992; Jelinek et al., 1992; Jelinek et al., 1994).

Increasing the dependencies on the context is the main feature of history based models. For instance, Johnson (1998) used the parent information of each non-terminal as the history information in the condition part of each rule. He showed that, instead of $P(A \rightarrow B|A)$, which is used in ordinary PCFG based parsing, using $P(A \rightarrow B|A, parent(A))$, where parent(A) is the nonterminal immediately dominating A, has a major positive impact on the accuracy of the parsing.

Based on the idea proposed by Johnson (1998), the so-called History based IO (HIO), improved the performance of IO especially in Persian (Feili and Ghassem-Sani, 2004). Parent based CCM (PCCM) is another history based method, which improved CCM (Mirroshandel and Ghassem-Sani, 2008). PCCM employs the parent's information of each context and constituent to prevent from divergence in the likelihood space.

There are also other techniques for improving the quality of an unsupervised grammar induction algorithm by considering some limitations, or additional information. For instance, Carroll and Charniak (1992) limit the set of non-terminals of the right hand side of rules with a given left-hand side.

3 Unsupervised Data Oriented Parsing

Unsupervised Data Oriented Parsing (UDOP) was introduced in (Bod, 2006a; Bod 2006b; Bod, 2007). In the first step, it generates all possible binary trees for each sentence of the corpus. This is followed by extracting all possible binary subtrees for parsing new sentences. In some methods, they convert each subtree to parsing rules. Number of rules will be increased exponentially. So these methods use Goodman reduction algorithm but we use subtree originally due to we want use Hidden Markov Model (HMM) for finding best parse tree for input sentence (Goodman, 2003).

UDOP uses a combination operator between the sub-trees for parsing a new sentence. We use "○" as the symbol of the combination operator.

Two sub-trees can be combined if the root of the right operand is equal to the leftmost nonterminal of the left operand. For example, let t_1 and t_2 be two sub-trees. Figure 1 shows t_1 and t_2 and the tree resulted from combining t_1 and t_2.

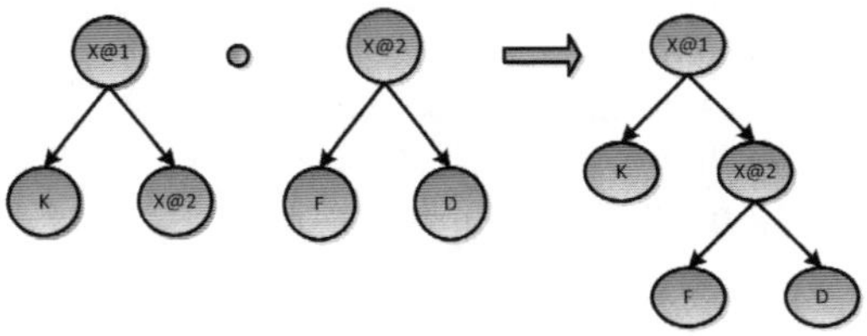

Figure 1. An example of the combination operator.

Let T be a parse tree for an input sentence resulted from combining sub-trees t_1, t_2, … , t_n (i.e., $t_1 \circ t_2 \circ \ldots \circ t_n$), then $t_1 \circ t_2 \circ \ldots \circ t_n$ is said to be a derivation of T (Rankin, 2007).

UDOP takes the shortest derivation as the best derivation. However, there may exist several shortest derivations. In such cases, in order to select the best derivation, UDOP uses probability.

The probability of any construction C is calculated by dividing the number of times C appears in the corpus by the number of times that any tree t with the same root appears in the corpus.

(1) $$P(C) = \frac{|C|}{\sum_{t:\,root(C)=root(t)} |t|}$$

The probability of a derivation is calculated by the product of probabilities of all the constructions in the derivation:

(2) $$P(t_1 \circ t_2 \circ \ldots \circ t_n) = \prod_j P(t_j)$$

Note that, there is an implicit assumption that, given root node root(t_i), each t_i is independent of every other t_j where j<>i. The probability of a parse tree T is calculated by the sum the probabilities of all the possible derivations of T.

(3) $$P(T) = \sum_{d \in D(T)} P(d)$$

D(T) is the set of all possible derivations of T. Let T_j be a member in the set of all possible parse trees of a given sentence s. Then the preferred parse tree of s is the one that maximizes $P(T_i|s)$ in:

(4) $$P(T_i \mid s) = \frac{P(T_i)}{\sum_j P(T_j)}$$

4 History-based UDOP

For computing all possible derivations of a new sentence, we can use the HMM, where each state corresponds to a sub-tree. The probability of each state is equal to the frequency of the subtree of that state. It means, the probability of the state that contains the sub-tree t_i is calculated similar to UDOP as follows:

(5) $$P(state_i) = \frac{|t_i|}{\sum_{t:\,root(t_i)=root(t)} |t|}$$

where $state_i$ corresponds to sub-tree t_i.

States in each step of HMM produce states in the next step, using the combination operator. Note that not all states can be combined. This is due to the definition of the combination operator. The transition probability between those states that cannot be combined will be set to zero. It means that if t_i and t_j cannot be combined, then $P(t_i \rightarrow t_{ij})$ and $P(t_j \rightarrow t_{ij})$, where $t_i \rightarrow t_{ij}$ to presents the transition between $state_i$ and $state_{ij}$, are set to zero. On the other hand, let t_x be a sub-tree with root X. Assume t_y is any other sub-tree that can be combined with t_x at node X. Also suppose that in tree t_y, there is a node P(x,y) that immediately dominates X (i.e., P(x,y) is parent of node X in tree t_y). In this case, there is a transition between t_x and

t_{xy} (i.e., $t_x \rightarrow t_{xy}$). The probability of $t_x \rightarrow t_{xy}$ is calculated as follows:

$$(6)\, P(t_x \rightarrow t_{xy} \mid Parent_{\forall i;ix}(t_x) = p_{(x,y)}) = \frac{|t_{xi} : parent(t_x) = p_{(x,y)}|}{|t_{xi}|}$$

We used top-down generative process to generate the HMM. By using parent information, the transition probabilities of HMM is calculated more accurately than in the case of UDOP. In HUDOP, the calculation of other probabilities, such as that of derivations and parse trees, is the same as UDOP.

Finally, in HUDOP, similar to UDOP, in order to find the most probable parse tree, we have used the Viterbi 100-best method, which uses 100 most probable states (sub-trees) in each step of HMM (Bod, 2006b).

5 Experimental results

Two kinds of experiments are presented in this section. At first, the result of applying HUDOP to two different English data sets are demonstrated and compared with that of related work. Then, we show the results of applying HUDOP to Persian, as a free-word order language.

5.1 Experimental result in English

HUDOP was tested on both ATIS (Hemphill et al., 1990) and WSJ-10 (Schabes et al., 1993). We used PARSEVAL to evaluate the quality of the output grammars. Part of speech tag sequences were used as the only lexical information of the training sets.

We executed two different experiments on the English sentences. At first, ATIS was divided in two distinct sets: the training set with almost 90% of the data and the test set including the rest. Although, HUDOP is an unsupervised approach and does not require any bracketing data set, we need the tree style syntactic information of the test data set for the evaluation purpose. We evaluated HUDOP using the ten-fold cross validation method. Similar to the original UDOP, we selected sentences with the length shorter than ten.

In the first experiment, we selected the spoken-language transcription of the Texas Instruments subset of ATIS (Hemphill et al., 1990), which is a part of Penn Treebank.

Method	UP	UR	F1
EMILE	51.9	16.81	25.35
ABL	43.64	35.56	39.19
LEFT	19.89	16.74	18.18
RIGHT	39.9	46.4	42.9
IO	42.19	35.51	38.56
HIO	46.85	40.9	43.67
CCM	55.4	47.6	51.2
PCCM	-	-	52.08
UDOP	58.90	58.50	58.70
HUDOP	63.90	62.89	**63.39**

Table 1. The results of HUDOP and other methods on ATIS data set.

The results of comparing HUDOP with other unsupervised methods, including EMILE (Adriaans and Haas, 1999), ABL (Van Zaanen, 2000), and CCM (Klein and Manning, 2005), on ATIS are shown in table 1. LEFT and RIGHT are the left and the right-branching baselines applied to ATIS. The results of left and right baselines have been taken from Klein and Manning (2005). As table 1 shows, the performance of HUDOP is superior to all the mentioned work.

We also tested HUDOP on WSJ-10 and compared its results with a number of related works including the state of the art (i.e., UDOP). The results are shown in Figure 2.

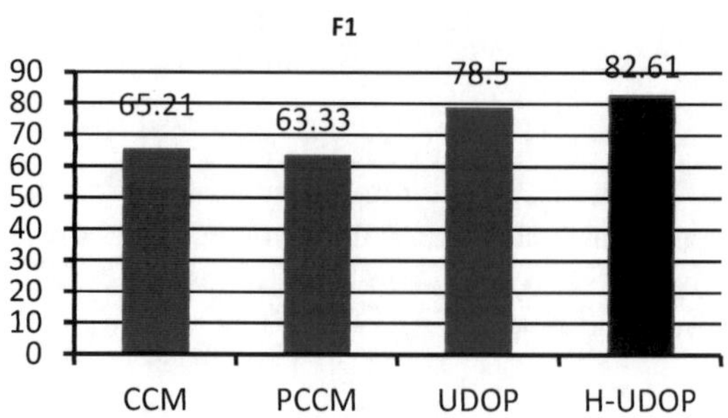

Figure 2. F1 scores for various models on WSJ-10.

5.2 Experimental results in Persian

We have also applied HUDOP to Persian, which is linguistically very different from English. Although many sentences in Persian have the form of SOV, it is generally considered to be a free-word-order language, especially in proposition adjunction and complements. It means that an adverb can be used at the beginning, in the middle, or at the end of sentences. This does not often change the meaning of the sentences.

In order to test HUDOP in Persian, we manually produced two different training corpora. All sentences of these corpuses contain less than 11 words, and have been extracted from a Persian corpus named Peykareh (Bijankhan, 2003; Megerdoomian, 2000). Peykareh has more than 32,255 sentences and uses a tag set similar to the tag set used in Amtrup et al. (2003). The first corpus included 3,000 sentences, which were manually changed in such a way that the structure of "S PP O V" was held. In other words, the common property of the sentences in this corpus was that the order of words were artificially fixed (i.e., they were not free in order). Table 2 shows main properties of the first corpus.

Property	Value
Number of sentence	3,000
Maximum length	10
Minimum length	2
Average Length	7
Number of words	22,153
Number of POS	18

Table 2. Main properties of first corpus.

The second corpus comprised 2,500 sentences with a high degree of free word orderness. Table 3 shows main properties of the second corpus.

Property	Value
Number of sentence	2,500
Maximum Length	10
Minimum Length	2
Average Length	7
Number of Words	18,482
Number of POS tags	18

Table 3. Main Properties of second corpus.

In Persian, we first ran both UDOP and HUDOP on each of the above corpora, separately. We also joined these corpuses to create a third mixed corpus, and repeated the experiments on this corpus, too. The results are shown in figure 3.

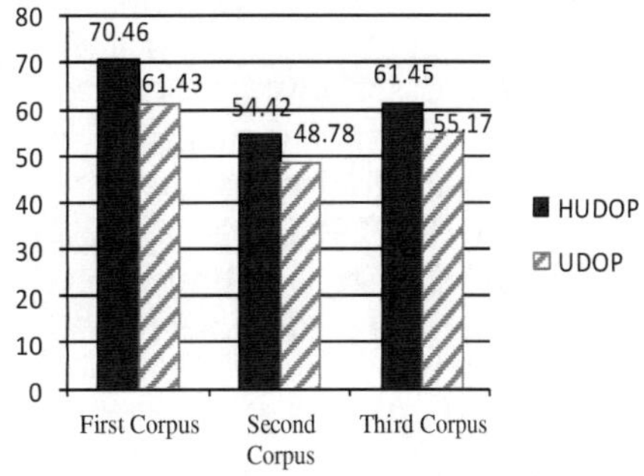

Figure 3. Comparison of UDOP and HUDOP methods in Persian (Based on the F1 measure).

Figure 3 shows the impact of the free word orderness property on the performance of both UDOP and HUDOP. The reduction in the performance of UDOP on the first corpus, in comparison to that of the second corpus, has been 13 percent in F1 score. The results of applying both UDOP and HUDOP to the combined corpus demonstrate little improvement. This shows that the free word orderness property of the input language has a negative effect on these methods.

The reason for this weakness is that these methods work based on the repetition of subtrees. Since in free word order languages, some words can freely appear in different places of sentences, the mentioned repetition decreases substantially, and as a result, the performance of the parsing is decreased.

The experiments also show that HUDOP outperforms UDOP in both languages.

6 Conclusion

Unsupervised Data Oriented Parsing (UDOP) is currently the state of the art in unsupervised grammar induction. UDOP works based on the repetition of possible sub-trees of parse trees of the input sentences. However, in free word order languages such as Persian, words can grammatically appear in different places of sentences. Thus, occurrence frequency of such sub-trees substantially decreases. In this paper, we proposed a novel approach, called History-based Unsupervised Data Oriented Parsing (HUDOP). We showed how by using parent nodes as a history notion of sub-trees, HUDOP outperforms UDOP. Parent information prevents from probability divergence and parsing will be more informative. To evaluate HUDOP, it was applied to both English and Persian (as a free word order language). The results of applying the new method to several corpuses with different degree of free word orderness showed that using parent information notably improves the performance of UDOP. One possible future work to improve the performance of HUDOP can be usage of other possible forms of history information. We are working on the idea implementing a semi-supervised HUDOP.

References

Adriaans, P. and Haas, E., (1999). Grammar induction as sub structural inductive logic programming. Proceedings of the 1st Workshop on Learning Language in Logic. Bled, Slovenia, pp. 117–127.

Allen, J., (1995). Natural Language Understanding. Benjamin/Cummings Pub.

Amaya, F., Benedi, J.M. and Sanchez, J.A., (1999). Learning of stochastic context-free grammars from bracketed corpora by means of re-estimation algorithms. The VIII Symposium on Pattern Recognition and Image Analysis, vol. 1, pp. 19–126.

Amtrup, J.W, Rad, H. R., Megerdoomian, K. and Zajac, R., (2000). Persian-English Machine Translation. An Overview of the Shiraz Project, NMSU, CRL.

Baker, J.K., (1979). Trainable grammars for speech recognition. Speech communication papers for the 97th Meeting of the Acoustical Society of America, pp. 547–550.

Bateni, M., (1995). Tosif-e Sakhtari Zaban-e Farsi (Describing the Persian Structure). Amir-Kabir Press, Tehran, Iran (in Persian).

Bijankhan, M., (2003). Emkansanji baraye Tarhe Modelsaziye Zabane Farsi (The feasibility study for Persian language modelling). The Journal of Literature. pp. 162–163.

Bijankhan, M., (2005). The role of corpus in generating grammar: presenting a computational software and corpus. Iranian Linguistic Journal 2 (19), pp. 48–67, (in Persian).

Black, E., Lafferty, J. and Roukos, S., (1992). Development and evaluation of a broad-coverage probabilistic grammar of English-language computer manuals. The Proceedings of the 30th Annual Meeting of the association for computational Linguistics, pp. 185–192.

Bod, R., (2006)a., Exemplar-based syntax: How to get productivity from examples? The Linguistic Review 23 (3), Special Issues on Exemplar- Based Models in Linguistics.

Bod, R., (2006)b., An All-subtrees Approach to Unsupervised Parsing. Proceedings ACL-COING, Sydney.

Bod, R., (2007)., A Linguistic Investigation into U-DOP. Proceeding ACL workshop on Cognitive Aspects of Computational Language Acquisition, pp.1-8.

BoonkWan, P. and Steedman. M., (2011)., Grammar Induction from Text Using Small Syntactic Prototypes. Proceedings of the 5th International Joint Conference on Natural language Processing, pp. 438-446.

Carroll, G. and Charniak, E., (1992). Two experiments on learning probabilistic dependency grammars from corpora. Technical Reports Department of Computer Science, Brown University, March.

Casacuberta, F., (1996). Growth transformations for probabilistic functions of stochastic grammars. IJPRAI 10 (3), pp. 183–201.

Charniak, E., (1996). Statistical Language Learning. MIT Press, Cambridge, London, UK.

Charniak, E., (1997). Statistical parsing with a context-free grammar and word statistics. Proceedings of the 14th National Conference on Artificial Intelligence, pp. 598–603.

Charniak, E., (1997). Statistical techniques for natural language parsing. AI Magazine 18 (4), pp. 33–44.

Charniak, E., (2000). A maximum-entropy-inspired parser. NAACL 1, pp. 132–139.

Church, K., (1988). A stochastic parts program and noun phrase parser for unrestricted text. Proceedings of the Second Conference on Applied Natural Language Processing, pp. 136–143.

Clark, A., (2001). Unsupervised induction of stochastic context-free grammars using distributional clustering. The Proceedings of 15th Conference on Natural Language Learning.

Collins, M., (1996). A new statistical parser based on bigram lexical dependencies. The Proceedings of the 34th Annual Meeting of the ACL, Santa Cruz.

Collins, M., (1997). Three generative, lexicalized models for statistical parsing. ACL 35/EACL 8, pp. 16–23.

Feili, H. and Ghassem-Sani G.,(2004). An Application of Lexicalized Grammars in English-Persian Translation. Proceedings of the 16th European Conference on Artificial Intelligence, pp. 596-600.

Goodman, J., (2003). Efficient algorithms for the DOP model. In R. Bod, R. Scha and K. Sima'an (eds.). Data-Oriented Parsing, The University of Chicago Press.

Hemphill, C.T., Godfrey, J. and Doddington, G., (1990). The ATIS spoken language systems pilot corpus. DARPA Speech and Natural language Workshop, Hidden Valey, Pennsylvania, June.

Jelinek, F., Black, E., Lafferty, J., Magerman, D.; Mercer, R. and Roukos, S. (1992). Towards history-based grammars: using richer models for probabilistic parsing. The Proceedings of the 5th DARPA Speech and Natural Languages Workshop, Harriman, NY.

Jelinek, F., Laferty, J.D., Magerman, D., Mercer, R.; Ratnaparakhi, A. and Roukos, S., (1994). Decision-tree parsing using hidden derivation model. The Proceedings of the Human Language Technology Workshop, pp. 272–277.

Johnson, M., (1998). The effect of alternative tree representations on treebank grammars. New Methods in Language Processing and Computational Natural Language Learning, ACL, pp. 39–48.

Klein, D. and Manning, C.D, (2005). The Unsupervised Learning of Natural Language Structure. Ph.D. Thesis, Department of Computer Science, Stanford University.

Klein, D. and Manning, C.D., (2001). Natural language grammar induction using a constituent-context model. Dietterich, T.G., Becker.

Koo, T., Carrera, X., and Collins, M., (2008). Simple Semi-Supervised Dependency Parsing. Proceeding of ACL 2008.

Magerman, D., (1995). Statistical decision-tree models for parsing. The Proceedings of ACL Conference.

Marcus, M.P., Santorini, B. and Marcinkiewicz, M.A., (1993). Building a large annotated corpus of English: the Penn Treebank. Computational Linguistics 19, pp. 313–330.

Megerdoomian, K., (2000). Persian Computational Morphology: A Unification-Based Approach. NMSU, CRL. Memoranda in Computer and Cognitive Science.

Mirroshandel, S. A. and Ghassem-Sani, G., (2008). Unsupervised Grammar Induction Using a Parent Based Constituent Context Model. 18th European Conference on Artificial Intelligence.

Pereira, F. and Schabes, Y., (1992). Inside-outside re-estimation from partially bracketed corpora. The Proceeding of 30th Annual Meeting of the ACL, pp. 128–135.

Radford, A., (1988). Transformational Grammar. Cambridge University Press, Cambridge.

Rankin, J., (2007). Data Oriented Parsing, Literature Review, November. pp. 4.

Schabes, Y., Roth, M. and Obsorne, R., (1993). Parsing the Wall Street Journal with the inside-outside algorithm. The Proceedings of the 6th Conference of the European Chapter of the ACL, pp. 341–347.

Van Zaanen, M. and Adriaans, P.W., (2001). Comparing two unsupervised grammar induction systems: alignment-based learning vs. EMILE. Technical Report: TR2001.05, School of Computing, University of Leeds.

Van Zaanen, M., (2000). ABL: alignment-based learning. COLING 2000, pp. 961–967.

Van Zaanen, M., (2002). Bootstrapping structure into language: alignment-based learning. Ph.D. Thesis, School of Computing, University of Leeds.

Contrasting and Corroborating Citations in Journal Articles

Adam Meyers
New York University
meyers@cs.nyu.edu

Abstract

Automatic recognition of CORROBORATE and CONTRAST relations between citations may enhance citation analysis. We describe a system that identifies these citation relations using predicate/argument and discourse structures.

1 Introduction

The citation of publications has been used to measure the impact of authors, publications, publishers, fields of study, etc., as represented in graphs in which nodes represent documents and edges connect documents if one refers to the other (citation graphs) or if a third document refers to both (co-citation graphs). NLP may be used to supplement these graphs with information about why documents are cited. While previous work (Teufel et al., 2009; Athar, 2011; Athar and Teufel, 2012) record positive and negative sentiment about cited work, we record information about how cited documents are compared to each other. CONTRASTing documents may describe different approaches or different opinions. Documents which CORROBORATE each other may follow a single approach. A document that is cited as corroborating with many other documents may be very salient. Some example instances of these CONTRAST/CORROBORATE relations are provided in Figure 1, the document containing the citations (represented as *we* or *this study*) contrasts with [1] and corroborates [2]; [3] and [4] contrast with each other; and [5] and [6] corroborate.

We use square brackets and numbers (IEEE style) to represent citations that are the object of this study (Figure 1). We use last name plus date (APA style) for works cited as part of this research effort. Examples in this paper (modified for brevity) are from the PubMed Central corpus[1]. As in Figure 1, arguments of relations are in bold and signals are underlined. Other important elements (Figure 3) have boxes drawn around them.

1. In contrast to **[1]**, **we** found clear detrimental effects of prophylaxis.
2. **This study** corroborates a study **[2]** finding no evidence of cross-hemisphere invasions.
3. FluA and FluB viruses have a common origin **[3]**. Thus, it is expected that aa residues of PA are conserved between FluA and FluB **[4]**.
4. Some species shed lots of virus, yet suffer few damaging effects **[5]**. On the other hand, species of swan, show 100% mortality within days of inoculation with HPAIV (H5N1) **[6]**.

Figure 1: CORROBORATE and CONTRAST

In this paper, we explore the relations between sentence-internal predicate relations, intersentential discourse relations and relations between citations. Then we describe and evaluate a system which derives CORROBORATE and CONTRAST relations between citations.

2 How Citation Relations are Encoded

2.1 The phrase/citation connection

(Abu Jbara and Radev, 2012) describes a system for identifying the **referential scope** of each citation, a text fragment that the citation is semantically related to–multiple citations can share the same referential scope. We assume that arguments of grammatical and discourse relations are essentially the referential scopes of the citations that we are concerned with. Like (Abu Jbara and Radev, 2012), we cover 2 cases. In the first case, the citation is an argument of some predicate (Figure 1, citation 1). In the second case, the citation is parenthetically linked to a constituent (Figure 1, ci-

[1] http://www.ncbi.nlm.nih.gov/pmc/

tations 2, 3 and 4) ((Abu Jbara and Radev, 2012) refers to this case as non-syntactic). We found the second case to be more common than the first for CORROBORATE and CONTRAST.

Authors use *we*, *our*, *this research*, and other phrases which we call **self-citations** to refer to their own work. These self-citations participate in the same citation relations as conventional citations. Thus, CORROBORATE and CONTRAST relations can have a self-citation arguments, e.g., Figure 1, **we** and **This study** in ex. 1 and 2. Self-citations occur in regular noun phrase positions (subject, object, etc.), but not parenthetically.

2.2 Citations, Discourse and Grammar

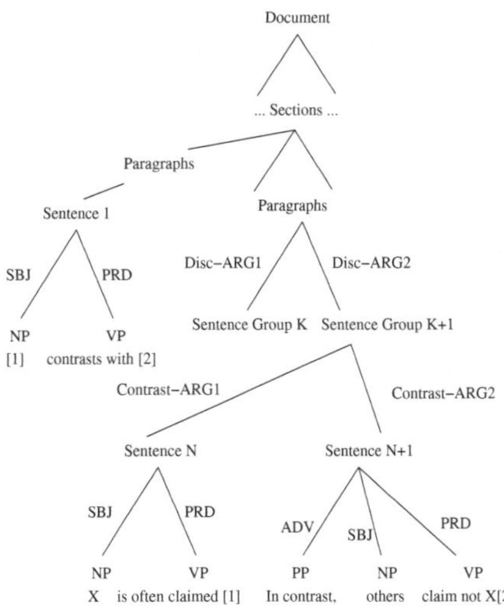

Figure 2: Constituent Structure of a Document

In Rhetorical Structure Theory (RST) (Mann and Thompson, 1988) and related approaches (Marcu, 2000), the discourse structure of a document forms a tree, with the root representing the document; internal nodes representing sections, paragraphs and multi-clause sentences, and leaves representing single clauses. The edge labels on the set of outgoing branches from a node collectively represent relations among the children of that node. As in Figure 2, substituting the leaves of a discourse tree with predicate argument representations (or parses) results in a rooted graph for a document with words as leaves. If the referential scopes of a pair of citations correspond to a pair of siblings at any level in this graph, the relation represented at the parent node can correspond to a citation relation. The sentence "*[1] contrasts with [2] regarding whether X is or is not true*" is analogous to the sentence "*X is often claimed [1]. In contrast, others claim not X [2]*" because the subject and object of the verb *contrast* correspond to the discourse arguments of *in contrast*. Taking this approach, we assume that discourse units and grammatical arguments are the referential scopes of citations. Furthermore, we limit our attention to citations scopes that are no more than a few sentences long (as in the Penn Discourse Treebank (PDTB) (Miltsakaki et al., 2004)).

We assume that: (1) there is a grammatical or discourse relation corresponding to each CORROBORATE and CONTRAST citation relation; (2) each such grammatical/discourse relation takes 2 arguments, each argument being a sequence of sentences, a sentence, a phrase or a word; and (3) more than one citation can be associated with each argument. Given these assumptions we seek to identify: (a) the candidate grammatical/discourse relation and its arguments; and (b) the sets of citations that correspond to these arguments. We then hypothesize the corresponding citation relation for each ARG1/ARG2 pair in the Cartesian product of the set of citations in the ARG1 domain and the set of arguments in the ARG2 domain.

This means that to identify CONTRAST and CORROBORATE citation relations, we need to identify syntactic and discourse signals that would imply that citations hold these relations. In the case of syntactic predicates, these turn out to be a list of words (*contrast, corroborate, endorse, ...*) that are idiosyncratic to this task. For discourse connectives, we can use some previous classifications: causal discourse connectives (*thus, therefore*) tend to be linked to CORROBORATE citation relations; and CONTRAST discourse connectives (*in contrast, on the other hand, however*) tend to be linked to CONTRAST citation relations. While all the cited work on discourse relations posit these same relations for consecutive sentences with no explicit connectives, we have not explored this avenue yet.[2]

2.3 Multi-Sentence Units

We recognize a third DISCOURSE relation, **EXPAND**, which does not directly link to either of our citation relations. Rather, 2 sentences in an EXPAND relation are treated as a single unit, which can, itself be a discourse argument. Fur-

[2](Prasad et al., 2007) reports annotating 16053 implicit and 18459 explicit discourse relations in their corpus.

A) Prior to the HPAI H5N1 virus epidemics, wild bird mortality from AI virus infection had been rare **[7]**, **[8]**.

B) In contrast, HPAIV H5N1 is unusual as high mortality rates have occurred in wild birds [9], [10].

C) Passerine birds have been naturally affected by HPAI H5N1 viruses [11]–[14].

D) Experimental infections of passerine [15], [16] characterized these birds as vulnerable.

E) Additionally, Gronesova et al., 2008 found that 18% of samples from 12 passeriform species tested positive for influenza A viral genome in a surveillance study [17].

Figure 3: Multi-S ARG2: (Kalthoff et al., 2009)

thermore, EXPAND relations can (transitively) link such units to additional sentences, producing larger multi unit chunks. Citations in 2 multi-sentence units can be in CORROBOATE or CONTRAST relations in the same manner as the single sentence cases described above. Figure 3 contains one such example. Sentences B, C, D and E are linked together into one unit by means of 3 EXPAND relations, holding between sentence pairs {B,C}, {C,D} and {D,E}. The discourse connective *In contrast* takes sentence A as one argument and the unit B through E as a second argument. Based on this CONTRAST discourse relation, we deduce that the citations in A (7 and 8) are in contrast with the citations in B through E (9–17), resulting in 18 CONTRAST citation relations.

Our EXPAND discourse relation approximately corresponds to several discourse relations in other frameworks (EXAMPLE, ELABORATION, LIST and others in (Marcu, 2000); CONJUNCTION, INSTANTIATION and others in PDTB). We collapse these relations in order to simplify the task. 2 mechanisms for identifying EXPAND relations both of which are evident in Figure 3: (i) using discourse connectives, e.g, the EXPAND relation between D and E is signaled by the connective *Additionally*; and (ii) based on the *cohesion* between 2 sentences – this is the case for the links connecting sentences {B,C} and {C,D}. Following (Marcu, 2000) (and others), cohesion can be determined by elements that indicate continuity between sentences such as anaphoric words (the demonstrative *these*) or repeated words from the previous sentence. In Figure 3, *birds, have, H5N1* and *viruses* are repeated in C, after occurring in B. D contains the demonstrative *these*, and repeats the word *birds* that is found in C. Our system takes these cohesive signals as evidence that an EXPAND relation holds between 2 consecutive sentences. Our Expand relations are used to approximate the larger citation context. (Athar and Teufel, 2012) uses similar methodology in their citation sentiment system.

3 DocRelate

3.1 Our Approach

Each file in our corpus of PubMed scientific articles has the citations premarked. Preprocessing includes the marking of all sentence and paragraph boundaries. Our citation relation system, DocRelate processes each document from beginning to end, one sentence at a time. All processing is based on regular expressions and simple string matches and is therefore both faster and less accurate than a syntactically-sophisticated approach would be. Nevertheless, we expect that aspects of DocRelate that deal with relations across sentence boundaries to be essentially the same as they would be in systems using deeper processing.

For each sentence, we find: (a) lexical signals; (b) sentence dividers (semi-colons, coordinate/subordinate conjunctions); and (c) citations (conventional and self-citations). For each lexical signal, we establish a $clause_1$ and a $clause_2$. If the lexical signal follows a sentence divider, $clause_1$ is the portion of the current sentence preceding the sentence divider, whereas $clause_2$ follows the sentence divider, e.g., the sentence divider is *and* in

> *The public considers frequently reported infectious diseases, to be the most severe* **[18]** *and therefore people's anxiety correlated with a negative perception of the disease* **[19]**.

Otherwise, the previous and current sentences are $clause_1$ and $clause_2$ (Figure 1 ex. 3 and 4).

We maintain a dictionary of lexical signals, which includes: surface forms, local disambiguating information, part of speech (POS) and CITATION relation (EXPAND, CORROBORATE or CONTRAST). For lexical signals with POS of 'adverb', $clause_1$ is assumed to contain the ARG1 citations and $clause_2$ is assumed to contain the

ARG2 citations: most examples discussed in this paper follow this pattern, e.g., Figure 1 ex. 3 and 4. For other POS: (preposition, verb, adjective and subordinate conjunction (SCONJ)) both arguments are inside clause$_1$. For most sentence-internal cases, the signal divides the clause into 2 parts: citations preceding the signal are candidate ARG1s and those following the signal are ARG2s, e.g., Figure 1 ex. 1 and 2. When an SCONJ occurs at the beginning of a clause, the clause must be divided at a centrally-located comma. Citations preceding that comma are ARG2 candidates, whereas citations following the comma are ARG1s. The 2 cases of SCONJ are:

Case 1 Limited studies have suggested dsRNA is an activator of NLRP3 inflammasome **[20]** although this has been disputed **[21]**.

Case 2 Although influenza strains resistant to NA inhibitors are less prevalent **[22]**, resistance to oseltamivir has been reported **[23]**,**[24]**.

For Case 1, ARG1 is 20 and ARG2 is 21; for case 2, both 23 and 24 are ARG1s and 22 is ARG2. Our approach to SCONJ is essentially the same as that of (Marcu, 2000) among others.

In the absence of discourse connectives, we can hypothesize an EXPAND relation between 2 sentences if the second sentence refers back to the first, as determined by: (a) the proportion of words in the second sentence also occurring in the first, ignoring a list of stop words; (b) the presence of abbreviations in the second sentence corresponding to word sequences in the first; (c) the presence of referring expressions found in the second sentence (*this, these, those, another, it, they, them, itself, themselves, their, here, latter*); and (d) the occurrence of self-citations in both the current sentence and the previous one.

Algorithm 1 is our approach for finding citation relations in an article. After each sentence is processed, citations that are not embedded in a sentence-internal ARG2 are recorded as potential ARG1s for the next sentence (the **cites** function) and each EXPAND relation causes the previous set of ARG1 citations to be stored as well (in St_ARG1). This makes analyses like that of Figure 4 possible: the (ARG1) citations preceding *However* are contrasted with the (ARG2) citations in the sentence containing *However*. The citations in sentence A are stored due to the Expand relation

```
foreach sentence in document do
  S ⟵ Sentence
  P ⟵ PreviousSentence
  SLink ⟵ DiscRel(S, P)
  Output Sentence-internal relations
  if SLink ∈ {CONTRA, CORROB} then
    ARG2 ⟵ cites(S)
    ARG1 ⟵ St_ARG1 ∪ cites(P)
    if Satisfy_Constraints(ARG1,ARG2) then
      Output SLink Relation for
      ∀{a1, a2} ∈ ARG1 × ARG2
    end
    Empty St_ARG1
    if ARG1 ≠ ∅ then
      St_SLink ⟵ SLink
      St_ARG1 ⟵ ARG1
    end
  end
  else if SLink = EXP then
    ARG1 ⟵ cites(P)
    ARG2 ⟵ cites(S)
    if St_SLink ≠ ∅ ∧ ARG2 ≠ ∅ then
      Output: St_Link relation for
      ∀{a1, a2} ∈ St_ARG1 × ARG2
    end
    else
      add cites(S) to st_ARG1
    end
  end
  else
    Empty St_ARG1 and St_SLink
  end
end
```

Algorithm 1: Identify Citation Relations

between sentences A and B, motivated by the referring expression *These* and abbreviation *HPAIV* (*highly pathogenic avian influenza virus*). When the procedure evaluates sentence C, the citations in A are potential ARG1s. However, as there is not an EXPAND relation between sentences B and C, these potential ARG1s are not stored for connectives in subsequent sentences.

Cross-sentence CONTRAST and CORROBORATE signals (**St_SLink** in Figure 1) are stored in addition to previous ARG1s up to that point. As long as there is a continuous sequence of EXPAND relations linking the subsequent sentences, citations in those sentences can fill the ARG2 slot for **St_SLink**. Figure 3 is one such example: the citations in the the sentence preceding *In contrast* are ARG1s and the citations following the signal are ARG2s: both citations in the sentence and in subsequent sentences. Storage of these elements is emptied in the absence of EXPAND.

We have implemented the following constraints on these procedures: (1) 2 clauses cannot be linked by multiple discourse relations. Conflicts favor the relations CONTRAST and CAUSE over EXPAND (where discourse CAUSE relations imply

A Recently, an H9N2 AIV was isolated from pigs in several provinces in China **[25]**,**[26]**,**[27]**, and a H5N1 HPAIV was identified in pigs in Asian countries **[28]**.

B These observations have led to the conclusion that swine can serve as direct and intermediate hosts for many subtypes of AIVs including the HPAIV of the H5 and H7 subtypes.

C However, there is recent evidence that domestic pigs show only low susceptibility to H5N1 HPAIV **[29]**, **[30]**.

Figure 4: Multi-S ARG1: (Ma et al., 2008)

POS	**BASE**	**Variants**	**Function**
VERB	*support*	+ed/s/ing	CORROB
Constraint: not after *the*|*a*; not before *vector*; not in FUNDING/ACKNOW Section			
VERB	*contrast*	+ed/s/ing	CONTRA
Constraint: before *with*; not after *by*|*in*			
PREP	*contrast*		CONTRA
Constraint: before *with*|*to*; after *in*|*by*			
ADV	*additionally*		EXPAND
ADV	*contrast*		CONTRA
Constraint: after *in*|*by*; not before *with*|*to*			
ADV	*roughly*		EXPAND
Constraint: sentence-initial only			
ADV	*thus*		CORROB

Figure 5: Sample Lexical Entries

CORROBORATE citation relations). This creates separate multi-sentence units for CONTRAST and CORROBORATE relations, since all storage is emptied in the absence of cross-sentence EXPAND relations; (2) the sets of citations for proposed ARG1 and ARG2 cannot have a member in common – this rules out relations that do not make sense (a document contrasting with itself) or that are uninformative (a document corroborating with itself). may be due to failures

3.2 Lexical Entries for Signals

We manually constructed a dictionary of signals licensing EXPAND, CORROBORATE and CONTRAST relations. The CORROBORATE and CONTRAST entries are signals which license citation relations, the entries being based on their roles in syntax and discourse structure. The EXPAND entries are signals that license EXPAND discourse relations. We have 246 entries for EXPAND, 48 for CONTRAST and 31 for CORROBORATE. This was feasible because there are a small number of these signals that cover most cases. We based our dictionary on previous work. We examined entries in COMLEX Syntax (Macleod et al., 1996) including the 7 coordinate conjunctions, 108 SCONJ, 96 adverbs marked as (META-ADV :CONJ T), and a few other adverb classes as well. We examined the set of discourse connectives marked in PDTB and classified in its manual (Prasad et al., 2007). We also did some manual annotation (unpublished work) and examined files from our training corpus while creating the system. Sample lexical entries (Figure 5) include: base forms, parts of speech (POS), relation licensed, and constraints. Multi-word expressions and POS disambiguation is implemented by requiring or excluding certain words before/after the key words. For example, *contrast* can be a verb; one of the multi-word prepositions {*in contrast with*, *in contrast to*, *by contrast to*}; or one of the multi-word adverbs {*in contrast*, *by contrast*}. Choice of POS for *contrast* determines the relative positions of ARG1 and ARG2, e.g., for the adverb, it is in the previous clause. Another constraint is the sentence-initial requirement, since some adverbs connect clauses when they occur initially, but not when they occur elsewhere in the sentence. For example, sentence-initial *roughly* can introduce a sentence that elaborates some aspect of the previous sentence (EXPAND), e.g., *Roughly, the chance that this would happen was 8 to 1.* However, the non-initial use of *roughly* still means something like *approximately*, but the connection with the previous sentence is no longer there, e.g., *The odds were roughly 8 to 1.*

3.3 System Evaluation

We ran DocRelate on a 20 document held-out test corpus. Figure 6 represent 216 correct answers out of 291 relations in the answer key (manual annotation by the author after the system was completed). We evaluated (CORROBORATE, CONTRAST) relations between citations, but not discourse relations between sentences (CAUSE, CONTRAST, EXPAND) or predicate argument relations.

4 Concluding Remarks

We achieve the highest accuracy for relations linking citations across adjacent sentences. Long-

Relation	Instances in Answer Key	All		Same Sentence		Next Sentence		2 or More Apart	
		Prec	Rec	Prec	Rec	Prec	Rec	Prec	Rec
Contra	156	90%	67%	75%	71%	99%	69%	53%	47%
Corrob	135	94%	83%	83%	57%	93%	92%	100%	79%
All	291	92%	74%	88%	76%	95%	66%	92%	74%
Instances in Answer Key		291		102		157		75	

Figure 6: Precision/Recall for Citation Relations

1. Dynamic models of epidemics are widely accepted **[31]**. So stochastic methods have emerged as the best way to model infectious diseases data **[32]**. [Missing CORROBORATE: *so* **NOT in lexicon**]

2. Age is not considered in **our model**, though it may affect behavior and, thus, risk of becoming infected [33]. [Marked CORROBORATE (*thus*) instead of CONTRAST (*though*)]

3. Fibroblasts transfected with ANGPT1 reduced expression of endothelial-selective adhesion molecules **[34]**. However, in **these studies** gene transfer was performed prior to lung injury. [Incorrect CONTRAST: *these studies* is not self-citation]

Figure 7: Example Sources of Error

distance citation relations were more difficult because: (a) they depend on additional (EXPAND) discourse relations; and (b) their relative rarity posed a challenge for evaluation (there were 17 contrast and 58 corroborate long-distance relations). While the single-sentence case is similar to the 1-sentence-apart case, our results for the latter case were lower because: (a) the inventory of same-sentence signals is larger and many are missing from our lexicon; (b) these signals are less reliable; and (c) our pattern-based approximations of syntactic rules did not work for the sentence-internal case – using parsing based rules would have helped. Our false negatives exceed our false positives. We observed errors due to the following: (1) missing entries in our dictionary; (2) defects in our sentence-internal syntactic analysis; and (3) false positives for self-citations. Some sample errors are provided as figure 7.

We presented an analysis of how authors of technical documents depict corroborations and contrasts between documents We have presented a syntactically naive system, that accounts for most aspects of this analysis. We showed that it was possible in many cases to derive relations between citations from predicate and discourse relations among the constituents that those citations link to. Our current system achieves accuracy of 92% precision and 74% recall for CORROBORATE/CONTRAST relations, with some variation based on relation type and the distance between the citations in terms of sentences. for citations not in adjacent sentences. The main contribution of this paper is the working out of the details of how to identify citation relations. Towards this goal, we described a robust system using simple, manually written string-based rules. In future work, we plan to identify properties of additional discourse structures that impact the problem of identifying citation relations. It is likely that a more elaborate system would achieve better results. Such systems could include features based on parsing, semantic role labeling and other text processing, thus making more precise rules available. Systems based on Machine Learning approaches could also be created based on the features described here, as well as text-processing-based features.

Acknowledgments

Supported by the Intelligence Advanced Research Projects Activity (IARPA) via Department of Interior National Business Center contract number D11PC20154. The U.S. Government is authorized to reproduce and distribute reprints for Governmental purposes notwithstanding any copyright annotation thereon. Disclaimer: The views and conclusions contained herein are those of the authors and should not be interpreted as necessarily representing the official policies or endorsements, either expressed or implied, of IARPA, DoI/NBC, or the U.S. Government. Approved for Public Release; Distribution Unlimited.

References

A. Abu Jbara and D. Radev. 2012. Reference scope identification in citing sentences. In *Proc. of NAACL:HLT 2012*.

A. Athar and S. Teufel. 2012. Detection of implicit citations for sentiment detection. In *ACL 2012 Workshop on Detecting Structure in Scholarly Discourse*, pages 18–26.

A. Athar. 2011. Sentiment analysis of citations using sentence structure-based features. In *Proc. of the ACL 2011 Student Session*.

D. Kalthoff, A. Breithaupt, B. Helm, J.P. Teifke, and M. Beer. 2009. Migratory status is not related to the susceptibility to hpaiv h5n1 in an insectivorous passerine species. *PLoS One*, 4(7):e6170.

W. Ma, R.E. Kahn, and J.A. Richt. 2008. The pig as a mixing vessel for influenza viruses: Human and veterinary implications. *J Mol Genet Med*, 3(1):158–66.

C. Macleod, A. Meyers, and R. Grishman. 1996. COMLEX Syntax: An On-Line Dictionary for Natural Language Processing. In *Proceedings of Euralex96*.

W. C. Mann and S. A. Thompson. 1988. Rhetorical structure theory: Toward a functional theory of text organization. *Text*, 8(3):243–281.

D. Marcu. 2000. *The Theory and Practice of Discourse Parsing and Summarization*. The MIT Press, Cambridge.

E. Miltsakaki, A. Joshi, R. Prasad, and B. Webber. 2004. Annotating discourse connectives and their arguments. In A. Meyers, editor, *NAACL/HLT 2004 Workshop: Frontiers in Corpus Annotation*, pages 9–16, Boston, Massachusetts, USA, May 2 - May 7. Association for Computational Linguistics.

R. Prasad, E. Miltsakaki, N. Dinesh, A. Lee, and A. Joshi. 2007. The Penn Discourse Treebank 2.0 Annotation Manual. `www.seas.upenn.edu/~pdtb/PDTBAPI/pdtb-annotation-manual.pdf`.

S. Teufel, A. Siddharthan, and C. Batchelor. 2009. Towards domain-independent argumentative zoning: Evidence from chemistry and computational linguistics. In *EMNLP-2009*.

CCG Categories for Distributional Semantic Models

Paramita Mirza
University of Trento
paramita.paramita@unitn.it

Raffaella Bernardi
University of Trento
bernardi@disi.unitn.it

Abstract

For the last decade, distributional semantics has been an active area of research to address the problem of understanding the semantics of words in natural language. The core principal of the distributional semantic approach is that the linguistic context surrounding a given word, which is represented as a vector, provides important information about its meaning. In this paper we investigate the possibility to exploit Combinatory Categorial Grammar (CCG) categories as syntactic features to be relevant for characterizing the context vector and hence the meaning of words. We find that the CCG categories can enhance the representation of verb meaning.

1 Introduction

The distributional semantic approach is based on the idea that the meaning of a word relies heavily on its context. Hence, the meaning of a word can be represented as a vector of its co-occurrence frequency with the neighbouring words. There have been several works that explore ways to improve the representation of word meaning by incorporating syntactic information in the context vector, dependency relations between words being the commonly used syntactic features. Dependency-based Distributional Semantic Models (DSMs) have been tested against several tasks and shown to be among the best performing word space models (Erk and Pado, 2008; Cruys, 2008; Baroni and Lenci, 2009; Baroni and Lenci, 2010).

In this paper we investigate an alternative view on the syntactic features that can be used to enrich the context vector, namely Combinatory Categorial Grammar (CCG) categories, which provide a transparent relation between syntactic category and semantic type of a linguistic expression. Hence, we propose to build a CCG-based DSM using a corpus annotated by a CCG parser.

We test the model on word categorization tasks, in particular concrete noun and verb categorization. We are interested in investigating how the role of context changes in capturing lexical meaning among the different word categories (nouns vs. verbs). Furthermore, we explore the performance of the model in capturing the different categories of verbs, based on several verb classifications studied in the literature.

By comparing the model based on CCG categories with an analogous one based on Part of Speech (PoS), we study the role of richer syntactic information in the task of word categorization. Finally, we include also function words (grammatical words) in the context vector instead of assuming that only content words (i.e. nouns, verbs, adjectives, adverbs) are relevant in capturing the word meaning. We find that for some cases function words are useful to distinguish different classes of verbs.

2 "Supertags" for Distributional Semantic Models

We propose to investigate the role of constituent structures and features encoding tense information, by building a distributional model with dimensions tagged by "supertags", namely by Combinatory Categorial Grammar (CCG) categories.

CCG is the categorial grammar version studied by the Edinburgh research group led by Steedman (2000), which has been used to theoretically analyse several linguistic phenomena. It has been used for building a CCGbank (Hockenmaier, 2003) and has been implemented into an efficient and wide coverage parser (Clark and Curran, 2007)[1]. Below we will briefly describe the CCG categories, without going into details about the grammar.

[1]However, for our experiments we used the revised version presented in Honnibal et al. (2007)

CCG language consists of atomic and complex categories where the latter are built out of the former by means of the directional implication operators $Output\backslash Input$ and $Output/Input$. For instance, an intransitive verb is assigned the category $S\backslash NP$, which means that it wants an NP-argument on its left.

The atomic categories considered are S, NP, N, and PP, but they are also enriched with features that further specify sub-categorization information. Bare nouns are distinguished from non-bare nouns by enriching the N-category: $N[nb]$ (non bare) and N (bare). Sentences and verb phrases are distinguished by means of the features enrichment of the S category. Sentences are distinguished into: $S[dcl]$ (declarative sentences), $S[wq]$ (wh-questions), $S[q]$ (yes-no questions), $S[qem]$ (embedded questions), $S[em]$ (embedded declaratives), $S[frg]$ (sentence fragments), $S[for]$ (small clauses headed by *for*), $S[intj]$ (interjections) and $S[inv]$ (elliptical inversion). Verbs carry tense features such as: $S[b]\backslash NP$ (bare infinitives, subjunctives and imperatives), $S[to]\backslash NP$ (to-infinitives), $S[pss]\backslash NP$ (past participles in passive mode), $S[pt]\backslash NP$ (past participles used in active mode) and $S[ng]\backslash NP$ (present participles).

3 Data Sets

In the following we describe the data sets that are used to carry out the experiments presented in Section 4. We will start with the classification of concrete nouns and then move to several verb classifications.

Concrete nouns: We take the data set developed for the shared task at the ESSLLI 2008 Workshop on Lexical Semantics[2]. The data set consists of 44 concrete nouns extracted from McRae et al. (2005). The nouns are grouped into 6 semantic categories, which are 4 categories of natural objects (*bird*, *groundAnimal*, *fruitTree*, and *green*) and 2 categories of man-made artifacts (*tool* and *vehicle*).

Furthermore, the nouns can also be classified into 3 classes: *bird* and *groundAnimal* are grouped together into *animal* class; *fruitTree* and *green* into *vegetable*; *tool* and *vehicle* into *artifact*. This hierarchical structure of the data set makes it possible to perform several tasks of categorization on one data set.

Verbs (classification based on Levin's criteria): Inspired by the classification originally proposed in Levin (1993) and further revised in Vinson and Vigliocco (2008), the organizers of the ESSLLI 2008 Workshop have proposed a data set of 45 verbs classified into 9 semantic classes (*communication*, *mentalState*, *motionManner*, *motionDirection*, *changeLocation*, *bodySense*, *bodyAction*, *exchange*, and *changeState*), further grouped into 5 classes: *communication* and *mentalState* into *cognition*; *motionManner*, *motionDirection*, and *changeLocation* into *motion*; *bodySense* and *bodyAction* into *body*; *exchange*; and *changeState*.

Verbs (argument structure distinctions): Merlo and Stevenson (2001) consider thematic relations to be crucial for verb classification, and hence propose a classification of verbs that is coarser than the one proposed by Levin and considered to be appropriate for numerous language engineering tasks. In particular, the relevant features to be considered are causativity, animacy, the passive vs. active voice, and the use of past-participle vs. simple past. They consider the argument-structure, which is the thematic roles assigned by the verbs, to be the discriminative main property. To this end, three classes of verbs are defined: *unergative*, *unaccusative*, and *object-drop*.

The *unergative* are intransitive *activity* verbs whose transitive form can be the causative counterpart of the intransitive form. The subject of an intransitive activity verb is specified by an *agent*, while the subject of the transitive form is indicated by the *agent of causation* (e.g. "The horse *raced* past the barn" and "The jockey *raced* the horse past the barn").

The *unaccusative* verbs are intransitive *change-of-state* verbs. The transitive counterpart of these verbs exhibits the causative/inchoative alternation. The subject of the transitive unaccusative verb is marked by the *agent of causation*, but the alternating argument becomes a *theme* (e.g. "The butter *melted* in the pan" and "The cook *melted* the butter in the pan").

The *object-drop* verbs are again *activity* verbs that exhibit a non-causative diathesis alternation in which the object is simply optional. The thematic assignment is *agent* for the subject and *theme* for the optional object (e.g. "The boy *played*" and "The boy *played* soccer").

[2] http://wordspace.collocations.de/doku.php/data:esslli2008:start

The data set comprises 18 unergative, 19 unaccusative, and 20 object-drop verbs.

Verbs (positive and negative): The distinction between these two classes of words is studied in sentiment analysis and used in opinion mining. To obtain the negative verbs, we started from the list provided by Hu and Liu (2004)[3]. We removed those verbs that were not among the target words of our models (see Section 4), and finally kept only the most frequent 500 verbs. The positive verbs were extracted by choosing the 500 most frequent verbs in the corpus that are not in the negative class.

Verbs (upward and downward monotonic): If we take a logical view on the verb classification issue, verbs can be divided into upward and downward monotonic. For instance, let us consider two sentences (1) "We *know* the epidemic spread quickly" and (2) "We *doubt* the epidemic spread quickly". From (1) we can infer the relaxed version "We know the epidemic spread" but we cannot infer the restricted one "We know the epidemic spread quickly via fleas". Whereas the reverse happens for (2), from which we cannot infer "We doubt the epidemic spread" but we can infer "We doubt the epidemic spread quickly via fleas".

In formal semantics, *doubt* is called a downward-entailing operator (it reverses the order of the arguments it takes) and *know* is called an upward-entailing operator (it preserves the order.) We take a data set of 29 downward-entailing verbs identified in Danescu-Niculescu-Mizil et al. (2009) based on Ladusaw (1980) (e.g. *avoid, block, decline*), and compare it to a set of non-downward-entailing verbs obtained by extracting verbs that do not belong to downward class and have similar frequencies in our corpus.

4 Experiments

We consider the unsupervised approach (i.e. clustering) to perform the word categorization tasks. Our goal is to bring to light the different role of syntactic information in capturing the meaning of nouns and verbs, and to investigate the role of function and content words, as well as tense features, in the different verb classifications previously discussed.

4.1 Distributional Semantics Models

Our two models, CCG-DSM and PoS-DSM, are harvested from two large corpora, Wikipedia and ukWaC. The former contains approximately 820 million words put together into 43.7 million sentences. While ukWaC (Ferraresi et al., 2008) is a very large (>2 billion words) corpus of British English built by web crawling, limited to the .uk Internet domain. For both models, we consider as target words the 10K most frequent nouns (excluding proper nouns and nouns containing numbers), the 5K most frequent verbs, and the 5K most frequent adjectives. The two models differ with respect to their dimensions as specified below.

PoS-based model (PoS-DSM): For building the PoS-DSM, the corpora have been tokenized and annotated with TreeTagger[4]. As dimensions we took 20K most frequent PoS tagged words (e.g. *fruit_NN, use_VBG)* considering both content and function words. There are 376 PoS tagged function words, 204 words of them are unique lemmas.

CCG-based model (CCG-DSM): For building the CCG-DSM, the corpora have been analyzed by the CCG parser (Honnibal et al., 2007), and the dimensions are 20K most frequent CCG tagged words (e.g. *fruit_N*, *use_(S[ng]\NP)/NP)*. There are 1,499 CCG tagged function words and 18,501 content words. Among the function words, there are many words with more than one CCG category, only 196 of them are unique lemmas; among the content words there are 8,812 unique lemmas. For example, *be* is associated with 61 different CCG categories which differ either in terms of features (e.g. *(S[b]\NP)/NP* vs. *(S[dcl]\NP)/NP*) or in terms of the arguments (e.g. *(S[dcl]\NP)/PP* vs. *(S[dcl]\NP)/S*).

For each model, we evaluate both the *complete model* (`compl`), which is the model containing both content and function words as the dimension, and the model built using only *content words* (`cont`). The latter model is obtained from the complete version by leaving in only nouns, verbs, adjective and adverbs as the dimension, based on their PoS tags.[5] Moreover, we observe two different context windows: *2 size context window* (`2win`) in which only 2 words before and

[3] `https://github.com/williamgunn/SciSentiment/blob/master/negative-words.txt`

[4] `http://www.ims.uni-stuttgart.de/projekte/corplex/TreeTagger/`

[5] As a consequence of this filtering method, the model based on only content words includes also negation, e.g. *not*, since it is tagged as an adverb.

Model	6-way		3-way		2-way		Average	Average
	Entropy	Purity	Entropy	Purity	Entropy	Purity	Entropy	Purity
Van de Cruys (dependency)	**0.173**	**0.841**	**0.000**	**1.000**	**0.000**	**1.000**	**0.058**	**0.947**
CCG-DSM-`cont-senwin-raw`	0.243	0.773	0.067	0.977	0.755	0.682	0.355	0.811
PoS-DSM-`cont-senwin-raw`	0.243	0.773	0.067	0.977	0.755	0.682	0.355	0.811
Van de Cruys (BoW)	0.334	0.682	0.539	0.705	0.983	0.545	0.619	0.644

Table 1: Concrete nouns clustering result

2 words after a given target word are considered to co-occur together with the target word and hence determine the context words; and *sentence size context window* (`senwin`) in which we assume that all words within the same sentence of a given target word are the context words. Finally, we consider the following different weighting schemas: Positive Point-wise Mutual Information (PPMI), Exponential Point-wise Mutual Information (EPMI), Positive Local Mutual Information (PLMI), and Positive Log Weighting (PLOG), besides the raw co-occurrence frequencies.

For the data sets developed by the organizer of the ESSLLI 2008 Workshop, which are the concrete noun categorization and the verb categorization based on Levin's classes, we report also the results of the dependency based model of Cruys (2008) – that resulted to be the one best performing at the workshop. Cruys (2008) compare the dependency based model with a Bag-of-Words model (BoW) to study the effects of syntactic information.

4.2 Clustering Algorithm

We follow the instructions given in the ESSLLI 2008 Workshop for all our experiments, using CLUTO toolkit (Karypis, 2003) for clustering. We use the k-means algorithm of CLUTO using the *rbr* parameter with global optimization, which repeatedly bisects the objects until the desired number of clusters is reached. As for the other parameters we use the default values.

4.3 Evaluation Measures

To evaluate the cluster quality, we use the two standard measures available in CLUTO: *entropy* measures the degree of "disorder" in a cluster (i.e. how many objects from different classes grouped into one cluster), the best result is obtained with value 0; while *purity* (Zhao and Karypis, 2001) measures the degree to which a cluster contains words from one class only (i.e. the proportion of the most frequent class in the cluster), the best result is obtained with value 1.

CLUTO also provides tools for analysing the discovered clusters, which can be used to gain a better understanding of the set of objects assigned to each cluster and to provide brief summaries about the cluster's contents. The set of *descriptive features* is determined by selecting the features that contribute the most to the average similarity between the objects of each cluster. For each descriptive feature, a certain number is given, which denotes the percentage of the within cluster similarity that this particular feature can explain.

5 Results and Analysis

We will present the experiment results and analysis for the various data sets explained in Section 3.

5.1 Concrete Nouns

As previously discussed, since the data set is organized hierarchically, it is possible to do several tasks of clustering, namely 6-way, 3-way, and 2-way clustering. Table 1 reports the detailed results for the three clustering tasks separately. For the CCG-DSM, we report the results only of the best performing version, which is the model with only content words as dimensions, the sentence as context window, and using raw frequency values (CCG-DSM-`cont-senwin-raw`).

For comparison, Table 1 shows also the results achieved at the ESSLLI 2008 Workshop by the other models previously described. CCG-DSM achieves better results than the BoW models (Cruys, 2008), but it is outperformed by the model based on the dependency relation – even though in 3-way clustering task the purity and entropy values of both models are comparable. Finally, in this particular experiment setup, PoS-DSM achieves exactly the same result, showing that the CCG categories are not really helpful in this particular task. Below we will present the qualitative analysis of the CCG-DMS and PoS-DSM for this task.

The CCG-DSM model successfully discriminates nouns of *vegetable* (cluster 0), *animal* (cluster 1), and *artifact* (cluster 2) classes. However, one noun from the *animal* class ("chicken") is grouped together with nouns of the *vegetable* class. Table 2 reports the top 10 descriptive features for each cluster obtained by the CCG-DSM in the 3-way clustering experiment, while Table 3 reports the PoS-DSM ones.

Cluster	Descriptive features
0	**other**_N/N 5.2%, **fruit**_N 4.1%, **apple**_N 3.0%, **not**_(S\NP)\(S\NP) 2.3%, **tomato**_N 2.3%, **potato**_N 2.2%, **crop**_N 2.2%, **tree**_N 2.2%, **onion**_N 1.7%, **also**_(S\NP)\(S\NP) 1.7%
1	**other**_N/N 6.0%, **not**_(S\NP)\(S\NP) 5.2%, **bird**_N 2.8%, **year**_N 2.3%, **animal**_N 2.2%, **also**_(S\NP)\(S\NP) 2.2%, **dog**_N 2.0%, **large**_N/N 1.9%, **many**_N/N 1.8%, **include**_(S[dcl]\NP)/NP 1.8%
2	**not**_(S\NP)\(S\NP) 5.9%, **other**_N/N 3.9%, **small**_N/N 2.4%, **first**_N/N 2.4%, **use**_(S[ng]\NP)/NP 2.3%, **time**_N 2.0%, **new**_N/N 1.9%, **water**_N 1.6%, **also**_(S\NP)\(S\NP) 1.6%, **year**_N 1.6%

Table 2: Descriptive features for 3-way concrete nouns clustering by CCG-DSM-`cont-senwin-raw`

Cluster	Descriptive features
0	**also**_RB 4.4%, **other**_JJ 4.1%, **not**_RB 4.0%, **fruit**_NN 3.0%, **then**_RB 1.7%, **small**_JJ 1.4%, **fresh**_JJ 1.3%, **vegetable**_NNS 1.2%, **apple**_NNS 1.2%, **large**_JJ 1.2%
1	**not**_RB 7.1%, **also**_RB 5.9%, **other**_JJ 4.4%, **species**_NNS 3.5%, **bird**_NNS 2.0%, **large**_JJ 1.4%, **many**_JJ 1.4%, **sea**_NN 1.4%, **animal**_NNS 1.3%, **first**_JJ 1.3%
2	**not**_RB 7.6%, **also**_RB 4.4%, **other**_JJ 2.8%, **then**_RB 2.8%, **use**_VBN 2.8%, **small**_JJ 2.0%, **use**_VBG 2.0%, **water**_NN 1.8%, **first**_JJ 1.8%, **time**_NN 1.7%

Table 3: Descriptive features for 3-way concrete nouns clustering by PoS-DSM-`cont-senwin-raw`

We can see that the descriptive features used by CCG-DSM and PoS-DSM are similar, most of them are nouns and adjectives. Thus, in this case CCG categories do not give more information than PoS tags.

5.2 Levin Inspired Verb Classification

Table 4 reports the comparison of models' performance on clustering the 45 verbs of the ESSLLI 2008 Workshop. The best performance of CCG-DSM is achieved using the following experiment setup: dimensions include both function and content words, context window is of size 2, and the weighting scheme is EPMI. Although the overall performance is lower than the one for the concrete nouns, with the average purity of 0.678 vs. 0.811, it is higher than one obtained by the best performing model at the Workshop, namely the model based on dependency relations (0.678 vs. 0.612). Moreover, the average entropy is reduced significantly: 0.323 vs. 0.436 for the CCG-based model and the dependency-based model respectively.

The confusion matrix for the 5-way verb clustering (Table 5) shows that the model obtains high purity and low entropy for the cluster 0 (10 verbs of the *motion* class out of 15), cluster 1 (7 verbs of the *cognition* out of 10) and cluster 3 (8 verbs of the *body* class out of 10). However, it confuses the verbs of the *motion* class and the verbs of the *changeState* class. Several verbs from the *motion* class, such as "fall", "pull", "push", and "rise" are considered as the verbs of the *changeState* class instead. The same confusion also happens between the *exchange* and *cognition* class: "evaluate", "request", and "suggest" are categorized as *exchange* verbs instead of *cognition*. The descriptive features for each cluster are described in Table 6.

Cluster	Classes					Entropy	Purity
	ex[1]	mo[2]	cs[3]	bo[4]	co[5]		
0	0	10	1	0	0	0.189	0.909
1	0	0	0	2	7	0.329	0.778
2	0	4	4	0	0	0.431	0.500
3	0	0	0	8	0	0.000	1.000
4	5	1	0	0	3	0.582	0.556

[1] exchange [2] motion [3] changeState [4] body
[5] cognition

Table 5: Confusion matrix for 5-way verbs clustering (ESSLLI Workshop 2008)

It is interesting to notice the change of the context-window parameter in the best performing model: while the meaning of concrete nouns are better captured by looking at the sentence window, verbs are more influenced by the surrounding words. From Table 6 we could see that the features which are found to be more descriptive of the classes mostly are not nouns and adjectives as before, but adverbs and auxiliary verbs.

5.3 Argument Structure Distinction

As what we have done so far, we report the results of the best performing CCG-DSM, which again is

Model	9-way		5-way		Average	Average
	Entropy	Purity	Entropy	Purity	Entropy	Purity
Van de Cruys (dependency)	0.408	0.556	0.464	0.667	0.436	0.612
CCG-DSM-`compl-2win-epmi`	**0.340**	0.600	**0.305**	**0.756**	**0.323**	**0.678**
PoS-DSM-`compl-2win-epmi`	0.351	**0.622**	0.364	0.733	0.358	**0.678**
Van de Cruys (BoW)	0.442	0.556	0.463	0.600	0.453	0.578

Table 4: Verbs clustering result (ESSLLI 2008 Workshop classification)

Cluster	Descriptive features
0	**upon**_(S/S)/(S[ng]\NP) 1.1%, **smoothly**_(S\NP)\(S\NP) 1.0%, **bicycle**_N 0.9%, **past**_((S\NP)\(S\NP))/NP 0.9%, **see**_(S[pss]\NP)/(S[ng]\NP) 0.9%,
1	**and**_(S\NP)/(S\NP) 3.4%, **password**_N/PP 2.1%, **worth**_(S[adj]\NP)/(S[ng]\NP) 2.1%, **have**_(S[dcl]/(S[pt]\NP))/NP 1.5%, **openly**_(S\NP)\(S\NP) 1.3%,
2	**damaged**_N/N 3.1%, **trigger**_N 2.9%, **wound**_S[pss]\NP 2.9%, **sharply**_(S\NP)\(S\NP) 2.7%, **apart**_S[adj]\NP 2.7%,
3	**eat**_S[b]\NP 5.7%, **make**_(S[b]\NP)/S[dcl] 3.3%, **deeply**_(S\NP)\(S\NP) 2.8%, **make**_(S[dcl]\NP)/S[dcl] 2.8%, **like**_PP/S[dcl] 2.5%,
4	**that**_S[bem]/S[b] 3.2%, **evidence**_N/(S[to]\NP) 2.4%, **Right**_N 2.1%, **effectiveness**_N/PP 1.7%, **tribute**_N 1.6%,

Table 6: Descriptive features for 5-way verbs clustering (ESSLLI Workshop 2008)

the model presented above: dimensions are both function and content words, the window context of size 2, with PPMI weighting schema (CCG-DSM-`compl-2win-ppmi`). The model obtains 0.544 entropy and 0.772 purity and it outperforms the PoS-DSM. Using the same experiment setup, PoS-DSM is able to cluster the verbs with 0.719 purity and 0.658 entropy.

Table 7 and Table 8 provide an error analysis of this task. The most common mistake is that verbs of the *object-drop* class, such as "carve", "clean", "knit", "pack", "swallow", and "wash" are considered to be of *unaccusative* class by the model. While "divide" and "open", which belong to *unaccusative* class, are clustered together into the *object-drop* class.

Interestingly, the descriptive features relevant for this classification task carry several tense features. Recall, the feature abbreviations are: $S[dcl]$ (declarative sentences), $S[b]$ (bare infinitives, subjunctives and imperatives), $S[to]$ (to-infinitives) $[pss]$ (past participles in passive mode), $S[ng]$ (present participles), $S[pt]$ (past participles used in active mode). Merlo and Stevenson (2001) theory indeed has foreseen the relevance of the distinction between passive vs. active voice, as well as the usage of past-participle vs. simple past.

From the descriptive features of each cluster we could infer that *unergative* verbs are verbs which tend to occur together with "around", "along", or

Cluster	Classes			Entropy	Purity
	unacc[1]	objdrop[2]	unerg[3]		
0	0	3	16	0.397	0.842
1	2	11	0	0.391	0.846
2	17	6	2	0.734	0.680

[1] unaccusative [2] object-drop [3] unergative

Table 7: Confusion matrix for argument structure distinction (Merlo & Stevenson)

Cluster	Descriptive features
0	**around**_PR 0.7%, **see**_(S[pss]\NP)/(S[ng]\NP) 0.7%, **around**_(S\NP)\(S\NP) 0.6%, **around**_((S\NP)\(S\NP))/(S[ng]\NP) 0.5%, **around**_PP/PP 0.5%, **along**_(S\NP)\(S\NP) 0.4%, **off**_PR 0.4%, **past**_((S\NP)\(S\NP))/NP 0.4%, **see**_((S[dcl]\NP)/(S[ng]\NP))/NP 0.3%, **backward**_N 0.3%
1	**begin**_(S[b]\NP)/(S[ng]\NP) 0.2%, **start**_(S[dcl]\NP)/(S[ng]\NP) 0.1%, **begin**_(S[dcl]\NP)/(S[ng]\NP) 0.1%, **eligible**_(S[adj]\NP)/(S[to]\NP) 0.1%, **continue**_(S[b]\NP)/(S[ng]\NP) 0.1%, **start**_(S[pt]\NP)/(S[ng]\NP) 0.1%, **start**_(S[b]\NP)/(S[ng]\NP) 0.1%, **continue**_(S[dcl]\NP)/(S[ng]\NP) 0.1%, **try**_(S[b]\NP)/(S[ng]\NP) 0.1%, **Manor**_N 0.1%
2	**partially**_(S\NP)/(S\NP) 0.3%, **gently**_(S\NP)/(S\NP) 0.3%, **slowly**_(S\NP)/(S\NP) 0.2%, **completely**_(S\NP)/(S\NP) 0.2%, **once**_(S/S)/(S[pss]\NP) 0.2%, **liquid**_N 0.2%, **begin**_(S[dcl]\NP)/(S[to]\NP) 0.2%, **start**_(S[dcl]\NP)/(S[to]\NP) 0.2%, **start**_(S[pt]\NP)/(S[to]\NP) 0.2%, **gently**_(S\NP)\(S\NP) 0.2%

Table 8: Descriptive features for argument structure distinction (Merlo & Stevenson)

"past"; the verbs of *object-drop* class tend to co-occur with "begin" or "start" in the form of gerund (e.g. "begin playing", "start studying"); whereas the verbs of *unaccusative* class usually occur together with "begin" or "start" in to-infinitive form (e.g. "start to melt", "begin to boil").

5.4 Positive and Negative Verbs

We report the results obtained by the best performing CCG-DSM, namely the one with both function and content words as dimensions, context window of size 2, and PLOG weighting scheme (CCG-DSM-`compl-2win-plog`). The model achieves 0.946 purity and 0.255 entropy. However, the same results are obtained also by the PoS-DSM using the same parameters.

Cluster	Classes		Entropy	Purity
	positive	negative		
0	500	54	0.461	0.903
1	0	446	0.000	1.000

Table 9: Confusion matrix for positive vs. negative verb clustering

Looking at the confusion matrix shown in Table 9, it can be seen that the model assign 54 negative verbs to the cluster of positive verbs (cluster 0). Some of the negative verbs that are failed to be clustered as negative verbs are not strictly negative, for instance, "blow", "hang", "issue", and "knock". However, there are also other verbs that the model fails to recognize as negative which obviously have negative nuance, such as "break", "die", "kill", and "reject".

Cluster	Descriptive features
0	**the**_NP/N 0.2%, **to**_(S[to]\NP)/(S[b]\NP) 0.2%, **and**_conj 0.2%, **a**_NP/N 0.2%, **be**_(S[dcl]\NP)/(S[pss]\NP) 0.2%, **have**_(S[dcl]\NP)/(S[pt]\NP) 0.2%, **it**_NP 0.2%, **in**_((S\NP)\(S\NP))/NP 0.2%, **of**_PP/NP 0.1%, **they**_NP 0.1%
1	**the**_NP/N 2.4%, **and**_conj 2.0%, **to**_(S[to]\NP)/(S[b]\NP) 1.9%, **be**_(S[dcl]\NP)/(S[pss]\NP) 1.6%, **a**_NP/N 1.5%, **have**_(S[dcl]\NP)/(S[pt]\NP) 1.3%, **by**_((S\NP)\(S\NP))/NP 1.3%, **he**_NP 1.2%, **it**_NP 1.2%, **they**_NP 1.2%

Table 10: Descriptive features for positive vs. negative verbs clustering

The descriptive features behind this clustering are reported in Table 10. Quite impressively, the descriptive features are dramatically changed with respect to the ones seen so far. They are all function words, we see for the first time an important role to be played by pronouns, prepositions, coordination and determiners.

5.5 Downward Monotonic Verbs

We report the results obtained by the best performing CCG-DSM (CCG-DSM-`compl-2win-empi`) with 0.732 entropy and 0.786 purity, and the confusion matrix is shown in Table 11. Out of the 28 downward monotonic verbs, CCG-DSM misses to consider only three verbs as such, namely "doubt", "luck", and "withstand". The verbs that are wrongly considered downward monotonic are: "acknowledge", "address","convince", "cooperate", "demand", "halt", "merge", "outline", and "reconstruct".

Cluster	Classes		Entropy	Purity
	non-DM	DM		
0	9	25	0.834	0.735
1	19	3	0.575	0.864

Table 11: Confusion matrix for non-DW vs. DW monotonic verb clustering

Cluster	Descriptive features
0	**rom**_PP/(S[ng]\NP) 1.3%, **suggestion**_N/S[em] 1.3%, **temporarily**_(S\NP)\(S\NP) 1.1%, **possibility**_N/S[em] 0.8%, **strictly**_(S\NP)\(S\NP) 0.7%, **until**_((S\NP)\(S\NP))/PP 0.7%, **relations**_N 0.7%, **act**_S[ng]\NP 0.6%, **strongly**_(S\NP)/(S\NP) 0.5%, **notion**_N/S[em] 0.5%
1	**seriously**_(S\NP)/(S\NP) 3.9%, **heavily**_(S\NP)\(S\NP) 2.0%, **knee**_N/PP 2.0%, **yourself**_NP 2.0%, **needle**_N 1.8%, **time**_N/(S[ng]\NP) 1.8%, **reward**_N/PP 1.5%, **siege**_N 1.4%, **reason**_N/(S[to]\NP) 1.4%, **duty**_(N/PP)/PP 1.3%

Table 12: Descriptive features for non-DW vs. DW monotonic verbs clustering

Interestingly, the downward entailing verbs are recognized mostly by means of preposition and adverbs as specified in Table 12. Using the same experimental set up, the PoS-DSM performs worse with 0.966 entropy and 0.607 purity. The model fails to recognize the downward monotonic verbs, assigning 12 downward entailing verbs in one cluster and 16 in the other.

6 Conclusions

We have shown that while the richer CCG tags encoding both constituent structures and some other information, such as verb tense features and bare vs. not-bare noun distinctions, they are not so relevant for noun classification. However, they indeed play an important role in distinguishing some classes of verbs. Thus, embedding CCG categories in the semantic space might be useful to give better representation of the meaning of verbs.

On the one hand, the CCG-DSM obtains equal results with PoS-DSM in distinguishing positive vs. negative verbs and concrete nouns, and on the later task the dependency model obtains better results. On the other hand, the CCG-DSM outperforms the dependency based one for the verb classification inspired by Levin's classes, with the average purity of 0.678 vs. 0.612 and the average entropy of 0.323 vs. 0.436. It outperforms PoS-DSM in the argument structure based distinction proposed by Merlo and Stevenson (2001) as well as in detecting downward entailing verbs.

Moreover, the experiments show that the size of context window have different impacts in the different classification tasks. The sentence context window is more informative for representing the meaning of nouns, whereas for verbs the more relevant information for distinguishing their classes is found within the context window of size 2.

Finally, while content words are the dimensions required by the semantic space of nouns to better picture them, verbs require to also consider function words. In particular, to distinguish negative from positive verbs (in the sense of sentiment analysis) a major role is played by grammatical words like coordination, pronouns, and prepositions; whereas adverbs seems to be more relevant for recognizing downward entailing verbs.

References

Marco Baroni and Alessandro Lenci. 2009. One distributional memory, many semantic spaces. In *Proceedings of the Workshop on Geometrical Models of Natural Language Semantics*, GEMS '09, pages 1–8, Stroudsburg, PA, USA. Association for Computational Linguistics.

Marco Baroni and Alessandro Lenci. 2010. Distributional memory: A general framework for corpus-based semantics. *Computational Linguistics*, 36(4):673–721, October.

Stephen Clark and James Curran. 2007. Wide-coverage efficient statistical parsing with CCG and log-linear models. *Computational Linguistics*, 33(4):493–552.

Tim Van de Cruys. 2008. A comparison of bag of words and syntax-based approaches for word categorizaiton. In M. Baroni, S. Evert, and A. Lenci, editors, *Proceedings of the ESSLLI Workshop on Distributional Lexical Semantics*, pages 47–54.

Cristian Danescu-Niculescu-Mizil, Lillian Lee, and Richard Ducott. 2009. Without a 'doubt'? Unsupervised discovery of downward-entailing operators. In *Proceedings of NAACL HLT*, pages 137–145.

Katrin Erk and Sebastian Pado. 2008. A structured vector space model for word meaning in context. In *Proceedings of EMNLP 2008*.

Adriano Ferraresi, Eros Zanchetta, Marco Baroni, and Silvia Bernardini. 2008. Introducing and evaluating ukwac, a very large web-derived corpus of english. In *In Proceedings of the 4th Web as Corpus Workshop*.

Julia Hockenmaier. 2003. *Data and Models for Statistical Parsing with Combinatory Categorial Grammar*. Ph.D. thesis, University of Edinburgh.

M. Honnibal, J. R. Curran, and J. Bos. 2007. Rebanking CCGBank for improved interpretation. In *Proceedings of the 48th annual meeting of ACL*, pages 207–215.

Minqing Hu and Bing Liu. 2004. Mining and summarizing customer reviews. In *Proceedings of the tenth ACM SIGKDD international conference on Knowledge discovery and data mining*, KDD '04, pages 168–177, New York, NY, USA. ACM.

George Karypis, 2003. *CLUTO: A Clustering Toolkit*.

William A. Ladusaw. 1980. *Polarity Sensitivity as Inherent Scope Relations*. Garland Press, New York. Ph.D. thesis date 1979.

Beth Levin. 1993. *English Verb Classes and Alternations. A Preliminary Investigation*. Chicago, Ill.: University of Chicago Press.

Ken McRae, George S. Cree, Mark S. Seidenberg, and Chris Mcnorgan. 2005. Semantic feature production norms for a large set of living and nonliving things. *Behavior Research Methods*, 37(4):547–559, November.

Paola Merlo and Suzanne Stevenson. 2001. Automatic verb classification based on statistical distributions of argument structure. *Comput. Linguist.*, 27(3):373–408, September.

Mark Steedman. 2000. *The Syntactic Process*. Cambridge, MA: MIT Press.

P. Vinson and G. Vigliocco. 2008. Feature norms for a large set of object and event concepts. *Behavior Research Methods*, 40(1):183–190.

Ying Zhao and George Karypis. 2001. Criterion functions for document clustering: Experiments and analysis.

Discourse-aware Statistical Machine Translation as a Context-Sensitive Spell Checker

Behzad Mirzababaei, Heshaam Faili and Nava Ehsan
School of Electrical and Computer Engineering
College of Engineering
University of Tehran, Tehran, Iran
{b.mirzababaei,hfaili,n.ehsan}@ut.ac.ir

Abstract

Real-word errors or context sensitive spelling errors, are misspelled words that have been wrongly converted into another word of vocabulary. One way to detect and correct real-word errors is using Statistical Machine Translation (SMT), which translates a text containing some real-word errors into a correct text of the same language. In this paper, we improve the results of mentioned SMT system by employing some discourse-aware features into a log-linear reranking method. Our experiments on a real-world test data in Persian show an improvement of about 9.5% and 8.5% in the recall of detection and correction respectively. Other experiments on standard English test sets also show considerable improvement of real-word checking results.

1 Introduction

Kukich (1992) has categorized errors of a text into five categories: 1. isolated error 2. syntactic error 3. real-word error 4. discourse structure and 5. pragmatic error. In this paper, we focus on the third category, which is also referred as context-sensitive spelling error. This type of error includes misspelled words that are converted to another word of the dictionary (e.g., typing "arm" instead of "are" in the sentence "we arm good"). In order to detect and correct this kind of error, context analysis of the text is crucial.

Here, we propose a language-independent method, which is based on a phrase-based Statistical Machine Translation (SMT). In this case, the input and output sentences are both in the same language and the input sentence contains some real-word errors.

Phrase-based SMT is weak in handling long-distance dependencies between the sentence words. In order to capture this kind of dependencies, which affects detecting the correct candidate word, mentioned SMT is augmented with a discourse-aware reranking method for reranking the N-best results of SMT.

Our work can be regarded as an extension of the method introduced by Ehsan and Faili (2013), in which they use SMT to detect and correct the spelling errors of a document. But here, we use the N-best results of SMT as a candidate list for each erroneous word and rerank the list by using a discourse-aware reranking system which is just a log-linear ranker.

Shortly, the contributions of this paper can be summarized as follow: The N-best results of SMT are regarded as a candidate list of suspicious word, which is reranked by using a discourse-aware reranking system. Two discourse-aware features are employed in a log-linear ranker. The keywords in whole document surrounding the erroneous sentence are considered as the context window. We have achieved about 5% improvement over the SMT-based approach in detection and correction recall and 1% in precision on English experiment. The state-of-the-art results are achieved for Persian context-sensitive spell checker respect to F-measure and Mean Reciprocal Rank metrics.

This paper is organized as follows: Section 2 presents an overview of related works. In Section 3, we explain attributes of Persian language. In section 4, we will describe how to use SMT for generating candidate words. In Section 5, we discuss the approach for reranking the N-best result of SMT. Finally, we illustrate the experimental results and compare the results with the SMT-based approach.

2 Related Works

Most of the previous works in real-word error detection and correction are classified into two categories : 1. based-on statistical approaches (Bassil & Alwani, 2012 and 2. based-on separate resource such as WordNet (Fellbaum, 2010) in (Pedler, 2007). Statistical methods use several features, such as N-gram models (Bassil & Alwani, 2012; Islam & Inkpen, 2009), POS tagging (Golding & Schabes, 1996), Bayesian classifiers (Gale, Church, & Yarowsky, 1992), decision lists (Yarowsky, 1994), Bayesian hybrid method (Golding, 1995), latent semantic analysis (Jones & Martin, 1997). The N-gram and POS-based method are combined by Golding and Schabes (1996) and a better result achieved.

Pedler (2007) used WordNet as a separate resource to extract the semantic relations of the words. These methods consider fixed-length windows instead of the whole sentence as the context window.

Most of these methods use confusion set for detecting real-word errors. The confusion set is a set of words that are confusable with the headword of the set. The words of the set are not necessarily confusable with each other (Faili, 2010). When the error checker comes across one of the words in a confusion set, it should select an appropriate word in the sentence. A machine-learning method and the Winnow algorithm is proposed in (Golding & Roth, 1999), to solve word disambiguities based-on surrounding words of the spelling errors. This method uses several features of surrounding words, such as POS tag. +/-10 words from the corresponding confusable word in confusion set are considered as the context window.

Wilcox-O'Hearn et al. (2008) report a reconsideration of the work of (Mays et al., 1991). They use three different lengths for the context window. Also, they use 6, 10 and 14 words as the context window and accommodate all the trigrams that overlap with the words in the window.

Some statistical methods use Google Web 1T N-gram data set to detect and select the best correct word for a real-word error (Bassil & Alwani, 2012; Islam & Inkpen, 2009). Google Web 1T N-gram consists of N-gram word sequences, extracted from the World Wide Web. 5-gram and 3-gram are used in these papers, thus the context window in these methods is 9 and 5 words respectively.

There are few spell checkers for Persian, such as the works presented by Ehsan and Faili (2013); Kashefi, Minaei-Bidgoli, and Sharifi (2010). In Kashefi et al. (2010), a new metric based-on string distance for Persian is presented to rank spelling suggestions. This ranking is based-on the effect of keyboard layout or on the typographical spelling errors.

A language-independent approach based on a SMT framework is presented by (Ehsan & Faili, 2013). This method achieved the state-of-the-art results for grammar checking and context-sensitive spell checking for Persian language. Here, we also use SMT as a candidate generator for spell checking of real word errors, but our approach is different from that work in the following causes: we consider the keywords of whole document as the context-aware features. SMT is used as a candidate generator. We train a log-linear reranking system as a post-processing system to rerank the candidate list.

Our experiments on a real-world test data in Persian show an improvement of about 9.5% and 8.5% in the recall of detection and correction respectively over the method of Ehsan and Faili (2013).

3 Persian Language

Persian or Farsi is an Indo-European language. It is mostly spoken in Iran, Afghanistan and Tajikistan with dialects Farsi, Dari and Tajik respectively. The Persian language has a rich morphology (Megerdoomian, 2000) in which words can be combined with a very large number of affixes. Combination, derivation, and inflection rules in Persian are uncertain (Lazard & Lyon, 1992; Mahootian, 2003).

The alphabet of Farsi is the same as Arabic with four additional letters. The alphabet contains 26 consonants and 6 vowels. Also there are some homophone and homograph letters. For example, "ز", "ذ", "ظ" and "ض" are homophones which all sound as "/z" and "ب"/*b*, "پ"/*p*, "ت"/t and "ث"/s are homograph letters which just differ in number and place of dots. These phonetic and graphical similarities cause many spelling errors. In the next section, we will describe how to use the SMT to detect context-sensitive spelling errors in a sentence and generate candidates.

4 SMT as a Candidate generator

SMT framework can be used to model context-sensitive spell checker, which translates a word that does not fit in a sentence with some suggestions for the suspicious word. SMT uses parallel corpora as the training data. It learns phrases of the language and some features such as phrase probability, reordering probability. In order to use SMT framework, a confusion set for each word is defined. Confusion set of a headword, w_i is a set of words $\{w_{i1}, w_{i2}, ..., w_{in}\}$, in which each word w_{ij} is a word that could be converted to w_i with one editing operation of insertion, deletion, substitution or transposition.

The Damerau-Levenshtein distance metric (Damerau, 1964) has been used for calculating the distance between two words. If their distance is lower than a pre-defined threshold, one editing operation, two words have been considered similar and then w_j is added to the confusion set of w_i. For example, confusable words in confusion set of the word روز ruz 'day' are as follows: روزه ruze 'fast', روش ravesh 'method', رود rud 'river', روح ruh 'spirit'.

If $E=\{w_1, w_2, ..., w_i, ..., w_n\}$ is a sentence and w_i is a real-word error in the sentence, it could appear in several confusion sets, thus, there are several headwords as candidates for the suspicious word. In other words, each headword that has w_i in its confusion set can be suggested as the correct word. To formulate this, consider $C=\{w_1, w_2, ..., w_i', ..., w_n\}$ is the correct sentence then w_i' is defined as follows (Ehsan & Faili, 2013):

$$w_i' = w_i \, or \, (w_{j,0} \; such \; that \; \exists_{j,k} w_{j,k} = w_i) \quad (1)$$

Equation (1) implies that the correct word, w_i', is either w_i or one of the headwords that contain w_i. For each erroneous sentence E, which contains real-word error w_i, we can define the N-best candidate sentences $\hat{C}$ as follows:

$$\hat{C} = N - argmax_C \frac{P(E|C)P(C)}{P(E)} \quad (2)$$

$P(E)$ in Equation (2) is probability of occurring the erroneous sentence, which is constant for each candidate sentence and can be removed from Equation (2). $P(E|C)$ can be defined as follows:

$$P(E|C) = P(w_1, ..., w_i, ..., w_n | w_1, ..., w_i', ..., w_n) \quad (3)$$

In Equation (3), each w is a word. In order to estimate $P(E|C)$ in Equation (3) we can convert E and C from word base to phrase base, $E = \bar{e_1}, \bar{e_2}, ..., \bar{e_I}$ and $C = \bar{c_1}, \bar{c_2}, ..., \bar{c_I}$. Using phrase-based SMT, we can capture some local dependencies among the words resulting better detection and correction on real-word errors. Let assume that w_i is in j-th phrase of E, then, we can estimate $P(E|C)$ as follows:

$$P(E|C) = P(\bar{e_j} \mid \bar{c_j}) = \frac{count\;(\bar{e_j},\bar{c_j})}{\sum_{\bar{e_j}} count\;(\bar{e_j},\bar{c_j})} \quad (4)$$

Equation (4) is the same as phrasal translation model in phrasal SMT systems. Therefore, we can use a phrasal SMT to correct context-sensitive spelling errors. In this paper, Moses (Koehn et al., 2007) is used as the phrasal SMT.

When using SMT as a context-sensitive spell checker, source and target sentences are in same language. The source sentences contain real-word error while the target sentences contain their correct form. After generating candidate sentences by retrieving the N-best results of the mentioned SMT, we rerank the candidate list by discourse-aware features, which are described in next section.

5 Discourse-aware Features

For any given sentence, SMT-based approach retrieves a list of candidate sentences. The phrasal SMT does not take the whole context of the sentence into account. Thus, in order to find the correct sentence from the candidate list and obtain a better ranking, we define other features that indicate the affinity of each word in candidate sentences with the whole context. Both the sentence and the whole document are considered as the context of the candidate sentences.

For example in the sentence: "This cat is black.", both "cat" and "car" could be meaningful. In this sentence, by considering just the sentence as context window, we cannot identify whether "cat" is correct or "car".

Discourse analysis may help us to detect the best candidate. If we know the document is about automobile or animal, then we can have better reranking on candidates. In other word, considering whole document as the context window is more helpful than considering just whole sentence for reranking the candidate.

Here, we get the benefit from discourse by capturing the relations among the words in a candidate sentence and with the keywords of whole document. In Subsection 5.1, we show that by selecting Point-wise Mutual Information (PMI) measure, we can find the long distance dependency between the words in a document.

Candidate	1 st	2 nd	3 rd	4 th	5 th	6 th	7 th
Detected word	دندان=>چندان	دندان=>دندان	دندان=>زندان	دندان=>مندان	**دندان=>دزدان**	ستر=>سصر	دندان=>بندان
$\mathbf{PMI_{sentence}}$	-10.8908	-10.8103	-10.8506	-10.9654	**-9.94**	-10.7639	-10.8488
$\mathbf{PMI_{discourse}}$	-7.1539	-7.1549	-7.1548	-7.1552	**-7.05**	-7.1606	-7.1523

Table 1: One erroneous sentence with 7 candidate sentences and their PMIs.

5.1 Contextual Features

We select some features that describe the information about the context of the sentences. PMI is used to measure the relation between candidate sentences and the document; and also to measure the co-occurrence among words of the sentence. Another feature that gives us useful information about fluency of candidate sentences is language model (LM) of sentence. A monolingual corpus is required to calculating PMI and LM. PMI of two words of *A* and *B* is calculated as follows:

$$PMI(A, B) = \frac{Doc\_Count\ (A,B)}{Doc\_Count\ (A) \times Doc\_Count\ (B)} \quad (5)$$

In Equation (5), *Doc_Count(A)* is number of documents that contain word A. *Doc_Count(A,B)* is number of documents that contain both *A*, *B*. We formulate two criteria based on PMI for each candidate sentence $PMI_{discourse}$ and $PMI_{sentence}$. $PMI_{discourse}$ is the PMI of the candidate sentence with its discourse while $PMI_{sentence}$ is the PMI of words candidate sentence. PMI for all words of the candidate sentence with the keywords of document is calculated as $PMI_{discourse}$. For extracting the keywords, term frequency (TF) and inverse document frequency (IDF) measure is like (Li & Zhang, 2007). For each sentence of the test data, 50 keywords are extracted from its discourse. To formulate this, consider *W* as a sentence in the test data and $S_j=\{w_{j1},w_{j2},\ldots,w_{jn}\}$ as j-th candidate sentence resulted from SMT-based approach. Let $C_w=\{c_1,c_2,\ldots,c_{50}\}$ is 50 keywords of the document containing W. $PMI_{discourse}$ for S_j is calculated as follow:

$$PMI_{discourse}\ (S_j) = \frac{\sum_{k=1}^{n}\sum_{m=1}^{50} \mathrm{PMI}\left(w_{jk};c_m\right)}{n*50} \quad (6)$$

In Equation (6), n is the number of sentence words. c_m is the m-th keyword of discourse and w_{jk} is k-th word of j-th candidate for *W*. Since PMI measures the co-occurrence of two different words, two identical words has maximum PMI in the sentence. In this case, if a word in the candidate is a keyword of the context, corresponding $PMI_{discourse}$ is increased. Consider S_j={This,cat,is,black} and S_k={This,car,is,black} are candidates of erroneous sentence of *W*. If discourse of *W* is about automobile then $PMI_{discourse}(S_k) > PMI_{discourse}(S_j)$, because the co-occurrence of "car" with the keywords of automobile related document is greater than the co-occurrence of "cat" with that keywords.

Second criterion is $PMI_{sentence}$, which refers to co-occurrence of sentence words with each other. To calculate $PMI_{sentence}$, the PMI of all words of the candidate sentence is calculated. To formulate this, consider $S_j=\{w_{j1},w_{j2},\ldots,w_{jn}\}$ is j-th candidate sentence for test sentence W. $PMI_{sentence}$ of S_j is calculated as follow:

$$PMI_{sentence}\ (S_j) = \frac{\sum_{k=1}^{n}\sum_{m=k}^{n} \mathrm{PMI}\left(w_{jk};w_{jm}\right)}{n*\frac{(n-1)}{2}} \quad (7)$$

In Equation (7), n is number of words of the sentence and w_{jk} is k-th word of j-th candidate of *W*. Table 1 shows an example of our Persian artificial test data in which $PMI_{discourse}$ and $PMI_{sentence}$ of correct candidate are more than that of SMT-based approach suggests. The input sentence is:

دندان قوي هيكل دو متر از ريل راه آهن اوكراين را دزديدند

dandaan-ghavi-hikal-dv-mtr-az-ril-raah-aahan-avkraain-raa-dozdidand

'Robust teeth stole two meters of railway of Ukrainian'.

There are two confusable words in the sentence, دندان dandaan 'teeth' and متر metr 'meter'. SMT generate 7 candidate sentences in which the 5th candidate is the correct one. As shown in Table 1, the first candidate, generated by SMT, has $PMI_{discourse}$ and $PMI_{sentence}$ score less than the correct sentence. By reranking SMT results using $PMI_{discourse}$ and $PMI_{sentence}$, we can put the correct sentence at better rank or the top of the list. The third contextual feature is LM, which is used to score the fluency of the candidate.

We consider surrounding words of suspicious word, whole sentence and whole document as the context, then, we use LM, $PMI_{sentence}$ and $PMI_{sentence}$ to extract information. After calculating $PMI_{sentence}$, $PMI_{discourse}$ and LM for all candidate sentences, a log-linear model is used to rerank the N-best results.

For reranking with log-linear model we need the weight of each feature. Support Vector Machine [1] (SVM) (Tsochantaridis, Joachims, Hofmann, Altun, & Singer, 2006) is used to weight each feature. SVM is a machine-learning algorithm based on statistical learning theory. It has been widely used, especially in function regression (Jeng, 2005) and pattern recognition (Tsai, 2005), in recent years for its better generalization performance (Burges, 1998).

5.2 Feature Weighting

Log linear model is used to rerank the N-best results of SMT. Like (Hayashi, Watanabe, Tsukada, & Isozaki, 2009), we use SVM-rank to obtain the weight of each feature. A corpus contains erroneous and correct sentence is developed. For each sentence of the corpus, $PMI_{sentence}$, $PMI_{discourse}$ and LM is calculated. We use the corpus a training data for SVM-rank to obtain the weight. In next section, the details of all data sets are described more precisely.

6 Experiment Result

We evaluate the accuracy of the approach by using the false positive and false negative rates as follows: *False positive* (FP) errors refer to real-word errors that were not identified by SMT-based system. *False negative* (FN) errors refer to appropriately written word that SMT-based approach detected as real-word error. *True positive* (TP) results are correct words that are considered as correct. *True negative* (TN) results refer to real-word errors that SMT-based approach detected and changed regardless of the correction. Finally *True negative with correction* (TNC) are real-word errors that SMT-based approach was able to replace them with the correct word. Evaluation metrics are computed as follows:

$$Precision = \frac{\#\ of\ TNC}{\#\ of\ TN} \quad (8)$$

$$Correction\ Recall = \frac{\#\ of\ TNC}{\#\ of\ FP\ and\ TN} \quad (9)$$

$$Detection\ Recall = \frac{\#\ of\ TN}{\#\ of\ FP\ and\ TN} \quad (10)$$

Another metric for evaluating our N-best result retrieved by SMT, is Mean Reciprocal rank. It is

calculated as follows:

$$MRR = \frac{1}{|Q|}\sum_{i=1}^{|Q|}\frac{1}{rank_i} \quad (11)$$

In Equation (11), $|Q|$ is the number of sentences of test data and $rank_i$ is the rank of correct sentence in 20-best result. We tested the SMT-based approach on two different languages, English and Persian. In the next subsections, we illustrate results on Persian and English languages.

6.1 Results on Persian Language

Our train data is generated from Peykareh (Bijankhan, 2004), Hamshahri[2] and IRNA[3] data sets. Hamshahri and IRNA are collections of news documents of Persian language. These corpora contain 814, 166,774 and 179,574 documents of general texts respectively. They have 56,241, 576,137 and 332,343 types and 2,530,772, 78,841,045 and 64,085,181 tokens respectively. All three corpora contain 923,744 types.

Our confusion set is generated from all mentioned data sets. It includes 5,000 headwords and each headword has about 4 confusable words in average. For our experiments on Persian, we have deployed two different test sets: an artificial and a real-world test sets.

Our Persian real-world test data for context-sensitive spelling errors contains 1,100 sentences. The test set selected manually from the Internet mostly from Persian weblogs[4]. Each sentence contains 16.7 words in average and only one real-word error. The test set contains 27 insertion errors, 266 deletion errors, 527 substitution errors and 91 transpositions errors. Only 89 errors, 8% of whole errors, need more than one editing action.

We also made an artificial test data for context-sensitive spelling errors. 1,500 sentences were selected randomly from Peykareh corpus. Length of each sentence is between 4 and 20 words. For each sentence in the artificial test set, one real-word error was inserted artificially, by replacing a random word with a word in its confusion set.

Our training corpus contains 381,007 sentence pairs which are selected form mentioned corpora. After generating training data, Moses is used as our SMT system, GIZA++ (Och & Ney, 2003) is used for word alignment and SRILM (Stolcke, 2002) is used as LM toolkit. Our LM is created from Hamshahri and IRNA and contains 329,607

[1] http://svmlight.joachims.org/

[2] The Hamshahri2 test collection is available on: http://ece.ut.ac.ir/DBRG/Hamshahri/.

[3] Islamic Republic News Agency-http://www.irna.ir

[4] The test set is available on: ece.ut.ac.ir/nlp/resources/

unigrams, 4,764,131 bigrams and 6,228,300 trigrams.

In order to develop training data for SVM, a confusion set is generated. The confusion set contains 26,891 headwords, which are selected from Hamshahri and Peykareh. Each headword has 4.6 confusable words.

5,000 sentences from Hamshahri and Peykareh are selected randomly. All sentences have at least one headword in the confusion set. For each sentence, one word of the sentence is selected and replaced with one of its headword. For each erroneous sentence maximum 20 candidates are generated by SMT. 56,320 sentences are generated and 3,728 of them are correct sentences. For each sentence of training data, $PMI_{sentence}$, $PMI_{discourse}$ and LM are calculated and their values normalized. We used 56,320 sentences as training data for SVM-rank to obtain the weights.

We generate a candidate list for each sentence of test sets by using the SMT and rerank the list in a post-processing step. In Table 2, results of discourse-aware reranking on real-world and artificial test data are shown. We selected the work of Ehsan and Faili (2013) as a baseline.

Experiments on Persian	Artificial test data	Real-world test data
Precision	0.97(-0.01%)	0.83(-0.01%)
Detection recall	0.70(+16%)	0.73(+9.5%)
Correction recall	0.69(+15%)	0.61(+8.4%)
F-measure	0.80(+8.4%)	0.70(+4.4%)
MRR	0.71(+8%)	0.67(+4%)

Table 2: Summarized results on Persian test sets (the improvements are mentioned in parentheses).

As it is shown in Table 2, in both test sets, the proposed ranker retrieved a significant superior result over the baseline with respect to recall metric with a comparable precision. Since the principle of discourse-aware SMT is language independent, we tested it on English language too.

6.2 Results on English Language

The test sets for English language were drawn from two corpora: Wall Street Journal (WSJ) and Brown corpus. For WSJ test set, a confusion set is generated with 73,437 headwords and each headword has 5.9 confusable words in average. We extract confusable words from WSJ based on one editing action. 1,500 sentences are selected from WSJ randomly similar to the test sets developed in (Islam & Inkpen, 2009; Wilcox-O'Hearn et al., 2008). For each sentence, a real-word error is inserted randomly. Rest of WSJ is considered as training data for SMT.

Similar work of Golding and Roth (1999); Jones and Martin (1997), we use 20% Brown corpus as test data and apply on 19 confusion sets. The test data contains 3015 erroneous sentences[1]. Train data for SMT, is generated from WSJ and rest of Brown corpus, 80%.

We have tested SMT based approach on both artificial English test data, generated candidates and reranked them with discourse-aware features. Table 3 shows results of discourse-aware.

Experiments on English	WSJ test data	Brown test data
Precision	0.97(+0.001)	0.96(+0.008%)
Detection recall	0.90(+5.4%)	0.81(+2.6%)
Correction recall	0.87(+5.6%)	0.78(+3.2%)
F-measure	0.92(+3%)	0.86(+2.1%)
MRR	0.88(+3%)	0.83(+1%)

Table 3: Summarized results on English test sets (the improvements are mentioned in parentheses).

As shown in Table 3, in WSJ and Brown test sets, our proposed system outperforms the baseline with respect to all metrics. We have a significant improvement over the baseline with respect to detection and correction recall.

7 Conclusion & Future work

We improved SMT-based approach by extracting some contextual features and using a learning algorithm, SVM-rank, for getting weights of each feature and reranking the N-best results by a log-linear model. The proposed ranker retrieved a significant superior result over the baseline with respect to recall metric with a comparable precision.

Real-word errors with two editing actions can be injected to training data. An ontology, named FarsNet (Shamsfard, 2008), can be used as an external resource to identify Persian semantic relationships between words. We can use discourse-aware reranking as a Learning To Rank, and apply it on every method that generate N-best result.

[1] The test set is available on: http://cogcomp.cs.illinois.edu/Data/Spell/

References

Bassil, Youssef, & Alwani, Mohammad. (2012). Context-sensitive Spelling Correction Using Google Web 1T 5-Gram Information. *arXiv preprint arXiv:1204.5852*.

Bijankhan, Mahmood. (2004). The role of the corpus in writing a grammar: An introduction to a software. *Iranian Journal of Linguistics, 19*(2).

Burges, Christopher JC. (1998). A tutorial on support vector machines for pattern recognition. *Data mining and knowledge discovery, 2*(2), 121-167.

Damerau, Fred J. (1964). A technique for computer detection and correction of spelling errors. *Communications of the ACM, 7*(3), 171-176.

Ehsan, Nava, & Faili, Heshaam. (2013). Grammatical and context - sensitive error correction using a statistical machine translation framework. *Software: Practice and Experience, 43*(2), 187-206.

Faili, Heshaam. (2010). *Detection and correction of real-word spelling errors in Persian language.* Paper presented at the Natural Language Processing and Knowledge Engineering (NLP-KE), 2010 International Conference on.

Fellbaum, Christiane. (2010). WordNet: an electronic lexical database. *WordNet is available from* http://www. *cogsci. princeton. edu/wn.*

Gale, William A, Church, Kenneth W, & Yarowsky, David. (1992). A method for disambiguating word senses in a large corpus. *Computers and the Humanities, 26*(5-6), 415-439.

Golding, Andrew R. (1995). *A Bayesian hybrid method for context-sensitive spelling correction.* Paper presented at the Proceedings of the third workshop on Very Large Corpora.

Golding, Andrew R, & Roth, Dan. (1999). A winnow-based approach to context-sensitive spelling correction. *Machine learning, 34*(1-3), 107-130.

Golding, Andrew R, & Schabes, Yves. (1996). *Combining trigram-based and feature-based methods for context-sensitive spelling correction.* Paper presented at the In Proceedings of the 34th Annual Meeting of the Association for Computational Linguistics, Santa Cruz, CA.

Hayashi, Katsuhiko, Watanabe, Taro, Tsukada, Hajime, & Isozaki, Hideki. (2009). Structural support vector machines for log-linear approach in statistical machine translation. *Proceedings of IWSLT, Tokyo, Japan.*

Islam, Aminul, & Inkpen, Diana. (2009). *Real-word spelling correction using Google Web IT 3-grams.* Paper presented at the Proceedings of the 2009 Conference on Empirical Methods in Natural Language Processing: Volume 3-Volume 3.

Jeng, Jin-Tsong. (2005). Hybrid approach of selecting hyperparameters of support vector machine for regression. *Systems, Man, and Cybernetics, Part B: Cybernetics, IEEE Transactions on, 36*(3), 699-709.

Jones, Michael P, & Martin, James H. (1997). *Contextual spelling correction using latent semantic analysis.* Paper presented at the Proceedings of the fifth conference on Applied natural language processing.

Kashefi, O, Minaei-Bidgoli, B, & Sharifi, M. (2010). A novel string distance metric for ranking Persian spelling error corrections. *Language Resource and Evaluation.*

Koehn, Philipp, Hoang, Hieu, Birch, Alexandra, Callison-Burch, Chris, Federico, Marcello, Bertoldi, Nicola, . . . Zens, Richard. (2007). *Moses: Open source toolkit for statistical machine translation.* Paper presented at the Proceedings of the 45th Annual Meeting of the ACL on Interactive Poster and Demonstration Sessions.

Kukich, Karen. (1992). Techniques for automatically correcting words in text. *ACM Computing Surveys (CSUR), 24*(4), 377-439.

Lazard, Gilbert, & Lyon, Shirley A. (1992). *A grammar of contemporary Persian*: Mazda Publishers.

Li, Juanzi, & Zhang, Kuo. (2007). Keyword extraction based on tf/idf for Chinese news document. *Wuhan University Journal of Natural Sciences, 12*(5), 917-921.

Mahootian, Shahrzad. (2003). *Persian*: Routledge.

Mays, Eric, Damerau, Fred J, & Mercer, Robert L. (1991). Context based spelling correction. *Information Processing & Management, 27*(5), 517-522.

Megerdoomian, Karine. (2000). *Unification-based Persian morphology.* Paper presented at the Proceedings of CICLing.

Och, Franz Josef, & Ney, Hermann. (2003). A systematic comparison of various statistical alignment models. *Computational linguistics, 29*(1), 19-51.

Pedler, Jennifer. (2007). Computer correction of real-word spelling errors in dyslexic text. *Unpublished PhD thesis. Birkbeck, University of London.*

Shamsfard, Mehrnoush. (2008). *Developing FarsNet: A lexical ontology for Persian.* Paper presented at the 4th Global WordNet Conference, Szeged, Hungary.

Stolcke, Andreas. (2002). *SRILM-an extensible language modeling toolkit.* Paper presented at the Proceedings of the international conference on spoken language processing.

Tsai, Chih-Fong. (2005). Training support vector machines based on stacked generalization for image classification. *Neurocomputing, 64*, 497-503.

Tsochantaridis, Ioannis, Joachims, Thorsten, Hofmann, Thomas, Altun, Yasemin, & Singer, Yoram. (2006). Large margin methods for structured and interdependent output variables. *Journal of Machine Learning Research, 6*(2), 1453.

Wilcox-O'Hearn, Amber, Hirst, Graeme, & Budanitsky, Alexander. (2008). Real-word spelling correction with trigrams: A reconsideration of the Mays, Damerau, and Mercer model *Computational Linguistics and Intelligent Text Processing* (pp. 605-616): Springer.

Yarowsky, David. (1994). *Decision lists for lexical ambiguity resolution: Application to accent restoration in Spanish and French.* Paper presented at the Proceedings of the 32nd annual meeting on Association for Computational Linguistics.

Cross-Lingual Information Retrieval and Semantic Interoperability for Cultural Heritage Repositories

Monti Johanna
University of Sassari
jmonti@uniss.it

Mario Monteleone
University of Salerno
mmonteleone@unisa.it

Maria Pia di Buono
University of Salerno
dibuono@unisa.it

Federica Marano
University of Salerno
fmarano@unisa.it

Abstract

This paper describes a computational linguistics-based approach for providing interoperability between multi-lingual systems in order to overcome crucial issues like cross-language and cross-collection retrieval. Our proposal is a system which improves capabilities of language-technology-based information extraction. In the last few years various theories have been developed and applied for making multicultural and multilingual resources easy to access. Important initiatives, like the development of the European Library and Europeana, aim to increase the availability of digital content from various types of providers and institutions. Therefore the accessibility to these resources requires the development of environments enabling to manage multilingual complexity. In this respect, we present a methodological framework which allows mapping both the data and the metadata among the language-specific ontologies. The feasibility of cross-language information extraction and semantic search will be tested by implementing an early prototype system.

1 Introduction

The growing need by users to access information on the web in languages different from their own is fostering the research in the field of Cross-language Information Retrieval (CLIR) applications.

Typically in state-of-the-art CLIR applications, information is searched by means of a query expressed in the user's mother tongue. This query is automatically translated in the desired foreign language and the results are translated back in the user's mother tongue.

This process is based on two different translation stages: query translation and document translation. The query translation concerns the translation in the desired foreign language of the query expressed in the user's mother tongue, whereas the document translation is the back translation in the user's language of the relevant documents found by means of the translated query.

CLIR success obviously depends on the quality of translation and therefore inaccurate translations may cause serious problems in retrieving the relevant information in a foreign language.

A very frequent source of mistranslations in specific domain texts is represented by multiword units (MWU). MWUs designate a wide range of lexical constructions, composed of two or more words with an opaque meaning, i.e. the meaning of a unit is not always the result of the sum of the meanings of the single words that are part of the unit. MWUs are not always easy to identify since co-occurrence among the lexemes forming the units may vary a great deal. A particular type of MWUs are term compounds, i.e. various types of compounds, but mainly noun compounds, which belong to a language for special purposes (LSP). In all languages there is a close relationship between terminology and multi-words and, in particular, word compounds. In fact, word compounds account in some cases for 90% of the terms belonging to an LSP.

Contrary to generic simple words, terminological word compounds are mono-referential, i.e. they are unambiguous and refer only to one specific concept in one special language, even if they may occur in more than one domain. Their meaning, similar to all compound words, cannot be directly inferred by a non-expert from the different elements of the compounds because it depends on the specific area and the concept it refers to.

Processing and translating these different types of compound words is not an easy task since their morpho-syntactic and semantic behavior is quite complex and varied according to the different types and their translations are practically unpredictable.

The main contribution of this paper is the experimentation of a bilingual ontology-based CLIR system designed to overcome the current limitations of the state-of the-art CLIR systems and in particular to take into account a proper processing and translation of MWUs. This experiment has been set up for the Italian/English language pair and it can be easily extended to other language pairs.

The remaining of this paper is organized as follows. The next section briefly explains the related work in the area of CLIR. Section 3 describes the methodology and the tools used in the experiment. Then, section 4 is devoted to the system overview, and in particular it presents the data modeling and the system architecture extension. Finally, experiments and conclusions and future work are reported in sections 5 and 6, respectively.

2 Related work

There are several approaches to CLIR: they are either based on bilingual or multilingual Machine Readable Dictionaries (MRD), Machine Translation (MT), parallel corpora and finally ontologies. For a description of the different approaches see Hull and Greffenstette (1996), Oard and Dorr (1996), Pirkola (1999) and more recently Oard (2009).

Both MRD-based and MT-based CLIR are very popular but they present several shortcomings especially in relation to domain-specific contexts because of the lack of consideration for MWUs, a very frequent and productive linguistic phenomenon in LSPs.

Various techniques have been proposed to reduce the errors due to the presence of MWU introduced during query translation. Among these techniques, phrasal translation, co-occurrence analysis, and query expansion are the most popular.

Concerning phrasal translation, techniques are often used to identify multi-word concepts in the query and translate them as phrases. Hull and Grefenstette (1996) showed that the performance achieved by manually translating phrases in queries is significantly better than that of a word-by-word translation using a dictionary. Davis and Ogden (1997) used a phrase dictionary extracted from parallel sentences in French and English to improve the performance of CLIR. Ballesteros and Croft (1996) performed phrase translation using information on phrase and word usage contained in the Collins machine readable dictionary. More recently, Gao et al. (2001) propose that noun phrases are recognized and translated as a whole by using statistical models and phrase translation patterns and that the best word translations are selected based on the cohesion of the translation words. Finally, Saralegi and López de Lacalle (2010) use a simple matching and translation technique based on a bilingual MWU list to detect and translate them.

Co-occurrence statistics is used to identify the best translation(s) among all translation candidates using text collections in the target language as a language model, assuming that correct translations occur more frequently than wrong ones (Maeda et al., 2000; Ballesteros and Croft, 1998; Gao et al., 2001, Sadat et al., 2001).

As for query expansion techniques, Ballesteros and Croft (1996 and 1997) assume that additional terms that are related to the primary concepts in the query are likely to be relevant and that phrases in query expansion via local context analysis and local feedback can be used to reduce the error associated with automatic dictionary translation.

Concerning MT-based CLIR, MWU identification and translation problems are far from being solved. Recently, increasing attention has been paid to MWU processing in MT since it has been acknowledged that MT cannot be effective without proper handling of MWUs of all kinds. MWU processing and translation in Statistical Machine Translation (SMT) started being addressed only very recently and different solutions have been proposed so far, but basically they are considered either as a problem of automatically learning and integrating translations or as a problem of word alignment.

Current approaches to MWU processing move towards the integration of phrase-based models with linguistic knowledge and scholars are starting to use linguistic resources, either handcrafted dictionaries and grammars or data-driven ones, in order to identify and process MWUs as single units. Monti (2013) provides a thorough overview of the problem.

Ontologies are also used in CLIR and are considered by several scholars a promising research area to improve the effectiveness of Information Extraction (IE) techniques particularly for technical-domain queries. Volk et al. (2003) use ontologies as interlingua in CLIR for the medical domain and show that the semantic annotation outperforms machine translation of the queries, but the best results are achieved by combining a similarity thesaurus with the semantic codes. Yapomo et al. (2012) perform ontology-based query expansion of the most relevant terms exploiting the synonymy relation in WordNet.

3 Methodology

Our linguistic methodology is based on the Lexicon-Grammar (LG) theoretical and practical analytical framework, formulated by the French linguist Maurice Gross (Gross, 1968; 1975; 1989).

LG presupposes that linguistic formal descriptions should be based on the observation of the lexicon and the combinatory behaviors of its elements, encompassing in this way both syntax and lexicon. Linguistic Resources (LRs) developed according to the LG framework are used in NLP applications and are helpful to achieve effective Information Retrieval (IR) Systems (Marano F., 2012).

In the field of MT-based CLIR, the LG methodology tries to overcome the shortcomings of statistical approaches as in *Google Translate* or *Bing* by Microsoft concerning MWU processing in queries, where the lack of context represent a serious obstacle to disambiguation. LG linguistic framework is grounded in the analysis of the so-called "simple sentence", achieved by considering rules of co-occurrence and selection restriction, i.e. distributional and transformational rules (active/passive, positive/interrogative, etc.) based on predicate syntactic-semantic properties in the wake of the Operator-Argument Grammar (Harris, 1982).

Thanks to the above-mentioned research studies, LG range of analysis concerns the concept of MWU as "meaning unit", "lexical unit" and "word group", for which LG identifies four different combinatorial behaviors (see De Bueriis et al., 2008).

Our LRs consist of (i) electronic dictionaries morphologically and semantically tagged, (ii) local grammars in the form of Finite State Transducers/Automata (FST/FSA) and (iii) tables in which the syntactic-semantic properties of lexical entries are described (see 5.1, 5.2).

4 System overview

In CLIR systems "the complexity of the grammatical structures and the quality of parsing are the main cause of the errors" (Vossen P. et alii, 2012). Indeed, the most frequent error is the assignment of wrong Part Of Speech (POS) to lexical meaning units. In this sense, as for IR and IE, we will see that our research framework allows to achieve major improvements both in recall and precision.

We propose an architecture, which when applied to a given language, maps data and metadata exploiting the morpho-syntactic and semantic information stored inside both electronic dictionaries and Finite State Automata/Finite State Transducers (FSA/FSTs) (presented in 5.2). Furthermore, this architecture can also map linguistic tags (i.e. POS) and structures (i.e. sentences, MWU) to domain concepts.

The first step performed by our system is a linguistic pre-processing phase in which natural language texts are analysed, tokenized and indexed and textual meaning units are assigned relevant morpho-grammatical and terminological information. During this first phase we also extract information from free-form user queries, and match this information with already available ontological domain conceptualizations.

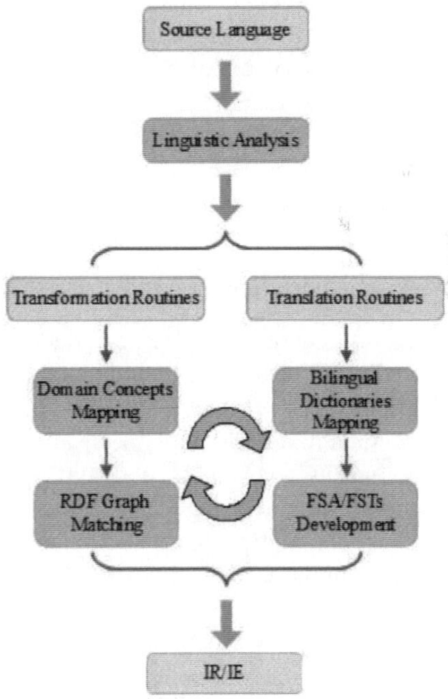

Figure 1: System Workflow

As described in Fig. 1, prior to the execution of a query against a knowledge base, it is necessary to apply the translation and transformation routines. The system is based on two workflows which are carried out simultaneously but independently.

The benefits of keeping separate these two workflows are (i) the development of an architecture with a central multilingual formalization of the lexicon, in which there is no specific target language, but each language can be at the same time target and source language, (ii) the development of extraction ontologies and SPARQL/SERQL adaptation systems which could represent a standard not only for our multilingual electronic dictionaries, but also for any lexical and/or language data-base for which translation is required.

With this dual-structure system, it is easier to successfully achieve the CLIR process since the separation of the RDF matching from the translation process allows to preserve semantic interoperability and translation quality.

5 Experiments

To test the feasibility of our architecture, we are carrying out a transfer experiment from Italian to English, using all ontological constraints defined for the Italian model.

We have chosen the Archaeological domain to test the applicability of our approach. This choice allows us to demonstrate that the modularity of our architecture may be applied to a domain which is variable by type and properties and is semantically interlinked.

In the next sections we will present the linguistic resources which have been developed for our experiment, together with the required semantic annotation and the translation system.

5.1 Electronic dictionaries

An electronic dictionary is a lexical database homogeneously structured, in which the morphologic and grammatical characteristics of lexical entries (gender, number and inflection) are formalized by means of distinctive and non-ambiguous alphanumeric tags (Vietri et al. 2004). The electronic dictionaries, used in this experiment and built according to the LG descriptive method, belong to the DELA system and are (i) the simple word dictionaries, which include semantically autonomous lexical units formed by character sequences delimited by blanks, such as *home*, and (ii) the compound word dictionaries, which include lexical units composed of two or more simple words with a non-compositional meaning, such as *rocking chair*. Terminological entries (the most common source of mistranslations in CLIR) are mainly lemmatized in compound word electronic dictionaries.

The following example represents an excerpt from the Italian-English dictionary of Archaeological Artifacts[1]

anfora di terracotta, N + NPN + FLX=C41 +DOM=RA1 + EN=earthenware amphora, N+AN+FLX=EC3
cerchi concentrici, N + NA + FLX=C601 + DOM=RA1 + EN=concentric ridges, N+AN+FLX=EC4
cottura ad alte temperature, N + NPAN + FLX =C611 + DOM=RA1 + EN=high fired, N+AN+FLX=EC4
fregio dorico, N + NA + FLX = C523 + DOM=RA1 + EN=doric frieze, N+AN+FLX=EC3
fusto a spirale, N + NPN + FLX = C7 + DOM=RA1 + EN=spiral stem, N+AN+FLX=EC3

For instance, the compound word *fregio dorico* («Doric frieze») is marked with the domain tag «DOM=RA1», which stands for «Archaeological Artifacts – Building – Architectural Elements – Structural Elements».

For each entry, a formal and morphological description is also given with (i) the internal structure of each compound, as in *fregio dorico* where the tag «NA» indicates that the given compound is formed by a Noun, followed by an Adjective and (ii) the inflectional class, for which the tag «+FLX=C523» indicates the gender and the number of the compound *fregio dorico*, together with its plural form. The inflectional class refers to a local grammar and indicates that *fregio dorico* is masculine singular, does not have any feminine correspondent form, and its plural form is *fregi dorici*.

Together with electronic dictionaries, local grammars are used in NLP routines to parse texts. Local grammar design is based on syntactic descriptions, which encompasses transformational rules and distributional behaviours (Harris, 1957). We develop local grammars in the form of FSA/FST (Silberztein, 1993; 2002).

[1]In order to develop the Italian-English dictionary of Archaeological Artifacts, we relied on the Thesauri and Guidelines of the Italian Central Institute for the Catalogue and Documentation (ICCD) available at http://www.iccd.beniculturali.it/index.php?it/240/vocabolari For each dictionary we developed a taxonomy, therefore all entries have a terminological and domain label usable for ontologies population.

5.2 Semantic annotation

As for ontologies, the formal definition we rely upon is the one given by the International Council of Museums - Conseil International des Musees (ICOM – CIDOC) Conceptual Reference Model (CRM), which states that “a formal ontology (is) intended to facilitate the integration, mediation and interchange of heterogeneous cultural heritage information” (Crofts N., Doerr M., Gill T., Stead S., Stiff M. 2008). The CIDOC CRM ontology is composed of two different hierarchies, one composed of 90 classes (which includes subclasses and superclasses) and another one of 148 unique properties (and subproperties). The object-oriented semantic model and its terminology are compatible with the Resource Description Framework (RDF)[2]. This ontology is constantly developed and updated. At the same time, our methodology shows that a given linguistic knowledge can be reused independently from the domain to which it pertains.

LRs are used for analyzing corpora to retrieve recursive phrase structures, in which combinatorial behaviours and co-occurrence between words identify properties, also denoting a relationship. Furthermore, electronic dictionaries also include all inflected verb forms allowing to process queries expressed also with passive and more generally non-declarative sentences.

Consequently we use FSA variables for identifying ontological classes and properties for subject, object and predicate within RDF graphs.

This matching of linguistic data to RDF triples and their translation into SPARQL/SERQL path expressions allows the use of specific meaning units to process natural language queries.

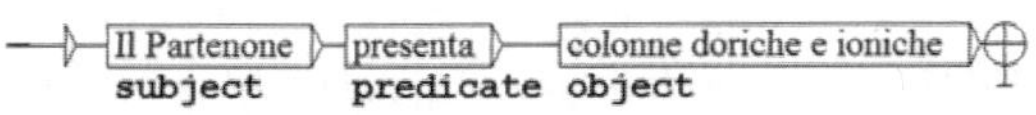

Figure 2: Simple FSA/FST with RDF Graph

Figure 2 is a sample of an automaton showing an associated RDF graph for the following sentence:

Il Partenone (subject) presenta (predicate) colonne doriche e ioniche (object)

According to our approach, electronic dictionaries entries (simple words and MWUs) are the subject and the object of the RDF triple.

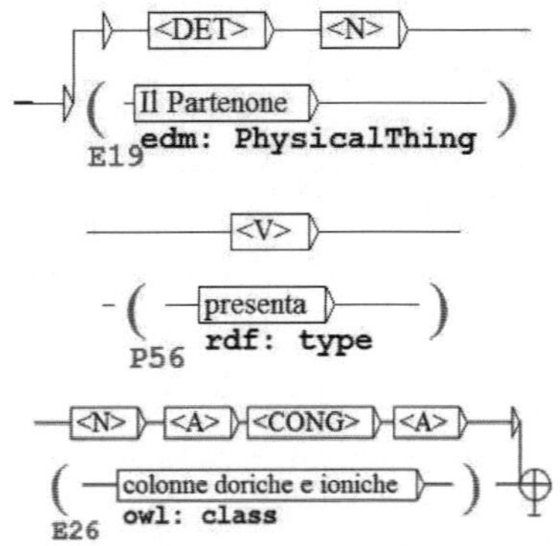

Figure 3: Sample of the use of the FSA variables for identifying classes for subject, predicate and object

In Figure 3 we develop an FSA with a variable which applies to the sentence the following classes and properties: (i) E19 indicates “Physical Object” class, (ii) P56 stands for “Bears Feature” property, (iii) E26 indicates “Physical Feature” class. So, the FSA variables transform our sentence into:

Il Partenone (E19) *bears feature* colonne doriche e ioniche (E26).

The role pairs *Physical Object/name* and *Physical Feature/type* are trigged by the RDF predicate *presenta.*

Besides in Fig. 3 we also indicate specific POS for the first noun phrase *Il Partenone* (DETerminer + Noun), the verb *presenta* (V) and the second noun phrase *colonne doriche e ioniche* (Noun+Adjective+Conjunction+Adjective).

By applying the automaton in Fig. 3 (built using the high variability of lexical class and not of the original form) we can recognize all instances included in E19 and E26 classes, the property of which is P56.

5.3 Query Translation

In our model, the Translation Routines are applied independently of the mapping process of the pivot language. This allows us to preserve the semantic representation in both languages.

Indeed, identifying semantics through FSA guarantees the detection of all data and metadata expressed in any different language.

Figure 4 shows a FST in which a translation process from Italian to English is performed on

[2] Information about the Resource Description Framework (RDF) can be found at http://www.w3.org/RDF/

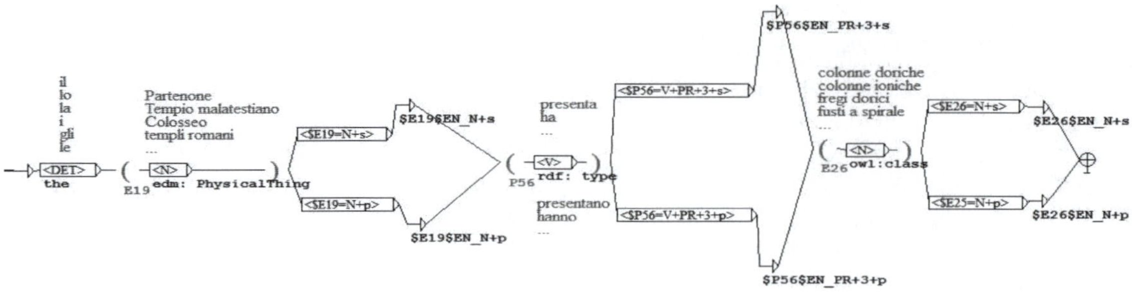

Figure 4: Translation FST with variables for identifying classes for subject, predicate and object

the basis of a dictionary look-up, a morpho-syntactic and semantic analysis. This translation FST, in fact, recognizes and annotates the different linguistic elements of declarative sentences such as "Il Partenone presenta fregi dorici", "I templi romani hanno fusti a spirale", etc, with their morpho-syntactic and semantic information and performs automatic translations on the basis of a well-crafted LG bilingual dictionary.

For instance, if a grammar variable, say $E26, holds the value "fusti a spirale", the output $E26$EN will produce the correct translation "spiral stems", on the basis of the value associated to the +EN feature in the bilingual entry "*fusto a spirale, N + NPN + FLX = C7 + OM=RA1 + EN=spiral stem,* N+AN+FLX=EC3" and the morpho-syntactic analysis performed by the graph in Figure 4, which identifies and produces the plural form of the compound noun "fusto a spirale".

5.4 Translation Quality Evaluation (TQE)

Often using smart technologies for MT involves the lowering of Translation Quality (TQ). In LG methodology, instead, we take advantage of well-formed LRs to maintain a high level of TQ. The Translation Quality Evaluation (TQE) methodology adopted to solve this problem is based on a hybrid approach, that encompasses human and automatic evaluation.

The process is composed of two cycles. The first cycle can be outlined as follows (i) a query expressed in a Source Language (SL) is the input of the CLIR application, (ii) the MT system produces sample queries (i.e. sample texts) in the Target Language (TL), (iii) the resulting translated queries are examined by humans (Linguists, Translators, Terminologists/Domain Experts) to evaluate their quality. The human judgements are based on common criteria of TQ – i.e. adequacy and fluency – and are expressed using a Likert scale with scores 1-5 (for instance using following judgements: 1. Strongly disagree, 2. Disagree, 3. Neither agree nor disagree, 4. Agree, 5. Strongly agree), (iv) only texts which obtained scores 4-5 become "validated" and "supervised" texts which represent the gold standard, (v) this gold standard is the training set for the Automatic Evaluation process, that can be carried out using METEOR[3] and GTM[4], that are the most suitable methods according to our opinion, as well as other ones[5].

During the second cycle, human evaluation is skipped and the SL queries directly become the input for automatic evaluation.

It is necessary to periodically repeat the first cycle in order to enrich the training set and to increase the quality cycle.

6 Conclusions

The proposed architecture ensures not only the coverage of a large knowledge portion but preserves deep semantic relations among different languages.

Future work aims at implementing further Linguistic Resources to achieve translation accuracy in CLIR applications and semantic search.

Note

Johanna Monti is author of sections 1, 2 and 5.3, Mario Monteleone is author of sections 5.1 and 6, Maria Pia di Buono is author of sections 4, 5 and 5.2 and Federica Marano is author of section 3 and 5.4.

---

[3] http://www.cs.cmu.edu/~alavie/METEOR

[4] http://nlp.cs.nyu.edu/GTM

[5] BLEU and NIST (based only on precision measure), F-Measure (based also on recall).

References

Ballesteros L. and Croft B. 1996. *Dictionary Methods for Cross-Lingual Information Retrieval*. Proc. of the 7th DEXA Conference on Database and Expert Systems Applications, Zurich, Switzerland, September 1996: 791-801.

Ballesteros L. and Croft B. 1997. *Phrasal translation and query expansion techniques for crosslanguage information retrieval*. In Proceedings of the 20th annual international ACM SIGIR conference on Research and development in information retrieval.

Ballesteros L. and Croft B. 1998. *Resolving Ambiguity for Cross-language Retrieval*. SIGIR'98, Melbourne, Australia, August 1998: 64-71.

Bloomfield L. 1933. *Language*. Henry Holt, New York.

Crofts N., Doerr M., Gill T., Stead S., Stiff M. (eds.). 2008. *Definition of the CIDOC Conceptual Reference Model, Version 5.0.*

Davis M. W., and Ogden W. C. 1997. *Free resources and advanced alignment for cross-language text retrieval*. In: The Sixth Text Retrieval Conference (TREC-6). NIST, Gaithersbury, MD.

De Bueris G., Elia, A. (eds.). 2008. *Lessici elettronici e descrizioni lessicali, sintattiche, morfologiche ed ortografiche*. Plectica, Salerno.

Gao J., Nie J., Xun E., Zhang J., Zhou M., Huang C. 2001. *Improving Query Translation for Cross-Language Information Retrieval using Statistical Models*. Proceedings of the 24th annual international ACM SIGIR conference on Research and development in information retrieval. ACM.

Gross M. 1968. *Grammaire transformationnelle du français. – I – Syntaxe du verbe*, Larousse, Paris.

Gross M. 1975. *Méthodes en syntaxe, régime des constructions complétives*, Hermann, Paris.

Gross M. 1989. *La construction de dictionnaires électroniques*. Annales des Télécommunications, vol. 44, n° 1-2: 4-19, CENT, Issy-les-Moulineaux/Lannion.

Harris Z.S. 1957. *Co-occurrence and transformation in linguistic structure*. Language 33,: 293-340.

Harris Z.S. 1964. Transformations in Linguistic Structure. *Proceedings of the American Philosophical Society* 108:5:418-122.

Harris Z.S. 1982. *A Grammar of English on Mathematical Principles*. John Wiley and Sons, New York, USA.

Hull D. A. and Grefenstette G. 1996. *Querying across languages: a dictionary-based approach to multilingual information retrieval*, Proceedings of the 19th annual international ACM SIGIR conference on Research and development in information retrieval: 49-57.

Knoth P., Collins T., Sklavounouy E., Zdrahal Z.. 2010. *Facilitating cross-language retrieval and machine translation by multilingual domain ontologies.*

Maeda, A., Sadat, F., et al. 2000. *Query Term Disambiguation for Web Cross-Language Information Retrieval using a Search Engine*. in Proc. of the Fifth Int'l Workshop on Info. Retrieval with Asian Languages, Hong Kong, China: 173-179.

Marano F. 2012. *Exploring Formal Models of Linguistic Data Structuring. Enhanced Solutions for Knowledge Management Systems Based on NLP Applications.* PhD Dissertation, University of Salerno, Italy.

Monti, J. 2013. *Multi-word unit processing in Machine Translation: developing and using language resources for multi-word unit processing in Machine Translation*. PhD dissertation. University of Salerno, Italy.

Oard D. W. 2009. *Multilingual Information Access*. in Encyclopedia of Library and Information Sciences, 3rd Ed., edited by Marcia J. Bates, Editor, and Mary Niles Maack, Associate Editor, Taylor & Francis.

Pirkola A. 1998. *The Effects of Query Structire and Dictionary Setups* in Dictionary-Based Cross-language Information Retrieval. In Croft, W.., et al., 21st Annual ACM SIGIR Conference on Research and Development in Information Retrieval (SIGIR 2008), Melbourne, Australia, August 24-28:55-63.

Sadat F., Maeda A., et al. 2002. *A Combined Statistical Query Term Disambiguation in Cross-language Information Retrieval*. Proc. of the 13th Int'l Workshop on Database and Expert Systems Applications, Aix-en-Provence, France, September 2002: 251-255.

Saralegi X. and de Lacalle M. L. 2010. *Dictionary and Monolingual Corpus-based Query Translation for Basque-English CLIR.*

Silberztein M. 1993. *Dictionnaires électroniques et analyse automatique de textes*, Masson, Paris.

Silberztein M. 2002. *NooJ Manual*. Available for download at: www.nooj4nlp.net.

Szpektor I., Dagan I., Lavie A., Shacham D., Wintner S. 2007. *Cross Lingual and Semantic Retrieval for Cultural Heritage Appreciation*. Proceedings of the ACL Workshop on Language Technology for Cultural Heritage Data, Prague, Czech Republic.

Vietri S., Elia A. and D'Agostino E. 2004. *Lexicon-grammar, Electronic Dictionaries and Local Grammars in Italian*, in Laporte, E., Leclère, C.,

Piot, M., Silberztein M. (eds.), Syntaxe, Lexique et Lexique-Grammaire. Volume dédié à Maurice Gross, Lingvisticae Investigationes Supplementa 24, John Benjamins, Amsterdam/Philadelphia.

Volk M., Vintar S., and Buitelaar P. 2003. *Ontologies in cross-language information retrieval.* Proceedings of WOW2003 (Workshop Ontologie-basiertes Wissensmanagement), Luzern, Switzerland.

Vossen P., Soroa A., Zapirain B. and Rigau G. 2012. *Cross-lingual event-mining using wordnet as a shared knowledge interface.* Proceedings of the 6th Global Wordnet Conference, C. Fellbaum, P. Vossen (Eds.), Publ. Tribun EU, Brno, Matsue, Japan, January 9-13:382-390.

Yapomo M., Corpas G., and Mitkov R. 2012. *CLIR- and ontology-based approach for bilingual extraction of comparable documents.* The 5th Workshop on Building and Using Comparable Corpora.

Improving Web 2.0 Opinion Mining Systems Using Text Normalisation Techniques

Alejandro Mosquera
University of Alicante
amosquera@dlsi.ua.es

Paloma Moreda
University of Alicante
moreda@dlsi.ua.es

Abstract

A basic task in opinion mining deals with determining the overall polarity orientation of a document about some topic. This has several applications such as detecting consumer opinions in on-line product reviews or increasing the effectiveness of social media marketing campaigns. However, the informal features of Web 2.0 texts can affect the performance of automated opinion mining tools. These are usually short and noisy texts with presence of slang, emoticons and lexical variants which make more difficult to extract contextual and semantic information. In this paper we demonstrate that the use of lexical normalisation techniques can be used to enhance polarity detection results by replacing informal lexical variants with their canonical version. We have carried out several polarity classification experiments using English texts from different Web 2.0 genres and we have obtained the best result with microblogs where normalisation contribution to the classification model can be up to 6.4%.

1 Introduction

Nowadays, Web 2.0 applications provide some of the most popular forms of communication between users on the Internet such as blogging, social networks or short text messaging platforms. This large daily amount of generated information contains valuable insights about user opinions and sentiments regarding almost any topic.

A basic task in opinion mining deals with determining the overall polarity orientation of a document about some topic. The polarity information extracted from user comments and consumer feedback from on-line product reviews can be used to increase the effectiveness of social media marketing campaigns, discover new market threats and opportunities or react faster to customer issues. Also, microblogging platforms such as Twitter include rich metadata about interactions which provides a way to measure the reputation of their users based on the number of followers or the publication popularity by counting the number of times one message has been shared.

However, the language used in social media is very informal, containing elements such as misspellings, slang, lexical variants, inconsistent punctuations, URLs or emoticons (Thurlow, 2003). Also, the presence of genre-specific terminology such as, *RT* for *re-tweet* and *#hashtags* can make any Natural Language Processing (NLP) task challenging. For this reason, a way to handle such challenges is needed in order to automatically understand the opinions and sentiments that people are communicating on the Internet. The use of lexical normalisation techniques has recently been the subject of research applied to short and noisy texts such as tweets or SMS, improving the performance of NLP tools that need to extract contextual and semantic information from this type of informal texts.

Moreover, not all Web 2.0 genres have the same level of informality, microblog posts have to be short so they tend to contain SMS-style contractions while blog entries are usually larger and more elaborated (Santini, 2006). For this reason, in this study we evaluate the contribution of text normalisation techniques to an opinion mining application using corpora from three different Web 2.0 genres, demonstrating that it can enhance the polarity classification of microblogs by a 6.4%.

This article is organised as follows: In Section 2 we review the state of the art. Section 3 describes the normalisation process. The polarity classification is explained in Section 4. In Section 5, the obtained results are analysed. Finally, our main conclusions and future work are drawn in Section 6.

2 Related Work

Both academic researches and commercial companies have increased their interests recently in mining user opinions on the Internet. After the initial works of (Pang et al., 2002) several applications of opinion mining have been developed in order to measure the word of mouth (Jansen et al., 2009), correlate polls with user opinion (Balasubramanyan et al., 2010) or predicting elections results (Tumasjan et al., 2010). Most of these studies have been focused on Twitter (Barbosa and Feng, 2010), (Bifet and Frank, 2010) using both machine learning (Turney, 2002) and lexicon-based approaches (Taboada et al., 2011). The real-time nature of tweets provides a large amount of metadata and content information such as hashtags and smileys (Davidov et al., 2010) that can be used as a training corpus for opinion mining systems (Pak and Paroubek, 2010) without requiring annotated corpora (Wiebe et al., 2005).

Text normalisation techniques (Liu et al., 2011), (Han et al., 2013) based on the substitution of out of vocabulary (OOV) words have been used in opinion mining systems before (Mukherjee et al., 2012), (Gutiérrez et al., 2013), (Sidorov et al., 2013) but this process is usually presented as an intermediate filtering step without explicitly detailing the contribution of normalisation to the classification results. On the other hand, there are different genres within the Web 2.0 and they do not have the same level of informality (Mosquera and Moreda, 2012), so the contribution of text normalisation techniques to polarity classification can be more or less relevant depending on that level. For this reason, in this study we evaluate the performance of an automated opinion classification system before and after using lexical normalisation techniques using annotated corpora from three different Web 2.0 genres.

3 Lexical Normalisation

We have used TENOR (Mosquera et al., 2012), a multilingual lexical normalisation tool for English and Spanish texts in order to transform noisy and informal words into their canonical form (see Table 1). After this step they can be easily processed by NLP tools and applications.

In order to do this, OOV words are detected with a dictionary lookup. TENOR uses a custom-made lexicon built over the expanded Aspell dictionary and then augmented with domain-specific knowledge from the Spell Checking Oriented Word Lists (SCOWL)[1] package.

The OOV words are matched against a phone lattice using the double metaphone algorithm (Philips, 2000) to obtain a list of substitution candidates. With the Gestalt pattern matching algorithm (Ratcliff and Metzener, 1988) a string similarity score is calculated between the OOV word and its candidate list.

Nevertheless, there are acronyms and abbreviated forms that can not be detected properly with phonetic indexing techniques *(lol - laugh out loud)*. For this reason, TENOR uses an exception dictionary with common Internet abbreviations and slang collected from online sources[2].

Moreover, a number transliteration lookup table and several heuristics such as word-lengthening compression, emoticon translation and simple case restoration are applied to improve the normalisation results. Finally, TENOR uses a trigram language model in order to enhance the clean candidate selection.

4 Polarity Classification

The methodology explained in (Boldrini et al., 2009) has been used in order to create a two-class polarity classifier (positive/negative) based on the bag of words model. We have tested two different machine learning algorithms: j48 (Quinlan, 1993) and Support Vector Machines (SVM) (Vapnik, 1997) with word unigrams and lemmas. Stopwords and URLs were replaced by static labels with aim to simplify the model and avoid extra noise.

4.1 Datasets

We have trained our polarity classification system using annotated English texts from three different Web 2.0 genres:

Microblog publications: Extracted from 5513 Twitter messages [3].

Blog posts: The Kyoto sub-set of the EmotiBlog[4]

[1] http://wordlist.sourceforge.net/

[2] http://en.wiktionary.org/wiki/Appendix:English_internet_slang

[3] http://www.sananalytics.com/lab/twitter-sentiment/sanders-twitter-0.2.zip

[4] The EmotiBlog corpus is composed by blog posts on the Kyoto Protocol and election processes in Zimbabwe and USA

	Informal English text	Normalised English text
a)	Gotta buy this asap	I am going to buy this as soon as possible.
b)	I will nevooor buy tis again :(	I will never buy this again I'm sad.
c)	Greeeeeeat product!!!	Great product!
d)	I dnt wnt to cmplain but reply me plz	I do not want to complain but reply me please.

Table 1: Example of raw and normalised pairs of English Web 2.0 texts.

corpus.

Product reviews: The phones sub-set of the EmotiBlog[5] corpus

5 Results

The polarity classification system has been evaluated using a ten-fold cross validation, see Table 2, before and after applying normalisation techniques. Analysing the results we can observe that the overall best classification is achieved using the SVM algorithm. For the microblog genre there are improvements when using the dataset normalised with TENOR and these are higher when using lemmas instead of unigrams with a 6.4% improvement over the original dataset. However, there is almost no improvement or even the performance is decreased in some cases when applying TENOR to both blogs and reviews genres. These contain a very low amount of lexical variants and misspellings, and because of that using lexical normalisation techniques can lead to false positives in the substitution process, thus decreasing the performance of the polarity classifier. On the other hand, the microblog dataset is substantially more informal, so the application of normalisation techniques has a positive impact in the classification results.

Corpus	Method	Precision	Recall	F1
micro	j48-unigram	0.705	0.706	0.705
micro-norm	j48-unigram	0.729	0.716	0.71
blog	j48-unigram	0.836	0.88	0.828
blog-norm	j48-unigram	0.8	0.866	0.812
review	j48-unigram	0.522	0.524	0.52
review-norm	j48-unigram	0.56	0.558	0.556
micro	j48-lemma	0.637	0.626	0.626
micro-norm	j48-lemma	0.656	0.655	0.654
blog	j48-lemma	0.836	0.88	0.828
blog-norm	j48-lemma	0.803	0.861	0.817
review	j48-lemma	0.554	0.555	0.547
review-norm	j48-lemma	0.551	0.55	0.549
micro	svm-unigram	0.804	0.795	0.795
micro-norm	svm-unigram	0.83	0.83	0.83
blog	svm-unigram	**0.849**	**0.88**	**0.854**
blog-norm	svm-unigram	0.803	0.848	0.819
review	svm-unigram	**0.679**	**0.679**	**0.679**
review-norm	svm-unigram	0.662	0.662	0.662
micro	svm-lemma	0.812	0.806	0.806
micro-norm	svm-lemma	**0.858**	**0.858**	**0.858**
blog	svm-lemma	0.847	0.877	0.854
blog-norm	svm-lemma	0.79	0.837	0.809
review	svm-lemma	0.667	0.667	0.667
review-norm	svm-lemma	0.671	0.671	0.671

Table 2: Polarity classification results before and after normalisation using corpora from three different Web 2.0 genres.

6 Conclusions and Future Work

In this paper we have presented the evaluation of the contribution of a text normalisation tool to an opinion mining system using corpora from three different Web 2.0 genres. The application of lexical normalisation techniques to short and very noisy texts such as tweets obtained a relatively 6.4% better F1 results than the classification baseline. On the other hand, it has been shown the need to determine the level of informality before applying normalisation techniques in order to avoid the loss of information when dealing with less informal genres. The use of informality analysis and exploring different polarity classification systems are left to a future work.

[5]It is an EmotiBlog extension with reviews of mobiles phones

Acknowledgments

This paper has been partially supported by Ministerio de Ciencia e Innovacion - Spanish Government (grant no. TIN2009-13391-C04-01), and Conselleria d'Educacion - Generalitat Valenciana (grant no. PROMETEO/2009/119, ACOMP/2010/286 and ACOMP/2011/001)

References

Ramnath Balasubramanyan, Bryan R. Routledge, and Noah A. Smith. 2010. From tweets to polls : Linking text sentiment to public opinion time series.

Luciano Barbosa and Junlan Feng. 2010. Robust sentiment detection on twitter from biased and noisy data. In *Proceedings of the 23rd International Conference on Computational Linguistics: Posters*, COLING '10, pages 36–44, Stroudsburg, PA, USA. Association for Computational Linguistics.

Albert Bifet and Eibe Frank. 2010. Sentiment knowledge discovery in twitter streaming data. In *Proceedings of the 13th international conference on Discovery science*, DS'10, pages 1–15, Berlin, Heidelberg. Springer-Verlag.

Ester Boldrini, Javi Fernández, José M Gómez, and Patricio Martínez-Barco. 2009. Machine learning techniques for automatic opinion detection in non-traditional textual genres. *Proceedings of WOMSA*.

Dmitry Davidov, Oren Tsur, and Ari Rappoport. 2010. Enhanced sentiment learning using twitter hashtags and smileys. In *Proceedings of the 23rd International Conference on Computational Linguistics: Posters*, COLING '10, pages 241–249, Stroudsburg, PA, USA. Association for Computational Linguistics.

Yoan Gutiérrez, Andy González, Roger Pérez, José I. Abreu, Antonio Fernández Orquín, Alejandro Mosquera, Andrés Montoyo, Rafael Muñoz, and Franc Cámara. 2013. Umcc_dlsi-(sa): Using a ranking algorithm and informal features to solve sentiment analysis in twitter. *Semeval 2013, Proceedings of the 7th International Workshop on Semantic Evaluations*.

Bo Han, Paul Cook, and Timothy Baldwin. 2013. Lexical normalization for social media text. *ACM Trans. Intell. Syst. Technol.*, 4(1):5:1–5:27, February.

Bernard J. Jansen, Mimi Zhang, Kate Sobel, and Abdur Chowdury. 2009. Twitter power: Tweets as electronic word of mouth. *J. Am. Soc. Inf. Sci. Technol.*, 60(11):2169–2188, November.

Fei Liu, Fuliang Weng, Bingqing Wang, and Yang Liu. 2011. Insertion, deletion, or substitution? normalizing text messages without pre-categorization nor supervision. In *Proceedings of the 49th Annual Meeting of the Association for Computational Linguistics: Human Language Technologies*, pages 71–76, Portland, Oregon, USA, June. Association for Computational Linguistics.

Alejandro Mosquera and Paloma Moreda. 2012. The study of informality as a framework for evaluating the normalisation of web 2.0 texts. In *Proceedings of 17th International conference on Applications of Natural Language Processing to Information Systems (NLDB 2012)*. Springer.

Alejandro Mosquera, Elena Lloret, and Paloma Moreda. 2012. Towards facilitating the accessibility of web 2.0 texts through text normalisation. In *Proceedings of the LREC workshop: Natural Language Processing for Improving Textual Accessibility (NLP4ITA) ; Istanbul, Turkey.*, pages 9–14.

Subhabrata Mukherjee, Akshat Malu, Balamurali A.R., and Pushpak Bhattacharyya. 2012. Twisent: a multistage system for analyzing sentiment in twitter. In *Proceedings of the 21st ACM international conference on Information and knowledge management*, CIKM '12, pages 2531–2534, New York, NY, USA. ACM.

Alexander Pak and Patrick Paroubek. 2010. Twitter as a corpus for sentiment analysis and opinion mining. In *Proceedings of the Seventh conference on International Language Resources and Evaluation (LREC'10)*, Valletta, Malta, May. European Language Resources Association (ELRA).

Bo Pang, Lillian Lee, and Shivakumar Vaithyanathan. 2002. Thumbs up?: sentiment classification using machine learning techniques. In *Proceedings of the ACL-02 conference on Empirical methods in natural language processing - Volume 10*, EMNLP '02, pages 79–86, Stroudsburg, PA, USA. Association for Computational Linguistics.

Lawrence Philips. 2000. The double metaphone search algorithm. *C/C++ Users Journal*, 18:38–43, June.

Ross Quinlan. 1993. *C4.5: Programs for Machine Learning*. Morgan Kaufmann Publishers, San Mateo, CA.

John W. Ratcliff and David E. Metzener. 1988. Pattern matching: The gestalt approach. *Dr. Dobb's Journal*, 13(7):46–72, July.

Marina Santini. 2006. Web pages, text types, and linguistic features: Some issues. *ICAME Journal*, 30.

Grigori Sidorov, Sabino Miranda-Jiménez, Francisco Viveros-Jiménez, Alexander Gelbukh, Noé Castro-Sánchez, Francisco Velásquez, Ismael Díaz-Rangel, Sergio Suárez-Guerra, Alejandro Treviño, and Juan Gordon. 2013. Empirical study of machine learning based approach for opinion mining in tweets. In *Proceedings of the 11th Mexican international conference on Advances in Artificial Intelligence - Volume Part I*, MICAI'12, pages 1–14, Berlin, Heidelberg. Springer-Verlag.

Maite Taboada, Julian Brooke, Milan Tofiloski, Kimberly Voll, and Manfred Stede. 2011. Lexicon-based methods for sentiment analysis. *Comput. Linguist.*, 37(2):267–307, June.

Crispin Thurlow. 2003. Generation txt? the sociolinguistics of young people's text-messaging. *Discourse Analysis Online*, 1(1).

Andranik Tumasjan, Timm O. Sprenger, Philipp G. Sandner, and Isabell M. Welpe. 2010. Predicting elections with twitter: What 140 characters reveal about political sentiment. In *ICWSM'10*, pages –1–1.

Peter D. Turney. 2002. Thumbs up or thumbs down?: semantic orientation applied to unsupervised classification of reviews. In *Proceedings of the 40th Annual Meeting on Association for Computational Linguistics*, ACL '02, pages 417–424, Stroudsburg, PA, USA. Association for Computational Linguistics.

Vladimir Vapnik. 1997. The support vector method. In Wulfram Gerstner, Alain Germond, Martin Hasler, and Jean-Daniel Nicoud, editors, *ICANN*, volume 1327 of *Lecture Notes in Computer Science*, pages 263–271. Springer.

Janyce Wiebe, Theresa Wilson, and Claire Cardie. 2005. Annotating Expressions of Opinions and Emotions in Language. *Language Resources and Evaluation*, 39(2-3):165–210.

Identifying Social and Expressive Factors in Request Texts Using Transaction/Sequence Model

Daša Munková[1], **Michal Munk**[1] and **Zuzana Fráterová**[2]
[1]Constantine the Philosopher University in Nitra, Slovakia
{dmunkova,mmunk}@ukf.sk
[2]University of Economics in Bratislava, Slovakia
zfraterova@gmail.com

Abstract

The paper focuses on requests in written forms, where we describe a novel approach to computational modelling of specific features of politeness in speech act of requesting. We examine the similarities and differences in the use of specific social and expressive factors in two languages (mother tongue and a foreign language). The requests collected from different social situations among students and their teachers in a university environment were used as data source for a research. Transaction/Sequence model for text representation was formulated and association rules analysis was applied as a research method. The findings are interesting mainly in terms of differences in the use of politeness features in foreign language and mother tongue. The results indicated that the requests written in mother tongue are less direct than in foreign language.

1 Introduction

Natural language is the most effective tool to perform speech acts in human communication (giving commands, making requests, apologies, thanks etc.). These speech acts are performed according to certain rules and principles. One of these principles is politeness, which has been discussed by many linguists (Awedyk, 2006; Blum-Kulka et al. 1989; Hill et al., 1986; Lakoff, 1973; Tannen, 1986; Wierzbicka, 1985; Watts at al., 1992, Munková et al., 2012) and others. Politeness communication represents one of the basic topics of successful implementation of language functionality and development of communicative competence (Hymes, 1996; Canale and Swain, 1980). Politeness functions and culture-specific features are associated with certain expressions, and grammatical constructions belong to language functionality in a given language. Based on them we may compare different languages. Researches examining various speech acts in many different languages have provided valuable insights into culture-specific features of politeness in many different languages (Liddicoat et al., 2003) and others.

The politeness theory we used when examining the production of speech acts of the requesters is the Brown and Levinson model (1987) that is, in various elaborated forms, still applicable today and forms the basis for newer models and definitions of politeness (Scollon and Scollon, 1995; Yabuuchi, 2006). Each interlocutor creates his/er own unique speech acts (Cohen, 1996; Searle, 1979) and within them s/he uses factors of politeness in various combinations and meanings.

We therefore believe that it is important to examine the rules of production of politeness speech acts, which the interlocutors use in the production of their spoken and written utterances.

The graphic form of the human communication is a written text, mostly unstructured, providing various kinds of information between the sender and the receiver, suitable mainly for a particular research or text mining.

Text mining includes several research areas. Similarly to KDD (Knowledge Discovery in Databases) statistical methods and methods of machine learning are tools for data analysis in text mining (Hearst, 1999; Sullivan, 2001). On the other hand, text mining is mainly based on theoretical and computational linguistics by data preprocessing (Neuendorf, 2002; Titscher et al., 2002; Hajičová et al., 2003; Weiss et al., 2005).

In our paper, we focus on an unstructured text - a request, where we try to find the similarities and differences in the use of chosen social and expressive factors in mother tongue (L1) and foreign language (English, L2). For this purpose, transaction/sequence model was formulated and the data - requests from the various social situations among students and their teachers in a university environment in both languages were collected. Cross-tabulation analysis and association rules were applied.

The rest of the paper is structured as follows. The next chapter deals with the request from the point of view of a speech act. The third chapter introduces some related papers written by authors doing research work in the same or similar field of interest. The methods and rules of data preprocessing are described in the fourth chapter, where we focus on information extraction from a text, specially the keywords - social and expressive factors were defined. The transaction/sequence model is described in the fifth chapter. The following chapter focuses on specific linguistic data analysis. At the end, we discuss the obtained results from the cross-tabulation analysis and association rules.

2 Request as a Speech Act

A request is a speech act whereby a requester conveys to a requestee that he/she wants the requestee to perform an act which is for the benefit of the requester (Trosborg, 1995). The act may be a request for an object, an action or some kind of service, etc. – a request for non-verbal items or services. Or it can be a request for information - a request for verbal items or services.

The speech acts of requesting become very popular in cross-cultural and interlanguage pragmatic studies. Their social function consists of getting the requestee to do something for the requester (Searle, 1979). According to Barron (2008) requests represent problematic areas for learners of all cultural backgrounds, even for advanced students.

The order, association and variability of the features of politeness are different in every language and culture, because they are based on different association rules in the given culture – based on general but also on individual level.

The requester has many features to formulate a request, which are usually classified according to a specific structure (culturally given). Blum-Kulka et al. (1989) defined three elements of a request sequence in addition to the Head Act: alerters, supportive moves (external modifiers) and internal modifications.

The function of alerters is to alert requestee's attention to the upcoming speech act (Blum-Kulka et al., 1989). External modifiers involve: preparators, disarmers, sweeteners, supportive reasons, and cost minimizing (Edmondson and House, 1981; House and Kasper, 1981; Faerch and Kasper, 1989; Trosborg, 1995). The function of internal modifications is to soften or increase the impact of a request. These devices are referred to as modality markers, and are divided into two groups: a) syntactic downgraders, lexical/phrasal downgraders – they decrease the impact of a request, and b) upgraders - intensify the force of a request (House and Kasper, 1981; Trosborg, 1995; Faerch and Kasper, 1989).

The emphasis which the requester makes in carrying out a request can be realised in several perspectives. Blum-Kulka and Olshtain (1984) distinguish the following perspectives of a request: a) Requester (Speaker) - oriented, b) Requestee (Listener) - oriented, c) Speaker and Listener - oriented and d) Impersonal.

3 Related Work

There is a considerable range of studies on culture-specific preferences of the Speech act of requesting, such as British English, American English, Irish English, Australian English (Barron, 2008), Canadian French (Blum-Kulka and House 1989), Argentinean Spanish (Faerch and Kasper 1989; House 1989), German (Faerch and Kasper 1989; House 1989; Barron 2008), Turkish (Marti 2006; Otcu and Zeyrek 2008) and many more.

There is also a number of studies which deals with requests illustrating the culture-specific discrepancies in carrying out the requests between two different languages (Barron, 2008; Awedyk, 2006; Byon, 2006; Márquez Reiter et al., 2002; Fukushima, 2000; Lubecka, 2000; Sifianou, 1992; Blum-Kulka et al., 1989; House, 1989) and others.

Interlanguage studies have proven that there are significant differences not only between two languages but also between mother tongue (L1) and foreign language (L2) in bringing across the intended illocutionary force of a request (Eslami and Noora, 2008; Woodfield, 2008; Otcu and Zeyrek, 2008; Félix-Brasdefer, 2007; Hassall, 2003; Trosborg, 1995).

Although a number of language researches has been conducted, especially for languages being so popular and dominant such as English, German or Spanish; little is known about the culture-specificity of Slovak requests. Therefore, one of the goals presented in this paper is to provide an insight into culture-specific preferences in Slovak requests.

4 Information Extraction from the Texts

Text sources in natural language offer lots of information, but not all of them are suitable for computational analysis. Though by using software for linguistic data preparation, large amounts of sources can be sorted out and useful information from the individual words, phrases or sentences can be extracted. Therefore the gist of information extraction is the identification of specific information, in our case the expressive and social factors. This identification helps us in computational modelling and understanding of the culture-specific features of politeness in speech acts of requesting not only in interlanguage (English) but also in mother tongue.

Methods based on rules and statistical methods are used to identify specific information. The methods based on rules, which we also used in our case, are based on fixed characteristics under which they are generated (e.g. association or sequence rules). We chose them because they are appropriate for specific tasks such as extraction of social and expressive factors. We used classification of politeness factors in line with Trosborg (1995) and Díaz-Pérez (2003) and we defined the following 9 factors:

- *Alerters* - a combination of salutations, a form to express a social role: e.g. addressing people (title, first name, last name, friendly appeal markers). - F1
- *Requester ' s perspective*: e.g. could I, may I etc. - F2
- *Requestee ' s perspective*: e.g. can you, would you etc. - F3
- *Politeness markers* - e.g. thank you, please - immediately before or after the request core. - F4
- *Pre-sequences* - elements before the core of a request. - F5
- *Post-sequences/supporting details* - features after the expressed request. - F6
- *Mitigating devices* - features expressing an apology for disturbing. - F7
- *Minimizers* - features minimising the impact of a request. - F8
- *Compliments* - features intensifying the likelihood of a request fulfilment. - F9

The first three represent social factors and the rest are expressive factors (supportive moves).

5 Transaction/Sequence Model

Text mining is analogous to Knowledge Discovery in Databases (KDD). Sometimes it is enough to slightly adapt the existing methods and procedures from other areas of knowledge discovery. In our case we chose a representation of examined request text similar to bag-of-words model. We used the Transaction/Sequence model for text representation, which allows us to examine the relationships between the examined attributes and search for associations among the identified keywords in texts of requests. Similarly, like in shopping cart analysis, a transaction represents one purchase, or in web analysis it represents the set of user's visited pages during one session, in our case it is a set of keywords in text of request. It is similar to bag of words model.

The structure and data character predetermine the use of specific methods for analysis – data modelling. In case of the use of transaction/sequence model for text representation, it is mainly association rule analysis and sequence rule analysis. The difference between the association and the sequence rule analysis is that we do not analyse the sequences but the transactions in association rule analysis, which means, we do not include the sequence variable representing the order of the key words in text into the analysis. The transaction represents a set of the key words of the text, whereby the order of occurrence of the identified key words in the given text is not taken into account.

Case	St.	Sit.	Lan.	T/S ID	Fac.	Seq.
:	:	:	:	:	:	:
1779	46	S5	FL	46#S5# FL	F4	1
1780	46	S5	FL	46#S5# FL	F2	2
1781	46	S5	FL	46#S5# FL	F5	3
1782	47	S5	MT	47#S5#MT	F1	1
1783	47	S5	MT	47#S5# MT	F2	2
1784	47	S5	MT	47#S5# MT	F5	3
:	:	:	:	:	:	:

Table 1. Transaction/Sequence Model of request texts.

Examined variables:

Student - Student ID who produced the given request.

Situation – Social situations- requests, the written requests were classified into five individual categories in line with Díaz-Pérez (2003) and Trosborg (1995).

Language - a language of request produced in (foreign language (FL) and mother tongue (MT)).

Transaction/Sequence ID - a set ID of key words in request text, it consists of previous three variables (Student ID, Situation and Language).

Factor - a key word represents social or expressive factors.

Sequence - an order of occurrence of key words in text of particular request.

6 Linguistic data analysis

6.1 Cross-tabulation analysis

In our case, a cross-tabulation analysis consists of an analysis of texts of requests formulated in mother tongue (MT) and in foreign language (FL, English). These texts of requests were collected from department of translations studies and department of American and English studies, where students studying linguistics have to communicate (in spoken and written form) among them and their teachers not only in a mother tongue but also in English language. We collected 1000 requests in total (500 English requests and 500 Slovak requests).

With the help of the cross-tabulation analysis we investigated whether there is a difference in the use of various factors in mother tongue (MT) and foreign language (FL, English).

	Chi-square	df	p
Pearson	114.9155	8	0.0000
Cont. coeff. C	0.2434		
Cramér's V	0.2509		

Table 2. Results of cross-tabulation analysis MT vs. FL.

The only requirement (a validity assumption) of the use of chi-square test is a large amount of expected frequencies. The requirement is not violated, the expected frequencies $eij = risj/n$ are large enough (i.e. they are positive and not more than 20% of eij are less than 5, $eij > 34.36$). The contingency coefficient represents the degree of dependence between two nominal variables. The value of coefficient (Table 2) is approximately 0.25, where 1 means perfect dependency and 0 means independency. There is a medium dependency between the occurrence of individual factors of politeness and the language in case of MT vs. FL, the contingency coefficient is statistically significant. The zero hypotheses (Table 2) are rejected, i.e. the occurrence (use) of individual factors of politeness depends on the language (MT or FL). The graph (Fig. 1) shows the interaction frequencies *Language* x *Factor*.

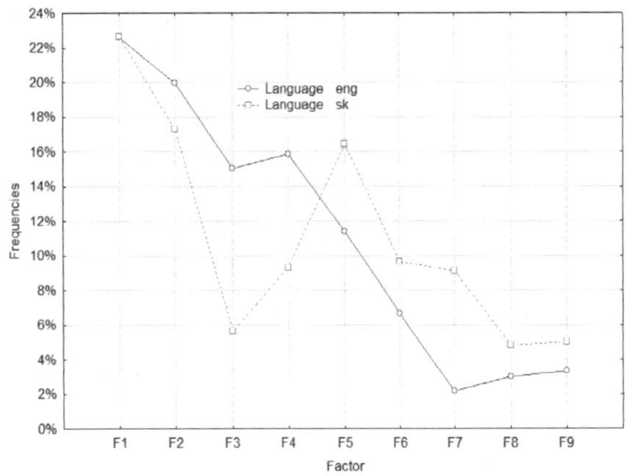

Figure 1. Interaction Plot - *Language* x *Factor* MT (red course) vs. FL (English, blue course)

The graph presents a categorized polygon, where the factors of politeness are on the x axis and the observed frequencies of their usage (the occurrence) are on the y axis; while for each level of the variable Language one polygon is depicted. If the curves copy each other – they show the same course, the use of individual factors of politeness does not depend on the selected language. And vice versa, if there is any defined degree of dependence, the curves would not copy each other – this is what the results of analysis have confirmed. We can observe different course for FL (English) and a different one for MT. As we can see on the graph (Fig. 1), the differences are mainly in factors F3, F4, F5 and F7. The factors F3 and F4 are considerably less used in MT than in FL. Factor F3 – the requestee's perspective represents a more direct and shorter utterance of a request. In terms of frequency, factor F2 – the requester's perspective is much more preferred in the decision of perspective in mother tongue and also in foreign language. It means that an indirect utterance of a request and an attempt to avoid a direct addressing of requestee is more preferred. Factor F2 reduces the impact of a request. Using these formulations a requester takes over a part of "the effort" needed to fulfil the request upon him/herself, assuming that the potential "alleviation" increases the likelihood of a request fulfilment. Factor F4 is considerably less used in mother tongue, that shows the requester's knowledge of politeness structures in FL with factor F4 - a politeness marker (with words such as please or thank you) - formulated in requests in comparison to MT. On the contrary, factors F5 and F7 are much more used in FL. These are expressive factors. When the requester uses factor F5, he/she assumes that by explaining the reasons to the requestee and the requestee's potential understanding of the reasons of his/her request may increase the likelihood of the fulfilment of a request. Consequently, the requester appeals to the empathy and imagination of the requestee, since he/she considers their influence as an effective strategy. Factor F7 - mitigating devices - reduce the impact of a request on the requestee, in terms of whether the requester does not interfere or over-interfere with his/her request in the requestee's time, space or decision making.

6.2 Association rule analysis

The association rule analysis represents a non-sequential approach to the data being analysed. We will not analyse the sequences but transactions, so we will not include the order of factors used into the analysis. In our case, a transaction represents the set of factors observed in the texts of requests separately for foreign language (FL) and mother tongue.

The web graph (Fig.2) depicts the discovered association rules for the texts of requests written in FL, specifically the size of node represents the support of occurrence of the politeness factor, the thickness of the line represents the support of rule – pairs of factors (probability of occurrence in the pair) and the darkness of the line colour presents a lift of the rule – the probability of a pair occurrence in transaction separately. We can see from the graph (Fig. 2) that the factors of politeness F2, F1, F4 and F3 (support > 51%) belong to the most frequently used factors. Similarly, like the combination of these factors` pairs F1, F2; F2, F4, and F1, F3 (support > 39%), the factors F5==>F3, F5==>F1, F2==>F4 and F1==>F3 occur in sets of factors of politeness more often together than as separate units (lift>1.11). In these cases the highest degree of interestingness was achieved – the lift, which defines how many times the selected factors of politeness occur more often together as if they were statistically independent. In case, that the lift is more than 1, the selected pairs occur more often jointly than separately in the set of used factors of politeness. It is necessary to take into account that in characterising the degree of interestingness – the lift, the orientation of the rule does not matter.

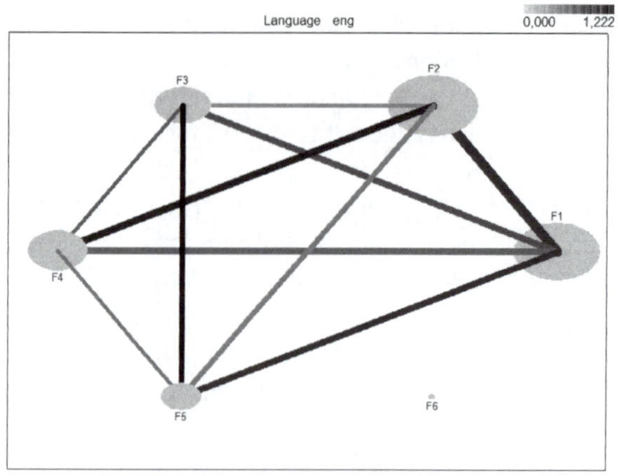

Figure 2. Web graph – a visualization of the discovered rules – Foreign language

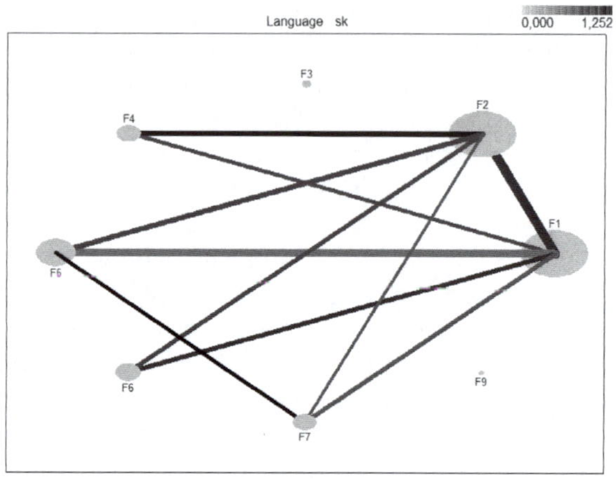

Figure 3. Web graph – a visualization of the discovered rules – Mother tongue

We found different association rules for texts of requests written in MT than for FL. The web graph (Fig. 3) illustrates the discovered association rules. The most frequently used factors of politeness are F1, F2 and F5 (support > 49%), as well as their pairs F1, F2 and F1, F5 (support > 43%). The factors F7==>F5, F5==>F1, F4==>F2, F1==>F7 and F6==>F1 occur more often together in transactions of used factors of politeness than separately (lift>1.02).

7 Discussion and Conclusion

Based on computational modelling, the present research compared the pragmalinguistic knowledge of speech act (culture-specific features) use of Slovak native speakers (L1) and advanced ESL learners, students studying linguistics (L2), in requests formulation. It identified significant differences in social and expressive factors, which help us to understand the influence of mother tongue, specially, requester's experience in L1, on request formulation in FL (L2), in interlanguage.

The politeness structure of the Slovak language has so far been investigated very peripherally. Therefore, in terms of comparison with Germanic and Romance languages this investigation is unique, and based on its results we can speculate not only about the decrease of transference regularities, but also about the politeness in Slovak language as such.

If we look at the results from the point of view of language used, in Slovak requests formulated by linguists the factors F1 (22.64%), F2 (17.30%) and F5 (16.46%) occurred most and the factors F8 (4.82%) and F9 (5.03%) least frequently. In English requests, the factors F1 (22.62%), F2 (19.98%) and F4 (15.84%) occurred most frequently and factors F7 (2.18%), F8 (2.99%) and F9 (3.33%) least frequently.

The results of cross-tabulation analysis showed (Tab. 2), that there is a difference between the language (Slovak or English) and the use of selected factors of politeness (the contingency coefficient is statistically significant (0.2434) at the level of $p<0.01$). This means that the occurrence of individual factors of politeness depends on the language used in the text of request.

It was proven (through the association rule analysis), that the factors F2, F1, F4 and F3 (support: 71.24%; 68.58%; 53.98%; 51.77%) occurred most frequently among all factors of politeness in examined requests formulations written in English.

The English requests are more direct with a politeness feature, which is a paradox. Linguists used more the *requestee's perspective* (F3 for Slovak is 5.66% and for English 15.04%), and similarly also the *politeness markers* (F4 for Slovak is 9.33% and for English 15.84%), and considerably less *pre-sequences* (F5 for Slovak is 16.46% and for English 11.34%), and *mitigating devices* (F7 for Slovak is 9.12% and for English 2.18%), which are typical features of politeness in Slovak language. The speaker uses them to "ensure" the request fulfilment, which seems to be a successful strategy to approach the requestee and his/her understanding of the request. In English, their occurrence is less frequent. We may discuss, whether the lower occurrence of these factors is due to different structure of politeness of requests, or if the requesters prefer directness to ensure that their request is comprehensible.

In terms of factor combination, the following factors were combined the most: *alerter* with *requester's perspective*, *requester's perspective* with *politeness marker* and *alerter* with *requestee's perspective* (support: 48.67%; 42.92%; 39.38%). From the point of view of pair occurrence F5==>F3, F5==>F1, F2==>F4 and F1==>F3 occurred more frequently jointly in transactions of used factors of politeness than as separate factors (lift: 1.22; 1.22; 1.12; 1.11).

In case of the couple pre-sequences ==> requestee's perspective, the association of direct factors of politeness is shown. This means that when the requester used a *pre-sequence*, he/she also used the *requestee's perspective* (to mitigate the directness of a request and its impact and effect on the requestee). The *pre-sequence* and *requestee's perspective* were associated with *allerters* (salutations and greetings) (F5 with F1) or (F3 with F1) by requesters. They reinforce the request with them, i.e. they express the respect to the introductory - opening communication structures in the specific language and will not risk the failure of supposed communicated expectations of the partner – a native speaker. The next pair was *requester's perspective* and the *politeness markers* (F2 with F4). In case of interlanguage (English), when requester used more direct utterance through factor F3, he/she mitigated this directness with expressive factor F4 (*politeness marker*). When he/she decided to express him/herself more indirectly, he/she used a combination with *politeness marker* (F2 with F4) reinforcing the likelihood of request fulfilment, which is confirmed by the last couple of factors.

The analysis results for the texts of requests written in Slovak were partially different. The most frequent factors used were: F1, F2 and F5 (support: 73.21%; 73.21%; 49.55%), contrary to English. As we mentioned before, Slovak language prefers indirect expressions with social factors of politeness that express the politeness model of requests in Slovak. Slovak language expresses the politeness through a more indirect utterance, explanation, compliments and avoiding the interruption of the image of his/her communication partner.

The most frequent factor combinations are: *alerter* with *requester's perspective* and *alerter* with *pre-sequences* (support: 52.68%; 43.30%); and F7==>F5, F5==>F1, F4==>F2, F1==>F7 and F6==>F1 occur in transactions of used factors more frequently together than separately (lift: 1.25; 1.19; 1.16; 1.11; 1.02). It is particularly interesting that there are combinations of *post-*

sequences with *mitigating devices* as combinations of expressive factors with social factors and the rules of their combinations, which are typical for Slovak language.

We can say that the requests in Slovak are less direct, using more *mitigating devices* (F7 - apologies for interference), *minimizers* (F8) and *compliments* (F9).

From our point of view, there are interesting pairs of expressive and social factors of politeness, i.e. *mitigating device* combined with *pre-sequences* but also with *attention getter* in a reverse order. It means that, when a requester used an *alerter* - a form of addressing, a specific greeting etc., it is more likely that he/she used an expressive factor, which raised the indirectness of utterance and decreased its possible negative effect. Similarly, if he/she used indirect expression of perspective – F2 then he/she combined it with *politeness markers*, so the most frequently occurred association rules were those indicating the preference of indirect expression is Slovak language.

The results are interesting mainly in terms of differences in the use of politeness factors in English and Slovak language.

We consider these findings interesting, because we examined the same requests (in context) but in different languages with different L1`s experience in speech acts of requesting and different L2 proficiency. Here, different patterns of request formulations are being created depending on the language used.

We used our own tool for requests pre-processing during which our self-created lists of particular factors for keywords identification were used.

Transaction/Sequence Model for text representation has proved to be suitable for short texts, because it allows us to examine the relationships among the examined attributes and search for associations among the identified keywords in texts of requests.

Acknowledgments

This work was supported by the Slovak Research and Development Agency under the contract No.APVV-0451-10.

References

W. Awedyk. 2006. *Politeness Markers in Norwegian and English. Contrastive Analysis of Speech habits among Norwegian Students of English.* Poznań: Uniwersytet im. Adama Mickiewicza

A. Barron. 2008. Contrasting requests in Inner Circle Englishes: a study in variational pragmatics. In *Developing Contrastive Pragmatics. Interlanguage and Cross-Cultural Perspectives*, Berlin and New York: Mouton de Gruyter

S. Blum-Kulka and J. House. 1989. Cross-cultural and situational variation in requesting behavior. In *Cross-cultural Pragmatics: Requests and Apologies*, Norwood, NJ: Ablex.

S. Blum-Kulka and E. Olshtain. 1984. Requests and Apologies: A Crosscultural study of speech act realization patterns (CCSARP). In: *Applied Linguistics*. Vol. 5, No. 3

S. Blum-Kulka, J. House and G. Kasper. (eds.) 1989. *Cross-cultural pragmatics: Requests and apologies*. Norwood: Ablex Publishing.

P. Brown and S. C. Levinson. 1987. *Politeness: Some universals in language usage*. Cambridge University Press, New York

A. S. Byon. 2006. The role of linguistic indirectness and honorifics in achieving linguistic politeness in Korean requests. In: *Journal of Politeness Research*. Vol. 2

M. Canale and M. Swain. 1980. Theoretical bases of communicative approaches to second language teaching and testing. In: *Applied Linguistics*. Vol. 1

A. D. Cohen. 1996. Speech acts. In *Sociolinguistics and Language Teaching*. Cambridge University Press, Cambridge

F. J. Diaz Pérez. 2003. *La cortesía verbal en inglés y en español.* Actos de habla y pragmática intercultural. Universidad de Jaén, Jaén

W. Edmondson and J. House 1981. *Let's Talk and Talk About It*. Munich: Urban and Schwarzenberg

Z. R. Eslami. and A. Noora. 2008. *In Developing Contrastive Pragmatics. Interlanguage and Cross-Cultural Perspectives*. Berlin and New York: Mouton de Gruyter

C. Faerch and G. Kasper. 1989. Internal and external modification in interlanguage request realization. In: *Cross-cultural Pragmatics: Requests and Apologies.* Norwood, N.J.: Ablex Publishing Corporation

J. C. Félix-Brasdefer. 2007. Pragmatic development in the Spanish as a FL classroom: a cross-sectional study of learner requests. In: *Intercultural Pragmatics*, Vol. 4

S. Fukushima. 2000. *Requests and Culture: Politeness in British English and Japanese*. Bern: Lang.

E. Hajičová, E., J. Panevová and P. Sgall. 2003. Úvod do teoretické a počítačové lingvistiky. Karolinum, Praha

T. Hassall. 2003. Requests by Australian learners of Indonesian. In: *Journal of Pragmatics*, Vol. 35, 1903-1928

M. A. Hearst. 1999. Untangling text data mining. In: *ACL '99 Proceedings of the 37th annual meeting of the Association for Computational Linguistics on Computational Linguistics*, 3-10

B. Hill, S. Ide, S. Ikuta, A. Kawasaki and T. Ogino. 1986. Universals of linguistic politeness. Quantitative Evidence from Japanese and American English. In: *Journal of Pragmatics*. Vol. 10

J. House. 1989. Politeness in English and German: the functions of please and bitte. In: *Cross-cultural Pragmatics: Requests and Apologies*, Norwood, NJ: Ablex

J. House and G. Kasper. 1981. Politeness markers in English and German. In: *Conversational Routine*. The Hague: Mouton

D. H. Hymes. 1996. On communicative competence. In: *The Communicative Approach to Language* Teaching, Oxford Univesity Press

R. Lakoff. 1973. The logic of politeness; or minding your p's and q's. Papers from the Ninth Regional Meeting of the Chicago Linguistic Society. Chicago: Chicago Linguistic Society, 292-305.

A. J. Liddicoat, L. Papademetre, A. Scarino and M. Kohler. 2003. Report on intercultural language learning. Report to the Australian Government Department for Education Science and Training

A. Lubecka. 2000. *Requests, Invitations, Apologies and Compliments in American English and Polish. A Cross-Cultural Communication Perspective*. Krakow: Ksiegarnia Akademicka

L. Marti. 2006. Indirectness and politeness in Turkish-German bilingual and Turkish monolingual requests. In: *Journal of Pragmatics*, Vol. 38

D. Munková, M. Munk, Z. Fráterová and B. Ďuračková. 2012. Analysis of Social and Expressive Factors of Requests by Methods of Text Mining. In: *Pacific Asia Conference on Language, Information and Computation, PACLIC 26*

K. A. Neuendorf. 2002. *The Content Analysis Guidebook*. Sage, London

B. Otcu and D. Zeyrek. 2008. Development of requests: a study on Turkish learners of English. In: *Developing Contrastive Pragmatics. Interlanguage and Cross-Cultural Perspectives*. Berlin/New York: Mouton de Gruyter

R. Scollon and S. Wong Scollon. 1995. *Intercultural Communication: A Discourse Approach*. Blackwell, Oxford

J. R. Searle. 1979. *Expression and meaning: Studies in the theory of speech acts*. Cambridge University Press, Cambridge

M. Sifianou. 1992. Politeness Phenomena in England and Greece. In: *A Cross-cultural Perspective*. Oxford, UK: Clarendon Press

D. Sullivan. 2001. *Document Warehousing and Text Mining: Techniques for Improving Business Operations*, Marketing and Sales. John Willey & Sons

D. Tannen. 1986. *That's not What I Meant! How Conversational Style Makes or Breaks Relationships*. New York: Ballantine Books

S. Titscher, M. Meyer, R. Wodak and E. Vetter. 2002. *Methods of Text and Discourse Analysis*. Sage, London

A. Trosborg. 1995. *Interlanguage pragmatics: Requests, complaints, and apologies*. Mouton de Gruyter, Berlin

R. J. Watts, S. Ide and K. Ehlich. 1992. *Politeness in Language: Studies in its History, Theory, and Practice*. Mouton de Gruyter, Berlin/New York

S. M. Weiss, N. Indurkhya, T. Zhang and F. J. Damerau. 2005. *Text Mining: Predictive Methods for Analyzing Unstructured Information*. Springer

A. Wierzbicka. 1985. Different cultures, different languages, different speech acts. In: *Journal of Pragmatics*. Vol. 9, 145-178

H. Woodfield. 2008. Interlanguage requests: a contrastive study. In *Developing Contrastive Pragmatics. Interlanguage and Cross-Cultural Perspectives*, Berlin and New York: Mouton de Gruyter

A. Yabuuchi. 2006. Hierarchy politeness: What Brown and Levinson refused to see. In: *Intercultural Pragmatics*, Vol.3, 323-351

Parameter Optimization for Statistical Machine Translation: It Pays to Learn from Hard Examples

Preslav Nakov, Fahad Al Obaidli, Francisco Guzmán and Stephan Vogel
Qatar Computing Research Institute, Qatar Foundation
Tornado Tower, floor 10, PO box 5825
Doha, Qatar
{pnakov,faalobaidli,fherrera,svogel}@qf.org.qa

Abstract

Research on statistical machine translation has focused on particular translation directions, typically with English as the target language, e.g., from Arabic to English. When we reverse the translation direction, the multiple reference translations turn into multiple possible inputs, which offers both challenges and opportunities. We propose and evaluate several strategies for making use of these multiple inputs: (a) select one of the datasets, (b) select the best input for each sentence, and (c) synthesize an input for each sentence by fusing the available inputs. Surprisingly, we find out that it is best to tune on the hardest available input, not on the one that yields the highest BLEU score. This finding has implications on how to pick good translators and how to select useful data for parameter optimization in SMT.

1 Introduction

Nowadays, statistical machine translation (SMT) systems are data-driven, and thus critically depend on the available resources for training, tuning and evaluation. These resources are hard to obtain, which has limited research to a small number of language pairs for which biligual sentence-aligned parallel corpora, called *bitexts*, are available.

What is often not realized is that SMT research has further been restricted to only some translation directions, e.g., those of interest to evaluation campaigns such as NIST and IWSLT or to funding agencies such as DARPA. This is because stable SMT evaluation requires multiple reference translations for the target language. Such multiple references are often available for the English (target) side of the tuning and the evaluation dataset, but not for the source language, e.g., Arabic, Chinese.

Reversing the translation direction yields (i) a single reference translation and (ii) multiple versions for each tuning/testing input sentence. There is little we can do about (i),[1] but (ii) offers interesting opportunities for tuning and evaluation.

Below we focus on the question of how to make best use of the multiple available inputs at *tuning* time. We propose and evaluate several strategies for making use of these multiple inputs: (a) select one of the datasets, (b) select the best input for each sentence, and (c) synthesize an input for each sentence by fusing the available inputs.

2 Related Work

One relevant line of research is on *multi-source translation*, which generates a single translation given multiple versions of the input. This line was started by Och and Ney (2001), who translated the different inputs in isolation and then selected one of them. It has been further extended with various strategies for generating a consensus translation by combining either the inputs (Schroeder et al., 2009) or the outputs (Matusov et al., 2006) of the SMT system. In contrast, we assume having multiple sources at tuning but not at testing time.

A related line focused on *data selection*. For *training* data, this includes filtering (Moore and Lewis, 2010; Foster et al., 2010), instance-weighting (Axelrod et al., 2011; Matsoukas et al., 2009) and model adaptation (Hildebrand et al., 2005). For *tuning* data, Liu et al. (2012) built a separate tuning dataset for each test sentence, which is too costly for real-world translation.

To the best of our knowledge, ours is the first attempt to make best use at *tuning* time of multiple input versions of the same tuning sentence and a single reference translation for it. Previous English–Arabic SMT has used the first input (Al-Haj and Lavie, 2012; Kholy and Habash, 2012).

[1] One could hire translators, but this would be costly.

3 Method

3.1 Choosing a dataset

We can select one of the input datasets.

Select-first. One possible baseline is to select randomly, e.g., the dataset that is listed first.

Concat-all. Another baseline is to concatenate all tuning datasets: using each of the available English versions of a given sentence as input, each paired with the only available Arabic reference.

Then, there are a number of strategies that select the dataset yielding the highest BLEU score:

Backtranslate. We can backtranslate the single target-language reference to English, then evaluate this translation with respect to each of the English inputs, and select the one yielding the highest BLEU score. We can do this using our own system, trained in the opposite, X-English direction; this makes the results potentially more relevant to a system trained and tuned on the same dataset, but in the English-X direction. Another option is to use Google Translate, which would avoid the bias to our datasets. One could argue in favor of either option, and we experiment with both.

X-vs-all-but-X. Here we pretend that one of the English inputs is in fact a translation, and we evaluate this "translation" with respect to the remaining English datasets. We calculate the BLEU score for each of the English datasets using the remaining English datasets as references, and we select the one with the highest BLEU. This minimizes the risk of selecting an outlier dataset for tuning.

Best-on-tuning. Given an English input, we use it to tune the parameters of our SMT system, then we use these learned parameters to translate each of the English inputs, and we evaluate them using BLEU. Then, we average the BLEU scores, where the averaging is over (a) the translations of all English inputs or (b) all but the one used for tuning. The rationale behind (a) is to make all BLEU scores comparable, while that for (b) is to clearly separate tuning from testing, i.e., not to test on the particular dataset that was used for tuning. In either case, we select the dataset that achieved the highest such average.

3.2 Synthesizing a dataset from full sentences

Instead of selecting an *entire* input dataset, we can *synthesize* a new dataset by fusing the available inputs. The easiest way is to do selection at the sentence-level: for each tuning reference sentence, we can select one of the available English inputs.

We will do the selection with respect to some English reference, e.g., backtranslation of the Arabic reference generated by our own system or by Google translate. Below, we present the similarity measures that we use for the selection.

BLEU+1 (B1). BLEU+1 (Lin and Och, 2004) is a smoothed version of BLEU (Papineni et al., 2002) used to address sparseness problems with n-gram matches when comparing sentences.

BLEU+1 BP smooth (B1-BP). The BLEU+1 approximation of BLEU smooths the n-gram counts but not the brevity penalty, thus destroying the balance between the two; it also assigns a non-zero precision to cases with zero matches. Thus, we experiment with a version of BLEU+1 from (Nakov et al., 2012) that smooths the brevity penalty and also uses a "grounding" factor.

BLEU+1 Sigmoid LP (B1-SG). Note that the brevity penalty of BLEU/BLEU+1 penalizes shorter but not longer sentences. Thus, we also experiment with a version of BLEU+1 with a symmetric length penalty, which penalizes the squared differences in length using a sigmoid function:

$$LP(s_i, r) = 3 - 4 * \texttt{sig}\left(\left[\frac{l(s_i) - l(r)}{\alpha}\right]^2\right)$$

where $l(s_i)$ and $l(r)$ are the length of the i-th input and of the reference, respectively, and α is a tolerance factor (set to 5 in our experiments).

Length Difference (DL). We also try to minimize the difference in length.

Minimum BLEU+1 (MIN-B1). Next, instead of maximizing BLEU+1, we can minimize it, i.e., pick the hardest input sentence, and tune the SMT system to perform well on such hard input.

Minimum Length (MIN-L). Finally, we can just pick the shortest sentence.

3.3 Synthesizing a dataset by fusing sentences

MEMT. Instead of selecting one of the possible inputs, we can synthesize a new input by mixing different inputs at the *sub-sentence* level. Here, we use the Multi-Engine Machine Translation system, or MEMT, (Heafield and Lavie, 2010) to merge different input sentences. It merges all input sentences into a lattice and then extracts a new candidate from that lattice using features such as length, language model, and n-gram matches; it tries to maximize BLEU with respect to a given reference: again, a backtranslation of the reference to English using own SMT system or Google Translate.

TEST ⇒	MT050		MT051		MT052		MT053		MT054		AVERAGE	
TUNE ⇓	BLEU	len	BLEU	len	BLEU	len	BLEU	len	BLEU	len	BLEU	len
MT040	**34.63**	0.984	**30.96**	0.984	**29.73**	0.973	~~40.40~~	1.014	**35.46**	0.988	**34.24**	**0.989**
MT041	34.37	0.969	30.59	0.966	29.44	0.954	**40.91**	0.999	35.31	0.972	34.12	0.972
MT042	34.34	0.967	30.57	0.964	29.08	0.952	40.64	0.998	35.12	0.970	33.95	0.970
MT043	33.99	0.957	30.23	0.952	29.06	0.943	40.62	0.988	~~34.81~~	0.960	33.74	0.960
MT044	~~33.87~~	0.961	~~30.18~~	0.957	~~28.96~~	0.947	40.51	0.992	34.82	0.965	~~33.67~~	0.964
MT04ALL	34.37	0.970	30.49	0.967	29.42	0.957	40.72	1.001	35.15	0.973	34.03	0.974
best−worst	0.76		0.78		0.77		0.51		0.65		0.57	

Table 1: **Tuning on MT04 and testing on MT05.** Shown are BLEU scores and hypothesis/reference length ratios. The best and the worst BLEU scores for each test MT05 dataset are in **bold** and ~~stroke out~~, respectively; the last row shows the absolute difference between them.

4 Experiments and Evaluation

4.1 Experimental Setup

We used the phrase-based SMT model (Koehn et al., 2003), as implemented in the Moses toolkit (Koehn et al., 2007), to train an SMT system translating from English to Arabic.

For tuning and evaluation, we used two multi-reference datasets, MT04 and MT05, from the NIST 2012 OpenMT Evaluation,[2] each with a single Arabic input and five English reference translations, which we inverted, ending up with five English inputs and one Arabic reference for each one.

We trained the English-Arabic system (translation, reordering, and language models) on all training data from NIST 2012 except for UN data. Following Kholy and Habash (2012), we normalized the Arabic training, development and test data using MADA (Roth et al., 2008), fixing automatically all wrong instances of *alef*, *ta marbuta* and *alef maqsura*. We segmented the Arabic words by splitting out conjunctions (MADA scheme D1). For English, we converted all words to lowercase.

We built our phrase tables using the standard Moses pipeline with max-phrase-length 7 and Kneser-Ney smoothing. We also built a lexicalized reordering model (Koehn et al., 2005): *msd-bidirectional-fe*. We used a 5-gram language model trained on the GigaWord v.5 with Kneser-Ney smoothing using KenLM (Heafield, 2011). For optimization, we used MERT. For evaluation, we used NIST's BLEU scoring tool v13a, which we ran on a desegmented Arabic output, where conjunctions are attached to the following word.

In order to ensure stability, we performed three reruns of MERT for each experiment, and we report evaluation results averaged over the three reruns, as suggested by Foster and Kuhn (2009).

[2] www.nist.gov/itl/iad/mig/openmt12.cfm

4.2 Tuning on MT04, testing on MT05

TEST ⇒	AVERAGE		AVG, no self	
TUNE ⇓	BLEU	len	BLEU	len
MT040	29.41	1.014	**30.30**	1.020
MT041	30.13	**0.993**	30.18	**0.993**
MT042	30.07	0.991	30.14	0.990
MT043	30.03	0.983	29.36	0.981
MT044	**30.14**	0.986	29.32	0.982

Table 2: **Tuning and testing on MT04.** We tune on the English input in the first column, then we translate all MT04x inputs. We report BLEU and hyp/ref length ratios averaged over (a) all MT04 datasets, and (b) all but the one used for tuning.

Table 1 shows the results when tuning on MT04 and testing on MT05. There are several interesting observations we can make. First, the choice of *test* dataset has a huge impact on the BLEU score: in some cases, more than 11 BLEU points, e.g., compare MT052 to MT053. Second, from the *tuning* dataset perspective, we can see 0.51-0.78 absolute difference in BLEU between the best (mostly MT040) and the worst choice (mostly MT044). These differences are large enough to justify our interest in tuning input selection.

Table 1 also allows us to assess the performance of the two baselines: *select-first* is optimal, achieving an overall BLEU score of 34.24, while *concat-all* is in the middle (would be third best if ranked with the rest) with a BLEU score of 34.03.

Table 2 shows the results when tuning on one MT04 dataset, and testing on all MT04 datasets. The results are averaged (a) over all MT04 datasets and (b) over all but the one used for tuning. In case (a) (see columns 2 and 3), MT044 is selected, which is the worst possible choice. However, in case (b) (see columns 4 and 5), the best score is achieved for MT040, which is the optimal choice, i.e., *best-on-tuning* yields optimal results when averaging over all but the tuning dataset.

Moreover, note that the BLEU scores in column 4 of Table 2 go in strictly decreasing order for MT040, MT041, MT042, MT043, MT044, and they do so also in Table 1. This suggests that the *best-on-tuning* strategy is very reliable here.

TEST	REF: all-but-X BLEU	len
MT040	52.81	0.976
MT041	57.16	**1.005**
MT042	58.55	1.007
MT043	**63.28**	1.008
MT044	62.56	1.013

Table 3: **X vs. all-but-X for MT04.** BLEU scores and hyp/ref length ratios when testing on each English input, using all the rest as references.

Table 3 implements *X-vs-all-but-X*. It shows the results when tuning on each English input, using all other inputs as references. The highest BLEU score is achieved by MT043, which is the second worst choice. Thus, this is a very poor strategy here; however, below we will see that it is quite reliable if we make a choice based on length ratio.

TEST	Our System BLEU	Our System len	Google BLEU	Google len
MT040	26.04	1.036	26.29	**0.992**
MT041	29.46	**0.979**	28.11	0.937
MT042	29.99	0.977	28.00	0.935
MT043	32.21	0.974	**30.36**	0.933
MT044	**32.27**	0.962	29.94	0.921

Table 4: **Backtranslate MT04.** BLEU scores and hyp/ref length ratios when backtranslating the Arabic reference to English, and then evaluating it with respect to each of the English inputs.

Table 4 shows the results when backtranslating the Arabic reference to English, and then scoring it with respect to each of the English inputs. The backtranslation uses (a) our own system trained to translate in the reverse direction, and (b) Google Translate. We can see that *backtranslate* performs poor: with (a), it selects MT044, the worst choice, and with (b), it selects MT043, the second worst; however, it works better if we use length ratios.

Table 5 shows the results when tuning on datasets synthesized from full sentences (all but the last line) or by fusing sentences (the last line), where we optimize some function with respect to a backtranslation obtained from (a) our own system or (b) Google Translate. We can see that no combination could improve over the best individual system, but the best synthesized dataset yielded a score matching that of the best individual system.

TUNE	Our System BLEU	Our System len	Google BLEU	Google len
B1	34.05	0.971	33.92	0.981
B1-BP	34.11	0.967	33.94	0.977
B1-SG	34.03	0.982	34.19	0.989
DL	34.21	0.982	34.07	0.990
MIN-L	33.53	1.020	**34.24**	1.005
MIN-B1	**34.23**	0.978	34.05	0.966
MEMT	33.71	**0.998**	33.47	**1.000**

Table 5: **Tuning on synthesized MT04 datasets, testing on MT05.** BLEU scores and hyp/ref length ratios averaged over all MT05 test datasets.

We believe that these results are due to our inability to choose a reliable reference translation: backtranslation generates an automatic translation, which most of the time is arguably worse in quality than the English inputs, which are *human*, after all. In future work, we plan to try other ways to generate a good reference translation.

4.3 Tuning on MT05, testing on MT04

Table 6 shows the results when tuning on MT05 and testing on MT04. Once again, the choice of *test* dataset has a huge impact on the BLEU score: this time up to 7 BLEU points, e.g., compare MT040 to MT044. We further see 0.5-1.5 absolute difference in BLEU between the best (mostly MT051) and the worst choice (mostly MT050).

This time, *select-first* does not work at all: it selects MT050, which is the worst possible choice (while it was best in the reverse, MT04-MT05, translation direction). However, the *concat-all* strategy performs reasonably well: it would be second best if ranked together with the individual inputs (it was third best in the reverse direction).

Table 7 shows that the *best-on-tuning* strategy once again works quite well, selecting MT051, which is the optimal choice. Note that this time the optimal choice is made regardless of whether the averaging is done over all datasets or over all but the tuning dataset (in the reverse direction, averaging over all made the worst possible choice, while averaging over all but the one used for tuning made an optimal choice).

Next, Table 8 shows that *X-vs-all-but-X* would select MT054, which is in the middle of the possible choices: not the worst, but also not the best (it was second worst in the reverse direction).

Table 9 shows that *backtranslate* does not work well: for both our SMT system and Google Translate, it selects MT053, the second worst choice (it was also second worst in the reverse direction).

TEST ⇒ TUNE ⇓	MT040 BLEU	MT040 len	MT041 BLEU	MT041 len	MT042 BLEU	MT042 len	MT043 BLEU	MT043 len	MT044 BLEU	MT044 len	AVERAGE BLEU	AVERAGE len
MT050	25.23	0.989	~~28.41~~	1.018	~~28.28~~	1.022	~~30.98~~	1.026	~~31.08~~	1.031	~~28.80~~	1.017
MT051	25.49	0.963	**29.38**	0.987	**29.23**	0.990	**32.22**	0.996	**32.61**	1.001	**29.79**	0.987
MT052	25.27	0.971	28.67	0.994	28.87	0.996	31.58	1.003	31.85	1.008	29.25	0.994
MT053	~~24.98~~	0.921	28.72	0.944	28.85	0.945	31.90	0.953	32.30	0.957	29.35	0.944
MT054	25.42	0.973	29.27	0.986	28.66	1.000	31.90	1.005	32.19	1.009	29.49	0.994
MT05ALL	**25.53**	0.964	29.17	0.986	29.03	0.989	32.06	0.996	32.37	1.002	29.63	0.987
best−worst	0.55		0.97		0.95		1.24		1.53		0.99	

Table 6: **Tuning on MT05 and testing on MT04.** Shown are BLEU scores and hypothesis/reference length ratios. The best and the worst BLEU scores for each test MT04 dataset are in **bold** and ~~stroke out~~, respectively; the last row shows the absolute difference between them.

TEST ⇒ TUNE ⇓	AVERAGE BLEU	AVERAGE len	AVG, no self BLEU	AVG, no self len
MT050	33.98	**0.995**	33.78	**0.996**
MT051	**34.28**	0.969	**35.11**	0.971
MT052	33.98	0.975	**35.11**	0.979
MT053	33.37	0.930	31.68	0.922
MT054	34.25	0.971	33.96	0.971

Table 7: **Tuning and testing on MT05.** We tune on the English input in the first column, then we translate all MT05x inputs. We report BLEU and hyp/ref length ratios averaged over (a) all MT05 datasets, and (b) all but the one used for tuning.

TEST	REF: all-but-X BLEU	REF: all-but-X len
MT050	63.38	**0.998**
MT051	58.20	0.992
MT052	62.73	0.994
MT053	66.88	1.026
MT054	**70.53**	1.005

Table 8: **X vs. all-but-X for MT05.** BLEU scores and hyp/ref length ratios when testing on each English input, using all the rest as references.

TEST	Our System BLEU	Our System len	Google BLEU	Google len
MT050	34.56	1.010	33.79	1.024
MT051	30.54	1.014	30.74	1.027
MT052	30.52	1.020	30.76	1.033
MT053	**38.66**	0.944	**37.66**	0.956
MT054	36.17	**0.992**	36.08	**1.005**

Table 9: **Backtranslate MT05.** BLEU scores and hyp/ref length ratios when backtranslating the Arabic reference to English, and then evaluating it with respect to each of the English inputs.

TUNE	Our System BLEU	Our System len	Google BLEU	Google len
B1	**29.64**	**1.011**	29.33	**1.017**
B1-BP	29.36	1.014	**29.43**	**1.017**
B1-SG	28.93	1.023	29.38	1.020
DL	28.76	1.032	29.08	1.022
MIN-L	27.07	1.068	28.18	1.055
MIN-B1	28.57	1.020	28.82	1.030
MEMT	28.68	1.031	28.69	1.036

Table 10: **Tuning on synthesized MT05 datasets, testing on MT04.** BLEU scores and hyp/ref length ratios averaged over all MT04 test datasets.

Table 10 shows the results when tuning on synthesized datasets. As before, this does not improve over the best individual system. Again, we can blame this on the bad selection of reference, but there could be also something else: selection strategies that synthesize input datasets based on what is *easiest* to translate might not be as useful as we have assumed. In the following section, we give some insight on why this might be the case.

5 Discussion

So far, we have explored input selection alternatives that make use of BLEU as a central criterion (while we have also experimented with some sentence selection strategies based on length, this was peripheral), and, in many cases, these strategies were very successful.

Below we explore two alternative strategies for best input dataset selection for tuning: (a) looking for the dataset that yields a tuning length ratio that is closest to 1, and (b) choosing the hardest input. We further explore the potential of using perplexity for tuning input selection.

5.1 Choosing length closest to 1

Above, we have considered the BLEU/BLEU+1 score as the main criterion for input dataset selection. This makes sense since this is the standard evaluation measure, which we are optimizing at test time. However, there are other reasonable criteria that could be considered. For example, recent work has suggested that length is an important factor for parameter optimization in statistical machine translation (Nakov et al., 2012).

Thus, we considered how the above strategies would work when selecting not the dataset yielding the highest BLEU, but that for which the source/reference length ratio is closest to 1. This turned out to work in some but not all cases.

When tuning on MT04: Table 2 shows that if looking for the best length instead of the best BLEU, the *best-on-tuning* strategy would select MT041, which is the second best choice.

The same choice would make *X-vs-all-but-X* (see Table 3) and *backtranslate* when using our system (see Table 4). With Google Translate, however, it would make the best choice: MT040.

When tuning on MT05: Table 7 shows that *best-on-tuning* would select MT050, which is the worst choice. The same choice would make *X-vs-all-but-X* (see Table 8). Both strategies made the second best choice for MT04. The *backtranslate* strategy, however, selects MT054, both with our SMT system and with Google Translate; this is the second best choice (see Table 9). On MT04, this strategy made an optimal choice.

Overall, the length ratio works great for *backtranslate* (best or second best choice), but for *best-on-tuning* and *X-vs-all-but-X* results are mixed.

5.2 Choosing the hardest dataset

A closer look at the strategies for *backtranslate* and *X-vs-all-but-X* reveals something unexpected: Tables 3, 4, 8, and 9 show that selecting the input dataset with the lowest BLEU would yield an optimal choice in all these cases.

We had assumed that the input that yields the highest BLEU score should be of highest quality, and thus the best to learn from. Instead, a closer inspection has found that the high-BLEU datasets were more literal translations, which were less fluent in English and thus ultimately of lower quality. So, we should really train on the hardest dataset.

In fact, this is not very surprising: a student would learn more from hard lessons than from easy ones. Thus, the best strategy to prepare for an exam is to learn hard rather than easy lessons.

It is reasonable to expect that hard inputs would have lower perplexity with respect to our language model, i.e., that they would be more similar to the training data, and thus that they should be also closer to the expected test time input. We tested this hypothesis by calculating the perplexity for all input MT04 datasets, and we found for MT040 the perplexity is indeed lower than for MT044.

The results are shown in Table 11, where we show the logarithm of the probability instead of the perplexity because the perplexity was too low.

These numbers offer yet another possible explanation about why combining inputs could not improve: it looks like MT040 is much better than the rest, and thus maybe there are simply no enough good translations in the remaining datasets.

INPUT	log P
MT040	**-98,862**
MT041	-106,022
MT042	-103,542
MT043	-104,780
MT044	-106,341

Table 11: **Log-probability of the different inputs** calculated with respect to the language model.

6 Conclusion and Future Work

We have studied the question of how to select/synthesize a good *tuning* dataset for SMT in the special case, when we have multiple possible input (English) versions of the same sentence and a single reference (Arabic) translation.

We have experimented with a number of strategies, and we have found that it is best to tune on the hardest available input, not on the one that yields the highest BLEU score (i.e., the easiest). We believe that this finding has implications on how we should pick good translators and how we should select useful data for parameter optimization. On the other hand, it might also indicate a problem with BLEU as an evaluation measure.

In future work, we plan to test our methods on other Arabic-English datasets that have multiple English references. We further plan experiments with other language pairs, e.g., Chinese-English, which are available from NIST and IWSLT. We also want to study the effect of the tuning dataset selection on evaluation measures other than BLEU, e.g., TER (Snover et al., 2006) and METEOR (Lavie and Denkowski, 2009). Looking at tuning dataset selection that takes the test data into account is another promising direction for future work. Features from quality estimation (Specia et al., 2010) might be also helpful to determine the best input to tune on.

Another related, but different, research direction is about how to best *evaluate* (as opposed to *tune*, which we have explored above) an SMT system in case multiple possible versions of the input sentences are available.

References

Hassan Al-Haj and Alon Lavie. 2012. The impact of Arabic morphological segmentation on broad-coverage English-to-Arabic statistical machine translation. *Machine Translation*, 26(1-2):3–24.

Amittai Axelrod, Xiaodong He, and Jianfeng Gao. 2011. Domain adaptation via pseudo in-domain data selection. In *Proceedings of EMNLP'11*, pages 355–362, Edinburgh, United Kingdom.

George Foster and Roland Kuhn. 2009. Stabilizing minimum error rate training. In *Proceedings of WMT'09*, pages 242–249, Athens, Greece.

George Foster, Cyril Goutte, and Roland Kuhn. 2010. Discriminative instance weighting for domain adaptation in statistical machine translation. In *Proceedings of EMNLP'10*, pages 451–459, Cambridge, MA.

Kenneth Heafield and Alon Lavie. 2010. Combining machine translation output with open source: The Carnegie Mellon multi-engine machine translation scheme. *The Prague Bulletin of Mathematical Linguistics*, 93(1):27–36.

Kenneth Heafield. 2011. KenLM: Faster and smaller language model queries. In *Proceedings of WMT'11*, pages 187–197, Edinburgh, Scotland.

Almut Silja Hildebrand, Matthias Eck, Stephan Vogel, and Alex Waibel. 2005. Adaptation of the translation model for statistical machine translation based on information retrieval. In *Proceedings of EAMT'05*, pages 133–142, Budapest, Hungary.

Ahmed El Kholy and Nizar Habash. 2012. Orthographic and morphological processing for English-Arabic statistical machine translation. *Machine Translation*, 26(1-2):25–45.

Philipp Koehn, Franz Josef Och, and Daniel Marcu. 2003. Statistical phrase-based translation. In *Proceedings of HLT-NAACL'03*, pages 48–54, Edmonton, Canada.

Philipp Koehn, Amittai Axelrod, Alexandra Birch Mayne, Chris Callison-Burch, Miles Osborne, and David Talbot. 2005. Edinburgh system description for the 2005 IWSLT speech translation evaluation. In *Proceedings of IWSLT'05*, Pittsburgh, PA.

Philipp Koehn, Hieu Hoang, Alexandra Birch, Chris Callison-Burch, Marcello Federico, Nicola Bertoldi, Brooke Cowan, Wade Shen, Christine Moran, Richard Zens, Chris Dyer, Ondrej Bojar, Alexandra Constantin, and Evan Herbst. 2007. Moses: Open source toolkit for statistical machine translation. In *Proceedings of ACL'07*, pages 177–180, Prague, Czech Republic.

Alon Lavie and Michael Denkowski. 2009. The METEOR metric for automatic evaluation of machine translation. *Machine Translation*, 23:105–115.

Chin-Yew Lin and Franz Josef Och. 2004. ORANGE: a method for evaluating automatic evaluation metrics for machine translation. In *Proceedings of COLING'04*, pages 501–507, Geneva, Switzerland.

Lemao Liu, Hailong Cao, Taro Watanabe, Tiejun Zhao, Mo Yu, and Conghui Zhu. 2012. Locally training the log-linear model for SMT. In *Proceedings of EMNLP-CoNLL'12*, pages 402–411, Jeju Island, Korea.

Spyros Matsoukas, Antti-Veikko Rosti, and Bing Zhang. 2009. Discriminative corpus weight estimation for machine translation. In *Proceedings of EMNLP'09*, pages 708–717, Singapore.

Evgeny Matusov, Nicola Ueffing, and Hermann Ney. 2006. Computing consensus translation from multiple machine translation systems using enhanced hypotheses alignment. In *Proceedings of EACL'06*, pages 33–40, Trento, Italy.

Robert Moore and William Lewis. 2010. Intelligent selection of language model training data. In *Proceedings of ACL'10*, pages 220–224, Uppsala, Sweden.

Preslav Nakov, Francisco Guzmán, and Stephan Vogel. 2012. Optimizing for sentence-level BLEU+1 yields short translations. In *Proceedings of COLING'12*, pages 1979–1994, Mumbai, India.

Franz Josef Och and Hermann Ney. 2001. Statistical multi-source translation. In *Proceedings of MT Summit*, volume 8, pages 253–258, Santiago de Compostela, Spain.

Kishore Papineni, Salim Roukos, Todd Ward, and Wei-Jing Zhu. 2002. BLEU: a method for automatic evaluation of machine translation. In *Proceedings of ACL'02*, pages 311–318, Philadelphia, PA.

Ryan Roth, Owen Rambow, Nizar Habash, Mona Diab, and Cynthia Rudin. 2008. Arabic morphological tagging, diacritization, and lemmatization using lexeme models and feature ranking. In *Proceedings of ACL'08*, pages 117–120, Columbus, OH.

Josh Schroeder, Trevor Cohn, and Philipp Koehn. 2009. Word lattices for multi-source translation. In *Proceedings of EACL'09*, pages 719–727, Athens, Greece.

Matthew Snover, Bonnie Dorr, Richard Schwartz, Linnea Micciulla, and John Makhoul. 2006. A study of translation edit rate with targeted human annotation. In *Proceedings of AMTA'06*, pages 223–231, Cambridge, MA.

Lucia Specia, Dhwaj Raj, and Marco Turchi. 2010. Machine translation evaluation versus quality estimation. *Machine translation*, 24(1):39–50.

Automatic Cloze-Questions Generation

Annamaneni Narendra, Manish Agarwal and Rakshit shah
LTRC, IIIT-Hyderabad, India
{narendra.annamaneni|manish_agrwal|rakshit_shah}@students.iiit.ac.in

Abstract

Cloze questions are questions containing sentences with one or more blanks and multiple choices listed to pick an answer from. In this work, we present an automatic Cloze Question Generation (CQG) system that generates a list of important cloze questions given an English article. Our system is divided into three modules: sentence selection, keyword selection and distractor selection. We also present evaluation guidelines to evaluate CQG systems. Using these guidelines three evaluators report an average score of 3.18 (out of 4) on Cricket World Cup 2011 data.

1 Introduction

Multiple choice questions (MCQs) have been proved efficient to judge students' knowledge. Manual construction of such questions, however, is a time-consuming and labour-intensive task. Cloze questions (CQs) are fill-in-the-blank questions, where a sentence is given with one or more blanks in it with four alternatives to fill those blanks. As opposed to MCQs where one has to generate the WH style question, CQs use a sentence with blanks to form a question. The sentence could be picked from a document on the topic avoiding the need to generate a WH style question. As a result, automatic CQG has received a lot of research attention recently.

1. *Zaheer Khan opened his account with three consecutive maidens in the world-cup final.*
   (a) Zaheer Khan (b) Lasith Malinga (c) Praveen Kumar (d) Munaf Patel

In the above example CQ, the underlined word (referred to as *keyword*) *Zaheer Khan* is blanked out in the sentence and four alternatives are given. In area of cloze questions, (Sumita et. al., 2005; Lee and Seneff, 2007; Lin et. al., 2007; Pino et. al., 2009; Smith et. al., 2010) have mostly worked in the domain of English language learning. Cloze questions have been generated to test students knowledge of English in using the correct verbs (Sumita et. al., 2005), prepositions (Lee and Seneff, 2007) and adjectives (Lin et. al., 2007) in sentences. Pino et. al. (2009) and Smith et. al. (2010) have generated questions to teach and evaluate student's vocabulary. Agarwal and Mannem (2011) have generated factual cloze questions from a biology text book through heuristically weighted features. They do not use any external knowledge and rely only on information present in the document to generate the CQs with distractors. This restricts the possibilities during distractor selection and leads to poor distractors.

In this work, we present an end-to-end automatic cloze question generating system which adopts a semi-structured approach to generate CQs by making use of a knowledge base extracted from a Cricket [1] portal. Also, unlike previous approaches we add context to the question sentence in the process of creating a CQ. This is done to disambiguate the question and avoid cases where there are multiple answers for a question. In Example 1, we have disambiguated the question by adding context *in the world-cup final*. Such a CQG system can be used in a variety of applications such as quizzing systems, trivia games, assigning fan ratings on social networks by posing game related questions etc.

Automatic evaluation of a CQG system is a very difficult task; all the previous systems have been evaluated manually. But even for the manual evaluation, one needs specific guidelines to evaluate fac-

[1] A popular game played in commonwealth countries such as Australia, England, India, Pakistan etc..

tual CQs when compared to those that are used in language learning scenario. To the best of our knowledge there are no previously published guidelines for this task. In this paper, we also present guidelines to evaluate automatically generated factual CQs.

2 Approach

Our system takes news reports on Cricket matches as input and gives factual CQs as output using a knowledge base on Cricket players and officials collected from the web.

Given a document, the system goes through three stages to generate the cloze questions. In the first stage, informative and relevant sentences are selected and in the second stage, keywords (or words/phrases to be questioned on) are identified in the selected sentence. Distractors (or answer alternatives) for the keyword in the question sentence are chosen in the final stage.

The Stanford CoreNLP tool kit is used for tokenization, POS tagging (Toutanova et. al, 2003), NER (Finkel et. al, 2005), parsing (Klein et. al, 2003) and coreference resolution (Lee et. al, 2011) of sentences in the input documents.

2.1 Sentence Selection

In sentence selection, relevant and informative sentences from a given input article are picked to be the question sentences in cloze questions.

Agarwal and Mannem (2011) uses many summarization features for sentence selection based on heuristic weights. But for this task it is difficult to decide the correct relative weights for each feature without any training data. So our system directly uses a summarizer for selection of important sentences. There are few abstractive summarizers but they perform very poorly, (Michael et. al., 1999) for example. So our system uses an extractive summarizer, MEAD [2] to select important sentences. Top 10 percent of the ranked sentences from the summarizer's output are chosen to generate cloze questions.

2.2 Keywords Selection

This step of the process is selection of words in the selected sentence that can be blanked out. These words are referred to as the keywords in the sentence. For a good factual CQ, a keyword should be the word/phrase/clause that tests the knowledge of the user from the content of the article. This keyword shouldn't be too trivial and neither should be too obscure. For example, in an article on Obama, Obama would make a bad keyword.

The system first collects all the potential keywords from a sentence in a list and then prunes this list on the basis of observations described later in this section.

Unlike the previous works in this area, our system is not bound to select only one token keyword or to select only nouns and adjectives as a keyword. In our work, a keyword could be a Named Entity (person, number, location, organization or date) (NE), a pronoun (that comes at beginning of a sentence so that its referent is not present in that sentence) or a constituent (selected using the parse tree). In Example 2, the selected keyword is a noun phrase, *carrom ball*.

2. *R Ashwin used his carrom ball to remove the potentially explosive Kirk Edwards in Cricket World Cup 2011.*

2.2.1 Observations

According to our data analysis we have some observations to prune the list that are described below.

- **Relevant tokens should be present in the keyword** There must be few other tokens in a keyword other than stop words[3], common words[4] and topic words [5]. We observed that words given by the TopicS tool are trivial to be keywords as they are easy to predict.

- **Prepositions** The preposition at the beginning of the keyword is an important clue with respect to what the author is looking to check. So, we keep it as a part of the question sentence rather than blank it out as the keyword. We also prune the keywords containing one or more prepositions as they more often than not make the question unanswerable and sometimes introduce a possibility for multiple answers to such questions.

[2]MEAD is a publicly available toolkit for multi-lingual summarization and evaluation. The toolkit implements multiple summarization algorithms (at arbitrary compression rates) such as position-based, Centroid[RJB00], TF*IDF, and query-based methods (http://www.summarization.com/mead)

[3]In computing, stop words are words which are filtered out prior to, or after processing of natural language data (text). http://armandbrahaj.blog.al/2009/04/14/list-of-english-stop-words/

[4]Most common words in English taken from http://en.wikipedia.org/wiki/Most_common_words_in_English.

[5]Topics (words) which the article talks about. We used the TopicS tool (Lin and Hovy, 2000)

We also use the observations, presented by (Agarwal and Mannem, 2011) in their keyword selection step, such as, a keyword must not repeat in the sentence again and its term frequency should not be high, a keyword should not be the entire sentence, etc. We use the score given by the TopicS tool to filter the keywords with high frequency.

The above criteria reduces the potential keywords' list by a significant amount. Among the rest of the keywords, our system gives preference to NE (persons, location, organization, numbers and dates (in order)), noun phrases, verb phrases in order. To preserve the overall quality of a set of generated questions, system checks that any answer should not be present in other questions. In case of a tie term frequency is used.

3 Distractor Selection

The previous two stages (*sentence selection* and *keyword selection*) are not domain specific in nature i.e. they work fine irrespective of the dataset and domain chosen. But the same is not true for *distractor selection* because the quality of distractors largely depends on the domain. We have performed experiments and presented the results on the domain Cricket. Consider Example 3.

3. *Sehwag had hit a boundary from the first ball of six of India's previous eight innings in Cricket World Cup 2011.*
   (a) Ponting (b) Sehwag (c) Zaheer (d) Marsh

In *Example 3*, although all the distractors are of the domain of Cricket, the distractors are not good enough to create confusion. We have some clues in the given sentence that can be exploited to provide distractors that pose a greater challenge to the students: (i) Someone hitting a boundary on the first ball must be a Top-order batsman and (ii) *India* in the sentence implies that the batsman is from Indian team. But out of the three distractors, one is an Indian bowler (*Zaheer*) and the other two are Australian Top-order batsmen (*Ponting* and *Marsh*). Hence answer of the question can easily be chosen which is *Sehwag*.

Player's name	Team	Playing Role	Batting Style	Bowling Style
Sachin Ramesh Tendulkar	India	Top-order batsman	Right hand	Right-arm, Off Break
Zaheer Khan	India	Fast bowler	Right hand	Left-arm, Faster
Virendra Sehwag	India	Top-order batsman	Right hand	Right-arm, Off Break
Ricky Ponting	Australia	Top-order batsman	Right hand	-

Table 1: Knowledge Base

To present more meaningful and useful distractors, the stage is domain dependent and also uses a knowledge base. The system extracts clues from the sentences to present meaningful distractors. The knowledge base is collected by crawling players' pages available at `http://www.espncricinfo.com`. Each page has a variety of information about the player such as name, playing style, birth date, playing role, major teams etc. This information is widely used to make better choices through out the system. Sample rows and columns from the database of players are shown in the Table 1. The Distractors are selected such that none of them already occur in the question sentence.

For the Cricket domain, the system takes only the NEs as keywords. So if a keyword's NE Tag is location/number/date/organization, then system selects three distractors from the database randomly. But in case when the NE tag is a person's name, three distractors are selected based on (i) the properties of the keyword and (ii) the clues in the question sentence. The distractor selection method is shown in Figure 1.

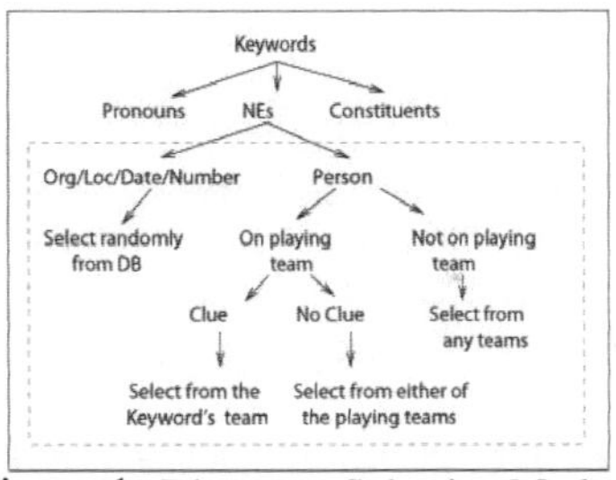

Figure 1: Distractor Selection Method

In case of a person's name *team name*, *playing role*, *batting style* and *bowling style* are the features of a keyword (Table 1). The system looks for clues in the sentence such as team names and other player names. According to the features and clues extracted by the system, three distractors are chosen either from the same team as that of the keyword or from both playing teams or from any team playing in the tournament. Distractors are selected such that none of them already occur in the question sentence. Remainder of this section describes different strategies incorporated in order to handle different cases.

3.1 Select distractors from a single team

The presence of a team name or of a team player of any of the two playing teams is a direct clue for selecting the distractors from the team of the keyword. It does not matter that the team name is of

Score	Sentence		Keyword	Distractor
4	Very informative	Very relevant	Question worthy	Three are useful
3	Informative	Relevant	Question worthy but span is wrong	Two are useful
2	Remotely informative	Remotely relevant	Question worthy but not the best	One is useful
1	Not at all informative	Not at all relevant	Not at all question worthy	None is useful

Table 2: Evaluation Guidelines

the player which is our keyword or of the team he is playing against as long as it is either of these two. Consider *Example 3* and *Example 4*.

4. ***MS Dhoni*** *trumped a poetic century from* <u>*Mahela Jayawardene*</u> *to pull off the highest run-chase ever achieved in a World Cup final.*
   (a) Kumar Sangakkara (b) Upul Tharanga
   (c) Mahela Jayawardene (d) Chamara Silva

In *Example 3*, the system finds explicitly *India*, the team name whereas in *Example 4*, the system finds a player of the opponent team, *MS Dhoni*. In both these cases, the distractors are selected from the team that the keyword belongs to.

3.2 Select distractors from both the teams

We observed that we could choose distractors from either of the teams if there are no features indicating a particular playing team and the keyword is from one of the two teams. So the system can select three distractors from any of the two playing teams, which is a larger source to select the distractors.

In *Example 1*, there are no features indicating that the distractors should all belong to either team *India* or team *Sri Lanka* knowing that the world cup final was played between India and Sri Lanka. So, we can select distractors from both the teams in such cases.

3.3 Select distractors from any team

If the keyword in a question does not belong to either of the teams then it could be a name of an umpire or a player from the other teams. In case of an umpire, we randomly select three umpires from the list of umpires for that tournament. And in case of a player that belongs to neither of the teams playing the match, we randomly pick three players with the same *playing role* as that of the keyword from any team, doesn't matter playing or not.

4 Evaluation Guidelines and Results

Automatic evaluation of any CQG system is difficult for two reasons i) agreeing on standard evaluation data is difficult ii) there is no one particular set of CQs that is correct. Most question generation systems hence rely on manual evaluation. However, there are no specific guidelines for the manual evaluation either. In this paper, we also present evaluation guidelines for a CQG system that we believe are suitable for the task. The proposed evaluation guidelines are shown in Table 2.

Evaluation is done in three phases: (i) Evaluation of selected sentences, (ii) Evaluation of selected keywords and (iii) Evaluation of selected distractors. The evaluation of the selected sentences is done using two metrics, namely, informativeness and relevance. Merging the two metrics into one can mislead because a sentence might be informative but not relevant and vice versa. In such a case, assigning a score of three for one possibility and two to the other will not do justice to the system. The keywords are evaluated for their question worthiness and correctness of their span. Finally, the distractors are evaluated for their usability (i.e. the score is the number of distractors that are useful). A distractor is useful if it can't be discounted easily through simple elimination techniques.

The overall score for every cloze question is calculated by taking the average of all the four metrics for a question. The overall score on the entire data is the mean of scores of each question.

Evaluator		4	3	2	1
Eval-1	Informativeness	8	10	3	1
	Relevance	4	15	3	0
	Keywords	16	0	5	1
	Distractors	11	4	4	3
Eval-2	Informativeness	13	7	2	0
	Relevance	9	11	2	0
	Keywords	7	0	15	0
	Distractors	6	14	1	1
Eval-3	Informativeness	9	9	4	0
	Relevance	8	10	4	0
	Keywords	7	0	15	0
	Distractors	14	5	3	0

Table 3: Results (Eval: Evaluator)

Cloze questions generated from news reports on two Cricket World Cup 2011 matches were used for evaluation. 22 questions (10+12) were generated and evaluated by three different evaluators using the above mentioned guidelines. The results are listed in Table 3. The overall accuracy of our system is 3.15 (Eval-1), 3.14 (Eval-2) and 3.26 (Eval-3) out of 4. The accuracy of the distractors is 3.05 (Eval-1), 3.14 ((Eval-2) and 3.5 (Eval-3) out of 4.

5 Conclusion & Future Work

This paper proposed the automatic generation of *Multiple Choice Questions*(MCQs). The proposed method generates MCQs using summarisation tool ,TopicS tool and knowledge base from the web.We have proposed a novel approach for distractor selection using knowledge base for the specific domain.The proposed constraints for the distractor selection makes questions effective.We have proposed the evaluation guidelines to evaluate multiple choice questions at three stages.

We believe that there is still much room for improvement.Firstly distractor selection proposal was done for specific domain ,these constraints can be generalised to any domain. Proposed evaluation guidelines do evaluation question by question only.The overall performance of the system,taking into account the entire document is not performed .This is left for future work.

References

Chin-Yew Lin and Eduard Hovy 2000 *The automated acquisition of topic signatures for text summarization.* In Proceedings of COLING 2000.

Dan Klein and Christopher D. Manning 2003 *Accurate Unlexicalized Parsing.* Proceedings of the 41st Meeting of the Association for Computational Linguistics, pp. 423-430.

Eiichiro Sumita, Fumiaki Sugaya, and Seiichi Yamamoto. 2005 *Measuring Non-native Speakers Proficiency of English by Using a Test with Automatically-Generated Fill-in-the-Blank Questions.* 2nd Wkshop on Building Educational Applications using NLP, Ann Arbor

Heeyoung Lee, Yves Peirsman, Angel Chang, Nathanael Chambers, Mihai Surdeanu, Dan Jurafsky. 2011 *Stanford's Multi-Pass Sieve Coreference Resolution System at the CoNLL-2011 Shared Task.* In Proceedings of the CoNLL-2011 Shared Task, 2011.

Jenny Rose Finkel, Trond Grenager, and Christopher Manning 2005 *Incorporating Non-local Information into Information Extraction Systems by Gibbs Sampling.* Proceedings of the 43nd Annual Meeting of the Association for Computational Linguistics (ACL 2005), pp. 363-370

John Lee and Stephanie Seneff. 2007 *Automatic Generation of Cloze Items for Prepositions.* CiteSeerX - Scientific Literature Digital Library and Search Engine [http://citeseerx.ist.psu.edu/oai2] (United States).

Juan Pino, Michael Heilman and Maxine Eskenazi. 2009 *A Selection Strategy to Improve Cloze Question Quality* Wkshop on Intelligent Tutoring Systems for Ill-Defined Domains. 9th Int. Conf. on ITS.

Kristina Toutanova, Dan Klein, Christopher Manning, and Yoram Singer 2003 *Feature-Rich Part-of-Speech Tagging with a Cyclic Dependency Network* In Proceedings of HLT-NAACL 2003, pp. 252-259.

Lin, Y. C., Sung, L. C., Chen and M. C.: 2007 *An Automatic Multiple-Choice Question Generation Scheme for English Adjective Understanding* CCE 2007 Workshop Proc. of Modeling, Management and Generation of Problems / Questions in eLearning, pp. 137-142.

Manish Agarwal and Prashanth Mannem 2011 *Automatic Gap-fill Question Generation from Text Book.* In the proceeding of, The 6th Workshop on Innovative Use of NLP for Building Educational Applications, ACL-HLT 2011.

Michael J.Witbrock and Vibhu O. Mittal. 1999 *Ultra-Summarization: A Statistical Approach to Generating Highly Condensed Non-Extractive Summaries.* In Proceedings of the 22nd annual international ACM SIGIR conference on Research and development in information retrieval.

Simon Smith, P.V.S Avinesh and Adam Kilgarriff. 2010 *Gap-fill Tests for Language Learners: Corpus-Driven Item Generation.*

High-Accuracy Phrase Translation Acquisition Through Battle-Royale Selection

Lionel Nicolas Egon W. Stemle Klara Kranebitter Verena Lyding
Institute for Specialised Communication and Multilingualism,
European Academy of Bozen/Bolzano
{lionel.nicolas,egon.stemle,klara.kranebitter,verena.lyding}@eurac.edu

Abstract

In this paper, we report on an unsupervised greedy-style process for acquiring phrase translations from sentence-aligned parallel corpora. Thanks to innovative selection strategies, this process can acquire multiple translations without size criteria, i.e. phrases can have several translations, can be of any size, and their size is not considered when selecting their translations. Even though the process is in an early development stage and has much room for improvements, evaluation shows that it yields phrase translations of high precision that are relevant to machine translation but also to a wider set of applications including memory-based translation or multi-word acquisition.

1 Introduction

This paper reports on work in progress to acquire contiguous phrase translations from sentence-aligned parallel corpora in an unsupervised way.

The described process has three key features: it allows to acquire multiple translations for each phrase, the acquired translations can comprise phrases of any length,[1] and it does not rely on any relation between the sizes of the phrases (no *fertility* criteria). In addition, its performance, especially its precision, allows for competition with the state-of-the-art. Furthermore, the acquired phrase translations can be used for performing machine translation, and memory-based translation; phrase/word alignment; multi-word, paraphrase, and synonymy acquisition; and error correction.

The process starts by generating an exhaustive set of candidate translations and coarsely filters them. It then provides the remaining set to a greedy fine-grained selection that processes one candidate translation at each iteration. The iteration stops when no candidate translations remain.

The main contributions of this paper are (1) to introduce a set of filters for the coarse filtering of candidate translations, and (2) to describe a greedy-style process for performing a fine-grained selection of translations.

In section 2 and 6, we describe the state-of-the-art and, in section 3 and 4, the process itself. We then present its results in section 5, compare it with related work in section 6, highlight future works in section 7 and conclude in section 8.

2 Related works

The process described here can be considered in between two lines of approaches: bilingual lexicon acquisition and phrase translations extraction from word alignments or translations.

Methods performing bilingual lexicon acquisition focus on short phrases, mostly with one or two tokens. They generally use association measures to rank candidate translations and apply several thresholds to decide which ones to keep (Gale and Church, 1991; Melamed, 1995; Wu and Xia, 1994). Most association measures used focus on recurrent occurrences, except methods like Widdows et al. (2002) which apply measures from semantic similarity approaches. Some approaches rely on either or both part-of-speech knowledge (Tufis, 2002; Ma et al., 2011) and transliterations (Tsuji and Kageura, 2004). As explained in Melamed (1997), incorrect translations can be generated because some phrases co-occur too often with the correct translation of a phrase[2]. The commonly used counter-measure is to discard a candidate translation in a bitext if it competes with another one with a higher score (Moore, 2001; Melamed, 1997; Melamed, 2000;

[1] We only use a loose maximum length restriction in order to limit exponential computation

[2] These are usually named *indirect associations*.

Tsuji and Kageura, 2004; Tufis, 2002; Yamamoto et al., 2003). The evaluation of the extracted lexica is mostly performed by classifying the generated translations into three categories: *wrong*, *correct* and *near misses*.

The line of approaches for extracting phrase translations from word alignments or translations are built on the outputs of the ones performing bilingual lexicon acquisition[3] (Neubig et al., 2011; Tillmann, 2003; Tambouratzis et al., 2012; Venugopal et al., 2003; Vogel, 2005; Moore and Quirk, 2007; Deng and Byrne, 2008; Koehn et al., 2003; DeNero and Klein, 2008). Some methods such as Zettlemoyer and Moore (2007) and Duan et al. (2011) work on top of the others by refining the phrase translations table acquired. While describing each of the numerous methods would go beyond the scope of this paper, we can summarize that most methods apply a similar set of ideas and combine them in a diversified manner. So as to evaluate a phrase translation, they usually combine features such as translation probabilities, expected size of the translation (often called *fertility*), expected position of the translation and number of word alignments included. Apart from the word alignments or translations, few methods rely on additional data such as part-of-speech. Performances are usually evaluated indirectly through the performance of a machine translation tool taking the phrase translations as input.

Since we could not find previous works for a direct comparison, a global one with related work is provided later in sect. 6.

3 Generation of candidates

3.1 Phrase collection

For each bitext bit : $sent\_l1 \parallel sent\_l2$ of the N available bitexts, we tokenize sentences $sent\_l1$ and $sent\_l2$, count their number of tokens and compute the two global values num_tok_l1 and num_tok_l2, i.e. the number of overall tokens in the $l1$ and $l2$ part of the corpus. Then, we add a start-of-sentence *-s-* token and e *-/s*-end-of-sentence *-/s-* one and generate all contiguous phrases in each bitext[4]. For each generated phrase ph of a language $lang$ we register four values.

(1) The number of tokens $size\_ph(ph)$.

(2) The global number of occurrences

$occ\_ph(ph) = \sum_{i=1}^{N\_bit} occ\_b\_ph(bit_i, ph)$

where $occ\_b\_ph(bit, ph)$ is the number of occurrences of ph in a bitext bit.

(3) The left and right diversity $left\_div\_ph(ph)$ and $right\_div\_ph(ph)$, i.e. the size of the set of different tokens/1-grams that occur next to ph.

(4) The value $num\_tok\_opp(ph)$ that corresponds to the number of tokens in the sentences of the other language (not $lang$) for the bitexts in which ph occurs.

We then discard phrases occurring less than min_occ times, i.e. when $occ\_ph(ph) < min\_occ$, and all l1 phrases with more than max_size_l1 tokens[5], i.e. when $size\_ph(ph\_l1) > max\_size\_l1$.

3.2 Candidate translations building

For every bitext bit : $sent\_l1 \parallel sent\_l2$ with l1 phrases $ph\_l1_1..ph\_l1_j$ and l2 phrases $ph\_l2_1..ph\_l2_l$, we compute the Cartesian product $[ct_1 : ph\_l1_1 \parallel ph\_l2_1], .., [ct_k : ph\_l1_j \parallel ph\_l2_l]$. A generated candidate translation $[ct : ph\_l1 \parallel ph\_l2]$ is said to occur in bit and two values are registered.

(1) The set of 1-grams occurring before and after ph_l1 and ph_l2 in the bitext.

(2) The number of occurrences $occ\_ct(bit, ct)$

$$occ\_ct(bit, ct) = min(occ\_bit\_ph(bit, ph\_l1) \quad occ\_bit\_ph(bit, ph\_l2))$$

Once every bitext has been processed, we compute the following values for every candidate translation $[ct : ph\_l1 \parallel ph\_l2]$.

(1) The size of ct.

$size\_ct(ct) = size\_ct(ph\_l1) + size\_ph(ph\_l2)$

(2) The global number of occurrences.

$glob\_occ\_ct(ct) = \sum_{i=1}^{N_{bit}} occ\_ct(bit_i, ct)$

(3) The original relative frequency of ct.

$orig\_freq\_ct(ct) = \frac{occ\_ph(ph\_l1)*occ\_ph(ph\_l2)}{num\_tok\_l1*num\_tok\_l2}$

(4) The values $num\_occ\_ph(ct, ph\_l1)$ and $num\_occ\_ph(ct, ph\_l2)$, which correspond to the number of occurrences of ph_l1 and ph_l2 in the set of bitexts where ct occurs.

(5) The conditional relative frequency of ct over the set of bitexts where it occurs.

$cond\_freq\_ct(ct) = \frac{num\_occ\_ph(ct,ph\_l1)*num\_occ\_ph(ct,ph\_l2)}{num\_tok\_opp(ph\_l2)*num\_tok\_opp(ph\_l1)}$

(6) The "strength", between 0 and 1, of ct, i.e. the likeliness of ct to be valid.

$str\_ct(ct) = cond\_freq\_ct(ct) - orig\_freq\_ct(ct)$

(7) The values $left\_div\_ct(ph, ct)$ and $right\_div\_ct(ph, ct)$ of ph_l1 and ph_l2, which

[3] The well known IBM models are a popular choice.

[4] The shortest phrase being one token and the longest phrase being the sentence itself.

[5] We do not apply such limits on the l2 phrases so as to not discard valid translations of the kept l1 phrases.

represent the size of the set of the different 1-grams occurring at their left or right side in all bitexts where ct occurs.

(8) The "context diversity" of ct[6].

$$context\_div(ct) = min(left\_div\_ct(ph\_l1, ct), right\_div\_ct(ph\_l1, ct), left\_div\_ct(ph\_l2, ct), right\_div\_ct(ph\_l2, ct))$$

3.3 Coarse filtering

Each candidate translation is submitted to four filters that aims at limiting computation by discarding the least likely ones [7] while leaving the selection of the remaining ones to the more sophisticated and computationally intense *battle-royale* method (see sect. 4).

Occurrence. This filter aims at dealing with candidate translations that combine completely unrelated phrases, i.e. candidate translations resulting from randomness[8]. A candidate translation ct is discarded if:
(1) it occurs in less than min_co_occ bitexts,
(2) in the bitexts where ct occurs, ph_l1 or ph_l2 occurs less than min_co_freq percents of their global number of occurrences.

If $occ\_ph(ph\_l1) * min\_co\_freq > num\_occ\_ph(ct, ph\_l1)$
Or $occ\_ph(ph\_l2) * min\_co\_freq > num\_occ\_ph(ct, ph\_l2)$

Context diversity. This filter has been designed to discard candidate translations that imply occurrences of either ph_l1 or ph_l2 with a limited left or right context.

This usually happens with indirect associations (Melamed, 1997) or candidate translations that combine a phrase with another one that is not the correct translation but includes the correct one. For example, for most occurrences of a candidate translation $[ct : the\ big \parallel la\ grande\ casa]$, the occurrences of $the\ big$ will have a low variability on its right context, i.e. it will almost always be followed by $house$. In order to detect that the context of a phrase ph is limited, we build on the assumption that values $left\_div\_ph(ph)$ and $right\_div\_ph(ph)$ follow a logarithmic curve as $occ\_ph(ph)$ augments. Therefore, the coefficient obtained from dividing the number of different contexts over the number of occurrences should decrease as the number of occurrences increases.

Since $occ\_ct(ct)$ is either inferior or equal to both $occ\_ph(ph\_l1)$ and $occ\_ph(ph\_l2)$, the following conditions should be fulfilled:

$$\frac{left\_div\_ct(ph\_l1, ct)}{glob\_occ\_ct(ct)} \geq \frac{left\_div\_ph(ph\_l1)}{glob\_occ\_ph(ph\_l1)}$$

$$\frac{left\_div\_ct(ph\_l2, ct)}{glob\_occ\_ct(ct)} \geq \frac{left\_div\_ph(ph\_l2)}{glob\_occ\_ph(ph\_l2)}$$

$$\frac{right\_div\_ct(ph\_l1, ct)}{glob\_occ\_ct(ct)} \geq \frac{right\_div\_ph(ph\_l1)}{glob\_occ\_ph(ph\_l1)}$$

$$\frac{right\_div\_ct(ph\_l2, ct)}{glob\_occ\_ct(ct)} \geq \frac{right\_div\_ph(ph\_l2)}{glob\_occ\_ph(ph\_l2)}$$

Conditional frequency. This filter relies on the idea that the occurrence of a phrase ph_l1 triggers the occurrence of a translation ph_l2 in the same bitext and vice-versa. The relative frequencies over the bitexts where ct occurs for both phrases should thus be greater than their global frequency. A candidate translation is thus discarded when:

$$\text{If } \frac{num\_occ\_ct\_ph(ct, ph\_l2)}{num\_tok\_opp(ph\_l1)} \leq \frac{glob\_occ\_ph(ph\_l2)}{num\_tok\_l1}$$

$$\text{Or } \frac{num\_occ\_ct\_ph(ct, ph\_l1)}{num\_tok\_opp(ph\_l2)} \leq \frac{glob\_occ\_ph(ph\_l1)}{num\_tok\_l2}$$

Maximum number of translations. This filters limits the number of candidate translations covering a given phrase ph to the $max\_translations$ best ones in term of strength str_ct.

4 Battle-royale selection

This core part of our approach is named after a 2000 Japanese film, the story of which metaphorically matches the approach applied for performing the selection of candidate translations. In this movie, young people are involved in a deadly game where only one is meant to survive. This results in group alliances and group conflicts that evolve as the game progresses. The same idea is applied here, conflicts and alliances are spotted among candidate translations and a greedy algorithm processes one candidate translation at a time. Depending on which one gets processed first, the situation of the remaining related ones can evolve drastically.

So as to illustrate how we spot conflicts and alliances, we provide candidate translations over the dummy English-Italian bitext:
$[the\ big\ house\ is\ new \parallel la\ grande\ casa\ è\ nuova]$

4.1 Detecting conflicts

We consider two candidate translations

$$ct_a : ph\_l1_a = t_i..t_j \parallel ph\_l2_a = T_k..T_l$$

[6] The higher it is, the more likely ct is to be valid.

[7] The values we used for configuration are provided in sect. 5.1.

[8] Usually one of the two phrases is a frequent one.

$ct_b : ph\_l1_b = t_m..t_n \parallel ph\_l2_b = T_o..T_p$
as being in conflict over one or several phrases $confl\_ph$ in a bitext bit when one of the following conditions is not met.

Non-concurrency condition. Two candidate translations should not cover the same phrase. E.g. $[the\ big \parallel la\ grande]$ and $[the\ big \parallel grande]$ conflict over $the\ big$.

$*$ If $ph\_l1_a = ph\_l1_b$ and $ph\_l2_a != ph\_l2_b$
Then $confl\_ph = ph\_l1_a$
$*$ If $ph\_l2_a = ph\_l2_b$ and $ph\_l1_a != ph\_l1_b$
Then $confl\_ph = ph\_l2_a$

Consistent inclusion condition. If a phrase in one language covered by a first candidate translation includes the phrase in the same language covered by a second candidate translation, then the two phrases in the other language should have the same relation. E.g. the two candidate translations $[the\ big \parallel la\ grande]$ and $[the\ big\ house \parallel grande\ casa]$ conflict since $the\ big\ house$ includes $the\ big$ but $la\ grande$ does not include $grande\ casa$.

$*$ If $incl(ph\_l1_a, ph\_l1_b)$ and $!incl(ph\_l2_a, ph\_l2_b)$
Then $confl\_ph = ph\_l1_b$
$*$ If $incl(ph\_l2_a, ph\_l2_b)$ and $!incl(ph\_l1_a, ph\_l1_b)$
Then $confl\_ph = ph\_l2_b$
$*$ If $incl(ph\_l1_b, ph\_l1_a)$ and $!incl(ph\_l2_b, ph\_l2_a)$
Then $confl\_ph = ph\_l1_a$
$*$ If $incl(ph\_l2_b, ph\_l2_a)$ and $!incl(ph\_l1_b, ph\_l1_a)$
Then $confl\_ph = ph\_l2_a$

Consistent overlap condition. We say that two phrases overlap when they share a sub-phrase that spans either the left-most or the right-most token of both phrases. For two candidate translations, if two phrases of the same language overlap then the two phrases in the other language should also overlap. E.g. $[the\ big\ house \parallel la\ grande\ casa]$ and $[house\ is\ new \parallel casa\ è\ nuova]$ do not conflict since they both overlap on $house$ and $casa$ but $[the\ big\ house \parallel la\ grande\ casa]$ and $[house\ is\ new \parallel è\ nuova]$ do conflict since they only overlap on $house$.

$*$ If $exists(t_q..t_r)$
with $(q = m$ and $r = j)$ xor $(q = i$ and $r = n)$
and $incl(ph\_l1_a, t_q..t_r)$ and $incl(ph\_l1_b, t_q..t_r)$
and $!exists(T_s..T_t)$
with $(s = o$ and $t = l)$ xor $(s = k$ and $t = p)$
and $incl(ph\_l2_a, T_s..T_t)$ and $incl(ph\_l2_b, T_s..T_t)$
Then $confl\_ph = t_q..t_r$.

$*$ If $exists(T_s..T_t)$
with $(s = o$ and $t = l)$ xor $(s = k$ and $t = p)$
and $incl(ph\_l2_a, T_s..T_t)$ and $incl(ph\_l2_b, T_s..T_t)$
and $!exist(t_q..t_r)$
with $(q = m$ and $r = j)$ xor $(q = i$ and $r = n)$
and $incl(ph\_l1_a, t_q..t_r)$ and $incl(ph\_l1_b, t_q..t_r)$
Then $confl\_ph = T_s..T_t$.

4.2 Detecting alliances

We consider two candidate translations ct_a and ct_b as being in alliance in a bitext bit if there exist pairs of phrases $[al\_ph_l1, al\_ph_l2]$ that are included or equal to the phrases combined by ct_a and ct_b and if ct_a and ct_b are not in conflict. For example, $[the\ big \parallel la\ grande]$ and $[big\ house \parallel grande\ casa]$ are in alliance because they do not conflict and their phrases both include big and $grande$.

4.3 Rating conflicts

If there are two candidate translations ct_a and ct_b conflicting over a phrase $confl\_ph$, and it occurs more than once in a bitext bit (i.e. $occ(bit, confl\_ph) > 1$), then, as we do not perform word/phrase alignment beforehand, we have no certainty that ct_a and ct_b do conflict over the same occurrences of $confl\_ph$.

For example, if in an English sentence the word car occurs twice but is translated to $macchina$ and $auto$ in the Italian counterpart, the candidate translations $[car \parallel macchina]$ and $[car \parallel auto]$ will be considered as conflicting over car even though they are both correct and cover two different occurrences.

For evaluating the strength of a conflict $conf$ between two candidate translations over a set of phrases $confl\_ph$ in a bitext bit, we compute the probability $ap\_cf(bit, ct, confl)$ that each candidate translation ct does apply on the phrases they conflict over.

$ap\_cf(bit, ct, confl) = max(\frac{occ\_ct(bit,ct)}{occ\_ph(bit,confl\_ph)})$

For two candidate translations ct_a and ct_b with a conflict $confl$ in a bitext bit, if $ap\_cf(bit, ct_b, confl) = 1$, we say that ct_a has a hard-conflict (is fully-incompatible) with ct_b.

For a conflict $confl$ in a bitext bit, we compute the impacts over ct_a and ct_b as:

$imp\_cf(bit, confl, ct_a) = ap\_cf(bit, ct_b, confl) * str\_ct(ct_b)$
$imp\_cf(bit, confl, ct_b) = ap\_cf(bit, ct_a, confl) * str\_ct(ct_a)$

Once all local conflicts of a candidate translation ct are rated, we calculate:

(1) the value $nb\_hard\_confl(ct)$ corresponding to the number of bitexts in which ct has at least one hard-conflict,
(2) the sum $sum\_confl(ct)$ of all imp_cf values of the local conflicts it is involved in,
(3) the value $avg\_confl(ct)$ indicating how much, in average, ct conflicts with other candidate translations.
$avg\_confl(ct) = \frac{sum\_confl(ct)}{occ\_ct(ct)}$

4.4 Rating alliances

For evaluating the strength of an alliance between two candidate translations regarding pairs of phrases $[al\_ph_{l1}, al\_ph_{l2}]$ in a bitext bit, we also compute the probability $ap\_al(bit, ct, al)$ that each candidate translation ct does apply on the phrases on which they are in alliance.
$ap\_al(bit, ct, al) = max(\frac{2*occ\_ct(bit,ct)}{occ\_ph(bit,al\_ph_{l1})*occ\_ph(bit,al\_ph_{l2})})$

For an alliance al in a bitext bit, we compute the impacts over ct_a and ct_b as:
$imp\_al(bit, al, ct_a) = ap\_al(bit, ct_b, al) * str\_ct(ct_b)$
$imp\_al(bit, al, ct_b) = ap\_al(bit, ct_a, al) * str\_ct(ct_a)$

Once all local alliances of each candidate translation ct are rated, we calculate:
(1) the sum $sum\_al(ct)$ of all imp_al values of the local alliances ct is involved in,
(2) the value $avg\_al(ct)$ indicating how much, in average, ct is in alliance with other candidate translations.
$avg\_al(ct) = \frac{sum\_al(ct)}{occ\_ct(ct)}$

4.5 Greedy-style selection

We start by computing the value $popularity(ct)$ of each candidate translation ct in order to perform the final selection.
$popularity(ct) = avg\_confl(ct) - str\_ct(ct) - avg\_al(ct)$

We then order the candidate translations according to, by order of importance, their $popularity$ (decrementally), str_c (incrementally), $context\_div$ (incrementally) an $size\_ct$ (incrementally) values[9].

Making use of this sorting procedure, a greedy-style selection is applied to the list of translation candidates that iterates as follows.
(1) Sort the list of candidate translations.
(2) Remove the first candidate translation ct.
(3) If $nb\_hard\_confl(ct) < \frac{occ\_ct(ct)}{2}$, then consider ct as valid and output it.
(4) Regardless of step 3, nullify its conflicts and alliances and update accordingly the avg_confl, avg_al and nb_hard_confl values of the related candidate translations.

At any iteration, even though a correct candidate translation can be ordered among the next candidates to be processed (and thus to be removed), its processing will be postponed as long as the ones with which it conflicts get selected before. Indeed, the more the values avg_confl and nb_hard_confl are updated, the more the candidate translation goes towards the end of the list. The exact opposite behaviour applies to the alliances: the more the values avg_al are updated, the more a candidate translation goes towards the beginning of the list. The later a candidate translation gets selected, the more likely it is to be considered as valid and kept in step 3.

5 Evaluation

5.1 Input corpora and configuration

To perform the evaluation, we used the 90345 bitexts of the *Catex* Corpus (Streiter et al., 2004). This bilingual corpus is a collection of Italian legal texts sentence-aligned with their German translations. Italian and German are a challenging pair since they have distinct word orders and handle gender, number and case in a rather different manner. The average length of Italian and German sentences are 23.2 and 21.8 tokens.

Regarding the thresholds used to coarsely limit the candidate translation generation (see sect. 3.1 and sect. 3.3), we chose very loose thresholds in order to evaluate the potential of the process. Therefore, a phrase had to occur only twice to be considered ($min\_occ = 2$), and, if German, could not have more than 10 tokens ($max\_size\_l1 = 10$). So as to be considered as possible translations, two phrases needed to co-occur in at least two bitexts ($min\_co\_occ = 2$) and co-occur in at least 5% of the bitexts of one another ($min\_co\_app = 0.05$). A phrase was allowed to have at maximum 20 possible translations ($max\_translations = 20$).

The process required 5 days of computation on a modern computer and the memory consumption raised up to 30 GB.

5.2 Formal Evaluation protocol

We decided to evaluate the phrase translations acquired with two metrics: an evaluation metric that we call hereafter *Scalable precision* that intends

[9] If two candidate translations have the same value for a given criterion, the next one is used for sorting.

to be as similar to the measures for evaluating the bilingual lexicon extraction methods described in Melamed (2000) and Moore (2001) and the well-known BLEU metric (Papineni et al., 2002).

We started from a manual evaluation where the evaluator, when necessary, corrects a candidate translation and count the minimum number of tokens $errors(ct)$ that are to be added or deleted in both phrases. For example, a candidate translation $[ct_b$: $landesgesetz\ vom\ 8.\ november \parallel provinciale\ 8\ novembre]$ requires to add $legge$ at the beginning of the Italian phrase and thus receives a score $errors(ct_b) = 1$. A total of 1000 randomly chosen candidate translations have been evaluated by a trained translator.

We then used the manually corrected candidate translations as gold standard to compute the *BLEU precision* both ways ($l1 \rightarrow l2$ and $l2 \rightarrow l1$) and the $errors(ct)$ values to compute the *Scalable precision* as follows.

$sca\_prec = 1 - \frac{errors(ct)}{size\_ct(ct)}$

5.3 Results

74771 candidate translations were considered as valid by the *battle-royale* selection.

As we can see in Table 1, among the phrases selected (see sect. 3.1), the coverage of the phrases, i.e. the number of phrases with at least one translation, drops quickly as the size of the phrases increases. The coverage is rather equivalent for small phrases of both languages. However, because of the max_size_l1 length threshold that filters out ($l1$) German phrases only, coverage is less important for Italian ($l2$) as the size of the phrases increases.

When studying the results more closely, we observe two phenomena limiting coverage. The first one is when all the translations of a phrase are not originally selected (see sect. 3.1). This happens with low frequency phrases with several translations due, overall, to the different way Italian and German handle gender, number and case. Dealing with lemmas instead of forms would avoid such issue. The second phenomenon limiting coverage is related to word order: contiguous phrases in one language are translated to non-contiguous ones in the other language. Our method does not yet cope with such aspect.

The vast majority of the phrases in both languages were associated with only one translation. However, 2857 phrases in German and 5131 Italian phrases have been associated with multiple translations (respectively 2.3 in average for both language).

As we can see in Table 2, of the candidate translations manually evaluated, 54.6% were perfect and correcting the other ones required to add or delete 2.3 tokens in average. The *Scalable* and the *BLEU precision* are very similar: when considering all candidate translations equivalent in weight ($weight(ct) = 1$), both metrics score an average precision around $83 \sim 85\%$. When we consider the weight of a candidate translation equal to its size multiplied by its number of occurrences ($weight(ct) = size(ct) * glob\_occ\_ct(ct)$), $Scalable_{bis}$ and $BLEU_{bis}$ values, average precision raises up to $93 \sim 94\%$[10].

5.4 Evaluating improvements

As it is designed, the process has the useful property that improving the selection improves both precision and coverage. Indeed, so as to illustrate the idea, we could compare it to the tetris-like task of ordering the content of a box: the more ordered the objects inside the box are, the more objects fit in this limited space. Since the number of phrases to be covered is also finite and since the biggest set of non-conflicting candidate translations should be the set including all correct ones, comparing two versions of the method can be straightforwardly estimated with no gold-standard, by observing if the number of candidate translations acquired has raised.

6 Comparison with related work

As layed out in sect. 2, the approach described here can be situated midway between methods for acquiring bilingual lexicon and methods for extracting phrase translations from word translations and/or alignments.

Comparing our method, on a global perspective, with the ones for acquiring bilingual lexica, we see five main aspects to highlight. First, we are able to acquire much longer phrases. Second, the step of our approach performing candidate translation generation and coarse filtering is similar to the other methods. Third, the threshold we use to validate or discard a candidate translation is

[10] Since we acquire translations instead of generating some, we don't have to deal with word order issues. This also explain why *BLEU* scores are way higher than usually reported in litterature

Phrase Size	1	2	3	4	5	6	7	8	9	10	11	12	13	14	15	16	17	18	19	≥ 20
German cov.	38.2	14.6	10.1	8.5	7.7	7.2	5.3	4.5	2.7	3.5	-	-	-	-	-	-	-	-	-	-
Italian cov.	43	13	8	6.6	6	5.4	4.1	3.3	2.2	1.5	1	0.8	0.4	0.3	0.2	0.1	< 0.1	< 0.1	< 0.1	< 0.1

Table 1: Coverage

Size	2	3	4	5	6	7	8	9	10	11	12	13	14	15	16	17	≥ 18	Total
Nb evaluated	115	65	168	87	108	75	79	51	61	40	41	24	22	19	15	6	24	**1000**
Nb perfect	78.3	16.9	76.2	36.8	63.0	41.3	62.0	25.5	50.8	35.0	75.6	45.8	50.0	52.6	13.3	33.3	50.0	**54.6**
Avg errors	1.7	1.5	1.9	2.0	2.2	1.8	3.3	2.7	2.5	3.0	4.0	2.9	2.7	1.7	2.9	2.8	3.9	**2.3**
Scalable	81.7	57.9	88.8	75.2	86.6	84.6	84.5	77.8	87.5	82.5	91.9	87.8	90.3	94.7	84.2	89.2	89.1	**83.2**
Scalable$_{bis}$	99.1	60.3	93.0	79.2	91.2	89.3	86.6	79.3	93.3	84.6	94.5	91.3	91.5	95.5	87.4	89.2	88.7	**93.6**
Bleu	84.5	71.6	91.8	79.5	88.3	84.2	83.9	76.9	85.9	82.1	91.2	86.9	89.0	94.2	86.2	88.2	90.2	**85.2**
Bleu$_{bis}$	99.2	74.1	95.0	83.0	92.5	89.1	85.7	78.1	92.5	84.3	94.1	90.5	90.3	95.4	88.8	88.2	90.0	**94.1**

Table 2: Candidate translations statistics and evaluation

dynamically adjusted and therefore less restrictive and prone to bias than manually set thresholds. Fourth, our *battle-royale* selection implements the selection algorithm used by other methods where concurrency conflicts are considered (Moore, 2001; Melamed, 1997; Melamed, 2000; Tsuji and Kageura, 2004; Tufis, 2002; Yamamoto et al., 2003) and extends it to a more sophisticated level. Fifth, even though a straight comparison with reported results is irrelevant, ours seem competitive and promising both in term of coverage and precision.

Comparing our method, on a global perspective, with the ones for extracting phrase translations from word translations and/or alignments, we see three main aspects to highlight. First, we do not take word alignments or translations as input. We believe that identifying word translations first would lead to diminished results. Indeed, in addition to the size issue, i.e. the translation of a word can have several tokens, translations of longer phrases are sometimes easier to identify than the translations of the phrases they contain. An example of this would be a non-ambiguous phrase containing a polysemous word. We thus aim at considering them all together at the same time. The second aspect to highlight is that we do use a feature similar to translation probabilities (i.e. $strength$ value) but do not directly intend to evaluate the expected size and position of the translation or the alignment of the sub-phrases included. We however indirectly rely on the *battle-royale* selection to exploit these concepts. If the size of a candidate translation, its position or the sub-phrases it includes are not compatible with the other candidate translations, conflicts will arise instead of alliances. The third aspect to highlight does not regard the method itself but the way to evaluate it. Indeed, no methods assessed directly, as we did, the quality of the phrase translations acquired. They were generally evaluated with respect to the differences in performance of a machine translation system. Thus the phrase translations are not themselves evaluated but their impact on a tool is. Unfortunately, evaluating phrase translations with machine translation only allows to evaluate how well machine translation systems manage to take advantage of this data at decoding time. However, it does not allow to evaluate how adequate such data would be for the other tasks that can benefit from such data (see sect. 7.2).

Last but not least, no methods mention the use of the left and right 1-gram of the phrases to filter or select candidate translations.

7 Future work

7.1 Planned improvements

Evaluation. We consider evaluating as we did for ours phrase translations generated by state-of-the-art tools. Also, as in most of the state-of-the-art, we strongly consider evaluating the phrase translations generated through a sophisticated machine translation system such as Moses (Koehn et al., 2007).

Performance. Depending on the configuration and the size of the input corpus, time and memory consumption can easily be a challenge even for modern computers and represent a scalability issue[11]. Parallelising the approach and adapting it to an incremental behavior could help tackling this aspect.

[11]However, since such data should not be generated often and modern HDDs provide decent swapping memory, these aspects are more drawbacks than issues.

Lemmatization. A pre-processing step that converts an input form-based parallel corpus into a lemmatized enhanced one could be added. All occurrences of different phrases with the same sequences of lemmas would be grouped and thus, both the average number of occurrences and the total number of occurrences would be higher[12]. Such improvement should increase both precision and coverage.

Beam-search. The greedy-style *battle-royale* selection can straightforwardly be adapted to a beam search driven by the sum of all the $popularity$ values.

Non-contiguous phrases. The approach could already cope with non-contiguous phrases. However, this would drastically increase the search space.

7.2 Possible applications

Thanks to the high precision achieved, a wider spectrum of applications than mentioned in the related work can be considered.

Machine translation. As proposed in most of the state-of-the-art, the candidate translations generated could be used to achieve machine translation.

Memory based translation. This task could be enhanced by using the candidate translations in a t9-style/auto-completion algorithms and propose typing suggestions. Such tools could both help saving time and standardizing translations.

Word/phrase alignment. Since high precision translations of both words and phrases are generated, a bottom-up or a top-down approach could take advantage of such data.

Multiword detection. A multiword in one language often corresponds to an unique word in another language[13]. Detecting multiwords could thus be achieved by selecting the candidate translation combining a single-token with a multi-token phrase matching certain part-of-speech patterns[14].

Paraphrase/synonyms acquisition. Two phrases that can be translated to the same phrase are possibly semantically equivalent. However, false positives can be generated from polysemous phrases.

Error acquisition. Error correction can be seen as the translation of an incorrect sentence into a correct one. Any parallel corpus for this task could thus be used as input and candidate translations combining two different phrases would represent errors.

8 Conclusion

In this paper, we have presented an unsupervised approach that is able to acquire phrase translations with great flexibility.

As it is a recent and on-going work, it has still much room for improvement. However, its performance already allows it to compete with the state-of-the-art.

We provided several tracks for improving it and described a set of applications that can be considered thanks to the precision achieved.

The evaluation performed confirms both its relevance and its potential.

References

John DeNero and Dan Klein. 2008. The complexity of phrase alignment problems. In *Proceedings of the 46th Annual Meeting of the Association for Computational Linguistics on Human Language Technologies: Short Papers*, pages 25–28. Association for Computational Linguistics.

Yonggang Deng and William Byrne. 2008. Hmm word and phrase alignment for statistical machine translation. volume 16, pages 494–507. IEEE.

Nan Duan, Mu Li, Ming Zhou, and Lei Cui. 2011. Improving phrase extraction via mbr phrase scoring and pruning. In *Proceedings of MT Summit*, volume 13, pages 189–197.

William A. Gale and Kenneth W. Church. 1991. Identifying word correspondence in parallel texts. In *Proceedings of the workshop on Speech and Natural Language*, HLT '91, pages 152–157, Stroudsburg, PA, USA. Association for Computational Linguistics.

Philipp Koehn, Franz Josef Och, and Daniel Marcu. 2003. Statistical phrase-based translation. In *Proceedings of the 2003 Conference of the North American Chapter of the Association for Computational Linguistics on Human Language Technology-Volume 1*, pages 48–54. Association for Computational Linguistics.

Philipp Koehn, Hieu Hoang, Alexandra Birch, Chris Callison-Burch, Marcello Federico, Nicola Bertoldi,

[12] The occurrences of non selected phrases could be taken into account in their lemmatized version.

[13] E.g. $pomme\ de\ terre\ (French)\ \|\ potato\ (English)$ or $landesgesetz\ (German)\ \|\ legge\ provinciale\ (Italian)$

[14] We expect high precision and, depending on the pair of languages considered, low recall. However, recall could be boosted by combining several pairs of languages, and a phrase labeled as multi-word can always be used in an adhoc fashion for further detection.

Brooke Cowan, Wade Shen, Christine Moran, Richard Zens, Chris Dyer, Ondřej Bojar, Alexandra Constantin, and Evan Herbst. 2007. Moses: open source toolkit for statistical machine translation. In *Proceedings of the 45th Annual Meeting of the ACL on Interactive Poster and Demonstration Sessions*, ACL '07, pages 177–180, Stroudsburg, PA, USA. Association for Computational Linguistics.

Qing Ma, Shinya Sakagami, and Masaki Murata. 2011. Extraction of broad-scale, high-precision japanese-english parallel translation expressions using lexical information and rules. In *PACLIC*, volume 25, pages 577–586.

I. Dan Melamed. 1995. Automatic evaluation and uniform filter cascades for inducing n-best translation lexicons. In *Proceedings of the Third Workshop on Very Large Corpora*, pages 184–198.

I. Dan Melamed. 1997. Automatic discovery of non-compositional compounds in parallel data. In *Proceedings of the 2nd Conference on Empirical Methods in Natural Language Processing*.

I. Dan Melamed. 2000. Models of translational equivalence among words. *Computational Linguistics*, 26:221–249.

Robert C Moore and Chris Quirk. 2007. An iteratively-trained segmentation-free phrase translation model for statistical machine translation. In *Proceedings of the Second Workshop on Statistical Machine Translation*, pages 112–119. Association for Computational Linguistics.

Robert C. Moore. 2001. Towards a simple and accurate statistical approach to learning translation relationships among words. In *Proceedings of the workshop on Data-driven methods in machine translation - Volume 14*, DMMT '01, pages 1–8, Stroudsburg, PA, USA. Association for Computational Linguistics.

Graham Neubig, Taro Watanabe, Eiichiro Sumita, Shinsuke Mori, and Tatsuya Kawahara. 2011. An unsupervised model for joint phrase alignment and extraction. In *Proceedings of the 49th Annual Meeting of the Association for Computational Linguistics: Human Language Technologies-Volume 1*, pages 632–641. Association for Computational Linguistics.

Kishore Papineni, Salim Roukos, Todd Ward, and Wei-Jing Zhu. 2002. Bleu: a method for automatic evaluation of machine translation. In *Proceedings of the 40th annual meeting on association for computational linguistics*, pages 311–318. Association for Computational Linguistics.

Oliver Streiter, Mathias Stuflesser, and Isabella Ties. 2004. Cle, an aligned tri-lingual ladin-italian-german corpus. corpus design and interface. *First Steps in Language Documentation for Minority Languages*, page 84.

George Tambouratzis, Michalis Troullinos, Sokratis Sofianopoulos, and Marina Vassiliou. 2012. Accurate phrase alignment in a bilingual corpus for ebmt systems. In *Proceedings of the 5th BUCC Workshop, held within the LREC2012 Conference*, volume 26, pages 104–111.

Christoph Tillmann. 2003. A projection extension algorithm for statistical machine translation. In *Proceedings of the 2003 conference on Empirical methods in natural language processing*, pages 1–8. Association for Computational Linguistics.

Keita Tsuji and Kyo Kageura. 2004. Extracting low-frequency translation pairs from japanese-english bilingual corpora. In Sophia Ananadiou and Pierre Zweigenbaum, editors, *COLING 2004 CompuTerm 2004: 3rd International Workshop on Computational Terminology*, pages 23–30, Geneva, Switzerland, August 29. COLING.

Dan Tufis. 2002. A cheap and fast way to build useful translation lexicons. In *Proceedings of the 19th International Conference on Computational Linguistics, COLING2002*, pages 1030–1036.

Ashish Venugopal, Stephan Vogel, and Alex Waibel. 2003. Effective phrase translation extraction from alignment models. In *Proceedings of the 41st Annual Meeting on Association for Computational Linguistics-Volume 1*, pages 319–326. Association for Computational Linguistics.

Stephan Vogel. 2005. Pesa: Phrase pair extraction as sentence splitting. In *Proceedings of the Machine Translation Summit X*, pages 251–258.

Dominic Widdows, Beate Dorow, and Chiu ki Chan. 2002. Using parallel corpora to enrich multilingual lexical resources. In *Third International Conference on Language Resources and Evaluation*, pages 240–245.

Dekai Wu and Xuanyin Xia. 1994. Learning an english-chinese lexicon from a parallel corpus. In *Proceedings of the First Conference of the Association for Machine Translation in the Americas*, pages 206–213.

Kaoru Yamamoto, Taku Kudo, Yuta Tsuboi, and Yuji Matsumoto. 2003. Learning sequence-to-sequence correspondences from parallel corpora via sequential pattern mining. In *Proceedings of the HLT-NAACL 2003 Workshop on Building and using parallel texts: data driven machine translation and beyond-Volume 3*, pages 73–80. Association for Computational Linguistics.

Luke S Zettlemoyer and Robert C Moore. 2007. Selective phrase pair extraction for improved statistical machine translation. In *Human Language Technologies 2007: The Conference of the North American Chapter of the Association for Computational Linguistics; Companion Volume, Short Papers*, pages 209–212. Association for Computational Linguistics.

Enriching Patent Search with External Keywords: a Feasibility Study

Ivelina Nikolova, Irina Temnikova, Galia Angelova
Institute of Information and Communication Technologies, Bulgarian Academy of Sciences
iva@lml.bas.bg, irina.temnikova@gmail.com, galia@lml.bas.bg

Abstract

This article presents a feasibility study for retrieving Wikipedia articles matching patents' topics. The long term motivation behind it is to facilitate patent search by enriching patent indexing with relevant keywords found in external (terminological) resources, with their monolingual synonyms and multilingual translations. The similarity between patents and Wikipedia articles is measured using various filtering techniques and patent document sections. The most similar Wikipedia articles happen to be the closest ones to the respective patent in 33% of the cases, otherwise they are within the top 12 ranked articles.

1 Motivations and Related Work

Patent documents exhibit structure uniformity (Alberts et al., 2011) and have assigned classification codes but patents search is not a trivial task. This is due to the large number of patents available worldwide (forty millions) (Hunt et al., 2007) and the specific language genre. Usually the invention descriptions aim at covering the widest possible application area and are intentionally left very vague. Thus patents do not follow a pre-established terminology but rather are written according to the specific lexicon and style of each inventor (Alberts et al., 2011). Patent applications are published before the granting decision, therefore their titles and abstracts are intentionally left very general (Adams, 2010a). Moreover, the internationally used classification hierarchies vary among institutions and are periodically changed.

The present NLP technologies provide insufficient support to patent searchers' needs (Lupu et al., 2011; Adams, 2010a). Full-text search is the most preferred type of patent search while examining a patent application in order to establish its novelty, patentability, and infringement (Adams, 2010a). Search is done through iterative attempts, using synonyms in order to catch the alternative expressions each inventor may use to describe the same concept (Hunt et al., 2007). It is known that it can take up to 40 hours (in average 12) for a specialist to complete the search task for 15 queries in 100 documents, including a minimum of 5 minutes for a single query formulation (Joho et al., 2010). Another specific requirement is that patent searchers need the highest possible recall because a single relevant missed document can invalidate an otherwise sound patent (Lupu et al., 2011).

Our original idea is to use Wikipedia as a free, multilingual and constantly updated terminology resource, in order to enrich patent indexing with monolingual term synonyms and their translations in multiple languages. This would allow increasing patent search recall, and it is the solution we propose to recognizing vague and inventor-specific term definitions. Wikipedia is constantly updated; besides the multiple critiques to the reliability of Wikipedia articles[1], its peer-review nature repays for it (Giles, 2005). Thus the automatic recognition of relevant to the patent's topic Wikipedia articles is a first experimental step towards enriching patents indexing with Wikipedia terms. As many Wikipedia article titles are homonyms (usually described in disambiguation pages[2]), full-text article recognition is necessary.

Related Work in NLP for patents. Most of the NLP approaches contributing to patent search have been published in the CLEF-IP[3], TREC-CHEM[4] tracks, the NTCIR workshops patents tracks for Japanese, and in the PaIR[5] workshops. Lupu et al. (2011) provides a very good overview of the state-of-the-art of IR technologies for patents and how well they respond to the users' needs. Multilinguality in patents search is

[1]http://en.wikipedia.org/wiki/Reliability_of_Wikipedia
[2]http://en.wikipedia.org/wiki/Wave_%28disambiguation%29
[3]http://www.ifs.tuwien.ac.at/ clef-ip/index.html.
[4]http://www.ir-facility.org/trec-chem.
[5]http://www.ir-facility.org/pair-workshops.

prevalently addressed by automatically translating whole patents in other languages into the language of the query. The existing approaches tackle a variety of specific patents retrieval tasks, ranging from patents language analysis (Shinmori, 2003), to patent retrieval evaluation (Lupu et al., 2011).

Among the closest to ours approaches is Pesenhofer et al. (2011), who assign new index terms to patents by retrieving relevant Wikipedia Science Portal pages. The difference with our work is that we plan to assign to patents as indexing terms only synonyms specified in the particular Wikipedia articles and translation equivalents from the linked pages, and that their approach takes into consideration only strictly scientific topics. Another relevant work is Magdy and Jones (2011) who generate synonyms for query terms using WordNet (Fellbaum, 1998). Compared to the approaches, currently known to us, the originality of our idea consists in the automatic generation of suggestions for (multilingual) synonyms with assigned similarity scores to be shown to the patentees when they perform patent searches.

2 Materials Used

The experimental dataset is a subset of patents from MAREC400k that belong to the MAREC corpus[6]. MAREC is a static collection of over 19 million patent documents provided as XML files, unifying 100,000 randomly selected patent applications and granted patents from four main patent authorities: the European Patent Office (EPO), the World Intellectual Property Organization, the US Patent and Trademark Office, and the Japan Patent Office. MAREC has been compiled specifically for NLP/IR/MT research by the IR Facility in Vienna [7]. We use only a subset of MAREC400k, which contains patents in English from the EPO collection, with the following subject categories (according to the International Patents Classification, IPC): *A43* – Footwear, *A44* – Haberdashery, Juwellery, *A45* – Hand or travelling articles, *A47* – Furniture and Domestic Articles, *G06* – Computing, *G07* – Checking Devices, and *G09* – Education, Cryptography.

We use only patent documents which contain the sections *Description* and *Claims* in addition to the patent *Invention title* and *Abstract*. A human judge collected our experimental corpus. He was asked to go manually through the patents, decide the topics and assign the most relevant Wikipedia articles to each of the patent documents as a whole, and to each of the patents' paragraphs, including claims. For this reason, in this experiment we use a restricted number of fifteen patent documents within the above-mentioned categories with length between 4 and 30 pages. It is known that most terms characterizing the invention are contained in the invention description and in the patent claims, while the patent title, abstract, and the context of the problem contain only very general information (2010a; 2010b).

In our experiment we used Wikipedia articles from the English Wikipedia. The corpus contains: *(i)* manually identified articles discussing the topics of the selected patents, with the best similarity match to the patents topics, 1-3 per patent (29); *(ii)* manually selected Wikipedia pages as distractors (articles discussing topic similar but not the same as the patent's ones), 2-20 per patent (153), and *(iii)* randomly selected Wikipedia articles (6,747).

All Wikipedia articles and patents are preprocessed within the GATE framework (Cunningham et al., 2011), (Cunningham et al., 2002), using the ANNIE processing resources (Cunningham et al., 2002). The XML- and MediaWiki-markups are ignored, the text is lemmatized and the calculation of similarity is done on lemmas only. Stopwords were marked and later we made experiments with both corpora - documents containing stopwords and documents with removed stopwords.

3 Experiments Design and Results

Our study includes identifying the closest Wikipedia article match with the currently processed patent document. As often there are Wikipedia pages with homonym titles, the "closest" article cannot be identified only by its title, e.g. *seat* (where one sits) vs *SEAT* (a car brand). In order to overcome homonym titles disambiguation, our approach uses the whole text of the Wikipedia articles, the patent document description, the patent categories and the patent claims. After calculating the similarity between a number of patent texts (or patent parts) and Wikipedia pages, we check if the closest match automatically identified by our method, corresponds to the closest match previously identified by a human judge.

[6] http://www.ir-facility.org/prototypes/marec

[7] http://www.ir-facility.org/home

Experiment 1 – Patent descriptions vs Wikipedia articles. To determine the best method for text similarity calculation, we performed several experiments with different algorithms for calculating the semantic distance between patent description texts and Wikipedia articles. We used the DKPro Similarity Framework (Bär et al., 2012) and applied most of the similarity measures available there, among which are *WordNGramJaccard measure*, *ExactStringMatch comparator*, *JaroSecondString comparator*, *JaroWinklerSecondString comparator*, *LevenshteinSecondString comparator*, and *LongestCommonSubstring comparator*. The best results were obtained with the classical *CosineSimilarity measure*. We used it in the study presented here.

A round of experiments has been done without using a stopwords list. The similarity was calculated on the basis of the words' lemmas. Although the highest similarity scores were quite close to 1, the results were rather discouraging, the documents having high scores were often not similar to the patents at all and the manually assigned as "most similar" documents were not given a high score. This is why we decided to use a stop word list in the further experiments, and it proved to be a better choice.

We made 2 separate runs of the similarity calculations. In Run 1 we measured the semantic distance between patent descriptions and a number of manually selected Wikipedia articles, annotated with the boolean values - *similar* or *distractor*. The results are illustrated in Table 1, Run 1, for each patent description. The 2nd column shows the position where the manually pre-defined "most similar" pages appeared among the top 20 highly ranked relevant Wikipedia pages. In all cases, except for the 11th patent, the "most similar" pages are recognised, and in the 3rd, 7th, 8th and 13th case they have the highest ranking. In the 4th and 12th cases, one of the Wikipedia articles was given highest score and in the rest of the cases the correct articles were with lower rank but still within the top 20 results. Unfortunately we see that the Wikipedia pages, intentionally selected as distractors, appear as highly similar documents as well, which means that the mere computation of similarity using bag-of-words techniques at this level is insufficient to ensure proper disambiguation.

In Run 2 we added some 6,747 randomly selected Wikipedia pages to the set of manually annotated pages. Many of these documents were given pretty high similarity score although they were irrelevant. Often they were about people, geographic locations and landmarks which are irrelevant to the patent data. We decided to remove such pages before running the similarity algorithm. We filtered them by their Wikipedia category and we ended up with 1,465 randomly selected Wikipedia pages. We note that the Wikipedia category tree is not consistently developed and it is not trivial to select all categories matching these types of articles thus some might be omitted. By augmenting the set of Wikipedia articles our goal was to check whether the algorithms will perform consistently and will assign higher score to the same pages as it did in the first run. The results are shown on Table 1, Run 2. We see that for the 2nd, 3rd, 4th, 7th, 8th, 12th and 13th patent the results are the same as in the case of the manually selected Wikipedia pages. For some cases there are slight shifts in the ranking, and for patent #11, the "most similar" pages do not appear at all among the top 20 closest documents in both Run 1 and Run 2. As a reason for that we see that the patent text is rather a functional description of the entertainment machine and the closest Wikipedia articles explain about the history and application of the entertainment machines.

The upper part of Table 2 shows the similarity scores calculated for the patent EP-0073116-A2 *Integrated data processing circuits* and the Wikipedia pages. The full patent text can be seen at the EPO site. The manually selected matching pages from Wikipedia are in bold. They appear in the top ranked results but without significantly higher similarity score. In addition to the manually selected pages here *Asynchronous circuit* and *Intel MCS-51* appear with very high similarity score. Indeed they are similar to the topic because *Intel MSC-51* is an implementation of integrated circuit and asynchronous circuit is also type of integrated circuit - sequential digital logic circuit. This is an example of gathering new potential indexing keyterms. The articles *Clock* and *Multiplication* have also been given pretty high score. Although the expert did not select them as closest matches to this patent, he did select them as "most similar" to some of the patent paragraphs, which means that they are also true positives and are appropriate to describe this patent.

The lower part of Table 2 shows the similarity

Pat. id	Rank in top 20 res	Wiki docs	Rank in top 20 res	Wiki docs	Rank in top 20 res	Wiki docs	Rank in top 20 res	Wiki docs	Rank in top 20 res	Wiki docs	Rank in top 20 res	Wiki docs	Rank in top 20 res
	Run 1		Run 2		Run 3		Run 4		Run 5		Run 6		Run 7
1.	2	156	3	1 465	N/A	1 465	3	1 465	3	1 465	3	1 465	2
2.	2, 4	156	2, 4	1 465	1, 3	1 465	2, 4	1 465	2, 8	1 465	2	1 465	2, 4
3.	1, 2	156	1, 2	1 465	1, 2	1 465	1, 2	1 465	1, 2	1 465	1, 2	1 465	1, 2
4.	1, 10	156	1, 10	1 465	2, 20	1 465	1, 10	1 465	1, 12	1 465	1	1 465	1, 12
5.	3, 12, 15	156	3	1 465	3, 13	1 465	3	1 465	2, 15	1 465	2	1 465	2, 12
6.	1, 2	156	1	1 465	3	1 465	1	1 465	2	1 465	2	1 465	1, 11
7.	1, 2	156	1, 2	1 465	1, 2	1 465	11, 20	1 465	1, 2	1 465	1, 2	1 465	1, 2
8.	1	156	1	1 465	6	1 465	1	1 465	1	1 465	1	1 465	1
9.	7	156	7	1 465	10	1 465	7	1 465	8	1 465	8	1 465	1
10.	1, 6	156	1, 10	1 465	6, 7	1 465	1, 10	1 465	1, 8	1 465	1, 8	1 465	1, 7
11.	N/A	156	N/A	1 465	7	1 465	N/A	1 465	N/A	1 465	N/A	1 465	N/A
12.	1, 4	156	1, 4	1 465	17	1 465	1, 4	1 465	1, 4	1 465	1, 4	1 465	1, 4
13.	1	156	1	1 465	6	1 465	1	1 465	1	1 465	1	1 465	1
14.	4, 6	156	7, 9	1 465	N/A	1 465	N/A	1 465	8, 10	1 465	8, 10	1 465	6, 8
15.	7, 11, 16	156	7, 11	1 465	6, 11	1 465	7, 11	1 465	6, 10	1 465	7, 11	1 465	6, 11

Table 1: Rank of the most similar documents according to cosine measure.
Run 1 - Patent descriptions and manually selected Wiki-articles; Run 2 - patent descriptions and both, manually and randomly selected Wiki-articles; Run 3 - patent categories and both, manually and randomly selected Wiki-articles; Run 4 - patent claims and both, manually and randomly selected Wiki-articles; Run 5 - combined patent description with claims and both, manually and randomly selected Wiki-articles; Run 6 - combined patent categories, description, claims and both, manually and randomly selected Wiki-articles; Run 7 - weighted similarity between Wiki-articles and a patent considering the scores from Runs 2–6.

Invention title: Integrated data processing circuits. Patent ID: EP-0073116-A2, Category: G06F.	
Wikipedia match: **Integrated circuit; Very-large-scale integration.**	
Run 1	Run 2
Rank of Wiki-pages sorted by cosine similarity:	
1. Asynchronous circuit (0.218) 2. Clock (0.207) 3. Multiplication (0.170) **4. Integrated circuit** (0.151) 5. Computer (0.151) **6. Very-large-scale integration** (0.147) ...	1. Intel MCS-51 (0.246) 2. Glia limitans (0.231) 3. Pennales (0.224) 4. Asynchronous circuit (0.218) 5. Clock (0.207) 6. Multiplication (0.170) **7. Integrated circuit** (0.151) 8. Computer (0.1506) **9. Very-large-scale integration** (0.147) ...
Invention title: Folding table or like structure. Patent ID: EP-0105957-A1, Category: A47B.	
Wikipedia match: **Table (furniture); Folding table.**	
Run 1	Run 2
Rank of Wiki-pages sorted by cosine similarity:	
1. Table (furniture) (0.509) **2. Folding table** (0.489) 3. Table (database) (0.339) 4. Table (parliamentary procedure) (0.270)	**1. Table (furniture)** (0.509) **2. Folding table** ([illegible]) 3. Table (database) (0.339) 4. Table (parliamentary 4. procedure) (0.270)

Table 2: Run 1 and 2 with patents EP-0073116-A2 and EP-0105957-A1

scores calculated for patent EP-0105957-A1. In this case the matching Wikipedia pages are the top closest results. We can view their Wikipedia categories as potential indices of EP-0105957-A1 as well: for the article *Table (furniture)* in Wikipedia these are *Tables (furniture)* and *Furniture*. So the latter term can be shown to a patent searcher as a potential descriptor. It reveals the semantics of EP-0105957-A1 despite the fact that it does not appear in the patent text at all.

Experiment 2 – Patent categories vs Wikipedia articles. We decided to observe the similarity between patents and Wikipedia articles from one more perspective: document categories versus document text contents. We extracted all categories of each patent (varying between 1 to 15 per patent), transformed their reference numbers into the titles of the categories, and pre processed them as a regular text document. Then we measured the similarity between these lemmatized texts and the Wikipedia articles.

We decided to use patents categories and Wikipedia texts, rather than the opposite (patent description and Wikipedia categories), because the IPO categorical tree is precisely elicited and the categories which are assigned to each patent are carefully chosen to make the patent easy to retrieve during search. Whereas Wikipedia categories are not really strictly organised and the depth of the categorical tree varies a lot from branch to branch. In Wikipedia it is very common that some articles on a topic, which is not popular, have only few categories listed (one or two), even if there are many other appropriate ones existing. In the same time articles like Barack Obama have 50 assigned categories. The process of assigning categories to patents is somehow better regulated.

We tested also this approach with and without using stop words and again only when we removed the stop words we could obtain meaningful results. The categories files are rather short, containing essential information and removing the stop words emphasises even more the keywords they contain. The presented results are only from the experiment when stop words are removed. We measured the similarity between the patent categories and the whole set of Wikipedia articles including manually selected and randomly added ones. The results are shown on Table 1, run 3.

Experiment 3 – Patent claims vs Wikipedia articles. We took also a third perspective in measuring the similarity between these two types of documents. We extracted all patent claims (varying between 4 and 36 per document) and preprocessed them as regular text documents. These differ from the patent description as they contain the synthesized essence of the invention, in bullet points, while the patents description contains also an overview of the problem background, and it is thus much more general. We applied the same similarity measure between these lemmatized texts and the whole collection of Wikipedia articles including the manually and randomly selected ones. The results, obtained after stop words removal, are presented on Table 1, Run 4.

Experiment 4 – Comparison of patent subsections with full text Wikipedia articles. The aim is to *(i)* find better matches to specific document sub-parts, describing specific techniques or methods, which may be used in other inventions. And thus adding new keywords describing these sub-parts, we augment the chance that the patent searcher will find those in order to prevent any infringement of the rights of previous patents. On the other hand, *(ii)* test if this helps to improve the match of the whole document to Wikipedia articles. Our hypothesis is that the description paragraphs would have more diverse matches than the claims, as manual analysis has shown that each claim tends to be more precise and mentions several times the object of the invention. Thus, by splitting the descriptions into paragraphs, we expect to find more Wikipedia article matches to the same patent. Further, a human judge has manually identified the best matches for some claims or paragraphs, to test if the short text of a paragraph is enough to have similarity between it and the appropriate Wikipedia article.

The motivation for this approach is that it often happens, that the same invention has parts describing specific and very concrete technologies, borrowed from other fields. For example, a patent application, describing a technology improving integrated data processing circuits (patent reference number EP-0073116-A2), can contain paragraphs, discussion specifically multiplication specificities, and clocks, operating with phase difference. While a patent application, discussing a spring seat invention (patent reference number EP-0090622-A1), can include paragraphs, discussing the interactions between human's ischial tuberosities with seating surfaces, or using webbing and clamps in a specific way to keep together parts of the invention. As, sometimes, the claims of a patent may contain these specific technologies, as part of the invention, it is necessary to check if they have not been used in previously granted patent applications or, if used, whether mentioning them in the claim can infringe previous patents rights. We consider that retrieving more patents, discussing these topics, will assist patent specialists in reviewing all possible applications which are related to this invention.

Initially we set-up a paragraph to be any sequence of characters between two new lines. These turned to be often very short, sometimes section titles and in general not informative enough to have a meaningful comparison with a full Wikipedia article. The results were rather discouraging and then we set up a minimum paragraph size of 500 chars. Thus paragraphs which were shorter than 500 chars were added to the next paragraph. In this Run again removing the stop words gave better results.

The obtained similarity scores between patent paragraphs and Wikipedia articles resemble quite a lot to the results obtained from the full patent descriptions and Wikipedia articles. The manually selected "most similar" Wikipedia articles are ranked within the top 20 results, however it is hard to distinguish them from the distractor articles. Indeed some Wikipedia articles which are similar with concrete paragraphs receive higher similarity score in this experiment, but it turns that they receive high similarity score also with the whole patent description. Some of the results are shown on Table 3. The expert has selected *Multiplication* and *Clock* as "most similar" pages to the 3rd paragraph of the patent however the rest of the top ranked articles are also true positives.

Experiment 5 – Combined patent parts vs Wikipedia articles. After running all comparisons of the separate patent parts we observed the results and decided to combine these parts and compare them once again to all Wikipedia articles. We made two separate runs. Once we combined only the patent description and claims because we noticed that the results when using these

Invention title: Integrated data processing circuits. Patent ID: EP-0073116-A2, Category: G06F Paragraph: 3
Wikipedia match: **Integrated circuit**, **Very-large-scale integration**
Rank of the Wikipedia pages sorted by cosine similarity: 1. **Multiplication** (0.169) 2. Asynchronous circuit (0.156) 3. Integrated circuit (0.139) 4. Very-large-scale integration (0.123) 5. **Clock** (0.122)

Table 3: Top results from matching paragraph 3 of EP-0073116-A2 with all Wikipedia articles.

two parts (Run 1,2 and 3) are more consistent that the ones obtained by the patent categories (Run 4). Then we combined also patent categories, description and claims (Run 6). We observed the change in the similarity score and ranking between the patents and the manually selected Wikipedia matches. The results from this experiment are presented on Table 1, Run 5 and Run 6.

Experiment 6 – Weighted Scoring of Wikipedia articles. To filter out the results obtained from all these experiments we calculated the weight of each Wikipedia article according to each patent, using the score obtained by the similarity algorithm and the number of times a Wikipedia article is ranked among the top 20 ones:

$$Weight = \sum_{i=1}^{i=n} Rank_i * Score_i$$

where n is the number of experiments, i.e. n=5 excluding Run 1 (without stopwords).

This way we give preference to the articles which appear more often than the others in the top results and to the ones with higher score. Although this technique is rather simple it allowed us to restrict the true positives within the top 12 results. In 8 of the cases they were within the top 5 results. We would like to mention that the fact that some manually selected Wikipedia articles appear with lower rank, often means that there are other very similar articles which were not selected by the human judge as such, and they appear with higher rank, and they are also appropriate to be used for indexing of that patent.

4 Discussion and conclusion

The results on Table 1 show the change in the ranking of the "most similar" manually selected Wikipedia articles when calculating similarity between different parts of the patents and Wikipedia articles. In Run 1 only 156 Wikipedia articles are used, in Run 2 - 10 times more (1 465), and there are still only slight differences in the ranking of the "most similar" articles in both runs. This stability in the performance of the cosine similarity algorithm in this task is encouraging for applying it for even bigger data sets. We see that the Wikipedia articles, which receive high similarity score and rank to some patent, retain it in all experiments (with claims, description, combined). The only experiment which gives somehow inconsistent results is (Run 3) where we map patent categories to Wikipedia articles. This must be due to the fact that patent categories are short expressions with rather general wording. Thus our feasibility study shows that the identification of the closest match is possible, but it is difficult to distinguish between closest and close results. In general the results are promising since the recall in patent search is more important than the precision, and thus the noise is not so disturbing. However much work remains to be done for improving the computation paradigm and refining the precision. Further, we aim at extracting synonyms and translation equivalents to enrich patents indexing, and this requires additional experiments with real users.

Another challenge is to elaborate the initial filtering of the Wikipedia articles in order to better restrict the categories of Wikipedia pages. For instance, pages for cities, states and provinces contain long descriptions about industries, communications etc. and therefore they might be identified as "similar" to various patents, so it is be reasonable to remove such pages from the experiment at all. Future work includes also experiments with assigning weight to the words in the patent description and claims, and processing multiword expressions. Last but not least, employment of multilinguality in decision making regarding similarity is possible as well. Wikipedia is multilingual and patents contain titles and abstracts in several languages, so patent fragments in another language can be used to calculate similarity with Wikipedia pages in the corresponding language.

Acknowledgements. The research work presented in this article is partially supported by the grant 316087 AComIn "Advanced Computing for Innovation". It is also related to the COST Action IC 1002 MUMIA "Multilingual and Multifaceted Interactive Information Access".

References

Adams Stephen 2010. *The text, the full text and nothing but the text: Part 1Standards for creating textual information in patent documents and general search implications.* World Pat Inf 32:22 29.

Adams Stephen. 2010. *The text, the full text and nothing but the text: Part 2The main specification, searching challenges and survey of availability.*. World Pat Inf 32:120128.

Alberts, D., C. B.Yang, D. Fobare-DePonio, K. Koubek, S. Robins, M. Rodgers, E. Simmons, and D. DeMarco. 2011. *Current Challenges in Patent Information Retrieval, Chapter 1: Introduction to Patent Searching-Practical Experience and Requirements for Searching the Patent Space.* The Information Retrieval Series, Volume 29. Springer-Verlag Berlin Heidelberg.

Bär, Daniel, Chris Biemann, Iryna Gurevych and Torsten Zesch. *UKP: Computing Semantic Textual Similarity by Combining Multiple Content Similarity Measures* In Proceedings of the 6th Int'l Workshop on Semantic Evaluation, in conjunction with the 1st Joint Conf. on Lexical and Computational Semantics pages 435-440, June 2012, Montreal, Canada.

Chen, L., Tokuda, N., & Adachi, H. 2003. *A patent document retrieval system addressing both semantic and syntactic properties.* In Proceedings of the ACL-2003 workshop on Patent corpus processing-Volume 20 (pp. 1-6). Association for Computational Linguistics..

Choi, Sung-Kwon, Oh-Woog Kwon, Ki-Young Lee, Yoon-Hyung Roh, and Young-Gil Kim. 2007. *Customizing an English-Korean Machine Translation System for Patent Translation.* In The 21st Pacific Asia Conference on Language, Information and Computation (PACLIC 21), pp. 105-114.

Cunningham, Hamish and Diana Maynard, Kalina Bontcheva, Valentin Tablan, Niraj Aswani, Ian Roberts, Genevieve Gorrell, Adam Funk, Angus Roberts, Danica Damljanovic, Thomas Heitz, Mark A. Greenwood, Horacio Saggion, Johann Petrak, Yaoyong Li and Wim Peters. 2011. *Text Processing with GATE (Version 6).* ISBN 978-0956599315, 2011, http://tinyurl.com/gatebook

Cunningham, Hamish, Diana Maynard, Kalina Bontcheva and Valentin Tablan. *GATE: A Framework and Graphical Development Environment for Robust NLP Tools and Applications,* In Proceedings of the 40th Anniversary Meeting of the Association for Computational Linguistics (ACL'02), 2002

H. Cunningham, Valentin Tablan, A. Roberts, K. Bontcheva (2013) *Getting More Out of Biomedical Documents with GATE's Full Lifecycle Open Source Text Analytics.* PLoS Comput Biol 9(2): e1002854. doi:10.1371/journal.pcbi.1002854 http://tinyurl.com/gate-life-sci/

Fellbaum, C. 1998. *WordNet: an Electronic Lexical Database.* MIT Press.

Joho, Hideo, Leif A. Azzopardi, and Wim Vanderbauwhede. 2010. *A survey of patent users: an analysis of tasks, behavior, search functionality and system requirements.* Proceedings of the third symposium on Information interaction in context, pp. 13-24. ACM.

Hunt, David, Long Nguyen, and Matthew Rodgers. (Eds). 2007. *Patent searching: Tools & techniques.* Wiley.

Giles, Jim. 2005. *Internet encyclopaedias go head to head.* Nature, vol. 438, 7070, pp.900-901 Nature Publishing Group.

Lu, Bin, and Benjamin K. Tsou 2009. *Towards bilingual term extraction in comparable patents.* In Proceedings of the 23rd Pacific Asia Conference on Language, Information and Computation (PACLIC), pp. 755-762.

Lupu, Mihai, Katja Mayer, John Tait, and Anthony Trippe. (Eds). 2011. *Current Challenges in Patent Information Retrieval.* The Information Retrieval Series, Volume 29. Springer-Verlag Berlin Heidelberg.

Magdy, W., & Jones, G. J. 2011. *A study on query expansion methods for patent retrieval.* In Proceedings of the 4th workshop on Patent information retrieval (pp. 19-24). ACM.

Andreas Pesenhofer, Helmut Berger, and Michael Dittenbach. 2011. *Current Challenges in Patent Information Retrieval, Chapter 18: 1Offering New Insights by Harmonizing Patents, Taxonomies and Linked Data.* The Information Retrieval Series, Volume 29. Springer-Verlag Berlin Heidelberg.

Sheremetyeva, Svetlana, Sergei Nirenburg, and Irene Nirenburg. 1996. *Generating patent claims from interactive input.* In Proceedings of the Eighth International Workshop on Natural Language Generation, pp. 61-70.

Shinmori, A., Okumura, M., Marukawa, Y., & Iwayama, M. 2003. *Patent claim processing for readability: structure analysis and term explanation.* In Proceedings of the ACL-2003 workshop on Patent corpus processing-Volume 20 (pp. 56-65). Association for Computational Linguistics.

Wood, Andrew, Kate Struthers, and Uk Edinburgh 2010. *Pathology education, Wikipedia and the Net generation.*. Medicine 38 (2010): 868-878.

A clustering approach for translationese identification

Sergiu Nisioi
Faculty of Mathematics and
Computer Science,
University of Bucharest
sergiu.nisioi@gmail.com

Liviu P. Dinu
Centre for Computational
Linguistics, Bucharest
ldinu@fmi.unibuc.ro

Abstract

Our paper is concerned with investigating the impact of translationese on the novels of a bilingual writer and asking whether one could determine the authorship of a translated document. The main part of our paper will be centered on selecting a good set of lexical features that can be considered characteristic for an author. We used in our research the novels of Vladimir Nabokov, a bilingual author, who wrote his works in both Russian and English. Each text is represented by a vector of function words. We are interested in determining how the results vary across different feature sets and which feature set could be considered the most representative. In order to inspect our results we used a hierarchical clustering method and draw conclusions based on the most frequent result.

1 Introduction

The term "translationese" proposed by Gellerstam (1986) currently means the entire sum of linguistic characteristics (Hansen, 2003) that a translation exhibits in comparison to a text written natively in a language. The existence of translationese has been discussed and more recently various methods (Koppel et al., 2011; Ilisei et al., 2010) for identifying translationese have been devised.

In the same context, an interesting discussion regards the equivalence in style between the translated and original text. As Boase-Beier (2006) suggests, among other factors, the stylistics of a translation is highly related to the choices made by the translator in re-creating the original style, the translator having a specific "fingerprint" (Wang and Li, 2012). Our concern is investigating the impact of translationese on a bilingual writer and asking whether one could determine the authorship of a translated document. The problem of authorship attribution is postulated on the grounds that the human stylome exists. The stylome is defined as "a linguistic fingerprint that can be measured, is largely unconscious, and is constant" (van Halteren et al., 2005). A fairly large amount of literature is dedicated to authorship problems and extensive overviews are provided by Juola (2006) or Stamatatos (2009).

We are mostly interested in finding the lexical features that can be used to discriminate or to characterize original and translated documents and once these words are presumably found, what is their role in authorship attribution for such documents? The main part of our paper will be centered on selecting a *good* set of lexical features to detect translations in a corpus of original documents.

In order to investigate our problems we have constructed two corpora from the novels of Vladimir Nabokov: a Russian corpus containing original Russian works and translations from English and a second corpus containing English original works and translations from Russian. The details with respect to each work included are to be found in Section 2. The fact that Vladimir Nabokov was bilingual (McKenna et al., 1999) certainly affects the interpretation of the results. On one side there exists a difference of style between author and translator and secondly a translation preserves enough translationese to make it different from any other original text.

For lexical feature sets, two quality criteria are commonly used in literature: one, the lexical features should have a relatively high frequency. Rybicki and Eder (2011) have reported better results with high frequency words. The second criterion is to consider function words instead of content words. Function words do not contain information about the topic of the text and are used unconsciously revealing important psychological aspects (Chung and Pennebaker, 2007). Moreover, these words are used to tie phrases and help making stylistic constructs that can be specific to one author. These two criteria were first attested by Mosteller and Wallace (1963) and remained an important decision factor until today.

2 Corpus

We have focused our analysis on the novels of Vladimir Nabokov by using two main corpora: one in Russian containing the original Russian novels (written before 1940) together with the translations of Nabokov's original English novels, and a second one containing the original English novels (written after 1940) together with various translations of his novels into English. Except for *Lolita* all the translations into Russian are done by Sergey Ilyin. This does not influence our results greatly for two main reasons: one *Lolita* is never clustered among the Russian novels although it was translated by Nabokov and two *Dar* is not always clustered among the Russian novels although it was originally written in Russian.

Traces of the author should exist in all the English translations since V. Nabokov collaborated in translating them.

Finally, the size of our Russian corpus reached 1,062,594 words and the size of the English corpus a smaller 904,712 number of words. Our hypothesis is that the original novels of Nabokov will be clustered separately from the translated ones without regarding the language.

We are confident that the works of Nabokov constitute two significant corpora on two different languages that are meaningful for comparisons.

In order to answer our second problem regarding the attribution of a translation we have added additional writers to our experiment. These authors are Alexey Tolstoy, Lev Tolstoy, Fyodor Dostoyevsky, Iury Olesha, Valery Bryusov, Ilf and Petrov, Boris Pasternak, Andrey Bely and Ivan Turgenev.

3 Using ranks and classification

Since we have a relatively small number of documents of significant size each (in both the Russian and the English corpus), we believe that hierarchical clustering will offer sufficient details to pursue our investigation and that it could determine homogenous groups providing additional information in comparison with a simple binary classification task.

We have used Burrows' Δ to calculate a similarity matrix as input for the clustering algorithm. This measure enjoyed a lot of attention (Argamon, 2008), producing results comparable with the ones of learning methods on authorship attribution. In our case, the use of Δ will be to distinguish between translated texts and original ones.

The equation of Δ is:

$$\Delta^{(n)}(D, D') = \frac{1}{n}\sum_{i=1}^{n}\frac{1}{\sigma_i}|f_i(D) - f_i(D')| \quad (1)$$

Where n is the size of our vectors or the number of words from our feature set, D and D' two vector documents, σ_i the standard deviation of word i in the whole corpus, f_i the frequency of word i in D and D'.

We can easily observe that if we remove the constant fraction $1/n$, the value of Δ is actually equal with the $l1$ distance between z-scores, defined as $\sum_{i=1}^{n}|z(x_i) - z(y_i)|$ where z is the z-score of a word equal to $z(x_i) = \frac{f_i - \mu_i}{\sigma_i}$.

In order to visualize the results we have used an $l1$ norm (Dinu and Nisioi, 2012) modified version of the hierarchical clustering algorithm proposed by Szekely and Rizzo (2005). Their algorithm is a bottom-up approach to generalize Ward's minimum variance method (Ward, 1963) by defining a cluster distance and objective function in terms of Euclidean distance. In addition it has the ability of identifying clusters with nearly equal centers and it was successfully used for classifying diseases (Szekely and Rizzo, 2005).

Dinu and Popescu (2008) introduced a ranking operation on the frequency vectors of each documents with the purpose of eliminating outliers (produced by large vs. small frequencies of words) thus making the distances between texts measurable and more stable. As a result, it produced confident results in a case of pastiche detection on Romanian (Dinu et al., 2012). We will further test this approach by applying it on Russian on a bilingual author in a different situation.

A ranking of a vector of n words is a mapping $\tau : \{1, 2, ..., n\} \rightarrow \{1, 2, ..., n\}$ where $\tau(f(i))$ will represent the place (rank) of the frequency (as in Equation 1) of the word indexed as i. If $\tau(f(i)) < \tau(f(j))$ then the word i is more frequent than word j. In our case of using Δ, no

Russian	Number of tokens	English	Number of tokens
Mashenka (1926) (O)	26,173	*Mary* (1970) (T: Michael Glenny and V. Nabokov)	34,906
Korol' Dama Valet (1928) (O)	57,123	-	-
Zashchita Luzhina (1930) (O)	54,013	*The (Luzhin) Defence* (1964) (T: Michael Glenny and V. Nabokov)	75,417
Podvig (1932) (O)	54,372	-	-
Camera Obskura (1933) (O)	45,245	*Laughter in the Dark* (1938) (T: V. Nabokov)	62,006
Otchayanie (1934) (O)	47,199	-	-
Priglasheniye na kazn (1936) (O)	42,429	*Invitation to a Beheading* (1959) (T: D. Nabokov and V. Nabokov)	60,195
Dar (1938) (O)	116,330	-	-
Podlinnaya zhizn Sebastyana Nayta (T: S. Ilyin)	54,180	*The Real Life of Sebastian Knight* (1941) (O)	62,390
Pod znakom nezakonnorozhdënnykh (T: S. Ilyin)	60,035	*Bend Sinister* (1947) (O)	73,075
Lolita (T: V. Nabokov)	117,287	*Lolita* (1955) (O)	117,185
Pnin (T: S. Ilyin)	48,984	*Pnin* (1957) (O)	52,628
Blednoye plamya (T: S. Ilyin)	81,816	*Pale Fire* (1962) (O)	85,164
Ada (T: S. Ilyin)	168,103	*Ada or Ardor: A Family Chronicle* (1969) (O)	181,346
Prozrachnyye veshchi (T: S. Ilyin)	25,898	*Transparent Things* (1972) (O)	29,073
Smotri na arlekinov! (T: S. Ilyin)	63,407	*Look at the Harlequins!* (1974) (O)	71,327
Russian Total	1,062,594	***English Total***	904,712

Table 1: Left, we have the Russian novels in original(O) and the translations of Sergey Ilyin. The size in words of the Russian corpus is 1,062,594. Right, we have the English novels in original together with a subset of translations from Russian. We could not obtain all the equivalent translations, the Eglish corpus having a smaller size of 904,712 words.

difference is made if the ordering relation is increasing or decreasing (Dinu and Nisioi, 2012).

This is our last operation onto the matrix of similarities before inputting it in the clustering algorithm. We have linearized the matrix (converted it into a vector of measurements obtained in this case from computing delta between each pair of novels). Each value was replaced by its tied rank in the entire vector (Dinu and Popescu, 2008). Then we have reordered the values back into the initial matrix. The reason for this operation is that small distances increase between each other and large distances decrease making the method more robust.

4 Feature set

On the English corpus, we have tested the feature set proposed by Mosteller and Wallace (1963) consisting from the words: a, been, had, its, one, that, was, all, but, has, may, only, the, were, also, by, have, more, or, their, what, an, can, her, must, our, then, when, and, do, his, my, shall, there, which, any, down, if, no, should, things, who, are, even, in, not, so, this, will, as, every, into, now, some, to, with, at, for, is, of, such, up, would, be, from, it, on, than, upon, your.

In this case each document becomes a vector of size 70 in which each entry represents the frequency for the corresponding feature. The text was preprocessed to remove punctuation marks and other signs.

4.1 Feature selection

The majority of the studies rely on the principle of the most frequent words from the corpus. However, finding the exact number of the most frequent words is subject of extensive debate which dates since the study of Mosteller and Wallace (1963). Rybicki and Eder (2011) correlate the number with the language properties, other studies (Hoover, 2004; Smith and Aldridge, 2011) eliminate certain classes of words and Jockers and Witten (2012) researched optimal thresholds for word frequencies. This problem persists in every case of word usage (Koppel et al., 2007) method. Overall, the problem of selecting an objective feature set does not have a straight forward solution.

For Russian, we have introduced a process of selecting a feature set based on quantitative aspects of the results produced.

We start with the premise that the clustering results are representative with respect to the distances measured. This is assured by the $l1$ change introduced by Dinu and Nisioi (2012) and by replacing the values with ranks inside the similarity matrix. Our comparisons depend on the clustering results obtained. Using various different lists of the most frequent function words, we have executed a computational process to produce for each list a dendrogram.

The outline of the algorithm is presented below:

Algorithm 1 - *for selecting the best feature set based on measured quality*

```
1.  let F = the function words
from a Language
```

```
2.  sort F decreasing by
frequency in the corpus
3.  exclude from F the words
that are missing in at least
one document from the corpus
4.  let n be the size of F and
h = n/2
for all i from h to n do
  4.1 F_i = the first i elements
  from F
  {the same as the first i
  function words from the
  corpus}
  4.2 for each document in the
  corpus construct vectors of
  frequencies using the list F_i
  4.3 for each vector
  representation of a document
  replace frequencies by ranks
  {as detailed in Section 3}
  4.4 let M = matrix obtained
  from Δ computed between each
  vector pair
  4.5 linearise M, replace the
  values by ranks (similar
  with 4.3), reconstruct M as
  a matrix
  4.6 let R_i = dendrogram
  obtained using hierarchical
  clustering algorithm with
  input M
  4.7 let U_i = un-weighted tree
  of dendrogram R_i
  4.8 let counter[U_i] =
  counter[U_i] + 1
  {increase the cardinal of each
  equivalence class generated by
  R_i}
  4.9 record that the feature
  set F_i produced the result R_i
end for
5.  let RESULT = R_i for which
counter[U_i] is maximum
6.  let FEATURE_SET = minimum
set F_i which generated R_i
```

The first step is to retrieve all the Russian conjunctions, determiners, particles, prepositions, pronouns and adverbs (function words) from ru.wiktionary.org. We have experimented with different classes of function words from Russian and the best results were obtained by partially removing pronouns. Previous studies like the one of Hoover (2004) also suggest this operation. The second step is to order the list descending, by frequency of appearance in the entire corpus. The third step is to select from this list only the words that appear individually at least once in each document.

The fourth step is about selecting a lower limit from which to start comparing the first, most frequent function words. Starting from the half of the entire function words list (notated as F) can be a good decision, especially if the list has a significant large size. It is not entirely clear what is the minimum number of words needed to characterize the style of a text. This is why the starting value of h will be left for the user to decide according to the case. In our case, let $F_{n/2}$ be the first $n/2$ function words sorted descending by frequency in corpus. Then for each $n/2 < i \leq n$ we create a set F_i by adding consecutively one more word found at position i in the entire set F. Thus the comparisons will be made between results computed with the lists of the first i most frequent function words F_i.

Moreover, for Russian the function words have a relatively high number of declensions, so in order to correctly count the features, all the text was POS-tagged and lemmatized using TreeTagger (Schmid, 1995). On English, this operation was not necessary since the list of words provided by Mosteller and Wallace contains un-lemmatized words (e. g. “been”, “had”, “were”, etc.).

The hierarchical clustering algorithm has as input a similarity matrix and the result is illustrated by a binary tree called dendrogram, as we can observe in Figure 1.

If we ignore the distances that the edges (also called weighted links) have between clusters, we obtain a simple binary tree that illustrates only the arrangements of the clusters. We will consider two dendrograms to be equivalent if their un-weighted binary trees are identical. This means that two dendrograms are equivalent if the arrangements of the clusters are identical. Other equivalence relations can be defined at this point, depending on the size of the corpus and the works which need to be emphasized.

Roughly, the algorithm constructs for each feature set the vector representation of the documents, replaces frequencies with ranks then computes the similarity matrix using Δ, cluster the documents,

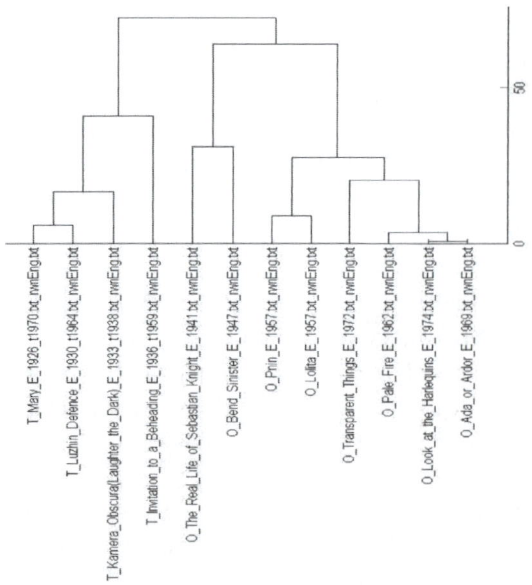

Figure 1: English corpus clustering result with the function words of Mosteller and Wallace. Translations (prefixed with T) are clustered separately from all the original works (prefixed with O). Moreover, we can observe a very small difference between the image with the original English novels and S. Ilyin's translations into Russian in Figure 2.

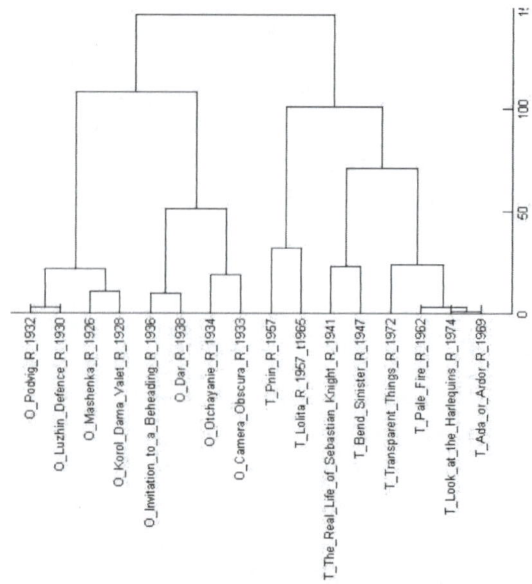

Figure 2: The most frequent Russian corpus clustering result. Translations (prefixed with T) are clustered separately from all the original works (prefixed with O). Furthermore, the original Russian novels are clustered chronologically two by two: 1932 - 1930, 1926 - 1928, 1936 - 1938, 1934 - 1933. The translations are clustered in a similar way as the originals in Figure 1.

obtains the dendrogram and based on the relation defined early it groups the equivalent results. Finally, we obtain, based on the arrangements of the clusters, different classes of results (equivalence classes).

A result is "better" (has a greater degree of quality) than another if the equivalence class of the result is larger than the equivalence class of the other.

The best result is the one with the most often produced un-weighted tree for various feature sets. Since the algorithm produces the same un-weighted tree with more words, we could just eliminate the surplus and keep only the smallest number of words.

Thus, from all the feature sets that produced the best result, we consider the smallest feature set to be the most representative for one specific corpus of text.

This criterion expresses the general tendency of the documents to be clustered in a particular way under an entire class of feature sets.

5 Results

In Figure 1 and Figure 2 we can observe that there are two main clusters of original (prefixed with O) and translated documents (prefixed with T). For Russian, the most frequent result was found with the minimum size of the list being $n = 94$ words. On English it produced the same RESULT as with the Mosteller and Wallace features Figure 1.

Using frequencies instead of ranks on both Russian and English failed to validate the hypothesis regarding translationese detection.

The RESULT of the algorithm can be seen in Figure 2 and the final FEATURE_LIST of 94 words, computed for Russian is: и, в, не, что, на, быть, с, как, а, это, но, к, по, же, так, то, из, за, у, бы, весь, от, о, только, да, уже, вот, когда, даже, до, или, для, если, другой, вдруг, время, ни, ли, чтобы, раз, во, под, со, чем, кто, два, без, потому, при, тогда, между, надо, через, над, сейчас, можно, будто, об, больше, всегда, хотя, перед, про, всякий, случай, именно, хоть, много, точно, довольно, пока, куда, давно, иногда, ко, иной, быстро, долго, едва, мало, завтра, также, сквозь,

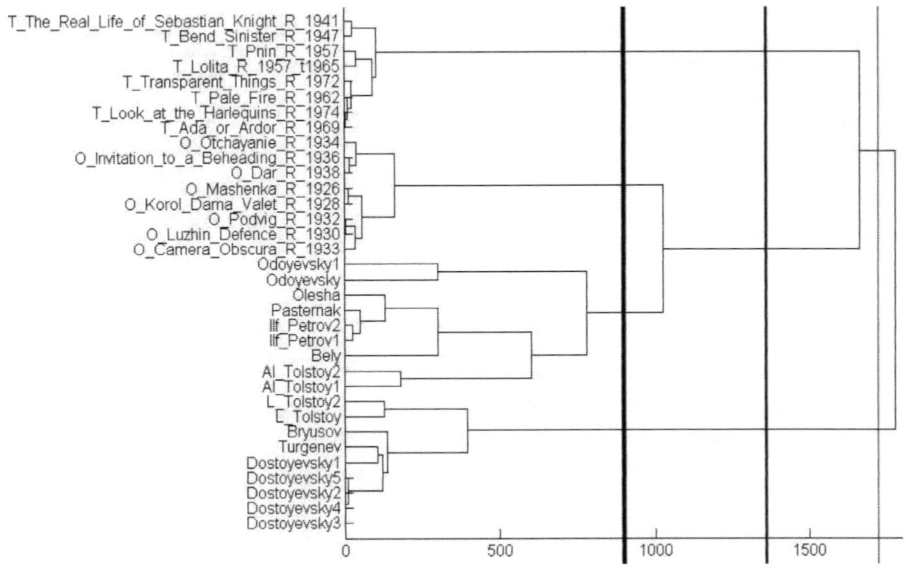

Figure 3: The result obtained from the first 94 function words (computed by the algorithm described) from the entire corpus. Nabokov is separated from other Russian authors and the translations are also separated. For each author the corresponding works are grouped in the same cluster.

мимо, домой, против, напротив, около, далеко, видно, вокруг, гораздо, вон, весело

Observation: Sometimes the counter of the "the best" result and the counter of the "second best" result could have similar values but this was not the case for us. In those situations, we would advise to analyze the differences between the results. Moreover, in thc case when a large number of files are analyzed the counters could be small and the clusters could differ by a small shift between one and other. We indicate choosing a different equivalence relation in this scenario.

Using the same feature set deduced early, we have obtained just the clustering result on Russian. Figure 3 is relevant in this sense. A first cut of this dendrogram (the rightmost thin vertical line) indicate that the early Russian novelists included (Dostoyevsky, Bryusov, L. Tolstoy, Turgenev) are clustered separately from all the other authors. A second cut (the middle-sized vertical line) indicate an answer to our second problem - if we can attribute a translation to an author. Giving the inter-cluster distance, we find the original works of Nabokov (prefixed with O) as being closest to the cluster containing translated works (prefixed with T). The third cut (the leftmost thick vertical line) suggests that translations (prefixed with T) are clustered separately from all the other Russian novels. This fact enforces the theory under which translations have distinctive features from text written natively in a certain language. Nevertheless, all the texts of various writers (including Nabokov) are clustered together, confirming the possibility of attributing translated documents to an author.

6 Conclusions and future work

We have reconsidered from a quantitative perspective the works of a bilingual writer. We have created a list of function words for Russian with respect to some quality factors described (frequency of words, frequency of results, word types and rankings) and tested it in a larger context by extending the initial corpus of Nabokov's works, see Figure 3. In the same figure the works of the other authors are grouped accordingly. The cluster of original works of Nabokov is the closest cluster to the translated from English documents (with respect to the inter-cluster distance). It seems that there is a tight relation between translationese identification and authorship attribution since features normally used to characterize the style of an author can be used to classify translated versus original documents.

As for of attributing a translation we can confirm that it is possible in a certain degree of fuzziness, Figure 3. We have to also consider fact that Nabokov, at the time of writing in English had assimilated the language perfectly as suggested by Gorski (2010).

The immediate priority is enlarging the English corpus for testing and extending the methods presented. Another chapter of interest is related to finding the linguistic resorts behind these feature sets and what other properties do they present with respect to the corpus. Analyzing the similarities between different translations of the same work is also on top of our list.

References

Argamon, S. 2008 Interpreting Burrows' Delta: Geometric and probabilistic foundations. *Literary and Linguistic Computing*, 23(2) 131-147

Boase-Beier, J. 2006 *Stylistic Approaches to Translation* Manchester: St Jerome, (2006).

Burrows, J.F. 2002 *Delta: A measure of stylistic difference and a guide to likely authorship.* Literary and Linguistic Computing 17 267–287

Chung, K.C. and Pennebaker, J.W. 2007 *The psychological functions of function words* Psychology Press, New York. 343–359

Dinu, L.P., Niculae, V., Şulea, O.M. 2012 Pastiche detection based on stopword rankings: exposing impersonators of a romanian writer. In: *Proceedings of the Workshop on Computational Approaches to Deception Detection. EACL 2012* Stroudsburg, PA, USA, Association for Computational Linguistics, 72–77

Dinu, L.P. and Nisioi, S. 2012 Authorial Studies using Ranked Lexical Features *Demos Proceedings of COLING 2012*, Mumbay, 125–130

Dinu, L.P. and Popescu, M. 2008 Rank distance as a stylistic similarity *Proceedings of COLING 2008*, Manchester, ELRA, 91–94

Hoover, D.L. 2004 Testing burrows's delta *Literary and Linguistic Computing*, 19, 453–475

Gorski, B. 2010 Nabokov vs. Набоков: A literary investigation of linguistic relativity *VESTNIK, THE JOURNAL OF RUSSIAN AND ASIAN STUDIES*

Gellerstam, M. 1986 Translationese in Swedish novels translated from English *Translation Studies in Scandinavia*, Lund: CWK Gleerup

Hansen, S. 2003 *The Nature of Translated Text* Saarbrucken: Saarland University

van Halteren, Hans and Baayen, R.H and Tweedie, F. and Haverkort, M. and Neijt, A. 2005 New machine learning methods demonstrate the existence of a human stylome *Journal of Quantitative Linguistics*, 65–77

Ilisei, I. and Inkpen, D. and Corpas Pastor, G. and Mitkov, R. 2010 Identification of translationese: a machine learning approach *Proceedings of the 11th international conference on Computational Linguistics and Intelligent Text Processing*, 503–511

Jockers, M.L. and Witten, D.M. 2012 A comparative study of machine learning methods for authorship attribution *Literary and Linguist Computing*, 215–223.

Juola, P. 2006 Authorship Attribution *Foundations and Trends in Information Retrieval*, Vol. 1, Nr. 3, 233-334

Koppel, M., Schler, J., Bonchek-Dokow, E. 2007 Measuring differentiability: Unmasking pseudonymous authors *Journal of Machine Learning* Res. 8, 1261–1276

Koppel, M., Ordan., N. 2011 Translationese and its dialects *Proceedings of the 49th Annual Meeting of the Association for Computational Linguistics: Human Language Technologies* Volume 1, 9, 1318–1326

McKenna, W., Burrows, J., Antonia, A. 1999 Beckett's "molloy": Computational stylistics and the meaning of translation *Variété: Perspectives in French Literature*, Society and Culture. Studies in Honour of Kenneth Raymond Dutton 79–92

Mosteller, F. and Wallace, L.D. 1963 Inference in an authorship problem *Journal of the American Statistical Association*, 58 275–309

Rybicki, J. and Eder, M. 2011 Deeper Delta across genres and languages: do we really need the most frequent words? *Journal of Litearary and Linguistic Computing*, 26, 3, 315 – 321

Schmid, H. 1995 Improvements in Part-of-Speech Tagging with an Application to German *Proceedings of the ACL SIGDAT-Workshop*. Dublin, Ireland

Smith, P.W.H. and Aldridge, W. 2011 Improving authorship attribution: Optimizing burrows' delta method*. *Journal of Quantitative Linguistics 18*, 63–88

Stamatatos, E. 2009 A survey of modern authorship attribution methods *J. Am. Soc. Inf. Sci. Technol.*, Vol. 60, Nr. 3, 538–556

Szekely, G.J. and Rizzo, M.L. 2005 Hierarchical clustering via joint between-within distances: Extending ward's minimum variance method. *Journal of Classification*, 151 – 183

Wang, Q. and Li, D. 2012 Looking for translator's fingerprints: a corpus-based study on chinese translations of ulysses. *Literary and Linguistic Computing*, 27, 81–93

s Ward, J.H. 1963 Hierarchical grouping to optimize an objective function. *J. of American Statistical Association*, 301, 236–244

PurePos 2.0: a hybrid tool for morphological disambiguation

György Orosz and **Attila Novák**
Pázmány Péter Catholic University, Faculty of Information Technology
MTA-PPKE Natural Language Processing Group
50/a Práter street, Budapest, Hungary
{oroszgy, novak.attila}@itk.ppke.hu

Abstract

We present PurePos, an open-source HMM-based automatic morphological annotation tool. PurePos can perform tagging and lemmatization at the same time, it is very fast to train, with the possibility of easy integration of symbolic rule-based components into the annotation process that can be used to boost the accuracy of the tool. The hybrid approach implemented in PurePos is especially beneficial in the case of rich morphology, highly detailed annotation schemes and if a small amount of training data is available. Evaluation of the tool was on a Hungarian corpus revealed that its hybrid components significantly improve overall annotation accuracy.

1 Introduction

Part-of-speech tagging is one of the basic and commonly studied tasks of natural language processing. High accuracy of morphosyntactic annotation is crucial since tagging is usually part of a language processing pipeline, thus tagging errors propagate. Several PoS tagging tools have been created and made available during the years, however, PoS tagging is just the subtask of morphological annotation: in addition to the morphosyntactic tag, the lemma needs to be identified for each token. For morphologically not very rich languages, like English, a cascade of a tagger and a stemmer may yield an acceptable performance, but in the case of morphologically rich languages, incorporating morphological knowledge in the form of a morphological analyzer (MA) into the tagging process seems to be necessary not only to obtain high tagging accuracy but also to provide correct lemmata.

Sequence tagging tasks are often solved using statistical modelling techniques, since having a huge amount of annotated data, a decent method can learn important regularities, and applying this knowledge can yield highly accurate results. Smoothing techniques are commonly used in statistical natural language processing applications to alleviate problems caused by data sparseness. However, this prevents purely statistical models from being able to exclude events from the model that are known to be impossible to occur. Rule-based tools can find their niche here: one can either use rules to filter out agrammatical sequences, or ones that do not occur in a given domain. Hybrid methods combining statistical and rule-based approaches are getting more and more popular, since these are often able to yield a level of performance not attainable by either the statistical or the rule-based component alone.

In this paper, we describe the improvements that we made to an open source tool, PurePos, which, combining statistical models with symbolic and rule-based components, can generate highly accurate morphological annotation. Our paper is structured as follows. First, we motivate the model with annotation scenarios where a hybrid approach can be expected to perform significantly better than a purely statistical solution. Then the components of the tool are introduced. We describe the disambiguation process implemented in the tool, focusing on methods that enable us utilize the knowledge of the built-in MA and algorithms that we use to lemmatize words unknown to the MA. Finally, we evaluate our tool in a scenario where the annotation task involves a language with a very rich agglutinating and compounding morphology, an annotation scheme with very detailed distinctions and a rather modest amount of training data.

2 The need of a hybrid annotation model

2.1 Agglutinating languages

If we compare an agglutinating language like Finnish with English in terms of the coverage of vocabulary by a corpus of a given size, we find that although there is a much higher number of different word forms in the Finnish corpus, these still cover a much smaller percentage of possible word forms of the lemmata in the corpus than in the case of English. Creutz et al. (2007) have compared the number of different word forms encountered in a corpus as a function of corpus size for English and agglutinating languages like Finnish, Estonian or Turkish. While a 10-million-word portion of their English newspaper corpus has less than 100,000 different word forms, a corpus of the same size for Finnish contains well over 800,000. On the other hand, however, while an open class English word has no more than 4–6 different forms, it has several hundred or thousand different productively suffixed forms in any of the agglutinating languages discussed in that paper. Moreover, there are much more different possible morphosyntactic tags in the case of agglutinating languages (corresponding to the different possible inflected forms) than in English (several thousand vs. a few dozen). Thus data sparseness is threefold:

- an overwhelming majority of possible word forms of lemmata occurring in the corpus is totally absent,
- word forms that do occur in the corpus have much less occurrences, and
- there are also much less examples of tag sequences, what is more, many tags may not occur in the corpus at all.

The identification of the correct lemma is not trivial either, especially in the cases of guessed lemmata. One such case from Hungarian is briefly discussed in (Orosz and Novák, 2012).

2.2 Resource-poor languages

A great proportion of resource-poor languages (that lack annotated corpora) is morphologically complex. To create an annotated corpus for these languages, an iterative workflow seems to be a feasible approach as it is proposed in (Orosz and Novák, 2012). First, a very small subset of the corpus is disambiguated manually, and the tagger is trained on this subset. Then another subset of the corpus is tagged automatically and corrected manually, yielding a new, bigger training corpus and this process is repeated. The higher the accuracy of the automatic annotation tool is, the less time human annotators need to spend manually correcting the results, and the less annotation errors are likely to remain in the resulting annotation.

2.3 Domain adaptation

Statistical models trained on a specific corpus, or even on balanced corpora, usually perform worse on texts from a different domain. The incorporation of symbolic morphological knowledge in the form of a high-coverage MA in the tagging procedure can successfully reduce the effect of domain differences. Miller et al. (2006) have shown that the incorporation of domain-specific lexical resources significantly improves performance. Such resources, however, can only increase accuracy in a consistent manner in the case of a morphologically rich language if the resource also covers suffixed forms of the domain-specific lexical items. Furthermore texts from a specific domain often have domain-specific syntactic and lexical patterns that can be made use of to gain accuracy.

Even in the case of ample training data, the tool may fail to generate correct annotation if the model implemented in it is not capable to capture some relevant generalization, e.g. a second-order HMM model may not capture long-distance agreement constraints, which results in random noise. In such a case, and for each of the use cases described above, applying additional linguistic constraints can improve accuracy. PurePos was made capable of incorporation of linguistic constraints and lexical knowledge both at its input and its output. It is capable of reading partially disambiguated input, where not only possible tags but their lexical probabilities can also be specified in the input for each individual token. In addition, it is capable of generating a k-best list of annotations with scores assigned to each annotated output, which can be used by either further parsing tools or machine learning systems.

3 Disambiguation model

The morphological annotation model performs lemma identification after determining the most probable morphosyntactic tag for each word. In this section, we describe the tagging and lemmatization models implemented in PurePos.

3.1 PoS tagging model

Our aim was to build a system that is not only highly accurate but has a short training time as well. Fast turnaround time is e.g. needed in the iterative corpus creation scenario described above. In order to achieve high accuracy and fast training time, PurePos uses methods introduced in TnT (Brants, 2000) and HunPos (Halácsy et al., 2007). The tagging model is a linearly interpolated n-gram-based contextual model[1], and it uses unigram or bigram lexical models.

$$P(t_k|t_{k-1,k-n+1}) = \sum_{i=1}^{n} \lambda_i \hat{P}(t_k|t_{k-1,k-i+1}) \quad (1)$$

In (1), $\hat{P}$'s are maximum-likelihood conditional probability estimates of different left context sizes, while the interpolation parameters (λ_i) are calculated in a context-independent way using deleted estimation. This algorithm iteratively increases the score of a model weight if that is the most confident one for a trigram found in the training data. PurePos, like HunPos and TnT, maintains a separate lexical model for special tokens, and employs a guessing algorithm for determining the tags for previously unseen words. This guesser estimates PoS tag probabilities for unknown words based on the suffix distribution of rare words. For decoding, HunPos offers a slightly sped-up version of the Viterbi algorithm, which, while it gains on speed, loses a little accuracy. Besides keeping the Viterbi decoder, beam search was added to PurePos, which can be selected as an alternative decoding algorithm. When using beam search, the updated version of PurePos is capable of providing k-best output, outputting for each candidate annotated sequence its score, which is used for ranking candidates:

$$\begin{aligned} &Score(w_{1,m}, t_{1,m}) \\ &= log \prod_{i=1}^{m} P(w_k|t_k) P(t_k|t_{k-1}, ..., t_{k-n+1}) \end{aligned} \quad (2)$$

[1]The software is able to incorporate higher-order models as well, but in practice, a smoothed trigram model is generally used.

Employing morphological knowledge

In addition to statistical modelling, the tagger can incorporate knowledge provided by a morphological analyzer. In a previous version of PurePos, this could only be done through integration of a symbolic component using a Java API. The updated version is capable to read pre-analyzed text from the input, which means that any morphological analyzer can be used. If possible analyses are specified in the input for a token, tagging options as well as lemmas are restricted to the ones in the input for that token.

While the usage of morphological information might seem at first sight to be simple, there are several corner cases that need to be handled. First of all, a problem arises when the model is requested to assign a probability mass (either lexical or contextual) to an unseen tag. This occurs when an unseen tag is input to the system either as user input or by the integrated analyzer: in the default implementation, there is no way to calculate a lexical probability for this event. The same problem arises when a new morphosyntactic tag is included as a candidate analysis for a word that was seen in the training data but was never observed with that tag. These annotations were ignored by the original algorithm implemented in HunPos thus yielding obviously erroneous tagging.

Simple settings described above make it impossible to estimate probabilities for unknown tags, thus they get zero probability (and negative infinity as a score), which affects the whole tagging sequence making it unreliable.

It is also important to note that in case of tagging morphologically rich languages, the cardinality of the tag set usually exceeds one thousand, which results in data sparseness. This is especially problematic when the amount of the training data is low. Adaptation to new domains or tasks may also lead to the expansion of the tag set, which is difficult to handle with other existing tools.

We employ the following method to deal with problematic cases: if a token has only one (unseen) candidate analysis, that one is selected, and the lexical probability of the word-tag pair is assumed to be 1, while the contextual probabilities of forthcoming tags are taken from a lower level (unigram) model. When multiple candidates exist and at least one label is missing from the training data, PurePos is able to estimate lexical and contextual probabilities through mapping it to a previously seen morphosyntactic tag. For this, the user must setup a configuration file in which morphosyntactic label mapping rules can be formulated using regular expressions.

3.2 Lemmatization model

The updated implementation of PurePos contains a lemma identification process that selects the lemma candidate that has the maximal probability according to following conditional model:

$$\arg\max_{l} P(l|t, w) \tag{3}$$

I.e. the most probable lemma given the token and part-of-speech tag is selected. In practice, this probability is estimated in two ways. First, assuming that the lemmata are independent from words and tags, their probability can be estimated with unigram maximum likelihood estimates $\hat{P}(l)$, which are derived from relative frequencies. In addition, reformulating the core of (3), we get

$$P(l|t, w) = \frac{P(l, t|w)}{P(t|w)} \tag{4}$$

As the task is to select an optimal lemma for a fixed word and label pair, $P(t|w)$ is constant and can be ignored. The rest is approximated by using smoothed suffix models as described in (Brants, 2000). In order to efficiently store *(lemma, tag)* pairs, they are represented as suffix transformations that are to be performed to get the lemma from the word form in case of the given tag. This model is not only used for calculating probabilities but also employed for generating the lemma candidates. To utilize the strengths of both models, we use log-linear interpolation:

$$P(l|w, t) = P(l)^{\lambda_1} P(l, t|w)^{\lambda_2} \tag{5}$$

The idea of estimating the $\lambda_{1,2}$ parameters is similar to that used for the interpolation of PoS n-gram models (see section 3.1), but instead using positive weights, negative penalty scores are added to the parameter for the model performing poorly for a given *(word, PoS tag, lemma)* triplet (see algorithm 1).

Having the $\lambda_{1,2}$ parameters calculated, lemmatization is performed after morphosyntactic disambiguation. If there are full morphological analyses provided by the MA, then the lemmata provided by the analyses are taken as candidates, otherwise the lemma-guesser provides them. Finally, PurePos selects the candidate that satisfies (3).

3.3 Hybrid components

In addition to the exhaustive use of the morphological knowledge described above, PurePos provides facilities for users to incorporate extra lexical or grammatical knowledge through the input to the tagger. One can provide pre-analyzed input that not only contains full morphological analysis of tokens but contains lexical distribution data, which can be used to locally override lexical distributions in the model used by the tagger coming from the training corpus. This facility can be used e.g. to provide domain-specific lexical distribution information if the distribution of analyses for a given lexical item are markedly different in the given domain from that in the training corpus. The same facility can be used to filter out candidates agrammatical in the given context, e.g. capturing long-distance agreement constraints that the trigram tagging model cannot handle.

Using the built-in k-best search algorithm and the variable beam size, it is possible to generate output that is apt for post-processing. Advanced machine learning techniques and further parsing algorithms can also benefit from the k-best output format, since the disambiguation scores for sentences are also output.

4 Evaluation

In this section, we present a tagging task that we used as a test case to evaluate the methods described above. In a project aiming at the creation of an annotated corpus of Middle Hungarian texts (Novák et al., 2013), [2] an adapted version of Hungarian HuMor (Prószéky and Novák, 2005; Prószéky, 1994) morphological analyzer was used. This tool was originally made to annotate contemporary Hungarian, but the grammar and lexicon were modified so that the tool can handle morphological constructions that existed in Middle Hungarian but have since disappeared from the language. In the experiments described here, we used a manually checked disambiguated portion of this corpus. The data was annotated using a rich variant of the HuMor tagset, the cardinality of which is over a thousand.

In order to simulate this annotation task, we split the corpus into three parts (Table 1). The tagger was trained on the biggest part, hybridization and adaptation methods were developed on a

[2] Historical corpus of informal language use [OTKA 81189]

Algorithm 1 Calculating parameters of the linear interpolated lemmatization model

for all (word, tag, lemma) **do**
  candidates ← generateLemmaCandidates(word, tag)
  maxUnigramProb ← getMaxProb(candidates, word, tag, unigramModel)
  maxSuffixProb ← getMaxProb(candidates, word, tag, suffixModel)
  actUnigramProb ← getProb(word, tag, lemma, unigramModel)
  actSuffixProb ← getProb(word, tag, lemma, suffixModel)
  unigramProbDistance ← maxUnigramProb − actUnigramProb
  suffixProbDistance ← maxSuffixProb − actSuffixProb
  if unigramProbDistance > suffixProbDistance **then**
    $\lambda_2 \leftarrow \lambda_2 +$ unigramProbDistance − suffixProbDistance
  else
    $\lambda_1 \leftarrow \lambda_1 +$ suffixProbDistance − unigramProbDistance
  end if
  normalize(λ_1, λ_2)
end for

Table 1: Characteristics of the used corpus

	Training	Dev.	Test
Documents	140	20	30
Clauses	12355	2731	2484
Tokens	59926	12656	11763

separate development subcorpus, while final evaluation was done on a test set. We used accuracy as a metric, with unambiguous punctuation tokens *not* taken into account (in contrast to how taggers are evaluated in general). The results were evaluated in a threefold way: PoS tagging accuracy and full morphological disambiguation accuracy were calculated for tokens, and the latter was also calculated to obtain a clause-level accuracy.

As baselines, we used the enhanced trigram-based algorithm derived from HunPos and implemented in PurePos (PP), while its combination with the HuMor analyzer (PPM) was also evaluated. As a lemmatization baseline, we used the unigram-based (UL) and the suffix-based model (SL) described in section 3.2. Performance of these systems is shown in Table 2. As the accuracy values indicate, suffix-based probability estimation could performed better when used together with a morphological analyzer, while when using no dedicated morphological component, the overall disambiguation accuracies applying either of the baseline lemmatization models were close to each other.

Basic lemmatization strategies can be improved through the model combination method described in Section 3.2. Results obtained by the com-

Table 2: Baseline disambiguation accuracies on the development set

	Tagging	Full	Clauses
PP+UL	93.20%	88.99%	55.58%
PP+SL	93.20%	89.01%	51.78%
PPM+UL	97.77%	97.22%	84.85%
PPM+SL	97.77%	97.50%	85.98%

bined approach are shown in Table 3. The presented algorithm yields an overall 3.2% relative error rate reduction compared to the best baseline (PPM+SL). The improvement is even more significant for in the case when a dedicated morphological analyzer is not used: the relative error rate reduction is 28.42% in this case (compared to PP+SL).

To demonstrate the strengths of the hybrid PurePos, we present three models to enhance the performance of the tool. To that end, we utilized a development set to analyze common error types and to test hypotheses.

Table 3: Full disambiguation accuracies with the proposed lemmatization model measured on the development set

	Tokens	Clauses
Using a MA	97.58%	86.48%
Without a MA	92.14%	65.40%

Mapping tags

In contrast to other Hungarian annotation projects, the tag set used for annotating the historical corpus distinguishes verb forms that have a verbal prefix from those that do not, because this is a distinction important for researchers interested in syntax.[3] This practically doubles the number of verb tags,[4] which results in data sparseness problems for the tagger. In case of a never encountered tag including a verbal prefix marking, mapping it to one without verbal prefix is a sensible solution since the distribution of prefixed and non-prefixed verbs largely overlap. Applying only this verbal mapping (TM), we could increase the clause level annotation accuracy to 86.53% that is 97.59% precision at token level.

Preprocessing

Another possible improvement is to employ rules that filter the input (FI). Exploiting the development set again, a preprocessing script was set up that employs five simple rules. Three of them catches frequent phrases such as *az a* 'that' in which *az* must be a pronoun. Another typical source of errors is the erroneous tagging or lemmatization of proper names that coincide with frequent common nouns or adjectives and the confusion of past participles as finite past verb forms. Implementing just a few rules for fixing these, we achieved 97.84% token accuracy and 86.77% clause accuracy on the development set.

k-best output

The k-best output of the tagger can either be used as a representation to apply upstream grammatical filters to or as candidates for alternative input to higher levels of processing. Five-best output for our test corpus has yielded an upper limit for attainable clause accuracy of 94.32%. While it is not directly comparable with the ones above, this feature could be successfully used also in self-training or in tagger combination schemes.

Applying the given hybridization steps to the test set, we can validate the performance improvements (see results in Table 4 [5]). Using 5-best output from the tagger, 92.30% of clauses have the golden annotation among the top 5 output.

Table 4: Disambiguation accuracies of the hybrid tool on the test set

	Tagging	Full	Clauses
Best baseline	96.72%	96.40%	80.52%
PurePos	96.72%	96.48%	80.95%
+TM	96.75%	96.51%	81.17%
+FI	96.83%	96.60%	81.55%
+FI +TM	96.87%	96.63%	81.77%

5 Conclusion

In this paper, we presented PurePos, an open-source full morphological annotation tool[6], which is based on simple and fast but effective models. The tagger is able to accommodate linguistic knowledge by using partially disambiguated input, including linguistic models that handle long-distance agreement constraints not covered by the core trigram HMM model. Its internal tag mapping interface can be used to handle problems caused by sparse tag data. Its data-driven lemmatization models are able to lemmatize words unseen in the training data and unknown to the morphological analyzer.

One can benefit from the usage of PurePos in cases of rich morphology, highly detailed annotation schemes or if a small amount of training data is available only. The possible application of linguistic knowledge makes it a feasible tool for rapid domain adaptation tasks as well.

Acknowledgement

Research reported in this paper was partially supported by the research project grants OTKA 81189, TÁMOP – 4.2.1.B – 11/2/KMR-2011-0002 and TÁMOP – 4.2.2/B – 10/1–2010–0014.

References

Thorsten Brants. 2000. TnT - A Statistical Part-of-Speech Tagger. In *Proceedings of the sixth conference on Applied Natural Language Processing*, pages 224–231.

Eric Brill. 1992. A simple rule-based part of speech tagger. In *Proceedings of the workshop on Speech and Natural Language*, pages 112–116.

[3]Hungarian verbal prefixes or particles behave similarly to separable verbal prefixes in most Germanic languages: they usually form a single orthographic word with the verb they modify, however, they are separated in certain syntactic constructions.

[4]320 different verb tags occur in the corpus excluding verb prefix vs. no verb prefix distinction. This is just a fraction of the theoretically possible tags.

[5]Results in Tables 2 and 3 were obtained on the development set.

[6]`http://nlpg.itk.ppke.hu/software/purepos`

Mathias Creutz, Teemu Hirsimäki, Mikko Kurimo, Antti Puurula, Janne Pylkkönen, Vesa Siivola, Matti Varjokallio, Ebru Arisoy, Murat Saraçlar, and Andreas Stolcke. 2007. Morph-based speech recognition and modeling of out-of-vocabulary words across languages. *ACM Transactions on Speech and Language Processing (TSLP)*, 5(1):3.

Jan Hajič, Pavel Krbec, Květoň, Karel Oliva, and Vladimír Petkevič. 2001. Serial combination of rules and statistics: A case study in Czech tagging. In *Proceedings of the 39th Annual Meeting on Association for Computational Linguistics*, pages 268–275.

Péter Halácsy, András Kornai, and Csaba Oravecz. 2007. HunPos: an open source trigram tagger. In *Proceedings of the 45th Annual Meeting of the ACL*, pages 209–212, Prague, Czech Republic.

Mans Hulden and Jerid Francom. 2012. Boosting statistical tagger accuracy with simple rule-based grammars. In *Proceedings of the Eight International Conference on Language Resources and Evaluation (LREC'12)*, Istanbul, Turkey.

John E Miller, Michael Bloodgood, Manabu Torii, and K Vijay-Shanker. 2006. Rapid adaptation of pos tagging for domain specific uses. In *Proceedings of the HLT-NAACL BioNLP Workshop on Linking Natural Language and Biology*, pages 118–119.

Attila Novák, György Orosz, and Nóra Wenszky. 2013. Morphological annotation of old and middle hungarian corpora. In *Proceedings of the 7th Workshop on Language Technology for Cultural Heritage, Social Sciences, and Humanities*, pages 43–48, Sofia, Bulgaria.

Csaba Oravecz and Péter Dienes. 2002. Efficient Stochastic Part-of-Speech Tagging for Hungarian. In *Third International Conference on Language Resources and Evaluation*, pages 710–717, Las Palmas, Spain.

György Orosz and Attila Novák. 2012. PurePos – an open source morphological disambiguator. In *Proceedings of the 9th International Workshop on Natural Language Processing and Cognitive Science*, pages 53–63, Wroclaw.

Gábor Prószéky and Attila Novák. 2005. Computational Morphologies for Small Uralic Languages. In *Inquiries into Words, Constraints and Contexts.*, pages 150–157, Stanford, California.

Gábor Prószéky. 1994. Industrial applications of unification morphology. In *Proceedings of the fourth conference on Applied natural language processing* -, page 213, Morristown, NJ, USA.

Adwait Ratnaparkhi. 1996. A maximum entropy model for part-of-speech tagging. In *Proceedings of the conference on Empirical Methods in Natural Language Processing*, pages 133–142, Somerset, New Jersey.

Kristina Toutanova, Dan Klein, Christopher Manning, and Yoram Singer. 2003. Feature-rich part-of-speech tagging with a cyclic dependency network. In *Proceedings of the 2003 Conference of the North American Chapter of the Association for Computational Linguistics on Human Language Technology*, pages 173–180, Edmonton, Canada.

More than Bag-of-Words: Sentence-based Document Representation for Sentiment Analysis

Georgios Paltoglou
Faculty of Science and Technology
University of Wolverhampton
Wulfruna Street, WV1 1LY, UK
g.paltoglou@wlv.ac.uk

Mike Thelwall
Faculty of Science and Technology
University of Wolverhampton
Wulfruna Street, WV1 1LY, UK
m.thelwall@wlv.ac.uk

Abstract

Most sentiment analysis approaches rely on machine-learning techniques, using a bag-of-words (BoW) document representation as their basis. In this paper, we examine whether a more fine-grained representation of documents as sequences of emotionally-annotated sentences can increase document classification accuracy. Experiments conducted on a sentence and document level annotated corpus show that the proposed solution, combined with BoW features, offers an increase in classification accuracy.

1 Introduction

Sentiment analysis is concerned with automatically extracting sentiment-related information from text. A typical problem is to determine whether a text is positive, negative or neutral overall. Most of the proposed solutions are based on supervised machine-learning approaches, with some notable exceptions (Turney, 2002; Lin and He, 2009), although unsupervised, lexicon-based solutions have also been used, especially in non review-based corpora (Thelwall et al., 2010).

This paper deals with the problem of detecting the overall polarity of a document. A common theme with a significant number of proposed solutions is the bag-of-words (BoW) document representation, according to which a document is represented as a binary or frequency-based feature vector of the tokens it contains, regardless of their position in the text. Nonetheless, significant semantic information is lost when all positional information is discarded. Consider, the following extract of a movie review (taken from Pang (2008)):

> This film should be brilliant. It sounds like a great plot, ... a good performance. However, it cant hold up.

Most of bag-of-words machine learning or lexicon-based solutions would be expected to classify the extract as *positive* because of the significant number of positive words that it contains. However, a human reader studying the review, recognizes the *change of polarity* that occurs in the last sentence, a change that is hinted at by the first sentence ("should be brilliant") but is only fully realized at the end. In fact, this phenomenon of "thwarted expectations" is particularly common in reviews and has been observed by both Pang et. al (2002) and Turney (2002) who noted that "the whole is not necessarily the sum of the parts".

In this work we propose a solution to the aforementioned problem by building a meta-classifier which models each document as a sequence of emotionally annotated sentences. The advantage of this modeling is that it implicitly captures word position in the whole document in a semantically and structurally meaningful way, while at the same time drastically reducing the feature space for the final classification. Additionally, the proposed solution is conceptually simple, intuitive and can be used in addition to standard BoW features.

2 Prior Work

The commercial potential of sentiment analysis has resulted in a significant amount of research and Pang (2008) provides an overview. In this section, we limit our presentation to the work that is most relevant to our approach.

McDonald et al. (2007) used structured models for classifying a document at different levels of granularity. The approach has the advantage that it allows for classifications at different levels to influence the classification outcome of other levels. However, at training time, it requires labeled data at all levels of analysis, which is a significant practical drawback. Täckström and McDonald (2011) attempt to elevate the aforementioned requirement, focusing on sentence-level sentiment analysis. Their results showed that this approach significantly reduced sentence classification errors over simpler baselines.

Although relevant to our approach, the focus of this paper is different. First, the overall purpose of our approach is to aid document-level classification. Second, the algorithm presented here utilizes sentence-level classification in order to train a document meta-classifier and explicitly retains the position and the polarity of each sentence.

Mao and Lebanon (2006) use isotonic Conditional Random Fields, in order to capture the *flow* of emotion in documents. They focus on sentence-level sentiment analysis, where the context of each sentence plays a vital role in predicting the sentiment of the sentence itself. They also present some results for predicting global sentiment, but convert the sentence-based flow to a smooth length-normalized flow for the whole document in order to compare documents of different length and use a k-nearest neighbor classifier using L_p distances as a measure of document similarity.

Our work can be seen as an extension of their solution, where the fine-grained sentiment analysis is given as input to the meta-classifier in order to predict the overall polarity of the document. Nonetheless, in our modeling we retain the structural coherence of the original document by representing it as a discrete-valued feature vector of the sentiment of its sentences instead of converting it to a real-valued continuous function.

3 Sentence-based document representation

The algorithm proposed in this paper is simple in its inception, intuitive and can be used in addition to standard or extended (Mishne, 2005) document representations. Although the approach isn't limited to sentiment classification and can be applied to other classification tasks, the fact that phenomena such as "thwarted expectation" occur mainly in this context, makes the approach particularly suitable for sentiment analysis.

3.1 Sentence classification

At the first level classification, the algorithm needs to estimate the affective content of the sentences contained in a document. The affective content of each sentence is characterized in two dimensions; subjectivity and polarity. The former estimation will aid in removing sentences which contain no or little emotional content and thus don't contribute to the overall polarity of the document and the latter estimation will be used in the final document representation as a surrogate for each sentence. Therefore, for each sentence we need to estimate its subjectivity and polarity, that is, build a *subjectivity* and a *polarity detector*.

Polarity detector: Given a set of positive and negative documents, the algorithm initially trains a standard unigram-based polarity classifier. In our experiments we tested Naive Bayes and Maximum Entropy classifiers, but focus on the former since both classifiers perform similarly, due to space constraints. The classifier utilizes the labels of the training documents as positive and negative instances. The trained classifier will be used at the second-level classification in order to estimate the polarity of individual sentences.

Subjectivity detector: As above, in this stage the algorithm trains a unigram-based subjectivity classifier, that will be used at a later stage for filtering out the sentences that don't contribute to the overall polarity of the document. Training such a classifier is less straight-forward than training the polarity classifier, because of the potential lack of appropriate training data. We propose two solutions to this problem. The first one is based on using a static, external *subjectivity* corpus. The second partly elevates the need for a full subjectivity corpus, by requiring only a set of objective documents, which are usually easier to come by (e.g. wikipedia). In the this case, we can use the training documents as subjective instances and the objective documents as objective instances[1]. We present results with both approaches in section 5.

3.2 Document classification

Having built the unigram-based subjectivity and polarity classifiers in the first stage of the process, the sentence of each training document is classified in terms of its subjectivity and polarity. The former estimation is used in order to remove objective sentences which do not contribute to the overall polarity of the document and also helps in "normalizing" documents to a common length.

More specifically, the sentences are ranked in reference to their probability of being subjective and only the top M are retained, where M is a predetermined parameter. In section 5 we present

[1]During n-fold cross-validation, we utilize only the documents in the training folds as subjective instances.

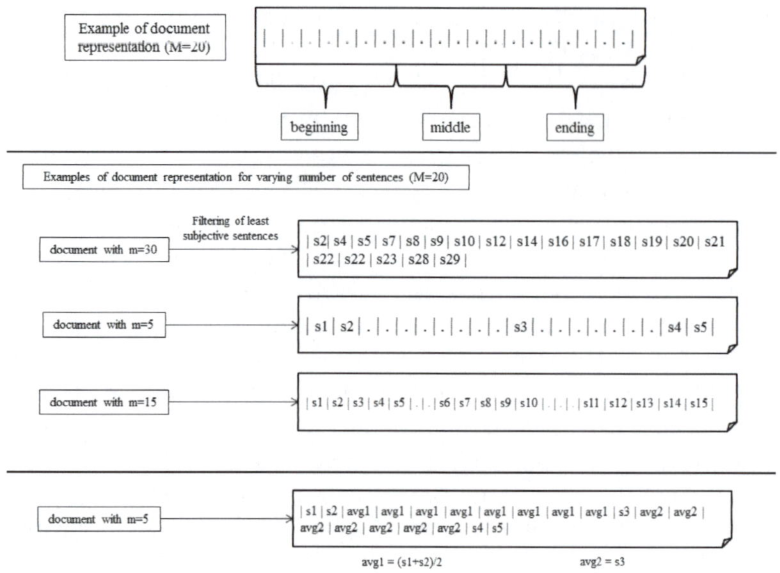

Figure 1: Examples of document representation.

results with various threshold values, but experiments show that a value for M in the $[15, 25]$ interval performs best. A natural question is how does the algorithm deal with documents which have less than M sentences. We provide the answer to this question subsequently, after we explain how the remaining sentences are ordered and utilized in producing the final document representation.

Having removed the least subjective sentences, the remaining are ordered in reference to their relative position in the original document, that is, sentences that precede others are placed before them (see first example in middle section of Figure 1). Using the polarity classifier built on the first stage of the algorithm, we estimate the polarity of each sentence and use this information in order to represent the document as a sequence of emotionally annotated sentences. Alternatively, we can use the probability of polarity of the sentences (e.g., $Pr(+1|sentence)$) in order to represent a document. In fact, the latter representation retains more information than the simple polarity, for example distinguishing between a "barely" positive and a "highly" positive sentence. Although the polarity of both sentences would be the same (i.e., +1) retaining information about the probability provides the document-level classifier with additional information. This decision contrasts with the way that sentence-based sentiment analysis is utilized by Mao and Lebanon (2006) and the experiments presented in section 5 indicate that it typically results in increased accuracy.

The modeling serves two purposes: first of all, by retaining only the more subjective sentences, we remove all sentences which do not contribute to the final polarity of the document. Secondly, by ordering the remaining sentences by their relative original position, we maintain positional information about the emotional content of the most subjective sentences in the document and thus may be able to extract useful positional patterns.

3.3 Dealing with small documents

One of the main problems with the aforementioned approach is the document "normalization" issue, that is, how to represent documents as an equal number of sentences. The retaining of only the most M subjective sentences solves the problem for longer documents and provides a predefined feature vector space, but the problem of effectively representing smaller documents remains.

In order to deal with the problem of small documents, we propose the following solution. Initially, we assume that each document can be represented on an abstract level as having a "beginning" section, a "middle" section and a "ending" section. Depending on the value of M each section is required to be populated by a specific number of sentences. If M is a multiple of 3, then each section will have an equal number of sentences ($M/3$). In the other cases, initially all sections are attributed the maximum equal number of sentences and the remaining sentences are attributed as follows: if $M mod 3 = 1$, then the extra sentence is added to the middle section and if $M mod 3 = 2$ then each one of the extra sentences are added to the beginning and last sections. For example if $M = 15$, then the distribution of sentences is $\{5, 5, 5\}$, if $M = 16$ then the distribution is $\{5, 6, 5\}$ and if $M = 17$ then $\{6, 5, 6\}$. Clearly, the decision of representing a document as three sections is ad-hoc, and some prior evidence suggests that a 4-way split is better for sentiment analysis (Pang et al., 2002), but we believe it is more in accordance with the intuitive interpretation of documents (Kress, 1999). See top section of Figure 1 for an example with $M = 20$.

Having determined the number of sentences that should be allocated to each section, the next logical step is distributing the existing document sentences to each[2]. We adopt the same process as above, using the number of sentences in the document m instead of M. Therefore, if for example a document has 7 sentences, then their distribution would be $\{2, 3, 2\}$. The placement of the sentences for the beginning and ending sections begin at the first and last position respectively while for the middle section, they are placed around the center. The middle section of Figure 1 provides examples for different m values.

Two final issues subsequently need to be resolved. The first one refers to the filling of the *empty* positions and the second refers to the distribution of sentences on the middle section when m and M differ in terms of their parity (odd vs. even). For the first issue we propose two solutions; the first one fills the empty positions with zeros and the second one fills them with the average of the proceeding polarities or probabilities (e.g., the average of $s1$ and $s2$ in the first example, see lower section of Figure 1). For the second problem, we propose two possible solutions; a "forward weighting" approach where the sentences in the middle section are placed one position toward the beginning of the document and the "backward weighting" approach in which the reverse happens. For example in the middle section of Figure 1 the former approach is used.

[2]Recall that this process is only adopted for documents with less than M sentences.

3.4 Training and testing

To summarize the whole process, during training the algorithm is given a set of positive and negative documents, and initially trains a unigram-based polarity classifier using the labels of the documents. A subjectivity classifier is also built either using a separate *subjectivity* corpus or alternatively, utilizing the documents in the training set as *subjective* instances and only a separate set of *objective* documents as objective instances. Using those classifiers, every sentence in the original training documents are classified in terms of subjectivity and polarity. The sentences are ranked in terms of their probability of being subjective and only the top M are retained, where M is a predefined threshold. Next, the sentences are ordered in reference to their position at the document and their polarity or probability of polarity is used to represent the document and train the second-level, sentence-based classifier.

During testing time, the unigram based classifiers that were built from the training corpus are utilized in order to classify all the sentences in the testing documents in terms of their subjectivity and polarity. As described previously, only the M most subjective sentences are kept and they are reordered in reference to their position in the original document. The learnt sentence-based classifier is applied and a final polarity prediction is made.

4 Experimental Setup

For our experiments, we used a corpus of customer reviews containing reviews of books, DVDs, electronics, music and videogames, split by polarity (henceforth referred to as the *consumer reviews* dataset). The dataset was introduced by Täckström and McDonald (2011) and is freely available[3]. It comprises 97 positive, 98 neutral and 99 negative reviews, annotated by two human assessors both at the document and at the sentence level. Overall inter-annotator agreement is 86% and Cohen's κ value is 0.79. More information about the dataset can be found at Täckström and McDonald (2011). The existence of a set of *neutral* documents and the fact that the corpus is also annotated at the sentence level make it very appropriate for our purposes. Alternatively, we could have utilized the corpus presented by McDonald

[3]The dataset can be obtained from `http://www.sics.se/people/oscar/datasets`.

Training Dataset	Naive Bayes	MaxEnt
Subjectivity corpus (whole documents)	60.75%	59.04%
Subjectivity corpus (filtered documents)	64.87%	62.00%
Consumer reviews (whole documents)	59.81%	63.12%
Consumer reviews (filtered documents)	62.69%	67.73%

Table 1: Subjectivity detection accuracy on the consumer reviews dataset. Result for the last two rows are based on 10-fold cross validation.

et al. (2007), but due to licensing issues, it is currently not publicly available.

For building the subjectivity classifier we use two different approaches. First, we utilize the objective documents of the corpus as objective instances and the training documents as subjective. Two parameterizations are tested: in the first case, we train the classifier on the whole documents and in the second we train the classifier only on the objective/subjective sentences for each category respectively. This way, we'll be able to test whether using much less noisy training data significantly aids the effectiveness of the classifier. In the second approach, we use a static, external corpus to train the subjectivity classifier. In this paper, we use the *subjectivity* corpus by Pang et al. (2002). The corpus is larger than the current dataset, but is only partly relevant to it, as it was built primarily for movie reviews while the consumer dataset that we are utilizing contains reviews from multiple domains.

As baselines, we use the standard unigram representation with presence-based features, with and without length normalization. The first-stage unigram based sentence classifiers are built using the MALLET toolkit (McCallum, 2002). For the final document classification, either using unigram or sentence-based features, we use the SVM implementation from Chang and Lin (2001). Experiments are based on 10-fold cross-validation.

5 Results

5.1 Sentence classification

We begin the analysis of the results by reporting the effectiveness of the subjectivity unigram classifiers in Table 1.

Approach	Accuracy (setting 1)	Accuracy (setting 2)
Baselines		
Unigrams	69.81%	69.81%
Unigrams (N.)	71.76%	71.76%
S-based (M=5)		
Standard	65.55%	64.55%
+ Unigrams	74.39%	72.81%
+ Unigrams (N.)	**75.39%**	72.81%
S-based (M=10)		
Standard	69.21%	69.71%
+ Unigrams	**74.86%**	**76.42%**
+ Unigrams (N.)	73.76%	72.31%
S-based (M=20)		
Standard	69.55%	65.10%
+ Unigrams	75.39%	74.42%
+ Unigrams (N.)	**77.42%**	**76.42%**
S-based (M=30)		
Standard	68.63%	65.60%
+ Unigrams	74.92%	74.92%
+ Unigrams (N.)	**76.92%**	**76.42%**
S-based (M=max)		
Standard	67.13%	67.13%
+ Unigrams	74.92%	74.9%
+ Unigrams (N.)	**76.42%**	**76.42%**

Table 2: 10-fold cross-validation accuracy. *S-based* denotes the sentence-based approach. For the $M = max$ setting we use the number of sentences of the longest document.

The results overall indicate that subjectivity detection on the specific dataset is particularly difficult. More specifically, training either a Naive Bayes or Maximum Entropy classifier on the subjectivity corpus and evaluating in on the consumer corpus, testing either on the whole documents (i.e., "whole documents") or only the objective and subjective sentences (i.e., "filtered documents") results in an accuracy of 64.87% at best. The results are slightly better using an subjectivity classifier trained on the same dataset. In this case, training and testing on only the objective and subjective sentences results in an accuracy of 67.73% at best, while using the whole documents produces an accuracy of 63.12% at best. It will be interesting therefore to see how the sentence-based document classification is affected by the subjectivity detection accuracy.

5.2 Document classification

Due to the number of variations of different document representations that can be explored (e.g., values of parameter M) and space constraints in this section we will present results with the optimal settings that we've discovered for those parameters[4]. Therefore in this section, all presented results are based on backward balancing where the documents are represented as a sequence of probabilities $Pr(+1|sentence)$ and the empty features for small documents are set to 0.

Table 2 presents results for various values of M, with and without additional unigram-based features. The *Standard* approach is based on using only sentences while the *+Unigrams* additionally adds unigram tokens as features. Lastly, we denote full document length-normalization with "*(N.)*". The results on the 2nd column of Table 2 (i.e., setting 1) are based on using the *objective* documents of the dataset for training the objectivity classifier while the results in the 3rd column are based on using the *subjectivity* corpus (i.e., setting 2).

The first rows of the tables present the unigram-based classification accuracy. As already stated, the proposed algorithm can be used in combination with other approaches, so we've opted to utilize this simple approach as a baseline in order to demonstrate its applicability. The baseline results indicate that the specific dataset offers particular challenges, with the standard unigram approach with a length-normalized document vector obtaining an accuracy of 71.76%, much lower that the typical 88% typically reported for other datasets (Pang et al., 2002). Using the sentence-based document representation of documents, initially doesn't provide any significant advantage, maintaining the accuracy effectiveness roughly at the same levels for most values of M. Especially when utilizing the external subjectivity corpus, the effectiveness seems to drop by approximately 6% (Table 2, 3rd column, *Standard* approach for $M = 20$ and $M = 30$).

Nonetheless, using the sentence-based document representation in combination with standard presence-based unigram features always results in an increase in classification accuracy, especially for values of M in the $[20, 30]$ range, reaching an accuracy of 76% in most cases, a rough increase of 6% and 77.42% at best, with $M = 20$. The results overall indicate that the algorithm is quite robust to the value of parameter M. The algorithm retains the high level of effectiveness even when M is set to the number of sentences of the longest document, that is, no sentences are removed and the approach presented in section 3.3 for small documents is applied to the rest of the documents.

The observed differences between using the external *subjectivity* corpus and the objective documents of the dataset aren't as pronounced as expected. Although the observed accuracy for a low value of M in this case is decreased, overall the accuracy levels for higher M values remain stable, typically higher than 76%. The results indicate the potential robustness of the algorithm in reference to the effectiveness of the subjectivity classifier and demonstrate that a static external subjectivity corpus can provide comparable performance.

Limitations: In addition to the experiments presented here, some experiments were also conducted on the MovieReview dataset (Pang et al., 2002) and initial results showed smaller improvements in accuracy. This fact may indicate that the proposed method is more suited for datasets with only limited training data or when unigram features alone attain reduced accuracy.

6 Conclusion

In this paper, we presented a simple and intuitive method of document representation that both implicitly retains word position in documents and explicitly trains a document classifier on the sequence of sentence-based opinions expressed in the document. The proposed algorithm aims to overcome some of the drawbacks of the standard bag-of-words representation, by offering a structurally and semantically meaningful way of effectively representing documents for sentiment analysis.

An obvious extension of the proposed algorithm is the utilization of sequential models, such as CRFs (Lafferty et al., 2001) and structurally-based features (Täckström and McDonald, 2011) in order to increase the effectiveness of the sentence polarity detection, as it was shown that increased sentence classification accuracy typically resulted in increased document classification accuracy.

References

Chih-Chung Chang and Chih-Jen Lin, 2001. *LIBSVM: a library for support*

[4]Detailed results with different parameter values are available from the authors upon request.

vector machines. Software available at http://www.csie.ntu.edu.tw/ cjlin/libsvm.

Nancy Kress. 1999. *Beginnings, Middles and Ends (The elements of fiction writing)*. Writer's Digest Books.

John D. Lafferty, Andrew McCallum, and Fernando C. N. Pereira. 2001. Conditional random fields: Probabilistic models for segmenting and labeling sequence data. In *Proceedings of the Eighteenth International Conference on Machine Learning*, ICML '01, pages 282–289, San Francisco, CA, USA. Morgan Kaufmann Publishers Inc.

Chenghua Lin and Yulan He. 2009. Joint sentiment/topic model for sentiment analysis. In *Proceeding of the 18th ACM conference on Information and knowledge management*, CIKM '09, pages 375–384, New York, NY, USA. ACM.

Y. Mao and G. Lebanon. 2006. Sequential models for sentiment prediction. *ICML Workshop on Learning in Structured Output Spaces*.

Andrew Kachites McCallum. 2002. Mallet: A machine learning for language toolkit. http://mallet.cs.umass.edu.

Ryan McDonald, Kerry Hannan, Tyler Neylon, Mike Wells, and Jeff Reynar. 2007. Structured models for fine-to-coarse sentiment analysis. In *Proceedings of the Association for Computational Linguistics (ACL)*, pages 432–439, Prague, Czech Republic, June. Association for Computational Linguistics.

G. Mishne. 2005. Experiments with mood classification in blog posts. In *1st Workshop on Stylistic Analysis Of Text For Information Access*.

B. Pang and L. Lee. 2008. *Opinion Mining and Sentiment Analysis*. Now Publishers Inc.

Bo Pang, Lillian Lee, and Shivakumar Vaithyanathan. 2002. Thumbs up? sentiment classification using machine learning techniques. In *Proceedings of the 2002 Conference on Empirical Methods in Natural Language Processing (EMNLP)*.

O. Täckström and R. McDonald. 2011. Discovering fine-grained sentiment with latent variable structured prediction models. In *Proceedings of the 33rd European Conference on Information Retrieval (ECIR 2011), Dublin, Ireland*.

Mike Thelwall, Kevan Buckley, Georgios Paltoglou, Di Cai, and Arvid Kappas. 2010. Sentiment strength detection in short informal text. *J. Am. Soc. Inf. Sci. Technol.*, 61:2544–2558, December.

Peter D. Turney. 2002. Thumbs up or thumbs down? semantic orientation applied to unsupervised classification of reviews. In *ACL*, pages 417–424.

Information Spreading in Expanding Wordnet Hypernymy Structure

Maciej Piasecki
Institute of Informatics
Wrocław Univ. of Technology
maciej.piasecki@pwr.wroc.pl

Radosław Ramocki
Institute of Informatics
Wrocław Univ. of Technology
rramocki@gmail.com

Michał Kaliński
Institute of Informatics
Wrocław Univ. of Technology
168023@student.pwr.wroc.pl

Abstract

The paper presents a wordnet expansion algorithm, which is based on lexico-semantic relations extracted from large text corpora. We do not assume that the extracted relation instances (i.e. word pairs) are described by probabilities. Thus, results produced by any method, including pattern-based and Distributional Semantics approaches can be used. The algorithm is based on a general spreading activation model. Support for word-to-word semantic associations is first mapped on the existing wordnet structure. Next, the support is spread over the wordnet network in order to find attachment areas for a new word. Evaluation and comparison with other approaches in experiments on Princeton WordNet 3.0 is presented.

1 Introduction

Wordnets became important large scale language resources providing relational description of lexical meanings. e.g. WordNet (Fellbaum, 1998), GermaNet (Hamp and Feldweg, 1997) or plWordNet (Maziarz et al., 2012). The required large amount of work on wordnet construction can be lessened by supporting manual work with automated tools for the extraction of lexico-semantic relations and wordnet expansion. A scheme for lexico-semantic network extraction from corpus includes, e.g. (Yang and Callan, 2009; Navigli et al., 2011): *term extraction*, extraction of *term associations* and *taxonomy induction*. A taxonomy structure is mostly a subset of the whole wordnet hyper/hyponynymy structure. Thus, a more general task, for the last phase, is *extraction of lexico-semantic relations* (*sensu stricto*), called *relation formation* in (Yang and Callan, 2009). In our work, we focus on the automated expansion of a such wordnet hypernymy structure.

Upper levels of a wordnet hypernymy describe more general, often highly abstract lexical units (i.e. pairs: lemma and its sense). Such fine grained distinctions are hard to trace in a corpus, but mostly it is this part of a wordnet that is created first. Thus, we assumed that upper hypernymic levels are already built manually, and what is needed is to expand the wordnet structure towards the lower levels. Our goal is to develop a method of automated expansion of wordnet hypernymy structure based on both lexico-semantic associations extracted automatically from a large text corpus and the prior partial wordnet structure. We do not assume the existence of any kind of semantic annotation or document structure, to make the proposed method general.

Most taxonomy induction methods use only the existing hypernymy structure as a basis for the incremental wordnet expansion, e.g. (Snow et al., 2006; Piasecki et al., 2009b). We explore all different types of wordnet links to identify the appropriate location for a new lemma sense.

2 Related works

(Alfonseca and Manandhar, 2002) and (Witschel, 2005) treat wordnet hypernymy as a kind of decision tree applied to word meanings described by Distributional Semantics. (Widdows, 2003) attaches words on the basis of their *semantic neighbours* – k most similar words according to their co-occurrence with the most frequent words.

(Snow et al., 2006) proposed Probabilistic Wordnet Expansion (PWE) method, which is based on a probabilistic model of the taxonomy expressed in terms of taxonomic relations. For WordNet expansion Snow *et al.* consider two type of relations: (transitive) *hypernymy* and (m,n)-*cousin*. To prevent adding a new word to overly-specific hypernym λ coefficient was introduced penalized by: λ^{k-1} factor, where k is number of links between attachment synset and its hypernym. (m,n)-cousinhood occurs between two word senses i and j if their *least common subsumer* is exactly m links from i and n links from j in the WordNet graph. Hypernymy and (m,n)-cousinhood instances imply sets of other instances, e.g. a direct hypernym of one word sense implies all other indirect hypernyms. To add a new word to the taxonomy, the whole taxonomy must be (locally) searched for an attachment place that maximises probabilities of all the implied relations. The attachment of new elements transforms the structure **T** into a new **T'**. The appropriate **T'** maximises the probability of the change in relation to the evidence at hand. *Multiplicative change* computation is based on all added relation links, including the links *implied* by hyponymy. Multiplicative change depends on the inverse odds of the prior k which is a constant independent of words and taxonomy **T**. (Snow et al., 2006) have not provided any value of k.

(Kozareva and Hovy, 2010) presented two step taxonomy induction. First, hyponym-hypernym pairs are extracted from Internet and ranked. The extraction mechanism is exclusively based on "doubly-anchored lexico-syntactic patterns" and a heuristic iterative algorithm. The process is weakly controlled by a *root* and *seed* lemmas. (Navigli et al., 2011) divided taxonomy induction into four steps. Three initial ones are devoted to the extraction of hypernymy instances. The process is focused on ontology learning, identification of overt definitions in text and the extraction of hypernymy instances from them. However, definitions are infrequent and occur only in specific text genres. The initial graph emerging from the extracted pairs is next weighted and pruned.

(Yang and Callan, 2009) proposed a *metric-based taxonomy induction framework* aimed at utilising different extraction methods: 15 methods in total were used. Each method produces a *feature function* a term pair $\rightarrow$ a real value or $\{0, 1\}$ value. The process starts with an initial partial taxonomy T^0, used also to estimate values of parameters, so it is a taxonomy expansion. The expansion is controlled by *Minimum Evolution Assumption* and *Abstractness Assumption* principles. The first results in minimising "the overall semantic distance among the terms" but also avoiding "dramatic changes" between the initial taxonomy and the expanded one. The total distance and change are characterised by the Information Function of a taxonomy T. Weights for different *feature functions* can be estimated in supervised training for each taxonomy level separately by approximating ontology metrics for term pairs:
$d(c_x, c_y) = \sum_{j \in features} w_j h_j(c_x, c_y)$
where $h_j()$ is a feature function and w_j its weight. The approximation was done by ridge regression, but it is not clear whether it was done separately for different taxonomy levels. Finally, Multi-Criterion Optimization Algorithm (MCOA) finds a place for each new term by joint application of both conditions, i.e. by minimising: the change in the taxonomy Information Function and the sum over the square error of the difference between new ontology metrics and their estimation based on the weighted feature functions. (Yang and Callan, 2009) performed evaluation on WordNet and an ontology. As far the first, 50 " hypernym taxonomies" were extracted from 12 topics (mostly concrete nouns) and 50 "meronymic taxonomies" from 15 topics (mostly concrete). The size of the test taxonomies and the way of their delimitation was not defined. Feature functions were built on the basis of a corpus including English Wikipedia and 1000 top documents per each term from Google. Precision and recall were calculated on the level of relation links. The number of the correctly attached terms is not known. MCOA achieved slightly better results in reconstructing of the hypernymic taxonomies than PWE.

(Piasecki et al., 2009a; Piasecki et al., 2011) proposed a heuristic wordnet expansion algorithm called *Area Attachment Algorithm* (AAA) which utilises different relation extraction methods. A modified version of AAA, was presented in (Piasecki et al., 2012). Our present work inherits several assumptions from AAA, but it based on a different model of spreading activation.

3 *Paintball* Algorithm

3.1 The idea of information spreading

A corpus is a very imprecise source of lexical semantics knowledge. Knowledge describing lexico-semantic relations that is extracted from it is always partial (not all word senses occur, most senses are infrequent) and may suggest erroneously accidental semantic associations between words. We cannot avoid errors, but we can to try to compensate them by combining word associations suggested by several extraction methods. Relations extracted automatically can be represented as sets of triples: $\langle x, y, w \rangle$, where y is a word already included in the wordnet, x is a 'new' word not included yet, and $w \in \Re$ is a weight. We call such a set a *knowledge source* (henceforth KS) extracted by a method from a corpus. A triple $\langle x, y, w \rangle$ from a KS K informs that x is semantically associated with y and w describes the strength of this association. In many approaches, e.g. (Snow et al., 2006), weights are interpreted as probabilities. However, many relation extraction methods are not based on statistics, and word-pairs extracted by them cannot be described by probabilities, e.g. the majority of pattern-based methods extract word pairs on the basis of a few occurrences. Nevertheless, as we need to 'squeeze' all available lexical knowledge out from the text, and we cannot loose any KS. We have to try to utilise those non-probabilistic KSs, too. Most if not all reliable extraction methods produce KSs for words, not word senses. Thus, we assume that w is a value of *support* for the given word pair x & y as semantically associated.

A triple $\langle x, y, w \rangle$ from a KS K_i suggests linking x to synsets including y. However, there are two problems: x and y can have several senses each, and the triple can express some error. In fact, the triple suggests linking x to different senses of y represented by synsets – each y synset describes a possible meaning of x. The triple does not disambiguate this, e.g. PWE hypernymy classifier generates ⟨*feminism*, *movement*, 1.0⟩, ⟨*feminism*, *theory*, 0.948⟩, ⟨*feminism*, *politics*, 0.867⟩, etc. As far the second, apart from clearly wrong, accidental triples, KSs very often include too general suggestions, e.g. y can be in fact an indirect hypernym of x or y can be associated with x by a kind of fuzzynymy. Combining information coming from several different triples describing x may solve both problems by identifying those parts of the wordnet hypernymy structures that are best supported by the evidence in KSs.

We proposed a wordnet expansion algorithm called *Paintball* which is based on a general model of *spreading activation* (Collins and Loftus, 1975; Salton and Buckley, 1988; Akim et al., 2011): the support from KS triples is the activation which is spread along the wordnet relations. *Paintball* algorithm is based on the metaphor of semantic support for x resembling drops of liquid paint that initially fall on some wordnet graph nodes (synsets) due to KSs and next the paint starts spreading over the graphs. Those regions that represent the highest amounts of paint after the spreading represent possible senses of x and include places for x.

The spreading model is motivated by the nature of KSs. KSs are typically extracted to represent selected wordnet relations, e.g. synonymy and hyper/hyponymy, but in practice KS triples represent a whole variety of relations, e.g. indirect hypernymy, but also meronymy, co-hyponymy (cousin or coordinate) or just stronger semantic association. A KS element $\langle x, y \rangle$ can suggest linking an x sense directly to a y sense by synonymy, but also indirectly by some other relation. KSs based on Distributional Semantics do not specify this relation, and pattern-based KS are mostly focused on hypernymy. So, a real attachment places for an x sense can be somewhere around the y synsets assuming that the given KS does not include too serious errors or too fuzzy semantic associations, e.g. triples generated by PWE hypernymy classifier: ⟨*feminism*, *relationship*, 0.768⟩, ⟨*feminism*, *study*, 0.951⟩, ⟨*feminism*, *idea*, 0.951⟩, etc. On the basis of the assumption that semantic similarity between a synset S, which is a proper attachment place for x, and y (suggested by the KS) is correlated with the length of the shortest path in the wordnet graph linking S and a synset of y, we can expect that the proper attachment places for a x sense is linked to y synset with relatively short path. For a KS triple we should consider a subgraph of potential synsets for x. Its shape should depend on the nature of a given KS. For instance, as it is easier to mismatch synonymy and hypernymy then hypernymy and antonymy, the subgraph is more likely to include hypo/hypernymic paths than paths including antonymy links, too. As we expect that KSs of some minimal accuracy include a large number of minor errors[1], we need to consider only subgraphs with limited length of paths corresponding to less serious errors. Thus, each KS triple marks whole wordnet subgraphs as potential attachment places for the senses of x.

Spreading activation model follows a general

[1]In the sense of a semantic difference between the suggested place and the proper one.

scheme, e.g. (Akim et al., 2011), in which initial activation is set at the start and then the node activation depends on the previous value and the activation coming from the connected nodes. The spreading is controlled by parameters representing the amount of *initial activation* and *activation decay*, respectively (Troussov et al., 2008). We identify activation with semantic support for x, the initial activation is called *direct support* while support coming from other nodes is called *indirect support*. Indirect support is intended to compensate errors of KSs and resolve the ambiguity of lemma-based information delivered in them.

Most frequent wordnet relations link synsets, but in every wordnet there are also many relations linking directly *lexical units* (LUs) (i.e. pairs word–sense number, e.g. antonymy. In order to use the whole wordnet graph structure, not only defined by synset relations, we treat LUs as nodes and synset relations are mapped to relations between all LUs from the linked synsets.

In Spreading Activation models, the activation decay parameter $\mu \in [0, 1)$ and have the same value for all links. In our approach the activation decay value depends on the link types due to different distribution of errors across KSs. Following (Piasecki et al., 2012), that part of the decay dependent on the link type is represented by two functions: *transmittance* and *impedance*. Transmittance is a function: *lexico-semantic relation* $\rightarrow \Re$ and describes the ability of links to transmit support. Link-to-link connection is characterised by the *impedance* function: *relation pair* $\rightarrow \Re$. The impedance describes how much indirect support can be transferred through the given connection, e.g. the transmission of support through holonymy–meronymy would mean that the direct support assigned to the whole (a holonym) via a part (a meronym) could be attributed to another whole (its second holonym), e.g. *car*–holo–*windscreen*–mero:substance–*glass*: indirect support could go from *car* to *glass* that is clearly too far. By an appropriate impedance function we can reduce the transmission or block it, i.e. we can shape the considered part of the wordnet graph.

3.2 Algorithm

The algorithm works in four main steps preceded by the preparatory Step 0. First, the initial local support for LUs is calculated on the basis of KSs. Next, the local support is recursively replicated from LUs to local subgraphs of connected LUs. Support for synsets is calculated on the basis of their LUs. Finally, following (Piasecki et al., 2012), connected wordnet subgraphs such that each synset in a subgraph has some significant support are identified. Such subgraphs are called *activation areas*. Top several activation areas with the highest support value are selected as *attachment areas* – descriptions of potential senses of x. In each attachment area, the synset with the highest support is a potential place to add x sense. Attachment areas are next presented to linguists to explain the suggested meanings of x.

Let x be a new word, J be a set of LUs, L – a set of lemmas, and $\mathbf{A} \subseteq 2^{J^2}$ – a set of lexico-semantic relations defined on J (including relations inherited from synsets like hypernymy and *lexical relations*). A knowledge source K is a set of triples of the type: $L \times L \times \Re$ where $\Re$ is a set of real numbers. Let $\mathbf{K}$ be a set of all KSs and $\sigma : J \times L \rightarrow \Re$; $\sigma(j, x) = \sum_{K \in \mathbf{K}} K(j, x)$ equals the sum of all weights assigned to the pair. The *transmitation* is represented by: $f_T : \mathbf{A} \times \Re \rightarrow \Re$ and the *impedance* is represented by: $f_I : \mathbf{A}^2 \times \Re \rightarrow \Re$.

Step 0 Constructing a graph of LUs on the basis of the graph of synsets

Step 1 Setting up the initial state

1. $\forall_{j \in J}.\mathbf{Q}[j] = \sigma(j, x)$
2. `for each` $j \in J$ `if` $\mathbf{Q}[j]) > \tau_0$ add j to the queue T

Step 2 Support replication across the LU graph

1. k = take first node from T
2. $supReplication(k, x, \sigma(k, x))$ – support for x is replicated from k onto the connected nodes
3. `if not` $empty(T)$ `then goto` 1

Step 3 Synset support calculation: `for each` s `in` Syn
`if` s does not have any support in any KS for `x then` $\mathbf{F}[s] = 0$
`else` $\mathbf{F}[s] = synsetSup(s, \mathbf{Q})$

Step 4 Identification of attachment areas

1. Recognition of connected subgraphs in WN, such that $G_m = \{s \in Syn : \mathbf{F}[s] > \tau_3\}$
2. `for each` G_m $score(G_m) = \mathbf{F}[j_m]$, where $j_m = max_{j \in G_m}(\mathbf{F}(j))$

3. Return G_m, such that $score(G_m) > \tau_4$ as activation areas.

In Step 1 only nodes that represent some meaningful value of local support (τ_0) are added to the queue as starting points for the replication in Step 2. The value of τ_0 depends on the KSs, but it can be set to the smallest weight value that signals good triples in the KS of the biggest coverage. All threshold values can be also automatically optimised, e.g., as in (Łukasz Kłyk et al., 2012).

In Step 2 support replication is run for nodes stored in the queue and is described by the following functions (where j is a LU to be processed and M support value to be replicated, $dsc(j)$ returns the set of outgoing relation links and $p|_1$ returns the first element – a relation link target node).
$supReplication(j, x, M)$:
1) `if` $M < \epsilon$ `then return`
2) `for each` $p \in dsc(j)$
$supRepTrans(p, x, f_T(p, \mu * M))$

$supRepTrans(p, x, M)$:
1) `if` $M < \epsilon$ `then return`
2) `for each` $p' \in dsc(p|_1)$
$supRepTrans(p', x, f_I(p, p', f_T(p', \mu * M)))$
3) $\mathbf{Q}[p|_1] = \mathbf{Q}[p|_1] + M$

Incoming support is stored in the given node and part of it is spread further on according to μ. The parameter μ together with the transmittance function f_T corresponds to activation decay. The spreading stops when the incoming support goes down below ϵ and is additionally blocked on connections of the predefined types by the impedance function f_I. The value of ϵ was heuristically set to $\tau_0/2$, but it can be obtained during optimisation. The parameters μ and ϵ control (together) the maximal distance of the support flow.

In Step 3, support for synsets is calculated on the basis of the support for LUs included in them. It can be done in many different ways, but the best results were obtained by using a function proposed in (Piasecki et al., 2009b):
$synsetSup(S, Q') =$
1) `sum` $= \sum_{s_i \in S} Q'[s_i]$
2) `if` $\delta(1, \texttt{sum}, |S|) > 0$ `then return sum else return 0`
where $\delta(h, n, s) = 1$ `if` $(n \geq 1,5 * h \wedge s \leq 2) \vee (n \geq 2 * h \wedge s > 2)$ `else 0`

The idea is to expect more support for larger synsets, but this dependency is not linear, as larger synset very often include many less frequent and worse described LUs. In Step 3, we also filter out synsets that do not have any local support in order to preserve only the most reliable data.

Finally, in Step 4, activation areas (subgraphs) are identified with the help of a subset of wordnet relations, which includes all relations defining the basic wordnet structure, e.g. in some wordnets a synset can be linked by a relation different then hyponymy as its only relation. The whole activation area expresses a location found by the algorithm for x: however, we also need one particular synset to attach a LU for x. Thus, we look for local maxima of the support value and use these values as the semantic support for the whole attachment areas. *Paintball* is focused on supporting linguists, recall is important, so up to max_{att} activation areas are finally returned as suggested *attachment areas*.

4 Evaluation

4.1 Methodology

The evaluation is based on wordnet reconstruction task proposed in (Broda et al., 2011): randomly selected words are removed from a wordnet and next the expansion algorithm is applied to reattach them. Removing of every word changes wordnet structure, so it is best to remove one word at a time, but due to the efficiency, small word samples are processed in one go. As the algorithm may produce multiple attachment suggestions for a word, they are sorted according to semantic support of the suggested attachments. A histogram of distances between a suggested attachment place and the original synset is built. We used two approaches to compute the distance between the proposed and original synsets. According to the first, called *straight*, a proper path can include only hypernymy or hyponymy links (one direction only per path), and one optional final meronymic link. Only up to 6 links are considered, as longer paths are not useful suggestions for linguists.

In the second approach, called *folded*, shorter paths are considered, up to 4 links. Paths can include both hypernymy and hyponymy links, but only one change of direction and an optional meronymic link must be final. In this approach we consider close cousins (co-hyponyms) as valuable suggestions for linguists.

The collected results are analysed according to three strategies. In the *closest path* strategy we analyse only one attachment suggestion per lemma that is the closest to any of its original locations. In the *strongest*, only one suggestion with the highest support for a lemma is considered. In the *all* strategy all suggestions are evaluated.

A set of test words was selected randomly from wordnet words according to the following conditions. Only words of the minimal frequency corpus 200 were used due to the applied methods for relation extraction. Moreover, only words located further than 3 hyponymy links from the top were considered, as we assumed that the upper parts are constructed manually in most wordnets.

4.2 Experiment setup

For the sake of comparison with (Snow et al., 2006) and (Piasecki et al., 2012) two similar KSs were built: a *hypernym classifier* and a *cousin classifier*. The first (Snow et al., 2004) was trained on English Wikipedia corpus (1.4 billion words) parsed by *Minipar* (Lin, 1993). We extracted all patterns linking two nouns in dependency graphs and occurring at least five times and used them as features for logistic regression classifier from *LibLINEAR*. Word pairs classified as hyperonymic were described by probabilities of positive decisions. Following (Piasecki et al., 2012), the cousin classifier was based on distributional similarity instead of text clustering as the clustering method was not well specified in (Snow et al., 2006). The cousin classifier is meant to predict (m, n)-cousin relationship between words. The classifier was trained to recognize two classes: $0 \leq m, n \leq 3$ and the negative. The measure of Semantic Relatedness (MSR) was used to produce input features to the logistic regression classifier. MSR was calculated as a cosine similarity between distributional vectors: one vector per a word, each vector element corresponds to the frequency of co-occurrences with other words in the selected dependency relations. Co-occurrence frequencies were weighted by PMI.

A sample of 1064 test words was randomly selected from WordNet 3.0. It is large enough for the error margin 3% and 95% confidence level (Israel, 1992). Trained classifiers were applied to every pair: a test word and a noun from WordNet.

As a *baseline* we used the well known and often cited algorithm PWE (Snow et al., 2006). Its performance strongly depends on values of predefined parameters. We tested several combinations of values and selected the following ones: minimal probability of evidence: 0.1, inverse odds of the prior: $k = 4$, cousins neighbourhood size: $(m, n) \leq (3, 3)$, maximum links in hypernym graph: 10, penalization factor: $\lambda = 0.95$.

In *Paintball* probability values produced by the classifiers were used as weights. The hypernym classifier produces values from the range $\langle 0, 1]$. Values from the cousin classifier were mapped to the same range by multiplying them by 4. Values of the parameters were set heuristically in relation to the weight values as follows: $\tau_0 = 0.4$, $\tau_3 = \tau_0$, $\tau_4 = 0.8$, $\epsilon = 0.14$ and $\mu = 0.65$.

Transmittance was used to define links for support spreading in *Paintball*. The graph was formed by hyper/hyponymy (H/h), holo/meronymy (o/m), antonymy (a) and synonymy (represented by synsets). Transmittance is $f_T(r, v) = \alpha * v$, where alpha was: 0.7 for hypernymy, 0.6 for mero/holonymy and 0.4 for antonymy. The parameter α was 1 for other selected relations and 0 for non-selected. Impedance allows for controlling the shape of the spreading graph. Here, the impedance function is defined as: $f_I(r_1, r_2, v) = \beta * v$, where $\beta \in \{0, 1\}$. We selected heuristically $\beta = 0$ for the following pairs: ⟨h, a⟩, ⟨h, m.⟩, ⟨H, h⟩, ⟨H, o⟩, ⟨a, a⟩, ⟨a, m⟩, ⟨a, o⟩, ⟨m, a⟩ and ⟨o, a⟩.

4.3 Results

Paintball and PWE algorithms were tested on the same word sample, the results are presented in Tab. 1 and 2. Test words were divided into two sub-samples: frequent words, >1000 occurrences (Freq in tables) and infrequent, ≤999 (Rare in tables), as we expected different precision and coverage of KSs. Statistically significant results were marked with a '*'. We rejected the null hypothesis of no difference between results at significance level $\alpha = 0.05$. The paired t-test was used.

Considering straight paths and their maximal length up to 6 links PWE performs slightly better than Paintball. Coverage for words and senses is also higher for PWE: 100% (freq.: 100%) 44.79% (43.93%) than for Paintball: 63.15% (freq.: 91.63%) and 24.66% (26.62%). However, a closer analysis reveals that PWE shows a tendency to find suggestions in larger distances from the proper place. If we take into account only suggestions located up to 3 links – the column [0,2] in Tab. 1, than the order is different: Paintball is significantly better than PWE. Paintball mostly suggests more specific synsets for new words and ab-

		Strategy	Hits distance [%]								
			0	1	2	3	4	5	6	**[0, 2]**	**total**
PWE	Rare	Closest	3.7	21.7	16.2	9.6	6.9	3.4	0.1	41.6	***61.5**
		Strongest	0.5	5.9	9.7	10.9	8.9	4.5	0.5	*16.1	**40.9**
		All	0.8	4.9	5.0	4.5	3.8	2.0	0.4	*10.7	**21.5**
	Freq	Closest	0.8	14.8	24.2	21.0	15.1	5.5	0.2	39.8	*81.6
		Strongest	0.1	2.7	9.4	16.1	15.7	13.2	0.8	*12.2	*58.0
		All	0.2	3.2	7.0	10.0	9.8	7.3	0.5	10.4	*38.0
Paintball	Rare	Closest	9.2	21.7	12.6	6.7	4.2	1.0	0.6	**43.5**	*56.1
		Strongest	4.8	13.1	10.0	6.5	3.4	1.2	0.4	***27.9**	39.4
		All	2.9	6.9	4.8	3.5	2.2	1.0	0.2	***14.6**	**21.5**
	Freq	Closest	6.3	20.5	15.0	11.9	6.7	2.6	0.5	**41.8**	*63.3
		Strongest	1.9	9.1	8.4	8.1	4.8	1.9	0.3	***19.4**	*34.7
		All	1.4	4.9	4.4	4.4	3.1	1.6	0.2	**10.7**	*20.0

Table 1: Straight path strategy: PWE and Paintball precision on WordNet 3.0.

		Strategy	Hits distance [%]					
			0	1	2	3	4	**total**
PWE	Rare	Closest	3.7	21.7	18.4	11.8	2.5	*58.2
		Strongest	0.5	5.9	10.7	12.6	2.3	*32.0
		All	0.8	4.9	6.6	6.9	1.5	*20.7
	Freq	Closest	0.8	14.8	25.2	22.9	4.0	67.7
		Strongest	0.1	2.7	9.6	17.0	3.4	*32.8
		All	0.2	3.2	7.9	12.2	2.9	*26.4
Paintball	Rare	Closest	9.2	21.7	21.9	10.7	1.9	***65.5**
		Strongest	4.8	13.1	15.3	13.1	1.5	***47.9**
		All	2.9	6.9	14.7	13.2	1.7	***39.4**
	Freq	Closest	6.3	20.5	20.7	18.6	2.8	**68.8**
		Strongest	1.9	9.1	11.5	13.5	3.1	***39.2**
		All	1.4	4.9	8.4	11.6	2.3	***28.5**

Table 2: Folded path evaluation strategy: PWE and Paintball precision on WordNet 3.0 .

stains in the case of the lack of evidence, e.g., for x=*feminism*, PWE suggests the following synset list: {*abstraction, abstract entity*}, {*entity*}, {*communication*}, {*group, grouping*}, {*state*}
while suggestions of *Paintball*, still not perfect, are more specific: {*causal agent, cause, causal agency*}, {*change*}, {*political orientation, ideology, political theory*}, {*discipline, subject, subject area, subject field, field, field of study, study, bailiwick*}, {*topic, subject, issue, matter*}.

PWE very often suggests abstract and high level synsets like: {entity}, { event}, {object}, {causal agent, cause, causal agency} etc. They dominate whole branches and are in a distance non-greater than 6 links to many synsets. *Paintball* outperforms PWE in the evaluation based on the folded paths. For more than half test words, the strongest proposal was in the right place or up to a couple of links from it. Suggestions were generated for 72.65% of lemmas and the sense recall was 24.63% that is comparable with other algorithms.

5 Conclusions

We presented a new wordnet expansion algorithm called *Paintball*. It is based on a spreading activation model applied to the wordnet and expanded with notions of transmittance and impedance. The model enables combining different heterogeneous and partial KSs extracted from corpora. Contrary to many approaches, e.g. PWE (Snow et al., 2006), *Paintball* can use any KS, as it does not assume the probabilistic character of KSs. *Paintball* includes several parameters (but the same is the case of PWE), but their values can be tuned on a wordnet sample. *Paintball* offers a simpler and less heuristic model than LAAA and is a general tool. There are almost no works on wordnet expansion by spreading activation, e.g. (Liu et al., 2005) presented rather an idea, not a solution, but this model was used for Word Sense Disambiguation, e.g. (Tsatsaronis et al., 2007). Contrary to (Yang and Callan, 2009) we do not assume any properties of the lexical semantic network, but we try to shape it according to the language data. We aim also at an unsupervised or very weakly supervised algorithm in which training is limited to finding only general properties of the wordnet relations. *Paintball* expressed significantly better results than well known PWE and LAAA algorithms in test on performed on on Princeton WordNet 3.0.

Acknowledgments

Co-financed by the European Union within European Innovative Economy Programme project POIG.01.01.02-14-013/09 and by by the Polish National Centre for Research and Development project SyNaT.

References

Nazihah Md. Akim, Alan Dix, Akrivi Katifori, Giorgos Lepouras, Nadeem Shabir, and Costas Vassilakis. 2011. Spreading activation for web scale reasoning: Promise and problems. In *Proceedings of WebSci '11, June 14-17, 2011, Koblenz, Germany*.

Enrique Alfonseca and Suresh Manandhar. 2002. Extending a lexical ontology by a combination of distributional semantics signatures. In *13th Int. Conf. Knowledge Eng. and Knowledge Management. Ontologies and the Semantic Web*, LNCS. Springer.

Bartosz Broda, Roman Kurc, Maciej Piasecki, and Radosław Ramocki. 2011. Evaluation method for automated wordnet expansion. In P. Bouvry, M. Kłopotek, F. Leprevost, M. Marciniak, A. Mykowiecka, and H. Rybiński, editors, *Security and Intelligent Information Systems*, LNCS. Springer.

Allan M. Collins and Elizabeth F. Loftus. 1975. A spreading-activation theory of semantic processing. *Psychological Review*, 82(6):407–428.

Christiane Fellbaum, editor. 1998. *WordNet — An Electronic Lexical Database*. The MIT Press.

Birgit Hamp and Helmut Feldweg. 1997. GermaNet – a Lexical-Semantic Net for German. In *Proceedings of the ACL Workshop on Automatic Information Extraction and Building of Lexical Semantic Resources for NLP Applications*, pages 9–15. Madrid.

G. Israel. 1992. Determining sample size. Tech. rep., University of Florida.

Zornitsa Kozareva and Eduard Hovy. 2010. A semi-supervised method to learn and construct taxonomies using the web. In *Proceedings of the 2010 Conference on Empirical Methods in Natural Language Processing, MIT, Massachusetts, USA, 9-11 October 2010*, pages 1110–1118. ACL.

Dekang Lin. 1993. Principle-based parsing without overgeneration. In *Proc. ACL-93, Columbus, Ohio*.

Wei Liu, Albert Weichselbraun, Arno Scharl, and Elizabeth Chang. 2005. Semi-automatic ontology extension using spreading activation. *Journal of Universal Knowledge Management*, 0(1):50–58.

Marek Maziarz, Maciej Piasecki, and Stan Szpakowicz. 2012. Approaching plWordNet 2.0. In Christiane Fellbaum and Piek Vossen, editors, *Proceedings of 6th International Global Wordnet Conference*, pages 189–196, Matsue, Japan, January. The Global WordNet Association. Book: `http://www.globalwordnet.org/gwa/proceedings/gwc2012.pdf`.

Roberto Navigli, Paola Velardi, and Stefano Faralli. 2011. A graph-based algorithm for inducing lexical taxonomies from scratch. In *Proceedings of IJCAI*.

Maciej Piasecki, Bartosz Broda, Maria Głąbska, Michał Marcińczuk, and Stan Szpakowicz. 2009a. Semi-automatic expansion of polish wordnet based on activation-area attachment. In *Recent Advances in Intelligent Information Systems*, pages 247–260. EXIT.

Maciej Piasecki, Stanisław Szpakowicz, and Bartosz Broda. 2009b. *A Wordnet from the Ground Up*. Oficyna Wydawnicza Politechniki Wrocławskiej, Wrocław.

Maciej Piasecki, Roman Kurc, and Bartosz Broda. 2011. Heterogeneous knowledge sources in graph-based expansion of the polish wordnet. In *Proc. of The 2nd Asian Conference on Int. Inf. and Database Systems*, number 6591 in LNAI. Springer.

Maciej Piasecki, Roman Kurc, Radosław Ramocki, and Bartosz Broda. 2012. Lexical activation area attachment algorithm for wordnet expansion. In Allan Ramsay and Gennady Agre, editors, *Proceedings of the 15th International Conference on Artificial Intelligence: Methodology, Systems, Applications*, volume 7557 of *Lecture Notes in Computer Science*, pages 23–31, Varna, Bulgaria. Springer.

G. Salton and C. Buckley. 1988. On the use of spreading activation methods in automatic Information Retrieval. In *Proceedings of ACM SIGIR*.

Rion Snow, Daniel Jurafsky, and Andrew Y. Ng. 2004. Learning syntactic patterns for automatic hypernym discovery. In *NIPS*.

Rion Snow, Dan Jurafsky, and Andrew Y. Ng. 2006. Semantic taxonomy induction from heterogenous evidence. pages 801–808. The Association for Computer Linguistics.

Alexander Troussov, Mikhail Sogrin, John Judge, and Dmitri Botvich. 2008. Mining socio-semantic networks using spreading activation technique. In *Proceedings of I-KNOW '08 and I-MEDIA '08 Graz, Austria, September 3-5, 2008*, pages 405–412.

George Tsatsaronis, Michalis Vazirgiannis, and Ion Androutsopoulos. 2007. Word sense disambiguation with spreading activation networks generated from thesauri. In *Proceedings of IJCAI-07*, pages 1725–1730.

Łukasz Kłyk, Paweł B. Myszkowski, Bartosz Broda, Maciej Piasecki, and David Urbansky. 2012. Metaheuristics for tuning model parameters in two natural language processing applications. In Allan Ramsay and Gennady Agre, editors, *Proceedings of the*

15th International Conference on Artificial Intelligence: Methodology, Systems, Applications, volume 7557 of *Lecture Notes in Computer Science*, pages 32–37, Varna, Bulgaria. Springer.

D. Widdows. 2003. Unsupervised methods for developing taxonomies by combining syntactic and statistical information. In *Proc. HLT of North American Chapter of the ACL*.

Hans Friedrich Witschel. 2005. Using decision trees and text mining techniques for extending taxonomies. In *Proc. of Learning and Extending Lexical Ontologies by using Machine Learning Methods, Workshop at ICML-05*.

Hui Yang and Jamie Callan. 2009. A metric-based framework for automatic taxonomy induction. In *Proceedings of the 47th Annual Meeting of the ACL and the 4th IJCNLP of the AFNLP*, pages 271–279. ACL.

Context Independent Term Mapper for European Languages

Mārcis Pinnis

University of Latvia
19 Raina Blvd., Riga, Latvia
marcis.pinnis@gmail.com

Tilde
Vienības gatve 75a, Riga, Latvia
marcis.pinnis@tilde.lv

Abstract

In this paper the author presents a new context independent method for bilingual term mapping using maximised character alignment maps. The method tries to particularly address mapping of multi-word terms and compound terms that are extracted from comparable corpora. The method allows integrating linguistic resources (e.g., probabilistic dictionaries and character based transliteration systems) that significantly increase the mapping recall while maintaining a stable precision. The term mapping method has been automatically evaluated using the *EuroVoc* thesaurus with varying availability of linguistic resources and on terms extracted from Latvian-English medical domain comparable corpus collected from the Web. The paper shows that the results significantly outperform previously reported results on the same evaluation corpus.

1 Introduction

Multi-lingual terminology is a valuable resource not only in human and machine translation (MT), but also in many other application domains, for instance, information retrieval, semantic analysis, question answering and others. Multi-lingual term glossaries can be automatically acquired from existing resources (monolingual lists of terms, parallel or comparable corpora, etc.) with the help of term mapping. Term mapping methods according to previous research in the field can be divided in two categories – context dependent methods and context independent methods.

The context dependent methods are applicable in situations when there is enough context from which to draw statistics. The necessary amount of context can differ depending on the methods. For instance, for term mapping in parallel data it can be enough to simply have one parallel document pair or a sentence-aligned parallel corpus (Federmann et al., 2012; Wolf et al., 2011; Lefever et al., 2009; Gaussier et al., 2000).

For under-resourced languages and numerous domains, however, parallel resources are scarce and not always available. Therefore, a more promising resource is comparable corpora, which has recently received much attention in the scientific community for its applicability in MT (Skadiņa et al., 2012). Most of the context-dependent methods designed for term mapping in comparable corpora, however, require relatively large corpora (e.g., hundreds or even thousands of documents) in order to calculate reliable cross-lingual association measures (Fung and Yee, 1998; Rapp, 1999; Shao and Ng, 2004; Morin and Daille, 2010). The proposed methods have also been focussed on language pairs with relatively simple morphology (e.g., German-English, French-English), but have not been thoroughly investigated for more complex languages (e.g., Finnish, Latvian, etc.). A recent study in the European Commission financed project TTC (2013) revealed that while the context-dependent methods by Morin et al. (2010) perform well for English-French, their applicability for English-Latvian is questionable because of a term mapping precision of below 5%. Laroche and Langlais (2010) also reported a relatively low precision (far below 50%) using context-dependent methods.

Context independent term mapping methods, however, are designed for situations when there is no context or the context is not large enough to draw statistics. Recent work on context independent term mapping has been done by Ştefănescu (2012) where a cognate similarity measure based on the Levenshtein distance (Levenshtein, 1966) was applied in order to estimate how similar two terms are. The method's weakness is a very limited term mapping recall.

Following previous work in context independent term mapping, this paper presents a new context independent term mapping method using maximised character alignment maps that has been created for term and term phrase mapping in term-tagged comparable corpora. The method allows mapping of multi-word terms and terms with different numbers of tokens in the source and target language parts – two term mapping scenarios that have not been sufficiently addressed by previous research. The mapper has been specifically designed to address term mapping between European languages (including languages with different alphabets based on Latin, Cyrillic and Greek) and it allows integrating linguistic resources to increase recall (while maintaining the same level of precision) of the mapped terms.

The mapper has been evaluated on the *EuroVoc* thesaurus (Steinberger et al., 2002) for 23 language pairs and for the Latvian-English language pair on a medical domain comparable corpus that was collected from the Web. The evaluation also shows benefits of having additional linguistic resources (e.g., probabilistic dictionaries, and transliteration support) with respect to having only some of the resources (or none at all) available.

The paper is structured so that section 2 describes the design of the term mapping system, section 3 describes the evaluation process and provides evaluation results with space constrained analysis, and the paper is concluded in section 4.

2 The Term Mapping Method

Given two lists of terms (in two different languages) the task of the term mapping system is to identify which terms from the source language contain translation equivalents in the target language. The system (as shown in Figure 1) consists of two main components – monolingual term pre-processing and term mapping. A possible third module that is not discussed in this paper is term pair consolidation – a language specific process that allows increasing term mapping precision by identifying morphological variability between term pairs and filtering out possible invalid mappings.

2.1 Term Pre-processing

Before mapping, all source and target language terms are tokenized and pre-processed using linguistic resources (if such are available). For each token the pre-processing module:

- Rewrites the token using lower-case letters;
- Rewrites the token with letters from the English alphabet (*simple transliteration*); letters that cannot be rewritten (e.g., the Russian softening and hardening marks "ь" and "ъ") are removed and letters that correspond to multiple letters in the English alphabet are expanded (e.g., the Russian "*ш*" and Latvian "*š*" are rewritten as "*sh*" in English).
- Finds top *N* translation equivalents in the other language using a probabilistic dictionary, e.g., in the *Giza++* format (Och and Ney, 2003).
- Finds top *M* transliteration equivalents in the other language using a *Moses* (Koehn et al., 2007) character-based SMT system.

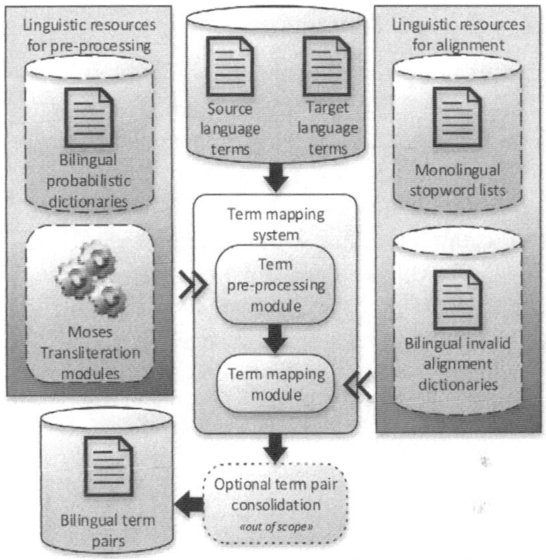

Figure 1: The overall design

Table 1 gives an example of a term in Latvian and English languages ("*extensive farming*") that has been pre-processed with direct *source-to-target* and *target-to-source* linguistic resources. If direct resources are not available, English can be used as an *Interlingua* for the dictionary-based look-up and the SMT-based transliteration.

The system allows limiting the retrieved candidates with confidence score thresholds, therefore, for the Latvian-to-English direction the example shows less than three transliteration candidates. For translation a limiting factor is also the available number of entries in the dictionary.

If for a language pair direct linguistic resources are not available, but there exist resources from the source and target languages to the English language, then the system allows using English as an *Interlingua* for term mapping.

Latvian term "*Ekstensīvā lauksaimniecība*"		
Lowercase form	ekstensīvā	lauksaimniecība
Simple translit.	ekstensiva	lauksaimnieciba
SMT translit.	extensiva extensive	-
Translation	-	agriculture farming
English term "*Extensive farming*"		
Lowercase form	extensive	farming
Simple translit.	extensive	farming
SMT translit.	ekstensīviem ekstensīvie ekstensīvai	farmēšana farmings farming
Translation	apjomīgam ekstensīvas izvērstāku	turēšanas saimniekošanas zemkopībā

Table 1: Examples of pre-processed terms

2.2 Term Mapping

After pre-processing the mapping module performs bi-directional term mapping. As shown in Figure 2 for each token in a term the mapping module operates with a set of constituents - *1* to *N* translation equivalents, *1* to *M* transliteration equivalents, one simple transliteration equivalent and one lowercased equivalent. The set of available constituents depends on the linguistic resources used (e.g., direct dictionaries, Interlingua dictionaries, no dictionaries, etc.).

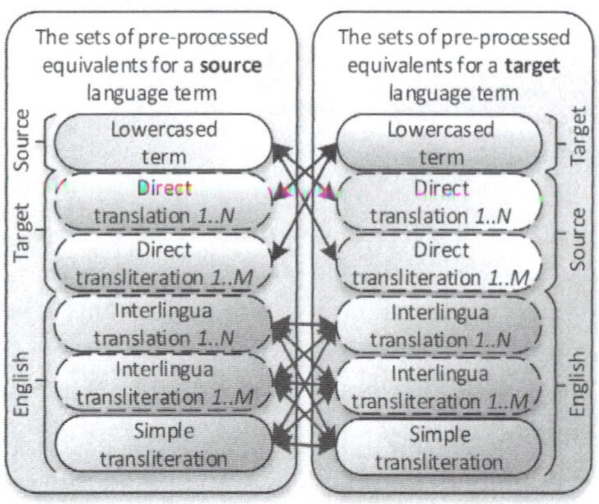

Figure 2: Bi-directional comparison sets for a single pre-processed term pair

The task of the mapping module is to decide whether a term pair can be mapped or not. The mapping process will be explained with the help of an example – the mapping of the English term "*dose of chemotherapy*" and its German translation "*chemotherapiedosis*". The mapping is performed in three steps.

2.2.1 Identification of Content Overlaps

At first, for every pre-processed token's constituent, we identify the *longest common substring* in all other term's pre-processed constituents that are in the same language (in Figure 2 comparison sets of the same language are connected with a bi-directional arrow). For the German-English example, the pre-processing module produced "*chemotherapiedosis*" as a simple transliteration of the German term. As the English lowercased term and the simple transliteration of the German term are within valid comparison sets, the mapper will analyse content overlaps between these constituents.

When identifying the *longest common substring* the positions of the substring within the constituents are preserved. If the length difference between the substring and the full source or target constituents exceeds a threshold (defined in a configuration file), the substring information is kept for the next step.

The results of the first step on the example are given in Figure 3. Two of the three English constituents ("*dose*" and "*chemotherapy*") can be nested within the German constituent. The third constituent's ("*of*") character overlap does not exceed the threshold (0.75 has been empirically selected as an appropriate default value), therefore, the substring information is ignored.

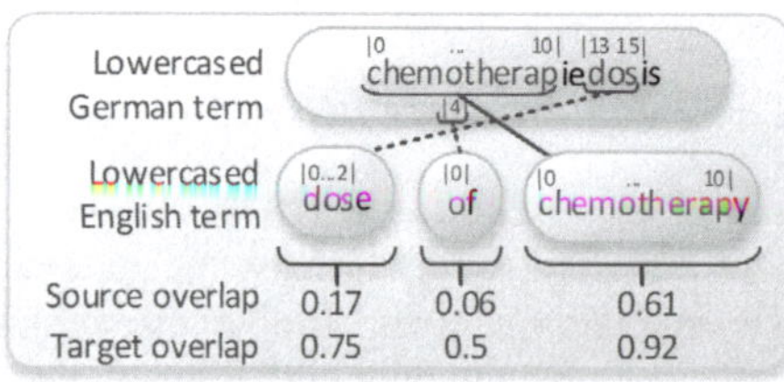

Figure 3: Longest common substring overlaps in German and English candidates

If the longest common substring overlap does not exceed the threshold, the mapper uses a fallback method based on the *Levenshtein distance* as applied by Ştefănescu (2012). The distance metric is transformed to a similarity metric:

$$Sim(s_1,s_2) = \frac{max(len(s_1),len(s_2))\text{-}LD(s_1,s_2)}{max(len(s_1),len(s_2))} \quad (1)$$

where *LD* is the *Levenshtein distance* between two strings, and *len* is a string length function. Each deletion, insertion and substitution is equally penalised with one point as in the first version of the *Levenshtein distance* (Levenshtein, 1966).

The motivation behind application of the alternative metric is that the SMT transliteration may introduce additional or different letters in a string and thus the longest common substring-based method can fail. However, this method has a limitation – it does not allow sub-word level mapping and if the similarity between two strings exceeds a predefined threshold, it is assumed that there is a complete overlap between the two strings. Assuming that the first comparison did not produce satisfactory results, Figure 4 shows the alternative comparison results for the example, however, none of the candidate pairs achieves a sufficient content overlap.

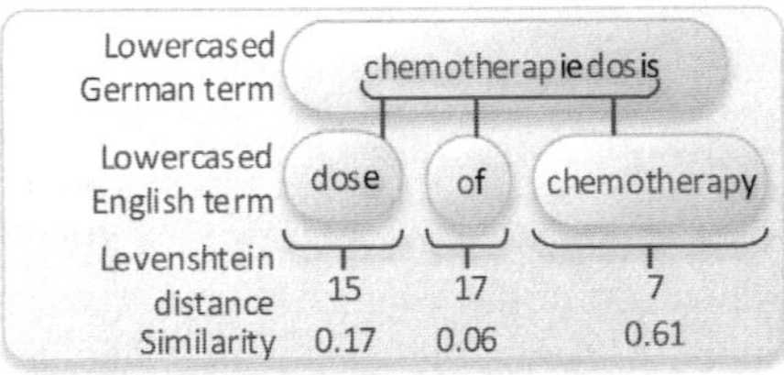

Figure 4: Levenshtein distance-based overlaps in German and English candidates

The result of this step is a list of binary alignment maps for constituent pairs. For instance, the binary alignment map for "*chemotherapiedosis*" and "*dose*" is "*000000000000011100*" (and "*1110*" for the target constituent).

2.2.2 Maximisation of content overlaps

In the next step the binary alignment lists are used to identify the mapping sequence that maximises the content overlap between the two terms. At first, the system iterates through the source term's tokens and tries to find for each token the constituent that has the highest overlap in a target term's constituent. At the same time the system maintains for each target term's token a binary one-dimensional alignment map that defines what part of the token has been already mapped in order not to allow conflicting and overlapping alignments. The length of the alignment map is determined by the longest constituent of the source and target terms. To find similar mappings from the target language, the iterative process is performed also for each token of the target term.

The example above contained two content overlaps (remember – the overlaps of the constituent "*of*" did not exceed thresholds). The overlap maximisation process in two iterations is shown in Figure 5.

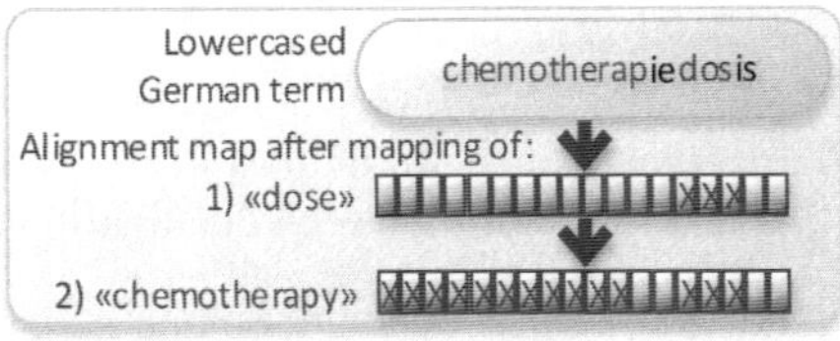

Figure 5: An example of the alignment map generation process for the German-English term pair

The goal of the mapper is to find term mappings that have a content overlap between terms in a way that restricts non-aligned segments (tokens or parts of tokens), but still allows a certain degree of imperfect mappings. For instance, we want the system to be able to decide that "*cost of treatment*" in English can be mapped to "*ārstēšanas izmaksas*" in Latvian (which is a direct translation) although it is evident that the token "*of*" does not have a mapping. However, we do not want the system to decide that "*β particles*" in English can be mapped to "*daļiņas*" in Latvian (transl. "*particles*") as well as we would not want "*electromagnetic field*" in English to be mapped to "*magnētiskais lauks*" in Latvian (transl. "*magnetic field*"). There is no perfect recipe that allows identifying all good and sufficient mappings from all bad and incomplete mappings in a language independent fashion, however, the mapper allows users to decide whether non-mapped segments at the beginning or the end of terms should be allowed or prohibited. Consequently the mapper can be executed in order to allow trimmed mappings, but not to limit non-mappings in-between of mapped segments. When trimmed mappings are allowed, it is important to disallow terms starting or ending with stopwords. Stopwords have shown to be very noisy in the probabilistic dictionaries (containing many false translations or context dependent translations). The mapper allows filtering out trimmed term mappings that start or end with stopwords if stopword lists are available.

2.2.3 Scoring of consolidated overlaps

In the final step the aligned constituents that produced character alignment map with the maximum content overlap are enrolled in two strings (source and target) in order to score the total overlap. The non-aligned source and target tokens (if there are any) are attached at the end of each string. At the same time, spaces are added to the other string to simulate non-aligned tokens.

As both the probabilistic dictionaries and the SMT-based transliteration systems provide confidence scores for each candidate, these scores are used as negative multipliers to filter out term pairs that may potentially result in invalid mappings.

The enrolled strings are scored using the *Levenshtein distance*-based similarity metric (described in section 2.2.1) multiplied by the negative multipliers. In the example the *Levenshtein distance* between "*chemotherapydoseof*" (representing the English term) and "*chemotherapiedosis$$*" (representing the German term; "*$$*" represent two space symbols) is *6*; the *Levenshtein distance*-based similarity is *0.7*. The simple transliteration does not have a negative multiplier, therefore, the term pair is considered to be mapped if the 0.7 is higher than a threshold.

2.3 How to Acquire Linguistic Resources?

The mapper is able to use four types of optional linguistic resources (probabilistic dictionaries, external *Moses* SMT-based transliteration modules, invalid mapping dictionaries, and stopword lists).

The resources integrated in the mapper have been built using *Giza++* probabilistic dictionaries extracted from the *DGT-TM* parallel corpus (Steinberger, 2012):

- The dictionaries have been filtered by removing translation entries below a certain threshold and entries that contain symbols that are not allowed in the source and target language alphabets (out-of-the-box support is provided for all official European languages).
- Dictionary entries with the *Levenshtein distance*-based similarity measure higher than a threshold are assumed to be transliterations. These entries are used as the training data for the character-based *Moses* transliteration module. The mapper has out-of-the-box support for transliteration of terms in 22 languages (see automatic evaluation) into English (and vice versa).
- Word pairs that have a high *Levenshtein distance*-based similarity, but are not defined as translation entries within the dictionary (i.e., the index of the line where the words are found in the dictionary differs), are extracted for the invalid mapping dictionary. For instance, "*pants*" in English has a similarity measure of 1.0 with "*pants*" in Latvian (transl. as "*article*" or "*paragraph*"). The invalid mapping dictionary is used to filter possible invalid source and target token pairs before the first step of the mapping module.

3 Evaluation

The mapper has been evaluated using two evaluation methods – automated evaluation and manual evaluation. The automated evaluation was performed for language pairs included in the *EuroVoc* thesaurus. It shows the applicability of the method for European languages and allows estimation of the upper level of recall that can be expected on comparable Web corpora.
The manual evaluation was performed on terms mapped in a Latvian-English comparable Web corpora in the medical domain. This evaluation allows estimating the expected performance of the method in terms of precision on noisy data.

3.1 Automatic Evaluation

The automatic evaluation has three goals: 1) to show how additional linguistic resources influence term mapping, 2) to evaluate the performance on European language pairs, and 3) to compare results with previous research using the same evaluation corpus. The *EuroVoc* thesaurus was selected as a suitable test corpus for the automated evaluation because it covers 24 European languages, it contains a relatively large number of terms (at the time of evaluation – 6,797 terms for all languages except Hungarian with 6,790, Italian with 6,643, and Maltese with 987 terms), and in average 65.5% of terms across all languages are multi-word terms.

For each evaluated language pair two monolingual lists of terms were created. Because the mapper sees only two independent lists of terms, the search space for mapping is not 6,797 term pairs, but rather 46.2 million term pairs (e.g., 6,797*6,797 for English-Latvian). In this evaluation the highest matching target term is retrieved for each source term. For the language pairs for which additional resources are available, for every token a maximum of five transliterations and 10 dictionary translations are retrieved.

At first, the mapping performance when using direct (*source-to-target* and *target-to-source*) linguistic resources, Interlingua-based (*source-to-English* and *target-to-English*) resources, and no resources was analysed. Figure 6 shows results (in terms of precision "*P*" and recall "*R*") for the Latvian-Lithuanian language pair. It is evident that direct resources allow achieving significantly higher recall than having Interlingua or no resources.

The results also suggest that the precision is stable at higher thresholds, however, it drops faster when using Interlingua-based resources. This can be explained by the noise that is introduced by the Interlingua-based resources. E.g., the term "*plakne*" (a type of a geometric figure) in Latvian can be wrongly be mapped to "*самолёт*" (a type of an aircraft) because both translate into English as "*plane*".

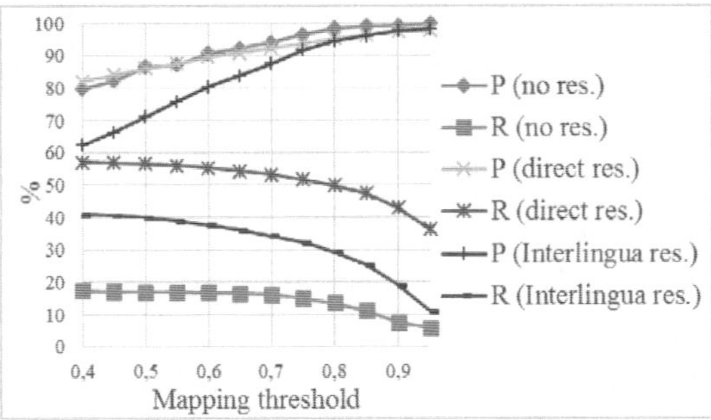

Figure 6: Latvian-Lithuanian evaluation results using direct, Interlingua, and no resources

Further, the benefits of having the probabilistic dictionaries and SMT-based transliteration modules were analysed. Figure 7 gives evaluation results for the Latvian-English language pair. The results show that without linguistic resources the recall is limited. This is due to the small number of terms that can be transliterated with the *simple transliteration* method. An analysis of 100 randomly selected unigram term pairs from the *EuroVoc* thesaurus revealed that 57 pairs were transliterations. 47 out of the 57 pairs were mapped using the *character-based transliteration* module. However, only 24 out of the 57 pairs were mapped using the *simple transliteration* method.

Evidently, adding resources allows significantly increasing the mapped term amount. It is also visible that the best results are achieved by using all linguistic resources.

Finally, term mapping was performed for 22 language pairs of the *EuroVoc* thesaurus with English as the source language. The results are given in Table 2. The evaluation was performed using direct *source-to-target* and *target-to-source* linguistic resources. The resources were built using *Giza++* probabilistic dictionaries extracted from the *DGT-TM* parallel corpus (Steinberger et al., 2012).

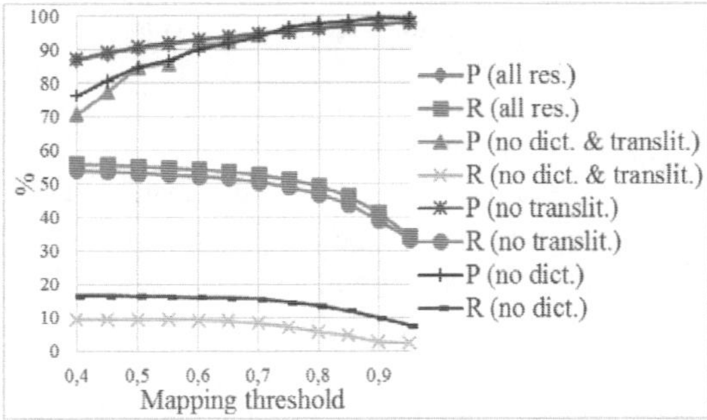

Figure 7: Latvian-English evaluation results using various resource configurations

The evaluation results show that the author's method significantly outperforms results reported earlier by Ştefănescu (2012) – an F1 score of 46.3 and 51.1 for English-Latvian and English-Romanian when using the same probabilistic dictionaries. The term mapping method proposed by Ştefănescu (2012) differs from the author's method in that it maps terms either with the *Levenshtein distance* based similarity metric or dictionary based exact match look-up. The author's proposed method, however, maps term tokens in sub-word level using maximised character alignment maps and applies Levenshtein distance just as a fall-back method and for scoring of the mapped term pairs.

Lang. pair	P	R	F1	Lang. pair	P	R	F1
en-mt	83.4	71.5	77.0	en-cs	85.9	53.4	65.8
en-fr	90.2	66.6	76.6	en-lt	86.1	52.6	65.3
en-ro	89.3	64.4	74.8	en-pl	86.0	52.1	64.9
en-es	91.1	63.2	74.6	en-el	86.0	49.6	62.9
en-pt	88.7	61.9	72.9	en-nl	82.0	50.7	62.7
en-it	87.4	62.0	72.6	en-sv	81.6	46.6	59.3
en-sk	90.8	58.8	71.4	en-da	81.4	45.3	58.2
en-lv	88.5	57.5	69.7	en-hu	78.5	45.7	57.8
en-sl	88.4	55.9	68.5	en-de	78.1	41.9	54.5
en-bg	88.0	55.2	67.9	en-et	74.5	39.0	51.2
en-hr	87.5	53.6	66.5	en-fi	72.3	33.7	46.0

Table 2: Evaluation results for *EuroVoc* language pairs with English as the source language (languages are given in the ISO 639-1 format).

The results suggest that the highest performance is achieved for the English-Maltese language pair, however, it is not comparable to the remaining results as they are based on only 987 term pairs from the *EuroVoc* thesaurus (covering mostly location and organisation named entities, which explains the relatively high recall).

An important aspect taken into account when designing the mapper was the mapping speed.

For the evaluation in Table 2 the mapper required in average 86.8 minutes (which is a speed of 8,868 term pairs per second) for one language pair on an 8 thread (4 core) Windows machine. The speed can be significantly improved by limiting the number of translation and transliteration candidates retrieved from the probabilistic dictionary and the character-based SMT module. The mapper requires in average less than 7 minutes for a language pair if no linguistic resources are used.

3.2 Manual Evaluation

The automatic evaluation was performed using terms in their base forms. The manual evaluation, therefore, has three goals: 1) to show the methods applicability on Web crawled comparable corpora 2) to show the methods performance in under-resourced conditions (the medical domain is out-of-domain for the DGT-TM corpus), 3) to show that the method can be applied for morphologically rich languages. The manual evaluation was performed for the Latvian-English language pair and for terms in the medical domain. Latvian was selected as one of the languages for this evaluation as it is a morphologically rich language and it is important to show that the method can be easily applicable to languages where terms are not always in their base forms.

Following the term mapping workflow proposed by Pinnis et al. (2012), two monolingual corpora were collected from the Web using the *Focussed Monolingual Crawler* (Mastropavlos and Papavassiliou, 2011). The acquired corpora (12,697 Latvian and 21,900 English documents) were then aligned in document level with the *DictMetric* (Su and Babych, 2012) comparability metric (59,600 document pairs were produced). The terms were tagged in the monolingual documents with *TWSC* (Pinnis et al., 2012). The term tagging step produced a total of 198,401 unique Latvian and 352,934 unique English terms. The reason why document alignment is a necessary step before mapping can be easily explained with the large number of monolingual terms. If the terms would be mapped between the two monolingual lists, the mapper would have to handle a search space of 70 billion term pairs and require over 91 days to complete (using direct linguistic resources). With document alignments the required time can be reduced to less than 2 days.

Finally, terms were bilingually mapped in the 59,600 document pairs. A maximum of three transliteration and translation candidates were retrieved for each token of a term. A total of 24,804 term pairs were produced above a threshold of 0.6 (for each source term only the target language term with the highest confidence score was returned). 1000 randomly selected term pairs were manually evaluated and the results are given in Table 3. The results are also compared with the method proposed by Ştefănescu (2012) using the same probabilistic dictionary.

The results suggest that the author's method performs significantly better for multi-word term mapping, which is the main goal of this method. It is also evident that the majority of true positives are scored with a mapping score of over 0.8. The results, however, require deeper analysis of why the unigram mapping score of the proposed method drops so fast.

Threshold	All terms		Multi-word terms		Single-word terms	
	Pairs	P	Pairs	P	Pairs	P
Author's method (random 1000/24,804 term pairs):						
1.0	17	88.2%	0	-	17	88.2%
0.9	601	91.3%	111	85.6%	490	92.7%
0.8	724	85.6%	160	73.8%	564	89.0%
0.7	880	74.8%	203	65.0%	677	77.7%
0.6	1000	66.6%	267	50.6%	733	72.4%
Ştefănescu (2012) (random 1000/2,330 term pairs):						
1.0	25	84.0%	2	0.0%	23	91.3%
0.9	44	90.9%	7	71.4%	37	94.6%
0.8	88	93.2%	12	83.3%	76	94.7%
0.7	186	87.6%	46	65.2%	140	95.0%
0.6	387	73.6%	173	49.7%	214	93.0%
0.5	1000	44.8%	697	25.1%	303	90.1%

Table 3: Manual evaluation results on the medical domain Latvian-English comparable corpus

Another important question left to answer is whether the mapper finds term pairs that are unknown to the linguistic resources integrated in the mapper. The mapping method is only useful if it is able to identify *out-of-vocabulary* (OOV) term pairs. Therefore, the 1000 randomly selected term pairs from the manual evaluation were looked up in the probabilistic dictionary (for the 733 single-word terms) and in a translation model of an SMT system (for the 267 multi-word terms) that was trained on the same parallel corpus from which the probabilistic dictionary was created. The results of the analysis in comparison with the method proposed by Ştefănescu (2012) are given in Table 4.

Table 4 shows that 76.3% of all multi-word term pairs, which were evaluated as "*correct*" during the manual evaluation, could not be found in the translation model of the SMT system. The results also suggest that the probabilistic dictionary introduces mapping errors as 24.75% of the wrongly mapped single-word term pairs were present in the dictionary.

	Single-word term pairs in the probabilistic dictionary		Multi-word term pairs in the Moses phrase table	
Evaluation:	**Correct**	**Wrong**	**Correct**	**Wrong**
Author's method:				
Source term OOV rate	13.94%	75.25%	76.30%	97.73%
Target term OOV rate	14.50%	75.66%	75.19%	97.73%
Term pair OOV rate	13.94%	75.25%	76.30%	97.73%
Ştefănescu (2012):				
Source term OOV rate	9.72%	76.00%	63.58%	99.58%
Target term OOV rate	12.09%	80.00%	62.86%	99.62%
Term pair OOV rate	12.09%	80.00%	62.86%	99.62%

Table 4: OOV analysis of randomly selected Latvian-English term pairs

4 Conclusion and Future Work

In this paper the author presented a new bilingual term mapping method using maximised character alignment maps. The method has been designed to address multi-word term pair as well as compound term pair mapping for European Languages that are based on Latin, Greek and Cyrillic alphabets.

The method has been automatically evaluated using the *EuroVoc* thesaurus for 23 language pairs. The paper discussed the impact of different linguistic resources on the term mapping performance. The method was also manually evaluated on terms mapped in a comparable corpus in the medical domain for the Latvian-English language pair, showing that the mapping method is suitable for handling noisy data collected from the Web. The evaluation also shows that up to 76.3% of the correctly mapped multi-word term pairs are out-of-vocabulary term pairs. The proposed term mapping method is able to find multi-word term alignments with a relatively high precision of up to 85.6%. It should, however, be noted that the scores depend on the corpus processed and may differ between language pairs as seen in the automatic evaluation.

The term mapping toolkit together with configuration and evaluation recipes is released under a non-commercial (free to use for scientific purposes) license. The toolkit can be downloaded from https://github.com/pmarcis/mp-aligner. The linguistic resources for the above-mentioned language pairs are also included in the release.

The future work on the term mapping method will involve a more in-depth error analysis of the mapped term pairs. Preliminary analysis suggests that simple filtering techniques could be applied to increase precision even further. For comparable corpora evaluation scenarios comparison with context-dependent methods is also necessary. The application of machine learning methods needs to be investigated in order to fine-tune the system's parameters for specific language pairs in order to achieve higher recall and precision. As the produced bilingual term pairs can be beneficial for MT systems, it is also necessary to evaluate the applicability of the method for MT system adaptation purposes to narrow domains. An important future step in order to improve the precision of term mapping and in order to provide term pairs for automated integration into terminology data bases in bilingual term extraction (of which term mapping is an integral component) is also term pair consolidation with knowledge rich term normalisation methods or language independent statistical methods that require presence of a large reference corpus.

Acknowledgement

This work has been supported by the European Social Fund within the project «*Support for Doctoral Studies at University of Latvia*». The research within the project TaaS leading to these results has received funding from the European Union Seventh Framework Programme (FP7/2007-2013), Grant Agreement no 296312.

References

Federmann, C., Gromann, D., Declerck, T., Hunsicker, S., Krieger, H., & Budin, G. (2012). Multilingual Terminology Acquisition for Ontology-based Information Extraction. In Proceedings of the 10th Terminology and Knowledge Engineering Conference (TKE 2012) (pp. 166–175). Madrid, Spain.

Fung, P., & Yee, L. Y. (1998). An IR approach for translating new words from nonparallel, comparable texts. In Proceedings of the 36th Annual Meeting of the Association for Computational Linguistics and 17th International Conference on Computational Linguistics - Volume 1 (pp. 414–420). Stroudsburg, PA, USA: Association for Computational Linguistics.

Gaussier, E., Hull, D. A., Salah, A., & Ait-Mokhtar, S. (2000). Term Alignment in Use: Machine-Aided Human Translation. Véronis, Jean: Parallel Text Processing. Alignment and Use of Translation Corpora. Dordrecht, 253–274.

Koehn, P., Hoang, H., Birch, A., Callison-Burch, C., Federico, M., Bertoldi, N., Cowan, B., Shen, W., Moran, C., Zens, R., Dyer, C., Bojar, O., Constantin, A., & Herbst, E. (2007). Moses: open source toolkit for statistical machine translation. In Proceedings of the 45th Annual Meeting of the ACL on Interactive Poster and Demonstration Sessions (pp. 177–180). Stroudsburg, PA, USA: Association for Computational Linguistics.

Laroche, A., & Langlais, P. (2010). Revisiting context-based projection methods for term-translation spotting in comparable corpora. In Proceedings of the 23rd International Conference on Computational Linguistics (pp. 617–625). Stroudsburg, PA, USA: Association for Computational Linguistics.

Lefever, E., Macken, L., & Hoste, V. (2009). Language-independent bilingual terminology extraction from a multilingual parallel corpus. In Proceedings of the 12th Conference of the European Chapter of the Association for Computational Linguistics (pp. 496–504). Stroudsburg, PA, USA: Association for Computational Linguistics.

Levenshtein, V.I. (1966). Binary codes capable of correcting deletions, insertions, and reversals. Soviet Physics Doklady 10: 707–10.

Mastropavlos, N., & Papavassiliou, V. (2011). Automatic acquisition of bilingual language resources. In Proceedings of the 10th International Conference of Greek Linguistics, Komotini, Greece.

Morin, E., & Daille, B. (2010). Compositionality and lexical alignment of multi-word terms. Language Resources and Evaluation, 44, 79–95.

Morin, E., Daille, B., Takeuchi, K., & Kageura, K. (2010). Brains, not brawn: The use of "smart" comparable corpora in bilingual terminology mining. ACM Transactions on Speech and Language Processing (TSLP), 7(1), 1.

Och, F. J., & Ney, H. (2003). A systematic comparison of various statistical alignment models. Computational Linguistics, 29, 19–51.

Pinnis, M., Ljubešić, N., Ştefănescu, D., Skadiņa, I., Tadić, M., & Gornostay, T. (2012). Term Extraction, Tagging, and Mapping Tools for Under-Resourced Languages. Proceedings of the 10th Conference on Terminology and Knowledge Engineering (TKE 2012) (pp. 193–208). Madrid.

Rapp, R. (1999). Automatic identification of word translations from unrelated English and German corpora. In Proceedings of the 37th annual meeting of the Association for Computational Linguistics on Computational Linguistics (pp. 519–526). Stroudsburg, PA, USA: Association for Computational Linguistics.

Shao, L., & Ng, H. T. (2004). Mining new word translations from comparable corpora. In Proceedings of the 20th international conference on Computational Linguistics. Stroudsburg, PA, USA: Association for Computational Linguistics. doi:10.3115/1220355.1220444

Skadiņa, I., Aker, A., Mastropavlos, N., Su, F., Tufiş, D., Verlic, M., Vasiļjevs, A., Babych, B., Clough, P., Gaizauskas, R., Glaros, N., Paramita, M.L., & Pinnis, M. (2012). Collecting and Using Comparable Corpora for Statistical Machine Translation. Proceedings of the Eight International Conference on Language Resources and Evaluation (LREC'12) (pp. 438–445). Istanbul, Turkey: European Language Resources Association (ELRA).

Steinberger, R., Eisele, A., Klocek, S., Pilos, S., & Schlter, P. (2012). Dgt-tm: A freely available translation memory in 22 languages. In Proceedings of the Eight International Conference on Language Resources and Evaluation (LREC'12) (pp. 454–459).

Steinberger, R., Pouliquen, B., & Hagman, J. (2002). Cross-lingual document similarity calculation using the multilingual thesaurus eurovoc. Computational Linguistics and Intelligent Text Processing, 101–121.

Su, F., & Babych, B. (2012). Measuring comparability of documents in non-parallel corpora for efficient extraction of (semi-)parallel translation equivalents. In Proceedings of the Joint Workshop on Exploiting Synergies between Information Retrieval and Machine Translation (ESIRMT) and Hybrid Approaches to Machine Translation (HyTra) (pp. 10–19). Stroudsburg, PA, USA: Association for Computational Linguistics.

Ştefănescu, D. (2012). Mining for Term Translations in Comparable Corpora. In The 5th Workshop on Building and Using Comparable Corpora (pp. 98–103).

TTC Project. (2013). Public deliverable D7.3: Evaluation of the impact of TTC on Statistical MT (p. 38). TTC Project: Terminology Extraction, Translation Tools and Comparable Corpora. Retrieved from http://ttc-project.eu/images/stories/TTC_D7.3.pdf

Wolf, P., Bernardi, U., Federmann, C., & Hunsicker, S. (2011). From Statistical Term Extraction to Hybrid Machine Translation. In Proceedings of the 15th Annual Conference of the European Association for Machine Translation (pp. 379–419).

Semi-supervised vs. Cross-domain Graphs for Sentiment Analysis

Natalia Ponomareva
University of Wolverhampton, UK
nata.ponomareva@wlv.ac.uk

Mike Thelwall
University of Wolverhampton, UK
m.thelwall@wlv.ac.uk

Abstract

The lack of labeled data always poses challenges for tasks where machine learning is involved. Semi-supervised and cross-domain approaches represent the most common ways to overcome this difficulty. Graph-based algorithms have been widely studied during the last decade and have proved to be very effective at solving the data limitation problem. This paper explores one of the most popular state-of-the-art graph-based algorithms - label propagation, together with its modifications previously applied to sentiment classification. We study the impact of modified graph structure and parameter variations and compare the performance of graph-based algorithms in cross-domain and semi-supervised settings. The results provide a strategy for selecting the most favourable algorithm and learning paradigm on the basis of the available labeled and unlabeled data.

1 Introduction

Sentiment classification is an active area of research concerned with the automatic identification of sentiment strength or valence in texts. Being a special case of topic classification, it can benefit from all well-known classification algorithms. However, as sentiment classification relies on sentiment markers rather than frequent topic words, it potentially needs more data for satisfactory performance. When a limited amount of labeled data is available, cross-domain learning (CDL) or semi-supervised learning (SSL) approaches are commonly used. CDL techniques endeavour to exploit existing annotated data from a different domain (i.e. different topic and/or genre) but their success largely depends on how similar the source and target domains are. In contrast, SSL relies on a small amount of labeled data from the same domain which requires additional annotations.

Graph-based (GB) learning has been intensively studied in the last ten years (Zhu et al., 2003; Joachims, 2003; Talukdar and Crammer, 2009; Subramanya and Bilmes, 2011) and applied to many NLP tasks. In particular, in the field of sentiment analysis GB models have been employed for sentiment classification (Pang and Lee, 2004; Goldberg and Zhu, 2006; Wu et al., 2009), automatic building of sentiment lexicons (Hassan and Radev, 2010; Xu et al., 2010), cross-lingual sentiment analysis (Scheible et al., 2010) and social media analysis (Speriosu et al., 2011). The popularity of GB algorithms is not accidental: they not only represent a competitive alternative to other SSL techniques (co-training, transductive SVM, etc.) but also feature a number of remarkable properties, including scalability (Bilmes and Subramanya, 2011) and easy extension to multi-class classification (Zhu et al., 2003). GB algorithms exploit the ability of the data to be represented as a weighted graph where instances are vertices and edges reflect similarities between instances. Higher edge weights correspond to more similar instances and vice versa. GB approaches assume smoothness of the label function on the graph so that strongly connected nodes belong to the same class. In this paper we focus on the adaptation of a widely used Label Propagation (LP) algorithm (Zhu and Ghahramani, 2002) to semi-supervised and cross-domain sentiment classification.

The goal of our research is two-fold. First, we attempt to formalise and unify the research on GB approaches in the field of sentiment analysis. In particular, we conduct a comparison between LP and its variants and study the impact of different graph structures and parameter values on algorithm performance. We also demonstrate that GB-SSL and GB-CDL accuracies are competitive or superior to the accuracies shown by other SSL and CDL techniques.

Second, most research on sentiment classification which deals with limited or no in-domain labeled data usually favours one learning paradigm

- SSL or CDL. However, in real life situations out-of-domain labeled data is often available, and therefore focusing only on SSL means overlooking the potential of already existing resources. At the same time, relying only on out-of-domain data might be risky as CDL accuracy largely depends on the properties of in-domain and out-of-domain data sets, e.g., domain similarity and complexity (Ponomareva and Thelwall, 2012a; Ponomareva and Thelwall, 2012b). Thus, it is important to investigate what data properties determine the choice of either CDL or SSL and what amount of in-domain labeled data is needed to outperform CDL accuracy. In light of this, the second objective of the paper is to develop a strategy for selecting the most appropriate learning paradigm under limited data conditions.

The paper is organised as follows. Section 2 presents the *LP* algorithm and its variants, some of which have been recently proposed for the sentiment classification task. Section 3 describes our approach to building the sentiment graph. Section 4 contains an extensive comparative analysis of *LP* and its variants in CDL and SSL settings. Section 5 lists some works on sentiment classification and GB learning related to our research. Finally, Section 6 defines the strategy suggesting the best algorithm and learning paradigm under limited data conditions and gives directions for further research.

2 Graph-based Approaches

2.1 Label Propagation

LP was one of the first GB algorithms to be developed, introduced by Zhu and Ghahramani (2002). It represents an iterative process that at each step propagates information from labeled to unlabeled nodes until convergence, i.e. when node labels do not change from one iteration to another. *LP* can be seen as weighted averaging of labels in a node neighbourhood where the influence of neighbours is defined by edge weights. In case of sentiment classification, the nodes are documents and the edge weights indicate the closeness of document ratings.

Let us introduce a formalism for a description of the algorithm. Let $G = (V, E)$ be an undirected graph with n vertices $V = \{x_1, ..., x_n\}$ connected through edges $E = \{(x_i, x_j)\}$. Assume that the first l nodes are labeled with $Y_l = \{y_1, ..., y_l\}$ while the remaining u nodes are unlabeled. Clearly $l + u = n$. We consider a binary classification problem, i.e. $y_i \in \{0, 1\}$, although the algorithm can be easily extended to multi-class cases. The task is to assign labels $\hat{Y}_u = \{\hat{y}_{l+1}, ...\hat{y}_n\}$ to unlabeled nodes. Let $W = (w_{ij})$ be a weight matrix on E with elements corresponding to the similarity between x_i and x_j, and let $\bar{W} = (\bar{w}_{ij})$ be its normalised version:

$$\bar{w}_{ij} = \frac{w_{ij}}{\sum_j w_{ij}} \quad (1)$$

LP is formally presented in Algorithm 1.

Algorithm 1. *LP*

1. Initialise $\hat{Y} = (y_1, ..., y_l, 0, ..., 0)$
2. Propagate $\hat{Y} \leftarrow \bar{W}\hat{Y}$
3. Clamp the labeled data: $\hat{Y}_l \leftarrow Y_l$
4. Repeat from 2 until convergence

Bengio et al. (2006) demonstrated that *LP* is equivalent to minimising a quadratic cost function:

$$C(\hat{Y}) = \sum_{ij} w_{ij}(\hat{y}_i - \hat{y}_j)^2 \rightarrow min \quad (2)$$

Zhu et al. (2003) showed that if we consider a continuous label space $\hat{y} \in \mathbf{R}$ instead of the discrete there exists a harmonic function delivering a closed form solution to the optimisation problem: Let us split the normalised weight matrix $\bar{W}$ into four sub-matrices:

$$\bar{W} = \begin{pmatrix} \bar{W}_{ll} & \bar{W}_{lu} \\ \bar{W}_{ul} & \bar{W}_{uu} \end{pmatrix} \quad (3)$$

The harmonic solution of (2) can be given by:

$$\hat{Y}_u = (I - \bar{W}_{uu})^{-1}\bar{W}_{ul}Y_l \quad (4)$$

Zhu et al. (2003) pointed out that if classes are not well-separated then the final distribution of classes can be highly skewed. To avoid unbalanced classification they adopt the class mass normalisation (CMN) procedure which scales the output values on the basis of the class priors. Let q be the desirable proportion for the classes and let $\sum_i \hat{y}_i$ and $\sum_i (1 - \hat{y}_i)$ be the masses of classes 1 and 0 respectively. The decision rule for $\hat{y}_i$ to belong to the class 1 can then be represented as:

$$q\frac{\hat{y}_i}{\sum_i \hat{y}_i} > (1 - q)\frac{1 - \hat{y}_i}{\sum_i (1 - \hat{y}_i)} \quad (5)$$

2.2 Modifications to the *LP* algorithm

The graph structure used in *LP* does not differentiate between labeled and unlabeled neighbours. However, in some cases it might be beneficial to give them different impacts. For example, in SSL

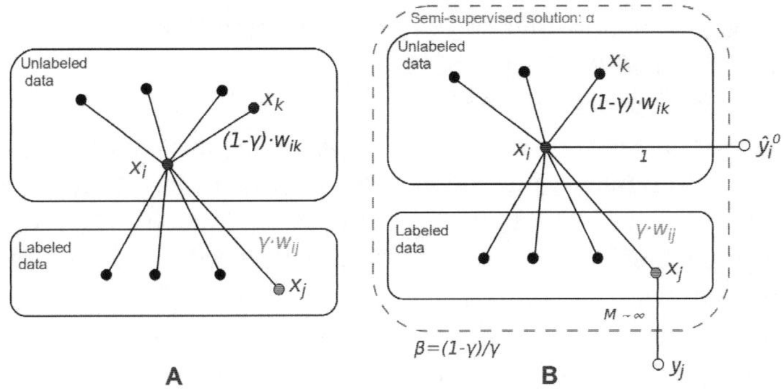

Figure 1: Modified graph structures for the LP algorithm.
A Different impact of labeled and unlabeled nodes; **B** incorporation of predictions by external classifiers

it is natural to rely more on labeled data whose labels are identified with a high level of confidence. In contrast, for CDL highly reliable labels do not help much when source and target data are very different and it might be better to prioritise unlabeled examples. Let us introduce a coefficient γ with $\gamma \in (0, 1)$ responsible for the proportion of influence between labeled and unlabeled data, so that $\gamma < 0.5$ gives preference to unlabeled and $\gamma > 0.5$ to labeled examples. This modification (LP_γ) leads to the redistribution of the weight function on graph edges (Figure 1A).

An approach very similar to LP_γ has been proposed by Wu et al. (2009) for cross-domain sentiment classification. The suggested method has two main differences from LP_γ. First, the weight matrices W_{uu} and W_{ul} are normalised separately instead of using the same scaling factor for labeled and unlabeled data. This difference has no effect as long as the scaling factors for both matrices are similar. However, this might not be the case for cross-domain graphs. Indeed, if source and target domains are very different so that out-of-domain neighbours are much farther away than in-domain neighbours, the scaling factors can have different orders of magnitude. Second, the updated values of unlabeled nodes are normalised after each iteration using the CMN procedure which fixes data skewing. As we will see in Section 4, these differences lead to a large performance increase in the results of GB-CDL. We formalise the method of Wu et al. (2009) (further called LP^n_γ, where "n" states for normalisation) in Algorithm 2.

We can further improve the graph structure in Figure 1A by incorporating external classifiers for unlabeled examples. This was implemented by Goldberg and Zhu (2006) in an application for semi-supervised multi-class sentiment classification (Figure 1B). In this modification, each labeled and unlabeled vertex is connected to a dongle node which is a labeled node with either the true value y_i or prediction $\hat{y}^0_i$ given by an external classifier. This LP variant (called $LP_{\alpha\beta}$) is able to take advantage of different sources of information. It relies on two main parameters, α and β. β is an analogue of γ in LP_γ, $\beta = \frac{1-\gamma}{\gamma}$. Parameter α controls the weight of the GB solution compared to the initial predictions. Specifically, α close to 0 gives more importance to the initial predictions whilst high values of α prioritise the GB solution. For further details about the implementation of $LP_{\alpha\beta}$ the reader is invited to refer to Goldberg and Zhu (2006).

Algorithm 2. LP^n_γ

1. Normalise separately W_{uu} and W_{ul}
2. Initialise Y_l and Y_u
3. Propagate $\hat{Y}_u \leftarrow (1-\gamma)\bar{W}_{uu}\hat{Y}_u + \gamma\bar{W}_{ul}\hat{Y}_l$
4. Normalise $\hat{Y}_u$ with CMN
5. Repeat from 3 until convergence

3 Sentiment Graph Construction

Construction of a good graph with an adequate approximation to similarity between data instances is key for the successful performance of GB algorithms (Zhu, 2005). Sentiment classification requires a similarity metric which assigns values to a pair of documents on the basis of their sentiments, so that documents with the same sentiment obtain high similarity scores and documents of opposite sentiments obtain low scores. This implies that vector representation of the data must contain sentiment markers rather than topic words. Previous research suggests several possible vector representations for documents. Pang and Lee

(2005) proposed PSP-based similarity and document representation as (PSP, 1-PSP), where PSP is the percentage of positive sentences in a document. They used an additional classifier for learning sentence polarity that was trained on external data with user-provided scores. As a result, the PSP values gave a high correlation with document ratings. Goldberg and Zhu (2006) also used in-domain labeled data to approximate sentiment similarity for semi-supervised sentiment classification. In particular, they constructed a vector representation based on document words. The weight of words was calculated using their mutual information with positive and negative classes from the external data set. The main disadvantage of both of the above approaches is that they require labeled in-domain data. The principal purpose of our research is to develop a learning strategy when a limited amount of labeled data is available.

Research on sentiment analysis suggests that certain parts of speech, e.g., adjectives, verbs and adverbs, are good sentiment markers (Pang and Lee, 2008). Thus, we represent a document as a vector of unigrams and bigrams and filter out those that do not contain above parts of speech. As nouns can also convey sentiments, we extend our feature space by the nouns listed in the SO-CAL-dictionaries (Taboada et al., 2010). The similarity between two documents is measured by the cosine similarity between their vector representations.

Another issue that needs to be tackled when constructing a graph is connectivity. Graphs can be fully connected or sparse. The former representation, besides its high computational cost, usually performs worse than sparse models (Zhu, 2005). The most common way to construct sparse graphs is to introduce either a threshold for the number of nearest neighbours k (kNN graphs) or a maximum proximity radius ϵ which removes edges with weights less than ϵ (ϵNN graphs). According to Zhu (2005) all kNN graphs tend to perform well empirically. Following this observation as well as our own experiments with ϵNN graphs, which showed no significant difference in the performance, we choose the kNN graph structure for all our models. Moreover, unlike much previous work we distinguish labeled and unlabeled nodes in a way that we connect each unlabeled node with k_l labeled and k_u unlabeled neighbours, where k_l and k_u can be different. This modification is justified empirically (see Section 4).

4 Experiments

4.1 Data and Experimental Objectives

In our experiments we use the popular multi-domain data set (Blitzer et al., 2007) comprising Amazon product reviews on 4 topics: books (BO), electronics (EL), kitchen appliances (KI) and DVDs (DV). Reviews are rated using a binary scale, 1-2 star reviews are considered as negative and 4-5 star reviews as positive. The data within each domain are balanced: they contain 1000 positive and 1000 negative reviews.

We experiment with these data in two different settings: CDL and SSL. In CDL settings we assume that there are 2 data sets: one labeled (source) and the other unlabeled (target). The task is to label the target data on the basis of the information given by the source data. In SSL settings we assume that we have a limited amount of labeled data and vast amount of unlabeled data and we aim to classify some test data belonging to the same domain. As both settings use some labeled data all algorithms described in Section 2 can be easily applied to these tasks. In our experiments we examine the performance of LP and its 3 variants: LP_γ, LP_γ^n and $LP_{\alpha\beta}$. We also compute normalise values of the obtained results: $LP_\gamma + CMN$ and $LP_{\alpha\beta} + CMN$.

Our experiments aim to answer four questions:

1. Which modifications of graph structure improve the algorithm performance and which algorithm delivers the best results?
2. Can GB-CDL approach fully-supervised in-domain accuracy levels?
3. How much labeled data does GB-SSL approach need to achieve the performance of fully-supervised classification?
4. Do GB algorithms provide results comparable with other state-of-the-art CDL and SSL techniques?

4.2 Cross-domain Learning

Previous studies on CDL agreed that properties of source and target data determine the results given by CDL algorithms. Asch and Daelemans (2010) and Plank and van Noord (2011) focused on the similarity between source and target data sets as the main factor influencing the CDL accuracy loss. Our previous research (Ponomareva and Thelwall, 2012a) brought forward another data

source-target	baseline	LP	LP_γ	LP_γ $+CMN$	$LP_{\alpha\beta}$	$LP_{\alpha\beta}$ $+CMN$	LP_γ^n	SCL	SFA	in-domain accuracy
EL-BO	65.5	68.5	69.0	70.3	69.2	70.5	72.3	75.4	75.7	78.6
KI-BO	64.7	68.8	69.2	69.9	69.2	71.5	73.9	68.6	74.8	78.6
DV-BO	74.4	**78.5**	**79.9**	**80.4**	**80.3**	**81.1**	**80.9**	**79.7**	**77.5**	78.6
BO-EL	70.0	69.8	70.0	73.8	73.2	74.1	77.4	77.5	72.5	81.2
KI-EL	79.7	**83.3**	**83.0**	**83.8**	**83.4**	**83.7**	**82.3**	**86.8**	**85.1**	81.2
DV-EL	67.2	74.1	74.3	74.9	74.1	76.2	78.9	74.1	76.7	81.2
BO-KI	69.5	73.0	74.8	76.3	76.1	77.0	81.4	78.9	78.8	82.9
EL-KI	81.6	**82.3**	**83.8**	**84.7**	**85.0**	**86.1**	**84.1**	**85.9**	**86.8**	82.9
DV-KI	70.2	75.3	75.5	76.2	77.3	77.6	80.9	81.4	80.8	82.9
BO-DV	76.5	78.0	77.0	**79.5**	**78.8**	**80.8**	**78.6**	75.8	**81.4**	79.6
EL-DV	71.3	71.3	72.3	73.0	74.7	74.6	74.6	76.2	77.2	79.6
KI-DV	70.1	71.0	72.5	72.8	72.8	75.2	76.3	76.9	77.0	79.6
average	71.7	74.5	75.1	76.3	76.2	77.3	78.4	78.1	78.7	80.6

Table 1: Accuracies (%) of GB algorithms in CDL settings (accuracies within the 95% confidence interval of the in-domain accuracies are highlighted).

property called domain complexity which we defined as vocabulary richness and approximated by the percentage of rare words. We showed a non-symmetry of the accuracy drop, specifically, that it tends to be higher when source data are more complex. We also demonstrated:

a) similarity between BO and DV on the one hand, and between EL and KI on the other hand;

b) a higher level of complexity of BO and DV with respect to EL and KI.

We exploit these findings to analyse the GB-CDL results. The four data sets give 12 combinations of source-target pairs and, therefore, 12 series of experiments. Our experimental setup includes 2 stages: parameter tuning and algorithm testing. We randomly extract 400 examples from the target data and use them as the development data set for tuning the parameters α, $\beta(\gamma)$, k_u and k_l. The parameter search is run over the following ranges: $k_u \in \{5, 10, 20, 50, 100\}$, $k_l \in \{5, 20, 50, 100, 200, 400\}$, $\beta \in \{0.2, 0.5, 1, 2, 5\}$, $\alpha \in \{1, 2, 5, 10, 50, 100, 200\}$. $LP_{\alpha\beta}$ also requires initial approximations for the labels which we obtain by applying a linear-kernel SVM[1] classifier trained on the source data. The best set of parameter values is established on the basis of the highest average accuracy over all source-target pairs.

Analysing the optimal set of parameter values we observe an overall agreement between the algorithms on the choice of $\beta(\gamma)$ with a preference for high values of $\beta = 5$ and correspondingly low values of $\gamma = 0.2$. This implies that GB algorithms in CDL settings heavily rely on labels provided by in-domain neighbours. Optimal value of α is obtained to be 200 as low values of α ($\alpha < 10$) keep output labels very close to the supervised solution. In most cases, the best results are achieved for low $k_u \leq 10$ and relatively high $k_l = 100$, which confirms the importance of separate parameters for the number of labeled and unlabeled neighbours. The obtained optimal parameter values are used in algorithms' testing conducted over the remaining 1600 examples from the target data.

GB-CDL accuracies are presented in Table 1. The baseline stands for the performance of a linear-kernel SVM classifier trained on the source data. The in-domain accuracies computed on the target data with 5-fold cross-validation give an estimation of the CDL performance upper bound. All LP variants improve the LP results, although the effect of some parameters is rather modest, e.g. γ. Incorporating external classifiers leads to an accuracy gain of more than 1% on average which is consistent over the domain pairs. The CMN procedure also brings a considerable contribution with overall accuracy increase of 1%. The highest results are achieved by LP_γ^n which outperforms $LP_\gamma + CMN$ by 2.5%.

All GB algorithms show a significant improvement over the baseline. Moreover, the accuracy gain given by the best two methods LP_γ^n and $LP_{\alpha\beta} + CMN$ reaches 5-6% on all domain pairs.

[1]We used the LIBSVM library (Chang and Lin, 2011).

GB-CDL demonstrates excellent results for pairs with similar source and target (DV-BO, BO-DV, KI-EL and EL-KI) outperforming in-domain supervised classification. At the same time, GB accuracies are rather low for pairs with large discrepancies between source and target data. In this respect, LP^n_γ is promising as it can "fix" the domain discrepancies for some source-target pairs: BO-EL, DV-EL, BO-KI and DV-KI. Keeping in mind that EL and KI have lower values of lexical richness than BO and DV, we can presume that LP^n_γ works better when the target domain is simple. This could be due to the fact that for simple domains the weight function better approximates the actual similarities between documents, but further research is necessary before such a conclusion can be drawn with high confidence.

GB algorithms demonstrate competitive performance with respect to other state-of-the-art approaches, namely SCL (Blitzer et al., 2007) and SFA (Pan et al., 2010). Indeed, Table 1 shows that the difference between average accuracies of SCL, SFA and the two best GB algorithms are not statistically significant. However, the GB approach is more beneficial for multi-class classification as its adaptation to this task is straightforward.

4.3 Semi-supervised Learning

SSL experiments are carried out separately for each domain. We randomly divide our data into 5 folds where one is used for parameter tuning and 4 for testing the algorithms in the cross-validation setup. Thus, in every experiment, 400 examples are used for testing/tuning and the remaining 1600 instances are split into labeled and unlabeled sets. We gradually increase the amount of labeled data from 50 to 800 to analyse the impact of the labeled data size on the algorithms' performance.

In contrast to the CDL experiments, we substitute k_l by the proportion of labeled neighbours Δ_l with respect to the labeled data size. We find this parameter more natural for variable sizes of labeled data. The best value for Δ_l is searched for in the range $\{0.05, 0.1, 0.2, 0.3, 0.4, 0.5\}$. The search for remaining parameters is run in the same ranges as for CDL and the optimal set is established on the basis of the highest average accuracy over all domains and labeled data sizes. Optimal value for β is found to be quite low: $\beta = 0.5$ ($\gamma = 0.7$) which is consistent with our expectations of the algorithms' preference for more reliable labeled data from the same domain. All algorithms agree on low values of k_u and Δ_l, showing best results for $k_u = 5$ and $\Delta_l = 0.1$ or 0.2.

GB-SSL accuracies are presented in Table 2[2]. The baseline corresponds to the accuracy given by a linear-kernel SVM classifier trained on the same portion of labeled data. We observe that GB-SSL algorithms outperform the in-domain results with 600-700 labeled examples. Moreover, relatively high accuracies (within the 95% confidence interval of the in-domain accuracies) can be achieved with only 500 labeled examples.

We also compare GB-SSL with two state-of-the-art SSL approaches tested on the same data (Dasgupta and Ng, 2009; Li et al., 2010) (Table 2). The method of Dasgupta and Ng (2009) combines spectral clustering with active learning. The authors report the accuracy for 100 and 500 labeled examples selected by active learning. The accuracies shown by $LP_{\alpha\beta} + CMN$ are significantly higher than the accuracies obtained by their method with an average difference of approximately 4% for both sizes of labeled data. Li et al. (2010) adopt a co-training approach which deploys classifiers trained on personal and impersonal view data sets. Although the co-training achieves very high accuracies for the KI domain it gives considerably worse results for the domains of BO and DV. Averaging accuracies across domains gives 71.4% for $LP_{\alpha\beta} + CMN$ vs. 64.5% for the co-training when 100 labeled examples are used and 77.2% vs. 74.7% for 300 examples. Moreover, unlike the proposed co-training approach the GB algorithms are much more robust delivering equally good results across all data sets.

5 Related Work

There are several fields related to our research. GB-SSL has received extensive attention from the research community (Zhu et al., 2003; Joachims, 2003; Talukdar and Crammer, 2009; Subramanya and Bilmes, 2011). Two of the most recent methods proposed in this field are Modified Adsorption (MAD) and Measure Propagation (MP), which present some advantages over LP. However, preliminary experiments we performed using MAD did not lead to very promising results and more experiments are necessary. Our paper is also re-

[2]We deliberately reduced the number of algorithms reported in this paper due to space constraints and similar behaviour of some LP variants.

No. labeled data	50	100	200	300	400	500	600	700	800	in-domain accuracy
					books					
SVM	60.3	65.2	71.8	71.8	73.2	74.9	76.1	76.8	76.3	78.6
$LP_\gamma + CMN$	68.0	71.1	72.7	75.5	**77.6**	**78.5**	**79.3**	**80.2**	**81.1**	
LP_γ^n	65.5	69.9	73.1	76.6	**78.0**	**78.7**	**80.0**	**80.1**	**79.7**	
$LP_{\alpha\beta} + CMN$	66.5	70.8	73.1	75.5	75.4	**78.2**	**79.3**	**79.9**	**80.1**	
Dasgupta and Ng (2009)	–	62.1	–	–	–	73.5	–	–	–	
Li et al. (2010)	–	60.1	73.0	71.6	–	–	–	–	–	
					electronics					
SVM	57.4	66.6	72.3	73.9	75.1	76.7	77.5	78.2	79.0	81.2
$LP_\gamma + CMN$	70.6	74.2	76.7	77.9	79.2	**80.6**	**80.1**	**80.6**	**81.5**	
LP_γ^n	66.7	72.8	77.4	79.4	**79.9**	**81.0**	81.0	**81.3**	**82.0**	
$LP_{\alpha\beta} + CMN$	69.9	74.1	77.8	78.4	78.9	**80.6**	**81.6**	**81.8**	**82.8**	
Dasgupta and Ng (2009)	–	70.6	–	–	–	77.5	–	–	–	
Li et al. (2010)	–	70.0	77.0	78.2	–	–	–	–	–	
					kitchen					
SVM	60.0	69.2	74.1	75.8	76.8	78.1	77.5	79.9	80.1	82.9
$LP_\gamma + CMN$	70.7	73.2	76.8	79.1	80.6	80.8	**81.8**	**82.5**	**82.2**	
LP_γ^n	68.3	71.4	76.7	80.1	81.0	**81.9**	**82.4**	**82.7**	**83.5**	
$LP_{\alpha\beta} + CMN$	71.4	74.2	76.5	79.5	80.3	**82.0**	**81.8**	**83.2**	**83.5**	
Dasgupta and Ng (2009)	–	74.1	–	–	–	78.4	–	–	–	
Li et al. (2010)	–	78.6	79.0	**83.3**	–	–	–	–	–	
					DVDs					
SVM	53.8	63.4	70.6	73.9	75.0	75.9	76.0	77.8	77.1	79.6
$LP_\gamma + CMN$	65.8	67.1	71.7	74.2	76.5	78.0	**80.0**	**80.8**	**81.4**	
LP_γ^n	65.2	66.3	72.3	75.1	**78.3**	**79.2**	**80.3**	**80.6**	**80.9**	
$LP_{\alpha\beta} + CMN$	65.2	66.3	72.1	75.3	77.3	**78.4**	**80.0**	**80.4**	**80.2**	
Dasgupta and Ng (2009)	–	62.7	–	–	–	73.4	–	–	–	
Li et al. (2010)	–	49.5	63.0	65.5	–	–	–	–	–	

Table 2: Accuracies (%) of GB algorithms in SSL settings (accuracies within the 95% confidence interval are highlighted; accuracies outperforming the in-domain accuracies are underlined).

lated to work in cross-domain sentiment classification and the results we obtain are comparable to those reported by (Blitzer et al., 2007; Pan et al., 2010). The SSL methods discussed in Section 4.3 (Dasgupta and Ng, 2009; Li et al., 2010) offer an interesting alternative to GB algorithms, but their results are substantially lower.

6 Conclusions and Future Work

This paper has explored GB algorithms in CDL and SSL settings. The evaluation of the GB-CDL algorithms has shown that the best methods, $LP_{\alpha\beta} + CMN$ and LP_γ^n, consistently improve the baseline by 5-6% for all domain pairs. Therefore, if source and target domains are similar (i.e. the baseline classifier loses less than 5% accuracy when adapted from the source to target domain) GB-CDL algorithms are a competitive alternative to the fully supervised techniques. Moreover, we have shown that if the target domain has low complexity, the LP_γ^n algorithm can deliver good performance even for quite different domain pairs.

For large discrepancies between source and target data GB-SSL can help to achieve good results with a reasonably small amount of labeled data. Specifically, even 500 labeled examples are enough to ensure performance within a 95% confidence interval of the in-domain accuracy.

In the future, we plan to compare GB-SSL and GB-CDL for multi-class sentiment classification. This extension should be straightforward as GB algorithms can be easily adapted to multi-class cases. In addition, we will include in our experiments other algorithms such as MAD and MP.

References

Vincent Van Asch and Walter Daelemans. 2010. Using domain similarity for performance estimation. In *Proceedings of the Workshop on Domain Adaptation for Natural Language Processing, ACL'10*, pages 31–36.

Yoshua Bengio, Olivier Delalleau, and Nicolas Le Roux, 2006. *Semi-Supervised Learning*, chapter 11. Label Propagation and Quadratic Criterion, pages 193–216. The MIT Press.

Jeff Bilmes and Amarnag Subramanya, 2011. *Scaling up Machine Learning: Parallel and Distributed Approaches*, chapter 15. Parallel Graph-Based Semi-Supervised Learning, pages 307–330. Cambridge University Press.

John Blitzer, Mark Dredze, and Fernando Pereira. 2007. Biographies, bollywood, boom-boxes and blenders: Domain adaptation for sentiment classification. In *Proceedings of ACL '07*, pages 440–447.

Chih-Chung Chang and Chih-Jen Lin. 2011. LIBSVM: A library for support vector machines. *ACM Transactions on Intelligent Systems and Technology*, 2:27:1–27:27. Software available at `http://www.csie.ntu.edu.tw/~cjlin/libsvm`.

Sajib Dasgupta and Vincent Ng. 2009. Mine the easy, classify the hard: A semi-supervised approach to automatic sentiment classification. In *Proceedings of ACL-AFNLP'09*, pages 701–709.

Andrew B. Goldberg and Xiaojin Zhu. 2006. Seeing stars when there aren't many stars: graph-based semi-supervised learning for sentiment categorization. In *Proceedings of TextGraphs '06*, pages 45–52.

Ahmed Hassan and Dragomir R. Radev. 2010. Identifying text polarity using random walks. In *Proceedings of ACL '10*, pages 395–403.

T. Joachims. 2003. Transductive learning via spectral graph partitioning. In *Proceedings of ICML'03*.

Shoushan Li, Chu-Ren Huang, Guodong Zhou, and Sophia Yat Mei Lee. 2010. Employing personal/impersonal views in supervised and semi-supervised sentiment classification. In *Proceedings of ACL '10*, pages 414–423.

Sinno Jialin Pan, Xiaochuan Niz, Jian-Tao Sunz, Qiang Yangy, and Zheng Chen. 2010. Cross-domain sentiment classification via spectral feature alignment. In *Proceedings of WWW '10*.

Bo Pang and Lillian Lee. 2004. A sentimental education: sentiment analysis using subjectivity summarization based on minimum cuts. In *Proceedings of ACL '04*, pages 271–278.

Bo Pang and Lillian Lee. 2005. Seeing stars: exploiting class relationships for sentiment categorization with respect to rating scales. In *Proceedings of ACL '05*, pages 115–124.

Bo Pang and Lillian Lee. 2008. Opinion mining and sentiment analysis. *Foundations and Trends in Information Retrieval*, 2(1-2):1–135.

Barbara Plank and Gertjan van Noord. 2011. Effective measures of domain similarity for parsing. In *Proceedings of ACL '11*, pages 1566–1576.

Natalia Ponomareva and Mike Thelwall. 2012a. Bibliographies or blenders: Which resource is best for cross-domain sentiment analysis? In *Proceedings of CICLing '12*.

Natalia Ponomareva and Mike Thelwall. 2012b. Do neighbours help? an exploration of graph-based algorithms for cross-domain sentiment classification. In *Proceedings of EMNLP '12*.

Christian Scheible, Florian Laws, Lukas Michelbacher, and Hinrich Schütze. 2010. Sentiment translation through multi-edge graphs. In *Coling 2010: Posters*, pages 1104–1112.

Michael Speriosu, Nikita Sudan, Sid Upadhyay, and Jason Baldridge. 2011. Twitter polarity classication with label propagation over lexical links and the follower graph. In *Proceedings of EMNLP '11*, pages 53–63.

A. Subramanya and J. Bilmes. 2011. Semi-supervised learning with measure propagation. *Journal of Machine Learning Research*, 12:3311–3370.

M. Taboada, J. Brooke, M. Tofiloski, K. Voll, and M. Stede. 2010. Lexicon-based methods for sentiment analysis. *Computational Linguistics*, 37(2):267–307.

Partha Pratim Talukdar and Koby Crammer. 2009. New regularized algorithms for transductive learning. In *Proceedings of ECML PKDD 2009*.

Qiong Wu, Songbo Tan, and Xueqi Cheng. 2009. Graph ranking for sentiment transfer. In *Proceedings of ACL-IJCNLP '09 (Short Papers)*, pages 317–320.

Ge Xu, Xinfan Meng, and Houfeng Wang. 2010. Build chinese emotion lexicons using a graph-based algorithm and multiple resources. In *Proceedings of Coling '10*, pages 1209–1217.

Xiaojin Zhu and Zoubin Ghahramani. 2002. Learning from labeled and unlabeled data with label propagation. Technical report, Carnegie Mellon University.

Xiaojin Zhu, Zoubin Ghahramani, and John Lafferty. 2003. Semi-supervised learning using gaussian fields and harmonic functions. In *Proceedings of the 20th International Conference on Machine Learning (ICML '03)*, pages 912–919.

Xiaojin Zhu. 2005. *Semi-Supervised Learning with Graphs*. Ph.D. thesis, Carnegie Mellon University.

Towards a Hybrid Rule-based and Statistical Arabic-French Machine Translation System

Fatiha Sadat
University of Quebec in Montréal
201 President Kennedy, Montréal
QC, Canada, H2X 3Y7
Sadat.fatiha@uqam.ca

Abstract

Arabic is a morphologically rich and complex language, which presents significant challenges for natural language processing and machine translation. In this paper, we describe an ongoing effort to build our first Arabic-French phrase–based machine translation system using the Moses decoder among other linguistic tools. The results show an improvement in the quality of translation and a gain in terms of Bleu score after introducing a pre-processing scheme for Arabic and applying some rules based on morphological variations of the source language. The proposed approach is completed without increasing the amount of training data or changing radically the algorithms that can affect the translation or training engines.

1 Introduction

Arabic is a morphologically rich and complex language, in which a word carries not only inflections but also clitics, such as pronouns, conjunctions, and prepositions. It is a highly inflectional language, which makes the morphological analysis complicated. In Arabic, many coordinating conjunctions, the definite article, many prepositions and particles, and a class of pronouns are all clitics that attach themselves either to the start or the end of words (Attia, 2008). This morphological complexity has consequences on NLP applications, such as machine translation and information retrieval.

One the one hand, developing an Arabic-French machine translation system is not an easy task, although there is a vast amount of training data nowadays. On the other hand, dealing with the complexity and ambiguity of the source language plays a major role in boosting the efficiency of the translation system.

In previous research, it was shown that morphological pre-processing of a morphologically rich language, such as Arabic does provide a benefit, especially in the case of limited volume of training data (Goldwater and McClosky, 2005), (Sadat and Habash, 2006), (Lee, 2004), (El Ishibani et al., 2006), (Hasan et al., 2003).

In Statistical Machine Translation (SMT) context, Habash et Sadat (Habash et Sadat, 2006) pre-processed Arabic texts using different segmentation schemes for translation into English and showed that the quality of translation is generally better than the baseline. Similar findings were reported by (El Ishibani et al., 2006) on Arabic-English SMT. In relation to Arabic-French SMT, few research and evaluations were reported, compared to Arabic-English SMT among other pairs of languages. One of the first statistically-driven machine translation systems for Arabic-French was reported by Hasan et al (Hasan et al., 2006) during the second Cesta evaluation campaign[1]. The proposed SMT system used a simple stemming algorithm based on finite-state automata to split Arabic words into prefixes, stem and suffixes. Nevertheless, this simple segmentation method showed a reduced OOV rate from 8.2% to 2.6% for the test data and thus a better quality of translation in terms of BLEU score (Papineni et al., 2001). Another research on Arabic-French SMT was focused on domain adaptation to the news domain and did not consider the pre-processing of the morphologically complex language such as Arabic (Schwenk and Senellart, 2009). An improvement of 3.5 BLEU points on the test set was realized. In relation to improving an SMT system using some language analysis rules, such as re-ordering and Arabic as a source language, there was no

[1] http://www.technolangue.net/article.php3?id_article=199

reported research on Arabic-French SMT. However, Carpuat et al. (Carpuat et al., 2010) showed that post-verbal subject (VS) constructions are hard to translate because they have highly ambiguous reordering patterns when translated to English. They proposed to reorder VS construction into SV order for SMT word alignment only. This strategy significantly improves BLEU and TER scores of the SMT using Arabic-English language pair.

In this paper, we report some experiments related to our first participation in the 2012 TRAD evaluation campaign[2], that was coordinated by the *Laboratoire National de métrologie et d'Essais (LNE)* and CASSIDIAN (*the defence and security subsidiary of the EADS group*), and was funded by the French General Directorate for Armament (DGA). Our main interest at this stage is related to the pre-processing of the source language, in order to improve the quality of translation, rather than the radical changes that might improve the translation or training engines or the increase of the amount of the training corpora. This paper is organized as follows. The morphology of Arabic language is described in section 2. In section 3, we discuss the proposed solutions of pre-processing Arabic through segmentation and different rules on morphological reduction of the source language. In section 4, we present the experiments on Arabic-French SMT with different evaluations. Section 5 concludes the present paper with a discussion and future extension.

2 The Morphology of Arabic Language

Before we delve into the methods, we need to discuss the nature of the Arabic language, which has a bearing on the text preparation stage.

The Arabic script is complicated in that each white-space-delimited unit may correspond to several syntactic units. The Arabic orthographic unit, a unit delimited by white space, usually carries more than one token. An example is a form like (*wsyktbwnhA*)[3] (In Eng. "and they will write it"). This grammatically complete sentence carries a conjunction w, a future particle s, a verbal token *yktbwn*, and a feminine singular third person object pronoun *hA*. The verbal token is made of a verb *ktb*, a masculine present third person inflection *y* and a plural indicative inflection *wn*. This nature entails that the type token ratio is much smaller than it is for a non-morphologically rich language like English for example. This means that the same word does not repeat often enough for the investigator to make valid observations. In order for any linguistic, especially lexical, investigation to be reliable, one needs to perform some sort of morphological analysis capable of reducing the word to its basic form. This has implications on machine translation as it means that no matter how big the training corpus is; the Arabic side will always suffer from scarcity.

3 Pre-processing Arabic for SMT

With Arabic being morphologically complex and rich, lexical scarcity comes as a natural result. In such cases it helps to reduce this morphological complexity in order to obtain better alignments and decoding for Statistical Machine Translation (Habash et al., 2010).

Our goal at this stage is related to the pre-processing of Arabic as a source language, in order to improve the quality of translation. First, in order to perform Arabic pre-processing, we used a machine learning approach that performs word segmentation and POS tagging at the segment level. We then use rules to derive the different pre-processing schemes required for the machine translation experiments. Thus, instead of using MADA (Habash et al., 2010), the well known morphological analyzer for Arabic, we choose another accessible morphological analyzer that is memory-based learning for both word segmentation and Part of Speech tagging (Emad and Kübler, 2010).

The segmentation and POS tagging modules above give a rich representation with enough information for almost any further required transformation. Given an input sentence like (a), the system produces (b) as a segmented and annotated sentence, as described in the following example:

(a) وقد ارتبطت الاضطرابات بترحيل السلطات الفرنسية للعديد من المهاجرين غير الشرعيين

(In Buckwalter transliteration: *wqd ArtbTt AlADTrAbAt btrHyl AlslTAt Alfrnsyp llEdyd mn AlmhAjryn gyr Al$rEyyn*).

(In English. The disorders have been linked to the deportation by French authorities for many illegal immigrants).

---

[2] http://www.trad-campaign.org/

[3] All Arabic transliterations are provided using the Buckwalter transliteration scheme (Buckwalter, 2002)

(In French. Les troubles ont été liés à la déportation par les autorités françaises pour de nombreux immigrants clandestins).

(b) w/**CONJ**+qd/**VERB_PART** ArtbT/**PV**+t/**PVSUFF_SUBJ:3FS** Al/**DET**+ADTrAb/**NOUN**+At/**NSUFF_FEM_PL** b/**PREP**+trHyl/**NOUN** Al/**DET**+slT/**NOUN**+At/**NSUFF_FEM_PL** Al/**DET**+frnsy/**ADJ**+p/**NSUFF_FEM_SG** l/**PREP**+l/**DET**+Edyd/**NOUN** mn/**PREP** Al/**DET**+mhAjr/**NOUN**+yn/**NSUFF_MASC_PL_GEN** gyr/**NEG_PART** Al/**DET**+$rEy/**ADJ**+yn/ **NSUFF_MASC_PL_GEN**

We set three different evaluations based on the variations on the output of the above example, as follows:

Basic. The Basic experiment is the baseline of all the work we are doing. In this experiment, the Arabic side undergoes minimal pre-processing in which we only separate the punctuation and remove the occasional diacritization (the short vowels). Short vowels do not normally occur in Arabic, but sometimes scattered ones are there mainly for disambiguation purposes; however since their use is not standardized and subjective, their removal usually leads to better agreement between the training and test sets.

Tokenized. In this context, tokenization means splitting the prefixes and suffixes that have a syntactic value and that usually stand as independent words in other languages. Examples of these include the possessive pronouns (-hm, -h, -y, -hA), conjunctions (w, f), and prepositions (l-, k-, t-). We have also chosen to split the Arabic definite article ***Al*** due to the perceived similarity in distribution between the Arabic and French definite articles.

The sentence above "wqd ArtbTt AlADTrAbAt btrHyl AlslTAt Alfrnsyp llEdyd mn AlmhAjryn gyr Al$rEyyn "

is thus tokenized as "**w/CONJ** qd/VERB_PART ArtbT/PV+t/PVSUFF_SUBJ:3FS Al/DET ADTrAb/NOUN+At/NSUFF_FEM_PL **b/PREP** trHyl/NOUN Al/DET slT/NOUN+At/NSUFF_FEM_PL Al/DET frnsy/ADJ+p/NSUFF_FEM_SG **l/PREP** **Al/DET** Edyd/NOUN mn/PREP Al/DET mhAjr/NOUN+yn/NSUFF_MASC_PL_GEN gyr/NEG_PART Al/DET $rEy/ADJ+yn/ NSUFF_MASC_PL_GEN".

Where the conjunction w, the prepositions b and l, and the definite article Al are no longer prefixes, but separate tokens. The process also normalized the definite article from ***l*** to ***Al***, which is the more frequent form.

MorpReduced. In the morphologically reduced experiment, we reduce the morphology of Arabic to a level that makes it closer to that of the French language. An example of this is the dual form, which does not occur in French and has thus been transformed to the plural. The following table (Table 1) lists the most common examples of Arabic morphological reduction.

Rule	Example before applying the rule	Example after applying the rule
Regular Plural Nominative → Regular Plural Accusative	mstwTn***wn***	AlmstwTn**yn**
dual Nominative → Regular Plural Accusative	lAEb***An***	lAEb***yn***
Jussive Mood → Indicative Mood	hn lm ylEb***n*** hm lm ylEb***wA*** hmA lm ylEbA	hm lm ylEb***wn*** hn lm ylEb***wn*** hm lm ylEb***wn***

Table 1: The most common rules for Arabic morphological reduction

4 Experiments on SMT

Our SMT system was trained on 3.5 million words of French and their parallel text in Arabic (equivalent to 108 300 sentences) in addition to 9700 parallel sentences that were extracted from the essentially comparable UN corpus of 2009. Thus, the total number of sentences is 118 000 for the training corpora. The development corpus contains 20,000 words, namely 40,000 words with the reference. The evaluation corpus contains 15,000 words with 4 references.

The common practice of extracting bilingual phrases from the parallel data usually consists of three steps: first, words in bilingual sentence pairs are aligned using state-of-the-art automatic word alignment tools, such as GIZA++ (Och and Ney, 2003), in both directions; second, word alignment links are refined using heuristics, such as Grow-Diagonal-Final (GDF) method; third, bilingual phrases are extracted from the parallel data based on the refined word alignments with predefined constraints (Och and Ney, 2003).

The trigram language models are implemented using the SRILM toolkit (Stolcke, 2002). Moses[4]

[4] Available on http://www.statmt.org/ moses/

(Koehn et al., 2007), an open source toolkit for phrase-based SMT system, was used as a decoder. These steps of building a translation system are considered as a common practice in the state-of-the-art of phrase-based SMT systems. Our research for improving the Arabic-French SMT system was emphasized more on the pre-processing part of the SMT system.

We have measured the effect of the proposed pre-processing steps on data sparseness, based on the percentage of unknown unigrams (OOVs) on a development set (dev set). Table 2 summarizes the findings on the dev set. We give numbers in terms of tokens (the total number of words) and types (the number of unique words in the text, i.e. no-redundant words in the text).

It can be noticed that the tokenization has a major effect on combatting data sparseness and consequently improving the quality of translation as measured by the BLEU score. Morphological normalization, which is a layer on top of tokenization, improves things even further, and this is reflected in the difference between the baseline BLEU score and the MorphReduced BLUE score which is 8.6 absolute points.

Table 3 compares the results, in term of BLEU scores, of the three experimental settings in 3 evaluations schemes, as follows:

(a) ***Standard***, which includes performing recasing and removing white space before punctuation,

(b) ***Nopunct***, in which punctuation is stripped and evaluation is performed on the lexical text only, and

(c) ***Nopunctcase*** in which, in addition to removing punctuation, all words are lower-cased.

We can see from Table 3 that the Baseline experiment produces the lowest results, and that the tokenization scheme is a big leap with a 7.2 BLEU scores of improvement (25.9 vs. 33.1), which means that performing tokenization is really a necessary step for translating from Arabic, and that the morphological complexity of Arabic could be a hindrance to quality automatic translation. While tokenization leads to considerable improvement, morphological reduction fares even better with a 7.4 BLEU score higher than the baseline. This could be due to the fact the morphological reduction reduces the number of unknown words even further than tokenization alone.

It is still an open question whether the positive effect of pre-processing will still carry over with increasing the amount of training data and to what extent this will help.

Experiment	% OOV (Types)	% OOV (Tokens)	BLEU score
Baseline	10.74	4.81	17.69
Tokenized	7.99	2.00	25.84
MorphReduced	7.87	1.98	26.33

Table 2: Effect of pre-processing on the development set

	Baseline	Tokenized	MorphReduced
Standard	25.9	33.1	**33.3**
Nopunct	23.8	31.5	**31.7**

Table 3: Results in terms of BLEU score

5 Conclusion

We have presented an ongoing project on developing our first machine translation for Arabic-French pair of languages, using the methods and data of the TRAD 2102 evaluation campaign. We have introduced pre-processing schemes for the source language (Arabic) and some rules of language analysis related to the target language (French). Our method for POS tagging and segmentation of Arabic texts showed a significant improvement in terms of BLEU score; however it does not assume the best results. The introduced morphological rule that reduces the morphology of Arabic to a level that makes it closer to that of the French language, showed the best results.

Our future work is focused on the introduction of extra swapping rules, to introduce some structural matching between the source language (Arabic) and the target language (French). Moreover, we are planning to introduce more rules for the recognition and transliteration of named entities; which makes our translation system a hybrid rule-based and statistical SMT system. We will also investigate the integration of more training data such as comparable corpora to make our MT system more competitive and reliable.

References

Attia, M. 2008. Handling Arabic Morphological and Syntactic Ambiguity within the LFG Framework with a View to Machine Translation. PhD Thesis. School of Languages, Linguistics and Cultures. The University of Manchester, UK.

Buckwalter, T. 2002. Buckwalter Arabic Morphological Analyzer Version 1.0. Linguistic Data Consortium, University of Pennsylvania. Catalog: LDC2002L49.

Carpuat, M., Marton, Y. et Habash, N. 2010. Reordering Matrix Post-verbal Subjects for Arabic-to-English SMT. In proceedings of the 17th Conference sur le Traitement des Langues Naturelles (TALN 2010). Montreal, Canada.

Diab, M., Hacioglu, K. et Jurafsky, D. 2004. Automatic Tagging of Arabic Text: From Raw Text to Base Phrase Chunks. In *Proc. of the North American Chapter of the Association for Computational Linguistics (NAACL)*, Boston, MA.

Emad, M. et Kübler, S. 2010. Is Arabic Part of Speech Tagging Feasible Without Word Segmentation? In HLT/ACL 2010, Human Language Technologies: The 2010 Annual Conference of the North American Chapter of the ACL, pages 705–708, Los Angeles, California, June 2010.

El Isbihani, A., Khadivi, S., Bender, O., et Ney, H. 2006. Morpho-syntactic Arabic Preprocessing for Arabic to English Statistical Machine Translation. In Human Language Technology Conf. / North American Chapter of the Assoc. for Computational Linguistics Annual Meeting (HLT-NAACL), Workshop on Statistical Machine Translation, New York City, pages 15-22.

Goldwater, S. et McClosky, D. 2005. Improving Statistical MT through Morphological Analysis. In *Proc. of Empirical Methods in Natural Language Processing (EMNLP)*, Vancouver, Canada.

Habash, N. et Sadat, F. 2006. *Arabic Preprocessing Schemes for Statistical Machine Translation*. In Proceedings of NAACL 2006, New York (USA). June 5-7.

Habash, N., Rambow, O. et Ryan R. 2010. *The MADA and TOKAN Manual*.

Hasan, S., El Isbihani, A. et Ney, H. 2006. Creating a Large-Scale Arabic to French Statistical Machine Translation System. In International Conference on Language resources and Evaluation (LREC), Genoa, Italy, pages 855-858.

Koehn, P., Shen, W., Federico, M,. Bertoldi, N., Callison-Burch, C., Cowan, B., Dyer, C., Hoang, H., Bojar, O. Zens, R., Constantin, A., Herbst, E., Moran C. et Birch, A. 2007. Moses: Open source toolkit for statistical machine translation. In Proceedings of ACL 2007.

Lee, Y. 2004. Morphological Analysis for Statistical Machine Translation. In *Proc. of NAACL*, Boston, MA.

Och, F., J. et Ney, H. 2003. A Systematic Comparison of Various Statistical Alignment Models. Computational linguistics 29 (1), pages 19-51.

Papineni, K., Roukos, S., Ward, T. et Zhu, W. 2001. Bleu: a Method for Automatic Evaluation of Machine Translation. Technical Report RC22176(W0109-022), IBM Research Division, Yorktown Heights, NY.

Sadat, F. et Habash, H. *Arabic Preprocessing for Statistical Machine Translation: Schemes and Techniques*. 2006. In Proceedings of COLING-ACL 2006, Sydney, Australia. July 17-21, 2006.

Schwenk, H. et Senellart, J. 2009. Translation Model Adaptation for an Arabic/French News Translation System by Lightly-Supervised Training. In *MT Summit*.

Stolcke, A. 2002. SRILM-An Extensible Language Modeling Toolkit. *In Proc. Of the International Conference on Spoken language Processing.*

Segmenting vs. Chunking Rules: Unsupervised ITG Induction via Minimum Conditional Description Length

Markus SAERS and **Karteek ADDANKI** and **Dekai WU**
Human Language Technology Center
Dept. of Computer Science and Engineering
Hong Kong University of Science and Technology
{masaers|vskaddanki|dekai}@cs.ust.hk

Abstract

We present an unsupervised learning model that induces phrasal inversion transduction grammars by introducing a minimum *conditional description length* (CDL) principle to drive search over a space defined by two opposing extreme types of ITGs. Our approach attacks the difficulty of acquiring more complex longer rules when inducing inversion transduction grammars via unsupervised bottom-up chunking, by augmenting its model search with top-down segmentation that minimizes CDL, resulting in significant translation accuracy gains. Chunked rules tend to be relatively short; long rules are hard to learn through chunking, as the smaller parts of the long rules may not necessarily be good translations themselves. Our objective criterion is a conditional adaptation of the notion of description length, that is conditioned on a fixed preexisting model, in this case the initial chunked ITG. The notion of minimum CDL (MCDL) facilitates a novel strategy for avoiding the pitfalls of premature pruning in chunking approaches, by incrementally splitting an ITG with reference to a second ITG that conditions this search.

1 Introduction

We describe an unsupervised approach to inducing phrasal inversion transduction grammars or ITGs (Wu, 1997) that employs a new theoretically well-founded minimum **conditional description length** (CDL) objective to explicitly drive two opposing, extreme ITGs towards one single ITG. Given one ITG initially composed of short rules learned by bottom-up chunking of short atomic rules, our method augments it with rules that are learned through top-down segmentation of long rules initialized by memorizing the parallel corpus. This offers an opportunity to capture longer non-compositional translations as explicit biterminal rules, which is hard for search to discover solely via bottom-up chunking. Iterative bottom-up chunking relies on composing two good translations into a longer good translation, which assumes that the long rules learned in this way are compositional. In contrast, iteratively segmenting an existing good translation into shorter good translations does not depend on assumptions about whether the resulting shorter rules can be further decomposed. Empirically, augmenting the chunked ITG with rules learned via top-down segmentation helps translation quality. However, the maximum likelihood objective is inadequate for this purpose; instead, we introduce the **minimum conditional description length** (MCDL) objective to drive the search for phrasal rules simultaneously from the two opposing types of ITG constraints, both of which have individually been empirically demonstrated to match phrase reordering patterns across translations well. In so doing, we aim to also provide an obvious basis for generalization to abstract translation schemas.

The necessity of MCDL as an alternative learning objective to standard maximum likelihood (ML) arises because the top-down rule segmentation search starts in a state where likelihood is already maximized, unlike bottom-up learning which can be driven with ML. The top-down search starts with all sentence pairs in the training corpus as biterminals, which maximizes the likelihood of the training data, but is guaranteed to generalize poorly to unseen data. There is no segmentation we can make to this grammar that would increase the likelihood of the training data, but we do nonetheless want to segment the existing rules so that the grammar has a chance to cover unseen data. The solution is to move away from pure ML; in this paper we will use minimum conditional description length, which has the likelihood of the training data as one component, but balances it with a notion of model size. MCDL allows us to make the training data less likely provided that the size of the grammar becomes smaller. Since the initial state of the top-down search has all the sentence pairs in the training data explicitly stored as biterminals, there is ample opportunity for shrinking the size of the grammar by segmenting the existing rules into reusable segments, and MCDL helps deciding when this is a good idea and when not. The difference between MCDL and minimum description length is that the lengths are subject to an external model. In our case, the external model is the bottom-up chunked ITG, which means that the auxiliary ITG being induced is tailored specifically towards augmenting it.

We choose to work with the well-defined and theoretically sound formalism of ITGs rather than over-engineered direct translation models (Koehn *et al.*, 2003) or feature-heavy transduction grammars (Chiang, 2005). The reason for this is twofold: (a) they allow for manual inspection, and (b) the assumptions stay the same through learning and testing. Being able to inspect the learned model is crucial for error analysis, but inspecting a typical state-of-the-art translation system is prohibitively hard. Phrasal direct translation systems rely heavily on the language model to compensate for the mistakes they make, as well as relying on a fine-tuned log-linear combination of several features to choose which lexical units to use. Pinning down exactly where and why an error occurred in this setup is very hard. The transduction grammar based approach is better in this respect, but the state-of-the-art typically relies on massive amounts, tens of thousands (Chiang *et al.*, 2009), of features. As a community, we still have no clear idea of why these features help translation, only that they do when the whole system pipeline is treated as a black box, but treating the system as a black box prevents effective error analysis. The state-of-the-art systems also relies on long and complicated learning pipelines that form ad-hoc models of how translation happens. These ad-hoc models differ significantly from the models of how translation happens that are used during actual translation, which violates the basic machine learning assumption that the same model should be used during training and testing. In contrast, the only difference between biparsing with ITGs (training) and decoding (testing) is that both sentences are given during biparsing, but only the input sentence during decoding—the model itself does not change, only the way it is used.

The space of possible ITG structures is intractably large, and there have been many attempts to introduce external constraints to guide the search. We do completely unsupervised search without introducing such constraints, which limits the scope of error analysis to the search strategy. Popular external constraints include word alignments (Chiang, 2005) and parse trees.

Word alignments are typically learned as a many-to-one function from one language into the other language (Brown *et al.*, 1993; Vogel *et al.*, 1996), but since no translation systems in use today actually rely on generating one output token at a time from zero or more input tokens, two opposing such functions are typically combined heuristically to form a many-to-many function between the input and output tokens. This is problematic, as it turns the alignments into hard constraints that are external to any model learned from them. Ironically, whenever transduction grammars are used to learn alignments these alignments are also treated as hard external constraints to the translation models that are learned from them (Cherry and Lin, 2007; Zhang *et al.*, 2008; Blunsom *et al.*, 2008, 2009; Haghighi *et al.*, 2009; Saers and Wu, 2009, 2011; Blunsom and Cohn, 2010; Burkett *et al.*, 2010; Riesa and Marcu, 2010; Saers *et al.*, 2010; Neubig *et al.*, 2011, 2012).

When parse trees are used to constrain the search they can be found on the input side only, making the resulting system a tree-to-string system, on the output side only, making it a string-to-tree system, or on both sides, making it a tree-to-tree system (Galley *et al.*, 2006). The grammarians who constructed the treebank—or the parser that it was created with, or the treebank that was used to train the parser—can and should not be expected to take into account the relationship between the language they are working with and all other languages on the planet, so the parse trees themselves run a real risk of matching the translation problem poorly.

We structure the paper so that we start by introducing conditional description length, which we will use to replace description length as the driving metric for the top-down rule-segmenting

ITG induction (Section 2). We then describe how we encode ITGs to measure their length in bits, which is a necessary component of any metric related to description length (Section 3). These two sections are the theoretical fundamental that we build the algorithms around. The first algorithm we describe is the baseline: top-down rule-segmenting ITG induction driven by minimum description length (Section 4). Although it is background, please bear with us as it serves an important role in contrasting conditional with unconditional, plain description length. This lays the ground work for the experimental contribution of the paper: Section 5 describes how we initialize an ITG by bottom-up rule-chunking, which is then augmented (Section 6) with rules learned through top-down rule segmentation as described in our second algorithm. This algorithm differs from the first in that it minimizes *conditional* description length rather than plain description length. We also test our model empirically in an experiment described in Section 7 and analyzed in Section 8. Finally, we offer some concluding remarks (Section 9).

2 Conditional Description Length

Conditional description length (CDL) is a general method for evaluating a model and a dataset given a preexisting model. This makes it ideal for augmenting an existing model with a variant model of the same family. In this paper we will apply this to augment an existing inversion transduction grammar (ITG) with rules that are found with a different search strategy. CDL is similar to description length (Solomonoff, 1959; Rissanen, 1983), but the length calculations are subject to additional constraints. When minimum CDL (MCDL) is used as a learning objective, all the desired properties of minimum description length (MDL) are retained: the model is allowed to become less certain about the data provided that it shrinks sufficiently to compensate for the loss in precision. MDL is a good way to prevent over-fitting, and MCDL retains this property, but for the task of inducing a model specifically to augment an existing model. Formally, CDL is:

$$DL(\Phi, D|\Psi) = DL(D|\Phi, \Psi) + DL(\Phi|\Psi)$$

where Ψ is the fixed preexisting model, Φ is the model being induced, and D is the data. The total unconditional length is :

$$\begin{aligned} &DL(\Psi, \Phi, D) \\ &\quad = DL(D|\Phi, \Psi) + DL(\Phi|\Psi) + DL(\Psi) \end{aligned}$$

In minimizing CDL, we fix Ψ instead of allowing it to vary as we would in full MDL; to be precise, we seek:

$$\begin{aligned} &\operatorname*{argmin}_{\Phi} DL(\Psi, \Phi, D) \\ &= \operatorname*{argmin}_{\Phi} DL(D|\Phi, \Psi) + DL(\Phi|\Psi) + DL(\Psi) \\ &= \operatorname*{argmin}_{\Phi} DL(\Phi, D|\Psi) \\ &= \operatorname*{argmin}_{\Phi} DL(D|\Phi, \Psi) + DL(\Phi|\Psi) \end{aligned}$$

To measure the CDL of the data, we turn to information theory to count the number of bits needed to encode the data given the two models under an optimal encoding (Shannon, 1948), which gives:

$$DL(D|\Phi, \Psi) = -\lg P(D|\Phi, \Psi)$$

The CDL of the model is not necessarily expressible as a probability, and in this paper we will measure its length as the number of bits required to encode the model using a theoretical encoding.

To determine whether a model Φ has a shorter conditional description length, than another model Φ', it is sufficient to be able to subtract one length from the other. For the model length, this is trivial as we merely have to calculate the length of the difference between the two models in our theoretical encoding. For data length, we need to solve:

$$\begin{aligned} &DL(D|\Phi', \Psi) - DL(D|\Phi, \Psi) \\ &\quad = -\lg P(D|\Phi', \Psi) - -\lg P(D|\Phi, \Psi) \\ &\quad = -\lg \frac{P(D|\Phi', \Psi)}{P(D|\Phi, \Psi)} \end{aligned}$$

3 Encoding ITGs

By encoding an ITG, we turn the relatively complex data structure into a series of symbols—a message, whose length can be measured in bits. This section describes how we device this encoding scheme. An ITG consists of a set of nonterminal symbols, a set of L_0 symbols, a set of L_1 symbols, a set of rules and a start symbol. We notice that the only significance of the sets of nonterminal, L_0 and L_1 symbols is to categorize the symbols that occur in the rules, and the identity of the start symbol constitutes a per-grammar constant. To measure the length of a grammar it is thus sufficient to measure and sum the lengths of all rules. We will measure the length by encoding the rule set as a sequence of symbols. We need one symbol for each of the nonterminal, L_0 and L_1 symbols of the ITG, as well as a meta symbol to separate rules and determine whether they are straight or inverted (unary rules are assumed to be straight). For conditional description length, rules that are found in Ψ can be excluded when measuring the length of Φ. Consider the following toy ITG:

$$S \rightarrow A, \qquad A \rightarrow \langle AA \rangle, \quad A \rightarrow [AA],$$
$$A \rightarrow \text{have/•} \;\; ; \;\; A \rightarrow \text{yes/•} \;\; ; \;\; A \rightarrow \text{yes/• •}$$

which is conditioned on the following ITG:

$$S \rightarrow A, \quad A \rightarrow \langle AA \rangle, \quad A \rightarrow [AA],$$
$$A \rightarrow \cdots, \qquad \cdots$$

Its serialized form would be:

$$[]A\text{have•} \;\; •[]A\text{yes•} \;\; •[]A\text{yes•} \;\; •$$

Assuming a uniform distribution over the symbols, each symbol will require $-\lg \frac{1}{N}$ bits to encode (where N is the number of different symbols in the ITG). The above toy ITG has 8 symbols, meaning that each symbol requires 3 bits. The encoded message is 12 symbols long, making the ITG 36 bits long.

4 Baseline ITG

The natural baseline to compare ITGs learned by minimizing *conditional* description length is ITGs learned by minimizing *unconditional* description length, which we will describe in this section. This is the same model as described in Saers *et al.* (2013), which is repeated here to highlight the minimum changes needed to switch the objective function from minimum description length to minimum conditional description length.

The ITG is initialized with all sentence pairs as biterminals:

$$\begin{aligned} S &\rightarrow A \\ A &\rightarrow e_{0..T_0}/f_{0..V_0} \\ A &\rightarrow e_{0..T_1}/f_{0..V_1} \\ &\;\;\ldots \\ A &\rightarrow e_{0..T_N}/f_{0..V_N} \end{aligned}$$

where S is the start symbol, A is the nonterminal, N is the number of sentence pairs, T_i is the length of the ith output sentence (making $e_{0..T_i}$ the ith output sentence), and V_i is the length of the ith input sentence (making $f_{0..V_i}$ the ith input sentence). After the ITG has been initialized, its preterminal rules are iteratively segmented until no segmentations can be found that would shorten its description length. The parameters of the model is initialized as relative frequency of the sentence pairs/biterminals.

The segmentation algorithm relies on identifying parts of existing biterminals that could be validly used in isolation, and allow them to combine with other segments. We do this by proposing a number of sets of biterminal rules and a place to segment them, evaluate how the description length would change if we were to apply one of these sets of segmentations to the grammar, and commit to the best set. That is: we do a greedy search over the power set of possible segmentations of the rule set. The key component in the approach is the ability to evaluate how the description length would change if a specific segmentation was made in the grammar. This can be extended to a set of segmentations, which only leaves the problem of generating suitable sets of segmentations.

The key to a successful segmentation is to maximize the potential for reuse, either by being able to identify a segment across multiple rules. Consider the terminal rule:

$$A \;\rightarrow\; \text{five thousand yen is my limit/}$$
$$\text{• • • • • • • • • • • • • • • •}$$

(Chinese romanization: wŏ zùi dūo chū wŭ qīan rì yúan). This rule can be split into three rules:

$$\begin{aligned} A &\rightarrow \langle AA \rangle, \\ A &\rightarrow \text{five thousand yen/• • • • ; • • •} \\ A &\rightarrow \text{is my limit/• • • • • • • •} \end{aligned}$$

Note that the original rule consists of 16 symbols (in our encoding scheme), whereas the new three rules consists of $4 + 9 + 9 = 22$ symbols. The bracketing inverted rule is likely to already be in the ITG, but the lexical rules still contain 18 symbols, which is decidedly longer than 16 symbols—and we need to get the length to be shorter if we want to see a net gain, since the length of the data is likely to be longer with the segmented rules. What we really need to do is find a way to reuse the lexical rules that came out of the segmentation. Now suppose the ITG also contained this terminal rule:

$A \rightarrow$ the total fare is five thousand yen/ •

(Chinese romanization: zǒng gòng de fèi yòng shì wǔ qīan rì yúan). This rule can also be split into three rules:

$A \rightarrow [AA]$,
$A \rightarrow$ the total fare is/• • • • • • • ; • • • • • •
$A \rightarrow$ five thousand yen/• • • • • • • •

Again, the structural rule is likely to already be present in the ITG, the old rule was 19 symbols long, and the two new terminal rules are $12 + 9 = 21$ symbols long. Again we are out of luck, as the new rules are longer than the old one, and three rules are likely to be less probable than one rule during parsing. The way to make this work is to realize that the two existing rules share a bilingual affix—a **biaffix**: five thousand dollars translating into • • • • • . If we make the two changes at the same time, we get rid of $16 + 19 = 35$ symbols worth of rules, and introduce a mere $9 + 9 + 12 = 30$ symbols worth of rules. Making these two changes at the same time is essential, as the length of the five saved symbols can be used to offset the likely increase in the length of the data. And of course: the more rules we can find with shared biaffixes, the more likely we are to find a good set of segmentations.

The top-down search algorithm takes advantage of the above observation by focusing on the biaffixes found in the training data. Each biaffix defines a set of lexical rules paired up with a possible segmentation. We evaluate the biaffixes by estimating the change in description length associated with committing to all the segmentations defined by a biaffix. This allows us to find the best set of segmentations, but rather than committing only to the one best set of segmentations, we will collect all sets which would improve description length, and try to commit to as many of them as possible. The pseudocode can be found in Algorithm 1. It uses the methods `collect_biaffixes`, `eval_dl`, `sort_by_delta` and `make_segmentations`. These methods collects all the biaffixes in an ITG, evaluate the difference in description length, sorts candidates by these differences, and commits to a given set of candidates, respectively. To evaluate the DL of a proposed set of candidate segmentations, we need to calculate the difference in DL between the current model, and the model that would result from committing to the candidate segmentations:

$$\begin{aligned} &DL(\Phi', D) - DL(\Phi, D) \\ &= DL(D|\Phi') - DL(D|\Phi) \\ &+ DL(\Phi') - DL(\Phi) \end{aligned}$$

The model lengths are trivial, as we merely have to encode the rules that are removed and inserted according to our encoding scheme and plug in the summed lengths in the above equation. This leaves the length of the data, which is:

$$DL(D|\Phi') - DL(D|\Phi) = -\lg \frac{P(D|\theta')}{P(D|\theta)}$$

where θ and θ' are the parameters of Φ and Φ' respectively. This lets us determine the probability through biparsing with the model being induced. Biparsing is, however, a very expensive operation, and we are making relatively small changes to the ITG, so we will further assume that we can estimate the DL difference in closed form based on the model parameters. Given that we are splitting the rule r_0 into the three rules r_1, r_2 and r_3, and that the probability mass of r_0 is distributed uniformly over the new rules, the new grammar parameters θ' will be identical to θ, except that:

$$\begin{aligned} \theta'_{r_0} &= 0 \\ \theta'_{r_1} &= \theta_{r_1} + \frac{1}{3}\theta_{r_0} \\ \theta'_{r_2} &= \theta_{r_2} + \frac{1}{3}\theta_{r_0} \\ \theta'_{r_3} &= \theta_{r_3} + \frac{1}{3}\theta_{r_0} \end{aligned}$$

We estimate the probability of the corpus given this new parameters to be:

$$-\lg \frac{P(D|\theta')}{P(D|\theta)} \approx -\lg \frac{\theta'_{r_1}\theta'_{r_2}\theta'_{r_3}}{\theta_{r_0}}$$

To generalize this to a set of rule segmentations, we construct the new parameters θ' to reflect all the changes in the set in a first pass, and then sum the differences in DL for all the rule segmentations with the new parameters in a second pass.

5 Initial ITG

The initial ITG that we start with is learned following the best bootstrapping approach reported in

Algorithm 1 Iterative rule segmenting learning driven by minimum description length.

1: Φ $\triangleright$ The ITG being induced
2: **repeat**
3: $\quad \delta_{sum} \leftarrow 0$
4: $\quad bs \leftarrow$ collect_biaffixes(Φ)
5: $\quad b\delta \leftarrow []$
6: $\quad$ **for all** $b \in bs$ **do**
7: $\quad\quad \delta \leftarrow$ eval_dl(b, Φ)
8: $\quad\quad$ **if** $\delta < 0$ **then**
9: $\quad\quad\quad b\delta \leftarrow [b\delta, \langle b, \delta \rangle]$
10: $\quad\quad$ **end if**
11: $\quad$ **end for**
12: $\quad$ sort_by_delta($b\delta$)
13: $\quad$ **for all** $\langle b, \delta \rangle \in b\delta$ **do**
14: $\quad\quad \delta' \leftarrow$ eval_dl(b, Φ)
15: $\quad\quad$ **if** $\delta' < 0$ **then**
16: $\quad\quad\quad \Phi \leftarrow$ make_segmentations(b, Φ)
17: $\quad\quad\quad \delta_{sum} \leftarrow \delta_{sum} + \delta'$
18: $\quad\quad$ **end if**
19: $\quad$ **end for**
20: **until** $\delta_{sum} \geq 0$
21: **return** Φ

Algorithm 2 Iterative rule segmenting learning driven by minimum conditional description length.

1: Φ, Ψ $\triangleright$ The auxiliary and initial ITG
2: **repeat**
3: $\quad \delta_{sum} \leftarrow 0$
4: $\quad bs \leftarrow$ collect_biaffixes(Φ)
5: $\quad b\delta \leftarrow []$
6: $\quad$ **for all** $b \in bs$ **do**
7: $\quad\quad \delta \leftarrow$ eval_cdl(b, Ψ, Φ)
8: $\quad\quad$ **if** $\delta < 0$ **then**
9: $\quad\quad\quad b\delta \leftarrow [b\delta, \langle b, \delta \rangle]$
10: $\quad\quad$ **end if**
11: $\quad$ **end for**
12: $\quad$ sort_by_delta($b\delta$)
13: $\quad$ **for all** $\langle b, \delta \rangle \in b\delta$ **do**
14: $\quad\quad \delta' \leftarrow$ eval_cdl(b, Ψ, Φ)
15: $\quad\quad$ **if** $\delta' < 0$ **then**
16: $\quad\quad\quad \Phi \leftarrow$ make_segmentations(b, Φ)
17: $\quad\quad\quad \delta_{sum} \leftarrow \delta_{sum} + \delta'$
18: $\quad\quad$ **end if**
19: $\quad$ **end for**
20: **until** $\delta_{sum} \geq 0$
21: **return** Φ

Saers *et al.* (2012). That is: we start by initializing a token-based bracketing finite-state transduction grammar, or FSTG, parameterized with relative frequencies from the training corpus. We then tune the parameters to the training corpus, and then change the structure of the grammar to include lexical rules that can be formed by chunking adjacent preterminals. The tune–chunk step is repeated twice, before transforming the FSTG into a bracketing linear inversion transduction grammar, or LITG (Saers *et al.*, 2010), whose parameters are also tuned to the training corpus. The LITG is then transformed into a full ITG whose parameters are again tuned to the training corpus. All parameter tuning is carried out with our in-house biparser, which is based on beam search (Saers *et al.*, 2009), and expectation maximization (Dempster *et al.*, 1977). We also prune away very improbable rules to reduce noise, which makes the model perform better than reported in the original paper, providing a more solid baseline for comparison.

6 Augmenting the initial ITG

To augment the initial ITG we will search top-down for rules that the chunking approach were unable to find. We do this by initializing an auxiliary ITG that merely contains all sentence pairs as biterminals. This auxiliary ITG is then iteratively segmented until we arrive at a set of rules which cannot be segmented to further reduce the conditional description length of the auxiliary ITG given the initial ITG. The initial and auxiliary ITGs are then combined to form the augmented ITG.

Learning the auxiliary ITG is very similar to learning the baseline ITG. The motivation and initialization are identical, but rather than driving the segmentation by evaluating description length, it is driven by evaluating conditional description length (CDL). Algorithm 2 is thus very similar to Algorithm 1, except that there is an initial ITG, and that Algorithm 2 calls `eval_cdl` on lines 7 and 14, where Algorithm 1 calls `eval_dl`. To evaluate the CDL of a proposed set of candidate segmentations, we now need to calculate the difference in CDL between the current model, and the model that would result from committing to the candidate segmentations:

$$
\begin{aligned}
&DL\left(\Phi', D|\Psi\right) - DL\left(\Phi, D|\Psi\right) \\
&\quad = DL\left(D|\Phi', \Psi\right) - DL\left(D|\Phi, \Psi\right) \\
&\quad\quad + DL\left(\Phi'|\Psi\right) - DL\left(\Phi|\Psi\right)
\end{aligned}
$$

The model lengths are still trivial, as we merely have to encode the rules that are removed and inserted according to our encoding scheme, but we

Table 1: The results of decoding.

ITG model	BLEU	NIST	Rules
Baseline	17.44	4.3909	47,298
Initial only	15.71	4.1267	251,947
Auxiliary only	16.11	3.9334	60,133
Augmented	19.32	4.4243	301,293

still need to calculate the change in the length of the data, which is:

$$DL\left(D|\Phi', \Psi\right) - DL\left(D|\Phi, \Psi\right) = -\lg \frac{P\left(D|\Phi', \Psi\right)}{P\left(D|\Phi, \Psi\right)}$$

For the sake of convenience in efficiently calculating this probability, we make the simplifying assumption that:

$$P\left(D|\Phi, \Psi\right) \approx P\left(D|\Phi\right) = P\left(D|\theta\right)$$

where θ is the model parameters, which allow us to approximate the difference in data CDL as:

$$-\lg \frac{P\left(D|\theta'\right)}{P\left(D|\theta\right)}$$

This is the same problem that we had for the baseline model, and we solve it in the same way: by assuming probability mass to be distributed uniformly over over the new rules and by approximating the change in corpus probability in closed form.

Although this simplifying assumption is reasonable for calculating the difference in probability of the data given the augmented model, it might not be such a good assumption during decoding. So, when using the augmented model for translation, we interpolate the initial and auxiliary ITG to produce the augmented ITG. The parameters of the augmented ITG are set such that:

$$\theta_r^{\Phi,\Psi} = \alpha\theta_r^{\Phi} + (1-\alpha)\theta_r^{\Psi}$$

for all rules r, where θ is the probability of a rule under a specific ITG, and α is a weighting parameter that determine which ITG we trust more. For the experiments in this paper, we fixed $\alpha = \frac{1}{2}$.

7 Experimental setup

To test the new learning algorithm, we will induce two ITGs: one using the baseline learning algorithm and one using the presented augmenting algorithm that relies on minimizing the introduced conditional description length. We use the Chinese–English translation task from IWSLT07 (Fordyce, 2007) as training and test data. In contains 46,867 sentence pairs of training data, and 489 sentence pairs of test data with 6 reference translations each. To decode with the learned model, we use our in-house ITG decoder with a trigram language model learned on the English part of the training data. The decoder uses CKY-style parsing (Cocke, 1969; Kasami, 1965; Younger, 1967) with cube pruning to integrate the language model (Chiang, 2007). The language model is trained with SRILM (Stolcke, 2002). To evaluate the output we use BLEU (Papineni *et al.*, 2002) and NIST (Doddington, 2002).

8 Results

The results (Table 1) show the baseline ITG and the proposed augmented ITG, as well as test scores for the two intermediate steps: the initial and auxiliary ITGs. The augmented ITG is significantly better (19.32 compared to 17.44 BLEU) than the baseline ITG, but also significantly larger (301,293 compared to 47,298). The number of rules is known to be somewhat correlated with the translation quality, so it is hard to draw any conclusions from these data. The fact that the augmented ITG is significantly better than the initial ITG (19.32 compared to 15.71 BLEU) with only a modest increase in the number of rules (49,346 extra rules) is, however, very interesting. It shows that the auxiliary ITG is indeed learning rules that complement the initial ITG well. This picture is further corroborated by the fact that the auxiliary ITG is far behind the full augmented ITG in terms of translation quality.

9 Conclusion

We have presented conditional minimum description length, a theoretically well-founded learning objective particularly suited for searching for a supplemental model tailored to augmenting a preexisting model, which we have applied to the task of inducing ITGs by augmenting a bottom-up chunked inversion transduction grammar with rules obtained by iteratively splitting existing rules into smaller rules. We have further shown empirically that the proposed augmentation strategy significantly boosts the quality of an initial ITG. The model provides an obvious foundation for generalization to more abstract transduction grammars with informative nonterminals.

Acknowledgements

This material is based upon work supported in part by the Defense Advanced Research Projects Agency (DARPA) under BOLT contract no. HR0011-12-C-0016, and GALE contract nos. HR0011-06-C-0022 and HR0011-06-C-0023; by the European Union under the FP7 grant agreement no. 287658; and by the Hong Kong Research Grants Council (RGC) research grants GRF620811, GRF621008, and GRF612806. Any opinions, findings and conclusions or recommendations expressed in this material are those of the authors and do not necessarily reflect the views of DARPA, the EU, or RGC.

References

Phil Blunsom and Trevor Cohn. Inducing synchronous grammars with slice sampling. In *NAACL HLT 2010*, pages 238–241, Los Angeles, California, Jun 2010.

Phil Blunsom, Trevor Cohn, and Miles Osborne. Bayesian synchronous grammar induction. In *NIPS 21*, Vancouver, Canada, Dec 2008.

Phil Blunsom, Trevor Cohn, Chris Dyer, and Miles Osborne. A gibbs sampler for phrasal synchronous grammar induction. In *ACL-IJCNLP 2009*, pages 782–790, Suntec, Singapore, Aug 2009.

Peter F. Brown, Stephen A. Della Pietra, Vincent J. Della Pietra, and Robert L. Mercer. The Mathematics of Machine Translation: Parameter estimation. *Computational Linguistics*, 19(2):263–311, 1993.

David Burkett, John Blitzer, and Dan Klein. Joint parsing and alignment with weakly synchronized grammars. In *NAACL HLT 2010*, pages 127–135, Los Angeles, California, Jun 2010.

Colin Cherry and Dekang Lin. Inversion transduction grammar for joint phrasal translation modeling. In *SSST*, pages 17–24, Rochester, New York, Apr 2007.

David Chiang, Kevin Knight, and Wei Wang. 11,001 new features for statistical machine translation. In *NAACL HLT 2009*, pages 218–226, Boulder, Colorado, Jun 2009.

David Chiang. A hierarchical phrase-based model for statistical machine translation. In *ACL-05*, pages 263–270, Ann Arbor, Michigan, Jun 2005.

David Chiang. Hierarchical phrase-based translation. *Computational Linguistics*, 33(2):201–228, 2007.

John Cocke. *Programming languages and their compilers: Preliminary notes*. Courant Institute of Mathematical Sciences, New York University, 1969.

Arthur Pentland Dempster, Nan M. Laird, and Donald Bruce Rubin. Maximum likelihood from incomplete data via the em algorithm. *Journal of the Royal Statistical Society. Series B (Methodological)*, 39(1):1–38, 1977.

George Doddington. Automatic evaluation of machine translation quality using n-gram cooccurrence statistics. In *HLT '02*, pages 138–145, San Diego, California, 2002.

C. S. Fordyce. Overview of the IWSLT 2007 evaluation campaign. In *IWSLT 2007*, pages 1–12, 2007.

Michel Galley, Jonathan Graehl, Kevin Knight, Daniel Marcu, Steve DeNeefe, Wei Wang, and Ignacio Thayer. Scalable inference and training of context-rich syntactic translation models. In *COLING/ACL 2006*, pages 961–968, Sydney, Australia, Jul 2006.

Aria Haghighi, John Blitzer, John DeNero, and Dan Klein. Better word alignments with supervised itg models. In *ACL-IJCNLP 2009*, pages 923–931, Suntec, Singapore, Aug 2009.

Tadao Kasami. An efficient recognition and syntax analysis algorithm for context-free languages. Technical Report AFCRL-65-00143, Air Force Cambridge Research Laboratory, 1965.

Philipp Koehn, Franz Joseph Och, and Daniel Marcu. Statistical Phrase-Based Translation. In *HLT-NAACL 2003*, volume 1, pages 48–54, Edmonton, Canada, May/Jun 2003.

Graham Neubig, Taro Watanabe, Eiichiro Sumita, Shinsuke Mori, and Tatsuya Kawahara. An unsupervised model for joint phrase alignment and extraction. In *ACL HLT 2011*, pages 632–641, Portland, Oregon, Jun 2011.

Graham Neubig, Taro Watanabe, Shinsuke Mori, and Tatsuya Kawahara. Machine translation without words through substring alignment. In *ACL 2012*, pages 165–174, Jeju Island, Korea, Jul 2012.

Kishore Papineni, Salim Roukos, Todd Ward, and Wei-Jing Zhu. BLEU: a method for automatic evaluation of machine translation. In *ACL-02*, pages 311–318, Philadelphia, Pennsylvania, Jul 2002.

Jason Riesa and Daniel Marcu. Hierarchical search for word alignment. In *ACL 2010*, pages 157–166, Uppsala, Sweden, Jul 2010.

Jorma Rissanen. A universal prior for integers and estimation by minimum description length. *The Annals of Statistics*, 11(2):416–431, Jun 1983.

Markus Saers and Dekai Wu. Improving phrase-based translation via word alignments from Stochastic Inversion Transduction Grammars. In *SSST-3*, pages 28–36, Boulder, Colorado, Jun 2009.

Markus Saers and Dekai Wu. Principled induction of phrasal bilexica. In *EAMT-2011*, pages 313–320, Leuven, Belgium, May 2011.

Markus Saers, Joakim Nivre, and Dekai Wu. Learning stochastic bracketing inversion transduction grammars with a cubic time biparsing algorithm. In *IWPT'09*, pages 29–32, Paris, France, Oct 2009.

Markus Saers, Joakim Nivre, and Dekai Wu. Word alignment with stochastic bracketing linear inversion transduction grammar. In *NAACL HLT 2010*, pages 341–344, Los Angeles, California, Jun 2010.

Markus Saers, Karteek Addanki, and Dekai Wu. From finite-state to inversion transductions: Toward unsupervised bilingual grammar induction. In *COLING 2012*, pages 2325–2340, Mumbai, India, Dec 2012.

Markus Saers, Karteek Addanki, and Dekai Wu. Iterative rule segmentation under minimum description length for unsupervised transduction grammar induction. In Adrian-Horia Dediu, Carlos Martín-Vide, Ruslan Mitkov, and Bianca Truthe, editors, *Statistical Language and Speech Processing, First International Conference, SLSP 2013*, Lecture Notes in Artificial Intelligence (LNAI). Springer, Tarragona, Spain, Jul 2013.

Claude Elwood Shannon. A mathematical theory of communication. *The Bell System Technical Journal*, 27:379–423, 623–656, Jul, Oct 1948.

Ray J. Solomonoff. A new method for discovering the grammars of phrase structure languages. In *IFIP*, pages 285–289, 1959.

Andreas Stolcke. SRILM – an extensible language modeling toolkit. In *ICSLP2002 - INTERSPEECH 2002*, pages 901–904, Denver, Colorado, Sep 2002.

Stephan Vogel, Hermann Ney, and Christoph Tillmann. HMM-based Word Alignment in Statistical Translation. In *COLING-96*, volume 2, pages 836–841, 1996.

Dekai Wu. Stochastic Inversion Transduction Grammars and Bilingual Parsing of Parallel Corpora. *Computational Linguistics*, 23(3):377–403, 1997.

Daniel H. Younger. Recognition and parsing of context-free languages in time n^3. *Information and Control*, 10(2):189–208, 1967.

Hao Zhang, Chris Quirk, Robert C. Moore, and Daniel Gildea. Bayesian learning of non-compositional phrases with synchronous parsing. In *ACL-08: HLT*, pages 97–105, Columbus, Ohio, Jun 2008.

A Combined Pattern-based and Distributional Approach for Automatic Hypernym Detection in Dutch

Gwendolijn Schropp
LT3, Language and Translation Technology Team
University College Ghent
Gent, Belgium
gwendolijn@gmail.com

Els Lefever, Véronique Hoste
LT3, Language and Translation Technology Team
Ghent University
Gent, Belgium
Els.Lefever@ugent.be
Veronique.Hoste@ugent.be

Abstract

This paper proposes a two-step approach to find hypernym relations between pairs of noun phrases in Dutch text. We first apply a pattern-based approach that combines lexical and shallow syntactic information to extract a list of candidate hypernym pairs from the input text. In a second step, distributional similarity information is used to filter the obtained list of candidate pairs. Evaluation of the system shows encouraging results and reveals that the distributional information particularly helps to improve the precision for context dependent hypernym pairs. The proposed hypernym module is considered an important step in building a semantic structure for automatically extracted terminology. As our approach does not require external lexical resources, it can be applied for any given Dutch input text and is particularly well suited for domain and user specific text.

1 Introduction

Recent work in knowledge-rich NLP tasks such as information retrieval, question answering, textual entailment and sentiment analysis have revealed a need for more structured data, where concepts are stored together with the semantic relationships that exist between these concepts and their corresponding surface forms. Structured lexical-semantic databases such as WordNet (Miller et al., 1990) or EuroWordNet (Vossen, 1998) have been deployed for a wide range of NLP tasks, but suffer from a number of shortcomings. Firstly, these manually crafted resources are very labour-intensive and costly to create. Secondly, existing lexical inventories contain more general vocabulary and have by consequence a low coverage for domain-specific terms. As a consequence, researchers have started to investigate how semantic resources such as ontologies can be learned from text instead of being created manually. For an overview we refer to (Biemann, 2005).

In this paper, we focus on the detection of hypernym relations between nouns and noun phrases. Automatic extraction of nouns or noun phrases which are semantically related has been successfully achieved in prior research, for example using coordination and co-occurrence information (Oh et al., 2009; Cederberg and Widdows, 2003; Roark and Charniak, 1998; Widdows and Borow, 2002). However, automatically distinguishing exactly which semantic relationship exists between them is not that straightforward. One of these semantic relationships is the hypernym relation which can be seen as a set-subset relation. In the literature the following description is adopted the most: *a(n) NP0 is a (kind of) NP1*; where NP1 is the *hypernym* of NP0 (which is in turn the *hyponym*) and the relationship is reflexive and transitive but not symmetric (Miller et al., 1990; Hearst, 1992). Note the subtle difference with meronymy (Girju et al., 2003), which is the part-whole relationship, and synonymy (Lin et al., 2003), which expresses equality.

Automatic hypernym detection has been explored in multiple ways. A clear distinction can be made between the pattern-based approaches and the statistical approaches. The aim of the present research is to present a hybrid approach in which distributional information acts as a filter on the pattern-based output. Although our current focus is on hypernym detection of noun-noun pairs, the final goal of this research is to use the automatic hypernym detection system to obtain a hierarchically structured term list for any kind of input text. Prior research in hypernym detection suggested the extracted hypernym-hyponym pairs could be used to extend general thesauri like WordNet (Snow et al., 2006; Roark and Charniak,

1998) or EuroWordNet (Van der Plas and Bouma, 2005). Our aim, however, is to make a hypernym detection system that can be used to structure automatically obtained term lists from domain and user specific texts. These texts typically contain a wide variety of technical terms that do not occur in general-purpose inventories like WordNet.

In the following sections, we will first discuss relevant related research in Section 2, describe our hypernym detection system in Section 3 and present our results in Section 4. Section 5 concludes the paper with some prospects for future research.

2 Related Research

Two main approaches are used to learn hypernym relations from text: pattern-based (or rule-based) approaches and distributional approaches.
Most of the pattern-based approaches were inspired by the seminal work of Hearst (1992) in which she identified a set of lexico-syntactic patterns for the identification of hyponymy relations in English text. Subsequently, various researchers continued working with this pattern-based approach for English (Cederberg and Widdows, 2003; Pantel and Ravichandran, 2004; Riloff and Shepherd, 1997; Roark and Charniak, 1998) as well as for other languages such as French (Malaisé et al., 2004) or Romanian (Mititelu, 2008). The patterns were further extended through translation and manually searching through texts (Kozareva et al., 2008), or by using more sophisticated methods of clustering related terms, starting from known hypernym pairs and features (Snow et al., 2006; Lin, 1998) or lists of seed words known to have the desired relationship (Roark and Charniak, 1998; Riloff and Shepherd, 1997; Widdows and Borow, 2002). Pantel and Pennacchiotti (2006) used generic patterns (broad coverage noisy patterns) to extract semantic relations and subsequently apply refining techniques to deal with the wide variety of such relations. Similar approaches that combine pattern extraction with post-processing techniques to enrich the system and improve the results have been investigated, for example, with Support Vector Machines and Hidden Markov Models (Ritter et al., 2009). A different approach has been used by Navigli et al. (2010), that use word class lattices, or directed acyclic graphs, to develop a pattern generalization algorithm that is able to extract definitions and hypernyms from web documents.
For Dutch, several methods have been investigated. Tjong Kim Sang et al. (2011; 2007) have tried to extract hypernymy information from text in three ways: comparing extraction of one pattern from the web with extraction from multiple patterns from a corpus, extraction with and without word sense tagging, and finally they also investigated the impact of using deep syntactic information for hypernym extraction. Bosma et al. (2010; 2011) applied different relation extraction methods in a way that the results of one method are used as input for another method, aiming to find the complete terminology of domain specific texts. In addition to applying a pattern-based and distributional approach, they also perform a morpho-syntactic analysis of compound terms and consider the longest known suffix of the term as a valid hypernym of the compound term. Van der Plas and Bouma (2005) present a searching method for semantically similar words on the basis of a parsed corpus of Dutch text and used these relations to boost the performance of an open-domain question answering system.

Other researchers have applied a distributional approach to automatically extract hypernym pairs from text. The latter approaches start from the distributional hypothesis, stating that words that occur in similar contexts tend to be semantically similar (Harris, 1968). In order to define the *context* of a given target word, both cooccurrence and syntactic information can be extracted from the surrounding words. Unsupervised learning methods like clustering to obtain taxonomies, definitions and semantically similar words have been applied by (Widdows, 2003; Pereira et al., 1993; Van de Cruys, 2010).
Clustering has also shown to be a valid approach to automatically detect hypernym relations between terms. By clustering words according to their contexts in text and assigning a label to each cluster, it is then also possible to extract $is-a$ relations between each cluster member and the cluster label. Caraballo (1999) uses syntactic dependency features (such as conjunction and apposition) to automatically build noun clusters. Pantel and Ravichandran (2004) extended his

work by including all syntactic dependency relations for each considered noun.

More recent distributional approaches rely on the *Distributional Inclusion Hypothesis*, according to which semantically narrower terms include a significant number of distributional features of their hypernyms (Lenci and Benotto, 2012).

The main advantage of the distributional approaches is that they allow to find semantically related terms, even when they do not explicitly occur in predefined patterns in text. The main disadvantage, however, is that these clustering approaches have difficulties to determine the exact semantic relationship (synonymy, antonymy, hyponymy) between the semantically related concepts.

In order to improve on precision for the automatic hypernym detection, we decided to combine the lexico-syntactic pattern-based approach with a distributional approach that filters candidate hypernym pairs containing noun pairs that are not semantically related (and that by consequence are not contained by the same sense cluster).

3 Dutch hypernym finder system

3.1 Pattern-based module

For our pattern detection system, we used the patterns from Hearst (1992), complemented with those from Mititelu (2008), and translated them into their Dutch equivalents. This resulted in a list of 42 patterns. If such equivalents did not logically exist in Dutch (e.g. *not least* and *become*), we either left them out or took a similar existing pattern instead. A few examples are the following:

English	Dutch
like	NP, zoals NP {, NP}* {(en|of) NP}
and/or other	NP {, NP} {,} (en|of) andere NP
(e)specially	NP, (voornamelijk|vooral|speciaal) NP {, NP}* {(en|of) NP}
including	NP, inclusief {NP, }* {(en|of) NP}
is a	NP is (een) NP
are	NP {, NP}* {(en|of) NP} zijn NP
for example	NP {,} bijvoorbeeld NP {, NP}* {(en|of) NP}
and/or similar	NP {, NP}* (en|of) soortgelijk(e)|dergelijk(e) NP

Some of the patterns were not as likely to occur in their Dutch translation as they might be in English (e.g. *in common with other*), but we decided to test all the patterns to get an idea which patterns would yield the correct noun pairs and which would more often result in false positives.

3.1.1 Datasets

The corpus used in the experiments is a one-million subcorpus of the 500-million word balanced reference corpus for contemporary (1954-present) Dutch texts: SoNaR (Oostdijk et al., 2012). It consists of 38 text types coming both from Flanders (1/3) and the Netherlands (2/3). The SoNaR-corpus was tokenized, lemmatized, Part-of-Speech-tagged and chunk-tagged using a preprocessing toolkit that was developed in-house (reference omitted). In order to develop and test our pattern detection system, we divided the one-million corpus in two parts: a development set of 250.000 words and a test set of 750.000 words. The development set was used to fine-tune the hypernym patterns and optimize the distributional model (See section 3.2).

3.1.2 Pattern-Based Approach

In order to define the patterns, a set of regular expressions was designed to match on both Part-of-Speech as well as chunk tags. Take for example the pattern *NP zoals NP* ((a(n) NP like NP). This is the simplified version of *NP (zo|even)als NP* {, *NP*}* {*(en|of) NP*}, in which NP is shorthand for at least one noun (PoS-tag 'N'). NP can also be a compound noun: a noun preceded by either another noun, an adjective (PoS-tag 'ADJ', chunk tag 'I-NP') or a verbal adjective (PoS-tag 'WW', chunk tag 'I-NP'). This allows us for example to capture hyponym/hypernym relations between phrases such as 'automatic gearbox', 'manual gearbox' and 'gearbox'. As patterns were often interrupted by adverbial phrases, we ignored adverbs (PoS-tag 'BW').

The detection system returns both the pattern matches (containing lemmas) as well as the hypernym-hyponym pairs themselves, as exemplified below:

```
['sector', 'als', 'biotechnologie', ',', 'farmacie'][1]
(sector, biotechnologie)
(sector, farmacie)
```

3.2 Distributional semantic module

Vector space models (VSMs) have been widely used for semantic processing of text (Turney and Pantel, 2010). These VSMs use statistical patterns of human word usage to build up an artificial

[1]English: 'sector', 'such as', 'biotechnology', ',', 'pharmacy'

understanding of a given text. In order to post-process the pattern-based hypernym pairs, we created a distributional semantic model for Dutch by applying following steps:

1. build a large *word-context matrix* for all words occurring in a Dutch reference corpus and convert this matrix into *context vectors*

2. *cluster* the resulting context vectors

The resulting clusters contain Dutch words occurring in similar lexical contexts and can by consequence be used to filter hypernym pairs that show little semantic relatedness.

We constructed a semantic model for part of the Twente News Corpus (TwNC), a multifaceted Dutch corpus that contains material from different sources such as national newspapers, television subtitles, broadcast news transcripts, etc. (Ordelman et al., 2007). The corpus was tokenized and contains around twenty million tokens.
In order to build a VSM model for our Dutch reference corpus, we first built a **word-context frequency matrix** storing for every word in the Dutch corpus how many times it occurred in a certain context. To define the context, we used cooccurring words. In a second step, we applied Pointwise Mutual Information (Church and Hanks, 1990) as a weighting function to discover informative semantic similarity relations between words. As we only want to consider contexts with a high semantic discrimination value, we smoothened the matrix by removing stop words and low frequent words (occurring less than 3 times in the corpus) from the context features. Finally, the cooccurrence matrix was converted into a vector of context features per target word. The matrix and vector construction was performed with the SenseClusters Package (Pedersen and Purandare, 2004).
We used the CLUTO clustering toolkit (Karypis, 2002) to group semantically related **words into clusters**. Similarity between the context vectors was computed by taking their cosine, the cosine of the angle between two vectors being the inner product of the vectors. We used a K-means clustering algorithm and ran experiments with a varying number of output clusters. The impact of the desired number of output clusters is discussed in section 4.

3.3 Filtering module

The filtering module uses distributional evidence to remove candidate hypernym pairs that are not semantically related; nouns that are considered to have a hypernym relationship (resulting from the pattern-based module) and that do not figure in the same semantic cluster (distributional semantic module) are removed from the hypernym pair list. In case one of the nouns does not appear in the clusters at all – because the word occurred less than three times in the reference corpus – we do not filter the given hypernym-hyponym pair. As our clusters are composed of single word terms, we only consider the last word of the hypernym/hyponym in case the pair contains multiword terms[2]. If we take for instance the hyponym *eerstelijns zorgverstrekker* [English: primary care provider], we only consider the last word "zorgverstrekker" [English: care provider] for comparison with the clustering output.

4 Experimental results

4.1 Experimental set-up

To evaluate the performance of both the pattern-based and combined approach, we extracted a test set from the Sonar corpus that contains 750.000 tokens. The output of the system was manually labeled by two annotators using the following labels:

- **strict**: correct hypernym-hyponym pair
- **context-specific**: there is context-specific hypernym relation between both noun phrases.
- **no**: not a correct hypernym pair

We included the context-specific class to cover hypernym relations between automatically extracted terms from domain or user-specific corpora, which is the ultimate goal of our work. Such a class can also cover domain-specific relations including proper names. Theoretically, proper names do not occur in a hypernym relation, since whether or not they would be considered correct is highly dependent on the context of the document: the hypernym pair (priest, John) can be correct in a text where John is in fact a priest, but if another non-priest John is referred to this pair would be

[2]In Dutch, the last word is usually the most meaningful part of a given multiword term.

incorrect. There are, however, pairs where the hypernym is more specific, which makes the pair less ambiguous. As an example, we can cite the pair '(queen, Beatrix)' or '(queen, Elisabeth)', which one might consider to be a correct hypernym pair. As many proper nouns occur in domain specific and technical texts, we decided to consider them as potential terms in a hypernym-hyponym relationship. Examples extracted from our corpus are: '(buurland, Nederland)' [English: neighboring country, The Netherlands] and '(concurrent, Inbev)' [English: competitor, Inbev].

Inter-annotator agreement We calculated inter-annotator agreement using Kappa on a subset of the test data containing 1000 hypernym-hyponym pairs (Carletta, 1996). The Kappa statistic was 0.687 for on the strict labeling task and 0.678 on the context-specific hyponyms. In addition, we also calculated inter-annotator agreement by measuring precision, recall and their harmonic mean $F1$ (van Rijsbergen, 1979). F-scores were calculated by taking one annotator as the gold standard and scoring the annotations of the other for precision and recall. This yields the same results as averaging the precision or the recall scores of both annotators, when using the other as a gold standard. A $F1$ score of 89% was obtained on the strict labeling task, whereas a 87% agreement was obtained on the labeling task in which also context-specific hypernyms were indicated.

Evaluation metrics In order to assess the performance of our hypernym extraction module, we calculated **Precision** by dividing the number of correct hypernym pairs by the total number of predicted hypernym pairs:

$$Precision = \frac{strict}{predicted} \quad (1)$$

We also measured the **Relaxed Precision** (*RelaxedP*) that measures the system performance on the context-specific hypernym relations:

$$RelaxedP = \frac{strict + context\ specific}{predicted} \quad (2)$$

4.2 Results of the pattern-based module

In the complete corpus, 13 patterns were found. As is shown in Table 1, there is a striking difference between the strict and relaxed precision.

Pattern	# tuples	Relaxed Precision	Precision
als NP zijn NP	1	0	0
NP, zoals NP	874	0.57	0.38
NP, inclusief NP	11	0.45	0.09
NP is (een) (soort (van)) NP	849	0.31	0.11
NP en gelijke / andere NP	8	0.875	0.875
NP, anders dan NP	7	0.57	0.14
NP, d.w.z. NP	2	0.5	0.5
NP, met uitzondering van NP	1	0	0
NP, ofwel NP	6	0.5	0.17
NP, genaamd NP	8	0	0
NP, die (een) NP zijn	32	0.19	0.06
NP, een NP	946	0.36	0.14
NP, maar niet NP	1	1	0

Table 1: Precision and Relaxed precision scores per pattern.

The relaxed scores are comparable to the 40% reported by Cederberg and Widdows (2003) and our *'zoals'*-pattern performs even better than the 52% reported by Hearst (1992) for the English version (*'such as'*). When comparing our results to those obtained for Dutch by Tjong Kim Sang and Hofmann (2009), several things can be noted. They report a 57,5% precision for the pattern *'such as'* on a Wikipedia corpus, whereas it only scored 25,1% on a Newspaper corpus. Our Sonar test corpus consists of both kinds of texts and others still, and also scored 57%. The other patterns we can compare with are *'N be N'*, scoring 22,9%, and *'N be a N'*, scoring 40,8%, which are both contained in our pattern *'NP is (een) (soort (van)) NP'*, scoring 31%.
Tjong Kim Sang et al. (2011) examined the effect of two text preprocessing approaches on the task of extracting hypernymy information, i.e. a pattern-based approach and a dependency parsing approach. Their pattern-based approach scores 43% precision on a newspaper corpus and 63,4% precision on a Wikipedia corpus.

We also calculated recall and precision of our hypernym pairs in comparison with the synsets of the Dutch part of EuroWordNet (EWN). Recall was 0.12 and precision 0.03. The reason for these low scores is mainly a coverage problem of the Dutch EWN. This caused a lot of correct pairs to be found incorrect (nonexistent) in EWN. As an example, the pair '(land, Nederland)' [English: country, The Netherlands] was considered correct since 'Nederland' is part of EWN, whereas the pair '(land, Rusland)' [English: country, Russia] was considered incorrect due to the fact that 'Rusland' is not incorporated in EWN.

We encountered some issues that are characteristic for a pattern detection system, such as words disturbing the pattern and preventing it from being matched, patterns that overgenerate and do not always indicate a hypernymy relationship (e.g. [NP, a NP]), or mistakes from preprocessing (e.g. nouns being tagged as verbs, or vice versa) yielding incorrect pairs or preventing correct ones from being matched. Furthermore, in running text, semantic relations are often left implicit, while a pattern-based approach can only handle the explicit instances. Were we to test on a text wherein conceptual relationships are explicit, like an encyclopedia, the system would probably perform better.

4.3 Results of the filtering module

The list of hypernym-hyponym pairs that resulted from the pattern-detection module was filtered by means of the distributional semantic module discussed in Section 3.2. By filtering hypernym pairs that do not appear in the same semantic cluster, we expect to partially solve the problem of overgeneration that is caused by very general patterns matching term pairs that are not semantically related.

Figure 1 confirms our hypothesis: although the strict precision is similar between the two methods, the combined system clearly improves the relaxed precision that also considers the context-specific hypernym pairs. The improved relaxed precision can be observed for all tested numbers of output clusters, but as can be expected slightly increases when grouping the nouns into smaller and thus semantically more narrow clusters[3].

Inspection of the results from the combined system revealed a couple of issues. First, the semantic model only covers part of the terms that appear in the hypernym-hyponym pairs. A matched hypernym pair such as for instance '(afvalproduct, stro)' [English: waste product, straw] is not filtered because the nouns are not contained in the semantic model. Second, we observed that semantically related words do not always appear in the same cluster. As a consequence, correct hypernym-hyponym pairs not occurring in the same clusters are erroneously eliminated by the filtering module. We detected for instance that the nouns in '(land, Rusland)' [English: country, Russia] are contained by different clusters (and are subsequently filtered by the distributional module), whereas the words in '(land, Nederland)' [English: country, Netherlands] do occur in the same cluster.

A possible explanation for both problems could be the modest size of our reference corpus (20 million words) where low frequent terms were filtered as well. We expect by consequence to solve these issues by using a much bigger reference corpus that allows us to store more contexts and examples for a broader range of words. In addition, we will also perform lemmatization and parsing of the reference corpus, in order to experiment with different kinds of features.

[3] A larger number of output clusters results into a smaller list of words contained by each cluster, and by consequence tighter semantic relations between these terms.

5 Conclusion and Future Research

We presented a first set of experiments for a Dutch hypernym detection system that combines a lexico-syntactic pattern-based and distributional approach. The experimental results show the effectiveness of the filtering step; adding a distributional model clearly improves the relaxed precision of the system.

Analysis of the test results revealed a number of shortcomings of the current approach that will be tackled in future research. Since at one hand the pattern detector purely matches on surface-syntactic forms, and on the other hand these patterns can also occur without actually representing a hypernym relation, we believe that a more flexible and sense-orientated approach is needed to amplify our pattern detector. Further experiments with a larger reference corpus are also needed to improve the semantic model for Dutch. Additional research is also needed to determine the best context representation (lexical or syntactic context, window size of the context) and clustering parameters (desired number of output clusters, clustering algorithm, etc.).

In future research, we will also develop gold standard corpora for different domains and different languages, in order to measure both precision and recall on technical and user specific data.

References

Chris Biemann. 2005. Ontology Learning from Text: A Survey of Methods. *LDV Forum*, 20(2):75–93.

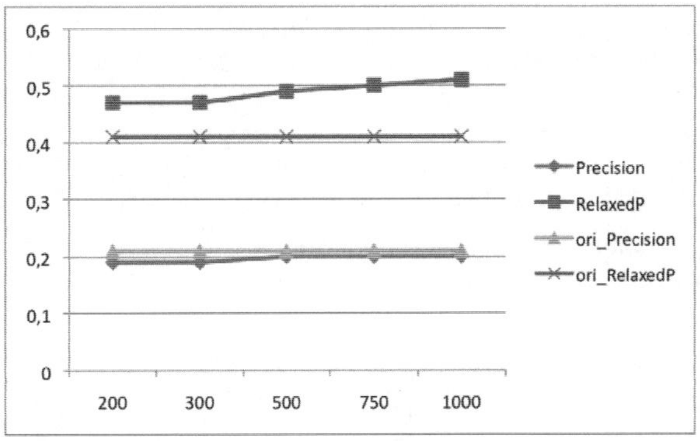

Figure 1: Precision and Relaxed precision scores for the pattern-based (*ori_Precision* and *ori_RelaxedP*) and combined module (*Precision/RelaxedP*) with a varying number of output clusters.

W. E. Bosma and P. Vossen. 2010. Bootstrapping language neutral term extraction. In *Proceedings of the 7th international conference on Language Resources and Evaluation (LREC2010)*, May.

W. E. Bosma, P. Vossen, and H. van der Vliet. 2011. Termextractie in kyoto. In *Terminologie in het Nederlandse Taalgebied*, volume 2010.

S. Caraballo. 1999. Automatic acquisition of a hypernym-labeled noun hierarchy from text. In *Proceedings of ACL-99*, pages 120–126, Baltimore, MD.

Jean Carletta. 1996. Assessing Agreement on Classification Tasks: The Kappa Statistic. *Computational Linguistics*, 22(2):249–254.

S. Cederberg and D. Widdows. 2003. Using lsa and noun coordination information to improve the precision and recall of automatic hyponymy extraction. In *Proceedings of the 7th CONLL at HLT-NAACL 2003*, volume 4, pages 111–118.

K. Church and P. Hanks. 1990. Word Association Norms, Mutual Information, and Lexicography. *Computational Linguistics*, 16(1):22–29.

R. Girju, A. Badulescu, and D. Moldovan. 2003. Learning semantic constraints for the automatic discovery of part-whole relations. In *Proceedings of HLT-NAACL*, volume 1, pages 1–8.

Zelig Sabbetai Harris. 1968. *Mathematical structures of language*. Wiley.

M. Hearst. 1992. Automatic acquisition of hyponyms from large text corpora. In *Proceedings of the International Conference on Computational Linguistics*, pages 539–545.

G. Karypis. 2002. CLUTO - a clustering toolkit. Technical Report 02-017, University of Minnesota, Department of Computer Science.

Z. Kozareva, E. Riloff, and E. Hovy. 2008. Semantic class learning from the web with hyponym pattern linkage graphs. In *Proceedings of the 46th Annual Meeting of the Association for Computational Linguistics (ACL)*, pages 1048–1056, Columbus, Ohio, USA.

A. Lenci and G. Benotto. 2012. Identifying hypernyms in distributional semantic spaces. In *Proceedings of the first Joint conference on Lexical and Computational Semantics (*SEM)*, pages 75–79, Montréal, Canada.

D. Lin, S. Zhao, L. Qin, and M. Zhou. 2003. Identifying synonyms among distributionally similar words. In *Proceedings of the 18th International Joint Conference on Artificial Intelligence*, pages 1492–1493.

D. Lin. 1998. Automatic retrieval and clustering of similar words. In *Proceedings of Coling-ACL*, pages 768–774.

V. Malaisé, P. Zweigenbaum, and B. Bachimont. 2004. Detecting semantic relations between terms in definitions. In *In the CompuTerm workshop 2004: 3rd International Workshop on Computational Terminology*, pages 55–62.

G.A. Miller, R. Beckwith, C. Fellbaum, D. Gross, and K.J. Miller. 1990. Introduction to wordnet: An online lexical database. *International Journal of Lexicography*, 3(4):235–244.

V. Mititelu. 2008. Hyponymy patterns. semi-automatic extraction, evaluation and inter-lingual comparison. *Text, Speech and Dialogue: Lecture Notes in Computer Science*, 5246:37–44.

R. Navigli and P. Velardi. 2010. Learning word-class lattices for definition and hypernym extraction. In *Proceedings of the 48th Annual Meeting of the Association for Computational Linguistics*, pages 1318–1327, Uppsala, Sweden.

J. Oh, K. Uchimoto, and K. Torisawa. 2009. Bilingual co-training for monolingual hyponymy-relation acquisition. In *Proceedings of ACL-09: IJCNLP*, pages 432–440.

N. Oostdijk, M. Reynaert, and I. Schuurman. 2012. The construction of a 500-million-word reference corpus of contemporary written Dutch. In P. Spyns and J. Odijk, editors, *Essential Speech and Language Technology for Dutch, Theory and Applications of Natural Language Processing*. Springer.

R. Ordelman, F. de Jong, A. Hessen, and H. Hondorp. 2007. TwNC: a Multifaceted Dutch News Corpus. *ELRA Newsletter*, 12(3-4).

P. Pantel and M. Pennacchiotti. 2006. Espresso: Leveraging generic patterns for automatically harvesting semantinc relations. In *Proceedings of the 21st International Conference on Computational Linguistics and the 44th Annual meeting of the Association for Computational Linguistics*, pages 113–120.

P. Pantel and D. Ravichandran. 2004. Automatically labeling semantic classes. In *Proceedings of HLT/NAACL-04*, pages 321–328, Boston, MA.

T. Pedersen and A. Purandare. 2004. SenseClusters - Finding Clusters that Represent Word Senses. In *Proceedings of Fifth Annual Meeting of the North American Chapter of the Association for Computational Linguistics (NAACL-04)*, pages 26–29, Boston, .A.

F. Pereira, N. Tishby, and L. Lee. 1993. Distributional clustering of English words. In *Proceedings of the 31st annual meeting on Association for Computational Linguistics*, pages 183–190.

E. Riloff and J. Shepherd. 1997. A corpus-based approach for building semantic lexicons. In *Proceedings of the 2nd Conference on Empirical Methods in NLP*, pages 117–124.

A. Ritter, S. Soderland, and O. Etzioni. 2009. What is this, anyway: Automatic hypernym discovery. In *Proceedings of Association for Advancement of Artificial Intelligence Spring Symposium on Learning by Reading and Learning to Read*, pages 88–93.

B. Roark and E. Charniak. 1998. Nound-phrase co-occurrence statistics for semiautomatic semantic lexicon construction. In *Proceedings of COLING and ACL*, volume 2, pages 1110–1116.

R. Snow, D. Jurafsky, and A.Y. Ng. 2006. Semantic taxonomy induction from heterogenous evidence. In *Proceedings of the 21st International Conference on Computational Linguistics and the 44th Annual meeting of the Association for Computational Linguistics*, pages 801–888.

E. Tjong Kim Sang and K. Hofmann. 2007. Automatic extraction of dutch hypernym-hyponym pairs. In *Proceedings of CLIN-2006*.

E.F. Tjong Kim Sang and K. Hofmann. 2009. Lexical patterns or dependency patterns: which is better for hypernym extraction? In *Proceedings of the Thirteenth Conference on Computational Natural Language Learning*.

Tjong Kim Sang, E. and Hofmann, K. and De Rijke, M. 2011. Extraction of hypernymy information from text. In A. Van den Bosch and G. Bouma, editors, *Interactive multi-modal question-answering*, Series: Theory and Applications of Natural Language Processing, pages 223–245. Springer-Verlag Berlin Heidelberg.

P. Turney and P. Pantel. 2010. From frequency to meaning: Vector space models of semantics. *J. Artif. Intell. Res. (JAIR)*, 37:141–188.

Tim Van de Cruys. 2010. *Mining for Meaning. The Extraction of Lexico-Semantic Knowledge from Text.* Ph.D. thesis, University of Groningen, The Netherlands.

L. Van der Plas and G. Bouma. 2005. Auotmatic acquisition of lexico-semantic knowledge for question answering. In *Proceedings of the IJCNLP Workshop on Ontologies and Lexical Resources*, Jeju Island, Korea.

C.J. van Rijsbergen. 1979. *Information Retrieval.* Buttersworth, London.

P. Vossen, editor. 1998. *EuroWordNet: a multilingual database with lexical semantic networks.* Kluwer Academic Publishers, Norwell, MA, USA.

D. Widdows and B. Borow. 2002. A graph model for unsupervised lexical acquisition. In *Proceedings of the 19th International Conference on Computational Linguistics*, volume 1, pages 1–7.

D. Widdows. 2003. Unsupervised methods for developing taxonomies by combining syntactic and statistical information. In *Proceedings of HLT-NAACL*, pages 197–204.

Exploiting Synergies Between Open Resources for German Dependency Parsing, POS-tagging, and Morphological Analysis

Rico Sennrich, Martin Volk and **Gerold Schneider**
Institute of Computational Linguistics
University of Zurich
Binzmühlestr. 14
CH-8050 Zürich
{sennrich,volk,gschneid}@cl.uzh.ch

Abstract

We report on the recent development of ParZu, a German dependency parser. We discuss the effect of POS tagging and morphological analysis on parsing performance, and present novel ways of improving performance of the components, including the use of morphological features for POS-tagging, the use of syntactic information to select good POS sequences from an n-best list, and using parsed text as training data for POS tagging and statistical parsing. We also describe our efforts towards reducing the dependency on restrictively licensed and closed-source NLP resources.

1 Introduction

German NLP tools such as part-of-speech taggers, morphology tools, and syntactic parsers often require licensing and suffer from usage restrictions, which makes the deployment of an NLP pipeline that combines several components cumbersome at best, impossible at worst (if no license can be obtained). Some restrictions are rooted in the copyright and/or licenses of the annotated corpora on which statistical taggers or parsers can be trained for German, such as TIGER (Brants et al., 2002) or Tüba-D/Z (Telljohann et al., 2004). There have been attempts to bypass these restrictions through corpus masking (Rehm et al., 2007), but for statistical models that require lexical information, this is not an option.

We discuss ParZu, a German dependency parser that relies on external tools for POS tagging and morphological analysis, and combines a hand-written grammar and a statistical disambiguation module that is trained on a treebank. We describe attempts to move towards components with freer licensing. We also discuss techniques to improve parsing performance by better exploiting the various resources, specifically by using morphological information in POS tagging, and through n-best POS tagging.

2 Parser Architecture

ParZu, first described in (Sennrich et al., 2009), is a hybrid dependency parser for German, which implements the grammar described by Foth (2005). It combines a hand-written grammar with a statistical disambiguation module, building on the same architecture as the English Pro3Gres parser (Schneider, 2008). The hand-written grammar is mostly unlexicalized and operates on the level of parts-of-speech.[1] To give the subject relation as example, the grammar constrains the possible parts-of-speech of the head (a finite verb) and the dependent (typically a noun or pronoun, but some other classes such as numbers are also allowed). The dependent must be in nominative case, and either agree with the verb in person and number, or be a coordinated structure. Since each word form may have multiple possible morphological analyses, the morphological constraints are unification-based and allow for underspecified representations. Also, at most one subject is allowed per finite verb, and some topological restrictions must be met, such as only one constituent being allowed in the Vorfeld.

The rules draw on part-of-speech information and morphological knowledge. For the former, Sennrich et al. (2009) use TreeTagger for POS tagging. For the latter, they use GERTWOL (Haapalainen and Majorin, 1995), a commercial morphology tool.

The statistical disambiguation module models lexical and positional preferences, and is trained on the TüBa-D/Z, a hand-annotated treebank of

[1] Among the lexicalized rules is a closed list of nouns which can head noun phrases with temporal function, such as *Er schläft* ***jeden Tag*** (English: 'he sleeps **every day**').

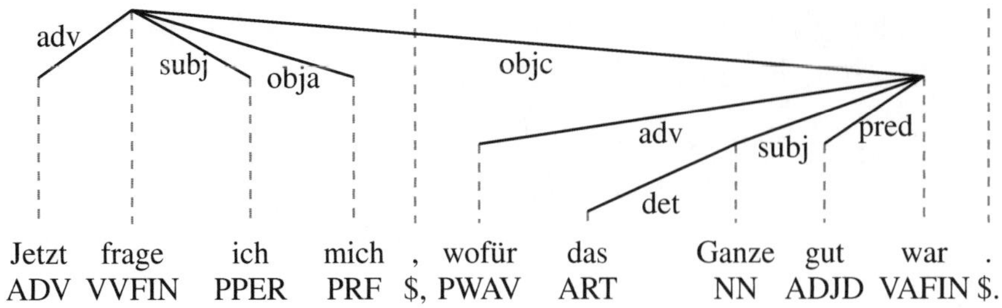

Figure 1: TüBa-D/Z parse tree in dependency format. (English: 'Now I ask myself what good it did.')

about 65 500 sentences from a German newspaper. Versley (2005) provides a conversion of the treebank into the dependency format that the parser implements. Figure 1 shows an example parse tree. Among others, the statistical disambiguation module performs a functional disambiguation of German noun phrases based on the verb's subcategorization frame, disambiguates the attachment of prepositional phrases and adverbs, and uses constant pseudo-probabilities to prefer some labels over others if both are permitted by the grammar.

In summary, ParZu requires three components with licensing restrictions, for which we will discuss alternatives: a morphology tool (GERTWOL), a POS tagger (TreeTagger) and an annotated treebank (TüBa-D/Z). First, we present a baseline evaluation that compares parser performance with a statistical parser, and shows improvements to the grammar and statistical disambiguation module since the evaluation in (Sennrich et al., 2009).

2.1 Evaluation

This first evaluation serves three purposes: comparing parsing performance of ParZu with that of a state-of-the-art statistical parser, comparing the version of ParZu that we use to that of earlier publications, and evaluating the performance loss when moving from gold POS tags to automatically predicted ones. Note that our initial comments on limited deployability also apply to statistical parsers. Even if a statistical parser is released under a permissive license, it requires an annotated treebank for model training, and thus its deployment is hampered by the licensing restrictions of the treebank.

Of the 65 500 sentences in version 7 of TüBa-D/Z (1 230 000 tokens), we use the first 1000 for development purposes, the next 3000 for this evaluation, and the remaining 61 500 sentences for training. To represent state-of-the-art statistical parsing, we use MaltParser (Nivre, 2009), with settings optimized with MaltOptimizer (Ballesteros and Nivre, 2012). MaltParser is a tool for data-driven dependency parsing which implements various algorithms. For TüBa-D/Z, MaltOptimizer selects the stack projective algorithm (Nivre, 2009) with pseudo-projective pre- and postprocessing. The algorithm generates a parse tree through a sequence of transitions from an initial configuration (a NULL word on the stack, all words of the sentence in the buffer, and an empty set of labelled dependency arcs) to a terminal configuration (a NULL word on the stack, an empty buffer, and a set of labelled dependency arcs which forms the parse tree). For each configuration, three transitions are possible, either shifting the first word in the buffer to the stack, or labelling the last word in the stack a dependent of the second-to-last (removing the dependent from the stack), or vice versa. Each transition is predicted by a classifier which is trained on the training treebank.

For ParZu, we present results for version 0.11 – evaluated in (Sennrich et al., 2009) – and the last released version 0.21. The difference between these represents improvements in the core grammar and statistical disambiguation module.[2]

We measure labelled precision and recall, i.e. for how many tokens both the head and the dependency label are correctly predicted, compared to either the total number of predictions, or the number of relations in the treebank. Punctuation marks and ROOT are not considered in the evaluation – this means that if a system does not predict a head for a token, this harms its recall, but not the precision. We also report the f_1 score, the harmonic mean between precision and recall. For the evaluation, we use tokenization and sentence splitting of the treebank, but not the lemmas or morphological features. For MaltParser, we predict lem-

[2]The evaluation set was not used during development of these components.

system	precision	recall	f_1
TreeTagger			
MaltParser	84.7	85.1	84.9
ParZu v. 0.11	83.5	75.8	79.4
ParZu v. 0.21	85.4	83.2	84.3
gold tags			
MaltParser	88.0	88.4	88.2
ParZu v. 0.11	86.6	81.1	83.7
ParZu v. 0.21	89.7	89.1	89.4

Table 1: Parsing performance baseline results with automatically predicted tags (TreeTagger) and gold POS tags.

mas with TreeTagger, and use no morphological features, neither for training nor for parsing, since most morphological analyses are ambiguous, and we cannot easily provide MaltParser with disambiguated morphological analyses for parsing; for ParZu, we predict lemmas and extract morphological analyses with GERTWOL. We also compare using POS tagging with TreeTagger to using the gold tags from the treebank to show how parsing performance degrades because of tagging errors.

Results are shown in table 1. For Maltparser, the loss in performance (f_1) is 3.3 percentage points when moving from gold POS tags to automatically predicted ones.[3] We found that the automatic prediction of lemmas is less problematic than that of POS tags, with a difference of 0.3 percentage points in f_1 score between automatically predicted and gold lemmas.

ParZu version 0.21 performs markedly better than version 0.11, which an improvement of about 3 percentage points in terms of precision, and 8 in terms of recall. This is mostly due to continued development on the core components, i.e. the grammar and the disambiguation module. With gold tags, ParZu outperforms MaltParser by 1.2 percentage points in f_1 score (88.2% $\rightarrow$ 89.4%). Note that, despite the similar total performance, the parsers have different strengths and weaknesses. ParZu is consistently better than MaltParser in the functional disambiguation of noun phrases, i.e. relations such as subject, object, and genitive modifier, while MaltParser finds more coordinations, albeit with lower precision. Some selected f_1 values (ParZu and MaltParser, respectively): SUBJ 94.5 vs. 90.3; OBJA 87.9 vs. 80.7; OBJD 77.8 vs. 49.6; GMOD 93.8 vs. 88.9.

[3]We follow the suggestion of Seeker et al. (2010) to tag the training data with the same tool used for decoding. With TreeTagger used only for parsing, but gold tags for training, performance is lower with 82.6% precision and 83.0% recall.

```
> Bewegungen
bewegen<V>ung<SUFF><+NN><Fem><Acc><Pl>
bewegen<V>ung<SUFF><+NN><Fem><Dat><Pl>
bewegen<V>ung<SUFF><+NN><Fem><Gen><Pl>
bewegen<V>ung<SUFF><+NN><Fem><Nom><Pl>
```

Figure 2: SMOR analysis of *Bewegungen*.

When moving from gold POS tags to automatically predicted ones, recall of ParZu drops by 5.9 percentage points, which is a bigger loss than that of MaltParser. Note that the drop is bigger in terms of recall than precision, which indicates that ParZu tends to make fewer labelling decisions, and generate more partial parses, when confronted with mistagged sentences. This is because the correct structure may be considered ungrammatical by the grammar on the basis of POS tags. While this can be perceived as a disadvantage compared to the data-driven MaltParser, which can learn the idiosyncrasies of the tagger when trained on automatically tagged data, we will try to exploit this behaviour to correct tagging errors in an n-best tagging workflow.

3 Morphology

For parsing, morphology tools provide two useful types of information. Lemma information allows for less sparse representation of statistical data, and inflectional analyses can be used to enforce agreement constraints, and for the functional disambiguation of German noun phrases.

As alternatives to GERTWOL, we investigate two morphology tools, both based on the SMOR grammar (Schmid et al., 2004), which is open source and licensed under GPL v2. The first is the SMOR grammar with the lexicon of the University of Stuttgart (consequently referred to as SMOR). The lexicon is closed-source, and can be licensed for research purposes. Secondly, we investigate Morphisto (Zielinski and Simon, 2009), which combines the SMOR grammar with an open-source lexicon, provided under the Creative Commons 3.0 BY-SA Non-Commercial license.

One problem with the SMOR grammar is that the morphology does not produce conventional lemmas, but derivational analyses as shown in figure 2. Specifically, the word form *Bewegungen* (English: 'movements') is shown to be composed

morphology tool	precision	recall	f_1
none	86.0	85.7	85.9
GERTWOL	89.7	89.1	89.4
SMOR	89.8	89.3	89.5
Morphisto	89.8	89.3	89.5

Table 2: ParZu parsing performance with different morphology tools (gold POS tags).

of the verb stem *bewegen* and the suffix *-ung*. In order to obtain a more traditional lemma, namely a form that corresponds to the nominative singular form (for nouns), we produce a pseudo-lemma by selecting the last morpheme in the analysis string, and concatenating it with the unnormalized stem. We separate the stem which we want to retain, and the ending which we substitute with the normalized form, through a longest common subsequence match between the original word form and the last morpheme in the SMOR analysis. In the example above, the last morpheme in the analysis is *ung*, which means that our pseudo-lemma is the concatenation of *Beweg* and *ung*, thus obtaining *Bewegung* as lemma.

Table 2 shows results for the three morphology systems. We can see that, for the purposes of parsing, the three tools perform similarly well, with SMOR/Morphisto performing 0.1 percentage points better than GERTWOL. The difference to not using any morphological information is about 3.5 percentage points. Note that ParZu relies heavily on these external analyses, and that some of the loss could be mitigated by using more lexicalized statistics instead. The performance difference is greatest for noun phrase relations, such as dative or accusative object.

We conclude that despite the unorthodox notion of lemmas, SMOR and Morphisto can be usefully deployed in a parser and are a suitable replacement for the commercial GERTWOL tool. This positive result is somewhat surprising given that, in a manual evaluation, a large performance gap between Morphisto and GERTWOL was found (Mahlow and Piotrowski, 2009). We plan to extract a fully free morphological lexicon from Wiktionary in future work, in order to have even more permissive licensing.

4 Tagging

The baseline experiments in table 1 show that tagging errors account for about a third of total parsing errors. As a consequence, we investigate ways to improve tagging, and mitigate the effect of tagging errors on parsing performance through n-best-tagging.

4.1 Conditional Random Field Tagging with Morphological Features

A major problem in statistical POS tagging for German is the complex morphology of German, which results in many inflected or compounded forms which have never been observed during training. We aim to improve performance by using a conditional random field (CRF) tagger that uses morphological features, similar to the first applications of CRFs described by Lafferty, McCallum and Pereira (Lafferty et al., 2001), and the model described in (Seeker et al., 2010). Conditional random fields are undirected graphical models that operate in a maximum entropy framework, and have the advantage over classical hidden Markov models (HMM) that they relax independence assumptions and allow for the inclusion of arbitrary features.

We use the following features:

- seven features representing the word form, the surrounding word forms (up to two words to the left and right), and the bigram of word plus left/right neighbour
- a bigram feature (on the level of labels)
- the lowercased word form
- is the word capitalized? (binary)
- is the word form alphanumeric (including dashes)? (binary)
- all possible POS tags of the word form as produced by a morphology tool

The set of possible POS tags is extracted from a morphology tool by mapping all analyses of the word form into the STTS tag set. Internally, all features are binarized.

4.2 Evaluation

We evaluate the CRF model without morphology, and with morphological analyses extracted from SMOR or Morphisto.[4] We use the CRF toolkit

[4]The feature extraction scripts, and configuration files necessary to reproduce our results are available on `https://github.com/rsennrich/clevertagger`.

tagger	morphology	TüBa	Sofies Welt
TreeTagger	-	94.9	95.0
TnT	-	97.0	94.7
CRF	-	96.2	94.7
CRF	Morphisto	97.6	96.6
CRF	SMOR	97.8	96.7

Table 3: POS tagging accuracy (in percent). N=53 935 (TüBa-D/Z) / 7416 (Sofies Welt).

tagger	morphology	TüBa	Sofies Welt	
				NE=NN
TnT	-	89.5	58.0	84.0
CRF	-	80.8	60.6	85.2
CRF	Morphisto	90.9	89.1	91.3
CRF	SMOR	92.6	89.6	91.3

Table 4: POS tagging accuracy for out-of-vocabulary words (in percent). N=3936 (TüBa-D/Z) / 393 (Sofies Welt).

Wapiti for training and decoding (Lavergne et al., 2010). We compare tagging performance to TreeTagger, a decision tree tagger, and TnT, a trigram HMM tagger.

We train TnT and the CRF models on the same 61 500 sentences from TüBa-D/Z that we used for the parsing evaluation; for TreeTagger, we use the published model for German. We evaluate performance on a 3000-sentence evaluation set from TüBa-D/Z, and a corpus of 529 sentences from "Sofies Welt", which is part of the Smultron parallel treebank (Volk et al., 2010).[5]

As the results in table 3 show, TnT performs better than TreeTagger on TüBa-D/Z (97% versus 94.9%), but slightly worse on Sofies Welt (94.7% versus 95.0%). This indicates that the TnT model is slightly domain-specific, and performance on Sofies Welt may better reflect out-of-domain performance. The CRF tagger without morphological features performs slightly worse than TnT, while the CRF models with morphological features perform best overall, with an accuracy of 97.6-8% on TüBa-D/Z, and 96.6-7% on Sofies Welt. This is an improvement of 1.6–2 percentage points compared to TreeTagger, TnT, and a CRF tagger without morphological features. The difference between using Morphisto and the original SMOR system to obtain morphological features is small.

[5]Both corpora use the STTS tag set, and we conflate non-standard tags: for pronominal adverbs, TüBa-D/Z uses *PROP*, Smultron *PROAV*, and TreeTagger *PAV*.

tagger	morphology	precision	recall	f_1
TreeTagger	-	85.6	83.7	84.6
TnT	-	87.1	85.2	86.2
CRF	-	86.3	84.8	85.5
CRF	Morphisto	87.9	86.7	87.3
CRF	SMOR	88.1	86.9	87.5

Table 5: Parsing performance with different POS taggers. ParZu with SMOR.

A large part of the performance difference can be attributed to the handling of unknown words. Table 4 shows tagging accuracy for words that do not occur in the TüBa-D/Z training set. TnT uses suffix analysis to estimate the class of unknown words, and on TüBa-D/Z, strongly outperforms a CRF model that has neither smoothing for unknown words nor morphological features. On Sofies Welt, TnT performs poorly due to frequent names (like *Sofie*) being tagged as *NN* instead of *NE*. We also present results with *NN* and *NE* conflated into a single POS tag.

The morphological features yield a big performance boost for the CRF tagger. With morphological features from SMOR, performance on TüBa-D/Z for out-of-vocabulary words is 12 percentage points better than without morphological features, and 3 percentage points better than that of TnT. On Sofies Welt, the difference is even more marked, with a gain of about 30 percentage points through morphological features, compared to either TnT or a CRF model without morphological features. Even if we conflate *NN* and *NE* into a single category, we observe a gain of 6-7 percentage points for the models with morphological features.

Improvements to POS tagging have a direct effect on parsing performance, as table 5 shows. we observe a difference of 3.2 percentage points in recall, and 2.5 percentage points in precision, between the worst tagger (TreeTagger) and the best one (CRF with SMOR).

4.3 N-best-tagging

While morphological analyses help the tagging of unknown words, the tag of some word forms cannot be predicted based on local features alone. Examples are the distinction between finite and infinitive verbs (e.g. *erhalten*), between relative pronouns and articles (e.g. *der*), and between prepositions and separated verb particles (e.g. *um*).

Consider examples 1–3 to see the single word form *erhalten* (English: 'receive') as three different parts-of-speech.

1. Sie feiern, wenn sie [...] erhalten/VVFIN.
   They celebrate if they receive [...]

2. Sie wollen [...] erhalten/VVINF.
   They want to receive [...]

3. Sie haben [...] erhalten/VVPP.
   They have received [...]

The gap [...] can be filled with a direct object and multiple adjuncts and thus be arbitrarily long, for instance *dieses Jahr viele Geschenke* (English: 'many gifts this year'). In such a case, a trigram Hidden Markov Model, which only considers a history of two words, would be unable to distinguish between the examples and assign the same label to *erhalten* in all of them.

The parser evaluation in table 1 shows that tagging errors affect the recall of ParZu more strongly than its precision. This indicates that ParZu tends to give no label at all, rather than the wrong label, if the POS sequence is ungrammatical. We propose to use this characteristic to choose the best tag sequence from an n-best list by preferring complete analyses over partial ones.

For each input sentence, we generate the n-best tag sequences with the CRF model, parse each, and then perform parse selection based on a number of features:

- The probability of the POS sequence
- The rank of the POS sequence
- The number of unattached nodes
- The number of "bad" labels (apposition or coordination, see below)

The features are combined into a single score in a log-linear framework, with weights set to optimize parsing performance on a development set of 1000 sentences. The probability feature obtains a positive weight (higher is better); all other features a negative one (higher is worse). Appositions and coordinations are considered bad labels because they are frequent in mistagged sentences. If a verb is mistagged as noun, noun phrases cannot be analyzed as subject, object etc., but will instead be labelled appositions of each others.

n-best	parsing performance precision	recall	f_1	tagging accuracy
1	(no parsing)			97.8
1	88.1	86.9	87.5	98.1
50	88.2	87.9	88.0	98.3

Table 6: Parsing performance and tagging accuracy with n-best tagging. CRF with SMOR for tagging, ParZu with SMOR for parsing.

In the following experiments, we perform n-best tagging with $n = 50$, then pruning all tag sequences which are less probable than the best sequence by a factor of 20 or more. This makes the size of the n-best list elastic in practice. If the tag sequence is unambiguous, all but the 1-best tag sequence are immediately discarded; for sentences with many ambiguities, we allow n of up to 50, which happens 13 times in the 3000-sentence evaluation set. On average, n (after pruning) is around 4, which also means that the number of sentences being parsed, and thus the runtime of the parser, is increased by a factor of 4. The baseline is the system with SMOR as morphology tool, both for the parser and the CRF tagging model.

We can see in table 6 that n-best tagging not only improves parsing recall by about 1 percentage point, but also improves tagging accuracy by 0.5 percentage points (97.8% $\rightarrow$ 98.3%). Some improvement in tagging accuracy is already visible with 1-best tagging, due to heuristic rules in the parser itself, i.e. forcing the last verb in a subordinated clause to be finite (VVFIN), even if the tagger predicts it to be infinite (VVINF) or a participle (VVPP), if the morphology system allows the analysis as VVFIN and the conjunction does not govern an infinitive.

With n-best tagging, parsing performance (f_1) is 88.0%, which is 1.4 percentage points below that with gold POS tags, and 3.7 percentage points better than in our baseline experiments in table 1 (84.3 $\rightarrow$ 88.0% $\rightarrow$ 89.4%). This means that n-best tagging, and the use of a CRF tagger rather than TreeTagger, has markedly reduced the number of parsing errors that are caused by tagging errors, compared to the baseline.

We will look more closely at the tagging results with SMOR and n-best tagging. The jump from 97.8% to 98.3% in tagging accuracy represents a relative reduction in tagging errors by 20%. Table 7 shows the change in tagging errors grouped

error type	tagging	+ parsing 1-best	+ parsing 50-best	change
verbs	299	146	112	-62.5%
nouns/names	372	372	381	+2.4%
pronouns	114	114	94	-17.5%
other	391	385	350	-10.5%
total	1176	1017	937	-20.3%

Table 7: Tagging errors grouped by gold POS. N=53935. CRF SMOR for tagging, ParZu with SMOR for parsing.

by different POS types. For verbs in German, tagging decisions are especially difficult to make locally because the part-of-speech tags encode some inflectional information, and the correct inflection may depend on non-local context. Both the heuristics in 1-best-tagging and tag sequence selection from n-best tagging help to reduce the number of verb tagging errors markedly, in total by 62.5%.

There are smaller improvements for pronouns and other parts-of-speech, including a better disambiguation between articles and pronouns. As an example of an ambiguity that is resolved through n-best-tagging, consider German *der*, which can mean 'the' (article), 'who' (relative pronoun), or 'this one' (demonstrative pronoun). 30–40% of tagging errors are due to confusions of NN (normal noun), NE (proper noun), and FM (foreign word). Parsing does not improve tagging accuracy for these parts-of-speech, mainly because ParZu makes little distinction between them.

In summary, we have demonstrated that we can perform n-best tagging, and use syntactic features extracted from ParZu for the selection of the best tag sequence. This allows us to disambiguate tagging ambiguities based on syntactic information, which improves both tagging accuracy and parsing performance.

5 Parsed Corpora as Training Treebanks

A third hurdle to the deployment of ParZu, and any data-driven parsers, is the limited availability of treebanks. We found that one complicating factor in the distribution of treebanks is that the creators of the treebank, i.e. the syntactic annotation layer, typically do not own the copyright to the original text. We thus investigate if it would be a viable alternative to use automatically annotated corpora as a training resource. Such an automatically annotated corpus would serve the same purpose as corpus masking (Rehm et al., 2007), i.e. allowing for the distribution of the annotation layer without infringing on the copyright of the original corpus, but while corpus masking loses lexical information, we can learn fully lexicalized statistics from automatically annotated corpora, at the cost of noise in the form of tagging/parsing errors.

In parsing, training on automatically parsed text is known as self-training. Self-training typically yields worse results than training on manually annotated data, with performance depending on the underlying parsing model (Steedman et al., 2003). There are, however, cases where self-training may be beneficial performance-wise, namely as a way to adapt systems to new domains (Steedman et al., 2003; Bacchiani et al., 2006), when using a re-ranker (Charniak and Johnson, 2005) or when considering the confidence score of the parser (Schneider, 2012).

We parsed the German portion of the Europarl corpus (Koehn, 2005) with ParZu, and extracted new statistics from this automatically parsed corpus. We chose Europarl because it has been used extensively in NLP research, especially in Statistical Machine Translation, and comes with no known usage restrictions. We compare three training sets: the original TüBa-D/Z, a training set of equal size (in terms of numbers of tokens: 1 million) from the parsed Europarl corpus, and the full Europarl corpus (1.8 million sentences; 47 million tokens).

We trained POS taggers and parsers on these corpora. For POS tagging, results are shown in table 8. While the taggers perform worse when trained on a segment of Europarl that is the same size as the TüBa-D/Z training corpus, this can be compensated by using the full Europarl corpus. For Sofies Welt, tagging accuracy almost reaches the level of the manually annotated training set, with a performance difference of 0.2-0.3 percentage points. On the TüBa-D/Z test set, the difference remains greater. However, this difference may be partially due to a second effect, namely that the TüBa-D/Z training corpus is in-domain in respect to the TüBa-D/Z test set, but Europarl is not.

Table 9 shows the performance for parsers trained on different training sets. We can see that the performance of MaltParser drops markedly when trained on parsed text, with a drop in f_1

tagger	treebank	TüBa	Sofies Welt
TnT	TüBa-D/Z	97.0	94.7
TnT	Europarl (1)	94.0	93.0
TnT	Europarl (47)	96.0	94.4
CRF	TüBa-D/Z	97.6	96.6
CRF	Europarl (1)	95.4	95.8
CRF	Europarl (47)	96.9	96.4

Table 8: POS tagging accuracy (in percent) with models trained on automatically annotated corpora. CRF with Morphisto.

system	treebank	parsing performance		
		precision	recall	f_1
ParZu	TüBa-D/Z	89.8	89.3	89.5
ParZu	Europarl (1)	89.0	88.5	88.7
ParZu	Europarl (47)	89.2	88.6	88.9
MaltParser	TüBa-D/Z	88.0	88.4	88.2
MaltParser	Europarl (1)	81.0	78.7	79.8
MaltParser	Europarl (47)	[training failed]		

Table 9: parsing performance (in percent) with models trained on automatically parsed text (gold POS tags; Morphisto).

by 8 percentage points. Performance of ParZu is more stable, and decreases by 0.6 percentage points when trained on the parsed Europarl corpus. The reason for this stability is that the role of statistical data in ParZu is limited to the disambiguation of some structures, with the grammar and morphology system constituting two other central knowledge sources for parsing, while MaltParser depends entirely on the data, and is thus more susceptible to noise. We also suspect that the fact that Europarl is from a different domain than the evaluation set accounts for some of the decrease in performance.

We conclude that the performance on self-trained data strongly depends on the statistical models, and also on the domains of the respective training and test sets. The CRF models with morphological features have shown to be more robust than a HMM tagger, and ParZu more robust than MaltParser in a self-training setting.

6 Conclusion

This paper discusses various interactions of three types of NLP tools: dependency parsers, POS taggers, and morphology tools. We demonstrate that the knowledge of morphology tools can be integrated into POS taggers through conditional random field (CRF) models, yielding very accurate models, which are also better at handling unknown words than conventional taggers. While the quality of POS tagging is important for parsing, POS tagging can also be improved with the help of a parser. We show that using n-best tagging, and parse selection based on syntactic features, can improve tagger accuracy. In our experiments, we measured an improvement of 0.5 percentage points in tagging accuracy, starting from a very competitive baseline of 97.8%. Our best system obtains a tagging accuracy of 98.3%, and labelled parsing f_1 of 88.0% on a TüBa-D/Z test set, compared to a baseline tagging accuracy of 94.9%, and labelled parsing f_1 of 84.9%, when using TreeTagger for POS tagging and MaltParser for parsing.

We also discuss and evaluate open alternatives to closed NLP resources. We perform an application-oriented evaluation of morphology tools, which shows that SMOR, both with the official Stuttgart lexicon and Morphisto, are competitive with GERTWOL for the purpose of extracting grammatical constraints, despite some technical challenges such as the idiosyncratic conception of lemmas in the SMOR grammar. Finally, we automatically annotate free corpora in order to use them for model training. These corpora can be distributed without infringing on the copyright of the corpora on which treebanks are based. Training models on these corpora leads to decreased performance compared to the manually annotated treebank, but performance is more robust with the models that integrate other knowledge sources, namely the CRF taggers with morphological features, and ParZu, which contains a hand-written grammar.

Acknowledgements

This research was funded by the Swiss National Science Foundation under grant 105215_126999.

References

Michiel Bacchiani, Michael Riley, Brian Roark, and Richard Sproat. 2006. Map adaptation of stochastic grammars. *Comput. Speech Lang.*, 20(1):41–68.

Miguel Ballesteros and Joakim Nivre. 2012. Malt-Optimizer: A system for MaltParser optimization.

In *Proceedings of the Eight International Conference on Language Resources and Evaluation (LREC'12)*, Istanbul, Turkey.

Sabine Brants, Stefanie Dipper, Silvia Hansen, Wolfgang Lezius, and George Smith. 2002. The TIGER treebank. In *Proceedings of the Workshop on Treebanks and Linguistic Theories*, Sozopol.

Eugene Charniak and Mark Johnson. 2005. Coarse-to-fine n-best parsing and MaxEnt discriminative reranking. In *Proceedings of the 43rd Annual Meeting of the Association for Computational Linguistics (ACL'05)*, pages 173–180, Ann Arbor, Michigan, June. Association for Computational Linguistics.

Killian A. Foth. 2005. *Eine umfassende Constraint-Dependenz-Grammatik des Deutschen*. University of Hamburg, Hamburg.

Mariikka Haapalainen and Ari Majorin. 1995. GERTWOL und Morphologische Disambiguierung für das Deutsche. In *Proceedings of the 10th Nordic Conference of Computational Linguistics*, Helsinki.

Philipp Koehn. 2005. Europarl: A parallel corpus for statistical machine translation. In *Proceedings of the 10th Machine Translation Summit*, pages 79–86, Phuket, Thailand.

John D. Lafferty, Andrew McCallum, and Fernando C. N. Pereira. 2001. Conditional random fields: Probabilistic models for segmenting and labeling sequence data. In *Proceedings of the Eighteenth International Conference on Machine Learning*, pages 282–289, San Francisco, CA, USA. Morgan Kaufmann Publishers Inc.

Thomas Lavergne, Olivier Cappé, and François Yvon. 2010. Practical very large scale CRFs. In *Proceedings the 48th Annual Meeting of the Association for Computational Linguistics*, pages 504–513, Uppsala, Sweden. Association for Computational Linguistics.

Cerstin Mahlow and Michael Piotrowski. 2009. A target-driven evaluation of morphological components for German. In *Searching Answers – Festschrift in Honour of Michael Hess on the Occasion of his 60th birthday*, pages 85–99. MV-Wissenschaft, Münster.

Joakim Nivre. 2009. Non-Projective Dependency Parsing in Expected Linear Time. In *Proceedings of the Joint Conference of the 47th Annual Meeting of the ACL and the 4th International Joint Conference on Natural Language Processing of the AFNLP*, pages 351–359, Suntec, Singapore. Association for Computational Linguistics.

G. Rehm, A. Witt, H. Zinsmeister, and J. Dellert. 2007. Corpus masking: Legally bypassing licensing restrictions for the free distribution of text collections. *Digital Humanities*, pages 166–170.

Helmut Schmid, Arne Fitschen, and Ulrich Heid. 2004. A German computational morphology covering derivation, composition, and inflection. In *Proceedings of the IVth International Conference on Language Resources and Evaluation (LREC 2004)*, pages 1263–1266.

Gerold Schneider. 2008. *Hybrid Long-Distance Functional Dependency Parsing*. Ph.D. thesis, Institute of Computational Linguistics, University of Zurich.

Gerold Schneider. 2012. Using semantic resources to improve a syntactic dependency parser. In *SEM-II workshop at LREC 2012*, pages 67–76, Istanbul, Turkey.

Wolfgang Seeker, Bernd Bohnet, Lilja Øvrelid, and Jonas Kuhn. 2010. Informed ways of improving data-driven dependency parsing for German. In *Proceedings of the 23rd International Conference on Computational Linguistics: Posters*, pages 1122–1130, Beijing, China. Association for Computational Linguistics.

Rico Sennrich, Gerold Schneider, Martin Volk, and Martin Warin. 2009. A New Hybrid Dependency Parser for German. In *Proceedings of the German Society for Computational Linguistics and Language Technology 2009*, pages 115–124, Potsdam, Germany.

Mark Steedman, Steven Baker, Jeremiah Crim, Stephen Clark, Julia Hockenmaier, Rebecca Hwa, Miles Osborne, Paul Ruhlen, and Anoop Sarkar. 2003. Semi-supervised training for statistical parsing. Technical Report CLSP WS-02 Final Report, Johns Hopkins University.

Heike Telljohann, Erhard W. Hinrichs, and Sandra Kübler. 2004. The TüBa-D/Z treebank: Annotating German with a context-free backbone. In *Proceedings of the Fourth International Conference on Language Resources and Evaluation*, Lisbon, Portugal.

Yannick Versley. 2005. Parser evaluation across text types. In *Fourth Workshop on Treebanks and Linguistic Theories (TLT)*, Barcelona, Spain.

Martin Volk, Anne Göhring, Torsten Marek, and Yvonne Samuelsson. 2010. SMULTRON (version 3.0) – The Stockholm MULtilingual parallel TReebank. http://www.cl.uzh.ch/research/paralleltreebanks.html.

Andrea Zielinski and Christian Simon. 2009. Morphisto – an open source morphological analyzer for German. In *Proceedings of the 2009 conference on Finite-State Methods and Natural Language Processing: Post-proceedings of the 7th International Workshop FSMNLP 2008*, pages 224–231, Amsterdam. IOS Press.

Using a Weighted Semantic Network for Lexical Semantic Relatedness

Reda Siblini
Concordia University
1400 de Maisonneuve Blvd. West
Montreal, Quebec, Canada, H3G 1M8
r_sibl@encs.concordia.ca

Leila Kosseim
Concordia University
1400 de Maisonneuve Blvd. West
Montreal, Quebec, Canada, H3G 1M8
kosseim@encs.concordia.ca

Abstract

The measurement of semantic relatedness between two words is an important metric for many natural language processing applications. In this paper, we present a novel approach for measuring semantic relatedness that is based on a weighted semantic network. This approach explores the use of a lexicon, semantic relation types as weights, and word definitions as a basis to calculate semantic relatedness. Our results show that our approach outperforms many lexicon-based methods to semantic relatedness, especially on the TOEFL synonym test, achieving an accuracy of 91.25%.

1 Introduction

Lexical semantic relatedness is a measurement of how two words are related in meaning. Many natural language processing applications such as textual entailment, question answering, or information retrieval require a robust measurement of lexical semantic relatedness. Current approaches to address this problem can be categorized into three main categories: those that rely on a lexicon and its structure, those that use the distributional hypothesis on a large corpus, and hybrid approaches.

In this paper, we propose a new lexicon-based approach to measure semantic relatedness that is based on a weighted semantic network that includes all 26 semantic relations found in WordNet in addition to information found in the glosses.

2 Related Work

Approaches to computing semantic relatedness can be classified into three broad categories: lexicon-based, corpus-based, and hybrid approaches.

Lexicon-based methods use the features of a lexicon to measure semantic relatedness. The most frequently used lexicon is Princeton's WordNet (Fellbaum, 1998) which groups words into synonyms sets (called synsets) and includes various semantic relations between those synsets, in addition to their definitions (or glosses). WordNet contains 26 semantic relations that include: hypernymy, hyponymy, meronymy, and entailment.

To measure relatedness, most of the lexicon-based approaches rely on the structure of the lexicon, such as the semantic link path, depth (Leacock and Chodorow, 1998; Wu and Palmer, 1994), direction (Hirst and St-Onge, 1998), or type (Tsatsaronis et al., 2010). Most of these approaches exploit the hypernym/hyponym relations, but a few approaches have also included the use of other semantic relations. Leacock and Chodorow (1998) for example, computed semantic relatedness as the length of the shortest path between synsets over the depth of the taxonomy. Wu and Palmer (1994) also used the hyponym tree to calculate relatedness by using the depth of the words in the taxonomy and the depth of the least common superconcept between the two words. Hirst and St-Onge (1998), on the other hand, used the lexical chains between words based on their synsets and the semantic edges that connect them. In addition to using the hypernym relations, they classified the relations into classes: "extra strong" for identical words, "strong" for synonyms, "medium strong" for when there is a path between the two, and "not related" for no paths at all. The semantic measurement is then based on the path length and the path direction changes. Tsatsaronis et al. (2010) used a combination of semantic path length, node depth in the hierarchy, and the types of the semantic edges that compose the path.

Figure 1: Example of the semantic network around the word *car*.

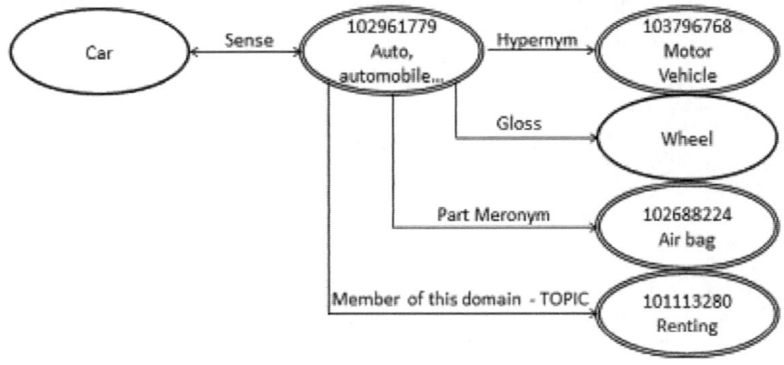

On the other hand, corpus-based approaches rely mainly on distributional properties of words learned from a large corpus to compute semantic relatedness. Such as the work of Finkelstein et al. (2001) that used Latent Semantic Analysis, and the work of Strube and Ponzetto (2006) and Gabrilovich and Markovitch (2007), which both used the distributional hypothesis on Wikipedia.

Finally, hybrid approaches use a combination of corpus-based and lexicon-based methods. For example, the approach proposed by Hughes and Ramage (2007) used a random walk method over a lexicon-based semantic graph supplemented with corpus-based probabilities. Another example is the work of Agirre et al. (2009) that used a supervised machine learning approach to combine three methods: WordNet-based similarity, a bag of word based similarity, and a context window based similarity.

The approach presented in this paper belongs to the lexicon-based category. However, as opposed to the typical lexicon-based approaches described above, our approach uses all 26 semantic relations found in WordNet in addition to information found in glosses. The novelty of this approach is that these relations are used to create an explicit semantic network, where the edges of the network representing the semantic relations are weighted according to the type of the semantic relation. The semantic relatedness is computed as the lowest cost path between a pair of words in the network.

3 Our Approach

Our method to measure semantic relatedness is based on the idea that the types of relations that relate two concepts are a suitable indicator of the semantic relatedness between the two. The type of relations considered includes not only the hyponym/hypernym relations but also all other available semantic relations found in WordNet in addition to word definitions.

3.1 WordNet's Semantic Network

To implement our idea, we created a weighted and directed semantic network based on the content of WordNet. To build the semantic network, we used WordNet 3.1's words and synsets as the nodes of the network. Each word is connected by an edge to its synsets, and each synset is in turn connected to other synsets based on the semantic relations included in WordNet. In addition each synset is connected to the content words contained in its gloss. For example, Figure 1 shows part of the semantic network created around the word *car*. In this graph, single-line ovals represent words, while double-line ovals represent synsets.

By mining WordNet entirely, we created a network of 265,269 nodes connected through a total of 1,919,329 edges. The nodes include all words and synsets, and the edges correspond to all 26 semantic relations in WordNet in addition to the relation between a synset and every content word of a synset definition.

3.2 Semantic Classes of Relations

To compute the semantic relatedness between nodes in the semantic network, it is necessary to take into consideration the semantic relation involved between two nodes. Indeed, WordNet's 26 semantic relations do not contribute equally to the semantic relatedness between words. The *hypernym* relation (relation #2), for example, is a good indicator of semantic relatedness; while the relation of *member of this domain - topic* (relation #15) is less significant. This can be seen in Fig-

Category	Weight	Semantic Relations in WordNet
$Similar$	α	antonym, cause, entailment, participle of verb, pertainym, similar to, verb group
$Hypernym$	$2 \times \alpha$	derivationally related, instance hypernym, hypernym
$Sense$	$4 \times \alpha + \beta$	lemma-synset
$Gloss$	$6 \times \alpha$	lemma-gloss content words
$Part$	$8 \times \alpha$	holonym (part, member, substance), inverse gloss, meronym (part, member, substance)
$Instance$	$10 \times \alpha$	instance hyponym, hyponym
$Other$	$12 \times \alpha$	also see, attribute, domain of synset (topic, region, usage), member of this domain (topic, region, usage)

Table 1: Relations Categories and Corresponding Weights.

ure 1, for example, where the word *car* is more closely related to *Motor vehicle* than to *Renting*. In order to determine the contribution of each relation, we compared a manually created set of 210 semantic relations for their degree of relatedness. For example, for the concept *car* we have compared the sense of *automobile* with the hypernym *motor vehicle*, the gloss word *wheel*, the part meronym *air bag*, the member of this topic *renting*, and another sense of *car* such as a *cable car*. This comparison has lead us to classify the relations into seven categories, and rank these categories from the most related category to the least related one as follows: *Similar* (highest contribution), *Hypernym*, *Sense*, *Gloss*, *Part*, *Instance*, and *Other* (lowest contribution). By classifying WordNet's relations into these classes, we are able to weight the contribution of a relation based on the class it belongs to, as opposed to assigning a contributory weight to each relations. For example, all relations of type *Similar* will contribute equally to the semantic relatedness of words, and will contribute more than any relations of the class *Hypernym*. Table 1 shows the seven semantic categories that we defined, their corresponding weight, and the WordNet relations they include. The weights[1] were simply assigned as a multiple of a small value α, representing the lowest weight, and an addition of 2 for each multiplier in the list in order to represent a higher cost of the less related categories. Let us describe each category in detail.

The category *Similar* includes WordNet's relations of *antonym*, *cause*, *entailment*, *similar to*, *participle of verb*, *pertainym* and *verb group*. This class of relations includes relations that are the most useful to compute semantic relatedness as per our manual corpus analysis and are the rarest available relations in the semantic network and hence was assigned the lowest weight of all categories of relations: α.

The second category of semantic relations is the *Hypernym* which includes WordNet's relations of *hypernym*, *instance hypernym* and *derivationally related*. Being less important than the *similar* relations to compute relatedness, as shown in Table 1, the *Hypernym* category was assigned a weight of $(2 \times \alpha)$.

The *Sense* category represents the relationship between a word and its synset. Because a word can belong to several synsets, in order to favor the most frequent senses as opposed to the infrequent ones, the weight of this category is modulated by a factor β. Specifically, we use $(4 \times \alpha + \beta)$, where β is computed as the ratio of the frequency of the sense number in WordNet over the maximum number of senses for that word.

The fourth category of semantic relations is the *Gloss* that covers relations between synsets and their glosses. A synset gloss contains a brief definition of the synset, which usually consists of a genus (or type) and one or more differentia (or what distinguishes the term from the genus). The genus relations is explicitly defined in WordNet as a hypernym relation, however the differentia is most of the time not defined. The differentia includes essential attributes to the term being defined, that makes it more semantically related to the main term than other attributes. For this reason, we explicitly included those relations in the semantic network. For example, the gloss of the synset *#102961779 car, auto, automobile ...* is *a*

[1]The weight can be seen as the cost of traversing an edge; hence a lower weight is assigned to a highly contributory relation.

Figure 2: Lowest Cost Path Between the Words *Monk* and *Oracle*.

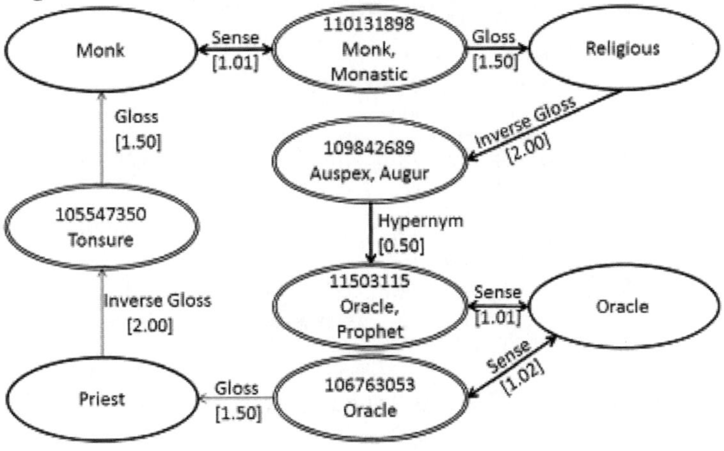

motor vehicle with four wheels, the hypernym of this synset is a *motor vehicle*, and the differentia is *four wheel*. There is no semantic relation explicitly defined in WordNet between *car* and *four wheel*, nor is there a relation with *wheel*. Even if a meronymy relation existed with *wheel* existed in WordNet, it also should be more related to it than the rest of the meronymy relations as it is a defining attribute. To include such relations to the semantic network, we create an edge between every content word in the gloss and the synset, but only consider words that have an entry in the lexicon. As this is a simplistic approach of adding the gloss relations, we gave it a high weight of $(6 \times \alpha)$, but less than the next category covering meronymy relations. The inverse of this edge (from a gloss word to a synset) is also included, but is considered to be less related and thus included in the next category.

The fifth category is the *Part* category that includes *holonymy*, *meronymy*, and *inverse gloss* relations which are all weighted as $(8 \times \alpha)$.

The sixth category, the *Instance* category, only includes the *hyponymy* and *instance of hyponymy* relations that are weighted as $(10 \times \alpha)$.

Finally, all others relations available in WordNet are grouped under the last category *Other* and given the maximum weight of $(12 \times \alpha)$.

3.3 Calculation of Semantic Relatedness

Given the weighted semantic network, the semantic relatedness, $S(w_1, w_2)$, between two words w_1 and w_2 is computed essentially as the weight of the lowest cost path[2] between the two words. However, because the network is directed, the lowest cost from w_1 to w_2, $P_{min}(w_1, w_2)$, may be different than from w_2 to w_1, $P_{min}(w_2, w_1)$. To account for this, we therefore consider the semantic relatedness $S(w_1, w_2)$ to be equal to the highest relatedness score in either direction. More formally, the semantic relatedness between w_1 and w_2 is defined as:

$$S(w_1, w_2) = \max\left(\frac{M - (P_{min}(w_1, w_2) - K)}{M}, \frac{M - (P_{min}(w_2, w_1) - K)}{M} \right)$$

Where, M is a constant representing the weight after which two words are considered unrelated, and K is constant representing the weight of true synonyms. In our implementation, we have set $M = 2 \times (12 \times \alpha)$ corresponding to the maximum of traveling twice the relation with the highest weight, and $K = 2 \times (4 \times \alpha)$ corresponding to the minimum of traveling from a word to its sense and back to the word itself.

3.4 An Example

Figure 2 shows an extract of the network involving the words *Monk* and *Oracle*. The lowest cost path from *Monk* to *Oracle* in highlighted in bold. As the figure shows, the word *Monk* is connected with a *Sense* relation to the synset *#110131898 [Monk, Monastic]*. As indicated in Table 1, the weight of this relation is computed as $(4 \times \alpha + \beta)$. Because

[2]The lowest cost path is based on an implementation of Dijkstras graph search algorithm (Dijkstra, 1959)

Approach	Category	Pearson
(Gabrilovich and Markovitch, 2007)	Corpus	0.72
(Hirst and St-Onge, 1998)	Lexicon	0.74
(Wu and Palmer, 1994)	Lexicon	0.78
(Resnik, 1995)	Hybrid	0.80
(Leacock and Chodorow, 1998)	Lexicon	0.82
(Lin, 1998)	Hybrid	0.83
(Bollegala et al., 2007)	Corpus	0.83
(Jiang and Conrath, 1997)	Hybrid	0.85
(Tsatsaronis et al., 2010)	Lexicon	0.86
(Jarmasz and Szpakowicz, 2003)	Lexicon	0.87
(Hughes and Ramage, 2007)	Lexicon	0.90
(Alvarez and Lim, 2007)	Lexicon	0.91
(Yang and Powers, 2005)	Lexicon	0.92
(Agirre et al., 2009)	Hybrid	0.93
Our approach	Lexicon	0.93

Table 2: Pearson Correlation of Various Approaches on the Miller and Charles Data Set.

this synset is the first sense (the most frequent sense given by WordNet) for the word *Monk*, then (β = 1/75 = 0.01, where 75 is the maximum number of senses for a word in WordNet. If α is set to 0.25, then, as shown in Figure 2, the weight of this edge is computed ($4 \times 0.25 + 0.01 = 1.01$). The synset *#11013898 [Monk, Monastic]* is connected to the word *Religious* through a *Gloss* relation type. In WordNet, the gloss of this synset is: *a male religious living in a cloister and devoting himself to contemplation and prayer and work*. The content words are: *male, religious, live, cloister, devote, contemplation, prayer*, and *work*, which are each related to this synset with the weight set to ($6 \times \alpha = 1.5$).
Overall, the weight of the lowest cost path $P_{min}(Monk, Oracle)$ is hence equal to the sum of the edges shown in Figure 1 (1.01+1.50+2.00+0.50+1.01 = 6.02). As the figure shows, in this example, $P_{min}(Monk, Oracle)$ is identical to $P_{min}(Oracle, Monk)$. With the constants M set to 6 and K to 2, $S(Monk, Oracle)$ will therefore be (6-(6.02-2))/6 = 0.33.

4 Evaluation

To evaluate our approach, we used two types of benchmarks: using human ratings and using synonym tests.

4.1 Evaluation using Human Ratings

In their study on semantic similarity, Miller and Charles (1991) (M&C) gave 38 undergraduate students 30 pairs of nouns to be rated from 0, for no similarity, to 4, for perfect synonymy. The noun pairs were chosen to cover high, intermediate, and low level of similarity and are part of an earlier study Rubenstein and Goodenough (1965) (R&G) which contained 65 pairs of nouns. The M&C test gained popularity among the research community for the evaluation of semantic relatedness. The evaluation is accomplished by calculating the correlation between the average student's ratings and one's approach. The commonly used correlation measurement for this test is the Pearson correlation measurement (Pearson, 1900), but some have also used the Spearman ranking coefficient (Spearman, 1904) as an evaluation measurement. Our approach achieved a Pearson correlation of 0.93 and a Spearman correlation of 0.87 with the M&C data set. In addition, it achieved 0.91 Pearson correlation and 0.92 Spearman correlation on the R&G data set.

For comparative purposes, Table 2 shows the Pearson correlation of several previous approaches to semantic relatedness measures against the same data set, as reported in their respective papers. For information, the table indicates the type of approach used: lexicon-based method, corpus-based method, or hybrid. As Table 2 shows, most other approaches achieve a correlation around 85%, while a few achieve a correlation above 90%. These results do not seem to be influenced by the type approach. Our approach compares favorably to the state of the art in the field on the Miller and Charles data set, with a high correlation of 93%. Our result is higher than any other lexicon based approach, however it must be noted that the Miller and Charles Data Set is quite small for empirical analysis.

WordSimilarity-353 is another set of human ratings that was introduced by Finkelstein et al.

Approach	Category	Spearman
(Strube and Ponzetto, 2006)	Corpus	0.48
(Jarmasz and Szpakowicz, 2003)	Lexicon	0.55
(Hughes and Ramage, 2007)	Lexicon	0.55
(Finkelstein et al., 2001)	Hybrid	0.56
(Gabrilovich and Markovitch, 2007)	Corpus	0.75
(Agirre et al., 2009)	Hybrid	0.78
Our approach	Lexicon	0.50

Table 3: Spearman Correlation of Various Approaches on WordSimilarity-353 Data Set.

Approach	Category	Accuracy
(Resnik, 1995)	Hybrid	32.66%
(Leacock and Chodorow, 1998)	Lexicon	36.00%
(Lin, 1998)	Hybrid	36.00%
(Jiang and Conrath, 1997)	Hybrid	36.00%
(Hirst and St-Onge, 1998)	Lexicon	62.00%
(Turney, 2001)	Corpus	74.00%
(Terra and Clarke, 2003)	Corpus	80.00%
(Jarmasz and Szpakowicz, 2003)	Lexicon	82.00%
(Tsatsaronis et al., 2010)	Lexicon	82.00%
Our Approach	Lexicon	84.00%

Table 4: Results with the ESL Data Set.

(2001). The data set is much larger than the Miller and Charles Data Set and includes 353 pairs of words, each rated by 13 to 16 subjects who were asked to estimate the relatedness of the words on a scale of 0 for "totally unrelated words" to 10 for "very much related or identical words". The common practice with this data set is to the use the Spearman coefficient.

Table 3 shows various approaches and their corresponding Spearman correlation as described in the literature. On this data set, our approach achieved a correlation of 0.50, which is quite lower than the current state of the art. After analysing our results, we identified several reasons why our approach did not perform as expected. First, all lexicon based methods seem to perform poorly on this data set because it includes a number of named entities that are typically not available in a lexicon. For example, in the word pair: *(Maradona – football)*, the word *Maradona* does not appear in WordNet, hence favoring corpus-based and hybrid approaches. Another difficulty is the high variance of human ratings for some word pairs, which could be due to the subjectivity required for this task, or the fact that the subjects who rated the data set were not native English speakers. That being said, perhaps the most important factors for the poor performance is that most of the pairs in that data set require general world knowledge that is not usually available in a lexicon. Nevertheless, other approaches were able to achieve a high correlation with this data set such as the machine learning approach of Agirre et al. (2009) that achieved a high correlation of 0.78.

4.2 Evaluation using Synonym Tests

To test the approach further, we also evaluated it on synonym identification tests. This type of test includes an initial word and a set of options from which the most synonymous word must be selected.

The first synonym test that we experimented with is the English as a Second Language (ESL) test. The test set was first used by Turney (2001) as an evaluation of algorithms measuring the degree of similarity between words. The ESL test includes 50 synonym questions and each having four choices. The following is an example question taken from ESL data set:

```
Text:  A rusty nail is not as strong as
a clean, new one.
Stem:  rusty
Choices:
(a) corroded
(b) black
(c) dirty
(d) painted
Solution:  (a) corroded
```

The results of our approach, along with other approaches, on the 50 ESL questions are shown

Approach	Category	Accuracy
(Resnik, 1995)	Corpus	20.31%
(Leacock and Chodorow, 1998)	Lexicon	21.88%
(Lin, 1998)	Hybrid	24.06%
(Jiang and Conrath, 1997)	Hybrid	25.00%
(Landauer and Dumais, 1997)	Corpus	64.38%
Average non-English US college applicant	*Human*	*64.50%*
(Padó and Lapata, 2007)	Corpus	73.00%
(Hirst and St-Onge, 1998)	Lexicon	77.91%
(Jarmasz and Szpakowicz, 2003)	Lexicon	78.75%
(Terra and Clarke, 2003)	Corpus	81.25%
(Ruiz-Casado et al., 2005)	Corpus	82.55%
(MaTveeva et al., 2007)	Corpus	86.25%
(Tsatsaronis et al., 2010)	Lexicon	87.50%
(Rapp, 2003)	Corpus	92.50%
(Turney et al., 2003)	Hybrid	97.50%
(Bullinaria and Levy, 2012)	Corpus	100.00%
Our Approach	Lexicon	91.25%

Table 5: Results with the TOEFL Data Set.

in Table 4. The results are measured in terms of accuracy - the percentage of correct responses by each approach. Our approach has achieved an accuracy of 84% on the ESL test, which is slightly better than the reported approaches in the literature. It should be noted that sometimes the difference between two approaches belonging to the same category are merely a difference in the data set used (Corpus or Lexicon) rather than a difference in the algorithms. Also, the ESL question set includes a sentence to give a context for the word, which some approaches (e.g. (Turney, 2001)) have used as an additional information source; we on the other hand, did not make use of the context information in our approach.

The second synonym test that we used is the Test of English as a Foreign Language (TOEFL) test. The test was first used by Landauer and Dumais (1997) as an evaluation for the algorithm measuring the degree of similarity between words. The TOEFL test includes 80 synonym questions each having four choices. The following is an example TOEFL question:

```
Stem:  levied
Choices:
(a) imposed
(b) believed
(c) requested
(d) correlated
Solution:  (a) imposed
```

The results on the 80 TOEFL questions are shown in Table 5, which also includes the results of other approaches for comparative purposes. Here again, the results are reported in terms of accuracy. As with the previous experiments, the category of the approach does not seem to have an impact on the results. It should be noted, however, that some of the approaches have been tuned specifically for the TOEFL questions.
Table 5 also includes an entry for the "Average non-English US college applicant" of 64.5%. The score that was originally reported in Landauer and Dumais (1997) is 52.5% for college applicants, however this figure penalizes random guessing by subtracting a penalty of 1/3. To provide a more fair comparison, this penalty has been removed leading to a score of 64.5%. Our approach has achieved an accuracy of 91.25% on the TOEFL test, which is better than any of the reported lexicon based approaches.

5 Conclusion

In this paper we have presented a state of the art semantic relatedness approach that is based on a weighted semantic network. The novelty of the approach is that it uses all 26 relations available in WordNet, along with information found in glosses, and the contribution of each relation to compute the semantic relatedness between pairs of words. This information was mined from WordNet to create a large semantic network consisting of 265,269 concepts connected through a total of 1,919,329 relations. To account for the different contribution of each semantic relation, each edge of the semantic network is assigned a weight according to the category of its semantic relation. All 26 of WordNet's semantic relations and the glosses have been categorised into seven categories, each carrying a weight. Computing the semantic relatedness between two words is now seen as computing the weight of the lowest cost path between the two words in the semantic network. However, because the semantic network is directed, we take the maximum weight among both directions that link the two words.

We evaluated the approach with several benchmarks and achieved interesting results, often among the best systems. Specifically, the approach achieved a Pearson correlation of 0.93 with the M&C human ratings, a Spearman correlation of 0.50 on the Word Similarity353 data set, an accuracy of 84% on the ESL synonym test, and an accuracy of 91.25% on the TOEFL synonym test.

Future work includes performing additional experiments to find the best values for the parameters α, β, and the class weights. Currently, the value of these parameters have been set empirically over several small experiments, but a more formal training to find the best combination of these parameters is necessary. In addition, the semantic information that we tried to include from the gloss have all been categorized into one single category with a unique weight. However, this should be modified to categorize the gloss relations further. For example, extensional types of definitions that specify extensions in the definition are usually less related than differentiating attributes. For example, in the *glow* definition: *have a complexion with a strong bright color, such as red or pink*, the extensions *red or pink* should have a lower relatedness than the attribute *bright* to the concept *glow*. Finally, some important issues in computing lexicon based semantic similarity in general must still be addressed. In particular, all words that are related to another word by the same path will have the same semantic relatedness. For example, a *take out* will have the same semantic relatedness to its sister terms *impulse-buy* and *buy out* by most of the lexicon based approaches as they all have the same path length and depth, however a *take out* can be more of an *impulse buy* than a *buy out* and thus should be more related. In addition, most lexicons do not have pragmatic relations that are important for calculating semantic relatedness, for example the pair *movie* and *popcorn* from the WordSimilarity data set has an average semantic relatedness by 13 different annotators of 6.19/10. however, the lowest cost path between the two in WordNet is through the *physical entity* concept, which means that a *movie* will have a shorter path to a *poison* through the *product* concept than to *popcorn*.

Acknowledgments

The authors would like to thank the anonymous reviewers for their comments on a previous version of this paper.

References

Eneko Agirre, Enrique Alfonseca, Keith Hall, Jana Kravalova, Marius Pasca, and Aitor Soroa. 2009. A study on similarity and relatedness using distributional and wordnet-based approaches. In *Proceedings of Human Language Technologies: The 2009 Annual Conference of the North American Chapter of the Association for Computational Linguistics*, pages 19–27, Boulder, June.

Marco A. Alvarez and SeungJin Lim. 2007. A graph modeling of semantic similarity between words. In *Proceedings of the First IEEE International Conference on Semantic Computing (ICSC 2007)*, pages 355–362, Irvine, September.

Danushka Bollegala, Yutaka Matsuo, and Mitsuru Ishizuka. 2007. Measuring semantic similarity between words using web search engines. In *Proceedings of the Sixteenth International World Wide Web Conference (WWW2007)*, volume 7, pages 757–786, Banff, May.

John A. Bullinaria and Joseph P. Levy. 2012. Extracting semantic representations from word co-occurrence statistics: stop-lists, stemming, and SVD. *Behavior Research Methods*, 44:890–907, September.

Edsger W. Dijkstra. 1959. A note on two problems in connexion with graphs. *Numerische mathematik*, 1(1):269–271.

Christiane Fellbaum. 1998. *WordNet: An Electronic Lexical Database*. MIT Press.

Lev Finkelstein, Evgeniy Gabrilovich, Yossi Matias, Ehud Rivlin, Zach Solan, Gadi Wolfman, and Eytan Ruppin. 2001. Placing search in context: The concept revisited. In *WWW '01: Proceedings of the 10th international conference on World Wide Web*, pages 406–414, New York, May.

Evgeniy Gabrilovich and Shaul Markovitch. 2007. Computing semantic relatedness using wikipedia-based explicit semantic analysis. In *Proceedings of the 20th international joint conference on Artifical intelligence (IJCAI 2007)*, pages 1606–1611, Hyderabad, January.

Graeme Hirst and David St-Onge. 1998. Lexical chains as representations of context for the detection and correction of malapropisms. *WordNet An electronic lexical database*, pages 305–332, April.

Thad Hughes and Daniel Ramage. 2007. Lexical semantic relatedness with random graph walks. In *Proceedings of the Conference on Empirical Methods in Natural Language Processing - Conference on Computational Natural Language Learning (EMNLP-CoNLL)*, pages 581–589, Prague, June.

Mario Jarmasz and Stan Szpakowicz. 2003. Roget's thesaurus and semantic similarity. In *Proceedings of Recent Advances in Natural Language Processing (RANLP 2003)*, pages 212–219, Borovets, September.

Jay J Jiang and David W Conrath. 1997. Semantic similarity based on corpus statistics and lexical taxonomy. In *Proceedings of International Conference on Research in Computational Linguistics*, pages 19–33, Taipei, Taiwan, August.

Thomas K. Landauer and Susan T. Dumais. 1997. A solution to plato's problem: The latent semantic analysis theory of acquisition, induction, and representation of knowledge. *Psychological Review*, 104(2):211–240.

Claudia Leacock and Martin Chodorow. 1998. Combining local context and wordnet similarity for word sense identification. *WordNet: An electronic lexical database*, 49(2):265–283.

Dekang Lin. 1998. An information-theoretic definition of similarity. In *Proceedings of the 15th international conference on Machine Learning (ICML 1998)*, volume 1, pages 296–304, Madison, July.

Irina MaTveeva, Gina-Anne Levow, and Ayman Farahat. 2007. Term representation with generalized latent semantic analysis. *Recent Advances in Natural Language Processing IV*, 292:45.

George A. Miller and Walter G. Charles. 1991. Contextual correlates of semantic similarity. *Language & Cognitive Processes*, 6(1):1–28.

Sebastian Padó and Mirella Lapata. 2007. Dependency-Based Construction of Semantic Space Models. *Computational Linguistics*, 33(2):161–199.

Karl Pearson. 1900. Mathematical contributions to the theory of evolution. On the correlation of characters not quantitatively measurable. *Philosophical Transactions of the Royal Society of London. Series A, Containing Papers of a Mathematical or Physical Character*, 195:1–405.

Reinhard Rapp. 2003. Word Sense Discovery Based on Sense Descriptor Dissimilarity. In *Proceedings of the Ninth Machine Translation Summit*, pages 315–322, New Orleans, September.

Philip Resnik. 1995. Using information content to evaluate semantic similarity in a taxonomy. In *International Joint Conference for Artificial Intelligence (IJCAI-95)*, pages 448–453, Montreal, August.

Herbert Rubenstein and John B. Goodenough. 1965. Contextual correlates of synonymy. *Communications of the ACM*, 8(10):627–633.

Maria Ruiz-Casado, Enrique Alfonseca, and Pablo Castells. 2005. Using context-window overlapping in synonym discovery and ontology extension. In *Proceedings of Recent Advances in Natural Language Processing (RANLP 2005)*, Borovets, September.

Charles Spearman. 1904. The proof and measurement of association between two things. *The American Journal of Psychology*, 15(1):72–101.

Michael Strube and Simone Paolo Ponzetto. 2006. WikiRelate! Computing semantic relatedness using Wikipedia. In *Proceedings of the National Conference on Artificial Intelligence*, volume 21, page 1419, Boston, July.

Egidio Terra and Charles LA Clarke. 2003. Frequency estimates for statistical word similarity measures. In *Proceedings of the 2003 Conference of the North American Chapter of the Association for Computational Linguistics on Human Language Technology (HLT-NAACL '03)*, volume 21, pages 165–172, Edmonton, May.

George Tsatsaronis, Iraklis Varlamis, and Michalis Vazirgiannis. 2010. Text relatedness based on a word thesaurus. *Journal of Artificial Intelligence Research*, 37(1):1–40.

Peter D. Turney, Michael L. Littman, Jeffrey Bigham, and Victor Shnayder. 2003. Combining Independent Modules to Solve Multiple-choice Synonym and Analogy Problems. In *Recent Advances in Natural Language Processing (RANLP 2003)*, pages 101–110, Borovets, September.

Peter Turney. 2001. Mining the Web for Synonyms: PMI-IR versus LSA on TOEFL. In *Proceedings of the Twelfth European Conference on Machine Learning (ECML-2001)*, pages 491–502, Freiburg, Germany, September.

Zhibiao Wu and Martha Palmer. 1994. Verbs semantics and lexical selection. In *Proceedings of the 32nd annual meeting on Association for Computational Linguistics*, pages 133–138, New Mexico, June.

Dongqiang Yang and David MW. Powers. 2005. Measuring semantic similarity in the taxonomy of wordnet. In *Proceedings of the Twenty-eighth Australasian conference on Computer Science*, volume 38, pages 315–322, Newcastle, January.

A New Approach to the POS Tagging Problem Using Evolutionary Computation

Ana Paula Silva
EST-IPCB
dorian@ipcb.pt

Arlindo Silva
EST-IPCB
arlindo@ipcb.pt

Irene Rodrigues
Universidade de Évora
ipr@di.uevora.pt

Abstract

The purpose of part-of-speech tagging is to automatically tag the words of a text, written in a certain language, with labels that usually take the form of acronyms that designate the appropriate parts-of-speech. In this paper we propose a new approach to the problem that divides it in two different tasks: a learning task and an optimization task. We tackled each of those tasks with evolutionary computation techniques: genetic algorithms and a particle swarm optimizer. We emphasize the use of swarm intelligence, not only for the good results achieved, but also because it is one of the first applications of such algorithms to this problem. We believe that this approach is generic enough so that it can be though as an alternative approach to solve other natural language processing tasks that share some fundamental characteristics with the part-of-speech tagging problem. The results obtained in two different English corpora are among the best published ones.

1 Introduction

In most languages, each word has a set of lexical categories that represent the roles that they can assume in a sentence. When the cardinality of this set is greater than one, we say that the word is ambiguous. Typically, the context of a word, i.e., the lexical categories of the surrounding words, is the fundamental piece of information for determining its role in a sentence. For instance, the word *fly* can assume the function of a **verb**, if it follows the word *to*, or can be used as a **noun** if it is preceded by a determiner like *the*. According to this, most taggers take into consideration the context of a word to decide which should be its tag. However, each of the words belonging to a word's context can also be used in different ways, and that means that, in order to solve the problem, a tagger should have some type of disambiguation mechanism that allows it to choose the proper POS tags for all the words of a sentence.

The methods used for solving the POS tagging problem can be divided into two distinct groups, based on the information they use. In one group, we can gather the approaches that use statistical information about the possible contexts of the various word tagging hypotheses. Most of the stochastic taggers are based on hidden Markov models. In the other group, we find rule based taggers (Brill (1995); Wilson and Heywood (2005); Nogueira Dos Santos et al. (2008)). The rules are usually discovered automatically, and its purpose is to correct errors resulting from an initial basic tagging. Brill's tagger (Brill (1995)) is perhaps the most popular tagger based on rules.

More recently, several works following an evolutionary approach have been published. These taggers can also be divided by the type of information they use to solve the problem: statistical information (Araujo (2002); Alba et al. (2006)), and rule-based information (Wilson and Heywood (2005)). In the former, an evolutionary algorithm is used to assign the most likely tag to each word of a sentence, based on a training table that basically has the same information that is used in the traditional probabilistic approaches. The later is inspired by Brill's rule based tagger. In this case a genetic algorithm (GA) is used to evolve a set of transformations rules, which will be used to tag a text in much the same way as in Brill's tagger. While in Araujo (2002) and Alba et al. (2006), the evolutionary algorithm is used to discover the best sequence of tags for the words of a sentence, using an information model based on statistical data, in Wilson and Heywood (2005) the evolutionary algorithm is used to evolve the information model itself, in the form of a set of transformation rules.

In this paper, we present a new evolutionary approach to the POS tagging problem. Our strategy implies a division of the problem into two different tasks: a learning task and an optimization task. These are tackled using not only evolutionary algorithms, but also particle swarm optimization (PSO), resulting, as far as we know, in the first attempt to approach this problem using swarm intelligence. Although focusing mainly on the POS tagging problem, we believe that this work may be the foundation for a new paradigm to solve other NLP tasks.

2 Rules Discovery Using Evolutionary Computation

It is our belief that the information stored in the training tables of the probabilistic approach can be interpreted as a set of instances. Each of these instances is typically described by a set of measurable attributes related to the tags of the surrounding words, and is associated with a numerical value that identifies the number of times each one occurs in the training corpus. Naturally, this information is specific to the corpus from which it was collected and does not show any degree of generalization, instead it can easily be interpreted as an extensive and comprehensive collection of information. Hence we are convinced that it is admissible to investigate the possibility of generalizing this information using a classification algorithm. From this generalization we expect to be able to reduce the amount of information needed to solve the problem and also to improve the tagging accuracy. The learned rules may be used, in a similar way to the training table, to guide the search of the POS tagging problem state space. They aim not to classify a given word, but rather assess the quality of a particular classification.

Previous experience with classification rules discovery (Sousa et al. (2004)), using evolutionary computation, has led us to define the classification algorithm based on a covering algorithm. We divided the problem into n distinct classification problems, n being the number of different tags used in the annotated corpus, from which the rules will be learned and that define the tag set E. Each tag $e \in E$ presented in the corpus determines a classifying object, with possible classes taking values from the discrete set $Y = \{Yes, No\}$. The covering algorithm receives as input a set of positive examples and a set of negative examples. It then invokes the search algorithm with the current sets of examples. This algorithm is responsible for determining the best classification rule for the set of training examples it receives as input. At each execution, the rule obtained is stored, along with its quality value, and the set of positive examples is updated by eliminating all the instances covered by the rule. The search algorithm will be executed as many times as necessary, so that all positive examples are covered, i.e., the set of positive examples is the empty set. Therefore, the complete set of rules is obtained by executing the search algorithm m times. Two different search algorithms were tested: one based on a GA and another based on a PSO.

2.1 Prediction attributes and representation

As prediction attributes we used two groups of information. The first group includes six attributes related with the context: the lexical categories of the third, second and first words to the left, and the lexical categories of the first, second, and third words to the right of a particular word. The second group comprises the following information about the words: if the word is capitalized, if the word is the first word of the sentence, if the word has numbers or '.' and numbers, and some words' terminations like ***ed***, ***ing***, ***es***, ***ould***, ***'s***, ***s***. The possible values for each of the first group's attributes are the values of the corpus tag set from which the search algorithm will learn the rules. This set will depend on the annotated corpus used, since the tag set will vary for different annotated corpora. The remaining attributes were defined as boolean.

The training sets were built from the Brown corpus. For each word of the corpus, we collected the values of every attribute in the rule's antecedent, creating a specific training example. Next, for each tag of the tag set, we built a training set made by positive and negative examples of that tag. The building process used to define each of the training sets was the following: for each example e_i of the set of examples, with word w and tag t, if w is an ambiguous word, with S the set of all its possible tags, then put e_i in the set of positive examples of tag t, and put e_i in the set of negative examples of all the tags in S, except t.

We used a binary representation for the rules. The attributes related with the context were codified, each one, by six bits. The first bit indicates whether the attribute should or should not be considered, and the following five bits represent the assumed value of the attribute in question. We adopted a table of 20 entries to store the tag set, and used the binary value represented by five bits to index this table. If the value exceeds the number 20, we used the remainder of the division by 20. The remaining attributes were encoded by 18 bits, two bits for each of the nine attributes. In the same way, the first bit indicates if the attribute should or shouldn't be considered, while the second bit, indicates whether the property is, or is not, present. We adopted a Michigan approach, thus, in both implementations of the search algorithm, each particle/individual represents a rule using the codification described. In short, each particle/individual was composed by $6 \times 6 + 2 \times 9 = 54$ bits.

2.2 Search Algorithm

As we said in the previous section, we implemented the search algorithm in two different ways: using a genetic algorithm and a particle swarm optimizer. For the PSO based search algorithm we adopted the binary version presented by Kennedy (Kennedy and Eberhart (2001)). The genetic algorithm based version follows the classical GA with binary representation (Holland (1992)). We used, as genetic operators, the two point crossover (with 0.75 probability) and the binary mutation (with 0.01 probability). The selection scheme used was a tournament selection with tournaments of size two and $k = 0.8$.

The formula used to evaluate each rule, and therefore to set its quality, is expressed by the well known F_β-measure (see Equation 1). The F_β-measure can be interpreted as a weighted average of precision and recall. We used $\beta = 0.09$, which means we put more emphasis on precision than recall. Each time the search algorithm is invoked by the covering algorithm it returns the best rule found and a numerical value that represents the value of the F_β-measure to that rule. This value will be used as the quality value of the rule by the POS-Tagger, which we will present in the next section.

$$F_\beta(X) = (1 + \beta^2) \times \frac{P(X) \times R(X)}{\beta^2 \times P(X) + R(X)} \quad (1)$$

$$P(X) = \frac{TP}{TP + FP} \quad (2)$$

$$R(X) = \frac{TP}{TP + FN} \quad (3)$$

In Equation 3 TP represents the number of true positives, i.e. the number of instances covered by the rule that are correctly classified; FP represents the number of false positives, i.e. the number of instances covered by the rule that are wrongly classified; FN the number of false negatives, i.e. the number of instances not covered by the rule, whose class matches the training target class.

3 POS-Tagger

By definition, a POS-tagger should receive as input a non annotated sentence, $\mathbf{w}$, made of n words, w_i, and should return the same sentence, but now with all the w_i marked with the appropriate tag. Assuming we know all the possibilities, W_i, of tagging each of the words w_i of the input sentence, the search space of the problem can be defined by the set $W_1 \times W_2 \times \cdots \times W_m$. Therefore the solution can be found by searching the problem state space. We believe that this search can be guided by the disambiguation rules found earlier. We tested two different global search algorithms: a genetic algorithm (GA-Tagger) and a binary particle swarm optimizer (PSO-Tagger).

The taggers developed were designed to receive as inputs a sentence, $\mathbf{w}$, a set of sets of disambiguation rules, D_t, and a dictionary, returning as output the input sentence with each of its words labeled with the correct POS tag. The search algorithm evolves a swarm/population of particles/individuals, that encode, each of them, a sequence of tags for the words of the input sentence. The quality of each particle/individual is measured using the sets of disambiguation rules given as input.

3.1 Representation

The representation used in the two implemented algorithms is slightly different. In the GA-Tagger, we adopted a symbolic representation. An individual is represented by a chromosome $\mathbf{g}$ made of a sequence of genes. The number of genes in a chromosome equals the number of words in the input sentence. Each gene, g_i, proposes a candidate tag for the word, w_i, in the homologous position. The possible alleles for gene g_i, are the elements of the set W_i.

Since we adopted the binary version of the PSO algorithm, we used, in this case, a binary representation. To encode each of the tags belonging to the tag set, we used a string of 5 bits. Therefore, a particle that proposes a tagging for a sentence with n ambiguous words will be represented by $n \times 5$ bits. Each five bits of a particle encode a integer number that indexes a table with as much entries as the possible tags for the correspondent ambiguous word. If the integer number, given by the binary string, exceeds the table size, we use as index the remainder of the division by the table size value.

3.2 Tagging Evaluation

The quality of the overall tagging, $\mathbf{t}$, is given by the sum of the evaluation results of each tag assignment, t_i for each word w_i. A particle/individual representing a sequence of n tags, $\mathbf{t}$, for a sentence with n words will give rise to a set of n pairs $\langle \mathbf{x}_i, t_i \rangle$, with $\mathbf{x}_i$ denoting the correspondent 15-tuple collecting the values of the 15 attributes presented in the disambiguation rule's antecedent. The quality of each tag assignment, t_i, is measured by assessing the quality of the pair $\langle \mathbf{x}_i, t_i \rangle$, with $\mathbf{x}_i$ using Equation 4.

$$h(\langle \mathbf{x}_i, t_i \rangle) = \begin{cases} q_k & \text{If } \langle r_k, q_k \rangle \in D_{t_i} \\ & \text{and } r_k \text{ covers } \mathbf{x}_i \\ 0 & \text{Otherwise} \end{cases} \quad (4)$$

The quality of a particle/individual is given by Equation 5, with T representing the set of all n pairs $\langle \mathbf{x}_i, t_i \rangle$.

$$Quality(T) = \sum_{j=1}^{n} h(T_j) \quad (5)$$

4 Experimental Results

We developed our system in Python and used the resources available on the NLTK (Natural Language Toolkit) package in our experiences. The experimental work was done in two phases. First the disambiguation rules were discovered and, after that, the POS taggers were tested. The results achieved in each phase are presented in the next subsections.

4.1 Disambiguation rules discovery

We used a simplified tag set, composed by 20 tags. This simplified tag set establishes the set of classes we use in our classification algorithm. We ran the covering algorithm for each one of these classes and built, for each one, the respective sets of positive and negative examples. We processed 90% of the Brown corpus in order to extract the training examples, and, for each word found, we built the corresponding instance. The total number of examples extracted from the corpus equaled 929286. We used 6 subsets of this set (with different cardinality) to conduct our experiments. We used sets of size: $3E4$, $4E4$, $5E4$, $6E4$, $7E4$ and $8E4$, which we identified with labels A, B, ..., F. For each subset, we built the sets of positive and negative examples for each tag, using the process described in the previous section.

We tested the classification algorithm both with the GA and the PSO implementation of the search algorithm. We ran the classification algorithm two times with each different implementation for each of the training sets. The GA was run with populations of size 200 for a maximum of 80 generations and the PSO with swarms of 20 particles over 200 generations. In table 1 we present the average number of rules achieved by both algorithms and the correspondent reduction, considering the total number of positive examples $(+)$ adopted.

Although the publications describing previous evolutionary approaches, based on training tables, do not clearly indicate the number of entries of those tables, their size is explicitly mentioned as a sensitive point concerning the algorithm time execution (Araujo (2002)). While unknowing these values, the total number of positive examples considered from each of the training sets adopted, can give us an idea of the size of these tables, since the information used is similar. However, while the large training set in our case has a total of$8E4$, the previous approaches use sets with typically more than $1.5E5$. As we can see in Table 1, the rules discovered by both algorithms, allowed a significant reduction (around 90%) in the number of positive examples considered. The results also show that there are no significant differences in the number of rules discovered by the GA and the PSO.

4.2 POS tagging results

We tested the PSO-Tagger and the GA-Tagger on a test set made of 22562 words of the Brown corpus using the best set of rules found (AG F.1). We ran the PSO-Tagger 20 times with swarms of 10 and 20 particles during 50 and 100 generations. The GA-Tagger was also executed 20 times with populations of 50 and 100 individuals during 10 and 20 generations. These values were chosen so that we could test both algorithms with similar computational effort, considering the number of necessary

Table 1: Average number of rules discovered by the classification algorithm.

			Average number of rules		
Set	+	GA	Reduction	PSO	Reduction
A	25859	2719	89.49%	2715.5	89.49%
B	33513	3081	90.81%	3124.5	90.68%
C	41080	3358.5	91.82%	3327.0	91.90%
D	48612	3735.5	92.32%	3696.5	92.39%
E	55823	4137	92.59%	4033.0	92.78%
F	63515	4399	93.07%	4288.5	93.25%

Table 2: Tagging accuracy results achieved by both POS-taggers on a test set made of 22562 words of the Brown corpus using as heuristic the set AG F.1.

Tagger	Part/Ind	Generations	Average	Best	Standard Deviation
PSO-Tagger	10	50	0.9672658	0.9679550	$2.6534E-4$
		100	0.9673123	0.9676004	$1.9373E-4$
	20	**50**	**0.9674896**	**0.9678220**	$1.9158E-4$
		100	0.9673921	0.9678663	$2.1479E-4$
GA-Tagger	50	10	0.9672170	0.9675561	$1.9200E-4$
		20	0.9672968	0.9674231	$1.1707E-4$
	100	10	0.9672591	0.9675561	$1.4097E-4$
		20	**0.9672835**	**0.9675117**	$1.0978E-4$

evaluations the effort measure.

The results achieved are shown in table 2. As we can see, the best average accuracy was achieved with the PSO-Tagger using a swarm of 20 particles evolving during 50 generations. The best accuracy result returned by the GA-Tagger is worst than the best result obtained with the PSO-Tagger and it needs the double number of evaluations required by the PSO-Tagger. However, the accuracy values displayed by the GA-Tagger are still very competitive when compared with others published using similar approaches.

We also tested the taggers on a test set of the WSJ corpus of the Penn Treebank. As expected, the results achieved by the two taggers on the WSJ corpus, using as heuristic the disambiguation rules learned from the Brown corpus, are inferior to the ones obtained on the Brown corpus. However, we believe that they allow us to conclude that the discovered rules are sufficiently generic so that they can be used in different corpora. This conviction emerges from comparing the obtained results with those published by other evolutionary approaches (see Table 3). Indeed, we found that the accuracy achieved is comparable with the best published results. It is also important to stress that this values are achieved with no previous training on this corpus. The accuracy values for the WSJ corpus presented in Table 3 were achieved using all the corpus available in the NLTK package, in a total of 100676 words.

Table 3, presents the accuracy values achieved by the taggers in both English corpora used, along with the results published by works using similar approaches. These results only reveal that the accuracy values obtained by the two taggers are competitive with those of past approaches. We can not directly compare our results with those published since we have no access to the test set used in the experiments made in the cited works. Nevertheless, we may conclude that for comparable size words sets (in the case of the evolutionary approaches), taken from the same corpora, the results obtained in this work are among the best published. The values shown in Table 3 were converted to percentage values and rounded to the second decimal place, so that they could be more easily compared with the ones presented in the publications cited.

5 Conclusions

We described a new evolutionary approach to the POS tagging problem, which we tested using two distinct algorithms from the evolutionary compu-

Table 3: Results achieved by the two taggers on two english corpora along with the ones published by similar approaches. (Araujo - Araujo (2002); Alba, Alba-GA, Alba-PGA, Alba - Alba et al. (2006); Wilson - Wilson and Heywood (2005); Brill - Brill (1995)).

Corpus	Tagger	Training set	Test set	Best
Brown	PSO-Tagger	80000	22562	**96.78**
	GA-Tagger	80000	22562	96.76
	Araujo	185000	2500	95.40
	Alba-GA	165276	17303	96.67
	Alba-PGA	165276	17303	96.75
WSJ	PSO-Tagger	∅	100676	96.67
	GA-Tagger	∅	100676	96.66
	Wilson	600000	=Training	89.80
	Brill	600000	150000	**97.20**
	Alba	554923	2544	96.63

tation field: a GA and a PSO. We would like to emphasize the fact that, to the best of our knowledge, this was the first attempt to apply a PSO to solve the POS tagging problem, and that, in general, there are few approaches based on swarm intelligence to solve NLP tasks.

The experiments made using the WSJ corpus and the disambiguation rules extracted from the Brown corpus gave us an idea of the degree of generalization achieved by the adopted classification algorithm. From those results, we were able to confirm that the rules obtained are sufficiently generic to be applied on different corpora. The attained generalization also reflected a substantial reduction in the information volume needed to solve the problem, while contemplating, besides the typical context information, other aspects related, not to the POS tags, but to the words' characteristics. Although we didn't present any example of the learned rules, we would like to point out the advantages of representing the information in the typical classification rule format, when compared to the numerical values used in the probabilistic approaches. The comprehensibility of the learned rules, which can be represented by predicate logic, allows its easy application in different contexts.

It is our conviction that the presented approach can be viewed as a new paradigm for solving a set of NLP tasks that share some of the features of the POS tagging problem and that are currently mainly solved by probabilistic approaches. Therefore, we are planning to extend this method to other tasks that also need some kind of disambiguation in the resolution process, like noun-phrase chunking, the named-entity recognition problem, sentiment analysis, etc.

References

Alba, E., Luque, G., and Araujo, L. (2006). Natural language tagging with genetic algorithms. *Inf. Process. Lett.*, 100(5):173–182.

Araujo, L. (2002). Part-of-speech tagging with evolutionary algorithms. In Gelbukh, A., editor, *Computational Linguistics and Intelligent Text Processing*, volume 2276 of *Lecture Notes in Computer Science*, pages 187–203. Springer Berlin / Heidelberg.

Brill, E. (1995). Transformation-based error-driven learning and natural language processing: a case study in part-of-speech tagging. *Comput. Linguist.*, 21:543–565.

Holland, J. (1992). Genetic Algorithms. *Scientific American*, 267(1).

Kennedy, J. and Eberhart, R. C. (2001). *Swarm intelligence*. Morgan Kaufmann Publishers Inc., San Francisco, CA, USA.

Nogueira Dos Santos, C., Milidiú, R. L., and Rentería, R. P. (2008). Portuguese part-of-speech tagging using entropy guided transformation learning. In *Proceedings of the 8th international conference on Computational Processing of the Portuguese Language*, PROPOR '08, pages 143–152, Berlin, Heidelberg. Springer-Verlag.

Sousa, T., Silva, A., and Neves, A. (2004). Particle swarm based data mining algorithms for classification tasks. *Parallel Computing*, 30(5):767–783.

Wilson, G. and Heywood, M. (2005). Use of a genetic algorithm in brill's transformation-based part-of-speech tagger. In *Proceedings of the 2005 conference on Genetic and evolutionary computation*, GECCO '05, pages 2067–2073, New York, NY, USA. ACM.

How Joe and Jane Tweet about Their Health: Mining for Personal Health Information on Twitter

Marina Sokolova
CHEO Research Institute
University of Ottawa
sokolova@uottawa.ca

Stan Matwin
Dalhousie University
University of Ottawa
stan@cs.dal.ca

Yasser Jafer
University of Ottawa
yjafe089@uottawa.ca

David Schramm
CHEO and University of Ottawa
dschramm@toh.on.ca

Abstract

With 19%–28% of Internet users participating in online health discussions, it became imperative to be able to detect and analyze posted personal health information (PHI). In this work we introduce two semantic-based methods for mining PHI on social networks which will warn the users about potential privacy breaches. One method uses WordNet as a source of health-related knowledge, another - an ontology of personal relations. We use Twitter data to empirically evaluate our methods. We also apply Machine Learning to demonstrate advantages of our extraction procedure when tweets containing PHI have to be automatically identified among other tweets.

Keywords: Text mining, Twitter, Personal Health Information, Machine Learning

1 Introduction

Online networking websites *Facebook, Twitter, PatientsLikeMe* became popular communication hubs connecting millions of individuals. In casually written messages (posts, tweets, updates), people discuss life experience (`i plan to stay home and watch christmas movies while I get better`) and comment on various events (`The discovery was made via CAT scans`) [1] amongst others.

While posting about personal health, a user reveals details that in pre-social network era were usually discussed during visits to a health care provider or in a family setting. This detailed health description is called Personal Health Information (PHI) (Hersh, 2009). Posted online PHI is used in several practical applications: formulating Web policies, including privacy and confidentiality concerns or information leak prevention (Ghazinour et al, 2013a), understanding population response on health care policies (vaccination, immunization)(Chew and Eysenbach, 2010), and an early detection of adverse health-related events (Lampos and Christianini, 2010).

Recent studies of 11,000 posts on a social network showed deficiencies of traditional electronic sources of medical information in the task PHI detection (Ghazinour et al, 2013b).

Our current work aims to show that it is possible to considerably improve accuracy of PHI extraction from social networks. Our approach uses the PHI ontology presented in (Sokolova and Schramm, 2011). The ontology's structure and terms reflect on patient communications in health care setting. In this paper, we present two semantic-based enhancements of the ontology and apply them to extract PHI in Twitter. One enhancement uses WordNet as a source of health-related knowledge, another – an ontology of personal relations.

We use manual analysis to demonstrate that incorporating semantic information significantly improves *Precision* and *Fscore* of the PHI text retrieval. We also apply Machine Learning methods to show the advantage of our approach in automated detection of PHI. Partial preliminary results of this work had been reported in (Sokolova et al, 2012).

2 Vocabulary Resources for PHI detection

It has been estimated that 19% – 28% of all Internet users participate in medical online forums, health-focused groups and communities and visit health-dedicated web sites (Baliccon and Paganelli, 2011),(Renahy, 2008). People share their health-related worries and medical conditions.

[1] All messages have authentical spelling and content.

Person		Diseases and Related Problems		Health Care System	
Anatomical parts	`head, kidneys`	Diseases	`arthritis, depression`	Providers	`dentist, surgeon`
Physiological functioning	`insomnia, pregnancy`	Symptoms	`fever, pain`	Setting	`ambulance, hospital`

Table 1: Examples of categories and terms of the PHI ontology

Automated text analysis often uses only a key word search to find PHI in the user posts. For example, in relation to the H1N1 pandemic in 2008–2009, occurrences of the PHI textual markers (`fever, temperature, sore throat, flu`) were traced in several geographic areas (Lampos and Christianini, 2010). The extracted tweets, however, were not analyzed if they indeed contain PHI, and all the retrieved messages were considered equally important.

A simple example illustrates limitations of the key word search. The following messages are extracted with a keyword `flu`: (`you are funny comparing the Iphone to a flu shot lol nice`) and (`I am trying to recover from my turn with the flu`).

Whereas the latter message is relevant to personal health, the former is not, but both were counted towards the flu symptoms.

The use of specialized resources of health-related terms can focus the analysis by refraining from the extraction of text irrelevant to PHI. In (Ghazinour et al, 2013b), the authors applied semantic analysis and domain knowledge, to find MedDRA and SNOMED terms related to personal health.

Below we compare the effectiveness of both resources with the PHI ontology (Sokolova and Schramm, 2011). The ontology contains a four–level hierarchy of concept categories corresponding to health discussions by the general public. The categories reference to anatomical parts and physiological functioning of body, diseases and symptoms, and the health care system. Extensive clinical experience of one of the authors was applied to empirically adapt the taxonomies to patients description of their health. As a result, the ontology contained 500 terms commonly used by patients in clinical setting. Table 1 lists two upper-level categories and examples of terms.

It should be emphasized that the presence of one or more health ontology term(s) does not necessarily guarantee that this tweet refers to personal health. In `well Im keeping my eye on you just so you know`, the word `eye` indicates "anatomical body part" but the message does not refer to personal health. Therefore, manual screening of the extracted messages is required in order to remove irrelevant messages.

We worked with the Twitter data from the Content analysis of Web 2.0 workshop [2]. The data was organized as threads, i.e. consecutive tweets posted by users. Only conversational tweets were present; spam, ads, organizational and promotional tweets were discarded. In this work, we use the tweet content, but not the meta characteristics (e.g., time and geo-locations of tweets).

We manually analyzed usefulness of health terms in extraction of tweets containing PHI. The original Twitter set has been organized in threads; hence, we used this unit in the selection step. To decrease an impact of a possible selection bias, we ran five rounds of random thread selection. Each round selected 200 threads. For each selected set, we extracted tweets with the health terms. 3017 tweets were extracted in total, from those 889 tweets contained PHI. Based on the manual analysis, the performance was evaluated by

$$Coverage = \frac{|Extracted\ texts|}{|Texts\ in\ corpora|} \quad (1)$$

$$Precision = \frac{|Extracted\ texts\ with\ PHI|}{|Extracted\ texts\ |} \quad (2)$$

$$Recall = \frac{|Extracted\ texts\ with\ PHI|}{|Texts\ with\ PHI|} \quad (3)$$

$$F - score = \frac{2PrecisionRecall}{Precision\ + Recall} \quad (4)$$

The extraction results were consistent across all the five subsets and significantly more accurate

[2]http://caw2.barcelonamedia.org/node/7

Tools	# of terms	Texts in corpora	Extracted texts	Extracted texts with PHI	*Coverage*	*Precision*	*F-score*
MedDRA-PHI	8561	11000	744	86	0.068	0.12	0.21
SNOMED-PHI	44802	11000	673	108	0.061	0.16	0.28
PHI ontology	500	36315	3017	889	**0.083**	**0.30**	**0.46**

Table 2: PHI extraction using MedDRA-PHI, SNOMED-PHI, and the PHI ontology terms. *Recall* = 1.00 for the three sources. MedDRA and SNOMED results are adapted from (Ghazinour et al, 2013b)

PHI ontology	Performance improvement		
vs	*Coverage*	*Precision*	*F-score*
MedDRA-PHI	122%	250%	220%
SNOMED-PHI	136%	188%	164%

Table 3: Advantage of the use of the PHI ontology in extraction of PHI texts

Data	*Precision*	*F-score*
All PHI tweets	0.30	0.46
PHI tweets with the PO	**0.41**	**0.58**
PHI tweets sans the PO	0.25	0.40

Table 4: Impact of the PO terms in extraction of PHI texts.

than those of MedDRA-PHI and SNOMED-PHI. Table 2 presents the results of the extraction, Table 3 exemplifies benefits of the PHI ontology over MedDRA-PHI and SNOMED-PHI in extraction of texts containing PHI.

Manual analysis of the extracted tweets revealed that most of tweets that do not reveal PHI were extracted with the PHI ontology terms from the Body and Organs categories. Among them, `head, hand, heart` were the top contributors to extraction of non-relevant messages (e.g., `back to work, lolo get outta my head`).

3 Semantic Enhancement of the PHI Extraction

In the current work we wanted to improve *Precision* of the extraction, without jeopardizing *Recall*, and reduce dependance on a manual analysis. We decided to reinforce the lexicon-based search with semantic enhancement. We used enhancement specific to PHI disclosure: a) a set of personal references organized as ontology of personal terms (Section 3.1), b) health terms' semantic information provided by WordNet (Section 3.2). We used *Precision(Pr)*, *Recall(R)*, *Fscore(F)* to evaluate the performance.

3.1 Ontology of Personal Terms

We observed that in messages discussing personal health, a user often directly refers to the person whose information is disclosed. This could be the user itself (e.g. `appointment at the plastic surgeon today for my scar from the accident`) or relatives (e.g. `my oldest had his th bday today & he had the stomach flu`).

We marked such references and then organized them in Ontology of Personal Terms (PO). At this point, the ontology includes terms representing the relationship between the user and family members. The terms were divided into four lexical categories, namely, Subjects, (e.g. `I, he, she`), Possessive Determiners (e.g. `my, his, her`), Relatives (e.g. `son, daughter, parents`), and verbs of belonging (e.g. `has, have, was`).

We expected a higher accuracy of detection and extraction of health information related to an individual when the health ontology is enhanced with the personal ontology. We started with incorporation of the PO terms into the tweet retrieval. On this step, we were looking for the impact of personal terms on retrieval of tweets with PHI. We grouped all the tweets retrieved with PHI terms into two sets: with explicit personal reference (i.e., with PO terms), such as (`I am trying to recover from my turn with the flu`), and without explicit personal reference (i.e., no PO terms), such as (`PSA tylenol cough & sore throat has more cough suppresant than all overthecounter cough syrups`).

We manually analyzed how PO terms contribute to the accuracy of extraction of tweets with PHI. Presence of the PO terms in PHI tweets increased *Precision* by 64%, *F-score* – by 45 % (Table 4).

terms	# of synsets
`Allergy, Hospital`	1
`Anxiety, Fever`	2
`Dizzy, Emergency`	3
`Sore, Panic`	4
`Tooth, Itching`	5
`Diet, Stomach`	6
`Infection, Pain`	7
`Hurt, Stress`	≥ 8

Table 5: Examples of the PHI terms and the number of their synsets.

3.2 Semantic Information from WordNet

WordNet[3] groups words in sets of cognitive synonyms (i.e., synsets), builds super-subordinate relations of the synsets, differentiates between common nouns and specific instances, etc. Each term has a number of corresponding synsets; the synsets are ordered from the most common to the least common. For example, the word `fever` has the representation:

- S: (n) fever, febrility, febricity, pyrexia, feverishness (a rise in the temperature of the body; frequently a symptom of infection);
- S: (n) fever (intense nervous anticipation) (in a fever of resentment).

The representation shows that `fever` more often signifies a rise in a body temperature than a nervous anticipation.

The number of synsets is a strong indicator of the number of different senses of the word (i.e. ambiguity). For health terms, a lesser number of synsets show a stronger correspondence of the term to personal health information. Table 5 lists examples of the health terms and the number of their synsets.

The rank of the health-related synset among the all synsets of the term is another strong indicator of the usefulness of the term in the given context. For example, `fever` has the rank 1 as its health-related synset is 1. Preliminary observations showed that 1st rank of the term's health synset is a strong indicator of the term relevance to personal health information.

3.3 Evaluation of Semantic Enhancement

To assess how accurate health terms are in the recognition of the tweets with PHI, we looked at the number of synsets and the health-related rank of the terms. We then manually analyzed tweets extracted with health terms and subdivided them into those with PHI and others. To follow the impact of the number of synsets and the health-realted rank, we divided health terms into 15 groups: those with 1 synset, those with 2 synsets and 1st health-related rank; other health terms with 2 synsets; ...; those with 7 synsets and 1st health -related rank; other health terms with 7 synsets; those with ≥ 8 synsets and 1st health-related rank; other health terms with ≥ 8 synsets.

[3]http://wordnet.princeton.edu/

PHI tweets with the PO terms	
Best Precision	0.774
Best F-score	0.652
PHI tweets without the PO terms	
Best Precision	0.738
Best F-score	0.649

Table 6: The best *F-score* and *Precision* of the PHI tweets extraction.

We computed *Precision* and *Fscore* of the extraction methods. Our empirical evidence showed that albeit the least ambiguous terms of synsets 1 and 2 give the highest *Precision*, the optimal *Fscore* is reached when the number of synsets reaches 6. Moreover, *Fscore*'s optimum at synset 6 is independent from the presence of personal ontology terms. In other words, it holds in both cases of personal health information extraction – with the PO terms and without them. Table 6 lists the best *F-score* and *Precision*. Note that our *Recall*= 100%.

The results showed that as the number of synsets associated with ontology terms increases, *Precision* of the extraction decreases but only slightly. This is an expected result of the word sense disambiguation, since, with more meanings associated with a given term, the more likely it is to be used in the non-health related contexts. This result, however, supported our premise of the importance of incorporating semantic information into the search.

4 Machine Learning of Tweets with PHI

On average, 200,000,000 tweets appear daily. [4] To be able to follow and extract tweets with PHI, we need to employ advanced automated software. In this section we show the advantage of using the

[4]https://blog.twitter.com/2011/200-million-tweets-day

Class	Relation to PHI	# of tweets
Class 1	the tweets with PHI	252
Class 2	tweets preceding PHI	251
Class 3	tweets following PHI	240

Table 7: Multi-class learning of PHI.

PHI ontology in Machine Learning of tweets containing PHI.

4.1 Classification problems

We apply classification technique to demonstrate that tweets with PHI are reliably differentiated from tweets without PHI if the extraction procedure used the PHI ontology. Hence, we classify the extracted tweets with PHI vs tweets without PHI. We use two types of tweets without PHI: a) those preceding the tweets with PHI, b) those following the tweets with PHI.

As a result, we state the learning experiments as a three-class classification problem. Classes are described in Table 7.

We applied Naive Bayes (NB) because of its reliable performance in previous Twitter classification studies (Bobicev et al., 2012).

4.2 Feature sets

Our next task was to define sets of words (i.e., features) that will represent tweets in classification. We contemplated between semantic PHI features and statistically selected features. We considered the use of semantic features to be undesirable. Semantic features were used to extract the tweets with PHI, thus representing tweets through them would bias an algorithm towards recognition of the tweets with PHI. On the other hand, we did not use the word statistic during the extraction procedure, thus, there would not be a pre-set classification bias if the features were selected statistically. Based on this consideration, we used four feature sets to represent the data:

Features I: all words with occurrence > 2;

Features II: words occur. > 2 that form the smallest subset of words which showed a better prediction of the class labels on the training set;

Features III: all words with occurrence > 5;

Features IV: words occur. > 5 that form the smallest subset of words which showed a better prediction of the class labels on the training set.

Three-class learning				
Features	*AUC*	*P*	*R*	*F*
I	**0.621**	0.459	0.448	0.452
II	0.569	0.386	0.388	0.386
III	0.607	**0.464**	**0.451**	**0.455**
I V	0.519	0.372	0.370	0.369
Baseline	0.497	0.115	0.339	0.172

Table 8: Classification of tweets with PHI. The best results are in **bold**.

4.3 Three-class learning

We used 10-fold cross-validation for the best classifier selection. We evaluated the performance by *Precision*, *Recall*, and *F-score*. Due to a relative imbalance of the data, we used *AUC* instead of a more traditional *Accuracy*. Also, *AUC*, representing a single point of the Reception Operating Characteristic curve, focuses on classifier's ability to avoid false classification (Sokolova and Lapalme, 2009).

Table 8 reports the average learning results. We computed baseline as the majority class classification.

The results show that classification beat the baseline on every feature set. The two-tailed t-test gives P equal to 0.067, 0.172, **0.064**, 0.220 on the four feature sets respectively. The most accurate identification of tweets with PHI happens when they are represented through words with occur. > 5, i.e., *P*, *R* and *F* are the highest. The most balanced identification of all the three classes happened on words with occur > 2, i.e. *AUC* is the highest. In the current case the feature selection substantially diminished the performance accuracy, unlike in previously reported studies of tweets with PHI(Bobicev et al., 2012).

We also wanted to know how well each class is differentiated among the three classes, depending on the features selected. Table 9 reports the classification results for each class separately.

We again see that the best identification of classes happens when the classifier can access words without any pre-selection. All the highest values but one were obtained on features representing words with occur. > 2 and > 5.

5 Related Work

We identify three major trends in mining for PHI on the Web.

Message boards In (Doing-Harris and Zeng-

Class I (Tweets with PHI)				
Features	*AUC*	*P*	*R*	*F*
I	**0.752**	0.607	**0.511**	0.555
II	0.624	0.426	0.458	0.442
III	0.700	**0.618**	0.508	**0.558**
I V	0.565	0.419	0.394	0.407
Class II (Tweets preceding PHI)				
Features	*AUC*	*P*	*R*	*F*
I	**0.580**	**0.408**	0.462	**0.433**
II	0.556	0.379	0.410	0.394
III	0.566	0.393	**0.470**	0.428
I V	0.500	0.347	0.414	0.377
Class III (Tweets following PHI)				
Features	*AUC*	*P*	*R*	*F*
I	0.531	0.362	**0.371**	0.366
II	**0.556**	0.351	0.295	0.32 0
III	0.554	**0.377**	**0.371**	**0.374**
I V	0.490	0.348	0.299	0.321

Table 9: Individual class recognition. The best results for each class are in **bold**.

Treiler, 2011), the authors extracted healthrelated terms from messages posted on PatientsLikeMe.com. To build a preliminary list of words, the authors applied entity recognition (dictionary look-ups, automated term recognition), N-gram modeling (frequency of consecutive words appearing in the messages) and symbolic processing (part-of-speech tagging and sentence parsing). User requests posted on an involuntary childlessness message board were studied (Himmel et al., 2009). In (Sokolova and Bobicev, 2011), the authors analyzed discussions about medications, treatment, illness and cure. Manual and automated methods were applied to recognize positive, negative and neutral opinions and positive and negative sentiments.

Blogsphere A keyword search was applied to the analysis of blogs written by military servicemen (Konovalov et al., 2010). The authors focused on finding terms that described clinically relevant combat exposure. In (Lagu et al., 2008), the authors manually examined blogs retrieved through Google searches medical blog, physician blog, doctor blog, nurse blog. The goal was to find blogs written by physicians or nurses that included some medical content (e.g., comments about health care system, laboratory studies).

Micro-blogosphere The occurrence of H1N1-related terms was studied in (Lampos and Cristianini, 2010).The extraction method traced tweets that contained H1N1 and its synonyms (e.g., swine flu). Numerical evaluation of the methods' accuracy were reported by the authors of the both papers. Bobicev et al (2012) studied tweets that reveal PHI. However, their work was focused on sentiment analysis of these tweets.

6 Conclusions and Future Work

In this work, we have presented a mining method for personal health information in Twitter. We have shown that the use of the PHI ontology considerably improves PHI extraction if compared with other electronic resources of health information. We also have analyzed the impact of term meanings (WordNet) and general semantics (ontology of personal relations) on the extraction of PHI. We have demonstrated that semantic enhancement allows a reliable identification of messages with the topic of personal health.

We applied Machine Learning to demonstrate the advantage of our extraction method in classification of tweets with PHI. The need for classification arises because of a large amount of tweets appearing daily (approx. 200 mil. per day). A three-class classification had shown considerable improvement over the baseline results.

The presented work for mining Twitter messages is novel in several ways. First, it is specific to personal health information. Second, we incorporate health-related semantics into the mining process, and third, we build language patterns indicative for discussion of personal health information. To the best of our knowledge, there has not been a similar effort in mining information in Twitter.

Our future work includes text mining of lists of tweets posted by the same user (threads), analysis of the health information dissemination among the users. We will apply our approach on a considerably bigger set of the Twitter data. Finally, we aim to use posts from other social networks to look for similarities in the discussion of personal health on the Web.

Acknowledgments

This work was in part supported by NSERC Strategic Projects grant and CHEO Department of Surgery Research grant.

References

The title, the publication venue, the year.

Balicco, L., and Paganelli, C. 2011. Access to health information: going from professional to public practices Information Systems and Economic Intelligence: 4th International Conference - SIIE'2011

Bobicev, V., M. Sokolova, Y. Jafer, D. Schramm. Learning Sentiments from Tweets with Personal Health Information, Proceedings of Canadian AI 2012, Springer, 2012.

Chanlekha, H. and Collier, N. Analysis of syntactic and semantic features for fine-grained event-spatial understanding in outbreak news reports, Journal of Biomedical Semantics, 1(3), 2010.

Chew, C. and G. Eysenbach. Pandemics in the Age of Twitter: Content Analysis of Tweets during the 2009 H1N1 Outbreak. PLoS One, 5(11), 2010.

Doing-Harris, K. and Q. Zeng-Treiler. Computer-Assisted Update of a Consumer Health Vocabulary Through Mining of Social Network Data. Journal of Medical Internet Research, 13(2):e37, 2011.

Ghazinour, K., S. Matwin, M. Sokolova. Monitoring and Recommending Privacy Settings in Social Networks, Proceedings of the 6th International Workshop on Privacy and Anonymity in the Information Society (PAIS 2013), p.p. 164 – 168, 2013.

Ghazinour, K., M. Sokolova, S. Matwin. Detecting Health-related Privacy Leaks in Social Networks Using Text Mining Tools, in Advances in Artificial Intelligence 26, Springer, 2013.

Himmel, W. and U. Reincke, H. Michelmann. Text Mining and Natural Language Processing Approaches for Automatic Categorization of Lay Requests to Web-Based Expert Forums. Journal of Medical Internet Research, 11(3):e25, 2009.

Hersh W., Information retrieval: a health and biomedical perspective, 3rd ed., Springer, 2009.

Konovalov, S., M. Scotch, L. Post, C. Brandt. Biomedical Informatics Techniques for Processing and Analyzing Web Blogs of Military Service Members. Journal of Medical Internet Research, 12(4):e45, 2010.

Lagu, T., E. Kaufman, D. Asch, and K. Armstrong. 2008. Content of Weblogs Written by Health Professionals. Journal of General Internal Medicine, 23 (10): 1642–1646, 2008.

Lampos, V. and N. Christianini. "Tracking the flu pandemic by monitoring the social web". 2nd Workshop on Cognitive Information Processing, 2010.

Renahy, E. 2008. Recherche bd'infomation en matiere de sante sur INternet: determinants, practiques et impact sur la sante et le recours aux soins., Paris 6.

Sokolova, M. and G. Lapalme. "A Systematic Analysis of Performance Measures for Classification Tasks", Information Processing and Management, 45, p. 427–437, Elsevier, 2009.

Sokolova, M. and V. Bobicev. Sentiments and Opinions in Health-related Web messages. Recent Advances in Natural Language Processing, p.p. 132–139, 2011.

Sokolova, M. and D. Schramm. Building a patient-based ontology for mining user-written content. Recent Advances in Natural Language Processing, p.p. 758–763, 2011.

Sokolova, M., Jafer, Y., Schramm, D. "Text Mining for Personal Health Information on Twitter", Proceedings of IEEE HISB 2012

Sutton, C. and McCallum, A."An Introduction to Conditional Random Fields". Foundations and Trends in Machine Learning 4 (4), 2012.

Witten, I, E., Frank, M. Hall. Data Mining: Practical Machine Learning Tools and Techniques, Morgan Kaufmann, 2011.

What Sentiments Can Be Found in Medical Forums?

Marina Sokolova
CHEOR Research Institute
University of Ottawa
sokolova@uottawa.ca

Victoria Bobicev
Technical University of Moldova
vika@rol.md

Abstract

In this work we present sentiment analysis of messages posted on a medical forum. We categorize posts, written in English, into five categories: *encouragement, gratitude, confusion, facts,* and *facts + sentiments*. Our study applies a manual sentiment annotation, affective lexicons in its sentiment analysis and machine learning classification of sentiments in these texts. We report empirical results obtained from analysis of 752 posts dedicated to infertility treatments. Our best results improve multi-class sentiment classification of online messages (*F-score* = 0.518, *AUC*= 0.685).

1 Introduction

User-friendly Web 2.0 technologies encourage the general public actively participate in the creation of the Web content. Blogs, social networks, message boards reach out to a global community of the Web users. The online texts discuss personal experience and convey sentiments and emotions of the authors. These emotion-rich posts are known to be important in setting interaction patterns among members of online communities as emotion-rich text has a strong influence on a public mood (Allan, 2005). Subjective information posted by a user may affect subjectivity in posts written by other users (Zafarani et al 2010).

Studies of online sentiments and opinions can help in understanding of sentiments and opinions of the public at large. Such understanding is especially important for the development of public policies whose success greatly depends on public attitudes. Among major policy issues (e.g., education, internal and foreign affairs), health care policies are those that directly affect everybody and cause many online discussions. A 2011 survey of the US population estimated that 59% of all adults have looked online for information about health topics such as a specific disease or treatment (Fox 2011). Reproductive technologies belong to a group of hotly debated health care issues in the modern societies (Zillen 2011). The systematic review of 19 studies from 1999-2009 listed several reasons for the use of medical forums: a) information searching - to learn about psychological, physical and social aspects of available treatments, evaluations of alternative treatments; b) in seeking emotional support - anonymous communication, immediate and constant community access, easy contact to peers.

We analyzed sentiments expressed by participants of *In Vitro Fertilization* (*IVF*) medical forum.[1] This forum brings together women who use IVF treatments with the hope to conceive. For the empirical analysis, we selected 752 posts that covered 74 topics related to IVF (e.g., *Over 40 and pregnant or trying to be*, *Odds of getting pregnant naturally on a cancelled IVf cycle*, *Going for a second opinion*). Starting with several possible sentiments, we finally categorized text into *encouragement, gratitude, confusion, facts + encouragement,* and *facts*. Texts in which the annotators disagreed on a class label were labeled as *uncertain*.

In the analysis, we applied a three-fold approach. First, we manually annotated the messages and then analyzed agreement between annotators. Second, we used affective lexicons for the sentiment analysis of the data. Next, we identified a multi-class classification problem and ran experiments to automatically classify posts into the five categories. The obtained results show a high agreement between the annotators (*Fleiss Kappa* = 0.73) and significant accuracy improvement over baseline (*F-score* = 0.518, *AUC*= 0.685 vs. the baseline *F-score* = 0.118, *AUC*= 0.491).

[1] http://ivf.ca/forums

2 Related works

Sentiment analysis has become a major research field in Text Data Mining and Computational Linguistics. Machine Learning (ML) methods, affective lexicons, and Natural Language Processing (NLP) apparatus are used to classify text units (e.g., words, sentences, paragraphs) into sentiment categories (Taboada et al, 2011). Availability of on-line data prompted sentiment analysis of user-written messages posted on the Web (Dodds et al. 2011; Thelwall at al., 2010; Jansen et al. 2009; Chmiel et al 2011). In this study, we worked with online messages posted on a medical forum. Hence a message is the main text unit on the Web forums we decided to keep it as our text unit.

Although empirical evidence strongly supports the importance of emotions in health-related messages (Pennebaker and Chung, 2006), there are few studies of the relationship between a subjective language and online discussions of personal health (Smith 2011). 16 categories of opinions and emotions in tweets were presented in (Chew and Eysenbach, 2010). The extraction method looked for tweets with references to H1N1 and its synonyms. However, numerical evaluation of the method was not reported by the authors. Sokolova and Bobicev (2011) studied positive and negative opinions and positive and negative sentiments in the health-related sci.med messages from *20 NewsGroups*.[2] For sentiments, Support Vector Machines obtained the best *Fscore* (70.8%). Sentiments in short health-related messages were studied in (Bobicev et al, 2012). The authors analyzed positive, negative and neutral sentiments expressed in tweets that discuss personal health. The Twitter data, however, contained a limited number of health-related tweets: among 409 analyzed tweets, only 124 tweets discussed personal health. In the current work, we obtained the results on 752 health-related messages, hence, gathered stronger empirical evidence.

Sentiment research often uses lexicons where words are assigned with opinion, sentiment, and emotion categories (Wilson et al, 2005; Strapparava et al, 2006; Strapparava and Mihalcea, 2008). The most popular resources are SentiWordNet[3], WordNetAffect[4] and the Subjectivity lexicon[5]. Although there was a study on the use of affective lexicons in discussion of prescriptive drugs (Goeuriot et al, 2012), to the best of our knowledge, there were no previous applications of affective lexicons to sentiment analysis of online discussions of personal health. In the current work, we experimented with the application of four affective lexicons in the sentiment analysis of online discussions of personal health.

Few publications focused on manual sentiment annotation of online messages. Topic-specific opinions in blogs were evaluated in Osman et al., (2010). Agreement among seven manual annotators was computed for five classification categories, including positive, negative, mixed opinions and non-opinionated and non-relevant categories. Sokolova and Bobicev (2011) evaluated concordance of the manual annotation of messages posted on a medical forum. The results show that annotators more strongly agree on what sentences do *not* belong to positive or negative subjective categories then on what sentences *do* belong to those categories. Bobicev et al (2012) used multiple annotators to categorize tweets into positive and negative sentiments and neutral tweets. The authors found that in annotation of health-related tweets annotators more strongly agreed on negative sentiments than on positive ones (p_{pos}= 0.22, p_{neg} = 0.35). The opposite was true for tweets that did not discuss personal health: annotators more strongly agreed on positive sentiments than on negative ones. Our current study addresses manual assignment of health-related texts with several classification labels.

3 Data

Our current research focuses on sentiment identification in messages posted on IVF forums. Such forums belong to an infertility outreach resource community created by prospective, existing and past IVF (In Vitro Fertilization) patients. The IVF.ca website includes forums: *Cycle Friends*, *Expert Panel*, *Trying to Conceive*, *Socialize*, *In Our Hearts*, *Pregnancy*, *Parenting*, and *Administration*.[6] Every forum hosts a few sub-forums, e.g. the *Cycle Friends* forum has six sub-forums:

[2] http://qwone.com/~jason/20Newsgroups/

[3] http://sentiwordnet.isti.cnr.it/

[4] http://wndomains.fbk.eu/wnaffect.html

[5] http://mpqa.cs.pitt.edu/#subj_lexicon

[6] www.ivf.ca/forums

Introductions, *IVF/FET/IUI Cycle Buddies*, *IVF Ages 35+*, *Waiting Lounge*, *Donor & Surrogacy Buddies*, and *Adoption Buddies*. On every sub-forum, topics are initiated by the forum participants. Depending on the interest among participants, a different number of messages is associated with each topic, e.g., *Human growth hormone & what to expect* has 120 messages posted from Oct 2012, while *Over 40 and pregnant or trying to be* has 3,455 messages posted from May 2010.

We wanted the forum to represent many discussions, and so forums were selected to ensure a high number of topics and large number of posts. The *IVF Ages 35+* sub-forum[7] satisfied both requirements.

In July 2012, it had 510 topics and 16388 messages. At this point, we discharged the largest four topics containing 7498, 2823, 1131 and 222 posts respectively; we will indentify the shortest topics and discharge them later on. Figure 1 presents the statistics for the rest of the topics in this subforum, i.e. the largest four topics are not shown in the chart. Topics are sorted by the number of posts in them in descending order. The topic's rank is its number in the sorted list.

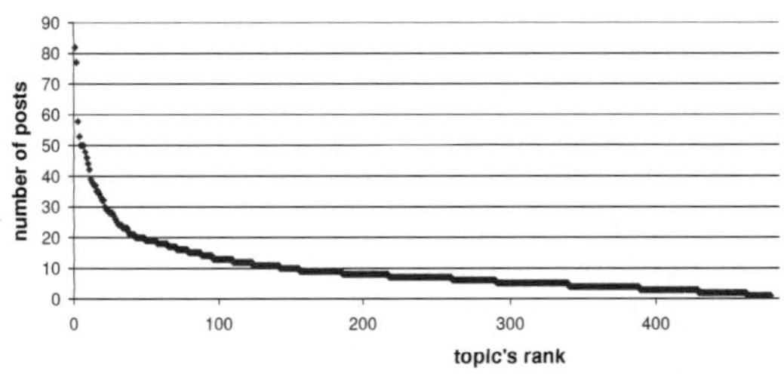

Figure 1: Number of posts per topic in the *IVF Ages 35+* sub-forum

Among the remaining 506 topics, we looked for those where the forum participants discussed only one theme. A preliminary analysis showed that discussions with $\leq$ 20 posts satisfied this condition. Also, we wanted discussions be long enough to form a meaningful discourse. This condition was satisfied when discussion had $\geq$ 10 messages. As a result, for further analysis, we analyzed 74 topics with 10 - 20 posts, with an average 12.5 messages per topic. Most of the topics had a similar structure:

a) a participant started the theme with a post;
b) the initial post usually contained some information about the participant's problem, expressed worry, concern, uncertainty and a request for help to the other forum participants;
c) the following posts:
 i) provided the requested information by describing their similar stories, knowledge about treatment procedures, drugs, doctors and clinics, or
 ii) supplied moral support through compassion, encouragement, wishing all the best, good luck, etc.
d) the participant who started the topic often thanked other contributors and expressed appreciation for their help and support.

4 Manual Annotation

4.1 Model

Annotation of subjectivity can be centered either on the perception of a reader (Strapparava, Mihalceal, 2008) or the author of a text (Balahur, Steinberger, 2009). In the current work, we aimed to detect sentiments conveyed by posts of the forum participants. Hence, we opted for the reader perception model and asked annotators to analyze the topic's sentiment as it was addressed toward the other forum participants.

We asked annotators to label the post with the dominant sentiment. Posts that combined factual information and sentiments usually expressed encouragement for specific participants, hence we suggested the label *"facts +encouragement"* for that category.

4.2 Identification of sentiments.

We wanted to know what types of sentiments were dominant in these forums and how these sentiments influence each other. Previously, analysis of the topics' content revealed that most posts referred to sharing personal experiences, provision of information or advice, expressions of gratitude/friendship, chat, requests for information, and expressions of universality (e.g. *"we're all in this together"*) (Malik, Coulson, 2010). Hypothesizing that binary sentiment categories (e.g., positive and negative polarity), would be too general and could not adequately cover emotions expressed in health-related messages, we intended to build a set of sentiments that

[7] http://ivf.ca/forums/forum/166-ivf-ages-35/

1. contains sentiment categories specific for posts from medical forums, and
2. makes feasible the use of machine learning methods for automate sentient detection.

To identify such a set, we asked annotators to read several topic discussions and describe sentiments expressed by the forum participants and the sentiment propagation within these discussions. More specifically, the annotators were told to indicate sentiments in sequences. For example, we asked annotators to answer groups of questions:

- What sentiment was expressed in the first post in the topic? How were the sentiments of the following posts affected by the initial sentiment?
- How long did an expressed sentiment last in the topic? If it was replaced by another one, how did the replacement happen?
- Did the participants joining the discussion try to change the previous sentiments? Did the participants succeed in such attempts?

We asked annotators not to mark descriptions of symptoms and diseases as subjective; in many cases they appear in the post as objective information for other forum participants that have encountered similar issues. In such cases only the author's sentiments toward other participant should be taken into consideration. For example, `I have had a few days now with heartburn/reflux - could be stress, a little achy tummy/pelvic and a tired aching back. More waiting, but getting more hopeful` is a description of symptoms and should not be annotated as subjective. In contrast, `I hope your visit with us infertilies is short and sweet and you get that baby soon!!!` exposes the author's sentiment towards another person.[8]

The data annotation was carried on by the Master's students as their practical work for the course "Semantic Interpretation of Text". The students already completed courses on "Computational Linguistics" and "Natural Language Processing". Based on the quality of annotations, eight annotators were selected after the first phase of the sentiment analysis. Most annotators already had experience in text annotation. Each annotator independently annotated a set of topics. Each annotator filled in a short questionnaire for every analyzed topic. After that, we merged and summarized all questionnaires.

4.3 The annotation scheme

Based on the responses to the questionnaires, we built three groups of sentiments:

1. **confusion**, which included worry, concern, doubt, impatience, uncertainty, sadness, angriness, embarrassment, hopelessness, dissatisfaction, and dislike;
2. **encouragement**, which included cheering, support, hope, happiness, enthusiasm, excitement, optimism;
3. **gratitude**, which included thankfulness.

A special case was presented by expressions of *compassion*, *sorrow*, and *pity* which did not appear individually but appeared in conjunction with encouragement; we treated them as a part of encouragement.

Also, we identified two types of posts with factual information: *facts* and *facts + encouragement*. Posts were marked as *facts* if they delivered factual information only. Posts were marked as *facts + encouragement* when they contained factual information supplemented by short emotional expressions; those expressions almost always conveyed encouragement ("*hope, this helps*", "*I wish you all the best*", "*good luck*").

As a result, our annotation schema was implemented as follows:

(a) annotation was performed on a level of individual posts; annotators were asked to select the most dominant sentiment in the whole post; descriptions of symptoms or diseases were omitted from the sentiment annotation;

(b) every post was marked with only one label; at this stage we did not aim to identify interrelations between sentiments; this task is delegated to the next stage of our study;

(d) finally, every post was labeled by two annotators.

We evaluated agreement between the annotators by using Fleiss Kappa (Nichols et al, 2010), a measure that evaluates agreement for a multi-class manual labeling.

Fleiss Kappa = $(P - P_{class})/(1-P_{class})$

where P is an average agreement per a post and P_{class} is an average agreement per a class. For a five-class problem, the annotators achieved a high agreement: Fleiss Kappa = 0.73 which indicates a strong agreement (Osman et al, 2010). Preparing our data for the machine learning experiments we assigned the five category labels

[8] All examples preserve original spelling and grammar.

only to posts that both annotators labeled with the same label, e.g., if a post was labeled *encouragement* by two annotators it was put into the *encouragement* category. We introduced a new class *uncertain* for the posts labeled with two different labels. The final number of posts per class was:
Encouragement – 206, *Gratitude* – 88, *Confusion* – 48, *Facts* – 187, *Facts + Encouragement* - 73, and *Uncertain*– 150; total – 752 posts.

5 HealthAffect

To the best of our knowledge, WordNet-Affect[9] is the only affective lexicon with a highly detailed hierarchy of sentiments (Strapparava et al 2006). Other affective lexicons assign words with positive and negative polarity labels only (e.g., SentiWordNet (Baccianella et al. 2010), Bing Liu's Opinion Lexicon [10] (Liu, 2010), MPQA subjectivity lexicon (Wiebe et al., 2005)).

However, comparison of the post vocabulary with WordNet-Affect words revealed that very few words from WordNet-Affect appeared in any given post's text. Consider a dialogue from Example 1.

Example 1. **post_id_140772** `The test is Positive!!! I'm giving you dancing banana's.`

post_id_140789 `I'm thinking that 64 sounds positive to me! I second Hopeful Flyer with the dancing bananas and raise her a for a BFP.`

post_id_141266 `thanks for your wishes The nurse at Edmonton called me and wants me to re-test`

post_id_141340 `yay! congrats! best of luck on test!`

post_id_141455 `Baby dust to you. Fingers crossed. Keep Positive.`

In Example 1, there was only one word - *positive* - which was found in WordNet-Affect; `thanks, congrats!, best of luck, Fingers crossed` were not found in the WordNet-Affect dictionary. On the other hand, some WordNet-Affect words were used in posts in the senses not related to sentiments (e.g. *get*, *move*, *close*, *cold*).

As those matching result were unsatisfactory, we created a specific lexicon which we named HealthAffect. To build HealthAffect, we adapted the Pointwise Mutual Information (PMI) of *word*1 and *word*2 (Turney, 2002):

$$\text{PMI}(word1, word2) = \log_2(\text{p}(word1 \ \& \ word2)/(\ \text{p}(word1)\ \text{p}(word2)))$$

First, we created a list of all words, bigrams and trigrams of words with frequency ≥ 5 from the unambiguously annotated posts (i.e., we omitted posts marked as *uncertain*). This was a list of candidates (aka *phrases*) to be included in our HealthAffect lexicon. Note that the Part-of-Speech tagging would be ineffective due to a high volume of textual noise (e.g., incomplete sentences, InternetSpeak jargon, loose grammar).

Next, for each class, we calculated PMI(*phrase*, *class*) as

$$\text{PMI}(phrase, class) = \log_2(\ \text{p}(phrase \text{ in } class)/(\ \text{p}(phrase)\ \text{p}(class))).$$

Finally, we calculated Semantic Orientation (SO) for each phrase and for each class as

$$\text{SO}(phrase, class) = \text{PMI}(phrase, class) - \Sigma\ \text{PMI}(phrase, other\_classes)$$

where *other_classes* are all the classes except for the class that Semantic Orientation is calculated for.

After all the possible SOs were computed, each HealthAffect candidate was assigned with the class that corresponded to its maximum SO. Consequently, each candidate was considered an indicator of the class that provided it with the maximum SO. It should be noted that each class got different numbers of indicative candidates. From 459 trigrams with frequency ≥ 5, 46 had their maximum SO for *encouragement*, 40 - for *gratitude*, 139 - for *confusion*, 95 - for *facts* and 139 for *facts + encouragement*.

For each class, we sorted all potential N-grams in decreasing order of SO and selected the equal number of N-grams to represent each class in the lexicon. The number of N-grams was determined as ½ of the minimum *per class* number of N-grams; for example, we used only 20 (=40:2) top trigram indicators for each class. Similarly, we selected 50 bigrams and 25 unigrams and added them to the lexicon.

A direct matching of HealthAffect to unambiguously annotated posts gave the following results:

- lexicon annotation matched the human annotation – 420 posts;
- lexicon annotation did not match the human annotation – 182 posts.

Thus, lexicon-based annotation matched 70% of unambiguously annotated posts. Therefore we used the created lexicon in Machine Learning experiments.

[9] http://wndomains.fbk.eu/wnaffect.html

[10] www.cs.uic.edu/~liub/FBS/opinion_lexicon_English.rar

6 Machine Learning Experiments

We used personal pronouns, short words, the WordNetAffect terms and the HealthAffect lexicon in four data representations:

- all semantic features (AllSem),
- WordNetAffect and pronouns features (WNAP),
- WordNetAffect features (WNA).
- HealthAffect lexicon (HAL)

We used Naïve Bayes (NB) and K-nearest neighbor (KNN) to classify the messages into 6 classes.

We assessed the learning methods by computing multi-class *Precision (Pr), Recall (R), F-score (F)* and *Accuracy Under the Curve (AUC).* We used 10-fold cross-validation to select the best classifier. Labeling all examples as the majority class gave the baseline for the performance evaluation: *Pr*= 0.075, *R* = 0.274, *F* = 0.118, *AUC* = 0.491. Table 1 and Table 2 report the empirical results.

NB results				
Features	*Pr*	*R*	*F*	*AUC*
AllSem	0.408	0.427	0.397	0.685
WNAP	0.324	0.395	0.333	0.661
WNA	0.322	0.350	0.303	0.605
HAL	0.527	0.541	0.518	0.799

Table 1: NB results in 6-class classification.

KNN results				
Features	*Pr*	*R*	*F*	*AUC*
AllSem	0.330	0.342	0.310	0.598
WNAP	0.287	0.319	0.284	0.591
WNA	0.279	0.322	0.275	0.571
HAL	0.377	0.376	0.340	0.619

Table 2: KNN results in 6-class classification.

Empirical evidence shows that while solving the multi-class classification problem, we significantly improved over the baseline ($P < 0.01$, paired t-test). HealthAffect provided a more accurate classification of sentiments, and NB outperformed KNN on all the data representations. However, for NB, the difference between the best and the worst F-score was as high as 60%, whereas for KNN the difference was < 10%.

7 Conclusions and Future Work

In this work, we have presented the sentiment analysis of messages posted on medical forums. We stated the sentiment analysis as a multi-class classification problem in which posts were classified into *encouragement, gratitude, confusion, facts, facts + encouragement* and *uncertain* categories. We applied the reader-centered manual annotation and achieved a strong agreement between the annotators: *Fleiss Kappa* = 0.73.

Sentiment analysis of online medical discussions differs considerably from the traditional studies of sentiments in consumer-written product reviews, financial blogs and political discussions opinion detection. While in many cases positive and negative sentiment categories are enough, such dichotomies are not sufficient for medical forums. The same can be said about the existing sentiment and affective lexicons: their general terms and labels do not adequately serve for the analysis of medical posts. Thus, new lexical resources sensitive to this specific domain should be created. We presented an ad-hoc method of the lexicon creation which is comparatively easy to implement. We have shown that the lexicon, which we call HealthAffect, provided the best accuracy in machine learning experiments. However, as many other lexical resources, the lexicon requires manual review and filtering. In the future, we plan to analyze and optimize this lexicon manually.

We used two algorithms, NB and KNN, to solve a multi-class sentiment classification problem. The probability-based NB demonstrated a better performance than KNN. The best F-score was achieved when posts were represented through HealthAffect, an affective lexicon built to identify sentiments in health-related online posts.

We present this work as the first phase of our analysis of medical forums. Our long term goal is to analyze health-related online discourses. We are interested in sentiment interaction, flow and propagation in these dialogues. To achieve this goal, we need a reliable tool for sentiment detection specifically in heath-related online texts. In the future, we aim to annotate more texts, enhance and refine our lexicon and achieve reliable automated sentiment detection in health-related messages. We plan to use the results obtained in this study to perform analyses of health-related discussions on medical forums related to highly debatable health care policies.

Acknowledgements

This work was in part supported by NSERC Discovery grant. The authors thank Brian Dewar for his assistance with the manuscript editing.

References

Allan, K. 2005. *Explorations in Classical Sociological Theory*: Seeing the Social World. Pine Forge Press, 2005.

Baccianella, S., A. Esuli, and F. Sebastiani. 2010. *SentiWordNet 3.0: an enhanced lexical resource for sentiment analysis and opinion mining*. Proceedings of the 7th LREC, 2200-2204.

Balahur, A. and R. Steinberger. 2009. *Rethinking Sentiment Analysis in the News: from Theory to Practice and back.* Proceedings of the 1st Workshop on Opionion Mining and Sentiment Analysis, 2009.

Bobicev, V., M, Sokolova, Y. Jaffer, D. Schramm. 2012. *Learning Sentiments from Tweets with Personal Health Information.* Proceedings of Canadian AI 2012, p.p. 37–48, Springer, 2012.

Chen, W. 2008. *Dimensions of Subjectivity in Natural Language (Short Paper).* In Proceedings of ACL-HLT, 2008.

Chew, C. and G. Eysenbach. 2010. *Pandemics in the Age of Twitter: Content Analysis of Tweets during the 2009 H1N1 Outbreak.* PLoS One, 5(11), 2010.

Chmiel, A., J. Sienkiewicz, M. Thelwall, G. Paltoglou, K. Buckley, A. Kappas, J. Holyst. 2011. *Collective Emotions Online and Their Influence on Community Life.* PLoS one, 2011.

Dodds, P., K. Harris, I. Kloumann, C. Bliss, C. Danforth. 2011. *Temporal Patterns of Happiness and Information in a Global Social Network: Hedonometrics and Twitter.* PLoS ONE, 6, e26752, 2011.

Fox, S. 2011. *The Social Life of Health Information.* Pew Research Center's Internet & American Life Project,http://pewinternet.org/Reports/2011/Social-Life-of-Health-Info.aspx

Goeuriot, L., J. Na, W. Kyaing, C. Khoo,Y. Chang, Y. Theng and J. Kim. 2012. *Sentiment lexicons for health-related opinion mining.* Proceedings of the 2nd ACM SIGHIT International Health Informatics Symposium, p.p. 219 – 225, ACM.

Jansen, B.J., Zhang, M., Sobel, K., and Chowdury, A. 2009. *Twitter power: Tweets as electronic word of mouth.* Journal of the American Society for Information Science and Technology, 60(11), 2169-2188, 2009.

Liu B. 2010. *Sentiment Analysis and Subjectivity.* Handbook of Natural Language Processing, Second Edition, 2010.

Malik S. and N. Coulson. 2010. *Coping with infertility online: an examination of self-help mechanisms in an online infertility support group.* Patient Educ Couns, vol. 81, no. 2, pp. 315–318, Nov. 2010.

Nichols, T., P. Wisner, G. Cripe, and L. Gulabchand. 2010. *Putting the Kappa Statistic to Use.* Qual Assur Journal, 13, p.p. 57-61, 2010.

Oakes, M. 2005. *Statistics for Corpus Linguistics.* Edinburgh University Press.

Osman, D., J. Yearwood, P. Vamplew. 2010. *Automated opinion detection: Implications of the level of agreement between human raters.* Information Processing and Management, 46, 331-342, 2010.

Pennebaker, J. and Chung, C. 2006. *Expressive Writing, Emotional Upheavals, and Health.* Handbook of Health Psychology, Oxford University Press.

Smith, C. 2011. *Consumer language, patient language, and thesauri: A review of the literature.* Journal of the Medical Library Association, 99(2), 135– 144, 2011.

Sokolova, M. and V. Bobicev. 2011. *Sentiments and Opinions in Health-related Web Messages.* Recent Advances in Natural Language Processing, p.p. 132- 139, 2011.

Strapparava, C. and R. Mihalcea. 2008. *Semeval-2007 task 14: Affective text.* Proceedings of the 2008 ACM symposium on Applied computing, 2008.

Strapparava, C., A. Valitutti, and O. Stock. 2006. *The affective weight of the lexicon.* Proceedings of the 5th International Conference on Language Resources and Evaluation, pages 474-481, 2006.

Taboada, M., J. Brooke, M. Tofiloski, K. Voll and M. Stede. 2011. *Lexicon-Based Methods for Sentiment Analysis.* Computational Linguistics 37 (2): 267-307.

Thelwall, M., K. Buckley, and G. Paltoglou. 2010. *Sentiment in Twitter events.* Journal of the American Society for Information Science and Technology, 62(2), 406-418, 2010.

Turney, P.D. 2002. *Thumbs up or thumbs down? Semantic orientation applied to unsupervised classification of reviews.* Proceedings of ACL'02, Philadelphia, Pennsylvania, pp. 417-424.

Wiebe, J., T. Wilson, and C. Cardie. 2005. *Annotating expressions of opinions and emotions in language.* Language Resources and Evaluation 39: 165-210.

Wilson, T., J. Wiebe, and P. Hoffmann. 2005. *Recognizing contextual polarity in phrase-level sentiment analysis.* Proceedings of EMNLP 2005. Association for Computational Linguistics

Zafarani, R., W. Cole, and H. Liu. 2010. *Sentiment Propagation in Social Networks: A Case Study in LiveJournal.* Advances in Social Computing (SBP 2010), pp. 413–420, Springer

Zillen, N. 2011. Internet Use of Fertility Patients: A Systemic Review of the Literature. *Journal of Reproductive Medicine and Endocrinology,* 8(4): 281–287.

Automated Learning of Everyday Patients' Language for Medical Blogs Analytics

Giovanni Stilo
Dipartimento di Informatica
stilo@di.uniroma1.it

Moreno De Vincenzi
Dipartimento di Informatica
devincenzi@di.uniroma1.it

Alberto E. Tozzi
Ospedale Pediatrico Bambin Gesù
albertoeugeniotozzi@opbg.net

Paola Velardi
Dipartimento di Informatica
velardi@di.uniroma1.it

Abstract

Analyzing how people discuss about health-related topics on dedicated forums and social networks such as Twitter, can provide valuable insight for syndromic surveillance and to predict disease outbreaks. In this paper we present a minimally trained algorithm to learn associations between technical and everyday language terms, based on pattern generalization and complete linkage clustering, and we then assess its utility on a case study of five common syndromes for surveillance purposes.

1. Introduction

Infodemiology is defined as "the science of distribution and determinants of information in an electronic medium, specifically the Internet, with the ultimate aim to inform public health and public policy" (Eysenbach, 2006). A seminal work in this area is (Ginsberg et al., 2009), in which the level of influenza in the U.S. is estimated using the relative frequency of search queries related to influenza-like illness. Similarly, in (Althouse et al., 2011), the authors demonstrate that query search volumes associated to Dengue fever can predict the incidence of Dengue. Another recent study (Xu et al., 2011) analyses the problem of predicting the tendency of hand-foot-and-mouth disease (HFMD), clustering HFMD-related search queries, medical pages and news reports. Query search volumes are estimated using Google Trends (GT) [1] or Google Flu, however, forums and micro-blogs (like Twitter) appear to be a better source of information, since keywords occur in contexts. Contexts make it possible to use text mining techniques for sense disambiguation, topic filtering and mood analysis (Berendt, 2011; Corley, 2009; Von Etter et al., 2010; Cohen and Hersh, 2005; Paul and Dredze, 2011). Among the others, the problem of tracing patient's naïve medical terminology is a very crucial one (Dahm, 2011; Molina Healthcare, 2004). Consider the following striking difference in the usage of terms describing the same health conditions, the first by a clinician, the second by a patient: "*Clinicians should maintain a high index of suspicion for this diagnosis in patients presenting with influenza-like symptoms that progress quickly to respiratory distress and extensive pulmonary involvement.*"[2] "*For the past 3 days I have had a stuffy, runny nose, congested chest, fever, sore ears and throat and burning eyes. I've been taking cold and flu medication, and it doesn't help*"[3]. Clearly, the patient's symptoms should induce "*a high index of suspicion*", but for an automated system to capture a similarity between the two symptom descriptions is not obvious. Being able to understand the way people talk about their health conditions in "peer to peer" communications is crucial for an effective monitoring of health-related behaviors based on social data.

In this paper we present a minimally supervised algorithm to learn patient's jargon and we apply it to the analysis of 5 common syndromes. We obtain an impressive correlation with existing official data, and furthermore, we are able to monitor not only a disease outbreak, but its related symptoms, which is a clear advancement over previous works in this area. The paper is organized as follows: in Section 2 we present the algorithm in detail, in Section 3 we describe the corpora and tools used to monitor patients' discussions and we analyze five cases of interest for epidemiologic surveillance. Section 4 is dedicated to the

[1] http://www.google.com/trends/

[2] *www.ncbi.nlm.nih.gov/pubmed/20085663*

[3] *ehealthforum.com*

analysis of related work, and Section 5 presents our concluding remarks.

2. Mapping Medical Jargon And Everyday Language

In this Section we present a minimally supervised algorithm to learn from the web (Wikipedia, Google snippets, and other resources) a set of generalized patterns to establish a correspondence between technical and naïve jargon, and to identify common expressions used by patients to describe their medical conditions. The algorithm starts with a relatively small learning set *MC* of medical conditions, composed by pairs (tt_i, nt_j), where tt_i is a technical term and nt_j a naïve term[4], e.g. <*myocardial infarction, heart attack*>, <*emesis, vomiting*> etc. The set *MC* is divided in three subsets S_o, S_1 and S_2 used for learning, refining and testing. The algorithm has four steps:

1. **Web mining step**: using S_0, we extract from the Web sentence snippets including both terms;
2. **Clustering step**: we generalize lexical patterns between a tt_i and an nt_j (or vice versa) and create weighted clusters of similar patterns; we also learn generalized expressions for tt_i and nt_j;
3. **Reinforcement step**: using S_1, we test the precision and recall of each pattern and adjust cluster weights;
4. **Testing phase**: The algorithm is tested on S_2 and the steps are repeated for any possible permutation of S_o, S_1 and S_2.

As a preliminary step, we define a policy to generalize lexical patterns and terminological expressions for medical conditions, as well as a distance measure to compute the similarity between patterns. Let tt_i and nt_j be single or multi-word expressions describing a technical or naïve medical condition, respectively, and let $p = w_1, w_2, \dots w_{|p|}$ be a word sequence between them, found on some document or web resource, e.g. "*abdominal obesity, colloquially known as belly fat*". Note that we can have $tt_i < p > nt_j$, as in previous example, or $nt_j < p' > tt_i$ as in "*belly fat is known clinically as abdominal obesity*". A pattern p is generalized as $p' = w_1', w_2' \dots w_{|p|}'$ where:

$$(1)\ w_i' = \begin{cases} w_i^* \ if\ POS(w_i) \in \{NOUN, VERB, PREP, PUNCT, "or"\} \\ POS(w_i)\ otherwise \end{cases}$$

where w_i^* is the word lemma and $POS(w_i)$ is the part of speech obtained with a POS tagger[5]. For example, if p="*is another word for*", then *p'=be #DT word for*. Since tt_i and nt_j are often multi-word expressions, e.g. "*high level of potassium*", we apply pattern generalization also to these terminological strings. A multi-word expression for a term describing a medical condition is generalized as follows:

$$(2)\ w_i' = \begin{cases} BODYPART\ if\ w_i \in \{eye, nose, skeleton..\} \\ DISCOMFORT\ if\ w_i \in \{pain, itch, ache, .miserable, ...\} \\ else\ w_i' = w_i\ if\ freq(w_i) > \vartheta \\ else\ w_i' = POS(w_i) \end{cases}$$

For example, *muscle weakness, heart attack, hair fungus*, generalize as BODYPART #NN. Discomfort words and body parts have been retrieved from publicly available Web resources[6]. The third generalization rule in (2) captures additional frequent words such as *illness, inflammation, infection, etc.* Rules in (2) are used to learn generalized sequences s_k for medical conditions, using the examples in *MC*, and group them by frequency. We denote with *T* the set of learned generalized medical condition patterns. Table 1 shows some of the most frequent sequences.

Sequence	Examples
NN	bilharzia, fainting, clenching, chickenpox
BODYPART NN	muscle weakness, heart attack, hair fungus
JJ BODYPART	crooked tooth, stuffy nose, crooked back, dry mouth
inflammation of BODYPART	inflammation of the heart, inflammation of the liver, inflammation of the skin

Table 1. Four most frequent generalized sequences for medical conditions (both *tt* and *nt*)

[4] In what follows, whenever a preposition applies to either a technical term or a naïve term, we use the notation *t* and *pt* (term and partner term) or *ct* (candidate partner term).

[5] We use the Treetagger *http://www.cis.uni-muenchen.de/~schmid/tools/TreeTagger/*

[6] E.g. for discomfort: http://www.macmillandictionary.com/thesaurus-category/british/Physically-painful-and-describing-pain

Given a pattern p, we define three categories for its elements w:

- $A := \{w_i \in p \mid POS(w_i) \in \{NOUN, \{VERB \neq be, can..\}\}\}$
- $B := \{w_i \in p \mid POS(w_i) \in \{PREP, ADJ, PUNCT\}\}$
- $C := \{w_i \in p \wedge w_i \notin \{A, B\}\}$

Let w^A, w^B and w^C be three experimentally tuned weights assigned to the word categories A, B and C. Given two patterns p_i and p_j, the *distance* between the patterns is defined as:

(3) $d(p_i, p_j) = 1 - (count(p_i, p_j, A) \times w^A + (count(p_i, p_j, B) \times w^B + (count(p_i, p_j, C) \times w^C)$

where $count(p_i, p_j, A)$ is the amount of common words in the two patterns belonging to category A. Matches in category A have a higher relevance wrt those in the other categories. For example, if the weights are 0.55, 0.3 and 0.15 respectively, *d*(", *known in medical terms as*", "*is another term for*")=0.725 and *d*(", *medical term for*", "*is fancy term for*")=0.25.

<u>*Learning Clusters Of Patterns*</u>

During step 1 of the algorithm (*web mining*), we start with S_o, and we extract from the Web text snippets including the pairs in S_o. Then, we take the *word sequence* between the two terms, and we apply pattern generalization using the rules in (1). To reduce noise, we also discard sequences whose length is more than 7 tokens, an experimentally selected threshold. Let *P* be the set of survived different patterns. For each pattern $p_i \in P$ we compute a score corresponding to the normalized count of different seed pairs that supported the pattern, e.g.:

(4) $weight(p_i) = \dfrac{|distinct\ seed\ pair\ with\ p_i|}{\max_j(|distinct\ seed\ pair\ with\ p_j|)}$

Next, we apply *pattern clustering* (step 2). For pattern clustering, we use an approach called *complete linkage* (Jain, 2010). The clustering literature is immense, and many other algorithms are available: however, complete linkage avoids the so-called *chaining phenomenon*, which causes one cluster to attract most of the population members. Furthermore, unlike the majority of clustering algorithms, complete linkage is not heavily parametric[7]. In complete linkage, the similarity of two clusters is defined as the similarity of the most dissimilar members, which is equivalent to choosing the cluster pairs whose merge has the smallest diameter. The algorithm starts with singleton clusters (e.g. each composed by one pattern $p \in P$) and then progressively merge two clusters C_i and C_j into larger ones, according to the distance function: $D(C_i, C_j) = \max_{p_i \in C_i, p_j \in C_j} d(p_i, p_j)$, where $d(p_i, p_j)$ is defined in our case by the formula (3). Using complete linkage we obtain balanced clusters, with low dissimilarity among the members of each cluster, for example: "*is a very broad term defining*" "*is a general medical term used for*" "*is a general term for*" "*is the common term for*", etc. Conversely, very specific patterns (e.g. "*your doctor would call it*") have the tendency to remain isolated. We define the following measure to weight the quality of the derived clusters: $score(C_i) = \sum_{p_j \in C_i} weight(p_j)$ where $weight(p_j)$ is computed as in formula (4).

<u>*Term Matching And Cluster Refinement*</u>

Term matching is the process of finding one or more candidate partner terms *ct* for a term *t*, where *ct* is technical if *t* is naïve, or vice versa. Once a clustering $C: \{C_1, C_2..C_k\}$ has been learned, it is used to find unknown technical or naïve terms in the following way: we take a term *t*, for example *belly fat*, and seek in the web for *domain relevant* sentences with this term. As a preprocessing step, we eliminate sentences not in the medical domain (e.g. if t=*plague*: "*The capacitor plague (also known as bad capacitors or "bad caps") was a problem with a large number of premature failures of aluminum electrolytic capacitors ...*") using a domain heuristics. The formula is the following: $DomainWeight(s) = \dfrac{|B(s) \cap D|}{|B(s)|}$ where *B(s)* is the bag of words of the retrieved snippet, and *D* is a set of singleton words (only nouns) extracted from a medical terminology[8]. Sentences with a domain weight lower than a threshold α are discarded. We then identify to the left or to the right of *t* the candidates partner terms *ct*. For example, given the sentence (retrieved for *t=belly fat*): "*abdominal obesity , colloquially known as* ***belly***

[7] For example, in many algorithms the number of clusters k is a parameter.

[8] We use Freebase http://www.freebase.com/view/medicine/disease, but any other medical terminology can be used.

***fat** or central obesity*" two candidates are selected, *abdominal obesity* and *central obesity*. To select candidates the algorithm uses a chunker[9] to identify noun phrases, and then select the best matching NP in terms of likeliness, using the set T of generalized learned sequences for medical conditions (see Table 1). This allows e.g. to prefer *central obesity* rather than *obesity* alone. For each candidate partner ct of t (e.g. *abdominal obesity)*, we take the pattern p between t and ct (*", colloquially known as"*), and compute its distance wrt the previously acquired cluster members, according to:

$$d'(p,C_j) = \frac{\sum_{p_i \in C_j} d(p,p_j)}{|C_j|}$$ the most similar cluster is

therefore: $$C_p^* = \begin{cases} C_k \text{ if } p \in C_k \\ \arg\min_{C_j \forall j} d'(p,C_j) \text{ otherwise} \end{cases}$$

Notice that the second rule says that p can be assigned to a cluster even though not only the pattern itself, but also its generalized structure p' has never been encountered during the learning phase. Furthermore, since the same candidate ct can be extracted from different sentences and patterns p_i, the global confidence in a candidate is computed as:

$$weight(ct) = \frac{\max_{p_i \in C^*_{p_i}} (score(C^*_{p_i}) \times (1 - d'(p_i, C^*_{p_i})) \times (1 + \ln(freq(ct))}{\max_{ct_n in\ EXP} weight(ct_n)}$$

The *max* function in the numerator selects the highest score obtained by any of the extracted patterns p_i that support *ct*, while the smoothing factor $(1 - d'(p, C_p^*))$ adjusts the weight of *ct* according to its membership in the selected cluster. Finally the factor $(1 + \ln(freq(ct))$ increases the weight of *ct* according to the number of patterns that supported *ct*. The denominator is a normalizing factor over all the weights calculated for all the terms t in a given run of the algorithm. A threshold β is experimentally tuned such that a *ct* is returned only if $weight(ct) \geq \beta$.

Term matching is used during the *reinforcement* phase (step 3 of the algorithm), which is aimed at refining cluster weights, according to their precision and recall. During the cluster refinement phase, we take the set S_1 in *MC* and, separately for each element of a pair $(tt_i, nt_j) \in S_1$, we test the recall and precision of the patterns belonging to the various clusters, in order to adjust cluster weights. In fact certain patterns, e.g. "*or*", as in "*hypoglycemia* _or_ *low blood sugar*" and "(", as in "*vomiting* _(_*emesis)*" are very frequent but have a low precision.

Given the terms in S_1 we test each pattern p_i in the following way: $n_{tp}(p_i)$ = number of true terms returned by p_i; $n_{fp}(p_i)$ = number of false terms returned by p_i; $n_{fn}(p_i)$ = number of true terms extracted by p_i but below the threshold β. We can then compute an additional weight for p_i that takes into account its performances: $weight_r(p_i) = (n_{tp}(p_i) + n_{fn}(p_i))$

and $weight^*(p_i) = weight(p_i) + weight_r(p_i)$

After this step, clusters weights are updated with the new pattern weights.

2.2 Evaluation

To test the algorithm we take S_2 and we perform term matching, using the adjusted clusters weights. We perform a six-fold cross evaluation, in which S_0, S_1 and S_2 are used interchangeably. Notice that in each run, the obtained clusters and weights can be different, since a different dataset is used to extract sentences from the Web. The global performances are averaged over all the runs.

For training, refining and testing purposes we use a set *MC* of 193 (tt,nt) pairs from Freebase.

To extract sentences we used the following web resources: Google snippets (up to the allowed query limits), Wikipedia, BMC BioMed Central Corpus[10], UKWaC British English web corpus[11].

During each run of a testing phase, we take a t_i from the dataset "playing the role" of S_2 and we try to extract from the previously listed web resources a set of correspondent partner terms, using the clusters and cluster weights learned in previous phases. We then compare them with the ground truth in S_2. Let *TT* the set of technical terms in the test set and $NT_i := \{nt_1^i, nt_2^i, nt_k^i\}$ the "true" set of naïve terms for each $tt_i \in TT$. To compute performances, we use standard measures such as *precision*, *recall* and *F-measure*, as well as the *mean reciprocal rank (MRR)*, a measure that prizes true positives if

[9] As for POS tagging, we use the Treetagger

[10] http://www.biomedcentral.com/about/datamining

[11] http://trac.sketchengine.co.uk/wiki/Corpora/UKWaC

they are top-ranked wrt the set of returned answers. *MRR* is defined as: $MRR = \frac{1}{|TT|} \sum_{nt^* \in NT_i \forall tt_i \in TT} \frac{1}{rank(nt^*)}$ where nt^* is a true positive for tt_i retrieved by the algorithm (e.g. $nt^* \in NT_i$), and $rank(nt^*)$ is the position of nt^* in the list returned by the algorithm. Since the test is repeated for any possible permutation of the three datasets S_0, S_1 and S_2, the performance is averaged over all the six experiments. The performance results are reported in Table 2 with $\alpha = 0.38$ and $(w^A, w^B, w^C) = (0.55, 0.30, 0.15)$. As expected, a higher threshold improves precision but reduces the recall. Furthermore, the high MRR shows that true positives are likely to receive a higher score wrt false positives, which is a desired property.

Since often for a technical term there might be many naïve terms, and Freebase is far from being complete, we asked two physicians (one is a co-author) to manually evaluate the extracted terms according to their expertise. In Table 3 the recall is computed considering the number of terms considered correct, both above and below the threshold. In the Table, *k-Fleiss* is the inter-annotator agreement[12]. The Table shows a higher precision, as expected, however there is quite a number of good terms below the threshold (recall is 0.49). In applications, the better strategy is to use no threshold and ask a physician to mark the correct terms. Given a disease under surveillance, this manual step is simple and requires few minutes, while there would be no easy way for a clinician to imagine, without the help of a text mining tool, the variety of expressions used by patients.

β	Precision	MMR	Recall
0	0.60	0.64	0.73
0.1	0.64	0.71	0.66
0.2	0.69	0.82	0.60

Table 2. Average system performance against golden-standard

β	Precision	Recall	F1	MMR	k-fleiss
0.2	0.76	0.49	0.59	0.74	0.53

Table 3. Manual Evaluation by domain experts

[12] http://en.wikipedia.org/wiki/Fleiss'_kappa#Interpretation

After the training phase, we selected the best performing clustering in the six experiments (namely, one with MRR=0,87) as the final model for extracting naïve medical language. We notice however that performances are not significantly variable and seem more related to the searched terms (i.e. whether they are more or less popular on the web) than to any of the clustering results.

3. Case Study On Five Syndromes

In this Section we apply the results of our algorithm to a case study of five common syndromes: influenza-like illness (with two sub-cases, ILI^{ECDC} and ILI^{FEVER}), common cold, allergic rhinitis, and gastroenteritis. Our clinical partnership used the results in (Rumoro et al., 2011) to create 5 queries, each testing for one of the following cases[13]: ILI^{ECDC}, ILI^{fever}, Gastroenteritis (GASTRO), allergic rhinitis (ALLERGY), common cold (COLD).

For example, the query for ILI^{ECDC} is:

((fever)OR(chills))OR(malaise)OR(headache)OR(myalgia))AND((cough)OR(pharyngitis)OR(dyspnea))

We used our algorithm to expand 17 symptom-related medical conditions (e.g. *rynhorrea, pharyngitis, myalgia, dyspnea, chills..*) mentioned in (Rumoro et al., 2011), and we retrieved an additional set of 62 naïve terms. Each symptom in a query was then expanded by adding its alternative retrieved terms. Using the available APIs[14], we collected a dataset of Twitter messages including at least one of the retrieved symptoms, from February 1st to May 6th 2013. To further extend the set of naïve terms, we used the patterns in Table 1 to extract additional candidates from our Twitter dataset. Overall, 29 additional terms are retrieved in this way.

Systematic keyword analysis has shown that being able to trace both technical and naïve terminology produces a much larger body of evidence. For example, as shown in Figure 1, on February 5th there have been 957 tweets including *watery eyes, bloodshot eyes*, etc, and 393 with *conjunctivitis* or *conjuntivitis*. Similarly, *pharyngitis or laryngitis* cumulated 47 tweets on the same day, while their correspondent set of naïve terms occurred 12,440 times.

[13] http://www.influenzanet.eu/en/results/?page=help

[14] https://dev.twitter.com/docs/streaming-apis

To evaluate the quality of retrieved tweets, for each of the five syndromes, we extract a set of 100 positive tweets (those matching the related query) and a random sample of 500 tweets not matching any query but including at least one symptom. Tweets are then examined by the physicians, to test whether they can be truly considered as reporting symptoms that match the considered case definition. Of course, it is impossible to verify if these users are truly affected by any of the 5 syndromes. The purpose is rather to assess the *confidence* we can have in our methodology as a mean to retrieve from Twitter messages that actually refer symptoms related to one of the analyzed syndromes. Examples of true positives, false positives and false negatives are:

tp: If this is the flu! I am going to be so pissed:/ ***fever****, nausea, neck pain,* ***sore throat****, all this* ***coughing****..its back to bed!*

fp: hate when people self diagnose no you haven't got 'depression' or ***'tonsillitis'*** *you've had a bad day and a* ***sore throat***

fn*: #****puking*** *#****stomachache*** *#imsorry*

The results of the evaluation (reported in Table 4) show a remarkable precision, furthermore we found no false negatives in the random set of 500 tweets (the Recall estimate is then 1). We provide hereafter an analysis of error causes, including those that possibly could produce false negatives:

1. Tweets that report news or someone else's condition: most of these errors are eliminated by simply canceling re-tweets or tweets including an url, but some still survive, e.g. "*Symptoms of H1N1 are like regular flu symptoms and include fever, cough, sore throat, runny nose, body aches, headache, chills, and fatigue.*"
2. Negation: the presence of a negation in a tweet is not enough to determine if it is a negative case. For example: "***Not*** *bad. Throat infection, fever and flu all at once!*" is a true positive for ILI^{ECDC}, while: "***No*** *fever, diarrhea, abdominal pain. On Tamiflu now!*" is a false positive. More complex treatment of negation is needed to handle these cases, however they are a minority.
3. There are naïve expressions for a medical condition that were not extracted by our algorithm. These may cause both false positive and false negative. For example, looking at the data we found that *puking* is an additional synonym of *emesis (vomiting)*. The previously cited example of false negative is precisely due to this type of error, since one of the positive conditions for gastroenteritis is: *(emesis) AND (abdominal pain)* where *puking* is a naïve term for *emesis* and *stomachache* for *abdominal pain*.

	total tweets	fp	Precision
ILI^{ECDC}	270,503	3/100	0.97
ILI^{fever}	24,575	1/100	0.99
ALLERGY	42,062	0/100	1.00
COLD	145,657	1/100	0.99
GASTRO	102,980	15/100	0.85
Total	585,777	20/500	0.96

Table 4. Evaluation of the ILI-related case study

Figure 2 shows the trends of the analyzed syndromes. Note that, given the time span under analysis there is a high predominance of COLD and ILI^{ECDC}, while ALLERGY is growing since April, as expected.

Finally, we aim to correlate our data with those reported by the U.S. Outpatient Influenza-like Illness Surveillance Network (ILINet), collected through the CDC Fluview website[15]. Figure 3 shows the time series for our Twitter messages, for Google Flu Trends, and the official ILINet data. All time series where smoothed by the *loss function* presented in (Cleveland and Devlin, 1988), to reduce the effect of daily fluctuations. The Pearson correlation Google/ILINet is 0.9927 and our geolocalized[16] time series ILI$^{ECDC\text{-}US}$ /ILINet is 0.9965.

4. Related Work

To the best of our knowledge (Elhadad and Sutaria, 2007) is the only paper in which the correspondence between technical and naïve terms is analyzed. The paper is however focused on pairing (tt_i, nt_j) terms when the set of technical and naïve terms is pre-determined, and defined in UMLS[17]. Another related area is synonym extraction, since naïve terms can be seen as synonyms or near synonyms of technical terms. In this area, most approaches are based on the so-called *distributional hypothesis*: words with similar contexts have a similar meaning. A very recent study on synonym extraction is described in (Henriksson et al., 2012), where random indexing and random permutation are applied to automatically extract variants of medical terms. We notice that performance is not

[15] http://gis.cdc.gov/grasp/fluview/fluportaldashboard.html

[16] http://www.jmir.org/2012/6/e156/

[17] *www.nlm.nih.gov/research/****umls****/*

very high: the best model for synonyms has a 0.42 recall while the precision is very low: 0.08 in the best experiment.

Semantic relation learning is also similar to our task at hand, since the objective is to identify sequences of words that imply a given relation between two terms, e.g. for causal relations: "*dengue fever is caused by which mosquito*". Patterns are either hand crafted, or they are automatically learned using some manually annotated set of sentences. Another difference among the various approaches is between fixed (or "hard") lexico-syntactic patterns, and generalized patterns, usually in the form of graphs. In her seminal work, Mart Hearst (1992) proposed a number of fixed lexical patterns to extract hypernyms from sentences, e.g. "X such as Y" . Snow et al (2004) first search sentences that contain two terms which are known to be in a taxonomic relation (term pairs are taken from WordNet), as we do for *tt-nt* pairs; then they parse the sentences, and automatically extract fixed patterns (features) from the parse trees. Finally, they train a hypernym classifer based on these features. The approach requires the annotation of a possibly very large set of sentence fragments to train the classifier, and final performance is not so high. Cui et al. (2007) propose the use of probabilistic lexico-semantic patterns, called soft patterns, to identify definitional sentences. Finally, Navigli and Velardi (2010) use word-class lattices (WCL) to identify definitional sentences, starting from a large dataset of annotated definitions, where the *definiendum* and *definiens* tems have been manually annotated. Like for soft matching, WCL provide a generalization of patterns, where nodes of a lattice are either words or part of speech tags. Our work builds on WCL's idea of replacing words in a sentence fragment with POS, while keeping nouns and functional words. The subsequent generalization steps are different, since we use semantic categories and pattern clustering rather than lattices, and furthermore, no manual annotation is needed.

Considering the literature on the use of web data for disease prediction, the most relevant work related to our study is reported in (Ginsberg et al., 2009). In this work the authors fit a linear model for predicting ILI epidemics using query volumes data and historical data from the CDC's US Influenza Sentinel Provider Surveillance Network. To automatically obtain relevant keywords they use a set of 5 years, 50 millions Google web search queries. To select the appropriate keywords from these queries, they perform a correlation study for each query, to test if it models accurately the CDC ILI data in nine regions. This study is certainly more accurate wrt previous similar works that use few manually defined keywords (Althouse et al., 2011), such as *flu* and *influenza*. However, first, the algorithm depends on the availability of critical resources: web query logs are a kind of data which is *not freely available*. Our algorithm instead, once the model is learned, allows it to extract the relevant keywords automatically (possibly with a quick manual post-editing), for any disease or symptom. Second, given the large amount of initial queries (50 millions), keyword selection and correlation estimation for each possible keyword becomes a very demanding task, and in principle, it should be repeated for any disease under surveillance, on continuously updated query log data, since new keywords may appear (e.g. this year the predominant flu strain is H3N2 and still lacks a nickname, previous names have been *swine flu, bird flu*, etc.). Third, measuring query search volumes has the problems that we outlined in the introduction (ambiguity, sensitivity to external events): blogs and forums provide keywords in contexts, fostering more interesting types of analyses, as shown in our ILI case study. Another recent work (Lamb et al. 2013) separates tweets reporting infection (*flu*) from those expressing concerns and fear ("*a little worried about flu epidemic*!"). To automatically separate these tweets, the authors use a log-linear model and a set of fine-grained manually identified features (e.g. expressions of concern, such as *afraid, worried, scared*). This method, which is complementary to our symptom-driven technique, is reported to obtain 0.9897 Pearson correlation with ILINET on a 2009 sample, but only 0.7897 in a 2011 sample (when also Google Flu obtained 0.8829).

5. Conclusions

Overall, the results of this study show that knowledge of patient's language fosters the exploitation of social media not only to predict disease outbreaks, but also to classify patient symptoms in more fine-grained cases. Our methodology is more powerful vrs. e.g. Google Flu Trends, since it may help estimating the seriousness of any disease outbreak, the incidence of individual symptoms (e.g. *cephalgia* was a predominant flu symptom this year), to classify an illness in sub-cases (ILI vrs common cold), to detect frequently – and possibly unexpected- co-occurring symptoms, etc. For the sake of space, we reported here only a fragment of our findings.

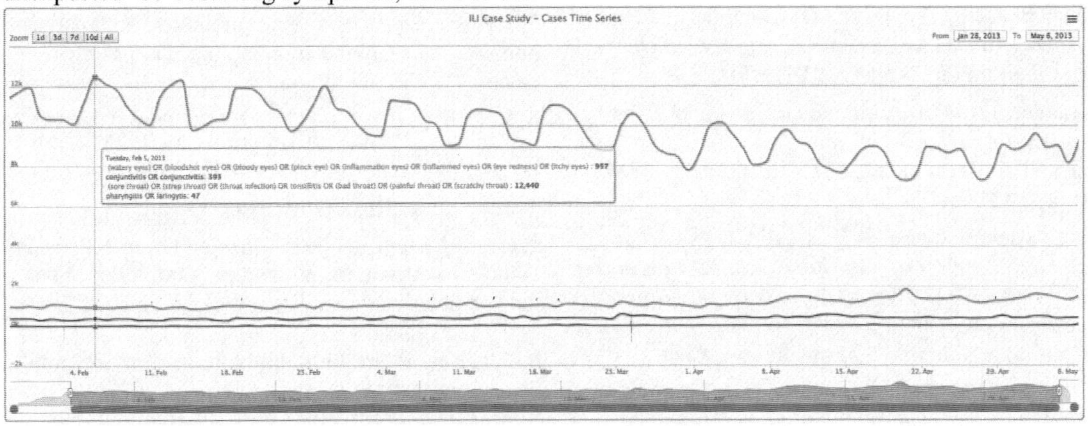

Figure 1. Total traffic for *laryngitis,pharyngitis* and correspondent naive terms, and for *conjuntivitis* and correspondent naive terms.

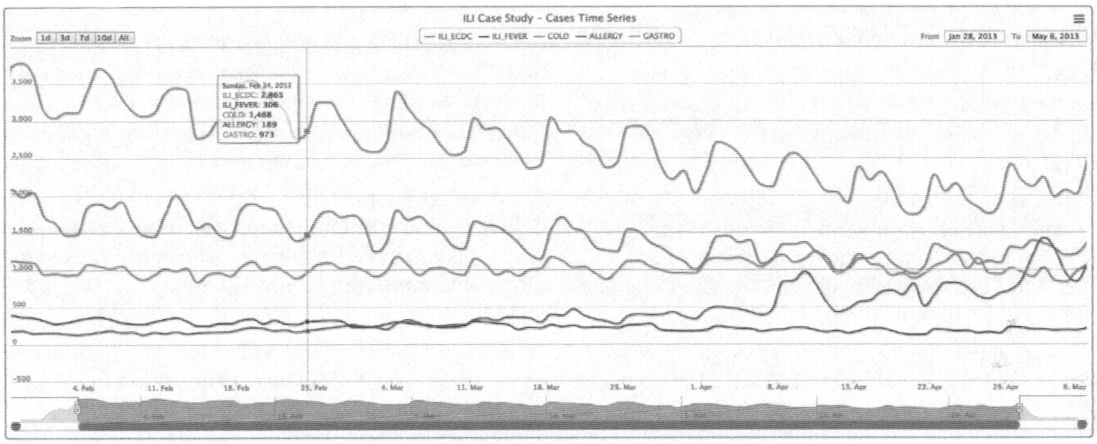

Figure 2. Total traffic for the five analyzed syndromes

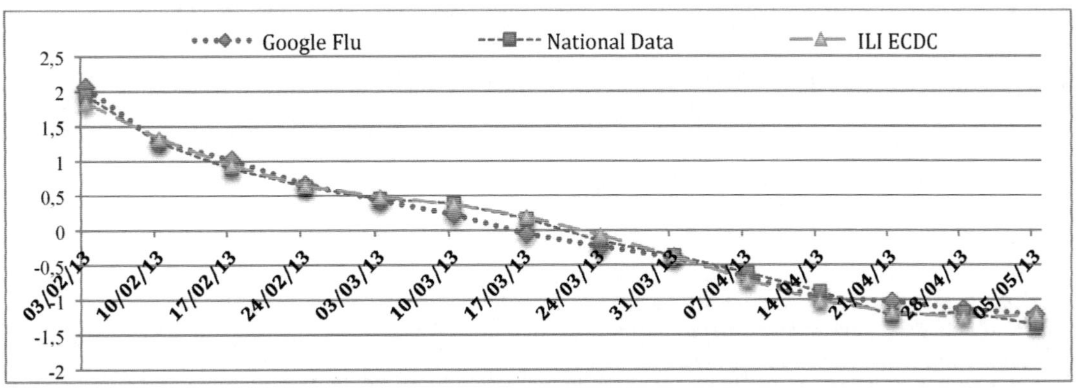

Figure 3. Correlation among Google Flu Trends, ILINet official data, and ILI^{ECDC} (US data)

References

B.M. Althouse, Y.Y. Ng, D.A.T. Cummings, (2011) *Prediction of Dengue Incidence Using Search Query Surveillance.* PLoS Negl Trop Dis 5(8)

B. Berendt (2011) *Text Mining for News and Blogs Analysis,* Encyclopedia of Machine Learning, Springer Science+ Business Media, LLC, 10.1007/978-0-387-30164-8_827

W. S. Cleveland and S. J. Devlin (1988), *Locally Weighted Regression: An Approach to Regression Analysis by Local Fitting,* Journal of the American Statistical Association, Vol. 83, No. 403 (Sep., 1988), pp. 596-610, American Statistical Association.

A. M. Cohen and W. R. Hersh (2005) *A Survey of current work in biomedical text mining*, Henry Stuart Publications *1467-5463, Briefings in Informatics*, Vol 6. NO 1. 57–71. March 2005

C. D. Corley (2009) *Social Network Simulation and mining social media to advance epidemiology*, PhD dissertation, University of North Texas

H. Cui, M. Kan, and T.Chua. (2007) *Soft pattern matching models for definitional question answering*, ACM Transactions on Information Systems (TOIS), vol. 25 n. 8

M. R. Dahm, (2011) *Exploring Perception and Use of Everyday Language and Medical Terminology* among International Medical Graduates in a Medical ESP Course in Australia, in: English for Specific Purposes, Elsevier v. 30 n. 3 pp186-197, Jul 2011

N. Elhadad and K. Sutraria (2007) *Mining a Lexicon of Technical Terms and Lay Equivalents.* Proceedings of the Workshop on BioNLP 2007

P. von Etter, S. Huttunen, A. Vihavainen, M. Vuorinen and R. Yangarber (2010) *Assessment of Utility in Web Mining for the Domain of Public Health*, Proc. of NAACL HLT 2010, pp 29-37

G. Eysenbach (2006) *Infodemiology: tracking flu-related searches on the web for syndromic surveillance.* AMIA Annual Symp Proc. pp 244–8.

J. Ginsberg, Mohebbi MH, Patel RS, Brammer L, Smolinski MS, et al. (2009) *Detecting influenza epidemics using search engine query data.* Nature 457:1012–4.

A. Henriksson, H. Moen, M. Skeppstedt,AM Eklund, V. Daudarvicius and M. Hassel (2012) *Synonym Extraction od Medical Terms from Clinical Text Using Combinations of Word Space Models*, in Proc. of the 5th International Symposium on Semantic Mining in Biomedicine (SMBM 2012)

M. Hearst (1992) *Automatic acquisition of hyponyms from large text corpora*, Proc. of the 14th International Conference on Computational Linguistics, Nantes , France.

A. K. Jain, (2010) *Data clustering: 50 years beyond K -means.* Pattern Recognition Letters , 31: 651–666, 2010

Alex Lamb, Michael J. Paul, Mark Dredze (2013). Separating Fact from Fear: Tracking Flu Infections on Twitter. North American Chapter of the Association for Computational Linguistics (NAACL), 2013.

Molina HealthCare and California Academy of Family Physicians, (2004) *Medical Jargon and Clear Communication*, CAFP's California Bureau of Registered Nursing Provider #1809

Roberto Navigli and Paola Velardi (2010) *LearningWord-Class Lattices for Definition and Hypernym Extraction*, Proc. of ACL 2010

Michael J. Paul and Mark Dredze (2011) *You Are What You Tweet: Analyzing Twitter for Public Health*, In the proceedings of the *5th International AAAI Conference on Weblogs and Social Media (ICWSM 2011)*, Barcelona, Spain. July 2011.

Dino Rumoro , Shital Shah , Julio Silva , Marilyn Hallock , Gillian Gibbs and Michael Waddell (2011) *Case definition for real-time surveillance of influenza-like illness*, Emerging Health Threats Journal 2011, **4**: 11123

R. Snow, D. Jurafsky, and A. Y. Ng. (2004) *Learning syntactic patterns for automatic hypernym discovery.* In Proceedings of Advances in Neural Information Processing Systems, pages 1297–1304

N. Zhong , Y. Li and S. Wu (2012) *Effective Pattern Discovery for Text Mining*, IEEE Transaction on Knowledge and Data Engineering, vol 24, n. 1 , January 2012

D. Xu, Y. Liu, M. Zhang, S. Ma, A. Ciu and L. Ru (2011) *Predicting Epidemic Tendency through Search Behaviour Analysis*, Proc. of 22nd IJCAI

How Symbolic Learning Can Help Statistical Learning (and vice versa)

Isabelle Tellier
Lattice / Lattice - UMR 8094
Lattice / 1 rue Maurice Arnoux
Lattice / 92120 Montrouge
isabelle.tellier@univ-paris3.fr

Yoann Dupont
Lattice / Lattice - UMR 8094
Lattice / 1 rue Maurice Arnoux
Lattice / 92120 Montrouge
yoa.dupont@gmail.com

Abstract

We describe in this paper how different learning strategies can be applied on the same NLP task, namely chunking. The reference corpus is extracted from the French Treebank, the symbolic learning strategy used is grammatical inference and the statistical one is CRFs (Conditional Random Fields). As expected, the symbolic approach allows readability but is less effective than the statistical one. We then propose two distinct ways to combine both approaches and show that in both cases they benefit from one another.

1 Introduction

Supervised machine learning approaches, especially when they have access to huge amounts of data, have now extensively proved their effectiveness for a lot of text mining tasks like text classification, sentence annotation and information extraction. Most effective learning approaches rely on a theoretical background which is either optimization (SVM), statistics (Naive Bayes) or both (HMMs, MaxEnt models, CRFs). But, however effective they may be, the main drawback of these techniques is that they usually do not provide any human-readable model.

There also exists other branches of Machine Learning, referred to as *symbolic*, whose particularity is to provide a more human-readable output. This is the case of decision trees, Inductive Logic Programming (ILP) or Grammatical Inference (GI in the following). The latter is our main interest here. It can be defined as the study of how it is possible to automatically learn a formal grammar or any other device able to represent a *language* (such as an automaton, a regular expression...) from a sample of (possibly enriched) sequences known to belong (or not) to this language (de la Higuera, 2010). This domain is often not very well known due to its roots in theoretical computer science and formal language theory. GI algorithms' known drawback is their lack of efficiency on real data: they are often time consuming, sensitive to errors and do not behave well with large alphabets (for example alphabets containing every word of a natural language).

In this article, we want to give some GI algorithms a chance to compete with the state of the art of statistical machine learning approaches. The task we deal with for this purpose is *chunking* (Abney, 1991) for French, which can be done with hand-made automata (Antoine et al., 2008; Blanc et al., 2010). To our knowledge, trying to *automatically learn these automata* instead of writing them by hand has never been tested for any language before. On the other hand, chunking can also be treated as an annotation task (cf. shared task of CoNLL2000) and thus been efficiently processed by a statistical machine learning approach . The state of the art in this domain are CRFs (Lafferty et al., 2001; Sha and Pereira, 2003). Chunking thus seems to be the ideal playground on which both approaches can be fairly compared.

But this comparison is not our only purpose. Our intuition is that both approaches are complementary, as they focus on very distinct properties of the dataset. We also provide in this article two distinct ways to combine them according to different purposes. The first one is effectiveness-oriented: it consists in enriching the CRF by automata-based features to improve again its effectiveness. The second strategy is readability-oriented: it consists in analyzing the behavior of an automaton produced by GI thanks to CRF-computed weights which are interpretable with respect to this automaton.

The paper is organized as follows. In the first section, we introduce the task of chunking and describe the dataset we have used in all our experiments. The second section is dedicated to grammatical inference. After a brief review, we focus on the k-RI-algorithms (Angluin, 1982) and provide the best experimental results we could reach with them on the task. In the next section, we apply CRFs (Lafferty et al., 2001) to the same task. As expected, CRFs give far better results than those obtained by GI, at the price of less readability. In the last section, we describe and evaluate two ways to combine automata and CRFs. The results of both combinations are promising and suggest original trails to associate symbolic and statistical learning.

2 Chunking: the Task and the Data

In this section, we describe the task of chunking as a labeling one and introduce the dataset we used for our experiments. As our purpose is to build a chunker for French, our starting point is the French Treebank (Abeillé et al., 2003).

2.1 The Task

The task of *chunking*, also called *shallow parsing* consists in identifying elementary (i.e. non recursive) syntactic phrases. Chunks are “contiguous and non-recursive lexical units sequences bound to an unique head” (Abney, 1991). Each chunk is characterized by the type (or syntactic category) of its unique head. So, there are as many different types of chunks as there are of considered heads. The chunks are thus intimately linked with the part-of-speech (POS in the following) tags associated with the lexical units of the sentences.

Chunking has been the target of the CoNLL shared task in 2000[1], in which the training set was composed of about 9 000 English sentences taken from the Penn Treebank with two levels of labels: a POS level provided by the Brill tagger and a chunk level. The winners used SVM and “Weighted Probability Distribution Voting”. The same corpus was used to show the effectiveness of CRFs (Sha and Pereira, 2003).

2.2 The Data

The French Treebank (FT in the following) has been built from a collection of sentences extracted from articles of the French newspaper “Le Monde”, published between 1989 and 1993 (Abeillé et al., 2003). The sentences are tokenized (with respect to some multi-word units), lemmatized, tagged and parsed. There exists multiple versions of the FT, the one we have used is made of about 8 600 XML trees, enriched by syntactic functions which were necessary to identify some chunks. For POS tags, we used the set of 30 morpho-syntactic tags defined by Crabbé and Candito (2008).

We consider 7 distinct types of chunks: AP (adjectival phrases), AdP (Adverbial phrases), CONJ, NP (noun phrases), PP (prepositional phrase), VP (verbal phrases) and UNKNOWN chunks (usually for those containing foreign words). Punctuation marks between chunks are considered as "out". Unlike Tellier et al. (2012), our CONJ chunk only contains the conjunction token(s) and, as opposed to Paroubek et al. (2006), the epithetic adjectives are always part of the NP containing the noun they qualify, whether they appear before or after this noun. Our AP chunk is thus relatively rare, as it only concerns detached or attribute adjectives (syntactic functions available in the XML trees are needed to identify some of them).

An example chunked sentence in our sense is shown in the following (it means "the depreciation against the dollar has been limited to 2.5%")[23]:
(la/DET dépréciation/NC)$_{NP}$ (par_rapport_au/P dollar/NC)$_{PP}$ (a/V été/VPP limitée/VPP)$_{VP}$ (à/P 2,5/DET %/NC)$_{PP}$

We extracted from the FT two distinct corpora:

- a corpus where every distinct chunk is extracted and labeled with the BIO (Begin/In/Out) convention. Chunks are distributed according to the following proportions: PP: 33,86%, AdP: 7,23%, VP: 17,11%, AP: 2,21%, NP: 32,95%, CONJ: 6,61%, UNKNOWN: 0,03%.

- a corpus where only NPs are labeled, every other token being considered as out (label O). Recognizing NPs only can be useful for the identification of co-reference chains. This corpus is not a subpart of the previous one, as many PPs include an NP. These "hidden NPs" become visible in the second corpus only, as in the previous example:
(la/DET dépréciation/NC)$_{NP}$ par_rapport_au/P (dollar/NC)$_{NP}$ a/V été/VPP limitée/VPP à/P (2,5/DET %/NC)$_{NP}$

[1] http://www.cnts.ua.be/conll2000/chunking

[2] In this example, NC is the French acronym for CN (common nouns) and VPP is for past participle verbs

[3] A Web page with every detail about the POS and chunk labels (illustrated by many examples) is available but we omit its address here to keep authors anonymous

3 Grammatical inference

Grammatical Inference (GI) is a domain of research which emerged in the 60s and thus has a long history which cannot be easily summed-up. We focus in this section on *GI of automata from positive examples*. After a brief review, we describe the k-RI algorithms (Angluin, 1982) that we used in our experiments and the results we could reach with them.

3.1 Brief state of the art

GI is the study of how it is possible to automatically learn a symbolic device able to represent a *language* (a formal grammar, an automaton...) from a sample of (possibly enriched) sequences known to belong (or not) to this language (de la Higuera, 2010). When only sequences belonging to the language are available, the problem is known as *GI from positive examples*. This is the case in our context, where no counter-example of any kind is available. This problem is much harder than when negative examples are available, because it is very difficult to avoid *over-generalization*. Ultimately, if a learning program hypothesizes that the language to be learned is the universal one (Σ^*, where Σ is the alphabet of the language), no positive example can disprove it, even if it over-generalizes.

The first concern of GI was to provide a precise definition of what it means for a program to be able to "learn a language". The criterion is theoretical and formal, not empirical. A parallel can be drawn with children's language acquisiton. A child is not "programmed" to learn any specific language, (s)he is able to learn whatever language is spoken in his(her) environment. Similarly, GI programs are required to learn *classes of languages*, that is to be able to characterize any member of such a class, when they are provided with examples known to be generated (or not) by this member. The main important "learnability criteria" (also called learning models) are known as "identification in the limit" (Gold, 1967) and "PAC learning" (Valiant, 1984). but we cannot describe them here.

Unfortunately, even for regular languages, the simplest class of the Chomsky hierarchy, those criteria are impossible to fulfill with positive examples only: there is no algorithm able to learn from positive examples the whole class of regular languages satisfying these criteria (Gold, 1967; Kearns and Vazirani, 1994). Researchers have thus tried to identify learnable smaller or transverse classes in Chomsky's hierarchy (Angluin, 1980). k-reversible languages (Angluin, 1982) are such classes, and were the starting point of our experiments. Many other learnable subclasses have been described and studied, for example in Garcia and Vidal (1990; Denis et al. (2002; Kanazawa (1998; Koshiba et al. (2000; Yokomori (2003).

Other advances in the domain concern the learnability of devices integrating probabilities, such as probabilistic automata and their links with HMMs (Thollard et al., 2000; Dupont et al., 2005). In parallel, challenges[4] allowed to test the effectiveness of the proposed algorithms when confronted with real data.

3.2 k-RI Algorithm

In this section, we describe the GI algorithms used for our experiments. They were applied to try and learn a chunk-specific automaton from the positive sequences of POS tags extracted from the training part of the dataset. GI algorithms from positive examples seem adapted to this problem, as the considered alphabet is limited (30 distinct tags at most) and each distinct kind of chunk can be described by a relatively limited number of syntactic constructions.

k-Reversible Inference (k-RI) algorithm (Angluin, 1982) has the property of identifying in the limit any k-reversible language, for any fixed $k \in \mathbb{N}$. The class of k-reversible languages is a subclass of regular languages, and its members can thus be represented by Deterministic Finite State Automata (DFA). An automaton is k-reversible if it is deterministic and its mirror [5] is *deterministic with a look-ahead of k*. When $k = 0$, a 0-reversible language can be represented by a DFA whose mirror is also deterministic, the algorithm being called Zero Reversible (ZR). If $k_1 < k_2$, the class of k_1-reversible languages is stricty included in the one of k_2-reversible lanugages.

Given a set of positive sequences S, the first step of k-RI is to build PTA(S), the Prefix Tree Acceptor of S. PTA(S) is a tree-shaped DFA, and it has the property of being the smallest tree-shaped DFA recognizing exactly the language defined by S. The root of PTA(S) is its initial state. The search

[4]The most recent ones were Stamina (http://stamina.chefbe.net) and Zulu (http://labh-curien.univ-st-etienne.fr/zulu)

[5]The mirror automaton is obtained by switching initial and final states and by reversing every transition

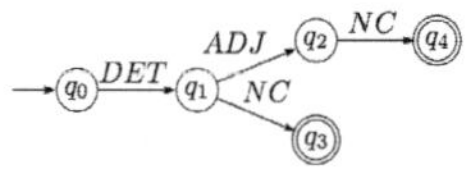

Step 1 : PTA(S)

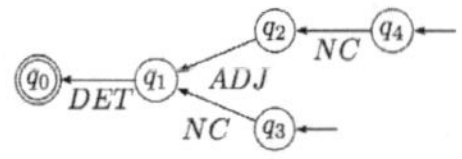

Step 1 : mirror of PTA(S)

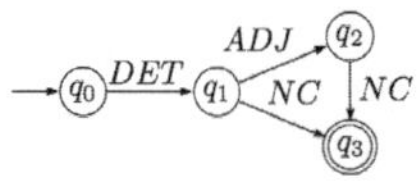

Step 2 : final states of PTA(S) are merged

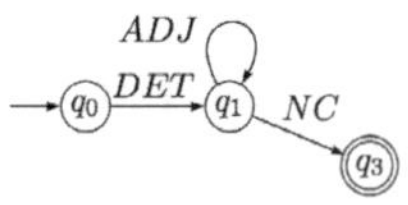

Step 3 : q_1 and q_2 are merged

Figure 1: Step by step demo of ZR

space of a GI algorithm for a given training set S of positive examples is a lattice whose bottom element is PTA(S) and top element is the universal language built from the alphabet of the examples (Dupont et al., 1994). Most GI algorithms start by building the PTA of the set of available positive examples, then try to generalize the recognized language by merging some of the states of this automaton. k-RI, detailled below, works accordingly. The merging operation here is deterministic, as it propagates recursively through the automaton to preserve determinism.

Algorithm k-RI
In : S : a set of (positive) sequences, k : natural;
Out : A : a k-reversible automaton;
begin
A := PTA(S);
while not(A k-reversible) **do**
// let N1 and N2 be two nodes
// violating k-reversibility of A.
Deterministic_Merge(A, N1, N2);
end while;
return A;
end k-RI;

In Figure 1, we illustrate how ZR behaves with the following set of positive examples of sequences of POS tags: $S = \{DET\ NC,\ DET\ ADJ\ NC\}$. On this example, we see that ZR already generalizes PTA(S) to output an automaton recognizing the language defined by the regular expression: $DET\ ADJ^*\ NC$. This generalization is linguistically relevant. But if we add to the previous positive sample the sequence made of NC alone, ZR will output an automaton recognizing the language $\{DET|ADJ\}^*NC$, which is a more doubtful generalization.

3.3 GI Experience Results on NP Chunking

We applied k-RI for different values of k ($k = 0, k = 1, k = 2$) on POS tags sequences matching NP chunks in the corpus of NP chunks only. This task is the one for which GI is the most appropriate. It is also possible to learn chunk-specific automata on the other corpus, but the application of multiple automata on new data pose a frontier covering problem. Therefore, we only use them in combination with a statistical model, in section 5.

ZR is really sensitive to the available data. A single incorrect sequence can force many states to merge. It was often the case with our dataset, where outliers or tagging errors are not absent. But some erroneous examples can be easily detected: for example, sequences of tags for a special kind on chunk which do not even contain any possible head tag of this chunk can be removed. Other cleaning strategies have been tried. Removing any sequence that occurs less than a fixed proportion was the most effective. Some information loss was nevertheless inevitable as there are heads that were rare (some clitics, for example).

Our experiments were made following a 5-fold cross-validation protocol. A learnt automaton is used as a regular expression on every new sequence of POS tags, looking for the smallest (resp. longest) matches (sm resp. lm). The correctness of a chunk is evaluated in a strict sense, i.e. it is correct if and only if both frontiers are correct. The precision, recall and F1-measure of NP-chunks are computed without taking into account O labels. Table 1 contains various F-measures that we managed to obtain by GI only on NP chunking, with a longest match strategy. Cleaned (c) versions are obtained by deleting every POS sequence that appeared strictly less than 0.01%. Values between parentheses are the medium sizes (in numbers of states) of the 5 automata sizes. PTA versions, whose performances are sometimes good, can be seen as "learning by heart" devices, as they are not generalized. Automata of size 1 are those, probably overgeneralized, that recognize the universal language of POS tags present at least once in NP chunks. $k \geq 2$ is necessary to obtain an automaton behaving better than the cleaned PTA.

4 Statistical learning for annotation

In this section, we focus on the best up-to-date statistical approach to perform an annotation task: Conditional Random Fields (or CRFs). We also

xp	pure PTA	cleaned PTA
F1-meas.	51.92	88.05

xp	c 0-RI (1)	c 1-RI (19)	c 2-RI (68.6)
F1	26.95	72.74	88.25

Table 1: GI results for NP chunking

recall how some HMMs can be "transformed" into a CRF, as it will be useful further.

4.1 Conditional Random Fields and HMMs

CRFs have been introduced by Lafferty et al. (2001). They belong to the family of graphical models. When the graph is linear (which is most often the case), the probability distribution that the annotation sequence y is associated with the input sequence x is expressed by:

$$p(y|x) = \frac{1}{Z(x)} \prod_t \exp\Big(\sum_{k=1}^{K} \lambda_k f_k(t, y_t, y_{t-1}, x)\Big)$$

Where $Z(x)$ is a normalization factor depending on x. This computation is based on K features f_k (usually binary functions), provided by the user. The feature f_k is activated (i.e. $f_k(t, y_t, y_{t-1}, x) = 1$) if a configuration occurring at the current position t in the sequence, concerning y_t, y_{t-1} (i. e. the values of the annotation at the positions t and $t-1$) and x is observed. Each feature f_k is associated with a weight λ_k which are the parameters of the model, to be estimated during the learning step. To define large enough a set of features, softwares implementing CRFs help users: they usually only require to provide *feature templates* which are automatically instanciated into as many features as there are positions in the training data where they can apply. The most current efficient implementation of linear CRFs is Wapiti[6], which uses a L1 penalization allowing to select the best features during the learning step (Lavergne et al., 2010). It is the software we have used.

CRFs have been applied with great success to various annotation tasks, among which POS labeling (Lafferty et al., 2001), named entity recognition (McCallum and Li, 2003), chunking (Sha and Pereira, 2003) and even full parsing (Finkel et al., 2008; Tsuruoka et al., 2009). Their main drawback is that they appear as "black boxes". A CRF model is simply characterized by a list of weighted features but it is not unusual that it contains thousands, even millions of such features. The result is therefore not easy to interpret.

HMMs, which were the previous state of the art for annotation tasks, have the merit to be more understandable. However, every discrete HMM can be "transformed" into a CRF model defining exactly the same probability distribution (Sutton and McCallum, 2006; Tellier and Tommasi, 2011). To do this, you have to define two families of features:

- features of the form $f(y_t, x_t)$ associating an individual label y_t with an individual input x_t: they correspond to the states y_t of the HMM where x_t can be emitted;
- features of the form $f(y_{t-1}, y_t)$ corresponding to the transitions of the HMM linking the states y_{t-1} and y_t.

If θ is a probability of emission or of transition of the HMM, then choose $\lambda = log(\theta)$ as the weight of the corresponding feature in the CRF. The computation of $p(y|x)$ then writes exactly the same in both cases. Discrete HMMs can thus been seen as a special case of CRFs. But CRFs are more general because they allow features to be more general than those used in this transformation. This transformation inspired us to use CRFs to *analyse* a discrete automaton learned by GI. This will be studied in section 5. Before, we provide the learning results obtained by using a CRF on our data.

4.2 Experimental Results

Tables 2 shows the feature templates and results obtained by using CRFs alone on both chunking tasks. For these experiments, we also followed a 5-fold cross-validation protocol and evaluated the chunks in a strict sense. For the complete chunking task, we computed both the micro-average of F-measures (i.e. the average of the F-measures of every kind of chunk weighted by their frequencies) and their macro-average (i.e. without any weight). As expected, CRFs provide excellent results. It is to be noted that they use words in their features along with POS tags, while GI algorithms have only access to the latter.

5 Combinations

In the previous sections, we have applied either pure symbolic learning or pure statistical learning. As expected, symbolic learning provides readable

[6]http://wapiti.limsi.fr/

Feat	Type	Window
Word	Unigram	[-2..1]
POS	Bigram	[-2..1]

chunking	Complete	NP only
micro	97.53	N/A
macro	90.49	N/A
F1-measure	N/A	96.43

Table 2: Template and obtained results with CRFs for each task

word	POS	NP	VP	PP	...	correct label
la	DET	B	O	O	...	B-NP
dépréciation	NC	I	O	O	...	I-NP
par_rapport_au	P	O	O	B	...	B-PP
dollar	NC	B	O	I	...	I-PP
a	V	O	B	O	...	B-VP
été	VPP	O	I	O	...	I-VP
limitée	VPP	O	I	O	...	I-VP
à	P	O	O	B	...	B-PP
2,5	DET	B	O	I	...	I-PP
%	NC	I	O	I	...	I-PP

Table 3: Dataset Enriched by the Output of the chunk-specific Automata

but not very effective programs, whereas it is the contrary for statistical learning. In this section, we want to combine both strategies. There are two different possible viewpoints for this combination:

• if we stand from the viewpoint of effectiveness, we will favor statistical leaning. But the automata provided by our GI algorithms capture long-distance relationships between POS tags that could be useful for a CRF. So, in this case, our combination strategy will consist in integrating the output provided by the automata into the features of the CRF as an external resource.

• if we stand from the viewpoint of readability, we will favor the automata produced by GI. As evoked in 4.1, it is possible to simulate a HMM (and, similarly, an automaton) with CRF's features. We will show that it is also possible to evaluate the states and transitions of an automaton with CRF-computed weights associated to the features that represent them in a CRF, suggesting ways to improve it.

5.1 Enriching a CRF by automata-based features

We attack here both types of chunking. The first combination consists in considering the automata as independent annotation tools, as in Constant and Tellier (2012). In the case of complete chunking, we applied GI on each distinct type of chunk, leading to as many automata as there are types of chunks. Each chunk-specific automaton provides an independent BIO tagging, as shown in Table 3. Therefore, there are as many new attributes as there are types of chunks in our data.

First tables in Tables 4 and 5 give the templates used to obtain the best results for the complete chunking, and similarly for the first one of Table 6 for the NP-chunks only. The lines "Automaton" take into account the output of each automaton independently, whereas "POS+Automata" represents the concatenation of POS columns along with the output of every single automaton.

Matching results are given in the other tables. They show that attributes taken from automata allow to significantly improve the results of CRFs. It is even more obvious for the macro-average, the one that gives equal importance to every chunk. This means that the information brought by the automata mostly improve the recognition of rare chunks. In the experiment leading to the best macro-average, the best improvements are the following: the F1-measure of UNKNOWN goes from 41.67 to 61.22, the one of AP from 96.78 to 97.44 and the one of AdP from 98.72 to 98.92.

Feature	Type	Window
Word	Unigram	[-2..1]
POS	Bigram	[-2..1]
Automaton	Bigram	[-2..1]

F-measure	pure 1-RI (lm)
micro	97.66
macro	92.22

Table 4: Best micro-aver. for complete chunking

Feature	Type	Window
Word	Unigram	[-2..1]
POS	Bigram	[-2..1]
Automaton	Unigram	[-1..1]
POS+Automata	Bigram	[-1..1]

F-measure	pure 1-RI (sm)
micro	97.62
macro	93.52

Table 5: Best macro-aver. for complete chunking

Feature	Type	Window
Word	Unigram	[-2..1]
POS	Bigram	[-2..1]
Automaton	Bigram	[-1..1]
POS+Automata	Bigram	[-1..1]

	pure 2-RI LM
F-measure	96.75

Table 6: Best F-measure for NP chunking

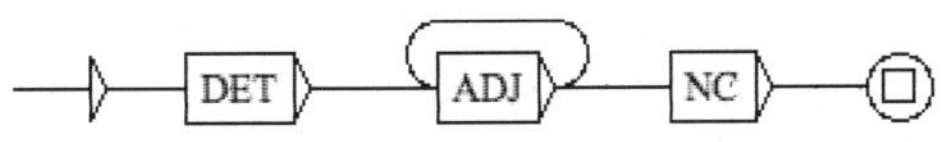

Figure 2: Unitex-generated automaton

5.2 Evaluating an automaton by CRF-computed weights

This time, we want to preserve the structure of the automata output by our GI strategies, but we use a CRF to evaluate some of their properties. We could build weighted automata, the way it is proposed by Roark and Saraclar (2004). Instead, we just propose a CRF-based diagnosis of a purely symbolic device. To illustrate our approach, we consider the NP-only chunking task, because only one automaton is to be considered. Our proposition is also easier to understand by representing automata in the alternative way of Figure 2 (representing the same automaton as the final one of Figure 1). This representation, which is favored in softwares like Unitex[7], has the advantage of displaying tags and transitions between tags as two distinct objects. To build a CRF based on such an automaton, we consider the BIO labeling effect of this automaton, as in section 5.1

Now, inspired by the relationship between discrete HMMs and CRFs (cf. section 4.1), we choose features which can be interpretable relatively to the automaton. We thus restrict ourselves to only two feature-templates:

• the unary feature-template only takes into account the current correct BIO NP-label together with the current POS tag and the current BIO label predicted by the automaton at the same position. Each POS tag matches one (or multiple) states of the automaton. If both BIO labels match for a given POS tag, then the features generated by this template express the correctness of the automaton at this position; if they are different they express its incorrectness

• the bigram feature-template only takes into account the current correct couple of BIO NP-labels together with the corresponding couple of consecutive POS tags as well as the corresponding couple of BIO automaton-predicted labels. The couples of consecutive POS tags characterize transitions of the automata. If the corresponding two couples of BIO labels coincide, it means that the automaton has correctly treated this transition, otherwise it has not.

Note that words, which do not appear in automata, are neither not taken into account in the feature-templates. The generated features have a constrained form to match the automaton structure. All of them are interpretable with respect to this automaton, as we will see now.

Table 7 is a confusion matrix comparing "automata-generated" BIO labels (AL) with the corresponding correct BIO label (CL), for a given POS tag. We can build as many such tables as there are distinct POS tags in NP chunks (the DET tag, in our example), each cell corresponding to an unigram feature. The cells of 7 are filled with the weights computed by the CRF for these features, where the colors display how they can be interpreted with respect to the initial automaton. As expected, weights on the diagonal, meaning a correct tagging, are positive and greater than those outside it, meaning a tagging error.

AL \CL	B	I	O
B	1.66	*-4.05*	*-0.84*
I	**-0.44**	0.46	*-2.51*
O	**-1.45**	**-1.02**	-0.17

Table 7: Confusion matrix for DET tag (2-RI, Table 1)

Where each cell can be interpreted as follows:

• no style : both outputs are identical.

• *italic* : premature chunk beginning.

• **bold** : missed chunk beginning.

• *italic* (underlined) : untimely chunk continuation.

• **bold** (underlined) : premature chunk ending.

Bigram features are a bit more complicated to interpret, but they can also give rise to confusion matrices. There are as many bigram confusion matrices as there are observed transitions between two tags, i.e. as many as observed couples of consecutive POS tags (at most $30 * 30$ in our case). A bigram confusion matrix for a specific transi-

[7] http://www-igm.univ-mlv.fr/ unitex/

Exp.	baseline (GI)	0-RI	1-RI	2-RI
chunk	88.25	93.00	93.07	93.08

Table 8: Labeling results of the CRFs based on the best automata for NP-chunking

tion has 9 lines and 9 columns, because there are $9 = 3 * 3$ distinct possible couples of BIO labels. Each cell corresponds to a bigram feature and is interpretable with respect to the transitions of the NP automaton. Each cell can thus also be filled with the weights associated to the corresponding feature by the CRF model.

The weights associated to the features in a CRF characterize their *discriminative power*. They are more relevant than the simple occurrence counts of how many times the features are satisfied in the training dataset. The content of diagonal cells can thus be seen as a measure of the effectiveness of the decision taken by the automaton at a state (resp. a transition) whereas the content of the other cells can be seen as the gain (or loss) taken by using an alternative decision at any time, during the labeling process. So, the whole set of confusion matrixes can be seen as a very precise evaluation of the relevance of the automaton.

Table 8 recalls the result of the best "pure GI" NP-automaton of section 3.3 and gives the labeling result of the CRFs defined as described above on the best automata output by k-RI, for each value of k. We see that the CRFs significantly improve the efficiency of the best automata, but are not as effective as a CRF using more attributes and features. This results can be interpreted as follows: it is sometimes beneficial to take labeling decisions which are not those of the automata. We still haven't taken the time to analyze the various confusion matrices produced by our CRFs in these cases, but we believe that they give very interesting indications about how, where and why the automata on which the features are based made right vs. wrong predictions, and possibly correct them.

6 Conclusion and perspectives

In this paper, we have applied two distinct machine learning approaches on the same dataset and proposed two distinct ways to combine them.

About GI alone, it is possible that other algorithms would give better results than k-RI, such as those of Garcia and Vidal (1990; Denis et al. (2002). The choice of a greater value of k could also improve our results, but at the cost of a greater time complexity[8]. More generally, it should be necessary be to define a learnable language class to which chunks are likely to belong. This would allow to define specific GI algorithms for this task, in which for example linguistic knowledge could be used to "control" state merges .

But the most original part of our work concerns CRFs and automata combinations. It is to be noted that they can both be applied to hand-made automata, likely to be more linguistically relevant than those obtained by GI. We focused here on automata produced by machine learning to show that, even without any linguistic expertise, it is possible to combine symbolic and statistical models. The intuition behind this work is that both machine learning techniques have complementary properties and should benefit from one another. CRFs are based on a huge number of weighted local configurations. It is theoretically possible to express in their features complex long-distance properties of the initial sequence x. In practice, it is rarely done. GI on the contrary applies to sequences and is able to provide a generalization of a set of sequences. It has already been observed that CRFs benefit from features expressing more general properties than simple local configurations (Pu et al., 2010). Our intuition was that GI could provide such useful generalizations. The obtained results confirm this intuition. It is also interesting to see that symbolic models enhance the treatment of rare cases, on which statistical models do not behave well.

CRF-generated confusion matrices for the analysis of an automaton still need to be further investigated. How to better interpret or take advantage of them is of particular interest. Some of the cells of these matrices are empty, either because the corresponding feature has not been observed in the training set or because it has been discarded by Wapiti during the learning step because of the penalty. It should be possible, thanks to this information, to modify the automaton on which the CRF is based by removing/adding states or transitions according to the diagnosis of the confusion matrices. A CRF-directed GI strategy still needs to be defined. This kind of GI challenge could also benefit from existing learning algorithms targeting probabilistic automata (Thollard et al., 2000).

[8] k-RI time complexity is of $|\Sigma|^k|Q|^{k+3}$ where $|Q|$ is the number of states of the PTA.

References

[Abeillé et al.2003] A. Abeillé, L. Clément, and F. Toussenel. 2003. Building a treebank for french. In A. Abeillé, editor, *Treebanks*. Kluwer, Dordrecht.

[Abney1991] S Abney. 1991. Parsing by chunks. In R. Berwick, R. Abney, and C. Tenny, editors, *Principle-based Parsing*. Kluwer Academic Publisher.

[Angluin1980] D. Angluin. 1980. Inductive inference of formal languages from positive data. *Information and Control*, 45(2):117–135, May.

[Angluin1982] D. Angluin. 1982. Inference of reversible languages. *Journal of the ACM*, 29(3):741–765, July.

[Antoine et al.2008] Jean-Yves Antoine, Abdenour Mokrane, and Nathalie Friburger. 2008. Automatic rich annotation of large corpus of conversational transcribed speech: the chunking task of the epac project. In *Proceedings of LREC'2008*, may.

[Blanc et al.2010] Olivier Blanc, Matthieu Constant, Anne Dister, and Patrick Watrin. 2010. Partial parsing of spontaneous spoken french. In *Proceedings of LREC'2010*.

[Constant and Tellier2012] M. Constant and I. Tellier. 2012. Evaluating the impact of external lexical resources unto a crf-based multiword segmenter and part-of-speech tagger. In *Proceedings of LREC 2012*.

[Crabbé and Candito2008] B. Crabbé and M. H. Candito. 2008. Expériences d'analyse syntaxique statistique du franÃ§ais. In *Actes de TALN'08*.

[de la Higuera2010] C. de la Higuera. 2010. *Grammatical Inference: Learning Automata and Grammars*. Cambridge University Press.

[Denis et al.2002] F. Denis, A. Lemay, and A. Terlutte. 2002. Some language classes identifiable in the limit from positive data. In *ICGI 2002*, number 2484 in Lecture Notes in Artificial Intelligence, pages 63–76. Springer Verlag.

[Dupont et al.1994] P. Dupont, L. Miclet, and E. Vidal. 1994. What is the search space of the regular inference. In Lecture Notes in Artificial Intelligence, editor, *ICGI'94 - Lectures Notes in Computer Science*, volume 862 - Grammatical Inference and Applications, pages 25–37, Heidelberg.

[Dupont et al.2005] Pierre Dupont, François Denis, and Yann Esposito. 2005. Links between probabilistic automata and hidden markov models: probability distributions, learning models and induction algorithms. *Pattern Recognition*, 38(9):1349–1371.

[Finkel et al.2008] Jenny Rose Finkel, Alex Kleeman, and Christopher D. Manning. 2008. Efficient, feature-based, conditional random field parsing. In *Proceedings of the 46th Annual Meeting of the Association for Computational Linguistics (ACL 2008)*, pages 959–967.

[Garcia and Vidal1990] P. Garcia and E. Vidal. 1990. Inference of k-testable languages in the strict sense and application to syntactic pattern recognition. *IEEE Transactions on Pattern Analysis and Machine Intelligence*, 12(9):920–925.

[Gold1967] E.M. Gold. 1967. Language identification in the limit. *Information and Control*, 10:447–474.

[Kanazawa1998] M. Kanazawa. 1998. *Learnable Classes of Categorial Grammars*. The European Association for Logic, Language and Information. CLSI Publications.

[Kearns and Vazirani1994] M. J. Kearns and U. V. Vazirani. 1994. *An Introduction to Computational Learning Theory*. MIT Press.

[Koshiba et al.2000] Takeshi Koshiba, Erkki Mäkinen, and Yuji Takada. 2000. Inferring pure context-free languages from positive data. *Acta Cybernetica*, 14(3):469–477.

[Lafferty et al.2001] J. Lafferty, A. McCallum, and F. Pereira. 2001. Conditional random fields: Probabilistic models for segmenting and labeling sequence data. In *Proceedings of ICML 2001*, pages 282–289.

[Lavergne et al.2010] Thomas Lavergne, Olivier Cappé, and François Yvon. 2010. Practical very large scale CRFs. In *Proceedings of ACL'2010*, pages 504–513. Association for Computational Linguistics, July.

[McCallum and Li2003] A. McCallum and W. Li. 2003. Early results for named entity recognition with conditional random fields. In *CoNLL'2003: Proceedings of The Seventh Conference on Natural Language Learning*.

[Paroubek et al.2006] P. Paroubek, I. Robba, A. Vilnat, and Ayache C. 2006. Data annotations and measures in easy, the evaluation campain for parsers of french. In *Proceedings of LREC'2006*, pages 315–320.

[Pu et al.2010] X. Pu, Q. Mao, G. Wu, and C. Yuan. 2010. Chineese named entity recognition with the improved smoothed conditional random fields. *Research in Computing Science*, 46:90–103. Special issue "Natural Language Processing and its Applications".

[Roark and Saraclar2004] Brian Roark and Murat Saraclar. 2004. Discriminative language modeling with conditional random fields and the perceptron algorithm. In *Proceedings of ACL*, pages 47–54.

[Sha and Pereira2003] F. Sha and F. Pereira. 2003. Shallow parsing with conditional random fields. In *Proceedings of HLT-NAACL 2003*, pages 213 – 220.

[Sutton and McCallum2006] Charles Sutton and Andrew McCallum, 2006. *Introduction to Statistical Relational Learning*, chapter An Introduction to Conditional Random Fields for Relational Learning. MIT Press, lise getoor and ben taskar edition.

[Tellier and Tommasi2011] Isabelle Tellier and Marc Tommasi. 2011. Champs Markoviens Conditionnels pour l'extraction d'information. In Eric Gaussier and François Yvon, editors, *Modèles probabilistes pour l'accès à l'information textuelle*. Hermès.

[Tellier et al.2012] I. Tellier, D. Duchier, I. Eshkol, A. Çourmet, and M. Martinet. 2012. Apprentissage automatique d'un chunker pour le français. In *Actes de TALN'12, papier court (poster)*.

[Thollard et al.2000] Franck Thollard, Pierre Dupont, and Colin de la Higuera. 2000. Probabilistic DFA inference using Kullback-Leibler divergence and minimality. In *Proc. 17th International Conf. on Machine Learning*, pages 975–982. Morgan Kaufmann.

[Tsuruoka et al.2009] Y. Tsuruoka, J. Tsujii, and S. Ananiadou. 2009. Fast full parsing by linear-chain conditional random fields. In *Proceedings of EACL 2009*, pages 790–798.

[Valiant1984] L.G. Valiant. 1984. A theory of the learnable. *Commun. ACM*, 27(11):1134–1142, November.

[Yokomori2003] T. Yokomori. 2003. Polynomial-time identification of very simple grammars from positive data. *Theoretical Computer Science*, 1.

Measuring Closure Properties of Patent Sublanguages

Irina P. Temnikova
Institute of ICT
Bulgarian Academy of Sciences
irina.temnikova@gmail.com

Negacy D. Hailu
Computational Bioscience Program
U. Colorado School of Medicine
negacy.hailu@ucdenver.edu

Galia Angelova
Institute of ICT
Bulgarian Academy of Sciences
galia@lml.bas.bg

K. Bretonnel Cohen
Computational Bioscience Program
U. Colorado School of Medicine
kevin.cohen@gmail.com

Abstract

Patent search is an important information retrieval problem in scientific and business research. Semantic search would be a large improvement to current technologies, but requires some insight into the language of patents. In this article we test the fit of the language of patents to the sublanguage model, focussing on closure properties. The research presented here is relevant to the topic of sublanguage identification for different domains, and to the study of the language of patents. We investigate the hypothesis that fit to the sublanguage model increases as one moves down the International Patent Classification hierarchy. The analysis employs a general English corpus and patent documents from the MAREC corpus. It is shown that patents generally fit the sublanguage model, with some variability between categories in the extent of the fit.

1 Introduction

The study presented in this article aims to contribute to two important Natural Language Processing (NLP) applications: patent search and sublanguage identification.

1.1 Patents and Patent Search

We define patents as "legal documents issued by a government that grant a set of rights of exclusivity and protection to the owner of an invention" (Alberts et al., 2011). Patent search is an important Information Retrieval (IR) problem due to the financial risks involved in accidentally breaking previously registered patent rights, and due to the complexity of the phenomenon. Patent search is carried out by a variety of users, including patent specialists, managers, researchers, attorneys, and inventors. There are multiple scenarios requiring patent search (Alberts et al., 2011), as well as multiple types of patent search tasks—state-of-the-art, novelty, patentability, infringement, freedom to operate, and due diligence (Hunt et al., 2007; Joho et al., 2010).

Different user types are prompted to adopt different and often complex search techniques, reflecting their different search aims and search tasks (Hunt et al., 2007). Search techniques include classification code search, keyword search, full-text search, forward and backward citation of related documents, inventor or author search, patent assignee search, patent family search, legal status, and cross-language search (Alberts et al., 2011). Among these, full-text search is considered to have relatively more advantages than the other types of search techniques, as it allows the user to access the full semantic contents of the patent document (Adams, 2010a). However, in its present state, full-text patent search still exhibits several shortcomings, such as poor precision and lack of disambiguation (Adams, 2010a; Adams, 2010b). Besides the increased IR field attention towards patent search (see the CLEF-IP[1], TREC-CHEM[2], NTCIR, and PaIR[3] tracks and workshops), full-text search still suffers from lack of linguistic processing, which prevents it from addressing real user needs (Adams, 2010a; Adams, 2010b).

1.2 Patents and Sublanguages

A major step forward in patent search could be achieved if patents could be indexed by semantic content. This could include indexing by semantic classes of named entities relevant to the domain of the patent, relationships between semantic classes of named entities, and the like. However, model-

[1]http://www.ifs.tuwien.ac.at/ clef-ip/index.html. Last accessed on May 16th, 2013.

[2]http://www.ir-facility.org/trec-chem

[3]http://www.ir-facility.org/pair-workshops

ing the appropriate semantics requires an in-depth understanding of the contents and the linguistic characteristics of the genre. This is a daunting task for unrestricted patents in general, but if patents in some domain only exhibit a limited number of semantic classes and relations, it becomes a practical undertaking. One could then apply the "information retrieval as information extraction" (Moens, 2006) approach to patent search. But, do patents exhibit such semantic limitations? And how can we tell?

The notion of the *sublanguage* has a long history in natural language processing. Definitions of "sublanguage" vary, but have some commonalities. They are contrasted with the general language (e.g. English as a whole) in terms of restrictions in a number of areas. Sublanguages (Kittredge, 2003) are generally thought to be restricted to communication by a limited community of experts, in a limited range of genres, using a limited vocabulary, with limits on the possible semantic classes of arguments to predicators and possibly limited or deviant syntax. Although it is logical to think that patents and patent applications discuss a restricted technical topic, it is known that every inventor uses his/her own language (Alberts et al., 2011), and thus the applicability of the sublanguage model to patents is not a given. This paper reports three experiments on the application of natural language processing techniques to the problem of determining whether or not patents fit the sublanguage model.

The approach taken here is to examine the closure properties of patents. The phenomenon of closure is related to the element of restriction in sublanguages. If a genre is restricted with respect to some linguistic characteristic, then that linguistic property will tend towards finiteness. We test for this by counting the incidence of some linguistic characteristic, such as the occurrence of novel lexical items, as increasing amounts of a body of documents are observed. If the linguistic characteristic tends towards finiteness, then at some point we will see no further growth as increasing amounts of the document collection are examined. When such growth stops, *closure* is said to have occurred. In this study, we experiment with three different levels of closure, described below.

For our experiment, we follow the International Patent Classification (IPC, recently revised to IPCR), which divides all areas of technology into eight sections (A-H), each hierarchically subdivided into several levels, including classes, subclasses, groups, and sub-groups (Alberts et al., 2011). Each patent has a code assigned, which indicates its membership at each of these classification levels (e.g. *"A63B 69/02"* corresponds to *training tools for fencing*).

It may be the case that sublanguages exist at the level of patents in general, or only at the lowest levels of the hierarchy, or at some level of abstraction between the lowest levels and the general category of "patent." For this reason, we experiment with categories at multiple levels in the hierarchy.

2 Related Work in Patent Language Studies and Sublanguage Identification

Besides the interest of the IR community, not much has been done on discussing the characteristics of patent language. The existing studies have noted very complex sentences, vague definitions, presence of multiple languages in the same patent, technical concepts, inventor-specific definitions, and a high number of spelling errors (Lupu, 2011; Itoh et al., 2003; Sheremetyeva et al., 1996). There is, however, also research focussing on the linguistic aspects of patent documents. Lin and Hsieh (2004) have investigated verb-noun collocations appearing in patent claims for developing resources for teaching English for Specific Purposes, and more specifically in the legal domain. The same authors (Lin and Hsieh, 2010) later conducted a corpus-based study with the purpose of collecting the most frequent technical terms using The United States Patent and Trademark Office (USPTO) Glossary. Shinmori et al. (2003) studied the syntactic and term complexities of Japanese patent claims using the NTCIR3 patent collection (Iwayama et al., 2003), with the aim of improving readability of Japanese patent claims.

The paper most related to our work is that of Oostdijk et al. (2010), who study the language differences between the different patent domains and the genre differences between the different patent sections (title, abstract, description, and claims) for purposes of tuning a patent search engine. They use the English-language European patent documents from the MAREC400k corpus. For preprocessing, they clean the XML tags, split the texts into sentences, and parse them with the Aegir parser. On average 1000 patents containing all four text sections, from three different classes (H01L – Semiconductor devices, A61K – Medical and dental preparations, and F06G – Electric digital data processing) were compared. Genre and domain differences were measured by calculating the average sentence length, the type-token ratio and the hapax ratio. They show that there are differences between the different domains, as well as that there are more differences at section than at subdomain level.

Our approach goes beyond the work of Oostdijk et al. (2010) by testing the hypothesis that the patent categories employed in their work fit the sublanguage model. To our knowledge, no study has tested this hypothesis on patents before. In addition to that, we also calculate the average sentence length and type:token ratio for all of the examined categories.

Our research hypothesis is that all of the levels of categories fit the sublanguage model, with the lowest (more specific ones) showing more closure, and the highest (more generic) ones having characteristics closer to general English.

Although there has been extensive work on recognizing and characterizing sublanguages, little has been done on recognizing sublanguages through closure properties. The classic study is (McEnery and Wilson, 2001). McEnery and Wilson (2001) compared two corpora which were thought to be representative of the general language with one corpus which was thought to represent a sublanguage. The general language corpora were a collection of works of fiction from the American Printing House for the Blind and a collection of proceedings from the Canadian Hansard. The corpus that was thought to represent a sublanguage was a collection of IBM technical manuals. They found evidence of lexical closure and type-POS closure (described below) in the IBM technical manuals, but no evidence of closure in sentence types. Temnikova and Cohen (2013) compared a sample of general English drawn from the British National Corpus with two biomedical corpora thought to represent two distinct sublanguages and found evidence of lexical and type-POS closure in both of the biomedical corpora. Like (McEnery and Wilson, 2001), they did not observe sentence type closure in either of the sublanguage corpora. Temnikova et al. (2013) examined the closure properties of clinical documents in Bulgarian, comparing a sample from the Bulgarian National Reference Corpus, representative of the general Bulgarian language, with a corpus of Bulgarian epicrises (a document type similar to discharge summaries). They found lexical and type-POS closure, and unlike the other studies just discussed, did observe sentence type closure.

3 Materials and Methods

For consistency with the work of Oostdijk et al. (2010), we use the MAREC400k corpus. MAREC400k is a subset of the MAREC corpus[4], which is a static collection of over 19 million patent applications written in 19 languages. The patents in the MAREC collection come from four different patent authorities: the European Patent Office[5] (patents from now on called **EP**), the World Intellectual Property Organization[6] (**WP**), the United States Patent and Trademark Office (USPTO[7], patents called **US**), and the Japan Patent Office[8] (**JP**). The patents are in a normalized XML format, which splits the patent in parts. MAREC400k is a subset of 100,000 randomly collected patents from each of the four patent collections (EP, WP, US, and JP). We utilized a 77,000 US patents of MAREC400k, as this is the amount we could process in time. The US patents were chosen, as according to MAREC's statistics, only in them both the abstracts and the descriptions were written fully in English[9].

The MAREC400k documents were stripped of the XML tags, with the title, abstract, description and claims extracted and left in text format. The texts were then split into sentences and enriched with part-of-speech tags with the help of the Natural Language ToolKit (NLTK) (Bird et al., 2009).

For consistency with Oostdijk et al. (2010), we extracted 1,000,000-word subsets of the 77,000 patents, containing text from patents, classified with the **A61K** and **H01L** IPC (International Patent Classification) categories. Although Oostdijk et al. also used the F06G documents, unfortunately, there were no F06G documents in our subset, so we restricted our experiment only to the first two patent categories. 1,000,000 words samples of the categories **A61**, **H01**, **A**, **H** were also collected from patents classified with the respec-

[4]http://www.ir-facility.org/prototypes/marec

[5]http://www.epo.org. Last accessed on June 10th, 2013.

[6]http://www.wipo.int/portal/index.html.en

[7]http://www.uspto.gov

[8]http://www.jpo.go.jp

[9]http://www.ir-facility.org/prototypes/marec/statistics

tive subcategories among the 77,000 documents. Finally, a 1,000,000 words subset of **All Patents (AP)** was also collected.

In order to collect an equal distribution of words from all sub-categories of a given category, we have split the 1,000,000 words between the sub-categories and collected 2000 words from file in each sub-category, until reaching the necessary number of words. In case of sub-categories with only a few files, we copied the whole file.

This has resulted in collecting 2000 words from on average 30 files from each subcategory. This approach has been followed to collect the 1,000,000 words for All Patents (subcategories A-H), A (subcategories A01-A99), H (subcategories H01-H99), A61 (subcategories A61B-A61Q), and H01 (subcategories H01B-H01T). The 1,000,000 words for A61K and H01L have been collected by simply getting the first 2000 words from each patent, classified with these categories.

Note that the result of this sampling is that the document collections at the higher levels are not composed by addition of the document collections at the lower levels–they are distinct.

Table 1 lists the IPC categories under study, along with their topics[10].

Category	Topics
A	Human Necessities.
H	Electricity.
A61	Medical or Veterinary Science, Hygiene.
H01	Basic Electric Elements.
A61K	(Chemical) Preparations for Medical, Dental, or Toilet Purposes.
H01L	Semiconductor Devices, Electric Solid State Devices.

Table 1: IPC Categories and topics.

In this categorization, the A categories are much wider than the H categories. The A sub-categories topics include: agriculture (A01), clothes and footwear (A41 and A43), furniture (A47), and fire-fighting (A61). In contrast, the H sub-categories are restricted to only electricity-related topics. At the lowest level, while A61K groups cleaning substances and drugs, H01L includes only semi-conductor devices.

In order to test our hypothesis of the sublanguage model fit (McEnery and Wilson, 2001), we needed a corpus of general English. We utilized a 1,000,000-word subset of the British National Corpus (BNC) (Leech et al., 1994), syntactically parsed by the Machinese Connexor's parser (Järvinen et al., 2004).

We do not consider here the differences between the NLTK and Connexor's parser tagsets, as Temnikova and Cohen (2013) have shown that differences in the tagset granularity do not affect the sublanguage model.

4 Results

The following subsections present the results of the three experiments, starting with the H class first, as its results are more straightforward to interpret.

4.1 Lexical Closure Properties

Figure 1 shows the lexical closure properties of the H class. The lexical *types* are the different types of words, while the lexical *tokens* are the single instances of these types occurring in the text. The 'type' is not the word lemma (i.e. the token 'stops' corresponds to the type 'stops' (which may have occurred 10 times in the text, which makes 10 tokens, but 1 type) and not to 'stop').

We display the growth in types for the BNC, for all patent classes combined, for the H class with all of its subclasses, for the H01 subclass with all of its subclasses, and for the H01L subclass of H01. Note that in the figures for the H class and for the A class, the curves for the BNC and for *all patents combined* are identical.

In the H class we see the prototypical results for lexical closure in a sublanguage and lack of closure in unrestricted text. As discussed in Temnikova et al. (2013), we consider tendency towards closure, with no evident closure as a sufficient sign of the sublanguage model fit. The clear closure in McEnery and Wilson (2001) is assumed to be due to the IBM manuals presumably being written in a controlled language, which, here, is not the case.

The number of types in the BNC continues to grow rapidly even after 1,000,000 tokens have been observed—there is no closure. In contrast, the number of types for all patents combined, for the H class, the H01 subclass of H, and the H01L subclass of H01 slows down in growth after about 200,000 tokens have been observed and after 1,000,000 tokens have been observed has

[10]Information taken from http://web2.wipo.int/ipcpub.

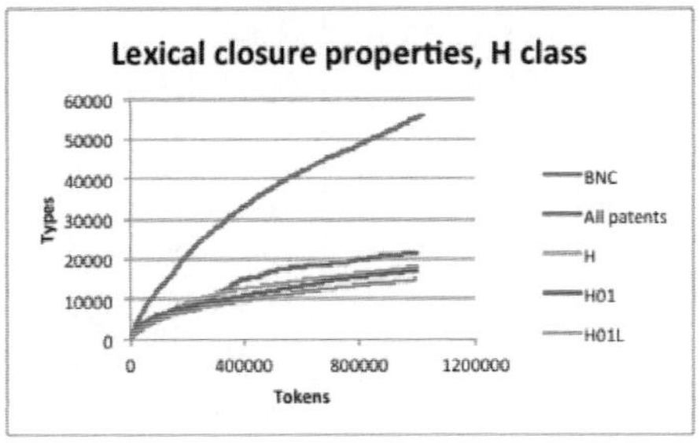

Figure 1: Lexical closure properties of the H class. Tick-marks on the x axis indicate increments of 400,000 tokens.

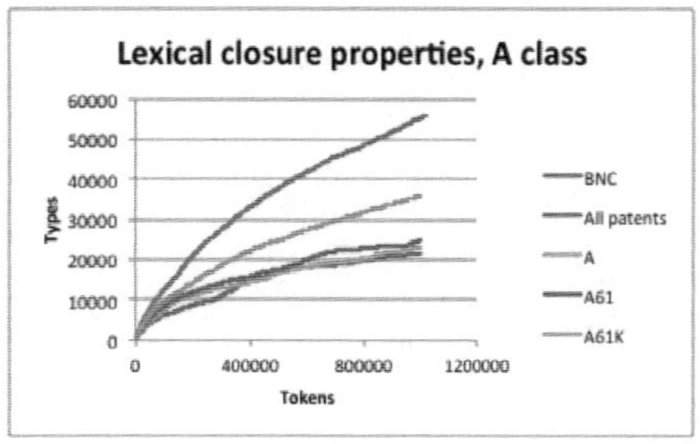

Figure 2: Lexical closure properties of the A class. Tick-marks on the x axis indicate increments of 400,000 tokens.

grown to a much smaller absolute number than the BNC. The evidence for closure is quite clear. In fact, closure is slightly more evident the further down the IPC hierarchy we go—looking at the ordering of the lines in Figure 1, we see that the ordering of the lines follows the descent into the hierarchy.

Figure 2 shows the lexical closure properties for the A class. Here, the picture is more complicated. Again, the BNC does not show closure. In contrast, the set of all patents, the A class, and the A61 subclass of A slow in growth after about 400,000 tokens have been observed and after 1,000,000 tokens have been observed have a much smaller absolute number of types than the BNC. However, the A61K subclass of A61 continues to exhibit rapid growth in the number of types as long as we continue to observe new tokens. After 1,000,000 tokens have been observed, the overall number of types is smaller than the BNC, but is about 1.5 times as large as the number of tokens in the classes that show closure. So, we can say that all patents, the A class, and its A61 subclass show lexical closure, but the A61K subclass does not appear to exhibit lexical closure.

The type to token ratios for lexical items for all the corpora as a whole are shown in Table 2. A lower ratio means that there is more variety in the specific corpus, while higher ratios mean more repetitiveness, and thus more restriction. Besides the differences in the 'type' interpretation between us and Oostdijk et al. (2010) (they looked at lemmas, while we do not), and thus the fact that they deal with much lower numbers, our findings confirm theirs in the fact that the average values for type:token ratios for A61K are lower than for H01L. As the sublanguage model would predict, all of the patent corpora have much higher ratios (i.e. exhibit more restriction) than the BNC.

Corpus name	Ratio
BNC	1: 18.20
All Patents	1: 46.36
H	1: 55.26
H01	1: 58.50
H01L	1: 65.23
A	1: 43.23
A61	1: 40.19
A61K	1: 27.87

Table 2: Lexical type-to-token ratios.

4.2 Type-Part-Of-Speech (POS) Closure Properties

Figures 3 and 4 show the type-POS set closure properties for the H and A classes, respectively. Here, the tokens are the single instances of lexical tokens, accompanied by their part-of-speech tag (e.g. 'stops – V', 'stops – N' are two tokens).

Again, the curves for the BNC and all patents are the same in both figures. We see similar patterns to the lexical closure properties: the BNC does not even come close to reaching closure; all patents tend to closure; the H class, its subclasses, the A class, and its subclass A61 tend to closure, with the H class and its subclasses beginning to slow in growth earlier than the A class and its subclass; the A61K class, in contrast, continues to grow rapidly even after 1,000,000 tokens have been observed.

The type-to-token ratios for token-POS pairs for all the corpora as a whole are shown in Table 3. Similarly to Table 2, we see much higher ratios for all the patents corpora, than for the BNC.

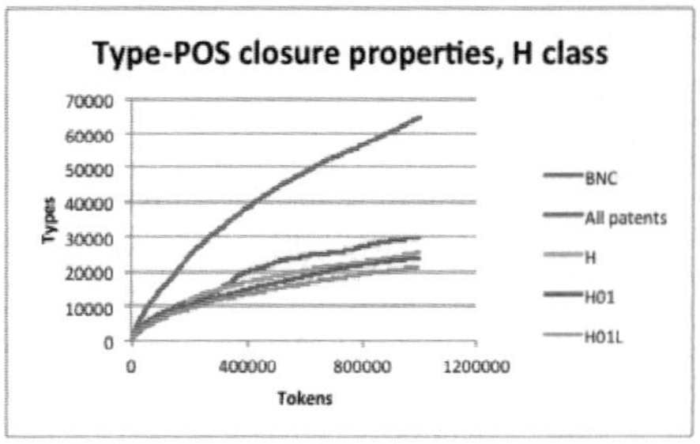

Figure 3: Type-POS closure properties of the H class. Tick-marks on the *x* axis indicate increments of 400,000 tokens.

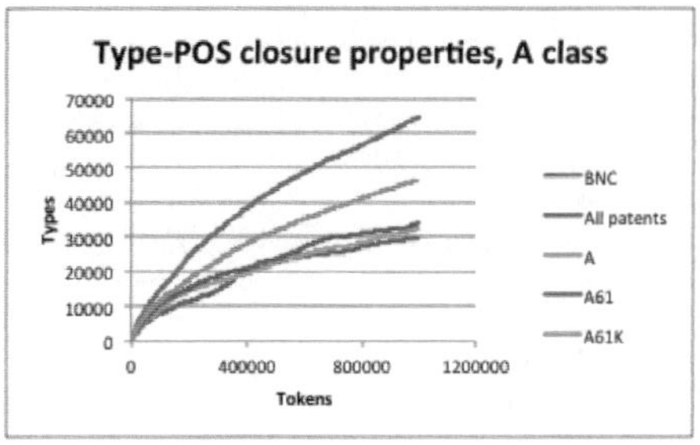

Figure 4: Type-POS closure properties of the A class. Tick-marks on the *x* axis indicate increments of 400,000 tokens.

4.3 Sentence Type Closure Properties

Figures 5 and 6 show the sentence type closure properties for the H class and the A class. Here, as in Temnikova and Cohen (2013), we define a sentence as a sequence of POS tags (every instance is a sentence token, the unique sentence is a sentence type). Again, the curves for the BNC and all patents are the same in both figures. Here we see no evidence for closure in the patents at all– the number of sentence types continues to grow rapidly even after 1,000,000 tokens have been observed.

The ratio of sentence types to sentence tokens and the average sentence lengths for the corpora as a whole are given in Table 4. As would be expected from the essentially linear growth observed in the graphics of all the corpora, all the ratios are close to 1:1. It can also be seen, that the average sentence lengths for all patents corpora are higher than the BNC, which confirms the findings of previous studies (Oostdijk et al., 2010; Shinmori et al., 2003).

Corpus name	Ratio
BNC	1: 15.46
All Patents	1: 33.36
H	1: 38.99
H01	1: 41.27
H01L	1: 46.34
A	1: 30.74
A61	1: 29.31
A61K	1: 21.41

Table 3: Type-to-token ratios for token/POS tags.

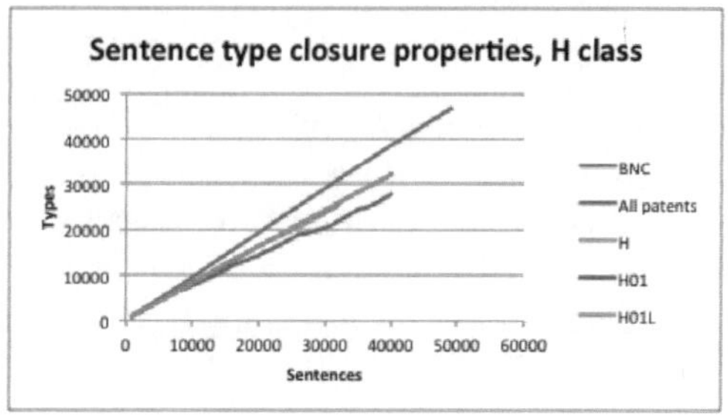

Figure 5: Sentence type closure properties of the H class. Tick-marks on *x* axis indicate increments of 50,000 tokens.

5 Discussion and Conclusions

The aim of the work reported here was to test the hypothesis that patent documents fit the sublanguage model. The motivation is that if we can detect sublanguages in any level of the patents, then there is the potential for developing methods for semantic search of patent collections.

Our most basic finding is that the patents do, in general, fit the sublanguage model. Tendency to closure at the lexical and type-POS levels were observed for all patents and for almost every class

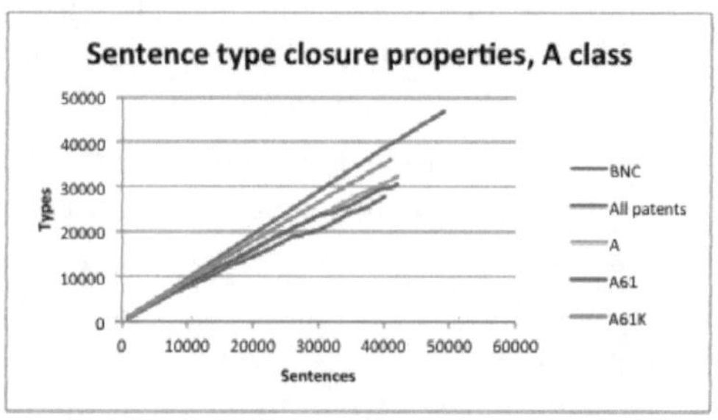

Figure 6: Sentence type closure properties of the A class. Tick-marks on *x* axis indicate increments of 50,000 tokens.

Corpus name	Ratio	Av. Sen. Length
BNC	1: 1.05	20.65
All Patents	1: 1.44	24.87
H	1: 1.27	30.95
H01	1: 1.24	24.78
H01L	1: 1.24	24.49
A	1: 1.30	23.42
A61	1: 1.37	23.53
A61K	1: 1.25	24.51

Table 4: Sentence type-to-token ratios and average sentence lengths.

and subclass that we examined, with the sole exception of A61K. Future linguistic analysis will clarify the unexpected behavior of A61K.

Sentence type closure was not observed; this result is consistent with the findings of McEnery and Wilson (2001) and Temnikova and Cohen (2013).

We examined the hypothesis that the further one descends down the IPC hierarchy, the closer the fit is to the sublanguage model. Here the results were more mixed. Descending the hierarchy of the H class, the hypothesis was supported. However, the behavior of the A class was not consistent with this hypothesis, and in fact it was unclear whether the A61K subclass fit the sublanguage model at all.

The type:token ratios showed different results for the A and the H categories. One fact that can be observed is, that in the case of H/H01/H01L the type:token ratios for lexical and token-POS pairs closures increase going down the hierarchy, as it would be expected from the increasing sublanguage specialization. The A/A61/A61K categories show the opposite: the type:token ratios are decreasing going down the hierarchy and approaching the general English values. These findings once again underline the unexpected nature of the A61K category.

The differing closure properties of the H class and the A class speak to a problem that we mulled over in the design of these experiments: is it meaningful to talk of the language of "patents" as a whole, or should we think in terms of there being many different kinds of languages of patents? The differences between the H and A class suggests that we should think of patents as representing a number of different language varieties. This raises the question of how well the language varieties line up with the IPC classification.

The size of the materials in this study allowed us to evaluate a hypothesis that has not been considered in any previous studies of the closure properties of language. McEnery and Wilson (2001) worked with samples of 200,000 words from each corpus. Temnikova and Cohen (2013) worked with samples of about 450,000 words. This study used samples of 1,000,000 words. Studies of closure properties have previously failed to consider the possibility that closure properties might be observed with small samples, but that there might be a "spikiness" to the distribution of lexical and other linguistic types that would reveal a lack of closure if larger samples were considered. The limiting factor in any study of closure properties is generally the size of the sublanguage sample; we considered here a sample more than twice the size of the previously largest sample, and still observed closure properties quite clearly. In this age of massive data sets, 1,000,000 words perhaps no longer qualifies as a "large" sample, but it is the most stringent test thus far of the ability of the sublanguage model to hold as sample size is increased beyond that of previous studies.

The results of this study hold out the promise of further development of semantic search for patents. However, they make it clear that this will be a broad problem, with the necessity to tackle different classes of patents separately, confirming the findings of Oostdijk et al. (2010). This study has shown that sublanguages exist in patents and that it is possible to recognize them using the techniques that we applied. Being able to recognize the presence of sublanguages in patents, the next step will be to develop techniques to characterize those sublanguages—to discover and describe *how* the patent sublanguages differ from the general language and from each other, and thence to develop methods of semantic search.

Acknowledgments

The work of Irina Temnikova and Galia Angelova was supported by the project AComIn "Advanced Computing for Innovation", grant 316087, funded by the FP7 Capacity Programme (Research Potential of Convergence Regions). The work of Kevin Bretonnel Cohen and Negacy D. Hailu was supported by grants NIH 5R01 LM009254-07 and NIH 5R01 LM008111-08 to Lawrence E. Hunter.

Finally, we would like to thank Mihai Lupu and Allan Hanbury for providing access to the MAREC400k corpus.

References

Stephen Adams. 2010a. The text, the full text and nothing but the text: Part 1–standards for creating textual information in patent documents and general search implications. *World Patent Information*, 32(1):22–29.

Stephen Adams. 2010b. The text, the full text and nothing but the text: Part 2–the main specification, searching challenges and survey of availability. *World Patent Information*, 32(2):120–128.

Doreen Alberts, Cynthia Barcelon Yang, Denise Fobare-DePonio, Ken Koubek, Suzanne Robins, Matthew Rodgers, Edlyn Simmons, and Dominic DeMarco. 2011. Introduction to patent searching. In *Current challenges in patent information retrieval*, pages 3–43. Springer.

Steven Bird, Ewan Klein, and Edward Loper. 2009. *Natural language processing with Python*. O'Reilly Media.

David Hunt, Long Nguyen, and Matthew Rodgers. 2007. *Patent searching: Tools and techniques*. Wiley.

Hideo Itoh, Hiroko Mano, and Yasushi Ogawa. 2003. Term distillation in patent retrieval. In *Proceedings of the ACL-2003 workshop on patent corpus processing-Volume 20*, pages 41–45. Association for Computational Linguistics.

Makoto Iwayama, Atsushi Fujii, Noriko Kando, and Akihiko Takano. 2003. Overview of patent retrieval task at NTCIR-3. In *Proceedings of the ACL-2003 workshop on Patent corpus processing-Volume 20*, pages 24–32. Association for Computational Linguistics.

Timo Järvinen, Mikko Laari, Timo Lahtinen, Sirkku Paajanen, Pirkko Paljakka, Mirkka Soininen, and Pasi Tapanainen. 2004. Robust language analysis components for practical applications. In *Robust and adaptive information processing for mobile speech interfaces: DUMAS final workshop*, pages 53–56.

Hideo Joho, Leif A. Azzopardi, and Wim Vanderbauwhede. 2010. A survey of patent users: an analysis of tasks, behavior, search functionality and system requirements. In *Proceedings of the third symposium on information interaction in context*, pages 13–24. ACM.

Richard I. Kittredge. 2003. Sublanguages and controlled languages. In Ruslan Mitkov, editor, *The Oxford Handbook of Computational Linguistics*, pages 430–447. Oxford University Press.

Geoffrey Leech, Roger Garside, and Michael Bryant. 1994. The large-scale grammatical tagging of text: experience with the British National Corpus. In N. Oostdijk and P. de Haan, editors, *Corpus based research into language*.

Darren Hsin-hung Lin and Shelley Ching-yu Hsieh. 2004. Collocation features of independent claim in US patent documents: Information retrieval from LexisNexis.

Darren Hsin-hung Lin and Shelley Ching-yu Hsieh. 2010. The specialized vocabulary of modern patent language: Semantic association in patent lexis. In *Proceedings of the 24th Pacific Asia Conference on Language, Information, and Computation (PACLIC 24)*.

Mihai Lupu. 2011. *Current challenges in patent information retrieval*, volume 29. Springer-Verlag Berlin Heidelberg.

Tony McEnery and Andrew Wilson. 2001. *Corpus Linguistics*. Edinburgh University Press, 2nd edition.

Marie-Francine Moens. 2006. *Information extraction: Algorithms and prospects in a retrieval context*. Springer.

Nelleke Oostdijk, Eva D'hondt, Hans Van Halteren, and Suzan Verberne. 2010. Genre and domain in patent texts. In *Proceedings of the 3rd international workshop on Patent information retrieval*, pages 39–46. ACM.

Svetlana Sheremetyeva, Sergei Nirenburg, and Irene Nirenburg. 1996. Generating patent claims from interactive input. In *Proceedings of the Eighth International Workshop on Natural Language Generation*, pages 61–70.

Akihiro Shinmori, Manabu Okumura, Yuzo Marukawa, and Makoto Iwayama. 2003. Patent claim processing for readability. In *Proceedings of ACL 2003 Workshop on Patent Corpus Processing Workshop*.

Irina Temnikova and K. Bretonnel Cohen. 2013. Recognizing sublanguages in scientific journal articles through closure properties. In *Proceedings of the 12th Workshop on Biomedical Natural Language Processing (BioNLP 2013)*.

Irina Temnikova, Ivelina Nikolova, William A. Baumgartner Jr., Galia Angelova, and K. Bretonnel Cohen. 2013. Closure properties of Bulgarian clinical text. In *Proceedings of RANLP 2013*.

Closure Properties of Bulgarian Clinical Text

Irina P. Temnikova
Institute of ICT
Bulgarian Acad. of Sciences

Ivelina Nikolova
Institute of ICT
Bulgarian Acad. of Sciences

William A. Baumgartner Jr.
Computational Bioscience Program
U. Colorado School of Medicine

Galia Angelova
Institute of ICT
Bulgarian Academy of Sciences

K. Bretonnel Cohen
Computational Bioscience Program
U. Colorado School of Medicine

Abstract

Sublanguages are specialized genres of language associated with specific domains and document types. When sublanguages can be recognized and adequately characterized, they are useful for a variety of types of natural language processing applications. Although there are sublanguage studies related to languages other than English, all previous work on sublanguage recognition has focused on sublanguages related to general English. This paper tests whether a sublanguage detecting technique developed for English can be applied to another language. Bulgarian clinical documents are an excellent test case, because of a number of unique linguistic properties that affect their lexical and morphological characteristics. Bulgarian clinical documents were studied with respect to their closure properties and were found to fit the sublanguage model and exhibit characteristics like those noted for sublanguages related to English. It was also confirmed that the clinical sublanguage phenomenon is not a coincidental phenomenon of English, but applies to other languages as well. Implications of this fact for natural language processing are proposed.

1 Introduction and Related Work

1.1 Sublanguages

The term *sublanguage* has various definitions, depending on criteria that will be discussed in a moment. However, descriptions of the sublanguage phenomenon generally have two things in common. One is that a sublanguage is the language used to communicate in a specific genre about a specialized domain. The other is that sublanguages are restricted in some way.

Sublanguages have been described for a variety of domains, including space events (Montgomery and Glover, 1986), recipes (Kittredge, 1982), legal documents (Charrow et al., 1982), and especially for clinical documents (Hirschman and Sager, 1982; Hiz, 1982; Friedman, 1986; Dunham, 1986; Stetson et al., 2002; Friedman et al., 2002).

Concomitantly with this domain restriction, sublanguages are typically characterized as being linguistically restricted in some way. For example, Kittredge (2003) describes sublanguages as having a restricted lexicon, relatively small number of lexical classes, restricted sentence syntax, deviant sentence syntax, restricted word co-occurrence patterns, and different frequencies of occurrence of words and syntactic patterns from the normal language.

Although sublanguage properties and sublanguage versus general language differences have been studied in various languages (e.g. (Laippala et al., 2009) and (Wermter and Hahn, 2004), for clinical language), all approaches to sublanguage recognition have been focussed on English. (We consider recognizing the existence of a sublanguage as a different task from learning the characteristics of a sublanguage; this paper is concerned with the problem of recognizing the existence of a sublanguage, although we also take preliminary steps to describe the data under investigation.) Sekine (1994) used an approach related to unsupervised learning, clustering documents and then calculating the ratio of the perplexity of the clustered documents to the perplexity of a random collection of words. Somers (1998) used weighted cumulative sums and showed that they are low in sublanguages. Stetson et al. (2002) used relative entropy and squared chi-square distance to demonstrate the existence of a sublanguage of cross-coverage notes. Mihaila et al. (2012) calculated distributions of a wide variety of biologically relevant semantic classes of named entities to identify and differentiate between a wide variety of scientific sublanguages in journal articles.

In addition to information-theoretic measures, non-information-theoretic, heuristic methods have been used to identify sublanguages, as well. In addition to the information-theoretic measures that they used, Stetson et al. (2002) also looked at such measures as sentence length, incidence of abbreviations, and ambiguity of abbreviations. Friedman et al. (2002) use semiautomatic and manual analyses to detect and characterize two biomedical sublanguages. McEnery and Wilson (2001) examine closure properties of differing genres; their approach is so central to the topic of this paper that we will describe it in some length separately.

One consequence of the various types of restrictions that can be seen in various researchers' conceptions of the notion of sublanguage is that various components of the language should tend towards finiteness. That is, if we examine sufficient quantities of a sample of the language, we should observe an eventual slowing or stoppage of growth in new items in that component of the language. Take, for instance, the case of lexical items, or words. As we examine increasing numbers of tokens, we would expect the number of types to increase. If a genre of language does not fit the sublanguage model, that growth will increase indefinitely. On the other hand, if a genre of language does fit the sublanguage model, that growth will asymptote towards zero. This slowing or stoppage of growth is known as closure. If growth in the number of types stops or asymptotes, we say that closure has occurred. If it does not, then there is no closure.

An early study of closure properties (although it did not use that term) was (Grishman et al., 1984). Grishman et al. (1984) utilized a broad-coverage syntactic grammar and three English-language document collections, each of which represented a presumed sublanguage. They charted the growth in the number of syntactic productions that was used as an increasing amount of the document collections was parsed. They found that for two of the three sublanguages, both consisting of medical documents, the growth curve flattened out, indicating closure. No non-sublanguage document collection was used for comparison. A revised grammar consisting just of productions that were observed in the sublanguage document collections was then used to re-parse the document sets, and a marked increase in the speed of parsing was obtained.

McEnery and Wilson (2001) first carried out a multi-faceted study of sublanguage closure properties, using two non-sublanguage document collections for comparison. Their experiment involved three document sets, one of which was suspected of fitting the sublanguage model and two of which were not. The document set that was suspected of fitting the sublanguage model consisted of a collection of IBM technical manuals. The document sets that were not suspected of fitting the sublanguage model were a collection of proceedings of the Canadian parliament known as the Hansard corpus, and a collection of works of fiction from the American Printing House for the Blind. They looked for closure on three levels: lexical closure, measured by growth in the number of word types as an increasing number of word tokens is examined; word-POS (part of speech) pair closure, where the number of different sets of combinations of a single word type with multiple POS tags is examined as an increasing number of POS-tagged words is observed; and sentence type closure, where the number of sentence types is examined as an increasing number of sentence tokens is observed.

In more recent work, Temnikova and Cohen (2013) applied similar techniques to two corpora of scientific journal articles, one from the genomics domain and one related to human blood cell transcription factors. They used the British National Corpus as the non-sublanguage comparison corpus. Scientific journal articles have been postulated to belong to a sublanguage since the seminal early work of (Harris et al., 1989). They found similar effects as in the (McEnery and Wilson, 2001) study of IBM technical manuals; lexical items and word-POS sets did not asymptote but had drastically smaller numbers than the BNC data and growth did slow considerably as the number of tokens increased. In addition, they found the type-token ratios for both of these to be consistent with the scientific journal articles fitting the sublanguage model, but not the BNC. The difference with the results of McEnery and Wilson (2001) was attributed to the fact that McEnery and Wilson (2001) probably employed a corpus of documents written in a controlled language. This factor would have restricted additionally the sublanguage corpus variety and would result in reaching closure much faster. For this reason, the significant slowing down of the growth of the specialized corpora's curves (compared with the general language corpus's), with tendency towards, but without reaching closure, was considered as a sufficient indicator of sublanguage model fit.

1.2 Relevance of Sublanguages to Natural Language Processing

The relevance of sublanguages to natural language processing is reviewed in (Temnikova and Cohen, 2013). The relevance of sublanguages to natural language processing has long been recognized in a variety of subfields. Hirschman and Sager (1982) and Friedman (1986) show how a sublanguage–based approach can be used for information extraction from clinical documents. Grishman et al. (1984) showed that a sublanguage grammar can be used to increase the speed of syntactic parsing. Finin (1986) shows that sublanguage characterization can be used for the notoriously difficult problem of interpretation of nominal compounds. Sager (1986) asserts a number of uses for sublanguage–oriented natural language processing, including resolution of syntactic ambiguity, definition of frames for information extraction, and discourse analysis. Sekine (1994) describes a prototype application of sublanguages to speech recognition. Friedman et al. (1994) uses a sublanguage grammar to extract a variety of types of structured data from clinical reports. McDonald (2000) points out that modern language generation systems are made effective in large part due to the fact that they are applied to specific sublanguages. Somers (2000) discusses the relevance of sublanguages to machine translation, pointing out that many sublanguages can make machine translation easier and some of them can make machine translation harder. Friedman et al. (2001) uses a sublanguage grammar to extract structured data from scientific journal articles.

1.3 Definition of and Prior Work on Epicrises

Since the putative sublanguage under consideration in this paper is that of Bulgarian epicrises, we define and describe them here, as well as the history of applying natural language processing techniques to them. The closest equivalents of the Bulgarian epicrises in English are discharge reports. The content of Bulgarian electronic health records is dictated by state regulatory agencies and is spelled out in Article 190 (3) of the legal agreement between the National Health Insurance Fund and the Bulgarian Medical and Dental Associations. Electronic health records must contain an *epicrisis*, or summation of the course of a medical case history. An epicrisis is typically 2-3 pages long and must contain the patient's personal details, diagnosis and comorbidities, anamnesis (personal medical history), patient status, physical examination and test findings, treatment, and recommendations. Epicrises are linguistically challenging input texts for natural language processing, for a variety of reasons. They may contain text in Latin (about 1%) and English, sometimes in the Cyrillic alphabet and sometimes in the Latin alphabet. About 3% of the text is abbreviations, both of Bulgarian and of Latin. Syntactically, the majority of the text consists of sentence fragments, rather than full sentences (Boytcheva et al., 2009).

There is some previous Natural Language Processing (NLP) work on Bulgarian epicrises which would benefit from insight into the sublanguage characteristics of Bulgarian epicrises. Boytcheva and Angelova (2009) describes a system architecture for processing Bulgarian epicrises, including a module for generating logical forms of conceptual graphs based on templates. Boytcheva et al. (2009) built a template-based system based on 106 epicrises, using it to extract structured information such as diagnoses, risk factors, and body parts. Georgiev et al. (2011) built a named entity recognizer to tag disease names in Bulgarian epicrises. Nikolova (2012) built a hybrid machine-learning-based and rule-based system to extract blood sugar levels and measures of body weight change from a collection of 2,031 sentences from 100 Bulgarian epicrises.

1.4 Hypotheses

The work presented in this article is based on the closure investigation method (McEnery and Wilson, 2001; Temnikova and Cohen, 2013). Our null hypothesis is that there are no differences in the closure properties of unrestricted text and epicrises. Neither might show closure, or both might show closure. If the null hypothesis turns out not to be true, then deviations from it could logically be observed in two directions. One is that the epicrises could demonstrate closure, while the unrestricted text does not. The other is that the unrestricted text could demonstrate closure, while the epicrises do not.

2 Materials and Methods

2.1 Materials

The experiments require two bodies of data: the collection of data that is being examined for fit to the sublanguage model, and a "background" corpus consisting of material in the general (i.e. not specialized) language. The data under examination in these experiments is a collection of de-identified epicrises. The background corpus is the Bulgarian National Reference Corpus (BNRC).

2.1.1 Epicrises

The collection of epicrises was de-identified by University Specialised Hospital for Active Treatment of Endocrinology "Acad. I. Penchev". It consists of 1,000 documents in total, containing 647,498 words.

2.1.2 Bulgarian National Reference Corpus

The Bulgarian National Reference Corpus (Savkov et al., 2012) is a collection of 400,000,000 tokens of spoken and written Bulgarian, composed of 50% fiction, 30% newswire text, 10% legal text, and 10% from other genres. Following the approach of the Brown corpus to obtain a balanced, representative subset of the same size as the collection of epicrises, 8,000 words were extracted from each BNRC file until 647,498 words were reached, which is the size of the epicrises corpus.

We note that it is reasonable to question whether the size of a corpus is necessary to detect or rule out closure properties. McEnery and Wilson (2001) were successful in doing both with collections of 200,000 words—one third the size of the corpora that we are using.

2.2 Methods

2.2.1 Data Preparation

The data was processed using the pipeline described in (Savkov et al., 2012). Both document sets were split into sentences, tokenized, part-of-speech tagged, and dependency parsed. All tokens were lower-cased.

2.2.2 Measuring Lexical Closure Properties

For each document set, the number of distinct lexical types was counted as increasing numbers of tokens were encountered.

2.2.3 Type-POS Closure

It is well known that a single word type might belong to more than one part of speech. We charted the number of new type/part-of-speech sets as increasing numbers of tokens were encountered. The motivation for examining the pattern of growth here is that if a sublanguage has a restricted lexicon, then words might be coerced into more parts of speech than is the case in unconstrained language.

2.2.4 Sentence Type Closure

Following (Temnikova and Cohen, 2013), we defined sentence types as sequences of part-of-speech tags. This is a very rough approximation of syntax—arguably, it is not syntactic per se—but it increases the sensitivity of the method to diversity in sentence types and has the advantage of being theory-neutral and easily generalizable.

2.2.5 Syntactic Deviance

Sublanguages have often been claimed to have deviant syntax (e.g. (Kittredge, 2003)). In an attempt to discover deviant syntactic structures, we looked for sentences that lack verbs, as discharge letters are expected to be characterized by this type of sentence.

2.2.6 Over-Represented Lexical Items in the Epicrises

Although the primary purpose of the work reported here is to recognize the existence of a sublanguage, rather than to learn its characteristics, we performed a preliminary investigation of the contents of the epicrisis corpus, using an algorithm known as simplemaths (Kilgarriff, 2012). Simplemaths is designed to find words that are over-represented in one corpus as compared to a reference corpus. It is based on the idea of calculating frequencies of occurrences of all words in both corpora, taking the ratio of the frequency of each word in both corpora, and ranking by ratio. To avoid the problem that words of widely differing frequencies might yield the same ratio—a word that occurs 100 times in the corpus of interest and 10 times in the reference corpus produce the same ratio as a word that occurs 10,000 times in one corpus and 1,000 times in the other, but they are not equally revealing as to the domain-related contents of the corpus, since one word is quite rare and the other quite common—we add a constant value to

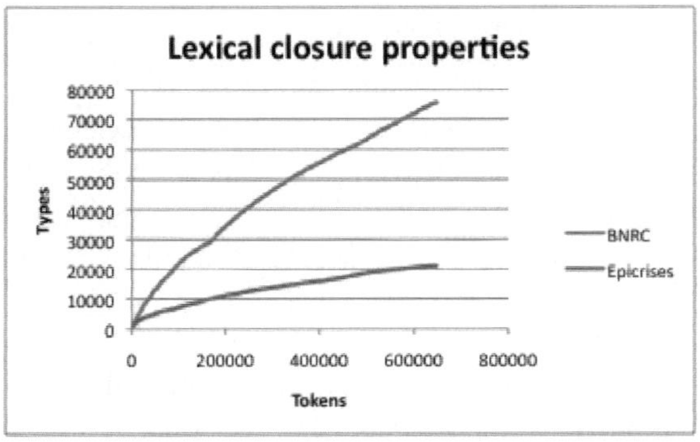

Figure 1: Lexical closure properties. Tick-marks on x axis indicate increments of 200,000 tokens.

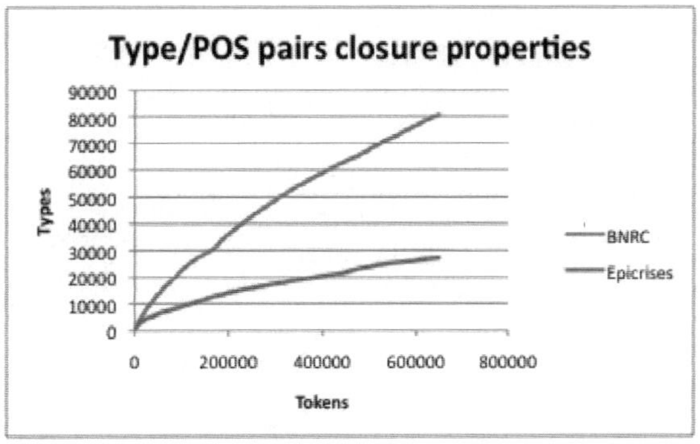

Figure 2: Type-POS closure properties. Tick-marks on x axis indicate increments of 200,000 tokens.

all counts. This has the effect of separating out the frequency ranges of rare and common words in the corpus. (It also takes care of smoothing zero counts.) The constant number is called the "simplemaths parameter." We used the suggested value of 100 for the simplemaths parameter.

3 Results

3.1 Lexical Closure

Figure 1 shows the lexical closure properties of the Bulgarian National Reference Corpus and the epicrises. As can be noted, there are drastic differences between the two. The BNRC has a much larger number of lexical types, and shows no tendency towards closure at all. In contrast, the epicrises have a much smaller number of lexical types and appear to show closure at a bit below 600,000 tokens.

The type/token ratio for lexical items in the BNRC and the epicrises is shown in Table 1. As the theory predicts, the type/token ratio of lexical items for the epicrises is much higher than that of the BNRC—more than three times higher.

Corpus	Ratio
BNRC	1:7.63
Epicrises	1:26.52

Table 1: Lexical type-to-token ratios.

3.2 Type-POS Closure

Figure 2 shows the type-POS set closure properties for the Bulgarian National Reference Corpus and the epicrises. Once again, we see drastic differences between the two. The BNRC has no tendency towards closure at all. In contrast, although the epicrises do not yet show closure, they show a clear tendency in that direction.

The type/token ratio for type-POS sets in the BNRC and the epicrises is shown in Table 2. Again, as the theory predicts, the type/token ratio of type-POS sets for the epicrises is much higher than that of the BNRC—more than two times higher.

Corpus	Ratio
BNRC	1:7.24
Epicrises	1:19.75

Table 2: Type/POS set type-to-token ratios.

3.3 Sentence Type Closure

Figure 3 shows the sentence type closure properties for the Bulgarian National Reference Corpus and the epicrises. Unlike the other two graphs, where the number of tokens is the same, in the case of this graph the number of sentence tokens is different between the two corpora, since sentence length varies between them. The results are notable for a number of reasons. We see drastic differences in the growth curves for the two corpora. In the case of the BNRC, growth in sentence types almost completely matches the number of sentence tokens—sentence types are rarely repeated. In contrast, we see drastically different growth in the epicrisis sentence types—there are many more epicrisis sentence tokens, and yet far fewer sentence types overall. Sentence types are frequently repeated in the epicrises. This is an important finding—McEnery and Wilson (2001) and Temnikova and Cohen (2013) did not find find any

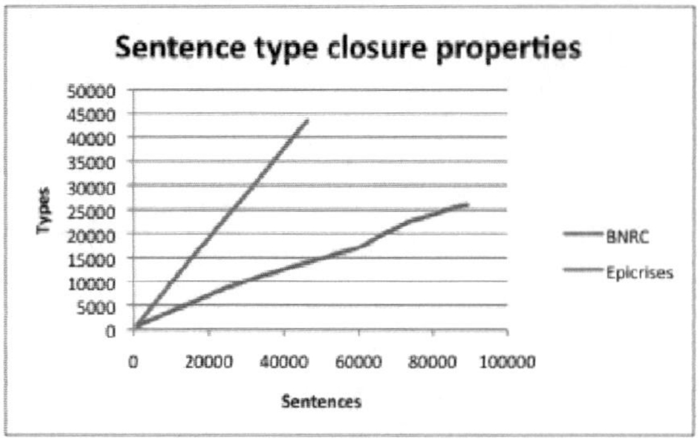

Figure 3: Sentence type closure properties. Tickmarks on x axis indicate increments of 20,000 tokens.

closure at the syntactic level. It is remarkable to note that this result was obtained in spite of the large number of part-of-speech tags assigned (680, due to the very complex morphology of Bulgarian). Such a large number would make the probability of any sequence of part-of-speech tags very low.

The type/token ratio for sentence types in the BNRC and the epicrises is shown in Table 3. Once again, as the theory predicts, the type/token ratio of sentences for the epicrises is much higher than that of the BNRC—more than three times higher. The type/token ratio for the BNRC is quite close to 1:1—sentence types in unrestricted text are almost never repeated.

Corpus	Ratio
BNRC	1:1.06
Epicrises	1:3.44

Table 3: Sentence type-to-token ratios.

It is likely that the presence of repeated sentence types in the epicrises as compared to the BNRC is related to the difference in the average length of sentences in the two corpora. The average sentence length in the BNRC is 14.16 words, while the average sentence length in the epicrises is 7.40–about half the length of the average BNRC sentence. This both explains the large difference in the number of sentences seen in Figure 3 (bear in mind that the number of words in the two sets of documents is the same) and helps explain why it might be more likely for sentence types to be repeated.

3.4 Syntactic Deviance

Our preliminary attempt at characterizing syntactic deviance through counting the number of sentences with no verbs shows a strong tendency towards syntactic deviance in the epicrises as compared to the Bulgarian National Reference Corpus. In the BNRC, we noted that 11% (4,943/46,549) of the sentences were verbless (probably mostly section headers and the like). In contrast, in the epicrises, a full 66% of sentences (58,753 out of 89,331 sentences) lacked a verb, e.g. Корем - мек, неболезнен. 'Abdomen - soft, painless.' The epicrises show a strong tendency towards syntactic deviance, as predicted for sublanguages.

3.5 Over-Represented Lexical Items in the Epicrises

Table 4 shows lexical items that are over-represented in the epicrises. Note that these are not the most *frequent* ones, but rather the ones that occur in the document set more often than would be expected. We display just the top ten most highly over-represented lexical items, with separate lists of the over-represented word types and over-represented lemmata. Examining the top 50 terms in each list, we see heavy representation of lexical items related to diabetes, body parts, and symptoms. Even in the short list of items displayed in Table 4, almost every item is relevant to either the semantics or the syntax of the domain. 'ч' is an abbreviation for 'часа' (hours), which occurs frequently to indicate the time at which one of a series of blood levels was drawn and is essential for extracting trends in lab results. '/' has a variety of uses, primarily syntactic, such as linking systolic and diastolic blood pressures. The clinical significance of the other items in the top-10 list is clear, with the exception of the semicolon ';' which occurs frequently in lists of lab values and of symptoms.

4 Discussion and Conclusions

This paper has presented the first attempt to detect a sublanguage in Bulgarian.

The data demonstrate that Bulgarian clinical records fit the model, as shown by the closure properties of the lexicon, morphology, and sentence types. Unlike the previous work of McEnery and Wilson (2001) and Temnikova and Cohen (2013), sentence type closure was demonstrated for the first time.

Word type		Lemma	
ч	hour	ч	hour
/	/	/	/
лечение	treatment	диабетна	diabetic, f. sg.
диабет	diabetes	лечение	treatment
;	;	диабет	diabetes
x	repetition, e.g. of dosage	захарен	sugar, m. sg. adj.
мг	mg	клиника	clinic
диабетна	diabetic, f. sg.	мг	mg
тип	type	полиневропатия	polyneuropathy
полиневропатия	polyneuropathy	анамнеза	anamnesis

Table 4: Word types and lemmata that are over-represented in the epicrises. Note that these are not the most frequent word types/lemmata, but rather the ones that occur more frequently than would be expected as compared to the reference corpus.

The finding that Bulgarian clinical documents are written in a sublanguage and the logical future work on closure with respect to arguments of predicators would aid Boytcheva and Angelova (2009) and Boytcheva et al. (2009) in the discovery of additional candidates for template representations.

Our finding that epicrises seem to be written in a very restricted sublanguage would also help understand how it was possible to achieve an F-measure of 0.81 on a test collection of only ten documents and why it took almost no time to build a named entity recognizer to tag disease names in Bulgarian epicrises (Georgiev et al., 2011).

The findings described here help us understand why that was possible, when building training sets for learning to recognize other biomedical classes of named entities has been so time-consuming. By virtue of fitting the sublanguage model, the epicrises represent a smaller set of lexical items to be classified and allow for the efficacy of a smaller number of features. Finally, as mentioned in the introduction, Nikolova (2012) built a hybrid machine-learning-based and rule-based symptom to extract blood sugar levels and measures of body weight change from a collection of 2,031 sentences from 100 Bulgarian epicrises. Insight into the sublanguage properties of the input data would have helped in determining which assays would best be extracted by rule-based methods and which would best be approached through machine learning.

This work has focused on detecting the existence of sublanguages. The important next step is to develop methods for determining the characteristics of sublanguages—determining the semantic, syntactic, and other restrictions that characterize the sublanguage and reporting them to the natural language processing researcher in a utilizable way. The work here lays the groundwork for that future work, helping us to determine when a genre or domain is likely to yield results that are susceptible to such research and when such research is less likely to be fruitful.

Acknowledgments

The work of Irina Temnikova, Ivelina Nikolova and Galia Angelova presented in this article was supported by the project AComIn "Advanced Computing for Innovation", grant 316087, funded by the FP7 Capacity Programme (Research Potential of Convergence Regions). The work of Kevin Bretonnel Cohen and William Baumgartner was supported by the grants NIH 5R01 LM009254-07 and NIH 5R01 LM008111-08 to Lawrence E. Hunter, NIH 1R01MH096906-01A1 to Tal Yarkoni, NIH R01 LM011124 to John Pestian, and NSF IIS-1207592 to Lawrence E. Hunter and Barbara Grimpe. We would like to specially thank Kiril Simov for the help with pre-processing the Bulgarian data.

References

Svetla Boytcheva and Galia Angelova. 2009. Towards extraction of conceptual structures from electronic health records. In *Conceptual structures: Leveraging semantic technologies*, pages 100–113.

Svetla Boytcheva, Ivelina Nikolova, and Elena Paskaleva. 2009. Context related extraction of conceptual information from electronic health records.

In *Conceptual structures for extracting natural language semantics*, pages 38–49.

Veda Charrow, Jo Ann Crandall, and Robert Charrow. 1982. Characteristics and functions of legal language. In Richard Kittredge and John Lehrberger, editors, *Sublanguage: Studies of language in restricted semantic domains*, pages 191–205. Walter de Gruyter & Company.

George Dunham. 1986. The role of syntax in the sublanguage of medical diagnostic statements. In Ralph Grishman and Richard Kittredge, editors, *Analyzing language in restricted domains: Sublanguage description and processing*, pages 175–194. Lawrence Erlbaum Associates.

Timothy W. Finin. 1986. Constraining the interpretation of nominal compounds in a limited context. In Ralph Grishman and Richard Kittredge, editors, *Analyzing language in restricted domains: sublanguage description and processing*, pages 85–102. Lawrence Erlbaum Associates.

Carol Friedman, Philip O. Anderson, John H.M. Austin, James J. Cimino, and Stephen B. Johnson. 1994. A general natural-language text processor for clinical radiology. *Journal of the American Medical Informatics Association*, 1:161–174.

Carol Friedman, Pauline Kra, Hong Yu, Michael Krauthammer, and Andrey Rzhetsky. 2001. GENIES: a natural-language processing system for the extraction of molecular pathways from journal articles. *Bioinformatics*, 17(Suppl. 1):S74–S82.

Carol Friedman, Pauline Kra, and Andrey Rzhetsky. 2002. Two biomedical sublanguages: a description based on the theories of Zellig Harris. *Journal of Biomedical Informatics*, 35:222–235.

Carol Friedman. 1986. Automatic structuring of sublanguage information. In Ralph Grishman and Richard Kittredge, editors, *Analyzing language in restricted domains: sublanguage description and processing*, pages 85–102. Lawrence Erlbaum Associates.

Georgi D. Georgiev, Valentin Zhikov, Borislav Popov, and Preslav Nakov. 2011. Building a named entity recognizer in three days: Application to disease name recognition in Bulgarian epicrises. In *Proceedings of the workshop on biomedical natural language processing, RANLP 2011*, pages 27–34.

Ralph Grishman, Ngo Thanh Nhan, Elaine Marsh, and Lynette Hirschman. 1984. Automated determination of sublanguage syntactic usage. In *Proceedings of the 10th International Conference on Computational Linguistics and 22nd annual meeting on Association for Computational Linguistics*, pages 96–100. Association for Computational Linguistics.

Zellig Harris, Michael Gottfried, Thomas Ryckman, Anne Daladier, Paul Mattick, T.N. Harris, and Susanna Harris. 1989. *The form of information in science: analysis of an immunology sublanguage*. Kluwer Academic Publishers.

Lynette Hirschman and Naomi Sager. 1982. Automatic information formatting of a medical sublanguage. In Richard Kittredge and John Lehrberger, editors, *Sublanguage: studies of language in restricted semantic domains*, pages 27–80. Walter de Gruyter.

Henry Hiz. 1982. Specialized languages of biology, medicine and science and connections between them. In Richard Kittredge and John Lehrberger, editors, *Sublanguage: Studies of language in restricted semantic domains*, pages 206–212. Walter de Gruyter & Company.

Adam Kilgarriff. 2012. Getting to know your corpus. In *Text, speech and dialogue*.

Richard Kittredge. 1982. Variation and homogeneity of sublanguages. In Richard Kittredge and John Lehrberger, editors, *Sublanguage: studies of language in restricted semantic domains*, pages 107–137.

Richard I. Kittredge. 2003. Sublanguages and controlled languages. In Ruslan Mitkov, editor, *The Oxford Handbook of Computational Linguistics*, pages 430–447. Oxford University Press.

Veronika Laippala, Filip Ginter, Sampo Pyysalo, and Tapio Salakoski. 2009. Towards automated processing of clinical Finnish: Sublanguage analysis and a rule-based parser. *International Journal of Medical Informatics*, 78(12):e7–e12.

David D. McDonald. 2000. Natural language generation. In Robert Dale, Hermann Moisl, and Harold Somers, editors, *Handbood of Natural Language Processing*, pages 147–179. Marcel Dekker.

Tony McEnery and Andrew Wilson. 2001. *Corpus Linguistics*. Edinburgh University Press, 2nd edition.

Claudiu Mihaila, Riza Theresa Batista-Navarro, and Sophia Ananiadou. 2012. Analysing entity type variation across biomedical subdomains. In *Third workshop on building and evaluating resources for biomedical text mining*, pages 1–7.

Christine A. Montgomery and Bonnie C. Glover. 1986. A sublanguage for reporting and analysis of space events. In Ralph Grishman and Richard Kittredge, editors, *Analyzing language in restricted domains: Sublanguage description and processing*, pages 129–161. Lawrence Erlbaum Associates.

Ivelina Nikolova. 2012. Unified extraction of health condition descriptions. In *Proceedings of the NAACL HLT 2012 student research workshop*, pages 23–28.

Naomi Sager. 1986. Sublanguage: linguistic phenomenon, computational tool. In Ralph Grishman and Richard Kittredge, editors, *Analyzing language in restricted domains: sublanguage description and processing*, pages 1–17. Lawrence Erlbaum Associates.

Aleksandar Savkov, Laska Laskova, Stanislava Kancheva, Petya Osenova, and Kiril Simov. 2012. Linguistic analysis processing line for Bulgarian. In *Proceedings of the eighth international conference on language resources and evaluation*, pages 2959–2964.

Satoshi Sekine. 1994. A new direction for sublanguage NLP. In *Proceedings of the international conference on new methods in natural language processing*, pages 123–129.

Harold Somers. 1998. An attempt to use weighted cusums to identify sublanguages. In *NeMLaP3/CoNLL98: New methods in language processing and computational natural language learning*, pages 131–139.

Harold Somers. 2000. Machine translation. In Robert Dale, Hermann Moisl, and Harold Somers, editors, *Handbook of Natural Language Processing*, pages 329–346. Marcel Dekker.

Peter D. Stetson, Stephen B. Johnson, Matthew Scotch, and George Hripcsak. 2002. The sublanguage of cross-coverage. In *Proc. AMIA 2002 Annual Symposium*, pages 742–746.

Irina Temnikova and K. Bretonnel Cohen. 2013. Recognizing sublanguages in scientific journal articles through closure properties. In *Proceedings of BioNLP 2013*.

Joachim Wermter and Udo Hahn. 2004. Really, is medical sublanguage that different? Experimental counter-evidence from tagging medical and newspaper corpora. *Studies in health technology and informatics*, 107(Pt 1):560.

Analyzing the Use of Character-Level Translation with Sparse and Noisy Datasets

Jörg Tiedemann
Department of Linguistics and Philology
Uppsala University
Uppsala, Sweden
jorg.tiedemann@lingfil.uu.se

Preslav Nakov
Qatar Computing Research Institute
Qatar Foundation, P.O. box 5825
Doha, Qatar
pnakov@qf.org.qa

Abstract

This paper provides an analysis of character-level machine translation models used in pivot-based translation when applied to sparse and noisy datasets, such as crowdsourced movie subtitles. In our experiments, we find that such character-level models cut the number of untranslated words by over 40% and are especially competitive (improvements of 2-3 BLEU points) in the case of limited training data. We explore the impact of character alignment, phrase table filtering, bitext size and the choice of pivot language on translation quality. We further compare cascaded translation models to the use of synthetic training data via multiple pivots, and we find that the latter works significantly better. Finally, we demonstrate that neither word- nor character-BLEU correlate perfectly with human judgments, due to BLEU's sensitivity to length.

1 Introduction

Statistical machine translation (SMT) systems, which dominate the field of machine translation today, are easy to build and offer competitive performance in terms of translation quality. Unfortunately, training such systems requires large parallel corpora of sentences and their translations, called *bitexts*, which are not available for most language pairs and textual domains. As a result, building an SMT system to translate directly between two languages is often not possible. A common solution to this problem is to use an intermediate, or *pivot* language to bridge the gap in training such a system.

A typical approach is a *cascaded translation* model using two independent steps of translating from the source to the pivot and then from the pivot to the target language. A special case is where the pivot is closely related to the source language, which makes it possible to train useful systems on much smaller bitexts using *character-level translation* models. This is the case we will consider below, translating Macedonian to English via related languages, primarily Bulgarian.

Our main contribution is the further analysis of such a setup. We show that character-level models can cut the number of untranslated words almost by half since translation involves many transformations at the sub-word level. We further explore the impact of character alignment, phrase table pruning, data size, and choice of pivot language on the effectiveness of character-level SMT models. We also study the use of character-level translation for the generation of synthetic training data, which significantly outperforms all cascaded translation setups. Finally, we present a manual evaluation showing that neither word- nor character-BLEU correlate perfectly with human judgments.

The remainder of the paper is organized as follows: Section 2 presents related work. Section 3 discusses technical details about using character-level SMT models. Section 4 describes the experiments, and Section 5 discusses the results. Section 6 concludes with directions for future work.

2 Related Work

SMT using pivot languages has been studied for several years. Cohn and Lapata (2007) used *triangulation* techniques for the combination of phrase tables. The lexical weights in such an approach can be estimated by bridging word alignments (Wu and Wang, 2007; Bertoldi et al., 2008).

Cascaded translation via pivot languages is used by various researchers (de Gispert and Mariño, 2006; Koehn et al., 2009; Wu and Wang, 2009). Several techniques are compared in (Utiyama and Isahara, 2007; de Gispert and Mariño, 2006; Wu and Wang, 2009). Pivot languages can also be used for paraphrasing and lexical adaptation (Bannard and Callison-Burch, 2005; Crego et al., 2010). None of this work exploits the similarity between the pivot and the source/target language.

The first step in our pivoting experiments involves SMT between closely related languages, which has been handled using word-for-word translation and manual rules for a number of language pairs, e.g., Czech–Slovak (Hajič et al., 2000), Turkish–Crimean Tatar (Altintas and Cicekli, 2002), Irish–Scottish Gaelic (Scannell, 2006), Cantonese–Mandarin (Zhang, 1998). In contrast, we explore statistical approaches that are potentially applicable to many language pairs.

Since we combine word- and character-level models, a relevant line of research is on combining SMT models of different granularity, e.g., Luong et al. (2010) combine word- and morpheme-level representations for English–Finnish. However, they did not assume similarity between the two languages, neither did they use pivoting.

Another relevant research combines bitexts between related languages with little or no adaptation (Nakov and Ng, 2009; Marujo et al., 2011; Wang et al., 2012; Nakov and Ng, 2012). However, that work did not use character-level models.

Character-level models were used for transliteration (Matthews, 2007; Tiedemann and Nabende, 2009) and for SMT between closely related languages (Vilar et al., 2007; Tiedemann, 2009a; Nakov and Tiedemann, 2012). Tiedemann (2012a) used pivoting with character-level SMT.

3 Character-level SMT Models

Closely related languages largely overlap in vocabulary and exhibit strong syntactic and lexical similarities. Most words have common roots and express concepts with similar linguistic constructions. Spelling conventions and morphology can still differ, but these differences are typically regular and thus can easily be generalized.

These similarities and regularities motivate the use of character-level SMT models, which can operate at the sub-word level, but also cover mappings spanning over words and multi-word units. Character-level SMT models, thus combine the generality of character-by-character transliteration and lexical mappings of larger units that could possibly refer to morphemes, words or phrases, to various combinations thereof.

One drawback of character-level models is their inability to model long-distance word reorderings. However, we do not assume very large syntactic differences between closely related languages. Another issue is that sentences become longer, which causes an overhead in decoding time.

In our experiments below, we use phrase-based SMT, treating characters as words, and using a special character for the original space character. Due to the reduced vocabulary, we can easily train models of higher order, thus capturing larger context and avoiding generating non-word sequences: we opted for models of order 10, both for the language model and for the maximal phrase length (normally, 5 and 7, respectively).

One difficulty is that training these models requires the alignment of characters in bitexts. Specialized character-level alignment algorithms do exist, e.g., those developed for character-to-phoneme translations (Damper et al., 2005; Jiampojamarn et al., 2007). However, Tiedemann (2012a) has demonstrated that standard tools for word alignment are in fact also very effective for character-level alignment, especially when extended with local context. Using character n-grams instead of single characters improves the expressive power of lexical translation parameters, which are one of the most important factors in standard word alignment models. For example, using character n-grams increases the vocabulary size of a 1.3M tokens-long Bulgarian text as follows: 101 single characters, 1,893 character bigrams, and 14,305 character trigrams; compared to 30,927 words. In our experiments, we explore the impact of increasing n-gram sizes on the final translation quality. We can confirm that bigrams perform best, constituting a good compromise between generality and contextual specificity.

Hence, we used GIZA++ (Och and Ney, 2003) to generate IBM model 4 alignments (Brown et al., 1993) for character n-grams, which we symmetrized using the *grow-diag-final-and* heuristics. We then converted the result to character alignments by dropping all characters behind the initial one. Finally, we used the Moses toolkit (Koehn et al., 2007) to build a character-level phrase table.

We tuned the parameters of the log-linear SMT model by optimizing BLEU (Papineni et al., 2002). Computing BLEU scores over character sequences does not make much sense, especially for small n-gram sizes (usually, $n \leq 4$). Therefore, we post-processed the character-level n-best lists in each tuning step to calculate word-level BLEU. Thus, we optimized word-level BLEU, while performing character-level translation.

4 Experiments and Evaluation

We used translated movie subtitles from the freely available OPUS corpus (Tiedemann, 2009b). The collection includes small amounts of parallel data for Macedonian-English (MK-EN), which we use as our test case. There is substantially more data for Bulgarian (BG), our main pivot language. For the translation between Macedonian and Bulgarian, there is even less data available. See Table 1.

dataset	# sentences	# words
MK-EN	160K	2.2M
MK-BG	102K	1.3M
BG-EN	10M	152M
MK-mono	536K	4M
BG-mono	16M	136M
EN-mono	43M	435M

Table 1: Size of the datasets.

The original data from OPUS is contributed by on-line users with little quality control and is thus quite noisy. Subtitles in OPUS are checked using automatic language identifiers and aligned using time information (Tiedemann, 2009b; Tiedemann, 2012b). However, we identified many misaligned files and, therefore, we realigned the corpus using `hunalign` (Varga et al., 2005). We also found several Bulgarian files misclassified as Macedonian and vice versa, which we addressed by filtering out any document pair for which the BLEU score exceeded 0.7 since it is likely to have large overlapping parts in the same language. We also filtered out sentence pairs where the Macedonian/Bulgarian side contained Bulgarian/Macedonian-specific letters.

From the remaining data we selected 10K sentence pairs (77K English words) for development and another 10K (72K English words) for testing; we used the rest for training. We used 10K pairs because subtitle sentences are short, and we wanted to make sure that the dev/test datasets contain enough words to enable stable tuning with MERT and reliable final evaluation results.

We further used the Macedonian–English and the Bulgarian–English movie subtitles datasets from OPUS, which we split into dev/test (10K sentence pairs for each) and train datasets. We made sure that the dev/test datasets for MK-BG, MK-EN and BG-EN do not overlap, and that all dev/test sentences were removed from the monolingual data used for language modeling.

Table 2 shows our baseline systems, trained using standard settings for a phrase-based SMT model: Kneser-Ney smoothed 5-gram language model and phrase pairs of maximum length seven.

Task	BLEU	NIST	TER	METEOR
MK-EN	22.33	5.47	63.57	39.19
MK-BG	30.70	6.52	50.94	70.44
BG-MK	28.01	6.24	51.98	69.89
BG-EN	37.60	7.34	47.41	58.89

Table 2: Phrase-based SMT baselines.

4.1 Translating Between Related Languages

We first investigate the impact of character alignment on the character-level translation between related languages. For this, we consider the extension of the context using character n-grams proposed by Tiedemann (2012a).

Another direction we explore is the possibility of reducing the noise in the phrase table. Treating even closely related languages by transliteration techniques is only a rough approximation to the translation task at hand. Furthermore, during training we observe many example translations that are not literally translated from one language to another. Hence, the character-level phrase table will be filled with many noisy and unintuitive translation options. We, therefore, applied phrase table pruning techniques based on relative entropy (Johnson et al., 2007) to remove unreliable pairs.

		PT Size		BLEU (%)	
n	align	std	fltd	std	fltd
1	2.5	5.1	1.0	30.47	31.13
2	2.6	5.2	0.9	30.87	31.32
3	2.9	6.9	0.9	30.32	31.03
4	3.0	10.4	1.1	29.76	30.42
5	3.1	12.0	1.2	29.25	30.19
6	3.2	10.8	1.2	28.81	29.68
7	3.4	8.1	1.1	28.73	29.73
8	3.5	6.4	1.0	28.40	29.45
9	3.6	5.4	0.9	27.67	29.19
10	3.6	5.1	0.9	27.11	28.78

Table 3: MK-BG character alignment points, phrase table sizes (in million of entries) and BLEU scores before (std) and after phrase filtering (fltd).

Table 3 shows the phrase table sizes for different settings and alignment approaches. We can see that, in all cases, the size of the filtered phrase tables is less than 20% of that of the original ones, which yields significant boost in decoding performance. More importantly, we see that filtering also leads to consistently better translation quality in all cases. This result is somewhat surprising for us: in our experience (for word-level models), filtering has typically harmed BLEU. Finally, we see that both with and without filtering, the best BLEU scores are achieved for $n = 2$.

The numbers in the table imply that the alignments become noisier for n-grams longer than two characters; look at the increasing number of phrases that can be extracted from the aligned corpus, many of which do not survive the filtering.

4.2 Bridging via Related Languages

Our next task is to use character-level models in the translation from under-resourced languages to other languages using the related language as a pivot. Several approaches for pivot-based translations have been proposed as discussed earlier.

We will look at two alternatives: (1) cascaded translations with two separate translation models and (2) bridging the gap by producing synthetic training corpora. For the latter, we automatically translate the related language in an existing training corpus to the under-resourced language.

Cascaded Pivot Translation

We base our translations on the individually trained translation models for the source (Macedonian) to the pivot language (Bulgarian) and for the pivot language to the final target language (English, in our case). As proposed by Tiedemann (2012a), we rerank k-best translations to find the best hypothesis for each given test sentence. For both translation steps, we set k to 10 and we require unique translations in the first step.

	BLEU	NIST	TER	METEOR
Model	individually tuned			
word-level pivot	22.48	5.46	64.11	47.77
char-based pivot	25.67	5.91	60.45	54.61
word+char+MK-EN	25.00	5.86	61.47	50.19
Model	globally tuned			
word-level pivot	23.38	5.44	64.33	48.31
char-based pivot	25.73	5.81	61.91	52.47
word+char+MK-EN	26.36	5.92	60.85	53.39

Table 4: Evaluating cascaded translation: Macedonian to English, pivoting via Bulgarian.

One possibility is to just apply the models tuned for the individual translation tasks, which is suboptimal. Therefore, we also introduce a global tuning approach, in which we generate k-best lists for the combined cascaded translation model and we tune corresponding end-to-end weights using MERT (Och, 2003) or PRO (Hopkins and May, 2011). We chose to set the size of the k-best lists to 20 in both steps to keep the size manageable, with 400 hypotheses for each tuning sentence.

Another option is to combine (i) the direct translation model, (ii) the word-level pivot model, and (iii) the character-level pivot model. Throwing them all in one k-best reranking system does not work well when using the unnormalized model scores. However, global tuning helps reassign weights such that the interactions between the various components can be covered. We use the same global tuning model introduced above using a combined system as the blackbox producing k-best lists and tuning feature weights for all components involved in the entire setup. Using the three translation paths, we obtain an extended set of parameters covering five individual systems. Since MERT is unstable with so many parameters, we use PRO. Note that tuning gets slow due to the extensive decoding that is necessary (five translation steps) and the increased size of the k-best lists (400 hypotheses for each pivot model and 100 hypotheses for the direct translation model).

Table 4 summarizes the results of the cascaded translation models. They all beat the baseline: direct translation from Macedonian to English. Note that the character-level model adds significantly to the performance of the cascaded model compared to the entirely word-level one. Furthermore, the scores illustrate that proper weights are important, especially for the case of the combined translation model. Without globally tuning its parameters, the performance is below the best single system, which is not entirely surprising.

Synthetic Training Data

Another possibility to make use of pivot languages is to create synthetic training data. For example, we can translate the Bulgarian side of our large Bulgarian–English training bitext to Macedonian, thus ending up with "Macedonian"-English training data. This is similar to previous work on adapting between closely related languages (Marujo et al., 2011; Wang et al., 2012), but here we perform translation rather than adaptation.

Model	BLEU	NIST	TER	METEOR
BG word-syn.	26.01	5.82	61.49	50.31
BG char-syn.	28.17	6.17	58.97	55.27
BG w+c-syn.	28.62	6.25	58.52	55.75
BG w+c-syn.+MK-EN	29.11	6.30	58.27	56.64
SR word-syn.	25.39	5.72	63.26	41.15
SR char-syn.	27.25	6.14	60.31	47.32
SR w+c-syn.	29.05	6.29	59.73	49.18
SR w+c-syn.+MK-EN	30.39	6.51	58.08	50.91
SL word-syn.	24.78	5.58	64.04	39.34
SL char-syn.	24.03	5.67	63.11	44.76
SL w+c-syn.	27.30	6.11	60.46	47.69
SL w+c-syn.+MK-EN	28.42	6.26	59.57	49.06
CZ word-syn.	26.48	5.83	62.52	41.02
CZ char-syn.	23.74	5.51	64.96	44.96
CZ w+c-syn.	28.03	6.08	61.12	48.41
CZ w+c-syn.+MK-EN	29.24	6.29	59.39	49.60
ALL-syn.	36.25	7.24	53.06	61.74
ALL-syn.+MK-EN	36.69	7.28	52.83	62.26

Table 5: Macedonian-English translation using synthetic data (by translating X-EN to MK-EN).

For translating from Bulgarian to Macedonian, we experimented with a word-level and a character-level SMT model. We also combined the two by concatenating the resulting MK-EN bitexts. We relied on the single best translation in all cases. Here, the character-level model was our best performing one, when using a filtered phrase table based on bigram alignments. Using k-best lists would be another option, but those should be properly weighted when combined to form a new synthetic training set. In future work, we plan to try the more sophisticated bitext combinations from (Nakov and Ng, 2009).

Table 5 shows the overall results. Experiments with word-level and character-level SMT are shown in rows 1 and 2, respectively. The result from the model trained on a concatenation of synthetic bitexts is shown in the third row. Finally, we also added the original MK-EN bitext to the combination (e.g., row 4). We can see from the top four rows that synthetic data outperforms cascaded translation by 2-3 BLEU points. Here again, the character-level model is much more valuable than the word-level one, which is most probably due to the reduction in the number of out-of-vocabulary (OOV) words it yields.

Another huge advantage over the cascaded approaches presented above is the reduced decoding time. Now, the system behaves like a traditional phrase-based SMT engine. The only large-scale effort is the translation of the training corpus, which only needs to be done once and can easily be performed off-line in a distributed setup.

4.3 Learning Curves and Other Languages

Observing the success of bridging via related pivot languages leads to at least two additional questions: (1) How much data is necessary for training reasonable character-level translation models that are still better than a standard word-level model trained on the same data? and (2) How strongly related should the languages be so that it is beneficial to use SMT at the character level?

Size of the Training Data

We investigated the first question by translating from Macedonian to Bulgarian with increasing amounts of training data. For comparability, we kept the model parameters fixed.

The top-left plot in Figure 1 shows the learning curves for word- and character-level models for MK-BG. We can see that the character-level models clearly outperform the word-level ones for the small amounts of training data that we have: the abstraction at the character level is much stronger and yields more robust models.

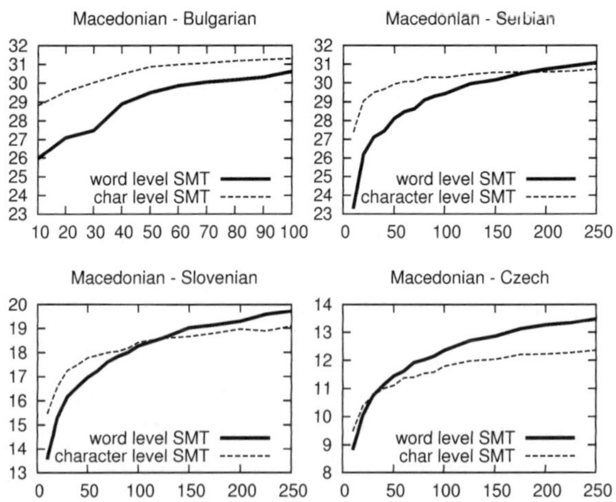

Figure 1: BLEU (in %) for word- and character-level SMT models with varying sizes of parallel training data (in thousands of sentence pairs).

Other Pivot Languages

We investigated the second question by experimenting with data from OPUS for two South-Slavic languages that are less related to Macedonian than Bulgarian. We selected Serbian and Slovenian from the Western group of the South-Slavic language branch (Bulgarian and Macedonian are in the Eastern group) from which Slovenian is the furthest away from Macedonian.

Note that while Bulgarian and Macedonian use Cyrillic, Slovenian and Serbian use the Latin alphabet (Serbian can also use Cyrillic, but not in OPUS). We have larger training datasets for the latter two: about 250-300 thousand sentence pairs.

To further contrast the relationship between South-Slavic languages (such as Bulgarian, Macedonian, Serbian, Slovenian) and languages from the Western-Slavic branch, we also experimented with Czech (about 270 thousand sentence pairs).

Note that we do not have the same movies available in all languages involved; therefore, the test and the development datasets are different for each language pair. However, we used the same amount of data in all setups: 10,000 sentence pairs for tuning and 10,000 pairs for evaluation.

Figure 1 also shows the learning curves for the three additional language pairs. For the South-Slavic languages, the character-level models make sense with sparse datasets. They outperform word-level models at least until around 100 thousand sentence pairs of training data.

Certainly, language relatedness has an impact on the effectiveness of character-level SMT. The difference between character- and word-level models shows that Slovenian is not the most appropriate choice for character-level SMT due to its weaker relation to Macedonian.

Furthermore, we can see that the performance of character-level models levels out at some point and standard word-level models surpass them with an almost linear increase in MT quality up to the point we have considered in the training procedures. Looking at Czech, we can see that character-level models are only competitive for very small datasets, but their performance is so low that they are practically useless. In general, translation is more difficult for more distant languages; this is also the case for word-level models.

Pivot-Based Translation

The final, and probably most important, question with respect to this paper is whether the other languages are still useful for pivot-based translation. Therefore, we generated translations of our Macedonian-English test set but this time via Serbian, Slovene and Czech. We used the approach that uses synthetic training data, which was the most successful one for Bulgarian, based on translation models trained on subsets of 100 thousand sentence pairs to make the results comparable with the Bulgarian case.

The pivot–English data that we have translated to "Macedonian"-English is comparable for Slovene and Serbian (1 million sentence pairs) and almost double the size for Czech (1.9 million).

Table 5 summarizes the results for all pivot languages: Bulgarian (BG), Serbian (SR), Slovenian (SL), and Czech (CZ). We can see that Serbian, which is geographically adjacent to Macedonian, performs almost as well as Bulgarian, which is also adjacent, while Slovenian, which is further away, and not adjacent to any of the above, performs worse. Note that with a Slovenian pivot, the character-level model performs worse than the word-level model.

This suggests that the differences between Slovenian and Macedonian are not that much at the sub-word level but mostly at the word level. This is even more evident for Czech, which is geographically further away and which is also from a different Slavic branch. Note, however, that we had much more data for Czech-English than for any other X-EN bitext, which explains the strong overall performance of its word-level model.

Overall, we have seen that as the relatedness between the source and the pivot language decreases, so does the utility of the character-level model. However, in all cases the character-level model helps when combined with the word-level one, yielding 1.5-4 BLEU points of improvement. Moreover, using all four pivots yields seven additional BLEU points over the best single pivot.

5 Discussion

Finally, we performed a manual evaluation of word-level, character-level and combined systems translating from Macedonian to English using Bulgarian. We asked three speakers of Macedonian and Bulgarian to rank the English output from the eight anonymized systems in Table 6, given the Macedonian input; we used 100 test sentences.

Model	word BLEU	char BLEU	Avg. rank	">" score	Untr. words
reference	—	—	1.57	0.73	—
baseline	22.33	50.83	3.37	0.25	4,959
word-pivot	23.38	53.26	2.81	0.42	3,144
char-pivot	25.73	56.00	2.51	0.52	1,841
comb-pivot	26.36	56.39	2.63	0.46	1,491
word-synth.	26.01	55.59	2.77	0.43	3,258
char-synth.	28.17	58.21	2.31	0.58	1,818
comb-synth.	28.62	58.53	2.11	0.65	1,712

Table 6: Comparing word- and character-level BLEU to human judgments for MK-EN using BG.

The results are shown in Table 6. Column 4 shows the *average rank* for each system, and column 5 shows the ">" *score* as defined in (Callison-Burch et al., 2012): the frequency a given system was judged to be strictly better than the rest divided by the frequency it was judged strictly better or strictly worse than the rest. We further include word- and character-level BLEU, and the number of untranslated words.

We calculated Cohen's kappas (Cohen, 1960) of 0.87, 0.86 and 0.83 between the pairs of judges, following the procedure in (Callison-Burch et al., 2012). This corresponds to almost perfect agreement (Landis and Koch, 1977), probably due to the short length of subtitles, which allows for few differences in translation and simplifies ranking.

The individual human judgments (not shown to save space) correlate perfectly in terms of relative ranking of (a) the three pivoting systems and (b) the three synthetic data systems. Moreover, the individual and the overall human judgments also correlate well with the BLEU scores on (a) and (b), with one notable exception: humans ranked *char-pivot* higher than *comb-pivot*, while word- and char-BLEU switched their ranks. A closer investigation found that this is probably due to length: the hypothesis/reference ratio for *char-pivot* is 1.006, while for *comb-pivot* it is 1.016. In contrast, for *char-synth.* it is 1.006, while for *comb-synth.* it is 1.002. Recent work (Nakov et al., 2012) has shown that the closest this ratio gets to 1, the better the BLEU score is expected to be.

Note also that word-BLEU and char-BLEU correlate perfectly on (a) and (b), which is probably due to tuning the two systems for word-BLEU.

Interestingly, the BLEU-based rankings of the systems inside (a) and (b) perfectly correlate with the number of untranslated words. Note the robustness of the character-level models: they reduce the number of untranslated words by more than 40%. Having untranslated words in the final English translation could be annoying since they are in Cyrillic, but more importantly, they could contain information that is critical for a human, or even for the SMT system, without which it could not generate a good translation for the remaining words in the sentence. This is especially true for content-baring long, low-frequency words. For example, the inability to translate the Macedonian лутам ('I am angry') yields "You don' лутам." instead of "I'm not mad at you."

Character models are very robust with unknown morphological forms, e.g., a word-level model would not translate развеселам, yielding "I'm trying to make a развеселам.", while a character-level model will transform it to the Bulgarian развеселя, thus allowing the fluent "I'm trying to cheer you up." Note that this transformation does not necessarily have to pick the correct Bulgarian form, e.g., развеселя is a conjugated verb (1st person, singular, subjunctive), but it is translated as an infinitive, i.e., all Bulgarian conjugated forms would map to the same English infinitive.

Finally, it is also worth mentioning that character models are very robust in case of typos, concatenated or wrongly split words, which are quite common in movie subtitles.

6 Conclusion and Future Work

We have explored the use of character-level SMT models when applied to sparse and noisy datasets such as crowdsourced movie subtitles. We have demonstrated their utility when translating between closely related languages, where translation is often reduced to sub-word transformations. We have shown that such models are especially competitive in the case of limited training data (2-3 BLEU points of improvement, and 40% reduction of OOV), but fall behind word-level models as the training data increases. We have also shown the importance of phrase table filtering and the impact of character alignment on translation performance.

We have further experimented with bridging via a related language and we have found that generating synthetic training data works best. This makes it also straightforward to use multiple pivots and to combine word-level with character-level SMT models. Our best combined model outperforms the baseline by over 14 BLEU points, which represents a very significant boost in translation quality.

In future work, we would like to investigate the robustness of character-level models with respect to domain shifts and for other language pairs. We further plan a deeper analysis of the ability of character-level models to handle noisy inputs that include spelling errors and tokenization mistakes, which are common in user-generated content.

Acknowledgments

We would like to thank Petya Kirova and Veno Pacovski for helping us with the manual judgments. We also thank the anonymous reviewers for their constructive comments.

References

Kemal Altintas and Ilyas Cicekli. 2002. A machine translation system between a pair of closely related languages. In *Proceedings of the 17th International Symposium on Computer and Information Sciences*, ISCIS '02, pages 192–196, Orlando, FL.

Colin Bannard and Chris Callison-Burch. 2005. Paraphrasing with bilingual parallel corpora. In *Proceedings of the 43rd Annual Meeting of the Association for Computational Linguistics*, ACL '05, pages 597–604, Ann Arbor, MI.

Nicola Bertoldi, Madalina Barbaiani, Marcello Federico, and Roldano Cattoni. 2008. Phrase-based statistical machine translation with pivot languages. In *Proceedings of the International Workshop on Spoken Language Translation*, IWSLT '08, pages 143–149, Honolulu, HI.

Peter Brown, Vincent Della Pietra, Stephen Della Pietra, and Robert Mercer. 1993. The mathematics of statistical machine translation: parameter estimation. *Computational Linguistics*, 19(2):263–311.

Chris Callison-Burch, Philipp Koehn, Christof Monz, Matt Post, Radu Soricut, and Lucia Specia. 2012. Findings of the 2012 workshop on statistical machine translation. In *Proceedings of the 7th Workshop on Statistical Machine Translation*, WMT '12, pages 10–51, Montréal, Québec, Canada.

Jacob Cohen. 1960. A Coefficient of Agreement for Nominal Scales. *Educational and Psychological Measurement*, 20(1):37–46, April.

Trevor Cohn and Mirella Lapata. 2007. Machine translation by triangulation: Making effective use of multi-parallel corpora. In *Proceedings of the 45th Annual Meeting of the Association for Computational Linguistics*, ACL '07, pages 728–735, Prague, Czech Republic.

Josep Maria Crego, Aurélien Max, and François Yvon. 2010. Local lexical adaptation in machine translation through triangulation: SMT helping SMT. In *Proceedings of the 23rd International Conference on Computational Linguistics*, COLING '10, pages 232–240, Beijing, China.

Robert Damper, Yannick Marchand, John Marsters, and Alexander Bazin. 2005. Aligning text and phonemes for speech technology applications using an EM-like algorithm. *International Journal of Speech Technology*, 8(2):149–162.

Adriá de Gispert and José Mariño. 2006. Catalan-English statistical machine translation without parallel corpus: Bridging through Spanish. In *Proceedings of the 5th Workshop on Strategies for developing Machine Translation for Minority Languages*, SALTMIL '06, pages 65–68, Genova, Italy.

Jan Hajič, Jan Hric, and Vladislav Kuboň. 2000. Machine translation of very close languages. In *Proceedings of the 6th Conference on Applied Natural Language Processing*, ANLP '00, pages 7–12, Seattle, WA.

Mark Hopkins and Jonathan May. 2011. Tuning as ranking. In *Proceedings of the 8th Conference on Empirical Methods in Natural Language Processing*, EMNLP '11, pages 1352–1362, Edinburgh, Scotland, United Kingdom.

Sittichai Jiampojamarn, Grzegorz Kondrak, and Tarek Sherif. 2007. Applying many-to-many alignments and hidden Markov models to letter-to-phoneme conversion. In *Human Language Technologies: The Conference of the North American Chapter of the Association for Computational Linguistics; Proceedings of the Main Conference*, NAACL '07, pages 372–379, Rochester, NY.

Howard Johnson, Joel Martin, George Foster, and Roland Kuhn. 2007. Improving translation quality by discarding most of the phrasetable. In *Proceedings of the Joint Conference on Empirical Methods in Natural Language Processing and Computational Natural Language Learning*, EMNLP-CoNLL '07, pages 967–975, Prague, Czech Republic.

Philipp Koehn, Hieu Hoang, Alexandra Birch, Chris Callison-Burch, Marcello Federico, Nicola Bertoldi, Brooke Cowan, Wade Shen, Christine Moran, Richard Zens, Chris Dyer, Ondrej Bojar, Alexandra Constantin, and Evan Herbst. 2007. Moses: Open source toolkit for statistical machine translation. In *Proceedings of the 45th Annual Meeting of the Association for Computational Linguistics. Demonstration session*, ACL '07, pages 177–180, Prague, Czech Republic.

Philipp Koehn, Alexandra Birch, and Ralf Steinberger. 2009. 462 machine translation systems for Europe. In *Proceedings of the Machine Translation Summit*, MT Summit XII, pages 65–72, Ottawa, Canada.

Richard Landis and Gary Koch. 1977. The measurement of observer agreement for categorical data. *Biometrics*, 33(1):159–74.

Minh-Thang Luong, Preslav Nakov, and Min-Yen Kan. 2010. A hybrid morpheme-word representation for machine translation of morphologically rich languages. In *Proceedings of the 7th Conference on Empirical Methods in Natural Language Processing*, EMNLP '10, pages 148–157, Cambridge, MA.

Luís Marujo, Nuno Grazina, Tiago Luís, Wang Ling, Luísa Coheur, and Isabel Trancoso. 2011. BP2EP - adaptation of Brazilian Portuguese texts to European Portuguese. In *Proceedings of the 15th Conference of the European Association for Machine Translation*, EAMT '11, pages 129–136, Leuven, Belgium.

David Matthews. 2007. Machine transliteration of proper names. Master's thesis, School of Informatics, University of Edinburgh.

Preslav Nakov and Hwee Tou Ng. 2009. Improved statistical machine translation for resource-poor languages using related resource-rich languages. In *Proceedings of the 6th Conference on Empirical Methods in Natural Language Processing*, EMNLP '09, pages 1358–1367, Singapore.

Preslav Nakov and Hwee Tou Ng. 2012. Improving statistical machine translation for a resource-poor language using related resource-rich languages. *Journal of Artificial Intelligence Research*, 44:179–222.

Preslav Nakov and Jörg Tiedemann. 2012. Combining word-level and character-level models for machine translation between closely-related languages. In *Proceedings of the 50th Annual Meeting of the Association for Computational Linguistics (Volume 2: Short Papers)*, ACL '12, pages 301–305, Jeju Island, Korea.

Preslav Nakov, Francisco Guzman, and Stephan Vogel. 2012. Optimizing for sentence-level BLEU+1 yields short translations. In *Proceedings of the 24th International Conference on Computational Linguistics*, COLING '12, pages 1979–1994, Mumbai, India.

Franz Josef Och and Hermann Ney. 2003. A systematic comparison of various statistical alignment models. *Computational Linguistics*, 29(1):19–51.

Franz Josef Och. 2003. Minimum error rate training in statistical machine translation. In *Proceedings of the 41st Annual Meeting of the Association for Computational Linguistics*, ACL '03, pages 160–167, Sapporo, Japan.

Kishore Papineni, Salim Roukos, Todd Ward, and Wei-Jing Zhu. 2002. BLEU: a method for automatic evaluation of machine translation. In *Proceedings of the 40th Annual Meeting of the Association for Computational Linguistics*, ACL '02, pages 311–318, Philadelphia, PA.

Kevin Scannell. 2006. Machine translation for closely related language pairs. In *Proceedings of the LREC 2006 Workshop on Strategies for developing machine translation for minority languages*, pages 103–108, Genoa, Italy.

Jörg Tiedemann and Peter Nabende. 2009. Translating transliterations. *International Journal of Computing and ICT Research*, 3(1):33–41.

Jörg Tiedemann. 2009a. Character-based PSMT for closely related languages. In *Proceedings of the 13th Annual Conference of the European Association for Machine Translation*, EAMT '09, pages 12–19, Barcelona, Spain.

Jörg Tiedemann. 2009b. News from OPUS - A collection of multilingual parallel corpora with tools and interfaces. In *Recent Advances in Natural Language Processing*, volume V, pages 237–248. John Benjamins, Amsterdam/Philadelphia.

Jörg Tiedemann. 2012a. Character-based pivot translation for under-resourced languages and domains. In *Proceedings of the 13th Conference of the European Chapter of the Association for Computational Linguistics*, EACL '12, pages 141–151, Avignon, France.

Jörg Tiedemann. 2012b. Parallel data, tools and interfaces in OPUS. In *Proceedings of the 8th International Conference on Language Resources and Evaluation*, LREC '12, pages 2214–2218, Istanbul, Turkey.

Masao Utiyama and Hitoshi Isahara. 2007. A comparison of pivot methods for phrase-based statistical machine translation. In *Human Language Technologies 2007: The Conference of the North American Chapter of the Association for Computational Linguistics; Proceedings of the Main Conference*, NAACL-HLT '07, pages 484–491, Rochester, NY.

Dániel Varga, László Németh, Péter Halácsy, András Kornai, Viktor Trón, and Viktor Nagy. 2005. Parallel corpora for medium density languages. In *Proceedings of the International Conference on Recent Advances in Natural Language Processing*, RANLP '05, pages 590–596, Borovets, Bulgaria.

David Vilar, Jan-Thorsten Peter, and Hermann Ney. 2007. Can we translate letters? In *Proceedings of the Second Workshop on Statistical Machine Translation*, WMT '07, pages 33–39, Prague, Czech Republic.

Pidong Wang, Preslav Nakov, and Hwee Tou Ng. 2012. Source language adaptation for resource-poor machine translation. In *Proceedings of the 2012 Joint Conference on Empirical Methods in Natural Language Processing and Computational Natural Language Learning*, EMNLP-CoNLL '12, pages 286–296, Jeju Island, Korea.

Hua Wu and Haifeng Wang. 2007. Pivot language approach for phrase-based statistical machine translation. In *Proceedings of the 45th Annual Meeting of the Association of Computational Linguistics*, ACL '07, pages 856–863, Prague, Czech Republic.

Hua Wu and Haifeng Wang. 2009. Revisiting pivot language approach for machine translation. In *Proceedings of the Joint Conference of the 47th Annual Meeting of the Association for Computational Linguistics and of the 4th International Joint Conference on Natural Language Processing of the Asian Federation of Natural Language Processing*, ACL-IJCNLP '09, pages 154–162, Singapore.

Xiaoheng Zhang. 1998. Dialect MT: a case study between Cantonese and Mandarin. In *Proceedings of the 17th International Conference on Computational Linguistics*, COLING '98, pages 1460–1464, Montréal, Québec, Canada.

A Feature Induction Algorithm with Application to Named Entity Disambiguation

Laura Toloşi, Valentin Zhikov, Georgi Georgiev, Borislav Popov
OntotextAD
laura.tolosi, valentin.zhikov, georgi.georgiev, borislav.popov@ontotext.com

Abstract

The performance of NLP classifiers largely depends on the quality of the features considered for prediction (feature engineering). However, as the number of features increases, the more likely overfitting becomes and performance decreases. Also, due to the very large number of features, only slimple linear classifiers are considered, thus disregarding potentially predictive non-linear combinations of features. Here we propose an automated method for feature induction, which selects and includes in the model features and feature combinations which are likely to be useful for the prediction.The resulting model relies on a smaller feature set, is non-linear and is more accurate than the baseline, which is the model trained on the entire feature set. The method uses a greedy filtering approach based on various univariate measures of feature relevance and it is very fast in practice. Also, our feature induction method is independent of the classifier used: we applied it together with Naïve Bayes and Perceptron models.

1 Introduction

NLP classification tasks are characterized by a very large number of features. When the number of available samples is smaller (for example several orders of magnitude less samples), overfitting can occur, leading to poor performance. In order to avoid overfitting, *feature selection* is commonly applied. In (Guyon and Elisseeff, 2003), the main approaches to feature selection are summarized: *filter*, *wrapper* and *embedded* methods. Filters use some scoring measure to quantify the predictivity of each feature independently. Then, features are ranked and only the top scoring ones are kept in the final model. The most popular measures for feature predictivity are Mutual Information (Lewis, 1992; Taira and Haruno, 1999), Information Gain (Uguz, 2011; Yang and Pedersen, 1997), Kullback-Leibler divergence (Lee and Lee, 2006; Schneider, 2004; Lee et al., 2011), Chi-squared statistics (Yang and Pedersen, 1997; Mesleh, 2007), Fisher statistics, Pearson correlation, etc. In (Yang and Pedersen, 1997) and (Forman, 2003), comparisons of the most popular methods are presented. Filter methods are computationally fast, but the univariate scoring can lead to the elimination of features that are useful only in combinations (Guyon and Elisseeff, 2003). Wrapper methods (Kohavi and John, 1997) can score subsets of features directly, by evaluating the performance of the classifier on the respective subset. A strategy of iteratively updating the subset of features is used, with the goal of finding a (close to) optimal subset. Forward selection, backward elimination, branch-and-bound (Narendra and Fukunaga, 1977), simulated annealing (Ekbal et al., 2011), genetic algorithms (Yang and Honavar, 1998) are among the most popular strategies. Wrapper methods tend to be slow in practice, because a classifier needs to be trained at each iteration. Embedded methods are explicitly optimizing an objective function that incorporates feature selection. In general, the objective is an expression of the trade-off between the goodness of fit and the number of variables that participate in the model. For example, l_1 penalties (Haffner et al., 2005) are combined with the likelihood objective in maximum entropy models in order to keep the number of predictors small.

For most NLP classification tasks, the number of features is very large. If no experts are available for selecting the most promising features for a specific task, the choice is really vast. In (Kamolvilassatian, 2002), the authors systemati-

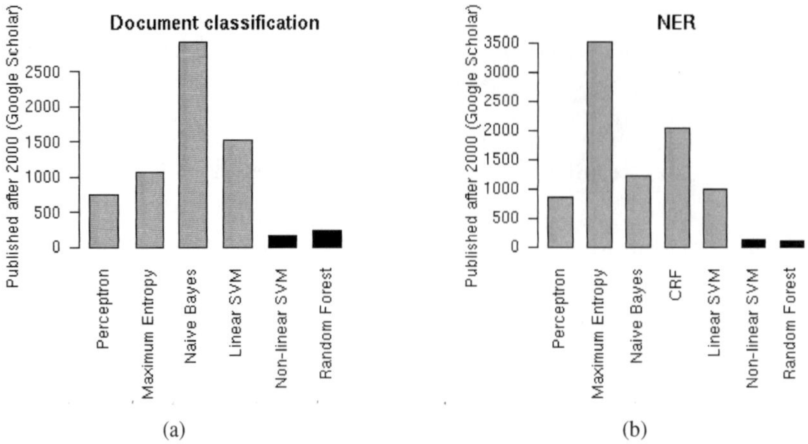

Figure 1: Classifier models used for a) document classification and b) named entity recognition. Linear models are represented with gray bars and non-linear models with black.

cally list of all features (with parameters), such as for example n-grams (n is a parameter), context of words, part of speech, lemmas, stems, etc. Owing to the very large number of features, linear (or log-linear) classifiers are preferred, because they are robust and can be trained fast. Simple search in Google Scholar shows that most frequently used models for document classification are Naive Bayes, linear SVMs (Cortes and Vapnik, 1995), Perceptrons (Rosenblatt, 1957) and Maximum Entropy (Berger et al., 1996) (Figure 1a). In contrast, non-linear models such as non-linear SVMs and Random Forest (Breiman, 2001) and Classification trees (Breiman et al., 1984) are significantly under-represented. For Named Entity Recognition, Maximum Entropy and CRFs (Lafferty, 2001) are mostly used, but other linear models like Perceptron, Naive Bayes and linear SVMs are employed (Figure 1b). Non-linear models are significantly less frequent. Feature induction can be used to efficiently introduce non-linearity in large models, in the form of feature conjunctions. As the space of all conjunctions of arbitrary length is very large ($2^{\#\text{features}}$), a greedy search approach is applied for selecting the most promising conjunctions with reasonable computational cost. In (McCallum, 2003), a method for inducing features and conjunctions especially tailored to CRF models is proposed. Iteratively, the most promising feature or conjunction to be added to the model is identified. To this end, a gain function is defined, for evaluating the improvement of the likelihood target upon the addition of the feature. Conjunctions are considered only among the top scoring feature candidates and the features already included in the model. In (Vens and Costa, 2011), the authors use random forests to form feature conjunctions, by traversing the trees from the root to the leaves.

In this article we present a method for feature selection and feature induction. The strengths of our method are fast running time and generality, in the sense that it can be used as preprocessing step to any classifier the user may choose.

2 Methods

Given are N pairs of observations and labels $(X_1, Y_1), (X_2, Y_2), ..., (X_N, Y_N)$. The observations X_i are over a set of p binary predicates (or terms) $T_1, ..., T_p$, which we call *atomic features*. For example, an atomic feature is an indicator of presence or absence of a particular word in a document. The class label can take the values from the set $\{c_1, c_2, ..., c_K\}$. In this article. we use the notion of 'features' to denote predicates, and not the classical feature functions $f(X_i, c_i)$ commonly used in NLP tasks. The reason is that we wish to be consistent with the established notions of 'feature selection' and 'feature induction', which otherwise would have to be called 'predicate selection' and 'predicate induction'.

The purpose of our method is to find a set of features consisting of atomic features or conjunctions of atomic features which can predict the class variable with high accuracy. The classification model is the user's choice.

Our algorithm is entitled Fast ITerative Selection and Induction (FITSI) and is a greedy heuristic search through the space of the atomic features and conjunctions. The main steps are described in Algorithm 1. A *feature selection* step and a *feature induction* step alternate in an iterative process. At each iteration, we rank the features according to some score σ that measures the univariate relevance of each feature w.r.t. the class variable. The choices for σ are described in Section 2.1. We keep only the top k features, where k is a generic parameter which can be either a percentage of the total number of features, or the number of features with scores larger than a threshold. Then, we add to the features set conjunctions between atomic features larger than a certain rank l and features or conjunctions from the entire list. The algorithm runs for m iterations, allowing for conjunctions of length up to m to be generated. Below we discuss in detail the two key ingredients of our algorithm: measures of feature relevance and the algorithm for generation of conjunctions.

2.1 Feature ranking and filtering

For ranking and filtering features (σ parameter in Algorithm 1), we implemented several measures: mutual information (MI), information gain (IG), symmetrical uncertainty (SU) and Fisher tests (FT). Each measure returns a score, which is an estimate of the predictive power of each feature w.r.t. the class variable. In a multi-class setting, there are several ways to compute scores: either globally, trying to capture the overall association of the feature with the class variable, or separately, computing a relevance score w.r.t. each class and then summing the scores. We prefer the later approach because it is equally fair to small and large classes. We summarize the class-specific scores by taking either the sum or their maximum value.

In what follows, we denote with Y_i the indicator variable of class c_i: $Y_i[k] = 1$, if $Y[k] = c_i$ and 0, otherwise.

Algorithm 1 Fast Iterative Selection and Induction

```
Require: {T_1, ..., T_p}, σ, k, l, m
  Initialize feature list Φ ← [T_1, ..., T_p]
  for i ∈ {1, ..., m − 1} do
      Feature selection:
      Φ ← sort(Φ, σ) ▷ Sort the list according to σ scores
      Φ ← Φ[1..k]              ▷ Keep only the top k features
      Feature induction:
      Γ ← generateConjunctions(Φ, l)
      if Φ == Φ ⋃ Γ then         ▷ No new conjunctions
          break
      else
          Φ ← Φ ⋃ Γ                      ▷ Append Γ to Φ
      end if
  end for
  return Φ
```

Algorithm 2 generateConjunctions(Φ, l)

```
  Γ ← ∅                          ▷ Initialize with empty list
  for i ∈ {1, ..., l} do
      if Φ[i] is atomic then
          for j ∈ {i + 1, ..., length(Φ)} do
              Γ ← Γ ⋃{Φ[i]&Φ[j]}    ▷ Add conjunction
          end for
      end if
  end for
  return Γ
```

Mutual information

Mutual information (Hamming, 1986) between a feature T and an indicator variable Y_i of class c_i is a quantity $\mathrm{MI}(T, Y_i)$ that measures the dependence between the two variables. It is calculated as:

$$\mathrm{MI}(T, Y_i) = \sum_{t\in\{0,1\}} \sum_{y\in\{0,1\}} \Pr(t, y) \log\left(\frac{\Pr(t, y)}{\Pr(t)\Pr(y)}\right)$$

where the joint probability $\Pr(t, y)$ and the marginals $\Pr(t)$ and $\Pr(y)$ are estimated using relative frequencies. $\mathrm{MI}(T, Y_i)$ is a positive quantity, with a value of zero if T and Y_i are independent. A large $\mathrm{MI}(T, Y_i)$ score indicates that T is predictive for class c_i.

Information gain

The information gain of feature T with respect to Y_i measures the decrease in entropy when the feature T is present versus absent from the set of features. We evaluate the information gain of feature T with respect to class c_i as in (Yang and Pedersen, 1997):

$$\begin{aligned}\mathrm{IG}(T, Y_i) = &- \Pr(Y_i = 1)\log(\Pr(Y_i = 1)) \\ &+ \Pr(T)\Pr(Y_i = 1|T)\log(\Pr(Y_i = 1|T)) \\ &+ \Pr(\bar{T})\Pr(Y_i = 1|\bar{T})\log(\Pr(Y_i = 1|\bar{T}))\end{aligned}$$

Symmetric uncertainty

Symmetric uncertainty between term T and class indicator variable Y_i is a normalized mutual information score, computed as follows:

$$\mathrm{SU}(T, Y_i) = \frac{2\mathrm{MI}(T, Y_i)}{\mathrm{H}(T) + \mathrm{H}(Y_i)}$$

where by $\mathrm{H}(X)$ we denote the entropy of variable X, computed in practice as $\mathrm{H}(X) = \sum_{x\in X} - \Pr(x)\log(\Pr(x))$.

Fisher test

Fisher's exact test (Fisher, 1928) is used to examine the significance of association between two binary variables. We apply it to the contingency table between feature T and class indicator Y_i and retrieve the significance p-value, which expresses the probability of the observed values of the table under the assumption of independence between the variables. If the probability is very small (i.e. p-value is small), then the independence assumption is rejected. We define the Fisher test score for feature selection as: $\text{FT}(T, Y_i) = 1 - p\text{-value}$. $\text{FT}(T, Y_i)$ always has values between 0 and 1. A typical threshold for significance is $p\text{-value} < 0.05$ or, more conservatively, $p\text{-value} < 0.01$.

2.2 Induction (generating conjunctions)

We include in the model feature conjunctions of maximum length m, which is a parameter of our method. At each iteration, the conjunctions are formed between atomic features that exceed some relevance threshold and any other feature or conjunction still present in the list of features.

Before adding a conjunction $T_i \& T_j$ to the the set Φ, we check if it has not been introduced already, for example as $T_j \& T_i$. If at a certain step all conjunctions that are generated are already in Φ, the algorithm stops (see step 8, Algorithm 1).

In typical applications, it is unlikely that very long conjunctions have a great impact on the classification performance. Therefore we suggest that m is kept small in practice, a value up to 3 should be sufficient for most applications.

2.3 Complexity of the algorithm

As we already argued in the introduction, computational complexity is one important bottleneck of feature selection and induction algorithms. Despite this, our method is fast. We run once through all samples in order to build the necessary data structures for evaluation of MI, IG, SU and FT scores, which takes $\mathcal{O}(pKN)$ time. The data structures esentially store the counts of samples in each class, for each feature. Thereafter, the complexity of scoring the set of p features and the sorting take place in $\mathcal{O}(pK)$ time, which is run m times. The overall time is thus $\mathcal{O}(pKm + pKN)$, which is $\mathcal{O}(pKN)$, in most applications. In practice the algorithm can become even faster by using sparse vectors to represent features.

2.4 Model training and evaluation

We use the FITSI Algorithm for generating a set Φ of atomic features and conjunctions of length up to $m = 2$. We use these features to represent the data and train a model $\mathcal{M}$, which in our experiments can be a Perceptron or a Naive Bayes model. The performance of the algorithm clearly depends on the parameters used for the feature induction and selection: σ, k and l.

If we exclude the scoring measure σ, which can be chosen by the user based on some subjective criteria, our algorithm has two numerical hyper parameters that can be estimated from data, in a way that the resulting model has optimal performance. We use B-fold cross-validation for this purpose. We first split the data into two subsets, for parameter selection and for testing. The part that is used for parameter selection is split into B bins (5 in our experiments). For each combination of parameters, we use $B - 1$ bins for feature induction and model training and we evaluate the performance of the classifier on the remaining bin. In consequence, for each combination of parameters, a set of B performance estimates are obtained, which allows to compute mean and standard deviation. We identify the model with largest mean performance and select the simplest model (smallest k) that has the mean within one standard deviation from the best model. This is known as the one-standard-error rule, proposed by (Breiman et al., 1984). The parameters of this model are the optimal parameters k_{opt} and l_{opt}. We test this model on the excluded samples and report a test performance.

We compare the performance of our model to that of a baseline model. To this end, we repeat the cross validation described above, but we do not perform any feature induction.

For evaluating the performance of a classifier, we use the F_1 measure, which is the harmonic mean of precision and recall.

3 Data

PA data: The "PA" dataset was developed by the Press Association[1] to enable the implementation of a system for recognition and semantic disambiguation of named entities in press releases. Given certain metadata for a number of overlapping candidate entities, an array of features derived from the textual context of their oc-

[1] http://www.pressassociation.com/

currence, and additional document-level metadata, the model recognizes which (if any) of the candidate entities is the one referenced in the text.

The corpus is annotated with respect to people, organization and location mentions; a special "negative" label denotes the candidates that can be considered irrelevant in the given context. In all cases, at most one of the overlapping candidates is annotated as positive. The dataset comprises a total of 2539 manually curated documents, and a total of 85602 concept mentions (this number represents the total of all candidate instances, including those annotated as non-entities).

For this dataset, the domain of the press releases is an important factor during classification, and specific features that express the belonging of a press release to a particular domain or category are also available. The dataset comprises articles from two domains: "General News" and "Olympics".

We remove non-location entity candidates, thus reducing the problem to the binary classification task of discerning locations from non-entities. We split the corpus into a training set (2369 documents) and a held-out test set (160 documents). As a result of this preprocessing, we have 2 classes (Location and Negative), 46273 instances, and a target to irrelevant instance counts ratio of 0.17.

From the training document set, we extracted 50455 atomic features.

As performance measure we report the F1 score of the positive class (i.e. 'Location').

4 Results

We performed feature induction using in turn all the measures of feature relevance mentioned in Section 2.1, followed by training Naive Bayes and Perceptron classifiers. The parameters k and l ($l > k$) of the feature induction step were iteratively selected from the set:

$$\{0.1\%, 0.25\%, 0.5\%, 0.75\%, 1\%, 2.5\%, 5\%, 7.5\%, 10\%, 25\%\}$$

of the total number of features p.

We used 5-fold cross-validation for selection of the optimal parameters k_{opt} and l_{opt}, as explained in section 2.4. Figure 2 illustrates the cross-validation search grid for the particular combination of feature induction with MI score and a Perceptron classifier. The intensity of the shade of gray is proportional to the average F1 measure over the 5 folds. The standard deviation for each combination of parameters is not shown in the image. The largest average F1 is 0.825 and is achieved for $k = 25\%$ and $l = 0.75\%$ of p.The standard deviation of this model is 0.009, estimated based on the 5 cross-validation folds. A simpler model, with $k = 25\%$ and $l = 0.1\%$ has average performance of 0.824, which is within one standard deviation from the maximum performance, hence there is no statistically significant difference between the two models. We thus chose the simpler model as optimal.

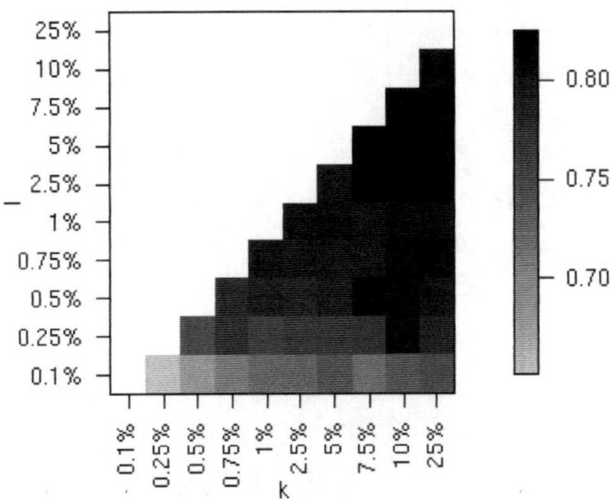

Figure 2: Parameter grid search by cross-validation.

	NB	Perc
MI	0.70	0.83
IG	0.70	0.83
SU	0.70	0.80
FT	0.75	0.83
Baseline	0.54	0.79

Table 1: Performance on the test dataset of classification models using various measures of feature relevance and comparison with the baseline.

In Table 1, we show the performance of the optimal models (determined by cross validation). The models that we investigated are various combinations of feature scoring measures (as rows) and classifiers (as columns). We compare to a Baseline model (last row), which is either a Naive Bayes or Perceptron, without any feature induction. Clearly, all our models outperform the Baseline, by a large margin: up to 20% in the case of Naive Bayes models and up to 4% for Perceptrons. In general, Naive Bayes classifiers are worse than the Perceptron. Fisher test ranking appears to work best for Naive Bayes classifiers, whereas for Perceptron models achieve similar performance for most of the scoring measures (apart from Symmetrical Uncertainty).

Table 2 shows for each model the optimal parameters k_{opt} and l_{opt} that were selected via cross

	NB (k_{opt}, l_{opt})	Perc (k_{opt}, l_{opt})
MI	$25\%, 0.25\%$	$25\%, 0.1\%$
IG	$25\%, 0.25\%$	$25\%, 0.1\%$
SU	$25\%, 0.1\%$	$10\%, 0.1\%$
FT	$25\%, 0.1\%$	$10\%, 0.25\%$

Table 2: Parameters of the resulting models.

validation. In general many atomic features are included in the model, indicated by the large values of k_opt, which are in general 25%. Only two models select 10% features, namely the Perceptron with FT and SU. The most common values for l_{opt} are 0.25% and 0.1%, which means that the useful conjunctions are those that comprise at least one high scoring atomic feature (from top 0.01% or 0.25%). In contrast, a larger l_{opt} would mean that the model benefits from conjunctions between two low scoring atomic features, which is not the case, according to our results.

5 Analysis of conjunctions

The purpose of feature induction is to generate useful combinations of features without the help of an expert in the domain of the application. Below we comment on interesting (types) of conjunctions that rank high ccording to the Perceptron model using the MI criterion for feature ranking, which showed highest performance.

- http://www.geonames.org/ontology#P.PPLC & ANNIES=location˙city

  The Geonames ontology[2] indicates that the candidate is a capital and Gate's ANNIE[3] suggests that the instance is a city. Therefore, the conjunction reinforces the recommendation for a location. The conjunction is very informative.

- PrevWord = "in" & MOST˙PROBABLE=true

  If the word preceding the candidate is 'in' and Location is most probable label of the entity, then there is a strong indication that the entity is indeed a Location.

- PrevWord = "in" & NoCandidates=1

  The conjunction between previous word being 'in' and the absence of other candidates at the specific location is a strong indicator for Location. This is a linguistic pattern that most experts would add to the model. Our algorithm automatically generates this pattern.

- ANNIES=location˙country & pacategory:Olympics

  A very interesting domain-specific conjunction is formed by the indication of ANNIE to a country and the category of the document being Olympics. Even though ANNIE points to a country, the fact that the document belongs to the Olympics category makes the Location less likely, because the candidate is most probably referring to a team. Such conjunctions are specific to domain adaptation tasks and our algorithm generates it automatically, without defining a domain adaptation problem explicitly. Only adding atomic domain features allows for generating of domain specific-conjunctions.

- multiple conjunctions including the domain name

  Our algorithm ranks high various conjunctions that include the domain of the document. As commented already above, our approach seems to implicitly perform domain adaptation, by adding conjunctions between features that play different roles in different domains and the respective domain features (very similar to the approach of (Daumé, 2009)).

6 Discussion

We introduced a greedy heuristic for feature selection and induction. The method is applied as a preprocessing step, prior to model fitting, therefore it is independent from the classifier chosen by the user. It is very fast in practice, having all the advantages of the filter-based methods over complex wrappers and embedded methods.

We applied the method on a custom dataset from Press Association, for named entity disambiguation. In particular, we recognized Locations from negative entities. The results, presented in the form of F1 measure corresponding to the Location class, show great improvements over the baseline.

We provided with a qualitative analysis of some of the highest ranking conjunctions and they appear to be strong predictors for Location, that a domain expert would also consider adding to the model.

[2] www.geonames.org

[3] http://gate.ac.uk/

References

Adam L. Berger, Vincent J. Della Pietra, and Stephen A. Della Pietra. 1996. A maximum entropy approach to natural language processing. *Comput. Linguist.*, 22(1):39–71.

Leo Breiman, Jerome Friedman, Charles J. Stone, and R. A. Olshen. 1984. *Classification and Regression Trees*. Chapman and Hall/CRC.

Leo Breiman. 2001. Random forests. *Machine Learning*, 45(1):5–32.

Corinna Cortes and Vladimir Vapnik. 1995. Support-vector networks. *Machine Learning*, 20(3):273–297.

H. Daumé. 2009. Frustratingly easy domain adaptation. *CoRR*, abs/0907.1815.

Asif Ekbal, Sriparna Saha, Olga Uryupina, and Massimo Poesio. 2011. Multiobjective simulated annealing based approach for feature selection in anaphora resolution. In *DAARC*, pages 47–58.

R.A. Fisher. 1928. *Statistical methods for research workers*. Oliver and Boyd.

George Forman. 2003. An extensive empirical study of feature selection metrics for text classification. *J. Mach. Learn. Res.*, 3:1289–1305.

Isabelle Guyon and André Elisseeff. 2003. An introduction to variable and feature selection. *J. Mach. Learn. Res.*, 3:1157–1182.

Patrick Haffner, Steven J. Phillips, and Robert E. Schapire. 2005. Efficient multiclass implementations of l1-regularized maximum entropy. *CoRR*, abs/cs/0506101.

Richard W. Hamming. 1986. *Coding and Information Theory*. Prentice-Hall, Inc., Upper Saddle River, NJ, USA.

Noppadon Kamolvilassatian. 2002. Property-based feature engineering and selection. Master's thesis, Department of Computer Sciences, University of Texas at Austin.

Ron Kohavi and George H. John. 1997. Wrappers for feature subset selection. *Artificial Intelligence*, 97(1–2):273–324.

John Lafferty. 2001. Conditional random fields: Probabilistic models for segmenting and labeling sequence data. pages 282–289. Morgan Kaufmann.

Changki Lee and Gary Geunbae Lee. 2006. Information gain and divergence-based feature selection for machine learning-based text categorization. (1):155–165.

Chang-Hwan Lee, Fernando Gutierrez, and Dejing Dou. 2011. Calculating feature weights in naive bayes with kullback-leibler measure. In *Proceedings of the 2011 IEEE 11th International Conference on Data Mining*, ICDM '11, pages 1146–1151.

David D. Lewis. 1992. Feature selection and feature extraction for text categorization. In *Proceedings of Speech and Natural Language Workshop*, pages 212–217. Morgan Kaufmann.

Andrew McCallum. 2003. Efficiently inducing features of conditional random fields.

A Moh'd A Mesleh. 2007. Chi square feature extraction based svms arabic language text categorization system.

P. M. Narendra and K. Fukunaga. 1977. A branch and bound algorithm for feature subset selection. *IEEE Trans. Comput.*, 26(9):917–922.

F. Rosenblatt. 1957. *The Perceptron, a Perceiving and Recognizing Automaton Project Para*. Cornell Aeronautical Laboratory report.

Karl-Michael Schneider. 2004. A new feature selection score for multinomial naive bayes text classification based on kl-divergence. In *Proceedings of the ACL 2004 on Interactive poster and demonstration sessions*, ACLdemo '04.

Hirotoshi Taira and Masahiko Haruno. 1999. Feature selection in svm text categorization. In *Proceedings of the AAAI '99*, pages 480–486.

Harun Uguz. 2011. A two-stage feature selection method for text categorization by using information gain, principal component analysis and genetic algorithm. *Knowledge-Based Systems*, 24(7):1024–1032.

Celine Vens and Fabrizio Costa. 2011. Random forest based feature induction. In *ICDM*, pages 744–753.

Jihoon Yang and Vasant Honavar. 1998. Feature subset selection using a genetic algorithm. *IEEE Intelligent Systems*, 13(2):44–49.

Yiming Yang and Jan O. Pedersen. 1997. A comparative study on feature selection in text categorization. In *Proceedings of the Fourteenth International Conference on Machine Learning*, ICML '97, pages 412–420.

Introducing a Corpus of Human-Authored Dialogue Summaries in Portuguese

Norton Trevisan Roman
School of Arts, Sciences and Humanities
University of São Paulo
São Paulo – SP, Brazil
norton@usp.br

Paul Piwek
Centre for Research in Computing
The Open University
Milton Keynes, UK
p.piwek@open.ac.uk

Ariadne M. B. Rizzoni Carvalho
Institute of Computing
University of Campinas
Campinas – SP, Brazil
ariadne@ic.unicamp.br

Alexandre Rossi Alvares
School of Arts, Sciences and Humanities
University of São Paulo
São Paulo – SP, Brazil
alexandre.alvares1@usp.br

Abstract

In this paper, we introduce a corpus of human-authored dialogue summaries collected through a web-experiment. The corpus features (i) one of the few existing corpora of written dialogue summaries; (ii) the only corpus available for dialogue summaries in Portuguese; and (iii) the only available corpus of summaries produced for dialogues whose participants' politeness alignment was systematically varied. Comprising 1,808 human-authored summaries, produced by 452 summarisers, for four different dialogues, this is, to the best of our knowledge, the largest individual corpus available for dialogue summaries, with the highest number of participants involved.

1 Introduction

As an important part of current mainstream research on automatic summarisation, corpora are used for a vast range of applications, from the construction of tutoring systems (*e.g.*, (Callaway et al., 2005)) to abstract production from extracts (*e.g.*, (Hasler, 2007)), to multi-document summarisation (*e.g.*, (Atkinson and Munoz, 2013)). Still, most corpora are available in English only, which may have an impact on the performance of automatic summarisation methods when applied to other languages (de Loupy et al., 2010). Also, there seems to be a preference for newswire (*e.g.*, (Amini, 2000; Copeck and Szpakowicz, 2004; Hasler, 2007; de Loupy et al., 2010)) and academic texts summaries (*e.g.*, (Teufel and Moens, 1997)), with fewer sources available for dialogue summaries, and those available mostly restricted to spoken dialogues (*e.g.*, (Murray et al., 2005; Carletta et al., 2006; Liu and Liu, 2008)).

In this paper we introduce a corpus of human-authored dialogue summaries, which we have released for use by the research community.[1] The corpus comprises 1,808 summaries, produced by 452 summarisers, for four different dialogues (each summariser produced a summary for each dialogue). To the best of our knowledge, this is the largest individual corpus available for dialogue summaries, with the largest number of participants involved. Collected through a web-experiment, where participants had to summarise a set of written dialogues, the corpus has the additional characteristic of being written in Portuguese (a language spoken by over 200 million people[2], if one accounts only for Brazil and Portugal), thereby helping reduce the dearth of corpora for written dialogue summaries in languages other than English.

Additionally, source dialogues were carefully chosen so they portray interactions with different degree of politeness, as measured in an experiment carried out by Roman et al. (2006b). Resulting summaries may therefore be used for a range of different tasks, such as (i) automatic dialogue summarisation, especially in Portuguese; (ii) studies

[1] At www.each.usp.br/norton/resdial/index_ing.html

[2] http://www.ibge.gov.br/home/estatistica/populacao/censo2010/default.shtm
http://censos.ine.pt/xportal/xmain?xpid=CENSOS&xpgid=censos2011_apresentacao

on reports of emotion in dialogue; and (iii) investigation of other properties of the language used in dialogue summaries, such as most frequent typing errors (which could be helpful in, for example, spelling correction systems). We intend our release of the corpus to the research community to lead to its use as set out above and, possibly, in many further ways.

The rest of this paper is organised as follows. Section 2 describes some of the currently available corpora, presenting their size, resulting documents, and set of summarisers. Section 3 introduces our corpus, along with the methodology followed during its construction. In Section 4 we present some examples of the documents that make the corpus, along with their codification. Finally, in Section 5 we present our conclusions and directions for future work.

2 Related Work

In the search for corpora of human-authored summaries, many strategies have been adopted along the years. One of the first ones (which is still in use) was to rely on already available datasets, such as the abstracts delivered with scientific papers and textbook chapters (*e.g.*, (Teufel and Moens, 1997; Silber and McCoy, 2002; Hasler, 2007)). With the growth of the information exchange through the Internet, yet another source for raw material has emerged: online newswire documents (*e.g.*, (Amini, 2000; Jing, 2002; Copeck and Szpakowicz, 2004; de Loupy et al., 2010)), in particular those that come with a summary by their editor.

However abundant, such sources have the drawback of being quite generic, making it harder for the researcher to control different phenomena. Alternative sources include summarising e-mail threads (*e.g.*, (Rambow et al., 2004)), line graphs (*e.g.*, (Greenbacker et al., 2011)) and dialogues (*e.g.*, (Murray et al., 2005; Carletta et al., 2006; Liu and Liu, 2008)). As for this last source, there seems to be no available corpus of summaries of written dialogues. The aforementioned corpora consist of transcriptions of naturally occurring spoken dialogues, which may differ from written scripted dialogue (for example, for films, plays and adverts), as a result of the way they are produced. Scripted dialogues are an important genre in their own right, which merits academic study and has a range of applications as a result of their wide use in the entertainment, education and information presentation industries.

Apart from the source data type, size is another important feature that influences the usage of corpora. Current corpora sizes may vary from as few as 15 summaries (*e.g.*, (Jing and McKeown, 1999)) to as many as 1,000 summaries (*e.g.*, (Amini, 2000)), and up to 9,086 summaries (*e.g.*, (Copeck and Szpakowicz, 2004)), if one includes collections of corpora (in this case, gathered from four Document Understanding Conferences – DUC). Along with the size of a corpus, yet another feature to be taken into account is the number of participants that produced it, since a small number of summarisers may lead to a sample that is not representative for the phenomenon to be measured. On this account, current corpora vary from a single summariser (*e.g.*, (Hasler, 2007)) to as many as 202 (*e.g.*, (Teufel and Moens, 1997)).

Our corpus is distinctive from all these in that it consists of a total of 1,808 human-produce dialogue summaries (to our knowledge, the largest collection of summaries produced in a single initiative), authored by 452 different summarisers (again, according to our knowledge, the largest amount of summarisers reported in the literature). A further distinctive property of our corpus is that it is entirely in Portuguese, which adds to the very few existing initiatives for languages other than English (*e.g.*, (de Loupy et al., 2010; Saggion and Szasz, 2012)).

Finally, to the best of our knowledge, the current corpus is the only summary corpus whose source was chosen so as to present instances of dialogues in which the politeness of the dialogue participants varied systematically, as determined by our choice of source dialogues (see Section 3). This allows researchers to examine how politeness in dialogue is reported when the dialogue is summarised. In the next Section, we describe our corpus in more detail. We explain how we selected the source dialogues, along with the instructions presented to summarisers.

3 Data Collection

The first problem we faced, when trying to build a corpus of dialogues with different degrees of politeness for the interlocutors, was that of where to find dialogues that might fulfil this requirement. Since most available corpora are built from meeting transcriptions, and the only alternative corpus that is available was automatically generated (see (Roman et al., 2006a)), we decided to go for human-authored (that is, scripted) dialogues. We then turned to film dialogues, given their availability through the web and the richness of situations they portray.

Once the source of dialogues was settled, we started to collect them from movie scripts and transcripts over the web. We collected a total of 16 dialogues, from 10 movies, which portray a customer-seller interaction.[3] This kind of interaction was chosen because (i) it delivers a situation where people would have an idea about what would be proper behaviour by the dialogue participants; and (ii) it allowed for any resulting conclusions on this subject to be compared to the existing corpus of machine-generated dialogues described in (Roman et al., 2006a), which also consists of customer-seller interactions. Dialogues were collected regardless of other features, such as genre, for example.

Given the scarcity of movie scripts and transcripts in Portuguese at the time of data collection, specially when considering the aforementioned requirements, the original materials were exclusively in English. Summarisers, on the other hand, were native speakers of Brazilian Portuguese. To overcome this mismatch, the dialogues were translated to Portuguese by one of the researchers. They were then presented to 153 subjects, in a web-experiment reported in (Roman et al., 2006b), where participants were asked to classify them according to one out of five categories on a Likert scale, ranging from "very impolite" to "very polite". The purpose of the study was to measure "first-order politeness" (Watts, 2003) (also called politeness$_1$ (Eelen, 2001)), that is, people's own interpretation of politeness (or, conversely, impoliteness). Of the original 153 participants, 89 finished the experiment, as a result of the precautions taken to avoid drop-out in the critical phase (*i.e.* the classification proper).

Finally, four dialogues were chosen from that experiment, where either one party was impolite, or both were polite (as in the experiment described in (Roman et al., 2006a)). The selected dialogues were those where the distribution of classifications was more skewed towards the positive or negative end of the scale. Although the dialogues varied considerably in size, being 54, 61, 125 and 320 words long, respectively, no statistically significant difference ($t = 0.9307$, $p = 0.5228$) was found between the dialogue length and its classification as polite or impolite.

[3] Dialogues were adapted so that proper names and contextual information referring to visual elements of the scene were removed.

3.1 Dialogue Summarisation – Building the Corpus

The four dialogues selected from the experiment described in (Roman et al., 2006a; Roman et al., 2006b) were presented, in a different web-experiment, to a set of 1,385 volunteers, recruited by e-mail from all students in a Brazilian university (see (Roman et al., 2005) for details). These participants were assigned a restriction (either their summary should be no longer than 10% of the number of words in the source dialogue, or they were free to write down as much as they felt like) and a viewpoint (either customer, vendor, or an observer), under which they should write the summary. These limits were arbitrarily chosen so as to frame the summarisers' choice when forced to produce a very short summary, compared to what they would do should they be given no constraint at all, in particular when it comes to the reporting of more subjective material, such as the behaviour demonstrated by the dialogue participants, of which politeness is the prototypical case. In the sequence, participants were asked to produce a summary for each of the dialogues, under the assigned point of view and size limit.

Even though the original dialogues were in English, both classification and summarisation tasks were carried out with their Portuguese version. This, in turn, helps reducing the effects of any loss in the original content of the dialogues, by linking each summary to its source dialogue's Portuguese version, instead of its original English content. Also, participants were free to chose their own summarising style, that is, they were not asked to specifically produce abstractive or extractive summaries (we are currently studying the data to find out what summarisation styles they actually adopted). Finally, in order to keep the data as bias-free as possible, the whole experiment was designed so that participants that summarised the dialogues were different from those who classified them (*cf.* (Roman et al., 2006b)).

The experiment followed the guidelines suggested in (Roman et al., 2006b), by presenting the participants with a good number of initial webpages, as a way to induce those that were more susceptible to giving up the experiment to drop out before the critical phase began (*i.e.* before they were asked to produce any summary). These measures seem to have worked since, of the original 1,385 participants who started the experiment, 598 finished it. However bad that may sound, drop-out concentrated in the pre-summarisation phase, where 658 participants abandoned the experiment, resulting in a set of 652 who started the critical phase (for a more comprehensive description of the technical details involved in this kind of experiment see (Roman et al., 2005)).

Drop-out rates at each step in the summarisation process are shown in Figure 1. At first, participants were shown a web page introducing the research (*Pres* in the figure), but without giving away much information about it. The number 1,385 indicates that, out of all participants that saw the web page, 1,385 decided to move on to the next page. In the next page (*Reg* in the figure), participants had to give some personal details. At this point, a total of 860 (*i.e.* a 38% reduction in the original set) filled in the form and decided to proceed with the experiment.

In the next pages, drop-out begins to slow down. At the Log-in page, 750 (from the 860 that registered for the experiment, *i.e.* a further 13% reduction) logged in the system. These participants were then shown a web page, saying a little more about the research, but with no mention of its real intent. Out of the 750 that logged in the experiment, another 23 gave it up (*i.e.* a 3% reduction). As a result, a total of 727 participants did actually see the first dialogue to be summarised, that is, they entered the critical phase of the experiment, of which 652 submitted their first summary (a 10% decrease).

The next three pages correspond to the submission of summaries for the remaining dialogues (*D2* to *D4* in the figure). Across this set, we lost a further 7%, leaving us with 604 participants who submitted all summaries (for a total drop-out rate of around 17% at the critical phase). In the sequence, participants were prompted to classify the dialogues about their politeness (so as to verify if their perception on the dialogues matched that of the classification experiment). At this step, another four were lost. Finally, they were asked about whether they recognised any of the dialogues (*Rec* in the figure), in which page we lost another couple of participants, ending up with 598.

The reason for moving both questions to the end of the experiment was to avoid giving the participants any information that might affect their decision on what to include in the summary. In this case, asking them about the politeness of dialogue participants right after each summary could have the participants focus on this facet of the interaction. Along the same lines, asking them whether they recognised the summarised dialogue would potentially have them effectively try to do it, which in turn might lead to false positives, whereby participants think they recognise some dialogue just because they are paying more attention to it.

Although the adopted measures succeeded in moving drop-out away from the experiment proper, it might be the case that drop-out occurred in a systematic way, in which case the experimental results could be themselves compromised (Reips, 2002). Figures 2 and 3 show the results of our analysis on drop-out according to the participants' gender, knowledge area, educational attainment and age, for all participants that provided that information. Amongst all these variables, only educational attainment was found to be related to drop-out in this experiment (χ^2 = 6.8327, p<0.0090), in that postgraduate students tended to drop out less often than undergraduate students (perhaps due to a better comprehension of the experimental dynamics in general). No differences were observed for the remaining variables.[4]

Since we were dealing with movie dialogues, some participants recognised the specific movies. These participants may have included information in their summary that went beyond the information that was present in the dialogue itself. For this reason, out of the 598 participants who finished the experiment, we removed the data from all 136 participants who indicated that they were already familiar with some of the dialogues, along with the single participant who did not provide such information. An analysis of the remaining data set led us to discard a further nine from the 461 remaining participants, resulting in a total of 452. Out of these nine, three were non-native speakers of Portuguese; two produced incomplete data sets, by leaving one or more summary empty; and four produced nonsense, by typing random charac-

[4] χ^2 = 2.0074, p = 0.1565, for gender; χ^2 = 0.2966, p = 0.8622, for area of knowledge; and χ^2 = 2.6390, p = 0.7554, for age.

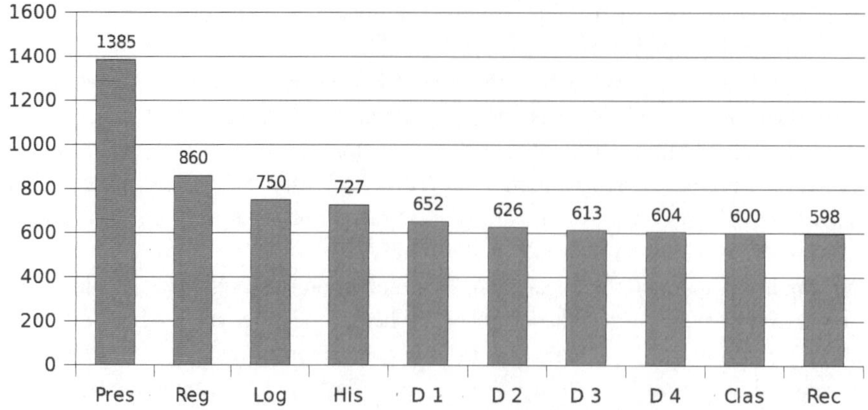

Figure 1: Number of participants at each webpage.

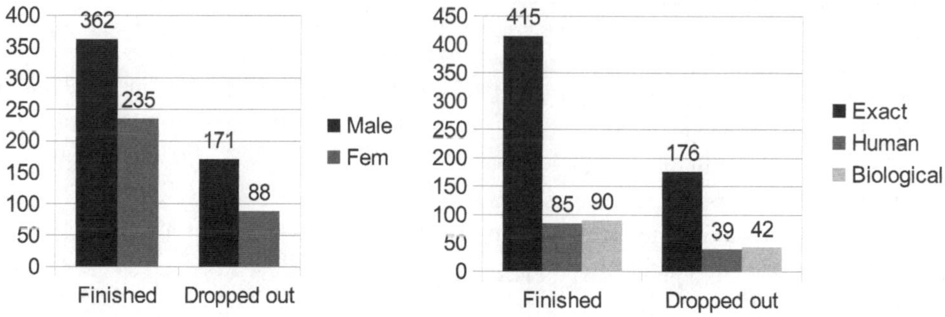

Figure 2: Dropout according to gender and knowledge area.

ters in the summary. All these correspond to mere 1.95% of the 461 participants, which adds to the trustworthiness of the data set.

Another source of bias in the experiment would be having an unbalanced number of participants recognise the dialogues, when compared to the 452 who did not recognise any of them. In this case, we found no statistically significant difference, between the participants who recognised any of the dialogues and those who did not, for the variables gender (χ^2 = 0.3656, p = 0.5454) and knowledge area (χ^2 = 3.4705, p = 0.1764). As for the remaining variables, once again, educational attainment showed a statistically significant difference, although borderline (χ^2 = 3.8726, p = 0.0491), whereby postgraduate students seem to have recognised the movies more often. Somewhat related to this finding is the statistically significant difference also found for the variable age (χ^2 = 23.8249, p = 0.0002), in which participants between 20-25 years old seem to have recognised proportionally less frequently the dialogues. Both results might be actually due to the participants' life experience, whereby the older they are, the higher the odds that they are both postgraduate students and have seen the movie before. Figure 4 shows the numbers for both variables.

After filtering out the data from the participants who recognised the dialogues and from the nine with problematic data, the resulting corpus comprised 1,808 human-made summaries, produced by 452 different participants, where each participant generated four different summaries, one for each dialogue. Due to the random distribution of participants amongst the experimental categories, out of the 1,808 summaries, 896 were produced by the group with no size restrictions, whereas the remaining 912 should be no longer than 10% of the number of words of their source dialogue. Finally, the entire corpus has a total of 62,858 words (mean of 34.7 words per summary), with 11,512 (mean of 12.6 per summary) in the 10% restriction set, and 51,346 (mean of 57.3 per summary) in the set with no size restriction at all.

Of the 452 participants, 270 (59.7%) were male and 181 (40%) female, with one abstention to the

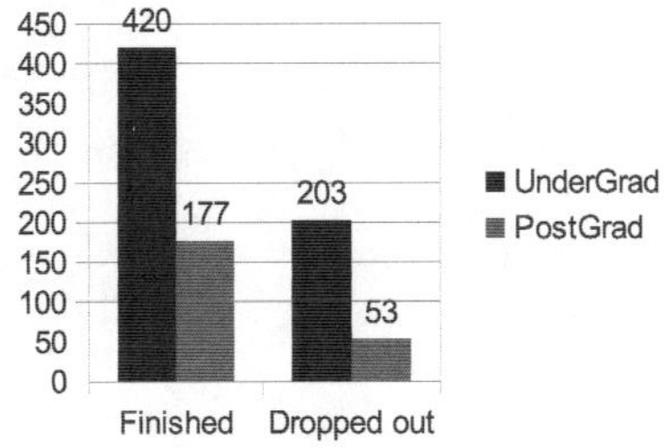

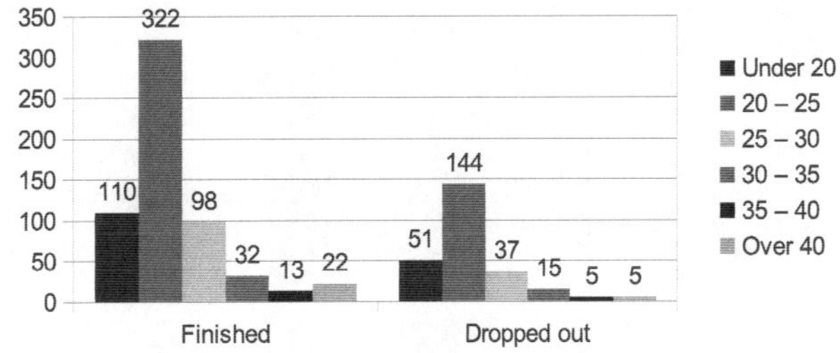

Figure 3: Dropout according to educational attainment and age.

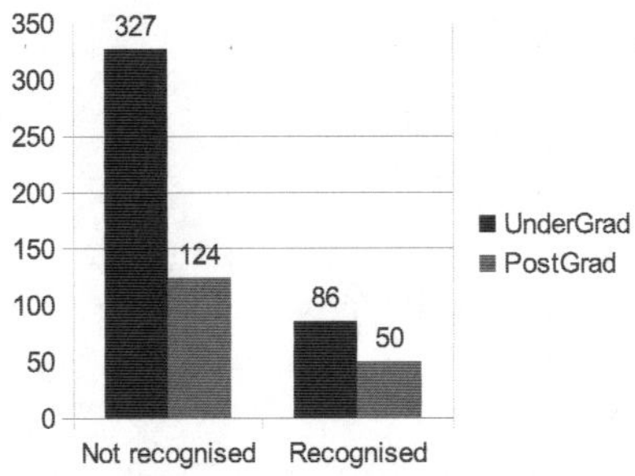

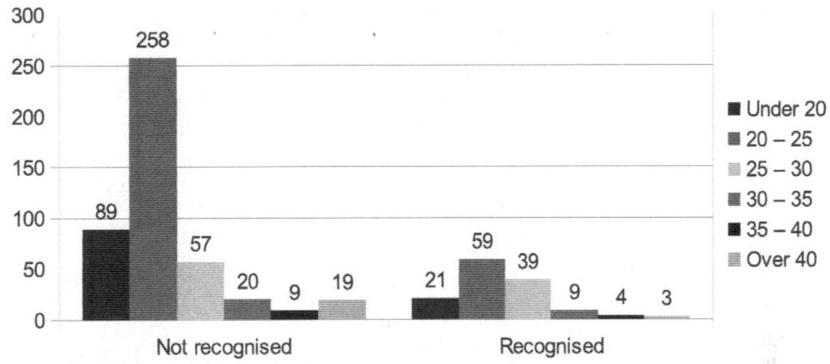

Figure 4: Distributions of participants that recognised the dialogues and those that did not.

question, 327 (72.3%) were undergraduate students, whereas 124 (27.4%) were postgraduate (and one abstention), with 322 (71.2%) pertaining to the exact sciences, 62 (13.7%) to the social sciences, other 62 to the biological sciences, and six abstentions. Ages varied from under 20 to over 40, distributed as shown in Figure 5.

Finally, regarding possible differences between the way people classified the dialogues' interaction (as reported in (Roman et al., 2006b)) and the way summarisers perceived it (in our experiment), we found no statistically significant difference[5] between both experiments, for any of the dialogues, with respect to whether participants perceived the dialogues as portraying a polite, neutral or impolite interaction. This is an indication that summarisers had understood the dialogues the same way as did those that classified them in the first experiment.

4 Corpus Delivery

The corpus is stored as a set of text files (UTF-8 encoded), in a single folder, where each file corresponds to a single summary. Within each file, data are represented using an XML compliant format[6], making them more independent of the process that created them (Müller and Strube, 2006; O'Donnell, 2008). Dialogue summaries are delivered as plain text, that is, with no further annotation added to them, so that future annotations can be made in a stand-off manner, whereby annotation and annotated data are kept in different XML files, with some link between them (Ide and Brew, 2000). Figure 6 illustrates a sample summary in the corpus.[7]

As can be seen in the figure, along with the summary, the XML includes its identification code ("R0001") and the identification of the corpus in which the summary is inserted (in this case, "C2"). There are also tags for the identification of the dialogue used to create the summary ("D1"), along with the identification of the corpus holding that dialogue (*i.e.* "Script2"). Given that summaries were produced under a viewpoint and possibly with a size constraint, both values are also recorded in their XML, followed by the summariser that produced this summary.

[5] χ^2 = 2.0926, p = 0.3512, for the first dialogue, χ^2 = 0.1038, p = 0.9494, for the second, χ^2 = 3.4405, p = 0.1790, for the third and χ^2 = 3.4225, p = 0.1806, for the fourth one.

[6] For a detailed description of the adopted XML codification, we refer the interested reader to (Roman, 2013).

[7] Main text may be translated as "The client in the pub wants the waitress Carol to serve him. That is not possible, because she is being replaced, since she would be better off with getting a job closer to her home. The client does not understand it at all, and he is ready to pay whatever it takes to get Carol to serve him".

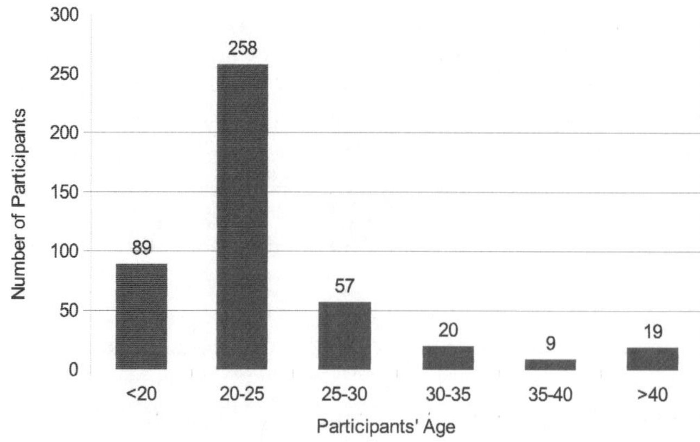

Figure 5: Distribution of participants according to their age.

```
<?xml version="1.0" encoding="UTF-8"?>
<plainDocument>
  <info type="id" value="R0001" />
  <info type="corpus" value="C2" />
  <info type="source" value="D1" />
  <info type="source-corpus"
        value="Script2" />
  <info type="viewpoint"
        value="attendant" />
  <info type="constraint" value="free"/>
  <info type="summariser"
        value="a30c92004183430935" />
  <text>O Cliente da lanchonete quer que
        a garçonete Carol atenda-o. Isso
        não é possivel pois ela está
        sendo substituida já que seria
        melhor ela arrumar um emprego
        mais perto da casa dela. O
        Cliente não entende de forma
        alguma, e está disposto a pagar
        o que for necessário
        para que a Carol o atenda.
  </text>
</plainDocument>
```

Figure 6: Codification of a plain summary.

Within this scheme, source dialogues are kept in a different folder, codified along the same lines as the corpus of summaries. Figure 7 shows a sample dialogue, adapted from the "As Good as it Gets" movie script.[8] Although following the same codification style, the stored information is different in this set. In this case, each file (and hence each source-dialogue) has, apart from its identification code and corpus identification, the identification of the source type ("Movie Script"), the movie title and the translator of the dialogue (a necessary step, since the summaries are in Portuguese whereas the script is in English). Finally, the politeness alignment of the dialogue, as determined by the majority of participants, both in the classification experiment carried out by Roman et al. (2006b) and ours, is also added to the summary, respectively, in the "classified-politeness" and "perceived-politeness" fields.

Inside each corpus folder, there is also a subfolder named "participants", which stores all the information regarding who was responsible for the production of that corpus. In the corpus of summaries, it corresponds to the characterisation of the human summarisers, while in the set of dialogues, it corresponds to the single person that translated them. Whatever the folder, the information about each participant is kept in separate files, one per participant, as with the corpus itself.

Figure 8 shows an example of such a file, in which we keep information about the participant's identification code (within the corpus), gender, area of knowledge, educational attainment, age and Brazilian State of origin. The last two tags in the figure refer to the time the participant registered and the time s/he actually logged in to carry out the experiment. Finally, we would like to emphasise that no information is kept that could be used to directly identify any of the participants. We only report on information that is useful for statistical purposes and to characterise the sample.

[8]The adapted dialogue is: "In a pub. Dialogue between a client and the waitress:
Waitress: How may I serve you?
Client: No. No. Get Carol.
Waitress: I'm filling in. I don't know if she's coming back. It might be better for her to get a job closer to home.
Client: What are you trying to do to me?
Waitress: What do you mean?
Client: Listen, elephant girl, call her or something... just let her do my one meal here. I'll pay whatever. I'll wait. Do it!!!"

```
<?xml version="1.0" encoding="UTF-8"?>
<plainDocument>
  <info type="id" value="D1" />
  <info type="corpus" value="Script2"/>
  <info type="source-type"
        value="Movie Script" />
  <info type="title"
        value="As Good as it Gets" />
  <info type="translator" value="t01"/>
  <info type="classified-politeness"
        value="very impolite" />
  <info type="perceived-politeness"
        value="very impolite" />
  <text>
   Em uma lanchonete. Diálogo entre um
   cliente e a garçonete.
     Garçonete:   Pois não.
     Cliente:     Não, não, vá chamar a
                  Carol.
     Garçonete:   Eu to substituindo
                  ela. Não sei se ela
                  vai voltar. Talvez
                  seja melhor ela
                  arrumar um emprego
                  mais perto da casa
                  dela.
     Cliente:     O que você tá tentando
                  fazer comigo?
     Garçonete:   Como assim?
     Cliente:     Escuta aqui, ô
                  elefanta, vá chamar
                  ela... só peça que ela
                  prepare minha refei-
                  ção. Eu pago o que
                  for. Eu espero. Vá!!!
  </text>
</plainDocument>
```

Figure 7: Codification of a source dialogue.

5 Conclusion

In this paper, we introduced a corpus of human-authored dialogue summaries. Collected through a web experiment, this is, to the best of our knowledge, the largest corpus available for dialogue summaries, with the highest number of participants involved. Amongst its main characteristics, are (i) it is one of the few existing corpora of dialogue summaries and, to our knowledge, the only one produced from written dialogues, as opposed to audio transcriptions; (ii) it is the only corpus available for dialogue summaries in Portuguese; and (iii) it is the only available corpus of summaries produced for dialogues whose participants' politeness alignment was systematically varied.

Amongst other possibilities, this corpus may serve as the basis for a range of projects, from studies in generation-based summarization (or its evaluation) to sentence compression, to research on the influence the dialogue participants' politeness has on the production of summaries for such dialogues. Since the dialogue summaries were directly typed in by the summarisers, more generic studies into language use can also be carried out, such as studies on spelling error frequencies, for example. As for future research, we intend to explore in more depth some of the topics described above.

```
<?xml version="1.0" encoding="UTF-8"?>
<participant>
  <info type="id"
        value="a30c92004183430935" />
  <info type="gender" value="m" />
  <info type="age" value="20-25" />
  <info type="area"
        value="exact sciences" />
  <info type="degree"
        value="undergraduate" />
  <info type="State of Origin"
        value="SP" />
  <info type="registration"
        value="Friday,1,October,2004.
        21h:0m:28s" />
  <info type="log-in"
        value="Friday,1,October,2004.
        21h:0m:58s"/>
</participant>
```

Figure 8: XML describing a summariser in the corpus.

Acknowledgements

This research was sponsored by CNPq – Conselho Nacional de Desenvolvimento Científico e Tecnológico – and CAPES – Coordenação de Aperfeiçoamento de Pessoal de Nível Superior. Part of it was also supported by the EC Project NECA IST-2000-28580 and the Programa de Educação Tutorial – MEC/SESu.

References

Massih-Reza Amini. 2000. Interactive learning for text summarization. In *Proceedings of the PKDD'2000 Workshop on Machine Learning and Textual Information Access*, Lyon, France, September 13-16.

John Atkinson and Ricardo Munoz. 2013. Rhetorics-based multi-document summarization. *Expert Systems with Applications*, 40:4346–4352.

Charles Callaway, Myroslava O. Dzikovska, Johanna D. Moore, David Reitter, and Claus Zinn. 2005. D11: Corpus collection and specification. Technical report, The LeActiveMath Consortium, May.

Jean Carletta, Simone Ashby, Sebastien Bourban, Mike Flynn, Mael Guillemot, Thomas Hain, Jaroslav Kadlec, Vasilis Karaiskos, Wessel Kraaij, Melissa

Kronenthal, Guillaume Lathoud, Mike Lincoln, Agnes Lisowska, Iain McCowan, Wilfried Post, Dennis Reidsma, and Pierre Wellner. 2006. The ami meeting corpus: A pre-announcement. In *Proceedings of the Second international Workshop on Machine Learning for Multimodal Interaction (MLMI'05)*, pages 28–39, Edinburgh, UK, July 11-13.

Terry Copeck and Stan Szpakowicz. 2004. Vocabulary usage in newswire summaries. In *Text Summarization Branches Out: Proceedings of the ACL-04 Workshop*, pages 19–26, Barcelona, Spain, July 25-26.

Claude de Loupy, Marie Guégan, Christelle Ayache, Somara Seng, and Juan-Manuel Torres Moreno. 2010. A french human reference corpus for multi-document summarization and sentence compression. In *Proceedings of the Seventh International Conference on Language Resources and Evaluation (LREC'10)*, Valletta, Malta, May, 19-21.

Gino Eelen. 2001. *A Critique of Politeness Theories*. St. Jerome, Manchester, England.

Charles F. Greenbacker, Sandra Carberry, and Kathleen F. McCoy. 2011. A corpus of human-written summaries of line graphs. In *Proceedings of the UCNLG+Eval: Language Generation and Evaluation Workshop (UCNLG+EVAL '11)*, pages 23–27, Edinburgh, UK, July 31.

Laura Hasler. 2007. From extracts to abstracts: Human summary production operations for computer-aided summarisation. In *Proceedings of the RANLP 2007 Workshop on Computer-Aided Language Processing (CALP)*, pages 11–18, Borovets, Bulgaria, 30 September.

Nancy Ide and Chris Brew. 2000. Requirements, tools, and architectures for annotated corpora. In *Proceedings of Data Architectures and Software Support for Large Corpora*, pages 1–5, Paris, France. European Language Resources Association.

Hongyan Jing and Kathleen R. McKeown. 1999. The decomposition of human-written summary sentences. In *Proceedings of the 22nd annual international ACM SIGIR conference on Research and development in information retrieval (SIGIR '99)*, Berkeley, USA, August 15-19.

Hongyan Jing. 2002. Using hidden markov modeling to decompose human-written summaries. *Computational Linguistics*, 28(4):527–543, December.

Fei Liu and Yang Liu. 2008. What are meeting summaries? an analysis of human extractive summaries in meeting corpus. In *Proceedings of the 9th SIGdial Workshop on Discourse and Dialogue*, pages 80–83, Columbus, Ohio, USA, June 19–20.

Christoph Müller and Michael Strube. 2006. Multi-level annotation of linguistic data with MMAX2. In Sabine Braun, Kurt Kohn, and Joybrato Mukherjee, editors, *Corpus Technology and Language Pedagogy: New Resources, New Tools, New Methods*, pages 197–214. Peter Lang, Frankfurt a.M., Germany.

Gabriel Murray, Steve Renals, and Jean Carletta. 2005. Extractive summarization of meeting recordings. In *Proceedings of the 9th European Conference on Speech Communication and Technology (Interspeech'2005-Eurospeech)*, Lisbon, Portugal, September 4-8.

Michael O'Donnell. 2008. The uam corpustool: software for corpus annotation and exploration. In *Proceedings of the XXVI Congreso de AESLA*, Almeria, Spain, April 3-5.

Owen Rambow, Lokesh Shrestha, John Chen, and Chirsty Lauridsen. 2004. Summarizing email threads. In *Proceedings Human Language Technology conference / North American chapter of the Association for Computational Linguistics annual meeting (HLT/NAACL 2004)*, Boston, USA, May 2-7.

Ulf-Dietrich Reips. 2002. Standards for internet-based experimenting. *Experimental Psychology*, 49(4):243–256.

Norton Trevisan Roman, Paul Piwek, and Ariadne Maria Brito Rizzoni Carvalho. 2005. A web-based experiment on dialogue summarisation. Technical Report IC-05-05, Computing Institute – State University of Campinas, Campinas, SP, Brazil, March.

Norton Trevisan Roman, Paul Piwek, and Ariadne Maria Brito Rizzoni Carvalho. 2006a. Politeness and bias in dialogue summarization: Two exploratory studies. In James G. Shanahan, Yan Qu, and Janyce Wiebe, editors, *Computing Attitude and Affect in Text: Theory and Applications*, volume 20 of *The Information Retrieval Series*, pages 171–185. Springer Netherlands, Dordrecht, The Netherlands, January 9. ISBN: 1-4020-4026-1.

Norton Trevisan Roman, Paul Piwek, and Ariadne Maria Brito Rizzoni Carvalho. 2006b. A web-experiment on dialogue classification. In Solange Oliveira Rezende and Antonio Carlos Roque da Silva Filho, editors, *Proceedings of the Fourth Workshop in Information and Human Language Technology (TIL'2006)*, Ribeir ao Preto, Brazil, October, 27–28. ICMC-USP.

Norton Trevisan Roman. 2013. Resdial – coding description (v.1.0). Technical Report PPgSI-001/2012, School of Arts, Sciences and Humanities – University of São Paulo, S ao Paulo, SP – Brazil, April.

Horacio Saggion and Sandra Szasz. 2012. The concisus corpus of event summaries. In *Proceedings of the Eight International Conference on Language Resources and Evaluation (LREC'12)*, Istanbul, Turkey, May 23–25.

H. Gregory Silber and Kathleen F. McCoy. 2002. Efficiently computed lexical chains as an intermediate representation for automatic text summarization. *Computational Linguistics*, 28(4):487–496.

Simone Teufel and Marc Moens. 1997. Sentence extraction as a classification task. In *Proceedings of the ACL/EACL Workshop on Intelligent Scalable Text Summarization*, pages 58–65, Madrid, Spain, July 11th.

Richard Watts. 2003. *Politeness*. Cambridge University Press.

Wikipedia as an SMT Training Corpus

Dan Tufiş
Institute for AI
Romanian Academy
Bucharest, Romania
tufis@racai.ro

Radu Ion
Institute for AI
Romanian Academy
Bucharest, Romania
radu@racai.ro

Ştefan Daniel Dumitrescu
Institute for AI
Romanian Academy
Bucharest, Romania
sdumitrescu@racai.ro

Dan Ştefănescu
University of Memphis
Memphis, USA
dstfnscu@memphis.edu

Abstract

This article reports on mass experiments supporting the idea that data extracted from strongly comparable corpora may successfully be used to build statistical machine translation systems of reasonable translation quality for in-domain new texts. The experiments were performed for three language pairs: Spanish-English, German-English and Romanian-English, based on large bilingual corpora of similar sentence pairs extracted from the entire dumps of Wikipedia as of June 2012. Our experiments and comparison with similar work show that adding indiscriminately more data to a training corpus is not necessarily a good thing in SMT.

1 Introduction

Wikipedia is one of the most accessed websites of the Internet according to Alexa.com with a global rank of 6 (being outrun only by major search engines such as Google, Yahoo and Baidu and by Face-book and YouTube). Approximately 14% of all Internet users use it on a daily basis and out of these, more than 50% browse through the English version of Wikipedia which is the most comprehensive one, judged by the number of articles. Wikipedia is not a real parallel corpus, although many documents in different languages are translations from English. Many documents in one language are shortened or adapted translations[1] of documents from other (not always the same) languages and this property of Wikipedia together with its size makes it the ideal candidate of a strongly comparable corpus from which parallel sentences can be mined. In the following, we use the term *MT useful data* to denote sets of bilingual sentences/phrases with a high level of cross-lingual similarity, out of which a word/phrase aligner can extract translation lexicons relevant for the SMT task. SMT engines like Moses (Koehn et al., 2007) produce better translations when presented with larger and larger training parallel corpora. For a given training corpus, it is also known that Moses produces better translations when presented with in-domain new texts (texts from the same domain as the training data, e.g. news, laws, medicine, etc.). Collecting parallel data from a given domain, in sufficiently large quantities to be of use for statistical translation, is not an easy task. To date, OPUS[2] (Tiedemann, 2012) is the largest **online** collection of parallel corpora, comprising of juridical texts (EUROPARL and EUconst)[3], medical texts (EMEA), technical texts (e.g. software KDE manuals, PHP manuals), movie subtitles corpora (e.g. OpenSubs) or news (SETIMES) but these corpora are not available for all language pairs nor their sizes are similar with respect to the domain.

In a previous paper (Ştefănescu et al., 2012) we described in details an open-source parallel data extractor from comparable corpora, developed within the ACCURAT EU-project[4]. Essentially, this extractor allows for identifying similar (translation-wise) sentences in a bilingual comparable corpus. A multi-variable function scores the similarity of each candidate pair, and depending on the level of similarity score (ranging between 0 and 1), one could compile different MT useful data sets. We showed elsewhere (Ion et al., 2011) that with the similarity threshold above 0.7, for all the languages we experimented with, our extracted data, human validated, is really parallel. However, depending on the comparability level of the extraction corpus, the quantity of parallel data extracted may range from 0.1% (weakly comparable corpora) to 29% (strongly comparable corpora) of the entire corpus (Ion et al., 2011). Setting a high similarity threshold has the disadvantage that a significant part of the MT

[1] http://en.wikipedia.org/wiki/Wikipedia:Translation

[2] http://opus.lingfil.uu.se/

[3] JRC-Acquis/DGT Translation Memories are other examples of large parallel juridical texts.

[4] http://www.accurat-project.eu/

useful data contained in the comparable corpora is lost.

The experiments we report in this article had multiple purposes:

a) to assess the usefulness of extracted data for SMT by investigating the contribution of less than parallel extracted data to the quality of the translations produced by a baseline SMT; this investigation was driven by iteratively lowering the similarity threshold for the extracted data and evaluating the translation quality for the system trained on the resulted MT useful data.
b) to assess the feasibility of better translating English documents absent from a foreign Wikipedia version; currently, Wikipedia does not offer an integrated translation engine to assist the translation task but this could be a worthy option to consider. With respect to this aim, all our experiments were conducted on in-domain (but unseen during the training) test sets.
c) to add a new domain (for many language pairs) – the encyclopedic domain – to the list of already existing domains for which MT useful data exists (e.g. Tiedemann's OPUS collection multilingual corpora).

In the rest of this paper, after reviewing the related research (Section 2), we provide some statistics on three large sets of similar sentence-pairs extracted from Wikipedia for the English-Spanish, English-German and English-Romanian language pairs (Section 3). In Section 4 we describe the Moses-based experiments with the extracted MT useful data and compare the results with those obtained in a similar scale experiment on Wikipedia. Section 5 describes the follow-up of the previously described experiments with even better results. We conclude with Section 6.

2 Related work

Due to its structure with linked articles on the same subject and because, frequently, articles in foreign languages contain adapted versions of the translations (or just the translation) of the English or other languages counterparts, Wikipedia is arguably the largest strongly comparable corpus available online. It has been the test bed of many attempts at parallel sentence mining.

Adafre and Rijke (2006) were among the first to attempt extraction of parallel sentences from Wikipedia. Their approach consists of two experiments: 1) the use of a MT system (Babelfish) to translate from English to Dutch and then, by word overlapping, to measure the similarity between the translated sentences and the original sentences and 2) with an automatically induced (phrase) translation lexicon from the titles of the linked articles, they measure the similarity of source (English) and target (Dutch) sentences by mapping them to (multiple) entries in the lexicon and computing lexicon entry overlap. Experiments were performed on 30 randomly selected English-Dutch document pairs yielding a few hundred parallel sentence pairs.

Mohammadi and GhasemAghaee (2010) continue the work of Adafre and Rijke (2006) by imposing certain limits on the sentence pairs that can be formed from a Wikipedia document pair: the length of the parallel sentence candidates must correlate and the Jaccard similarity of the lexicon entries (seen as IDs) mapped to source (Persian) and target (English) must be as high as possible. As with Adafre and Rijke, the work performed by Mohammadi and GhasemAghaee does not actually generate a parallel corpus but only a couple of hundred parallel sentences intended as a proof of concept.

Another experiment, due to Smith et al. (2010), addressed large-scale parallel sentence mining from Wikipedia. Based on binary Maximum Entropy classifiers, in the spirit of Munteanu and Marcu (2005), they automatically extracted large volumes of parallel sentences for English-Spanish (almost 2M pairs), English-German (almost 1.7M pairs) and English-Bulgarian (more than 145K pairs). According to Munteanu and Marcu (2005), a binary classifier can be trained to distinguish between parallel sentences and non-parallel sentences using features such as: word alignment log probability, number of aligned/unaligned words, longest sequence of aligned words, etc. To enrich the feature set, Smith et al. proposed to automatically extract a bilingual dictionary from the Wikipedia document pairs and use this dictionary to supplement the word alignment lexicon derived from existing parallel corpora. Since the work of Smith et al. (2010) is the only one we know of that extracted parallel corpora of similar sizes to ours, we will reserve a detailed comparison with their work in the evaluation section (Section 4.4). Furthermore, they released their English-Spanish and English-German Wikipedia test sets and so, a direct comparison is made possible. Unfortunately, the large amounts of extracted parallel corpora are not available online for the SMT research community.

3 The Extracted Wiki Datasets

Using LEXACC (Ştefănescu et al., 2012) we mined (Ştefănescu and Ion, 2013) for parallel sentence pairs from selected documents belonging to full dumps of English, Romanian, Spanish and German Wikipedias as of December 2012. Table 1 lists, for different similarity scores (**Sim**) as extraction thresholds, the number of MT useful sentence pairs (P) found in each language pair dataset, as well as the number of words (ignoring punctuation) per language (EnW, DeW, RoW, EsW) in the respective sets of sentence pairs. Data extracted with a given similarity score threshold is a proper sub-set of any data extracted with a lower similarity score threshold.

Sim	En-De	En-Ro	En-Es
0.9	P: 38,390 EnW: 0.695 M DeW: 0.543 M	P: 42,201 EnW: 0.814 M RoW: 0.828 M	P: 91,630 EnW: 1.126 M EsW: 1.158 M
0.8	P: 119,480 EnW: 2.077 M DeW: 2.010 M	P: 112,341 EnW: 2.356 M RoW: 2.399 M	P: 576,179 EnW: 10.504 M EsW: 11.285 M
0.7	P: 190,135 EnW: 3.494 M DeW: 3.371 M	P: 142,512 EnW: 2.987 M RoW: 3.036 M	P: 1,219,866 EnW: 23.730 M EsW: 25.931 M
0.6	P: 255,128 EnW: 4.891 M DeW: 4.698 M	P: 169,662 EnW: 3.577 M RoW: 3.634 M	P: 1,579,692 EnW: 31.022 M EsW: 33.706 M
0.5	P: 322,011 EnW: 6.453 M DeW: 6.186 M	P: 201,263 EnW: 4.262 M RoW: 4.325 M	P: 1,838,794 EnW: 36.512 M EsW: 39.545 M
0.4	P: 412,608 EnW: 8.470 M DeW:8.132 M	P: 252,203 EnW: 5.415 M RoW: 5.482 M	P: 2,102,025 EnW: 42.316 M EsW: 45.565 M
0.3	P: 559,235 EnW: 13.740M DeW: 11.353M	P: 317,238 EnW: 6.886 M RoW: 6.963 M	P: 2,656,915 EnW: 54.932 M EsW: 58.524 M
0.2	P: 929,956 EnW: 25.485M DeW: 21.492M	P: 449,640 EnW: 9.956 M RoW:10.056 M	P: 3,850,782 EnW: 88.567 M EsW: 93.047 M
0.1	P: 1,279,166 EnW: 37.076M DeW: 31.537M	P: 683,223 EnW: 16.275 M RoW:.16.420 M	P: 5,025,786 EnW: 122.760 M EsW: 128.132 M

Table 1: Number of parallel sentences and words extracted for each language pair, for a given threshold (Ştefănescu and Ion, 2013)

From Table 1, one could easily calculate the average word length for the extracted sentences for each language and each threshold value. It is not surprising that longer the sentences their similarity scores get lower. For the En-De language pair, the sentence word length varied for En from 28.98 to 18.11 while for De it varied from 24.65 to 14.43. A similar variation may be noticed for En-Es pair: from 24.42 to 12.28 (En) and from 25.49 to 12.63 (Es). For En-Ro the average sentence word length varied less: from 23.82 to 19.27 (En) and from 24.03 to 19.63 (Ro).

By random manual inspection of the generated sentence pairs, we confirmed earlier evaluations (Ion et al., 2011) that, in general, irrespective of the language pair, sentence pairs with a translation similarity measure of at least 0.7 are entirely parallel (e.g. "In 2003, Africa 2 Africa was merged with SABC Africa." ⇔ "En 2003, Africa 2 Africa fue fusionada con SABC Africa.", score 0.97), those with a translation similarity measure of at least 0.5 have extended parallel fragments which an accurate word or phrase aligner easily detects (e.g. "Besides regular repairs of the existing runways, Prague Airport (Letiště Praha s.p." ⇔ "Además de las habituales refacciones de las pistas, Letiště Praha s.p.", score 0.59). Below 0.5, sentences usually become strongly comparable. Further down the threshold scale, below 0.3, we usually find sentences that roughly speak of the same event but are not actual translations of each other (e.g. "Slaves were previously introduced by the British and French who colonized the island in the 18th century."⇔ "Los esclavos ya habían sido introducidos un siglo antes por los británicos y franceses que trataron de conquistar la isla.", score 0.29). The noisiest data sets were extracted for the 0.1 similarity threshold and we drop them from further experiments.

4 SMT experiments with Wiki datasets

There is a strong opinion, empirically supported, that parallel data extracted from comparable corpora leads to improvements of the translation quality of a baseline MT system when it incorporates this data. This has been exemplified by showing that a baseline MT system trained on data covering one or more domains, when tested on texts out of the respective domain(s), performed significantly worse. Translation models adaptation with data extracted from comparable corpora from the test domain improved the translation quality, but in general not reaching the same quality as in the baseline MT translation of the in-domain texts. One can naturally raise the following question: given a large and continuously growing multilingual collection of documents (such as Wikipedia) what would be a good approach for enhancing a SMT trained to translate Wikipedia-like documents (let's call it Wiki-translator)? The question calls to the limited available in-domain parallel data for any language pair (the sizes of pair-wise parallel Wikipedias are limited, even for the best represented languages) but suggest the benefits of in-domain adaptation by using comparable data extracted from Wikipedia. This issue is placed into operational terms, by asking the question: what level of sentences comparability is useful for improving the quality of Wiki-translator's output? The experiments described in this section try to provide some hints to the questions above.

We argued that with a high value (0.7) for the similarity threshold, the extracted sentence-pairs can safely be considered truly parallel. However, in Table 1, we showed that the number of sentences pairs with a similarity score of at least 0.7 represents a small portion (ranging from 14% to a maximum of 24%) of the potentially MT useful sentence pairs (corresponding to the threshold 0.1) from the interlinked documents.

In what follows, we give experimental insights by observing how translation improves/degrades when training on parallel sentences with different translation similarity thresholds.

4.1 Experimental setup

As mentioned in Section 4, the English, German and Spanish Wikipedias are the largest ones with substantial cross-lingual coverage. Romanian Wikipedia is medium-sized but containing many translations or adaptations of articles from other languages (mainly English). Consequently, we could find in En-De, En-Es and En-Ro Wikipedias a number of parallel sentences (190,135 for En-De with more than 6.86 million words, 142,512 for En-Ro with more than 6 million words and 1,219,866 for En-Es with almost 50 million words) allowing for building baseline Wiki-translators for these language pairs. The large sets of comparable sentences allowed us to conduct experiments on assessing the translation quality improvement/degradation when the parallel core training corpora were gradually extended with comparable but less and less parallel sentence pairs.

As the standard SMT system we chose Moses[5] with the default parameters for factorial optimization. We used it with the following parameters:

- surface-to-surface translation;
- phrase length of maximum 4 words;
- lexical reordering model with parameters `wbe-msd-bidirectional-fe`.

[5] http://www.statmt.org/moses/

The **language model** (LM) for all experiments was trained on entire monolingual, sentence-split English Wikipedia, after removing the administrative articles as described in Section 4. The language model was limited to 5-grams and the counts were smoothed with the interpolated Knesser-Ney method.

The **test sets for the three language pairs** were created by concatenating randomly extracted 2500 sentence pairs from each similarity interval ensuring parallelism ([0.6, 1], [0.7, 1], [0.8, 1] and [0.9, 1]). The sentence pairs extracted from each similarity interval were manually checked for parallelism. Thus we obtained 10,000 parallel sentence pairs for each language pair. These sentences were removed from the training data. In compiling the test sets, we were careful to observe the Moses' filtering constraints: both the source and target sentences must have at least 4 words and at most 60 words and the ratio of the longer sentence (in tokens) of the pair over the shorter one must not exceed 2.

Once the test sets were ready, we further trained **eight translation models** (TM), for each language pair, over cumulative threshold intervals beginning with 0.2: $TM_{[0.2,\ 1]}$ for [0.2, 1], $TM_{[0.3,\ 1]}$ for [0.3, 1] …, $TM_{[0.9,\ 1]}$ for [0.9, 1]. The training data for $TM_{[0.2,\ 1]}$ was the largest but the noisiest, while the training data for $TM_{[0.9,\ 1]}$ was the smallest but fully parallel. The resulting eight training corpora have been filtered with Moses' cleaning script with the same restrictions mentioned above. For every language, both the training corpora and the test set have been tokenized using Moses' tokenizer script and true-cased.

We are interested in finding out if the quality of the translation system based on the translation model TM_i were significantly different from the quality of the translation system based on the translation model TM_{i+1}, where TM_i and TM_{i+1} are translation models built as described in the previous sub-section. The quality of the translation systems was measured as usual in terms of their BLEU score (Papineni et al., 2002) on the same test data (10,000 parallel sentence pairs).

4.2 SMT results for Spanish-English and German-English

Table 2 shows the variations of the BLEU scores on the Spanish-English test set for the SMTs with different translation models. The shaded lines indicate the translation models built on fully parallel data. The better score of $TM_{[0.7,\ 1]}$ as compared to those of $TM_{[0.8,\ 1]}$ and $TM_{[0.9,\ 1]}$ is not surprising: the parallel training data is significantly larger: 190,135 pairs for $TM_{[0.7, 1]}$, 119,480 pairs for $TM_{[0.8, 1]}$ and only 38,390 for $TM_{[0.9, 1]}$. However, with additionally more 369,100 sentence pairs less parallel, $TM_{[0.3, 1]}$ achieves the best performance, with an statistically significant increase of 0.31 BLEU points and a much larger lexical coverage.

One can further see from Table 2, that in spite of the major reduction of the size of the training data, a significant increase in the BLEU score is achieved from the 0.2 translation model to 0.3.

The explanation is that most of the eliminated data was noisy; the training corpus became cleaner. This is a clear indication that comparable data existing in the respective training sets: **1)** does not degrade SMT performance; **2)** it makes the translation model more robust.

TM	BLEU SCORE
TM $_{[0.2, 1]}$	47.22
TM $_{[0.3, 1]}$	**47.59**
TM $_{[0.4, 1]}$	47.52
TM $_{[0.5, 1]}$	47.53
TM $_{[0.6, 1]}$	47.44
TM $_{[0.7, 1]}$	47.28
TM $_{[0.8, 1]}$	46.27
TM $_{[0.9, 1]}$	39.68

Table 2: Experimental SMT results on Es-En

Similar comments can be made for the English-German experiment. Table 3 presents the experimental results. This time the best BLEU score is obtained using TM $_{[0.5, 1]}$.

TM	BLEU SCORE
TM $_{[0.2, 1]}$	37.61
TM $_{[0.3, 1]}$	39.16
TM $_{[0.4, 1]}$	39.46
TM $_{[0.5, 1]}$	**39.52**
TM $_{[0.6, 1]}$	39.5
TM $_{[0.7, 1]}$	39.24
TM $_{[0.8, 1]}$	38.57
TM $_{[0.9, 1]}$	34.73

Table 3: Experimental SMT results on De-En

4.3 SMT results for Romanian-English

Translation for Romanian-English language pair has also been studied in Dumitrescu et al. (2013) with explicit interest for the in-domain/out-of-domain test/train data, using Moses in various configurations for surface-to-surface and factored translation. Out of the seven domain specific corpora (legal, transcribed speech, parliamentary debates, literature, medicine, news and encyclopedic) the encyclopedic corpus was based on Wikipedia. They have experimented with English-Romanian parallel sentence pairs extracted from Wikipedia using LEXACC at a fixed threshold: 0.5 (called "WIKI5"). A random selection of unseen 1000 Wikipedia Romanian test sentences has been translated into English using combinations of:

- a WIKI5-based translation model (240K sentence pairs)/WIKI5-based language model;
- a global translation model (1.7M sentence pairs)/global language model named "ALL", made by concatenating all specific corpora.

Table 4 gives the details, giving the BLEU scores for the Moses configuration similar to ours: surface-to-surface translation, with the language/translation model combinations described above.

	WIKI5 TM	ALL TM
WIKI5 LM	**29.99**	29.95
ALL LM	29.51	29.95

Table 4: BLEU scores on 1000 sentences Wikipedia test set of Dumitrescu et al. (2013)

Dumitrescu et al.'s results confirm the conclusion we claimed earlier: the ALL system performs worse than the in-domain WIKI5 system.

Our present results show the same characteristics as those of the Spanish-English and German-English experiments presented earlier. They are summarized in Table 5.

TM	BLEU SCORE
TM $_{[0.2, 1]}$	36.1
TM $_{[0.3, 1]}$	37.24
TM $_{[0.4, 1]}$	37.71
TM $_{[0.5, 1]}$	**37.99**
TM $_{[0.6, 1]}$	37.85
TM $_{[0.7, 1]}$	37.39
TM $_{[0.8, 1]}$	36.89
TM $_{[0.9, 1]}$	32.76

Table 5: Experimental SMT results on Ro-En

The almost eight BLEU points difference between our results and those in (Dumitrescu et al., 2013) may be explained by:

1) our language model was entirely in-domain for the test data and much larger: our language model was built from entire Romanian Wikipedia (more than 220,000 documents) while the language model in (Dumitrescu et al., 2013) was built only from the Romanian doc-

ument paired to English documents (less than 100,000 documents);

2) different Moses filtering parameters (e.g. the length filtering parameters),

3) different test sets.

4.4 Comparison with Smith et al. (2010)

As mentioned in Section 2, Smith et al. (2010) mined for parallel sentences from Wikipedia producing parallel corpora of sizes similar to ours Furthermore, they have made their Wikipedia test set available for Spanish-English and German-English (500 sentence pairs per language pair). We have translated these test sets (after being true-cased) with our best translation models (0.3 for Spanish-English and 0.5 for German-English) and also with Google Translate (as of mid-February 2012). Table 6 summarizes the results.

In this table, "Large+Wiki" denotes the best translation model of Smith et al. which was trained on many corpora (including Europarl and JRC Acquis) and on more than 1.5M parallel sentences mined from Wikipedia. "0.3 TM" and "0.5 TM" are our translation models as already explained. "Train data size" gives the size of training corpora in multiples of 1,000 sentence pairs.

Language pair	Train data size	System	BLEU
Spanish-English	9642K	Large+Wiki	43.30
	2288K	TM $_{[0.4,\ 1]}$	**50.19**
	N/A	Google	44.43
German-English	8388K	Large+Wiki	23.30
	306K	TM $_{[0.5,\ 1]}$	**23.34**
	N/A	Google	21.64

Table 6: Comparison between SMT systems on the Wikipedia test set provided by Smith et al. (2010)

It is thus empirically supported the finding that indiscriminately adding more out-of domain data, when large enough in-domain data already exists (as in these compared experiments), produces worse results.

5 Bootstrapping experiments

The astute reader may have noticed that the dictionaries used by LEXACC for mining MT useful data were extracted by GIZA++ from out-of-domain corpora (JRC-Acquis and Europarl). After obtaining the sets of in-domain MT useful data for the three language pairs discussed above, it was a natural decision to go one step further: compute new translation dictionaries by merging the old ones with the dictionaries generated by GIZA++ from in-domain data (extracted as described in Section 4) and re-do the SMT experiments described in Section 5. Since the full chain of experiments for the three language pairs is extremely time consuming, at the time of this writing we have the new results only for En-Ro language pair, which has the smallest datasets.

5.1 English-Romanian new extracted data

The earlier experiments empirically showed that the Similarity Score below 0.2 produced too much noisy data to be useful in SMT experiments. Therefore, we proceed with the LEXACC extraction process considering Similarity Score (**Sim**) higher or equal to 0.2.

Table 7 shows a significant increase of the number of extracted bilingual sentence pairs when the out-of-domain translation dictionary is extended by the in-domain translation lexicon.

Sim	Initial En-Ro	Boosted En-Ro
0.9	P: 42,201 EnW: 0.814 M RoW: 0.828 M	P: 66,777 EnW: 1.077 M RoW: 1.085 M
0.8	P: 112,341 EnW: 2.356 M RoW: 2.399 M	P: 152,015 EnW: 2.688 M RoW: 2.698 M
0.7	P: 142,512 EnW: 2.987 M RoW: 3.036 M	P: 189,875 EnW: 3.364 M RoW: 3.372 M
0.6	P: 169,662 EnW: 3.577 M RoW: 3.634 M	P: 221,661 EnW: 3.961 M RoW: 3.970 M
0.5	P: 201,263 EnW: 4.262 M RoW: 4.325 M	P: 260,287 EnW: 4,715 M RoW: 4,722 M
0.4	P: 252,203 EnW: 5.415 M RoW: 5.482 M	P: 335,615 EnW: 6.329 M RoW: 6.324 M
0.3	P: 317,238 EnW: 6.886 M RoW: 6.963 M	P: 444,102 EnW: 8.712 M RoW: 8.700 M
0.2	P: 449,640 EnW: 9.956 M RoW:10.056 M	P: 811,113 EnW: 171.425 M RoW: 171.109 M

Table 7: Boosting: comparison between the number of parallel sentences and words extracted for En-Ro

The new extracted corpus was used for the similar SMT experiments as described in Section 5. The test set was selected from completely parallel documents, not contained into the data extraction space. We changed the test set construction strategy using entire parallel documents and not sentence pairs from the parallel documents.

The first strategy could be suspected of biasing, since the contexts of the tested sentences (the documents from where the test sentence-pairs were extracted) were used for training.

The test set contains 1,000 Ro-En parallel sentences. Table 8 shows the results.

Again, we outline the differences in BLEU scores for the initial SMT experiments and the boosted ones.

TM	Initial BLEU score	Boosted BLEU score
TM $_{[0.2, 1]}$	36.10	47.31
TM $_{[0.3, 1]}$	37.24	49.83
TM $_{[0.4, 1]}$	37.71	49.83
TM $_{[0.5, 1]}$	**37.99**	50.74
TM $_{[0.6, 1]}$	37.85	**50.78**
TM $_{[0.7, 1]}$	37.39	50.52
TM $_{[0.8, 1]}$	36.89	49.85
TM $_{[0.9, 1]}$	32.76	45.52

Table 8: Boosting: BLEU comparisons on Ro-En

We made also translation experiments for the other direction, Ro-En, and as expected the translation accuracy (in terms of BLEU scores) was significantly lower. The best BLEU score for En-Ro translation direction was **44.09**, but this time for the translation model trained on the bilingual corpus with the similarity score equal or higher than 0.5 (TM $_{[0.6, 1]}$).

The last step in our experimental chain was to optimize the translation parameters using the usual MERT procedure. The development set used to tune the translation parameters had 1,000 parallel sentences, not used in the training or test sets. Not surprisingly, the BLEU scores further improve. Table 9 summarizes the new results:

TM	Boosted BLEU score	MERT Boosted BLEU score
TM $_{[0.2, 1]}$	47.31	48.92
TM $_{[0.3, 1]}$	49.83	50.61
TM $_{[0.4, 1]}$	49.83	50.48
TM $_{[0.5, 1]}$	50.74	**51.05**
TM $_{[0.6, 1]}$	**50.78**	50.97
TM $_{[0.7, 1]}$	50.52	50.65
TM $_{[0.8, 1]}$	49.85	50.65
TM $_{[0.9, 1]}$	45.52	46.69

Table 9: Optimized Boosting: BLEU comparisons on Ro-En

So far, we obtained our best result of 51.05 BLEU for the Ro-En direction, using the MERT-enhanced Boosted method.

6 Conclusions

We have shown that Wikipedia is a rich resource for parallel sentence mining in Statistical Machine Translation. Comparing different translation models containing MT useful data ranging from comparable, through strongly comparable, to parallel, we concluded that there is sufficient empirical evidence not to dismiss sentence pairs that are not fully parallel on the suspicion that because of the inherent noise they might be detrimental to the translation quality. On the contrary, our experiments demonstrated that in-domain comparable data are strongly preferable to out-of-domain parallel data. However, there is an optimum level of similarity between the comparable sentences, which according to our similarity metrics (for the language pairs we worked with) is around 0.4 or 0.5.

Additionally, the two step procedure we presented, demonstrated that an initial in-domain translation dictionary is not necessary, it can be constructed subsequently, starting with a dictionary extracted from whatever out-of-domain data. The parallel Wiki corpora (before and after the boosting step), including the two test sets (containing 10,000 and respectively 1,000 sentences) are freely available on-line[6]. We want to clarify one aspect though: it is not the case that our extracted data is the maximally MT useful data. We evaluated and extracted only full sentences. A finer-grained (sub-sentential) extractor would likely generate more MT useful data.

Acknowledgments

This work has been supported by the EU under the Grant Agreements no. 248347 and no. 270893.

[6] http://ws.racai.ro:9191/repository/search/

References

Sisay Fissaha Adafre and Maarten de Rijke. 2006. Finding similar sentences across multiple languages in Wikipedia. In *Proceedings of the 11th Conference of the European Chapter of the Association for Computational Linguistics* (EACL 2006), April 3-7, 2006. Trento, Italy, pp. 62—69.

Qin Gao and Stephan Vogel. 2008. Parallel implementations of a word alignment tool. In *Proceedings of ACL-08 HLT: Software Engineering, Testing, and Quality Assurance for Natural Language Processing,* June 20, 2008. The Ohio State University, Columbus, Ohio, USA, pp. 49—57.

Radu Ion, Mārcis Pinnis, Gregor Thurmair, Ahmet Aker, Rob Gaizauskas, Mateja Verlic, and Nikos Glaros. 2011. Extracted data for translation models of SMT and RBMT lexicon from aligned comparable corpora. Deliverable D2.5 of the ACCURAT Project. Available online at http://www.accurat-project.eu/index.php?p=deliverables

Philipp Koehn. 2005. Europarl: A Parallel Corpus for Statistical Machine Translation, In Proceedings of the tenth *Machine Translation Summit,* Phuket, Thailand, pp. 79-86.

Philipp Koehn, Hieu Hoang, Alexandra Birch, Chris Callison-Burch, Marcello Federico, Nicola Bertoldi, Brooke Cowan, Wade Shen, Christine Moran, Richard Zens, Chris Dyer, Ondřej Bojar, Alexandra Constantin, and Evan Herbst. 2007. Moses: open source toolkit for statistical machine translation. In *Proceedings of the 45th Annual Meeting of the ACL on Interactive Poster and Demonstration Sessions* (ACL '07). Association for Computational Linguistics, Stroudsburg, PA, USA, 177-180.

Mehdi Mohammadi and Nasser GhasemAghaee. 2010. Building bilingual parallel corpora based on Wikipedia. In Computer Engineering and Applications (ICCEA 2010), In Proceedings of the *Second International Conference on Computer Engineering and Applications,* Vol. 2, pp. 264—268. IEEE Computer Society Washington, DC, USA.

Dragoş Munteanu and Daniel Marcu. 2005. Improving machine translation performance by exploiting comparable corpora. *Computational Linguistics*, 31(4): 477–504.

Kishore Papineni, Salim Roukos, Todd Ward and Wei-Jing Zhu. 2002. BLEU: A method for automatic evaluation of machine translation. In *Proceedings of the 40th Annual Meeting of the Association for Computational Linguistics* (ACL), July 2002. Philadelphia, USA, pp. 311—318.

Jason R. Smith, Chris Quirk and Kristina Toutanova. 2010. Extracting parallel sentences from comparable corpora using document level alignment. In Proceedings of *the Human Language Technologies: The 2010 Annual Conference of the North American Chapter of the Association for Computational Linguistics*, pp. 403—411. © Association for Computational Linguistics (2010).

Ralf Steinberger, Bruno Pouliquen, Anna Widiger, Camelia Ignat, Tomaž Erjavec, Dan Tufiş. The JRC-Acquis: A multilingual aligned parallel corpus with 20+ languages. In *Proceedings of the 5th LREC Conference*, Genoa, Italy, 22-28 May, 2006, pp.2142-2147, ISBN 2-9517408-2-4, EAN 9782951740822

Dan Ştefănescu, Radu Ion and Sabine Hunsicker. 2012. Hybrid parallel sentence mining from comparable corpora. *In Proceedings of the 16th Conference of the European Association for Machine Translation* (EAMT 2012), pp. 137—144, Trento, Italy, May 28-30, 2012

Dan Ştefănescu, and Radu Ion. 2013. Parallel-Wiki: A collection of parallel sentences extracted from Wikipedia. In *Proceedings of the 14th International Conference on Intelligent Text Processing and Computational Linguistics (CICLING 2013),* March 24-30, 2013, Samos, Greece.

Jörg Tiedemann. 2012. Parallel data, tools and interfaces in OPUS. In *Proceedings of the 8th International Conference on Language Resources and Evaluation* (LREC 2012), May 23-26, 2012. Istanbul, Turkey, pp. 2214—2218.

DutchSemCor: in Quest of the Ideal Sense Tagged Corpus

Piek Vossen, Rubén Izquierdo and **Attila Görög**
VU University Amsterdam
piek.vossen/ruben.izquierdobevia/a.gorog@vu.nl

Abstract

The most-frequent-sense and the predominant domain sense play an important role in the debate on word-sense-disambiguation. This discussion is, however, biased by the way sense-tagged corpora are built. In this paper, we argue that current sense-tagged corpora neglect rare senses and contexts and, as a result, do not represent a good corpus for training and testing word-sense-disambiguation. We defined three quality criteria for sense-tagged corpora and a methodology to satisfy these criteria with minimal effort. Following this method, we built a Dutch sense-tagged corpus that tried to meet these criteria. The corpus was evaluated by deriving word-sense-disambiguation systems and testing these on different subsets of the corpus in different ways. The performance of our systems and the quality of the derived data are equal to state-of-the-art English systems and corpora. Finally, we used the systems to create a Dutch corpus of over 47 million sense-tagged tokens spread over a large variety of genres, domains and usages of Dutch. The results of the project can be downloaded freely from the project website.

1 Credits

The DutchSemCor project was an NWO Humanities medium investment subsidy project with a subsidy period of September 2009 - August 2012. We would like to thank NWO for making it possible to carry out the project.

2 Introduction

Word Sense Disambiguation (WSD) research in the last decade demonstrated a number of important insights (Agirre and Edmonds, 2006): 1. evaluation results are strongly dependent on the corpus and the lexicons used, 2. the most-frequent-sense derived from SemCor (Miller et al., 1993) is a strong baseline that is not easy to beat in evaluations like SensEval or SemEval and 3. predominant senses in specific domains give the best WSD results by far (McCarthy et al., 2007). From these observations, one may conclude that we need to collect large sets of (sense-tagged) domain- and probably genre-specific corpora to determine predominant senses. Obtaining sufficient data without ignoring rare or low-frequent senses, however, requires an enormous effort. Manually tagged data is still very sparse and evaluation results vary from task to task, hence we still do not know where we stand in the area of WSD.

This raises the question: how should the ideal sense-tagged corpus for WSD look like, to enable detection of any sense in any type of corpus? Existing sense-tagged corpora have different design properties that make them good corpora in some aspects but not in others. In this paper, we will define quality criteria for sense-tagged corpora and will describe a novel method for building a large-scale sense-tagged Dutch corpus that meets these criteria with as little manual effort as possible. We argue that an ideal sense-tagged corpus should be balanced for the different senses, for the different contexts and should provide information on sense-frequencies, preferably across a wide range of domains and genres.

In the DutchSemCor[1] project we tried to meet these three criteria by using large corpora that cover a wide range of language-use, including spoken and written language, Flemish and Dutch standard language and dialects, and numerous genres and domains. Furthermore, we tagged these corpora through a mixture of manual and automatic annotations and selections of word tokens. We first aimed at a corpus that represents the meanings of an existing lexicon including sufficient examples for rare senses. Secondly, we extended this corpus to acquire a wider representation of contexts when needed and, finally, in order to acquire sense-distributions, the full corpus was annotated automatically applying three WSD systems. The resulting annotations (both manual and automatic) were tested for all three criteria. As a side result,

[1] http://www2.let.vu.nl/oz/cltl/dutchsemcor/

we obtained three WSD systems for Dutch that can be freely used for research and that perform at state-of-the-art level of English WSD systems.

The paper is structured as follows. In section 3, we describe related work and different types of sense-tagged corpora that are commonly used. After a discussion of the advantages and disadvantages of each type of corpus, we define the main criteria that a sense-tagged corpus should meet. In 4, we outline our overall approach. In 5, a short overview of the resources (tools and corpora) is given. We describe the different phases of the annotation process including their evaluation in the subsequent sections: 6, 7, 8. In section 9, we discuss the overall results.

3 Related Work

Roughly speaking, there are two methods to annotate a corpus with senses: sequential tagging and targeted tagging. In the case of sequential tagging, annotators read a text word by word while annotating each occurrence. In the case of targeted tagging, the annotators will get a list (usually a KWIC index) of sentences for a single word and they annotate all the occurrences of the word. In the former case, annotators read each context only once but they need to reconsider the possible meaning of a word over and over again, each time they come across it. In the latter case, the annotators can tag all the occurrences of a word in one task and even apply contrastive analysis when considering all the contexts. The drawback is that they may have to read the same context again when another word of the same context is annotated. The two approaches usually produce different annotation results for the same text and usually targeted tagging is more systematic and faster.

In addition to the annotation method, we can also distinguish sense-tagged corpora by their textual coverage. Sequential tagging usually results in an **all-words corpus** that contains annotations for all content words in texts. Targeted tagging usually results in a **lexical sample corpus**, a selection of target word occurrences with different contexts annotated with senses. The most famous example of an all-words corpus is SemCor (Miller et al., 1993), which was created through sequential tagging of parts of the Brown corpus (186 texts have all-words annotation, while in 166 texts only the verbs are annotated). An example of a lexical-sample corpus is the so-called line-hard-serve corpus (Mooney, 1996)[2], which contains 4,000 instances of the noun *line* (six meanings), 4,000 instances of the verb *serve* (four meanings), and 4,000 instances of the adjective *hard* (three meanings).

Another lexical-sample corpus is DSO which has annotations only for the most frequent and ambiguous nouns (121) and verbs (70) in parts of the Brown corpus and a selection of Wall Street Journal articles, but is comparable in size to SemCor. For evaluation purposes, many other small all-words and lexical-sample corpora have been produced (cf. Senseval and SemEval competitions).

Lexical-sample and all-words corpora can often differ in the range and selection of their texts. Usually, all-words corpora cover a small number of texts, limited genres and domains and, as a result, a small number of senses, while lexical sample corpora usually represent a large number of different contexts and meanings of the target word. SemCor and DSO partly inherit the balanced nature of the Brown corpus. The corpora used in the Senseval evaluations: BNC, Wall Street Journal, Penn Treebank, part of Brown, show a variety of text types but do not provide systematic coverage neither of senses nor of different text types. Not surprisingly, the evaluation results of the Senseval competitions vary with the variation of corpora[3]. The lexical sample results vary from 64% to 77% and the all-words results vary from 45% to 69% (Agirre and Edmonds, 2006). Interestingly, the inter-annotator-agreements (IAA) vary also a lot across the different tasks: 67% to 86% for the lexical sample tasks and 62% to 75% for the all-words task, as reported by (Agirre and Edmonds, 2006). In all the competitions, the most-frequent-sense (MFS) in SemCor turned out to be a strong baseline (used as a fallback by many systems) that scores only a few points below the best systems (Agirre and Edmonds, 2006).

These results raise a number of questions on how to annotate corpora with senses and how to develop WSD systems. Are the corpora for training and testing diverse enough in terms of contexts since they show so much variation in results? If MFS defines the ceiling for most systems, does this imply that we are neglecting low-frequent senses? Very often, annotators choose for repre-

[2] See also the *interest* (Bruce and Wiebe, 1994) corpus

[3] Only Senseval-1 used a different lexical database. Senseval2&3 used WordNet1.7 and subsequent competitions used other versions of WordNet (Fellbaum, 1998).

senting the corpus rather than representing the resource. Consequently, low frequent senses are not well represented in the training data. Besides, systems (and often also the evaluations) are too much skewed towards the most frequent senses. Depending on the evaluation set, a corpus that is not balanced for the different senses could give totally different results.

4 Our overall approach

We believe that sense-tagged corpora should be designed more carefully to provide answers to the above questions. We suggest three different desiderata for a sense-tagged corpus:

1. balanced-sense corpus: provide tokens and contexts for words that clearly illustrate the meaning of a word and provide equal numbers of examples for each meaning;

2. balanced-context corpus: provide tokens and contexts that represent the different usages of words in a representative corpus;

3. sense-probability corpus: provide a representative sample of the true frequency of a word meaning in a representative corpus.

To get a balanced-sense (1) and balanced-context (2) corpus, annotators need to build a lexical sample corpus by selecting or searching examples that fit the given senses best, where they can ignore unclear and problematic tokens of a word and avoid annotating the same contexts twice. To get a sense-probability corpus, a representative sample of language use from different styles, genres and domains needs to be annotated. The annotators have to assign senses to all the tokens selected by the sampler and they cannot discard tokens.

Obviously, the larger an annotated corpus the better. The question is how to build a corpus that tries to meet the above criteria using as little manual effort as possible. We propose a mixture of manual and automatic annotations:

1. Manually create a balanced-sense corpus (criterion 1). This corpus has an equal number of corpus examples for each sense, also for rare senses, and as-much-as-possible representing the variety of contexts rather than dominantly selecting examples with the same context.

2. Use this lexical sample corpus to train a WSD system that automatically annotates the remainder of a very large and diverse corpus. This corpus represents a large variety of contexts (criterion 2), while the WSD does not suffer from over-fitting for the MFS or for contexts and properties of the training corpus. Likewise, the system can detect rare senses equally well as frequent senses.

3. We use the complete set of annotations (manual and automatic) to obtain information on the sense-distributions (criterion 3) and to develop a MFS approach.

4. We evaluate a random sample of the tagged corpus to evaluate the automatic annotation and we test the WSD and the MFS on an all-words evaluation set. This will tell us how well the automatic annotation through the WSD system can handle the different contexts and how well it reflects the sense-distributions.

Below, we will describe how we implemented this approach in the DutchSemCor project and what the results are. In the next section, we will first describe the resources we used.

5 Resources

We used the Cornetto database (Vossen et al., 2007) as the sense repository for the annotation. Cornetto combines a Dutch wordnet database with a traditional lexical-unit database that has detailed information on lexical units (synonyms in the Dutch wordnet). For the annotation, we made a selection of the 2,870 most polysemous and frequent content words in the database. The words together represent 11,982 word meanings with an average polysemy of around 3 senses per word.

As our primary corpus, we used the SoNaR corpus (Oostdijk et al., 2008), which contains circa 500 million tokens of written Dutch and covers a wide range of different genres and topics (34 different categories including discussion lists, subtitles, books, legal texts, sms, chats, autocues, etc). SoNaR is fully tokenised, part-of-speech tagged, and lemmatised. Another corpus used was CGN (Corpus Gesproken Nederlands) which contains about nine million words of transcribed spontaneous Dutch adult speech. SoNaR is a very large corpus, however, it appeared not big enough to offer sufficient examples for a number of possibly rare senses (even if lexicographers agreed that these senses did exist). We developed a tool in order to search additional examples on Web mediated through the WebCorp platform[4]. The annotators could make a selection of Internet examples and add these to the corpus. The web-snippets were then automatically tokenised, part-of-speech tagged and lemmatised. The final DutchSemCor corpus is, thus, a subset of SoNaR, CGN, and the manually-selected web-snippets.

During the project, we developed three Word-sense-disambiguation (WSD) systems, all three based on Machine Learning. The first one, called **DSC-TiMBL**, is a supervised Machine Learning system based on TiMBL (Daelemans et al., 2007). It implements a K-nearest neighbor algorithm (Aha et al., 1991). TiMBL has been widely used in NLP tasks. In the project, we used three different types of features. From the local context, we selected the word forms, lemmas and part-of-speech tags. The global context was modelled through bag-of-words contained in the same sentence as the target word. Finally, the system made use of information on SoNaR text type and of the token identifier to which the example belonged. Some filtering for the bag-of-words was performed in order to ensure the quality of the word predictors following the approach in (Ng and Lee, 1996).

The second system (**DSC-SVM**) uses a supervised Machine Learning approach based on Support Vector Machines, which belongs to the family of linear separators (Cortes and Vapnik, 1995). This technique was extensively used in automatic classification tasks applying WSD systems and showed excellent performance in very high dimensional and sparse feature spaces, which is typically the case for WSD. In the project, we used the library SVMLight[5]. In this case the features were a bag-of-words around the target words. We also carried out a filtering process similar to the one mentioned above.

The third system (**DSC-UKB**) was an unsupervised Machine Learning system based on the UKB algorithm (Agirre and Soroa, 2009). This algorithm implements a so-called Personalized Page Rank algorithm similar to the one used by Google. It considers Wordnet as a graph where each synset is a node in the graph and the relation between the synsets are seen as edges between the nodes. Disambiguation is performed through the ranking of the candidate nodes following the Personalized Page Rank algorithm. We used different sets of relations to build the graph: relations of the Dutch WordNet, English Wordnet, equivalence relations from Dutch synsets to English synsets, WordNet Domain relations and co-ocurrence relations extracted from the mannual annotations of our corpus (i.e. relations between monosemous words and annotated polysemous examples)[6].

6 Building a balanced-sense corpus

To create a balanced-sense corpus, a team of annotators (trained student assistents) used an annotation tool developed within the project (SAT) (Reference removed for double blind reviewing) that loads data on the word meanings from the Cornetto lexical database and examples from the corpora mentioned in 5. The annotators could use various search strategies to find examples matching the selected meanings. Annotators needed to reach a high agreement (IAA 80% or higher) and were instructed to select 25 examples per sense.

6.1 Initial balanced-sense corpus

The annotation process took about two years. In this time span, 282,503 tokens were double annotated by 4 teams of two annotators, each annotator working 12 hours per week. As a result, 80% of the senses received 25 annotated examples or more, and 90% of the lemmas received 25 examples for each sense. The distribution of annotated examples over the different resources is 67% SoNaR, 5% CGN, and 28% web-snippets. This shows that even a 500-million-token corpus like SoNaR is not big enough to provide a balanced-sense corpus, since 28% of the examples had to be derived from the Internet. Nonetheless, a small but significant portion of senses is still not well represented in the corpus even after Web search. These are mostly very rare senses belonging to specific domains or registers (e.g. one of the senses of the Dutch word *crisis* refers to a *specific critical medical state*). Nevertheless, we can conclude that we achieved a satisfactory result on the first quantitative requirement to represent all the senses of

[4] http://www.webcorp.org.uk/live

[5] http://svmlight.joachims.org

[6] 1.8 million relations were used in total: 1 million derived from Cornetto and WordNet and 800,000 derived from the manually-tagged data

the top 2,870 most frequent and most polysemous Dutch words. The average IAA for this corpus was 94%. This high IAA score can be explained by our working method: annotators did not tag all tokens presented to them, but were given the instruction to select contexts that clearly represented the senses and to avoid vague, problematic and unclear cases. This is another indication that the annotated tokens represent the senses well[7].

6.2 WSD from balanced-sense data

After creating an initial balanced-sense corpus through manual annotation, we trained and evaluated a WSD system using this data to obtain an estimation of the performance of each word. The result of this evaluation was then used to automatically conduct further annotation for weakly performing words. For this purpose, only the system **DSC-TiMBL** was used as described in section 5.

We followed a 5-fold cross validation. It was very important to test the system both for high- and low frequent senses under the same conditions. This enabled us to obtain a balanced evaluation for all senses. (Recall that in the initial annotation phase, annotators were asked to tag all senses for each word with at least 25 examples.) The folds were created at the word-sense level and not at the word level: for each word, each fold contained the same number of examples for each of its senses (randomly selected).

Since our main objective was to build a system to annotate the remainder of the corpus, we could exploit all SoNaR metadata as features. Our experiments showed, for instance, that the token identifier of SoNaR at the paragraph level, the document identifier and the genre of the annotated instances are all strong features for WSD. The effect is comparable to the one-sense-per-discourse/domain/genre heuristic.

We ran the first evaluation for all words but focusing mainly on the nouns. The accuracy of the system for all nouns was 82.76. From this evaluation, we selected a set of 82 lemmas performing below 80%. The output of the system for the 82 lemmas was validated by human annotators in three different cycles till we reached 81.62% for a total of 8,641 instances in the last evaluation round.

[7]Note that annotators could propose new senses to be added to the database or senses to be removed.

7 Making the corpus more balanced for context

In the second phase of the project, we tried to improve the range of contexts for the different senses. If we could annotate the full corpus, the range of contexts would be as broad as the diversity of the corpus. To minimise the effort, we thus decided to improve the WSD for the automatic annotation task by adding more examples and contexts for words that are problematic for the system. We applied the following procedure for this:

1. Select all words that perform with less than 80% accuracy on the folded-cross validation;

2. Automatically annotate the remainder of the tokens of these words using the TiMBL-WSD system;

3. From the automatically annotated tokens, we selected 50 new tokens belonging to senses that performed weakly and that had a context different from the training data. We measured this by selecting tokens with both high-confidence scores for the sense and high-distance from the k-nearest-neighbour;

4. Annotators had to annotate all the 50 tokens, i.e. they could not choose tokens that fit the senses well but had to link senses to the respective tokens;

The last point constitutes an important difference between annotation performed for the balanced-sense and the balanced-context corpus. For the former, the annotators search tokens that fit the senses, while for the latter they fit the senses to the preselected tokens. The balanced-context tokens are therefore mainly determined by the characteristics of the SoNaR corpus.

The annotators were presented with 50 tokens that the system considers to belong to a 'weak' sense with high confidence. Some words have several weak senses, which results in more than 50 tokens for a word to annotate. The students independently assigned the proper senses to the tokens, without knowing the choice of the system. While annotating, they may agree or disagree with the system. In total 114,162 tokens were annotated this way. The annotators also encountered errors in lemmatization and part-of-speech tagging, figurative and idiomatic usage and unknown senses which were marked accordingly and were

Type	Accuracy	# Examples
BS	81.62	8,641
BS + LD	78.81	13,266
BS + LD_agree	85.02	11,405
BS + HD	76.24	19,055
BS + HD_agree	83.77	13,359
BS + LD_agree + HD_agree	85.33	16,123

Table 1: Evaluating the extension with more contexts

excluded from the process (this represented 18% of the selected tokens).

7.1 Evaluating the extension with more contexts

We experimented with various selections of the new annotations to measure how much the WSD system will improve using the new annotations. We divided the new annotations into two groups:

- Low Distance[8] (LD): those with a low distance to the training instances (only marginally different contexts)
- High Distance (HD): with a high distance to the training distance (very different contexts)

We also split the new data based on the agreement of the annotators with the suggestions of the system. Considering the above divisions of the newly annotated examples, different sets were added to the initial balanced-sense (BS) corpus. We calculated the accuracy of the **DSC-TiMBL** system for the selected 82 lemmas trained with the different sets. Each time, the same 5-fold cross validation was carried out. The results can be seen in table 1.

Interestingly, the best results are achieved using all the new training data (low- and high-distance) where the WSD system and the students agreed. Including all annotations or just low- or high-distance examples did not lead to major improvements.

7.2 Optimized WSD systems on the whole balanced-context corpus

Next, we used the optimal set of annotations to finally build the final versions of the 3 different WSD systems explained above. We also defined a majority voting among the three systems that was evaluated on the same data. Table 2 shows the overall accuracy for the systems on the complete balanced-context corpus[9].

System	Nouns	Verbs	Adjs.
DSC-timbl	83.97	83.44	78.64
DSC-svm	82.69	84.93	79.03
DSC-ukb	73.04	55.84	56.36
Voting	88.65	87.60	83.06

Table 2: Evaluation of the WSD systems on the balanced-context corpus

7.3 Evaluating corpus representativeness

To test the performance of the WSD systems on the remainder of the corpus, we carried out a random evaluation. The training data was still skewed towards a balanced-sense corpus. A random selection from SoNaR shows how optimal these systems perform on all other cases. For the random evaluation, we selected a stratified sample of lemmas for each performance range. We considered the following four ranges of accuracy based on the folded cross evaluation: [90% - 100%] , [80% - 90%] , [70% - 80%] and [60% - 70%]. From each of these performance ranges, 5 nouns, 5 verbs and 3 adjectives were randomly selected: a total of 52 lemmas. For all these lemmas, 100 untagged examples in SoNaR were automatically tagged by our system and then manually validated. Table 3 shows the results for the 3 systems and the voting heuristic.

System	Nouns	Verbs	Adjs.
DSC-timbl	54.25	48.25	46.50
DSC-svm	64.10	52.20	52.00
DSC-ukb	49.37	44.15	38.13
Voting	60.70	53.95	50.83

Table 3: Performance of our WSD systems on the random evaluation

Clearly, the result for the random evaluation are much lower than for the folded-cross validation. This shows the difference in approach between representing the senses and representing the corpus. Still, the results are comparable to state-of-the-art results reported for English in Senseval/Semeval.

[8]Timbl provides the distance to the closest training instance then classifying a new instance

[9]We also developed a set of sense groups based on properties of synsets and relations. For instance, if two senses of the same word share the hyperonym, they are related and can be merged into a broader sense without semantic loss. Evaluation using these sense-groups can be found at the webpage of the project: (URL removed for double blind reviewing). Overall, the sense-groups lead to an improvement of 5% in accuracy

8 Obtaining sense-probabilities

The manually annotated portion of the corpus does not exhibit sense-distributions. Mostly, the annotation was limited to 25 tokens per sense to make it balanced-sense and the extension was based on selections of 50 tokens per sense. Sense-frequencies could however be derived by automatically annotating the remainder of the corpus and assuming that the automatic annotation still reflects the true distribution. We thus applied the final WSD systems to the remainder of SoNaR and extracted the sense frequencies according to each system.

To evaluate the frequency distribution, we needed an independent sample reflecting similar distribution. Since the random sample contains only a small selection of words, a more natural sense distribution would follow from an all-words corpus. We created an all-words corpus from the part of the corpus that was kept separate from our selections (i.e. it had not been used for training purposes). This corpus consists of 23,907 tokens and represents 1,527 of our original lemmas (more than 53%).

We evaluated the three WSD systems on the all-words corpus applying 3 different baselines: the 1st sense in Cornetto, a random sense baseline and the most-frequent automatically annotated sense (MFS) by DSC-SVM[10].

System	Nouns	Verbs	Adjs.
1st sense	53.17	32.84	52.17
Random sense	29.52	24.99	32.16
Most frequent	61.20	50.78	54.02
DSC-timbl	55.76	37.96	49.0
DSC-svm	64.58	45.81	55.70
DSC-ukb	56.81	31.37	35.93
Voting	66.09	45.68	52.24

Table 4: Performance of our WSD systems on the random evaluation

The MFS performance for Dutch is similar to the results known for English. It thus seems that the MFS for Dutch according to our approach is performing equally well as a predictor. Our approach generates reasonable sense-probabilities in addition to our approach to obtain balanced-sense annotations.

The MFS baseline performs considerably higher than the 1st sense baseline for verbs (18 points) and nearly 30 points higher than the random baseline (57.54 against 28.26). We also experimented with using only high-confidence annotations but this does not lead to a significant difference. Finally, we got 6.36 points improvement by excluding the 5 most frequent verbs (auxiliary verbs)[11].

[10] The most-frequent sense baseline for DSC-TiMBL and DSC-UKB are performing less

9 Project results and discussion

The DutchSemCor project resulted in numerous data sets and software tools, among which:

- 274,344 tokens for 2,874 lemmas manually annotated by two annotators with an IAA of 90% with the aim of obtaining a balanced-sense corpus
- 132,666 tokens for 1,133 lemmas, manually annotated by a single annotator but agreeing with the WSD-system for IAA 44%
- 47,797,684 automatic annotations by 3 WSD systems
- 28,080 sense groups, representing 6,903 word meanings, which improve performance by 5%
- corpora for random evaluation and all-words evaluation
- 3 WSD systems based on machine-learning
- 800,000 semantic relations between synsets derived from the annotations
- an improved version of the Cornetto database
- an annotation tool and web search tool that can be used to annotate more data
- statistics on figurative, idiomatic and collocational usage of words
- data and statistics on phrasal verbs

Most of these results can be downloaded from the project website as open source data or can be licensed for research without a fee. The central question remains to what extent the sense-tagged corpus satisfies all 3 criteria, being: balanced-sense, balanced-context and reflecting

[11] Note that the corpus characteristics carried over by the token identifier in SoNaR is not useful for the all-words evaluation since the identifiers are completely different. Likewise, the all-words evaluation can be seen as a good indication of quality of the systems for generic WSD which is different from the automatic annotation of SoNaR.

sense-distributions. The first criterion was definitely met and was the starting point of the project. Senses that do not occur in SoNaR were retrieved using web search. Finally, a small set of senses were under-represented. We think that a balanced-sense corpus like DutchSemCor that, at the same time, represents the contexts and distributions of senses well is a unique data set. We tried to obtain a balanced-context corpus in two steps. First, we added new contexts to weak senses and secondly we annotated the remainder of SoNaR which covers a wide range of language use. The random evaluation shows that our performance is lower than the cross-fold evaluation on the balanced-sense corpus but the results are still in line with state-of-the-art results for English. We think that future research is needed to find out whether the drop in results is due to context diversity or other facts. Finally, the sense-probabilities were tested against an all-words corpus. Again, the results are compatible with state-of-the-art results for English. As such, we can expect that the sense-probabilities derived from DutchSemCor will also provide as strong a baseline as the MFS from SemCor is now for English. Last but not least, SoNaR provides many opportunities to differentiate these distributions over different domains and genres (McCarthy et al., 2007).

10 Conclusion

In this paper, we presented a classification of different sense-annotated corpora and described their (dis-)advantages. We proposed a method for meeting three different requirements for sense-tagged corpora. From a manually annotated seed corpus, we automatically extended the representative annotations through WSD, where we used high-confidence results and active learning for low-performing words. A small proportion of the words and word-senses will always be poorly represented, as their usage can only be found on the Web or their senses cannot be discriminated. Finally, we trained three WSD-systems using annotation data created manually and semi-automatically in the first and second phase of the project in order to extend the corpus with new tokens. Apart from cross-fold validation, we used an independent all-words corpus and a random corpus to validate the quality of the WSD system based on our lexical-sample corpus. We demonstrated the feasibility of our approach to efficiently build a balanced-sense lexical-sample corpus in a semi-automatic way that also reflects a variety of contexts and proper sense-distributions. We showed that our results are in line with state-of-the-art results for English which are mostly based on corpora that show sense-distributions or context-distributions. While our balanced-sense approach is important for modeling low frequent senses, we can still obtain good results for context-diversity and sense-probability. In future research, we would like to further define the diversity of contexts in relation to the performance of different words in WSD systems. Especially, the rich and diverse genre and domain classification of SoNaR can be exploited to derive more precise knowledge about sense distributions. Along the same line, the tokens annotated for figurative, metaphoric and idiomatic usage will provide valuable data to research. Finally, we will further experiment with different behaviors of supervised and unsupervised systems by inserting sense-probabilities assigned by the supervised systems into the graphs of the unsupervised system. We hope to implement the learned data in a system that is more robust to changes of genre and domain.

References

Eneko Agirre and Philip Edmonds. 2006. *Word sense disambiguation : algorithms and applications*. Text, speech and language technology. Springer, Dordrecht, NE.

Eneko Agirre and Aitor Soroa. 2009. Personalizing pagerank for word sense disambiguation. In *Proceedings of the 12th Conference of the European Chapter of the Association for Computational Linguistics*, EACL '09, pages 33–41, Stroudsburg, PA, USA. Association for Computational Linguistics.

DavidW. Aha, Dennis Kibler, and MarcK. Albert. 1991. Instance-based learning algorithms. *Machine Learning*, 6:37–66.

Rebecca F. Bruce and Janyce Wiebe. 1994. Word-sense disambiguation using decomposable models. In *ACL*, pages 139–146.

Corinna Cortes and Vladimir Vapnik. 1995. Support-vector networks. In *Machine Learning*, pages 273–297.

W. Daelemans, J. Zavrel, K. Van der Sloot, and A. Van den Bosch. 2007. Timbl: Tilburg memory based learner, version 6.1, reference guide. Technical report, ILK Research Group Technical Report Series no. 07-07.

Christiane Fellbaum. 1998. *WordNet: An Electronic Lexical Database*. Bradford Books.

Diana McCarthy, Rob Koeling, Julie Weeds, and John Carroll. 2007. Unsupervised acquisition of predominant word senses. *Computational Linguistics*, 33(4):553–590.

George A. Miller, Claudia Leacock, Randee Tengi, and Ross T. Bunker. 1993. A semantic concordance. In *Proceedings of the workshop on Human Language Technology*, HLT '93, pages 303–308, Stroudsburg, PA, USA. Association for Computational Linguistics.

Raymond J. Mooney. 1996. Comparative experiments on disambiguating word senses: An illustration of the role of bias in machine learning. *CoRR*, cmp-lg/9612001.

Hwee Tou Ng and Hian Beng Lee. 1996. Integrating multiple knowledge sources to disambiguate word sense: An exemplar-based approach. In *IN PROCEEDINGS OF THE 34TH ANNUAL MEETING OF THE ASSOCIATION FOR COMPUTATIONAL LINGUISTICS*, pages 40–47.

N. Oostdijk, M. Reynaert, P. Monachesi, G. van Noord, R.J.F. Ordelman, I. Schuurman, and V. Vandeghinste. 2008. From d-coi to sonar: A reference corpus for dutch. In *Proceedings on the sixth international conference on language resources and evaluation (LREC 2008)*, pages 1437–1444. ELRA. ISBN=2-9517408-4-0.

Piek Vossen, Katja Hofmann, Maarten de Rijke, Erik T. Sang, and Koen Deschacht. 2007. The Cornetto database: Architecture and user-scenarios. In M. F. Moens, T. Tuytelaars, and A. P. de Vries, editors, *Proceedings DIR 2007*, pages 89–96.

Towards detecting anomalies in the content of standardized LMF-dictionaries

Wafa WALI
MIR@CL Laboratory,
FSEGS,Sfax,Tunisia
wafa.wali
@fesgs.rnu.tn

Bilel GARGOURI
MIR@CL Laboratory,
FSEGS,Sfax,Tunisia
bilel.gargouri@
fesgs.rnu.tn

Abdelmajid BEN HAMADOU
MIR@CL Laboratory,
ISIMS,Sfax,Tunisia
abdelmajid.benhamadou
@isimsf.rnu.tn

Abstract

Dictionaries are reference resources for learning and diffusing natural languages. Their contents must be enriched carefully due to their importance. However, such contents might contain errors and inconsistencies that are hard to detect manually. Several researches have been made in recent years in order to perform this step automatically. However, they have dealt with the problem in a superficial way. The present paper deals with the detection of anomalies in the content of LMF-standardized dictionaries that covers lexical knowledge at the morphological, syntactic and semantic levels. Thus, we are proposing an approach based on a typological study of the potential anomalies that can occur in editorial dictionaries in general. This approach takes advantage of the LMF fine structure that highlights all kinds of relationships between entries' knowledge and distinguishes the role of each available text such as giving definitions and examples. An experiment of the proposed approach was carried out on an available LMF-standardized dictionary of the Arabic language. This experiment has been related to the morphological and syntactic levels.

1 Introduction

Dictionaries are important linguistic resources for learning and diffusing natural languages. They can be used for several purposes such as to find the meaning, the translation, the synonym or antonym of a word. Moreover, they can help to check the spelling or to find out grammatical information about a word.

For ages, editorial dictionaries (for human use) have been developed in paper versions for many natural languages. With the advent of the computer science, several editorial electronic dictionaries have been constructed to be released from the constraint of their paper versions. Thus, the use of the electronic dictionaries has been expanded to meet the NLP (Natural Language Processing) needs. Then, several models have been proposed to represent the dictionary knowledge. In addition, some projects have suggested a common representation of dictionaries such as TEI (Veronis and Ide, 1996), GENELEX (Antoni-Lay et al., 1994), EAGLES (Calzolari et al., 1996) and ISLE (Calzolari et al., 2003). Moreover, an ISO standard has been proposed for modeling lexical resources and electronic dictionaries accordingly. This standard, named Lexical Markup Framework (LMF: ISO 24613), provides a finely structured representation of large and common lexical knowledge (Francopoulo et al., 2008).

On the other hand, a good dictionary must contain accurate knowledge to give the right answers for any use. Thus, it is very important to assess the quality of dictionaries' contents, which is expensive to perform manually and requires high linguistic expertise (Fersoe and Morachina, 2004). In this context, a few works have been devoted to the evaluation of electronic dictionaries for many Latin and bilingual dictionaries (Zagic et al., 2011), (Rodrigues et al., 2011). For some other languages such Arabic, the published works still deal with paper versions (Alkhatib, 1967), (Alchidyâq, 1899), and (Hamzaoui, 1986). Thus, we can qualify the evaluation of dictionaries content as very important, notably with an automatic process.

In this paper, we are dealing with the automatic detection of anomalies in the content of standardized LMF dictionaries starting from a typological study of pertinent anomalies. In fact, we propose an approach that takes advantage of the fine structure of LMF. Indeed, LMF highlights all kinds of relationships between entries knowledge and distinguishes the role of each available text such as giving definitions and examples. In order to experiment the proposed approach, we applied it on an available standardized dictionary for the Arabic language (Khamekhem et al., 2012). This experiment is related to the morphological and syntactic levels.

We are going to start with presenting some works related to the evaluation of dictionaries' contents. Then, we are reporting a typological study on the pertinent anomalies in the standardized dictionaries. Thereafter, we are describing the proposed approach. Finally, we are detailing the experiment that we carried out and we are giving the obtained results.

2 Related works

In this section, we have presented the most rele- -vant works related to the evaluation of dictionaries. Some works are proposed to evaluate content of monolingual and bilingual dictionaries in paper versions. For monolingual dictionaries, most of the works focused on problems such as false derivation, incoherence of definition and incoherence between the example and the definition. These works deal with paper versions of dictionaries and are relatively old such as (A. Alkhatib, 1967), (A.F.alchidyâq, 1899), (I.Ben Mrad, 1987) and (M.Hamzaoui, 1986) that are dedicated for the Arabic dictionaries. Other works (M.Asfour, 2003), (M.Khoury, 1996), (A.Kasimi, 1998) dealt with the evaluation of bilingual dictionaries. They specially deal with translation problems.

Moreover, a few efforts are made to detect anomalies for electronic dictionaries as (Zagic et al., 2011) and (Rodrigues et al., 2011). The authors elaborated methods for detecting and correcting OCR problems in Urdu- English digital dictionaries using Dictionary Language Modeling (DML). However, these dictionaries are poorly structured resulting in the digitalization of paper versions. Furthermore, this situation generates a handicap for the evaluation of electronic dictionaries that require fine structure of the dictionary entries.

Finally, we believe that the lack of works on automatic detection of anomalies in the contents of dictionaries can be explained by the complexity of this task.

3 Study of anomalies in LMF standardized dictionaries

Based on subtle, powerful, universal LMF metamodel and applied to all natural languages, the present study was carried out on LMF standardized models of dictionaries for three languages used in the world (English, French and Arabic).

The dictionaries that we will evaluate, resulting from the conversion a paper dictionary in electronic version or went through a strict acquisition system. In this section, we will aim to give an overview of the standard LMF and to identify and classify pertinent anomalies in such dictionaries. We focused mainly on the morphological, syntactic and semantic linguistic levels.

3.1 Lexical Markup Framework-ISO 24613

The Lexical Markup Framework (LMF) (Francopoulo et al., 2008) provides a generic metamodel that can be applied for most natural Languages. It is composed of a core and several optional extensions as indicated in Figure 1 given below. The core and the extensions contain several classes detailing all lexical knowledge and the relationships between them. We can select the extensions and/or the classes with respect to a specific need to construct a dictionary. The selected model will be decorated by data categories from the DCR (Data Categories Registry) standardized with respect to the ISO 12620 standard.

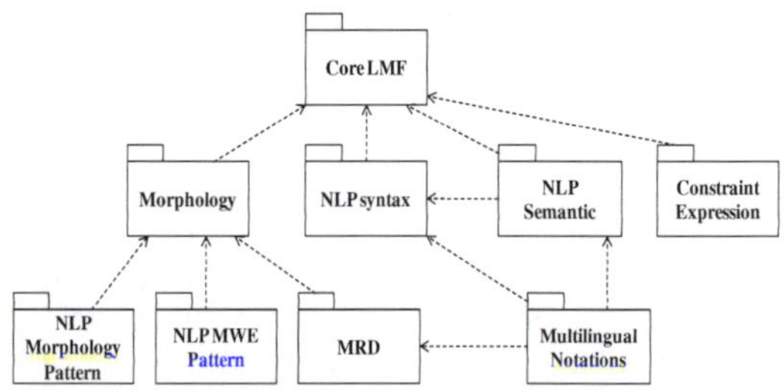

Figure 1: The LMF core and its extensions

3.2 Morphological anomalies

In the morphological model, each lexical entry has one lemma, many word forms that represent their inflected forms and morphological features (grammatical number, grammatical gender, person…) and many ordered stems. Indeed, each root or derived form in separate lexical entry are connected them by the class RelatedForm which has a Data Category (DC) type. This DC allows us to specify the type of relationship between the lexical entries whether it has a stem or a root. Thus, two kinds of anomalies can occur. The first one has something to do with false values of properties as shown in Figure 2.
Normally, the inflected form Muslims "مُسْلِمُون" is the plural of word Muslim "مُسْلِمْ" as described in figure2. But it can find the anomaly mentioned in figure 3 such as the value of the attribute

"grammatical number" of the inflected form is singular.

Lemma	مُسلِمٌ	Muslim
Inflected form in the plural	مُسلِمُون	Muslims

Figure 2: Example of Muslims"مُسْلِمُون "

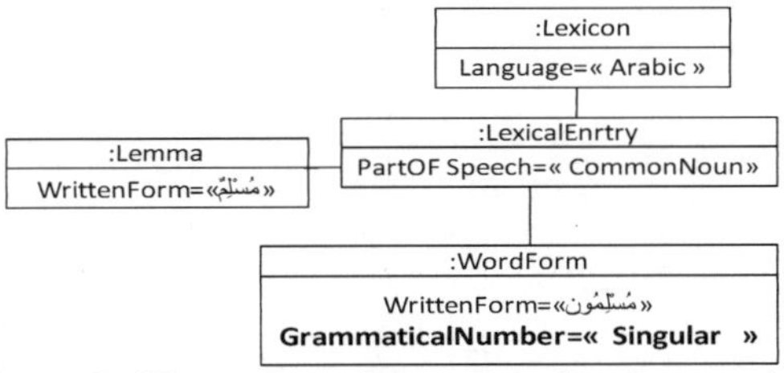

Figure 3: Illustration of the anomalies in proprieties values

The second anomaly is related to false morphologic links like incoherence between stem and lemma or incoherence between root and lemma. The Arabic word" مَكْتَبٌ - bureau" has a root "كَتَبَ - write" like the one presented in figure 4. Although, it can induce an anomaly as shown in figure 5 such as the root of the word" مَكْتَبٌ - bureau" is "كبت - inhibit".

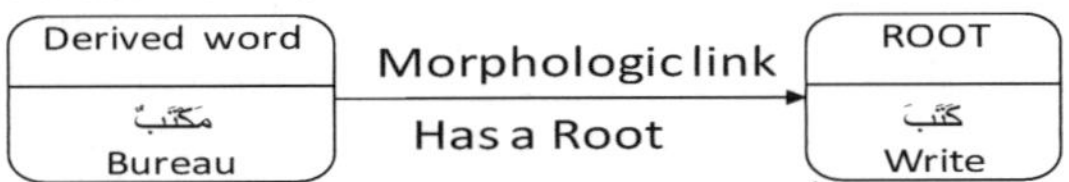

Figure 4: Example of derivation " مَكْتَبٌ -bureau"

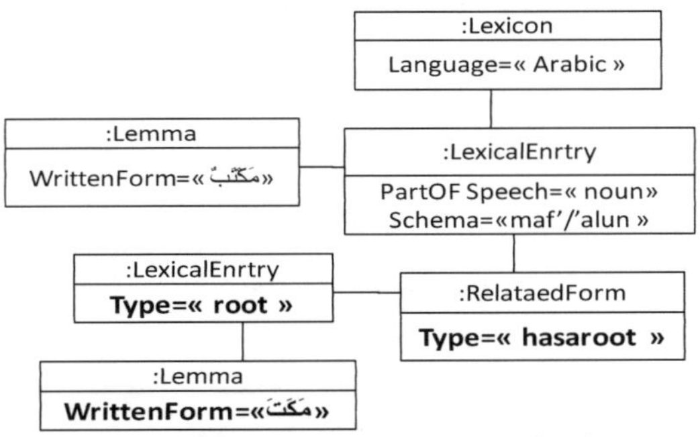

Figure 5: Illustration of anomalies in morphologic links

3.3 Syntactic anomalies

The syntactic model presents the syntax of sentences through sub-categorization frames. Then, it specifies the possible frames of a LexicalEntry (LE) and for each frame it specifies the various senses of the LE. The main class of syntactic model is SubcategorizationFrames that is a syntactic behavior of LE. This class is composed of a set of Syntactic Arguments and a LexemeProperty that include the characteristics of the central node of this frame.

In this syntactic model, we can find two types of anomalies like the incoherence between syntactic behavior and example. Indeed, the example" أَخَذَ الوَلَدُ الكِتَابَ-the boy takes the book" given in figure 6 has a syntactic behavior "verb subject object (VSO)". However, it can cause an error as indicated in figure 7 and present the syntactic behavior of the example like "subject verb (SV)".

Example	أَخَذَ الوَلَدُ الكِتَابَ	the boy takes the book
Syntactic behavior	O S V	

Figure 6: Example of syntactic behavior "VSO"

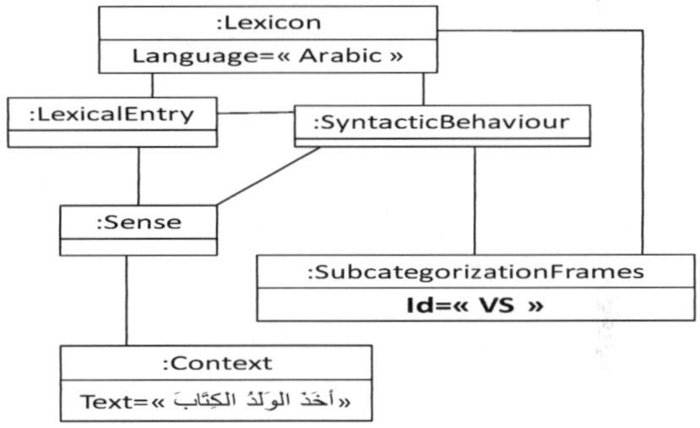

Figure 7: Illustration of the anomaly "incoherence between example and syntactic behavior"

The second anomaly related to the syntactic level is the incoherence between example and information in the LexemeProprety class. The example presented in figure 8 "أَخَذَ الوَلَدُ الكِتَابَ- the boy takes the book" is in the active voice. But, it can have an anomaly as it was mentioned in figure 9 such as the voice of example is passive voice.

Example	أخَذَ الوَلَدُ الكِتَابَ	the boy takes the book
Voice of example	Active Voice	

Figure 8: Example in active Voice

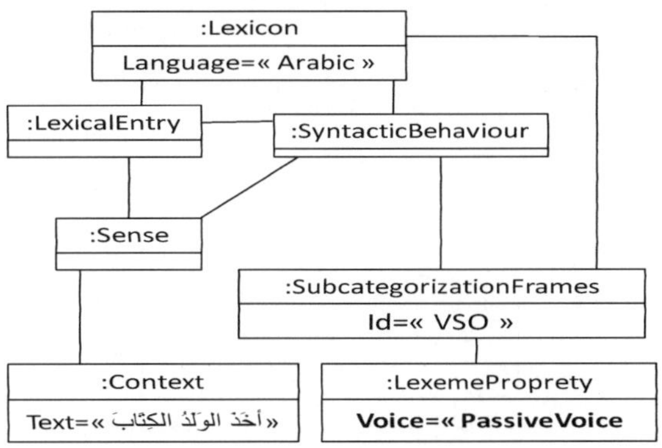

Figure 9: Illustration of anomalies of propriety values related to context and Lexeme Proprety class

3.4 Semantic anomalies

The senses of word may be general or specific to one field and may belong to a semantic class. In addition, The SenseRelation allows us to connect the senses belonging to different lexical entries with several types of relationships such as the synonym, the antonym. The SenseExample represents an instance of a given sense. SubjectField and Context are two classes from MRD extension. The first class is used when the meaning is specific to a particular area and the second one represents an example of using a LE in the frame of a given sense. Furthermore, the standard has represented the overlap between syntax and the semantics in the semantic extension.

For this model, we might find the following anomalies: incoherence sense (in Definition class), incoherence domain (in SubjectFieled class), redundancy of examples and senses, incoherence between example (in Context class) and sense, lack of explanation like definitions based on references (null pointer, synonymy or antonym), false semantic relations and incoherence between example and semantic class. Figure 10 shows semantic relations between three lexical entries. The sense 1 of word 1 is a synonym with the sense 3 of word 2 and the sense 2 of word 3 is a synonym with the sense 3 of word 2. Therefore, transitively speaking, the sense 2 of word 3 and the sense 1 of word 1 are synonyms. Nevertheless, in figure 11 presents the two senses (sense 2of word 3 and sense 1 of word 1) described previously as antonyms.

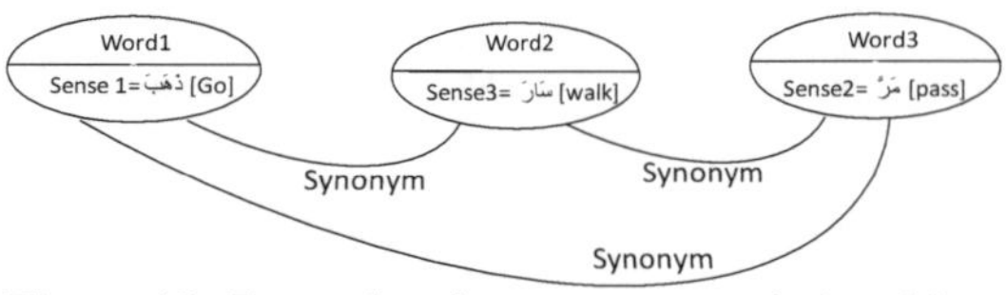

Figure 10: Example of synonymous relationships

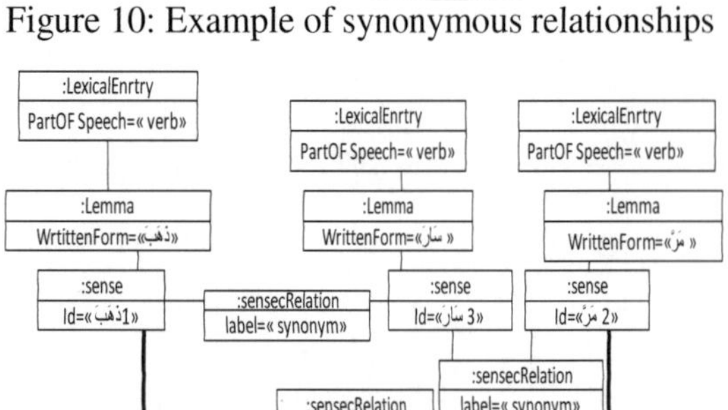

Figure 11: Illustration of semantic relations anomaly

The figure12 schematized below, presents an attribute value of semantic class" human" for the subject "the boy الوَلَدُ". But, it can cause an anomaly as shown in figure13 and presented the semantic class of subject like inanimate concrete.

Example	أكل الولد	the boy eats
Semantic class	human	

Figure 12: Example of semantic class

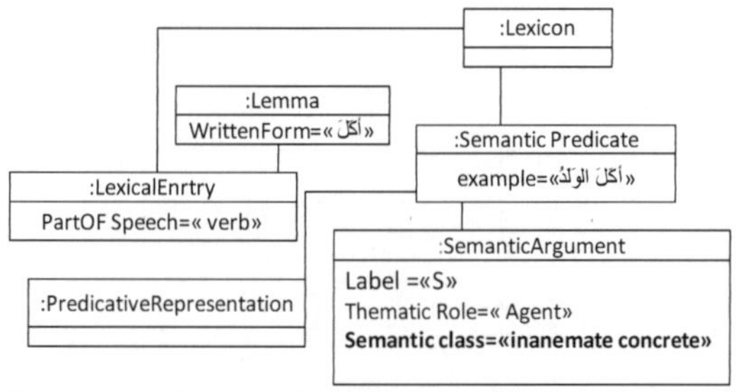

Figure 13: Illustration of anomalies attribute values for a semantic class

4 Overview of the approach

In this section, we give an overview of the approach that we propose for detecting anomalies in the content of LMF-standardized dictionaries. This approach consists mainly of three stages as shown in Figure 14. Firstly, we check the structure of dictionaries according to the DTD of LMF. Secondly, we proceed to verify the validity of the properties inside classes and finally we deal with coherence of properties that have connections outside classes. In the following figure, we detail the three stages of the proposed approach.

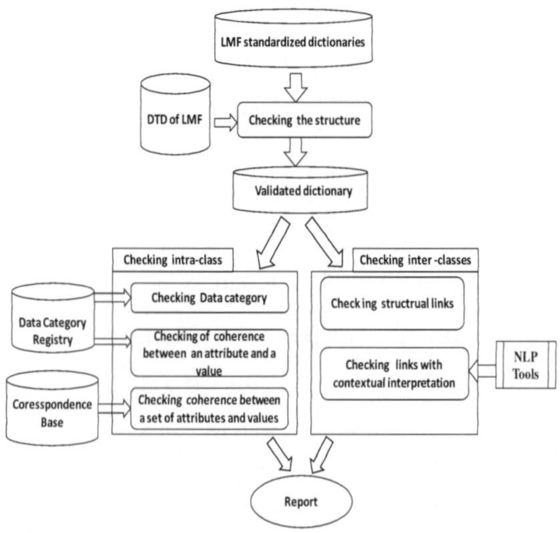

Figure 14: The approach overview for detecting anomalies in LMF-standardized dictionaries

4.1 Check of the structure

In this initial stage, we intend to check the structure of the dictionary dealt with. In the case of encoding with XML (eXtensible Markup Language), this step is simple to perform. It consists of verifying the dictionary structure with respect to the DTD (Data Type Description) of the standard LMF. In the case of a relational encoding of the dictionary database, an appropriate reference schema should be used.

4.2 Check intra-class

The second stage consists in verifying the properties (Attributes and values) inside each class by checking at the beginning the used Data Category (DC) with respect to the Data Category Register (DCR). Then, we check the coherence between the used attributes and the associated values. Each selected attribute from the DCR has its appropriate values which are also specified in the DCR. Finally, we check the coherence between two DC, using a set of correspondence rules according to language specificities.

4.3 Check inter-classes

The purpose of this final stage is to verify the coherence between properties (attributes and values) situated in different classes. To achieve this, we inspect all existing links between the classes of the LMF-standardized dictionaries. For instance, in the morphological extension, we can have false structural links like LE1, which has a root LE2 and has a stem LE3, LE2 has a stem LE3. Also, in the semantic extension, we might have structural links anomaly such as LE1 is synonym with LE2, LE2 is synonym with LE3 and LE3 is antonym with LE1. Afterwards, for each extension of LMF-standardized dictionary, we verify the links with contextual interpretation by applying various NLP tools. For example, the verification of coherence between example and syntactic behavior requires primarily the use of a parser to obtain the syntactic tree of the example and then verify this structure with syntactic behavior described in the Syntactic Behavior class.

5 Case study: detection of morphological and syntactic anomalies in LMF-standardized Arabic dictionary

The proposed approach was applied to a case study and the experiment was carried out on the Arabic language. This choice is explained both by the great deficiency of work in evaluating electronic Arabic dictionaries and the availability within the research team of an LMF standardized Arabic dictionary containing about 37.000 entries.

To automatically perform the stages of the proposed approach, we developed a system using Java and NetBeans IDE7.2 environment (see Figure 16).

5.1 Fundamentals of the Arabic morphology

Arabic is a derivational and a flexional language. The base of the derivation process is a root composed of three out of four letters. Then, the obtained lemma can be a stem for another lemma. Each one is characterized by a schema that consists of presenting the model of its derivation. The base of the schema is composed of the three letters f [ف], E [ع], l [ل]. The schemas are classified according to the Parts Of Speech (POS).
Moreover, in the Arabic standard, the words contain vowels associated with their letters. The vowels are used to distinguish words that are composed of the same sequence of consonants but they are semantically different such as "kabar" [كَبَرَ], "kabur" [كَبُرَ] and "kabir" [كَبِرَ] [16]. Moreover, these vowels must be coherent to the indicated schema and can have an influence on the flexion process.
These characteristics are, among others, considered in the LMF normalized model of the used dictionary.

5.1.1 Steps of the morphological detecting process

The proposed process is composed of the following four steps: (i) the verification of vowels, (ii) the verification of the coherence between POS and schemas, (iii) verification of the coherence between the stems and the lemmas (iv) the verification of the coherence between the roots, the schemas and the lemmas. The two first steps belong to the stage of validity intra-classes whereas the third and the fourth steps belong to the stage of inter-classes coherence. Figure 15 given below synthesizes the morphological detection process.

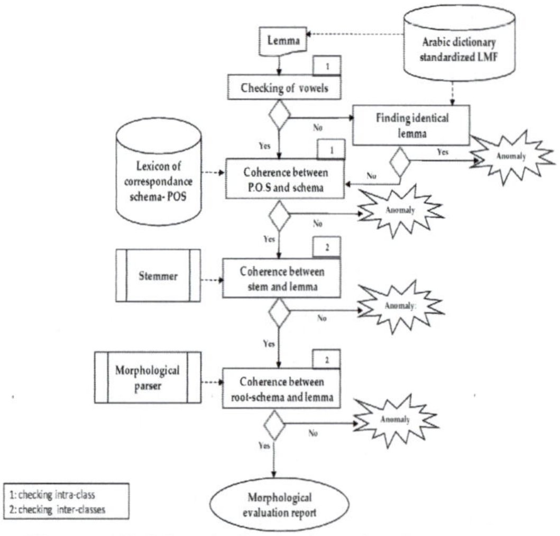

Figure 15: Morphological evaluation process

Verification of vowels: The aim of this step is to verify the used vowels of all the lemmas in the dictionary. In this step, we detect an anomaly if there are two lemmas like LE, that are using the same sequence of letters and one of them or both have no vowels.

Verification of the POS-schema coherence: The second step is to verify the coherence between POS and schema. To check this coherence, we need a lexicon of correspondence between Arabic schemas and its POS. At this phase, we used a lexicon which is enriched manually by an expert.

Verification of the stem- lemma coherence: This step consists of checking the coherence between stems and lemmas. According the standard LMF-ISO 24613, the stem is a sequence of morphs that is smaller than or equal to the form of a single lexeme and that may be affected by an inflectional, agglutinative, compositional or derivative process.

Moreover, the link between a lemma and its stem is presented through the RelatedForm class of the morphological extension. The stem does not need to be identical to the root of the word. In this stage, we used the "khoja Arabic stemmer" (S.Khoja, 2001) developed in Java. It removes the longest suffix and prefix. It then matches the remaining word with verbal and noun patterns to extract the stem.

Verification of the root-schema-lemma coherence: The last step consists of verifying the coherence between the root, the schema and the lemma that are based on the available information in the LexicalEntry (schema), Lemma (lemma) and RelatedForm (root) classes. For checking this coherence, we need a morphological parser. In our work, we used the MORPH parser (Chaabane et al., 2010).

5.1.2 The obtained results

Figure 16 illustrates the detection process and gives the obtained results at the end of this process. The percentage of incoherent entries can be due either to an inconsistency or absence of entry in the data base of the systems used (MORPH, khoja Arabic stemmer).

As shown in this Figure:

- The verifying of vowels: 96% of the entries contain vowels and 4% of them are without vowels.
- The coherence between schema and POS: the rate of coherent entries is 69% and the rate of incoherent entries (incorrect entries + unrecognized entries) is 31%.
- The coherence between stem and lemma: the rate of coherent entries is 75% and the rate of incoherent entries (incorrect entries + unrecognized entries) is 25%. This is explained by the absence, until now, of links between lemmas and their stems in the available dictionary.
- The coherence between root, schema and lemma: the rate of coherent entries is 57, 14% and the rate of incoherent entries (incorrect entries + unrecognized entries) is 42, 85%.

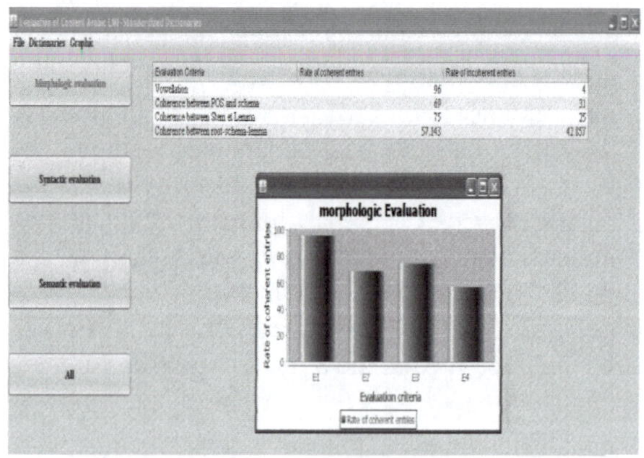

Figure 16: System outputs

5.2 The bases of the Arabic syntax

Parsing Arabic sentences is a difficult task due to the following reasons (Othman et al., 2003): first, the Arabic sentences are long and complex. Second, the Arabic sentence is syntactically ambiguous and complicated due to the frequent usage of grammatical relations, the order of words and phrases, conjunctions, etc. For the last two decades, concentration of the Arabic language processing has focused on morphological analysis. In contrast, there were fewer works related to on syntactic analysis of Arabic.

To detect the anomalies of the syntactic level, we use the platform NOOJ[1].

NOOJ is a linguistic environment of development that can analyze a large corpus in real time. It includes tools to build, test and maintain formalized descriptions of natural languages (in the form of electronic dictionary or grammar) (M.Salbeztein, 2005).

NOOJ can build lemmatized concordances for a large text using finite state grammar, and can also perform transformations on texts hidden in order to annotate or produce paraphrases. The lexical module of NOOJ used in the detection of syntactic anomalies, is based on syntactic grammar.

This grammar is represented in the form a finite-state nodes. It represents sequences of grammatical categories corresponding to the production of a sentence. Although these grammatical categories are predefined by NOOJ (e.g. <V> verb, <S> subject, <PREP> preposition, <PRON> pronoun, <LOC> noun of place, etc.)

5.2.1 Steps of the syntactic detecting process

The proposed detection process is based primarily on the study of an example in order to compare the structure of the example with the syntactic behavior described in the Arabic standardized LMF dictionary and verifies the coherence between the voice of the example (passive voice or active voice) and the information presented in the Lexeme Proprety class.

Figure 17 given below synthesizes the syntactic detection process.

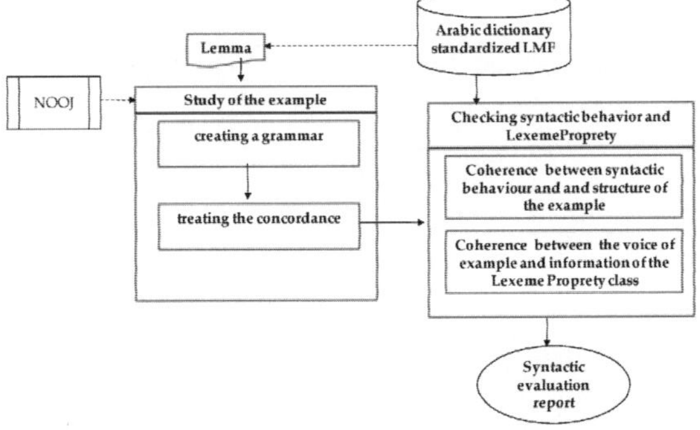

Figure 17: Syntactic evaluation process

Study of the example: in the platform NOOJ, we create a grammar corresponding to the examples presented in the Arabic standardized LMF dictionary so generate the concordance for verify the coherence with syntactic behavior and the information of the Lexeme Proprety class. This grammar is formed by seven nodes, besides to the two nodes: start and end. The nodes that are used: <V> verb, <N> noun, <PRON> pronoun, <PREP> preposition, <PREF> prefix, <ADJ> adjective, <LOC> noun of place.

Verification of syntactic behavior and Lexeme Proprety: in this step, we check the coherence between the syntactic behavior presented in the Arabic standardized LMF dictionary and the syntactic behavior described in the concordance table.

Also, NOOJ annotates for each verb the voice which is appropriate. This information is compared to information in *lexeme Proprety* class in the Arabic standardized LMF dictionary.

6 Conclusion

In this paper, we proposed an approach based on a typological study of the potential anomalies that can occur in LMF standardized dictionaries. The originality of this approach lies in the use of a unique, finely-structured source, rich in lexical and conceptual knowledge at the morphological, syntactic and semantic levels. Our method consists of three stages. It starts with verifying the structure of LMF dictionaries with respect to the DTD of LMF. Then, it performs the verification of properties in each class. Finally, it verifies the inter-classes links. In addition to, the experiment of the proposed approach carried out on an available LMF-standardized dictionary of Arabic language.

This experiment is related to the morphological and syntactic levels. For future works, we aim to deal with the automatic detection of semantic anomalies. In addition to that, we plan to extend the experiment to cover other languages.

References

Akhatib A. 1967. "*Arabic dictionary between the past and the present*". Nachiroun library, Liban

Alchidyâq A. F.1899‹*The spy on the dictionary*". Sâdir library, Beirut

Antoni-lay MH. Francopoulo G. and Zayssern L. 1994. *A generic model for reusable lexicons: The genelex project*, Literary and Linguistic Computing, 1994.

[1] The download free and the user manual of a linguistic platform NOOJ are available at: http://www.nooj4nlp.net

Asfour M. 2003 *Problems in modern English-Arabic lexicography*, journal of Zeitschrift für arabische Linguistik, 2003, N°42, pp 41-52.

Ben Mrad I. 1987 *"Studies in the Arabic dictionary"*, dar Algharb Alislâmi, Beirut, Liban.

Calzolari N. Bertagna F. Lenci A. Monachini M. 2003. *Standards and best Practice for Multilingual Computational Lexicons. MILE (The Multilingual ISLE Lexical Entry)*. ISLE CLWG Deliverable D2.2 et 3.2 Pisa.

Calzolari N. McNaught J. Zampolli A. 1996. *Eagles, editors introduction.* http://www.ilc.cnr.it/EAGLES96/edintro/edintro.html

Chaâben N. Hadrich Belguith L. and Ben Hamadou A. 2010. *The MORPH2 new version: A robust morpholgical analyser for Arabic texts*. In the proceedings of the 10 international days on statistical analysis of data (JADT 2010), Rome,Italy, 9-11 June 2010.

Fersoe H. and Morachina M. 2004. *ELRA Validation Methodology and Standard Promotion for Linguistic Resources*, LREC 2004, Lisbon, Portugal.

Francopoulo G. and George M. 2008. *Language Resource Management.*2008. *Lexical Markup Framework (LMF). Technical report, ISO/TC 37/SC 4 N453 (N330 Rev.16)*, 2008.

Hamzaoui M. 1986. *"Arab dictionary issues"* Dar Algarb alislâmi, Beirut, Liban.

Kasimi A. 1998. *"Problematic in Arabic lexicographical significance"*. Articles literary forum integraeted and literary library.

Khemakhem A. Gargouri B. and Ben Hamadou A. 2012 *LMF standardized dictionary for Arabic language*. In the proceedings of the 1st International Conference on Computing and Information Technology (ICCIT 2012), Al-Madina, Saudi Arabia, 12-14 March 2012.

Khoja S. 2001. *Stemming Arabic Text.* http://zeus.cs.pacificu.edu/shereen/research.htm, 2001

Khoury M. 1996. *Dictionnaires arabes bilingues, présentation historique et étude comparative*, thèse de maîtrise présentée à l'école des études supérieures et de la recherche de l'université de Ottawa, Ontario, 1996

Othman E. Shaalan K. and Refea A. 2003. *Achart parser for analysing modern standard Arabic sentence*. In proceedings of the MT summit IX workshop on machine translation for semetic languages : issues and approaches, USA , pp 33-39, 2003.

Rodrigues P. Zagic D. Buckwalter T. Maxwell M. and AntonRytting C. 2011. *Quality control for digitized dictionaries*. The 9th conference of the Association for Machine Translation in the Americas, workshop on developing up dating and coordination technologies, Dictionary and Lexicons for Terminological Consisentency, October 2011.

Salibeztein M. 2005. *NOOJ's dictionaries*. In actes LTC 2005, Poznan.

Veronis J. and Ide N. 1996. *"Encodage des dictionnaires électroniques: problèmes et propositions de la TEI"*. In D. Piotrowsky (Ed.), Lexicograpbie et informatique - Autour de l'informatisation du Trésor de la Langue Française. Actes du Colloque International de Nancy (pp. 239-261). Paris: Didier Erudition, 1996.

Zagic D. Maxwell M. Doermann D. Rodrigues P. and Bloodgood M. 2011. *Correcting Errors in Digital Lexicograhic Resources Using a Dictionary Manipulation Language*. Proceedings of eLex 2011, pp. 297-301.

Edit Distance: A New Data Selection Criterion for Domain Adaptation in SMT

Longyue Wang[1], Derek F. Wong[1],
Lidia S. Chao[1], Junwen Xing[1], Yi Lu[1], Isabel Trancoso[2]
[1]Natural Language Processing & Portuguese-Chinese Machine Translation Laboratory, University of Macau, Macau S.A.R., China
[2]L2F Spoken Language Systems Lab, INESC-ID, Lisboa, Portugal
{mb15505,derekfw,lidiasc,mb15470,mb25435}@umac.mo,
isabel.trancoso@inesc-id.pt

Abstract

This paper aims at effective use of training data by extracting sentences from large general-domain corpora to adapt statistical machine translation systems to domain-specific data. We regard this task as a problem of filtering training sentences with respect to the target domain[1] via different similarity metrics. Thus, we give new insights into when data selection model can best benefit the in-domain translation. Based on the investigation of the state-of-the-art similarity metrics, we propose edit distance as a new data selection criterion for this topic. To evaluate this proposal, we compare it with other methods on a large dataset. Comparative experiments are conducted on Chinese-English travel dialog domain and the results indicate that the proposed approach achieves a significant improvement over the baseline system (+4.36 BLEU) as well as the best rival model (+1.23 BLEU) using a much smaller training subset. This study may have a significant impact on mining very large corpora in a computationally-limited environment.

1 Introduction

A well-known problem of statistical machine translation (SMT) (Brown et al., 1993) is that the data-driven system is not guaranteed to perform optimally if the data for training and testing are not identically distributed. Domain adaptation for SMT has been explored at different component levels: word level, phrase level, sentence level and model level. For example mining unknown words from comparable corpora (Daume III and Jagarlamudi, 2011), weighted phrase extraction (Mansour and Ney, 2012), mixing multiple models (Civera and Juan, 2007; Foster and Kuhn, 2007; Eidelman et al., 2012), etc. Recently, data selection as a simple and effective way for this special task has attracted attention.

Under the assumption that there exists a large general-domain corpus (general corpus) including sufficient domains, the task of data selection is to translate a domain-specific text using the optimized translation model (TM) or language model (LM) trained by less but more suitable data retrieved from the general corpus. To state it formally, R is an abstract model of target domain and s_G is a sentence or a sentences pair in the general corpus G. The score of each s_G is given by

$$Score(s_G) \rightarrow Sim(s_G, R) \quad (1)$$

which means if we could find a better function to measure the similarity between s_G and R, G could be replaced by a new sub-corpus G_{sub} for training a domain-specific SMT system.

We focus on two data selection criteria that have been explored for domain adaptation. One comes from the realm of information retrieval (IR), which is defined as the cosine of the angle between two vectors based on term frequency-inverse document frequency (TF-IDF). Hildebrand et al. (2005) showed that it is possible to apply this standard IR technique for both TM adaptation and LM adaptation. It is also similar to the offline data optimization approach proposed by Lü et al. (2007), who re-sample and re-

[1] It could be modeled by an in-domain corpus or text to be translated.

weight sentences in general corpus, achieving an improvement of about 1 BLEU point over the baseline system. This simple co-occurrence based matching only considers keywords overlap, which may result in weakness in filtering irrelevant data. Thus, it needs a large size of the selected subset (more than 50% of general corpus) to obtain an ideal performance. The other data selection criterion is a perplexity-based model which can be found in the field of language modeling. This has been explored by Gao et al. (2002) and more recently by Moore and Lewis (2010), who used cross-entropy to score text segments according to an additional in-domain LM. Axelrod et al. (2011) employed these perplexity-based variants for SMT adaptation and showed that the fast and simple technique allows to discard over 99% of the general corpus resulting in an increase of 1.8 BLEU points. By considering not only the distribution of terms but also the collocation, perplexity-based metrics perform better than the IR techniques in general.

We show that constraint factors in similarity measuring such as word overlap and word order may have a major impact on the quality of selected data as well as the translation quality. The stricter selection criteria may have stronger ability in filtering noises, resulting in a better domain-specific translation. Edit distance is much stricter than the former two criteria. The factors of words overlap, order and position are all comprehensively considered. This distance able to retrieve more similar sentences from the general corpus. Actually, edit distance has been widely used for example-based MT (EBMT) (Leveling et al., 2012) and convergence of translation memory (TM) and SMT (Koehn and Senellart, 2010), but it was not previously applied to this topic. This proposal is under the assumption that the general corpus is large and broad enough to cover highly similar sentences with respect to the target domain. We compared it with the baseline and other two state-of-the-art methods on a large Chinese-English general corpus. Using BLEU (Papineni et al., 2002) as an evaluation metric, we obtained a significant improvements over the baseline system and the best of other methods.

This paper is organized as follows. Section 2 describes the related models for data selection. The resources and configurations of experiments for are detailed in Section 3. Finally, we compare and discuss the results in Section 4 followed by a conclusion to end the paper.

2 Model Description

This section will briefly describe the three data selection models to be considered: standard IR model, perplexity based model and the proposed model.

2.1 IR Model

Each document D_i is represented as a vector (w_{i1}, w_{i2},..., w_{in}), and n is the size of the vocabulary. So w_{ij} is calculated as follows:

$$w_{ij} = tf_{ij} \times \log(idf_j) \tag{2}$$

where tf_{ij} is term frequency (TF) of the j-th word in the vocabulary in the document D_i, and idf_j is the inverse document frequency (IDF) of the j-th word calculated. The similarity between two documents is then defined as the cosine of the angle between two vectors.

In practice, we only use the sentences in the source language for indexing and query generation. Each sentence in the general corpus is indexed as one document by Apache Lucene[2]. Every sentence without the stop words from the reference set is used as one separate query. As in (Hildebrand et al. 2005), we allow duplicated sentences during the selection which is similar with. All retrieved sentences with their corresponding target translations are ranked according to their similarity scores.

2.2 Perplexity-Based Model

The perplexity of a string s with empirical n-gram distribution p given a language model q is:

$$2^{-\sum_x p(x)\log q(x)} = 2^{H(p,q)} \tag{3}$$

in which $H(p, q)$ is the cross-entropy between p and q. Selecting segments based on a perplexity threshold is equivalent to selecting based on a cross-entropy threshold, which is more often used for this task (Moore and Lewis, 2010; Axelrod et al., 2011). Supposed that $H_I(s)$ and $H_O(s)$ are the cross-entropy of a string s according to an in-domain language model LM_I and non-in-domain LM_G respectively trained on in-domain data set I and a partition of general-domain data set G. Considering both source (src) and target (tar) side of parallel training data, there are three variants. The first is basic cross-entropy given by:

$$H_{I-src}(s) \tag{4}$$

[2] Available at http://lucene.apache.org.

and the second is cross-entropy difference (Moore and Lewis, 2010):

$$H_{I-src}(s) - H_{G-src}(s) \quad (5)$$

which tries to select the sentences that are more similar to the target domain but different to others in general corpus. The third one is to sum the cross-entropy difference over both source and target side of the corpus:

$$\begin{aligned} &[H_{I-src}(s) - H_{G-src}(s)] \\ &+[H_{I-tar}(s) - H_{G-tar}(s)] \end{aligned} \quad (6)$$

The third variant has been is proven to achieve the best result among the three cross-entropy variants (Axelrod et al., 2011).

2.3 Edit-Distance-Based Model

Given a sentence s_G from a general corpus and a sentence s_R from the test set or in-domain corpus, the edit distance for these two sequences is defined as the minimum number of edits, i.e. symbol insertions, deletions and substitutions, for transforming s_G into s_R. There are several different implementations of the edit-distance-based retrieval model. We used the normalized Levenshtein similarity score (fuzzy matching score, FMS) proposed by Koehn and Senellart (2010):

$$FMS = 1 - \frac{LED_{word}(s_G, s_R)}{Max(|s_G|, |s_R|)} \quad (7)$$

in which LED_{word} is a distance function and $|s|$ is the number of tokens of sentence s. In this study, we employed a word-based Levenshtein edit distance function instead of additionally using a letter-based one. If the score of a sentence exceeds a threshold, we will further penalize it according to space and punctuations edit differences.

3 Experimental Setup

3.1 Corpora

Two corpora are needed for the domain adaptation task. Our general corpus includes 5 million English-Chinese parallel sentences comprising various genres such as movie subtitle, law literature, news and novel. The in-domain corpus and test set are randomly selected from the IWSLT2010 (International Workshop on Spoken Language Translation) Chinese-English Dialog task[3], consisting of transcriptions of conversational speech in a travel setting. All of them were segmented [4] (Zhang, 2003) and tokenized [5] (Koehn, 2005). The sizes of the test set, in-domain corpus and general corpus we used are summarized in Table 1.

Data Set	Sentences	Tokens	Ave. Len.
Test Set	3,500	34,382	9.60
In-domain	17,975	151,797	9.45
Training Set	5,211,281	53,650,998	12.93

Table 1: Corpora statistics.

In practice, we followed the experiments conducted by Lü et al. (2007) and Hildebrand et al. (2005), where the test set was used to select in-domain data from general corpus. The only difference is that an additional in-domain corpus is employed to build the LM for perplexity-based retrieval (Moore and Lewis, 2010; Axelrod et al., 2011).

3.2 System Description

The experiments presented in this paper are carried out with the Moses toolkit (Koehn et al., 2007), a state-of-the-art open-source phrase-based SMT system. The translation and the reordering model relied on "*grow-diag-final*" symmetrized word-to-word alignments built using GIZA++ (Och and Ney, 2003) and the training script of Moses. A 5-gram language model was trained on the target side of the training parallel corpus using the IRSTLM toolkit (Federico et al., 2008), exploiting improved Modified Kneser-Ney smoothing, and quantizing both probabilities and back-off weights.

3.3 Baseline System

The baseline system was trained on the general corpus with toolkits and settings as described above. The baseline BLEU is **29.34** points. This low value is occurred by the fact that he general corpus does not consist of enough sentences on the travel domain and has a lot of out-of-domain data, which can be regarded as noise for this task.

4 Results and Discussions

A number of experiments have been conducted to investigate five data selection methods: standard IR (IR), source-side cross-entropy (CE),

[3] http://iwslt2010.fbk.eu/node/33.

[4] IC-TCLAS2013 is available at http://ictclas.nlpir.org/.

[5] Scripts are available at http://www.statmt.org/europarl/.

source-side cross-entropy difference (CED), bilingual cross-entropy difference (B-CED) and the fuzzy matching (FMS_{ours}) methods. Supposed that M is the size of the test set or in-domain corpus and N is the number of sentences retrieved from the general corpus according to each query. Thus, the size of the subset we selected is $M \times N$.

We investigate each method in a step of 2x starting from 0.25% of the general corpus (0.29%, 0.52%, 1.00%, 2.30%, 4.25% and 12.5%) where K% means K percentage of general corpus are selected as a subset.

Firstly, we evaluated IR which improves by at most 1.03 BLEU points when using 4.25% of the general corpus as shown in Fig. 1. Then the performance begins to drop when the size is more than 4.25%. This shows that keyword overlap plays a significant role in retrieving sentences in a similar domain. However, it still needs a large amount of selected data to obtain an ideal performance due to its weakness in filtering noise.

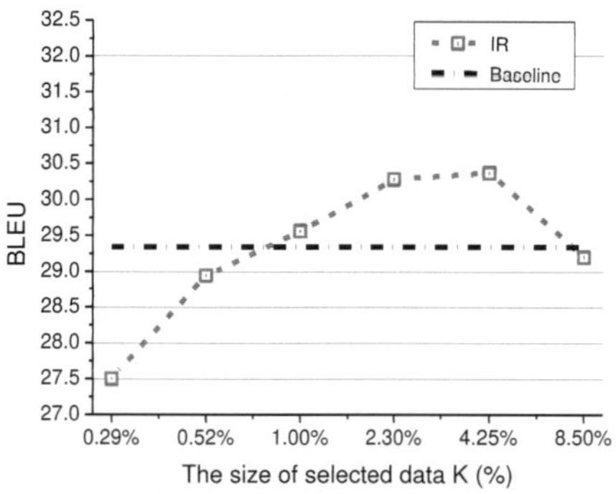

Figure 1: Translation results using subset of general corpus selected by standard IR model.

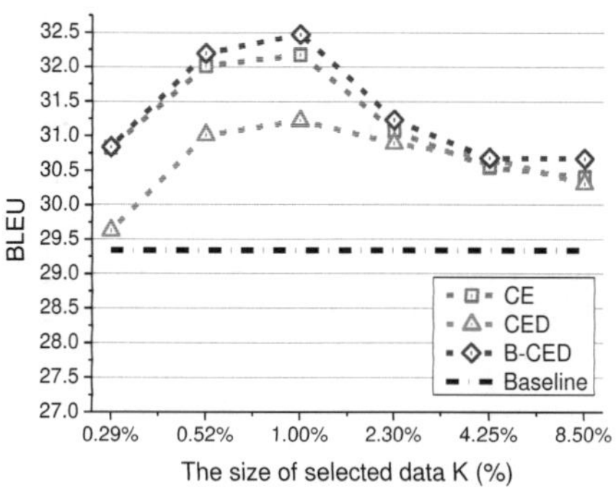

Figure 2: Translation results using subset of general corpus selected by three perplexity-based variants.

Secondly, we compared three perplexity-based methods. As illustrated in Fig. 2, all of them were able to significantly outperform the baseline system using only 1% of the entire training data. The size threshold is much smaller than the one of IR when obtaining the equivalent performance. Moreover, the curve drops slowly and is always over the baseline. This shows a better ability of filtering noises. Among the perplexity-based variants, the B-CED works best, which is similar to the conclusion drawn by Axelrod et al. (2011). It proves that bilingual resources are helpful to balance OOVs and noises. Next we will use B-CED to stand for perplexity-based methods and compare with other selection criteria.

Finally, we evaluated FMS and compared it with IR, B-CED and the baseline system, which are shown in Fig. 3. FMS seems to give an outstanding performance on most size thresholds. It always outperforms B-CED over at least 1 point under the same settings. Even using only 0.29% data, the BLEU is still higher than baseline over 0.66 points. In addition, FMS is able to conduct a better in-domain SMT system using less data than other selection methods. This indicates that it is stronger to filter noises and keep in-domain data when considering more constrain factors for similarity measuring.

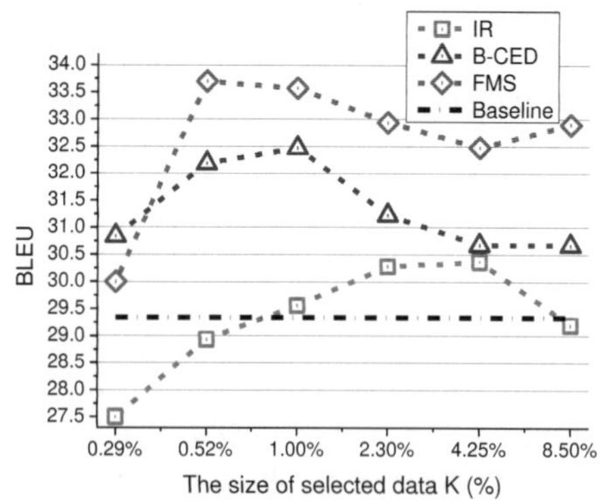

Figure 3: Translation results using subset of general corpus selected by different methods.

Corpus	Size (%)	BLEU
Baseline	100	29.34
IR	4.25	30.37 (+1.03)
CE	1.00	32.17 (+2.83)
CED	1.00	31.22 (+1.88)
B-CED	1.00	32.47 (+3.13)
FMS_{ours}	**0.52**	33.70 (**+4.36**)

Table 2: Best result of each method with corresponding size of selected data.

To give a better numerical comparison, Table 2 lists the best result of each method. As expected, FMS could use the smallest data (0.52%) to achieve the best performance. It outperforms the baseline system trained on the entire dataset over 4.36 BLEU points and B-CED over 1.23 points.

5 Conclusions

In this paper, we regard data selection as a problem of scoring the sentences in a general corpus via different similarity metrics. After revisiting the state-of-the-art data selection methods for SMT adaptation, we propose edit distance as a new selection criterion for this topic. In order to evaluate the proposed method, we compare it with four other related methods on a large data set. The methods we implemented are standard information retrieval model, source-side cross-entropy, source-side cross-entropy difference, bilingual cross-entropy difference as well as a baseline system. We can analyze the results from two different aspects:

Translation Quality: The results show a significant performance of the proposed method with increasing 4.36 BLEU points than the baseline system. And it also outperforms other four methods over 1-3 points.

Filtering Noises: Fuzzy matching could discard about 99.5% data of the general corpus without reducing translation quality. However, other methods will drop their performance when using the same size of data. The proposed metric has a very strong ability to filter noises in general corpus.

Finally, we can draw a composite conclusion that edit distance is a more suitable similarly model for SMT domain adaptation.

Acknowledgments

The authors are grateful to the Science and Technology Development Fund of Macau and the Research Committee of the University of Macau for the funding support for our research, under the reference No. 017/2009/A and MYRG076(Y1-L2)-FST13-WF. The authors also wish to thank the anonymous reviewers for many helpful comments.

References

Amittai Axelrod, Xiaodong He, and Jianfeng Gao. 2011. Domain adaptation via pseudo in-domain data selection. In: *Proceedings of EMNLP*. pp. 355–362.

Peter F. Brown, Vincent J. Della Pietra, Stephen A. Della Pietra, and Robert L. Mercer. 1993. The mathematics of statistical machine translation: Parameter estimation. *Computational Linguistics*. 19:263–311.

Jorge Civera and Alfons Juan. 2007. Domain adaptation in statistical machine translation with mixture modelling. *Proceedings of the Second ACL Workshop on Statistical Machine Translation*. pp. 177–180.

Hal Daumé III and Jagadeesh Jagarlamudi. 2011. Domain adaptation for machine translation by mining unseen words. In: *Proceedings of ACL-HLT*. pp. 407–412.

Vladimir Eidelman, Jordan Boyd-Graber, and Philip Resnik. 2012. Topic models for dynamic translation model adaptation. *Proceedings of ACL: Short Papers*. Vol. 2. pp. 115–119.

Marcello Federico, Nicola Bertoldi, and Mauro Cettolo. 2008. IRSTLM: an open source toolkit for handling large scale language models. *Proceedings of Interspeech*. pp. 1618–1621.

G. Foster and R. Kuhn. 2007. Mixture-model adaptation for SMT. *Proceedings of the Second ACL Workshop on Statistical Machine Translation*. pp. 128 – 136.

Jianfeng Gao, Joshua Goodman, Mingjing Li, and Kai-Fu Lee. 2002. Toward a unified approach to statistical language modeling for Chinese. *ACM Transactions on Asian Language Information Processing* (TALIP). 1:3–33.

Almut Silja Hildebrand, Matthias Eck, Stephan Vogel, and Alex Waibel. 2005. Adaptation of the translation model for statistical machine translation based on information retrieval. *Proceedings of EAMT*. pp. 133–142.

Johannes Leveling, Debasis Ganguly, Sandipan Dandapat and Gareth J.F. Jones. 2012. Approximate Sentence Retrieval for Scalable and Efficient Example-based Machine Translation. *Proceedings of COLING 2012*. pp. 1571-1586.

Philipp Koehn. 2005. Europarl: A parallel corpus for statistical machine translation. *MT Summit*. Vol. 5. pp. 79–86.

Philipp Koehn, Hieu Hoang, Alexandra Birch, Chris Callison-Burch, Marcello Federico, Nicola Bertoldi, Brooke Cowan, Wade Shen, Christine Moran et al. 2007. Moses: Open source toolkit for statistical machine translation. *Proceedings of ACL*. pp. 177–180.

Philipp Koehn and Jean Senellart. 2010. Convergence of translation memory and statistical machine translation. *Proceedings of AMTA Workshop on MT* Research and the Translation Industry. pp. 21–31.

Yajuan Lü, Jin Huang, and Qun Liu. 2007. Improving statistical machine translation performance by training data selection and optimization. *Proceedings of EMNLP-CoNLL*. pp. 343–350.

Saab Mansour and Hermann Ney. 2012. A Simple and Effective Weighted Phrase Extraction for Machine Translation Adaptation. *Proceedings of IWSLT*. pp. 193-200.

Robert C. Moore and William Lewis. 2010. Intelligent selection of language model training data. *Proceedings of ACL: Short Papers*. pp. 220–224.

Franz Josef Och and Hermann Ney. 2003. A systematic comparison of various statistical alignment models. *Computational Linguistics*. 29:19–51.

Kishore Papineni, Salim Roukos, Todd Ward, and Wei-Jing Zhu. 2002. BLEU: a method for automatic evaluation of machine translation. *Proceedings of ACL*. pp. 311–318.

Hua-Ping Zhang, Hong-Kui Yu, De-Yi Xiong, and Qun Liu. 2003. HHMM-based Chinese lexical analyzer ICTCLAS. *Proceedings of the 2nd SIGHAN Workshop on Chinese Language processing*. Vol. 17. pp. 184–187.

Automatic Enhancement of LTAG Treebanks

Farzaneh Zarei, Ali Basirat*, Heshaam Faili and Maryam Sadat Mirian
School of Electrical and Computer Engineering
College of Engineering
University of Tehran, Tehran, Iran
{zareeifarzaneh,hfaili,mmirian}@ut.ac.ir
*a.basirat@srbiau.ac.ir

Abstract

The Treebanks as the sets of syntactically annotated sentences, are the most widely used language resource in the application of Natural Language Processing. The occurrence of errors in the automatically created Treebanks is one of the main obstacles limiting the using of these resources in the real world applications. This paper aims to introduce an statistical method for diminishing the amount of errors occurred in a specific English LTAG-Treebank proposed in Basirat and Faili (2013). The problem has been formulated as a classification problem and has been tackled by using several classifiers. The experiments show that by using this approach, about 95% of the errors could be detected and more than 77% of them could successfully be corrected in the case of using Adaboost classifier. In addition, it has been shown that the new treebank could reach a high of 76% F-measure which is 8% higher than the original treebank.

1 Introduction

Treebanks, as special corpora annotated with syntactic structures, play a crucial role in the recent success of natural language processing applications like speech recognition, spoken language systems (Xue et al, 2005), parsing (Mirroshandel et al, 2012), and machine translation (Kotze et al, 2012).

Regarding the development methods of the treebanks, generally, they can be placed in either manually crafted or automatically extracted treebanks. Due to the large number of sentences, the manual creation of the treebanks can be very expensive and time consuming. For instance, Penn English treebank as one of the outstanding handmade ones took eight years (1989-1996) to be completed. The difficulties, raised in the manual creation of Treebanks, led the researchers to use automatic and semi-automatic methods of treebank development methods. On the other hand, the automatically extracted Treebanks are not as accurate as manual versions. In fact, these resources mostly suffer from the occurrence of error in the annotated sentences that in turn reduces the applicability of these resources in the real world applications.

A large number of researchers tried to improve the quality of the automatically extracted Treebanks in order to increase the applicability level of these resources in the NLP tasks (Xue et al, 2005).

For instance Dickinson and Meurers (2003) proposed an n-gram based approach for detecting Part-of-Speech errors in Penn English Treebank. In other works, Agarwal et al. (2012) proposed a hybrid approach to improve the mechanism of error detection introduced by Ambati (2011) for detecting the errors in a dependency treebank. Ule and Simov (2003) also could find unexpected tree productions by using a method called Directed Treebank Refinement (DTR).

In this paper, we try to correct the errors occurring in the treebank automatically generated from the approach proposed by Basirat and Faili (2013). This Treebank named *LTAG Treebank* is a corpus of supertag annotated sentences. A supertag is an abstract concept of the syntactic structures defined by the elementary structures of the lexicalized grammars like LTAG, HPSG, and CCG. This concept, as an extension of a simple part-of-speech tag, provides a rich and complex linguistically motivated description for the lexical items of language. A concrete instance of this concept is the elementary tree of a Lexicalized

Tree-Adjoining Grammars (LTAG), which gives a comprehensive description of the syntactic environment on which a word can be appeared.

In the supertag annotated corpus, the supertags are considered as the elementary trees of a typical LTAG of English, called XTAG grammar. The main interesting point of this grammar is the linguistically motivated descriptions provided by the elementary trees of this grammar for the syntactic environments of the words. Each sentence in the LTAG Treebank is associated with a sequence of elementary trees of XTAG grammar that directly defines a set of parse trees for the sentence, regarding the standard tree attachment operations defined in the LTAG formalism called substitution and adjunction.

In order to correct the miss-annotated words in the LTAG Treebank, a discriminate based formulation of the problem working in two main steps: *error detection* and *error correction* have been proposed. The error detection phase is responsible for detecting the miss-annotated words by employing some contextual features of the words. The output of this phase beside the other contextual features of the word then would be used by the error correction phase in order to find the best candidate among all elementary trees that can be assigned to the word.

To do so, two main classes have been considered for the error detection phase, *correct* and *incorrect*. Regarding this fact that in LTAG Treebank the number of miss-annotated words is much less than correct ones, the classes are imbalanced.

To the purpose of error detection and correction, three different classification methods have been employed: Adaboost (Freund and Schapire, 1998), Multilayer perceptron (MLP) and C4.5 (Quinlan, 1993). These classifiers are chosen due to the following justifications:

- Adaboost is a strong classifier in handeling imbalanced data (Japkowicz and Stephen, 2002).
- MLP is a universal function approximator.
- C4.5 is a decision tree approach which facilitates visualization of the found rules.

To handle the aforementioned class imbalance problem, these classifiers have been suggested. Japkowicz and Stephen studied several resampling methods and established the relation among concept complexity, size of the training set and class imbalance level.

We selected C4.5 among decision tree classifiers as it is a typical classification approach and has some superiorities to ID3 such as handling missing values and different feature costs.

On the other hand, there have been a number of studies on extending Adaboost to imbalanced datasets(Japkowicz and Stephen, 2002).

By applying these classifiers on the LTAG Treebank in the best case the precision increased by 8% and reached 76%.

The rest of this paper would be as follows: Sec. 2 gives brief information about the LTAG Treebank used in this work. Sec. 3 deals with the feature selection of the classifiers. In the next section, Sec. 4, the classification methods is expressed in details. Finally, Sec. 5 elaborates the numerical results of the error detection and correction. It also represents the quality of the resultant LTAG-Treebank according to different evaluation criterion.

2 LTAG Treebank

An LTAG-Treebank can formally be defined as a set of sentences annotated with the elementary trees of a lexicalized tree-adjoining grammar each of which defines a set derived/derivation trees for the sentences. The LTAG on which this work is focused has been developed as a part of a grammar development system, called XTAG. The importance of this grammar can be seen in the linguistic notions and rich feature structures like semantic representations that are embedded in its elementary trees. Nevertheless, lack of enough statistical information of co-occurrence elementary trees of XTAG grammar has limited its usage in the powerful statistical and machine learning approaches proposed in the recent decades.

It is expected that the LTAG-Treebank, can significantly compensate this weakness of the XTAG grammar by providing the empirical probability distributions of the co occurring elementary trees.

The idea of automatic error detection and correction mentioned in this work, has been applyied on the LTAG treebank introduced in Basirat and Faili (2013). This treebank has been developed based on the hidden relationship between two LTAGs of English, XTAG grammar and an automatically extracted LTAG used by MICA parser (Bangalore et al, 2009).

We have applied this method on a subset of sentences of Wall Street Journal (WSJ) in order to annotate them with the elementary trees of the

XTAG grammar. The result was a set of English sentences and their related XTAG elementary tree sequences each of which could define a set of parse trees for their sentences.

One of the difficulties raised in using this approach is the occurrence of errors in the elementary trees assigned to the words. Regarding the standard tree attachment operations defined in TAG, the existence of these errors would lead to the following problems: i) The sequence of elementary trees that cannot attach to each other to create a parse tree for the sentence. ii) The sequences of elementary trees that can attach to each other but the resultant parse tree is not correct.

In principle, the occurrence of these errors is the direct consequence of the weakness of the classifier used by Basirat and Faili (2013) for assigning the XTAG elementary trees to the sentences. The assignment was based on a Hidden Markov Model (HMM) and due to the inherent weaknesses of the HMM, some miss-annotations in the generated Treebank have occurred.

As a specific example, the sentence "I believe in the system" is labeled by the approach proposed by Basirat and Faili (2013). Table 1 shows the output of this approach and its correct version.

word	Output of the HMM	Correct version
I	alphaNXN	alphaNXN
believe	alphanx0V	alphanx0V
in	betavxPnx	betavxPnx
the	alphaD	betaDnx
system	alphaDnx0V	alphaNXN

Table 1: the output of the HMM for the sentence "I believe in the system" and its corrected version

Figure 1 also shows the elementary trees resulted from the HMM proposed by Basirat and Faili (2013). As it can be seen, these elementary trees cannot attach to each other in order to create full parse tree. Because miss annotating occurred in two last word of the sentence. But after correcting these errors, we would have a full parsed tree.

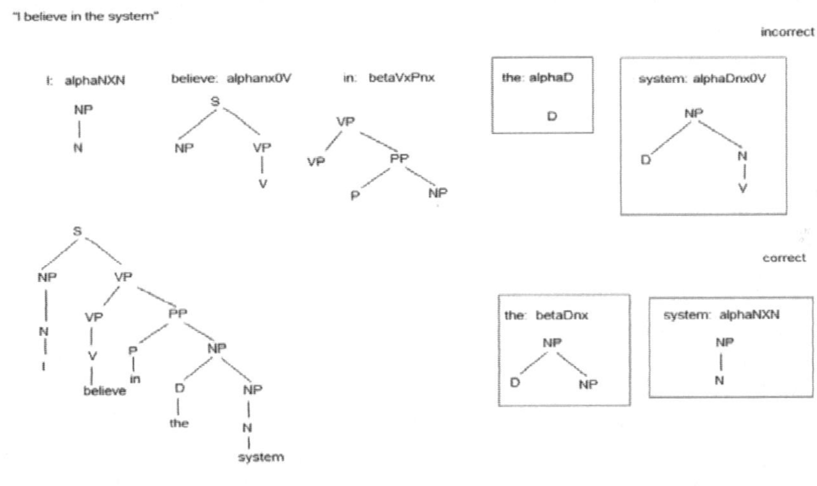

Figure 1: the output of the HMM for the sentence "I believe in the system" and its corrected version

3 Feature Selection

Depending on the type of errors occurred in the LTAG tree bank, several features can be used to detect them. For instance, the erroneous sequences that cannot lead to full parse trees can be analyzed by using the contextual information of the words (e.g., POS tag of the word and its neighbors, the morphological information of the word, the word itself and its neighbors, etc). The dependency information of the words can also be helpful for finding the errors in the sequences that might result in parse trees but incorrect parse trees.

Because of the huge size of the set of language words, among all contextual information of the words, three features were selected including the *Part Of Speech tag*, the *XTAG elementary tree*, and *supertag* of the words. Here the *supertag* is selected from the set of elementary trees of another LTAG used by the MICA parser. The XTAG elementary tree also is the elementary tree initially assigned to the word by using the aforementioned LTAG treebank builder. The main reason for using these features is their ability in encapsulating the complexity of the syntactic environment of the words in the structural objects to be used by the discriminant based classifiers like neural networks.

The dependency information of the words can also be encoded into the feature vector by using an extra input item representing the information of governor/dependent relationship of the words. This information can be extracted from the dependency tree of the sentence generated by the MICA parse. Just like what was done for the contextual information of the words, here also instead of using the governor *word*, its MICA supertag is used.

To summarize, the feature vector used by the classifier would contain contain the following elements:

- The XTAG elementary tree of the word
- The POS tag of the word
- The MICA supertag of the word (dependent)
- The MICA supertag of the governor

Using this set of features, the only extra tool for development of the set of feature vectors is the MICA parser. The POS tag also is extractable from the MICA supertag sequences generated by the MICA parser.

4 Classification

As mentioned before, the LTAG treebank creation method introduces in Basirat and Faili is based on the hidden markov model which does not provide any clear solution for using extra information of the word such as syntactic environment information. The suggested classification approach proposed in this paper, however enables us to easily use a lot of essential information of the word such as POS tag and its dependency information.

The task of correcting annotations can be done in two steps: i) Detecting the XTAG elementary trees that are incorrectly assigned to the words. ii) finding the correct labels for them.

Detecting the errors can be considered as a binary classification problem in which each word is classified *correct* or *incorrect* with respect to the XTAG elementary tree. Despite the detection, in the correction phase the number of the classes is equal to the number of the XTAG elementary trees appeared used in the Treebank.

Although the number of XTAG elementary trees is more than 1000, just 115 trees out of them were used in our corpus (before and after correction).

The rest of this section, would elaborate the implementation of each of these classification algorithms.

4.1 Adaboost

In boosting algorithms training data are classified by some weak classifiers iteratively. In each iteration, Boosting reweights the training data, such that the weights of correctly classified instances are decreased and the others are increased.

The week classifier used in our algorithm is Random Forest. Although, Random Forest is not as weak as a naïve bayse[1], we coupled them with Adaboost in order to utilize their power to conquer the imbalanced problem we face here. The combination of Adaboost and Random Forest has been used in the traffic flow (Leshem, and Ritov, 2007) and cancer survivability (Thongkam et al, 2008) and improve the performance of them.

4.2 Multilayer Perceptron (MLP)

A three-layered feed-forward neural network (one hidden layer containing 30 neurons) was trained, using back propagation algorithm. The back propagation training algorithm with generalized delta learning rule is an iterative gradient algorithm designed to minimize the mean square error between the actual output of a multilayered feed-forward neural network and a desired output.

4.3 C4.5

One of the famous algorithms which divides and conquers a problem for constructing a decision tree is C4.5. The model describes the condition of independent attributes that leads to each class prediction. The approach selects and places an attribute at the root node to generate one branch for each possible value of the attribute. The criterion for attribute selection involves obtaining a maximum information gain using the information theorem (Quinlan, 1993). And then, the branches can split the instances into numerous partitions, including one for every attribute value. Finally, each partition recursively repeats the splitting process until all instances at a node are in the same class. A pruning strategy is applied to reduce size of the decision tree.

[1] We tried NB as the weak learners and the resulting performance was not satisfactory.

In the next section we elaborate the numerical results obtained from correcting the proposed LTAG Treebank.

5 Evaluation

The classification method has been run on a subset of sentences of Wall Street Journal (WSJ) annotated with the elementary tree of the XTAG grammar. To this end, among the all sentences shorter than 40 words, 1393 sentences were randomly selected to be annotated with the XTAG elementary tree. The annotation process has been done according to the Treebank creation method introduced in Basirat and Faili (2013). Then, output of the annotation process has been manually corrected in order to be used as the gold standard in the evaluation phase.

Table 2 gives some statistical information of these sentences.

	train	test
Total number of sent	1,293	100
Total number of words	12,630	1,042
Avg length of sent	9.7	10.42
Avg number of errors per sent	1.57	1.46
Total number of correct annotated words	10,600	896
Total number of miss-annotated words	2,030	146

Table 2: selected sentences annotate with XTAG elementary trees

We employed some standard metrics in error detection and correction in order to evaluate the output of the classifiers. The measures are as follows:

- *False positive* (FP): refers to real errors that were not identified by the classifier.
- *False negative* (FN): refers to correct annotated word that the classifier detected as real errors.
- *True positive* (TP): refers to correct annotated words that are also considered as correct in the gold data.
- *True negative* (TN): refers to correct annotated words that the classification method changed regardless of the correction.
- *True negative with correction* (TNC): are real errors that the classification method was able to replace with the correct XTAG elementary trees.

By comparing the result of each classifier to the gold data, all the mentioned measures are calculated. Table 3 contains the evaluation results of each classifier.

	Adaboost	MLP	C4.5
False positive	30	57	48
False negative	12	6	13
True positive	768	801	785
True negative	116	89	98
True negative with correction	113	89	97

Table 3: output statistical information of the classifiers

Fig. 2, 3, 4 demonstrate performance of each selected classifiers.

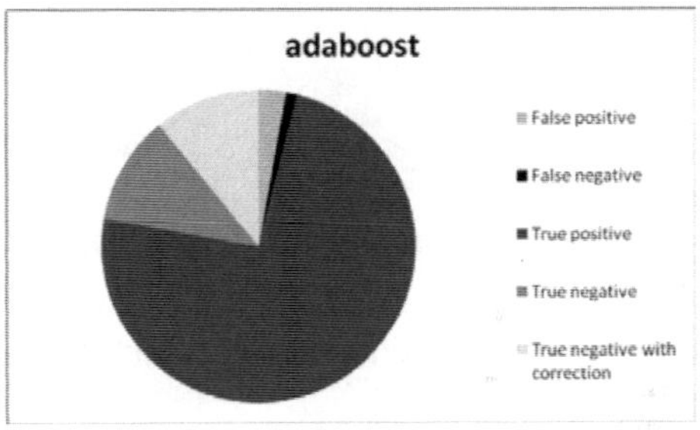

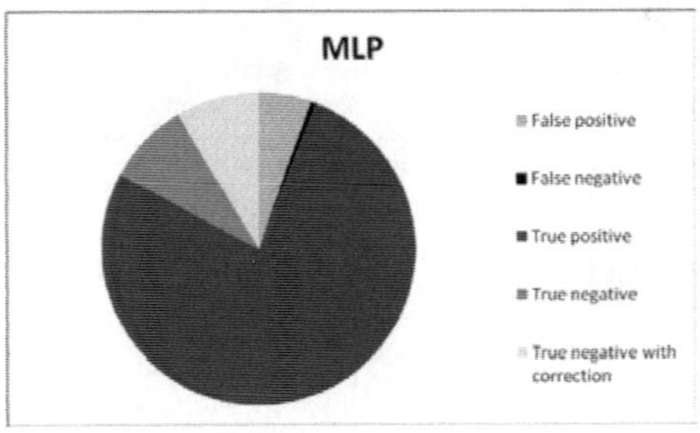

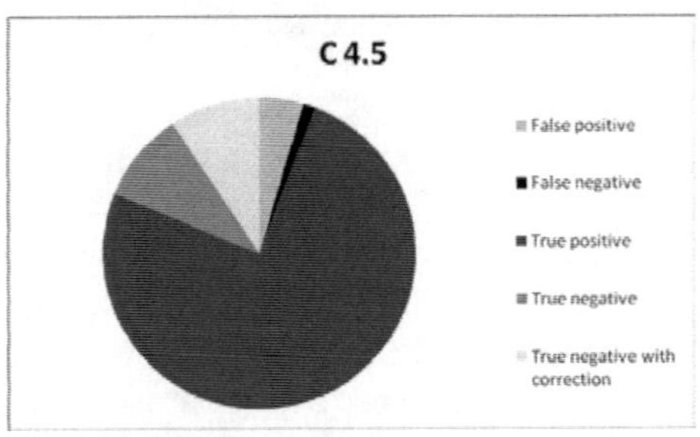

As we expected, the selected classifiers are strong enough to detect and correct a large proportion of errors correctly.

By using these metrics, we define four evaluation measures.

- Precision: The proportion of the correctly detected errors. That is, how many errors that the classifier detects were actually correct

$$precision = \frac{TP}{TP + FP}$$

- Detection Recall: The fraction of real errors detected by the classifier. That is, how many errors that have been detected by the classifier is actually error.

$$Detection\,\mathrm{Re}call = \frac{TN}{FP + TN}$$

- Correction Recall: The fraction of real errors corrected by the classifier. That is, how many errors that have been corrected by the classifier is actually error.

$$Correction\,\mathrm{Re}call = \frac{TNC}{FP + TN}$$

- Accuracy (A): the total number of correctly detected word divided by the total number of the word

$$Accuracy = \frac{TP + TN}{TP + TN + FP + FN}$$

Precision, detection recall, correction recall and accuracy of each classifier is calculated and shown in Figure 5.

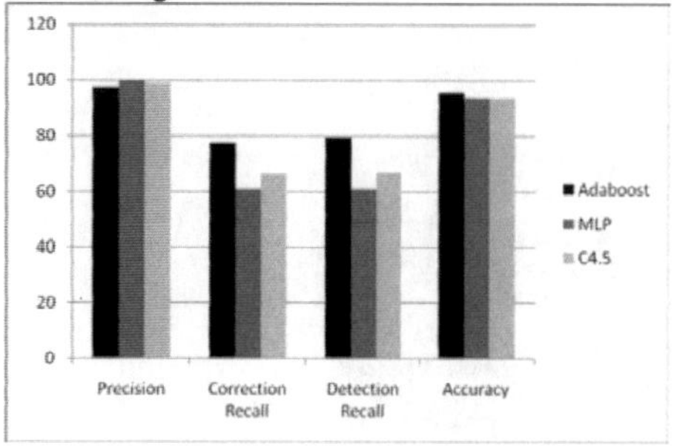

Figure 5: Precision, recall and accuracy of each classifier

According to Figure 5 although the MLP has a highest precision (100%), its recall is slightly lower than the C4.5 classifier. The accuracy of the C4.5 and MLP classifiers are almost equal. The Adaboost classifier appeared to outperform the others. It has the best detection and correction recall but its precision is only slightly lower than the best case (97.41%).

The rest of this section deals with the evaluation of the developed Treebank.

5.1 Evaluation of LTAG treebank

Precision, recall and F-measure are three primary evaluation criteria to measure the quality of a parse tree.

Table 4 represents quality of the LTAG-Treebank before applying the error correction. It shows the values of precision, recall and F-measure of the parse trees generated from the elementary tree sequences with respect to the gold parse trees available in the Penn-Treebank.

	Before correction
Precision	54.78
Recall	88.80
F-measure	67.76

Table 4: precision, recall and F-measure of LTAG treebank before correction

Table 5 shows same criteria for the parse trees after applying error detection and correction methods.

	precision	recall	F-measure
Adaboost	63.99	94.72	76.38
MLP	63.67	94.33	76.03
C4.5	63.40	94.84	76.00

Table 5: precision, recall and F-measure of LTAG treebank after correction

As can be seen, the value of F-measure of the parse trees after applying the error detection and correction could significantly be improved.

6 Conclusion

In this paper, we proposed an error detection and correction method for improving the quality of automatically created LTAG Treebank introduced in Basirat and Faili (2013). The problem was formulated as a sequence classification problem and tackled by using three classifiers Adaboost, Multi Layer perceptron (MLP) and C4.5.

Because of the imbalanced situation of the problem in which the ratio of correctly annotated words was much higher than the miss-annotated words, the Adaboost classifier with random forest as a week learner could provide better results in comparison with the other classifiers. By applying the classifiers on the LTAG treebank, in the best case, the value of F-measure of the treebank could be increased by 8 % compared with the initial treebank.

References

Ali Basirat and Hesham Faili. 2013. *Bridge the gap between statistical and hand-crafted grammars*, Computer Speech and Language, volume 27, Pages 1085-1104

Gideon Kotze, Vincent Vandeghinste, Scott Martens, Jorg Tiedemann. 2012. Large aligned treebanks for syntax-based machine translation. Proceedings of the Eight International Conference on Language Resources and Evaluation (LREC'12). European Language Resources Association (ELRA).

Guy Leshem, Yaacov Ritov, 2007, *Traffic flow prediction using adaboost algorithm with random forests as a weak learner*, in: Proceedings of World Academy of Science, Engineering and Technology, vol. 19, Bangkok, Thailand, 193–198

Jaree Thongkam, Guandong Xu, and Yanchun Zhang. 2008. *AdaBoost algorithm with random forest for predicting breast cacer survivability*, IJCNN, 3062-3069. IEEE(2008)

John Ross Quinlan, 1993. *C4.5 programs for machine learning*. San Mateo, CA: Morgan Kaufmann

Naiwen Xue , Fei Xia, Fu-Dong Chiou, Marta Palmer. 2005. *The penn chinese treebank: Phrase structure annotation of a large corpus*. Natural Language Engineering , 11(2), 207-238.

Nathalie Japkowicz and Shaju Stephen.2002. *The class imbalanced problem: A systematic study*. Intelligent Data Analysis. Volume 6. 429-449.

Markus Dickinson, and W.Detmar Meurers, 2003 , *Detecting Errors in Part-of-Speech Annotation.* In The 10th Conference of European Chapter of the Associa-tion for Computational Linguistics(EACL-03).

Mitchell P. Marcus, Mary Marcinkiewicz, Beatrice Santorini.1993. *Building a large annotated corpus of english: The penn treebank*. Computational Linguistics - Special issue on using large corpora 19(2), 313 – 330.

Rahul Agarwal, Bharat Ambati, and Dipti Sharma. 2012, *A Hybrid Approach to Error Detection in a Treebank and its Impact on Manual Validation Time*, volume 7. Linguistic Issues in Language Technology.

Seyed Abolghasem Mirroshandel, Nasr Alexis, Joseph Le Roux. 2012. *Semi-supervised dependency parsing using lexical affinities*. ACL '12 Proceedings of 50th Annual Meeting of the Association for Computational Linguistics. Volum 1, 777-785

Srinivas Bangalore, Anoop Sarkar, Christine Doran, Beth Ann Hockey, 1998, *Grammar & parser evaluation in the xtag project*. In: Proceedings of the Workshop on Evaluation of Parsing Systems, Granada ,Spain. Language Resources and Evaluation Conference.

Srinivas Bangalore, Patrick Haffner, and Ga¨el Emami. 2005. *Factoring global inference by enriching local representations*. Technical report, AT&T Labs – Reserach.

Srinivas Bangalor, Pierre Boullier, Alexis Nasr, Owen Rambow, Benoit Sagot. 2009. *Mica: A probabilistic dependency parser based on tree insertion grammar*. NAACL-Short '09 Proceedings of Human Language Technologies: The 2009 Annual Conference of the North American Chapter of the Association for Computational Linguistics, vol. Short Papers, 185–188.

Yoav Freund and Robert E. Schapire, 1996, *Experiments with a New Boosting Algorithm*, Proc. of 13th International Conference on Machine Learning, pp. 148—156.

Inductive and deductive inferences in a Crowdsourced Lexical-Semantic Network

Manel ZARROUK
LIRMM
manel.zarrouk@lirmm.fr

Mathieu LAFOURCADE
LIRMM
lafourcade@lirmm.fr

Alain JOUBERT
LIRMM
alain.joubert@lirmm.fr

Abstract

In Computational Linguistics, building lexical-semantic networks and validating contained relations are paramount issues as well as adding some reasoning skills in order to enrich these knowledge bases. In this paper we devise an inference engine which aims at producing new "potential" relations from already existing ones in the JeuxDeMots network. This network is constructed with the help of a GWAP (game with a purpose) thanks to thousands of players. It handles terms and weighted relations between these terms, and currently contains over 2 million relation occurences. Polysemous terms may be refined in several senses (*bank* may be a *bank>financial institution* or a *bank>river*) but as the network is indefinitely under construction (in the context of a Never Ending Learning approach) some senses may be missing at a given time. The approach we proposed here is founded on the triangulation method through two kinds of inference schemes: deduction (top-down from generic to specific terms) and induction (bottom-up from specific to generic terms). A blocking mechanism, whose purpose is to avoid proposing highly dubious new relations, is based on logical and statistical constraints. Automatically inferred relations are then proposed to human contributors to be validated. In case of invalidation, a reconciliation dialog is undertaken to identify the cause of the wrong inference: an exception, an error in the premises or a previously undetected confusion due to polysemy on the central term common to both premises.

1 Introduction

Developing resources in NLP is one of the crucial issue of the field. Most of the existing lexico-semantic networks have been constructed manually, like for instance the famous WordNet. Of course some tools are generally designed for consistency checking, but nevertheless the task remains time consuming and costly. Fully automated approaches are generally limited to term coocurrences as extracting precise semantic relations between terms from text remains really difficult. New approaches involving crowdsourcing are flowering in NLP especially with the advent of Amazon Mechanical Turk or in a broader scope Wikipedia and Wiktionnary, to cite the most well known examples. WordNet ((**?**) and (**?**)) is such a lexical network based on synsets which can be roughly considered as concepts. EuroWordnet (**?**) a multilingual version of WordNet and WOLF (**?**) a French version of WordNet, were built by automated crossing of WordNet and other lexical resources along with some manual checking. (**?**) constructed automatically BabelNet a large multilingual lexical network from term coocurrences in the Wikipedia encyclopedia.

A highly lexicalized lexical-semantic network can contain concepts but also plain words (and multi-word expressions) as entry points (nodes) along with word meanings. The idea itself of *word senses* in the lexicographic tradition may be debatable in the context of resources for semantic analysis, and we generally prefer to consi..0 der word usages. By *word usages* we mean refinements of a given word which is clearly identified by locutors. A polysemic term has several usages that might differ substantially from word senses as classically defined. A given usage can also in turn have several deeper refinements and the whole set of usage can take the form of a decision tree. In the context of a collaborative construction, such a lexical resource should be considered as being constantly evolving and a general rule of thumb is to have no definite certitude about the state of an entry.

The building of a collaborative lexical network (or any similar resource) can be devised according to two broad strategies. First, it can be designed as a contributive system like Wikipedia where people willingly add and complete entries (like for Wiktionary). Second, contributions can be made indirectly thanks to games (better known as GWAP (?) and (?)) and in this case players do not need to be aware that while playing they are helping building a lexical resource. In any case, the lexical network that is built is not free of errors which are corrected along their discovery. Thus a large number of obvious relations are not contained in the lexical network but are indeed necessary for a high quality resource usable in various NLP application and notably semantic analysis. For example, contributorsdo not indicate that a particular bird type can fly, as it is considered as an obvious generality. Only notable facts which are not easily deductible are naturally contributed. Well known exceptions are also generally contributed and take the form of a negative weight for the relation (for example, *fly* $\xrightarrow{agent:-100}$ *ostrich*).

In order to consolidate the lexical network, we adopt a strategy based on a simple (if not simplistic) inference mechanism to propose new relations from those existing. The approach is strictly endogenous as it doesn't rely on any other external resources. Inferred relations are submitted either to contributors for voting or to expert for direct validation/invalidation. A large percentage of the inferred relations has been found to be correct. However, a non negligible part of them are found to be wrong and understanding why is both relevant and useful. The explanation process can be viewed as a reconciliation between the inference engine and the validator who is guided through a dialog to explain why he found the considered relation as incorrect. A wrong inferred relation may come from three possible origins: false premises used by the inference engine, exception or confusion due to polysemy.

In this article, we first present the principles behind of lexical network construction with crowdsourcing and *games with a purpose* (also know as human-based computation games) and illustrated them with the JeuxDeMots (JDM) project. Then, we present the outline of an *elicitation engine* based on an *inference engine* using deduction and induction schemes and a *reconciliation engine*. An experimentation is then reported on the performances of the system.

2 Lexical Network and Crowdsourcing

There are many ways for building a lexical network considering some crucial factors as the quality of data, cost and time. Beside manual or automated strategies, contributive approaches are more and more popular as they are both cheap to set up and efficient in quality. More specifically, there is an increasing trend of using on-line GWAPs ((?) and (?)) method for feeding such resources.

The JDM lexical network is constructed through a set of on-line associative games. In these games, players are appealed to contribute on lexical and semantic relations between terms or verbal expressions which are presented in the network by the arcs interconnecting nodes in a graph. The informations in the JDM network are gathered by an unnegotiated crowd agreement (classical contributive systems rely on a negotiated crowd agreement).

2.1 JeuxDeMots: a GWAP for Building a Lexical-Semantic Network

JeuxDeMots[1] is a two player GWAP which aims to build a large lexical-semantic network (?). The network is composed of terms (as vertices) and typed relations (as links between vertices). It contains terms and possible refinements in a similar way to the WordNet synset (?). The semantic network is constructed by connecting terms by typed and weighted relations, validated by pairs of players. These relations are labelled according to the instructions given to the players and weighted according to the number of pairs of players who choose them. Other Web-based systems exist, such as Open Mind Word Expert (?), which aims at creating large sense-tagged corpora with the help of Web users, and SemKey (?) which makes use of WordNet and Wikipedia to disambiguate lexical forms referring to concepts, thus identifying semantic keywords.

[1] http://jeuxdemots.org

2.2 Diko as a Contributive Tool

Diko[2] is a web based tool for displaying the information contained in the JDM lexical network which can also be used as a contributive tool. The necessity to not rely only on the JDM game for building the lexical network comes from the fact that many relation types of JDM are either difficult to grasp for a casual player or not very productive (not many terms can be associated).

The principle of the contribution process is that a proposition made by a user will be voted pro or con by other users then included or excluded by an expert validator. What we propose in this paper falls under this type of scenario of contributions/validations.

3 Elicitation by Inference and Reconciliation

We designed a system for augmenting the number of relations in the JDM lexical network having two main components: (a) an inference engine and (b) a reconciliator. The inference engine proposes relations as if it was a contributor, to be validated by human contributors or experts. In case of invalidation of an inferred relation, the reconciliator is invoked to try to assess why the inferred relation was found wrong. Elicitation here should be understood as the process to transform some implicit knowledge of the user into explicit relations in the lexical network.

3.1 Making Inferences

The core ideas about inferences in our system are the following:

- for the engine, inferring is to derive new premises (under the form of relations between terms) from previously known premises, which are existing relations;
- candidate inferences may be logically blocked on the basis of the presence or absence of some other relations;
- candidate inferences can be filtered out on the basis of a strength evaluation.

3.1.1 Deduction Scheme

In this paper, the first type of inference we are working with is the deduction or top-down scheme, which is based on the transitivity of the ontological relation *is-a* (hypernym). If a term A is a kind of B and B holds some relation R with C, then we can expect that A holds the same relation with C. The scheme can be formally written as follows:

$$\exists A \xrightarrow{is-a} B \ \wedge \ \exists B \xrightarrow{R} C \ \Rightarrow \ A \xrightarrow{R} C$$

Global processing - Let us consider a term T with a set of weighted hypernyms. From each hypernym, the inference engine deduces a set of inferences. Those inference sets are not disjoint in the general case, and the weight of an inference proposed in several sets is the incremental geometric mean of each occurrence.

Logical filtering - Of course, this scheme above is far too naive, especially considering the resource we are dealing with. In effect, B is possibly a polysemous term and ways to block inferences that are certainly wrong can be devised. If there are two distinct meanings of the term B that hold respectively the first and the second relation, as in the Figure ?? below, then most probably the inference is wrong.

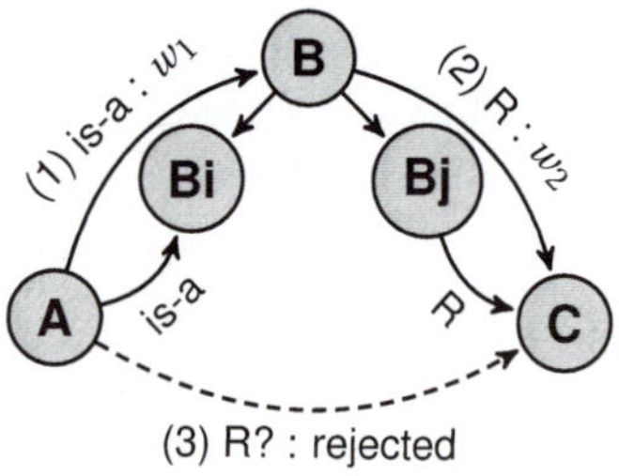

Figure 1: Triangular inference scheme with logical blocking based on the polysemy of B.

In this case, a relation R -to be inferred- must fulfill some constraints as formulated below:

$$\begin{aligned} & A \xrightarrow{is-a} B \ \wedge \ B \xrightarrow{R} C \\ \wedge \ & (\exists B_i \xrightarrow{meaning-of} B \ \wedge \ \exists B_j \xrightarrow{meaning-of} B) \\ \wedge \ & (\nexists A \xrightarrow{is-a} B_i \ \vee \ \nexists B_j \xrightarrow{R} C) \\ & \Rightarrow \ A \xrightarrow{R} C \end{aligned}$$

Moreover, if one of the premises is tagged as *true but irrelevant*, then the inference is blocked. ***Statistical filtering*** - It is possible to evaluate a confidence level (on an open scale) for each produced inference, in a way that dubious inferences can be filtered out. The weight w of an inferred relation is the geometric mean of the weight of the premises (relations (1) and (2) in Figure ??). If the second premise has a negative value, the weight is not a number and the proposal is discarded. As the geometric mean

[2] http://www.jeuxdemots.org/diko.php

is less tolerant to small values than the arithmetic mean, inferences which are not based on two rather true relations (premises) are unlikely to pass.

$$w(A \xrightarrow{R} C) = (w(A \xrightarrow{is-a} B) * w(B \xrightarrow{R} C))^{1/2}$$
$$\Rightarrow \quad w3 = (w1 * w2)^{1/2}$$

3.1.2 Induction Scheme

As for the deductive inference, induction exploits the transitivity of the relation *is-a*. If a term A is a kind of B and A holds a relation R with C, then we might expect that B could hold the same type of relation with C. More formally we can write:

$$\exists A \xrightarrow{is-a} B \;\wedge\; \exists A \xrightarrow{R} C \;\Rightarrow\; B \xrightarrow{R} C$$

This scheme is a generelization inference. The ***global processing*** is similar to the one applied to the deduction scheme and similarly some logical and statistical filtering may be undertaken.

The term joining the two premises (called *central term,* in this case term A) is possibly polysemous. If the term A is presenting two distinct meanings which hold respectively the premises (as shown in Figure **??**), then the inference done from that term may be probably wrong.

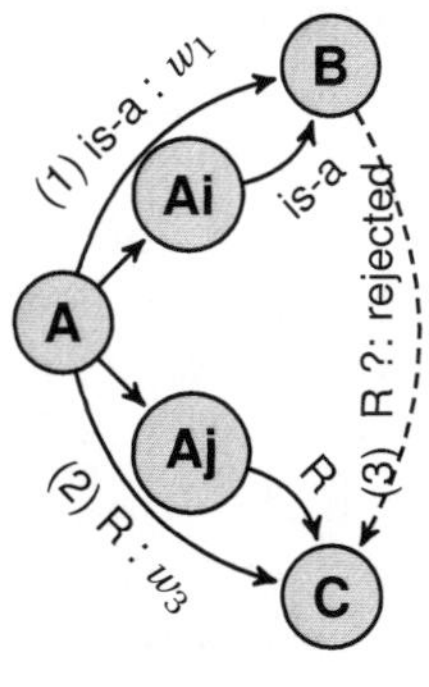

Figure 2: (1) and (2) are the premises, and (3) is the logical induction proposed for validation. Central term A may be polysemous with meanings holding premises, thus inducing a probably wrong relation.

Logical filtering can be formalized as follows:

$$A \xrightarrow{is-a} B \;\wedge\; A \xrightarrow{R} C$$
$$\bigwedge \; (\exists A_i \xrightarrow{meaning-of} A \;\wedge\; \exists A_j \xrightarrow{meaning-of} A)$$
$$\bigwedge \; (\nexists A_i \xrightarrow{is-a} B \;\vee\; \nexists A_j \xrightarrow{R} C)$$
$$\Rightarrow \; B \xrightarrow{R} C$$

Statistical filtering is possible, as for the deductive scheme to evaluate a confidence level. According to the weight evaluation from the deductive diagram, the estimated weight for the induced relation is:

$$w(B \xrightarrow{R} C) = (w(A \xrightarrow{R} C))^2 \;/\; w(A \xrightarrow{is-a} B)$$
$$\Rightarrow \quad w2 = \frac{(w_3)^2}{w_1}$$

3.2 Performing reconciliation

Inferred relations, further to both induction and deduction, are presented to the validator to decide of their status: *rather true, rather true but irrelevant, possible* or *mostly false.* In case of invalidation, a reconciliation procedure is committed in the purpose to try to diagnose the reasons: error in one of the premises (previously existing relations are false), exception or confusion due to polysemy (the inference has been made on a polysemous central term) and initiates a dialog with the user. The latter is free to choose to pursuit the dialog partially, entirely or to choose not to start it. To know in which order to proceed, the reconciliator determines if the weights of the premises are rather strong or weak. This confidence is done by comparing the relation weight to a confidence threshold which is computed as the starting point of the long tail in the distribution of the relation. For the whole set of the outgoing relations from a term the long tail starts at the point where the cumulated weights of the relations of the tail is equal the cumulated weights of the relations which do not belong to the tail (**?**).

- If $w(A \xrightarrow{is-a} B) >= conf - thr(A)$ ⇒trusted relation
- If $w(A \xrightarrow{is-a} B) < conf - thr(A)$ ⇒dubious relation

In the case we have both relations (1) and (2) as trusted, the reconciliator tries, by initiating a dialog with the validator, to check at first if the relation inferred is an exception. If not, it proceeds by checking if term B is polysemous and finally checks if it is an error case. We check the error case in the final step because the confidence level of relations (1) and (2) made them trusted.

In the case of having a dubious relation either for (1) and (2), the reconciliator suspects that it is an error case and this relation was the cause of a wrong inference. So, the validator is asked to confirm or to disprove it. In case of refutation of one of the relations, we have an error. If not, we proceed with checking if it's an exception case or a polysemy.

3.2.1 Errors in the premises

In this case, suppose that relation (1) has a relatively low weight. The reconciliator asks the validator about the relation (1) .

- If is false, a negative weight is attributed to (1) and the reconciliation is completed. As such, this relation will not be used later on as premises on further inferences;
- If it is true, ask if relation (2) is true and proceed as above if the answer is negative;
- Otherwise, move to checking the other cases (exception, polysemy).

3.2.2 Errors as exceptions

For the *deduction*, if the validator indicates that the inferred relation is an exception relatively to the term *B*, the relation is stored in the lexical network with a negative weight along with a meta-information which indicates that it is an exception. [3]

For the *induction*, if the alidator indicates that the relation ($A \xrightarrow{R} C$) (which served as premise) is an exception relatively to the term *B*, in addition to storing the false inferred relation ($B \xrightarrow{R} C$) in the network with a negative weight, the relation ($A \xrightarrow{R} C$) is tagged with a meta-information indicating it as an exception. In the induction case, the exception is a true premise which leads to a false induced relation. [4]

In both cases of induction and deduction, the *exception* tag concerns always the relation ($A \xrightarrow{R} C$). Once this relation is tagged as an exception, it will not participate as a premise in inferring generalized relations (bottom-up model) but can still be used in inducing specified relations (top-down model).

3.2.3 Errors due to Polysemy

In this case, if the middle term (*B* for deduction and *A* for induction) presenting a polysemy is mentioned as polysemous in the network, the refinement terms $term_1$, $term_2$, ..., $term_n$ are presented to the validator so he can choose the appropriate one. The validator can propose new terms as refinements if he is not satisfied with the listed ones (inducing the creation of new appropriate refinements). After this procedure, two new relations ($A \xrightarrow{is-a} B_i$ and $B_j \xrightarrow{R} C$ in the case of deduction, or $A_i \xrightarrow{is-a} B$ and $A_j \xrightarrow{R} C$ in the induction case) will be included in the network with positive values and the inference engine will use them later on as premises.

[3]For example, suppose we have ($ostrich \xrightarrow{agent} fly$) inferred by *deduction* with the central term *B*. In this case, it's true that an ($ostrich \xrightarrow{is-a} bird$) and that a ($bird \xrightarrow{agent} fly$), but the inferred relation an *ostrich can fly* is *false* and it is considered as an *exception* considering the central term *"bird"*.

[4]As for the relation ($fish \xrightarrow{agent} fly$) which is a false inferred relation based on the central term *exocet*. The ($exocet \xrightarrow{is-a} fish$) and ($exocet \xrightarrow{agent} fly$) are true but the latter one is an *exception* in the form of a *true* relation.

4 Experimentation

We made an experiment with a unique run of the engine over the lexical network of JDM. The purpose is to measure the production of the inference engine along with the blocking and filtering. From the set of supposedly valid inferred relations (both by induction and deduction), we took a random sample of 400 propositions for each relation type and undertook the validation/reconciliation process. The experiment conducted is for evaluation purpose only, as actually the system is running iteratively along with contributors and games.

4.1 Unleashing the Inference Engine

We applied the inference engine on around 23 000 randomly selected terms having at least one hypernym or one hyponym and thus produced by deduction 1 484 209 inferences (77 089 more were blocked). The threshold for filtering was set to a weight of 25. This value is relevant as when a human contributor proposed relation is validated by an expert, it is introduced with a default weight of 25. For induction, the inference engine produced 353 371 relation candidates. The table **??** presents the number of relations proposed by the inference engine through deduction. The different types for the second premise are variously productive. Of course, this is mainly due to the number of existing relations and the distribution of their type in the network.

The transitive relation *is-a* is the less productive which might seems surprising at first glance. In fact, this relation is already quite populated in the network, and as such, fewer new relations can be inferred. The figures are inverted for some other relations that are not so well populated but still are potentially valid. The agent semantic role (the *agent-1* relation) is by far the most productive, with 30 time more propositions than what currently exists in the lexical network.

Relation type	Proposed	Blocked	Filtered
is-a	91k (6,1)	4 k (5.2)	53 k (26,3)
has-parts	372k (25.1)	31 k (40.7)	100 k (49.3)
holonym	108k (7.2)	17 k (23.3)	26 k (13.2)
place	271k (18.3)	11 k (15)	14 k (7)
charac	203k (13.7)	2 k (3.4)	6 k (3.2)
agent-1	198k (13.3)	9 k (11.7)	1122 (0.5)
instr-1	24k (1.7)	127 (0.2)	391 (0.2)
patient-1	14k (1)	7 (0.01)	13 (0)
place-1	145k (9.8)	129 (0.2)	206 (0.1)
place >action	50k (3.4)	91 (0.1)	132 (0.06)
obj >mater	4k (0.3)	135 (0.2)	262 (0.1)
Total	**1 484k**	**77 k**	**203 k**

Table 1: Numbers and percentages for inferences (proposed, blocked or filtered) by the deduction.

4.2 Figures on Reconciliation

Table **??** contains some evaluation of the status of the inferences proposed by the inference engine through deduction. Inferences are valid for an overall of 80-90% with around 10% valid but not relevant (like for instance *dog* $\xrightarrow{has-parts}$ *proton*). We observe that error number in premises is quite low, and nevertheless errors can be easily corrected. Of course, not all possible errors are detected through this process.The reconciliation allows in 5% of the cases to identify polysemous terms. Globally false negatives (inferences voted false but are true) and false positives (inferences voted true but are false) are evaluated to less than 0,5%. For the induction process (table **??**), the relation *is-a* is not obvious (a lexical network is not reductible to an ontology and multiple inheritance is possible). Result seems about 5% better than for the deduction process: inferences are valid for an overall of 80-95%. The error number is very low. The main difference with the deduction process is on errors due to polysemy which is lower with the induction process.

5 Conclusion

We presented some issues about inferring new relations from existing ones in a contributed lexical-semantic network in which word usages are discovered incrementally along its construction. Errors are naturally present as they might originate from games played on difficult relations, but they are usually spotted and corrected by contributors for terms they are interested in. To be able to enhance the network quality, we proposed an elicitation engine based on inferences and reconciliations. Inferences are here proposed with two different schemes (induction and deduction), along with a logical blocking and statistical filtering. If an inferred relation is proven wrong, a reconciliation is conducted to identify the underlying cause. As global figures, we can conclude that inferred deductive relations are correct and relevant in about 78% of the cases and correct but irrelevant in 10% of the case. Overall wrong deductive inferences is about 12% with at least one error in the premises of about 2%, exceptions about 5% and polysemy confusion about 5%. Induction is naturally less productive but more reliable. Beside a tool for increasing relations in a lexical network, the elicitation engine is both an error detector and a polysemy identifier. Actions taken during the reconciliation forbid an inference proven wrong or exceptional to be proposed again. Such an approach should be pushed forward with other types of inference scheme like abduction, and possibly with distribution evaluation of term semantic classes on which inferences are conducted. Indeed, some classes like concrete objects or living beings may be substantially more productive for certain relation types than abstract nouns of processes or events. Anyway, such discrepancies of inference productivity between classes are worthy to investigate further.

Deduction	% valid		% error		
Relation type	**rlvt**	**¬ rlvnt**	**prem**	**excep**	**pol**
is-a	76%	13%	2%	0%	9%
has-parts	65%	8%	4%	13%	10%
holonym	57%	16%	2%	20%	5%
typical place	78%	12%	1%	4%	5%
charac	82%	4%	2%	8%	4%
agent-1	81%	11%	1%	4%	3%
instr-1	62%	21%	1%	10%	6%
patient-1	47%	32%	3%	7%	11%
typical place-1	72%	12%	2%	10%	6%
place >action	67%	25%	1%	4%	3%
object >mater	60%	3%	7%	18%	12%

Table 2: Results of the validation/reconciliation according to relation types in the deduction. Valid relations can be relevant or not, and errors can be in **prem**ises, **excep**tions or **pol**ysemy.

Induction	% valid		% error		
Relation types	**rlvt**	**¬rlvnt**	**prem**	**excep**	**pol**
has-parts	78%	10%	3%	2%	7%
holonym	68%	17%	2%	8%	5%
typical loc	81%	13%	1%	2%	3%
carac	87%	6%	2%	2%	3%
agent-1	84%	12%	1%	2%	1%
instr-1	68%	24%	1%	4%	3%
patient-1	57%	36%	3%	2%	2%
typical loc-1	75%	16%	2%	5%	2%
lieu-action	67%	28%	1%	3%	1%
object mater	75%	10%	7%	5%	3%

Table 3: Results of the validation/reconciliation according to relation types in the induction. The relation *is-a* is inappropriate for Induction.

References

von Ahn, L. and Dabbish, L. (2008) *Designing games with a purpose.* Communications of the ACM, number 8, volume 51. pp. 58-67.

Chamberlain, J., Fort, K., Kruschwitz, U., Lafourcade, M. and Poesio, M. (2013) (2013) Using Games to Create Language Resources: Successes and Limitations of the Approach. Gurevych, Iryna; Kim, Jungi (Eds.), Springer, ISBN 978-3-642-35084-9, 2013, 42 p.

Fellbaum, C. (1988, ed.) WordNet: An Electronic Lexical Database. The MIT Press.

Law, E., Luis von Ahn, L. and Mitchell, T. (2009) *Search war: a game for improving web search.* KDD Workshop on Human Computation 2009. 31p.

Law, E., Luis von Ahn, L., Dannenberg, R. B. and Crawford, M.. (2007) *TAgATune: A Game for Music and Sound Annotation.* ISMIR 2007. pp. 361-364.

Lafourcade, M. and Joubert, A. (2012) *Long Tail in Weighted Lexical Networks.* In proc of Cognitive Aspects of the Lexicon (CogAlex-III), COLING, Mumbai, India, December 2012. 16 p.

Lafourcade, M. (2007) *Making people play for Lexical Acquisition.* In Proc. SNLP 2007, 7th Symposium on Natural Language Processing. Pattaya, Thailande, 13-15 December. 8 p.

Marchetti, A., Tesconi, M., Ronzano, F., Mosella, M and Minutoli, S. (2007) *SemKey: A Semantic Collaborative Tagging System.* in Procs of WWW2007, Banff, Canada. 9 p.

Mihalcea, R. and Chklovski, T. (2003) *Open Mind-Word Expert: Creating large annotated data collections with web users help..* In Proceedings of the EACL 2003, Workshop on Linguistically Annotated Corpora (LINC). 10 p.

Miller, G.A., Beckwith, R., Fellbaum, C., Gross, D. and Miller, K.J. (1990) *Introduction to WordNet: an on-line lexical database.* International Journal of Lexicography. Volume 3, pp. 235-244.

Miller, G.A. (1995) *WordNet: A Lexical Database for English.* Communications of the ACM Vol. 38, No. 11, pp. 39-41.

Navigli, R. and Ponzetto, S. (2010) *BabelNet: Building a very large multilingual semantic network.* In Proceedings of the 48th Annual Meeting of the Association for Computational Linguistics, Uppsala, Sweden, 11-16 July 2010. pp: 216-225.

Navigli, R. and Ponzetto, S. (2012) *BabelNet: The Automatic Construction, Evaluation and Application of a Wide-Coverage Multilingual Semantic Network.* , Artificial Intelligence, 193: pp. 217-150.

Sagot, B. and Fier, D. (2010) *Construction d'un wordnet libre du français à partir de ressources multilingues.* In Proceedings of TALN 2008, Avignon, France, 2008.12 p.

Thaler, S., Siorpaes, K., Simperl, E. and Hofer, C. (2011) *A Survey on Games for Knowledge Acquisition.* STI Technical Report, May 2011.19 p.

Vossen, P. (1998) *EuroWordNet: a multilingual database with lexical semantic networks..* Kluwer Academic Publishers.Norwell, MA, USA. 200 p.

Machine Learning for Mention Head Detection in Multilingual Coreference Resolution

Desislava Zhekova
CIS, University of Munich
zhekova@cis.uni-muenchen.de

Sandra Kübler
Indiana University
skuebler@indiana.edu

Abstract

This work introduces a machine learning approach to the identification of mention heads needed for multilingual coreference resolution (MCR). We evaluate the method and compare it to a heuristic baseline and a rule-based approach, which are widely used in coreference resolution systems. We use the CoNLL-2012 shared task data sets, which include data for Arabic, Chinese, and English. We show that for MCR, machine learning offers a competitive, flexible, and robust solution for mention head detection.

1 Introduction

Coreference Resolution (CR) aims to detect all linguistic expressions in a given discourse that refer to real world entities. Such expressions are generally called *mentions*. They need to be grouped into equivalence classes so that each class contains only mentions that refer to the same entity. The classes are called *coreference chains*. The task of CR includes not only the identification of coreference links between mentions, but also the detection of the mentions themselves. This subtask of CR has not been a main topic of interest, since most of the standard data sets for CR contained gold mention information. This situation changed in the most recent shared tasks on the topic of CR: SemEval-2010 Task 1 (Recasens et al., 2010), CoNLL-2011 (Pradhan et al., 2011) and CoNLL-2012 (Pradhan et al., 2012). The data distributed by these tasks included syntactic annotations, and it was considered an integral part of the task for the participating systems to develop their own methods to detect mention boundaries.

Statistical approaches to the CR problem often recast the task to a binary classification exercise. For the latter, coreference is represented by a decision model, such as the mention-pair model (Soon et al., 2001). The mention-pair model, which is the most widely used model for CR, pairs the anaphor with a potential antecedent, and determines whether they are coreferent or not. Since the decisions are taken independently for each possible antecedent, a global heuristic can be used to decide between multiple positive decisions or in cases where no antecedent was found.

The use of the mention-pair model implies that an instance consists of a pair of mentions, and, since vectors for machine learning (ML) need to be of a fixed length, each mention is generally represented by its syntactic head, plus informative features that describe the phrases and their context. As a consequence, there is an additional subtask of CR that needs to be performed before the actual resolution process: *mention head detection* (MHD). This is usually done by the use of simple heuristics or manually defined sets of rules (see section 2). In this work, we will investigate a novel ML method for multilingual MHD.

Multilinguality has presented additional issues to the coreference task, which were discussed and addressed by the two multilingual shared tasks on the topic SemEval-2010 Task 1 and CoNLL-2012. In general, MCR is faced with the same problems as monolingual CR: we have to optimize the 3 main stages in CR, the actual detection of mentions (MD), the detection of the syntactic heads of the latter and classification, based on a selection of features that can represent the phenomena. In our current work, we assume a mention-pair coreference model.

Identifying the head of a phrase is closely related to detecting the grammatical structure of sentences. Thus, the annotation layers provided in the two shared tasks led to the development of successful methods for MD that were mostly based on the underlying syntactic structure of the sentences. To our knowledge most state-of-the-art CR systems have not regarded MHD as a stand-alone subtask of CR, but rather as part of the feature extraction process. Since mentions often correspond to NPs, most approaches use variants of head finding rules, which were made popular by Collins (1999). Such rules are manually written and specify where to find the head for an individual syntactic category.

In this work, we pursue the goal of MCR in the sense that we are developing an architecture that allows CR for multiple languages with only a minimal adaptation to the individual language. This means that we also need a multilingual approach to MHD that does not require the development of head-finding rules for every language to be added to the system. Thus, we introduce a novel method for MHD based on a ML approach, and we compare it to two widely used approaches.

In section 2, we give a short overview of the state of the art, then we present the problems with respect to multilinguality and the head detection problem (section 3). In section 4, we describe the two existing approaches to MHD and propose our own ML method. Section 5 describes the data set and evaluation settings and presents a comparison of the ML approach with respect to the other two approaches. In section 6 we conclude our observations and delineate future directions for this task.

2 Related Work

While there is a bulk of literature on CR for English (Soon et al., 2001; Ng and Cardie, 2002; Ng, 2007, for example), MCR has only been addressed recently. The majority of work in this area was carried out in the context of the two shared tasks, the SemEval-2010 (Recasens et al., 2010) and the CoNLL-2012 (Pradhan et al., 2012) tasks. We focus on MHD for the data from CoNLL-2012.

The majority of the systems participating in the two shared tasks used approaches that were fairly language dependent with respect to MHD. In the context of the CoNLL-2012 task, the systems by Chen and Ng (2012), Martschat et al. (2012), and Uryupina et al. (2012) used manually created sets of rules, based on head-finding models following (Collins, 1999). This means that every language other than English, which is targeted by these systems, would need other, language specific, sets of rules. Björkelund and Farkas (2012) employed Choi and Palmer (2010)'s percolation rules for Arabic and English and the rules of Zhang and Clark (2011) for Chinese. Li et al. (2012) used the head-finding rules from Penn2Malt, for English and for Chinese. The system by Martschat et al. (2012) relies on the Stanford SemanticHeadFinder (also an implementation of the rules by Collins (1999)) for English while the head detection for Chinese is provided by the SunJurafskyChineseHeadFinder (an implementation of the rules presented by Sun and Jurafsky (2004)). Martschat et al. (2012) did not work on CR for Arabic.

Uryupina et al. (2012) created their own heuristic rules for the Arabic and Chinese; for English, they used Collins (1999)'s rules. For Arabic, the first noun/pronoun was selected as head; in Chinese, the last noun/pronoun was chosen as the head. Uryupina et al. (2012) also made the observation that the absence of expert linguistic knowledge can become an important obstacle when rules are to be developed manually for each separate language. Additionally, depending on the language, the collection of such rules may be a rather expensive task.

3 Issues in Multilingual MHD

The concept of a mention is closely related to NPs in syntax. The reason for this relation is that CR at present focuses on entities and often ignores event coreference. As a consequence, finding the head of a mention generally corresponds to identifying the syntactic head of the corresponding NP. The major difference lies in the fact that mentions often correspond to maximal rather than to base NPs.

If we approach the task of finding the mention heads by identifying syntactic heads, the task would be trivial if we had a full syntactic analysis, as provided in X-bar theory (Chomsky, 1970; Jackendoff, 1977) or in *head-driven phrase structure grammar* (Sag et al., 2003; Levine and Meurers, 2006). However, treebanks are generally annotated in a more surface-oriented and flat annotation, in which heads of phrases are often not marked as such. The Penn Treebank (Marcus et al., 1993), which is the standard for training statistical parsers for English, for example, uses a flat annotation scheme for NPs, as shown in the examples in (1). The annotation in the Penn Treebank for English also served as the model for the annotations in the Penn Arabic and Chinese treebanks.

(1) a. [$_{NP}$ The average seven-day compound yield]
  b. [$_{NP}$ [$_{NP}$ the ceiling] [$_{PP}$ on [$_{NP}$ government debt]]]
  c. [$_{NP}$ [$_{NP}$ executives] and [$_{NP}$ their wives]]

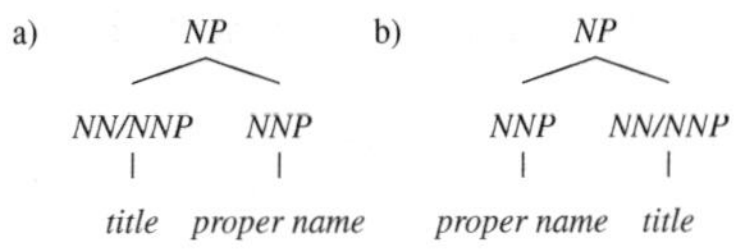

Figure 1: The structure of NPs with titles; with the head in phrase-initial or -final position.

Phrase directionality, which describes the position of the syntactic head in a phase, is fairly regular for most languages, which is mainly why MHD is generally performed via heuristics or language dependent sets of rules. The languages in the CoNLL-2012 shared task represent a good variation of directionalities: Arabic is a consistently head-initial language; Chinese is a consistently head-final language; and English represents a language with mixed directionality since it places specifiers before the head and heavier constituents, such as prepositional phrases or relative clauses, after the syntactic head. Thus, English is the most difficult case: it requires knowledge of the internal structure of the NP in order to correctly identify the head of a higher-order NP, which is non-trivial to capture in a heuristic or in rules.

In the context of the CoNLL-2012 shared task, one simple type of NP that is difficult to capture by heuristics across languages consists of phrases containing a combination of titles, such as *Mr.*, or *Dr.*, and proper names. In all three data sets, proper names are part-of-speech (POS) tagged as NNP, titles can be tagged as either NN or NNP depending on the language: In English, titles are NNP, in Chinese NN, and in Arabic, they are NOUN_PROP in the gold annotations, but the automatically assigned tag is NN. Generally, there are two possibilities where to place titles: either directly before or directly after the proper name, which is visually represented in figure 1. In both cases, the proper name is the head of the full NP. While in Arabic and English, titles are placed before the proper names, in Chinese, they are in phrase-final position. A simple heuristic approach to MHD, using either the first or the last token in the mention, would not capture the proper token as a head of such phrases. For Arabic, for example, as a head-initial language, the heuristic will pick the first token of the phrase to be the head. However, in that position, Arabic places the titles and not the proper names. In contrast, for Chinese, the last token will be selected, but this language places the titles after the names.

Titles and proper names are not the only phrase type that is difficult to be covered by heuristics. Other such types include full person names with the use of given and surname or more complex cases, involving coordinated phrases that need to elicit more than one head. Such complex cases cannot be covered by a simple heuristic, but rather need to be defined via language dependent rules in order to be captured properly across languages. However, as mentioned before, this requires linguistic knowledge of the language in question.

4 Methods for Multilingual MHD

In this section, we discuss 2 baseline methods and our novel ML method.

Heuristic MHD (HeuristicH) Detecting the head of the phrase via a heuristic considers only the predominant language directionality. For example, since Arabic is consistently head-initial, the heuristic will choose the first noun/pronoun to be the head of each NP. For head-final languages, the last noun/pronoun is selected. Since English has a mixed directionality, we treat it as a head-initial language. We are aware that this is not a good fit for English, but we aim at modeling lesser resourced languages with mixed directionality, for which no language specific knowledge is available. We employ the heuristic without improvement as a language independent baseline for which the only knowledge needed is the predominant directionality of the NPs in that language.

Rule-based MHD (RuleH) The rule-based approach uses a set of rules: every set consists of language dependent rules that cover MHD for coordinated phrases and the occurrence of proper names and titles. For English, we include a rule defining the head to be the last noun/pronoun in a sequence of nouns/pronouns, which addresses the problem of nominal premodification. We also restrict the search for the head to words before postmodifier clauses. Our rule set is similar to the one by Collins (1999). However, since we extract heads for mentions rather than for (often nested) phrases, we modified the rules so that they consider context to account for the mixed directionality of English NPs (i.e., the search stops at e.g. prepositions).

Machine Learning for MHD (MLH) Our machine learning method is based on memory-based learning (MBL), which has been shown to have a

#	Feature Description
1	the target token
2	part-of-speech tag of the target token
3	part-of-speech tag of token$_{-1}$
4	part-of-speech tag of token$_{+1}$
5	Y if it is the only token in the mention; else N
6	Y if it is not in a PP, SBAR, VP, S; else N
7	Y if it is the first token in the mention; else N
8	Y if it is the last token in the mention; else N
9	Y if the target token is a noun
10	Y if the target token is a pronoun
11	Y if the target token is a noun or a pronoun
12	Y if the target token is followed by a noun
13	Y if the target token is followed by a pronoun
14	Y if the following token is possessive and the last token in the mention

Table 1: The 14 features for the MLH classifier.

good bias for a variation of NLP problems (Daelemans and van den Bosch, 2005), more specifically TiMBL (Daelemans et al., 2010), an efficient implementation of the k-nearest neighbor (k-NN) approach. MBL classifies a new instance based on the k closest examples from the training set. If the k nearest examples are distributed over different classes, the majority of the set is used. We do not perform parameter optimization.

In the current task of MHD, we create an instance for every word in a mention, and decide for this word whether it is the head of the mention or not. As mentions we select the set of *gold* mentions provided by the task. Since mention head information is not provided in standard data distributions and was not included in the CoNLL-2012 data, we manually annotated a small data set.

In order to create the training/test data sets, all mentions from the training data are extracted, and each of the tokens for each of the mentions is represented as a feature vector containing information about the context of the given token in the current mention. As features, we collect 14 language independent values, listed in table 1. The features are extracted from the POS annotation layer.

One problem that is not handled by the MLH approach is that the tokens are classified individually, i.e., it is possible that more than one token is classified as the head. However, mentions that do not contain coordinating conjunctions should be assigned exactly one head. Correspondingly, the existence or type of the coordinating conjunction could be used in order to restrict the output of the classifier, which can be also regulated via a weighted classification procedure. In our work, we did not postprocess the output of the classifier, i.e., the output may contain multiple heads per mention.

5 Mention Head Detection Experiments

The evaluation of MHD is not a trivial task, since as noted before, mention heads are not included in standard linguistic annotation layers. It is also not part of the evaluation software provided by the shared tasks.

First, in section 5.1, we describe the data set and the experimental setup, including the CR system that we use. Then, we perform two different types of evaluation: In section 5.2, we assess the performance of the three MHD methods on the manually annotated data sets in an intrinsic evaluation, without integrating them into the full CR pipeline. And in section 5.3, we perform an extrinsic evaluation by using each of the three methods in an MCR system and compare the CR performance achieved by the approaches.

5.1 Data Set and Experimental Setup

For the following experiments, we used the CoNLL-2012 training and test data sets. In order to be able to assemble training data for the ML approach, we manually annotated a subset of the data for each of the three languages in the task. The data for Arabic includes an excerpt of 42 documents for training and 8 for testing. For English, we consider 100 documents for training and 20 documents for testing. Finally, for Chinese, 84 documents are annotated as a training set, and 16 are used as a test set. Note that Arabic has a significantly lower number of annotated documents, which is not only the result of its smaller data sets, but rather a consequence of the fact that Arabic has a highly NP-rich syntactic structure, which accounts for substantially more training instances per document than for English and Chinese. The annotations for English were performed by the first author, the ones for Chinese and Arabic by linguistically educated native speakers. The mentions used for the experiments are *gold* mentions, thus only coreferent mentions. Overall, the number of instances extracted are similar across all three languages. On average, the annotation of the data set required approximately two person-days per language.

For the intrinsic evaluation in section 5.2, we calculate precision, recall, and F_1-score. For the extrinsic evaluation in section 5.3, we asess the results in the full pipeline of a MCR system. We use the UBIU architecture (Zhekova and Kübler, 2010). UBIU is based on the mention-pair model

language	metric	HeuristicH	RuleH	MLH
AR	R	0.79	0.83	**0.85**
excerpt	P	0.87	0.88	**0.91**
	F_1	0.83	0.85	**0.88**
EN	R	0.65	**0.92**	0.87
excerpt	P	0.70	0.97	**0.98**
	F_1	0.67	**0.95**	0.92
ZH	R	0.84	0.96	**0.97**
excerpt	P	0.98	0.98	**0.99**
	F_1	0.90	0.97	**0.98**

Table 2: MHD for excerpt data for all languages, Arabic (AR), English (EN), and Chinese (ZH), for all spans of mentions.

and uses TiMBL for classification. Since we are more interested in the effects of the MHD methods on the full CR system rather than in the optimal performance that can be achieved by UBIU, we do not aim at language dependent system optimization on any system component. We use the official CoNLL-2012 scorer, which provides five evaluation metrics: MUC (Vilain et al., 1995), B^3 (Bagga and Baldwin, 1998), the two variants of CEAF (Luo, 2005), $CEAF_E$ and $CEAF_M$, and BLANC (Recasens and Hovy, 2011). For comparison, we calculate a TOTAL score as the average of the F-score of all metrics.

5.2 Intrinsic Evaluation

The results in table 2 show an interesting outcome: HeuristicH, which requires only minimal language specific knowledge, leads to the lowest performance across all three languages, with an F-score of 0.83 for Arabic, 0.90 for Chinese, and 0.67 for English. This outcome shows that for Arabic and Chinese, we reach a very competitive performance with a rather simple heuristic. Remember that both Arabic and Chinese have a clearly unidirectional NP structure. For English, however, with its mixed directionality in NPs, the results are far below the results for the other two languages, with a difference of 23 percent points between Chinese and English. This difference is a direct consequence of the various issues specific to English that we introduced in section 3, such as nominal premodification. Therefore, HeuristicH should only be used when it is known that a language is unidirectional. Even in such cases, we cannot expect a high performance in every case.

The rule-based approach partially addresses the shortcomings of the HeuristicH baseline. It achieves an F-score of 0.85 for Arabic, 0.95 for English, and 0.97 for Chinese. This shows that we can reach very reliable results for English and Chinese; especially for English, which shows an improvement by 28 percent points, from an F-score of 0.67 to 0.95. For Arabic, however, the gain from the heuristic to the rule-based approach is minimal: it only gains 2 percent points, and it is far from reaching 90%.

The results for MLH show that this method is highly competitive: For Arabic (with an F-score of 0.88) and Chinese (with an F-score of 0.98), the ML approach reaches the best performance on the task. For English, the overall performance is 0.92, which is only 3 percent points lower than for the rule-based variant. Moreover, the scores for this language show that RuleH reaches a higher recall while precision is better for MLH. Part of the low recall for English may be due to the fact that the training set is restricted in size, which is detrimental for English since there the task is more difficult because of the mixed directionality in NPs.

Note also that overall, for all languages, precision is always higher than recall, which allows the conclusion that our simplistic approach in the ML method, allowing more than one head, does not harm the method's performance. Overall, we can conclude that the MLH approach is capable of learning the different directionalities, and it is highly competitive, especially given that it is a language independent method that can be employed for any language for which POS information is provided, given a small annotated data set.

5.3 Extrinsic Evaluation

For the extrinsic evaluation, we integrate all methods for MHD into the complete MCR pipeline. This shows whether the MHD methods have an effect on CR. The results are listed in table 3. As upper bound, we use *gold standard* heads. The results show the same trends as in our intrinsic evaluation: HeutisticH consistently reaches the lowest scores across all languages, with TOTAL scores as follows: Arabic: 30.54, English: 40.10 and Chinese: 37.53.

RuleH again achieves higher scores in comparison to the heuristic across all languages. This again confirms our observations that HeuristicH is not a good fit for a multilingual environment. RuleH reaches a TOTAL score of 31.74 for Arabic, 48.40 for English and 48.21 for Chinese. This leads altogether to the best observed performance for the English language. However, for Arabic and Chinese, MLH once more performs best with

		AR			EN			ZH		
		R	P	F_1	R	P	F_1	R	P	F_1
HeuristicH	MD	4.85	43.05	8.72	42.18	51.39	46.33	58.73	40.43	47.89
	MUC	1.70	18.18	3.11	24.31	28.87	26.39	42.29	30.33	35.32
	B^3	31.82	94.60	47.63	52.29	62.17	56.81	61.54	45.82	52.53
	$CEAF_M$	29.11	29.11	29.11	34.96	34.96	34.96	28.78	28.78	28.78
	$CEAF_E$	49.33	16.36	24.58	32.06	27.16	29.41	15.92	24.02	19.15
	BLANC	50.05	51.54	48.25	52.60	53.66	52.94	52.09	51.79	51.89
	TOTAL			30.54			40.10			37.53
RuleH	MD	7.35	48.95	12.78	57.09	57.57	57.33	71.80	65.37	68.44
	MUC	3.41	27.11	6.06	43.80	42.30	43.03	59.31	58.90	59.10
	B^3	33.10	93.43	48.88	61.49	59.08	60.26	51.39	62.79	56.52
	$CEAF_M$	29.79	29.79	29.79	42.55	42.55	42.55	40.59	40.59	40.59
	$CEAF_E$	49.04	17.07	25.32	32.90	34.24	33.56	24.83	25.16	25.00
	BLANC	50.22	54.74	48.66	63.94	61.59	62.61	58.93	68.44	59.83
	TOTAL			31.74			**48.40**			48.21
MLH	MD	8.76	61.53	15.34	56.97	58.59	57.76	72.12	65.37	68.58
	MUC	4.05	35.18	7.26	42.51	42.10	42.30	59.54	58.90	59.22
	B^3	31.90	94.26	47.66	59.05	59.56	59.30	51.57	62.67	56.58
	$CEAF_M$	30.41	30.41	30.41	41.38	41.38	41.38	40.65	40.65	40.65
	$CEAF_E$	52.28	17.28	25.98	33.40	33.77	33.58	24.78	25.29	25.03
	BLANC	50.37	60.43	48.83	59.09	59.44	59.26	58.92	68.38	59.81
	TOTAL			**32.03**			47.16			**48.26**
gold heads	MD	13.30	51.51	21.14	57.09	58.49	57.78	71.66	65.94	68.68
	MUC	4.69	20.18	7.61	42.83	42.28	42.56	58.61	58.90	58.76
	B^3	36.24	87.14	51.19	59.40	59.54	59.47	49.33	62.52	55.15
	$CEAF_M$	30.87	30.87	30.87	41.65	41.65	41.65	39.37	39.37	39.37
	$CEAF_E$	46.06	18.87	26.77	33.48	33.97	33.72	24.77	24.54	24.60
	BLANC	50.26	52.50	49.09	59.28	59.50	59.38	58.08	67.40	58.51
	TOTAL			33.11			47.36			47.28

Table 3: MHD performance of HeuristicH, RuleH and MLH compared to the use of *gold* heads.

32.03 for Arabic and 48.26 for Chinese. For English, RuleH is marginally better than the MLH approach. This mirrors the performance of both methods in the intrinsic evaluation. Moreover, the performance of the system when given gold mention heads for this language is 47.36, which is only 0.2 percent points higher than MLH's performance. This shows that the latter approach already achieves a close to optimal performance.

The results of this experiment show that improvements in MHD translate directly into improvements of the overall CR system. Since the ML approach outperforms the rule-based approach for two languages, we can conclude that MLH is highly competitive for MHD in a MCR context, as it is language independent in that it does not require any language specific knowledge or annotation layers, apart from POS information and a small data set annotated for heads. Note also that the RuleH total scores for English and Chinese as well as the MLH total score for Chinese are higher than the respective values given *gold standard* heads. This is due to an increased recall across the different metrics.

6 Conclusion and Future Work

We propose a machine learning approach to mention head detection in the context of multilingual coreference resolution. We conducted an in-depth intrinsic and extrinsic evaluation of the method and compared it to a heuristic and a language dependent rule-based approach, generally used in CR systems. Our results show that the ML approach is language independent, given a small annotated set, and that it performs competitively in a multilingual setting.

The proposed ML method for MHD includes a basic set of language independent features. Like any ML approach, features are very important to the overall performance of the learner. For this reason, one very promising direction of further investigation is the thorough evaluation and extension of the feature set used for classification. In order to keep the language independent nature of MLH, only language independent features should be added to the current set of 14 values.

As discussed in section 4, the MLH approach does not control the number of heads allowed per mention. Thus, a possible improvement of this method can be achieved by an additional restriction on the number of heads allowed per phrase that is bound by the type of NP and the existence of coordinating conjunctions used in the phrase.

Acknowledgments

We are grateful to the organizers of the shared task for providing the data sets and to Marwa Ragheb and Yuyin Hsu for the the mention head annotations in Arabic and Chinese.

References

Amit Bagga and Breck Baldwin. 1998. Algorithms for scoring coreference chains. In *Proceedings of the LREC Workshop on Linguistic Coreference*, Granada, Spain.

Anders Björkelund and Richárd Farkas. 2012. Data-driven multilingual coreference resolution using resolver stacking. In *Joint Conference on EMNLP and CoNLL-Shared Task*, pages 49–55, Jeju, Korea.

Chen Chen and Vincent Ng. 2012. Combining the best of two worlds: A hybrid approach to multilingual coreference resolution. In *Joint Conference on EMNLP and CoNLL-Shared Task*, pages 56–63, Jeju, Korea.

Jinho D. Choi and Martha Palmer. 2010. Robust constituent-to-dependency conversion for English. In *Proceedings of the Ninth International Workshop on Treebanks and Linguistic Theories (TLT)*, pages 55–66, Tartu, Estonia.

Noam Chomsky. 1970. Remarks on nominalization. In R. Jacobs and P. Rosenbaum, editors, *Reading in English Transformational Grammar*, pages 184–221. Ginn and Co., Waltham.

Michael Collins. 1999. *Head-Driven Statistical Models for Natural Language Parsing*. Ph.D. thesis, University of Pennsylvania, Philadelphia, PA, USA.

Walter Daelemans and Antal van den Bosch. 2005. *Memory Based Language Processing*. Cambridge University Press, Cambridge, UK.

Walter Daelemans, Jakub Zavrel, Ko van der Sloot, and Antal van den Bosch. 2010. TiMBL: Tilburg Memory Based Learner, version 6.3, reference guide. Technical Report ILK 10-01, Induction of Linguistic Knowledge, Computational Linguistics, Tilburg University.

Ray Jackendoff. 1977. *X-Bar Syntax: A Study of Phrase Structure*. MIT Press, Cambridge.

Robert D. Levine and W. Detmar Meurers. 2006. Head-driven phrase structure grammar: Linguistic approach, formal foundations, and computational realization. In Keith Brown, editor, *Encyclopedia of Language and Linguistics*. Elsevier, 2nd ed. edition.

Xinxin Li, Xuan Wang, and Xingwei Liao. 2012. Simple maximum entropy models for multilingual coreference resolution. In *Joint Conference on EMNLP and CoNLL-Shared Task*, pages 83–87, Jeju, Korea.

Xiaoqiang Luo. 2005. On coreference resolution performance metrics. In *HLT '05: Proceedings of the Conference on Human Language Technology and Empirical Methods in Natural Language Processing*, pages 25–32, Vancouver, Canada.

Mitchell Marcus, Beatrice Santorini, and Mary Ann Marcinkiewicz. 1993. Building a large annotated corpus of English: The Penn Treebank. *Computational Linguistics*, 19(2):313–330.

Sebastian Martschat, Jie Cai, Samuel Broscheit, Éva Mújdricza-Maydt, and Michael Strube. 2012. A multigraph model for coreference resolution. In *Joint Conference on EMNLP and CoNLL-Shared Task*, pages 100–106, Jeju, Korea.

Vincent Ng and Claire Cardie. 2002. Improving machine learning approaches to coreference resolution. In *Proceedings of the 40th Annual Meeting of the Association for Computational Linguistics*, pages 104–111, Philadelphia, PA.

Vincent Ng. 2007. Shallow semantics for coreference resolution. In *Proceedings of the 20th International Conference on Artificial Intelligence (IJCAI'07)*, Hyderabad, India.

Sameer Pradhan, Lance Ramshaw, Mitchell Marcus, Martha Palmer, Ralph Weischedel, and Nianwen Xue. 2011. CoNLL-2011 shared task: Modeling unrestricted coreference in OntoNotes. In *Proceedings of the Fifteenth Conference on Computational Natural Language Learning (CoNLL): Shared Task*, pages 1–27, Portland, OR.

Sameer Pradhan, Alessandro Moschitti, Nianwen Xue, Olga Uryupina, and Yuchen Zhang. 2012. CoNLL-2012 shared task: Modeling multilingual unrestricted coreference in OntoNotes. In *Joint Conference on EMNLP and CoNLL-Shared Task*, pages 1–40, Jeju, Korea.

Altaf Rahman and Vincent Ng. 2009. Supervised models for coreference resolution. In *Proceedings of EMNLP 2009*, pages 968–977, Singapore.

Marta Recasens and Eduard Hovy. 2011. BLANC: Implementing the Rand Index for Coreference Evaluation. *NLE*, 17(4):485–510.

Marta Recasens, Lluís Màrquez, Emili Sapena, M. Antònia Martí, Mariona Taulé, Véronique Hoste, Massimo Poesio, and Yannick Versley. 2010. Semeval-2010 task 1: Coreference resolution in multiple languages. In *Proceedings of the 5th International Workshop on Semantic Evaluation*, pages 1–8, Uppsala, Sweden.

Ivan A. Sag, Thomas Wasow, and Emily M. Bender. 2003. *Syntactic Theory: A Formal Introduction*. CSLI Publications, Stanford, 2 edition.

Wee Meng Soon, Hwee Tou Ng, and Daniel Chung Yong Lim. 2001. A machine learning approach to coreference resolution of noun phrases. *Computational Linguistics*, 27(4):521–544.

Honglin Sun and Daniel Jurafsky. 2004. Shallow Semantic Parsing of Chinese. In *North American Chapter of the ACL: Human Language Technologies (NAACL-HLT)*, pages 249–256, Boston, MA.

Olga Uryupina, Alessandro Moschitti, and Massimo Poesio. 2012. BART goes multilingual: The UniTN / Essex submission to the CoNLL-2012 shared task. In *Joint Conference on EMNLP and CoNLL-Shared Task*, pages 122–128, Jeju, Korea.

Marc Vilain, John Burger, John Aberdeen, Dennis Connolly, and Lynette Hirschman. 1995. A Model-Theoretic Coreference Scoring Scheme. In *Proceedings of the 6th Message Understanding Conference*, Columbia, MD.

Yue Zhang and Stephen Clark. 2011. Syntactic Processing Using the Generalized Perceptron and Beam Search. *Computational Linguistics*, 37(1):105–151.

Desislava Zhekova and Sandra Kübler. 2010. UBIU: A language-independent system for coreference resolution. In *Proceedings of the 5th International Workshop on Semantic Evaluation*, pages 96–99, Uppsala, Sweden.

Combining POS Tagging, Dependency Parsing and Co-referential Resolution for Bulgarian

Valentin Zhikov and Georgi Georgiev
Ontotext AD
Sofia, Bulgaria
valentin.zhikov@ontotext.com
georgiev@ontotext.com

Kiril Simov and Petya Osenova
Linguistic Modelling Department
IICT-BAS, Sofia, Bulgaria
kivs@bultreebank.org
petya@bultreebank.org

Abstract

This paper proposes a combined model for POS tagging, dependency parsing and co-reference resolution for Bulgarian — a pro-drop Slavic language with rich morphosyntax. We formulate an extension of the MSTParser algorithm that allows the simultaneous handling of the three tasks in a way that makes it possible for each task to benefit from the information available to the others, and conduct a set of experiments against a treebank of the Bulgarian language. The results indicate that the proposed joint model achieves state-of-the-art performance for POS tagging task, and outperforms the current pipeline solution.

1 Introduction

Advanced language technology applications depend on various forms of preprocessing, such as POS tagging, parsing, co-reference resolution, word sense disambiguation, etc. Although in ideal settings these tasks have satisfactory solutions on their own, their combination in a pipeline is related to a significant decrease in accuracy at each consequent stage of analysis. Recently, models that enable the single-step handling of multiple tasks have gained popularity, as they improve on the performance achieved by pipeline approaches. They take advantage of the interaction among the various levels of linguistic knowledge. Here we propose a model that challenges three tasks simultaneously: POS tagging, dependency parsing and co-reference resolution (within a sentence). The experiments are performed on data from the Bulgarian HPSG-based treebank — BulTreeBank. Our motivation to attempt solving these particular problems via a single model is many-fold: (1) avoiding the accumulation of errors inherent to pipeline processing, (2) overcoming the low speed of model-chaining approaches, (3) confirming the success of previous developments in joint modeling; and last but not least, (4) assessing the benefits of modeling the interactions that exist among morphology, syntax and discourse.

Pipeline approaches follow a sequence of processing that reflects the traditional levels of analysis within linguistics: syntax depends on morphology; co-reference resolution depends on morphology and syntax. Thus, dependency arcs are determined by the grammatical features of the wordforms; co-reference chains depend on the grammatical features of wordforms and the configuration of the dependency arcs. Unfortunately, this style of processing does not necessarily lead to optimal results. One should keep in mind that some alternative interaction paths and interdependencies exist among the linguistic levels, and this interdependence can be accounted for in order to achieve a better solution for each task. Two phenomena in Bulgarian that illustrate this statement are: (1) co-reference links between dative verbal clitics and nouns (within a prepositional phrase, expressing the indirect object of the same verb) have common number and gender features; (2) unexpressed subjects participate in co-reference chains of control, binding, etc. constructions. We propose a model capable of handling such interactions among the different linguistic levels. We define an extended dependency tree that incorporates service nodes and links, through which additional knowledge, such as POS tag candidates, correct POS tags and co-reference relations, can be fed into the MST-Parser algorithm for non-projective dependency parsing (McDonald et al., 2005). The sentences in the treebank are projected as extended dependency trees, and the parser is applied to their new representation. Although the proposed model addresses the Bulgarian language, it is also applicable to other languages, provided that all necessary resources are available.

The structure of this paper is as follows: in Section 2, we introduce related work; in Section 3, we discuss the relevant annotations available in the Bulgarian treebank; Section 4 presents the proposed approach for joint modeling, Section 5 elaborates on our experimental settings and the obtained results; Section 6 concludes the paper.

2 Related work

We are not aware of other studies that propose joint models for Bulgarian, and to the best of our knowledge, attemps at combining the three tasks (POS tagging, dependency parsing and co-reference resolution) in a joint model have not been described in the literature either.

Our approach is inspired by works such as (Finkel and Manning, 2010), (Bohnet and Nivre, 2012) and (Qian and Liu, 2012). Finkel and Manning (2010) report on combining NER and parsing tasks in a joint model. One similarity with our task is the understanding that the separate tasks can help each other in various not-always-subsequent executions. Another one is the fact that the explored algorithm is extended. The difference is that the authors rely on a feature-rich CRF parser, while our algorithm is based on an online large-margin learning algorithm.

Bohnet and Nivre (2012) studies the combination of two tasks (POS tagging and Dependency labeled non-projective parsing) against datasets in four languages, and the reported results indicate an improvement over the pipeline-generated output for all considered languages. The algorithm behind their architecture is transition-based.

The reported results indicate that combining POS tagging and dependency parsing could be a successful step not only for morphologically rich languages (such as Czech and German), but also for languages where POS ambiguities are abundant (such as Chinese). This work illustrates the superiority of joint models in settings rather similar to our own. The authors added features for improving the POS tagging task within the combined model. We also followed this strategy.

Our work differs in the choice of an algorithm (Maximum Spanning Tree Model), and in the greater number of problems tackled by the proposed model. The motivation for choosing the approach of the MSTParser is that two of the tasks that we handle can be non-local, and the algorithm may require information from distant nodes in order to find an appropriate solution. Therefore, a straight adaptation of the transition-based model is not possible.

Qian and Liu (2012) focuses on the modelling of three tasks for Chinese - word segmentation, POS tagging and parsing. The models for each task are trained separately, while the unification of predictions is performed during the decoding phase. As in the previous paper, the authors report improvements over the pipeline results for Chinese. The similarity is that our approach also considers three tasks in one model for one language with a modified algorithm.

Our approach differs in the following aspects: the third task is not identical. In our case it is the addition of co-reference chains instead of the specific for Chinese word segmentation module. Bulgarian is a morphologically rich language in comparison to Chinese - hence, the POS tagging model is more complex. The parsing task uses dependencies instead of the CFGs used in the case of the Chinese parser. Our model does not train the tasks separately, with specific models, before combining them, and the joint model is used during the development and exploitation of the proposed parser. Our aim is to combine 3 closely related tasks, which have not been addressed widely in NLP, and to evaluate their impact on the processing of Bulgarian. The complexity of the joint task is high not only due to the number of modules incorporated in the model, but also to the morphosyntactical richness of the language addressed in our work.

Below we describe our dataset, before we continue discussing the algorithm that handles the joint modeling task.

3 The Linguistic Annotation of the Bulgarian Treebank (BulTreeBank)

BulTreeBank provides rich linguistic information that goes beyond syntactic annotation. It comprises the full grammatical tags, lemmas for all wordforms, syntactic relations (HPSG), named entities, as well as co-references within each sentence. Since parts of speech, syntactic and co-reference relations have been incorporated in our joint modeling effort, we will outline the specifics of their annotation within the dataset.

As we have already mentioned, Bulgarian is a morphologically rich language. Morphological richness has many varieties from a typological point of view. Bulgarian has a very rich verb system, and it is an inflective language, whose complete part of speech tagset comprises about 680 tags[1]. As this circumstance causes sparseness and increases the modeling complexity, we opt in for filtering the input with the aid of a rich morphological lexicon and morphological guessers. Besides the original HPSG-based corpus, there is a dependency version of BulTreeBank, derived from the original dataset. More details regarding the types of dependency relations available in it are enlisted at http://www.bultreebank.org/dpbtb/.

In Figure 1, an HPSG-based tree of the sentence "Vednaga odobri namerenieto na sestra si" ('Immediately approved intention of sister his', He approved his sister's intention immediately) is shown. This example illustrates the way in which the HPSG-based version of the dataset encodes dependency information (the "NPA" tag stands for nominal phrases of type head-adjunct). Another noteworthy detail is the co-reference link between the un-expressed subject and the reflexive possessive pronoun. In the HPSG-based version of the treebank, the unexpressed subject is represented explicitly only in cases when it participates in a co-reference chain, as shown in the sample sentence. It is considered to be a property of the verb node, and not part of the constituent structure.

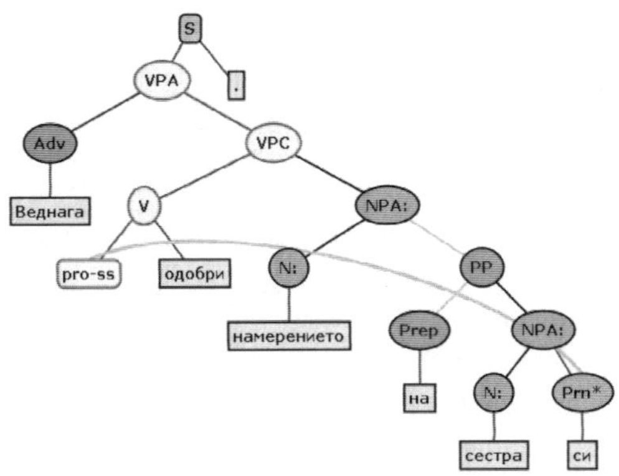

Figure 1. HPSG-based tree.

Figure 2 provides a view on the same sentence after its conversion to dependency format. The head-adjunct relation found within the lowest NPA in the tree has been projected into a head-modifier relation. Co-reference arcs have not been transferred into the dependency version of the treebank used within the CoNLL 2006 shared task. We have added them specially for the modeling effort reported in this paper. Here, co-references are represented as secondary edges connecting the word nodes, and arc labels are represented as ovals situated between the connected word pairs.

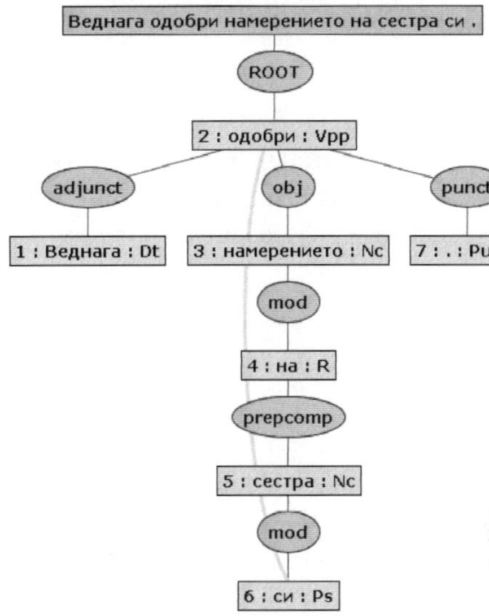

Figure 2. Dependency tree.

The annotation of BulTreeBank complies with the definition of co-reference resolution as the identification of expressions that reference a common discourse entity (Recasens et al., 2010). From a semantic perspective, co-references include three types of relations: "equality", "member-of" and "subset-of". Reflected linguistic phenomena include: pro-dropness (when co-referentially bound), subject and object control, secondary predication, binding, and nominalizations. Co-references are found in the following set of dependency relations: coordination, subordination, complementation, adjunction and modification. The annotated co-reference chains within the treebank amount to 5,312. On average every third sentence contains at least one co-reference chain. Thus, the impact of the co-references within Bulgarian grammar is clearly indicated.

4 Maximum Spanning Tree Model of the Joint Task

4.1 Extended dependency tree model

In this section we introduce a method for incorporating part-of-speech and co-reference tags into the tree-representation of a sentence. This transformation enables the direct application of the maximum spanning tree non-projective parser developed by McDonald et al. (2005). We define the

[1] http://www.bultreebank.org/TechRep/BTB-TR03.pdf

#	System	POS	Co-reference			Dependency		
		Accuracy (%)	Prec (%)	Recall (%)	F	LAS (%)	UAS (%)	LA (%)
1	features&morph	95.99	80.90	33.08	46.96	81.22	85.12	88.96
2	features&decomp. morph*	95.52	81.04	32.08	45.96	80.50	84.55	88.59
3	1&word context	95.95	80.97	33.23	47.12	81.42	85.35	88.95
4	3&distances	95.98	82.03	37.06	**51.05**	81.82	85.70	89.32
5	4&context-bigrams	97.12	81.77	35.38	49.39	82.29	86.19	89.65
6	5&additional conjunctions	**97.13**	81.16	34.30	48.22	**82.39**	86.17	89.64

Table 1: Evaluation results on the test dataset.
Labeled Arc Score (LAS): Accuracy computed over both correctly connected and properly labeled arcs.
Unlabeled Arc Score (UAS): Accuracy computed over correctly connected arcs.
Label Accuracy (LA): Accuracy computed over correctly labeled arcs.
Prec(ision), Recall, F: Correspond to the standard F1 metric and its components.

analysis of a sentence as a tree that includes some new types of service nodes in addition to the nodes that represent words. Service nodes connect to either words or other service nodes, in accordance with a set of rules that we describe in detail in 4.2.

Let us have a set G of POS tags, and a set D of dependency tags ($ROOT \in D$). Let us have a sentence $x = w_1, ..., w_n$. A *tagged dependency graph with co-reference relations* is a directed tree $T = (V, A, \pi, \delta, C)$ where:

1. $V = \{0, 1, ..., n\}$ is an ordered set of nodes, that corresponds to an enumeration of the words in the sentence (the root of the tree has index 0);
2. $A \subseteq V \times V$ is a set of arcs;
3. $\pi : V \to G$ is a partial labeling function from nodes to POS tags;
4. $\delta : A \to D$ is a labeling function for arcs;
5. 0 is the root of the tree
6. $C \subseteq V \setminus \{0\} \times V \setminus \{0\}$ is a set of undirected arcs representing the co-reference equality relation over the nodes of the dependency tree;

We will hereafter refer to this structure as a parse graph for the sentence x. Figure 2 illustrates one such parse graph.

As a first step of extending the tree, we assume a range of possible POS tags for each wordform in the sentence. Such a range of tags has to contain the correct tag for the wordform in the given context. The straightforward solution of assigning all the tags available in the tagset to each wordform makes the subsequent task of obtaining the correct tag infeasible, due to the great number of tags available in BulTreeBank. In order to deal with this issue, we incorporate an inflectional lexicon (including a substantial set of entity names), which provides all possible tags for the wordforms available in it. Furthermore, we enable the handling of unknown words by applying a morphological guesser that suggests up to ten possible tags per wordform. Thus, we use the described components to yield a highly accurate and compact set of candidate POS tags.

These tags are included in the tree as service nodes. In the linear representation of the sentence, they are inserted after the node for the corresponding wordform, and before the node for the next wordform to the right. They are connected to the corresponding wordform with a special link $TAG.

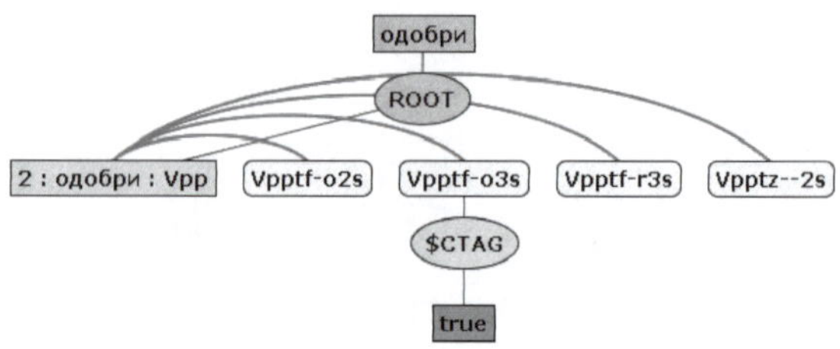

Figure 3. Subtree of the candidate POS tags and the correct tag for one word.

In order to indicate the correct tag, we introduce another type of service node. In the linear representation of the sentence, it is inserted after the last POS tag candidate node, and before the one corresponding to the next wordform to the right. This node is connected to the correct tag via a special arc $CTAG (correct tag). In this way, all information about the potential tags and the correct tag is represented in the form of a subtree, attached to the wordform. Figure 3 depicts the encoding of a word with POS tag ambiguity. The correct tag is indicated: verb, personal, perfective, transitive, finite, aorist, third person, singular. The $TAG arcs are represented as red links without labels. The $CTAG arc is represented as an oval.

The next problem is representing the co-referencial relations via the dependency tree. In order to do this, we introduce yet another type of service node, denoted as $CR. Such nodes are inserted on the right side of the corresponding wordform node, and to the left of the first POS-tag candidate node in the linear representation of the sentence. We classify these nodes into two groups. The first group consists of nodes, attached to wordforms that do not participate in a co-reference relation with another wordform that precedes them in the sentence. These $CR nodes are linked to their wordform with an arc labeled $DI (discourse index), which might be linked to an entity in thc discourse.

Figure 4. Representation of co-references as tree fragments.

The second group of $CR nodes are those participating in a co-reference relation between their corresponding wordform and another wordform that precedes them in the sentence. We say that such nodes share a discourse index with a word preceding them in the sentence, and assign the $SDI label to the arcs that interconnect such pairs service nodes. The nodes in the second group are not connected to their corresponding wordform nodes, but are instead connected to the co-reference nodes of the referenced entities. This approach allows us to represent the co-reference relations as supplementary tree fragments, attached to the original tree. Figure 4 presents an example of a sentence tree that contains both kinds of co-reference nodes and the means through which they are connected to the graph.

$DI arcs are depicted as dark blue links. In cases where a word participates in a co-reference chain with a word that precedes it, there is no link between the word and it's $CR node. Instead, its $CR node is connected to the $CR node of the first word in the co-reference chain. Such arcs ($SDI) are depicted as light blue links.

Applying the described transformations allows us to obtain a tree representation of a tagged dependency graph that includes co-reference relations.

4.2 Constraining the edge generation mechanism of the MSTParser

Inference on the complex graph structures output by the proposed sentence representation technique leads to a significant computational overhead, given the specifics of the original MST algorithm that generates edges among all nodes in the graph. In order to reduce the feature space and simplify the learning task, we take advantage of the circumstance that service node connectivity is subject to a set of rules, and we eliminate edges that do not conform to these rules by modifying the feature-generation mechanism of the MSTParser.

To this end, we assign empty feature vectors to the dependency arcs that do not comply with either of the following preconditions: (i) root nodes can only be linked to word nodes; (ii) word nodes can only be linked to their corresponding co-reference ($CR) and POS candidate ($TAG) nodes, other word nodes, or root nodes; (iii) co-reference ($CR) nodes can only be linked to their corresponding wordform nodes (via a $DI arc), or to the co-reference nodes of wordforms preceding them in the sentence (via a $SDI arc); (iv) POS-candidate ($TAG) nodes can be linked to their corresponding word node, and to the node that denotes the true POS tag ($CTAG); and (v) node denoting true POS tags ($CTAG) can only be linked to one of the POS candidate nodes ($TAG) of the corresponding wordform.

Additionally, we introduce a set of linguistic rules to further reduce the number of co-reference arcs. Given a list of parts of speech that cannot take part in co-reference relations, and the set of candidate POS tags for a pair of wordforms, we assign empty feature vectors to the edges that connect the co-reference nodes of the two words, when it is clear that they cannot be involved in a co-reference relation. In order to do so, we inspect the candidate tag set of each node, and check whether all of its candidate tags belong to either of the following part-of-speech classes (regular expressions that cover all tag variations available within BulTreeBank are provided in the brackets that follow the names of the individual classes): (1) particles ("T.*"); (2) adverbs ("D.*"); (3) interjections ("I"); (4) prepositions ("R"); (5) impersonal verbs ("Vn.*); (6) conjunctions ("C.*"); (7) punctuation ("punct"); (8) gerunds ("V.*g").

4.3 Features incorporated in the joint model

In this section, we outline the set of features available to the algorithm during our joint modeling effort. Feature vectors are extracted on a per-edge basis, by applying a common set of rules over each pair of nodes that remains after the filtering step described earlier.

We use a feature naming convention that allows the classifier to discern six groups of features on the basis of the types of the interconnected nodes, i.e. different weights are learned for edges that connect different types of nodes. In this way, our model is aware of sets of features that correspond to the following dependency arc types: (i) word → sentence root; (ii) word → word; (iii) co-reference → word ($SDI); (iv) co-reference → co-reference ($DI); (v) POS candidate → word; (vi) correct POS node → candidate POS node. Furthermore, the features reflect the individual characteristics of the head and dependent nodes in each of these types of pairs. We provide details regarding each subset of features below.

Attachment distance is computed for each pair of interconnected nodes. Our algorithm provides two alternative modes for calculating the attachment distance - one that accounts for the presence of service nodes among the words, and one that ignores such nodes. The obtained attachment distance undergoes additional discretization before it is assigned as a feature, but we omit the details regarding the concrete discretization routine due to space limitations.

In the below description, the term "context features" is introduced as a convenient means of referencing the characteristics of a group of ordered word nodes: the node corresponding to a word at a given sentence position, and the nearest two word nodes to its left and right (i.e., context windows always span over 3 adjacent word nodes).

The complete list of features for each edge type follows:

1. Word → sentence root: attachment distance; node types; POS tag candidates (word nodes only); context word strings (word nodes only); conjunctions between: (i) the attachment distance feature and the node type and candidate POS tag features; (ii) the word node's string and its corresponding POS tag candidates; (iii) the POS-tag candidates in the word's context window.

2. Word → word: attachment distance; node types; POS tag candidates; context word strings (head and dependent are modeled separately); conjunctions between: (i) the attachment distance feature and the node type and candidate POS tag features; (ii) the head and dependent nodes' word forms; (iii) the candidate POS tags of the head and dependent nodes and their context; (iv) the context words of the head and dependent nodes; (v) the word strings and the POS tag candidates of the head and dependent nodes.

3. Co-reference → word: node types; word string; POS-tag candidates for the corresponding word form.

4. Co-reference → co-reference: attachment distance; node types; POS tag candidates; context word strings (head and dependent are modeled separately); conjunctions between: (i) the attachment distance feature and the node type and candidate POS tag features; (ii) the head and dependent nodes' word forms; (iii) the candidate POS tags of the head and dependent nodes and their context; (iv) the context words of the head and dependent nodes; (v) the word strings and the POS tag candidates of the head and dependent nodes.

5. POS candidate → word: node types.

6. Correct POS node → candidate POS node: node types; context word strings; context POS-tag candidates; conjunctions between: (i) the context words; (ii) the POS tag candidates in the word's context window; (iii) the word and its corresponding POS tag candidates.

5 Results and Discussion

Our dataset comprises 190,000 tokens from the dependency version of the BulTreeBank. Of these, we used 90% for training, and 10% – for testing. We compiled the two subsets by allocating every tenth sentence to the test split, and putting all remaining sentences into the training split.

We trained and evaluated two versions of the MSTParser using the original version of the algorithm (and tree representation model) that constitute our baseline results. For the first experiment, we excluded all available information other than the word forms, to observe an accuracy of 65.21% (LAS). Next, we incorporated the gold standard morphosyntactic tagset of BulTreeBank, and noticed a dramatic increase in accuracy – 83.93% (LAS) for dependency parsing.

Georgiev et al. (2012) reported POS tagging accuracy between 95.72% (for guided learning without added linguistic resources) and 97.98% (for guided learning with an inflectional lexicon and applying linguistic rules over the output). In order to provide a meaningful comparison to the results yielded by our system on the dependency parsing subtask, we trained a separate model in a pipeline-like setting, using the predictions of the best tagger model described in (Georgiev et al., 2012).

When given the gold standard POS tags as input, the described dependency parsing algorithm yielded 87.6% LAS. However, training it with predicted POS tags decreased its accuracy to only 82.1% LAS against the test set for the joint task, owing to the errors of the tagger component.

We evaluated the proposed joint model through a number of experiments, whose results are summarized in Table 1. Its first instantiation took into account the word forms and the tags predicted by the inflectional lexicon, and excluded all features modeling the word context and all feature conjunctions. It yielded 95.99% (Accuracy), 46.96 (F) and 81.22% (LAS) for the POS tagging, co-reference and dependency parsing respectively (line 1 in Table 1).

As the sparseness of observations stemming from the great number of POS tags available in the BulTreeBank may lead to various issues, we attempted a different approach for handling the POS tags. We decomposed them to atomic characteristics – such as the part of speech and grammatical features such as person, gender, and number – that convey the meaning of the complete tags. We replaced the POS tag features incorporated in the first model with the new set of features that reflects their atomic counterparts, and repeated the experiment. However, we observed a small drop in accuracy (line 2).

We continued experimenting by complementing our first model with word context features (line 3). For our next model, we revised the graph distance features, and stopped accounting for service nodes in their computation (line 4). Following that, we added all conjunct features, including combinations between the head and dependent morphosyntactic tags and the bigrams generated over the context of the head and child nodes' words (line 5, respectively). Line 6 shows the results yielded after adding the full set of conjunctions between the POS candidates and the wordform strings of the head and child nodes. Using this final feature set, we obtained the highest scores of 97.13% and 82.39% for POS tagging and dependency parsing respectively. However, the F-score computed for co-reference results decreased for this feature set.

At the dependency parsing task, we achieved a dramatic improvement over the scores yielded by our baselines, and slightly outperformed the pipeline-based model described earlier. Our results for the POS tagging task are aligned with the current state-of-the-art for Bulgarian. However, a direct comparison to (Georgiev et al., 2012) is not possible, since their POS tagging component was trained on the morphosyntactic subset of BulTreeBank that is two times larger than the dependency subset we used, and it was evaluated against a different collection of test sentences.

Our results for the co-reference subtask are in line with the results reported in (Recasens et al., 2010) for other languages. Our dataset is bigger than the datasets for Dutch, English and Italian, and similar in size to the datasets for Catalan and Spanish. The annotations available in our dataset are also comparable to theirs: POS, morphosyntactic information, heads, dependency relations, named entities, etc. However, semantic roles are missing in BulTreeBank. Our experimental settings resemble the singleton co-reference settings described in the cited work. If we take F-measure as a comparison criterion, our results (51%) are similar to the results for Catalan (56.2% SUKRE[2]), Spanish (55% SUKRE), Italian (50.4% SUKRE). We mention these results only for illustrative purposes, and this comparison has no pretension for completeness. However, in our case the precision is very high (around 80%), while the recall is low (around 30%). It should be noted that in (Recasens et al., 2010) balanced values prevail, and recall usually dominates precision. Our con-

[2]SUKRE is the system that performed the task.

clusion is that the features included in our model need to be carefully revised.

6 Conclusion and Future Work

The results reported in this paper indicate that three core tasks, namely POS (morphosyntactic) tagging, co-reference resolution and dependency parsing, can be solved via a combined model based on the MSTParser. Our approach is language independent. The model depends on the availability of a dependency treebank with annotated co-reference chains and morphosyntactic information. The model would be better manageable if the number of the possible POS tags for each wordform remained small. In our experiments we use a morphosyntactic lexicon and a guesser. Thus, we expect similar resources to be available for other languages. We expect also some of the interactions observed for Bulgarian to hold for a number of other languages, at least with respect to the connection between phenomena like binding, control, pro-drop, on the one hand, and rich morphology, on the other. Since the co-reference might be dependant mainly on morphological features (in morphologically rich languages) and/or syntactic positions and dependencies (both - in morphologically rich and morphologically poor languages), the difference would be rather explicated in the degrees of mutual interaction. Our expectation would be that the morphologically poorer the language, the bigger role of the word order and syntactic dependencies.

The joint model achieves performance similar to that of the current state-of-the-art for the POS-tagging task, and the combined model outperforms the dependency parsing in the pipeline currently available for Bulgarian.

The features used for single-task modeling cannot be easily ported to the joint modeling setting, and further design and experimentation with regard to the feature sets are required in order to improve the performance of the system. Such an effort may as well support the incorporation of other tasks in the proposed joint modeling framework. Some ideas we have in this regard include the addition of semantic class annotations to the individual wordforms, as well as features derived by some form of shallow analysis, such as chunking. We expect that such extensions will improve the performance of the system with respect to the dependency and co-reference resolution tasks.

Still, in future work we plan to attempt modeling the three tasks via a transition-based model that will require the simultaneous consideration of more than two non-adjacent nodes in the sentence. For example, in the Bulgarian sentence: "Toj mu_1 ya_2 podade $kartinata_2$ na $Ivan_1$." ("He him it gave picture-the to Ivan", *He gave the picture to Ivan*), a co-reference chain exists between the dative clitic 'mu' and the person name 'Ivan' which is interacting with the dependency relations between the clitic, the proper name, and the verb 'podade'.

We also intend to experiment with alternative encodings of the co-reference chains in order achieve a better use of the information available in our resources. Another direction of future work is the application of the described approach to treebanks of other languages.

Acknowledgments

The contribution of Kiril Simov and Petya Osenova is partially supported by the FP7 Capacity Project AComIn: Advanced Computing for Innovation (316087).

References

Bernd Bohnet and Joakim Nivre. 2012. A transition-based system for joint part-of-speech tagging and labeled non-projective dependency parsing. In *EMNLP-CoNLL*, pages 1455–1465.

Jenny Rose Finkel and Christopher D. Manning. 2010. Hierarchical joint learning: Improving joint parsing and named entity recognition with non-jointly labeled data. In *Proceedings of ACL 2010*.

Georgi Georgiev, Valentin Zhikov, Kiril Ivanov Simov, Petya Osenova, and Preslav Nakov. 2012. Feature-rich part-of-speech tagging for morphologically complex languages: Application to Bulgarian. In *EACL'12*, pages 492–502.

Ryan McDonald, Koby Crammer, and Fernando Pereira. 2005. Online large-margin training of dependency parsers. In *Proceedings of ACL'05*, pages 91–98.

Xian Qian and Yang Liu. 2012. Joint chinese word segmentation, pos tagging and parsing. In *EMNLP-CoNLL*, pages 501–511.

Marta Recasens, Liu Màrquez, Emili Sapena, M.Antònia Martí, Mariona Taulé, Véronique Hoste, Massimo Poesio, and Yannick Versley. 2010. SemEval-2010 task 1: Coreference resolution in multiple languages. *Journal of the Association for Computing Machinery*, 28(3):114–133.

magyarlanc: A Toolkit for Morphological and Dependency Parsing of Hungarian

János Zsibrita[1], **Veronika Vincze**[1,2] and **Richárd Farkas**[1]
[1]Department of Informatics, University of Szeged
{zsibrita,rfarkas}@inf.u-szeged.hu
[2]Hungarian Academy of Sciences
Research Group on Artificial Intelligence
vinczev@inf.u-szeged.hu

Abstract

Hungarian is the stereotype of morphologically rich and free word order languages. Here, we introduce magyarlanc, a natural language toolkit developed for the linguistic preprocessing – segmentation, morphological analysis, POS-tagging and dependency parsing – of Hungarian texts. We hope that the free availability of the toolkit fosters the research not just on the Hungarian language but on all the morphologically rich languages in general. The main novelties of the tool are the application of a new harmonized morphological coding system of Hungarian, the data-driven approach and the integration of a dependency parser. The system is implemented in JAVA, hence it can be used in a platform-independent way.

1 Introduction

For end user natural language processing applications, it is essential to have access to a basic linguistic analyzer tool on the target language, in order to prevent reinventing the wheel every time. In this paper, we present magyarlanc, a basic linguistic analyzer toolkit developed for Hungarian.

Hungarian is a morphologically rich language with free word order (i.e. leaving aside the issue of the internal structure of NPs, most sentence-level syntactic information in Hungarian is conveyed by morphology, not by configuration). A large part of the methodology for morphosyntactic analysis has been developed for English. However, the linguistic analysis of morphologically rich and free word order languages requires special techniques. Hence, it was not sufficient to simply employ available tools and retrain on Hungarian corpora, we had to modify/adapt them. We hope that our findings and experiences gained during this adaptation process are useful for everybody dealing with morphologically rich – especially agglutinative – languages.

magyarlanc is enriched with a sentence splitter and tokenizer, a morphological analyzer, a POS-tagger and a dependency parser, each of them fine-tuned for the characteristics of Hungarian. The main novelties of magyarlanc are the following (each of the three criteria is unique among Hungarian-oriented linguistic analyzers):

- It is data-driven. Every module was systematically trained and evaluated on the Szeged Corpus and Szeged Dependency Treebank (82K sentences with manual annotation).
- It is an integrated toolkit, starting from raw text outputs to dependency parses.
- It is implemented fully in JAVA (incorporation to big systems is straightforward).

magyarlanc is freely available for research purposes at http://www.inf.u-szeged.hu/rgai/magyarlanc.

The structure of the paper is the following. First, we provide a summary of the grammatical features of Hungarian, which is followed and a short description of Hungarian morphological coding systems. Then we present the modules of magyarlanc. We also test the efficiency of magyarlanc and provide results on morphological and dependency parsing.

2 Grammatical Features of Hungarian

In this section, we provide a basic description of the Hungarian language with special emphasis on the phenomena that are important for morphological and syntactic parsing, based on Farkas et al. (2012). For a better understanding of the phenomena described, English will be used as a contrast language.

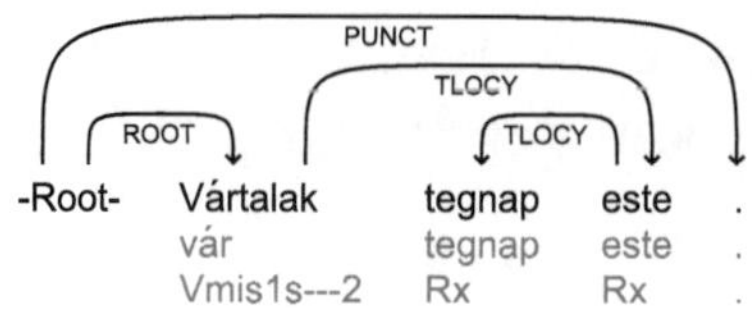

Figure 1: Dependency graph of the sentence *Vártalak tegnap este* "I was waiting for you last night".

Hungarian is an agglutinative language, thus a word can have hundreds of word forms due to inflectional or derivational affixation. Grammatical information is usually encoded in morphology and Hungarian is a typical morphologically rich language. Word order is free in the sense that the positions of the subject, the object and the verb are not fixed within the sentence, but word order is related to information structure, e.g. new (or emphatic) information (the focus) always precedes the verb and old information (the topic) precedes the focus position. Thus, the position relative to the verb has no predictive force as regards the syntactic function of the given argument: while in English, the noun phrase before the verb is most typically the subject, in Hungarian, it is the focus of the sentence, which itself can be the subject, object or any other argument (É. Kiss, 2002).

The grammatical function of words is determined by case suffixes as in *lánc* "chain" – *lánccal* (chain-INS) "with (a/the) chain". Hungarian nouns can have about 20 cases[1] and – being a head-final language – case suffixes always occur at the right end of the word as in *lánc* "chain" – *láncaikkal* (chain-3PLPOSS-PL-INS) "with their chains". Case suffixes mark the relationship between the head and its arguments (subject, object, dative etc.).

Verbs are inflected for person and number and the definiteness of the object. Conjugational information is sufficient to deduce the pronominal subject or object, hence they are mostly omitted from the sentence: *Vártalak tegnap este.* (wait-PAST-1SG2OBJ yesterday evening) "I was waiting for you last night". This pro-drop feature of Hungarian leads to the fact that there are several clauses without an overt subject or object, however, the first person singular subject and the second person object can be reconstructed on the basis of the grammatical features of the verb (see Figure 1).

Hungarian is characterized by vowel harmony, which means that most of the suffixes exist in two different forms – one with a front vowel and another one with a back vowel – and it is the vowels within the stem that determine which form of the suffix is attached to the word. For instance, the verb *fut* "run" is inflected as *futnak* "they run" in the third person plural because the stem contains a back vowel but the same form of the verb *mer* "dare" is *mernek* "they dare" since there is a front vowel in the stem.

There are several other linguistic phenomena that are syntactic in nature in English but they are encoded morphologically in Hungarian. For instance, causation and modality are expressed by derivative suffixes and so is passive (although the passive voice is rare in modern Hungarian): e.g. *csináltathatjátok* (make-CAUS-MODAL-2PL-OBJ) "you can have it made".

Another peculiarity of Hungarian is that the third person singular present tense indicative form of the copula is phonologically empty, i.e. there are apparently verbless sentences in Hungarian: *A ház nagy* (the house big) "The house is big". However, in other tenses or moods, the copula is present as in *A ház nagy lesz* (the house big will.be) "The house will be big".

According to these facts, a Hungarian syntactic parser must rely much more on morphological analysis than e.g. an English one since in Hungarian it is morphemes that mostly encode morphosyntactic information.

3 Morphological Coding Systems for Hungarian

There are three widely used morphological coding systems for Hungarian: Humor, MSD and KR and they make use of different tagsets. The coding system Humor is based on unification, which means that stems and morphemes are assigned features that allow or prohibit their attachment to other morphemes. One word form can contain only morphemes the features of which are not contradictory (Prószéky and Tihanyi, 1993).

[1] Some Hungarian grammars and morphological coding systems treat some rare suffixes as derivational suffixes while others treat them as case suffixes; see e.g. Farkas et al. (2010).

The MSD morphological coding system was developed for a bunch of languages including Hungarian (Erjavec, 2004). Within the codes the first position determines the part-of-speech while other positions offer other types of linguistic information (e.g. in the case of verbs, the type, mood, tense, number and person are provided).

The KR coding system was developed with respect to the morphology of the Hungarian language, however, its basic syntax is language-independent (Trón et al., 2006b). Linguistic information is encoded in hierarchical attribute value matrices: there are default values (e.g singular or 3rd person) and only those that differ from these manifest in the code.

Recently, there has been a successful attempt to harmonize the linguistic principles behind the coding systems MSD and KR (Farkas et al., 2010). The harmonization of Hungarian morphological coding systems was necessary due to the following reasons. *morphdb.hu* is one of the most widely used morphological databases for Hungarian, which makes use of the KR morphological annotation system (Trón et al., 2006a). However, the only manually POS-tagged corpus, the Szeged Corpus (Alexin et al., 2003) is annotated with MSD codes. The two coding systems are not compatible, which entails that if we want to exploit both resources in a statistical language parser (POS tagger, constituency parser, dependency parser etc.), we have to fall back to conversion rules, which leads to the loss of information. In order to avoid this, the two coding systems (MSD and KR) were harmonized and their basic principles were also made compatible. When harmonizing the two coding systems, the following principle was observed: morphological codes should include only those types of information that are useful for later processing (syntax, applications). For instance, in the case of derived verbs, only those pieces of derivational information are explicitly marked that are expressed with syntactic tools in other languages. Recall the example of *csináltathatják* (make-CAUS-MODAL-2PL-OBJ) "you can have it made", where the lemma is *csinál* "make", the derivational suffixes *-tat* and *-hat* denote causativity and modality, respectively, and the morphological code of the word form includes information on causativity and modality as well. However, no derivational information is marked in the case of the denominal verb *kezel* "treat, handle", which is derived from *kéz* "hand", since this information is irrelevant from a syntactic point of view.

4 Related Work

There have been some solutions implemented for the tokenization and morphological analysis of Hungarian texts, which we briefly summarize now.

For tokenizing Hungarian texts, we are aware of the MtSeg segmentation tool developed in the framework of the MULTEXT project (Ide and Véronis, 1994), which was later adapted to Hungarian with the help of specific lists and lexicons (of abbreviations). In addition, the *huntoken* tool also segments Hungarian texts into sentences and tokens and is widely used in many language processing applications (Halácsy et al., 2004).

One of the first morphological analyzer developed for Hungarian was Humor (Prószéky and Tihanyi, 1993). However, the tool is not freely available and is not open source. On the other hand, *hunmorph* is an open source tool, which can be used for lemmatization, morphological analysis and spellchecking in various languages including Hungarian (Trón et al., 2005).

As for Hungarian POS-tagging, *hunpos* was developed on the basis of *hunmorph* (Halácsy et al., 2006). It is based on a Hidden Markov Model, is also free to use and is an open source tool. There is also a POS-tagger based on the morphological analyzer Humor (Prószéky and Tihanyi, 1993), which is enhanced by statistical information gathered from the Hungarian National Corpus (Váradi, 2002). Recently, PurePOS has been implemented (Orosz and Novák, 2012), which is an open source morphological tagger based on a Hidden Markov Model.

Although there are a handful of morphological taggers for Hungarian, their performances are not directly comparable since they rely on different coding systems. However, the harmonized morphology (see Section 3) enable us to build a morphological parser, which is now integrated into `magyarlanc` and the output of which is in total harmony with the Szeged Corpus.

Besides being the first morphological tool that makes use of the harmonized morphological coding system – thus enables the training and evaluation on a large manually annotated corpus –, the most novel feature of *magyarlanc* is that to the best of our knowledge, it contains the first dependency parser adapted to Hungarian.

5 The System

magyarlanc consists of a sentence splitter and a tokenizer, a morphological analyzer and POS-tagger and a dependency parser. In the following, these modules will be presented.

5.1 Sentence Splitting and Tokenization

The first step of text processing is to split the text into sentences, for which we applied the sentence splitter built in MorphAdorner, a language toolkit developed at Northwestern University[2]. Its dictionary was extended with specific Hungarian abbreviations, which end in a dot but they do not signal the end of the sentence, e.g. *kft.* "ltd." or *szül.* "born" and the abbreviations of months. As a second step, tokens within the sentence are identified, which is carried out by the tokenizer module of MorphAdorner. During tokenization, special emphasis is paid to abbreviations consisting of double letters (in Hungarian spelling, some sounds are denoted by a combination of letters, e.g. *cs* denotes the palatal voiceless affricate [tʃ]).

5.2 Morphological Analysis

Lemmatization and morphological analysis is carried out by a morphological analyser based on the lexical resource *morphdb.hu* (Trón et al., 2006a). Originally, the analyzer yields KR morphological codes but they are then converted to the harmonized MSD-style codes (see Section 3). As a result of the morphological analysis, pairs of lemmas and morphological codes are provided for each word. For instance, for the word *egyed* entity / eat-2SG-IMP-OBJ / one-2SGPOSS "entity" / "you should eat" / "your one" we get the following analyses:

egyed@Nn-sn
eszik@Vmmp2s—y
egy@Mc-snd—-s2

where the lemma and the morphological code are separated by an @ sign.

5.3 POS-tagging

POS-tagging is executed by a modified version of the Stanford POS-tagger (Toutanova et al., 2003), which is based on a Maximum Entropy classifier and makes use of the possible tags provided by the morphological analysis (see above). The POS-tagger was trained on the Szeged Corpus, a manually POS-tagged corpus of 1.2 million words (Csendes et al., 2005). For training, we applied only a reduced set of the original MSD-codes, however, at the end of the analysis, full MSD-codes are provided, which are in accordance with the harmonized Hungarian morphology (Farkas et al., 2010). The reduction of POS-codes was necessary as discriminative POS-taggers are not prepared to deal with thousands of different POS-codes. The reduced tagset consisted of only about 60 elements, which proved to be manageable for the POS-tagger.

When reducing the original tagset, we followed the main principle of preserving an unambiguous mapping between the output of the POS-tagger using a reduced tagset on the one hand and the original (full) MSD tagset on the other hand. For instance, a noun ending in the *-nak/-nek* suffix may be in the genitive or in the dative case, thus the MSD codes `Nc-sd` (a singular noun in the dative) and `Nc-sg` (a singular noun in the genitive) will be reduced in a different way. However, the codes `Nc-sd` and `Nc-sd---s3` will be reduced to the same form since there is no such Hungarian lemma that would have the same word form for a dative singular and a dative singular with a third person singular possessor (and thus, the POS-tagger would not have to choose between these possibilities).

As default, MSD codes of nouns, adjectives, numerals and pronouns are reduced to the main part of speech (i.e. the first element of the MSD code). Their forms in dative and genitive, however, coincide that is why in these cases the reduced codes also preserve the case of the noun (e.g. `Nd`, `Ng`). Essive and superessive forms of nominals may also coincide, e.g. *szépen* nice-ESS or nice-SUP "nicely" or "on a nice one". In such cases, the reduced codes preserve the case as well, e.g. `Ap`. The form of nouns with a third person singular possessor may coincide with the non-possessive form of the noun, e.g. *Ajkán* Ajka-SUP (a town in Hungary) or lip-SUP "in Ajka" or "on his lip" and here the reduced codes also differ from each other. An inflected form of a third person singular possessive form of a noun with front vowels may coincide with the inflected possessed form of the same noun, e.g. *énekét* song-3SGPOSS-ACC or song-POSS-ACC "his song" or "that of his song",

[2]http://morphadorner.northwestern.edu/

Feature	N	V	V	A	P	T	R	R	S	C	M	I	I	X	Y	Z	O	O
SubPOS	•	•	•	•	•	•	•	l	•	•	•		o				•	e/d/n
Num	•	•	•	•	•			•			•						•	•
Cas	•			•	•						•						•	•
NumP	•			•	•						•						•	•
PerP	•			•	•						•						•	•
NumPd	•			•	•						•						•	•
Mood		•	n															
Tense		•																
Per		•	•		•			•										
Def		•																
Deg				•			•	•										
Clitic																		
Form										•	•							
Coord										•								
Type																		•

Table 1: Relevant features for each part of speech and subtypes of parts of speech: type – SubPOS, number – Num, case – Cas, number of possessor – NumP, person of possessor – PerP, number of possessed – NumPd, mood/form – Mood, tense – Tense, person – Per, definiteness – Def, degree – Deg, clitic – Clitic, form – Form, type of coordination – Coord, subtype – Type.

having the reduced codes `Ns` and `Nz`, respectively. In addition, reduced codes for pronouns belonging to the most important subclasses also preserve their types: `Pe` for personal pronouns, `Pq` for interrogative pronouns and `Pr` for relative pronouns. Fractions also preserve their types (`Mf`).

The default reduced code of a verb is simply `V` and codes of auxiliaries are reduced to `Va`. The present conditional first and second person plural forms of verbs coincide in the objective and subjective conjugation thus the codes of the objective forms are reduced to `Vcp` (e.g. *olvasnánk* read-COND-1PL or read-COND-1PL-OBJ "we would read (an indefinite object)" or "we would read (a definite object)"). For certain verbs, the first person singular forms coincide in subjective and objective conjugation and thus the objective forms are reduced to `Vip` (e.g. *iszom* drink-1SG or drink-1SG-OBJ "I drink (an indefinite object)" or "I drink (a definite object)"). The present conditional first person singular subjective form and the present conditional third person plural objective form of verbs with front vowels also coincide, hence the third person plural form is reduced to `V3p` (e.g. *ennék* eat-COND-1SG or eat-COND-3PL-OBJ "I would eat (an indefinite object)" or "they would eat (a definite object)"). The subjective and objective forms of past indicative first person singular verbs coincide, thus the MSD code of the objective forms is reduced to `Vy` (e.g. *osztottam* divide-PAST-1SG or divide-PAST-1SG-OBJ "I divided (an indefinite object)" or "I divided (a definite object)"). The codes of imperative verbs are reduced to `Vm`. In certain cases the past tense of a verb coincides with the present tense of another verb, thus the MSD codes of present tense verbs for which none of the previous rules hold are reduced to `Vp` (e.g. *ért* (understand) or (reach-PAST-3SG) "understand" or "reached").

MSD codes of adverbs are reduced to `R` by default, however, the most important subtypes of adverbs preserve their types: `Rp` for preverbs, `Rq` for interrogative adverbs, `Rr` for relative adverbs and `Rl` for personal pronominal adverbs. The reduced code of articles is `T`. In the case of conjunctions, postpositions, interjections, abbreviations and misspelled or unknown words, the original MSD code functions as the reduced code as well.

Table 1 shows the relevant features for each part of speech. It is also noted in the table if a specific subclass of a given part of speech has different features than the main part of speech, e.g. not all the grammatical features are relevant for infinitives that are relevant for main verbs.

5.4 Syntactic Parsing

There are two mainstream approaches to syntactic parsing: the one based on constituency grammar and the other one based on dependency grammar. Dependency parsers are believed to be especially useful for parsing languages with free word order such as Hungarian since these parsers are able to connect grammatically related words that are not adjacent.

Farkas et al. (2012) made the first experiments on applying state-of-the-art dependency parsers to Hungarian. Since their results indicated that the Bohnet parser (Bohnet, 2010) was the most efficient on Hungarian dependency parsing, we integrated this parser into `magyarlanc`. The applied model was trained on the Szeged Dependency Treebank, which consists of 82,000 sentences, is manually POS-tagged and contains manually annotated dependency parses for each sentence (Vincze et al., 2010).

Multiword named entities (e.g. *Coca Cola Ltd.*) and multiword numbers (e.g. *42 million*) are treated in a special way. We consider the last word as the head because the last word of multiword units gets inflected in Hungarian and all the previous elements are attached to the succeeding word, i.e. the penultimate word is attached to the last word, the antepenultimate word to the penultimate one etc. with an NE relation for named entities and a NUM relation for numbers.

In the verbless clauses the Szeged Dependency Treebank introduces virtual nodes. This solution means that a similar tree structure is ascribed to the same sentence in the present third person singular / plural and all the other tenses / persons (see Figure 2). A further argument for the use of a virtual node is that the virtual node is always present at the syntactic level since it is overt in all the other forms, tenses and moods of the verb. Seeker et al. (2012) experimented with several methods for inserting virtual nodes into the verbless clauses. Although their results indicate that this issue still requires further investigation, in `magyarlanc`, we follow their complex label approach, which means that children of a virtual node are assigned a complex dependency label (e.g. ROOT-VAN-SUBJ), referring to the fact that the specific node is the subject of a virtual node (here VAN) which is itself not present in the sentence but functions as the root. Figure 2 shows variations of a sentence in the past tense and in the present tense with a virtual node and with complex dependency labels.

In order to represent the dependency parses of the sentences visually, we also integrated the `whatswrong`[3] visualizer into the system.

5.5 The Output of the Toolkit

As an input, `magyarlanc` requires a raw text in a txt format. The linguistic processing can be used in three possible modes. First, it is only tokenization and POS-tagging that is carried out. Second, dependency parsing also takes place beside the above-mentioned two processing steps. Third, it is only morphological analysis that is carried out.

[3]`https://code.google.com/p/whatswrong/`

Borpancsolókra	borpancsoló	Nn-ps
,	,	,
zajongókra	zajongó	Nn-ps
és	és	Ccsw
állatkínzókra	állatkínzó	Nn-ps
nagyon	nagyon	Rx
számítanak	számít	Vmip3p—n
.	.	.

Table 2: POS-tagging of the sentence *Borpancsolókra, zajongókra és állatkínzókra nagyon számítanak.* "They heavily count on wine forgers, noise makers and animal torturers."

The output file produced by `magyarlanc` has the following structure. One line corresponds to one token and sentences are separated by an empty line. When there is no dependency parsing carried out, the first column contains the word form, the second one contains the lemma and the third one contains the MSD code. A sample of the output is shown in Table 2.

When there is also dependency parsing, the first column contains the identifier of the word within the sentence, the second column contains the word form, the third one the lemma, the fourth one the MSD code, the fifth one the part of speech, the sixth one the morphological features, the seventh one the identifier of the parent node, and finally the eighth one contains the dependency label. Table 3 shows a sample output of a sentence parsed both morphologically and syntactically.

Figure 3 shows a sample dependency graph visualized by the `whatswrong` tool. The dependency parse of the sentence is denoted by arrows and the coarse-grained morphological analysis can also be found under the word forms.

6 Results

In order to evaluate the performance of `magyarlanc`, we experimented both with POS-tagging and dependency parsing. For this purpose, we made use of the Szeged Dependency Treebank (Vincze et al., 2010). Sentences of the treebank were randomly divided into training and test sets in a ratio of 80:20%, respectively. Below, we show

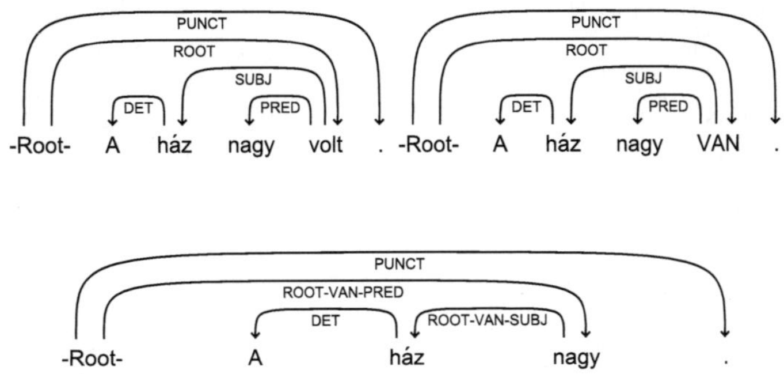

Figure 2: Dependency graphs with overt and covert virtual nodes of the sentences *A ház nagy (volt).* "The house is/was big."

1	Az	az	Tf	T	SubPOS=f	2	DET
2	elnök	elnök	Nn-sn	N	SubPOS=n—Num=s|Cas=n| NumP=none|PerP=none|NumPd=none	3	SUBJ
3	megígérte	megígér	Vmis3s—y	V	SubPOS=m|Mood=i|Tense=s|Per=3|Num=s|Def=y	0	ROOT
4	,	,	,	,	_	3	PUNCT
5	az	az	Tf	T	SubPOS=f	7	DET
6	észlelt	észlelt	Afp-sn	A	SubPOS=f|Deg=p|Num=s|Cas=n| NumP=none|PerP=none|NumPd=none	7	ATT
7	hibákat	hiba	Nn-pa	N	SubPOS=n|Num=p|Cas=a| NumP=none|PerP=none|NumPd=none	14	OBJ
8	a	a	Tf	T	SubPOS=f	9	DET
9	szövetség	szövetség	Nn-sn	N	SubPOS=n|Num=s|Cas=n| NumP=none|PerP=none|NumPd=none	10	ATT
10	vezetése	vezetés	Nn-sn—s3	N	SubPOS=n|Num=s|Cas=n| NumP=s|PerP=3|NumPd=none	14	SUBJ
11	45	45	Mc-snd	M	SubPOS=c|Num=s|Cas=n|Form=d| NumP=none|PerP=none|NumPd=none	12	ATT
12	napon	nap	Nn-sp	N	SubPOS=n|Num=s|Cas=p| NumP=none|PerP=none|NumPd=none	13	OBL
13	belül	belül	St	S	SubPOS=t	14	TLOCY
14	kijavítja	kijavít	Vmip3s—y	V	SubPOS=m|Mood=i|Tense=p|Per=3|Num=s|Def=y	3	ATT
15	.	.	.	.	_	0	PUNCT

Table 3: Morphological and dependency analysis of the sentence *Az elnök megígérte, az észlelt hibákat a szövetség vezetése 45 napon belül kijavítja.* "The president promised that the leadership of the federation would correct the recognized errors within 45 days."

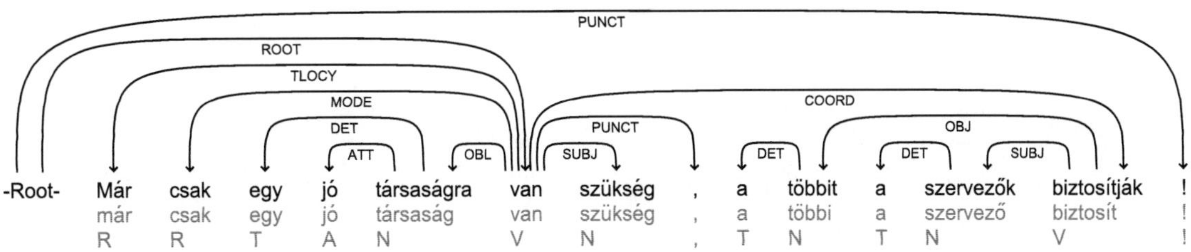

Figure 3: Dependency graph of the sentence *Már csak egy jó társaságra van szükség, a többit a szervezők biztosítják*! "Now you just need a good company, everything else will be provided by the organizers."

POS-tagging	96.33%
Dependency parsing (LAS)	91.42%
Dependency parsing (ULA)	93.22%

Table 4: Results achieved by `magyarlanc`.

and discuss the results of our experiments.

6.1 Results on POS-tagging

In order to determine the efficiency of POS-tagging, we applied an accuracy score. An analysis was considered correct if both the lemma and the deep morphological information (i.e. the part of speech and all the morphological features) of the token were correct. In this way, *magyarlanc* achieved an accuracy of 96.33%.

6.2 Results on Dependency Parsing

For the evaluation of dependency parsing, we applied the metrics Labeled Attachment Score (LAS) and Unlabeled Attachment Score (ULA). In the case of LAS, it is both the parent node and the dependency label that must be the same as the gold standard while in the case of ULA, it is only the parent node that counts (i.e. a wrong dependency label does not yield an error). `magyarlanc` obtained the scores of 91.42% (LAS) and 93.22% (ULA) on the test set.

6.3 Speed of Linguistic Processing

We also tested how fast `magyarlanc` can parse texts. For this purpose, we selected *Stars of Eger*, a historical novel written by Géza Gárdonyi. Running the whole processing chain from segmentation till dependency parsing, 1000 sentences are analyzed per minute by using 1 GB RAM, running on a single thread. If just segmentation and POS-tagging are performed, it results in an analysis of 3000 sentences per minute.

7 Conclusions

In this paper, we presented `magyarlanc`, a natural language toolkit developed for the linguistic preprocessing – segmentation, morphological analysis, POS-tagging and dependency parsing – of Hungarian texts. The main novelties of the tool are the usage of the harmonized morphological coding system of Hungarian and the integration of a dependency parser, which makes it unique among NLP tools developed for Hungarian. It is also data-driven as every module was systematically trained and evaluated on the Szeged Corpus and Szeged Dependency Treebank. The system is implemented in JAVA, hence it can be used on all kinds of platforms. `magyarlanc` is freely available for research purposes at `http://www.inf.u-szeged.hu/rgai/magyarlanc`.

Acknowledgments

This work was supported in part by the European Union and the European Social Fund through the project FuturICT.hu (grant no.: TÁMOP-4.2.2.C-11/1/KONV-2012-0013). Richárd Farkas was partially funded by the Hungarian National Excellence Program (TÁMOP 4.2.4.A/2-11-1-2012-0001).

References

Zoltán Alexin, János Csirik, Tibor Gyimóthy, Károly Bibok, Csaba Hatvani, Gábor Prószéky, and László Tihanyi. 2003. Annotated Hungarian National Corpus. In *Proceedings of the EACL*, pages 53–56.

Bernd Bohnet. 2010. Top accuracy and fast dependency parsing is not a contradiction. In *Proceedings of the 23rd International Conference on Computational Linguistics (Coling 2010)*, pages 89–97.

Dóra Csendes, János Csirik, Tibor Gyimóthy, and András Kocsor. 2005. The Szeged Treebank. In *TSD*, pages 123–131.

Katalin É. Kiss. 2002. *The Syntax of Hungarian*. Cambridge University Press, Cambridge.

Tomaš Erjavec. 2004. *MULTEXT-East morphosyntactic specifications. Version 3.*

Richárd Farkas, Dániel Szeredi, Dániel Varga, and Veronika Vincze. 2010. MSD-KR harmonizáció a Szeged Treebank 2.5-ben [Harmonizing MSD and KR codes in the Szeged Treebank 2.5]. In *VII. Magyar Számítógépes Nyelvészeti Konferencia*, pages 349–353.

Richárd Farkas, Veronika Vincze, and Helmut Schmid. 2012. Dependency Parsing of Hungarian: Baseline Results and Challenges. In *Proceedings of the 13th Conference of the European Chapter of the Association for Computational Linguistics*, pages 55–65, Avignon, France, April. Association for Computational Linguistics.

Péter Halácsy, András Kornai, László Németh, András Rung, István Szakadát, and Viktor Trón. 2004. Creating open language resources for Hungarian. In *Proceedings of the 4th International Conference on Language Resources and Evaluation.*

Péter Halácsy, András Kornai, and Csaba Oravecz. 2006. HunPos - an open source trigram tagger. In *Proceedings of the 45th Annual Meeting of the Association for Computational Linguistics Companion Volume Proceedings of the Demo and Poster Sessions*, pages 209–212, Prague, Czech Republic. Association for Computational Linguistics.

Nancy Ide and Jean Véronis. 1994. MULTEXT: Multilingual Text Tools and Corpora. In *Proceedings of the 15th conference on Computational linguistics*, pages 588–592.

György Orosz and Attila Novák. 2012. PurePos – an open source morphological disambiguator. In *Proceedings of the 9th International Workshop on Natural Language Processing and Cognitive Science.*

Gábor Prószéky and László Tihanyi. 1993. Humor: High-speed unification morphology and its applications for agglutinative languages. *La tribune des industries de la langue*, 10:28–29.

Wolfgang Seeker, Richárd Farkas, Bernd Bohnet, Helmut Schmid, and Jonas Kuhn. 2012. Data-driven dependency parsing with empty heads. In *Proceedings of COLING 2012: Posters*, pages 1081–1090, Mumbai, India, December. The COLING 2012 Organizing Committee.

Kristina Toutanova, Dan Klein, Christopher D. Manning, and Yoram Singer. 2003. Feature-rich part-of-speech tagging with a cyclic dependency network. In *Proceedings of the 2003 Conference of the North American Chapter of the Association for Computational Linguistics on Human Language Technology - Volume 1*, pages 173–180.

Viktor Trón, László Németh, Péter Halácsy, András Kornai, György Gyepesi, and Dániel Varga. 2005. Hunmorph: open source word analysis. In *Proceedings of ACL.*

Viktor Trón, Péter Halácsy, Péter Rebrus, András Rung, Eszter Simon, and Péter Vajda. 2006a. Morphdb.hu: Hungarian lexical database and morphological grammar. In *Proceedings of 5th International Conference on Language Resources and Evaluation (LREC '06).*

Viktor Trón, Péter Halácsy, Péter Rebrus, András Rung, Eszter Simon, and Péter Vajda. 2006b. The annotation system of HunMorph. Technical report, The Media Research center of the Budapest University of Technology and Economics.

Tamás Váradi. 2002. The Hungarian National Corpus. In *Proceedings of the Third International Conference on Language Resources and Evaluation (LREC-2002)*, pages 385–389, Las Palmas de Gran Canaria. European Language Resources Association.

Veronika Vincze, Dóra Szauter, Attila Almási, György Móra, Zoltán Alexin, and János Csirik. 2010. Hungarian Dependency Treebank. In *Proceedings of the Seventh Conference on International Language Resources and Evaluation (LREC'10).*

Author Index